Latvian-English Dictionary

Latvian-English Dictionary

Volume I
A-M

Compiled by
Leonard Zusne

CONTENTS

PREFACE

A translating dictionary, like the present one, is a practical dictionary that translates words in existing texts. It does not, as a rule, provide descriptions or explanations, nor does it set norms of how words should be spelled. The aim of dictionary users can be either to understand the source language (the language of the headwords) or to translate it into the target language (the language of the translation equivalents). The user's first language can be either the source language or the target language. This makes for four possible types of interlingual dictionaries (descriptive, prescriptive, or translating). Existing Latvian-English dictionaries indicate that they are intended for users whose first language is Latvian and whose purpose is to translate it into English. The present dictionary is intended primarily for users whose first language is English and who wish to understand texts written in Latvian. This, of course, does not preclude Latvian speakers from using it to translate from Latvian into English, i.e., to produce English texts. English-speaking Latvians may, in fact, find it helpful for accurate and natural translation. Other features of this dictionary are: the number of entries, over 106,000, which is more than double that of any other Latvian-English dictionary; the use of American rather than British English; an extensive coverage of technical terms from all fields of science and technology; the comprehensive inclusion of spelling variants; and the inclusion of colloquialisms, common speech words, vulgar terms, slang, barbarisms, selected regionalisms, and terms found in folkloric language. (A dictionary of Latvian proverbs is included in the back.)

The entries of this dictionary were collected from various extant monolingual and bilingual Latvian dictionaries, general and specialized: spelling dictionaries, technical dictionaries, etymological dictionaries, general encyclopedias, periodical literature, and many Latvian speakers. Of the latter, I want to single out the contribution of the late sea captain Inats Lejnieks. In his time, the captain had commanded full-rigged sailing ship with Latvian crews, and he supplied the Latvian equivalents of the names of sails and principal ropes, spars, and parts of the hull. I was fortunate to have captain Lejnieks share his expertise with me as this material was not available anywhere else. The contribution of Rasma Sināte should also be noted for editorial assistance on an earlier unpublished edition.

INTRODUCTION

PRONUNCIATION AND ALPHABET

In Latvian pronunciation, the vowels a, e, i, u have and open or "Italian" quality. The vowel o is pronounced as a diphthong, uo. In words of foreign origin it is sounded like an Italian o. A printed macron above a vowel indicates that it is long. No macron is placed above an o.

The letter e can be pronounced either as a "broad" e [æ] or a "narrow" e [ɛ]. No diacritic is used to indicate this difference, however. In this dictionary, homographs are discriminated with a notation that indicates which one is pronounced with the [æ] sound.

All vowels can have the additional quality of being sounded with a glottal stop. There is no diacritic to signal this quality, and homographs are discriminated with a notation that indicates, with a circumflex (ˆ), which one is pronounced with a glottal stop.

The diphthongs are ai (pronounced as in eye), au (as in now), ei (as in may), ie (as in Pieta), ui (as in Lewis), iu (as in peeoo), o (as in duo), and oi (as in boy).

The consonants b, d, f, h, k, l, m, n, p, r, s, t, v, z are pronounced approximately as in English. The consonant c is pronounced as ts in pots, č as ch in church, š as sh in dish, and ž as si in vision. The palatalized consonants ļ, n, ģ, ķ, and ŗ have the same sound quality as the Russian l, n, d, t, and r when these are followed by an e, i or the palatalization symbol.

There are 34 letters in the Latvian alphabet. The letters and their pronunciations when naming them are as follows:

a (ā), ā (garais ā), b (bē), c (cē), č (čē), d (dē), e (ē), ē (garais ē), f (ef), g (gā), ģ (ģē), h (hā), i (ī), ī (garais ī), j (jē), k (kā), ķ (ķē), l (el), ļ (eļ), m (em), n (en), ņ (eņ), o (uo; o in foreign words), p (pē), r (er), ŗ (eŗ), s (es), š (eš), t (tē), u (ū), ū (garais ū), v (vē), z (zē), ž (žē).

The grapheme ch (pronounced cehā in naming it but sounded like an h with a word) occurs only in words of foreign origin. Although it may be perceived as a unit (representing either the German ch or Greek chi), for purposes of alphabetization it is treated as two separate letters and placed between ce and ci. During the Soviet rule in Latvia, ch was replaced with a simple h. While this makes spelling more phonetic it also makes it more difficult to find a word if the dictionary user is not a native speaker. Anything printed in Latvian before 1946 contains the ch, and it was never abandoned by Latvian writers and the press outside Latvia. It is also retained in the present dictionary.

SPELLING

This lexicon provides alphabetic access to most Latvian words that have appeared in print during the past three quarters of a century, hence all spelling variants are entered, and appear in their proper places alphabetically. Spelling changes have been introduced by language authorities several times during the last 75 years. These involve: (1) long and short vowels (macron or no macron); (2) single or geminated consonants in words borrowed from other languages; (3) the use of ch or h to represent the aspirate in words originating in Latin, Greek, and German; and (4) the palatalization of r. Spelling variants that have been addressed by language authorities are treated by placing the affected letter or letters in brackets, both within the word and immediately following it. Thus, met[all]org[a]nisks [āl][ā] is read as metallorganisks or metālorgānisks. Other spelling variants are entered fully. A word that has a variant whose spelling puts it in a different place alphabetically appears in two places. If the difference does not place a variant elsewhere alphabetically, the two forms appear together, connected with an "or." Otherwise the less common variant appears in its alphabetic order and is referred to the more common one with an equal sign (=).

THE ELEMENTS OF AN ENTRY

- An entry consists of either a single line or a paragraph with a hanging indent.

- All Latvian words are set in bold face letters.

- Homonyms are identified by Roman numerals.

- The headword, when repeated unchanged within an entry, is indicated by its first letter (e.g., ā. for ābols). Derivations are formed by replacing the unchanged portion of the word with a swung dash (~), followed by the appropriate ending or suffix. The unchanged portion of the word is separated from the rest with a diagonal (e.g., ābol/s). This portion is not necessarily the stem or some other grammatical unit. It is chosen only for convenience as a space-saving device.

- The headword is immediately followed by its grammatical category in italics. In the case of a noun, the grammatical category, n, is followed by an indication of the grammatical gender of the noun, nf (feminine) or nm (masculine). The reflexive feminine nouns ending in -šana are further identified with an r.

- The abbreviations vt and vi identify transitive and intransitive verbs, respectively. The abbreviation vr, reflexive verb, refers both to the verb form and its voice. Latvian reflexive verbs indicate that the action reverts to the actor, that interaction is taking place, that the action is repeated a number of times (iterative verbs), or they can be purely intransitive. The abbreviation irr denotes an irregular verb. It appears after each of the three irregular verbs (būt, dot, iet), their various inflected forms, and their combinations with prefixes.

- The headword is followed by its English equivalent or an explanation. Abbreviations and other text in parentheses before the English equivalent further clarify the headword. The abbreviations bot. and zool. are used only in cases where the English word may also have a non-biological meaning. The text in parentheses that follows the English equivalent clarifies the latter. If more English equivalents than one are provided, they are separated by commas, semicolons, or numbers. A comma indicates synonymity or near-synonymity. In some instances a synonym is given only to clarify a word that may have more than one meaning in English. A semicolon separates related but distinct English equivalents, and boldface numbers separate unrelated or only remotely related meanings. Under a given number, further separation of meanings is made by the use of lower-case letters (a., b., etc.). The symbol ◊ precedes idiomatic expressions.

- Most headwords are single words. Terms consisting of two or three words are treated as follows: Reduplicated words (as in interjections, eponyms, and names of holidays) present no special problem. Two- and three-word combinations in an inflected language, such as Latvian, do present a problem. These combinations are: (1) terms in which a (preceding) adjective qualifies a noun, and (2) terms in which a noun in its genitive form serves as a qualifier of a nominative noun. Should such terms be subsumed in an entry under a headword that is the first noun, or should it be given the status of an independent headword? Most Latvian translating dictionaries choose the first option. There are no clear criteria for deciding whether a particular two- or three-word combination should be given the status of an independent entry. The criterion chosen here is whether the combination is a bona fide term, that is, a fixed, established name of a thing or process. Relatively few terms in category (1), mentioned above, qualify to be headwords (e.g., aklā zarna); the majority in category (2) do. The alphabetic placing of terms in the second category is determined by the following considerations. When both the qualifying and qualified nouns are fused, the genitive ending of the qualifying noun may be preserved (e.g., mājasvieta) or not (e.g., mājvieta). When both forms are in use, each appears in its proper alphabetic order and one is cross-referenced to the other. If the qualifying and qualified nouns are written separately, and the combination does not constitute a fixed term, the term appears in the entry where the headword is the qualifying noun of the term. If the combination is a fixed term, it appears alphabetically as an independent entry under the first word. Some two-word terms are used both in their fused and separate forms, in which case the dictionary lists only the fused form.

- As a general rule, participles are not listed in the those that have a distinct English equivalent.

- All adverbs are listed as headwords.

- The following categories of proper nouns are included: (1) Persons and places that are parts of eponyms; (2) The planets and the twelve constellations of the zodiac; (3) Holidays; (4) A few names from folklore and literature that are well known and used generically.

DICTIONARY OF LATVIAN PROVERBS

A proverb is a generalization that is in the form of a rule, advice, prescription, or description. Proverbs differ from idiomatic expressions, comparisons, alliterative jokes, and metaphoric descriptions and characterizations in that they do not refer to a single, specific thing, act or situation but are generalizations. The former are included in the main body of this dictionary. The proverbs proper are presented in this addendum.

In the main body of this dictionary the English words and phrases are the equivalents of the corresponding Latvian linguistic units, not translations. Proverbs are also fixed linguistic units, not just ordinary sentences. Correspondingly, the English equivalents, not translations, are provided here for Latvian proverbs. Not every Latvian proverb has an English equivalent, of course. Yet there are far more such equivalents than the dozen or two suggested by dictionaries and language instruction materials. The problem is to identify them and bring together Latvian and English proverbs that mean the same thing but may differ drastically in the use of words that convey their imagery. The following pairs of proverbs were established by classifying Latvian and American proverbs into categories according to the proverb themes and then searching for equivalents within each category. The proverbs were then listed again alphabetically by the initial letter of the first significant Latvian noun or verb. If a proverb does not contain a noun or a verb, it is listed according to the first significant adjective, adverb, or pronoun. The negative verbal prefix ne- and the debitive prefix jā- are ignored in alphabetizing. Variations within a proverb are included between brackets and separated by a slash. A slash also separates variant versions of the English equivalents.

A

Kāda **ābele**, tāds ābols. *Like begets like.*

Arī sarkanam **ābolam** tārps vidū. *Many a rosy apple is rotten to the core.*

Ābols nekrīt tālu no ābeles. *An apple never falls far from the tree.*

Otra **acī** skabargu ierauga, pats savā baļķi nepamana. *Cast the beam out of your own eye before you try to cast the mote from the eyes of your neighbor.*

Acīm vien amatu neiemācīsies. *Dexterity comes by experience.*

Acīm zagt nav grēks. *Steal all you can with your eyes but never with your hands.*

Kad no **acīm** nost, tad vairs nepiemin. *Seldom seen, soon forgotten.*

Acis grib, vēders nepieņem. *The eyes are bigger than the stomach.*

Acis melo. *Men's faces are not to be trusted.*

Acis vaļā, muti ciet! *Keep your mouth shut and your eyes open.*

Kad **acis** sāp, tad dūmiem vaina. *"Sour grapes," said the fox when he could not reach them. / If you don't know how to dance, you say that the drummer is bad.*

Ko **acis** neredz, to sirds aizmirst. *Out of sight, out of mind.*

Ko **acis** redz, to sirds tic. *Seeing is believing.*

Tavas **acis** rāda, kāds blēdis tu esi. *It's in the looks that conscious guilt appears.*

Kam **āda** niez, lai kasās. *Scratch where it itches.*

Katram sava **āda** mīļa. *Close sits my shirt, but closer my skin.*

Adata maza, bet strādā lielu darbu. *Little axe cuts down a big tree.*

No **adatas** iesāk, pie zirga pēcgalā ķeras. *He that will steal a pin will steal a better thing.*

Labāk **agrāk** nekā vēlāk. *It's better to be an hour too early than a minute too late.*

Ar divi **aiŗiem** vien nekad nedrīkst braukt jūŗā—otrs pāris jāņem līdz atsargam. *It's good to have two strings to one's bow.*

Viena kraupaina **aita** aplaiž visu baru ar kraupi. *One scabbed sheep will mar a flock.*

Arī **aitiņa** var nikna tapt. *Dread the anger of a cornered sheep.*

Labāk ar **aitu** meža braukt nekā ar muļķi runāt. *Arguing with a fool shows there are two.*

Vieglāk **aizdot** nekā atpakaļ dabūt. *Let the lender beware.*

Ko šodien **aizkavēsi**, to vairs nemūžam nepanāksi. *Defer not till tomorrow to be wise: tomorrow's sun to you may never rise.*

Akmens, kas daudz ritināts, lēti neapsūno. *A rolling stone gathers no moss.*

Amatam zelta pamats. *He that has a trade has an estate, and he that has a calling has an office of profit and honor.*

Deviņi **amati**, desmitais bads. *A man of many trades begs his bread on Sunday.*

Amats netop lamāts. *He that has a trade has an office of profit and honor.*

Daudz **amatu**, daudz nelaimes. *Jack of all trades and master of none.*

Anci, nesaki ui, kamēr neesi pāri grāvim! *Don't halloo till you're out of the woods.*

Bez **apdoma** krīt nelaimē, ar apdomu nāk svētība. *Caution is the parent of safety.*

Apdomā papriekšu, tad pēc nebūs žēl. *Planning your future saves you from regretting your past.*

Divreiz **apdomā**, vienreiz runā! *Think twice; speak once.*

Apdomājies labi, iekams ko uzņemi. *Think before you leap.* / *Think—then act.*

Labāk **apdomāt** papriekšu nekā pēc tam. *Have not the cloak made when it begins to rain.*

Kas dos **arāja** mētelim zīda oderi. *Cut the coat according to the cloth.*

Ja **arkla** netaisīsi, tad maizes nedabūis. *Plow your furrows deep while sluggards sleep, and you shall have corn to sell and keep.*

Asinis biezākas nekā ūdens. *Blood is thicker than water.*

Ļaunam ar labu **atmaksā**—gan viņš dabūs savu algu! *Requite injury with kindness.*

Atzīšanās—ceļš uz labošanos. *Confession is good for the soul.*

Aizliegts **auglis** salds. *Forbidden fruit is the sweetest.*

Augļi nāks savā laikā. *Time ripens all things.*

Aukstums māca tecēt, bads strādāt. *Necessity sharpens industry.*

Kur **auša** runā, tur gudrais cieš klusu. *When the argument flares up, the wise man quenches it by silence.*

Vai **avens** pie vēža ies vilnas prasīt! *Don't go to a buzzard's nest to find a dove.*

Avis būs cirpt, nevis dīrāt. *Don't kill the goose that lays the golden egg.*

B

Bada laikā velns mušas ķeŗ. *When the devil hungers, he will eat scraps.*

Bads dara rūgtumu saldu. *All's good in a famine.*

Kad **bads** pa durvīm iekšā, tad mīlestība pa logu ārā. *When want comes in at the door, love flies out of the window.*

Bagātais liels arī bez galvas. *A rich man's foolish sayings pass for wise ones.*

Bailēm lielas acis. *The fear is greater than the reason for it.*

Kas **bailīgs**, tas vainīgs. *The guilty one always runs.*

Pārlieku **bargam** būt neder. *Chide not severely nor punish hastily.*

Baro nu suni, kad vilks jau kūtī! *There is no use in closing the barn door after the horse is stolen.*

Kam tuvāk **baznīca**, tam tālāk Dievs. *The nearer the church, the farther from God.*

Visi nav svēti, kas **baznīcā** iet. *All are not saints that go to church.*

Bēdas līdz ar laiku skrien. *There is no pain so great that time will not soften.*

Bēdas nenāk bez biedriem. *Sorrow never comes singly.* / *Trouble loves company.*

Bēda pie bēdas. *Trouble comes in bunches.*

Dalītas **bēdas**—pusbēdas, dalīti prieki—divkārši prieki. *Two in distress make sorrow less.*

Katram savas **bēdas**. *Everybody has his troubles.*

Tikko vienas **bēdas** nobēdātas, otras klāt. *Trouble comes in bunches.*

Kas citam **bedri** rok, pats iekrīt. *If you dig a ditch for your neighbor, you will fall into it yourself.* / *He that mischief hatches, mischief catches.*

Kas beigts, no tā nav ko **bīties**. *Dead men never bite.*

Vecam maza **bērna** prāts. *An old man is twice a boy.*

13

Bērni ir kā kociņi, ko var locīt. *Bend the tree while it is young.*

Bērni un muļķi runā patiesību. *Children and fools speak the truth.*

Mazi **bērni**, maza bēda; lieli bērni, liela bēda. *Little children, little troubles; big children, big troubles.*

Mazi **bērni** spiež ceļus, lieli—sirdi. *Little children step on your toes; big children step on your heart. / When a child is little, it pulls at your apron strings; when it gets older, it pulls at your heart strings.*

No **bērniem** prāta ļaudis nāk. *Wanton kittens may make sober cats.*

Bērns, kas vienreiz pirkstu apdedzinājis, bīstas uguns. *A burned child dreads the fire.*

Ieglabāts **bērns** grib glabājams. *Give a child his will and help his fill, and neither will thrive. / With seven nurses a child will be without eyes.*

Jau **bērns** rāda, kāds būs vīram tikums. *Bad boys make bad men.*

Kad **bērns** nomiris, tad vecmātes gudras. *Hindisght is better than foresight.*

Kamēr **bērns** vēl jauns, vari viņu kā kociņu locīt. *A young tree is easier twisted than an old tree.*

Katram savs **bērns** tas mīļākais. *Each old crow thinks her young are the blackest. / Every mother's duck is a swan.*

Ko **bērns**, jauns būdams, redz un dzird, to viņš patur visā savā mūžā. *What is learned in the cradle lasts to the grave.*

Viena **bezdelīga** vasaru nenes. *One swallow does not make a summer.*

Bībele padusē, bet brauc velna darbos. *An angel on the street, a devil at home.*

Kas **bijis**, izbijis. *Let bygones be bygones.*

Ne**bīsties** no nāves—vienreiz tā kā tā jāmirst. *Dying is as natural as living.*

Zagtas bites nepadosies. *He who steals will always fail.*

Blēdība pati sev rīkstes griež. *Chickens will always come home to roost.*

Blēdis blēdi pazīst. *A thief knows a thief as a wolf knows a wolf.*

Ātri tikai **blusas** ķeŗ. *Attempt not too hastily nor pursue too eagerly.*

Tukša **blusa** augstu lec. *The balloon with the most air makes the loudest noice when it bursts.*

Pie pilnas **bļodas** draugu daudz. *In time of prosperity, friends will be plenty; in time of adversity, not one in twenty.*

Pie sasistas **bļodas** draugu nav. *When fortune frowns, friends are few.*

Priekš **bojā** iešanas nāk lepns prāts. *Pride comes before a fall.*

Brālis brāli ienīst. *The wrath of brothers is the wrath of devils.*

Vienādi **brāļi** kopā rodas. *Each kind attracts its own. / Birds of a feather flock together.*

Kam **brandvīns** galvā, tam prātiņš vējā. *When the ale is in, wit is out.*

Kas pirmais **brauc**, pirmais maļ. *He who comes first grinds first. / First come, first served.*

Kad iz**braucis**, tad jābrauc; kad ko iesācis, tad jāpabeidz. *Do a thing and have done with it.done with it.*

Lēnāk **brauksi**, tālāk tiksi. *Make haste slowly. / Slow and easy wins the race.*

Ne**brēc**, kamēr rīkste vēl pacelta. *Don't holler before you are hurt.*

Liela **brēka**, maza vilna. *Great cry but little wool. / Much ado about nothing.*

Vecam **bukam** stīvi ragi. *The older the buck, the stiffer the horn.*

C

Cāļus skaita rudenī. *Don't count your chickens before they are hatched.*

Cālis grib vistu mācīt! *Eggs can't teach the hen.*

Ne**cel** āzi par dārznieku! *Don't set a wolf to watch the sheep.*

Kāds **celms**, tāda atvase. *Like begets like.*

Ko nevar **celt**, to nevar nest. *Undertake no more than you can perform.*

Ko nevar **celt**, to var pavilkt. *By hook or by crook.*

Kas augstu **ceļas**, tas dziļi dubļos veļas. *The higher they go, the lower they fall. / A man on a pinnacle has nowhere to go but down.*

Vistaisnākais **ceļš** visīsākais. *The shortest distance between two points is a straight line.*

Akls aklam **ceļu** rāda, abi iekrīt grāvī. *If the blind lead the blind, both shall fall into the ditch.*

Nekur ar gataviem **cepešiem** pretī nenāk. *There is no free lunch.*

Ne**ceri** uz to, kas vēl nav rokā! *Do not anxiously hope for what is not yet come; do not vainly regret what is already past.*

Cerība cilvēku spēcina. *Hope keeps the heart from breaking.*

Cerība neatstāj kaunā. *He who has hope has everything.*

Kur **cērt**, tur skaidas lec. *Let the chips fall where they may.*

Kāda **cibiņa**, tāds vāciņš. *There is a lid for every pot.*

Ciema kukulis allaž gards. *Vegetables from your neighbor's garden are always the best.*

Cilvēka mūžs raibs kā [pupas zieds/dzeņa vēders]. *Life is just one damned thing after another.*

Nav **cilvēka**, kas visiem spētu iztapt. *You can't please everybody.*

Cilvēkam jāmācās kamēr dzīvs. *Live and learn.*

Nevienam **cilvēkam** nevar iekšā ielīst. *None knows where the shoe pinches like the one who wears the shoe.*

Cilvēki mirst kā lapas birst. *Here today, gone tomorrow.*

Cilvēks domā, Dievs dara. *Man proposes, God disposes.*

Cilvēks mācās, līdz kāju kapā speŗ. *Live and learn.*

Cilvēks nedzīvo no maizes vien. *Man cannot live by bread alone.*

Cilvēks niknāks nekā zvērs. *Man is a wolf to man.*

Cilvēks var atmest ieradumu, bet ne dabu. *Nature passes nurture.*

Izsalcis **cilvēks** daudz nedzird. *A hungry stomach has no ears.*

Kas tas **cilvēks** ir : te viņš ir, te viņa nav. *Here today, gone tomorrow.*

Katrs **cilvēks** maldās. *Mistakes will happen.*

Cilvēku pazīst, kad kopā puds sāls apēsts. *Before you make a friend, eat a peck of salt with him.*

Daudz **cilvēku**, daudz prātu. *As many men, so many opinions.*

Kādu tik to **cilvēku** pasaulē nav! *It takes [all kinds of people/all sorts of folk] to make up the world.*

Sader kā **cimds** ar roku. *Hand in glove.*

Mazs **cinītis** gāž lielu vezumu. *A little stone may upset a large cart. / One lose pebble can start a landslide. / Small leaks sink big ships.*

Labāk **cirvis** bez kāta nekā vīrs bez prāta. *Better sense in the head than cents in the pocket.*

Bez **cirvja** ne paegli nenocirtīsi, bez padoma ne pirti neizkurināsi. *You can't go far in a rowboat without oars.*

Cūka galvu nokož, ķēniņš nepieliek. *What is done cannot be undone.*

Izpeldināta **cūka** no jauna dubļos vārtās. *Wash a hog and it will return to its wallow.*

Kāda **cūka**, tādi sivēni. *The she-goat brings no sheep into the world.*

Kas nu **cūkai** dos kartupeļus dēstīt! *Don't set a wolf to watch the sheep.*

Nekaisi **cūkai** pērles priekšā! *Don't cast your pearls before swine.*

Cūku maisā nevar pirkt. *Don't buy a pig in a poke.*

Č

Kas **čīkst**, tas jāsmērē. *The wheel that does the squeaking is the one that gets the grease.*

Kas **čukst**, tas melo. *Where there is whispering, there is lying.*

D

Labs, ko **dabon**. *Be content with your lot.*

Ko **dabūjis**, par to pateicies. *Be content with your lot.*

Kur **dabūsi** suņu kūtī maizi. *The doghouse is no place to keep a sausage.*

No skopa var vēl ko **dabūt**, no tukša nekā. *Sue a beggar, and you'll get a louse.*

Kas labprāt **danco**, tam labprāt spēlē. *Everyone lays the burden on the willing horse.*

Ko ar klibu **dancot**, ko ar muļķi runāt. *Arguing with a fool shows there are two.*

Labāk ar klibu **dancot** nekā ar muļķi runāt. *Arguing with a fool shows there are two.*

Dar' nu velnam labu! *No gratitude from the wicked.*

Jā**dara**, vai patīk vai nepatīk. *Do what you ought, come what may. / Hew to the line; let the chips fall where they may.*

Kas jā**dara**, tas jādara—vai raudi, vai dziedi. *Do what you ought, come what may. / Hew to the line; let the chips fall where they may.*

Mudīgi pie **darba**, mudīgi pie ēšanas. *Quick at meat, quick at work.*

Paliec pie **darba**, ko tu proti. *Every man to his trade. / Do not meddle with business you know nothing about.*

Katram **darbam** savs ķēriens. *There are tricks in all trades.*

Labam **darbam** labi augļi. *A good deed bears a blessing for its fruit.*

Labi **darbi** ierakstīti jūrmalas smiltīs. *Good deeds are easily forgotten, bad deeds never.*

Ne visi **darbi** veicami ar spēku. *Skill is better than strength.*

Darbs ceļ vīru. *No man e'er was glorious who was not laborious.*

Darbs dara dzīvi saldu. *There is no greater cure for misery than hard work. / Taste the joy that springs from labor.*

Darbs darina meistaru. *Practice makes perfect.*

Darbs darītāju māca. *We learn by doing, achieve by pursuing.*

Kāds darbs, tādas drēbes. *Only the witless one expects the blacksmith to wear a white silk apron.*

Kamēr vēl **darbs** darāms, nevar gavilēt. *Never say "whoopee" before you jump.*

Jo **dārgs**, jo labs; jo lēts, jo slikts. *Cheap things are not good, good things are not cheap.*

Dari daudz, runā maz! *Less said, more done.*

Dari, kas jādara, un nebēdā! *Do what you ought, come what may. / Hew to the line; let the chips fall where they may.*

Dari ko dari, uz reizes padari! *Do a thing and have done with it.*

Dari ko darīdams, apdomā galu. *Action without thought is like shooting without aim.*

Dari sunim labu! *Rub a hog and he'll lay down on you.*

Ko **dari**, to dari ar rokām! *Do nothing by halves. / Anything worth doing is worth doing well.*

Ko **dari**, to dari kā vīrs! *Do boldly what you do at all. / Do what you do with all your might.*

Ko **dari**, to dari pie laika! *He acts well who acts quickly.*

Tā **dari**, ka vilks paēdis un kaza dzīva. *Live and let live.*

Daudzreiz **darīts** viegls top. *Repetition is the mother of skill.*

Kas **darīts**, padarīts. *What is done cannot be undone.*

Kas par **daudz**, tas par skādi. *Too much of a good thing is worse than none at all. / Nothing in excess is best.*

Dāvanas neliek uz svariem. *Don't look a gift horse in the mouth.*

Dāvanas nevajaga pelt. *Don't look a gift horse in the mouth.*

Kas man ne**deg,** to es nedzēšu. *If it ain't broke, don't fix it.*

Viss, kas pārlieku, ne**der** nenieku. *Nothing in excess is best. / Moderation in all things.*

Katrai **desai** divi gali. *Every path leads two ways.*

Desas nemeklē suņu stallī. *The doghouse is no place to keep a sausage.*

Dots **devējam** atdodas. *Give and you shall receive. / The hand that gives, gathers.*

Priecīgu **devēju** Dievs mīlē. *God loves the cheerful giver.*

Ar **diegiem** nav aršana. *You can't saw wood with a hammer.*

Laba tā **diena**, kuŗa pagājusi. *Praise a fine day at night.*

Ļauna **diena** paliek atmiņā. *A bad day never has a good night.*

Katra **diena** nav svētdiena. *Every day is not a holiday.*

Rītu ar vēl **diena**. *Tomorrow is a new day.*

Katrai **dienai** savas bēdas. *No day passes without some grief.*

Katrai **dienai** sava nakts. *Every day has its night, every weal its woe.*

Dieva darbi—pašam jāstrādā. *Pray to God, but keep hammering.*

Dieva dzirnavas maļ lēni, bet labi. *God's mill grinds slowly, but it grinds exceedingly fine.*

Dieva klētiņa allaž vaļā. *God is always opening his hand.*

Dieva roka zaļa, bagāta. *God is always opening his hand.*

Dievam viss iespējams. *All things are possible with God.*

Kur **Dievam** baznīca, tur arī velns savu skolu uzturēs. *Where God has a church, the devil has a chapel.*

Dievs deva saules gaismu, Dievs ir lietu dos. *The Lord sends sun at one time, rain at another.*

Dievs dod, Dievs ņem. *The Lord who gave can take away.*

Dievs dzīvo un gādā. *The Lord will provide. / God is in heavens and wll is well with the world.*

Dievs mutē, velns sirdī. *An angel on top but a devil underneath.*

Dievs pasargi mani no drauga! No ienaidnieka pats atsargāšos. *God protect me from my friends; my enemies I know enough to watch.*

Katrs par sevi, **Dievs** par visiem. *Every man for himself.*

Kur **divi**, tur trešais lieks. *Two is company, three is a crowd.*

Nedižojies ar to, kas vēl nav sasniegts. *Catch before hanging.*

Dod man, es došu tev. *Give a little, take a little.*

Dod sunim desu glabāt! *The doghouse is no place to keep a sausage.*

Jo **dod**, jo grib. *Give some people everything you have and they still want the moon. / The more you have, the more you want.*

Domā lēni, strādā drīz! *Whatsoever is well resolved on should be quickly performed.*

Ko nedzēris **domā**, to piedzēris runā. *What soberness conceals, drunkenness reveals.*

Domāt nevienam nevar aizliegt. *A man can't be hanged for his thoughts.*

Kas kaunīgam ko **dos**. *It is only the bashful that lose.*

Kā to var otram **dot**, kas pašam labi smeķ. *Every man drags water to his own mill.*

Kas **drabenēs** maisās, to cūkas ēd. *If you get mixed up in swill, you'll be eaten up by the swine. / If you mix with the bran, the cows will eat you.*

No **draudiem** neviens nemirst. *Sticks and stones may break my bones, but names will never hurt me.*

Esi **draugs**, bet ne uzreiz. *Of chance acquaintance beware. / Short acquaintance brings repentance.*

Labs **draugs** ir tā lielākā manta pasaulē. *A good friend is a great treasure.*

Labs **draugs**—reta manta pasaulē. *A faithful friend is better than gold.*

Neīsts **draugs** nav labāks par īstu ienaidnieku. *Better an open enemy than a false friend.*

Kāda **drēbe**, tāds ielāps. *The hole and the patch should be commensurable.*

Pa **dubļiem** vārtoties, pats dubļains paliksi. *You can't play in the dirt without getting dirty.*

Piedzēris izguļ **dullumu**, muļķis nekad. *A drunk man will sober up, but a damn fool never.*

Kur **dūmi**, tur uguns. *Where there is smoke, there is fire.*

Kur lieli **dūmi**, tur maz siltuma. *He that makes a fire of straw has much smoke but little warmth.*

No **dūmiem** kapiju vārīt nevar. *You can't make bricks without straw.*

Dusmas ir grūti valdīt. *Be master of your anger.*

Dusmās sirds neprot, kas labs, kas ļauns. *Anger and folly walk cheek by jowl.*

Dusmība paīsina dzīvību. *Quick resentments are often fatal.*

Kal **dzelzi** kamēr vēl karsta! *Strike while the iron is hot.*

Kā **dzen**, tā lien. *Action and reaction are equal.*

Nedzen dievu kokā, pēc ne lūgdams nenolūgsi. *Don't burn your bridges behind you.*

Nedzen vēju ar dūri! *Strive not against the stream.*

Katrs **dzied** savā meldijā. *Every man to his own opinion.*

Kāda **dzija**, tāda drēbe. *You can't make a good coat out of bad wool.*

Kas **dzimst**, tas mirst. *The first breath is the beginning of death.*

Daudz ko **dzirdēt**, maz ko runāt. *Listen much, speak little. / Talk less, listen more. / Have a wide ear and a short tongue./ Hear all and say nothing.*

Dzirdi daudz, runā maz. *Listen much, speak little. / Talk less, listen more. / Have a wide ear and a short tongue. / Hear all and say nothing.*

Kur **dzirkstele**, tur uguns. *Sparks become flame.*

Maza **dzirkstele** nodedzina lielu meēu. *A little spark kindles a great fire.*

No mazas **dzirksteles** liela uguns izceļas. *A little spark kindles a great fire.*

Pirmais **dzirnavās**—pirmais maļ. *He who comes first grinds first. / First come, first served.*

Būs tam, kas **dziŗas**. *Strive and succeed.*

Kāda **dzīve**, tāds gals. *An ill life, an ill end.*

Dzīvo tā, ka arī citi var dzīvot. *Live and let live.*

Dzīvo taupīgi, lai arī priekšdienām kas būtu. *He who does not economize must agonize.*

Kā **dzīvo**, tā mirst. *An ill life, an ill end.*

Kamēr **dzīvo**, tikmēr mācies. *Live and learn; die and forget all.*

Ne visi, kas kristīti, kristīgi **dzīvo**. *All are not saints that go to church.*

Ikviens grib **dzīvot**. *Everyone has to live.*

E

Ēd ko ēzdams, neapēd godu! *Desire nothing that would bring disgrace.*

Ēd ko ēzdams, neapēd sēklu! *Don't eat your father's seed potatoes.*

Jo **ēd**, jo gribas. *The more you eat, the more you want.*

Labāk **ēdiens** uz ēdiena nekā sitiens uz sitiena. *Honey catches more flies than vinegar. / Correction does much, but encouragement everything.*

Ēdis vai neēdis, turi galvu gaisā. *Hold up your head even if your tail does drag in the mud.*

Kādā **ēnā** sēdi, tādā priecājies. *Be content with your lot.*

Katram **ērmam** patīk paša bērni. *Every mother's duck is a swan.*

Ērms paliek ērms, kaučču zelta drēbes nēsājis. *An ape is an ape, a varlet is a varlet, though they be clad in silk and scarlet.*

Es citam, cits man. *Tit for tat.*

Kam gribas **ēst**, tam viss gards. *Appetite furnishes the best sauce*

Ēstgriba rodas ēdot. *The appetite comes while eating.*

Kur **ezi** aizkaŗ, tur bada. *Don't kill a hedgehog or porcupine with your bare fists.*

G

Gādā, bet ne pārlieku! *Care killed the cat.*

Ir labākajam **gadās**. *It happens to the best of us.*

Pirmie desmit **gadi** tie grūtākie. *The first hundred years are the hardest.*

Gaidi gaili pautu izdējam! *You can't get blood out of a turnip.*

Gaidi vien kā akmenim bērnu! *You can't get blood out of a turnip.*

Gaidīdams uz Dievu, ātri badā nomirsi. *God helps those who help themselves.*

Labs nāk ar **gaidīšanu**, silts ar sildīšanu. *All good things come to those who wait.*

No zila **gaisa** neviens nevar dzīvot. *A man cannot live on air.*

Viss nāk **gaismā**. *There is nothing covered that shall not be revealed, nor hidden that shallnot be known.*

Gals labs, viss labs. *All's well that ends well.*

Gals rāda, kāds tas darbs. *At the end of the work, you may judge the workman.*

Gals rādīs, kur būs. *It will all work out in the end.*

Labs **gals**, laba slava. *The end crowns the work.*

Kad **galva** rokā, ko par asti bēdā! *If you can get over the horse, you can get over the tail.*

Sirma **galva** jāgodā. *Respect your elders.*

Viena **galva**, viena bēda. *Single blessedness.*

Kas nav **galvā**, tas ir kājās. *What your head forgets, your heels must remember.*

Tukšā **galvā** allaž daudz lepnības. *The less the brains, the bigger the hat.*

Ja nav gudras **galvas**, turi vieglas kājas. *If you don't use your head, you must use your legs. / What your head forgets, your heels must remember.*

Daudz **galviņu**, daudz padomu. *So many heads, so many wits.*

Kur **gaļa**, tur kauli; kur āda, tur spalva. *Conveniences have their inconveniences, and comforts their crosses.*

Pats **gans**, pats vilks. *Don't set a wolf to watch the sheep.*

Glāb vien kaķi no nāves: viņš tev ieplēsīs rokā. *Rub a hog and he'll lay down on you.*

Kad **govij** astes vairs nav, tad tik zina, kam tā derējusi. *The cow knows not the value of her tail till she has lost it. / Cows don't know the good of the tail till fly time.*

Tas tikpat kā **govij** sedli. *You can't put a round peg in a square hole.*

Pati **govs** pienu deva, pati izspēra. *The cow gives a good pail of milk and then kicks it over.*

Kas **grasi** netaupa, pie rubļa netiek. *Take care of the dimes and the dollars will take care of temselves.*

Grasis pie graša iztaisa rubli. *Penny and penny laid up will be many.*

Katram savs **graustiņš** mīļš. *Each bird likes his own nest best.*

Pašam **grēka** maiss uz muguras, citam kulīti ierauga. *Men often condemn others for what they see no wrong in doing themselves.*

Grēks **grēku** dzemdē. *One sin another does provoke.*

Kāds **grēks**, tāda sodība. *Every sin carries its own punishment.*

Jo ātri **grib**, jo nevar. *The greater hurry, the worse speed.*

Ko pats ne**gribi**, to otram nedari. *Do unto others as you would have them do unto you.*

Ar labu **gribu** visu var panākt. *Nothing is impossible to a willing [heart/mind].*

Ne**grozait** velnam cepeti, ziemas laikā uz rijas krāsns staipīdamies. *The devil is always at the elbow of an idle man.*

Katram savas **grūtības**. *Everybody has his troubles.*

Kas **grūtumu** panes, dabū vieglumu. *Where the cross is, there is light.*

Vieglāk **gudram** būt priekš cita nekā pašam priekš sevis. *It is easier to give advice than to take it.*

Gudrība labāka par zeltu. *Intelligence is worth more than richness. / Better sense in the head than cents in the pocket.*

Gudrību nevar atsvērt ne ar naudu. *Wisdom is better than rubies.*

Guļot maizi necep. *No pains, no gains; no sweat, no sweet.*

Ko līdz lieli **gurķi**, kad tukši vidi. *Outside show, inside woe.*

Ģ

Ko **ģeld** pēc launaga karote. *After meat comes mustard.*

I

Jo vairāk **iegribas**, jo mazāk dabū. *All covet, all lose.*

Iejūdzies—velc! *Fish or cut bait.*

Labāk **iekod** mēli zobos nekā nevajadzīgu vārdu izteic. *Be silent if you have nothing worth saying.*

Labāk **ielāps** nekā caurums. *A patch is better than a hole.*

Viens **ienaidnieks** ir par daudz, simts draugu par maz. *He that has a thousand friends has not a friend to spare.*

Ko pats **ienīsti**, nedari citam. *Don't do to other what you would not have done to you.*

Ieradums ir otra daba. *Custom is a second nature.*

Ne**iesāc** nekā bez laika! *There is a time and place for everything.*

Ko slikti **iesāk**, to labi pabeidz. *A bad beginning makes a good ending.*

Reiz **iesāktais** jābeidz. *Don't start anyting you can't finish./ Never leave a task until it is done.*

Labi **iesākts** darbs ir jau pus padarīts. *Well begun is half done.*

Iesākumā nes ūdeni ar sietu, pēc ne ar spaini nevīžo atnest. *Alert in the beginning, negligent in the end.*

Kam **iesākumā** grūti iet, tam beigās laime smaida. *Bad start, good ending.*

Iesim vienu ceļu, kausim vienu teļu. *You scratch my back; I'll scratch yours.*

Kas skriešus **ieskrien**, tas lēkšus aizlec. *Hasty climbers have sudden falls.*

Kas ne**iet**, tas arl nekrīt. *It is better to sit still than to rise and fall.*

Kam **ir**, tam pieliek klāt; kam nav, no tā vēl atņem. *To him who has shall be given.*

Kam kas **ir**, no tā plēš; kam nekā nav, ko no tā plēsīs? *If you have nothing, you've got nothing to lose.*

Kad pirmo reizi **izdodas**, viss izdodas. *If you miss the first buttonhole, you will not succeed in buttoning up your coat.*

Kas labāk **izkliedz**, tas vairāk pārdod. *It pays to advertise.*

Ne**izlej** netīru ūdeni, kamēr tīra nav. *Don't throw away your dirty water until you get clean.*

Ne**izlej** pirms vecu ūdeni, kamēr jauns nav iesmelts. *Don't throw away your dirty water until you get clean.*

Izsalkušam viss gards. *Hunger makes hard beans sweet. / Hungry dogs will eat dirty pudding.*

Izskats pieviļ. *Appearances are deceiving./ Looks often deceive.*

Visiem **iztikdams**, sev sariebsi. *He labors in vain who tries to please everybody.*

Izvelc suni no ūdens, viņš tev iekož rokā. *Rub a hog and he'll lay down on you.*

J

Katram ir savs **jājamzirdziņš**. *Every man has his hobby.*

Ne**jauc** vecus mēslus! *Don't wake a sleeping lion. / It is best to let a sleeping dog lie.*

Kad **jaunībā** izpriecāsies, tad būs vecumā ko atminēt. *Every man must sow his wild oats.*

Ko **jaunumā** nemācies, vecumā nepratīsi. *What we learn early we remember late.*

Kad viens **jūrā** noslīkst, vai tamdēļ tur nebrauks? *He that fears leaves must not come into a wood.*

K

Labāk labs **kaimiņš** nekā slikts draugs. *Who has a good neighbor has a good friend.*

Kāda **kaite**, tāda zāle. *For every ill beneath the sun, there is a remedy or none.*

Katram sava **kaite** sāp. *Every man thinks his own burden the heaviest.*

Kaķim deviņas dzīvības. *A cat has nine lives.*

Kaķim gribas zivtiņu ēst, bet negribas kāju slapināt. *The cat that would eat fish must wet her feet.*

Kaķim spēle, pelei nāve. *One man's pleasure is another man's poison.*

Kaķis ar cimdiem peļu neķeŗ. *The cat in gloves catches no mice.*

Kaķis pieglaudies plēš. *He who plays with a cat must expect to be scratched.*

Kad **kaķis** nav mājās, tad peles danco. *While the cat's away, the mice will play.*

Kas **kalējam** par zāli, tas skroderim par nāvi. *One man's meat is another man's poison.*

Kapā līdzi neņemšu. *You can't take it with you.*

Kapā paliek zelta kalns, kapā arī nabaga tarba. *The grave levels all distinctions. / Death is a great leveler.*

Kapā visām bēdām gals. *Only in the grave is there rest.*

Kapam neviens gaŗām nav ticis. *The grave will receive us all.*

Kapeika pati no griestiem nekrīt. *Money does not grow on trees.*

Bez **kapeikas** rublis nav pilns. *Pennies make dollars.*

Kas **kapeiku** netaupa, pie rubļa netiek. *Take care of the dimes and the dollars will take care of themselves.*

Kas uz **kapiem** aizvests, tam tur jāpaliek. *From the cemetery no one is brought back.*

No **kapiem** augšā necelsies. *Death is permanent.*

Kaps visus samierina. *A piece of churchyard fits everybody.*

Jo augstu **kāpj**, jo zemu krīt. *Climb not too high lest the fall be great.*

Kas rāmi **kāpj**, droši iet. *Do what you do carefully.*

Pie ielauztas **karašas** visi ķeŗas. *All dogs bite the bitten dog.*

Ne**kāro** visiem iztikt. *You can't please everybody. / He labors in vain who tries to please everybody.*

Vienas **kārtas** putni kopā skrien. *Birds of a feather flock together.*

Kam nav **kauna**, tam nav goda. *He who has no shame has no honor.*

Kas vairs ne**kaunās**, ar tādu viss pagalam. *Past shame, past grace.*

Kaunēdamies tālu netiksi. *Bashfulness is a great hindrance to a man.*

Kam ar stiprāku **kauties**, kad no tā var izbēgt. *Discretion is the better part of valor.*

Dažai **kazai** āža ragi, tomēr kaza paliek kaza. *An ass is an ass though laden with gold.*

Pēc **kāzām** visi gudri. *Hindsight is better than foresight.*

Kam labi **klājas**, tas top pārgalvīgs. *Too much prosperity makes most men fools.*

Ne**kliedz** urrā, kad vilks vēl purā. *Don't halloo till you're out of the woods.*

Klusēšana arī ir atbilde. *No answer is also an answer.*

Kļūdīties ir cilvēciski. *To err is human.*

Ar ļaunu ne**kļūsi** projām. *He who does evil comes to an evil end.*

Mazs **kociņš** lokāms, neba vairs liels. *A young twig is easier twisted than an old tree.*

Ne no katra **koka** var svilpes griezt. *You can't make a silk purse out of a sow's ear.*

Katram **kokam** divi gali. *There are two sides to everything.*

Veci **koki** grūti lokāmi. *An old tree is hard to straighten.*

Koks, kas čīkst, tik ātri nelūst. *A squeaking gate hangs the longest.*

Koks nekrīt ar pirmo cirtienu. *The first blow does not fell the tree.*

Kāds **koks**, tādas lapas. *Like begets like.*

Kāds **koks**, tādi augļi. *A tree is known by its fruit.*

Pārdēstīts **koks** labi neaug. *A tree often transplanted neither grows nor thrives.*

Augstus **kokus** visi vēji aizķeŗ. *Tall trees catch much wind. / The highest branch is not the safest roost.*

Kopu cūka nebarojas. *The common horse is worst shod.*

Netaisns **krājums** atkal izput. *Ill-gotten goods prosper not long.*

Ja **krāsni** nekurināsi, istabu nesildīsi. *Action is the basis of success.*

Krauklis krauklim acis ārā neknābs. *A crow does not pull out the eye of another crow.*

Krekls tuvāks nekā svārki. *The shirt is nearer than the coat.*

Katram savs **krekls** tuvākais. *Close sits my shirt, but closer my skin.*

Katram savs **krusts** jānes. *Every man must bear his own burden.*

Katrai **krūzītei** sava osiņa. *Every bullet has its billet.*

Kāds **kubulītis**, tāds vāciņš. *There is a lid for every pot.*

Lielam **kuģim** dziļa peldēšana. *A great ship asks for deep water.*

Kukuļu nesējs visur mīļš. *Every man loves a man who gives gifts. / Liberal hands make many friends.*

Kulē bāžams maisā nelien. *You can't put a round peg in a square hole.*

Apēstu **kumosu** nevar atrīt. *You can't eat the same bread twice.*

Kunga dots—jāēd, vai čīkst vai nečīkst. *The dependent man must dine late and eat leftovers.*

Ar **kungiem** nav labi dalīties. *Those that eat cherries with great persons shall have their eyes squirted out with stones.*

Diviem **kungiem** nevar kalpot—viem iztiks, otram sariebs. *No man can serve two masters.*

Lieliem **kungiem** ir gaŗas rokas. *Kings have long arms.*

Kāds **kungs**, tāds kalps. *Like master, like man.*

Kurpniek, kur lieste! *Shoemaker, stick to your last.*

Kas dos **kurpniekam** labus zābakus. *All cobblers go barefoot. / He that makes shoes goes barefoot. / The shoemaker's child goes barefoot.*

Lai **kurpnieks** paliek pie savām liestēm. *Shoemaker, stick to your last.*

Kad nav **kviešu** maizes, tad garda arī rudzu maize. *If you have no bacon, you must be content with cabbage.*

Ķ

Šodien **ķēniņš**– rītu mironis. *Kings and queens must die, as well as you and I.*

Ķer nu vilku pi astes! *It is difficult to take a wolf by the ears.*

Neķer ezi ar plikām rikām. *Don't kill a hedgehog or porcupine with your bare fists.*

Kur **ķerru** stumj, tur ķerra iet. *Where the needle goes, the thread follows.*

Kas ātri ķeŗ, tam pirksti deg. *Careless hurry may cause endless regrets.*

Kur ķīli dzen, tur ķīlim jālien. *Where the needle goes, the thread follows.*

L

Laba daudz nevajag. *Good things come in small packages.*

Labs nav bez ļauna. *Where there is light there is shadow.*

Labs pats no sevis labs. *Virtue is its own reward.*

Labāk ar **labu** nekā ar ļaunu. *Honey catches more flies than vinegar.*

Divi ir **lāci** veic. *Four hands can do more than two.*

Lācim ikreizes nevar teikt, ka viņš ir lācis. *The truth cannot always be told.*

Lācis vēl nav rokā, kad ādu jau pārdod. *Don't count your chickens before they are hatched. / First catch your hare before you skin it.*

Nelaid maizi gar durvīm! *Opportunities neglected are lost.*

Laiki mainās. *Times change, and we change with them.*

Citi laiki, citi tikumi. *Other times, other customs.*

Veci laiki, veci darbi; jauni laiki, jauni darbi. *Times change, and we change with them.*

Laiks matus balina, bet prātu nebriedina. *Age makes a man white but not better.*

Laiks padomu spriež. *Good counsel never comes too late.*

Laiks paņem visas bēdas. *Time erases all sorrows. / Time heals all wounds. / Time is a true friend to sorrow.*

Laiks pārgroza daudzas lietas. *Time changes the oak into a coffin. / Time and patience change the mulberry leaf to satin.*

Laiks pieved augļus. *Time ripens all things.*

Laiks rādīs. *Time will tell.*

Laiks visu atklāj. *Time brings everything to light.*

Nāks laiks, nāks padoms. *Good counsel never comes too late.*

Visam savs laiks. *Everything has its time.*

Laima nepalīdz, ja pats nepalīdzas. *Fortune helps him that is willing to help himself.*

Laime aizskrien skriešus, nelaime lien līšus. *Misfortune arrives on horseback but departs on foot.*

Laime ar nelaimi blakus turas. *Fortune and misfortune are next door neighbors.*

Laime [drīz mainās/nav pastāvīga]. *Fortune is fickle.*

Laime nenāk viena—nelaime nāk viņai līdz. *Sorrow treads upon the heels of mirth.*

Laime padara glēvu, nelaime dūšīgu. *Adversity makes men; prosperity monsters.*

Laime un glāze vārīgas lietas. *Fortune is like glass: it breaks when it is brightest.*

Kad laime ir klāt, tad viss vedas. *If you are lucky, even your rooster will lay eggs.*

Kam laime rokā, tas var lēti iebandoties. *He dances well to whom fortune pipes.*

Kam laime, tam draugs. *The friends of the unlucky are far away.*

Kam ir laime, tam ir vērsim teļš atneseas. *If luck is with you, even your ox will give birth to a calf.*

Kam **laimes** nav kāršu spēlē, tam laime mīlestībā. *Lucky at cards, unlucky in love.*

Katrs pats savas **laimes** kalējs. *Every man is the architect of his own fortune. / No one else will do it for you.*

Nelaid garām **laimes** brīdi. *When fortune knocks, open the door. / When fortune smiles, embrace her.*

Negaidi **laimi** ar cimdiem rokā. *Depend not on fortune but on conduct.*

Lakstīgalai nesmukas spalvas, bet smuka dziesma. *A pearl is often hidden in an ugly shell.*

Lepnība ceļ kaunu. *Prides goes before, and shame follows after.*

Lepnība nāk uz krišanu. *Pride comes before fall.*

Lepnība un kauns ir abi rada gabali. *Pride goes before, and shame follows after.*

Lepnums un posts nav tālu viens no otra. *Pride and poverty go hand in hand.*

Ne**lepojies** ar vārdiem, bet ar darbiem. *Let your actions be equal to your promises.*

Kur **līdz** darbs, neskaiti pātarus. *Pray to God, but keep hammering.*

Ne**liec** runci piena podam par sargu. *Don't put the fox to guard the henhouse.*

Nelieli dienu pirms vakara, mūžu pirms nāves. *Praise a fine day at night.*

Kā tie **lielie**, tā tie mazie. *As the old cock crows, the young cock learns. / As the dogs bark, the young ones learn.*

Laba **lieta** ne tik ātri izdarāma. *Good and quickly seldom meet.*

Katrai **lietai** divas puses. *Everything has two sides. / There are two sides to everything. / There is a good and a bad side to everything.*

Katrai **lietai** savas beigas. *All things [have/come to] an end.*

Vaļā **lietas** zaglim ceļu rāda. *Lock your door and keep your neighbors honest.*

Visas labas **lietas** trīs. *What happens twice, happens thrice.*

Pēc **lietus** saule spīd. *Sun follows the rain. / After the clouds, the sun shines.*

Arī mazs **lietutiņš** slapina. *A small rain lays a great dust.*

Kas **likstā** dodas, likstā aiziet. *He that loves danger shall perish therein.*

Katram savs **liktenis**. *You cannot escape your fate.*

Kas grib **linus** plūkt, tam nevajag grečus sēt. *He who sows brambles reaps thorns.*

Lišķim salda mēle. *Flattery is sweet food to those who can swallow it.*

Loki koku, kamēr vēl mazs. *Bend the [twig/tree] while it is [green/young].*

Loks, pārāk liekts, lūst. *A bow too much bent will break.*

Jaunam **lopa** dienas. *Youth will have its fling.*

Nedar' pāri **lopiņiem**: pirmie Dievam sūdzētāji. *Be kind to dumb animals.*

Lops paliek lops. *You cannot take the grunt out of a pig.*

Ļ

Veciem **ļaudīm** vājas kājas, bet stiprs prāts. *Men grow weaker and wiser.*

Kad nedari **ļauna**, tad nebīsties kauna. *Do no evil and fear no harm.*

Ļauns ļaunam atdodas. *He who does harm should expect harm.*

M

Nemāci kaķi peles ķert. *Don't try to teach your grandmother how to suck eggs.*

Viltīga **mācība** ievelkas. *An evil lesson is soon learned.*

Cauru **maisu** nepiepildīsi. *A broken sack will not hold corn.*

Kas **maita** bijis, tas maita paliek. *Once a crook, always a crook.*

Kur **maita**, tur kraukļi. *Where the carcass is, there the eagles gather.*

Apēsta **maize** grūti pelnāma. *It is hard to pay for bread that has been eaten.*

Kas izsalcis, tam rūgta **maize** salda. *For a good appetite there is no hard bread. / Hunger sweetens what is bitter.*

Kur **maize** bez garozas, gaļa bez kauliem! *You have to take the bitter with the sweet. / Every sweet has its bitter.*

Nav **maizes** bez garozas, nav darba bez grūtuma. *You must take the sour with the sweet.*

Kā **maizi** ēd, tā dziesmu dzied. *Whose bread I eat, his song I sing.*

Kas **māk**, tam nāk. *He who has an art has a place anywhere.*

Solīts **makā** nekrīt. *Promises fill no sack.*

Bez **mākas** nevar ne cūku sapīt. *It's all in knowing how.*

Ikviens var maldīties. Mistakes will happen.

Sausa **malka** drīz kaist. *Wood half-burnt is easily kindled.*

Kur **maļ**, tur birst. *There is no corn without chaff.*

Kam liela **manta**, tam liela bēda. *Anxiety attends increase of wealth.*

Kur **manta**, tur liela sirds. *Where your treasure is, there will your heart be also.*

Netaisna **manta** rokā izkūst. *Ill-gotten goods prosper not long.*

Netaisni iegūta **manta** augļus nenes. *Treasures of wickedness profit nothing.*

Kas pēc **mantas** prec, tas mantu apprec. *He that marries for money earns it.*

Mantu zaudēt—nekas nav zaudēts; godu zaudēt—daudz zaudēts; dūšu zaudēt—viss zaudēts. *Money lost, nothing lost; courage lost, much lost; honor lost, more lost; soul lost, all lost.*

Māņu cerības dažu nerro. *A false-grounded hope is but a waking man's dream. / A vain hope flatters the heart of a fool. / Don't feed yourself on false hopes.*

Kāda **māte**, tāda meita. *As is the mother, so is the daughter.*

Ne ikdienas **māte** raušus cep. *Everyday is not a holiday.*

Gaŗi **mati,** īss padoms. *Long hair, little brains.*

Lai **mazs**, kad tik labs. *Quality is better than quantity.*

Kas **mazumu** nesmādē, dabū daudz. *Many littles make a lot. / Many a mickle makes a muckle.*

Kas nesāk ar **mazumu**, tas savu mūžu netiks pie lieluma. *He that will not stoop for pin will never be worth a pound. / Add little to little and there will be a great heap.*

Daudzi **meistari** darbu saķēzī. *Too many cooks spoil the broth.*

Meistars no debesīm nekrīt. *Masters are made, not born.*

Neviens par **meistaru** nav piedzimis. *Masters are made, not born.*

Meita bez tikuma kā putra bez aizdara. *A fair woman without virtue is like stale wine.*

Meklē, tad atradīsi—klaudzini, tad atvērs. *Seek and you shall find; knock and it shall be opened unto you.*

Kas **meklē**, tas atrod. *Seek and you shall find.*

Mēle bez kauliem. *Man's tongue is soft and bone does lack, yet a stroke therewith may break a man's back.*

Mēle maza, bet lielas lietas pastrādā. *The tongue is a little thing, but fills the universe with trouble.*

Mēle nokauj, mēle pakaŗ. *The tongue wounds more than the arrow.*

Asa **mēle** ātri atgriežas. *Ridicule is a weak weapon.*

Asa **mēle** griež vairāk nekā nazis. *Slander is sharper than the sword. / No sword bites so fiercely as an evil tongue.*

Gaŗa **mēle** piesolīt, īsa roka padot. *Men apt to promise are apt to forget.*

Ja **mēle** mutē—nepazudīsi. *He who uses his tongue will reach his destination.*

Meli ir velna bērni. *A liar is worse than a thief.*

Ar **mēli** mutē nevar maldīties. *He who uses his tongue will reach his destination.*

Ar **mēli** var otram muguru pārlauzt. *Man's tongue is soft and bone does lack, yet a stroke therewith may break a man's back.*

Kas **mēli** palaiž, tam slikti iet. *The jawbone does the mischief.*

Ka **mēli** satur, tad labi iet. *Confine your tongue, lest it confine you.*

Meliem īsas kājas: drīz var panākt. *A liar has no legs. / Liars have short wings. / A liar is sooner caught than a cripple.*

Ar **meliem** tālu netiek. *You can get far with a lie, but not come back. / A lie runs until it is overtaken by the truth.*

No **meliem** ausis kust. *Liar, liar, pants on fire.*

Melnums baltumā labi atspīd. *The darker the night, the brighter the candle.*

Kas deviņreiz **melo**, tam netic, kaut desmitoreiz taisnību runā. *No one believes a liar when he tells the truth.*

Kas **melo**, tas zog. *A liar is worse than a thief.*

Melus drīz daudzina. *A lie can go a mile before truth can put its boots on.*

Ne**mērī** citus ar savu olekti. *Don't measure my corn by our bushel. / Don't judge others by yourself.*

Ne**mēro** visus pēc vienas mērauklas. *Don't measure my corn by your bushel.*

Ar kādu **mēru** mērīsi, ar tādu tev atmērīs. *The measure you give will be the measure you get.*

Jo **mēslus** rakā, jo mēsli smird. *The more you stir a stink, the louder it smells.*

At**mēz** papriekšu savas nama durvis, tad otra. *Sweep in front of your own door first.*

Lai katrs **mēž** savu durpriekšu, tad visas malas būs tīras. *Sweep in front of your own door first. / Sweep the dirt from in front of your own door, and don't worry about your neighbor's.*

No **meža** ābeles gardus ābolus nesagaidīt. *Plant the crab tree where you will, it will never bear pippins.*

Uz **meža** zemi nevajaga mēslus vest. *The man who carries coal to Newcastle will pour water on a drowned mouse.*

Uz **mežu** malku neved. *The man who carries coal to Newcastle will pour water on a drowned mouse.*

Miers baro, nemiers posta. *Peace feeds, war wastes; peace breeds, war consumes.*

Ko **mīlē**, tas tiek pārmācīts. *He who loves well chastises well.*

Mīlestība ir akla. *Love is blind.*

Mīlestība nav pērkama, bet iegūstama. *Love can neither be bought nor sold; its only price is love.*

Mīlestība neļaunojas, kad arī tiek ar suni rīdīta. *A blow from a lover is as sweet as eating raisins.*

Kur papriekšu liela **mīlestība**, tur pēc liela ienaidība. *Love is akin to hate.*

Pirmā **mīlestība** nerūsē, kaut septiņus gadus renstelē gulējusi. *First love, last love, best love.*

Veca **mīlestība** nerūs. *Old love does not rust.*

Mīlestībai nav neviens žogs par augstu. *Love knows no obstacles and grows with them.*

Mīlestības dāvanas nedara nabagu. *No one becomes poor through giving alms.*

Mīlestību, uguni un kāsuli nevar paslēpt. *Love and smoke cannot be hidden.*

Milti gaisā, sēnalas maisā. *Don't put the cart before the horse.*

Nevienam **milti** nebirst nemaļot. *No one else will do it for you.*

Neskaties uz **mirdzumu**, bet uz labumu! *Judge not according to appearances.*

Miris neizpļāpās. *Dead men tell no tales.*

Kas **miris**, augšā necelsies. *Death is permanent.*

Vecam jāmirst, jauns nomirst. *Old men go to death, but death comes to young men. / The young men die; the old must die.*

Visiem reiz jā**mirst**. *All men must die.*

žēl bij **mirt** bajāram, paliek mantas pakaļā. *A rich man is happy while he is alive but sorry when he dies.*

Mori nevar baltu nomazgāt. *Soap and water will not make a Negro's face white. / A crow is no whiter for being washed.*

Tukša **muca** tālu skan. *An empty barrel makes the most noise.*

Muižinieks brauc ar sešiem zirgiem, nabags iet ar diviem spieķiem, bet pie kapa panāk to. *Death is no respecter of persons.*

Mūk kā žurkas no grimstoša kuģa. *Rats desert a sinking ship.*

Kad **muļķi** runā, tad gudrie stāv klusu. *When the argument flares up, the wise man quenches it by silence.*

Ko ar **muļķi** runāt, ko ar pliku plūkties. *Never argue with a child or a fool.*

Muļķim dienu mūžu/vienmēr laime. *Fortune favors fools.*

Muļķim muļķības atliku likām. *There is no ass but brays.*

Muļķis paliek muļķis. *If an ass goes traveling, he'll not come back a horse.*

Katrai **mušai** savs zirneklis. *There is no flying from fate.*

Klusa **mute** neizpļāpās. *A still tongue tells no tales.*

Piedzērusi **mute** izpļāpā visu, kas uz sirds. *All alcohol shows the inner man.*

Skaista **mute** un skaista sirds reti gadās kopā. *A fair face may hide a foul heart.*

Ar **muti** Rīgā, ar darbiem aizkrāsnē. *Long on promise, short on performance. / He who talks boldly is quick to run away.*

Mutē medus, sirdī ledus. *Soft of speech, hard of heart.*

Mūža galu neviens nevar saredzēt. *There is no way of knowing when death will come; it just does.*

Mūžā jāredz daža diena gan balta, gan nebalta. *Life is subject to ups and downs.*

Mūžs sūrs kā vērmeles. *Tears and troubles are the lot of all.*

Mūžu dzīvo, mūžu mācies. *Live and learn.*

N

Nabadzība nav grēks. *Poverty is no sin.*

Kas viegli **nācis**, tas viegli iet. *Easy come, easy go.*

Kas **nagus** un mēli savalda, tam visur dzīvība salda. *He who conquers himself conquers the world.*

Sadedzinātus nagus pie uguns nebāzīs. *Once burned, twice shy.*

Kas lēni **nāk**, tas labi nāk. *Slow things are sure things./ Slow but sure.*

Kas pirmāk **nāk**, tas pirmāk dabū. *First come, first served.*

Naktī visi kaķi melni. *All cats are black at night.*

Nauda gudra—vīra rokā. *An arm and money require good hands.*

Nauda naudu pelna. *Money begets money.*

Nauda rokā visus loka. *Money talks.*

Nauda spēj daudz, mīlestība spēj visu. *Against love and fortune there is no defense.*

Nauda stiprāka par taisnību. *When money speaks, truth keeps its mouth shut.*

Kāda **nauda**, tāda prece. *You get what you pay for.*

Par **naudu** ir velns danco. *Money makes the pot boil. / Money makes the mare go.*

Par **naudu** viss dabūjams. *Money will do anything.*

Nāve nāk negaidāma. *Death keeps no calendar.*

Nāve nelūko gadus. *You are never too young to die.*

Nāves ceļš visiem jāstaigā. *Every man dies as he must.*

Priekš **nāves** zāļu nav. *There is a remedy for all things but death.*

Ar neasu **nazi** nevar pagriezt. *Dull scissors can't cut straight.*

Atgriezts **nazis** nekož. *Dull scissors can't cut straight.*

Kur **nekas** nav, tur nekas neiznāks. *From nothing, nothing is made. / Nothing happens for nothing.*

Nelaime ar nelaimi biedrojas. *Fortune and misfortune are next door neighbors. / Joy is kin to sorrow.*

Nelaime nenāk brēkdama. *Trouble arises when you least expect it.*

Nelaime nenāk viena. *Misfortunes seldom come alone.*

Kad **nelaime** notikusi, tad visi gudri. *Hindsight is better than foresight.*

Kas **nelaimē** dodas, tas nelaimē aiziet. *He that loves danger shall perish therein.*

Otra **nelaimei** nepriecājies! *Never find your delight in another's misfortune. / Rejoice not in another's sorrow.*

Nelaimes brīdi i vabole gaļa. *Hunger never saw bad bread.*

Kur **nelaimes** negaidi, tur nelaime notiek. *Trouble arises when you least expect it.*

No cita **nelaimes** galva nesāp. *Another's cares will not rob you of sleep.*

No **nelaimes** neizbēgsi! *Man is born unto trouble.*

Pēc **nelaimes** netrūkst padoms. *Hindsight is better than foresight.*

Nepateicība ir pasaules alga. *Ingratitude is the way of the world.*

Labāk **netaisnību** ciest nekā darīt. *It is better to suffer injustice than to do it.*

Nezāles neiznīkst. *Ill weeds always grow apace.*

Nezāles visur ielasās. *There's a bad apple in every box.*

Nieki nelīdz, darīšana līdz. *Doing is better than saying.*

Kas **niekiem** tic, tas pievilts kļūs. *He who believes easily is easily deceived.*

Kam **niez**, tas kasās. *Scratch where it itches.*

Septiņas reizes **nomēro**, vienreiz nogriez. *Measure twice bfore you cut once. / Measure your cloth ten times: you can cut it but once.*

Notes laikā velns mušas ēd. *When the devil hungers he will eat scraps.*

Kas noticis, tas noticis. Things done cannot be undone.

Pēc, kad **noticis**, visi gudri. *Hindsight is better than foresight.*

Notiek daudz kas, ko nedomā. *The unexpected often happens.*

Katrai **nūjai** divi gali. *Every medal has its reverse.*

Ņ

Ņem, kas rokā krīt. *Take while the taking is good.*

Ņēmējs nekad nebūs devējs. *A good borrower makes a poor lender.*

No tukša nevar daudz **ņemt**. *Where nothing is, no thing can be had.*

O

Kad **ozols** pie zemes guļ, tad katrs grib skaidas lasīt. *When the tree is fallen, everyone goes to it with his hatchet.*

P

Ar **pacietību** viss iespējams. *Everything comes to him who waits. / He that can have patience can have what he will.*

Pacietības zālīte visu neaug. *Patience is a flower that grows not in every garden.*

Ko tu bagātam **padarīsi**! *A rich man has the world by the tail.*

Ko pats vari **padarīt**, ar to nemoki citus. *Never trouble another for what you can do yourself.*

Ko vari **padarīt** šodien, to neatstāj uz rītu. *Never put off until tomorrow what you can do today.*

Kas **padarīts**, to nevar atdarīt. *What is done cannot be undone.*

Labs **padoms** dārgs. *Advice that ain't paid for ain't no good.*

Labs **padoms** vairāk vērts nekā nauda. *Good advice is beyond price.*

Viena **pagale** vien nedeg. *One actor cannot make a play. / One flower makes no garland.*

Kas pie **pagāzas** nāk, tam mieles jādzeŗ. *The devil takes the hindmost.*

Viena **pakava** nagla var zirgu nopostīt. *For the want of a nail, the shoe was lost; for want of a shoe, the horse was lost; for want of a horse, the rider was lost.*

Ar **paldies** vien nepietiek. *You can't put thanks into your pocket.*

Ko **palīdz** gailim pērle. *Don't cast your pearls before swine.*

Kas pirmais pamanās, tam tiek. First come, first served.

Pamātes sirds nav mātes sirds. *There are as many good stepmothers as white ravens.*

Izsalkušu ne**pamielosi** ar vārdiem. *Words never filled a belly. / Fair words butter no cabbage.*

Parāds grūta nasta. Debt is a hard taskmaster.

Paradumam liels spēks. *It is a thousand times easier to contract a new habit than to get rid of an old one.*

Labāk viens **paraugs** nekā simts vārdu. *Practice what you preach.*

Ne**pārdod** ādu, kad lācis vēl meēā! *Don't count your chickens before they are hatched.*

Pārgudrs sev pašam par skādi. *He who would be too clever makes a fool of himself.*

Pašslava—neslava. *The worst praise is self-praise. / Self-praise is no recommendation.*

Ar **pātagu** neizdabūsi no bērna tik daudz kā ar vārdiem. *Never take the whip when a word will do the turn.*

Ar **pātariem** vien nedzīvosi. *Pray to God, but keep hammering.*

Cik ir, tik jā**pateic**. *Be content with your lot.*

Viegli **pateikt**, ne tik viegli izdarīt. *It is easier said than done.*

Patiesība neslīkst ūdenī, nedeg ugunī. *Truth and oil always come to the top.*

Patiesība top reti uzņemta. *Truth is too heavy for most people to bear.*

Katram **patīk** sava dziesma. *Every bird likes to hear himself sing. / Every ass loves to hear himself bray. Everyone prefers his own.*

Vienam **patīk** māte, otram meita. *There is no accounting for taste. / Everyone to his own taste.*

Kur **patikšana**, tur satikšana. *If you'd be beloved, make yourself amiable.*

Labs jā**patur**, slikts jāatmet. *Cease to do evil, learn to do well.*

Kad **pavada** pilna, tad trūkst. *The tighter the burden strap, 'tis most likely to break.*

Kur daudz **pavāru**, tur putra piedeg. *Too many cooks spoil the broth.*

Tam jā**pazemojas**, kas nepatiesi paaugstinājies. *He who exalts himself shall be humbled.*

Ir **pelīte** čīkst, kad to min. *Even a rat, when cornered, will turn and fight.*

Mazai **pelītei** arīdzan ausis. *Little pitchers have big ears.*

Pērc, pērc no suņa desu! *The doghouse is no place to keep a sausage.*

Kas lēti **pērk**, tas dārgi maksā. *Cheap goods always prove expensive. / Cheapest is dearest.*

Pērkons sausu laiku apducina. *When the thunder is very loud, there's very little rain.*

Ja jāpeŗ, per, žēlodams ātrāk nobeigsi. *Spare the rod and spoil the child.*

Ne**pieber** vecu aku, kamēr jauna nav izrakta! *Cast no dirt in the well that gives you water.*

Ko negribi **piemirst**, to aizliec aiz auss. *What is well learned is not forgotten.*

Nevienam nav **pierē** rakstīts, kāds tas ir. *It is well that our faults are not written on our faces.*

Ar **pieri** caur sienu neizskriesi. *You can't fly with one wing.*

Bagāts ir tas, kam **pietiek**. *The poor are rich when they are satisfied. / Contentment is better than riches.*

Kam **pietiek** tā, ko Dievs devis, tam allaž dievsungan. *He who is content has enough.*

Kas **piķi** aiztiek, tas nosmērē sev pirkstus. *He who touches pitch will get black.*

No **pirksta** nevar neko izzīst. *You can't get feathers off a toad. / String cannot be made from stone.*

Kas vienreiz **pirkstu** ugunī bāzis, tas otrreiz vairs nebāzīs. *A burnt child dreads the fire.*

Noplucinājis **pirkstus**, sāksi pūst arī aukstu ūdeni. *Once bitten, twice shy.*

Plēs—vai tevi plēsīs! *Life is a matter of dog eat dog.*

Grūti ar pliku **plūkties**, ar muļķi runāt. *It is impossible to defeat an ignorant man in an argument.*

Ko **podā** liksi, to atkal izņemsi. *There comes nothing out of the sack but what was in it.*

Kāds **podiņš**, tāds vāciņš. *There is a lid for every pot. / Every pot has its cover.*

Pods katlam smejas—abi divi melni. *The pot calls the kettle black.*

Pods podu vārta—abi vienā melnumā. *The pot can't call the kettle black.*

Prasi sunim desu! *The doghouse is no place to keep a sausage.*

Prāts līdz ar cilvēku aug. *Sense comes with age.*

Prāts nāk ar gadiem. *Sense comes with age.*

Godīgs **prāts** visur iztiek. *Honesty is the best policy.*

Lepns **prāts** netāl no posta. *Self-conceit may lead to self-destruction.*

Mudrs **prāts** vairāk ģeld nekā visas skolas mācības. *A handful of common sense is worth a bushelful of learning.*

Ar **prātu** vairāk padara nekā ar spēku. *Brain is worth more than brawn.*

Ar gudru **prātu** var visu padarīt. *A good mind possesses a kingdom.*

Katrs savu **preci** slavē. *Every cook praises his own broth.*

Ja gribi daudz **pretinieku**, tad saki taisnību acīs. *Truth finds foes where it makes none.*

Ne**priecājies** par otra nelaimi, drīz pats vari tādā iekrist. *Don't rejoice about your neighbor's misfortune, for the same may happen to you.*

Nav **prieka** bez bēdām. *Every day has its night, every weal its woe. / No joy without annoy. / Into each life some rain must fall.*

Dalīti **prieki**—divkārši prieki. *A joy that's shared is a joy made double.*

Kad **put**, lai put—šauj pa jaunu! *Stick to your guns.*

Ir **putnam** spalva nokrīt. *Even a monkey will fall from a tree sometimes.*

Putniņu nenoķersi, ar roku mezdams. *Frightening a bird is not the way to catch it. / Without bait you can't catch fish.*

Kuŗš **putns** skrien, tas atmetas. *Every high-flying bird must at some time light.*

Tas ir slikts **putns**, kas savu ligzdu apgāna. *It's an ill bird that fouls its own nest.*

Ne ikkatrs **puisis**, kas var panest cirvi. *All are not hunters that blow the horn.*

Kas **purvā** iet, tam kājas mirkst. *He who would catch fish must not mind getting wet.*

Katram sava labā un kreisā **puse**. *Every man has his faults.*

Pusmutes laid, pusmutes satur'! *Short answers save trouble.*

Pūt nu pret vēju! *Puff not against the wind.*

Katram **putnam** sava ligzda mīļa. *Each bird likes his own nest best.*

Jaunie **putni** veco putnu dziesmu dzied. *As the old bird sings, so the young ones twitter.*

Putniņš, kas agri ceļas, agri degunu slauka. *The early bird catches the worm.*

Kāds **putns**, tāda lizda. *Little bird, little nest.*

Kur **putns** ligzdu taisa, tur tam arī jātup. *As one makes his bed, so must he lie.*

Putnu pazīst no dziesmas. *A bird is known by its note and a man by his talk.*

Kādu **putru** izvārīsi, tādu izstrēbsi. *He that makes himself an ass must not complain if men ride him.*

Kas karstu **putru** strebj, sadedzina lūpas. *A quick decision may speed you into disaster.*

R

Divi vairāk **redz** nekā viens. *Four eyes see more than two.*

Ko viens ne**redz**, to redz otrs. *Four eyes see more than two.*

Ikkatram sava **reize** nāk. *Every dog has his day.*

Pirmā **reizīte** tā grūtākā. *The first attempt is the most difficult.*

Kur divi **rejas,** tur trešais rij. *Two dogs fight for a bone, and third runs away with it.*

Otra **riebdams**, pats sev sariebsi. *Malice drinks its own poison.*

Nogriezts **rieciens** nepielīp. *You can always cut more wood off, but you cannot put it on again. / You can't unscramble eggs.*

Ko līdz lieli **rieksti**, ja vidū tārpi. *Outside show, inside woe.*

Rīga nav celta vienā dienā. *Rome was not built in a day.*

Asa **rīkste** dara bērnus rāmus. *A lot of child's welfare can be done with a razor strap.*

Kas otram **rīksti**, griež pats dabū pērienu. *He who lays a snare for another, himself falls into it. / He that mischief hatches, mischief catches. / When you plot mischief for others, you're preparing trouble for yourself.*

Aizsviesta **ripa** un izrunāts vārds vairs nenāk atpakaļ. *Time and words can never be recalled.*

Rīta darbs sokas. *He who rises early makes progress in his work.*

Rīta laiks—zelta laiks. *Morning hour has gold in its mouth.*

Rīta stunda—zelta stunda. *He who gets up early has gold in his mouth.*

Rīta stundai zelts mutē. *Morning hour has gold in its mouth.*

Rītā nezina, kāds būs vakars. *No day is over until the sun has set.*

Jāgaida, ko **rītdiena** sacīs. *Tomorrow is a new day. / There is always a tomorrow.*

Jo **riteņus** smērē, jo tie viegli skrej. *To make the cart go you must grease the wheels.*

Rīts gudrāks nekā vakars. *An hour in the morning is worth two in the evening.*

Visam savas **robežas**. *There is a limit to everything.*

Maza **rocība**, maz rūpju. *Little goods, little care.*

Roka rokai palīdz. *One knife sharpens another.*

Roka roku mazgā, abas baltas. *One hand washes the other.*

Labā **roka** nezina, ko kreisā dara. *Never let your left hand know what your right hand is doing.*

Trīcošām **rokām** nekā nepadarīsi. *Do boldly what you do at all.*

Rokas klēpī maizi nepelna. *A lazy dog finds no bone.*

Rokas pie arkla pielicis, neskaties atpakaļ! *He who puts his hand to the plow should never look back.*

Aukstas **rokas**, silta sirds. *A cold hand, a warm heart.*

Daudzas **rokas** darbu skubina. *Many hands make light work.*

Rublis apaļš—tas rit. *Money is round and rolls away.*

Runā ar apdomu! *Think twice; speak once.*

Ne**runā** gaŗi, bet dari! *Deeds, not words.*

Runāt—sudrabs, klusēt—zelts. *Speech is silver; silence is golden.*

Mazāk **runāt**, vairāk strādāt. *Few words, many deeds.*

Ne vienmēr runcim krējuma pods. *Every day is not a holiday.*

Kad ru**nča** nav mājās, tad peles pa galdu lēkā. *While the cat's away, the mice will play.*

Rūsa maitā dzelzi, slinkums—cilvēku. *If you rest, you rust.*

Izsalkušam pat **rutku** miza salda. *Hunger makes hard beans sweet. / Hunger sweetens what is bitter. / Hunger is the best sauce.*

S

Sacīšana nav darīšana. *Saying and doing are two different things.*

Tāds ar tādu **saderas**. *Like attracts like. / Everyone to his equal.*

Kas skaidri **saderēts**, to nevar pārkāpt. *A bargain is a bargain.*

Saimniece ar padusi vairāk iznes nekā saimnieks ar vezumu ieved. *The wife can throw more out the back window than a man can bring in the front door with a shovel.*

Saimnieka acis vairāk padara nekā kalpa rokas. *The eye of the master does more than his hand. / No eye like the master's eye.*

Kāda **sakne**, tāda atvase. *What is in the cat will come out in the kitten. / Bad bird, bad eggs.*

Kādu **saknīti** cūciņa izrok, tāda jāēd. *Gnaw the bone which has fallen to your lot.*

Labāk **sakod** mēli zobos nekā pļāpā. *Keep your tongue within your teeth.*

Katrs **sākums** grūts. *The beginning is the hardest. / The hardest part of a job is the beginning.*

Samaitāt var ātri, sataisīt grūti. *It is easier to pull down than to build up.*

Paēdis neēdušu ne**saprot**. *The full do not believe the hungry.*

Sargies no ļauna, tad meli paliks kaunā. *Shun wickedness.*

Sargies pats, tad Dievs tevi sargās. *Heaven helps those that help themselves.*

Citur arī **saule** spīd. *In every country the sun rises in the morning. / The sun shines on all the world.*

Ne ikdienas **saule** spīd, ne ikdienas lietus līst. *Life is subject to ups and downs.*

Kādā **saulē** sēdi, tādā sildies. *Be content with your lot.*

Nav nekā jauna zem **saules**. *There's nothing new under the sun.*

Sēdies, kur tev Dieviņš liek, ēd, kas tev rokā tiek! *Be content with your lot.*

Ko **sēj**, to pļauj. *As you sow, so shall you reap.*

Kāda **sēkla**, tāda raža. *If you want to raise corn, plant corn seed, not cotton seed.*

Kādu **sēklu** sēsi, tādus augļus pļausi. *As you sow, so shall you reap.*

Kā **sēsi**, tā pļausi. *As you sow, so shall you reap.*

Jo augstāka **sēta**, jo mīļāki kaimiņi. *Good fences make good neighbors. / A fence between makes friends more keen. / A hedge between keeps fellowship green.*

Kur zema **sēta**, tur visas kazas pāri lec. *A low hedge is easily leaped over.*

Sieva klēpī vairāk var no sētas iznest nekā vīrs ar vezumu ievest. *The wife can throw more out the back window than a man can bring in the front door with a shovel.*

Sieva un krāsns paliek mājās. *A woman, a cat, and a chimney should never leave the house. / A woman's place is in the home.*

Laba **sieva** ir dārga manta. *A good wife and health are a man's best wealth.*

Laba **sieva** nav ar zeltu atsveŗama. *Better a fortune in a wife than with a wife.*

Tikla **sieva** ir vīra kronis. *A true wife is her husband's [flower of beauty/better half]. / A worthy woman is the crown of her husband. / A virtuous woman is a source of honor to her husband; a vicious one causes him disgrace.*

Sievas ir īstas valodnieces. *A woman's strength is in her tongue.*

Kas ar **sieviešiem** ķīvējas, nes ūdeni sietā. *Never quarrel with a woman.*

Siksnai divi gali. *Every path leads two ways.*

Sīkstulis mūžam nabags. *A rich miser is poorer than a poor man.*

Silts nāk ar **sildīšanu**, labs ar gaidīšanu. *All things come to him who waits.*

Cita **sirdi** nevar redzēt. *You can look in the eyes but not in the heart.*

Kad **sirds** pilna, mute runā. *Out of the abundance of the heart the mouth speaks.*

Kam droša **sirds**, tam laimējas. *Good courage breaks bad luck. Fortune favors the brave. / No guts, no glory.*

Kas nāk no **sirds**, tas iet pie sirds. *Hearts may agree, though heads differ.*

Kas uz **sirds**, tas uz mēles. *Don't wear your heart on your sleeve.*

Pa trīs, lai **sirds** netrīs! *There is strength in numbers.*

Skaidra **sirds**—dārgākā manta pasaulē. *A clear conscience is God's greatest gift.*

Guļošu ne**sit**. *When a man is down, don't kick him lower.*

Sitiens ir grūts, bet atsitiens vēl grūtāks. *Bad actions lead to worse reactions.*

Sivēnu maisā nepērk. *Don't buy a pig in a poke.*

Viss, kas pārlieku, tas **skādē**. *Nothing in excess is best. / Moderation in all things.*

Viss, kas **skaists**, ātri zūd. *All that's fair must fade.*

Skaistuma ziedi pirmie birst. *Beauty is a fading flower.*

Skaistums aiziet, vecums pienāk. *Beauty is the bloom of youth.*

Skaistums nepilda vēderu. *Beauty doesn't make the pot boil.*

Skaistums vīst, tikums zied un nes augļus. *Beauty vanishes, virtue endures. / Beauty is the flower of life, but virtue is the fruit.*

Ko palīdz **skaistums,** ja sirdī nemīt labums. *Beauty is no longer amiable than while virtue adorns it.*

Skaldi un valdi. *Divide and conquer.*

Ne**skatieties** uz maniem darbiem, klausieties uz maniem vārdiem! *Don't do as I do, but as I say.*

Skauģim sāp, kad cits ir priecīgs. *Envy has smarting eyes.*

Labāk lai mani **skauž** nekā nožēlo. *Better be envied than pitied.*

Ja **skola** neizmācīs, tad izmācīs teļāda. *A lot of child's welfare can be done with a razor strap.*

Kas ātri **skrej**, tas pārskrejas. *A hasty man is seldom out of trouble.*

Kas čakli **skrej,** tas drīz piekūst. *They stumble that run fast.*

Jo ātri **skrien**, jo drīz klūp. *They stumble that run fast./ Walk too fast and stumble over nothing.*

Kāda **slaka,** tāds tikums. *What is bred in the bone will come out in the flesh.*

Slapjumu neredzēs—sausumu nebaudīs. *We know the sweet when we have tasted the bitter.*

Slauc, kamēr pienu dod. *Get while the getting's good.*

Laba **slava** iet kājām, slikta jāj jāšus. *A good reputation stands still; a bad one runs.*

Slēdz stalli, kad zirgs jau vējā. *There's no use in closing the barn door after the horse is stolen.*

Slēp slēpdams, tak reiz nāks gaismā. *What goes on in the dark must come out in the light. / What is done in the night appears in the day.*

Slīcējs ķeras pie salmiņa. *A drowning man will catch at a straw.*

Jauns **slinko**, vecs mocies. *A young man idle, and old man needy.*

Slinkums ir pereklis, kur top perēts nelietis. *Idleness is the mother of evil.*

Slinkums ir visa ļaunuma pereklis. *Idle hands are the devil's tools.*

Slinkums laba nemāca. *Of idleness comes no goodness.*

Slinkums maitā kā rūsa dzelzi. *If you rest, you rust.*

Jauns **sliņķis**, vecs zaglis. *A young idler, an old beggar.*

Jauna **slota** tīri slauka. *A new broom sweeps clean.*

Kas daudz **smejas**, negudrs rādās. *Laugh and show your ignorance.*

Kas pēdējais **smejas**, tas gardāki smejas. *He that laughs last laughs best.*

Smejies vien, gan tu pēc raudāsi. *After laugter, tears.*

Smiekli kaklu nelauž, smiekli gurnu negrauē. *Laughter does not spoil the skin.*

Pēc **smiekliem** raudas nāk. *After joy comes sorrow.*

No **smilgas** citreiz pils aizdegas. *Little sticks kindle large fires. / Behold what a fire a little matter kindles.*

No **smilgas** piekrauj lielu siena vezumu. *Many small makes a great. / Every pea helps to fill the rack. / Many drops of water make an ocean.*

Otram redz **smilgu**, sev pašam baļķi neredz. *Cast the beam out of your own eye before you try to cast the mote from the eyes of your neighbor.*

Kur **smird**, tur deg. *Where there is smoke, there is fire.*

Nelīdz **smukums**, ja nav tikums. *Beauty without virtue is a rose without fragrance.*

Smulis paliek smulis, mazgā cik gribi! *Wash a hog and it will return to its wallow.*

Sodība grēkam pakaļ iet. *Every sin carries its own punishment.*

Kas pirmo **soli** spēris, lai speŗ arī otru. *If you say A, they'll make you say B.*

Ko **soli**, to turi. *Perform whatever you promise.*

Pirmais **solis** tas grūtākais. *The first step is the hardest. / The first attempt is the most difficult.*

Daudz **solīt**, maz iedot. *The more you promise, the less you will have to deliver.*

Arī lēni **soļi** ved uz priekšu. *Little by little one goes far./ Step by step, one goes a long way.*

Jauns ar **spēku**, vecs ar prātu. *Age should think and youth should do.*

No āra **spīd**, no iekšas smird. *Outside show, inside woe.*

Nespļauj akā—pašam būs jādzeŗ! *Do not spit into the well: you may have to drink out of it.*

Nespļauj pret vēju! *Who spits against the wind spits in his own face.*

Nespļauj spainī, pats dabūsi izstrēbt. *Do not spit into the well: you may have to drink out of it.*

Jo **steidz**, jo ķeŗas. *Hasty bird makes hasty nest. / More haste, worse speed.*

Steidzies, bet lēnam! *Make haste slowly.*

Strādā ar rokām, ne ar muti! *Deeds, not words.*

Jauns būdams, **strādā**, pietaupi, tad vecs bez maizes nebūsi! *Spare when you are young and spend when you are old. / For age and want, save while you may, for no morning lasts all day.*

Kas **strādā**, tas ēdīs. *No bees, no honey; no work, no money.*

Kas nestrādā, tam nav jāēd. *Those who will not work shall not eat.*

Kas negrib **strādāt**, lai cieš badu. *Those who will not work shall not eat. / The indolent man draws his breath but does not eat.*

Pieēdušam grūti **strādāt**. *When the belly is full, the bones are at rest.*

Pa **straumei** viegli peldēt. *It's easy going with the stream.*

Pret **straumi** grūti peldēt. *We must run with the stream.*

Nestreb karstu putru! *A quick decision may speed you into trouble.*

Kas ātri **strebj**, tam mute deg. *Careless hurry can cause endless regrets.*

Kas pirmāk pie **sudmalām** braucis, lai uzbeŗ savu labību. *He who comes first grinds first.*

Kāda **suga**, tāds tikums. *What is bred in the bone will come out in the flesh.*

Kas **suni** pārkāpis, pārkāps arī asti. *If one gets over the dog, one gets over the tail.*

Vienreiz **suni** pievil ar kaulu, otrreiz ne ar gaļu nepievils. *A fox is not caught twice in the same place.*

Kas **sunim** asti pacels, ja pats nepacels. *Toot your own horn lest the same be never tooted.*

Suns, kas daudz zaķu ķeŗ, nevienu nenoķeŗ. *The grayhound that starts many hares kills none.*

Suns, kas desu dabūjis, atpakaļ jau nedod. *A dog with a bone knows no friend.*

Suns, kas rej, lēti nekož. *A barking dog never bites.*

Suns sunim [kājā nekož/uz astes nemīs]. *Wolves never prey upon wolves.*

Suns suņa gaļu neēd. *Dog will not eat dog.*

Suns zina, ko izēdis. *A guilty dog always barks.*

Pats **suns** zina, kas viņu baro. *A dog knows his own master.*

Gulošs **suns** zaķi neķeŗ. *The sleeping fox catches no poultry.*

Kāds **suns** iekodis, tāds lai atkož. *The hair of the dog is good for the bite.*

Viens **suns** vien ilgi nerej. *One dog barks at nothing; the rest bark at him.*

No **suņa** nevar desu pirkt. *The doghouse is no place to keep a sausage.*

Beidzamo **suņi** rej. *The devil takes the hindmost.*

Divi **suņi** pie viena kaula nesader. *Two dogs over one bone seldom agree.*

Pēdējam **suņi** ķeŗas pie stilbiem. *The devil takes the hindmost.*

Suņu kūtī gaļu neglabā. *The doghouse is no place to keep a sausage.*

Kas labi **svaida**, labi brauc. *He who greases well drives well.*

Kādi **svārki**, tāda odere. *Cut the coat according to the cloth.*

Izpūsta **svece** neiedegas. *What is done cannot be undone.*

Neturi **sveci** zem pūra. *Don't hide your light under a bushel.*

Sviest kātu cirvim pakaļ. *Don't throw good money after bad.*

Š

Šodien man, rītu tev. *Your turn today, mine tomorrow. / Turnabout is fair play.*

Šuj ko šūdams, aizmet mezglu! *Do what you do carefully.*

Kāds **šūpulī**, tāds arī kapā. *He who is born round cannot die square.*

T

Tikai tad **taisa** vāku akai, kad bērns tanī jau iekritis. *It is too late to cover the well when the child is drowned.*

Taisnība nav noslēpjama. *The truth will out.*

Taisnība patur virsroku. *Right makes might.*

Taisnība tomēr vienmēr gaismā nāk. *The truth will out.*

Kas stiprāks, tam **taisnība**. *Might makes right.*

Katrreiz **taisnību** nevar teikt. *Always tell the the truth, but don't always be telling the truth.*

Tauki allaž peld pa virsu. *Cream always comes to the top.*

Jo **taukus** pieliek, jo viegla braukšana. He *who greases well drives well.*

Taupi jaunumā—būs vecumā. *Save when you are young to spend when you are old.*

Taupība labāka par bagātību. *Economy is the road to wealth.*

Kas sevi jauns ne**taupīs**, tas nevar vecumu piedzīvot. *The excesses of our youth are draughts upon our old age.*

Ko līdz **taupīt**, kad visas malas tukšas. *It is too late to spare when the bottom is bare.*

Cits **teic**, cits smādē. *Everybody to his own taste. / Everybody to their own notion.*

Lai tevi citi **teic**, bet ne paša mute. *Let another man praise you, not your own mouth.*

Neteic tauku nedīrātu. *Hear the evidence before you pass sentence.*

Ne**teic** treknu, kamēr neesi dīrājis. *Hear the vidence before you pass sentence.*

Ne**teic** visu, ko zini: vēders no tā nesāp. *Don't tell all you know nor all you can.*

Šodien **teikts**, rīt jau beigts. *Fame one day, zero the next.*

Mīlīgu **telīti** divas govis zīda. *If you'd be beloved, make yourself amiable.*

Labāk dzīvs **telš** nekā beigts lauva. *Better live dog than dead lion. / It is better to be a live rabbit than a dead tiger.*

Tēva mājās garoza gardāka nekā svešās cepetis. *Dry bread at home is better than roast meat abroad.*

Gudram **tēvam** gudri bērni. *A wise man has wise cildren.*

Kas **tēvam** neklausa, [klausa meēam/neklausa pat ne velnam]. *A wise son hears his father's instruction.*

Kāds **tēvs**, tāds dēls. *Like father, like son.*

Ko **tēvs** ar sviedriem sapelnī, to dēls ar meitām nodzīvoi. *A thrifty father rarely has a thrifty son.*

Kur **tēvs** krājējs, tur dēls izšķērdētājs. *A miserly father makes a prodigal son.*

Klaus' **tēvu**! *A wise son hears his father's instruction.*

Kas lēti **tic**, tas pievilts kļūs. *He who believes easily is easily deceived.*

Ne visam jā**tic**, ko dzird. *Season all you hear with salt.*

Ne**tici** visu, ko ļaudis runā. *Put no faith in tale bearers.*

Kur tie ātrie **tikuši**, kur tie lēnie palikuši. *Haste not, rest not.*

Trakam traka valoda. *A cracked vessel is known by its sound, a cracked mind by the tongue's speech.*

Ar **trakiem** pa labam! *Get out of the way of a mad dog.*

Jo **trin**, jo spodrāks. *The used key is always bright.*

Trūkums kājas aun. *Need makes the old wife trot. / Want is the mother of industry.*

Kā **tu** citam, tā cits tev. *Expect to be treated as you have treated others.*

Kā **tu** man, tā es tev. *Tit for tat.*

Kad vienreiz **tukšs**, vai tādēļ nezvejos? *Strive though you fail.*

Tumsā tāds viens kaķis, kāds otrs. *All cats look alike in the dark.*

Tupiņam jau vārpu nesagaidīsi. *You can't grow figs from thistles. / You can't raise grain by sowing grass. / Lilies don't spring from thistles.*

Katrs pats sev **tuvākais**. *Everyone speaks for his own interest.*

U

Kas **ubagam** slieksni liedz, nepelna dievpalīgu. *He who closes his door to the poor will find the gates of heaven closed.*

Ūdeni Daugavā liet. *The man who carries coal to Newcastle will pour water on a drowned mouse.*

Ūdeni sietā neiesmelsi. *The sea cannot be scooped up in a tumbler. / All is lost that is poured into a cracked dish.*

Izlijušu **ūdeni** nesasmelsi. *Spilled water cannot be gathered up. / You can't pick up spilled milk.*

Jo duļķaināks **ūdens**, jo labāka zvejošana. *It's good fishing in troubled waters.*

Kad **ūdens** nāk mutē, jāmācās peldēt. *Sink or swim.*

Kur dziļāks **ūdens**, tur vairāk zivju. *The best fishing is in the deepest water.*

Klusie **ūdeņi** dziļi. *Still waters run deep.*

Lieli **ūdeņi**, lielas zivis. *Big fish are caught in a big river. / Great fishes are caught in great waters.*

Ar **uguni** nevar spēlēties. *If you play with matches, you will get burned.*

Kas **uguni** ķeŗ, tam pirksti deg. *If you hold the frying pan, don't blame it if you burn yourself. / They who play with edged tools must expect to be cut.*

Kas **ugunī** iet, ugunī sadeg. *He that loves danger shall perish therein.*

Uguns ar ūdeni vienā traukā nestāv. *Fire and water don't mix.*

Uguns nav puķe. *Don't play with fire.*

Uguns salmos lēti metas. *Fire and flax agree not.*

Ko **uguns** neiznīcina, to tā norūda. *Difficulty strengthens the mind as labor does the body.*

Kur **uguns** jau deg, tur kurstīt nevajag. *A clean hand needs no washing.*

Es vairāk **uzticos** acīm nekā ausīm. *It is better to trust the eye than the ear.*

V

Kad **vadzis** pilns, tad tas lūst. *Too much in the vessel burst the lid. / Weight broke the wagon down.*

Ne visi **vagari**, kam pātaga rokā. *All are not hunters who blow the horn. / Not every one who carries a long knife is a cook. / If the beard were all, the goat might preach.*

Kur skaisti **vaigi**, tur lepna sirds. *Beauty is vain.*

Nelūko skaistu **vaigu**, bet skaistu sirdi. *Beauty comes from the soul. / A homely form oft holds a handsome heart.*

Cita **vaina** acīs duŗas. *Nothing is easier than fault finding.*

Kas **vainīgs**, tas bailīgs. *The guilty one always runs. / Guilt makes the bravest man coward.*

Svešu **vainu** redz, pats savu nē. *We see the faults of others but not our own.*

Vakars gudrāks nekā rīts. *The evening brings all home.*

Vakars rāda, kāda diena bijusi. *The evening brings all home.*

Valdi muti un rokas, tad dzīvosi simts gadu. *Govern yourself and you'll be able to govern the world.*

Pašam sevi valdīt ir tā vislielākā valdīšana. *No man is such a conqueror as the man who has defeated himself. / He who overcomes others is strong; he who overcomes himself is mightier.*

Valdniekam gaŗas rokas—tālu sniedz. *Kings have long arms.*

Liela **valoda**, maz augļu. *Great braggarts are little doers.*

Gudram ir maz **valodas**. *An intelligent person is one who knows when to keep his mouth shut. / A still tongue makes a wise head. / No wisdom like silence.*

Pēc **valodas** var pazīt, kāds katrs ir. *Your conversation is the mirror of your thoughts.*

Varas darītāju neiens neieredz. *Violence breeds hatred, and hatred dissension.*

Labam **vārdam** laba vieta. *A kind word goes a long way.*

Ir **varde** pīkst, kad virsū min. *Even a rat, when cornered, will turn and fight.*

Vārdi nemaksā parādus. *Words never filled a belly.*

Kādi **vārdi**, tādi darbi. *Suit the actions to the word.*

Kur nelīdz **vārdi**, tur līdz pātaga. *A child that won't hear will feel.*

No **vārdiem** līdz darbiem labs gabals. *Saying and doing are two different things.*

Izteikts **vārds** nav atsaucams. *Words once spoken you can never recall. / Spoken words are like flown birds: neither can be recalled.*

Labs **vārds** atrod labu sirdi. *A word of kindness is seldom spoken in vain.*

Laipns **vārds** mūžam gards. *A kind thought is never lost.*

Rupjš **vārds** sāp ilgāk nekā pļiķis. *The hard words cut the heart.*

Labu **vārdu** labprāt pieņem. *A word of kindness is seldom spoken in vain.*

Mazāk **vārdu**, vairāk darbu! *Few words, many deeds.*

Ko pats **vārīsi**, to pats ēdīsi. *You must drink beer of your own brewing, no matter how bitter.*

Vārna vārnai acis ārā neknābj. *A crow does not pull out the eye of another crow. / The ravens don't peck one another's eyes out.*

Pilna **vārpa** noliekusies. *A full ear of corn will bend its head; an empty ear will stand upright.*

Tukšas **vārpas** augstu stāv. *A full ear of corn will bend its head; an empty ear will stand upright.*

Ar **varu** nevar būt otram mīļš. *He who forces love where none is found remains a fool the whole year round.*

Jo mazāk **vāti** plēš, jo ātrāk sadzīst. *Don't nurse your sorrows.*

Katram sava **vāts** sāp. *To everyone his cross is heaviest.*

Kādi **vecāki**, tādi bērni. *As mother and father, so is daughter and son.*

Kas **vecāku** vārdu klausa, pilnu abru maizes mīca. *Obedience is the first duty of a child.*

Vecums kaulus grauž. *Age breeds aches.*

Vecums pienāk nemanot. *Old age comes uncalled.*

Pilns **vēders** kūtrs pie grāmatām. *Full stomachs make empty heads.*

Labāk ar tukšu **vēderu** gulēt nekā ar parādiem piecelties. *Better go to bed supperless than rise in debt. / Sleep without supping and wake without owing.*

Vai tādēļ, ka vienreiz **vēja** nav, zēģeles jāpārdod? *Strive though you fail.*

Vējam nevar pretī atpūst. *You can't hinder the wind from blowing. / Puff not against the wind.*

Kā **vējiņš** pūš, tā salmiņš danco. *The reed does blow at every blast.*

Kā **vējš** skrien, kā miets atduras. *Haste is slow. / Haste may trip up its own heels.*

Kā **vējš** pūš, tā grozās. *As the wind blows, so bends the twig.*

Kā **vējš** un ūdens ir sieviešu prāts. *Women are as fickle as April weather.*

Uz kuŗu pusi **vējš** pūš, tur jāliecas kokam. *As the wind blows, so bends the twig.*

Kas **vēju** sēj, tas vētru pļauj. *Sow the wind and reap the whirlwind.*

Iedod **velnam** pirkstu, viņš tev paņems visu roku. *Give the devil an inch and he will take an ell.*

Kas **velnam** vienu matiņu atļauj, tam viņš rauj visu galvu. *Give the devil an inch and he will take an ell.*

Velns nav tik melns kā to mālē. *The devil is not as black as he is painted.*

Ko **velns** nezin, to bābas zin. *A woman knows a bit more than Satan.*

Par velti pat **velns** savu māti nedod. *If you want to dance, you must pay the fiddler.*

Ielaid **velnu** baznīcā, viņš grib kāpt uz kanceli. *He that takes the devil into his boat must carry him over the sound.*

Kas par **vēlu,** tas par skādi. *Delay is dangerous.*

Labāk par **vēlu** nekā nekad. *Better late than never.*

Kas **vērdiņu** taupa, tam nāk dālderis rokā. *Take care of the dimes and the dollars will take care of themselves.*

Vērsi tur pie ragiem, vīru pie vārda. *A man is no better than his word.*

Vienu **vērsi** nevar diviem miesniekiem pārdot. *You can't dance at two weddings with one pair of feet.*

Vērsis nav tādēļ dārgāks, ka tas raibs. *A golden bit does not make the horse any better.*

No viena **vērša** nevar divas ādas dīrāt. *You can't get a quart out of a thimble.*

Veselība labāka nekā manta. *Give me my health and take my wealth. / Good health is priceless.*

Veselība pārāka par bagātību. *Good health is priceless. / Give me my health and take my wealth.*

Veselība visdārgākā manta pasaulē. *Health is wealth.*

Nekas nav dārgāks par **veselību**, nekas nav labāks par mīlestību. *The first wealth is health.*

Veselais ikreiz **veselību** neprot cienīt. *Health is not valued till sickness comes.*

Šodien **vesels**, rītu trūds. *Here today and gone tomorrow.*

Kur nu **vieglums** bez grūtuma, saldums bez rūgtuma. *Honey is sweet but bees sting. / If you want to gather honey, you must bear the sting of bees.*

Kā **vietu** taisa, tā guļ. *As one makes his bed, so must he lie.*

No **vilka** neizmācīs lopu suni. *You can't make a racehorse out of a mule.*

Vilkam mežā ceļu nerāda. *Don't try to teach your grandmother how to suck eggs.*

Kad **vilkam** nav gaļas, tad ēd plieņus. *They that have no other meat gladly bread and butter eat.*

Ar **vilkiem** jākauc. *Who keeps company with a wolf learns to howl.*

Vilks ganam neprasa, vai ļaus jēru ņemt. *It never troubles the wolf how many the sheep may be.*

Vilks katru gadu met spalvu un tomēr paliek vilks. *Wolves may lose their teeth, but they never lose their nature.*

Vilks nav tik liels kā vilka kauciens. *The devil is not as black as he is painted.*

Vilks neaudzina jēru. *Don't set a wolf to watch the sheep.*

Vilks neprasa, kam tās avis pieder. *It never troubles the wolf how many the sheep may be.*

Vilks paliek vilks. *In every country dogs bite.*

Vilks spalvu met, bet ne tikumu. *Wolves may lose their teeth, but they never lose their nature.*

Beigts **vilks** nekož. *Dead men never bite.*

Solītu ir **vilks** neēd. *Promises don't fill the belly.*

Vilku par ganu celt. *Don't set a wolf to watch the sheep.*

Kā **vilku** piemin, tā vilks klāt. *Speak of the devil and he'll appear.*

Labāk zem veca **vīra** bārdas nekā zem jauna pātagas. *Better an old man's darling than a young man's slave.*

Vīrs domā: viņš zin, bet sieva zin labāk. *A man thinks he knows, but a woman knows better.*

Vīrs paliek pie sava vārda! *A man is no better than his word.*

Vīrs pie vārda, [kā cirvis pie kāta/kuģis pie enkura/vērsis pie valga]. *A man is no better than his word.*

Vīrs sievas galva, kakls to groza, kā grib. *The husband is the head of the house, but the wife is the neck—and the neck moves the head.*

Vīrs sola, vīrs dara. *A man is no better than his word.*

Labs **vīrs** savu vārdu neatrauс. *Straight folk never make broken promises.*

Liels **vīrs** nedara mazas ģeķības. *Great actions speak great minds.*

Neskaties **vīru** no cepures! *Judge not according to appearances. / Clothes and looks don't make the person.*

Visādi ir un visādu vajag! *It takes all kinds of people to make the world.*

Vista kasa, atrod graudu. *Where the hen scratches, there she expects to find a bug.*

Akla **vista** arī graudu atrod. *Even a blind pig occasionally picks up an acorn. / A blind man may sometimes shoot a crow by accident.*

Kā **vista** klukst, tā cāļi āiepst. *As the old bird sings, so the young ones twitter.*

Kam nu **vistilbas** dziesmu dziedāt, kad par cīruli piedzimis. *If you've got it, flaunt it.*

Z

Zagli no zagšanas neatradināsi. *Once a thief, always a thief.*

Zaglis dabū savu algu: savā kaklā cietu valgu. *The end of the thief is the gallows.*

Zaglis un saņēmējs—viens tāds kā otrs. *The receiver is as bad as the thief.*

Mazos **zaglus** ķeŗ, lielos ceļ amatos. *We hang little thieves and take off our hats to great ones. / There is one law for the rich and another for the poor.*

Nezāģē zaru, uz kuŗa pats sēdi. *Don't cut the limb which bears your weight.*

Zaķi pakaŗ, vilku palaiž. *We hang little thieves and take off our hats to great ones.*

Divus **zaķus** reizē ķerdams, neviena nenoķersi. *He who chases two hares catches neither.*

Kas [liks **zaldāta** šinelim/dos arāja mētelim] zīda oderi. *Cut the coat according to the cloth.*

Jo rūgta **zāle**, salda veselība. *Bitter pills may have blessed effects.*

Slimam ne **zelta** gulta nepalīdz. *Wealth can buy no health.*

Ne viss ir **zelts**, kas spīd. *All that glitters is not gold.*

Zeltu pārbauda ugunī, cilvēku—ciešanās. *Gold is tested by fire, men by gold.*

Jo taukāka **zeme**, jo vairāk lieka zāle aug. *A good garden always has weeds.*

Tā **zeme** jūŗas dibenā, tā zeme kapā. *Any soil will do to bury in.*

Zemes ieražas top cienītas. *When in Rome, do as the Romans.*

Kā **zemi** kopsi, tā zeme atlīdzēs. *It's the farmer's care that makes the field bear.*

Zemniekam zelta pamats. *Agriculture is the most certain source of wealth.*

Zemniekam zemnieka prāts. *You can take the farmer out of the country, but you can't take the country out of the farmer.*

Ziema prasa, ko vasarā darījis. *Winter eats what summer gets.*

Labāk **zīle** rokā nekā mednis kokā. *A bird in hand is better than two in the bush.*

Ko divi **zina**, to visi zina. *A secret shared is no secret.*

Kas var **zināt**, kur citam sāp. *No one knows the weight of another's burden. / None knows where the shoe pinches like the one who wears the shoe.*

Ko es **nezinu**, tas man nedara raizes. *What one doesn't know won't hurt him. / Ignorance is bliss.*

Kam nav **zirga**, jāiet kājām. *Feet were made before wheels.*

Zirgam četras kājas—tomēr klūp. *It is a good horse who never stumbles.*

Ātram **zirgam** piešu nevajag. *Don't spur a willing horse.*

Šķiņķotam **zirgam** zobos neskatās. *Don't look a gift horse in the mouth.*

Ne visi **zirgi** vienādi velk. *Different strokes for different folks.*

Zirgs zobus met, bet niķus neatmet. *The fox changes his skin, but not his habit.*

Zirgu aiz ratiem jūdz. *Don't put the cart before the horse.*

Zirgu tur pie pavadas, vīru pie vārda. *A man is no better than his word.*

Ja par **zirgu** esi uzņēmies—velc! *Do boldly what you do at all.*

Zivis bez darba nenāk laivā. *No pains, no gains; no sweat, no sweet.*

Zivs un ciemiņi trešā dienā smird. *Fish and callers smell in three days.*

Zivs sāk pūt no galvas. *Fish begin to stink at the head, men at the feet.*

Pamazām, pamazām—ir pie **zivs** jau ar ļaunu nevar pietikt. *Honey catches more flies than vinegar.*

Kas **zobus** saulē silda, tam nav kas bļodu pilda. *The man with the lazy hand has an empty mouth.*

Zoss nu dos tev auzas! *The doghouse is no place to keep a sausage.*

No **zosu** tēviņa nevar auzas pirkt. *The doghouse is no place to keep a sausage.*

Daudz **zvirbuļu** vienā perēklī nesader. *Two sparrows upon one ear of corn are not likely to agree.*

Ž

Kam **žults** mutē, tam viss rūgts. *Everything looks blue to the jaundiced eye.*

GRAMMATICAL ABBREVIATIONS

act	active	*nf*	feminine noun
adj	adjective, adjectival	*nm*	masculine noun
adv	adverb	*nom*	nominal
aux	auxiliary	*nomin*	nominative case
comp	comparative	*num*	numerical
cond	conditional mode	*paren*	parenthetic word
conj	conjunctive	*part*	participle
copul	copulative	*partic*	particle
dat	dative case	*past*	past tense
deb	debitive	*perf*	perfective
decl	declinable	*pers*	person, personal
def	defective	*pl*	plural
defin	definitive	*poss*	possessive
dem	demonstrative	*pref*	prefix
dim	diminutive	*prep*	preposition
emph	emphatic form	*pres*	present tense
f	feminine	*pron*	pronoun
fut	future tense	*prop*	proper
gen	genitive case	*r*	reflexive
i	intransitive	*sg*	singular
imper	imperative	*sub*	subjunctive
indecl	indeclinable	*super*	superlative
indef	indefinite	*t*	transitive
instr	instrumental case	*v*	verb
interj	interjection	*var*	variant
irr	irregular	*vi*	intransitive verb
iter	iterative	*virr*	irregular verb
loc	locative case	*voc*	vocative case
m	masculine	*vt*	transitive verb
neg	negative		

GENERAL ABBREVIATIONS

abb.	abbreviated, abbreviation	forest.	forestry term
aeron.	aeronautics	geod.	geodetic term
agr.	agriculture	geog.	geography
alpha.	alphabetic	geol.	geology
anat.	anatomy	geom.	geometry
anthr.	anthropology	gram.	grammatical term
arch.	architecture	hist.	historical term
archa.	archaic	hort.	horticulture
astr.	astronomy	hum.	humorously
bact.	bacteriology	hydr.	hydrology, hydraulics
barb.	barbarism	iron.	ironically
Bibl.	Biblical term	jur.	juridical term
biol.	biology	ling.	linguistics
bookk.	bookkeeping term	lit.	literature, literary term
bot.	botany	math.	mathematics
bus.	business term	mech.	mechanics
cent.	century	med.	medical term
chem.	chemistry	metall.	metallurgy
child.	children's language	meteor.	meteorological term
col.	colloquialism	mfg.	manufacturing term
com.	common speech	mil.	military term
Comm.	Communist term	mus.	music, musical term
compu	computer term	myth.	mythology
constr.	construction trade term	naut.	nautical term
cont.	term of contempt	n. u.	not used
cul.	culinary term	obj.	objectionable form
dial.	dialectal	obs.	obsolete
econ.	economy	parl.	parliamentary term
educ.	education	pharm.	pharmaceutical term
el.	electricity, electronics	phil.	philosophy
esp.	especially	phot.	photography
ethnogr.	ethnography	phys.	physics
fig.	figuratively	physiol.	physiology
folk.	folkloric	poet.	poetic language

pol.	political term	stat.	statistics
psych.	psychology	sth.	something
rare.	rarely so used	tech.	technical term
reg.	regionalism	text.	textile manufacturing
rel.	religious term	theat.	theatrical term
RR	railroads	typ.	typographical term
sbd.	somebody	usu.	usually
sl.	slang	vulg.	vulgar term
s.o.	someone	weav.	weaving term
soc.	sociology	zool.	zoology

A

à *adv* (in price markings) each, ea.

ā *interj* oh; ā, pas look at him (her) (used to refer to a person's unwillingness to perform); ā re there you are; you see?

aa or āā *interj* aha

abadona *nf* Abaddon

abadons *nm* angel of death

abaka *nf* abaca

abaks *nm* (arch.) abacus

abandons *nm* (jur.) abandonment

abasīds *nm* Abbasid

abate *nf* abbess

abatija *nf* abbey

abats *nm* abbot

abazija *nf* abasia

abaēūrs *nm* lampshade

ab[ch]az/s [h] *nm*, ~iete nf Abkhasian

abderits *nm* Abderite

abdikācija *nf* abdication

abdikants *nm* abdicant

abdomens *nm* abdomen

abdomināls *adj* abdominal

abdukcija *nf* (physiol.) abduction

abduktors *nm* (anat.) abductor

ābece *nf* ABC's, primer; the rudiments; ~s patie-sība truism

ābecisks *adj* elementary, simpleminded

ābecnie/ks *nm*, ~ce *nf* abecedarian, (col.) first-grader; beginner

ābečnieks *nm* = (col.) ābecnieks

abējādi *adv* in both ways

abējādība *nf* dual nature

abējāds *adj* of both kinds

abējādums *nm* dual nature

abēji *adj* both

abējpus *adv* on both sides

ābele *nf* apple tree

ābelnīca *nf* 1. apple tree; 2. orchard

ābeļdārzs *nm* apple orchard

ābeļu lapu blusiņa *nf* jumping plant louse

ābeļu laputs *nf* apple aphid

ābeļu tinējs *nm* codling moth

ābeļu ziedu dūrējs *nm* apple blossom weevil

ābeļzieds *nm* apple blossom

abe[r]ācija [rr] *nf* aberration

abesin/is *nm*, ~iete *nf* Abyssinian

abet *conj* (reg.) but

abgregācija *nf* ostracism, expulsion

abhazs *nm* See abchazs

abi *adj* both; abi divi both of them; viens no abiem one of the two; neviens no abiem neither one; abos gadījumos in either case ◊ mēs pa abiem between the two of us; abi labi either will do; two of a kind

abietins *nm* abietine

abietinskābe *nf* abietic acid

abiniek/s *nm* amphibian

abinieku sūrene *nf* willow-weed

abiog[e]nisks [ē] *adj* abiogenic

abiog[e]ns [ē] *adj* abiogenic

abioģen[e]ze [ē] *nf* abiogenesis

abiotisks *adj* abiotic

abioze *nf* abiosis

abisāle *nf* abyss–

abisāls *adj* abyssal

abit[u]rient/s [ū] *nm*, ~e *nf* graduating high school senior

abit[u]rijs [ū] *nm* graduation from high school

abit[u]rs [ū] *nm* = abiturijs

ablācija *nf* ablation

ablaktācija *nf* ablactation

ablaktēšana *nf* (hort.) inarching

abl[a]tīvs [ā] *nm* (gram.) ablative

ablauts *nm* ablaut

ablegats *nm* ablegate

abnormāli *adv* abnormally

abnormāls *adj* abnormal

abnormi *adv* abnormally

abnorms *adj* abnormal

ābolaine *nf* mowed clover field

ābolainis *nm* dapple-gray horse

ābolains *adj* dapple-gray

ābolaite *nf* (reg.) mowed clover field

ābolājs *nm* mowed clover field

ābolaugļi *nm* pl pome fruit

abol[i]cija [ī] *nf* abolition

abolicionisms *nm* abolitionism

abolicionists *nm* abolitionist

ābolinājs *nm* (reg.) mowed clover field

āboliņa vija *nf* clover dodder

āboliņa ziedu smecernieks *nm* clover weevil

āboliņ/š *nm* 1. clover; 2. *dim* of **ābols**, little apple

ābolītis *nm dim* of **ābols**, little apple

ābolkūka *nf* apple strudel, apple cake

ābolmaize *nf* flat sheetbread with apple topping

ābolots *adj* dapple-gray

ābol/s *nm* apple ◊ **vesels kā ā.** fit as a fiddle; **sīvā ~ā kost** bite the bullet

ābolskābe *nf* malic acid

āboltains *adj* (reg.) dapple-gray

āboltiņš *nm dim* of **ābols**, little apple

ābolu biezenis *nm* applesauce

ābolu zāģlapsene *nf* apple sawfly

ābolu roze *nf* apple rose

ābolu serēu duŗamais *nm* apple corer

ābolu tārps *nm* apple worm; codling moth caterpillar

ābolvīns *nm* apple wine

abonements *nm* subscription

abonentmaksa *nf* price of subscription

abonent/s *nm*, ~e *nf* subscriber; holder of a season ticket

abonentu saraksts *nm* list of subscribers; telephone directory

abonēt *vt* subscribe to

abordāēa *nf* boarding (of a ship)

abordāēas kāsis *nm* grapnel

abor[i]gēns [ī] *nm* aborigine

abortēt *vt* abort

abortist/s *nm*, ~e *nf* abortionist

abortīvi *adv* abortively

abortīvs *adj* abortive

aborts *nm* abortion; **mākslīgais a.** induced abortion; **spontānais a.** miscarriage

abpus *adv* on both sides

abpusass *adj* double-edged

abpusēji *adv* mutually

abpusējs *adj* mutual

abpusgriezīgs *adj* double-edged

abpusība *nf* mutuality

abpusīgi *adv* mutually

abpusīgs *adj* mutual

abpusīgums *nm* mutuality

abra *nf* kneading trough

abrakadabra *nf* abracadabra

abrakasis *nm* = **abrkasis**

abraskrāpis *nm* = **abrskrāpis**

abrāzija *nf* abrasion

abrāzijas līdzenums *nm* (geol.) abrasion platform, wave-cut platform

abrazīvs *nm* abrasive

abrazīvs *adj* abrasive

abreaģēt *vi* abreact

abreakcija *nf* abreaction

abreviācija *nf* abbreviation

abrevi[a]tors [ā] *nm* abbreviator

abrevi[a]tūra [ā] *nf* abbreviation

abriss *nm* outline

abrkasis *nm* 1. kneading trough scraper; 2. small loaf of bread (made of dough remnants); 3. (hum.) last-born child

abrocīgā grūšana *nf* two hands clean and jerk

abrocīgā raušana *nf* two hands snatch

abrocīgā spiešana *nf* two hands military press

abrocīgi *adv* with two hands

abrocīgs *adj* two-hand

abrogācija *nf* abrogation

abroma *nf* devil's cotton

abrskrāpis *nm* kneading trough scraper

abrumaiškis *nm* small dough mixing spoon

abrupcija *nf* abruption

abrupti *adv* abruptly

abrupts *adj* abrupt

abrurags *nm* kneading trough handle

abruskrāpis *nm* = abrskrāpis

abscess *nm* abscess

abscisa *nf* abscissa

absentisms *nm* absenteeism

absintisms *nm* absinthism

absints *nm* 1. absinth; 2. wormwood

absolūcija *nf* absolution

absolūtais *nom adj* the absolute

absolūti *adv* absolutely

absolūtisms *nm* absolutism

absolūtist/s *nm*, ~e *nf* absolutist

absol|u|tizēt [ū] *vt* absolutize

absolūts *adj* absolute

absolvent/s *nm*, ~e *nf* graduate

absolvēt *vt* graduate (from college, high school); finish a course

absorbcija *nf* absorption

absorbents *nm* absorbent

absorbers *nm* absorber

absorbēšana nf absorption

absorbēšanas spēja *nf* power of absorption

absorbēt *vt* absorb

absorbēties *vr* become absorbed

absorbētspēja *nf* power of absorption

abstarpēji *adv* reciprocally, mutually

abstarpējs *adj* reciprocal, mutual

abstencionisms *nm* abstentionism

abstinence *nf* 1. abstinence; 2. withdrawal syndrome

abstinents *nm* abstainer

abstinents *adj* abstinent

abstrahēt *vt* abstract

abstrahēties *vr* abstract

abstrakcija *nf* abstraction

abstrakcionisms *n*m abstractionism

abstrakcionist/s *nm*, ~e *nf* abstractionist

abstrakti *adv* abstractly

abstraktisms *nm* abstractionism

abstrakts *adj* abstract

abstraktums *nm* abstractness

abstrūzi *adv* abstrusely

abstrūzs *adj* abstruse

absurdi *adv* absurdly

absurds *nm* absurdity

absurds *adj* absurd; smieklīgi a. preposterous

abudi *nm* pl sourkraut and pork soup

abūlija *nf* abulia

abulis *nm* (of a pair of pants) crotch

abundācija *nf* abundance

abutilons *nm* abutilon, Indian mallow

abvērs *nm* Abwehr

acābols *nm* eyeball

acainais sfings *nm* eyed hawk moth

acaines *nf* pl 1. eyeglasses; 2. a type of broach

acainis *nm* reticulum

acains *adj* 1. (of bread) porous; (of potatoes) eyed; 2. having an eyelike pattern

acaiņi *nm* pl 1. dotted mittens; 2. (weav.) slubs

acālija *nf* azalea

aceknis *nm* 1. reticulum; 2. linen cloth of a special weave pattern; 3. eye of a mesh

acelaīnskābe *nf* azelaic acid

acenes *nf* pl eyeglasses

acetāls *nm* acetal

acetamidīns *nm* acetamidine

acetam|i|ds [ī] *nm* acetamide

acetanhidr|i|ds [ī] *nm* acetic anhydride

acetātplēve *nf* acetate film

acetāts *nm* acetate

acetātšķiedra *nf* acetate fiber

acetātzīds *nm* acetate fabric

acetetiķesteris *nm* ethyl acetoacetate

acetilbrom|i|ds [ī] *nm* acetyl bromide

acetilceluloze *nf* cellulose acetate

acetil|ch|lor|i|ds [h]|ī] *nm* acetyl chloride

acetilēns *nm* acetylene

acetil|i|ds [ī] *nm* acetylide

acetils *nm* acetyl

acetilsalicilskābe *nf* acetylsalicylic acid

acetons *nm* acetone

a|ch|aj/s [h] *nm*, ~iete *nf* Achaean

a|ch|alāzija [h] *nf* achalasia

a|cha|ts [hā] *nm* agate

A[ch]ileja dzīsla [h] *nf* Achilles tendon
A[ch]ileja papēdis [h] *nm* Achilles' heel
a[ch]ilija [h] *nf* achylia gastrica
a[ch]imenas [h] *nf* pl achimenes
a[ch]olija [h] *nf* acholia
a[ch]ondrīts [h] *nm* achondrite
a[ch]romatija [h] *nf* achromatism
a[ch]romatiski [h] *adv* achromatically
a[ch]romatisks [h] *adj* achromatic
a[ch]romatisms [h] *nm* achromatism
a[ch]romatopsija [h] *nf* achromatopsia
a[ch]romats [h] *nm* achromatic lens
a[ch]romija [h] *nf* achromia
a[ch]tele [h] *nf* (sl., vulg.) ass
acība *nf* 1. keen eyesight, alertness;
   2. porosity
acidācija *nf* acidification
acidifikācija *nf* acidification
acidimetrija *nf* acidimetry
aciditāte *nf* acidity
acidofilija *nf* eosinophilia
acidofils *adj* acidophilous
acidometrs *nm* acidometer
acidoze *nf* acidosis
acīgi *adv* with a keen eye
acīgs *adj* keen-eyed
acīgums *nm* alertness
aciklisks *adj* acyclic
acilācija *nf* acylation
acils *nm* acyl
acīmredzami *adv* evidently
acīmredzams *adj* evident
acīmredzot *adv* evidently
aciņa *nf dim* of aka, little well
acīte *nf* vingt-et-un
acojums *nm* (hort.) budding
acošana *nf* (hort.) shield budding
acot *vt* (hort.) bud
acotnis *nm* a year-old shoot from a grafted scion
acots 1. part of acot; 2. *adj* = acains

ac/s *nf* 1. eye; labas (or gaišas) ~is good eyesight; laba a. a sharp eye; ļauna a. the evil eye; sliktas (or tumšas) ~is poor eyesight; zila a. black eye ◊ aiz acīm behind one's back; ~i pret ~i (1) an eye for an eye (2) face to face; zem četrām ~īm tête-a-tête; (skatīties) ar baltu ~i cast a baleful eye; (būt) ar ~īm keep one's eyes open; kamēr man ~is platas while I am alive; ar raibām ~īm drunk; raibs gar ~īm to see stars; bez ~īm (fig.) blind; līdz ~īm full, up to here; (neieredz) ne ~u galā (cannot stand) the sight of; tumšs gar ~īm blank out, (of sight) blur; ar neapbruņotu ~i with the naked eye; tik, cik a. var nest almost nothing; prom no manām ~īm! out of my sight! (sargāt) kā ~i pierē (cherish) as the apple of one's eye; pa ~u galam casually; ~is pārgriezis with great effort; par skaistām ~īm for love; ~i pret ~i face to face; (tam) ~is slapjā vietā (his) eyes are watering; (ka vai) ~is zaļas paliek (till you are) blue in the face; zem ~īm being watched over; ~u priekšā within eyesight; visu ~u priekšā publicly; (ir) ~is pierē (have) eyes to see; ne ~ī duŗams pitch dark; 2. (fig.) face; uz ~īm prone; ~is rādīt show one's face; 3. stitch; 4. mesh; 5. pip; 6. point (in a game); 7. (sl.) power of observation
acs bults *nf* eyebolt
acsskrūve *nf* eyebolt, eye screw
actains *adj* (of crops) spotty, with bare spots
actek/s *nm*, ~iete *nf* Aztec
actenes *nf* pl eyeglasses
actiņa *nf* 1. *dim* of acs, eyelet; 2. (of a gun) touch-hole; 3. well (depression, for gravy, in mashed potatoes, porridge)
acu apmānīšana *nf* sleight of hand, trickery
acu apmānītājs *nm* legerdemaine artist
acu ārsts *nm* oculist, ophthalmologist
acu baltums *nm* white of the eye
acu dioptrs *nm* peep sight

acu dobums *nm* (anat.) orbit

acu dzirnums *nm* (anat.) pupil

acu gaisma *nf* eyesight

acu gneiss *nm* augengneiss

acu klape *nf* blinder

acu lēca *nf* crystalline lens

aculiecinie/ks *nm*, ~ce *nf* eyewitness

acumēr/s *nm* visual estimate; **labs a**. sure eye; **slikts a**. faulty eye; **pēc ~a** by the eye

acumirklīgi *adv* momentarily; immediately, in-stantaneously

acumirklīgs *adj* momentary;immediate, instantaneous

acumirklīgums *nm* momentariness

acumirkl/is *nm* moment, instant; ~i ! just a moment! ~ī instantly

acu nervs *nm* optic nerve

acuplaksti *nm* pl 1. eyelids; 2. sundew

acuplakstiņi *nm* pl *dim* of **acuplaksti**, eyelids

acu rauds *nm* (obs., anat.) pupil

acuraugs *nm* apple of one's eye

acu redzoklis *nm* (anat.) pupil

acu stikli *nm* pl (obs.) eyeglasses

acu uzmetiens *nm* glance

acu vāki *nm* pl eyelids

acu zirnītis *nm* (anat.) pupil

acuzobs *nm* eyetooth

acu zvītriņa *nf* (anat.) pupil

āče *interj* look

ačele *nf* (cont.) eye

ačgārni *adv* the wrong way; inside out; upside down

ačgārnība *nf* absurdity; perversity; ~s gars contrariness, perverseness

ačgārnis *nm* 1. one who does things the wrong way; 2. one who moves backwards

ačgārniski *adv* = **ačgārni**

ačgārnisk/s *adj* = **ačgārns**

ačgārniskums *nm* absurdity; perversity

ačgārns *adj* 1. reversed, inverted, turned the wrong way; inside out; upside down; 2. absurd, preposterous, wrong

ačgārnums *nm* absurdity

ači *nm* pl (col.) eyeglasses

ačk/a *nf* 1. one-eyed person, half-blind person; 2. a person with poor vision; a blind person; 3. weirdo; 4. ~u dzīt play blindman's buff

ačka *interj* heck

ačkups *nm* a Latvian folk dance

ačtele *nf* (cont.) eye

ād/a *nf* 1. skin, hide; fell; pelt; 2. leather; **mākslīga ā**. imitation leather ◊ **ā. pār kārti** end, finish, death; **aiz ~as** up one's sleeve; **ar veselu ~u** a narrow escape; **(būt kāda) ~ā** be in s.o.'s shoes

adadēo indecl *nm* adagio

ādainis *nm* hack, nag

ādains *adj* thick-skinned

ādaiņi *nm* pl leather gloves

ādamābols *nm* Adam's apple

adāmadata *nf* knitting needle

adāmais *nom adj* knitting (work in progress)

Ādama kostīmā *adv* (col.) in one's birthday suit

adamantāns *nm* adamantane

adāmmašīna *nf* knitting machine; ~s slēgs cam box

adamsīts *nm* adamsite

adapcija *nf* adaptation

adapcija tumsai *nf* dark adaptation

adaptācija *nf* adaptation

adapters *nm* (tech.) adapter; phono pickup

adaptēšanās *nfr* adaptation

adaptēt *vt* adapt

adaptēties *vr* adapt

adaptīvs *adj* adaptive

ādas krāsa *nf* complexion

ādas laka *nf* leather varnish

ādas slimības *nf* pl 1. diseases of the skin; 2. dermatology

ādas slimību ārsts *nm* dermatologist

adat/a *nf* needle; **adāmā a**. knitting needle; **gravējamā a**. engraving needle; **piespraueamā a**. safety pin; **tamborējamā**

a. crochet hook; ~**as dūriens** stitch; prick of a needle, (fig.) pinprick ◊ **kā uz ~ām** on pins and needles

adatādaiņi *nm* pl echinoderms

adatains *adj* covered with spines or needles, prickly

adatcūka *nf* porcupine

adatene *nf* (bot.) butcher's-broom

adatiņa *nf dim* of **adata**, small needle

adatiņas *nf* pl (sensation) pins and needles

adatnīca *nf* pincushion

adatniece *nf* needlewoman

adatnieks *nm* pincushion

[a]dats [ā] *nm* adat

adatterapija *nf* acupuncture

adatu dzniedniecība *nf* acupuncture

adatu gultnis *nm* needle bearing

adatu spilvens *nm* pincushion

adatveida indecl *adj* needle-shaped, acerose

adatveidīgs *adj* needle-shaped, acerose

adatvīle *nf* needle file

adatzivs *nf* pipefish

ādbruņrupucis *nm* (zool.) leatherback

adeklis *nm* unfinished piece of knitting (with needles)

adekļi *nm* pl socks or mits given as wedding gifts

adekvāti *adv* adequately

adekvāts *adj* adequate

adekvātums *nm* adequacy

adelfog[a]mija [ā] *nf* adelphogamy

adempcija *nf* ademption

adenektomija *nf* adenectomy

ādenieks *nm* (col., of a horse) jade

adenija *nf* adenoma

adenīns *nm* adenine

ādenis *nm* (col., of a horse) jade

adenīts *nm* adenitis

adenofora *nf* ladybell

adeno[i]ds [ī] *nm* adenoid

adeno[i]ds [ī] *adj* adenoid

adenoma *nf* adenoma

adenotomija *nf* adenoidectomy

adenovīruss *nm* adenovirus

adenoze *nf* adenosis

adenozīns *nm* adenosine

adepts *nm* adept

adepts *adj* adept

ader *conj* (col.) or

ādere *nf* (obs.) vein

āderēšana *nf* venesection, bloodletting

āderēt *vt* venesect

ādermanis *nm* phlebotomist

ādernieks *nm* phlebotomist

āderu zāle *nf* centaury

ādgrauēi *nm* pl dermestids

adhērents *nm* adherent

adhērents *adj* adherent

adhēzija *nf* adhesion

adh[e]zīvs [ē] *nm* adhesive

adh[e]zīvs [ē] *adj* adhesive

adhibicija *nf* adhibition

adhortācija *nf* exhortation

adiabāte *nf* adiabat

adiabātiski *adv* adiabatically

adiabātisks *adj* adiabatic

adiafora *nf* adiaphoron

adiaforisms *nm* adiaphorism

adiaforist/s *nm*, ~**e** *nf* adiaphorist

adiagnostisks *adj* adiagnostic

adiantpaparde *nf* maidenhair fern

adicija *nf* aditio

adieņi *nm* pl spring rye

adījums *nm* knitting (finished work)

adīklis *nm* knitting (work in progress)

ādiņa *nf* **1.** *dim* of **āda**, skin; pelt; **spodrināmā ā.** chamois; **2.** pellicle, film

adinamija *nf* adynamia

ādinieks *nm* (col., of a horse) jade

adipīnskābe *nf* adipic acid

adīt *vt* knit; (of fishnets) weave; **a. kreiliski** purl; **a. labiski** knit

adītāj/a *nf*, ~**s** *nm* knitter

adītava *nf* knitting workshop

adīties *vr* 1. knit for oneself; 2. compete in knitting; 3. knit itself

aditivitāte *nf* additivity

aditīvs *nm* additive

adjektivācija *nf* adjectivization

adjektīvisks *adj* adjectival

adjektivizācija *nf* adjectivization

adjektīvs *nm* adjective

adjicēt *vt* add

adjudikācija *nf* adjudication

adjunkts *nm* adjunct

adjunkts *adj* adjunct

adjustēt *vt* adjust

adjutants *nm* aid-de-camp; **vecākais a.** adjutant

ādminība *nf* leather tanning

ādminis *nm* tanner

administrācija *nf* administration

administr[a]tīvi [ā] *adv* administratively

administr[a]tīvs [ā] *adj* administrative

administr[a]tor/s [ā] *nm*, ~e *nf* administrator

administrēt *vt* administer

admirālis *nm* 1. admiral; 2. (zool.) red admiral

admir[a]litāte [ā] *nf* admiralty

admirālkuģis *nm* flagship

admisija *nf* admission

admitance *nf* (el.) admittance

admonicija *nf* admonition

adonijs *nm* adonic verse

adonisi *nm* pl (pharm.) adonises; (bot.) Adonis

adonitols *nm* adonitol

adopcija *nf* adoption

adoptācija *nf* adoption

adoptēt *vt* adopt

adoptētais *nom adj* adoptee

adoptīvbērns *nm* adoptive child

adorācija *nf* adoration

adrenalīns *nm* adrenalin

adrenāls *adj* adrenal

adrenerģisks *adj* adrenergic

adrenoģenitāls *adj* adrenogenital

adrenoinhibitors *nm* adrenal inhibitor

adrenokortikotropisks *adj* adrenocorticotropic

adrenomimetisks *adj* adrenomimetic

adresants *nm* sender

adresāts *nm* addressee

adres/e *nf* address; **pēc ~es** in care of, c/o ◊ **tas ir uz tavu ~i** that's a dig at you

adresēt *vt* address

adreskarte *nf* address card

adreslapa *nf* address label

adresu birojs *nm* addressing service

adresvedība *nf* (compu.) address administration

ādsiene *nf* leather strap

adsorbāts *nm* adsorbate

adsorbcija *nf* adsorption

adsorbents *nm* adsorbent

adsorbents *adj* adsorbent

adsorbēt *vt* adsorb

adstrāts *nm* (ling.) adstratum

aduktors *nm* adductor

adukts *nm* adduct

ādveida indecl *adj* leather-like

advekcija *nf* advection

advente *nf* advent

adventisms *nm* Adventism

adventist/s *nm*, ~e *nf* Adventist

adventīvs *adj* adventitious

advents *nm* Advent

adverbiāli *adv* adverbially

adverbializācija *nf* adverbialization

adverbializēt *vt* adverbialize

adverbializēties *vr* be adverbialized

adverbiāls *adj* adverbial

adverbs *nm* adverb

adversatīvs *adj* adversative

advokāts *nm*, ~e *nf* lawyer, counsel; **zvērināts a.** attorney at law

advokātu kollēģija *nf* the bar

advok[a]tūra [ā] *nf* the bar; law profession

adzī *interj* (reg.) look

adēār/s *nm*, ~iete *nf* Adzhar

aerācija *nf* aeration

aer|a|tors [ā] *nm* aerator

aeren|ch|īma [h] *nf* aerenchyma

aerēt *vt* aerate

aerobāka *nf* beacon

aeroballistika *nf* aeroballistics

aerobātika *nf* aerobatics

aerobāts *nm* stunt flier

aerobika *nf* aerobics

aerobioloģija *nf* aerobiology

aerobisks *adj* aerobic

aerobs *nm* aerobe

aerobs *adj* aerobic

aerobuss *nm* aerobus

aerodinamika *nf* aerodynamics

aerodinamiski *adv* aerodynamically

aerodinamisks *adj* aerodynamic

aerodroms *nm* airfield, airport

aerof|āg|ija [aģ] *nf* aerophagia

aerofilters *nm* aerofilter

aerofits *nm* epiphyte

aeroflote *nf* air fleet

aerofobija *nf* aerophobia

aerofors *nm* air pump (for diving)

aerofotoaparāts *nm* aerial camera

aerofotogr|a|fija [ā] *nf* aerial photography

aerofotogrammetrija *nf* aerophotogrammetry

aerofotoizlūkošana *nf* aerial photoreconnaissance

aerofototopogr|a|fija [ā] *nf* aerophototopography

aerofotouzņemšana *nf* aerial photography

aerofotouzņēmums *nm* aerial photograph

aerog|e|nisks [ē] *adj* (med.) airborne

aerogr|a|fija [ā] *nf* meteorology

aerogr|a|fs [ā] *nm* meteorograph

aeroģeodēzija *nf* aerial survey

aerokamanas *nf* pl airsleigh

aeroklubs *nm* flying club

aerolaiva *nf* airboat

aerolits *nm* aerolite

aerologs *nm* aerologist

aeroloģija *nf* aerology

aeroloģisks *adj* aerological

aerome|cha|nika [hā/ *nf* aeromechanics

aerometrs *nm* aerometer

aeromobils *adj* (mil.) airmobile

aeronautika *nf* aeronautics

aeronauts *nm* aeronaut

aeronavigācija *nf* aerial navigation

aeronomija *nf* aeronomy

aeropasts *nm* airmail

aeroplāns *nm* (obs.) airplane

aeroponika *nf* aeroculture

aeroreklāma *nf* aerial advertising

aerosēja *nf* aerial sowing

aerosmaile *nf* (of aircraft, projectiles) nose

aerosols *nm* aerosol

aerospidometrs *nm* air speed indicator

aerostatika *nf* aerostatics

aerostats *nm* aerostat

aerotanks *nm* aeration tank

aerote|ch|nika [h] *nf* aeronautics

aeroterapija *nf* aerotherapeutics

aerotransports *nm* air transportation

aerotriangulācija *nf* aerial triangulation

aerotropisms *nm* aerotropism

aerouzņēmums *nm* aerial photograph

aezojs *nm* Aezoic

afaģija *nf* aphagia

afalīna *nf* bottlenose dolphin

afanītisks *adj* aphanitic

afanīts *nm* aphanite

af|a|zija [ā] *nf* aphasia

afekcija *nf* affection

afektācija *nf* affectation

afektēt *vt* affect

afektēti *adv* in a studied manner

afektēts *adj*, part of afektēt studied, affected

afektīvs *adj* affective

afekts *nm* strong emotion; fit of passion

afekta stāvoklis *nm* temporary insanity

afēlijs *nm* aphelion

afēra *nf* shady deal

aferentācija *nf* afferentation

aferents *adj* afferent

afēristiski *adv* by means of a shady deal

afēristisks *adj* crooked

afērist/s *nm*, ~e *nf* swindler

afgān/is *nm*, ~iete *nf* Afghan

afgāns *nm* (currency) afghani

aficēt *vt* affix

afidāvits *nm* affidavit

afiksācija *nf* affixation

afikss *nm* affix

afiliācija *nf* affiliation

afinācija *nf* affination

afināēa *nf* affinage

afinitāte *nf* affinity

afirmācija *nf* affirmation

afirm|a|tīvi [ā] *adv* affirmatively

afirm|a|tīvs [ā] *adj* affirmative

afirmēt *vt* affirm

afiša *nf* poster, playbill

afišēt *vt* (of bills) post; (fig.) broadcast

afišu dēlis *nm* billboard

afišu stabs *nm* poster pillar

afonija *nf* aphonia

afonisks *adj* aphonic

aforisms *nf* aphorism

aforistiski *adv* aphoristically

aforistisks *adj* aphoristic

afotisks *adj* aphotic

afrikāner/is *nm*, ~iete *nf* Afrikaner

afrikān/is *nm*, ~iete *nf* African

afrikānistika *nf* African studies

afrik|a|nizācija [ā] *nf* Africanization

Afrikas bifelis *nm* Cape buffalo

Afrikas desukoks *nm* sausage tree

Afrikas sāre *nf* pearl millet; fountain grass

Afrikas skudrulācis *nm* aardvark

Afrikas sparmanija *nf* African hemp

afrikāta *nf* affricate

afroamerikān/is *nm*, ~iete *nf* Afro-American

afrodīzijs *nm* aphrodisiac

afronts *nm* affront

afta *nf* aphtha

aga *nm* aga

agalaktija *nf* agalactia

agalmatol|i|ts [ī] *nm* agalmatolite

ag|a|mija [ā] *nf* agamy

agamogonija *nf* agamogony

agams *adj* agamous

agape *nf* (love) agape

agaragars *nm* agar-agar

agaricīns *nm* choline

agars *nm* agar-agar

agarskābe *nf* agaric acid

agatoloģija *nf* agathology

agave *nf* agave

agenda *nf* agenda

agerāts *nm* ageratum

aglomerācija *nf* agglomeration

aglomerāts *nm* agglomerate

aglomerēt *vt* agglomerate

aglutinācija *nf* agglutination

aglutin|a|tīvs [ā] *adj* agglutinative

aglutinētājs *nm* agglutinative

aglutinīns *nm* agglutinin

agnātisks *adj* agnate

agnāts *nm* agnate

agni *adv* eagerly

agnosticisms *nm* agnosticism

agnostick/is *nm*, ~e *nf* agnostic

agnostiski *adv* agnostically

agnostisks *adj* agnostic

agnozija *nf* agnosia

agns *adj* eager

agoģika *nf* agogics

agone *nf* agonic line

agonija *nf* agony

agonisks *adj* agonal

agora *nf* agora

agorafobija *nf* agoraphobia

agrafe *nf* agrafe

agr|a|fija [ā] *nf* agraphia

agrains *adj* early

agraiņa *nf* early hour

agrais grīslis *nm* vernal sedge

agrais sikspārnis *nm* noctule

agrāk *adv* earlier; sooner; before; formerly

agrākais *adj* earlier; former; (super of **agrs**) the earliest; *adv* at the earliest

agrāks *adj* (comp of **agrs**) earlier; previous

agramatisms *nm* agrammatism

agranulocīts *nm* agranulocyte

agrārbanka *nf* agricultural bank

agrārietis *nm* agrarian

agrārjautājums *nm* agrarian issue

agrārlikums *nm* agrarian law

agrārmuita *nf* agricultural tariff

agrārpol[i]tika [ī] *nf* agrarian policy

agrārreforma *nf* agrarian reform

agrārs *adj* agrarian; agricultural

agrārvalsts *nf* agricultural state

agrās dedestiņas *nf* pl spring vetchling

agre *nf* (poet.) early hour

agregācija *nf* aggregation

agregāts *nm* **1.** aggregate; **2.** component; **3.** (tech.) unit, assembly

agregātstāvoklis *nm* state of matter

agregātveids *nm* state of matter

agrējs *adj* early

agremāns *nm* (diplomacy) agrément

agresija *nf* aggression; **pārnestā a.** displaced ag-gression; **pastarpinātā a.** mediated aggression

agresivitāte *nf* aggressiveness

agresīvi *adv* aggressively

agresīvs *adj* aggressive

agresīvums *nm* aggressiveness

agresor/s *nm*, ~e *nf* aggressor

agreēē *indecl nm* agrégé

agri *adv* early; **a. un vēlu** at all hours

agriena *nf* **1.** early hour; **2.** early times

agriene *nf* = **agriena**

agrīgs *adj* early rising

agrikultūra *nf* agriculture

agrīnība *nf* early ripeness

agrīns *adj* early; early ripe

agrīnums *nm* early ripeness

agripnija *nf* agrypnia

agrītiņām *adv* very early

agrobioloģija *nf* agrobiology

agrobizness *nm* agrobusiness

agrofizika *nf* agrology

agrofons *nm* soil condition

agroģeoloģija *nf* agricultural geology

agrojautājums *nm* agrarian issue

agroklimatisks *adj* agroclimatic

agroklimatoloģija *nf* agroclimatology

agroķīmija *nf* agricultural chemistry

agroķīmisks *adj* agrochemical

agroloģija *nf* agrology

agromeliorācija *nf* farm drainage and soil improvement

agrometeoroloģija *nf* agricultural meteorology

agrometeoroloģisks *adj* pertaining to agricultural metereology

agromuita *nf* agricultural tariff

agronomija *nf* agronomy

agronomisks *adj* agronomic

agronom/s *nm* ~e *nf* agronomist

agropilsēta *nf* agricultural town

agropol[i]tika [ī] *nf* agrarian policy

agroserviss *nm* farm aid service

agrot *vi* get up early

agrote[ch]nika [h] *nf* agrotechnology

agrote[ch]niķ/is [h] *nm*, ~e *nf* agrotechnologist

agrote[ch]nisks [h] *adj* agrotechnological

agroties *vr* **1.** get up early; **2.** ripen early

agrs *adj* early

agrtecīte *nf* (folk.) "early riser", an epithet for the bee

agrumeļļa *nf* citrus oil

agrum/s *nm* early hour; **rīta ~ā** early in the morning

agutis *nm* agouti

aģenda *nf* agendum

aģentēšanas līgums *nm* agency contract

ağent/s *nm*, ~e *nf* agent

ağentūra *nf* agency

ağitācija *nf* propaganda, agitation

ağitātor/s *nm*, ~e *nf* agitator, propagandist

ağitbrigāde *nf* propaganda team

ağitēt *vi* agitate, carry on propaganda

ağitkolektīvs *nm* propaganda agency

ağitpunkts *nm* campaign headquarters; propaganda center

ağittrupa *nf* theatrical propaganda troupe

ah- See ach-

ahoi *interj* ahoy

ai *interj* oh; ouch; alas

aicinājums *nm* 1. call, appeal; summons; challenge; 2. invitation; 3. vocation, calling

aicināt *vt* 1. call; summon; subpoena; 2. invite, ask

aicināties *vr* invite one another

aidā *interj* let's go

aidenieks *nm* (of horses) pacer

aideniski *adv* pacing; a. iet pace

aideniska gaita *nf* (of horses) pace

aidēt *vi* sound; make noise

aidinieks *nm* (of horses) pacer

aids (also Aids, AIDS) *nm* (med.) AIDS

aigida *nf* aegis

aijā *interj* a., bērniņ rockaby baby; iet a. (child.) go to sleep

aijas *nf* pl (child) cradle, bed

aijāt *vt* lull to sleep; rock

aijāties *vr* rock

aiju *interj* = aijā

aikido indecl *nm* aikido

aila *nf* opening (for a window or door)

ailants *nm* tree-of-heaven

ail/e *nf* 1. column (of writing); šai ~ē under this heading; 2. passageway; 3. = aila

ailis *nm* pole (for supporting fishgarths or in-creasing the carrying capacity of haywagons); roller (for moving heavy objects)

ailī—te *nf dim* of aile, column (of writing)

aiļot *vt* set up columns

aimaks *nm* aimak

aimanas *nf* pl lamentation, vailing

aimanāt *vi* lament, vail

aina *nf* 1. scene, sight; image; landscape; 2. (theat.) scene

ainava *nf* landscape

ainavisks *adj* landscape; scenic

ainavist/s *nm*, ~e *nf* landscape painter

ainavnie/ks *nm*, ~ce *nf* 1. landscape painter; 2. regional geographer

ainavzinātne *nf* regional geography

ainiņa *nf dim* of aina, scene

ainojums *nm* depiction

ainoties *vr* (of images) form

ain/s *nm*, ~iete *nf* Ainu

ainu meklētājs *nm* viewfinder

Aiola kokle *nf* Aeolian harp

|ai|oliet/is |e| *nm*, ~e *nf* Aeolian

aions *nm* eon

airans *nm* airan

airas *nf* pl hair grass

aire *nf* supporting member of a swing set

airēklis *nm* rudder

airene *nf* ryegrass

airēšana *nf* rowing; sculling; akadēmiskā a. rowboat racing; ~s sacīkste rowboat race

airēt *vt*, *vi* row; scull

airētāj/s *nm*, ~a *nf* rower, oarsman

airinie/ks *nm*, ~ce *nf* rower, oarsman

airis *nm* oar, scull

airīt *vt* a. zobus show one's teeth, grin, smile

airīties *vr* cut up, clown

airkāji *nm* pl pinnipeds

airkājvēži *nm* pl copepods

airsols *nm* rower's seat, thwart

airu laiva *nf* rowboat

aisbergs *nm* iceberg

aisīt *vt* a. zobus show one's teeth, grin, smile

aisīties *vr* cut up, clown

|ai|stētika |e| *nf* aesthetics

[ai]stētiski [e] *adv* aesthetically

[ai]stētisks [e] *adj* aesthetic

[ai]stētisms [e] *nm* aestheticism

[ai]stetizācija [e] *nf* aesthetic idealization

[ai]stēt/s [e] *nm*, ~e *nf* aesthete

aisti *nm pl* Aestii

aita *nf* sheep; (fig.) muttonhead; see also **resn-ragu a.**

aitāda *nf* sheepskin; fleece

aitainis *nm* sheepskin coat

aitasgalva *nf* (col.) muttonhead, oaf

aitas gaļa *nf* mutton

aitaspiere *nf* (col.) muttonhead, oaf

aitašķi *nm pl* yarrow

aitcirpis *nm* sheep shearer

aitene *nf* **1.** (bot.) poison pax; **2.** ~s bugloss

aitēns *nm* lamb

aitērisks *adj* etheric

[ai]t[ē]rs [ē][e] *nm* (phys.) ether

aitieši *nm pl* (obs.) sheep

aitiņa *nf* **1.** *dim* of **aita**, lambkin; **2.** ~s a. fleece clouds; b. rabbit-foot clover

aitioloģija *nf* = **etioloģija**

aitioloģiski *adv* = **etioloģiski**

aitioloģisks *adj* = **etioloģisks**

aitkopēj/s *nm*, ~a *nf* sheep farmer

aitkopība *nf* sheep farming

aitkop/is *nm*, ~e *nf* sheep farmer

aitnīca *nf* sheep farm

aitniece *nf* shepherdess

aitnieks *nm* shepherd

aitu āboliņš *nm* rabbit-foot clover

aitu asins sūcējs *nm* sheep ked

aitu auzene *nf* sheep fescue

aitu beka *nf* cauliflower mushroom

aitu dundurs *nm* sheep botfly

aitu dziras *nf pl* yarrow

aitu gans *nm* shepherd

aitu kūts *nf* sheepfold

aitu zāle *nf* yarrow

aiviekstenājs *nm* (reg.) raspberry bushes

aiviekstene *nf* (reg.) raspberry

aiz *prep* **1.** behind, on the other side of, round (the corner); **viens a. otra** one after the other; **2.** (touch, grasp) by; **3.** *conj* because of; **a. ko** why; **a. piesardzības** as a precaution; **a. tā** be-cause

aiza *nf* gorge, canyon; cleft, chasm; crevasse; **zemūdens a.** submarine trough

aizacīs *adv* behind one's back

aizači *nm pl* blinders

aizadi *nm pl* a piece of knitting that has been just cast on

aizaicināt *vt* call away

aizaijāt *vt* carry away rocking

aizains *adj* clefted

aizairēt *vt, vi* row away, row to

aizairēties *vr* row away; row to

aizāķēt *vt* hook up, fasten with a hook

aizāķēties *vr* get hooked, catch

aizalvot *vt* tin over

aizara *nf* cross-furrows (the portion of a field that has been plowed across rather than lengthwise because of some obstacle)

aizars *nm* = **aizara**

aizart *vt* **1.** cover up by plowing; **2.** begin to plow; **3.** plow away; **4.** plow to a certain point

aizasarot *vi* fog up

aizāt *vt* develop crevasses

aizaudi *nm pl* (weav.) start of a weave

aizaudzēt *vt* allow to or make (a plant) cover sth.; allow to overgrow; (of a wound) make heal

aizauga *nf* bushes

aizaugt *vi* overgrow (with plants); become co-vered (with plants); grow (reaching a certain place); heal (filling with new tissue)

aizaulekšot *vi* gallop away, race away

aizauļot *vi* gallop away, race away

aizaurēties *vr* begin to howl, begin to cry; cry out

aizause *nf* **1.** place behind the ears; **2.** space be-tween the inner and outer openings of an oven

aizauss *indecl adj* parotic

aizauss dziedzeris *nm* parotid gland

aizauss paugurs *nm* mastoid bone

aizaust I *vi* begin to dawn

aizaust II *vt* **1.** cover, close by weaving; **2.** begin to weave

aizbadēties *vr* fast a long time

aizbadīt *v* **1.** *vt* butt away; **2.** *vi* miss in butting; **3.** *vt* (col.) tuck in

aizbadojies *adj, part* of **aizbadoties** hungry

aizbadoties *vr* fast a long time

aizbaidīt *vt* scare away; shoo away

aizbailes *nf pl* fright

aizbakstīt *vt* caulk

aizbalstīt *vt* tuck in

aizbalzīt *vt* tuck in

aizbangot *v* **1.** *vi* (of waves) move away, move to; **2.** *vt* (of waves) carry away

aizbarikādēt *vt* barricade, block

aizbarikādēties *vr* barricade oneself

aizbars *nm* **1.** narrowing of the swath during mowing; newly begun swath; **2.** a dusting of flour (on risen dough, before baking); **3.** grits, groats; a dish of boiled grits

aizbārstīt *vt* pour behind sth.

aizbauroties *vr* moo, begin to moo

aizbāzeknis *nm* stuffing material, caulking; stopper

aizbāzis *nm* = **aizbāzs**

aizbāzīt *vt* tuck in

aizbāznis *nm* stopper, plug, bung, wadding, tampion

aizbāz/s *nm* **1.** stopper, plug, bung, wadding, tampion; **2.** reserve, stopgap; **3.** ~i a. bribe; b. charms (used in malevolent magic)

aizbāzt *vt* **1.** cork, stopper, plug, bung, stop; **2.** stick, push behind sth.; hide; **a. muti** (col.) shut so up, squelch

aizbāzties *vr* **1.** stick behind sth. (on one's person); **2.** get plugged up, get stopped

aizbāžamais *nom adj* stopper, plug, bung

aizbāžburtnīca *nf* stock book

aizbēdzināt *vt* make flee

aizbēgt *vi* run away; flee; escape; elope; abscond; desert

aizbēgušais *nom adj* escapee; runaway

aizbere *nf* fill, backfill; filling

aizbērt *vt* fill, backfill; pour (into); **a. garām** miss (in pouring)

aizbest *vt* fill, backfill; pour (into)

aizbīdeklis *nm* bar, bolt

aizbīdene *nf* door bolt

aizbīdes *indecl adj* push, slide

aizbīdes ārdu kurtuve *nf* onward-feed furnace

aizbīdīt *vt* push, shove (away, aside, in front of); (of a drawer) close; **a. aizšaujamo** bolt the door; **a. ciet** close, push to close

aizbīdnis *nm* door bolt; (chimney) damper; (tech.) gate; slide valve

aizbīdņa vārstulis *nm* gate valve

aizbiedēt *vt* scare away

aizbikstīt *vt* stick, push behind sth.

aizbildinājums *nm* excuse, apology; pretext

aizbildināšanās *nfr* excuse, apology; pretext

aizbildināt *vt* excuse

aizbildin/āties *vr* excuse oneself; **a. ar nezināšanu** plead ignorance; ~oties ar . . . under the pretext of . . . ; ~oties, ka . . . under the plea that . . .

aizbildnība *nf* guardianship, wardship, trusteeship, tutelage

aizbildnības territorija *nf* trust territory

aizbildniecība *nf* guardianship

aizbildniecisks *adj* pertaining to guardianship; like a guardian

aizbildn/is *nm*, ~e *nf* guardian; trustee

aizbilst *vt* mention; **a. vārdu (kāda labā)** put in a good word

aizbilstam/ais *nom adj*, ~ā *f* ward; protégé

aizbirdināt *vt* (of granular matter) pour (behind)

aizbirt *vi* (of granular materials) fall, drop behind sth.; (of holes, excavations) fill up, cave in

aizbizināt *vt* make (cattle) bolt

aizbizot *vi* bolt (away)

aizblākšēt *vi* = **aizblākšķēt**

aizblākšķēt *vi* (of a door) slam

aizblandīties *vr* (com.) stray, traipse away

aizbliest *v* **1.** *vt* carry away furtively; **2.** *vt* **a. muti** squelch; **3.** *vi* scamper

aizbliesties *vr* slink away

aizblīkšķināt *vi* **a. gaŗām** miss (in shooting)

aizblīvēt *vt* caulk

aizbļaut *vt* **1.** outshout; **2.** (folk., of birds) utter a cry (as an ill omen)

aizbļauties *vr* begin to shout

aizbode *nf* river bend; cove

aizbojāt *vt* damage slightly

aizborta *indecl adj* outboard

aizborta traps *nm* accomodation ladder

aizbraucēj/s *nm*, **~a** *nf* departing person

aizbraukšana *nf* departure

aizbraukt *vi* leave, depart, drive off, drive away; go (by train, by boat); *vt* drive to; **a. ciemos** go visiting

aizbrāzt *vi* dash off; thunder past

aizbrāzties *vr* dash off, thunder past

aizbrēkt *vt* outshout; (folk., of birds) utter a cry (as an ill omen)

aizbrēkties *vr* begin to cry

aizbrikšķēties *vr* snap, crack

aizbrist *vi* **1.** wade away; wade to; **2.** (of the sun, moon) set amid clouds

aizbrukt *vi* cave in

aizbruzdēt *vi* rumble away

aizbubināt *vi* begin to whinny

aizbubināties *vr* begin to whinny

aizbultēt *vt* (of doors, gates) bolt

aizbultēties *vr* **1.** lock o.s. in; **2.** (of bolts) slide by itself to lock the door

aizburbēt *vi* **1.** begin to decay; **2.** overgrow with soft, porous vegetation; **3.** swell

aizburbis *adj, part* of **aizburbēt 1.** partly rotten; **2.** overgrown with soft, porous vegetation; **3.** swollen

aizburbuļot *vi* bubble away

aizbūvēt *vt* build in front of; fill with buildings

aizbūvēties *vr* **1.** build a house and move into it; **2.** build in front of

aizcelt *vt* **1.** move, transfer, relocate; **2.** (of a gate, window) close

aizcelties *vr* **1.** move, relocate; **2.** withdraw

aizceļot *vi* leave on a journey, go off on a trip

aizcementēt *vt* fill with cement

aizceple *nf* place behind the oven

aizceplis *nm* = **aizceple**

aizcerēt *vt* hope for, have designs for, have an eye on

aizcerot *vt* overgrow

aizciest *vt* get over the loss of

aizciesties *vr* hold back; restrain oneself for too long

aizcietējums *nm* constipation

aizcietēt *vi* constipate; harden

aizcilas *nf pl* **1.** collateral, security, forfeit; **2.** pole gate

aizcilpot *vi* bound away; take to one's heels, get away

aizcinis *nm* place behind a tussock

aizcīnīties *vr* get to a place by struggling

aizcipt *vi* (reg.) get stuck and be late; stumble

aizcirst *vt* **1.** notch, make a notching cut; **2.** (of a door, lid) slam; **a. muti** shut so up; **a. kāju priekšā** trip up; **3. a. ceļu** make an abatis; **~s** abatised; **4.** *vi* dash

aizcirsties *vr* **1.** (of doors, lids) slam; **2.** become breathless, become speechless; **3.** get caught on sth.; **4. a. priekšā** cut s.o. off

aizcirtnis *nm* abatis

aizcirtums *nm* (of horses) injury to the coronet

aizcits *adj* (of a day, month or year) one after the next

aizcitu *adv* after the next (day, month or year)

aizčabēt *vi* move away rustling

aizčabēties *vr* rustle briefly

aizčabināt *vi* (col.) move away, patter away

aizčākstēties *vr* (of birds) begin to call

aizčalot *vi* **1.** flow away murmuring; **2.** move away chattering

aizčāpāt *vi* toddle away; (with **līdz, uz**) toddle to

aizčāpot *vi* = **aizčāpāt**

aizčaukstēt *vi* rustle away, rustle past

aizčaukstēties *vr* rustle briefly

aizčauvēt *vt* (reg.) scare away

aizčerkstēt *vi* (col.) become hoarse

aizčiepstēties *vr* chirp briefly

aizčīkstēties *vr* creak briefly

aizčinkstēties *vr* jingle briefly

aizčīpstēties *vr* chirp briefly

aizčirkstēties *vr* (of birds) sing briefly

aizčokurēt *vt* repair the ridge (of a roof)

aizčučināt *vt* (child.) put to sleep

aizčūlot *vi* (of a suppurating wound) scab over

aizčunčināt *vi* trot away

aizdabūt *vt* get (or lug) to a place

aizdaga *nf* (reg.) kindling

aizdambējums *nm* dam, dike; obstruction, jam

aizdambēt *vt* dam

aizdambēties *vr* dam up

aizdārdēt *vi* thunder away, rumble away

aizdārdēties *vr* thunder briefly

aizdārdināt *v* **1.** *vi* move away rumbling; **2.** *vt* move away with a rumble

aizdare *nf* fastener

aizdarīt *vt* **1.** close, shut; **a. acis uz mūžu** (poet.) die; **neaizdarīt ne aci** keep awake; **2.** add fat or dairy products to food; **3.** do sth. for s.o. beforehand; **4. a. dusmas** make mad; **5.** dirty

aizdarīties *vr* close, shut

aizdars *nm* fat or dairy products added to food

aizdauzīties *vr* (col.) traipse away

aizdāvāt *vt* give away

aizdāvināt *vt* give away

aizdedze *nf* (tech.) ignition; **agrā a.** preignition; **priekšlaicīga a.** preignition; **vēlā a.** retarded ignition

aizdedzes ierīce *nf* igniter

aizdedzes kārtība *nf* firing order

aizdedzes laiks *nm* (of fluorescent lamps) start period

aizdedzes magnets *nm* magneto

aizdedzes punkts *nm* ignition point

aizdedzināmība *nf* ignitability

aizdedzināms *adj, part* of **aizdedzināt; viegli a.** flammable

aizdedzināt *vt* light (a match, fire), kindle, ignite, set on fire; **a. ugunis** turn on the lights

aizdedzinātājs *nm* igniter

aizdedzinošs *adj, part* of **aizdedzināt** incendiary

aizdedzis *nm* igniter

aizdedzis *adj, part* of **aizdegt** on fire

aizdedzkapsele *nf* blasting cap, ignitor cap

aizdegs *nm* (tech.) igniter

aizdegšanās *nfr* ignition; **sekundārā a.** secondary fires

aizdegšanās spēja *nf* ignitability

aizdegšanās temper[a]tūra [ā] *nf* fire point

aizdegt *v* **1.** *vt* light, kindle, set on fire, ignite, (of lights) turn on; (fig.) inflame; **2.** *vi* (of a cow's udder) become inflamed; **3.** *vi* catch fire and burn

aizdegties *vr* catch fire; (of lights) come on; **a. dusmās** (fig.) flare up

aizdegune *nf* nasopharynx

aizdejot *vi* dance away

aizdelverēt *vi* traipse away

aizdelverēties *vr* traipse away

aizdenderēt *vi* (col.) leave

aizderēt *vi* hire out

aizdevas *nf pl* loan

aizdevēj/s *nm*, ~a *nf* creditor, lender

aizdevu kase *nf* savings and loan association

aizdevum/s *nm* loan; ~a ņēmējs borrower

aizdiebt *vi* run away

aizdiegt *vi* 1. stitch, baste; 2. scurry away

aizdiegties *vr* scurry away

aizdīgt *vi* germinate, sprout

aizdikāt *vi* (col.) scurry away

aizdilināt *vi* trot away

aizdimdēt *vi* rumble away

aizdimdināt *v* 1. *vi* rumble away; 2. *vt* make sth. sound

aizdimēt *vi* rumble away

aizdimīt *vt* (reg.) drag away

aizdimt *vi* rumble away

aizdipēt *vi* scurry away

aizdipināt *vi* scurry away

aizdipt *vi* scurry away

aizdīrāt *vt* begin to skin

aizdirbt *vi* scurry away

aizdirst *vt* (com.) dirty, befoul

aizdomas *nf pl* suspicion

aizdomāt *vi* a. uz priekšu think ahead

aizdomāties *vr* get lost in thought

aizdomīgi *adv* suspiciously

aizdomīgs *adj* suspicious

aizdomīgums *nm* suspiciousness

aizdot *vt* 1. give away, send away; 2. loan; a. bailes frighten; a. dusmas make angry

aizdoties *vr* take off (depart) quickly

aizdragāt *vt* 1. fling violently away; 2. damage slightly

aizdrāzt *v* 1. *vt* sharpen, scrape to a point; 2. *vi* dash away, rush away

aizdrāzties *vr* dash away, rush away

aizdrebēt *vi* begin to shiver; begin to rattle

aizdrebēties *vr* begin to shiver; begin to rattle

aizdrīģēt *vt* bar

aizdrīvēt *vt* caulk

aizdrunēt *vi* weather partly

aizducināt *vi* (of a tumble, thunder) move away

aizducināties *vr* rumble briefly

aizdūdoties *vr* coo briefly

aizdudzēt *vi* rumble

aizdudzis *adj* hazy

aizdūkt *v* 1. *vi* buzz away; 2. *vt* deafen by buzzing; (of a sound) drown in a buzz

aizdūkties *vr* buzz briefly

aizduļķot *vt* muddy up

aizdūmakot *vi* become hazy

aizdūmakots *adj, part* of aizdūmakot hazy

aizdumējis *adj, part* of aizdumēt hazy

aizdumēt *vi* become hazy

aizdūmot *v* 1. *vt* (of bees) smoke ; 2. *vi* become hazy

aizdundurot *vi* buzz away

aizdunēt *vi* (of booming sound, footsteps) move away

aizdunēties *vr* boom briefly

aizdu[r]amais [ŗ] *nom adj* plug, bung

aizdurs *nm* bar (for a door lock or hasp)

aizdurt *vt* 1. stick; fasten (by sticking); 2. injure (by sticking)

aizdurve *nf* place behind the door

aizdusa *nf* short breath; man ir a. I am shortwinded

aizdvesties *vr* suffocate

aizdzelt *vt* sting

aizdzeltēt *vi* yellow

aizdzelžot *vt* bar, install bars

aizdzenāt *vt* shoo away, drive away

aizdzert *vt* 1. celebrate an engagement; 2. have celebrated already

aizdziedāt *vt* 1. outsing; 2. (folk., of birds) bring bad luck (to one who wakes in the morning hearing their song); 3. (folk., of a cock) crow before the devil has finished his evil deed

aizdziedāties *vr* sing briefly

aizdziedēt *vt* heal

aizdziedināt *vt* heal

aizdzīres *nf pl* party after a feast

aizdzirkstīt *vi* begin to sparkle, light up

aizdzirkstīties *vr* begin to sparkle, light up

aizdzīt I *vt* **1.** drive away; chase away; **2.** (of plugs, stoppers, pins) drive in

aizdzīt II *vi* heal, skin over

aizdzīties *vr* (with **pēc**) chase after; run (drive, ride) away at full speed

aizdzīvot *vt* **1.** lose by loose living; **2.** live (to a certain age)

aizdzīvoties *vr* (of a nursing mother) become pregnant

aizdžinkstēt *vi* **1.** buzz past; whizz by; **2.** (of ears) begin to ring

aizdžungļoties *vr* overgrow

aizecēt *vt* **1.** harrow (to a certain point); **2.** cover in harrowing

aizēda *nf* snack

aizeja *nf* departure

aizejošs *adj, part* of **aiziet** (RR) departing

aizelsa *nf,* usu. *loc* **aizelsā** out of breath

aizelsies *adj, part* of **aizelsties** out of breath

aizelsties *vr* be out of breath

aizelša *nm, nf* one out of breath

aizēna *nf* shadow; lee side

aizēnot *vt* cast a shadow; overshadow, eclipse

aizēst *vt* **1.** snack (before a main meal); **2.** finish eating before another person; **3.** begin to corrode

aizēsts *adj, part* of **aizēst** chewed-on, moth-eaten

aizezere *nf* place across the lake

aizezerieši *nm pl* people living across the lake

aizfantazēties *vr* become lost in fantasy

aizfronte *nf* (mil.) rear

aizgādāt *vt* (with **prom**) get rid of; (with **līdz, uz**) get to, deliver to; **a. no ceļa** get rid of; **a. pie malas** kill

aizgadgadā *adv* from year to year, always

aizgādīb/a *nf* care; protection; **būt ~ā** be in s.o.'s charge; **~as iestāde** social welfare bureau

aizgādīgi *adv* solicitously

aizgādīgs *adj* solicitous

aizgādnība *nf* **1.** guardianship; **2.** care, protection

aizgādniecība *nf* = (obs.) **aizgādnība**

aizgādniecisks *adj* solicitous

aizgādnie/ks *nm,* ~ce *nf* guardian

aizgādn/is *nm,* ~e *nf* guardian

aizgāds *nm* stock, supply, reserve, provision

aizgailēties *vr* flare up

aizgainīt *vt* drive away, shoo away; (fig.) dispel

aizgaiņāt *vt* drive away, shoo away; (fig.) dispel

aizgaita *nf* (reg.) **1.** trouble, bad luck; **2.** excuse, pretext; **3.** errand for another person

aizgaite *nf* = **aizgaita**

aizgaitne *nf* **1.** side trip; **2.** old disability

aizgājēj/s *nm,* ~a *nf* **1.** departing person; **2.** the deceased

aizgājība *nf* the past

aizgājis *adj, part* of **aiziet** past

aizgājuš/ais *adj* **1.** past; **2.** *nom adj* the deceased; ~ā *f*

aizgalde *nf* **1.** place on the other side of the table; **2.** side boards of a wagon

aizgaldīt *vt* board up

aizgaldnīca *nf* porker, market hog

aizgaldnieks *nm* a young animal that is being fatted in a pen

aizgalds *nm* pen, stall, sty

aizgalēties *vr* endure

aizgani *nm pl* substituting for another herdsman

aizganīt *vt* **1.** chase away; **2.** herd cattle early (to quiet them)

aizgansts *nm* pretext

aizgaņģis *nm* **1.** refuge; **2.** slew; **3.** alley; **4.** narrow strip of land

aizgārgties *vr* begin to rattle in one's throat

aizgarot *vi* begin to steam

aizgātnis *nm* emigrant

aizgaudoties *vr* howl briefly

aizgavēnis *nm* Sunday after Shrove Tuesday

aizgavilēties *vr* begin to cheer, begin to jubilate

aizgāzelēties *vr* wobble away

aizgāzt *vt* dump in front of, block (by dumping, tipping)

aizgāzties *vr* (of a pit) collapse; (with **priekšā**) fall in front of

aizglabāt *vt* hide; keep

aizglābties *vr* hide oneself

aizglaudīt *vt* (of hair) push behind (the ears)

aizglaust *vt* (of hair) push behind (the ears)

aizgludināt *vt* smooth

aizglumēt *vi* clog up

aizgniezt *vt* carry away

aizgore *nf* (reg.) **1.** (of peasant dwellings) space between the oven and the wall; **2.** narrow alley between buldings

aizgorīties *vr* walk away swinging one's hips

aizgoze *nf* sunny lee side

aizgrabēt *vi* rattle away

aizgrabēties *vr* begin to rattle

aizgrābīgs *adj* thrilling, moving

aizgrabināt *vi* rattle away

aizgrābjošs *adj, part* of **aizgrābt** thrilling, moving

aizgrābstīt *vt* rake away; rake to

aizgrābt *vt* **1.** thrill, transport, move; **2.** grab; **3.** rake (to a place)

aizgrābtība *nf* thrill, transport, ecstasy

aizgrābties *vr* be thrilled

aizgrandēt *vi* rumble away

aizgrausties *vr* begin to thunder

aizgraut *vt* block by tumbling or collapsing

aizgrauties *vr* **1.** drop down heavily behind sth.; **2.** (of a sound) roll

aizgrauzdēt *vt* roast lightly

aizgrauzt *vt* begin to gnaw

aizgrauzties *vr* gnaw (one's way) to

aizgrāvot *vt* surround with ditches

aizgrēda *nf* place behind a woodpile

aizgrieznis *nm* **1.** faucet valve; tap, cock; **2.** river bend; **3.** tie connecting the thill to a sled; **4.** (reg.) grass blades or stalks left unmowed under a swath

aizgriezt I *vt* **1.** shut (by turning), turn off; **2.** turn away; **3.** block

aizgriezt II *vt* notch; cut

aizgriezties *vr* **1.** turn, turn away from, turn off (to one side); **2.** lock (by turning)

aizgrīļot *vi* stagger away

aizgrīļoties *vr* stagger away

aizgrimt *vi* sink, sink behind, sink out of sight

aizgrozīties *vr* move away twisting and turning

aizgrudzināties *vr* begin to whinny

aizgrūst *vt* **1.** push, push away; **2.** push shut

aizgrūt *vi* **1.** cave in, become blocked; **2.** (of loose material) slide down and in front of

aizgruvumezers *nm* landslide lake

aizgruvums *nm* cave-in, slide

aizgruzdēt *vi* begin to smolder

aizguldināt *vt* **1.** put to sleep; **2.** allow to oversleep

aizguldīt *vt* allow to oversleep

aizguldzenēties *vr* choke

aizgulēt *vi* miss by oversleeping

aizgulēties *vr* oversleep

aizgult *vi* lie down, settle down (in front of sth.)

aizgulte *nf* place behind the bed

aizgulties *vr* lie down, settle down (in front of sth.)

aizgurkstēt *vi* (of the sound of footsteps on crunchy snow) move away

aizgurkstēties *vr* (of the sound of footsteps on crunchy snow) be heard briefly

aizgūt *vt* **1.** borrow; **2.** grab; overwhelm; bewilder

aizgū/ties *vr* **1.** grab; **2.** stumble over one's words; **~damies** eagerly, stumbling in one's eagerness

aizgūtn/e *nf* **1.** eagerness; ~ēm a. eagerly; **dzert** ~ēm gulp; b. in snatches, by fits and starts; **2.** stock, supply

aizgūtnība *nf* eagerness, greed

aizgūtnīgi *adv* eagerly, passionately

aizgūtnīgs *adj* eager, ardent, passionate

aizgūtnis *nm* greedy person, miser

aizguvuma vārds *nm* loan word

aizguvums *nm* borrowing

aizģeņģerēt *vi* stagger away

aizīdēties *vr* bleat briefly

aiziešana *nf* **1.** going away, departure; **2.** dying, death

aiziet *vi irr* **1.** go, go away, leave, depart; take off; (*3rd pers*, theat.) exit; **a. no darba** leave work; resign; **a. ciemos** go visiting; **a. gulēt** go to bed; **a. pensijā** retire; **2.** go (up) to, lead to; **3. a. pēc** go for, go and get, fetch; **4.** (of time) pass; **5.** die; **6.** (of odors, fame, rumors) spread; **7.** get to; **8.** be lost; **9.** close ◊ **a. aizsaulē** leave this world; **a. badā** starve; **a. bojā** perish; **a. dibenā** sink; **a. gar degunu** (of vehicles, transport) just miss; **a. garu ceļu** (col.) be lost, be stolen; **a. kapā** (poet.) die; **a. karā** (of persons) go to war; **a. mūēīgā** (or **Dieva**) **mierā** (poet.) pass on; **a. nebūtībā** die; **a. nelietā** spoil, be damaged, perish; **a. neceļos** (fig.) go astray; **a. nīkā** perish; disappear; be destroyed; **a. pazušanā** (or **pa-zudā**) perish; disappear; be destroyed; **a. priek-šā** a. walk in front of; b. pass by; surpass; **a. pie tēviem** (or **senčiem**) (iron.) die; **a. pie veļiem** die; **a. postā** perish; **a. savās darīšanās** (sl.) go see a man about a dog; **a. secen** miss; **a. uz mūēiem** die; **a. uz viņpasauli** (or **viņā saulē**) die; **a. vējā** (or **niekā**) (col.) be wasted, be lost, perish; **a. pa gaisu** (fig.) be lost, evaporate; **a!** let's go! **a. jūriņā!** there it goes!

aizieties *vr irr* **1.** begin to hurt; **2. valoda aizgā-jās** he (she) stuttered

aizirt I *vi, vt* row away; row to

aizirt II *vi* begin to unravel

aizirties *vr* row to

aizjādelēt *vi* ride away; ride to

aizjāt *vi, vt* ride away; ride to; **a. priekšā** overtake (in riding)

aizjauda *nf* premonition

aizjemt *vt* = **aizņemt**

aizjoņot *vi* gallop away, rush away

aizjozt I *vi* run away, dash away

aizjozt II *vt* (of a belt) put on, don

aizjūg/s *nm* **1.** harness; ~a animal-drawn; **2.** team (of horse and wagon)

aizjūgt *vt* harness; yoke

aizjūgties *vr* put oneself in harness

aizjumt *vt* (of roofs) repair

aizjūra *nf* overseas

aizjūras telegramma *nf* cablegram

aizkabināt *vt* hook on

aizkabināties *vr* get caught on

aizkacēt *vt* **1.** hook; **2.** reach

aizkaisīt *vt* scatter, broadcast

aizkaitīgs *adj* easily offended, irritable

aizkaitinājums *nm* irritation, annoyance

aizkaitināmība *nf* irritability

aizkaitināt *vt* irritate, annoy, offend

aizkājot *vi* hoof it (to)

aizkakl/e *nf*, usu. *loc* ~ē behind the collar

aizkakte *nf* remote corner

aizkakts *nm* = **aizkakte**

aizkalēties *vr* fast; be thirsty, be hungry

aizkalne *nf* the other side of the mountain

aizkalst *vi* **1.** dry; dry out; **2.** begin to dry, wither

aizkaltēt *vt* stop milking

aizkamāt *v* **1.** *vi* stomp; **2.** *vt* hitch up

aizkāmējis *adj* starving, very hungry

aizkapa *indecl adj* from beyond the grave, sepulchral; **a. dzīve** life after death

aizkapāt *vt* hack

aizkaplēt *v* **1.** *vi* hoe (to a place); **2.** *vt* begin to hoe

aizkāpt *vi* 1. reach in climbing; 2. (with **uz**, iron.) sashay to

aizka|r|amais |ŗ| *nom adj* hanging, curtain, blind; padlock

aizka|r|amība |ŗ| *nf* touchiness

aizkarene *nf* (col.) padlock

aizkarināt I *vt* hang

aizkarināt II *vt* tease, annoy

aizkārpīt *vt* (of a hole in the ground) cover, fill

aizkars *nm* curtain; blind

aizkārstīt *vt* bar

aizkarst *vi* heat up; catch fire

aizkāršot *vt* 1. bar with poles; 2. fence with poles

aizkar/t *vt* 1. touch; **a. (kāda) tiesības** encroach upon s.o.'s rights; 2. offend; **a. vārdiem** abuse verbally; **a. vārīgā vietā** touch a sore spot; **viegli ~ams** easily offended

aizkārt *vt* hang, (with **priekšā**) hang in front of

aizkartne *nf* (bot.) great burnet

aizkārtne *nf nm* (of railroad crossing, toll gate) bar; gate

aizkārtnis *nm* = **aizkārtne**

aizkārtnīte *nf* padlock

aizkārtņot *vt* bar, barricade

aizkārums *nm* offense; infringement

aizkāsēt *vi* clear one's throat; clear one's throat meaningfully

aizkāsēties *vr* clear one's throat

aizkasīt *vt* cover up by scratching

aizkašāt *vt* = **aizkašņāt**

aizkašņāt *vt* (of a hole in the ground) fill

aizkātot *vi* (col.) stride away

aizkaukt *vi* move (away, by) howling

aizkaukties *vr* howl briefly

aizkausēt I *vt* tire, tire out

aizkausēt II *vt* weld shut, solder shut

aizkaustīt *vt* fasten by wedging

aizkaut *vt* wound in the process of slaughter; **~s** in the process of being slaughtered, stuck

aizkavējums *nm* delay

aizkavēšana *nf* delay; **~s uguns** dilatory fire

aizkavēt *vt* 1. delay, detain; keep; 2. slow down, retard; postpone

aizkavēties *vr* be delayed, be held up, be behind schedule

aizklabēt *vi* clatter away

aizklabēties *vr* clatter briefly

aizklabināt *v* 1. *vt* rattle briefly; 2. *vi* rattle away

aizkladzināt *vt* **a. ausis** deafen with one's cackling

aizkladzināties *vr* cackle briefly

aizklaiņāt *vi* wander away

aizklaiņot *vi* = **aizklaiņāt**

aizklājs *nm* covering, screen

aizklakstēt *v* 1. *vt* shut with a clatter; 2. *vi* move away with a clatter

aizklakšķināt *vi* clip-clop away

aizklančot *vi* shamble away

aizklapēt *vt* close

aizklāt *vt* cover, veil, screen

aizklāti *adv* secretly

aizklātība *nf* secrecy

aizklāties *vr* cover o.s.; be covered up

aizklāts *adj, part* of **aizklāt** (of votes, ballots) secret; (of meetings) executive

aizklaudzēt *vi* clatter away, rattle away

aizklaudzēties *vr* knock briefly

aizklaudzināt *vt* (coll, of auctioning) hammer away

aizklausīt *vt* please (by obeying or serving)

aizklausīties *vr* (usu. in the phrase **ka nevar ne a.**) be unable to hear, think, or open one's mouth (because of s.o.'s excessive talking or crying)

aizkleberēt *vi* move away clumsily, move away with a clatter

aizklejot *vi* wander away, wander off

aizkleķēt *vt* fill (with clay, plaster)

aizklenderēt *vi* (com.) traipse away

aizklengot *vi* wander off

aizklepot *vi* clear one's throat; clear one's throat as a signal

aizklepoties *vr* clear one's throat

aizklibot *vi* limp away

aizklīdināt *vt* disperse, drive apart

aizklidzināt *vi* clip-clop away

aizkliedēt *vt* drive away

aizkliegt *vt* deafen (by shouting); outshout

aizkliegties *vr* call out

aizklikstināt *vi* clip-clop away

aizklimst I *vi* vibrate with the sound of

aizklimst II *vi* wander off

aizklimstēt *vi*= **aizklimst**

aizklinkāt *vi* wobble away

aizklīst *vi* wander off, stray

aizkluburot *vi* = **aizklumburot**

aizklūgot *vt* fasten with a withe

aizklukstēties *vr* cackle briefly

aizklumburot *vi* waddle away

aizklunčot *vi* (col.) shamble away

aizklunkšķēties *vr* gurgle briefly

aizklunkurot *vi* waddle away

aizkļūdīties *vr* wander off

aizkļūt *vi* get to, reach

aizknābāt *vt* peck here and there

aizknābt *vt* miss in pecking

aizknakstīties *vr* creak briefly

aizknakšēties *vr* creak briefly

aizknakšķēties *vr* creak briefly

aizknaukšķēties *vr* creak briefly

aizkniedēt *vt* rivet shut

aizknikšķēties *vr* crackle briefly

aizknikšķināt *vi* click away

aizkniepēt *vt* fasten with pins

aizkņopēt *vt* (barb.) button up

aizkomandēt *vt* send, dispatch, (mil.) detail

aizkore *nf* barrier

aizkorēt *vt* bar

aizkorķēt *vt* stopper

aizkost *vt, vi* take a bite; have a snack

aizkrāce *nf* place on the other side of a rapids

aizkrāciet/is *nm,* ~**e** *nf* Zaporozhie Cossack

aizkrakstēties *vr* begin to creak; creak briefly

aizkrakšķēties *vr* begin to creak; creak briefly

aizkrākties *vr* snore briefly

aizkrāmēt *vt* remove

aizkrāmēties *vr* (barb.) move (to another residence)

aizkrampēt *vt* fasten with a hook

aizkrampēties *vr* lock oneself in (with a door hook)

aizkrāpt *vt* lure away

aizkrāsne *nf* (obs., of peasant dwellings) space between the oven and the wall

aizkrāsot *vt* cover with paint

aizkrāt *vt* save

aizkrāties *vr* accumulate

aizkratīt *vt* shake; empty by shaking behind sth.

aizkratīties *vr* 1. fall into (or behind) because of shaking; 2. take a shaky ride (to a place)

aizkraut *vt* 1. stack (away, behind, up to); 2. block (by stacking)

aizkravāt *vt* 1. remove; 2. barricade

aizkravāties *vr* move away

aizkrebināt *vt* fasten loosely

aizkrekl/e *nf,* usu. *loc* ~**ē** behind one's shirt, in one's bosom

aizkrekstēties *vr* cough a little; begin to cough

aizkrēslis *nm* twilight

aizkrēšļot *vi* disappear in the twilight

aizkriet *vt* begin to skim milk

aizkrimst *vt* begin to gnaw, begin to eat

aizkrist *vi* 1. fall (drop) behind sth.; 2. drop (and shut sth. off); (of voice) lose; (of nose, ears) be stuffed, congested

aizkritināt *vt* shut

aizkritis *adj, part* of **aizkrist** hoarse

aizkritne *nf* trap door

aizkritnis *nm* catch, snap

aizkritņa atslēga *nf* snap lock

aizkruķēt *vt* push with a poker (to a place)

aizkrūmojis *adj* overgrown (with bushes)

aizkrustīt *vt* bar passage or entry (with a cross or symbolic tree branches)

aizkrustojums *nm* barricade

aizkrustot *vt* block, bar, barricade

aizkrūts *indecl adj* located behind the breastbone

aizkrūts dziedzeris *nm* thymus gland

aizkuģot *vi* sail away, sail to

aizkūkot *vt* (folk., of cuckoo's song) signal bad luck (if heard on an empty stomach in the morning); foretell the future by counting the cuckoo's calls

aizkūkoties *vr* (of a cuckoo) begin to call

aizkūlāt *vi* grow over with poor, tough grass

aizkulcenēt *vi* waddle away

aizkūlējs *nm* (hist., in the corvée system) day shift thresher

aizkūleņot *vi* tumble away

aizkuli/ses *nf pl* backstage; ~sēs backstage, be-hind the scenes; ~šu sarunas behind-the-scenes negotiations

aizkulties *vr* (col.) make one's way (with difficulty) to; stray, blunder

aizkunkstēties *vr* begin to moan

aizkunkuļ-ot *vi* waddle away

aizkuņģa *indecl adj* pancreatic

aizkuņģa dziedzeris *nm* pancreas

aizkuņģa dziedzera saliņas *nf pl* islands of Langerhans

aizkūnāties *vr* = **aizkūņoties**

aizkūņoties *vr* dodder away

aizkupeņot *vt* cover with snowdrifts

aizkūpēt *vi* 1. begin to steam; 2. become covered with soot; 3. (fig.) evaporate; (of smoke) subside

aizkupināt *vt* (of wind) block with snow

aizkūpināt *vt* (of pipe, cigarette) light

aizkūpis *adj* sooty

aizkurēties *vr* begin to burn

aizkurināt *vt* start the fire

aizkurkstēties *vr* begin to croak

aizkurkšķēties *vr* begin to croak

aizkurkt *vt* deafen by shouting

aizkurs *nm* 1. kindling; 2. mouth of a baking oven

aizkurst *vi* become deaf

aizkurstīt *vt* start the fire

aizkurt *vt* start the fire

aizkusīgs *adj* easily fatigued

aizkusis *adj, part* of **aizkust** out of breath

aizkust *vi* get tired, lose one's breath

aizkustēt *vi* 1. move away; 2. move briefly

aizkustēties *vr* 1. move away; 2. move briefly

aizkustinājums *nm* emotion

aizkustināt *vt* touch, move, affect

aizkusums *nm* fatigue

aizkvarkstēties *vr* begin to croak

aizkvēlināt *vt* fire; make glow

aizkvēloties *vr* 1. glow briefly; 2. begin to glow; get fired up

aizkvēpināt *vt* soot

aizkvēpis *adj, part* of **aizkvēpt** sooty

aizkvēpt *vi* become sooty

aizkviekt *vt* deafen with one's squealing

aizķēdēt *vt* (of a door) fasten with a chain

aizķeksēt *vt* hook

aizķepējums *nm* clog, plug

aizķepēt *vt* close, plug up (with a plastic substance); *vi* become clogged

aizķepināt *vt* fill, close, plug, seal, cover

aizķept *vi* become clogged

aizķepuroties *vr* struggle to (a place)

aizķere *nf* catch

aizķērkstēties *vr* begin to croak, begin to caw

aizķērkties *vr* begin to croak, begin to caw

aizķert *vt* grab; brush against, catch, touch; **a. vā-rīgā vietā** touch a sore spot

aizķerties *vr* (col.) catch, get stuck, get caught, stick, hang up; be held up, be delayed; (of voice) shake; **lai darbs neaizķeras** so that the work go smoothly; **a. prātā** (or **atmiņā**, **galvā**, **apziņā**) stick with one (in memory)

aizķēzīt *vt* dirty

aizķibelēt *vt* hinder, create difficulties, put obstacles in s.o.'s path

aizķibināt *vt* hook on, hang loosely

aizķīlāt *vt* put a lien on

aizķīlēt *vt* wedge, drive in a wedge

aizķitējums *nm* putty seal

aizķitēt *vt* putty over

aizlabināt *vt* entice

aizlāčot *vi* waddle away

aizlaide *nf* roller shutter, roller door

aizlaidnes *nf pl* venetian blind

aizlaidnis *nm* 1. curtain, blind; 2. damper

aizlaidnītes *nf pl* miniblinds

aizlaiki *nm pl* ancient times

aizlaiku or **aizlaikus** *adv* (obs.) 1. beforehand; 2. at the proper time

aizlaipot *vi* pick one's way (to a place)

aizlaist *vt* 1. let go; **a. garām** let pass by; **a. gar degunu** (col.) miss an opportunity; 2. dismiss, send off; **a. pensijā** retire; 3. drop; 4. neglect; 5. (of farm animals, before they drop their young) stop milking; 6. fling; 7. (col.) squander; sell too cheap; **a. vējā** (or **niekā**) (col.) squander; 8. (col., of a message) send; 9. (col.) go, run, drive quickly to

aizlaisties *vr* 1. fly away; 2. (col.) dash away; flee

aizlaists *adj, part* of **aizlaist** neglected

aizlaivot *vt* take to (by boat)

aizlaiēamais *nom adj* curtain, blind

aizlakojums *nm* seal

aizlakot *vt* seal

aizlāpīt *vt* darn, mend, patch up

aizlapot *vi* overgrow with leaves, become covered with leaves

aizlāpot *vi* (col.) lumber away

aizlasīt *vt* read (to a place)

aizlasīties I *vr* become engrossed in reading

aizlasīties II *vr* (col.) make oneself scarce

aizlāsot *vi* fog over

aizlauzt *vt* 1. crack; 2. damage; 3. (of voice) cut off

aizlauzties *vr* fight one's way to

aizlauzts *adj, part* of **aizlauzt** (of voice) feeble, cracked

aizlavīties *vi* sneak away

aizleja *nf* = **aizlejs**

aizlejs *nm* fat or dairy product added to food

aizlēkāt *vi* hop away

aizlēkšot *vi* gallop away

aizlēkt *vi* jump away, hop away

aizlemperēt *vi* (col.) toddle away

aizlempēt *vi* = **aizlemperēt**

aizlidināt *vt* 1. (of wind, aircraft) carry away; 2. throw

aizlidināties *vr* fly away

aizlidot *vi* fly away

aizlīdzēt *vi* loan, help out with money

aizlīdzināt *vt* 1. pay, pay off; 2. smooth

aizliedēt I *vt* solder, solder shut, repair (by soldering)

aizliedēt II *vt* (of hay, grain) allow to get wet

aizliedzīgi *adv* unaccomodatingly

aizliedzīgs *adj* unaccomodating

aizliegt *vt* 1. forbid, prohibit, ban; 2. (obs.) deny; (mil.) interdict

aizliegties *vr* refuse, turn down

aizliegums *nm* prohibition, ban; (mil.) interdiction

aizliekt *vt* bend (around, in front of); bend slightly

aizlienēt *vt* 1. (col.) loan; 2. (col.) borrow

aizlienētāj/s *nm*, ~a *nf* 1. (col.) creditor; 2. (col.) borrower

aizliesmoties *vr* flare up

aizliet *vt* 1. pour behind; **a. aiz apkakles** pour down the collar; 2. **a. putru** add milk to porridge; 3. fill (by pouring)

aizlīgot *vi* 1. float behind; float away; move away swaying; 2. (of songs) resound; 3. outdo in the singing of Ligo songs

aizlīkot *vi* move along a curved path, meander

aizlikt *vt* **1.** put (away, aside, behind, in front of); block; **a. aiz auss** make a note of; **a. kāju priekšā** trip up; **a. labu vārdu** put in a good word; **2.** *vi* (col.) pay for s.o.; **3.** *vi* (col.) scamper away; **4.** block; close; bring to a halt; **a. acis** fall asleep

aizlīkt *vi* bend down in front of sth.

aizlikties *vr* scamper

aizlīkumot *vi* wind into the distance, meander; zigzag

aizlīmējums *nm* glued-on seal

aizlīmēt *vt* seal, stick, close (by gluing)

aizlīmēties *vr* (of surfaces with glue) get stuck

aizlingot *vt* fling, sling

aizlinkāt *vi* scamper

aizlinot *vi* run away, run to

aizlipināt *vt* seal, stick, close (by gluing)

aizlipt *vi* get stuck together

aizlīst *vi* **1.** crawl away; (with **līdz**, **uz**, **aiz**) crawl to, crawl behind; **2.** slink away

aizlīt *vi* **1.** pour, spill or rain behind sth.; **2.** (of hay) get spoiled by rain

aizlobt *vi* scamper

aizlocīt *vt* bend (around, behind), tuck behind; fold; mark (a page by folding a corner)

aizlocīties *vr* wind into the distance, meander; zigzag; (of snakes) crawl away

aizlodāt *vi* crawl away; (fig.) spread

aizlodējums *nm* soldering, a soldered place

aizlodēt *vt* solder, solder shut, repair (by soldering)

aizloeņāt *vi* crawl away

aizlūgšana *nf* prayer

aizlūgt *vi* **1.** pray for; **2.** put in a good word, intercede; **3.** *vt* ask, invite

aizlūgums *nm* prayer service

aizlūgums par mirušiem *nm* office for the dead

aizlumpačot *vi* waddle away

aizlūzt *vi* crack; (of voice) break

aizlūzums *nm* break, crack

aizļekāt *vi* walk away fast

aizļenkāt *vi* walk away; hop away, lope away

aizļepatot *vi* = **aizļepot**

aizļepināt *vt* (col.) close (by gluing)

aizļepot *vi* flee, depart hurriedly, lope away

aizļēpot *vi* = **aizļepot**

aizļinkāt *vi* slouch away

aizļipot *vi* walk away; trot away, lope away

aizļodzīties *vr* totter away

aizmaitāt *vt* damage

aizmākoņots *adj* cloudy, overcast

aizmaksa *nf* payment; bill; account; **uz (kāda) ~s** at s.o.'s expense

aizmaksāt *vt* pay

aizmākties *vr* **1.** become overcast; **2.** be out of breath

aizmākuļot *vi* (of light clouds) move in

aizmaldināt *vt* lure away

aizmaldīties *vr* go astray, lose one's way

aizmānīt *vt* lure away

aizmanīties *vr* slip away, sneak away; **a. no stundām** cut classes

aizmargojums *nm* banisters; (in a courtroom) dock

aizmargot I *vt* put up banisters; enclose

aizmargot II *vt* spatter

aizmārša *nf, nm* **1.** forgetful or absentminded person; **2.** oblivion

aizmaršēt *vi* march away

aizmāršība *nf* forgetfulness; absentminded-ness

aizmaršīgi *adv* absentmindedly

aizmaršīgs *adj* forgetful; absentminded

aizmaršīgums *nm* forgetfulness; absentmind-edness

aizmaskēt *vt* mask, disguise; camouflage

aizmaskēties *vr* camouflage oneself

aizmaskot *vt* = **aizmaskēt**

aizmaskoties *vr* = **aizmaskēties**

aizmastīt *vt* **1.** (knitting) cast on; **2.** fence in; **3.** darn

aizmatot *vi* scamper

aizmaukt *vi* scamper

aizmauroties *vr* begin to low

aizmaut *vi* swim (to a place)

aizmeijot *vt* **1.** decorate with branches; **2.** mark with branches

aizmeimurot *vi* stagger to, stagger away

aizmēles *indecl adj* postlingual

aizmēles iedobe *nf* foramen caecum

aizmelnēt *vi* become grimy, blacken

aizmelnot *vi* = **aizmelnēt**

aizmelzt *vi* sand up

aizmērdēt *vt* starve

aizmērdēties *vr* starve oneself

aizmērēt *vi* starve, be hungry or thirsty for

aizmērēties *vr* starve, be hungry or thirsty for

aizmest *vt* **1.** throw away, discard, trash; **a. vecos dzelēos** scrap; **2.** throw, fling (to a point); **a. ciet** close; **a. garām** miss; **a. kādu vārdu** put in a good word; **a. Dievu** (or **Dieva vārdu**) (col.) swear to God; **a. krustu** cross oneself; **3.** throw, drop (behind sth.); **4.** fill (a hole in the ground); **5.** (of loops, knots) cast, tie; **a. zirgu** hitch up; **6. a. pumpurus** bud

aizmesties *vr* **1.** (of clothing, feet, voice, food in the throat) catch; **2.** (of fruit, buds) begin to form; **3.** dash away; **4.** be thrown

aizmētāt *vt* stitch, baste

aizmetiens *nm* **1.** throw, casting; **2.** hindrance

aizmetināt *vt* **1.** weld, weld shut, fill with a weld; **2. a. ilksis** harness hurriedly; **3.** have a snack before a meal; **4.** fasten, stitch lightly

aizmetnis *nm* (bot.) germ

aizmezglot *vt* knot

aizmēzt *vt* sweep away

aizmeēs *nm* place on the other side of the forest

aizmīdīt *vt* trample down

aizmidzināt *vt* put to sleep

aizmidzis *adj, part* of **aizmigt** asleep

aizmiegs *nm* nap

aizmiegt *vt* (of eyes) close

aizmiglot *vt* fog up, cloud; dim

aizmigloties *vr* fog, grow misty, dim

aizmigt *vi* fall asleep; **a. mūēīgā miegā** (poet.) pass away

aizmiģelis *nm*, **~e** *nf* one who falls asleep on the job

aizmīlēt *vt* take a liking to

aizmīlēties *vr* take a liking to; **a. garām** fail to become fond of

aizmilzt *vi* **1.** sand up, silt up; **2.** fester; **3.** (of glass) become discolored

aizmilzums *nm* **1.** build-up (of sand or silt); **2.** boil

aizmīņāt *vt* trample down

aizmirdzēt *vi* (of a shining, brilliant object) move away

aizmirdzēties *vr* begin to shine, shine briefly

aizmirdzināt *vi* (of rain, sprinkles) move away, move by

aizmirgot *vi* move away twinkling

aizmirgt *vt* (of one's eyes) close

aizmirkšt *vt* (of one's eyes) close

aizmirsa *nf* oblivion

aizmirsība *nf* forgetfulness

aizmirsīgs *adj* forgetful

aizmirst *vt* forget

aizmirstams *adj, part* of **aizmirst** forgettable

aizmirstība *nf* oblivion

aizmirsties *vr* **1.** forget; **2.** become absorbed in; **3.** forget oneself; **4.** lose control of oneself

aizmirstīgs *adj* forgetful

aizmirša *nf, nm* forgetful person

aizmiršanās *nfr* absorption (in sth. to the exclusion of everything else); oblivion

aizmirt *vi* **1.** be close to death; **2.** keep s.o. from dying by dying first

aizmīt I *vt* **1.** trample down; **2. a. garām** miss (a stop); **3.** injure (by stepping)

aizmīt II *vt* trade away

aizmizot *vt* begin to peel

aizmocīt *vt* (of a burden) drag, struggle with

aizmocīties *vr* struggle (to get to a place)

aizmotora braukšana *nf* bicycle racing behind a motor vehicle

aizmuguras *indecl adj* (jur., of a judgment) by default

aizmugure *nf* **1.** (mil.) rear area; **2.** back side; **no ~s** from behind; **3.** (of a chair, seat) back; **4.** (soccer, hockey) off side; **5.** (fig., col.) backing, connections

aizmugures varonis *nm* braggart (concerning military exploits)

aizmuguriski *adv* (jur.) in absentia

aizmugurisks *adj* (jur., of a judgment) by default

aizmukt *vi* (col.) flee; bolt; hide

aizmuldēt *vi* (col.) wander away

aizmurdzīt *vt* drag, pull

aizmūrēt *vt* wall up

aizmurīt *vt* **1.** cut, wound (in slaughtering); **2.** lug

aizmūžīgs *adj* eternal; immemorial

aizmūžs *nm* **1.** eternity; **2.** ancient times

aiznadze *nf* hangnail

aiznaglot *vt* nail shut

aiznags *nm* hangnail

aiznākamais *adj* one after the next

aiznākamgad *adv* two years from now

aiznākošais *adj* one after the next

aiznākt *vi* come behind

aiznāvēt *vt* wound mortally

aiznesējvads *nm* (anat.) vein

aiznest *vt* carry away; take to; **a. kukuli** bribe

aiznesties *vr* dash away; dash to

aiznirt *vi* dive to

aizņaudēties *vr* begin to meow, meow briefly

aizņaukstēties *vr* begin to meow, meow briefly

aizņēmēj/s *nm*, **~a** *nf* borrower

aizņemt *vt* **1.** (of space, time, mind) occupy; keep busy; **a. elpu** take one's breath away; **a. rindu** take a place in a line; **2.** reserve

aizņemtība *nf* **1.** area occupied; **2.** bysyness

aizņemties *vr* **1.** borrow; **2.** (in speech) get into; **3.** begin; **4.** imagine

aizņemts *adj, part* of **aizņemt 1.** filled; occupied; taken; (of persons, telephone lines) busy; **2.** borrowed

aizņēmums *nm* loan

aizņerkstēties *vr* whimper briefly

aizņirbēt *vi* flash by

aizņirbt *vi* flash by

aizņurdēties *vr* begin to growl; begin to grumble

aizoke[a]na [ā] *indecl adj* overseas

aizorēt *vt* (col.) cart away; *vi* move away slowly

aizpagājis *adj* one before last

aizpagājušais *adj* one before last

aizpagātne *nf* ancient past

aizpaijāt *vt* remove by stroking, stroke away

aizpaļāt *vt* bad-mouth

aizpampt *vi* swell, swell shut

aizpampums *nm* swelling

aizpārdevums *nm* provisional sale, forward sale contract

aizpārdošana *nf* provisional sale, forward sale

aizpārdot *vt* sign a preliminary sales contract

aizparīt *adv* the day after tomorrow

aizpasaule *nf* the other side, spirit world

aizpeldēt *vi* swim to; float away

aizpeldināt *vt* float to

aizpelēt *vi* begin to mold

aizpelnīt *vt* **1.** deserve; **2.** earn

aizpelt *vt* bad-mouth, run down

aizperēt *vt* begin to brood; have been brooding for some time

aizperēts *adj, part* of **aizperēt** (of eggs) addled

aizpērn *adv* the year before last

aizpērnais *adj* of two years ago, two years old

aizpērngad *adv* two years ago

aizpērt *vt* overtake (in a carriage, by whipping the horse)

aizpērties *vr* struggle through to

aizpīkstēties *vr* begin to squeal

aizpiķēt *vt* fill with tar

aizpildījums *nm* filling

aizpildīt *vt* fill; fill up

aizpildīties *vr* fill; fill up

aizpilēt *vi* drip behind sth.

aizpilināt *vt* let drops fall behind sth.; miss in putting in drops

aizpīpēt *vt* (of tobacco) light; *vi* light up

aizpīpot *vt* = **aizpīpēt**

aizpirkums *nm* (bus.) preemption

aizpīt *vt* **1.** weave shut; cover with sth. woven; **2.** weave (to a point)

aizplaisāt *vi* begin to crack

aizplakt *vi* make oneself flat behind sth.

aizplanēt *vi* glide away; glide off to one side

aizplaukt *vi* (of buds) begin to open

aizplest *vt* spread out

aizplēst *vt* make a tear; begin to tear

aizplesties *vr* block the way (by spreading oneself across the way)

aizplēsties *vr* be taken along (because of incessant pleading)

aizplīst *vi* begin to tear, begin to crack

aizplivināt *vi* flutter away

aizplivināties *vr* flutter away

aizplīvot *vi* flutter away

aizplīvoties *vr* flutter briefly

aizplīvurojums *nm* veil, cover

aizplīvurot *vt* veil; **a. bilanci** doctor the books

aizplīvurotība *nf* secrecy, veil

aizplīvuroties *vr* cover oneself with a veil

aizplombēt *vt* (of teeth) fill; (of doors, containers) seal

aizplūde *nf* outflow

aizpludināt *vt* float to

aizplūdināt *vt* let (water) run (to, along)

aizpludināties *vr* float away

aizplūst *vi* **1.** flow away; **2.** float away; **3.** fill with water, flood

aizpļāpāt *vi* forget oneself in chatting, spend a long time chatting

aizpļāpāties *vr* forget oneself in chatting, spend a long time chatting

aizpļaut *vi* **1.** begin to mow; **2.** (with **līdz**) mow to; **a. gaŗām** mow past; **3.** *vt* nick, cut (partly through, with a scythe)

aizpļauties *vr* dash off to

aizpogāt *vt* button, button up

aizpogāties *vr* button oneself up

aizposāt *vi* begin to suppurate

aizpost *vi* hurry away

aizprasīt *vt* enquire (prior to doing sth. else); ask for

aizprasīties *vr* ask for permission to go

aizprāta *indecl adj* incomprehensible; transcendental

aizprātot *vi* (of thinking) lead to

aizprātoties *vr* get lost in thought

aizprecēt *vt* give away in marriage (to s.o. living far away)

aizprecēties *vr* marry and move away

aizpūdēt *vt* allow to begin to mold

aizpukstēties *vr* (of the heart) begin to beat

aizpukšķināt *vi* put-put to

aizpumpēt *vt, vi* (sl.) **1.** borrow; **prasīt a.** cadge; **2.** lend

aizpumpēties *vr* (sl.) borrow

aizpurināt *vt* (of snow, dust) shake behind sth.

aizpurvietis *nm* one living on the other side of the swamp

aizpurvs *nm* place on the other side of the swamp

aizpuse *nf* back side

aizpūst *vt* **1.** blow away; **2.** (of wind) block with snow or sand; **3.** hurry (to, by)

aizpuškot *vt* decorate

aizpūt *vi* begin to rot

aizputeņot *v* **1.** *vt* block or cover with snow or sand; **2.** *vi* move away (during a snowstorm)

aizputēt *vi* **1.** become covered with dust; become snowbound; **2.** (of dust particles) be blown away; **a. vējā** turn to nothing

aizputinājums *nm* blockage by snow or sand

aizputināt *vt* **1.** block or cover (with snowdrifts or sand); **2.** (of sand, snow) blow away

aizputināts *adj, part* of **aizputināt** (of roads) snowbound

aizputne *nf* pantry

aizpūžņot *vi* become covered with pus

aizrādījums *nm* **1.** reprimand; **2.** instruction; **3.** allusion, hint; **4.** comment

aizrādīšana *nf* reprimanding; **~s pienākums** duty to reprimand

aizrādīt *vt* **1.** reprimand; **2.** point out; **3.** direct, instruct; **4. netieši a.** hint, allude to

aizraidīt *vt* send off; turn away, (of thoughts) turn off, dismiss; **a. uz viņpasauli** send to kingdom come; **a. nāvē** kill; **a. uz elli** a. send packing; b. kill

aizrakstīt *vt* write to

aizrakt *vt* **1.** (with **līdz**) dig to; **2.** (of a hole in the ground) fill

aizrakties *vr* dig to (a place)

aizrāpot *vi* crawl away; (with **aiz**) crawl behind; **a. garām** crawl past; (with **līdz**) crawl to

aizrāpties *vr* crawl away; (with **aiz**) crawl behind; **a. garām** crawl past; (with **līdz**) crawl to

aizrasot *vi* fog up

aizrasoties *vr* fog up

aizrast *vi* unlearn, forget through disuse

aizraudāties *vr* cry briefly

aizraujoši *adv* thrillingly, engrossingly

aizraujošs *adj, part* of **aizraut** thrilling, engrossing

aizraust *vt* **1.** cover (by raking); **2.** rake away

aizrausties *vr* make one's way to

aizraušanās *nfr* enthusiasm; infatuation; becoming engrossed (in an activity)

aizraut *vt* **1.** pul, drag along; pull, drag away; **a. ciet** close, shut; **a. elpu** take away one's breath; **2.** fascinate, thrill; **ar ~u elpu** with bated breath; **3.** (of zippers, curtains) pull (to close)

aizrautība *nf* enthusiasm, eagerness

aizrauties *vr* **1.** be carried away, be swept away; become engrossed, become absorbed (in an activity); take a fancy to, become infatuated; **aiz-raudamies** eagerly, enthusiastically; (of laughter) to the point of losing one's breath; **2.** (of voice) choke; **man aizrāvās elpa** it took my breath away; **3.** (suddenly) pull forward, start, move with a start

aizrautīgs *adj* = **aizrāvīgs**

aizrautīgums *nm* = **aizrāvīgums**

aizrāvīgi *adv* thrillingly, engrossingly

aizrāvīgs *adj* thrilling, engrossing

aizrāvīgums *nm* enthusiasm

aizredze *nf* providence

aizredzība *nf* care, consideration, concern

aizrekstēties *vr* begin to grunt; utter a short grunt

aizrekšēties *vr* = **aizrekstēties**

aizrekšķēties *vr* = **aizrekstēties**

aizrepēt *vi* scab over

aizrestot *vt* (of windows) bar

aizrētot *vi* heal

aizrežģot *vt* (of windows) bar

aizrībēt *vi* rumble away; begin to rumble; **a. garām** rumble past

aizrībēties *vr* begin to rumble, rumble briefly

aizrībināt *vi* roll with a rumble

aizridāt *vt* block

aizridāties *vr* (reg.) move (to another dwelling)

aizrīdināt I *vt* drive s.o. away by siccing dogs

aizrīdināt II *vt* stuff with food to the point of choking

aizrīdīt I *vt* = **aizrīdināt** I

aizrīdīt II *vt* = **aizrīdināt** II

aizriebt *vi* antagonize

aizriebties *vr* become repugnant

aizriest *v* **1.** *vi* grow in clumps; **2.** *vt* (weav.) beam the warp

aizriesties *vr* grow in clumps

aizriet *vt* scare away by barking

aizrietēt *vi* (of a cow's udder) harden, run dry

aizrieties *vr* begin to bark, bark briefly

aizrietināt *vt* make a cow run dry

aizrīkot *vt* send to, order to (a place)

aizrikšot *vi* trot away; **a. garām** trot past; (with **līdz**) trot to

aizripināt *vt* roll away; (with **aiz**) roll behind; **a. garām** roll past; (with **līdz**) roll to

aizripot *vi* roll away; (with **aiz**) roll behind; **a. garām** roll past; (with **līdz**) roll to

aizrisināt *vt* unroll, unreel

aizrisināties *vr* unroll, unreel

aizrīt *vt* swallow

aizritēt *vi* roll away; (with **aiz**) roll behind; (with **garām**) roll past; (with **līdz**) roll to; (of time) go by

aizrīties *vr* choke, swallow the wrong way

aizritināt *vt* roll away; roll together; (with **aiz**) roll behind; **a. garām** roll past; (with **līdz**) roll to

aizritināties *vr* 1. roll to; 2. roll together

aizrobeža *nf* lands on the other side of the border; foreign land

aizrobežu *indecl adj* foreign

aizrobs *nm* 1. reason or pretext for ill will or anger; 2. shortfall

aizrosīties *vr* get ready and go

aizrotīt *vt* (of sacks) close (by twisting)

aizrožot *vi* become covered with frost flowers

aizrubināties *vr* (of a male grouse) call briefly

aizrūcināt *vi* 1. rumble away; 2. (col., of engines) start

aizruden *adv* the fall before last

aizrūgt *vi* begin to ferment

aizrukstēties *vr* begin to grunt

aizrūkt *vi* rumble into the distance

aizrūkties *vr* begin to rumble, begin to growl

aizrūķēt *vt* move carefully; squirrel away

aizruna *nf* pretext, excuse

aizrunāt *vt* 1. outtalk; 2. put in a word for; 3. reserve; **4. a. par tālu** talk too much

aizrunātāj/s *nm*, **~a** *nf* defender

aizrunāties *vr* 1. keep on talking, forget oneself in a conversation; waste one's time in talking; 2. make excuses; **aizrunājoties ar . . .** under the pretext of . . .; **a. ar nezināšanu** plead ignorance; 3. say too much, let spill

aizrunāts *adj, part* of **aizrunāt** taken (reserved)

aizrūsējis *adj, part* of **aizrūsēt** rusty

aizrūsēt *vi* begin to rust

aizrušināt *vt* cover (with friable material)

aizsācēj/s *nm*, **~a** *nf* instigator; initiator

aizsainis *nm* bundle, package

aizsaiņot *vt* pack

aizsaite *nf* bandage

aizsaitēt *vt* tie; bandage

aizsākt *vt* 1. begin; start; 2. introduce

aizsākties *vr* begin

aizsākums *nm* beginning; (of a battle) initial engagement

aizsaldēt *vt* freeze, freeze over

aizsalis *adj, part* of **aizsalt** frozen over, icebound

aizsalkt *vi* get hungry

aizsalt *vi* freeze over, ice over

aizsanēt *vi* buzz away

aizsanēties *vr* buzz briefly

aizsāpēt *vi* 1. begin to hurt; 2. (of pain) abate

aizsāpēties *vr* begin to hurt

aizsapņot *v* 1. *vt* waste time in daydreaming; 2. *vi* (in dreaming) retrace one's life to a point

aizsapņoties *vr* become lost in a reverie

aizsardzība *nf* 1. protection; **~s** protective; 2. (mil., sports, games, psych.) defense; **ātrā a.** (mil.) hasty defense; **daudzvienību sastāva a.** coherent defense; **elektroniskā a.** electronic security; **pretgaisa a.** antiaircraft defense; **riņķveida a.** perimeter defense

aizsardzības me[cha]nisms [hā] *nm* (psych.) defense mechanism

aizsargacenes *nf pl* safety goggles

aizsargapmetnis *nm* protective cloak

aizsargapstādījumi *nm pl* windbreak

aizsargapvalks *nm* **1.** protective covering; **2.** fingerstall

aizsargāt *vt* protect; defend

aizsargāties *vr* protect oneself; defend oneself

aizsargātāj/s *nm,* ~**a** *nf* protector

aizsargbrilles *nf pl* goggles

aizsargbrusa *nf* (RR) scotch beam

aizsargbūve *nf* defensive structure

aizsargcimdi *nm* pl protective gloves

aizsargdambis *nm* levee, dike; breakwater; mole

aizsarggrāvis *nm* protective ditch

aizsargierīce *nf* protective device, protector

aizsargjosla *nf* **1.** defense zone; **2.** shelterbelt

aizsargjosta *nf* = **aizsargjosla**

aizsargjums *nm* awning

aizsargkārtiņa *nf* protective film

aizsargkavēšana *nf* (physiol.) protective inhibition

aizsargkoki *nm pl* windbreak

aizsargkrāsa *nf* protective coloration; protective paint; ~**s** camouflage (*adj*)

aizsargķivere *nf* safety helmet

aizsarglīdzeklis *nm* preventive; protective substance; repellent

aizsargmargas *nf pl* guardrail

aizsargmarka *nf* trademark

aizsargmaska *nf* protective mask

aizsargme[cha]nisms [hā] *nm* protective mechanism, protective device; safeguard

aizsargmeēs *nm* protective forest zone

aizsargmuita *nf* protective tariff

aizsargorg[a]ns [ā] *nm* protective organ

aizsargpārklājums *nm* protective layer

aizsargpote *nf* prophylactic vaccine

aizsargpotēšana *nf* prophylactic vaccination

aizsargreakcija *nf* protective reaction

aizsar/gs *nm* **1.** protector; defender; (basketball) guard; (soccer) back; **2.** protective cover; **3.** (el.) fuse; **4.** (hist.) member of the Aizsargi organization; ~**dze** *nf*

aizsargsala *nf* traffic island

aizsargsavienība *nf* defensive alliance

aizsargsega *nf* protective covering

aizsargskārds *nm* (sheet metal) flashing

aizsargskava *nf* (of a firearm) trigger guard

aizsargskrūve *nf* safety bolt

aizsargstabiņš *nm* (highway) guard post

aizsargstādījums *nm* protective planting, windbreak

aizsargstieple *nf* sheathing wire

aizsargstikls *nm* protective glass shield; safety glass

aizsargtapa *nf* (of weapons) safety pin

aizsargtērps *nm* protective suit

aizsargtīkliņš *nm* (el.) screen grid

aizsarguguns *nf* (mil.) protective fire

aizsarguztvērējs *nm* cow catcher

aizsargvalnis *nm* levee, dike; breakwater; bulwark; **pretšķembu a.** revetment

aizsargviela *nf* protective substance

aizsargzeķes *nf pl* protective socks

aizsargziede *nf* protective lubricant

aizsargēogs *nm* snow fence

aizsarkt *vi* **1.** turn red; **2.** (of a red glow) fade

aizsarmot *vi* become covered with frost

aizsārtis *adj* reddened

aizsaukt *vt* **1.** call away; **2. a. sev līdz** invite (to come along); **3.** summon

aizsaukties *vr* call out

aizsaule *nf* the other world

aizsēdēties *vr* sit too long

aizsēdināt *vt* seat (away, further away)

aizsega *nf* = **aizsegs**

aizsegs *nm* screen, cover; (mil.) defilade; ~**a uguns** screening fire

aizsegt *vt* cover up; eclipse; **a. skatu** block the view

aizsegties *vr* cover oneself up

aizsēklis I *nm* seeds that remain after sowing or are kept for sowing

aizsēklis II *nm* place beyond a shallow or a sandbank

aizsēkties *vr* cry out

aizsens *adj* ancient

aizsērējums *nm* siltation, (of pipes) obstruction

aizsērēt *vi* silt up; clog up

aizsēr(s)t *vt* dam up; silt up; clog up

aizsēst *vi* change one's seat

aizsēsties *vr* change one's seat

aizsēt *vt* block passage by sowing

aizsētīt *vt* fence in

aizsienamais *nom adj* tie, cord

aizsiet *vt* tie; **a. acis** blindfold

aizsieties *vr* **1.** put on oneself, tie on oneself; **2.** tie oneself; be tied

aizsijāt *vt* miss (the sieve in sifting)

aizsiksnot *vt* strap down

aizsīkt *vi* buzz away, buzz past

aizsīkties *vr* buzz briefly

aizsile *nf* place beyond a large forest

aizsilietis *nm* inhabitant of a place beyond a large forest; hermit

aizsilnieks *nm* = **aizsilietis**

aizsi/st *vt* **1.** close; **a. ar naglām** nail shut; **a. ar dēļiem** board up; **2.** (of a door, window) slam; **a. ausis** deafen; **a. ciet** slam shut; **a. elpu** take one's breath away; **a. muti** shut so up; **3.** kick (further, to); **4.** dawn; **austra ~tusi** it has dawned

aizsi/sties *vr* **1.** slam shut; **man elpa ~tās** it took my breath away; **2.** hide (quickly)

aizskaitīt *vi* count to

aizskalot *vt* wash away

aizskaloties *vr* be washed away

aizskandināt *vt* **1.** begin to play; **2.** make resound

aizskanēt *vi* **1.** (of sound) carry; **2.** (of a sound source) move away

aizskanēties *vr* begin to sound; sound briefly

aizskape *nf* place behind the cupboard (or cabinet, wardrobe)

aizskapēt *vt* (com.) get sth. to (a place), move

aizskarošs *adj, part* or **aizskart** offensive, in-sulting

aizskart *vt* **1.** touch; touch upon; **a. vārīgā vietā** touch to the quick; **2.** offend, insult; **a. godu** put s.o.'s honor at stake; **3.** affect; infringe upon

aizskārums *nm* offense; infringement

aizskrabināties *vr* make brief gnawing noises

aizskraidīt *vi* get to a place (in running around)

aizskrambāt *vt* scratch

aizskriet *vi* run away; (of time) go by; (with **aiz**) run behind sth.; **a. garām** run past, hurry past; (with **līdz, uz**) run to; (with **pēc**) go get sth., fetch; **a. pie (kāda)** go see s.o., drop in; **a. priekšā** overtake

aizskrubināt *vi* begin to gnaw

aizskrūvēt *vt* screw shut, close (by turning)

aizskubināt *vt* urge (to go somewhere)

aizskūpstīt *vt* kiss better

aizskūt *vt* half-finish one's shaving

aizslacināt *vt* = **aizslacīt**

aizslacīt *vt* splash (to a place behind)

aizslacīties *vr* get splashed (to, on, behind)

aizslaistīties *vr* wander away while loafing

aizslampāt *vi* trudge away

aizslamstīties *vr* wander away while loafing

aizslānīt *vt* barricade

aizslapēt *vt* wet a little

aizslapstīties *vr* sneak away, get to a place by skulking

aizslāpt *vi* **1.** begin to suffocate; **2.** almost die of thirst

aizslāt *v* **1.** *vt* cover, conceal; protect; **2.** *vi* slink away

aizslaucīt *vt* **1.** sweep away; **2.** (of one's tracks) cover

aizslaukt *vt* **1.** miss one's aim in milking; **2.** be-gin to milk

aizslavēt *vt* lavish praise on s.o.

aizslēgs *nm* (of firearms) bolt, breechblock; **~a aizturis** slide stop, bolt hold-open catch; ~a **kāts** breechlock stop; ~a **me[cha]nisms [hā]** breech mechanism; ~a **rāmis** (small arms) operating rod

aizslēgt *vt* **1.** lock, lock up; **2.** close

aizslēgties *vr* **1.** lock itself; **2.** close

aizslēģēt *vt* shutter

aizslempties *vr* waddle away

aizslēpēt *vi* = **aizslēpot**

aizslēpot *vi* ski away; ski to

aizslēps *nm* shelter

aizslēpt *vt* hide

aizslēpties *vr* hide

aizslēptuve *nf* hiding place

aizslīdēt *vi* glide away, drift away; (with **aiz**) slide behind, slip behind; **a. gaŗām** glide past, slide past, slip by; (fig.) miss; **a. priekšā** slip or drift in front of

aizslidināt *vt* push (to, away along a slippery surface)

aizslīdināt *vt* slide (to, away)

aizslidot *vi* skate (to, away)

aizslieksnis *nm* place beyond the threshold

aizsliekties *vr* lean (over, to)

aizsliet *vt* **1.** block, barricade; **2.** lean (behind sth.)

aizslietnis *nm* movable partition; screen

aizslīgt *vi* droop

aizslodzīt *vt* barricade

aizsmacināts *adj* hoarse

aizsmacis *adj, part* of **aizsmakt** hoarse

aizsmakt *vi* become hoarse, lose one's voice

aizsmakums *nm* hoarseness

aizsmaržot *vi* stop smelling; (fig.) come to an end

aizsmaržoties *vr* begin to smell

aizsmēķēt *vt* (of tobacco) light; light up

aizsmelgt *vi* begin to smart, begin to ache

aizsmeldzēties *vr* begin to ache

aizsmelgties *vr* begin to ache

aizsmērēt *vt* (col.) fill (with a plastic material); besmear

aizsmiet *vt* forfeit

aizsmirdināt *vt* stink up

aizsnaust *vi* doze off

aizsnausties *vr* doze off

aizsnidzis *adj, part* of **aizsnigt** snowed in, snowbound; covered with snow

aizsniedzams *adj, part* of **aizsniegt** within reach, attainable

aizsniegt *vt* reach; attain

aizsniegties *vr* reach

aizsnigt *vi* **1.** be covered with snow, become snowbound; **2.** (of snow) fall behind sth.

aizsoļot *vi* walk away, march away; **a. gaŗām** march past; (with **līdz**, **uz**) walk to

aizspārdīt *vt* kick away

aizspert *vt* kick away; (with **līdz**) kick to; (with **pāri**) kick across, kick over; **a. gaŗām** miss (in kicking)

aizsperties *vr* make one's way to (with effort)

aizspēt *vt* **1.** overtake; manage to catch (a train or boat); **2.** befall (before sth. else)

aizspīdēt *vi* (of light) reach, be visible

aizspiednis *nm* snap fastener

aizspiegties *vr* squeal

aizspiest *vt* **1.** push away; push to; **2.** press shut, close, stop; **a. dziesmu** (sl.) shut up; choke

aizspiesties *vr* **1.** (with **līdz**) press one's way to; **a. gaŗām** press, squeeze oneself past; **2.** (of rubber tubing) pinch; **3.** (of food) stick (in one's throat)

aizspietot *vi* run away

aizspindzēt *vi* buzz away

aizspļaut *vt* spit (to, as far as)

aizspolēt *vi* scamper

aizspostot *vt* stopper, plug

aizsprādzēt *vt* buckle up

aizsprādzēties *vr* buckle up

aizsprāgt *vi* be blown away or to (by an explosion); fly off; jump behind sth.

aizspraišļot *vt* bar (install bars)

aizsprakstēt *vi* pop away with a crackle

aizsprakšķēt *vi* pop away with a crackle

aizspraudīt *vt* tuck in; stick in (behind sth., repeatedly)

aizspraukties *vr* squeeze oneself through to, squeeze oneself behind sth.

aizsprauslāt *vt* drive away (insects) by snorting or sputtering

aizsprauslot *vt* = **aizsprauslāt**

aizspraust *vt* **1.** stick behind sth.; **2.** fasten

aizsprausties *vr* **1.** tuck in; stick in (behind sth., repeatedly); be fastened; **2.** squeeze oneself be-hind sth.

aizspriedīgi *adv* in a prejudiced way

aizspriedīgs *adj* prejudiced, biased; preconceived

aizspriedumaini *adv* in a prejudiced way

aizspriedumains *adj* prejudiced, biased; preconceived

aizspriedum/s *nm* prejudice, bias; **bez ~iem** un-prejudiced, unbiased

aizspriest *vt* bar, bolt

aizspriesties *vr* get stuck, stick

aizsprosta balons *nm* barrage balloon

aizsprosta baļķis *nm* stoplog

aizsprosta cekuls *nm* crest of a weir

aizsprosta ezers *nm* weir basin

aizsprosta gultne *nf* (hydr.) apron

aizsprosta mugura *nf* downstream face

aizsprostojums *nm* obstruction, barricade; barrage; traffic jam; (med.) thrombosis, embolism

aizsprostot *vt* block

aizsprostoties *vr* jam, become clogged

aizsprostpunkts *nm* (mil.) blocking point

aizsprosts *nm* **1.** dam, weir; **2.** barrage; **3.** abatis

aizsprostsiena *nf* bulkhead wall

aizsprostuguns *nf* barrage fire

aizsprūdot *vt* (of clothing) fasten (with plugs used in place of buttons)

aizsprudzināties *vr* get stuck

aizsprukt *vi* slip away

aizsprūst *vi* get stuck; clog up; (of words) choke on

aizspundēt *vt* bung up

aizspurgt *vi* flutter away, flit away

aizstādināt *vt* set behind, set away

aizstādīt *vt* plant in front of

aizstaigāt *vi* walk to

aizstājēj/s *nm*, **~a** *nf* substitute

aizstājamība *nf* substitutability; **savstarpēja a.** interchangeability

aizstājums *nm* (jur.) fungible

aizstāklis *nm* substitute

aizstāstīt *vt* (of a story) tell (only) to a point

aizstāšana *nf* substitution

aizstāt *vt* replace, substitute for; displace

aizstāties *vr* (with **aiz**) position oneself behind; **a. priekšā** position oneself in front of; **a. ceļā** block the way

aizstatnis *nm* screen (folding partition)

aizstāvamais *nom adj* (jur.) defendant

aizstāvams *adj, part* of **aizstāvēt** defensible

aizstāvēšana *nf* defense; advocacy

aizstāvēšanās *nfr* **1.** self-defense; **nepieciešamā a.** (jur.) self-defense; **2.** (mil.) defense; **a. pasā-kumi** defensive measures; **a. līdz pēdējam** last-ditch defense

aizstāvēšanas runa *nf* defense summation

aizstāvēt *vt* defend

aizstāvētāj/s *nm*, **~a** *nf* defender; protector

aizstāvēties *vr* defend oneself

aizstāvība *nf* (jur.) defense; **~s runa** speech for the defense

aizstāv/is *nm*, **~e** *nf* defender; advocate; (jur.) counsel for the defense

aizstāvniecība *nf* defense

aizstāvnieks *nm* (col.) defense attorney

aizsteberēt *vi* hobble away

aizsteigt *vi* (of time) go by quickly

aizsteigties *vr* **1.** rush, rush off, leave hurriedly; (with **aiz**) rush behind; (with **pa**) hurry along;

(with **uz**) rush off to, hurry to; **a. uz priekšu** run ahead; **2.** (of time) go by quickly; **3. a. garām** pass, overtake; **priekšā** overtake, get ahead of; **a. notikumiem priekšā** forestall events, anticipate events

aizstibīt *vt* lug away, drag away

aizstīdzēt *vi* stretch out, reach

aizstiept *vt* **1.** stretch across, stretch in front of; **2.** lug, drag away

aizstiepties *vr* **1.** stretch to reach; **2.** stretch (to, from one place to another); **3.** move away slowly

aizstīgt *vi* (of a road) stretch

aizstiklot *vt* (of windows) glaze

aizstiknīties *vr* (of voice) shake

aizstrādāt *vt* **1.** beat s.o. at work, surpass; **2.** be-gin to work on sth.; **3.** pay in advance by labor

aizstraume *nf* **1.** place on the other side of a river; **2.** current in a river bend

aizstreipuļot *vi* stagger away; stagger to

aizstrinkšķēties *vr* (of strings) sound, twang, strum, tinkle briefly

aizstrinkšķināt *vt* pluck, thrum

aizstrinkšķināties *vr* = **aizstrinkšķēties**

aizstumt *vt* push away, move away; push shut; push, move (to, behind, past)

aizstumties *vr* push oneself to (a place)

aizstūrēt *vt, vi* steer, steer to; **a. garām** steer past

aizstū/ris *nm* place behind the corner; **no ~ra** from behind the corner

aizsūbēt *vi* (of glass) cloud

aizsūkstēties *vr* begin to hurt

aizsūnot *vi* overgrow with moss

aizsūrkstēties *vr* = **aizsūrstēties**

aizsūrstēties *vr* begin to hurt

aizsūtīt *vt* send, send away; (with **pēc**) send for; (with **uz**) send to; **a. atpakaļ** send back, return; **a. pie tēviem** do in

aizsvaidīt *vt* scatter

aizsvelpt *vi* whiz past

aizsvelpties *vr* begin to whistle; whistle briefly

aizsvempties *vr* slog away, plod away

aizsviest *vt* **1.** throw away, throw (to, behind; **a. prom** throw away, discard; **a. garām** miss (in throwing); **2.** (of a hole in the ground) fill

aizsviesties *vr* **1.** get thrown unintentionally; **2.** dash away

aizsvilināt *vt* set fire to

aizsvilpot *vi* whiz past

aizsvilpt *vi* whiz past

aizsvilpties *vr* begin to whistle; whistle briefly

aizsvilt *vi* redden

aizsvilties *vr* **1.** catch fire; **2.** get mad; **3.** redden

aizsvīst *vi* **1.** steam up; **2.** dawn

aizšalkoties *vr* = **aizšalkties**

aizšalkt *vi* **1.** move away rustling; **2.** (poet.) pass

aizšalkties *vr* begin to rustle; rustle briefly

aizšaujamais *nom adj* bolt, door bolt

aizšaut *vt* **1.** (of gunfire) reach; **a. garām** miss (in shooting); **2.** wound (with a firearm); **3.** (of door bolts) bolt; **4.** push quickly in front of; **a. kāju priekšā** trip up; **a. roku mutei priekšā** clap one's hand over one's mouth; **5.** *vi* (col.) run quickly to

aizšauties *vr* **1.** dash off, dart away; dash off to; **a. priekšā** dart in front of; **a. garām** dash past; **2.** bolt itself; **3.** forget

aizšautne *nf* door bolt; (chimney) damper

aizšautra *nf* door bolt

aizšķaudīt *vi* (folk.) sneeze away (negate an expected, hoped for, or feared outcome by sneezing)

aizšķaudīties *vr* sneeze suddenly and briefly

aizšķelt *vt* begin to split

aizšķelties *vr* begin to split

aizšķērsis *nm* barrier

aizšķērslis *nm* obstacle

aizšķērsot *vt* bar, block

aizšķēršļot *vt* bar, block

aizšķiest *vt* splash (to, as far as)

aizšķilt *vt* strike fire

aizšķilties *vr* strike fire

aizšķindēt *vi* (of ringing, jingling) die away

aizšķindēties *vr* ring (or jingle) briefly

aizšķirt *vt* 1. (of books, bound pages) close; lose one's place (in a book); 2. leaf through to (a place in a book); 3. avert

aizšķirties *vr* 1. (of books) close; 2. lose one's place in a book

aizšķīst *vi* (of loose matter) fly away

aizšķīt *v* 1. *vt* (of vegetation) begin to strip; 2. *vi* decamp

aizšķūrēt *v* 1. *vt* shovel away; 2. *vi* get away; get to

aizšķūtēt *vt* transport

aizšlenderēt *vi* (barb.) wander to, amble to

aizšlepēt *vt* (barb.) drag away, drag to

aizšļakstēt *v* 1. *vt* splash full; 2. *vi* (of a splash) reach

aizšļakstināt *vt* make a splash reach (a place)

aizšļakstīt *vt* make a splash reach (a place)

aizšļākt *v* 1. *vi* (of waves, splashes) reach; 2. *vt* splash as far as

aizšļākties *vr* (of waves, splashes) reach

aizšļūcināt *vt* slide to, drag to

aizšļukt *vi* slip behind

aizšļūkt *vi* toddle away; toddle to

aizšmaukt *vi* (col.) slip away

aizšņākt *v* 1. *vi* whiz past; run away snorting, run past snorting; 2. *vi* begin to hiss, snore, or blow; 3. *vt* outsnore

aizšņākties *vr* begin to snore; begin to roar; snore briefly

aizšņirkstēties *vr* begin to grate, creak, or gnash

aizšņorēt *vt* (col.) lace, tie

aizšūpot *vt* carry away rocking

aizšūpoties *vr* (of swinging on a swing) push oneself to (a certain height)

aizšūt *vt* sew up; mend

aizšvīkstēt *vi* swish away, swish past

aizšvīkstēties *vr* begin to rustle; begin to swish

aizšvīkstināt *vi* drive away

aizšvirkstēt *vi* sputter briefly; begin to sputter

aiztaisīt *vt* 1. close; 2. button; 3. fill; 4. add milk to porridge

aiztaisīties *vr* close

aiztapināt *vt* borrow

aiztapot *vt* bung up, close

aiztapt *vi* get to (a place)

aiztarkšķēt *vi* chug away; rattle away

aiztarkšķēties *vr* chug briefly; begin to chug; rattle briefly, begin to rattle

aiztaupījums *nm* savings

aiztaupīt *vt* save; spare

aiztaupīties *vr* remain, be saved; be spared

aiztaurēt *v* 1. *vi* go away honking; 2. *vt* deafen (by blowing a horn)

aiztaurēties *vr* (of a horn) begin to blow; blow briefly

aiztaustīties *vr* grope one's way

aiztecējušais *adj* past, last

aiztecēt I *vi* 1. flow away; flow to; (with **aiz**) drip behind; 2. (of time) pass

aiztecēt II *vi* trip, run to

aiztenterēt *vi* stagger away, toddle away

aiztepēt *vt* putty, putty over

aiztērpis *adj* swollen

aiztīklot *vt* veil

aiztikšķēt *vi* tick away

aiztikšķēties *vr* begin to tick

aiztikt I *vt* 1. touch; 2. bother

aiztikt II *vi* get to

aiztikums *nm* (folk.) violation of a touch taboo

aiztinkšķēt *vi* leave tinkling or clinking

aiztinkšķēties *vr* jingle briefly; begin to jingle

aiztipināt *vt* trip away; trip to

aiztīstīt *vt* bundle up

aiztīstīties *vr* bundle up

aiztīt *vt* wrap, cover up

aiztīties *vr* wrap oneself up

aiztramdīt *vt* scare away

aiztransportēt *vt* transport to

aiztraucēt *vt* scare away; disturb

aiztraukt *v* **1.** *vt* shoo away, scare away; ward off; blow away; **2.** *vi* run, flee, fly

aiztraukties *vr* speed away; **a. garām** speed past; (of time) fly

aiztrenkt *vt* chase away, drive away; **a. ratā** banish, drive out

aiztrīcēties *vr* begin to tremble

aiztriekt *vt* drive away

aiztriept *vt* fill (with a plastic substance)

aiztrinkšķēties *vr* = **aizstrinkšķēties**

aiztrinkšķināt *vi* = **aizstrinkšķināt**

aiztrīsēties *vr* begin to tremble

aiztrīsināt *vt* make vibrate

aiztrūdēt *vi* begin to decay

aiztrūkt *vi* **1.** begin to tear, (of buttons) begin to come off; (of voice) begin to crack; **2.** (of suckling female animals) begin to run dry

aiztrunējis *adj, part* of **aiztrunēt** partly rotten

aiztrunēt *vi* begin to rot

aiztrupēt *vi* begin to rot

aiztukšīt *vt* begin to empty

aiztūkt *vi* swell, puff up; grow fat

aiztūkums *nm* swelling

aiztumšojums *nm* blackout

aiztumšot *vt* black out

aiztuntuļot *v* **1.** *vt* bundle up; **2.** *vi* (col.) waddle away

aiztuntuļoties *vr* bundle up

aiztupt *vi* squat behind sth.

aiztupties *vr* squat behind sth.

aizture *nf* (physiol.) inhibition; (med.) retention; retardation

aizturējums *nm* detention

aizturēšana *nf* **1.** retention; **2.** detention; **3.** suppression

aizturēt *vt* **1.** detain; **2.** stop hold up; **3.** keep; keep in; keep out; retain; **4.** suppress; **a. elpu** hold one's breath; **ar ~u elpu** with bated breath

aizturētais *nom adj*, **~ā** *f* detainee

aizturētājs *nm*, **~a** *nf* **1.** detainer; **2.** (in combination with nouns) resistant; retaining

aizturis *nm* block, stop, wedge; **pēdējais a.** dog-shore

aizturķīlis *nm* locking wedge

aizturs *nm* stop; door stop

aizturvārsts *nm* backpressure valve

aiztusnīt *vi* walk away panting

aiztversme *nf* obstacle, impediment

aiztvert *vt* **1.** catch, grab; **2.** stop, intercept

aiztverties *vr* find refuge

aizugune *nf* place behind the fire, place behind the hearth

aizugunis *nm* = **aizugune**

aizupe *nf* the other side of the river

aizupiet/is *nm*, **~e** *nf* dweller on the other side of the river

aizurbt *vt* start a hole (by drilling); drill to

aizurbties *vr* drill to (a certain depth)

aizurdzēt *vi* purl away, bubble away

aizurgt *vi* purl away, bubble away

aizurkstēties *vr* begin to grunt

aizurkšķēties *vr* = **aizurkstēties**

aizvadāt *vt* transport (in several trips)

aizvadāties *vr* move away

aizvadīt *vt* **1.** (of water, sewage) drain; **2.** see off; take s.o. to; **a. pēdējā gaitā** attend s.o.'s funeral; **a. uz viņpasauli** be the death of s.o.; (of a time period) spend

aizvadīts *adj, part* of **aizvadīt** past, last

aizvaidēties *vr* moan briefly

aizvainojums *nm* hurt feelings

aizvainot *vt* hurt s.o.'s feelings

aizvainotība *nf* hurt feelings

aizvainoties *vr* take offense

aizvairīt *vt* ward off, shut off; **a. visu pasauli** shut off the world

aizvairoga dziedzeris *nm* parathyroid gland

aizvakar *adv* the day before yesterday; **a. vakarā** the evening before last

aizvakardien *adv* the day before yesterday

aizvakardiena *nf* day before yesterday

aizvakarējs *adj* from the day before yesterday

aizvakarnakt *adv* the night before last

aizvakarrīt *adv* the morning before last

aizvākojums *nm* lid, cover, covering

aizvākot *vt* put a lid on, cover up

aizvākt *vt* remove, put away

aizvākties *vr* **1.** move away; **2.** (col.) make oneself scarce; **a. pie laika** go while the going is still good

aizvara *nf* (reg.) tie, drawstring

aizvārdot *vt* defend (verbally)

aizvārdzis *adj* feeble

aizvārīt *vt* stew, braise

aizvars *nm* **1.** (of a sluice, lock) gate; **2.** bar; **3.** drawstring

aizvārstāms *adj* (of footwear, clothing) laced

aizvārstījums *nm* (superficial) stitching

aizvārstīt *vt* stitch together, mend (superficially)

aizvārša *nf* (of a door, gate) bar

aizvārte *nf* place behind the gate

aizvaskojums *nm* wax seal

aizvaskot *vt* seal with wax

aizvaukšēties *vr* (col.) begin to bark; move away yapping

aizvaukšķēties *vr* = **aizvaukšēties**

aizvazāt *vt* carry off

aizvazāties *vr* (com.) traipse to

aizvāzt *vt* **1.** close the lid of; **2.** (of a folding knife) fold

aizvaēot *vi* drive away, ride away

aizvedējs *nm* abductor

aizvedināt *vt* lure away, entice

aizvēdināt *vt* shoo away (by waving)

aizvēdīt *vt* blow away

aizvējīgs *adj* sheltered

aizvējot *vi* (of an air current) move away

aizvējš *nm* **1.** lee; **2.** shelter

aizvelkams *adj, part* of **aizvilkt**, usu. *defin* **aizvelkamais** (of curtains) draw

aizvelmēt *vt* (metall.) cog

aizvelt *vt* roll away; roll to; **a. priekšā** roll in front of

aizvelties *vr* roll away; roll to; **a. priekšā** roll in front of

aizvēnis *nm* **1.** lee; **2.** protection

aivēņots *adj* sheltered

aizvēre *nf* open space beyond a forest

aizveris *nm* handle

aizvērpt *vt* **1.** close by spinning; **2.** begin to spin

aizvērpties *vr* (of a thought, conversation) begin to spin

aizvērst *vt* (of eyes) avert

aizvērsties *vr* turn away

aizvērt *vt* close, shut; **a. acis** (fig.) shut one's eyes, overlook; **a. acis uz mūēu** breathe one's last; **a. acis mirējam** attend s.o. on his (her) deathbed; **ne acu neaizvērt** be unable to sleep

aizvērties *vr* close, shut

aizvērtnis *nm* shutter

aizvest *vt* **1.** take away, drive away, cart away; take (back, behind, along, to); **2.** abduct; kidnap; deport; **3.** (of roads, paths) lead

aizvēsture *nf* prehistoric times

aizvēsturisks *adj* prehistoric

aizvešana *nf* abduction; kidnapping; deportation

aizvien *adv* **1.** always; **2.** increasingly; **a. ātrāk** faster and faster; **3.** still

aizvienējs *adj* customary; steady

aizviet/a *nf* place behind a place; **katrā ~ā** in every nook and cranny

aizvietot *vt* **1.** put back; **2.** replace, substitute for

aizvietotāj/s *nm*, **~a** *nf* substitute, replacement

aizvīksnīties *vr* take off, scram

aizvilināt *vt* lure away

aizvilk/t *vt* **1.** pull away, drag away, pull to, drag to; **a. valodu** a. stammer; b. change the subject; **2.** pull together, pull tight; **3.** (of curtains) draw; **4. a. priekšā** pull in front of, stretch across; **5.** cover up (with snow, sand)

aizvilk/ties *vr* **1.** drag oneself to; **2.** *(3rd pers)* slide or glide away, slide or glide behind; **3.** *(3rd pers)* tighten; **4.** *(3rd pers)* slowly be-come overcast; slowly become covered or filled (with snow, sand); **5.** *(3rd pers, of time)* drag; **6.** run out of breath; **~damies** out of breath

aizvilnīt *vi* billow away

aizvilt *vt* lure away

aizviļņot *v vi* billow away; *vt* carry or spread on waves

aizviļņoties *vr* billow away

aizviņdien *adv* day before yesterday, the other day

aizviņgad *adv* the year before last

aizviņjūru *indecl adj* overseas

aizviņnakt *adv* two nights ago

aizviņnedēļ *adv* the week before last

aizviņsvētdien *adv* the Sunday before last

aizvirmot *vi* whirl away

aizvirpināt *vt* whirl away

aizvirpot *vi* whirl away

aizvirpuļot *vi* whirl away

aizvirst *vi* flow away

aizvirt *vi* bubble away

aizvirtnis *nm* window shutter

aizvirze *nf* deflection; diversion; drainage

aizvirzīt *vt* divert; **a. sarunu** change the topic of conversation

aizvirzīties *vr* move (away, aside, back, to)

aizvīst *vi* wilt partly

aizvīt *vt* **1.** close by weaving; **2.** weave to a point; **3.** begin to weave

aizvīterot *vi* fly away warbling

aizvīteroties *vr* begin to warble

aizvīties *vr* **1.** (of a road, stream) wind its way, meander; (of vines, tendrils) twist (up to, be-hind); (of snakes, worms) slither away

aizvizēt *vi* **1.** begin to shimmer; flash; **2.** freeze over (with a thin coat of ice)

aizvizēties *vr* flash briefly

aizvizināt *vt* take s.o. to (in a boat or vehicle, for fun)

aizvizināties *vr* go to (in a boat or vehicle, for fun)

aizvizmot *vi* move away in a glitter

aizzagties *vr* sneak away; sneak behind; steal to

aizzāģēt *vt* saw halfway through

aizzālināt *vt* put under grass

aizzāļot *vi* overgrow (with plants)

aizzarot *vi* (of trees, shrubs) spread branches in front of sth.

aizzaroties *vr* branch off

aizzēģelēt *vi* sail to

aizzelt *vi* **1.** begin to green; **2.** overgrow

aizzemdēt *vi* silt up

aizzibēt *vi* flash by

aizzibināt *vi* dash away

aizzibināties *vr* dash away

aizzibsnīt *vi* flash by

aizzibsnīties *vr* flash briefly

aizzieģelēt *vt* (obs.) seal

aizziest *vt* cover or fill with grease (or other plastic material)

aizzilējis *adj, part* of **aizzilēt** (of eyes) bleary; covered with a film

aizzilēt *vi* (of eyes) become bleary; (of glass) film over

aizzilgmējis *adj* bluish

aizzilināt *vt* add a little milk

aizzīmēšana *nf* marking, scoring

aizzīmēšanas adata *nf* scorer

aizzīmēt *vt* mark, score

aizzīmētāj/s *nm*, **~a** *nf* marker, scorer

aizzīmogot *vt* seal

aizziņot *vt* (col.) give notice to appear

aizzobe *nf* place behind the teeth

aizzust *vi* disappear behind sth.

aizzuzēt *vi* buzz past

aizzvanīties *vr* ring briefly; begin to ring

aizzviest *vt* fill (with plastic material)

aizžiglot *vi* run to

aizžilbināt *vt* dazzle

aizžmauga *nf* a narrow place

aizžmaugt *vt* throttle, strangle

aizžmiegt *vt* throttle, strangle

aizžņaudze *nf* throttle

aizžņaugt *vt* throttle, strangle

aizžņaugties *vr* (of voice) choke

aizžogojums *nm* fencing, hoarding; enclosure; (barbed wire) entanglement

aizžogot *vt* fence in, put up a fence

aizžogoties *vr* fence oneself in

aizžogs *nm* fencing, hoarding; enclosure; (barbed wire) entanglement

aizžuburot *vi* reach, spread

aizžuburoties *vr* reach, spread

aizžvadzēt *vi* jangle away, rattle away

aizžvakstēties *vr* begin to rattle

aizžvīkstēt *vi* swish by, whiz by

aizžvīkstēties *vr* begin to swish

aizžvinkstēt *vi* whiz by

|a]jato|l]a [ā]|lll] *nm* ayatollah

ak *interj* oh; **ak tā** oh, I see; **ak jā** oh, by the way; **ak nu** oh, come now; **ak vai** oh, dear

ak/a *nf* well; **kā ~ā iekritis** vanished without a trace

akācija *nf* acacia

akacis *nm* sinkhole in a swamp

akačainība *nf* abundance of sinkholes

akačains *adj* dotted with sinkholes

akačainums *nm* abundance of sinkholes

akadēmija *nf* academy

akadēmiķ/is *nm*, **~e** *nf* academician

akadēmiski *adv* academically

akadēmisks *adj* academic

akadēmiskums *nm* academicism

akadēmisms *nm* academism

akadēmist/s *nm*, **~e** *nf* academic

akalkulija *nf* acalculia

akantolimoni *nm pl* Acantholimon

akants *nm* (plant, ornament) acanthus

akaricīds *nm* tick and mite killer

akaroloģija *nf* acarology

akata *nf* sinkhole in a swamp

akatalektisks *adj* acatalectic

akate *nf* (reg.) sinkhole in a swamp

akatists *nm* acathistus

akaēu *indecl nm* acajou (cashew; mahogany)

akcelerācija *nf* acceleration

akcelerātors *nm* accelerator

akcelerāts *nm* precocious child

akcelerometrs *nm* accelerometer

akcentējums *nm* stress

akcentēt *vt* (of speech) stress; accentuate

akcents *nm* accent

akcentšķīvis *nm* crash cymbal

akcentuācija *nf* accentuation

akceptants *nm* (bus.) acceptor

akceptēt *vt* (bus.) accept

akceptkred|i]ts [ī] *nm* (bus.) acceptance credit

akceptors *nm* (bus.) acceptor

akcepts *nm* (bus.) acceptance, accepted bill

akcesija *nf* accession

akcesorisks *adj* accessory

akcesors *nm* accessory

akcidence *nf*, usu. *pl* **~s** 1. incidental income; 2. small printing jobs

akcidentāls *adj* accidental

akcidentpapīrs *nm* jobbing paper

akcija I *nf* share (of stock); **parastā a.** common share; **priviliģētās ~s** preferred stock

akcija II *nf* campaign; (mil.) operation

akciju banka *nf* banking corporation

akciju īpašnieks *nm* stockholder

akciju izlaidum/s *nm* share issue; **a. ~a uzcenojums** share premium

akciju kapitāls *nm* (econ.) stock

akciju kontrolpakete *nf* (econ.) majority interest

akciju kurss *nm* stock price

akciju pakete *nf* (econ.) portfolio

akciju sabiedrība *nf* joint stock company

akciju tirgus *nm* stock market

akciju tirgotājs *nm* stock broker

akcionār/s *nm*, ~e *nf* stockholder; ~u **kapitāls** stockholders' equity

akcīze *nf* excise tax

akinēzija *nf* akinesia

aklacis *nm* cleg

akl/ais *nom adj*, ~ā *f* blind person; ~ie the blind

aklais dundurs *nm* cleg

aklais koks *nm* (bot.) ash

aklamācija *nf* acclamation

aklamēt *vt* acclaim

aklā zarna *nf* blind gut, caecum; ~s ~s **iekaisums** appendicitis; ~s ~s **piedēklis** appendix

aklene *nf* columbine

aklenis *nm* cleg

aklenīte *nf* columbine

akles *nf pl* hemp nettle

akli *adv* blindly

aklība *nf* blindness

aklimatizācija *nf* acclimatization

aklimatizēt *vt* acclimatize

aklimatizēties *vr* become acclimatized

aklināt *vt* dazzle

aklis *nm* mole rat

aklīši *nm pl* red hemp nettle

aklo raksts *nm* Braille

akls *adj* blind; (of night, darkness) pitch-dark; (of obedience) implicit ◊ **ne a.** not for anything; **vai a.!** wow!

aklums *nm* blindness

akļi *nm pl* hemp nettle

akmeisms *nm* acmeism

akmeists *nm*, ~e *nf* acmeist

akmenājs *nm* stony ground; rock formation

akmenčakstis *nm* wheatear

akmenisks *adj* (fig.) stony

akme/ns *nm* stone, rock; boulder; gemstone, jewel; **kalts a.** stone block; **a. bruģis** stone block pavement; ~ņu **bērums** rockfill; ~ņu **šķembas** crushed stone ◊ **kā a. no sirds novēlās** it was a load off my mind

akmens bute *nf* turbot

akmensdārzs *nm* = **akmeņdārzs**

akmensizņemšana *nf* lithotomy

akmens krāvuma kaps *nm* cairn

akmens laikmets *nm* stone age; **jaunākais a. l.** neolithic period; **vecākais a. l.** paleolithic period; **vidējais a. l.** mesolithic period

akmenslauztuve *nf* = **akmeņlauztuve**

akmensmasa *nf* stoneware; **tumšā a.** common stoneware

akmens milti *nm pl* stone dust

akmens zīme *nf* bound stone

akmentiņš *nm dim* of **akmens**, little stone, pebble

akmeņainība *nf* stoniness

akmeņains *adj* stony

akmeņainums *nm* stoniness

akmeņčakstīte *nf* wheatear

akmeņdārzs *nm* rock garden

akmeņdruka *nf* lithography

akmeņgrauzis *nm* 1. loach; 2. gudgeon

akmeņkalis *nm* stonemason

akmeņkaltuve *nf* stonemason's shop

akmeņkalve *nf* boulder belt

akmeņkoks *nm* hackberry

akmeņķirsis *nm* mahaleb cherry

akmeņlauze *nf* burnet saxifrage

akmeņlauzējs or **akmeņlauzis** *nm* quarryman

akmeņlauzīte *nf* burnet saxifrage

akmeņlauztuve *nf* stone quarry

akmeņogle *nf*, usu. *pl* **akmeņogles** coal

akmeņots *adj* stony

akmeņozols *nm* holm oak

akmeņplekste *nf* turbot

akmeņpluka *nf* yellowish brown dye (obtained from stone lichen)

akmeņsāls *nf* rock salt

akmeņskaldis *nm* stone crusher

akmeņskaldītājs *nm* stone crusher

akmeņslīpētājs *nm* stone polisher; lapidary

akmeņtārtiņš *nm* turnstone

akmeņu apogs *nm* little owl

akmeņu bute *nf* turbot

akmeņu cauna *nf* stone marten

akmeņu čipste *nf* rock pipit

akmeņu lauks *nm* field of stone; (geol.) blockfield, boulder field

akmeņveidīgs *adj* stonelike

aknainis *nm* gutsy person

aknains *adj* crumbly

aknas *nf pl* liver; (fig., col.) guts

akne *nf* acne

aknu dēle *nf* liver fluke

aknu desa *nf* liverwurst

aknu sūnas *nf pl* liverwort

aknu vārti *nm pl* (anat.) portal fissure

akolāde *nf* accolade

akomodācija *nf* accomodation

akomodēt *vt* accomodate

akompanements *nm* accompaniment

akompanēt *vt* (mus.) accompany

akompanētāj/s *nm*, **~a** *nf* accompanist

akonitins *nm* aconitine

akonīts *nm* wolfsbane

akonītskābe *nf* aconitic acid

akonskābe *nf* aconic acid

a konto *adv* (bus.) on account

akordalga *nf* piecework pay

akorddarbs *nm* piecework

akordeonist/s *nm*, **~e** *nf* accordionist

akordeons *nm* accordion

akordeonveida *indecl adj* accordion-like

akordnie/ks *nm*, **~ce** *nf* pieceworker

akords *nm* **1.** (mus.) chord; **2.** piecework

akordstrādnie/ks *nm*, **~ce** *nf* pieceworker

akosmisms *nm* acosmism

akotains *adj* awned, bearded

akotiņš *nm dim* of **akots**, awn, beard; guard hair

akotmati *nm pl* guard hair

akotnie/ks *nm*, **~ce** *nf* furrier

akots *nm* **1.** awn, beard; **2.** guard hair; **3.** (fig.) skill

akracis *nm* well digger

akrēcija *nf* (geol.) accretion

akreditācija *nf* accreditation

akreditēšanās *nfr* presentation of credentials; **a. raksts** credentials

akreditēt *vt* accredit

akreditēties *vr* present one's credentials

akreditīvs *nm* **1.** letter of credit; **2.** credentials

akrībija *nf* meticulousness, painstaking care

akrilāns *nm* acrylic fabric

akrilijs *nm* = **akrils**

akrils *nm* acrylic

akrilskābe *nf* acrylic acid

akrilsveķi *nm pl* acrylic resin

akrilšķiedra *nf* acrylic fiber

akrob[a]tija [ā] nf acrobatics

akrob[a]tika [ā] *nf* acrobatics

akrob[a]tiski [ā] *adv* acrobatically

akrob[a]tisks [ā] *adj* acrobatic

akrob[a]tiskums [ā] *nm* acrobatism

akrob[a]t/s [ā] *nm*, **~e** *nf* acrobat

akrocefālija *nf* acrocephaly

akrodonts *nm* acrodont

akrofobija *nf* acrophobia

akrofobs *nm* acrophobe

akrokefalija *nf* acrocephaly

akroklinijas *nf pl* acrocliniums

akrole[i]ns [ī] *nm* acrolein

akrolekts *nm* acrolect

akromatisks *adj* acromatic

akromeg[a]lija [ā] *nf* acromegaly

akropole *nf* acropolis

akrosti[ch]s [h] *nm* acrostic

akroterijs *nm* acroterion

akrs *nm* acre**

akselbante *nf* aiguilette, shoulder cord; **kājnieku a.** infantry cord

akselerators *nm* accelerator

akselerogr[a]fs [ā] *nm* accelerograph

akselerometrs *nm* accelerometer

aksels *nm* axel

aksesuārs *nm* (theat.) prop; accessory

aksesuārs *adj* accessory

aksiālgultnis *nm* thrust bearing

aksiāli *adv* axially

aksiāls *adj* axial

aksioloģija *nf* axiology

aksioma *nf* axiom

aksiomatika *nf* axiomatics

aksiomatisks *adj* axiomatic

aksiometrs *nm* axometer

aksires *nf pl* axyris

aksis *nm* axis deer

aksonometrija *nf* axonometric projection

aksons *nm* axon

ākstība *nf* buffoonery

ākstīgs *adj* buffoonish

ākstīgums *nm* buffoonery

ākstīt *vt* (obs.) ridicule

ākstīties *vr* **1.** clown; (col.) play pranks, fool around; **ā. pakaļ** ape; **2.** (col.) vomit

aksts *nm* (of a pen, feather, sting) point

aksts *adj* nimble

āksts *nm* buffoon, clown, jester

aktierene *nf* (col.) actress

aktieris *nm* actor, player

aktieriski *adv* (of an actor) professionally

aktierisks *adj* **1.** affected, false, put-on; **2.** having stage presence

aktinīds *nm pl* actinide

aktinīdija *nf* silvervine

aktīnija *nf* actinia

aktīnijs *nm* actinium

aktīnisks *adj* actinic

aktīnisms *nm* actinism

akt[i]nogr[ā]fs [ī][a] *nm* actinograph

akt[i]nogramma [ī] *nf* X-ray photograph

akt[i]nolīts [ī] *nm* actinolite

akt[i]nometrija [ī] *nf* actinometry

akt[i]nometrisks [ī] *adj* actinometric

akt[i]nometrs [ī] *nm* actinometer

akt[i]nomicēte [ī] *nf* actinomycete

akt[i]nomicīns [ī] *nm* actinomycin

akt[i]nomikoze [ī] *nf* actinomycosis

aktīns *nm* actin

aktis *nf pl* See **akts** II

akt[i]vācija [ī] *nf* activation

akt[i]vācijas [ī] anal[i]ze [ī] *nf* activation analysis

akt[i]vators [ī] *nm* activator

akt[i]vēšana [ī] *nf* (chem., biol.) activation

akt[i]vēt [ī] *vt* activate

akt[i]vēties [ī] *vr* become activated

aktīvi *adv* actively

aktīvist/s *nm*, **~e** *nf* activist

akt[i]vitāte [ī] *nf* activity

akt[i]vizācija [ī] *nf* activation

akt[i]vizācijas [ī] pulss *nm* indicator gate

akt[i]viz[a]tor/s [ī][ā] *nm*, **~e** *nf* activator

akt[i]vizēšana [ī] *nf* activation

akt[i]vizēt [ī] *vt* make more active, stir to activity, (chem.) activate; (physiol.) stimulate

akt[i]vizēties [ī] *vr* become more active

aktīvs *nm* **1.** (pol.) most active members; **2.** (bus.) assets; **materiālais a.** tangible assets; **nemateriālais a.** intangible assets; **3.** (gram.) active voice

aktīvs *adj* active

aktīvums *nm* activity

aktrise *nf* actress

akts I *nm* **1.** act; **2.** official document; statement; documentary evidence; **3.** ceremony; **svinīgs a.** solemn assembly; **4.** (art) nude

akts II *nf*, usu. *pl* **~is** file

aktuāli *adv* currently

aktu[a]litāte [ā] *nf* topicality; our times; **~s jautājumi** current events; **~s samazināšanās** (of classified information) loss of sensitivity

aktu|a]lizācija [ā] *nf* actualization
aktu|a]lizēt [ā] *vt* actualize
aktuāls *adj* current, topical, of the day; urgent
aktuārs *nm* actuary; clerk; court reporter
aktu āzis *nm* pigeonhole rack
aktu vāks *nm* file folder
aktu zāle *nf* assembly hall
akūdens *nm* well water
akult|u]rācija [ū] *nf* acculturation
akumetrija *nf* hearing test
akumulācija *nf* accumulation
akumul|a]tors [ā] *nm* storage battery
akumulft *vt* accumulate
akumulēties *vr* accumulate
akupresūra *nf* acupressure
akupunktūra *nf* acupuncture
akurāti *adv* accurately, precisely; punctually; neatly; correctly
akurātība *nf* accuracy, precision; punctuality; tidiness, neatness
akurāts *adj* accurate, precise; punctual; tidy, neat; correct
akurātums *nm* accuracy
akustika *nf* acoustics
akustiķ/is *nm*, ~e *nf* acoustician
akustiski *adv* acoustically
akustisks *adj* acoustic
akustoelektronika *nf* acoustoelectronics
akušier/e *nf* (barb.) midwife
akušieris *nm* (barb.) accoucheur
akutēt *vt* acute
akūti *adv* acutely
akūts *nm* acute accent
akūts *adj* (med.) acute; (of problems, questions) urgent, vital, burning
akūtums *nm* acuteness; orgency
akuz|a]tīvs [ā] *nm* (gram.) accusative
akvadags *nm* Aquadag
akvaforts *nm* aquafortis
akvakultūra *nf* aquiculture
akvalangisms *nm* skin diving

akvalangist/s *nm*, ~e *nf* aqualunger, skin diver, (mil.) frogman
akvalangs *nm* Aqua-Lung
akvamanils *nm* aquamanile
akvamarīns *nm* aquamarine
akvametrija *nf* aquametry
akvanautika *nf* undersea exploration
akvanauts *nm* aquanaut
akvaplāns *nm* water ski
akvarelējums *nm* watercolor painting
akvarelēt *vi* paint in watercolors
akvarelis *nm* aquarelle, painting in water color
akvarelist/s *nm*, ~e *nf* watercolorist
akvareļgleznieciība *nf* watercolor painting
akvareļkrāsa *nf* watercolor
akvarīdas *nf pl* Aquarids
akvārijs *nm* aquarium
akvatinta *nf* aquatint
akvatipija *nf* aquatone
akvatorija *nf* territory covered by water; defined waters
akvavits *nm* aquavit
akvedukts *nm* aqueduct
akvifolija *nf* holly
akvizīcija *nf* acquisition
akvizīts *nm* acquisition
āķēt *vt* hook
āķīgi *adv* 1. trickily; 2. cleverly
āķīgs *adj* 1. (of a problem) tricky, involved; 2. (of a person) sly, tricky, crafty; clever
āķīgums *nm* trickiness
āķis *nm* hook; (fig.) snag, rub, catch; ā. un cilpa hook and eye
āķītis *nm* 1. *dim* of āķis, little hook; 2. (bot., zool.) burr, hook
āķveida *indecl adj* hook-shaped
āķveidīgs *adj* hook-shaped
ala *nf* cave, cavern; burrow, den
alabastrs *nm* alabaster
alains *adj* filled with caves
al|a]lija [ā] *nf* alalia, mutism

al|a|liķis [ā] *nm* mute

alanīns *nm* alanine

alān/s *nm*, ~e *nf* Alan

ālanta *nf* elecampane

alantoīns *nm* allantoin

alantojs *nm* allantois

ālants *nm* ide

alarmēt *vt* alarm

alarmisms *nm* alarmism

alarms *nm* alarm

alarod/s *nm*, ~iete *nf* Alarod

Alaskas ciedrs *nm* Alaska cedar

ālata *nf* grayling

alauns *nm* alum

ālava *nf* 1. dry cow; 2. barren female animal

ālave *nf* = ālava

ālavība *nf* (of female animals) infertility

ālavnīca *nf* (reg.) 1. dry cow; 2. barren female animal

ālavniece *nf* = ālavnīca

alba *nf* (lit.) alba

albān/is *nm*, ~iete *nf* Albanian

albatross *nm* albatross

albedo *indecl nm* albedo

albedometrs *nm* albedometer

alberēties *vr* (barb.) fool around, act silly

albicija *nf* albizzia

albieši or albiģieši *nm pl* Albigenses

albīniķis *nm* albino

albīnisms *nm* albinism

albīns *nm* albino

albīts *nm* albite

alborāda *nf* alborada

albumināts *nm* albuminate

albuminoids *nm* albuminoid

album|i|ns [ī] *nm* albumin

albuminūrija *nf* albuminuria

albumoze *nf* albumose

albums *nm* album

alcēj/s *nm*, ~a *nf* one that longs (or thirsts) for sth.

Alcheimera slimība *nf* Alzheimer's disease

alckupes *nf pl* thongs (that harness the pole to the hames in a two-horse wagon)

alda *nf* Aldine

aldar/is *nm*, ~e *nf* brewer

aldazīns *nm* aldazine

aldehīdamonjaks *nm* aldehyde ammonia

aldehīds *nm* aldehide

aldermanis *nm* alderman

aldīna *nf* Aldine

aldoheksoze *nf* aldohexose

aldonskābe *nf* aldonic acid

aldosterons *nm* aldosterone

aldoze *nf* aldose

aldrovandas *nf pl* Aldrovanda

aldzinieks *nm* wage earner

aleatorika *nf* aleatoric music

aleatorisks *adj* aleatoric

aleatorisms *nm* aleatoric music

alebarde *nf* halberd

alebardnieks *nm* halberdier

alegācija *nf* allegation

alegorija *nf* allegory

alegoriski *adv* allegorically

alegorisks *adj* allegoric

alegoriskums *nm* allegoricalness

alegorisms *nm* allegoricalness

alegreto *adv, indecl nm* = **allegreto**

alegri *indecl nm* = **allegri**

alegro *adv, indecl nm* = **allegro**

aleirometrs *nm* aleurometer

aleirons *nm* aleurone

aleja *nf* avenue; tree-lined lane

aleksandrietis *nm* alexandrine

Aleksandrijas lapa *nf* Alexandria sennna

aleksandrisks *adj* alexandrine

aleksandrīts *nm* alexandrite

aleksija *nf* alexia

alektorijas *nf pl* horsehair lichen

alektriomantija *nf* alectryomancy

alēle *nf* = **allēle**

alēlisms *nm* = **allēlisms**

alelomorfa *nf* = **allēlomorfa**

alelopatija *nf* = **allēlopatija**

aleluja [ā] *interj* hallelujah

alemande *nf* = **allemande**

alemaņi *nm pl* Alemanni

alene *nf* 1. bumblebee; 2. sand martin

alenis *nm* a forest rich in caves

alēns *nm* = **allēns**

alergēns *nm* allergen

alergologs *nm* = **allergologs**

alergoloģija *nf* = **allergoloģija**

alerģija *nf* = **allerģija**

alerģisks *adj* = **allerģisks**

ālestība *nf* silliness

ālēt *vt* fish with a drift net

ālēties *vr* romp; (col.) bluster, raise havoc

alētisks *adj* alethic

aleut/s *nm*, ~iete *nf* Aleut

alfa *nf* alpha

alfabētiski *adv* alphabetically

alfabētisks *adj* alphabetic

alfab[e]tizēt [ē] *vt* alphabetize

alfabēt/s *nm* alphabet; **pēc ~a** in alphabetic order

alfa sabrukšana *nf* alpha decay

alfaskaitlisks *adj* alphanumeric

alfonss *nm* gigolo

alga I *nf* 1. salary, wage, pay; remuneration ◊ **vie-na a.** or **a. viena** it makes no difference; 2. (fig.) reward

alga II *nf* alga

algādzēt *vr* hire daily workers

algādzība *nf* employment of daily workers

algādz/is *nm*, ~e *nf* 1. daily worker, hired hand; 2. hireling

algādžot *vt* hire daily workers

algas puisis *nm* hired hand

algebra *nf* algebra

algebriskā anal[i]ze [ī] *nf* calculus

algebriski *adv* algebraically

algebrisks *adj* algebraic

algezimetrs *nm* algesimeter

algicīds *nm* algicide

algīns *nm* algin

algofilija *nf* algophilia

algojums *nm* remuneration

algolagnija *nf* algolagnia

algoloģija *nf* algology

algols *nm* (compu.) Algol

algometrs *nm* algometer

algonkijs or **algonkins** *nm* (geol.) Algonkian

algoritmisks *adj* algorithmic

algoritmizēšana *nf* algorithmic solution of a problem

algoritms *nm* algorithm

algot *vt* hire; pay wages

algotnis *nm* mercenary; (fig.) hireling

algots *adj, part* of **algot** paid

algr[a]fija [ā] *nf* algraphy

algu saraksts *nm* payroll

alianse *nf* alliance

alias *nm indecl* alias

alibi *nm indecl* alibi

aliciklisks *adj* alicyclic

alid[a]de [ā] *nf* alidade

alienācija *nf* alienation

alif[a]tisks [ā] *adj* aliphatic

aligācija *nf* = **alligācija**

aligators *nm* alligator

alignīns *nm* lignin

alīgs *adj* (obs.) erroneous

ālīgs *adj* (col.) boisterous

alikvants *adj* aliquant

alikvots *adj* aliquot

āliķis *nm* (sl.) drink

alilhlorīds *nm* = **allilchlorīds**

alimentācija *nf* 1. (hist.) alimentation; 2. alimony payments

alimentārs *adj* alimentary

alimenti *nm pl* alimony

alinieks *nm* cave dweller

āliņģis *nm* hole in ice

aliņš *nm dim* of **alus**, little beer

alīrs *nm* (of horses) gait

alises *nf pl* alyssum

aliterācija *nf* = **alliterācija**

aliterēt *vi* = **alliterēt**

alitēt *vt* aluminize

alizar[i]ns [ī] *nm* alizarin

alka *nf* craving, desire; (poet.) hunger

alkacis *nm* frivolous, thoughtless person

alkadiēns *nm* alkadiene

alkahests *nm* alkahest

alkaini *adv* passionately; lustfully

alkains *adj* passionate; lustful

alkaisks *adj* alcaic

alkalds *nm* alcalde

alkalice[ll]uloza [l] *nf* alkalicellulose

alkalijs *nm* alkali

alkalimetrija *nf* alkalimetry

alk[a]lisks [ā] *adj* alkaline

alkalitāte *nf* alkalinity

alkalizācija *nf* alkalinization

alkaloīds *nm* alkaloid

alkaloze *nf* alkalosis

alkani *adv* avidly

alkanna *nf* alkanet

alkans *adj* **1.** avid; **2.** passionate, lustful

alkāns *nm* alkane

alkanums *nm* avidity

alkata *nm, nf* greedy person

alkataini *adv* greedily

alkatains *adj* greedy

alkatība *nf* greed

alkatīgi *adv* greedily

alkatīgs *adj* greedy

alkatīgums *nm* greediness

alkatis *nm* greedy person

alkatnie/ks *nm*, **~ce** *nf* greedy person

alkazars *nm* alcazar

alkēns *nm* alkene

alk[i]ds [ī] *nm* alkyd

alk[i]dsveķi [ī] *nm* alkyd resin

alkilācija *nf* alkylation

alkilfluorids *nm* alkyl fluoride

alkils *nm* alkyl

alkme *nf* (poet.) longing, desire

alkoholāts *nm* alcoholate

alkoholiķ/is *nm*, **~e** *nf* alcoholic

alkoholisks *adj* alcoholic

alkoholisms *nm* alcoholism

alkoholizēt *vt* alcoholize; (of wines) fortify

alkoholometrs *nm* alcoholometer

alkohols *nm* alcohol

alkovs *nm* alcove

alks *adj* (poet.) **l.** avid; **2.** passionate

alks *nm* auk; razorbill

alksme *nf* (poet.) desire

alksnaine *nf* alder growth

alksnājs *nm* alder growth, alder woods

alksnene *nf* **1.** red hot milk cap; **2.** mallow

alksniens *nm* alder growth

alksnis *nm* alder

alksnīte *nf* red hot milk cap

alkšņa *nf* (reg.) alder growth

alkšņains *adj* overgrown with alders

alkšņu blusiņa *nf* alder psylla

alkšņu ķeģis *nm* redpoll

alkšņu lapgrauzis *nm* an alder leaf chafer, Melasoma aenae

alkt *vt* long for, thirst for

alktin *emph* of **alkt; a. alkt** thirst mightily

alkums *nm* **1.** avidity; **2.** greed

alkveidīgie *nom adj* auks

alķīmija *nf* alchemy

alķīmiķis *nm* alchemist

alķīmisks *adj* alchemical

allantoiss *nm* allantois

allaž *adv* always

allažība *nf* (poet.) everyday commonness

allažiņ *adv* always

a[ll]egreto [l] *adv, indecl nm* allegretto

a[ll]egri [l] *indecl nm* raffle

a[ll]egro [l] *adv, indecl nm* allegro

a[ll]ēle [l] *nf* allele

a[ll]ēlisms [l] *nm* allelism

a[llē]lomorfs [le] *nf* allele

a[llē]lomorfisms [le] *nm* allelism

a[llē]lop[a]tija [le][ā] *nf* allelopathy

a|ll|emande [l] *nf* allemande

a|ll|ēns [l] *nm* allene

a|ll|ergolo/gs [l] *nm*, ~ģe *nf* allergist

a|ll|ergoloģija [l] *nf* allergology

a|ll|erģija [l] *nf* allergy

a|ll|erģisks [l] *adj* allergic

a|ll|igācija [l] *nf* alloy

a|ll|il|ch|lorids [l][h] *nm* allyl chloride

a|ll|iterācija [l] *nf* alliteration

a|ll|iterācijas [l] pantmērs *nm* alliterative verse

a|ll|iterēt [l] *vi, vt* alliterate

a|ll|og|a|mija [l][ā] *nf* allogamy

a|ll|ogr|a|fs [l][ā] *nm* allograph

a|ll|okācija [l] *nf* allocation

a|ll|oksāns [l] *nm* alloxan

a|ll|oksantīns [l] *nm* alloxantine

a|ll|okūcija [l] *nf* allocution

a|ll|omorfoze [l] *nf* allomorphosis

a|ll|ometrija [l] *nf* allometry

a|ll|on|i|ms [l][ī] *nm* allonym

a|ll|onēs [l] *nm* allonge, extension slip

a|ll|op|a|tija [l][ā] *nf* allopathy

a|ll|op|a|tisks [l][ā] *adj* allopathic

a|ll|opatrija [l] *nf* allopatry

a|ll|op|a|ts [l][ā] *nm* allopath

a|ll|oplastika [l] *nf* alloplasticity

a|ll|otriofaģija [l] *nf* allotriophagy

a|ll|otropija [l] *nf* allotropy

a|ll|otropisks[l] *adj* allotropic

a|ll|otrops [l] *nm* allotrope

a|ll|oze [l] *nf* allose

almana[ch]s [h] *nm* almanach

almenda *nf* (hist.) common land

almandīns *nm* almandine

almukantarats *nm* almucantar

alnis *nm* elk

alo|ch|tons [h] *nm* allochton

alodifikācija *nf* alodification

alods *nm* alodium

alofons *nm* allophone

alogains *adj* (reg.) springy, rich in springs

alogāmija *nf* = **allogamija**

alogrāfs *nm* = **allografs**

alogs *nm* (reg.) spring (of water)

aloģiski *adv* alogically

aloģisks *adj* alogical

aloģisms *nm* alogism

aloja *nf* aloe

aloje *nf* = **aloja**

alokācija *nf* = **allokācija**

aloksāns *nm* = **alloksāns**

aloksantīns *nm* = **alloksantīns**

alokūcija *nf* = **allokūcija**

alomorfoze *nf* = **allomorfoze**

alometrija *nf* = **allometrija**

alonims *nm* = **allonims**

alonžs *nm* = **allonžs**

alopātija *nf* = **allopatija**

alopātisks *adj* = **allopatisks**

alopatrija *nf* = **allopatrija**

alopāts *nm* = **allopats**

alopecija or alopekija *nf* alopecia

aloplastika *nf* = **alloplastika**

alot I *vt* tunnel, burrow, bore

alot II *vi* (folk.) to sing herdsmen's songs with the "alo" refrain

alotājkodes *nf pl* leaf-mining moths

aloties *vr* (obs.) err

alotigēns *adj* allothogenic

alotriofaģija *nf* = **allotriofaģija**

alotropija *nf* = **allotropija**

alotropisks *adj* = **allotropisks**

alotrops *nm* = **allotrops**

aloze *nf* = **alloze**

alp/a *nf* time, instance, spell, period; ~ām at times; ~ām . . . ~ām now . . . then

alpains *adj* (of wind, moods) changeable

alpaka *nf* (animal, fabric) alpaca

alpaks *nm* German silver

alpari *adv* at par

alp|i|nārijs [ī] *nm* display of Alpine flora

alpīnisms *nm* alpinism

alpīnist/s *nm*, ~e *nf* alpinist

alpīns *adj* Alpine, alpine

Alpu baltegle *nf* Alpine fir
Alpu baltirbe *nf* ptarmigan
Alpu bezdelīga *nf* red-rumped swallow
Alpu doņi *nm pl* Richardson's rush
Alpu glīvene *nf* northern pondweed
Alpu kovārnis *nm* yellow-billed chough
Alpu kreimule *nf* butterwort
Alpu miltenes *nf pl* Alpine bearberry
Alpu raganu puķe *nf* smaller enchanter's night-shade
Alpu roze *nf* 1. edelweiss; 2. rhododendron
Alpu rūgtlape *nf* Alpine sawwort
Alpu vārna *nf* red-billed chough
Alpu vijolīte *nf* cyclamen
Alpu ziemastere *nf* Michaelmas daisy
Alpu zvaigznīte *nf* edelweiss
alsine *nf* starwort
alsofila *nf* alsophila
alsunģietis *nm* 1. an inhabitant of Alsunga; 2. a Latvian folk dance
Altaju vijolīte *nf* Altaian violet
altajiet/is *nm*, **~e** *nf* Altaian
alta rags *nm* alto saxhorn
altā[r]glezna [ŗ] *nf* altarpiece
altāris *nm* altar
altā[r]niša [ŗ] *nf* apse
altā[r]telpa [ŗ] *nf* chancel
altā[r]trauki [ŗ] *nm pl* communion silver
altazimuts *nm* altazimuth
alteja *nf* marshmallow
altejs *nm* = **alteja**
alterācija *nf* (mus.) alteration
alterācijas zīmes *nf pl* (mus.) accidentals
alternācija *nf* alternation
altern[a]tīva [ā] *nf* alternative
altern[a]tīvi [ā] *adv* alternatively
altern[a]tīvs [ā] *adj* alternative
altern[a]tors [ā] *nm* alternator
alternāts *nm* 1. alternate; 2. (diplomacy) alternat
alternēt *vi* alternate
altigr[a]fs [ā] *nm* altigraph

altimetrija *nf* altimetry
altimetrs *nm* altimeter
altings *nm* Althing
altins *nm* (hist.) three-copeck piece
altiste *nf* 1. alto singer; 2. viola player
altists *nm* viola player
altroze *nf* altrose
altruisms *nm* altruism
altruistiski *adv* altruistically
altruistisks *adj* altruistic
altruist/s *nm*, **~e** *nf* altruist
alts *nm*, *nf* 1. alto; 2. viola
altvijole *nf* viola
alu cilvēks *nm* caveman
alumināts *nm* aluminate
alum[i]nijs [ī] *nm* aluminum
alum[i]nija [ī] oksīds *nm* alumina
aluminotermija *nf* aluminothermy
alumosilikāts *nm* aluminum silicate
alunds *nm* Alundum
al[u]n[i]ts [ū][ī] *nm* alunite
alūns *nm* alum
alu pētniecība *nf* speleology
alus *nm* beer; **gaišais a.** weiss beer; **tumšais a.** dark beer
alus darītava *nf* brewery
alusmuca *nf* beer keg; (col.) drunk
alus muša *nf* barfly
alus nesēju brālība *nf* (hist.) beer carriers' guild
alus raugs *nm* brewer's yeast
alusvāts *nf* beer barrel; (col.) drunk
alutiņš *nm dim* of **alus**, beer
aluviāls *adj* alluvial
al[u]vijs [ū] *nm* alluvium
alūzija *nf* allusion
alva *nf* tin
alvacis *nm* (folk.) person with poor eyesight
alvas akmens *nm* tin stone
alvas folija *nf* tinfoil
alvas krāsa *nf* vermilion
alvas papīrs *nm* tinfoil

alvas skārds *nm* tinplate
alveja *nf* aloe
alveola *nf* alveolus
alveolārs *nm* alveolar
alvojums *nm* tinning, coating of tin
alvot *vt* tin
alvskābe *nf* stannic acid
alžīriet/is *nm*, ~e *nf* Algerian
alze *nf* (naut.) tack
aļaskiet/is *nm*, ~e *nf* Alaskan
aļģe *nf* alga
aļģsēnes *nf pl* water mold, Phycomycetes
āļoties *vr* (col.) make a row
āma *nf* (obs.) a liquid measure
amakos/s *nm*, ~e *nf* Xhosa
amaleķiet/is *nm*, ~e *nf* Amalekite
amalgama *nf* amalgam; (fig.) amalgamation
amalgamēt *vt* amalgamate
amarants *nm* amaranth
amarantveida aksires *nf pl* upright axyris
āmarija *nm* (reg.) glutton
amarilis *nm* amaryllis
amata lāde *nf* tool chest
amata kāzas *nf pl* professional jubilee
amata svārki *nm pl* official robe
amatāt *vt* make by hand
amata zvērasts *nm* oath of office
amatbiedrība *nf* trade union, guild
amatbrālis *nm* fellow professional
amatier/is *nm*, ~e *nf* amateur
amatieriski *adv* amateurishly
amatierisks *adj* amateurish
amatierisms *nm* amateurism
amatistaba *nf* office
amatniecība *nf* craft, trade; ~s izstrādājumi
   hand-made goods
amatnieciski *adv* in a pedestrian or unimaginative fashion
amatniecisks *adj* related to trades and crafts;
   (fig.) pedestrian, unimaginative
amatnieciskums *nm* craftsmanship; (fig.)
   pedestrianism

amatnie/ks *nm*, ~ce *nf* craftsman, artisan
amatnieku savienība *nf* trade union
amatnieku skola *nf* vocational school, trade
   school
amatnolaidība *nf* nonfeasance
amatnoziegums *nm* malfeasance
amatols *nm* amatol
amatot *vt* make by hand
amatpārkāpums *nm* misfeasance
amatpersona *nm*, *nf* official, functionary
amats *nm* 1. trade; 2. craft; profession; 3. office,
   position; ~a official; 4. guild; 5. (col.) habit
   ◊ a. rokā get the knack
amatu savienošana *nf* pluralism (holding down
   more than one office)
amatveidīgi *adv* professionally
amatviltojums *nm* forgery (by an official)
amatvīrs *nm* (obs.) official, functionary
amauroze *nf* amaurosis
amazone *nf* 1. (myth.) Amazon; 2. amazon,
   virago; 3. horsewoman
ambarkadera *nf* embarcadero
amb[i]cija [ī] *nf* ambition
ambiciozs *adj* ambitious
ambigvitāte *nf* ambiguity
ambilineārs *adj* ambilineal
ambiloģija *nf* ambiguity
ambilokāls *adj* ambilocal
ambivalence *nf* ambivalence
ambivalents *adj* ambivalent
ambliopija *nf* amblyopia
ambons *nm* ambon
ambra *nf* ambergris
ambrazūra *nf* embrasure
ambrozija *nf* 1. ambrosia; 2. ~s ragweed
ambroziju balanda *nf* Mexican tea
ambulance *nf* outpatient clinic; dispensary
ambulances vāģis *nm* ambulance
ambulants *adj* ambulant
ambulatorijs *nf* veterinary clinic
ambulatoriski *adv* on an outpatient basis
ambulatorisks *adj* outpatient

ambušurs *nm* embouchure

amēba *nf* amoeba

āmeklis *nm* clown

ameliorācija *nf* amelioration

āmen *interj, nm indecl* amen; **kā ā. baznīcā** invariably

amencija *nf* amentia

amendaments *nm* amendment

amenoreja *nf* amenorrhea

ameraziāts *nm* Amerasian

amer[i]cijs [ī] *nm* americium

Amerika *prop nf* **1.** America; **2.** (sl.) wonderland

amerikāniski *adv* in an American fashion

amerikānisks *adj* American

amerikāniskums *nm* Americanism; American character

amerikānisms *nm* (ling.) Americanism

amerikān/is *nm*, ~e *nf* American

amerikānistika *nf* American studies

amerikanizēt *vt* Americanize

amerikanizēties *vr* Americanize

Amerikas dārza plūme *nf* wild goose plum

Amerikas dzeltenais koks *nm* American yellow-wood

Amerikas kastanis *nm* American chestnut

Amerikas lapegle *nf* American larch

Amerikas lazda *nf* filbert

Amerikas liepa *nf* basswood

Amerikas osis *nm* white ash

Amerikas paltuss *nm* arrow-toothed flounder

Amerikas plūme *nf* wild yellow plum

Amerikas skābarde *nf* American beech

Amerikas vīksna *nf* American elm

ametists *nm* amethyst

ametropija *nf* ametropia

amfetamīns *nm* amphetamine

amf[i]bija [ī] *nf* **1.** amphibian; **2.** amphibious vehicle

amf[i]bijlidmašīna [ī] *nf* amphibian airplane

amf[i]bijtanks [ī] *nm* amphibious tractor

amfibiotisks *adj* amphibiotic

amfībisks *adj* amphibious

amfibolija *nf* amphibology

amfibolīts *nm* amphibolite

amfibols *nm* amphibole, hornblende

amfibra[ch]s [h] *nm* amphibrach

amfibrahijs *nm* = **amfibrachs**

amfiktionija *nf* amphictyony

amfiktionis *nm* amphictyon

amfimakrs *nm* amphimacer

amfimikse *nf* amphimixis

amfiokss *nm* amphioxus

amfipodi *nm pl* Amphipoda

amfiprostils *nm* amphiprostyle

amfiteātris *nm* amphitheater

amfora *nf* amphora

amfotērisks *adj* amphoteric

amfotērs *adj* amphoteric

amhariet/is *nm*, ~e *nf* Amhara

amidopirīns *nm* aminopyrine

amīds *nm* amide

amigdalīns *nm* amygdalin

amikrons *nm* amicron

amilalkohols *nm* amyl alcohol

amilāze *nf* amylase

amilēns *nm* amylene

amilodekstrīns *nm* amylodextrin

amiloids *nm* amyloid

amilopektīns *nm* amylopectin

amiloze *nf* amylose

amils *nm* amyl

amilspirts *nm* amyl alcohol

amīmija *nf* amimia

aminācija *nf* amination

am[i]nopirīns [ī] *nm* aminopyrine

am[i]noskābe [ī] *nf* amino acid

am[i]notiazols [ī] *nm* aminothiazole

amīns *nm* amine

amīnskābe *nf* amino acid

āmiņš *nm* (naut.) draft mark

amis *nm* doggie

āmis I *nm* prankster, clown

āmis II *nm* (of a trawl) cod end

āmīties *vr* clown, romp

amītis *nm* (col.) American

amitoze *nf* amitosis

amizanti *adv* amusingly, entertainingly

amizants *adj* amusing, entertaining

amizēt *vt* amuse, entertain

amizēties *vr* enjoy oneself; flirt

amizieris *nm* (sl.) ladies' man

amma *nf* (child.) food

ammāt *vt, vi* (child.) eat

ammija *nf* bishop's-weed

ammins *nm* ammine

a|mm|onīts |m| *nm* 1. ammonite; 2. ammonium
    nitrate

amnestēt *vt* grant amnesty, pardon

amnestija *nf* amnesty

amn|e|zija|ē| *nf* amnesia

amnijs *nm* amnion

amnions *nm* amnion

amobijas *nf pl* winged everlasting

amodenijas *nf pl* seabeach sandwort

amoks *nm* amok

amoliņš *nm* 1. clover; 2. sweet clover; 3. *dim* of
    amols; mistletoe; daisy; clover

amols *nm* 1. mistletoe; 2. daisy; 3. clover

amoltiņš *nm* (col.) daisy

amoms *nm* amomum

amonāls *nm* ammonal

amonijmēsli *nm pl* ammonium fertilizer

amonijs *nm* ammonium

amonīts *nm* = ammonīts

amonizēt *vt* ammonate

amonjaka sāls *nf* sal ammoniac

amonjaks *nm* ammonia; ammonium hy-
    droxide

amonjakūdens *nm* ammonium hydroxide

amorālība *nf* amorality

amorālisms *nm* amoralism

amorālitāte *nf* amorality

amorāls *adj* amoral

amorālums *nm* amorality

amorets *nm* amoretto

amorfa *nf* amorpha

amorfisms *nm* amorphism

amorfs *nm* amorphous substance

amorfs *adj* amorphous

amorfums *nm* amorphism

amors *nm* cupid

amortizācija *nf* 1. depreciation; amortization;
    2. (mech.) damping, absorption of shocks

amortizācijas fonds *nm* sinking fund

amortiz|a|tors |ā| *nm* shock absorber

amortizēt *vt* 1. depreciate; amortize; 2. (mech.)
    dampen

ampelis *nm* (barb.) clown

ampelmanis *nm* jumping jack; (barb.) clown

amperāēa *nf* amperage

ampērmetrs *nm* ammeter

Ampēra likums *nm* Ampere's law

ampērs *nm* ampere

ampersands *nm* ampersand

ampērsekunde *nf* ampere-second

ampērstunda *nf* ampere-hour

ampērvijums *nm* ampere-turn

ampīrs *nm* Empire (style)

amplēties *vr* (col.) act silly, gesture with hands
    and feet

amplība *nf* silliness

amplidīns *nm* amplidyne

amplificēt *vt* amplify

amplifikācija *nf* amplification

amplīgs *adj* silly, clownish

ampl/is *nm*, ~e *nf* (col.) fool

amplitūda *nf* amplitude

ampluā *indecl nm* role type; strong suit

ampula *nf* ampule

amputācija *nf* amputation

amputēt *vt* amputate

āmrija *nm* 1. (com.) glutton; wolfer; 2. (zool.)
    glutton; wolverine

āmrijīgs *adj* (com.) gluttonous

āmrīļa *nm* = āmrija

āms I *nm* (reg.) prankster; clown

āms II *nm* small fishing net

amtmanis *nm* (hist.) bailiff
amulets *nm* amulet
āmuļi *nm pl* mistletoe
āmura pārtraucējs *nm* hammer breaker
Amūras korķkoks *nm* cork tree
Amūras līdaka *nf* Amur pike
āmura sviešana *nf* hammer throwing
āmurgalva *nm* (col.) blockhead
āmurhaizivs *nf* (zool.) hammerhead
āmuriņš *nm* 1. *dim* of āmurs, little hammer;
    2. (anat.) malleus; 3. (telegraph) sounder
āmurraja *nf* (zool.) hammerhead
amūrs *nm* See baltais a., melnais a.
āmur/s *nm* hammer; mallet; atskaldāmais ā.
    miner's pick; šķeltzoba ā. claw hammer;
    uzsitamais ā. sledgehammer ◊ zem ~a
    (col.) under the hammer
āmurzivs *nf* (zool.) hammerhead
amutulis *nm* hothead
amūzija *nf* amusia
anabaptisms *nm* Anabaptism
anabaptist/s *nm*, ~e *nf* Anabaptist
anabazīns *nm* anabasine
anabiotisks *adj* anabiotic
anabioze *nf* anabiosis
anabolika *nf* anabolic substance
anabolisks *adj* anabolic
anabolisms *nm* anabolism
ana[ch]orets [h] *nm* anchorite
ana[ch]ronisks [h] *adj* anachronistic
ana[ch]ronisms [h] *nm* anachronism
anacikle *nf* German pellitory
anadiploze *nf* anadiplosis
anaerobisks *adj* anaerobic
anaerobs *nm* anaerobe
anaerobs *adj* anaerobic
anafilakse *nf* anaphylaxis
anafilaksija *nf* anaphylaxis
anafora *nf* anaphora
anafrod[i]zija [ī] *nf* anaphrodisia
anaglifija *nf* anaglyphy
anaglifs *nm* anaglyph

anagnostiķ/is *nm*, ~e *nf* anagnostic
anagoģija *nf* anagoge
anagramma *nf* anagram
anah- See anach-
anakardija *nf* cashew; ~s Anacardiaceae
anakolūtija *nf* anacoluthia
anakolūts *nm* anacoluthon
anakonda *nf* anaconda
anakreontika *nf* anacreontic
anakreontisks *adj* anacreontic
anakrūze *nf* anacrusis
anāldziedzeris *nm* anal gland
analektes *nf pl* analects
analeptika *nf* analeptic
analeptisks *adj* analeptic
analfabētiski *adv* analphabetically
analfabētisks *adj* analphabetic; illiterate
analfabētisms *nm* illiteracy
analfabēt/s *nm*, ~e *nf* illiterate
analgētika *nf* analgetic
analgētisks *adj* analgetic
analg[e]zija [ē] *nf* analgesia
analitika *nf* analytics
analitiķ/is *nm*, ~e *nf* analyst
anal[i]tiski [ī] *adv* analytically
anal[i]tisks[ī] *adj* analytic, analytica
anal[i]tiskums [ī] *nm* analyticity
analiz[a]tors [ā] *nm* analyzer
anal[i]ze [ī] *nf* analysis
analizēt *vt* analyze; (gram.) parse
analogdati *nm pl* analog data
analogi *adv* analogously
analogmodelis *nm* analog model
analogs *nm* analog
analogs *adj* analogous
analogu dators *nm* analog computer
analoģija *nf* analogy
analoģijas burvība *nf* sympathetic magic
analoģiski *adv* analogically
analoģisks *adj* analogical
analoģiskums *nm* analogism
analoģisms *nm* analogism

anāls *adj* anal

anamiet/is *nm*, ~e *nf* Annamese

anamnēze *nf* anamnesis

anamorfisks *adj* anamorphic

anamorfoza *nf* anamorphosis

anamorfs *adj* anamorphic

ananasa zemene *nf* Ananassa strawberry

ananass *nm* pineapple

anap|ai|sts [e] *nm* anapest

anaptikse *nf* anaptyxis

anar|ch|ija [h] *nf* anarchy

anar|ch|iski [h] *adv* anarchically

anar|ch|isks [h] *adj* anarchic

anar|ch|isms [h] *nm* anarchism

anar|ch|istiski [h] *adv* anarchistically

anar|ch|istisks [h] *adj* anarchistic

anar|ch|ist/s [h] *nm*, ~e *nf* anarchist

anar|ch|osindikālisms [h] *nm* syndicalism

anar|ch|osindikālists [h] *nm* syndicalist

anarh- See anarch-

anartrija *nf* anarthria

anasarka *nf* anasarca, dropsy

anastatisks *adj* anastatic

anastigmatisks *adj* anastigmatic

anastigmatisms *nm* anastigmatism

anastigmats *nm* anastigmatic lens

anastomoze *nf* anastomosis

anastrofa *nf* anastrophe

anat|e|ma [ē] *nf* anathema

anatocisms *nm* anatocism, compound interest

anatomēt *vt* anatomize

anatomija *nf* anatomy

anatomikums *nm* anatomical theater

anatomiski *adv* anatomically

anatomisks *adj* anatomic, anatomical

anatom/s *nm*, ~e *nf* anatomist

ancestrāls *adj* ancestral

ancila laiks *nm* Holocene

ancīši *nm pl* agrimony

anckapele *nf* (barb.) (harness) neck strap

ancuks *nm* (sl.) suit

ančars *nm* antiar

ančara koks *nm* upas tree

andaluziet/is *nm*, ~e *nf* Andalusian

andaluzīts *nm* andalusite

andante *adv, indecl nm* (mus.) andante

andele *nf* (col.) haggling

andelēties *vr* (sl.) 1. sell, deal; 2. haggle, bargain

andelētāj/s *nm*, ~a *nf* (barb.) seller

andezins *nm* andesine

andezīts *nm* andesite

andogs *nm* trawl bag

androcentrisks *nm* androcentric

androcentrisms *nm* androcentrism

androfobija *nf* androphobia

androg|e|ns [ē] *nm* androgen

androginija *nf* androgyny

androids *nm* android

androloģija *nf* andrology

andromeda *nf* andromeda

andropogone *nf* beard grass

androsterons *nm* androsterone

andrs or andrus *nm* (reg.) keel

Andu lācis *nm* spectacled bear

andžiņš *nm* a Latvian folk dance

aneirisms *nm* = aneurisms

anekdote *nf* anecdote

anekdotiski *adv* anecdotally

anekdotisks *adj* anecdotal

anekdotiskums *nm* anecdotism

aneksija *nf* annexation

aneksionistisks *adj* annexational

anektēt *vt* annex

anēmija *nf* anemia

anēmisks *adj* anemic

anemobiogr|a|fs [ā] *nm* anemobiograph

anemofilija *nf* anemophily

anemofils *adj* anemophilous

anemog|e|ns [ē] *adj* anemogenic

anemogr|a|fs [ā] *nm* anemograph

anemoloģija *nf* anemology

anemometrija *nf* anemometry

anemometrs *nm* anemometer

anemone *nf* anemone
anemotropisms *nm* anemotropism
anero[i]ds [ī] *nm* aneroid barometer
anestētika *nf* anesthetic
anest[e]zēt [ē] *vt* anesthetize
anestēzija *nf* anesthesia
anest[e]ziolo/gs [ē] *nm*, ~ġe *nf* anesthesiologist
anest[e]zioloģija [ē] *nf* anesthesiology
anestēzist/s *nm*, ~e *nf* anesthetist
anetols *nm* anethole
aneurisms *nm* aneurysm
anfilāde *nf* enfilade
angārs *nm* hangar
angaēements *nm* (theat.) contract engagement
angaēēt *vt* (theat.) engage
angīna *nf* tonsillitis
angio[ch]olīts [h] *nm* angiocholitis
angioloģija *nf* angiology
angioma *nf* angioma
angioplastija *nf* angioplasty
angiospermas *nf pl* Angiospermae
anglezīts *nm* anglesite
anglicisms *nm* anglicism
anglicist/s *nm*, ~e *nf* Anglicist
angliete *nf* Englishwoman
anglificēt *vt* anglicize
anglikān/is *nm*, ~iete *nf* Anglican
anglikānisms *nm* Anglicanism
anglis *nm* Englishman
angliski *adv* in English, (speak) English
anglisks *adj* English
angliskums *nm* Englishness
anglistika *nf* Anglistics
anglofilija *nf* anglophilia
anglofil/s *nm*, ~e *nf* anglophile
anglofobija *nf* anglophobia
anglofob/s *nm*, ~e *nf* anglophobe
anglofonisks *adj* English-speaking
anglomānija *nf* anglomania
anglosaks/is *nm*, ~iete *nf* Anglo-Saxon
angļu atslēga *nf* monkey wrench

angļu dārzs *nm* formal garden
angļu dogs *nm* mastiff
angļu gotika *nf* (arch.) perpendicular style
angļu jūdze *nf* statute mile;
angļu kvieši *nm pl* cone wheat
angļu plāksteris *nm* adhesive plaster
angļu radziņš *nm* English horn
angļu raizāle *nf* ryegrass
angļu sāls *nf* Epsom salts
angļu skābene *nf* patience dock
angļu slimība *nf* rickets
angļu valsis *nm* hesitation waltz
angoba *nf* engobe
Angoras kaķis *nm* Angora cat
Angoras kaza *nf* Angora goat
Angoras trusis *nm* Angora rabbit
Angoras vilna *nf* mohair
angstrēms *nm* angstrom
angulātors *nm* angulator
anhidr[i]ds [ī] *nm* anhydride
anhidrisks *adj* anhydrous
anhidrīts *nm* anhydrite
anhidrobioze *nf* anhydrobiosis
anihilācija *nf* annihilation
anilids *nm* anilide
anilings *nm* anilingus
anilīnkrāsa *nf* aniline dye
anilīns *nm* aniline
anīls *nm* anil
animācija *nf* animation
animālisms *nm* animalism
animālistisks *adj* (of art) animalistic
animālist/s *nm*, ~e *nf* animalier
animāls *adj* animal
animisms *nm* animism
animistisks *adj* animistic
animists *nm* animist
anionisks *adj* anionic
anions *nm* anion
anīsa sēne *nf* blue-green anise mushroom
anīss *nm* anise
anizols *nm* anisole

anizofillija *nf* anisophylly

anizogamija *nf* anisogamy

anizokorija *nf* anisocoria

anizotropija *nf* anisotropy

anizotropisks *adj* anisotropic

anizotropisms *nm* anisotropy

anjons *nm* anion

ankambaris *nm* (com.) pantry

anketa *nf* questionnaire

anketaptauja *nf* questionnaire survey

anketēšana *nf* questionnaire method of research

ankilostoma *nf* ancylostome

ankiloze *nf* ankylosis

anklāvs *nm* enclave

ankons *nm* ancon

ankravas *nf pl* ruts (in the road)

anksāris *nm* deep place in a river

anksters *nm* maggot

anķins *nm* (col.) gadget, thingamajig

annāles *nf pl* annals

annālists *nm* annalist

annātes *nf pl* annates

annona *nf* annona, custard apple

annuitāte *nf* annuity

anoa *nf* anoa

anodbaterija *nf* B battery, plate battery

anodizēt *vt* anodize

anods *nm* anode

anodslodze *nf* plate load

anodspriegums *nm* plate voltage

anodstari *nm pl* anode rays

anodstrāva *nf* plate current

anofeļi *nm pl* Anopheles

anoftalmija *nf* anophthalmia

anoksija *nf* anoxia

anom[a]li [ā] *adv* anomalously

anom[a]lija [ā] *nf* anomaly

anom[a]ls [ā] *adj* anomalous

anomers *nm* anomer

anomija *nf* anomie

anon[i]mi [ā] *adv* anonymously

anon[i]mitāte [ī] *nf* anonymity

anon[i]ms [ī *nm* anonym

anon[i]ms [ī] *adj* anonymous

anonse *nf* classified ad; notice

anonsēt *vt* publish a classified ad, advertise

anonss *nm* = anonse

anopistogr[a]fiski [ā] *adv* anopistographically

anopistogr[a]fisks [ā] *adj* anopistographic

anopsija *nf* anoopsia

anoraks *nm* parka, anorak

anoreksija *nf* anorexia

anorganisks *adj* inorganic

anormalitāte *nf* abnormality

anormāli *adv* abnormally

anormāls *adj* abnormal

anortīts *nm* anorthite

anortozīts *nm* anorthosite

anosmija *nf* anosmia

anotācija *nf* annotation

anotēt *vt* annotate

ansamblis *nm* (mus.) ensemble; (theat.) troupe, company

anserīns *nm* anserine

ansītis *nm dim* of *prop n* Ansis; **garais a.** middle finger; **mazais a.** little finger

anšluss *nm* Anschluss

anšovs *nm* anchovy

anštalte *nf* (sl.) government office

anštellēties *vr* (col.) pretend

anštendīgs *adj* (sl.) polite, decent

antablements *nm* entablature

antagonisks *adj* antagonistic

antagonisms *nm* antagonism

antagonistiski *adv* antagonistically

antagonistisks *adj* antagonistic

antagonist/s *nm*, ~e *nf* antagonist

antante *nf* entente

Antarktikas efejvīns *nm* kangaroo vine

antarktisks *adj* Antarctic

antecedencija *nf* antecedence

antecedents *nm* antecedent

antedatēt *vt* antedate
antefikss *nm* antefix
antefleksija *nf* anteflexion
antena *nf* antenna
antenas slēdzis *nm* antenna grounding switch
antenna *nf* = antena
anterīdijs *nm* antheridium
antialkoholiķ/is *nm*, ~e *nf* antialcoholic
antiamerikānisks *adj* anti-American
antiariss *nm* upas tree
antibak[ch]s [h] *nm* antibacchius
antibakt[e]riāls [ē] *adj* antibacterial
antibarions *nm* antibaryon
antibiotika *nf* antibiotic
antibiotiski *adv* antibiotically
antibiotisks *adj* antibiotic
antibioze *nf* antibiosis
antiblastisks *adj* antiblastic
anticiklonisks *adj* anticyclonic
anticiklons *nm* anticyclone
anticipācija *nf* anticipation
anticip[a]tīvi [ā] *adv* anticipatorily
anticip[a]tīvs [ā] *adj* anticipatory
anticipēt *vt* anticipate
antidaļiņa *nf* antiparticle
antidemokratisks *adj* antidemocratic
antidepresants *nm* antidepressant
antidetonators *nm* antiknock
antidiabētisks *adj* antidiabetic
antidots *nm* antidote
antielektrons *nm* antielectron
antifašistiski *adv* in an antifascist manner
antifašistisks *adj* antifascist
antifašist/s *nm*, ~e *nf* antifascist
antifebrīns *nm* Antifebrin, acetanilide
antifeodāls *adj* antifeudal
antifona *nf* antiphon
antifrīze *nf* or antifrīzs *nm* antifreeze
antigēns *nm* antigen
antihelminti *nm pl* antihelminthics
antihigiēnisks *adj* unhygienic
antihistamīns *nm* antihistamine

antihormons *nm* antihormone
antihumānistisks *adj* antihumanistic
antihumāns *adj* antihumanistic
antiimperiālistiski *adv* anti-imperialistically
antiimperiālistisks *adj* anti-imperialistic
antīka *nf* antiquity
antikatalizātors *nm* anticatalyst
antiklerikālisms *nm* anticlericalism
antiklerikāls *adj* anticlerical
antiklināle *nf* anticline
antiklināls *adj* anticlinal
antikoagulanti *nm pl* anticoagulants
antikodons *nm* anticodon
antikoloniāls *adj* anticolonial
antikom[u]nisms [ū] *nm* anticommunism
antikom[u]nistiski [ū] *adv* anticommunistically
antikom[u]nistisk/s [ū] *adj* anticommunisti
antikom[u]nist/s [ū] *nm*, ~e *nf* anticommunist
antikonstitucionāls *adj* anticonstitutional
antikorozīvs *adj* anticorrosive
antikrists *nm* antichrist
antīks *adj* antique
antīkums *nm* antiqueness
antīkva *nf* (typ.) Roman
ant[i]kvariāts [ī] *nm* second-hand bookstore; antique shop
ant[i]kvār/s [ī] *nm*, ~e *nf* second-hand bookseller; seller of antiques; antiquary
ant[i]kvitāte [ī] *nf* antiquity; ~s antiquities
antilogaritms *nm* antilogarithm
antiloģija *nf* antilogy
antiloģiski *adv* antilogically
antiloģisks *adj* antilogical
antilope *nf* antelope
anti-mao viela *nf* monoamine oxidase inhibitor
antimateriālistiski *adv* antimaterialiastically
antimateriālistisks *adj* antimaterialistic
antimetabolīts *nm* antimetabolite
antimilitārisms *nm* antimilitarism
antimilitārist/s *nm*, ~e *nf* antimilitarist

antimilitārs *adj* antimilitary

antimona blende *nf* kermesite

antimonar[ch]istisks [h] *adj* antimonarchistic

antimona spīde *nf* stibnite

antimonāts *nm* antimonate

antimona ziedi *nm pl* antimony bloom

antimonīds *nm* antimonide

antimonīts *nm* antimonite, stibnite

antimonopolisks *adj* antimonopolistic

antimonopolu *indecl adj* antimonopolistic

antimons *nm* antimony

antimonskābe *nf* antimonic acid

antimutagēns *nm* antimutagenic agent

antinacionālsociālistisks *adj* anti-Nazi

antineitrino *nm indecl* antineutrino

antineitrons *nm* antineutron

antineoplastisks *adj* antineoplastic

antinomija *nf* antinomy

antinuklons *nm* antinucleon

antiņš *nm* (col.) simpleton

antioksidants *nm* antioxidant

antipartejiski *adv* directed against the party

antipartejisks *adj* directed against the party

antipasāts *nm* antitrades

antip[a]tija [ā] *nf* antipathy

antip[a]tiski [ā] *adv* antipathetically

antip[a]tisks [ā] *adj* antipathetic

antipirēns *nm* fire retardant

antipirētika *nf* antipyretic

antipirētisks *adj* antipyretic

antipirīns *nm* antipyrine

antipods *nm* antipode

antipols *nm* antipole

antiprotons *nm* antiproton

antireliģiski *adv* antireligiously

antireliģisks *adj* antireligious

antisanitāri *adv* in an unsanitary manner

antisanitārs *adj* insanitary

antisemītiski *adv* anti-Semitically

antisemītisks *adj* anti-Semitic

antisemītisms *nm* anti-Semitism

antisemīt/s *nm*, ~e *nf* anti-Semite

antis[e]ptika [ē] *nf* antisepsis

antis[e]ptiski [ē] *adv* antiseptically

antis[e]ptisks [ē] *adj* antiseptic

antis[e]ptiskums [ē] *nm* antisepsis

antis[e]ptizēt [ē] *vt* antisepticize

antisociāli *adv* antisocially

antisociāls *adj* antisocial

antispasts *nm* antispast

antistatiķis *nm* antistatic

antistatisks *adj* antistatic

antistrofa *nf* antistrophe

antitetiski *adv* antithetically

antitetisks *adj* antithetic

antit[e]ze [ē] *nf* antithesis

antitipija *nf* antitypy

antitireoidāls *adj* antithyroid

antitireoīds *adj* antithyroid

antitoksīns *nm* antitoxin

antitoksiski *adv* antitoxically

antitoksisks *adj* antitoxic

antitoksiskums *nm* antitoxicity

antiviela *nf* 1. antibody; 2. antimatter

antivīruss *nm* antivirotic

antizinātniski *adv* antiscientifically

antizinātnisks *adj* antiscientific

antizinātniskums *nm* antiscientific bias

antolo/gs *nm*, ~ģe *nf* anthologist

antoloģija *nf* anthology

anton[i]mija [ī] *nf* antonymy

anton[i]ms [ī] *nm* antonym

antonomāze *nf* antonomasia

antonomāzija *nf* antonomasia

antonovka *nf* a variety of apple

antons *nm* (sl.) dumbbell

antracens *nm* anthracene

antra[ch]ionons [h] *nm* anthraquinone

antracītisks *adj* anthracitic

antracīts *nm* anthracite

antraflāvskābe *nf* anthraflavic acid

antragallols *nm* anthragallol

antraknoze *nf* anthracnose

antrakoze *nf* anthracosis

antrakss *nm* anthrax
antrakts *nm* entracte; intermission
antranols *nm* anthranol
antrapurpurīns *nm* anthrapurpurin
antrarufīns *nm* anthrarufin
antrašā *indecl nm* entrechat
antreja *nf* entryway
antrekots *nm* entrecote
antreprenier/is *nm*, ~e *nf* entrepreneur
antresols *nm* 1. mezzanine; 2. upper shelf
antrilēns *nm* anthrylene
antrils *nm* anthryl
antropisks *adj* anthropic
antropocentriski *adv* anthropocentrically
antropocentrisk/s *nm* anthropocentric
antropocentrisms *nm* anthropocentrism
antropofags *nm* anthropophagus
antropofaģija *nf* anthropophagy
antropofobija *nf* anthropophobia
antropogēns *adj* anthropogenic
antropogr[a]fija [ā] *nf* anthropography
antropoģen[e]ze [ē] *nf* anthropogenesis
antropoģeogr[a]fija [ā] *nf* anthropogeo-
      graphy
antropo[i]ds [ī] *nm* anthropoid
antropolatrija *nf* anthropolatry
antropolo/g/s *nm*, ~ģe *nf* anthropologist
antropoloģija *nf* anthropology
antropoloģiski *adv* anthropologically
antropoloģisk/s *adj* anthropological
antropometrija *nf* anthropometry
antropometriski *adv* anthropometrically
antropometrisks *adj* anthropometric
antropomorfiski *adv* anthropomorphically
antropomorfisks *adj* anthropomorphic
antropomorfisms *nm* anthropomorphism
antropomorfs *nm* anthropoid
antropon[i]mija [ī] *nf* anthroponymy
antropon[i]mika [ī] *nf* anthroponymy
antropon[i]ms [ī] *nm* anthroponym
antropopatisms *nm* anthropopathism
antropoteisms *nm* anthropotheism

antropozofija *nf* anthroposophy
ants *nm* (arch.) anta
anturāža *nf* entourage
anturija *nf* anthurium
anuitāte *nf* = annuitāte
anulējams *adj, part* of anulēt defeasible
anulēšana *nf* annulment; rescission; cancellation;
      abolition; abrogation; nullification
anulēt *vt* annul; rescind; cancel; abolish;
      abrogate; nullify
anulis *nm* 1. annulus; 2. (arch.) annulet
ānungs *nm* (sl.) notion, idea
anūrija *nf* anuria
anuss *nm* anus
āņķēns *nm* spigot
aorists *nm* aorist
aorta *nf* aorta
aortāls *adj* aortic
ap I *prep* around; about
ap II *prep* (folk.) under
apač/s *nm*, ~iete *nf* Apache
apadīt *vt* 1. knit around; knit an edging;
      2. provide with knitted items
apagoģiski *adv* apagogically
apagoģisks *adj* apagogic
apairēt *vt, vi* row around
apairēties *vr* row around sth.
apakš *prep* under; beneath
apakš/a *nf* underside; bottom; place underneath;
      no ~as from below, from the bottom; uz ~u
      down, downwards; no pašas ~as from the
      very bottom; (griezt) ~u uz augšu (turn)
      upside down
apakšā *adv* 1. underneath; down; below; at the
      bottom of; (es,) a. parakstījies (I,) the un-
      dersigned; te a. down here; 2. downstairs
apakšaudze *nf* undergrowth
apakšaugs *nm* underplanting
apakšaugsne *nf* subsoil
apakšbikses *nf pl* underpants, drawers, shorts
apakšbiksītes *nf pl* panties
apakšbruņči *nm pl* underskirt

apakšbūve *nf* substructure
apakšcentrāle *nf* branch telephone exchange
apakšdaļa *nf* lower part, bottom
apakšdelma kauls *nm* (anat.) radius
apakšdelms *nm* forearm
apakšdevons *nm* Lower Devonian
apakšdrānas *nf pl* undergarments
apakšdrēbes *nf pl* undergarments
apakšdzimta *nf* subfamily
apakšējais *adj* lower
apakšgals *nm* lower end
apakšgaroza *nf* bottom crust
apakšgarums *nm* (typ.) descender
apakšgrunts *nf* subsoil
apakšgrupa *nf* subgroup
apakšģints *nf* subgenus
apakšīpašnieks *nm* part owner
apakšīre *nf* subrent; subrenting
apakšīrnie/ks *nm*, **~ce** *nf* subtenant
apakškārta *nf* subsoil
apakšklājs *nm* (naut.) lower deck
apakškomisija *nf* subcommittee
apakškomiteja *nf* subcommittee
apakškopa *nf* subset
apakškrekls *nm* undershirt
apakškultūra *nf* subculture
apakšķīla *nf* subcollateral
apakšlūpa *nf* lower lip
apakšmala *nf* lower edge; (of a skirt) hem
apakšmīna *nf* belly attack mine, tilt-rod mine
apakšnams *nm* (pol.) lower house
apakšnie/ks *nm*, **~ce** *nf* subordinate
apakšnodaļa *nf* subsection
apakšnoma *nf* (of a piece of land) subtenancy
apakšnomnieks *nm* subtenant (of a piece of land)
apakšnozare *nf* subbranch
apakšpakš/i *nm pl* place under the eaves; **~os iet** a children's game
apakšpalāta *nf* (pol.) lower house
apakšpamats *nm* subgrade
apakšpasaule *nf* underworld

apakšprogramma *nf* subprogram
apakšpulkvedis *nm* lieutenant colonel
apakšpunkts *nm* (of a text) subsection
apakšpus *prep* below, beneath
apakšpuse *nf* lower half; underside
apakšrajons *nm* subdistrict
apakšraugs *nm* bottom yeast
apakšsekcija *nf* subsection
apakšsistēma *nf* subsystem
apakšspridzeklis *nm* base fuze
apakšstacija *nf* substation
apakšstāvs *nm* ground floor
apakšstilbs *nm* shank
apakšstraume *nf* undercurrent
apakšstrāva *nf* undercurrent
apakšstrāvojums *nm* undercurrent
apakšsuga *nf* subspecies
apakšsvārki *nm pl* underskirt, petticoat
apakššķira *nf* lower class
apakštase *nf* saucer
apakšteikums *nm* (gram.) minor
apakštīkls *nm* (compu.) subnetwork
apakštituls *nm* subtitle
apakštonis *nm* undertone
apakšuzņēmējs *nm* subcontractor
apakšveids *nm* subtype
apakšveļa *nf* underwear
apakšvienība *nf* subunit; **galvenā a.** (mil.) principal subordinate command
apakšvilenis *nm* (weav.) cloth beam
apakšvirkne *nf* (compu.) subsequence
apakšvirsnieks *nm* noncommissioned officer
apakšvirsraksts *nm* subtitle; subheading
apakšvirziens *nm* (math., of vectors) sense
apakšzāles *nf pl* low-growing grasses
apakšzeme *nf* underground, underworld
apakšzemes *indecl adj* subterranean, underground
apakšzemes dzelzceļš *nm* subway
apakšzobs *nm* lower tooth
apakšzona *nf* subzone
apakšžoklis *nm* lower jaw

apalis *nm* round timber

apālis *nm* (reg.) thick windrow of drying hay

apaliski *adv* around, in a circle

apalisks *adj* 1. roundish; (of pelts) whole, uncut; 2. unfettered (unmarried)

apalītis *nm* 1. small, round tub for milk or soup; 2. bread roll

apaloties *vr* (obs.) lose one's way

apalvojums *nm* tinning

apalvot *vt* tin

apaļakmens *nm* uncut paving stone

apaļāmurs *nm* machinist's hammer, ball peen hammer

apaļdzelzs *nf* steel round

apaļēvele *nf* 1. beading plane; 2. compass plane

apaļi *adv* round; **a. veidots** made round

apaļīgi *adv* **a. veidots** of rounded contours

apaļīgs *adj* roundish, rounded; (of persons) plump, chubby

apaļīgums *nm* roundness; plumpness, chubbiness

apaļināt *vt* round, make round

apaļiski *adv* around, in a circular fashion

apaļisks *adj* round

apaļkniebes *nf pl* round-nose pliers

apaļkoks *nm* round timber

apaļkolba *nf* round flask

apaļlapu *indecl adj* round-leaved

apaļlapu pulkstenīte *nf* harebell

apaļlapu rasene *nf* European sundew

apaļlapu ūdensgundega *nf* stiff white water crowfoot

apaļlapu ziemciete *nf* larger wintergreen

apaļmutes *nf pl* cyclostomes

apaļot *vt* round, make round; (of numbers) round off

apaļraksts *nm* round hand (handwriting)

apaļš *adj* 1. round; 2. (of numbers) a. rounded to the nearest number ending in zero) round; b. whole; (col., of an orphan) complete;

(col., of a dozen) even; 3. (col., of a male or female) single

apaļtērauds *nm* steel round

apaļums *nm* roundness

apaļvaidz/is *nm*, **~e** *nf* round-cheeked person

apaļvīle *nf* round file

apanāēa *nf* appanage

apara *nf* small, untillable or unmowable area in a field or meadow

aparas *nf pl* end of plowing; end-of-plowing feast

aparātbūve *nf* instrument manufacture

aparāts *nm* instrument; apparatus

apar[a]tūra [ā] *nf* apparatus; equipment; (compu.) hardware

apar[a]tūrpārbaude [ā] *nf* (compu.) hardware check

apar[a]tūrpārtraukums [ā] *nm* (compu.) hardware interrupt

apar[a]tūrsader¬ba [ā] *nf* (compu.) hardware compatibility

apārdīt *vt* 1. unravel; 2. ted

apārdnis *nm* = (reg.) **apārnis**

apārds *nm* = (reg.) **apārnis**

apārnis *nm* thick windrow of drying hay

apars *nm* 1. fallow; 2. a strip of field left unplowed

apārstēt *vt* heal partly, cure partly

apārstēties *vr* receive partial medical treatment

apart *vt* 1. plow, plow up; 2. turn over in plowing; 3. furrow, cultivate; 4. *vi* plow around

apartaments *nm* suite

aparte[i]ds [ī] *nm* apartheid

aparts *nm* separate, reprint

aparvilis *nm* (reg.) skirt chaser

apasarot *vi* sweat, gather surface moisture

apašs *nm* apache, ruffian

ap[a]tija [ā] *nf* apathy

ap[a]tiski [ā] *adv* apathetically

ap[a]tisks [ā] *adj* apathetic

ap[a]tiskums [ā] *nm* apathy

apatīts *nm* apatite

apatrīds *nm* stateless person

apauda *nf* ornamental border of a **sagša**

apaudi *nm pl* = **apauda**

apaudzēt *vt* let grow on sth.; **a. ar mežu** afforest

apaudzēties *vr* (of one's hair) let grow

apauglojums *nm* fecundation, impregnation

apauglošanās *nfr* fecundation, impregnation

apauglot *vt* fecundate, fertilize, impregnate

apaugloties *vr* become fertilized, become impregnated

apaugt *vi* **1.** overgrow, become overgrown, become covered with; (of wounds) heal, skin over; **a. ar taukiem** accumulate fat; **2.** become too small (**mētelītis bērnam apaudzis** the child has outgrown its coat)

apaugums *nm* growth

apauklēt *vt* (of several babies) rock (sequentially)

apauklot *vt* tie (around)

apaukstējums *nm* chill

apaukstēt *vt* chill

apaukstēties *vr* catch a slight cold

apaulekšot *vi* gallop around sth.

apaulot *vi* gallop around sth.

apaust *vt* weave around, weave an edge; cover with (woven material); weave (for many)

apausties *vr* finish weaving

apauši *nm pl* headstall

apaut *vt* (of shoes, socks) put on; **a. kājas** put on shoes

apauties *vr* put on shoes

apavi *nm pl* footwear

apavnieks *nm* shoemaker

apavrūpniecība *nf* shoe industry

apavu krēms *nm* shoe polish

apavu spodrinātājs *nm* bootblack

apbadīt *vt* **1.** punch a circular pattern of holes; **2.** (of animals) toss around with horns; **3.** (of bedding) tuck in

apbakstīt *vt* (of bedding) tuck in

apbalēt *vi* fade partly

apbalvojums *nm* award

apbalvot *vt* present an award; **a. ar medaļu** decorate with a medal

apbalzīt *vt* (of bedding) tuck in

apbārstīt *vt* bestrew, sprinkle with

apbārstīties *vr* be sprinkled on (with flour, sand)

apbāzīt *vt* (of bedding) tuck in

apbēdas *nf pl* a pork and cabbage meal (taken after the slaughter of a pig)

apbedījums *nm* burial

apbēdinājums *nm* (emotional) hurt

apbēdināt *vt* hurt (emotionally), sadden

apbedīšana *nf* burial

apbedīšanas birojs *nm* funeral home

apbedīt *vt* bury, inter

apbēdot *vt* mourn

apbēdzināt *vt* hide

apbērēt *vt* (obs.) bury, inter

apbērnoties *vr* produce children; (of animals) drop, calve, litter, cub, foal, kitten

apbērot *vt* (obs.) bury, inter

apbērt *vt* bestrew, sprinkle with; cover with (earth, sand); pour around; (fig.) shower (with questions, gifts)

apbērties *vr* pour (sand, debris) on oneself

apberzt *vt* rub, scour

apbest *vt* bury, inter

apbetonēt *vt* cover with concrete

apbīdīt *vt* push sth. around (to surround sth.)

apbikstīt *vt* poke (around, all over)

apbirdināt *vt* bestrew, sprinkle with

apbirt *vi* **1.** be covered (with friable material); **2.** (*3rd pers*) drop, fall

apblāzmot *vt* light, illuminate

apbolīt *vt* (com.) look over, ogle

apbraucams *adj, part* of **apbraukt** bypass, detour

apbraucīt *vt* massage, knead, rub

apbraukāt *vt* travel from place to place, travel all over

apbraukt *vt* drive around sth.; **a. lielu līkumu** make a long detour; travel around

apbriest *vi* dry

apbrīna *nf* admiration

apbrīnojams *adj, part* of **apbrīnot** admirable

apbrīnot *vt* admire

apbrīnotāj/s *nm*, ~a *nf* admirer

apbrīns *nm* admiration

apbrist *vi* wade around sth.

apbrucināt *vt* scald

apbrucināties *vr* scald oneself

apbrukt *vi* collapse, slide down

apbrūnināt *vt* brown

apbruņojums *nm* armament

apbruņot *vt* **1.** arm; **2.** equip

apbruņoties *vr* **1.** arm oneself; **2.** equip oneself

apbružāt *vt* scuff; crumple; wear; soil; tatter

apbružāties *vr* become soiled, scuffed, or worn

apbūbēt *vi* mold

apbučot *vt* kiss

apburāt *vt* sail, sail around (a place)

apburbēt *vi* develop pores, turn pithy (all around)

apburošs *adj, part* of **apburt** (col.) enchanting, bewitching

apburt *vt* **1.** put a spell on, enchant, spellbind; **2.** (fig., col.) charm, enchant

apburtība *nf* enchantment

apbūrums *nm* spell

apburzīt *vt* crumple

apburzīties *vr* **1.** be crumpled, be shopworn; **2.** (col.) get used to, adapt to

apbūve *nf* construction; **brīva a.** open development

apbūves gabals *nm* lot

apbūves kvartāls *nm* housing development

apbūves laukums *nm* building site

apbūves zeme *nf* land zoned for construction

apbūvēt *vt* build up, fill with buildings; (of a housing site) develop

apbūvēties *vr* get built up

apcelt *vt* **1.** exploit, take advantage of; **2.** (col.) tease; **3.** (of game) raise, flush; find; **4.** (folk.) realize

apcelties *vr* be teased

apceļot *vt* visit, travel across, travel around

apceļš *nm* bypass, detour

apcepināt *vt* brown (in cooking)

apcepināties *vr* (col.) get sunburned

apcept *vt* brown (in cooking)

apcepties *vr* get browned (in cooking)

apcepums *nm* crust

apcere *nf* **1.** essay; **2.** reflection, contemplation

apcerējums *nm* essay; treatise

apcerēt *vt* consider; reflect upon; conceive of

apcerīgi *adv* reflectively, contemplatively

apcerīgs *adj* reflective, contemplative

apciemojums *nm* visit

apciemot *vt* visit

apciemoties *vr* visit each other

apciems *nm* neighboring farms, group of farms

apciesties *vr* (reg.) become inured to cold

apcietinājum/s *nm* arrest, detention; ~ā arrested, detained

apcietināšana *nf* arrest, detention

apcietināšanas pavēle *nf* arrest warrant

apcietināt *vt* arrest, detain

apcietināt/ais *nom adj*, ~ā *f* detainee

apcietinātājs *nm* detaining officer

apcietināties *vr* dig in, take fortified positions

apcilāt *vt* pick over

apcilāties *vr* (of animals) conceive

apcilnis *nm* ridge

apcinkot *vt* galvanize

apcirknis *nm* storage bin; compartment

apcirpaļāt *vt* = **apcirpt**

apcirpt *vt* **1.** cut; shear; trim; prune; dock; clip; **a. īsi** crop; **a. spārnus** (fig.) clip s.o.'s

wings; **a. štatus** cut staff; **a. tiesības** dock
s.o.'s rights; **2.** dupe, trick, take in

apcirpties *vr* be shorn

apcirst *vt* **1.** lop off, chop off; dock; cut down;
trim; **2.** shape by hewing; **3.** turn or flip
around sharply

apcirsties *vr* **1.** turn around sharply; **2.** wind
around; **3.** capsize

apciršana *nf* trimming

apcirtējs *nm* trimmer

apcirtums *nm* felled trees, cut shrubs, lopped-
off branches

apcūkot *vt* (com.) soil, dirty

apcukurot *vt* sugar, sugarcoat; candy; ice

apcukuroties *vr* (of sugar) crystallize

apčabināt *vt* rustle

apčamdīt *vt* **1.** finger; **2.** ransack, go through

apčamdīties *vr* search one's pockets

apčāpāt *vi* toddle around

ap-či *interj* ahchoo

apčubināt *vt* **1.** fluff up; **2.** fuss with (a baby's
bedding and the baby)

apčūlot *vi* blister

apdabt *vt* get around sth.

apdaidzīt *vt* (sewing) baste

apdainot *vt* (of folk singing) sing about s.o.

apdaiņot *vt* = **apdainot**

apdalīt *vt* pass out gifts

apdāļāt *vt* pass out gifts

apdancināt *vt* dance with everyone

apdancot *vt* **1.** (col.) serve hand and foot;
2. dance around; dance in circles

apdare *nf* **1.** (interior, exterior) finish; **2.** adaptation (to screen, stage); (mus.) arrangement;
mākslinieciskā a. design; **skatuviskā
a.** staging; **3.** (tech.) dressing

apdarene *nf* **1.** fenced-in meadow; **2.** (eyeglass)
frames; **3.** ornamental window frame

apdares nagla *nf* finishing nail

apdares veseris *nm* dressing hammer

apdarināt *vt* **1.** trim, (of a log) dress; **2.** finish
(by polishing, decorating, trimming); hem;

3. design; **4.** (mus.) harmonize, provide
with harmony

apdarīt *vt* **1.** finish doing; **2.** fence in

apdarīties *vr* **1.** work for oneself; **2.** soil
oneself

apdarvot *vt* tar

apdārzs *nm* **1.** (meteor.) halo; **2.** circle

apdauzīt *vt* **1.** batter, bruise; scuff, dent;
2. hammer lightly

apdauzīties *vr* suffer bruises; get damaged by
being knocked about

apdauzīts *adj, part* of **apdauzīt** bruised,
battered, dented, scuffed; (com.) dumb;
crazy

apdāvāt *vt* = **apdāvināt**

apdāvināt *vt* give presents to; heap presents
upon

apdāvinātāj/s *nm*, **~a** *nf* gift giver

apdāvinātība *nf* giftedness

apdāvināties *vr* exchange gifts

apdāvināts *adj, part* of **apdāvināt** gifted,
tal-ented

apdedzinājums *nm* burn

apdedzināt *vt* **1.** burn; **a. mēli** let one's tongue
run away with one; **2.** burn or scorch all
around; **3.** (of bricks, ceramics) bake; (of
ore) roast

apdedzināties *vr* burn oneself, get burned

apdedži *nm pl* burnt sticks of wood

apdegt *vi* **1.** burn all around; burn in spots;
2. (of chimneys) become covered with soot;
3. get singed; **4.** tan; **5.** be burned out

apdegulis *nm* **1.** firebrand; scorched timber;
2. fire victim

apdegums *nm* burn, scorch; scald

apdejot *vt* **1.** dance around; **2.** dance attendance

apdeldēt *vt* wear, scuff, soil

apdēstījums *nm* planting

apdēstīt *vt* **1.** plant around sth.; surround with
plants; **2.** plant, fill with plants; **a. no jauna**
replant; reforest

apdēstīties *vr* finish planting

apdiega *nf* overhand stitching

apdiegt *vt* overhand; stitch around

apdienēt *vt* (barb.) wait on hand and foot

apdiet *vt* 1. dance around; 2. dance attendance

apdīgt *vi* sprout

apdilis *adj, part* of **apdilt** shabby, threadbare, worn

apdilt *vi* become shabby, become threadbare

apdilums *nm* wear

apdirst *vt* (vulg.) shit upon, soil

apdirsties *vr* (vulg.) go in one's pants

apdobe *nf* garden bed (around a tree or shrub)

apdoma *nf* = **apdoms**

apdomāt *vi* consider, think it over; **iepriekš ~s** premeditated; **labi ~s** well thought out; **ja ap-domā, ka . . .** to think that . . .

apdomā/ties *vr* 1. think it over; **~jies!** just think of it! well, what do you know! 2. reconsider, change one's mind

apdomība *nf* caution, circumspection

apdomīgi *adv* carefully, cautiously

apdomīgs *adj* cautious, careful

apdomīgums *nm* caution, circumspection

apdom/s *nm* thought, deliberation; prudence, circumspection; forethought; **ar ~u** deliberately; thoughtfully, with circumspection; **bez ~a** thoughtlessly; rashly; **nav nekāda ~a** it makes no sense

apdot *vt* pass around; **a. ziņu** spread the news

apdraiskāt *vt* wear thin

apdraudējums *nm* jeopardy, danger; endangerment

apdraudēt *vt* endanger, imperil, jeopardize

apdraudi *nm pl* threat

apdrāvēt *vt* (reg.) scold

apdrāzt *v* 1. *vt* whittle, pare; 2. *vi* dash, tear around

apdrāzties *vr* dash around sth.

apdrīksnāt *vt* scratch, score; underline

apdriskājies *adj, part* of **apdriskāties** shabby, worn

apdriskāt *vt* wear thin

apdriskāties *vr* wear thin

apdrošinājuma līgums *nm* insurance policy

apdrošinājums *nm* insurance

apdrošināšana *nf* insurance

apdrošināt *vt* insure

apdrošinātais *nom adj* the insured, policyholder

apdrošinātāj/s *nm*, **~a** *nf* insurer

apdrošināties *vr* get insurance

apdrukāt *vt* print (all over)

apdrupināt *vt* cover with crumbs

apdrupis *adj, part* of **apdrupt** crumbly

apdrupt *vi* crumble, crumble away

apdudzis *adj* hazy

apdugt *vi* (of air, sky) turn hazy

apdūkt *vi* 1. (of the skies) become overcast; 2. become giddy, benumbed

apdūkums *nm* giddiness

apdullināt *vt* stun; narcotize; deafen

apdullināties *vr* numb one's senses

apdullinošs *adj, part* of **apdullināt** (of noise) deafening

apdullt *vi* be stunned; become dizzy, stupefied; **a. no trokšņa** be deafened by noise

apdullums *nm* stupefaction

apduļķojums *nm* cloudiness (of an otherwise transparent substance)

apduļķot *vt* muddy; cloud

apduļķoties *vr* get muddied, turn cloudy

apdūmējis *adj, part* of **apdūmēt** covered with smoke; overcast

apdūmēt *vi* become covered with smoke

apdumis *adj, part* of **apdumt** hazy

apdūmojis *adj* hazy

apdūmot *vt* smoke, fumigate

apdūmoties *vr* become smoky

apdumt *vi* become hazy

apdūņot *vt* cover with muck

apdūņoties *vr* be covered with muck

apdūre *nf* embroidered shirt cuff

apdurstīt *vt* **1.** pin down; **2.** injure or damage by poking around

apdurt *vt* **1.** stake out; **2.** stab (all, many)

apdvest *vt* breathe upon; (of air, atmosphere) envelop; (fig.) inspire

apdzejojums *nm* poem (about an event)

apdzejot *vt* write poems about, sing of; sing the praise of

apdzelt *vt* (of nettles) sting (all around, in many places)

apdzeltējums *nm* yellowing

apdzeltēt *vi* yellow

apdzenāt *vt* (col., of logs, branches) trim

apdzert *vt* **1.** empty (by drinking), drink up; **2.** drink away, lose by drinking

apdzerties *vr* get drunk

apdzesēt *vt* **1.** cool; **2.** (of thirst) quench

apdzēst *vt* extinguish, put out

apdziedāšanās *nfr* war of songs

apdziedāt *vt* **1.** sing the praise of; **2.** tease, mock in song

apdziedāties *vr* engage in a war of songs

apdziedēt *vt* heal a little or superficially

apdziedēties *vr* heal over

apdziesmot *vt* write poems about; sing the praise of

apdzira *nf* intent

apdziras *nf pl* **1.** ground fir; **2.** (folk., in Latgale) drinking party to celebrate an engagement

apdzirdināt *vt* make s.o. drunk

apdzirdīt *vt* make s.o. drunk

apdzirenes *nf pl* ground fir

apdzirties *vr* intend, propose

apdzisme *nf* (poet., fig.) dying out

apdzist *vi* (of fire) go out

apdzisums *nm* extinction

apdzīt I *vt* **1.** drive around; **2.** (of a furrow) plow; **3.** overtake, pass, outrun; **4.** drive (posts) into the ground around sth.

apdzīt II *vi* heal (partly, around the edges)

apdzīvināšana *nf* settlement, settling

apdzīvojams *adj, part* of **apdzīvot 1.** habitable; **2.** residential

apdzīvojums *nm* settlement

apdzīvot *vt* inhabit; populate; occupy

apdzīvotāj/s *nm*, **~a** *nf* inhabitant, resident; lodger, tenant

apdzīvotība *nf* **1.** density of population; **2.** inhabitation

apdzīvoties *vr* accustom oneself to new living conditions

apdzīvotne *nf* settlement

apecējums *nm* harrowing

apecēt *vt* harrow

apeirons *nm* apeiron

apeja *nf* **1.** bypass; **2.** (hist.) external upper floor walk of a granary

apek[s] [ss] *nm* apex

ape[l]ācija [ll] *nf* (jur.) appeal

ape[l]ācijas [ll] tiesa *nf* appellate court

ape[l]ants [ll] *nm* apellant

ape[la]tīvs [llā] *nm* appellative, common noun

ape[l]ējums [ll] *nm* appeal

ape[l]ēt [ll] *vi* (jur., fig.) appeal

apelsīns *nm* orange

apenāji *nm pl* black currant (bushes)

apendektomija *nf* appendectomy

apendicīts *nm* appendicitis

apendik[s] [ss] *nm* (anat.) appendix

apēnojums *nm* shadow; shade

apēnot *vt* shade; overshadow; darken

apercepcija *nf* apperception

aperceptēt *vt* apperceive

aperceptīvs *adj* apperceptive

apercipēt *vt* apperceive

aperenes *nf pl* powdery mildew

aperitīvs *nm* aperitif

aperkots *nm* uppercut

apērmot *vt* disfigure

apertūra *nf* lens opening, aperture

apēst *vt* eat up; devour

apēsties *vr* **1.** consume oneself; **2.** eat one's fill apetīte *nf* appetite; ~s **ierosinātājs** appetizer

apetīts *nm* = **apetīte**

apēvelēt *vt* plane, trim with a plane

apgabalis *adv* (of buying or selling) the lot; in large amounts; by leaps and bounds

apgabals *nm* region; province; **mežonīgs a.** wilderness

apgabaltiesa *nf* regional court

apgādājam/ais *nom adj*, ~ā *nf* dependent

apgādāt *vt* 1. supply, supply with, provide, provide with, furnish, furnish with, equip with; 2. provide for, support; 3. (obs.) publish

apgādātājs *nm* 1. supplier; 2. provider, breadwinner; 3. (obs.) publisher

apgādātība *nf* supply

apgādāties *vr* supply oneself with, lay in supplies

apgāde *nf* 1. supply, provision; provisioning; **atkārtota a.** resupply; **materiāli techniskā a.** logistics; ~s **priekšmeti** supplies; 2. welfare department

apgādes grāmatiņa *nf* ration booklet

apgādes vilciens *nm* supply train

apgādība *nf* 1. support; 2. (obs.) publishing house

apgādīgs *adj* provident

apgādniecība *nf* 1. support; 2. (obs.) publishing house

apgādnie/ks *nm*, ~ce *nf* 1. provider; 2. supplier

apgāds *nm* publishing house

apgaisma *nf* 1. surrounding light; 2. enlightenment

apgaisme *nf* 1. enlightenment; 2. lighting

apgaismība *nf* enlightenment

apgaismības laikmets *nm* Age of Enlightenment

apgaismniecība *nf* enlightenment

apgaismniecisks *adj* of or pertaining to enlightenment

apgaismnie/ks *nm*, ~ce *nf* enlightener

apgaismojuma mērītājs *nm* exposure meter

apgaismojum/s *nm* lighting, illumination; (fig.) elucidation; ~am to shed light on a subject

apgaismošana *nf* lighting; (photo.) exposure; (obs.) education

apgaismošanas ķermenis *nm* lighting fixture

apgaismot *vt* light, illuminate; (fig.) elucidate

apgaismotāj/s *nm*, ~a *nf* 1. enlightener; 2. lighting director; gaffer

apgaismoties *vr* be illuminated, be exposed to light

apgait/a *nf* beat, round; tour; **iet** ~ā make the rounds

apgaitnie/ks *nm*, ~ce *nf* beat walker

apgājiens *nm* round

apgājīgs *adj* (reg.) dashing

apgāle *nf* glaze of ice

apgalēt *vt* 1. realize; 2. overcome, manage; finish

apgālēt *vi* glaze over

apgalve *nf* headrest

apgalvene *nf* 1. head of a runner (of a sled); 2. head scarf

apgalvenis *nm* = **apgalvene**

apgalvojuma teikums *nm* declarative sentence

apgalvojums *nm* assertion; **apgriezts a.** contrary assertion; **nepatiess a.** false statement

apgalvot *vi* assert, maintain, declare

apgānīšana *nf* desecration

apgānīt *vt* graze partly

apgānīt *vt* defile; profane; desecrate; (col.) befoul

apgarojums *nm* inspiration

apgarot *vt* inspire; (of an emotion showing in one's face) shine

apgaroti *adv* in an inspired manner

apgarotība *nf* inspiration

apgarots *adj*, *part* of **apgarot** inspired

apgarotums *nm* inspiration

apgatavenis *nm* (tech.) blank, billet

apgausināt *vt* (folk.) bless

apgaust *vt* bemoan

apgāzēt *vt* fumigate

apgāzt *vt* **1.** topple, upset; overthrow; capsize; **a. uz mutes** turn upside down; **2.** (fig.) refute, dis-prove

apgāzties *vr* topple, tip over, fall; capsize

apgāztuve *nf* tipple

apglabāšana *nf* burial

apglabāt *vt* bury, inter

apglāstīt *vt* pet, stroke

apglaudīt *vt* pet, stroke

apglaust *vt* stroke

apglausties *vr* envelop

apglemēt *vi* become slimy

apgleznot *vt* cover with a painting

apglīdēt *vi* become slimy

apglotēt *vi* become slimy

apgludināt *vt* smooth

apglumēt *vi* become slimy, become covered with clay or silt

apglumt *vi* become slimy

apglūnēt *vt* examine, scrutinize

apgļototies *vr* become slimy

apgodīt *vt* **1.** show respect; **2.** take care of; tidy up

apgrābāt *vt* (col.) **1.** finger, paw; fumble, search clumsily; **2.** rake down; rake lightly

apgrābstīt *vt* **1.** finger, paw; fumble, search clumsily; **2.** rake down; rake lightly

apgrābt *vt* rake down; rake lightly

apgraizas *nf pl* clippings

apgraizelēt *vt* trim; clip; prune

apgraizīt *vt* **1.** trim; clip; prune; **2.** circumcise

apgramstīt *vt* **1.** finger, paw; fumble, search clumsily; **2.** feel, touch

apgraušļāt *vt* gnaw on; chew up

apgrauzdēt *vt* roast lightly

apgrauzīt *vt* = **apgrauzt**

apgrauzt *vt* **1.** gnaw, gnaw all around; **2.** chew up

apgrāvjot *vt* surround with ditches

apgrāvot *vt* = **apgrāvjot**

apgrebt *vt* carve

apgrēcība *nf* sin, sinfulness, fault

apgrēcīgi *adv* sinfully

apgrēcīgs *adj* sinful

apgrēcināt *vt* (Bibl.) offend

apgrēcināties *vr* (Bibl.) commit a sin

apgredzenot *vt* (of birds) band; (of trees) ring

apgrēkoties *vr* sin, fall into sinful ways

apgriešanās *nfr* turning; **a. baseins** turning basin

apgrieze *nf* (bus.) circulation

apgriezējmašīna *nf* trimmer

apgriezniski *adv* reversibly

apgriezenisks *adj* (chem.) reversible

apgrieziens *nm* **1.** turn, rotation, revolution; **~u skaits** rotational speed; **2.** a rope for fastening a thill to the strut of a sled

apgrieznība *nf* (biochemistry) Walden inversion

apgriezt I *vt* **1.** turn; **a. riņķī** (or **apkārt**) turn completely around; turn upside down (in searching); **2.** turn around, reverse; **3.** reverse, turn inside out; **4.** (math., ling.) invert; **a. otrādi** turn upside down; **a. visas malas** turn everything upside down (in looking for sth.); **5.** *vi* **a. ap stūri** turn the corner

apgriezt II *vt* **1.** pare, clip, trim; **a. spārnus** pinion; (fig.) clip one's wings; **a. kaklu** (col.) kill; **2.** cut a lot, cut all

apgriezti *adv* the other way, upside down, inversely

apgriezties *vr* **1.** turn around; **2.** turn over; turn about (and come back); **ka nevar ne a.** (of a room) jam-packed

apgriezts *adj, part* of **apgriezt** I turned; reversed; (math.) inverse; (ling.) inverted

apgriezums *nm* cut edge

apgropēt *vt* groove around

apgrozāmība *nf* liquidity; salability

apgrozāms *adj, part* of apgrozīt (of money, capital) working; liquid

apgrozība *nf* 1. circulation; trade; transactions; trading; turnover; 2. traffic

apgrozības kapitāls *nm* negotiable capital; working capital

apgrozības nodoklis *nm* sales tax

apgrozījumlaiks *nm* (compu.) turnaround time

apgrozījum/s *nm* (bus.) turnover; ~i sales; transactions

apgrozīt *vt* 1. turn over; turn around; 2. turn over repeatedly

apgrozīties *vr* 1. turn around; 2. circulate; come and go; 3. frequent

apgrūst *vt* topple, upset; overthrow

apgrūt *vi* collapse, crumble

apgrūtinājum/s *nm* burden, bother, nuisance, trouble; ja nav par ~u if it isn't too much trouble

apgrūtināt *vt* bother, trouble, be a burden

apgrūtinošs *adj, part* of apgrūtināt burdensome, onerous, troublesome

apgruzdēt *vi* become scorched

apgubenis *nm* fine cloth kerchief

apgudrot *vi* consider, think it over

apguldināt *vt* put to bed; lay down

apguldīt *vt* put to bed; lay down

apgulējies *adj, part* of apgulēties dirty

apgulēties *vr* (of animals) get dirty (by lying in a dirty place)

apgulināt *vt* put to bed

apgult *vi* lie down

apgulties *vr* lie down; go to bed

apgultiņa *nf* = apgultne

apgultne *nf* poorly drained depression in a ground moraine

apgumzīt *vt* wrinkle

apgurdināt *vt* tire

apgurt *vi* grow tired

apgurums *nm* tiredness

apgūsme *nf* learning

apgūt *vt* 1. learn; a. zināšanas get an education; 2. develop

apgūtība *nf* degree of development

apguve *nf* 1. learning; 2. development

apģērb/s *nm* clothes, clothing; attire; gatavi ~i ready-to-wear clothes; siltais a. (mil.) cold weather gear; ~a piederumi trimmings

apģērbt *vt* dress, clothe; (of a garment) put on

apģērb/ties *vr* get dressed; labi ~ies well dressed

apģībt *vi* (of several persons) pass out

apģieda *nf* realization

apģist *vi* realize

apģisties *vr* bethink oneself, realize suddenly

apiešana *nf* (mil.) envelopment; dubultā a. double envelopment, pincer movement

apiešanās *nfr* treatment (of people); slikta a. maltreatment

apiet *vi irr, vt irr* 1. go around; round; a. mājas soli do house chores; 2. bypass; (mil.) envelop; a. no flanga outflank; 3. (fig.) avoid, circum-vent, bypass, sidestep; a. ar līkumu give a wide berth; 4. (fig.) pass over; 5. crisscross

apieties *vr irr* 1. treat; 2. handle; slikti a. maltreat; a. ar prasmi have a way with; a. taupīgi use sparingly

apietīgi *adv* sociably

apietīgs *adj* sociable

apija *nf* plow handles

apikāls *adj* apical

apikāts *nm* (obs.) lawyer

apīnājs *nm* hop field

apīnis *nm* (bot.) hop

apīnītis *nm dim* of apīnis, hop

apīņi *nm pl* hops

apīņskābardis *nm* hop hornbeam

apirda *nf* fingertip abscess

apirdināt *vt* loosen the soil (around sth.)

apirt *vi* row around (a place)

apirties *vr* row around (a place)

apiterapija *nf* bee venom therapy

apīžas *nf pl* plow handles

apjāšus *adv* astride

apjāt *vt* **1.** ride around sth.; **2.** visit on horseback; **3.** (vulg.) take in, deceive

apjaucēt *vt* accustom

apjaukt *vt* stir

apjausma *nf* mental capacity, mental horizons

apjaust *vt* **1.** realize, perceive (dimly); **2.** sense (vaguely)

apjauta *nf* perception; **jutekliskā a.** sensation

apjautāt *vt* question

apjautāties *vr* enquire

apjavs *nm* flour added to a horse's drinking water

apjēga *nf* sense, comprehension, realization

apjēgt *vt* comprehend, realize

apjemt *vt* = **apņemt**

apjemties *vr* = **apņemties**

apjērošanās *nfr* lambing

apjēroties *vr* lamb

apjomība *nf* bulkiness, bulk, volume

apjomīgi *adv* voluminously

apjomīgs *adj* bulky, voluminous; (of writings) long

apjomīgums *nm* bulkiness

apjom/s *nm* volume; size, dimension; extent; **plaša ~a** large-scale

apjoņot *vi* dash around (a place)

apjozt I *vt* gird; buckle on

apjozt II *vi* dash around (a place)

apjozties *vr* gird oneself

apjucība *nf* confusion

apjucināt *vt* confuse

apjukt *vi* become confused

apjūkt *vi* get used to

apjukums *nm* confusion

apjuma *nf* roofing

apjumības *nf pl* harvest home

apjūmības *nf pl* party to celebrate the end of a roofing job

apjums *nm* **1.** vault of the sky; **2.** roofing

apjumt *vt* roof, thatch

apjumts tilts *nm* covered bridge

apjūsma *nf* enthusiastic praise; adoration

apjūsmot *vt* extoll

apkaime *nf* vicinity; environs

apkaimība *nf* neighborhood

apkaisīt *vt* strew, sprinkle, besprinkle; **a. ar pūderi** powder; **a. ar smiltīm** sand

apkaitināt *vt* make mad

apkājām *adv.* (reg.) indirectly

apkakāties *vr* (child., col.) go in one's pants

apkakle *nf* collar; **atlokāmā a.** turn-down collar

apkakles maãiņš *nm* ring ouzel

apkakles podziņa *nf* collar stud

apkakles sīga *nf* Houbara bustard

apkakles strazds *nm* ring ouzel

apkaklis *nm* (hist.) metal collar, torque

apkaklīte *nf* collar (men's detachable); **nolocīta a.** wing collar; **stāva a.** stand-up collar

apkala *nf* sheet of ice

apkaldinājums *nm* (horse) shoeing; (mech.) fitting; ferrule; (jewelry) setting

apkaldināt *vt* = **apkalt**

apkaldīt *vt* = **apkalt**

apkālība *nf* evasiveness

apkalpe *nf* **1.** crew; **2.** service; servicing; maintenance

apkalpes tilts *nm* catwalk, service bridge

apkalpes lifts *nm* service elevator

apkalpošana *nf* service; servicing, maintenance

apkalpot *vt* **1.** serve, wait upon; **2.** service; **3.** operate

apkalpotāja *nf* **1.** waitress; **2.** maid; **3.** cleaning woman

apkalpotāj/s *nm* **1.** waiter; **2.** janitor, caretaker; **3.** attendant; operator; **~i** domestic servants

apkalpotība *nf* level of service

apkalpoties *vr* serve oneself

apkalst *vi* **1.** dry; (of bread) become stale; **2.** (of vegetation) wither apkalt *vt* (of horses) shoe; (of wooden objects) sheet; attach metal ornaments

apkaltēt *vt* dry slightly

apkaltis *adj, part* of **apkalst** dried up, crusted; stale

apkalums *nm* (horse) shoeing; (mech.) fitting; ferrule; (jewelry) setting

apkāļām *adv* (reg.) indirectly; **a. runāt** beat about the bush

apkāļas *nf pl* evasive speech

apkaļķojums *nm* coat of whitewash; calcification; boiler scale

apkaļķošanās *nfr* calcification; sclerosis

apkaļķot *vt* whitewash; paint with milk of lime

apkaļķoties *vr* become coated with calcareous scale; calcify; (of arteries) narrow

apkāļš *adj* (reg., of speech) evasive

apkampiens *nm* embrace, hug

apkampt *vt* **1.** clasp, enfold; **2.** embrace, hug

apkampties *vr* embrace, hug each other

apkankarāt *vt* **1.** dress in old clothes, rags; **2.** put on accessories

apkankarāties *vr* **1.** put on old, ragged clothes; **2.** put on accessories

apkankarot *vt* = **apkankarāt**

apkankaroties *vr* = **apkankarāties**

apkantējums *nm* edge, border, trim

apkantēt *vt* (of garments) edge, border

apkapāt *vt* chop all around

apkaplēt *vt* hoe all around

apkāre *nf* honeycomb frame

apkarināt *vt* hang all around; hang with many items

apkarināties *vr* hang on oneself, bedeck oneself with

apka[r]ošana [ŗ] *nf* fight, struggle against

apka[r]ot [ŗ] *vt* (of diseases, deficiencies) combat, wage war on; (of pests, weeds) control

apka[r]oties [ŗ] *vr* fight among themselves

apkārpīt *vt* bury (like a dog)

apkarsēt *vt* warm

apkarst *vi* get rather hot

apkārstīt *vt* hang (all around, in excess, carelessly)

apkārstīties *vr* hang on oneself, bedeck oneself with

apkāršot *vt* enclose with a pole fence

apkārt *vt* hang all around; hang with many items

apkārt *adv, prep* **1.** around, round; **a. griezties!** about face! **pa kreisi a.!** left about turn! **a., marš!** about face, march! **2.** (of time) up, passed

apkārtaršana *nf* plowing that follows a spiral pattern

apkārtceļojošs *adj* itinerant

apkārtceļš *nm* detour

apkārtdauza *nm* (col.) tramp

apkārtēj/ais *nom adj* surroundings; ~ie bystanders

apkārtējs *adj* surrounding, neighboring

apkārtgriešanās *nfr* about-face

apkārties *vr* bedeck oneself with

apkārtklejojošs *adj* wandering

apkārtklīstošs *adj* wandering

apkārtlidojums *nm* round flight

apkārtmērs *nm* circumference, length of perimeter, girth

apkārtne *nf* **1.** vicinity, neighborhood; environs; **2.** environment

apkārtnes mācība *nf* (educ.) natural science (in elementary school curriculum)

apkārtnes piesārņošana *nf* environmental pollution

apkārtraksts *nm* circular

apkārtskraida *nm, nf* gadabout

apkārtskrējiens *nm* round race

apkārtstaiga *nm, nf* **1.** tramp; **2.** (hist.) traveling craftsman

apkārtstaigul/is *nm*, ~e *nf* tramp

apkārtstāvošais *adj* surrounding

apkārtstāvošie *nom adj* bystanders

apkārttecis *nm* gadabout

apkārtteķis *nm* swollen finger

apkases *nf pl* rakings (obtained in smoothing a haystack or hay wagon)

apkasīt *vt* rake down, smooth with a rake

apkaunē/ties *vr* feel ashamed; ~**jies!** you ought to be ashamed!

apkauninât *vt* shame, make one feel ashamed

apkaunojošs *adj, part* of **apkaunot** shameful, disgraceful

apkaunojums *nm* shame, disgrace

apkaunot *vt* shame, disgrace

apkauns *nm* shame

apkausēt *vt* melt the surface of

apkaustīt *vt* (of horses) shoe

apkaut *vt* kill, slaughter

apkauties *vr* kill each other

apkautrēties *vr* turn shy

apkāzoties *vr* (col.) marry

apklaiņot *vi* roam

apklājs *nm* cover

apklāt *vt* cover; **zvaigznēm** ~**s** star-studded

apklāties *vr* cover oneself; *(3rd pers)* become covered; **a. ar mākoņiem** become overcast

apklausīties *vr* pick up information (by listening)

apklaušināt *vt* question

apklaušināties *vr* ask around

apklejot *vt* wander all over

apklibot *vt* limp around sth.; *vi* limp through

apkluburot *vi* toddle around sth.

apklumburot *vi* toddle around sth.

apklunkurot *vi* waddle around sth.

apklusa *nf* stopping, pause

apklusināt *vt* 1. silence; hush, quiet; 2. assuage, allay

apklust *vi* (of persons) fall silent; (of noise) die down

apkļaut *vt* embrace, enfold; (of clothes) fit tightly, cling

apkļauties *vr* wind around, entwine, cling to, envelop

apkļūt *vi* **a. apkārt** get around sth.

apknābāt *vt* peck, peck here and there

apknaibīt *vt* pinch (in a number of places, all around)

apknibināt *vt* pick around

apkniebt *vt* pinch off

apkodelēt *vt* take bites here and there

apkodīt *vt* take bites here and there

apkope *nf* (mech.) maintenance; care

apkopēja *nf* maid; cleaning woman; (in hospitals) practical nurse

apkopēj/s *nm* janitor

apkopes zona *nf* service area

apkopjam/ais *nom adj* patient; (nursing home) inmate; ~**o mītne** nursing home

apkopojums *nm* summary, generalization, general conclusion

apkopot *vt* 1. collect; 2. summarize, draw general conclusions

apkopoties *vr* unite

apkopt *vt* 1. do chores, clean; **a. mājas soli** do housekeeping chores; 2. (of plants, land) tend; 3. (of people, animals) take care of

apkopties *vr* clean up

apkorām *adv* indirectly

apkost *vt* 1. bite, gnaw; (of frost) nip; 2. (of predators) kill

apkošļāt *vt* nibble on, chew, gnaw

apkožļāt *vt* nibble on, chew, gnaw

apkrāmēt *vt* 1. pile on top of, pile around; 2. (col.) rob

apkrampēt *vt* clamp around; **a. pirkstus** grasp firmly

apkrāpēj/s *nm*, ~**a** *nf* deceiver

apkrāpt *vt* deceive

apkrāpties *vr* allow to be deceived

apkrāsot *vt* paint

apkraukļāt *vt* spit on, hawk on, soil with phlegm

apkraupējis *adj, part* of **apkraupēt** rough

apkraupēt *vi* (of hands) become rough

apkraustīt *vt* pile up

apkraut *vt* pile up; load down, burden; **a. ar darbiem** swamp with work; **a. ar lāstiem** curse

apkrauties *vr* load oneself down

apkrecēt *vi* congeal, harden

apkrēpot *vt* soil with phlegm

apkrevējis *adj, part* of **apkrevēt** rough

apkrevelējis *adj, part* of **apkrevelēt** rough

apkrevelēt *vi* = **apkrevēt**

apkreveļojis *adj* rough

apkrevēt *vi* become covered with thick, rough skin, crust, or bark

apkrimst *vt* gnaw

apkrist *vi* **1.** fall (in large quantities); **2.** (*3rd pers*) fall around sth.; **3.** fall, tumble; **a. ap kak-lu** throw one's arms around s.o.'s neck

apkuģot *vt* circumnavigate; go around (on a sea voyage)

apkūlas *nf pl* = **apkūlības**

apkūlības *nf pl* end of threshing; feast to celebrate the end of threshing

apkulstas *nf pl* finished scutching

apkulstīt *vt* finish scutching

apkult *vt* finish threshing

apkulties *vr* **1.** finish threshing; **2.** grow; put on weight; **3.** (of bad company) get mixed up with

apkūpēt *vi* become covered with soot, become blackened with smoke

apkūpināt *vt* **1.** blacken with smoke or soot; **2.** smoke lightly

apkūpt *vi* = **apkūpēt**

apkure *nf* heating

apkurināt *vt* heat

apkurinātāj/s *nm*, ~a *nf* stoker

apkurlināt *vt* deafen

apkurlt *vi* be deafened

apkurtēt *vi* (of vegetables) turn somewhat pithy

apkust I *vi* **1.** melt on all sides; **2.** become tired

apkust II *vi* become tired

apkvēpēt *vt* blacken with smoke

apkvēpināt *vt* blacken with smoke

apkvēpt *vi* become blackened with smoke or soot

apkvēpums *nm* coating of soot

apkverpis *adj, part* of **apkverpt** gnarled; underdeveloped

apkverpt *vi* grow deformed, become gnarled

apķellēt *vt* (com.) dirty

apķēpāt *vt* (col.) dirty

apķepēt *v* **1.** *vi* get sticky; **2.** *vt* cover with a sticky substance

apķepināt *vt* (of mud, glue) get on (clothes, other surfaces)

apķept *vi* get sticky, get muddy, get covered with a sticky substance

apķērība *nf* presence of mind, ready wit, ingenuity

apķēriens *nm* (col.) presence of mind, ready wit, ingenuity

apķērīgi *adv* ingeniously

apķērīgs *adj* quick-witted, ingenious

apķērīgums *nm* presence of mind, ready wit, ingenuity

apķērnāt *vt* (col.) dirty

apķerstīt *vt* touch, handle, pat

apķert *vt* **1.** clasp around, grip, grasp; **2.** (fig.) grasp, realize

apķerties *vr* **1.** cling to; **2.** (fig.) realize suddenly

apķēzīt *vt* (com.) dirty

apķīlājums *nm* distraint; impoundment; confiscation

apķilas *nf pl* **1.** foot rags; **2.** footless kneesocks

apķīlas *nf pl* distress, seized goods

apķīlāt *vt* distrain, impound, confiscate

apķirmēt *vi* mold around the edges

aplabināt *vt* (of animals) calm, quiet

aplādēt *vt* curse

aplāgiem *adv* once in a while

aplaidelēties *vr* fly around sth.

aplaidināt *vt* (of a disease) give to s.o.

aplaikiem *adv* once in a while

aplaiku *adv* in time, in a timely manner

aplaimojums *nm* happiness, bestowal of happiness

aplaimot *vt* make happy, gladden; benefit

aplaipot *vi* pick one's way around sth.

aplaiskoties *vr* grow lazy

aplaist *vt* 1. move in a circle; **a. acis** look around; **a. loku** go around (once), make a round, circle; 2. pass around; (of a disease) give, infect; **a. ziņu** send word around

aplaisties *vr* 1. (of a disease, with **ar**) catch; allow to be infected; 2. become covered with

aplaistīt *vt* water

aplaistīties *vr* pour water on oneself

aplaišana *nf* infection

aplaizīt *vt* lick; slicken

aplaizīties *vr* lick one's lips, (of animals) lick one's nose; (fig.) lick one's chops

aplakstīt *vt* (col.) dangle after; make court

aplakstot *vt* = **aplakstīt**

aplam *adv* 1. wrong, incorrectly; 2. too, excessively; uncommonly; 3. very frequently

aplami *adv* incorrectly, erroneously

aplamība *nf* error; absurdity, nonsense

aplamīgi *adv* erroneously

aplamīgs *adj* erroneous; foolish

aplam/is *nm*, **~e** *nf* fool

aplamnieks *nm*, **~ce** *nf* fool

aplams *adj* incorrect, wrong, erroneous; foolish

aplāms *nm* area

aplanāts *nm* aplanatic lens

aplāpīt *vt* mend, darn (everything, for everyone)

aplāpīties *vr* 1. do one's own mending; 2. finish mending

aplapot *vi* leaf out

aplapoties *vr* leaf out

aplāsināt *vt* spot, bespot

aplasīt *vt* 1. pick (all, many); 2. pick over; 3. (col.) pick off

aplāsot *vi* dew over

aplatot *vt* lath

aplaudēt *vi* applaud

aplaupīšana *nf* robbery

aplaupīt *vt* rob

aplausi *nm pl* applause

aplauzējs *nm* 1. one that breaks off; 2. (typ.) makeup man

aplauzīt *vt* break off (in a number of places)

aplauzt *vt* 1. break off (many, all); **a. ragus** (col.) put one in one's place, cut down to size; 2. (typ.) make up

aplauzums *nm* 1. break; 2. (typ.) makeup

apl[a]zija [ā] *nf* aplasia

aplecināt *vt* arrange (for a farm animal) to be served

apledojis *adj, part* of **apledot** ice-covered

apledojums *nm* ice cover, coat of ice

apledošana *nf* icing

apledot *vi* become ice-covered

aplēkāt *v* 1. *vi* jump all around sth.; 2. *vt* wait on hand and foot

aplēkt *v* 1. *vi* jump or hop around sth.; 2. *vt* (of farm animals) cover

aplēkties *vr* (of farm animals) settle

aplenkt *vt* surround, encircle; besiege

aplenkuma stāvoklis *nm* state of siege

aplenkums *nm* siege

aplēpēt *vi* become covered with sth. sticky

aplēse *nf* calculation; estimate

apleskāt *vt* (com.) spot, bespot

aplēst *vt* calculate; estimate

aplēsums *nm* calculation; estimate

aplicējs *nm* (typ.) lockup man

aplidināt *vt* fly around; hover around

aplidināties *vr* fly around (repeatedly)

aplidojums *nm* round flight; circumnavigation (by aircraft or spacecraft)

aplidot *vt, vi* 1. fly around; circumnavigate (by aircraft or spacecraft); fly from place to place; 2. (of news) spread; 3. dangle after

aplidotāj/s *nm* 1. circumnavigator (by aircraft or spacecraft); ~a *nf*; 2. suitor, swain

aplīdzināt *vt* smooth; even; trim

apliecība *nf* certificate; ~s **raksts** certification, certificate

apliecinājums *nm* 1. certification; **a. zvērasta vietā** affidavit; 2. assurance, expression

apliecināt *vt* 1. certify; testify; attest; witness; **to apliecinot** in witness whereof; 2. (*3rd pers*) prove; show; confirm; 3. assure, express

apliecinātāj/s *nm*, ~a *nf* 1. witness; 2. affirmer

apliekamais *nom adj* 1. compress; 2. wrapper; dust jacket

apliekamais papīrs *nm* wrapper; dust jacket

apliekt *vt* 1. bend around; 2. go around; turn a corner

apliesmot *vt* light, illuminate

apliet *vt* 1. pour over; **a. ar gaismu** shed light on; **kā ar ūdeni** ~s unpleasantly surprised; stunned; 2. water; 3. spill

aplieties *vr* pour or spill on oneself

aplietot *vt* wear

aplieva *nf* sapwood

aplīgošana *nf* teasing with Ligo songs

aplīgošanās *nfr* mutual teasing with Ligo songs

aplīgot *vt* tease with Ligo songs

aplīgoties *vr* mutually tease with Ligo songs

aplīk *adv* (reg.) around

aplikācija *nf* 1. appliqué; 2. (med.) compress

aplikant/s *nm*, ~e *nf* applicant

aplik[a]tīvs [ā] *adj* appliquéd

aplik[a]tūra [ā] *nf* (mus.) fingering

aplīkāt *vt* wait on

aplīki *adv* (reg.) around

aplikšana *nf* imposition

aplīkšus *adv* (reg.) indirectly

aplikt *vt* 1. put around; 2. cover; 3. impose; **a. ar nodokļiem** tax

aplīkt *vi* bend

aplikties *vr* put around oneself

aplikts *adj, part* of **aplikt** (of tongue) coated; (of throat) strep

aplīkumot *vi* detour; circle

aplīkumoties *vr* wind around

aplikums *nm* 1. compress; 2. dust jacket; 3. cover; 4. (of mucous membranes) coating

aplīkum/s *nm* curve; **ar** ~u indirectly

aplīmēt *vt* paste over; cover with, stick on

aplingot *vt* (reg.) fence in

aplinkām *adv* indirectly

aplink/i *nm pl* evasive speech; **bez** ~iem straight to the point, straightforward; ~u **ceļā** indirectly

aplinkiem *adv* indirectly

aplinks *adj* indirect, roundabout

aplinku(s) *adv* indirectly

aplipināt *vt* 1. cover with (by sticking, pasting); 2. (col.) infect

aplipt *vi* 1. become covered with sth. sticky; 2. (col.) become infected

aplipums *nm* coating, film

aplis *nm* circle; hoop; (sports) round; see also **apļi; loģiskais a.** circular reasoning

aplīst *vi* crawl around; crawl under; (fig.) circumvent

aplīt *vi* get wet

aplītis *nm dim* of **aplis**, small circle

aplīts *nm* (geol.) aplite

aplobīt *vt* peel

aplobt *vi* make the rounds; run through

aploce *nf* 1. circle (line); 2. circular frame; (of a wheel) rim; felly

aplocene *nf* (tinsmith's) folding tool

aplocīt *vt* bend around

aplocīties *vr* twist around

aploda *nf* door frame; window case

aplodāt *vi* (of small creatures) scurry around

aplodēt *vt* tin

aplokāms *adj, part* of **aplocīt** folding

aploks *nm* **1.** corral, pen, paddock; **2.** (of a wheel) rim; **3.** (of a hat) a. brim; b. band

aploksne *nf* envelope

aplombs *nm* aplomb

apložņāt *vt* sneak around; scurry about

aplūgt *vt* invite

aplūkojums *nm* examination

aplūkošana *nf* examination; (police) lineup

aplūkot *vt* **1.** look at; inspect, examine; **2.** see, visit

aplūkoties *vr* look around

aplupināt *vt* peel

aplupīt *vt* **1.** (col.) eat up; **2.** (fig.) fleece

aplupt *vi* peel

aplūza *nf* thaw

aplūzt *vi* break off

apļi *nm, pl* of **aplis** (sports) rings

apļot *vi* turn (on an axle or pivot)

apļveida *indecl adj* circular

apļveidīgi *adv* in a circle

apļveidīgs *adj* circular

apmācība *nf* instruction, training; **a. darba vietā** on-the-job training; **atkārtota a.** retraining; praktiskā a. hands-on training

apmācības brauciens *nm* training cruise; shake-down cruise

apmācības kuģis *nm* training ship

apmācies *adj, part* of **apmākties** overcast

apmācīt *vt* train, instruct; drill

apmaidīt *vt* mark, stake out with branches or saplings

apmaināmība *nf* exchangeability; **savstarpēja a.** interchangeability

apmaināms *adj, part* of **apmainīt** exchangeable; **savstarpēji a.** interchangeable

apmainīt *vt* exchange; trade; barter; **a. pa vārdam** chat a little

apmainīties *vr* exchange; **a. domām** exchange ideas

apmaiņa *nf* exchange; trade; barter; **līdzvērtīga a.** equivalent exchange; (mil.) replacement in kind

apmaiņas tirdzniecība *nf* barter trade

apmaisīt *vt* stir

apmaksa *nf* **1.** pay; payment; **2.** fee; **brīvs no ~s** duty-free; **3.** postage

apmaksāt *vt* pay; **~s** (of postage) prepaid; **nepietiekami ~s** insufficient postage

apmākt *vt* overwhelm, overcome

apmāktība *nf* gloominess

apmākties *vr* become overcast; turn gloomy

apmākulis *nm* overcast skies

apmākuļojies *adj* (of the skies) overcast

apmalām *adv* (reg.) indirectly

apmaldīties *vr* lose one's way, get lost

apma/le *nf* **1.** border, edge; edging; hem; fringe; **~ļu ļaudis** neighbors; **2.** contour; **3.** window sill; **4.** (naut.) coaming

apmalene *nf* (mech.) folding brake

apmālis *nm* (reg.) thick windrow of drying hay

apmalojums *nm* frame; edging

apmalot *vt* border, edge, trim

apmalotājs *nm* edger

apmalt *vt* finish grinding

apmalties *vr* finish grinding

apmaļdzega *nf* band cornice

apmaļu dzelzs *nf* bordering tool

apmanīt *vt* notice

apmānīt *vt* deceive

apmāns *nm* illusion

apmantot *vt* (reg.) cast a spell on s.o.

apmāņa *nf* = **apmāns**

apmargojums *nm* railing, balustrade, banisters

apmargot *vt* rail in, enclose with a railing

apmarkot *vt* affix a stamp

apmāt *vt* overwhelm; possess

apmātība *nf* daze; insanity

apmatojums *nm* amount of hair

apmāts *adj* insane

apmaukt *vt* 1. (of shoes, gloves) put on; 2. (fig.) overwhelm; possess; 3. (reg.) fool, deceive

apmaut *vt* = apmaukt

apmaukties *vr* (of shoes, gloves) put on

apmazgāt *vt* 1. wash lightly; 2. wash all or most of sth.

apmazgāties *vr* wash up

apmāžot *vt* deceive, trick; (obs.) cast a spell on s.o.

apmēbelēt *vt* furnish

apmeijot *vt* mark or decorate with boughs

apmeklējums *nm* visit

apmeklēt *vt* visit; (of school, lecture) attend

apmeklētāj/s *nm*, ~a *nf* visitor; ~u stundas visiting hours

apmeklētība *nf* attendance; number of visitors

apmelnēt *vi, vt* blacken; (metall.) blackwash

apmelnot *vt* = apmelnēt

apmelojums *nm* slander, libel, defamation

apmelot *vt* slander, libel, defame

apmelotāj/s *nm*, ~a *nf* slanderer, libeler, defamer

apmēļot *vt* gossip, spread rumors about s.o.

apmēram *adv* approximately

apmērcēt *vt* dip

apmērcēties *vr* take a dip

apmēr/s *nm* 1. circumference; dimensions; 2. ex-tent; plašā ~ā on a wide scale; 3. amount

apmesli *nm pl* (weav.) warp

apmēslot *vt* fertilize

apmest *vt* 1. cover (with dirt, sand); 2. throw around; a. acis take a quick look around; a. audeklu (weav) beam the warp; a. līkumu a. take a walk; b. go around, give a wide berth; 3. flip; 4. plaster

apmesties *vr* 1. settle; stay; (of birds) alight; 2. encamp; 3. turn sharply; 4. (*3rd pers*) (of weather) change suddenly; 5. (of garments) throw around one's shoulders

apmešanās *nfr* settling, settlement; a. atļauja residence permit

apmētāt *vt* 1. throw at, pelt with; a. akmeņiem stone; a. ar dubļiem cuss out; 2. (sewing) overcast, whipstitch

apmētāties *vr* throw at each other

apmetēj/s *nm*, ~a *nf* plasterer

apmetināt I *vt* overcast, whipstitch

apmetināt II *vt* put up temporarily

apmetne *nf* 1. settlement, colony; 2. camp

apmetnis *nm* cape; poncho

apmetuma ģipsis *nm* stucco plaster

apmetums *nm* 1. plaster, plastering; 2. (knitting) loop

apmežojums *nm* new forest

apmežošana *nf* afforestation

apmežot *vt* afforest

apmežotība *nf* degree of afforestation

apmīcīt *vt* knead again

apmīdīt *vt* trample down

apmiegoties *vr* become sleepy

apmielot *vt* feed (a large number of people)

apmierinājums *nm* satisfaction

apmierināt *vt* 1. satisfy; a. vajadzību a. satisfy a need; b. relieve oneself; 2. calm, quiet

apmierinātība *nf* 1. satisfaction; 2. complaisance

apmierināties *vr* 1. be satisfied, be content; 2. calm down

apmierinoši *adv* satisfactorily; (grade) satisfactory

apmierinošs *adj, part* of apmierināt satisfactory

apmiet *vt* pale, fence, encircle

apmiga *nf* light nap; a nap taken after sleeping

apmiglojums *nm* spraying

apmiglot *vt* 1. fog, fog up, mist; 2. (fig.) cloud; 3. fumigate, spray

apmiglotājs *nm* sprayer

apmigloties *vr* 1. become covered with fog; 2. fog up; become blurred; 3. (*3rd pers*, of weather) become foggy; 4. (fig.) cloud

apmīlēt *vt* caress, pet, fondle

apmīlināt *vt* pet

apmilzināt *vt* make blurry, fog up

apmilzt I *vi* (of eyes) turn blurry, fog up

apmilzt II *vi* swell

apmilzums *nm* swelling

apmīļot *vt* caress, pet, fondle

apmīņāt *vt* trample

apmirdzēt *vt* light, illuminate

apmirdzināt *vt* light, illuminate

apmirgot *vt* **1.** light, illuminate; **2.** spray

apmirkt *vi* get wet

apmirt *vi* die out

apmīt I *vt* trample, step on; stomp out

apmīt II (with **î**) *vt* exchange, trade

apmitot *vt* exchange, trade

apmizēt *vi* (of teeth) be covered with a film

apmizēties *vr* (of teeth) be covered with a film

apmizot *vt* peel; bark

apmizoties *vr* (of teeth) be covered with a film

apmīzt *vt* (col.) urinate on

apmīzties *vr* (col.) wet one's pants

apmīžļāt *vt* (col.) spray with urine

apmudžināties *vr* wind around

apmuldēties *vr* misspeak

apmulsa *nf* confusion; embarrassment; perplexity

apmulsināt *vt* confuse; embarrass; perplex

apmulst *vi* become confused; be perplexed; be embarrassed

apmulsums *nm* confusion; embarrassment; perplexity

apmuļināt *vt* slubber over

apmuļķot *vt* fool, make a fool of s.o.

apmuļļāt *vt* **1.** dirty; **2.** slubber over

apmuļļāties *vr* **1.** get dirty; **2.** get a smattering of

apmurcīt *vt* rumple

apmurdzīt *vt* rumple

apmūrējums *nm* masonry

apmūrēt *vt* wall in, build a wall around; face (with bricks, stonework)

apmutēt *vt* kiss (repeatedly)

apnaglot *vt* stud with nails

apnākt *vi* come around

apnēsāt *vt* **1.** wear; **2.** serve around

apnēsāties *vr* wear out, become worn

apnēsāts *adj, part* of **apnēsāt** (of clothes) worn

apnest *vt* **1.** carry around; **2.** cover with (silt, sand), deposit on

apnesties *vr* stand, tolerate

apnicība *nf* tediousness

apnicīgi *adv* boringly, tediously

apnicīgs *adj* boring, tedious

apnicīgums *nm* tediousness

apnicināt *vt* disdain

apnicis *part* of **apnikt** bored; **tas man ir a.** I am bored by it

apnika *nf* boredom, tedium

apnikt *vi* be bored with

apnikties *vr* be bored with

apnīkt *vi* die

apnikums *nm* boredom, tedium

apņēmība *nf* resoluteness, determination

apņēmīgi *adv* resolutely

apņēmīgs *adj* resolute, determined

apņēmīgums *nm* resoluteness

apņemšanās *nfr* resolution, decision; promise

apņemt *vt* **1.** put around; **2.** engulf; surround; **3.** (obs.) take; **a. par sievu (vīru)** marry (her, him); **a. sievu** (of a man) get married

apņemties *vr* **1.** resolve, decide; undertake; **2.** put sth. around oneself

apņirgt *vt* mock

apņurcīt *vt* rumple

apocentrs *nm* apocenter

apodiktiski *adv* apodictically

apodiktisks *adj* apodictic

apodziņš *nm* **1.** *dim* of **apogs**, little owl; **2.** Eurasian pygmy owl

apofiza *nf* apophysis; (arch.) apophyge

apofīze *nf* = **apofiza**

apogamija *nf* apogamy

apogams *adj* apogamic

apogeja *nf* apogee

apogejs *nm* = apogeja

apogļošana *nf* carburization

apogļot *vt* char; (tech.) carburize

apogļoties *vr* char, become charred

apogļots *adj, part* of apogļot (metall.) carbonized

apogs *nm* little owl

apokalipse *nf* apocalypsis

apokaliptika *nf* apocalyptic

apokaliptiski *adv* apocalyptically

apokaliptisks *adj* apocalyptic

apokope *nf* apocope

apokopēt *vt* apocopate

apokrifi *nm pl* apocrypha

apokrifs *adj* apocryphal

apokšķerēt *vi* (fig.) sniff around

apol[i]tiski [ī] *adv* apolitically

apol[i]tisks [ī] *adj* apolitical

apol[i]tiskums [ī] *nm* apolitical stance, indifference to politics

apol[i]tisms [ī] *nm* = apolitiskums

Apollo tauriņš *nm* Apollo butterfly

apoloģētika *nf* apologetics

apoloģētiski *adv* apologetically

apoloģētisks *adj* apologetic

apoloģēt/s *nm*, ~e *nf* apologist

apoloģija *nf* apology

apoloģisks *adj* apologetic

Apolonija riņķa līnija *nf* Apollonian circle

apolonisks *adj* apollonian

apomiksija *nf* apomixis

apomorfijs *nm* apomorphine

apopleksija *nf* apoplexy

aporija *nf* aporia

aports *nm* a variety of apple

aposelēnijs *nm* aposelene, apolune

apost *vt* sniff at

apostats *nm* apostate

aposteriori *adv* a posteriori

aposteriors *adj* a posteriori

apostīt *vt* sniff around, sniff at

apostīties *vr* sniff at each other

apostolisks *adj* apostolical

apostrofēt *vt* apostrophize

apostrofs *nm* apostrophe

apošņāt *vt* sniff around, sniff at

apošņāties *vr* sniff at each other

apotegma *nf* apothegm

apot[e]ma [ē] *nf* apothem

apoteoze *nf* apotheosis

apoz[i]cija [ī] *nf* apposition

apozitīvi *adv* appositively

apozitīvs *adj* appositive

appaijāt *vt* caress

appampt *vi* swell all around

appampums *nm* swelling

appārslot *vi* become covered with flakes

appeldēt *vi* swim around sth.

appeldināt *vt* make swim around sth.

appelējis *adj, part* of appelēt moldy

appelēt *vi* mold, grow moldy

apperēt *vt* hatch

appērt *vt* flap all over (with a leafy besom
  while bathing)

appērties *vr* 1. (of birds) get covered with dust;
  2. make one's way with difficulty (around a
  sandy or muddy place)

appesteļot *vt* cast a spell on

appētīt *vt* check, check around

appētīties *vr* ask around, make enquiries

appilēt *vi* be dripped on

appilināt *vt* spot (with drops of liquid)

appilināties *vr* let sth. drip on oneself

appirkt *vt* buy up

appirkties *vr* make a mistake in buying

appīt *vt* wrap around, wind around

appīties *vr* twist around

applāt *vt* 1. (of dough pockets) fill and smooth;
  2. (of distance) cover

applaucējums *nm* scald

applaucēt *vt* scald

applaucēties *vr* scald oneself

applēnēt *vi* (of embers) become covered with white ash

applēst *vt* tear around the edges

applēsties *vr* spread around oneself, spread over oneself

applēvēt *vi* (of heated milk, liquids) skin over; (of embers) become covered with white ash

applicināt *vt* (of soil) exhaust

applīsis *adj, part* of applīst shabby

applīst *vi* become torn around the edges, become shabby

applīvurot *vt* veil

applucināt I *vt* scald

applucināt II *vt* pluck (a bird) superficially

applucis *adj, part* of applukt shabby; mangy; threadbare; run-down

applūdināt *vt* flood

applūkāt *vt* pluck here and there

applukt *vi* 1. (of colors) fade; 2. be scalded lightly

applūkt *vt* 1. pluck or pick here and there; 2. pluck or pick all

appluskāt *vt* wear out

appluskāties *vr* become mangy

appluskāts *adj, part* of appluskāt worn-out, shabby

applūst *vi* flood

applaustīt *vt* mow (quickly, superficially) around sth.

applaut *vt* 1. mow around sth.; 2. mow all; 3. (of grass) shorten (by mowing)

applauties *vr* finish mowing

applāvības *nf pl* end of grain harvest; feast at the end of the harvest, harvest home

applūtīt *vt* (vulg.) shit upon

appoetizēt *vt* write poems about s.o. or sth.

appogāt *vt* button around

appost *vt* tidy up

apposties *vr* 1. finish tidying up; 2. fix oneself up

apprasīt *vt* question (many, all)

apprasīties *vr* ask about; ask around

apprašņāt *vt* question (many, all)

apprašņāties *vr* ask about; ask around

apprātot *vi* consider, think it over

apprecēšanās *nfr* marriage

apprecēt *vt* marry

apprecēties *vr* get married

apprecināt *vt* give away in marriage, marry off

appūdēt *vt* (of hay) allow to mold

appuišot *vt* (col.) wait on

appumpot *v* 1. *vi* break out in pimples; 2. *vt* provide with a knob, pommel, boss, or stud

appuņķot *vt* (col.) cover with snot

appūst *vt* 1. blow on; (of an injury) kiss better; 2. (*3rd pers*, of wind) cover (with sand, snow); 3. cast a spell by blowing

appūsts *adj, part* of appūst (of faces) weather-beaten

appušķot *vt* adorn, decorate

appušķoties *vr* adorn oneself

appūšļot *vt* cast a spell by blowing

appūt *vi* rot in spots

appute *nf* pollination

apputeksnēt *vt* pollinate

apputeksnēties *vr* be pollinated

apputekšņot *vt* pollinate

apputekšņoties *vr* be pollinated

apputēt *vi* become dusty

apputināt *vt* 1. snow under; (of wind) cover with sand; 2. dust; 3. (obs.) pollinate

apputinātājs *nm* duster (person or device)

apputināties *vr* get covered with (dust, flour)

apradi *nm pl* distant relatives

aprādījums *nm* pointing out, calling attention to

apradināt *vt* accustom

apradināties *vr* get accustomed to

aprādīt *vt* point out; demonstrate

apradums *nm* habit, habituation

apraibināt *vt* mottle, speckle; variegate

apraibīt *vt* cast a medicinal spell

apraknāt *vt* dig up

apraksija *nf* apraxia

prakste *nf* (jur.) distraint, distress

aprakstījums *nm* description

aprakstīšana *nf* (jur.) distraint, distress; (of a plot) description

aprakstīt *vt* 1. cover with writing; 2. describe; 3. (jur.) distrain, levy a distress; 4. embroider; decorate with designs

aprakstniek/s *nm*, **~ce** *nf* documentary writer

aprakstošs *adj, part* of **aprakstīt** descriptive

apraksts *nm* 1. description; 2. documentary; 3. record

aprakstveida *indecl adj* descriptive

aprakstveidīgi *adv* descriptively

aprakstveidīgs *adj* descriptive

aprakt *vt* 1. bury; 2. dig around

aprakties *vr* bury oneself

aprāmējums *nm* frame

aprāmēt *vt* frame

aprāpot *vi* crawl around

aprāpties *vr* climb around sth.; creep around

aprasināšana *nf* watering; **~s iekārta** sprinkler system

aprasināt *vt* spray; sprinkle; water

aprasot *vi* be covered with dew; steam up

aprasoties *vr* be covered with dew; steam up

aprast *vi* accustom oneself to, get used to

aprasts *adj, part* of **aprast** accustomed

aprāt *vt* rebuke, scold

apraudāt *vt* 1. bemoan; mourn over; 2. wet with tears

apraudāties *vr* begin to cry; cry a short while, shed a few tears

apraudzīt *vt* 1. examine, inspect, test, check; 2. visit

apraudzīties *vr* visit

apraukt *vt* pull together, gather

apraust *vt* cover (with sand, soil, ashes); (of potatoes) hill

apraustīt *vt* pluck or pick here and there

aprausums *nm* hill (around a plant)

apraušana *nf* (of plants) hilling

apraut *vt* 1. tear off, pick or pluck most or all; 2. cut short, stop, check; 3. (*3rd pers*, of wind, sun) wither, scorch; 4. (of clothes) put on quickly; 5. pull together, gather

aprautība *nf* discontinuity; (of speech) clipped character

aprauties *vr* 1. cut oneself short; 2. (*3rd pers*) stop suddenly; 3. (col.) dry superficially; 4. (of clothes) put on quickly

aprauti *adv* abruptly

apraut/s *adj, part* of **apraut** 1. (of speech, thought) interrupted; abrupt, clipped; 2. (of movement) brief; 3. weather-beaten

aprāvains *adj* gusty

apravēt *vt* 1. weed around sth.; 2. weed all

apravēties *vr* finish weeding

aprāvības *nf pl* the end of flax pulling; celebration of the end of flax pulling

aprebt *vi* (of wounds) close; scab

aprecēt *vi* scab

aprēda *nf* forest circuit (under a forest conservator)

apredzams *adj, part* of **apredzēt** surveyable

apredze *nf* 1. visual field; vista; 2. scope

apredzēt *vt* survey, encompass in one's view

apreibināšanās *nfr* intoxication

apreibināt *vt* intoxicate; make drunk; (fig.) go to one's head

apreibināties *vr* becoome intoxicated, get oneself drunk

apreib/is *adj, part* of **apreibt** 1. intoxicated; 2. dizzy; **man galva ~usi** I am dizzy

apreibt *vi* 1. become intoxicated; 2. become dizzy

apreibums *nm* intoxication

apreizot *vt* (barb.) travel across, see (in traveling)

aprēķina grāmatiņa *nf* paybook

aprēķina laulība *nf* marriage of convenience

aprēķināt *vt* calculate, compute; figure

aprēķina tabula *nf* calculation table

aprēķināts *adj, part* of **aprēķināt** premeditated

aprēķināties *vr* settle accounts

aprēķinātāj/s *nm,* ~a *nf* calculator; estimator

aprēķin/s *nm* **1.** calculation, computation; (bookk.) settling; **aptuvens a.** estimate; **saimnieciskais a.** a. cost accounting; b. (socialist economy) recovery of cost of production from an enterprise's own returns (without state subsidy); ~**a bilance** balance of payment; **2.** advantage; **3.** ulterior motive, calculations

apremdēt *vt* = **apremdināt**

apremdināt *vt* still, soothe; (of anger) control; (of cold water) warm up

aprepēt *vi* (*3rd pers,* of hands, feet) become rough, grow a crust, become encrusted

aprept *vi* = **aprepēt**

apretētāj/s *nm,* ~a *nf* dresser (of textiles or furs); finisher

apretūra *nf* (of textiles or furs) dressing

apriebt I *vt* heal or ease suffering by stroking and the use of magic formulae; bewitch

apriebt II *vi* become repulsive, become intolerable

aprieb/ties *vr* become repulsive, become intolerable; **man tas ir ~ies** I am disgusted with it; ~**ies līdz nāvei** sick and tired of it

apriecenis *nm* (whole) slice of bread

aprieks *nm* (whole) slice of bread

apriepojums *nm* tires

apriepot *vt* put on tires

apriet *vt* bark at; (fig.) vilify

aprika *nf* (whole) slice of bread

aprīkojums *nm* (mil.) equipment; kit

aprīkot *vt* **1.** harness; **2.** equip; **3.** order

aprikoze *nf* apricot

apriks *nm* = **aprika**

aprikšot *vt* (col.) wait on

april, april *interj* April fool

aprīlis *nm* April; **pirmais a.** April Fool's Day

aprima *nf* cessation, rest

aprimis *adj, part* of **aprimt** (geol.) stagnant; abated; quiescent

aprimt *vi* **1.** quiet down; die down; abate; diminish; **2.** stop

aprimties *vr* **1.** quiet down; die down; abate; diminish; **2.** stop

aprindas *nf pl* (of society) circles; **valdošās a.** ruling circles, the Establishment

apriņķa ārsts *nm* district chief medical officer

apriņķa pašvaldība *nf* district government

apriņķa priekšnieks *nm* district internal security chief

apriņķa skola *nf* (hist.) junior high school

apriņķa vecākais *nm* district chief executive

apriņķis *nm* (first administrative subdivision of an **apgabals**) district

apriņķot *vt* circle

apriori *adv* a priori

apriorisms *nm* apriorism

aprioristisks *adj* aprioristic

aprioritāte *nf* apriority

apriors *adj* a priori

apripināt *vt* roll around sth.

apripot *vi* roll around

apri/se *nf* contour; outline; ~**šu mācīšana**s **metode** case method

aprist *vi* (of time) roll around

aprīt *vt* devour, gulp down, swallow; eat up; (com.) eat the whole thing

aprite *nf* (econ.) turnover; (econ., physiol.) circulation

apritēt *vi* **1.** roll around; (of time) pass; **2.** circulate

apritināt *vt* **1.** roll around sth.; **2.** dog-ear

apritināties *vr* wrap oneself around, wind oneself around

aprīvēt *vt* rub a little

aprobācija *nf* approbation, official approval

aprobatīvs *adj* aprobative

aprobēt *vt* approbate, approve officially

aprobežojums *nm* limitation, restriction

aprobežot *vt* limit, restrict

aprobežoti *adv* with limitations

aprobežotība *nf* narrow-mindedness

aprobežoties *vr* limit or confine oneself

aprobežots *adj, part* of **aprobežot 1.** (of means) limited, scanty; **2.** narrow-minded; **3.** mentally limited

aprobīt *vt* mark, notch

aproce *nf* **1.** cuff; **2.** bracelet

aproces podziņa *nf* cufflink

aprocīte *nf dim* of **aproce**, cuff; bracelet

aproksimācija *nf* approximation

apropriācija *nf* appropriation

aprota *nf* (of books) edge ornament

aprubināt *vt* gnaw

aprumbāties *vr* **1.** grow fat (instead of tall), put on bulk; **2.** bundle up; **3.** (of bones) knit

aprumulēt *vt* (folk.) splash with water (those doing a chore the first time in the year)

apruna *nf* gossip; slander

aprunāt *vt* gossip about; slander

aprunāties *vr* have a talk, talk things over; consult with

aprunīgs *adj* gossipy; slanderous

aprūpe *nf* providing (for the elderly, indigents), caretaking; welfare work; **garīgā a.** providing for spiritual needs

aprūpēt *vt* take care of, care for

aprūpība *nf* care

aprūsējums *nm* rust, rusty place

aprūsēt *vi* rust

aprūsināt *vt* rust

apruslis *nm* gravel pit

aprušināt *vt* cover with soil, (of potatoes) hill

apsaimniekot *vt* run a farm; manage

apsaine *nf* aspen grove

apsainis *nm* bandage

apsaišķis *nm* bandage

apsaite *nf* bandage

apsaitējums *nm* bandage

apsaitēt *vt* bandage

apsājs *nm* aspen grove

apsakņot *vt* root

apsakņoties *vr* put down roots

apsākt *vt* begin

apsākums *nm* first steps (in the completion of a job or project)

apsaldējums *nm* frostbite

apsaldēšanās *nfr* hypothermia

apsaldēt *vt* **1.** freeze; **2.** cover with frost or ice; **3.** chill

apsaldēties *vr* catch a cold; get chilled

apsālīt *vt* salt lightly

apsalt *vi* **1.** winter-kill; freeze to death; **2.** get frozen, be nipped by the frost; **3.** frost over, ice over

apsaluma āūla *nf* chillblain

apsalums *nm* frostbite

apsāpēt *vi* begin to ache

apsāpēties *vr* begin to ache

apsardze *nf* **1.** guards; **2.** guarding, security

apsardzība *nf* **1.** protection; **2.** guard; custody; **3.** defense

apsardzības kārtība *nf* (jur.) procedure for nonactionable cases

apsardznieks *nm* guard

apsargāt *vt* **1.** guard; **2.** keep watch over, stand guard over; **3.** defend

apsargātāj/s *nm*, **~a** *nf* guard; custodian; defender

apsargpostenis *nm* sentry

apsar/gs *nm*, **~dze** *nf* sentinel

apsarkt *vi* redden

apsarkums *nm* reddening, redness

apsarme *nf* **1.** mildew; **2.** bloom

apsarmojums *nm* **1.** frost; **2.** mildew

apsarmot *vi* frost, become frosted

apsārtināt *vt* (of red fruit) ripen; rouge

apsārtis *adj, part* of **apsārtot** reddened

apsārtot *vi* redden

apsauciens *nm* warning call

apsaukāt *vt* call names

apsaukāties *vr* call each other names

apsaukt *vt* call to order; scold

apsaukums *nm* call to order

apsauļošanās *nfr* sunbathing

apsauļot *vt* expose to the sun; sunbathe

apsauļoties *vr* sunbathe

apsausēt *vt* dry superficially

apsausināt *vt* dry superficially

apsaust *vi* dry

apsautēt *vt* (cul.) sear; **tikai ~s** (fig.) he has learned only a little

apse I *nf* aspen

apse II *nf* (arch.) apse

apsebēt *vi* be late

apseboties *vr* be late

apsēdēt *vt* (reg.) soil

apsēdināt *vt* seat; make sit down

apsedlot *vt* = **apseglot**

apsedziņš *nm dim* of **apsegs**, cover; bedspread

apsega *nf* = **apsegs**

apseglot *vt* saddle

apsegs *nm* cover; bedspread; counterpane; (tech.) casing, housing

apsegt *vt* cover

apsegties *vr* cover oneself

apsēja I *nf* sowing

apsēja II *nf* 1. bandage; 2. armband

apsējas *nf pl* feast at the close of sowing

apsējības *nf pl* = **apsējas**

apsējiņš *nm dim* of **apsējs**, bandage; armband

apsējs *nm* 1. bandage, dressing; 2. armband; brassard

apsējums *nm* bandage

apsēklošana *nf* insemination

apsēklot *vt* inseminate; (biol.) fertilize

apsekojums *nm* survey

apsekot *vt* 1. follow s.o., spy on; 2. follow, study; survey; check, inspect

apsekt *vt* (of game) track down

apsene *nf* orange boletus; rough boletus

apserde *nf* sapwood

apsērot *vt* mourn

apsērsēj/s *nm*, **~a** *nf* (obs.) visitor

apsērsnot *vi* (of snow) crust

apsērst *vt* (obs.) visit

apsērsums *nm* (obs.) visit

apsēst *vt* 1. mob, surround; 2. plague; 3. obsess; 4. possess; 5. *vi* (poet.) sit down; 6. (obs.) besiege

apsēstība *nf* obsessiveness

apsēsties *vr* sit down; (col.) be floored; (of birds, bugs) alight, land

apsēt *vt* sow

apsēta *nf* encircling fence

apsēties *vr* finish sowing

apsētot *vt* fence in

apsīda *nf* apsis

apsidrabot *vt* = **apsudrabot**

apsīds *nm nf* apsis

apsiekalot *vt* beslobber

apsiekaloties *vr* drool

apsiens *nm* aspen grove

apsiet *vt* tie around; wrap, cover; (of a tie, apron) put on

apsieties *vr* put on (oneself by tying)

apsietne *nf* headband

apsievojies *adj, part* of **apsievoties** married

apsievoties *vr* (col.) take a wife

apsijāt *vt* besprinkle

apsikas *nf pl* stuttering

apsīkstēt *vi* become tough

apsikt *vi* 1. run dry; run out of; fizzle out; 2. dwindle

apsīkt *vi* = **apsikt**

apsikums *nm* (of strength) exhaustion; (of ideas) impoverishment

apsīkums *nm* = **apsikums**

apsilde *nf* heating

apsildīšana *nf* heating

apsildīt *vt* 1. warm; 2. heat; **a. degunu** (fig.) get one's feet wet apsildītājs *nm* heater

apsildīties *vr* warm oneself

apsilt *vi* get warm

apsirgt *vi* become ill

apsirmot *vi* (of hair) turn gray

apsirmoties *vr* (of hair) turn gray

apsirot *vt* maraud (through an area)

āpsis *nm* badger; **kā ā.** (of sleeping) like a log

apsist *vt* **1.** line, cover with; attach, nail down; **2.** kill, slaughter; (of hail) beat down (crops)

apsisties *vr* **1.** (of clothes) wrap around; **2.** develop a rash; **3.** fog up; **4.** become weather-beaten; **5.** change direction suddenly; flip around

apsitām *adv* unevenly; (of wind) in gusts

apsīte *nf dim* of **apse**, little aspen

apsitīgi *adv* adroitly

apsitīgs *adj* **1.** adroit; **2.** (of winds) variable

apsitnis *nm* cape

apsitums *nm* (seat) cover, covering; siding

apskābe *nf* acid in the lowest state of oxidation; usu in compound words, e.g., **chlorapskābe** hy-pochlorous acid

apskābēt *vt* sour slightly

apskabīt *vt* (reg., of a log) dress

apskābļot *vt* acidulate; acidify

apskābt *vi* sour slightly

apskādēt *vt* (obs.) damage, harm

apskaidre *nf* enlightenment

apskaidrība *nf* enlightenment

apskaidrot *vt* enlighten; clear one's mind

apskaidrotība *nf* enlightenment

apskaidroties *vr* clear up; (of face) become serene

apskaisties *vr* get angry

apskaišanās *nfr* getting angry

apskaitīgs *adj* easily offended, irritable

apskaitīt *vt* count; compute

apskaits *nm* count; computation

apskaldīt *vt* chop (to shape)

apskalot *vt* **1.** wash superficially; **2.** slosh around; **3.** (of waves) wash, wash against

apskaloties *vr* wash oneself off

apskaņošana *nf* acoustic irradiation

apskaņot *vt* irradiate acoustically

apskapstējis *adj, part* of **apskapstēt** patinaed

apskapstējums *nm* patina

apskapstēt *vi* patinate

apskarājies *adj, part* of **apskarāties** tattered, in tatters

apskarbalājies *adj* tattered, in tatters

apskarāties *vr* become tattered all around

apskare *nf* frame

apskaris *adj* tattered, in tatters

apskārst *vt* comprehend, realize

apskate *nf* inspection; **medicīniskā a.** physical examination

apskatīgi *adv* observantly

apskatīgs *adj* observant

apskatīt *vt* **1.** view; inspect; look at; (med.) examine; (of an exhibition) visit; **a. pilsētu** see the sights of a city; **sīki a.** examine, scrutinize, in-spect closely; **2.** consider, discuss

apskatīties *v* **1.** *vi* look around; check to see; **2.** *vt* look at, view, inspect

apskats *nm* review

apskaudība *nf* **1.** envy; **2.** (folk.) bad luck (brought by an envious person)

apskaust *vt* envy

apskaut *vt* embrace

apskauties *vr* embrace each other

apskaueams *adj, part* of **apskaust** enviable

apskava *nf* circular clamp

apskave *nf* = **apskava**

apskāviens *nm* embrace

apskolot *vt* educate superficially

apskraidīt *vt* run through, run to (a number of places in search of sth.)

apskrambāt *vt* scratch

apskrambāties *vr* get scratched

apskramstīt *vt* nibble, nibble away

apskrandāties *vr* become tattered

apskrandējis *adj* tattered, ragged

apskrandis *adj* tattered, ragged

apskrandojis *adj* tattered, ragged

apskrāpēt *vt* scratch a little

apskrāpēties *vr* get a few scratches

apskretis *adj* encrusted with dirt

apskribināt *vt* = **apskrubināt**

apskriet *vt, vi* **1.** run around sth.; **2.** see on the run, run through (a number of places); make a round of calls; **3.** (of news) spread

apskrieties *vr*, usu. in phrase **man dūša** (or **sirds, žults**) **apskrējās** I was annoyed; I really got mad

apskrīpāt *vt* scratch all over

apskrotele *nf* waistband

apskrubināt *vt* nibble on, gnaw on, (of a bone) pick

apskrubis *adj* crumbling

apskujot *vt* cover with fir (spruce, pine) branches

apskumt *vi* grow somewhat sad

apskūpstīt *vt* kiss all over

apskurbināt *vt* intoxicate

apskurbināties *vr* become intoxicated

apskurbt *vi* become intoxicated

apskurbums *nm* intoxication

apslābt *vi* diminish, weaken, wane

apslābums *nm* weakening, waning

apslacināt *vt* sprinkle repeatedly

apslacīt *vt* sprinkle, spray; (fig.) celebrate, make it an occasion; **a. putekļus** beat down the dust

apslacīties *vr* **1.** splash (a liquid) on oneself; **2.** bespatter oneself

apslāga *nf* one trouble after another; disaster

apslaka *nf* sprinkling, spraying

apslaktēt *vt* (barb.) slaughter

apslānīt *vt* slaughter

apslapēt *vt* wet, moisten

apslāpēt *vt* (of fire) quench, smother; (of sound) muffle; (of emotions, uprisings) suppress, stifle; (of vibrations) damp

apslapināt *vt* moisten, wet

apslapināties *vr* become wet, (col., of an infant) wet oneself

apslapt *vi* become wet

apslāpt *vi* (of fire) go out; (of sound) die down, die away

apslaucīt *vt* wipe on all sides; wipe dry; sweep

apslaucīties *vr* dry oneself

apslaukt *vt* finish milking; (col., fig.) fleece, take to the cleaners

apslēpēj/s *nm*, ~a *nf* concealer

apslepkavot *vt* massacre

apslēpt *vt* hide, conceal

apslēpties *vr* hide oneself

apslēpts *adj, part* of **apslēpt 1.** hidden; covert; **2.** latent

apslīcināt *vt* submerge, flood

apslidināties *vr* skate around sth.

apslidot *vt* skate around sth.

apsliedēt *vt* leave tracks

apsliekot *vt* beslobber

apslienāt *vt* beslobber

apsliet *vt* put up, erect around sth.

apslīkt *vi* drown

apslimt *vi* fall ill

apslinkoties *vr* give oneself to laziness

apslinkt *vi* become lazy

apslīpēt *vt* polish, (of gems) cut

apslīpēties *vr* be polished; (fig.) become polished

apslist *vi* die down, stop

apslodzīt *vt* weigh down

apslogas *nf pl* (of shingle roofs) ridge boards

apsludināt *vt* proclaim far and wide

apsmacēt *vt* (of fire) put out

apsmādēt *vt* disdain

apsmadzeņot *vt* (sl.) consider, think it over

apsmakt *vi* 1. (of fire) die down; 2. acquire the smell of sth.

apsmalstīt *vt* skim partly

apsmējēj/s *nm*, **~a** *nf* mocker, ridiculer; banterer

apsmelt *vt* dip (partly or superficially), skim (repeatedly, all containers)

apsmērēt *vt* (col., of butter, grease) spread; smear on

apsmidzināt *vt* spray

apsmidzināties *vr* spray oneself

apsmiekls *nm* 1. ridicule; mockery; 2. object of ridicule, laughing stock

apsmiet *vt* ridicule, laugh at, mock

apsmieties *vr* **ļauties a.** allow to be laughed at

apsmirst *vi* stink, stink up

apsmulēt *vt* dirty

apsmulēties *vr* dirty oneself

apsmulis *adj* (col.) dirty

apsmurgāt *vt* 1. (com.) soil with nasal mucus; 2. slubber, do a sloppy job

apsnausties *vr* fall asleep

apsniegt *vt* 1. pass around; 2. reach all around

apsnidzis *adj, part* of **apsnigt** snow-covered

apsnigt *vi* become covered with snow

apsolījums *nm* promise

apsolīt *vt* promise; pledge, vow

apsolīties *vr* promise; pledge, vow

apsoļot *vi, vt* 1. walk around sth.; 2. walk all over

apspaidīt *vt* 1. poke, feel; (metall.) shingle; (metall.) cog (in rolling); 2. oppress; 3. heal (magically)

apspaidītājs *nm* healer, witchdoctor

apspaidīties *vr* 1. (of fruit) become bruised; 2. **viņš neļauj a.** he doesn't let anyone touch him

apspaids *nm* (metall.) shingling

apspaidu stāvs *nm* shingler; cogging stand

apspalvojums *nm* (of birds) feathers, plumage, indumentum; (of quadrupeds) fur

apspalvoties *vr* grow feathers

apspēle *nf* superior maneuver; **tā bija veikla a.** they outmaneuvered (their opponents) beautifully

apspēlēt *vt* 1. beat at a game; outmaneuver; 2. play up, emphasize

apspīdēt *vt* shine upon, illuminate

apspīdināt *vt* shine upon, illuminate

apspiedēj/s *nm*, **~a** *nf* oppressor; suppressor

apspiest *vt* oppress; suppress; repress; stifle

apspiestais *nom adj*, **~ā** *f* the oppressed

apspiestība *nf* oppression

apspiešana *nf* oppression; **~s uguns** suppressive fire

apspīlēt *vt* clamp; squeeze in

apspļaudīt *vt* spit upon (repeatedly)

apspļaut *vt* spit upon

apspļāvas *nf pl* fly specks

apsprādzēt *vt* buckle all around

apsprāgt *vi* 1. burst all around; 2. (of animals) die in large numbers

apspraudīt *vt* 1. mark with stakes; adorn with branches or saplings; 2. (of bedding) tuck in

apsprauslot *vt* sputter on s.o.

apspraust *vt* 1. mark with stakes; adorn with branches or saplings; 2. (of bedding) tuck in

apsprēgāt *vi* crack

apsprendzēt *vt* (folk.) saddle

apspriede *nf* conference

apspriedelēt *vt* pick on, criticize

apspriest *vt* discuss; **rūpīgi a.** give careful consideration

apspriesties *vr* confer; deliberate; consult with

apspulgot *vt* shine upon, illuminate

apspulgs *nm* essay

apspuris *adj, part* of **apspurt** frayed

apspuroties *vr* become frayed

apspurt *vi* fray

apstādījumi *nm pl* trees and shrubs; green belts, parks apstādināt *vt* stop; stall; **a. šaušanu** (mil.) stand fast

apstādīt *vt* plant, plant with; plant trees and shrubs; **kokiem ~s** tree-lined

apstaiga *nf* beat, round

apstaigāt *vt* make the rounds; walk through; (of news) spread; *vi* walk around

apstāja *nf* interruption; **bez ~s** without cease, nonstop; **~s** *pl* a. retention of urine; b. missing a period

apstāj/i *nm pl* **1.** = **apstājas**; **2. ar ~iem** (of a horse) restive; **3.** imaginary illness

apstājies *adj, part* of **apstāties** stopped; still; **laiks ir a.** time is standing still

apstājš *adj* restive

apstāklenis *nm* adverb

apstāk/lis *nm* **1.** circumstance; **2. ~ļi** circumstances; conditions; **labos ~ļos** in good circumstances; **labvēlīgi ~ļi** favorable conditions; **mīkstinoši ~ļi** extenuating circumstances; **ne-paredzēti ~ļi** unforeseen circumstances; contingency; **spaidīgi ~ļi** straits, bind; money difficulties

apstākļa palīgteikums *nm* adverbial clause

apstākļa vārds *nm* adverb

apstarojums *nm* irradiance

apstarošana *nf* irradiation

apstarot *vt* **1.** shine upon illuminate; **2.** ir-radiate, treat with radiation

apstaroties *vr* undergo radiation therapy

apstāstīt *vt* tell all about

apstāsts *nm* recounting

apstāšanās *nfr* stop, halt; stoppage; **bez a.** without stopping, nonstop

apstāt *v* **1.** *vt* surround; mob; descend in swarms upon; **2.** *vi* stop

apstāties *vr* **1.** stop, halt; pause; **a. pie jautājuma** dwell on the question; **2.** surround

apstāvēt *vt* (obs.) (of a deceased person) eulogize; (of a corpse) bury

apstāvētājs *nm* (obs.) reader of a eulogy (at a funeral)

apstāvēties *vr* **1.** get stiff legs (from standing too long); **2.** spoil (after being kept too long)

apsteidze *nf* = **apsteiga**

apsteidzējuguns *nf* leading fire

apsteidzošs *adj, part* of **apsteigt** (of an attack) preemptive

apsteiga *nf* (ballistics, el.) lead; **~a attālums** leading distance

apsteigt *vt* overtake

apstiept *vt* stretch around

apstiepties *vr* extend around sth.

apstigot *vt* **1.** mark with posts; **2.** (fig.) border

apstīgot *vt* (of musical instruments) string

apstīpot *vt* hoop

apstiprinājums *nm* **1.** confirmation; corrobora-tion; **2.** ratification; certification

apstiprināt *vt* **1.** confirm; corroborate; **2.** ratify; certify; attest; approve; **a. autentiskumu** authenticate

apstiprināties *vr* be confirmed

apstotēt *vt* (of skirts) hem

apstrādājamība *nf* (of materials) workability

apstrādājums *nm* (of products) finish

apstrādāšana *nf* processing; finishing

apstrādāt *vt* **1.** treat, work, process, finish; (land) work, prepare, till, cultivate; edit; **2.** (col.) de-ceive; (col.) rob; **3.** (col.) try to convince; **4.** (col.) work over, attack, beat up

apstrāde *nf* processing; **atkarīga a.** (compu.) on-line processing; **ideoloģiska a.** brain-washing; **neatkarīga a.** off-line processing; **a. ar skrotīm** shotblasting

apstraume *nf* stream

apstrāvot *vt* **1.** waft over; **2.** permeate

apstrēbt *vt* (of soup, porridge) eat up

apstrīdamība *nf* questionability

apstrīdams *adj, part* of **apstrīdēt** questionable, disputable, arguable

apstrīdēt *vt* question, dispute; challenge; (of a will) contest

apstrupot *vt* dull

apstulbināt *vt* stun, daze

apstulbt *vi* be stunned, be dumbfounded, be dazed

apstulbot *vt* stupefy

apstulbums *nm* daze, stupefaction

apstūrēt *vi* steer around

apstutēt *vt* prop up

apsūbējums *nm* tarnish

apsūbēt *vi* tarnish; (fig.) mold

apsudrabot *vt* silver, silver-plate

apsūdzēt *vt* accuse; bring action against; complain against

apsūdzēt/ais *nom adj*, ~ā *f* the accused, defendant; ~o sols dock

apsūdzētāj/s *nm*, ~a *nf* accuser, plaintiff; (officer of the court) prosecutor

apsūdzība *nf* accusation, charge; **dubulta a.** double jeopardy; **melīga a.** false charge

apsūdzības raksts *nm* indictment

apsūdzības runa *nf* prosecutor's charge

apsukāt *vt* (col.) eat up, clean the platter

apsūkāt *vt* suck all around

apsula *nf* hardened birch sap

apsulājs *nm* aspen grove

apsūlāt *vi* suppurate

apsūnojis *adj, part* of **apsūnot** moss-covered

apsūnot *vi* gather moss, become covered with moss

apsusēt *vi* dry on the surface

apsusināt *vt* blot, dry

apsust *vi* stew on the outside

apsutināt *vt* stew lightly

apsūtīt *vt* 1. (rare.) send around; 2. (obs.) order, subscribe to

apsvaidīgi *adv* adroitly

apsvaidīgs *adj* 1. adroit; 2. shifty; (of winds) variable

apsvaidīt *vt* besprinkle (ritually)

apsveicēj/s *nm*, ~a *nf* congratulator

apsveiciens *nm* greeting, salutation

apsveicinājums *nm* greeting, salutation

apsveicināšanās *nfr* exchange of greetings

apsveicināt *vt* greet

apsveicināties *vr* exchange greetings

apsveikt *vt* 1. congratulate; wish many happy returns; **a. Jaunajā gadā** wish a happy New Year; 2. welcome

apsveikties *vr* congratulate each other

apsveikum/s *nm* 1. congratulation; 2. greeting; ~a runa welcoming speech

apsvēpēt *vt* 1. smoke out; 2. blacken with smoke; 3. treat with smoke

apsvēpināt *vt* 1. smoke out; 2. blacken with smoke; 3. treat with smoke

apsvēpis *adj* blackened with smoke, sooty

apsvērīgi *adv* cautiously, carefully

apsvērīgs *adj* cautious, careful

apsvērīgums *nm* caution

apsvērt *vt* consider, weigh in consideration

apsvērties *vr* tilt; flip around

apsvērums *nm* consideration

apsvētīt *vt* bless

apsvīdis *adj, part* of **apsvīst** steamed up, fogged

apsvīdums *nm* steam (on windows)

apsviedīgi *adv* adroitly

apsviedīgs adj 1. adroit; **valodiski a.** verbally fluent; 2. (of winds) variable

apsviest *vt* 1. turn over rapidly, turn on the side, flip; throw s.o. on one's back; 2. cover (with dirt, sand); 3. (of a garment) throw on one's shoulders

apsviesties *vr* swing around, turn around suddenly; (of weather) change suddenly

apsviķot *vt* tar

apsvilināt *vt* singe; burn; **a. pirkstus** (fig.) burn one's fingers over sth.

apsvilināties *vr* burn oneself

apsvil/t *vi* get singed, get burned; **kā ~is** as if on fire

apsvīst *vi* 1. perspire; 2. get steamed up

apšalkot *vt* (of rustling, soughing, the sound of the surf) envelop

apšalkt *vt* = **apšalkot**

apšaubāmi *adv* questionably

apšaubāmība *nf* doubtfulness; dubiousness

apšaubāms *adj, part* of **apšaubīt 1.** questionable, doubtful; **2.** dubious, suspicious; **3.** (of compliments) equivocal

apšaubīt *vt* doubt, question

apšaude *nf* (mil.) fire; bombardment, shelling; **savstarpēja a.** fire fight; ~s **lauks** field of fire; **a. pāri galvai** low angle fire

apšaudīšana *nf* (mil.) fire; shelling

apšaudīšanās *nfr* exchange of gunfire

apšaudīt *vt* fire upon; shell; **a. ar ložmetēju** machine-gun; **tikt ~am** be under fire, take fire

apšaudīties *vr* exchange fire

apšaut *vt* shoot down, kill off

apšauties *vr* **1.** exchange fire; **2.** become covered with fog or clouds; **3.** turn quickly; do a complete switch

apškundziņš *nm* orange boletus

apšķaidīt *vt* bespatter

apšķaidīties *vr* bespatter oneself

apšķaudīt *vt* sneeze on

apšķebināt *vt* make sick

apšķebinā/ties *vr*, usu. *3rd pers* **man ~jās dūša** (col.) I felt sick

apšķērēt *vt* cut off, trim

apšķibīt *vt* (col.) cut off, break off

apšķiest *vt* bespatter

apšķiesties *vr* bespatter oneself

apšķiņķot *vt* (barb.) shower with gifts

apšķīst *vi* get spattered on

apšķīt *vt* pick off

apšķūnis *nm* (col.) shed

apšlakošana *nf* (barb.) impounding, confiscation

apšlakot *vt* (barb.) impound, confiscate

apšļacināt *vt* splash on, bespatter

apšļakstēt *vi* get splashed on, get bespattered

apšļakstināt *vt* splash on

apšļakstināties *vr* splash on oneself

apšļakstīt *vt* splash on, bespatter

apšļākt *vt* splash on

apšļākties *vr* splash on oneself

apšļircināt *vt* spray

apšļūkt *vi* slide around

apšmaukt *vt* (col.) trick, deceive

apšmaukties *vr* be taken in

apšņāpt *vt* (col.) cut, trim

apšņīpāt *vt* (col.) cut, trim

apšpricēt *vt* (barb.) spray

apšu beka *nf* **1.** orange boletus; **2.** rough boletus

apšu kokgrauzis *nm* poplar borer

apšu lapgrauzis *nm* an aspen leaf chafer, Melasoma populi

apšu sfings *nm* poplar hawk moth

apšust *vi* **1.** become furious; **2.** revolt, rebel

āpšu suns *nm* dachshund

apšūt *vt* **1.** hem; edge, border; **2.** do the sewing for (all, many); **3.** (tech.) board, panel; veneer; plate; sheath; line, face; cover

apšutis *adj, part* of **apšust** shocked; furious

apšuve *nf* facing; revetment

apšuvuma ķieģelis *nm* facing brick

apšuvums *nm* paneling, veneer; plating; sheathing; lining; facing; siding; covering; fairing

aptaisīt *vt* **1.** make (sth. to go around), build around; **a. sētu** fence in; **2.** dirty

aptaisīties *vr* dirty oneself; (of small children) soil one's diapers, mess one's pants

aptaka *nf* circulation; circuit

aptakelēt *vt* rig, fit out with tackle

aptamborēt *vt* **1.** crochet around, make a crocheted edge; **2.** do the crocheting for (all, many)

aptašķīt *vt* bespatter

aptašķīties *vr* bespatter oneself

aptaucis *adj* fat

aptauja *nf* **1.** enquiry; **2.** poll

aptaujas lapa *nf* questionnaire

aptaujāšana *nf* inquiry

aptaujāšanās *nfr* inquiry

aptaujāt *vt* put the question to; poll

aptaujāties *vr* inquire

aptaukošanās *nfr* putting on fat, (med.) fatty degeneration

aptaukot *vt* cover with fat, spread fat on

aptaukoties *vr* put on weight, get fat; develop fatty deposits

aptaustīt *vt* feel (with one's hands); **a. sānus** beat

aptecēt I *vi* **1.** flow around; **2.** run down (the sides)

aptecēt II *vi, vt* **1.** trip, trot, run around; **a. mājas soli** do housework; **2.** (of time) pass; **3.** serve on s.o., serve hand and foot

aptecē/ties *vr* **1.** fog up; **2. man sirds ~jās** I got really mad

aptecināt *vt* let drip on

aptēgāties *vr* (reg.) inquire

aptekāt *vt* serve hand and foot

aptekāties *vr* (of animals) settle

apteksne *nf* housemaid, hotel maid

aptēlot *vt* depict, describe, portray

apteļoties *vr* calf

aptenkot *vt* gossip about

aptērpt *vt* dress, attire

aptērpties *vr* clothe oneself

aptēse *nf* one of the rough-hewn sides of a squared log

aptēst *vt* roughhew

aptieciņa *nf* **1.** *dim* of **aptieka**, pharmacy; **2.** first aid kit; **3.** medicine chest

aptieka *nf* pharmacy; **~s** apothecary; **~s preces** pharmaceuticals

aptieku anacikle *nf* German pellitory

aptieku indaines *nf pl* white swallowwort

aptieku žodzene *nf* hedge mustard

aptiekar/s *nm*, **~e** *nf* pharmacist

aptieķnie/ks *nm*, **~ce** *nf* (col.) pharmacist

aptiesāt *vt* (col., of food) polish off

aptikt *vi* get around

aptinums *nm* wrapping

apt|i|ņāt [ī] *vt* wrap, wrap around

apt|i|ņāties [ī] *vr* wrap, twist around

aptipināt *vi* tiptoe around

aptīrīšana *nf* refuse collection; cleanup

aptīrīt *vt* **1.** clean, tidy up; dust, brush; cleanse; **a. dzīvokli** do housecleaning; **2.** (col.) burglarize, clean out

aptīrīties *vr* clean oneself

aptīrītāj/s *nm*, **~a** *nf* janitor

aptīstīt *vt* wrap around

aptīstīties *vr* wrap oneself

aptīt *vt* wrap; twine around, twist around; **a. ap pirkstu** wrap around one's little finger

aptīties *vr* wrap, twine, or twist around

aptītlīgs *adj* (sl.) appetizing, tasty

aptraipīt *vt* spot, stain, (fig.) soil; **a. rokas** (fig.) stain one's hands

aptraipīties *vr* get dirty; **a. ar asinīm** have blood on one's hands

aptraukt *vt* knock down (fruit, leaves)

aptrenkt *vt* drive s.o. around sth.

aptriekt *vt* drive s.o. around sth.

aptriekties *vr* have a long chat

aptriept *vt* smear, besmear; grease, tar, paint; (of butter, honey) spread

aptriepties *vr* besmear oneself

aptrīt *vt* grind all around

aptrūdēt *vi* begin to rot

aptrūkt *vi* **1.** run out of, be short of; **2.** (of a conversation) stop

aptrūkties *vr* **1.** run out of, be short of; **2.** (of a conversation) stop

aptrulis *adj* dull, dulled

aptrult *vi* become dull

aptrunēt *vi* **1.** rot all around; **2.** rot a little

aptrupēt *vi* **1.** rot all around; **2.** rot a little

aptrupt *vi* = **aptrupēt**

aptrust *vi* (of hair, wool) break

aptūcis *adj, part* of **aptūkt** fat

aptūkt *vi* grow fat; swell somewhat

aptūkums *nm* swelling

aptumsa *nf* dusk

aptumst *vi* **1.** grow dark; **2.** (of mind) be disturbed

aptumsums *nm* **1.** eclipse; **2.** mental disturbance

aptumšojums *nm* (mil.) blackout; (mental) disturbance

aptumšošana *nf* (mil.) blackout

aptumšošanās *nfr* eclipse

aptumšot *vt* darken, obscure, cloud; (mil.) black out

aptumšoties *vr* **1.** grow dark; become overcast; **2.** eclipse; **3.** (of mind) become disturbed

aptuntulēt *vt* (col.) wrap

aptuntuļot *vt* (col.) wrap

aptuntuļoties *vr* bundle up

aptupties *vr* hunker down

aptura *nf* stopping

apture *nf* barricade, checkpoint

apturēšana *nf* stopping; suspension; (jur.) postponement (of trial); (jur.) reprieve, respite, stay (of execution)

apturēt *vt* stop; suspend; (jur.) postpone, reprieve, stay; (of an attack) check, stall; **a. asiņošanu** stanch

apturvārsts *nm* shutoff valve

aptuveni *adv* approximately

aptuvenība *nf* approximation

aptuvens *adj* approximate

aptuvenums *nm* imprecision

aptuviene *nf* environs

aptuvis *adv* approximately

aptuvu *adv* approximately

aptuvumis *adv* approximately

aptvars *nm* **1.** contour; outline; **2.** volume

aptvarste *nf* (police) bust

aptveramība *nf* conceivability

aptvere *nf* **1.** clamp; (tech.) stirrup; **2.** cartridge clip, magazine clip

aptvērējlīkne *nf* (tech.) envelope

aptvēriens *nm* grasp, grip; (dance) hold

aptveršana *nf* **1.** comprehension; **2.** (mil.) flanking attack

aptvert *vt* **1.** grasp, grip; clasp, embrace; envelop; (mil.) flank; **2.** involve, include; **3.** encompass; **4.** grasp, comprehend, conceive

apūdeņojums *nm* **1.** irrigation; **2.** irrigation water

apūdeņošana *nf* irrigation

apūdeņot *vt* irrigate

apuguņot *vt* illuminate

apustulis *nm* apostle

apustulisks *adj* apostolic

apustuļu biedrība *nf* company of Apostles

Apustuļu darbi *nm pl* The Acts

apustuļu ticības apliecība *nf* Apostles' Creed

apvada *nf* border of ornamental design

apvadāt *vt* lead around; **kā ap kāsi ~s** a frequent guest

apvadāties *vr* (of female animals) settle

apvadceļš *nm* detour

apvade *nf* = **apvada**

apvadvārsts *nm* bypass valve

apvagot *vt* furrow

apvaicāties *vr* inquire; ask around

apvainojums *nm* **1.** insult; **2.** accusation; **3.** offense

apvainošana *nf* **1.** insult; **2.** accusation

apvainošanas akts *nm* indictment

apvainot *vt* **1.** insult; **2.** accuse; **3.** offend

apvainot/ais *nom adj*, **~ā** *f* defendant

apvainotāj/s *nm*, **~a** *nf* accuser; plaintiff

apvainotība *nf* offense

apvainoties *vr* take offense

apvaiņagot *vt* put a wreath on; (fig.) crown

apvaislot *vt* inseminate

apvaisloties *vr* become inseminated

apvākas *nf pl* harvest home (feast)

apvākojums *nm* covers; dust jacket

apvākot *vt* (of books) jacket; attach a lid

apvāks *nm* dust jacket; cover; wrapper

apvākt *vt* harvest

apvalda *nf* control; self-control

apvalds *nm* = **apvalda**

apvaldīgi *adv* with self-control

apvaldīgs *adj* self-controlled, restrained

apvaldīt *vt* control; suppress; keep in

apvaldīties *vr* control oneself

apvālis *nm* (reg.) thick windrow of drying hay

apvalkāt *vt* wear

apvalkāties *vr* become worn

apvalkāts *adj, part* of apvalkāt worn, threadbare, shabby

apvalkcaurule *nf* casing

apvalkdūmenis *nm* fireplace chimney

apvalkošana *nf* (tech.) jacketing

apvalks *nm* 1. cover; 2. casing, jacket, shell; hull; 3. (bot.) pericarp; 4. (fig.) envelope

apvalstīt *vt* roll in sth.

apvāļāt *vt* drag through dirt

apvaļņot *vt* wall in

apvandīt *vt* ransack

apvārdot *vt* 1. cast a (healing) spell, charm away; 2. talk s.o. into doing sth., persuade; a. zobus fool with fine words, put one over

apvārdoties *vr* ļaut a. allow oneself to be sweet-talked

apvārīt *vt* boil briefly

apvārīties *vr* be slightly boiled; turn color (through boiling)

apvārsmot *vt* write poems about

apvārsnis *nm* horizon

apvārstīt *vt* stitch on; stitch around; (of a string, lace) run through (holes) and around

apvārtīt *vt* 1. soil; ~s shopworn; 2. dip, roll in sth.

apvārtīties *vr* get dirty (by rolling in sth.)

apvarzāt *vt* 1. entangle; 2. slubber over

apvaskot *vt* wax

apvazāt *vt* (col.) bedraggle

apvazāties *vr* become bedraggled

apvāznis *nm* visor

apvāzt *vt* 1. cover, put a lid on; 2. turn upside down; 3. gird; hoop

apvedceļš *nm* 1. beltway; 2. bypass

apvēdināt *vt* 1. air; fan; 2. waft around

apvēdināties *vr* fan oneself

apvēdīt *vt* 1. air; fan; 2. waft around

apveids *nm* contour; configuration

apvējot *vt* (of gentle breezes) caress

apveldzēt *vt* moisten

apvēlies *adj, part* of apvelties corpulent

apvelt *vt* 1. roll around sth.; 2. turn over

apvelties *vr* 1. roll around; 2. turn over; 3. (col.) put on weight

apveltīt *vt* 1. give gifts; 2. endow; 3. regale

apvemt *vt* bevomit

apvemties *vr* 1. vomit; 2. begin to vomit

apventēt *vt* (col.) throw to the ground

apvēris *nm* area, region

apvērot *vt* view; inspect; look at

apvērpt *vt* spin (much or all)

apvērpties *vr* 1. twist around sth.; 2. spin (all that is required)

apvērse *nf* turning around, reversa

apvērses termometrs *nm* tipping thermometer

apvērsiens *nm* reversal

apvērst *vt* turn over; turn inside out; invert

apvērsties *vr* turn around; turn over

apvērsums *nm* 1. revolution; coup (mil.) subversion; 2. (mus.) inversion

apvēršana *nf* reversal; ~s ierīce reversing device

apvērt *vt* run a string or lace around (the edge of a purse, bag, bast shoe)

apvērtēt *vt* evaluate

apvērties *vr* look around

apverzelēt *vt* (col.) wrap around

apverzelēties *vr* (col.) wrap oneself around

apvēsmot *vt* blow on gently

apvest *vt* lead, take around; a. ap stūri (col.) lead up the garden path

apvēstīt *vt* inform, notify

apvēziens *nm* (gymnastics) turn; lielais a. grand circle (on the horizontal bar)

apvēzt *vt* turn over

apvicināt *vt* wind by swinging

apvicot *vt* enclose with withes or wickers

apvidus *nm* **1.** terrain; **aizaudzis a.** close country; **mazšķēršļots a.** flat ground; **nepārredzams a.** dead space; **šķēršļots a.** broken country, rough terrain; **2.** region, locality

apvidus apmācība *nf* (mil.) field exercises

apvidus ātrums *nm* four-wheel drive

apvidus mašīna *nf* (mil.) tactical vehicle, all terrain vehicle

apvidus skrējiens *nm* cross-country race

apvidus vāģis *nm* four-wheel drive vehicle

apvidvārds *nm* (ling.) regionalism, localism

apviedēt *vt* (reg.) take a look around

apvienība *nf* union, society, confederation

apvienojums *nm* combination

apvienot *vt* unite; combine, pool; (of computer files) merge; (of large groups) mass

apvienoties *vr* unite; join; **atkal a.** reunite

apvija *nf* **1.** (bot.) hop; **2.** garland

apvīkstīt *vt* wrap; bandage

apvildzis *adj, part* of **apvilgt** damp

apvīlēt I *vt* file, file around, smooth with a file

apvīlēt II (with î) *vt* hem, edge

apvilgt *vi* become damp

apvilkt *vt* **1.** pull or drag around sth.; **2.** encircle (with a fence, wires); (of wire, rope) stretch all around; **3.** draw a line around, circle; **a. apli** draw a circle; **4.** cover with fabric, upholster; **5.** (col.) put on (clothes, footwear)

apvilkties *vr* **1.** (col., of clothes, footwear) put on **2.** enclose, cover

apvilkums *nm* **1.** covering; **2.** drawn line

apviļāt *vt* roll (in flour, sand, mud)

apviļāties *vr* get dirty, get muddy (by rolling in dirt, mud)

apviņķelēt *vt* (col.) wrap around

apvirde *nf* boil, abscess

apvirināt *vt* parboil

apvirpot *vt* turn on a lathe

apvirt *vt* parboil

apvirzīt *vt* guide around

apvirzīties *vr* be guided around

apvīst *vi* wilt

apvīstīt *vt* wrap up

apvīstīties *vr* bundle up

apvīt *vt* wind around, twine around, wrap around; **a. ar lauriem** crown with laurels

apvīties *vr* wind around, twine around

apvītināt *vt* wilt

apvizēt *v* **1.** *vt* cast a shimmering light on sth.; **2.** *vi* glaze over (with ice)

apvizmot *vt* = **apvizēt**

apvizuļot *vt* = **apvizēt**

apzadzēj/s *nm*, ~a *nf* robber

apzagt *vt* rob

apzagties *vr* (col.) commit a robbery

apzāģēt *vt* saw off; cut (by sawing) all (or many)

apzaimot *vt* slander, defame

apzaļot *vi* green, leaf out

apzāļot *v* **1.** *vi* overgrow with grass; **2.** *vt* bewitch (using herbs)

apzaļumot *vt* plant greenery

apzarnis *nm* mesentery

apzavēt *vt* bewitch, cast a spell on

apzelēt *vt* suck and chew on, mouth

apzelt *vi* overgrow with grass

apzeltījums *nm* gilding

apzeltīt *vt* gild, gold-plate

apzibēt *vi* be dazzled

apzibināt *vt* dazzle

apziedēt *vi* mold

apziednis *nm* perianth

apziedot *vt* (folk.) shower with gifts

apziepējams *adj* saponifiable

apziepēšana *nf* **1.** soaping; **2.** saponification

apziepēt *vt* **1.** soap; **2.** saponify

apziest *vt* (of butter, grease, ointment) spread, apply

apziesties *vr* apply (an ointment) to one's skin; besmear oneself apzilēt *vi* turn blue

apzilt *vi* turn blue

apzīmējums *nm* 1. designation, name; 2. label; insignia; **pieņemtais a.** legend (symbols); 3. notation; (compu.) representation

apzīmēt *vt* 1. draw around; 2. draw all over, cov-er with drawings; 3. mark, label; call; 4. stand for, symbolize

apzīmētāja palīgteikums *nm* adjective clause

apzīmētājs *nm* (gram.) qualifier; (philos.) designator

apzīmogot *vt* stamp; seal and stamp; brand

apzināšanās *nfr* consciousness; realization

apzināt *vt* study; study and record, collect and study

apzināti *adv* deliberately, intentionally; consciously

apzināties *vr* realize, be aware, know

apzināts *adj* deliberate, intentional; conscious

apzinība *nf* conscientiousness

apzinīgi *adv* conscientiously

apzinīgs *adj* conscientious

apzinīgums *nm* conscientiousness

apziņa *nf* 1. consciousness; **primārā a.** the preconscious; ~s **stāvoklis** state of consciousness; 2. sense

apziņot *vt* notify, inform (all concerned)

apzobis *nm* weaving defect (caused by the omission of a thread)

apzvanīt *vt* 1. call around (on the telephone); 2. toll the passing bell

apzveja *nf* fishing

apzvejot *vt* fish (all, a large area)

apzvelt *vt* turn over

apzvelties *vr* tip

apzvērēt *vt* swear under oath

apžāklis(ki) *adv* (col.) astride

apžaut *vt* hang out laundry all over sth.

apžāvēt *vt* dry (partly, superficially); (of food products) cure, smoke, dry

apžāvēts *adj, part* of **apēāvēt** (of fish) bloated; partly cured, smoked, or dried

apžāvēties *vr* dry oneself (superficially, quickly)

apžeibt *vi* become dizzy

apžēlošana *nf* amnesty; clemency

apžēlot *vt* grant amnesty; (mil.) give quarter

apžēlotāj/s *nm,* ~a *nf* the merciful one

apžēlo/ties *vr* take pity, have mercy on; ~jies! mercy me! good heavens!

apžilbināšana *nf* dazzling; (mil.) flash blindness

apžilbināt *vt* dazzle

apžilbinošs *adj* dazzling

apžilbt *vi* be dazzled

apžmaugt *vt* tighten

apžmaugties *vr* cling to

apžņaugt *vt* 1. wring the necks of (many, all), strangle; 2. squeeze, hug tightly

apžņaugties *vr* encircle, embrace; coil oneself around

apžogojums *nm* fencing

apžogot *vt* fence in, enclose

apžūt *vi* dry partly

ar *prep* 1. with; (of painting, drawing) in (**zīmēt ar tušu** draw in ink); 2. what with; 3. (mus., with **pavadīt**) on

ar *partic* (col.) also

ara *nf* (zool.) Ara

āra *nf* (obs.) fields and meadows; outside

ārā *adv* 1. out; **ā. metams** useless; 2. outside; outdoors

arabāns *nm* araban

āra bērzs *nm* 1. white birch; 2. wart birch

arabes *nf pl* rock cress

arabeska *nf* arabesque

Arabijas akācija *nf* gum arabic tree

arabinoze *nf* arabinose

ar[a]biski [ā] *adv* in Arabic

ar[a]bisk/s [ā] *adj* Arabic, Arabian

ar[a]bisms [ā] *nm* Arabism

ar[a]bistika [ā] *nf* Arab studies

ar[a]bist/s [ā] *nm,* ~e *nf* Arabist

arabitols *nm* arabitol

arabonskābe *nf* arabonic acid

ar|a|b/s [ā] *nm*, ~iete *nf* Arab

ar|a|bu [ā] gumija *nf* gum Arabic

ara|ch|idonskābe [h] *nf* arachidonic acid

ara|ch|īnskābe [h] *nf* arachidic acid

ara|ch|iss [h] *nm* arachis

ara|ch|nofobija [h] *nf* arachnophobia

ara|ch|noloģija [h] *nf* arachnology

aragonīts *nm* aragonite

arah- See **arach-**

araiometrs *nm* = **areometrs**

arājiņš *nm dim* of **arājs**, plowman; (folk.) bridegroom, husband

arājs *nm* plowman; (poet.) husbandman, peasant

araks *nm* arrack

arālija *nf* (bot.) aralia

a|r|amderīgums [ŗ] *nm* arability

aramiet/is *nm*, ~e *nf* Aramaean

a|r|amkārta [ŗ] *nf* topsoil

a|[r|ams [ŗ] *adj, part* of **art** arable

a|[r|amzeme [ŗ] *nf* arable land, cropland, farmland

aranžējums *nm* (mus.) arrangement

aranžēt *vt* (mus.) arrange

ārapšuve *nf* (naut.) shell

aras *nf pl* (hist.) plowable land, property of the lord of the manor under the corvée system

ārāsviedējs *nm* bouncer

araubruņrupucis *nm* arrau

araukārija *nf* araucaria; Norfolk Island pine

āravietis *nm* (hist.) a peasant living on **aras**

arba *nf* (carriage) araba

arbaleta *nf* or **arbalets** *nm* arbalest

arbitrāža *nf* arbitration

arbitrs *nm*, ~e *nf* arbitrator; (sports) referee; umpire

arborētums *nm* arboretum

arboricīds *nm* herbicide

ārborta *indecl adj* outboard

arbovīruss *nm* arbovirus

arb|u|zs [ū] *nm* watermelon

arceitobija *nf* mistletoe

ārceļš *nm* side road between fields

ar|ch|aika [h] *nf* (of Greek art) Archaic period

archaio- See **archeo-**

ar|ch|aiski [h] *adv* archaically

ar|ch|aisks [h] *adj* archaic

ar|ch|aisms [h] *nm* archaism

ar|ch|aizēt [h] *vt* archaize

ar|ch|ajs [h] *nm* Archean (age)

ar|ch|egonijs [h] *nm* archegonium

ar|ch|eogr|a|fija [h][ā] *nf* paleography

ar|ch|eogr|a|f/s [h][ā] *nm*, ~e *nf* paleographer

ar|ch|eolo/gs [h] *nm*, ~ģe *nf* archeologist

ar|ch|eoloģija [h] *nf* archeology

ar|ch|eoloģisks [h] *adj* archeological

ar|ch|eopteriks [h] *nm* archeopteryx

ar|ch|etipisks [h] *adj* archetypal

ar|ch|etips [h] *nm* archetype

ar|ch|ibīskapija [h] *nf* archbishopric

ar|ch|ibīskaps [h] *nm* archbishop

ar|ch|idiakons [h] *nm* archdeacon

ar|ch|idiecēze [h] *nf* archdiocese

ar|ch|ierejs [h] *nm* (Greek Orthodox) bishop

ar|ch|iloģija [h] *nf* archelogy

ar|ch|imandr|i|ts [h][ī] *nm* archimandrite

Ar|ch|imeda [h] skrūve *nf* Archimedes' screw

ar|ch|ipelags [h] *nm* archipelago

ar|ch|itektonika [h] *nf* architectonics

ar|ch|itektoniski [h] *adv* architectonically

ar|ch|itektonisks [h] *adj* architectonic

ar|ch|itekt/s [h] *nm*, ~e *nf* architect

ar|ch|itektūra [h] *nf* architecture

ar|ch|itravs [h] *nm* architrave

ar|chī|vālijas [hi] *nf pl* files

ar|chī|vāls [hi] *adj* archival

ar|ch|īvār/s [h] *nm*, ~e *nf* archivist

ar|ch|īvēt [h] *vt* file

ar|ch|īvolts [h] *nm* archivolt

ar|ch|īvs [h] *nm* archives; files

ar|ch|īvu [h] skapis *nm* filing cabinet

ar|ch|onts [h] *nm* archon

ārcilvēks *nm* stranger, outsider

ārcūka *nf* pig, hog (kept outdoors)

ārdavs *adj* fluent

ārdeklis *nm* two-pronged pitchfork; **(iet) kā ā.** (it moves) upsetting everything in its way

ardenis *nm* (horse) Ardennes

ārdēt *vt* harden, temper

ārdēties *vr* be hardened, be tempered

ārdi *nm pl* **1.** grate; **2.** poles for drying crops or clothes

ardievas *nf pl* parting words, farewells, good-bye

ardievoties *vr* say goodbye, bid farewell

ardievu *interj* goodbye

ārdīklis *nm* hay tedder

ārdināt *vt* harden, temper

ārdīt *vt* **1.** (of seams) rip, (of knitting) unravel; **2.** (of hay) ted, (of manure) spread out; **3.** tear down, demolish; **4.** destroy

ārdītājiedarbība *nf* high explosive effect

ārdītāj/s *nm*, **~a** *nf* **1.** ripper; demolisher, destroyer; **2.** tedder

ārdīties *vr* **1.** unravel; **2.** storm, rage, brawl, (of children) romp

ārdonis *nm* **1.** braggart; **2.** powerful worker

ārdošs *adj, part* of **ārdīt** destructive

ārdstienis *nm* grate bar, fire bar

ārdurvis *nf pl* outside door

āre *nf*, usu. *pl* **āres** (poet.) fields; open, tilled fields

āre *interj* (col.) look, see

areāllingvistika *nf* areal linguistics

areāls *nm* surface area, acreage, area

āreāe *interj* (col.) look, see

areiopags *nm* areopagus

ārēji *adv* on the outside, externally

ārējs *nm* plower

ārējs *adj* outer, outward, outside, external, exterior; surface, superficial; foreign

areka *nf* areca

arēna *nf* arena

ārenieks *nm* stranger, outsider

arenīts *nm* arenite

areometrs *nm* hydrometer

arestants *nm*, **~e** *nf* prisoner

arestantu rota *nf* convict labor gang

arestēt *vt* arrest

arestētais *nom adj*, **~ā** *f* detainee

arest/s *nm* arrest; (jur.) attachment, seizure; **~ā** under arrest

aresttelpa *nf* detention room

arfa *nf* harp

arfist/s *nm*, **~e** *nf* harpist

ārgalība *nf* foolishness, silliness

ārgalīgs *adj* foolish, silly

ārgalis *nm* fool

ārgaloties *vr* cut up, clown

argals *nm* argali

ārgals *nm* outer end

argānija *nf* argan tree

argemone *nf* argemone

argentāns *nm* nickel silver

argilīts *nm* argillite

arginīns *nm* arginine

argo *nm* argot

argonauts *nm* Argonaut

argons *nm* argon

argotisms *nm* argot word

argumentācija *nf* argumentation

argumentēt *vi* argue

arguments *nm* argument

arģentīniet/is *nm*, **~e** *nf* Argentinian

arh- See **arch-**

arī *partic* also, as well, too, likewise; (with a negation) either, neither

ariānisms *nm* Arianism

arīds *adj* arid

arīdzan *partic* (obs.) also

āriene *nf* exterior, outside, (of a person) appearance

ārietis *nm*, **~e** *nf* Aryan

arieta *nf* arietta

arīg *partic* (obs.) also

ārīgi *adv* externally, outwardly

ārīgs *adj* external, outward

ārija *nf* aria

ariozo *indecl nm* arioso

āriski I *adv* well; beautifully

āriski II *adv* the Aryan way

ārisks I *adj* (folk.) good; beautiful; cultivated

ārisks II *adj* Aryan

aristidas *nf pl* Aristida

aristoġen|e|ze [ē] *nf* aristogenesis

aristokr|a|tija [ā] *nf* aristocracy

aristokr|a|tiski [ā] *adv* aristocratically

aristokr|a|tisks [ā] *adj* aristocratic

aristokr|a|tisms [ā] *nm* aristocratism

aristokr|a|ts [ā] *nm*, ~e *nf* aristocrat

aristolo[ch]ija [h] *nf* birthwor

ārišķība *nf* affectation, pretense

ārišķīgi *adv* ostentatiously

ārišķīgs *adj* ostentatious, affected, pretentious

ārišķīgums *nm* affectation, pretentiousness

aritmētika *nf* arithmetic

aritmētiķis *nm* arithmetician

aritmētiski *adv* arithmetically

aritmētisks *adj* arithmetic, arithmetical

aritmija *nf* arrhythmia

aritmiski *adv* arrhythmically

aritmisks *adj* arrhythmic

aritmiskums *nm* arrhythmia

aritmometrs *nm* arithmometer

arjegard/s *nm* rear guard; ~a kauja rearguard action

arka *nf* arc, arch

ārkabata *nf* outside pocket

arkāde *nf* arcade

arkāns *nm* lariat

arkāns *adj* arcane

ārkārtas *indecl adj* = ārkārtējs

ārkārtēji *adv* preferentially, specially

ārkārtējs *adj* extraordinary, extra, of emergency; (of a professorship) assistant

ārkārtība *nf* the unusual, the extraordinary

ārkārtīgi *adv* 1. extremely, immensely, supremely; 2. exceptionally

ārkārtīgs *adj* 1. very unusual, special, exceptional; emergency; 2. extreme; very great, enormous

arkebuza *nf* harquebus

arkkosekanss *nm* arc cosecant

arkkosinu|s| [ss] *nm* arc cosine

arkkotangenss *nm* arc cotangent

arkla tiesa *nf* (hist.) corvées reelles exacted from a one-arkls farmer

arkla tiesnesis *nm* (hist.) magistrate in charge of fugitive peasant cases

arkla vīrs *nm* (hist.) farmer of a one-arkls farm

arklinieks *nm* (hist.) owner of one arkls of land

arkls *nm* 1. plow; **abpusvērsējs a.** lister; **piekabināmais a.** trailer plow; **rušināmais a.** ridge plow, lister; 2. (hist.) unit of land value

arkoze *nf* arkose

arkozīts *nm* arkosite

arksekanss *nm* arc secant

arksinu|s| [ss] *nm* arc sine

arktangenss *nm* arc tangent

arktika *nf* arctic regions

arktisks *adj* arctic

arktotes *nf pl* Arctotis

arkveida *indecl adj* arch-shaped

arkveidīgi *adv* like an arch

arkveidīgs *adj* arch-shaped

arlabudien *interj* goodbye

arlabunakti *interj* good night

arlaburītu *interj* goodbye

arlabvakar *interj* good night

ārlaidars *nm* corral (unattached to a building)

ārlaulība *nf* cohabitation; ~s *gen* a. illegitimate; b. extramarital

arlekīns *nm* Harlequin

ārleņķis *nm* external angle

ārlietas *nf pl* foreign affairs

ārlietu ministrija *nf* Ministry of Foreign Affairs; (British) Foreign Office; (USA) State Department

ārlietu ministrs *nm* Minister of Foreign Affairs; (British) Foreign Secretary; (USA) Secretary of State

ārlīnijas *indecl adj* (compu.) off-line

ārlogs *nm* outer window frame of a double window

ārļaudis *nm pl* outsiders, strangers

armāda *nf* armada

armadils *nm* armadillo

armadors *nm* ship owner

ārmala *nf* outer edge; outside, exterior

armanjaks *nm* armagnac

ārmaņ/a *nf* (reg.) madness; **kā ~ā** crazy

armators *nm* ship owner

armatūra *nf* (el.) armature; fittings; (concrete) reinforcement

armatūras dēlis *nm* switchboard, instrument board

arm|e|n/is [ē] *nm*, **~iete** *nf* Armenian

armērija *nf* (bot.) thrift

armēt *vt* (tech.) reinforce

armija *nf* armed forces; **aktīvā a.** army in the field; **regulārā a.** standing army; **~s parauga** government-issue; **~s veikals** Army exchange

armijas mācītājs *nm* chaplain

armijas pavēle *nf* army field order

ārmisija *nf* (rel.) foreign mission

arnika *nf* arnica

ārnovadnie/ks *nm*, **~ce** *nf* a person from outside a region

ārnovads *nm* area outside a region

arnozere *nf* lamb succory

arodbiedrība *nf* trade union

arodgrupa *nf* trade club

arodizglītība *nf* vocational education

arodizvēle *nf* vocational choice

arodkomiteja *nf* executive committee of a trade union

arodkustība *nf* labor movement

arodmirstība *nf* professional mortality

arodnieciski *adv* professionally

arodniecisks *adj* professional

arodnie/ks *nm*, **~ce** nf 1. professional; 2. union member

arodorganizācija *nf* trade union local

arodprakse *nf* practice of a trade

arod/s I *nm* trade; occupation, profession; **pēc ~a** by trade

arods II *nm* (obs.) storage bin

arodskola *nf* trade school

arodskolēns *nm* trade school student

arodskolnie/ks *nm*, **~ce** *nf* trade school student

arodslimība *nf* occupational disease

arogance *nf* = **arrogance**

arogants *adj* = **arrogants**

aroma *nf* aroma

arom|a|tiski [ā] *adv* aromatically

arom|a|tisks [ā] *adj* aromatic

arom|a|tiskums [ā] *nm* aromaticity

aromatizators *nm* aromatic substance

aromatizēt *vt* aromatize

aromatizēties *vr* acquire an aroma

arom|a|ts [ā] *nm* aroma

aromorfoze *nf* aromorphosis

aromviela *nf* aromatic substance

Årona nūja *nf* arum

aronija *nf* chokeberry

ārosta *nf* outport

arpa *nf* harp

ārpagastniek/s *nm*, **~ce** *nf* a person from outside a township

ārpagasts *nm* area outside a township

ārpasaule *nf* outside world

arpents *nm* arpent

ārpilsēta *nf* suburb

ārpilsonis *nm* non-citizen

arpist/s *nm*, **~e** *nf* harpist

ārpol|i|tika [ī] *nf* foreign policy
ārpol|i|tiski [ī] *adv* in one's foreign policy
ārpol|i|tisks [ī] *adj* foreign-policy
ārpol|i|tiķis [ī] *nm* foreign policy expert
ārprātība *nf* insanity, madness
ārprātīg/ais *nom adj*, ~ā *f* lunatic, madman
ārprātīgi *adv* insanely
ārprātīgs *adj* insane
ārprātīgo nams *nm* insane asylum
ārprātīgums *nm* insanity, madness
ārprāt/s *nm* insanity, madness; **trakojošs ā.**
    raving madness; **līdz ~am** to the point of
    madeness
ārpus *prep* outside, out of; beyond; over and
    above; (of eating) out; **ā. mājas** out of
    doors
ārpusdarba *indecl adj* (of one's job or pro-
    fession) extracurricular; (of non-working
    hours) off
ārpusdienesta *indecl adj* 1. unofficial; 2. ex-
    tracurricular
ārpusdzemdes *indecl adj* extrauterine
ārpus/e *nf* outside, exterior; ~ē outside,
    outdoors, out; **uz ~i** outward
ārpusēji *adv* from the outside, externally
ārpusējs *adj* outside, external
ārpusgalaktisks *adj* extragalactic
ārpusjuteklisks *adj* extrasensory
ārpuskārtas *indecl adj* extraordinary; super-
    numerary
ārpusklases *indecl adj* extracurricular
ārpusledāja *indecl adj* extraglacial
ārpusnie/ks *nm*, ~ce *nf* outsider
ārpusplāna *indecl adj* outside the plan, over
    and above the plan
ārpusreglamenta attiecības *nf pl* (col.) bul-
    lying; hazing
ārpussituatīvs *adj* extrasituational
ārpusskolas *indecl adj* nonschool
ārpusstundu *indecl adj* extracurricular
ārpusštata *indecl adj* non-staff
ārpustiesas *indecl adj* extrajudicial

ārpuszemes *indecl adj* extraterrestrial
arpveida *indecl adj* harp-shaped
ārrīdznieks *nm* non-Rigan
ārrindas *indecl adj* noncombatant
ārrindas dienests *nm* (mil.) desk job; inactive
    duty
ārrindnieks *nm* noncombatant soldier
arrogance *nf* arrogance
arroganti *adv* arrogantly
arrogants *adj* arrogant
ars *nm* (area unit) are
ār/s *nm* 1. outdoors; 2. outside; **uz ~u** outward,
    out; 3. fields and meadows
arse *nf* arsis
ārsēja *nf* a field planted out of the rotational
    order
arsenāls *nm* 1. arsenal; 2. armory
arsenāts *nm* arsenate
arsēna ūdeņradis *nm* arsine
arsēna ziedi *nm pl* arsenic bloom
arsen|i|ds [ī] *nm* arsenide
arsēniks *nm* arsenic trioxide
arsenīts *nm* arsenite
arsēnniķeļspīde *nf* gersdorffite
arsēnpaskābe *nf* arsenious acid
arsēnpirīts *nm* arsenopyrite
arsēns *nm* arsenic
ārsiena *nf* exterior wall
arsīns *nm* arsine
arsīnskābe *nf* arsinic acid
ārskats *nm* exterior view, (film) exterior shot
ārsta palīdzība *nf* medical assistance; **ātrā
    ā. p.** emergency medical assistance
ārstēšana *nf* medical treatment
ārstēšanās *nfr* medical treatment (received);
    ā. izdevumi medical expenses
ārstēt *vt* treat (medically)
ārstēties *vr* undergo medical treatment; **es
    ārstējos pie Dr. N.** I am under Dr. X's care;
    ā. ar dū-ņām take a mud cure; **ā. ar mājas
    līdzekļiem** use home remedies
ārstniecība *nf* medicine, medical arts

ārstniecības augs *nm* medicinal herb

ārstniecības iestāde *nf* hospital, clinic

ārstniecības līdzekļi *nm pl* medicines

ārstniecības mugurene *nf* angular Solomon's seal

ārstniecisks *adj* medicinal

ārsts *nm* physician, doctor; **~e** *nf*; **praktizējošs ā.** general practitioner

aršana *nf* plowing

aršīna *nf* arshin (Russian unit of length)

ārštata *indecl adj* not on the regular staff; freelance

ārštatnie/ks *nm*, **~ce** worker not on the manning table; freelancer

art *vt* plow

ārtausts *nm* outside caliper

artava *nf* 1. (hist.) heller (a small copper coin); 2. (Bibl.) mite

ārtava *nf* = **artava**

ārtecis *nm* domestic animal that is kept outdoors

artefakts *nm* artifact

artelis *nm* artel, cooperative craft society

ārtelpu *indecl adj* outdoor

art|e|riāls [ē] *adj* arterial

artērija *nf* artery

artēriju apkaļķošanās *nfr* atherosclerosis

art|e|riola [ē] *nf* arteriole

art|e|rioskleroze [ē] *nf* arteriosclerosis

art|e|rīts [ē] *nm* arteritis

artēzisks *adj* artesian

artikulācija *nf* articulation

artikulēt *vt* articulate

artikulēti *adv* articulately

artikulēts *adj, part* of **artikulēt** articulated, articulate

artikuls *nm* (gram., bus.) article

artiķelis *nm* article (a written piece)

artil|e|rija [ē] *nf* artillery; **~s apšaude** cannonade; **~s uguns** shellfire

artil|e|rists [ē] *nm* artillerist

artistiski *adv* artistically

artistisks *adj* artistic

artistiskums *nm* artistry

artist/s *nm*, **~e** *nf* artist, artiste

artišoks *nm* artichoke

artralģija *nf* arthralgia

artrīts *nm* arthritis

artroks *nm* art rock

artroplastika *nf* arthroplasty

artropods *nm* arthropod

artroze *nf* dystrophic arthritis

ārturziņa *nf* outer case

arumains *adj* furrowed

āruma ūdeņi *nm pl* runoff water (from the fields)

arum/s *nm* area plowed; work done in plowing; **~i** plowed field

arumsloksne *nf* upturned furrow slice

arumu sīkausīte *nf* field vole

arundinarijas *nf pl* Arundinaria

ārup *adv* outward

āru vārdi *nm pl* place names (for places that are not settlements)

ārvalstnie/ks *nm*, **~ce** *nf* (jur.) alien

ārvalsts *nf* foreign country

ārvidē *adv* outside

arvien(u) *adv* 1. always; **vēl a.** still; **kā a.** as usual; 2. increasingly; **a. labāk** better and better

ārzem/es *nf pl* foreign countries; **~ēs** abroad; **uz ~ēm** (going) abroad; **~ju** foreign; international; (of a passport) external, travel

ārzemnieciski *adv* like a foreigner

ārzemniecisks *adj* foreign

ārzemnieks *nm*, **~ce** *nf* foreigner

ārzemnieku leģions *nm* Foreign Legion

ārzemnieku likumi *nm pl* alien laws

ārzemnieciskums *nm* foreignness

ārzona *nf* outer zone; **~s** offshore

aṛ- See **ar-**

asaciņa *nf dim* of **asaka**, small fishbone

asā dzelzszāle *nf* Goodenough's sedge

asā egle *nf* blue spruce

asafetida *nf* asafetida (plant)

asais dadzis *nm* bull thistle

asais dievkrēsliņš *nm* leafy spurge

asais grīslis *nm* acute carex

asaka *nf* fishbone ◊ ļauna a. (fig.) shrew

asakainība *nf* (of fish) boniness

asakains *adj* (of fish) bony

asakainums *nm* (of fish) boniness

asambleja *nf* assembly; international conference

asambleris *nm* (compu.) assembler

asamblervaloda *nf* (compu.) assembly language

asā pulkstenīte *nf* a bellflower, Campanula cervicaria

asara *nf* tear

asarainība *nf* teariness

asaraini *adv* with tears in one's eyes, tearfully

asarains *adj* tearful

asarainums *nm* teariness

asariņa *nf* 1. *dim* of asara; 2. ~s bird's-eye primrose

asaris *nm* (zool.) perch

asarītis *nm dim* of asaris, little perch

asarot *vi* (of eyes) water, run

asarots *adj* teary

asaru maisiņš *nm* lacrymal sack

asarveidīgs *adj* percoid

asā spireja *nf* (bot.) bridal wreath

asā tauksakne *nf* rough comfrey

asbests *nm* = azbests

ascendents *adj* ascendant

ascidija *nf* ascidian

ascīts *nm* ascites

aseismisks *adj* aseismic

asējums *nm* etching

aseksuāli *adv* asexually

aseksuāls *adj* asexual

asemblers *nm* (compu.) assembler

asenizācija *nf* sanitation, trash collection

aseniz[a]tors [ā] *nm* trash collector

aseptika *nf* asepsis

aseptiski *adv* aseptically

aseptisks *adj* aseptic

asertorisks *adj* assertoric

asesors *nm* (jur.) assessor, assistant judge

asēt *vt* etch

asfalta papīrs *nm* tar paper

asfaltbetons *nm* asphalt macadam

asfaltēns *nm* asphaltene

asfaltēt *vt* asphalt, pave with asphalt

asfalts *nm* asphalt

asfiksija *nf* asphyxia

asfodele *nf* asphodel

asfodeline *nf* (bot.) Jacob's rod

asgalīgs *adj* pointed

asgals *nm* point, peak, tip

asi *adv* sharply

asibilācija *nf* assibilation

asibilēt *vt* assibilate

asie jānīši *nm pl* fleabane

asignācija *nf* 1. assignation, assignment; 2. bank note

asignants *nm* assigner

asignāts *nm* asignee

asignējums *nm* assignment; allocation, allotment

asignēšana *nf* (of funds) allocation

asignēt *vt* assign, allocate, allot

asimetrija *nf* asymmetry

asimetriski *adv* asymmetrically

asimetrisks *adj* asymmetric

asimetriskums *nm* asymmetry

asimilāts *nm* assimilate

asimilācija *nf* assimilation

asimilēt *vt* assimilate

asimilēties *vr* become assimilated

asimptote *nf* asymptote

asinājums *nm* 1. sharpening; 2. sharpened edge

asināt *vt* sharpen; whet, strop

asināties *vr* grow sharper; get sharpened

asin[ch]ronisks [h] *adj* asynchronous

asin[ch]ronitāte [h] *nf* asynchrony

asin|ch|ronizēt [h] *vt* make asynchronous

asin|ch|ronmašīna [h] *nf* asynchronous machine

asin|ch|rons [h] *adj* asynchronous

asindetisks *adj* asyndetic

asindetons *nm* asyndeton

asindets *nm* asyndeton

asinerģija *nf* asynergy

asines *nf pl* Saint-John's-wort

asinīgs *adj* rich in blood

asins *nf*, usu. *pl* asinis blood ◊ **a. balss** blood is thicker than water

asinsaina *nf* blood picture

asinsanal|i|ze [ī] *nf* blood test

asinsapgāde *nf* blood supply

asinsatriebība *nf* blood vengeance

asinsbrālība *nf* blood brotherhood

asinsbrālis *nm* blood brother

asinscirkulācija *nf* blood circulation

asinsdarbs *nm* bloody deed

asins dēle *nf* medicinal leech

asinsdesa *nf* blood sausage

asinsdevēj/s *nm*, ~a *nf* blood donor

asinsdziras *nf pl* yarrow

asinsdzīres *nf pl* bloodbath

asinsdzīsla *nf* vein

asinsgrēks *nm* incest

asins grimšana *nf* (col.) precipitin reaction

asinsgrupa *nf* blood group

asinzizliešana *nf* bloodshed

asinsizplūdums *nm* hemorrhage

asinskāre *nf* bloodthirstiness

asinskāri *adv* bloodthirstily

asinskārīgi *adv* bloodthirstily

asinskārīgs *adj* bloodthirsty

asinskārīgums *nm* bloodthirstiness

asinskārs *adj* bloodthirsty

asinskauja *nf* bloody battle

asinskāzas *nf pl* massacre

asinsķermenītis *nm* blood corpuscle

asinslapas *nf pl* oxeye daisy

asinslāse *nf* drop of blood

asinsloks *nm* blood circulation

asinsmilti *nm pl* blood meal

asinsnauda *nf* blood money

asins nolaišana *nf* bloodletting

asins noplūdums *nm* loss of blood

asins pārliešana *nf* blood transfusion

asinspieplūdums *nm* engorgement with blood, congestion, rush of blood

asinspiliens *nm* drop of blood

asinspirts *nf* bloodbath, massacre

asinsplatnīte *nf* blood platelet

asinsplazma *nf* blood plasma

asinsplūdi *nm pl* bloodbath

asinspuķe *nf* Saint-John's-wort

asinsrade *nf* production of blood

asinsradniecība *nf* blood relationship

asinsradnie/ks *nm*, ~ce *nf* kinsman, kin; ~ki blood kin

asinsradošs *adj* hematogenic

asinsriņķošana *nf* blood circulation

asinsrite *nf* blood circulation

asinssaindēšanās *nfr* blood poisoning

asinssāls *nf* See **dzeltenā a., sarkanā a.**

asinssarkans *adj* bloodred

asinssārtā ģerānija *nf* crimson cranesbill

asinssārtais grimons *nm* red dogwood

asinssērga *nf* (obs.) dysentery

asinssikspārnis *nm* vampire bat

asinsspalvas *nf pl* pinfeathers

asinsspiediens *nm* blood pressure; **paaugstināts a.** hypertension; **pazemināts a.** hypotension

asinsstindzinošs *adj* bloodcurdling

asinssūcēj/s *nm*, ~a *nf* bloodsucker

asinssuns *nm* 1. bloodhound; 2. (fig.) bloodsucker, extortioner; sponger

asins uts *nf* woolly apple aphid

asinsvads *nm* blood vessel

asinsvadu *indecl adj* vascular

asinszāle *nf* Saint-John's-wort

asinszāļu spireja *nf* a spirea, Spiraea hypericifolia

asinszīdēj/s *nm*, **~a** *nf* bloodsucker

asintiņas *nf pl dim* of asinis (asins)

asiņaini *adv* in a bloody fashion

asiņains *adj* bloody; blood-stained; blood-colored

asiņošana *nf* bleeding; **neredzamā a.** occult bleeding

asiņot *vi* bleed

asiņu ģerānija *nf* crimson cranesbill

as[i]riet/is [ī] *nm*, **~e** *nf* Assyrian

asistent/s *nm*, **~e** *nf* assistant

asistēt *vi* assist

asistolija *nf* asystole

asīt/e *nf dim* of ass I; **(paņemt) uz ~i** (sl.) (give) a ride (to a person standing on the rear axle of a bicycle)

askarels *nm* askarel

askarīda *nf* ascarid

askaridols *nm* ascaridole

askaridoze *nf* ascariasis

askētiski *adv* ascetically

askētisks *adj* ascetic

askētiskums *nm* asceticism

askētisms *nm* asceticism

askēt/s *nm*, **~e** *nf* ascetic

askēze *nf* ascesis, ascetism

asklepija *nf* common milkweed

askniebes *nf pl* cutters

askomicētes *nf pl* Ascomycetes

askorbīnskābe *nf* ascorbic acid

asku sēnes *nf pl* Ascomycetes

aslaiviņa *nf* oxytropis

aslapainā paparde *nf* shield fern

aslapes *nf pl* twig rush

aslapu flokši *nm pl* moss pink

aslapu grīslis *nm* lesser prickly sedge

asme *nf* (geog.) point

asmēl/is *nm*, **~e** *nf* sharp-tongued person

asmenītis *nm dim* of asmens, (safety razor) blade

asmens *nm* **1.** blade; knife; **2.** (of cutting tools) edge; **3.** (RR) tongue, point rail (of a switch)

asmeņkaplis *nm* pick, pickax

asmeņvīle *nf* taper file

asmīte *nf* (hist.) one-eighth of an **arkls** (arkls 2)

asmītnieks *nm* owner of an **asmīte**

asnains *adj* covered with shoots

asnainums *nm* excess of shoots

asnot *vi* sprout, shoot

asns *nm* sprout, shoot

asociācija *nf* association

asociāciju psīcholoģija *nf* associationism

asociāls *adj* asocial

asoci[a]tīvi [ā] *adv* associatively

asoci[a]tīvs [ā] *adj* associative

asociēt *vt* associate

asociēties *vr* associate

asonance *nf* assonance

asorti *indecl nm* mix

asortiments *nm* assortment

asparaginӣze *nf* asparaginase

asparagīns *nm* asparagine

asparagīnskābe *nf* aspartic acid

aspar[a]gs [ā] *nm* asparagus

aspekts *nm* aspect

aspermija *nf* aspermia

aspidistra *nf* aspidistra

aspiks *nm* aspic

aspirācija *nf* breathing in; (gram., med.) aspiration

aspirant/s *nm*, **~e** *nf* graduate student

aspirantūra *nf* graduate study

aspirāta *nf* aspirate

aspirātors *nm* aspirator

aspirēt *vt* aspirate

aspirēts *adj* aspirate

aspirīns *nm* aspirin

asprātība *nf* **1.** wit; **2.** witticism

asprātīgi *adv* wittily; cleverly

asprātīgs *adj* witty; clever

asprātīgums *nm* wittiness

asprāt/is *nm*, **~e** *nf* (person) wit

ass I *nf* **1.** axle; pivot; **2.** axis; **pirmās šķiras a.** (bot.) rachis, principal axis

ass II *nf* **1.** (archa., unit of length) fathom; **2.** (unit of measure for piled wood) ass, cord

ass III *nm* ace (outstanding performer)

ass *adj* **1.** sharp; keen, acute; **2.** clean-cut, sharply cut; **3.** pungent, biting; acrid; **4.** rough, prickly; **5.** hostile; (of a battle) pitched; (of a remark) cutting

assgals *nm* axle end

asskoks *nm* (archa.) cord (of wood)

asspurains *adj* sharp-finned

asšķautnains *adj* sharp-edged

astainais amarants *nm* love-lies-bleeding

astainie abinieki *nm pl* Caudata, caudates

astains *adj* tailed, caudate

astaksantīns *nm* astaxanthin

astatīns *nm* astatine

astatisks *adj* astatic

astats *nm* astatine

ast/e *nf* **1.** tail, train; (of a tailcoat) tails; **2.** (waiting) line ◊ **ar ~i** (of distance) just over; **a. piesieta** (of mothers of young children) tied down; **kā a. pakaļā** dodge s.o.'s footsteps

ast[e]nija [ē] *nf* asthenia

ast[e]niķ/is [ē] *nm*, **~e** *nf* asthenic

ast[e]nisks [ē] *adj* asthenic

astenopija *nf* asthenopia

astenosf[ai]ra [ē] *nf* asthenosphere

astere *nf* **1.** aster; **2.** China aster

asterisks *nm* asterisk

asteroīds *nm* asteroid

astes kaul/s *nm* tailbone; coccyx; **a. ~a** coccygeal

astes vagons *nm* caboose

astes zvaigzne *nf* (col.) comet

astgal/s *nm* **1.** tip of a tail; **2.** *pl* **~i** remnants, dregs

astigmatisks *adj* astigmatic

astigmatisms *nm* astigmatism

astigmats *nm* astigmatic lens

astilbe *nf* astilbe

astīte *nf dim* of **aste**, little tail; short line

astma *nf* asthma

astmatiķ/is *nm*, **~e** *nf* asthmatic

astmatisks *adj* asthmatic

astoņacis *nm* (of cards) the eight

astoņai[r]u [ŗ] *indecl adj* eight-oared

astoņdesmit *indecl adj* eighty

astoņdesmit/ais *adj* eightieth; **~ie gadi** the eighties

astoņdesmitgadīgais *nom adj*, **~ā** *f* octogenarian

astoņdesmitgadīgs *adj* eighty years old

astoņgadīgs *adj* eight years old, eight-year

astoņ/i *adj* **1.** *indecl, decl* eight; **2.** *decl* eight o'clock; **~os** at eight

astoņkājis *nm* octopus

astoņkārt *adv* eightfold

astoņkārtējs *adj* eightfold

astoņkārtīgs *adj* eightfold

astoņkrāsains *adj* of eight colors

astoņnieks *nm* (digit, card) the eight; group of eight

astoņpadsmit *indecl adj* eighteen

astoņpadsmitais *adj* eighteenth

astoņpadsmitgadīgs *adj* eighteen years old

astoņplaknis *nm* octahedron

astoņplāksnis *nm* octahedron

astoņreiz *adv* eight times

astoņsimt *indecl adj* eight hundred

astoņsimtais *adj* eight hundredth

astoņskaldnis *nm* octahedron

astoņstāvu *indecl adj* eight-story

astoņstundu *indecl adj* eight-hour

astoņstū[r]ains [ŗ] *adj* octogonal

astoņstūris *nm* octagon

astotais *adj* eighth

astotdaļa *nf* one eighth

astotdaļloksne *nf* octavo

astotdaļnots *nf* (mus.) eighth note

astotdaļpauze *nf* (mus.) eighth rest

astotkārt *adv* eight times

astotnieks *nm* the eight

astra *nf* aster

astragals *nm* astragal

astrains *adj* horsehair

astrāls *adj* astral

astrancija *nf* masterwort

astrobotanika *nf* astrobotany

astrodinamika *nf* astrodynamics

astrofizika *nf* astrophysics

astrofizikāli *adv* astrophysically

astrofizikāls *adj* astrophysical

astrofiziķ/is *nm*, ~e *nf* astrophysicist

astrofotogr|a|fija [ā] *nf* astrophotography

astrofotometrija *nf* astrophotometry

astrofotometrs *nm* astrophotometer

astrogr|a|fs [ā] *nm* astrograph

astrogr|a|fisks [ā] *adj* astrographic

astroģeoloģija *nf* space geology

astrokompass *nm* astrocompass

astrolabija *nf* astrolabe

astrolatrija *nf* astrolatry

astrolo/gs *nm*, ~ģe *nf* astrologer

astroloģija *nf* astrology

astroloģiski *adv* astrologically

astroloģisks *adj* astrological

astrometrija *nf* astrometry

astronautika *nf* astronautics

astronaut/s *nm*, ~e *nf* astronaut

astronavigācija *nf* astronavigation

astronomija *nf* astronomy

astronomiski *adv* astronomically

astronomisks *adj* astronomical

astronom/s *nm*, ~e *nf* astronomer

astrs *nm* horsehair

astru drāna *nf* haircloth

asum/s *nm* 1. sharpness; acuteness, keenness; pungency; 2. sharp point; prickle; 3. ~i acrimonious exchange, bitter quarrel, row

ašenes *nf pl* scouring rush

aši *nm pl* scouring rush

aši *adv* fast; promptly

ašķ/i *nm pl* 1. horsehairs; 2. scouring rush

ašs *adj* fast; prompt

ašums *nm* speed; promptness

atā *interj* (child.) bye-bye

atadīt *vt* unravel a knitting

atadīties *vr* knit to the point of weariness

ataicināt *vt* invite, call

ataijāt *vt* bring (while rocking or lulling)

ataina *nf* depiction

atainojums *nm* depiction

atainot *vt* depict

atainoties *vr* be depicted; (of memory images) appear

atairēt *vt, vi* row to

atairēties *vr* row to

ataksija *nf* ataxia

atāķēt *vt* unhook

atāķēties *vr* come unhooked

atāla puķe *nf* grass-of-Parnassus

ataleja *nf* Attalea

atālene *nf* grass-of-Parnassus

atalgojums *nm* remuneration, pay, salary; reward, recompense

atalgot *vt* reward; recompense; remunerate, pay

atalgoties *vr* pay off

atāls *nm* aftermath, second crop

atamans *nm* hetman

atara *nf* unplowed part of a field (because it is adjacent to a ditch or fence)

ataraksija *nf* ataraxy

atārdīt *vt* rip open

atārdīties *vr* unravel

atāre *nf* second-crop rye field

atašejs *nm* attaché

ataudi *nm pl* warp ends

ataudze *nf* = atauga

ataudzēt *vt* grow back

atauga *nf* 1. second growth forest; 2. shoot, sprout; 3. offspring

ataugsme *nf* renewal, recrudescence

ataugt *vi* grow back

atauklēties *vr* rock (a baby) to the point of weariness

ataukstēt *vt* cool

ataukstēties *vr* cool

ataulekšot *vi* come galloping

ataulot *vi* come galloping

ataurēt *vt* call together

ataurēties *vr* respond to a call

ataurot *vt* = **ataurēt**

atauroties *vr* = **ataurēties**

atausma *nf* dawn

ataus/t I *vi* dawn, (of daylight) break; **cerība a.** there is a gleam of hope; **a. atmiņā** flash on one's mind; **man gaisma ~a** it dawned on me

ataust II *vt* (weav.) undo a weave; even out uneven warp using the batten

ataut *vt* (of footwear) take off

atavisms *nm* atavism

atavistisks *adj* atavistic

atbadīt *v* **1.** *vt* (of pointed instruments) dull; **2.** *vi* butt back

atbadīties *vr* **1.** (of pointed instruments) get dull; **2.** grow tired of butting

atbaidāmviela *nf* repellent

atbaidīgi *adv* repulsively

atbaidīgs *adj* repugnant, repulsive, repellent; forbidding

atbaidīšanas līdzeklis *nm* deterrent

atbaidīt *vt* **1.** repel; scare off; **2.** deter; **3.** antagonize

atbakstīt *vt* dull

atbalsojums *nm* echo

atbalsot *vi* echo, reverberate, resound

atbalsoties *vr* echo, reverberate, resound

atbalspārbaude *nf* (compu.) echo check

atbalss *nf* echo; (fig.) response

atbalss lote *nf* echo sounder

atbalstenes *nf pl* step ladder

atbalstīšana *nf* support; (of crime) abetting

atbalstīt *vt* support

atbalstītāj/s *nm*, **~a** *nf* supporter

atbalstīties *vr* lean against, lean on

atbalstmūris *nm* retaining wall

atbalstnis *nm* (of a chair) arm

atbalstprogramma *nf* (compu.) support program

atbalsts *nm* **1.** support; prop; footing; **2.** (mil.) base

atbalsta gredzens *nm* trunnion

atbalsta plātne *nf* base plate

atbalstpunkts *nm* point of support; (of a lever) fulcrum; (mil.) stronghold; footing, foothold

atbalsta rats *nm* carrier roller

atbalsta stabs *nm* supporting post

atbalsta terapija *nf* supportive therapy

atbalstrāmis *nm* rack frame

atbalstsiena *nf* retaining wall

atbalstuguns *nf* supporting fire

atbalšņi *nm pl* (mus., organ) swell

atbangot *vi* arrive on waves

atbaras *nf pl* (hist.) impost of grain

atbari *nm pl* = **atbaras**

atbarot *vt* fatten

atbaroties *vr* put on weight

atbāzt *vt* (of skirts) pin up; shore back

atbēgt *vi* flee back, run back

atberes *nf pl* (hist.) repayment of a debt of grain (owed the granary of a township); amount of grain paid as interest on borrowed grain

atbēres *nf pl* (obs.) repeat celebration of a funeral feast

atbērt *vt* **1.** pour back; **2.** pour off, measure off; **3.** (of a memorized piece) rattle off

atbērties *vr* be poured back

atberzt *vt* rub off

atbīde *nf* pushing back, pushing aside

atbīdes ārdu kurtuve *nf* backward-feed furnace

atbīdīt *vt* push aside; push apart; **a. atpakaļ** push back atbīdīties *vr* be pushed aside (or back, to, open)

atbiedēt *vt* scare away

atbilde *nf* answer, reply, response; retort; **asprātīga a.** repartee; **noraidoša a.** rebuff, refusal, a no for an answer; **~s uguns** returned fire

atbildēt *vt, vi* **1.** answer, reply, respond; retort; **a. uzdoto** say one's lesson; **a. ar jā** say yes; **a. uz jautājumu** answer the question; **a. jautājumu** answer the question (on a test); **2.** take the responsibility; **a. par sekām** bear the consequences

atbildētāj/s *nm*, **~a** *nf* **1.** responder; **2.** (jur.) de-fendant, respondent

atbildība *nf* responsibility; **(saukt) pie ~s** (call) to account

atbildības apdrošināšana *nf* liability insurance

atbildības pienākums *nm* liability

atildības trūkums *nm* irresponsibility;

atbildīgi *adv* responsibly

atbildīgs *adj* **1.** responsible; **2.** crucial

atbildīgums *nm* responsibility

atbilsme *nf* correspondence, fit, match; counterpart; (philos.) reference

atbilst *vi* correspond; answer, fit

atbilstība *nf* correspondence, fit, match

atbilstīgi *adv* correspondingly, to correspond, to fit

atbilstīgs *adj* corresponding to

atbiras *nf pl* screenings

atbirt *vi* be screened out; (fig.) drop out

atbirum/s *nm* **1.** number of dropouts; **2.** **~i** screenings

atbirzt *vi* crumble

atbizināt *vt* (of cattle) make run home

atbizot *vi* (of cattle) stampede back, stampede home

atblandīties *vr* return from wandering

atblāzma *nf* glow; afterglow; reflection; (fig.) reverberations

atblāzmojums *nm* glow; afterglow; reflection

atblāzmot *vi* (of a glow) reflect; light up

atblāzmoties *vr* (of a glow) reflect; light up

atblēdīt *vt* entice (to a place); cheat out of

atblēt *vi* answer (by bleating)

atblokošana *nf* (compu.) deblocking

atblusot *vt* deflea

atbļaut *vi* (col.) shout back in reply

atbode *nf* backflow, backwash, backwater

atbradāties *vr* wade to one's heart's content

atbrangt *vi* **1.** recover from illness; **2.** gain weight

atbraucēj/s *nm*, **~a** *nf* arrival (one arriving); newcomer

atbrauciens *nm* arrival

atbraucīt *vt* roll back, pull back; **a. piedurknes** roll up one's sleeves

atbraucīties *vr* **1.** roll up one's sleeves; **2.** (of sleeves) roll up by themselves

atbraukas *nf pl* **1.** stripped leaves; **2.** tow and combings

atbraukāt *vi* **1.** come repeatedly, arrive repeatedly; **2.** (of sleeves) roll up repeatedly

atbraukšana *nf* arrival

atbraukt *vi* **1.** arrive; **a. ciemā** come visiting; **2. a. atpakaļ** drive back, come back

atbrāzt *vi* storm in

atbrāzties *vr* storm in

atbrēkt *vi* scream back, yell back

atbrēkties *vr* **1.** (of animals) call back (in reply); **2.** be through crying

atbremzēt *vt* release the brake

atbrist *vi* wade (up) to, come wading

atbristies *vr* be done wading

atbrīve *nf* (poet.) liberation

atbrīvojošs *adj, part* of **atbrīvot** relaxing

atbrīvojums *nm* furlough

atbrīvošana *nf* release; liberation; dismissal (from work); **a. no soda** suspended sentence

atbrīvošanās *nfr* liberation; riddance

atbrīvot *vt* free, release, liberate; exempt; clear, vacate; relax; **a. no darba** dismiss, lay off; **a. ceļu** clear the way; **a. vietu** make room for

atbrīvotāj/s *nm*, **~a** *nf* liberator

atbrīvotība *nf* relaxation

atbrīvoties *vr* free oneself; get rid of; (*3rd pers*) be freed, become free; become vacant; **a. no aiz-bildnības** become one's own master

atbruka *nf* yarn that has spilled over the ends of a spool

atbrukt *vi* crumble and fall off

atbruņošanās *nfr* disarmament

atbruņot *vt* disarm

atbruņoties *vr* disarm

atbubināt *vi* 1. whinny in response; 2. mumble in response

atbultēt *vt* unbolt

atburāt *vi* arrive in a sailboat

atburkšķēt *vi* grunt in reply

atburt *vt* turn back into (by magic), reverse a magic spell; get back (by magic)

atburtot *vt* decipher

atbust *vi* awake

atbūtne *nf* absence

atcēlējs *nm* 1. abolitionist; 2. repealer

atcelmot *vt* remove stumps, grub

atcelšana *nf* 1. abolition; 2. repeal, abrogation; 3. cancellation; 4. rescision, countermand; 5. dismissal

atcelt *vt* 1. abolish; 2. repeal, abrogate; 3. cancel; 4. rescind, countermand; 5. dismiss; 6. pick up and move away; 7. pick up and put back

atcēlums *nm* = **atcelšana**

atceļa biļete *nf* return ticket

atceļot *vi* travel back

atceļš *nm* the way back

atcepināt *vt* (of baking bread) overdo (so that the crust separates)

atcept *vi* (of baking bread) be overdone (so that the crust separates)

atcepties *vr* bake to the point of weariness

atcere *nf* (poet.) remembrance; commemoration; **~s akts** commemorative act; **~s** memories

atcerēties *vr* remember, recall

atcerīgs *adj* 1. retentive; 2. mindful

atcilpot *vi* come running, come loping

atcīnīties *vr* fight one's way to (a place)

atcirst *vt* 1. cut off, chop off; 2. blunt; 3. retort, snap back

atcirsties *vr* (of an axe) become blunt

atcirsts *adj, part* of **atcirst** dull

atcirties *adj, part* of **atcirsties** dull

atcirtnis *nm* cut-off

atcirtums *nm* cleared right-of-way in a forest; severance, cutting

atčabināt *vi* come toddling

atčāpot *vi* come toddling

atčivināt *vi* reply merrily, chirp back

atčukstēt *vi* whisper a reply

atdabūt *vt* 1. get back, retrieve; 2. lug or drag to; 3. get sth. off (with difficulty); 4. **a. vaļā** get sth. open (with difficulty)

atdairīt *vt* push away, fend off; keep away

atdale *nf* partitioned section

atdalījum/s *nm* 1. (partitioned) section; 2. **~i** (physiol.) secretion; discharge

atdalīšanās *nfr* 1. separation; 2. secretion; 3. secession

atdalīt *vt* 1. separate; split off; partition off; segregate; 2. (physiol.) secrete, discharge

atdalīties *vr* 1. separate; split off; 2. leave; 3. (physiol.) secrete; 4. stand out; 5. (pol.) secede

atdalīts *adj, part* of **atdalīt** separate

atdaļa *nf* section, subdivision

atdārdēt *vi* 1. arrive rumbling; 2. (of a thundering sound) be heard (from a given direction)

atdārdināt *v* 1. *vi* come rumbling; 2. *vt* drive to with a thundering noise

atdarinājums *nm* imitation; copy

atdarināt *vt* imitate; copy

atdarināts *adj, part* of atdarināt copied; fake

atdarīt *v* 1. *vt* open; 2. *vt, vi* repay, pay back; get back at; take revenge

atdarīties *vr* open

atdarīts *adj, part* of atdarīt open

atdauzīt *vt* 1. hammer loose; split off, knock off; 2. hurt oneself; 3. blunt

atdauzīties *vr* (col.) drop in

atdāvāt *vt* give away

atdāvināt *vt* give away

atdegt *vi* burn off

atdejot *vi* dance to

atdelverēt *vi* arrive, get to (romping)

atderēt *vt* (of agreements) nullify, cancel, void

atdēstīt *vt* plant back

atdevas *nf pl* repayment (with interest)

atdeve *nf* 1. devotion; dedication; 2. yield; (physiol.) secretion; (phys.) radiation; (bus.) return

atdevēj/s *nm*, ~a *nf* he that gives back

atdevības *nf pl* return

atdevīgi *adv* devotedly

atdevīgs *adj* devoted; self-sacrificing

atdiebt *vi* scurry back

atdiegt *vi* 1. come in a rush; 2. overhand

atdiene *nf* a cow that calves in her second year

atdienēt *vt* (obs.) work off

atdieņi *nm pl* spring rye

atdievoties *vr* say goodbye

atdimdēt *vi* thud, (of thuds) resound, echo

atdimdināt *vi* approach with a great noise

atdimt *vi* thud, (of thuds) resound, echo

atdipēt *vi* (of the sound of small footsteps) approach

atdipināt *vi* come scurrying, come running pit-a-pat

atdipt *vi* (of light, rapid footfalls) approach

atdīrāt *vt* skin back

atdomas *nf pl* memories

atdomāt *vt* remember, recall

atdomāties *vr* remember, recall

atdošan/a *nf* return; uz ~u to be returned; I will return it

atdošanās *nfr* devotion, dedication

atdošas *nf pl* (obs.) 1. return; 2. (ancient form of marriage) exchange of females between two clans; 3. borrowed grain, bread, or other food

atdot *vt* 1. give back, return; refund, reimburse; a. godu salute; return a salute; 2. give; a. izlabot have sth. repaired; a. pārtaisīt have sth. altered; 3. give up; 4. dedicate, devote; 5. send (to a place of work, school)

atdoties *vr irr* 1. devote oneself to, abandon oneself to, (fig.) surrender to; 2. receive in return

atdragāt *vt* knock off

atdrāzt *v* 1. *vi* come rushing; 2. *vt* shave off (with a knife)

atdrāzties *vr* come rushing, rush to

atdrēgnis *nm* mild weather (following a hard freeze)

atdrēģis *nm* = atdrēgnis

atdrupināt *vt* crumble away

atdrupt *vi* crumble off

atducināt *vi* (of a rumbling sound) be heard, reach

atdudināt *vi* respond in a cooing voice

atdūdot *vi* respond in a cooing voice

atdūkt *vi* 1. come flying and buzzing; 2. answer in a deep voice

atduļķošana *nf* clarification; (of cement) elutriation

atdunēt *vi* (of a rumble) echo

atdūņošana *nf* sludge removal; desilting

atdūņot *vt* remove sludge; desilt

atdure *nf* backstop

atdurstīt *vt* 1. (of a needle) blunt; 2. separate with a spade

atdurt *vt* 1. cut off; 2. (of pointed instruments) blunt

atdurties *vr* bump into, bump against; run into

atdusa *nf* rest

atdusēt *vi* rest

atdusēties *vr* rest

atdusinât *vt* let rest

atdvēst *vi* answer almost inaudibly

atdzeja *nf* translation of a poem

atdzejojums *nm* translation of a poem

atdzejot *vt* translate a poem

atdzejotāj/s *nm*, ~a *nf* translator of poems

atdzelt *vi* come back (with a retort)

atdzelzošana *nf* iron removal

atdzemdināšana *nf* revival; rebirth; renascence

atdzemdinât *vt* revive

atdzenât *vt* shoo away

atdzert *vt* 1. take sips off the top (of a glass) **a. paģiras** the hair of the dog; **2.** celebrate a second time

atdzerties *vr* 1. drink one's fill; **2.** over-indulge in drink

atdzesēt *vt* cool

atdzesēties *vr* cool off, cool oneself

atdzesinât *vt* cool

atdzesināties *vr* cool off, cool oneself

atdziedāt *vi* answer with a song

atdzimstošs *adj, part* of **atdzimt** resurgent

atdzimšana *nf* rebirth, revival, renascence

atdzimšanas laikmets *nm* Renaissance

atdzimt *vi* revive, be reborn

atdzimtne *nf* revival; rebirth; renascence

atdzirdīt *vt* quench s.o.'s thirst

atdzīres *nf pl* party after a party

atdzirknis *nm* (of fishnets) trap

atdzisinât *vt* cool

atdzist *vi* cool

atdzīt I (with î) *vt* drive (to a place); drive away; push (to a place); (of wind, water) blow away, push away

atdzīt II *vi* recover from illness

atdzīties *vr* get home with great effort

atdzīvināšana *nf* resuscitation

atdzīvinât *vt* 1. revive, bring back to life, resuscitate; **2.** revitalize; **3.** enliven

atdzīvošanâs *nfr* 1. revival; reanimation; **2.** animation; bustle, stir

atdzīvoties *vr* 1. revive; **2.** become animated

āte *nf* turbot

atēdas *nf pl* leavings

atēdinât *vt* stuff s.o. with food

ateisms *nm* atheism

ateistiski *adv* atheistically

ateistisks *adj* atheistic

ateist/s *nm*, ~e *nf* atheist

ateja *nf* restroom; (mil.) latrine; **pagaidu a.** cat hole

atejas papīrs *nm* toilet paper

atejošs *adj, part* of **atiet** (RR) departing

ateljē *nm indecl* atelier, studio; workshop

atelpa *nf* respite, breathing space

atelpēties *vr* = **atelpoties**

atelpot *vi* take a breath; catch one's breath; **brīvi a.** breathe freely again

atelpoties *vr* catch one's breath

atelsas *nf pl* sobbing (after crying)

atelsoties *vr* catch one's breath

atelst *vi* catch one's breath

atelsties *vr* catch one's breath

at[e]matisks [ē] *adj* athematic

atēna *nf* shadow, shadowy reflection

atēniet/is *nm*, ~e *nf* Athenian

atēnojums *nm* shadow, shadowy reflection

atēnot *vt* (of shadows) reflect

atēnoties *vr* (of shadows) be reflected

atentāts *nm* assasination attempt

ateroma *nf* atheroma

aterosklerotisks *adj* atherosclerotic

ateroskleroze *nf* atherosclerosis

atestācija *nf* 1. certification; **2.** employee evaluation; (mil.) officer review; ~s **komisija** (mil.) promotion board

atestāts *nm* certificate

atestēt *vt* 1. certify; 2. evaluate

atēsties *vr* eat one's fill

atetoze *nf* athetosis

atēvelēt *vt* (of a plane) dull

atgabalus *adv* (obs.) from afar

atgāda *nf* (obs.) memory

atgādāšana *nf* delivery

atgādāt *vt* 1. bring, take to, deliver; 2. (obs.) re-member

atgādāties *vr* (obs.) remember

atgadījums *nm* incident; **nelaimīgs a.** accident

atgādinājums *nm* reminder

atgādināt *vt* remind

atgadīties *vr* happen

atgādne *nf* reminder

atgainīt *vt* drive away, keep off

atgainīties *vr* protest (the expression of thanks)

atgaiņāt *vt* drive away, keep off; (fig.) fight back

atgaiņāties *vr* ward off; (fig.) fight back; protest

atgaisma *nf* glow; afterglow; reflection

atgaismis *nm* lampshade

atgaisot *vt* deareate

atgaisotājs *nm* deareator

atgaita *nf* 1. (hist) corvée labor performed for a neighbor; 2. contretemps, mishap; impediment

atgaitīgs *adj* hindering, difficult

atgājies *adj, part* of **atieties** recovered (from an illness)

atgalēt *vt* manage, accomplish

atgalēties *vr* ward off

atgalīgi *adv* wittily

atgalīgs *adj* quick-witted; witty

atgalis *nm* great talker

atgalotņot *vt* (of trees) top; pollard

atgalotņošana *nf* (of trees) topping; pollarding

atgalvene *nf* head of a runner (of a sled)

atgalvenis *nm* = **atgalvene**

atgalvnieks *nm* (bus.) countersecurity

atganīt *vt* 1. drive back; shoo away; 2. graze to satiety; 3. do one's turn as a herdsman; 4. tend cattle as a substitute herdsman

atganīties *nr* 1. (of grazing animals) regain weight; 2. shoo away; 3. tend cattle to the point of weariness; 4. (of cattle) move to a place in grazing

atgarēt *vi* = **atgarēties**

atgarēties *vr* cool off

atgarot *vi* = **atgaroties**

atgaroties *vr* (of beer) go flat

atgarozēties *vr* (of the crust of baking bread) separate

atgarša *nf* aftertaste

atgātnis *nm* returnee

atgavilēt *vi* (yodeling) respond

atgāze I (with **â**) *nf* steep slope

atgāze II *nf* exhaust gas

atgāzene *nf* (of a chair) back; ~s krēsls recliner

atgāzeniski *adv* backward, leaning backward

atgāzēšana *nf* degassing

atgāzēt *vt* degas

atgāznis *nm* diagonal (member of a truss); strut

atgāzt *vt* 1. (of the head) throw back; push back (causing a fall); 2. dump back

atgāzties *vr* 1. lean against, lean back; recline; 2. fall back

atglāstīt *vt* (of hair) smooth back

atglaudīt *vt* (of hair) smooth back

atglaust *vt* (of hair) smooth back

atgode *nf* repeat celebration of a feast or holiday

atgrābt *vt* rake away

atgraizas *nf pl* cuttings, ends, remnants

atgrātēt *vt* deburr

atgrauzt *vt* gnaw off

atgrēmas *nf pl* sick feeling

atgremošana *nf* (physiol.) rumination

atgremot *vt* regurgitate; ruminate, chew a cud; (fig.) rehash

atgremotāj/s *nm*, ~**a** *nf* **1.** ruminant; **2.** (fig.) re-gurgitator

atgremu *indecl adj* recycled, regurgitated, unoriginal

atgriešanās *nfr* return; homecoming

atgriezējatspere *nf* buffer spring

atgrieznis *nm* (fabric, carpet) remnant

atgrieznisks *adj* **1.** reflexive; feedback; **2.** reverse

atgriezt I *vt* **1.** unscrew; **a. krānu** turn on the faucet; **2.** turn sth. around; **3.** turn so back; **4.** bring back (from the past); **5.** (rel.) convert; **6.** turn away from

atgriezt II (with **iê**) *vt* **1.** cut off; **2.** cut open; **3.** blunt, dull

atgriezties I *vr* **1.** turn around; **a. no grēkiem** re-pent; **2.** return, come back, go back; **a. pa pēdām** retrace one's footsteps; **3.** unscrew

atgriezties II (with **iê**) *vr* become blunt, dull

atgriezum/s *nm* (of fabric) length; **a. kleitai** dress length; ~**i** cuttings, ends, remnants

atgrīļoties *vr* stagger to

atgrimēt *vt* (theat.) remove makeup

atgrimēties *vr* (theat.) remove one's makeup

atgrims *nm* makeup remover

atgrimt *vi* sink back

atgrožot *vt* give free rein

atgrūde *nf* recoil

atgrūdes bremze *nf* recoil brake

atgrūdien/s *nm* push, push back, repulse, thrust; recoil; ~**a motors** repulsion motor

atgrūst *vt* **1.** push back; **2.** push to, push aside; **3.** push open; **4.** rebuff, repulse

atgrūsties *vr* push off; (*3rd pers*) repel

atgrūšana *nf* repulsion; rebuff

atguldināt *vt* lay down, put to bed; put back to bed

atguldīt *vt* lay down, put to bed

atgulēt *vt* **1.** catch up on one's sleep; **2.** (of a part of the body) get bedsores

atgulēties *vr* get plenty of sleep

atgulties *vr* lie down

atgultne *nf* couch, bed

atgulu *adv* apart

atguļa *nf* relapse

atguļas drudzis *nm* relapsing fever

atguļas tīfs *nm* recurrent typhus

atgundums *nm* glut, surfeit

atgūt *vt* recover, get back, retrieve; regain; make up (for time lost)

atgūta *nf* (obs.) rest, stopping

atgūties *vr* **1.** recover, snap back; **2.** realize suddenly; **3.** catch one's breath

atgūtne *nf* (obs.) rest, stopping

atguve *nf* recovery, (compu.) retrieval

atģērbt *vt* undress

atģērbties *vr* undress (oneself)

atģida or **atģieda** *nf* **1.** consciousness; **2.** com-prehension

atģist *vi* **1.** realize suddenly; **2.** remember

atģisties *vr* **1.** recover consciousness; **2.** come to one's senses; **3.** realize

atīdēt *vi* (of calves) bleat back (in response)

atierosināt *vt* deenergize

atiest *vt* (of teeth) bare

atiešana I *nf* **1.** stepping back, stepping aside; **2.** (folk.) return; **3.** (of transportation) departure; sailing; **4.** (mil.) retreat

atiešana II *nf* baring of teeth

atiet *vi irr* **1.** step back, step aside; **2.** (folk.) return; **3.** (of transportation) leave, depart, sail; **4.** (of roads) branch off; **5.** (mil.) retreat

atieties *vr* **1.** recover (from illness); **2.** do enough walking

atiezt *vt* (of teeth) bare

atiezties *vr* bare one's teeth

atika *nf* (arch.) attic; ~**s stāvs** attic

atindēšana *nf* detoxification; decontamination

atindēt *vt* detoxify; decontaminate

atindustrializēt *vt* deindustrialize

ationizēt *vt* deionize

162

atipiski *adv* atypically

atipisks *adj* atypical

atirdināt *vt* (of seams) rip, undo

atireoze *nf* athyreosis

atirt I *vi* (of seams) come undone

atirt II *vt* 1. row away from; 2. row to; a. krastā row ashore

atirties *vr* 1. row away from; 2. row to; 3. a. kras-tā row ashore

atirzt *vt* (of teeth) bare

atitīda *nf* (ballet) attitude

atizolēt *vt* (el., of insulation) strip

atjāt *vi* come riding (on horseback)

atjaucēt *vt* wean

atjauda *nf* (obs.) memory

atjaudāties *vr* 1. come to one's senses; realize suddenly; 2. regain consciousness

atjaukt *vt* take apart, pull apart; unscramble

atjauninãms *adj* renewable

atjauninãšana *nf* = atjaunošana

atjauninãt *vt* = atjaunot

atjauninãties *vr* = atjaunoties

atjaunojams *adj* renewable

atjaunojums *nm* renewal; (theat.) revival

atjaunošana *nf* 1. renewal; 2. resumption; 3. revival; 4. rebuilding, restoration, renovation; 5. rehabilitation; 6. (compu.) updating

atjaunošanãs *nfr* 1. renewal; 2. revival; 3. resumption

atjaunot *vt* 1. renew; 2. resume; 3. revive; 4. rebuild, restore, renovate; 5. (jur.) rehabilitate; 6. (bus.) revolve; 7. (compu.) update

atjaunotãj/s *nm*, ~a *nf* renovator, restorer, rebuilder

atjaunoties *vr* 1. be restored; be renewed; 2. re-vive; 3. resume

atjaunotne *nf* (poet.) renewal

atjausma *nf* realization

atjaust *vt* know; dawn on one, realize

atjausties *vr* come to one's senses

atjauta *nf* 1. quick wit; 2. resourcefulness, ingenuity

atjautãt *vt* answer a question with a question

atjautība *nf* 1. quick wit; 2. resourcefulness, in-genuity

atjautīgi *adv* 1. wittily; 2. resourcefully, ingeniously

atjautīgs *adj* 1. witty; 2. resourceful, ingenious

atjautīgums *nm* 1. quick wit; 2. resourcefulness, ingenuity

atjēdzināt *vt* bring to one's senses

atjēga *nf* 1. comprehension; 2. awareness; 3. sense

atjēgt *vt* comprehend; realize

atjēgties *vr* 1. come to one's senses; 2. regain consciousness; 3. realize suddenly

atjēlēt *vi* soften, become mushy

atjemt *vt* = atņemt

atjokot *vi* make a funny reply, come back with a joke

atjokoties *vr* get away with a joke, laugh it off

atjoņot *vi* come tearing

atjozt I *vi* come tearing

atjozt II *vt* unbuckle

atjozties *vr* (of belts) come undone; unbuckle (one's belt)

atjūgt *vt* unharness

atjūgties *vr* come unharnessed

atjukt *vi* separate, fall off

atjūkt *vi* become disaccustomed, become estranged

atkabe *nf* release; ~s vãrsts releasing gear

atkabināt *vt* unhook, uncouple, (RR) detach

atkabināties *vr* come unhooked, come uncoupled

atkailināt *vt* bare, lay bare, uncover, expose

atkailinãtība *nf* nakedness

atkailinãties *vr* strip

atkailot *vt* bare, lay bare, uncover, expose

atkaitēt *vt* retaliate, get even

atkãjot *vi* come afoot

atkal I *adv* **1.** again, once more; **a. un a.** time and time again; **2.** in turn

atkal II *conj* **1.** however, but; then again; **2.** (with **tad**, to indicate sth. is a matter of course) and; **kādēļ tad a. nē ?** and why not?

atkala *nf* sleet, ice sheet

atkalapdzīvināšana *nf* repopulation

atkalapvienošana *nf* reunification

atkalapvienošanās *nfr* reunification

atkalapvienot *vt* reunite

atkalatnākšana *nf* return, (rel.) second coming

atkalēties *vr* **1.** recover; **2.** (with **no**) become estranged, become disaccustomed

atkaliņ *adv* (col.) again

atkalītēs *adv* (obs.) again

atkalizmantošana *nf* recycling

atkalne *nf* slope

atkalnis *adv* **1.** backwards; **a. adīt** purl; (of the needle in stitching) eye first; **2.** downhill

atkalnu *adv* = **atkalnis**

atkalpārdevējs *nm* reseller, retailer

atkalpārdošana *nf* resale

atkalpārdot *vt* resell

atkalpazīšana *nf* recognition

atkalpot *vt* (of a debt) work off

atkalredzēšan/ās *nfr* reunion; **uz drīzu ~os!** see you again soon!

atkalsavienošana *nf* reunification

atkalt *vt* **1.** chisel off; **2.** open (by chiseling)

atkalties *vr* wear off, become blunt (from repeated impacts)

atkaļķošana *nf* decalcification

atkaļķot *vt* decalcify

atkaļņi *adv* = **atkalnis**

atkapāt *vt* **1.** chop off, hack off; **2.** dull (in hacking or hoeing)

atkapāties *vr* **1.** dull (in hacking or hoeing); **2.** hoe or hack to the point of weariness

atkāp/e *nf* **1.** indentation; **ar ~i** indented; **2.** deviation; **3.** digression; **4.** (of buildings) setback

atkapināt *vt* (of a scythe) dull (in an attempt to sharpen)

atkāpināt *vt* **1.** (of horses) make step back; **2.** (typ.) indent

atkāpšanās *nfr* **1.** (mil.) retreat; **2.** deviation; **3.** digression; **4.** resignation

atkāpšanās nauda *nf* buyoff

atkāpt *vi* (col.) stop by

atkāpties *vr* **1.** step back, step aside; back off; **2.** recede; **3.** leave alone; **4.** (mil.) retreat; **5.** give up; **6.** go back on (a promise); set aside, ignore; **7.** resign

atkar/a *nf* **1.** dependence; **~ā no** depending on; **2.** overhang, jut

atkarāties *vr* **1.** hang from, dangle; **2.** depend

atkare *nf* dislike

atkareni *adv* hanging loosely; pendulously

atkarens *adj* loose hanging, pendulous, drooping

atkarīb/a *nf* dependence; **savstarpēja a.** interdependence; **~ā no** depending on

atkāries *adj, part* of **atkārties** hanging loosely, pendulous, drooping

atkarīgi *adv* depending on; dependently

atkarīgs *adj* dependent

atkarme *nf* reason, grounds

atka[r]ot [ŗ] *vt* reconquer, win back

atkarpains *adj* barbed

atkarpe *nf* barb

atkārpīt *vt* **1.** dig, lay open by scraping or scratching; **2.** scrape, scratch away

atkārpīties *vr* escape, free oneself

atkarpjains *adj* barbed

atkars *adj* loose hanging, pendulous, drooping

atkārt *vt* **1.** put back to hang; **2.** let hang down

atkārta *nf* repetition; **~s ecēt** harrow a second time

atkārties *vr* hang down

atkārtojuma zīme *nf* (mus.) repeat (sign)

atkārtojums *nm* repetition; reiteration

atkārtošana *nf* repetition; (compu.) rollback, re-run

atkārtošanās *nfr* repetition

atkārtot *vt* repeat; reiterate

atkārtotāja programma *nf* (compu.) rollback program

atkārtotājs *nm*, ~a *nf* repeater

atkārtoti *adv* repeatedly

atkārtoties *vr* be repeated; repeat itself; happen again

atkārtots *adj, part* of **atkārtot** repeated; ~a (gram., of discourse) direct

atkaru *adv* backwards; (of the manner of fastening the blade of a scythe) at a wide angle

atkasas *nf pl* scraping

atkāsas *nf pl* phlegm

atkāsēt *vt* cough up; clear one's throat; expectorate

atkāsēties *vr* clear one's throat

atkasīt *vt* scratch off, scrape off

atkāst *vt* (of milk) decant and filter

atkašāt *vt* scrape off; rake off; dig up (by scraping)

atkašļot *vt, vi* expectorate

atkašņāt *vt* scrape off; rake off; dig up (by scraping)

atkātot *vi* (col.) come, come by

atkaukt *vi* arrive howling

atkaukties *vr* **1.** howl back; **2.** get tired howling

atkaulēt *vt* haggle down

atkauliņot *vt* (of fruit) pit

atkauliņotājs *nm* pitter

atkausēt *vt* thaw, melt

atkauties *vr* (col.) fight off; **a. no miega** overcome sleepiness; **no viņa nevar a.** there is no getting rid of him

atkautrība *nf* repulsion

atkāzas *nf pl* repeat wedding feast (on Sunday after the wedding)

atklaiņāt *vi* come tramping

atklaiņot *vi* = **atklaiņāt**

atklājums *nm* discovery

atklanīties *vr* return a bow

atklāsme *nf* (rel.) revelation

atklāšana *nf* **1.** revelation disclosure; **mīlestības a.** declaration of love; **2.** discovery; detection; **3.** opening; inauguration; unveiling

atklāt *vt* **1.** uncover, reveal; **a. savas kārtis** put one's cards on the table; **a. mīlestību** declare one's love; **2.** discover; detect; **a. Ameriku** (iron.) reinvent the wheel; **3.** open; inaugurate; unveil; **a. uguni** open fire; **a. pretuguni** return fire; **a. sprostuguni** lay down a barrage

atklāti *adv* **1.** openly; **2.** publicly; **3.** frankly

atklātība *nf* **1.** openness, frankness; **2.** publicity; the public

atklāties *vr* **1.** be revealed; (of a view) open; **2.** turn out (to be), be found (to be)

atklātne I *nf* postcard

atklātne II *nf* (chess, checkers) opening

atklāts *adj, part* of **atklāt 1.** open; **2.** public; (of a vote) by show of hands, by acclamation; **3.** frank; **4.** unprotected

atklātums *nm* openness

atklausīt *vt* (hist.) render corvée labor

atklausīties *vr* **1. nevar ne a.** have an earful; **2. grūti a.** can't get enough of (s.o.'s singing, music, speech)

atklejot *vi* come tramping

atklenderēt *vi* (col.) come tramping

atklepot *vt, vi* cough up, expectorate

atklepoties *vr* clear one's throat

atklibot *vi* come limping

atklīdenis *nm* stray

atklidzināt *vi* come clip-clopping

atkliegt *vi* shout back

atkliegties *vr* shout back

atklīst *vi* **1.** come tramping; wander hither; **2.** wander away, stray

atkluburot *vi* stumble home, stumble to a place, come stumbling

atklumburot *vi* = **atkluburot**

atklunkurot *vi* stumble home, stumble to a place, come stumbling

atklupt *vi* come stumbling

atkļūdošana *nf* (compu.) debugging

atkļūt *vi* get to (a place), arrive

atknibināt *vt* unravel, undo

atkniebt *vt* pinch off, nip off

atkniedēt *vt* 1. unrivet; 2. (of rivets) upset

atknopēt *vt* (barb.) unbutton

atknubināt *vt* unravel, undo

atkņopēt *vt* = **atknopēt**

atkodēšana *nf* decoding

atkodēt *vt* decode

atkodētāj/s *nm*, **~a** *nf* decoder

atkomandēt *vt* send on an assignment

atkopt *vt* restore to former state of health or wellbeing

atkopties *vr* recover, recuperate; gain back weight

atkorķēt *vt* uncork

atkost *vt* 1. bite off; 2. dull, blunt; 3. neutralize a bite with a counterbite; 4. get back at s.o.

atkosties *vr* 1. become dull, blunt; 2. get back at s.o.

atkrāmēt *vt* shove away; put away

atkrampēt *vt* unhook

atkrāsot *vt* discolor, decolorize

atkrāsotājs *nm* decolorant

atkrāsoties *vr* become discolored or decolorized

atkratīt *vt* shake off, shake loose

atkratīties *vr* 1. slide (to a place as a result of shaking); 2. (col.) shake so, get rid of so; 3. (col.) refuse; 4. (col.) arrive (along a bumpy road or in an uncomfortable vehicle)

atkraukāt *vi* clear one's throat, hawk up

atkraukāties *vr* clear one's throat

atkraut *vt* 1. stack or pile in another place; 2. pile back, load back

atkrava *nf* junk

atkravāt *vt* clear, clear away

atkravāties *vr* move (here)

atkrekstēties *vr* clear one's throat

atkrekšķēties *vr* clear one's throat

atkrēpas *nf pl* phlegm

atkrēpot *vt, vi* expectorate

atkrēpoties *vr* expectorate

atkrēsloties *vr* throw a shadow

atkrist *vi* 1. fall off, fall away; 2. fall back; 3. drop out; desert a cause; 4. become unnecessary; 5. (col.) get sth. out of a thing, profit; 6. (of doors, lids) open (rapidly and with a bang); 7. (col.) lie down to rest

atkristies *vr* (of liquid levels) drop

atkristīt *vt* (col.) water down

atkrišņas *nf pl* garbage, refuse; trash

atkritalas *nf pl* garbage, refuse; trash

atkritēj/s *nm*, **~a** *nf* renegade

atkritumi *nm pl* garbage, refuse; trash; waste materials; (fig.) dregs; (ore) tailings

atkritumprodukti *nm pl* waste products

atkritumu bedre *nf* refuse pit

atkritumu šachta *nf* refuse chute

atkritumu tvertne *nf* garbage can

atkritumu vācējs *nm* refuse collector

atkritumvads *nm* refuse chute

atkritumvielas *nf pl* waste materials

atkropļošana *nf* (audio) correction of distortion

atkruķēt *vt* (barb.) unscrew

atkuģot *vi* come sailing, steam home

atkūkot *vi* answer the call of a cuckoo

atkukulis *nm* gift given in exchange (at a wedding)

atkūleņot *vi* come tumbling

atkūlības *nf pl* feast at the close of threshing

atkulties *vr* (col.) arrive, get to a place (with difficulty or from far away and unexpectedly)

atkūņoties *vr* **1.** leave the cocoon (with difficulty); **2.** drag oneself to

atkūpēt *vi* (of smoke, dust) come billowing

atkupināt *vt* curdle

atkurst *vi* obey, mind

atkusa *nf* = **atkusnis**

atkusnis *nm* thaw

atkust *vi* thaw

atkustēt *vi* move, move further away; (col., of transportation) leave

atkustēties *vr* = **atkustēt**

atkusums *nm* **1.** thawing; **2.** thawed place

atkušņains *adj* thawy

atkvēlināt *vt* anneal

atkvēpināt *vt* drive away with smoke

atķēdēt *vt* unchain

atķeksēt *vt* (col.) check off

atķemmēt *vt* comb (away from, back)

atķepuroties *vr* **1.** (col.) recover; **2.** crawl to

atķērkt *vi* answer cawing; (of humans) screech (angrily) in reply

atķert *vi* **1.** (col.) catch it, comprehend; **2.** remember

atķerties *vr* realize; realize suddenly

atķibināt *vt* untie, untangle

atlabināt *vt* **1.** appease; **2.** reconcile

atlabot *vt* repair; restore

atlaboties *vr* get better, recover

atlabt *vi* get better, recover; (of s.o.'s attitude) improve

atlaida *nf* **1.** thaw; **2.** (hist., rel.) indulgence; ~ **as** a. remission of sins; b. (rel.) day of remission of sins

atlaice *nf* spare time

atlaid/e *nf* **1.** rebate, discount; **ar** ~**i** (of selling) at a discount; **2.** special consideration

atlaidenis *nm* thaw

atlaidens *adj* thawy

atlaidi *nm pl* (rel.) day of remission of sins

atlaidība *nf* complaisance

atlaidiens *nm* (weav.) length of warp advanced at one time

atlaidies *adj, part* of **atlaisties** soft, thawed

atlaidīgi *adv* complaisantly, compliantly

atlaidīgs *adj* complaisant, compliant

atlaidinājums *nm* relaxation

atlaidināšana *nf* tempering

atlaidināšanas krāsa *nf* oxide tint

atlaidināt *vt* **1.** (metall.) temper; **2.** thaw slowly; **3. a. muguru** (col.) rest

atlaidināties *vr* thaw

atlaidinošs *adj, part* of **atlaidināt** relaxing

atlaidu krāsa *nf* annealing color

atlaidus *adv* reclining

atlaipot *vi* come picking one's way

atlaist *vt* **1.** (usu. **laist vaļā**) let go of sth., release; **2.** let s.o. go; **a. no stundām** cancel classes; **a. atvaļinājumā** give a vacation; **a. pensijā** retire; **3.** dismiss, fire; (of legislative bodies, assemblies) dissolve; **4.** (of debt) cancel; (of sentences) suspend; (of sins) remit; **5. a. no cenas** (col.) reduce the price; **6.** loosen; **a. gro-ēus** give rein; **7. a. kaulus** (col.) stretch out (by lying down); **8. a. lopus mājās** drive cattle home; **9.** (col.) send (a message); **10.** *vi* get to a place quickly (in a vehicle)

atlaisties I *vr* **1.** release; unclench; **2.** give up; **3.** (*3rd pers*) thaw; soften; **4.** (*3rd pers*) diminish, abate; (of weather) turn milder; **5.** lie down (to rest, briefly), recline

atlaisties II *vr* (of birds) arrive, come home; fly here

atlaistīt *vt* dilute

atlaiža *nf* remission of sins

atlalināt *vi* answer (happily)

atlampaāot *vi* come waddling

atlampot *vi* (col.) come tramping

Atlantijas grinda *nf* pilot whale

atlantisks *adj* **1.** Atlantic; **2.** Atlantean

atlants *nm* (geog., arch., anat.) atlas

atlapot *v* **1.** *vi* leaf back; **2.** *vt* strip of leaves

atlasas *nf pl* remainders

atlase *nf* selection

atlasināt *vt* test for reading skills

atlasīt *vt* **1.** select, pick out; **2.** say one's reading lesson

atlass *nm* satin

atlatviskot *v* **1.** *vt* re-Letticize; **2.** *vi* become alienated from Latvian culture

atlaulāt *vt* (obs.) divorce

atlaulāties *vr* (obs.) get a divorce

atlaulene *nf* (obs.) divorcée

atlaulenis *nm* (obs.) divorced man

atlaupīt *vt* peel

atlauzt *vt* **1.** break off; **2.** break open; **3. a. roku** twist s.o.'s arm behind his back

atlauzties *vr* **1.** break off; **2.** struggle to (a place)

atlavīties *vr* **1.** sneak away; **2.** come sneaking

atlēce *nf* ricochet

atlēcība *nf* elasticity; elastic tension

atlēciens *nm* jump-off

atlēcīgs *adj* **1.** elastic; **2.** (of bark) easily separable

atlecināt *vt* **1.** (of bark) tap to loosen; **2.** deduce, infer

atledot *vt* deice, defrost

atledotājs *nm* deicer

atlējums *nm* casting

atlēkšot *vi* come galloping

atlēkt *vi* **1.** jump back; jump aside; **2.** jump to; **3.** (*3rd pers*) fall off, pop off; **4.** (*3rd pers*) re-bound, bounce back, ricochet; **5.** (*3rd pers*) pop open; **6.** (*3rd pers*) (col., usu. with **labums, peļ-ņa**) profit

atlēkties *vr* **1.** take after (a relative); **2.** bounce back; **3.** jump to exhaustion

atlētika *nf* athletics

atlētiski *adv* athletically

atlētisks *adj* athletic

atlētiskums *nm* athleticism

atlēt/s *nm*, **~e** *nf* athlete

atlicējs *nm* (typ.) type distributor

atlicen *adv* enough and to spare

atlicināt *vt* (of money, time) set aside

atlidināties *vr* flutter hither

atlidot *vi* (of birds, missiles) come flying, (of aircraft, air passengers) arrive, arrive by air; (of sounds) float, be heard

atlīdze *nf* = **atlīdzība**

atlīdzēt *vt* = **atlīdzināt**

atlīdzīb/a *nf* **1.** compensation; recomense; **par mazu ~u** for a small fee; **bez ~as** without compensation, for nothing; **2.** remuneration; **3.** re-ward; **4.** reimbursement

atlīdzinājums *nm* = **atlīdzība**

atlīdzināt *vt, vi* **1.** compensate; recompense; **2.** re-munerate; **3.** reimburse

atliecējmuskulis *nm* (anat.) extensor

atliekām *adv* = **atlikām**

atliekas *nf pl* remnants; remains; leavings; residue; scraps

atlieks *nm* remnant, remainder, rest

atliekt *vt* **1.** bend back, bend aside; **2.** straighten, unbend; **a. muguru** (col.) rest; **muguru neatliecis** without unbending one's back

atliekties *vr* **1.** bend back; **2.** straighten, unbend

atliekums *nm* turndown

atliet *vt* **1.** pour off; **2.** pour back; **3.** cast (in a mold)

atlīgot *vt, vi* **1.** come swaying; **2.** entice with song; respond to a Ligo song; **3.** (of sounds) float to

atlīgoties *vr* come swaying

atlīgt *vt* keep (part of sth., according to an agreement)

atlija *nf* (of waves after a storm) subsidence

atlikām *adv* plenty, enough and to spare

atlik/as *nf pl* remants; remains; **~u likām** plenty, in great quantities, enough and to spare

atlikšana *nf* postponement

atlikšanas pulss *nm* reset pulse

atlikt I *vt* **1.** put aside; **2.** put back; **a.!** as you were! **3.** set aside, save; **4.** postpone

atlikt II *vi* remain, be left over

atlikties I *vr* remain, be left over

atlikties II *vr* lie down (to rest, briefly)

atlikums *nm* remnant, remainder, rest

atlīmēt *vt* unstick, unglue

atlīmēties *vr* come unglued; come off

atlingot *v* **1.** *vi* come in a big hurry; **2.** *vt* fling, hurtle

atlipināt *vt* unglue

atlipt *vi* come off, come unstuck

atlīst *vi* **1.** crawl to, creep to; **2.** crawl away or aside; **3.** (com.) come (slowly, quietly, hiding)

atlīt *vi* **1.** pour back; **2.** soften

atlobīt *vt* peel away; (metall.) descale

atlobīties *vr* peel away

atlobt *vi* come running

atloce *nf* cuff, turnup

atlocene *nf* cotter pin

atlocījums *nm* fold

atlocīt *vt* **1.** unfold; **2.** bend back; turn up; (of sleeves) roll back

atlocīties *vr* **1.** become bent (in the opposite or unwanted direction); (of pages) become dogeared; **2.** unfold; **3.** roll up one's sleeves; **4.** slither

atlodēt *vt* unsolder

atloks *nm* (of trousers, sleeves) cuff; (of a jacket) lapel; turnup; (tech.) flange

atlūgt *vt* **1.** invite; **2.** return an invitation

atlūgties *vr* ask to be excused; beg off; **a. no amata** resign one's post

atlūgumies, usu. *acc* **atlūgumos** *nmr* resignation

atlūgums *nm* resignation

atlūkoties *vr* **1.** look back; **2.** look enough

atlumpaāot *vi* come waddling

atlupināt *vt* **1.** peel off; **2.** peel open

atlupt *vi* peel off

atlūza *nf* fragment

atlūznis *nm* fragment

atlūzt *vi* break off

atļauja *nf* permission; permit, authorization

atļaut *vt* permit, allow; authorize; **vai ~s smēķēt?** do you mind if I smoke?

atļauties *vr* **1.** afford; **2.** permit oneself, allow oneself; **3.** venture; presume; **a. vaļības** take liberties

atļecis *adj* (of ears) pendulous

atļepatot *vi* come loping

atļēpot *vi* = **atļepatot**

atļinkāt *vi* come loping

atļepot *vi* come loping

atļucis *adj, part* of **atļukt** (of ears) pendulous; droopy

atļukt *vi* droop

atļutis *adj* = **atļucis**

atmācība *nf* repeat course

atmācīt *vt* wean, disaccustom

atmagnetizēt *vt* demagnetize

atmagnetizēties *vr* become demagnetized

atmagnetizētājs *nm* demagnetizer

atmaidzināt *vt* (fig.) soften

atmaigt *vi* soften; relent, be mollified

atmainīt *vt* trade back

atmainīties *vr* trade back

atmaiņa *nf* trade-back, exchange

atmaksa *nf* **1.** repayment; **2.** retribution; revenge

atmaksāšanās *nfr* returns

atmaksāt *vt* **1.** repay, pay back; **2.** avenge

atmaksāties *vr* **1.** pay; **2.** pay for itself; **3.** be worthwhile, be worth (sth.)

atmaldīties *vr* come wandering, come tramping

atmaļus *adv* apart

atmanīt *vt* **1.** (col.) feel; **2.** remember

atmānīt *vt* **1.** entice back; **2.** lure away

atmanīties *vr* **1.** sneak to; **2.** feel, sense; grasp; **3.** remove oneself

ātmans *nm* atman

atmaņa *nf* consciousness

atmaršēt *vi* come marching

atmāršīgi *adv* attentively

atmāršīgs *adj* attentive

atmaskojums *nm* exposé

atmaskot *vt* unmask; expose

atmaskoties *vr* be unmasked

atmāt *vi* 1. wave back; 2. wave it off

atmat/a *nf* fallow; ~ā fallow (*adj*)

atmatains *adj* interspersed with fallows

atmatene *nf* meadow mushroom, champignon

atmaukt *vt* (of a piece of clothing) roll back, push back

atmaurot *vi* moo back

atmauroties *vr* moo back

atmaut *vi* moo back

atmauties *vr* moo back

atmazgāt *vt* (of money) launder

atmēdīt *vi* answer mockingly

atmeimurot *vi* (col.) 1. come traipsing; stagger to; 2. stagger away

atmēļot *vi* reply carelessly

atmērcēt *vt* 1. soak; moisten; 2. soak off, loosen by soaking

atmērīt *vt* measure off

atmērot *vt* 1. repay, pay back; 2. avenge

atmest *vt* 1. throw to, throw as far as; 2. throw back; toss back; throw aside; **a. ar roku** a. wave it off; b. give up; **a. ķepalas** (vulg.) die; 3. drop, discard; give up; 4. throw, give (disdainfully); 5. answer curtly; 6. throw open

atmesties *vr* 1. drop oneself (on a chair, bed); (of a bird) alight; 2. lean on, lean against; stem oneself against; 3. catch on sth.; hit; 4. (of weather) change, turn; 5. (of cards) discard; 6. give up; (of birds and nests) abandon

atmešņas *nf pl* garbage, refuse; trash

atmetas *nf pl* garbage, refuse; trash

atmeteklis *nm* foundling

atmetināt *vt* untie

atmetumi *nm pl* garbage, refuse; trash

atmezglot *vt* unravel, disentangle, (of a knot) untie

atmēzt *vt* 1. sweep to (a place); 2. sweep away

atmežošana *nf* deforestation

atmežot *vt* deforest

atmīdīt *vt* 1. trample down; 2. hurt one's feet (in trampling, walking)

atmiecēt *vt* soak

atmiedze *nf* = atmiegs

atmiedzis *nm* = atmiegs

atmiegs *nm* light nap, a nap taken after sleeping

atmiekšķenis *nm* thaw

atmiekšķēt *v* 1. *vt, vi* soften; 2. *vt* loosen by soaking

atmiekšķēties *vr* 1. soften; 2. (of bones) become brittle

atmiga *nf* = (reg.) atmiegs

atmigloties *vr* (of fog) rise

atmīkne *nf* thaw

atmīksne *nf* = atmīkne

atmīkstens *adj* thawy

atmīkšķēt *vi* = atmiekšķēties

atmīkšt *vi* = atmiekšķēties

atmīkt *vi* thaw; (of weather) turn milder

atminējums *nm* (of a riddle) solution, answer; (of a secret) correct guess

atmīnēšana *nf* mine clearance

atminēt *vt* 1. (of a riddle) solve, riddle; (of a secret) guess; 2. remember

atmīnēt *vt* clear of mines

atminēties *vr* remember, recall; reminisce

atmīnētājs *nm* mine remover

atminība *nf* retentiveness

atminīgs *adj* retentive

atmiņa *nf* memory; recall; retention; **ilgstošā a.** long-term memory; **īslaicīgā a.** short-term memory; (el.) storage

atmīņāt *vt* trample down

atmircināt *vt* soak, soak off

atmirdza *nf* 1. gleam; 2. reflection

atmirdzējums *nm* 1. gleam; 2. reflection

atmirdzēt *vi* 1. gleam; shine forth; (of faces) shine (with joy, pride); 2. be reflected

atmirdzums *nm* 1. gleam; 2. reflection

atmirgot *vi* 1. be reflected; 2. twinkle

atmiris *adj, part* of atmirt necrotic

atmirkšķināt *vi* wink back

atmirkt *vi* 1. soften; 2. come off (after soaking)

atmiršana *nf* necrosis

atmirt *vi* 1. die off; wither away; 2. (of a limb) go numb, go to sleep

atmist *vi* soften; (of weather) become thawy

atmīt I *vt* trade back

atmīt II *vt* wear down; bend back (by wearing); (of feet) hurt (from stepping)

atmitināt *vt* (reg.) soak

atmitis *adj, part* of **atmist** thawy

atmitrināt *vt* dehumidify

atmitrinātājs *nm* dehumidifier

atmizot *v* 1. *vt* peel; 2. *vi* (of teeth) set on edge

atmizoties *vr* (of teeth) set on edge

atmocīt *vt* (col.) wrestle (sth. to a place)

atmoda *nf* awakening, waking up; (fig.) revival, renascence

atmodināt *vt* awaken

atmometrs *nm* atmometer

atmosf[ai]ra [ē] *nf* atmosphere

atmosf[ai]ras [ē] traucējumi *nm pl* atmospheric static

atmosf[ai]risks [ē] *adj* atmospheric

atmosties *vr* wake up

atmudžināt *vt* disentangle

atmudžināties *vr* become disentangled

atmugura *nf* back of a chair

atmugure *nf* = **atmugura**

atmuguris *adv* backward

atmuguriski *adv* backward

atmugurisks *adj* backward

atmukas *nf pl* fallen-off bark; loose yarn, unraveled threads

atmukt *vi* 1. come fleeing; 2. come undone, unravel; fall off

atmūķēt *vt* (of locks) pick

atmuldēt *vi* answer groggily

atmulst *vi* awaken; regain consciousness; (of one's mind) clear up

atmurkšķēt *vt, vi* mumble back

atmurmināt *vt, vi* mumble back

atnācēj/s *nm*, ~a *nf* arrival, comer

atnadzis *nm* hangnail

atnākt *vi* 1. come, arrive; a. ciemā come to see, call on; a. (kādam) pakaļ pick (s.o.) up; 2. a. vaļā (*3rd pers*, col.) open, come open; 3. (of animals) be born

atnākties *vr* (of farm animals) bring forth young; calve, lamb, farrow, foal

atnest *vt* 1. bring; 2. (of animals) bear (young)

atnesties *vr* (of farm animals) bring forth young; calve, lamb, farrow, foal

atnešanās *nfr* calving, lambing, farrowing, foaling

atņēmien/s *nm* spurt; ~iem repeatedly, periodically, in spurts

atņemšana *nf* 1. taking away; deprivation; 2. subtraction

atņemšanas zīme *nf* minus sign

atņemt *vt* 1. take away, take back; deprive; a. advokāta tiesības debar; a. dienesta pakāpi de-mote; a. drosmi unnerve; a. elpu recover one's breath; rest, take five; a. ilūzijas disenchant; neatņemot elpu in the same breath; a. no krūts wean; a. pilsoņa tiesības disfranchise; a. vārdu (parl.) deprive of the floor; 2. (math.) subtract; 3. (of time) demand; 4. (of a greeting) return

atņem/ties *vr* 1. (col.) recover one's breath; rest; 2. resume; ~damies pausing; 3. claim; 4. get tired of, get sated; ~as jau arī in the end one gets tired

atņemu ņemām or atņemu atņēmām *adv* time and again

atņirgt *vt* 1. (of one's teeth) bare; 2. (com.) sneer in reply

atņirgties *vr* bare one's teeth

atņurdēt *vi* growl in reply

atogļošana *nf* decarburization

atogļot *vt* decarburize

atols *nm* atoll

atomārs *adj* atomic

atombaterija *nf* atomic battery

atombumba *nf* atom bomb

atomdegviela *nf* nuclear fuel

atomdzinējs *nm* nuclear engine

atomeksplozija *nf* atomic blast

atomelektrostacija *nf* nuclear power plant

atomenerģētika *nf* nuclear energetics

atomenerģija *nf* atomic energy

atomfizika *nf* nuclear physics

atomfiziķ/is *nm*, ~e *nf* nuclear physicist

atomierocis *nm* nuclear weapon

atomisms *nm* atomism

atomistika *nf* atomic theory

atomka[r]š [ŗ] *nm* nuclear war

atomkodols *nm* atomic nucleus

atomkuģis *nm* nuclear ship

atomlādiņš *nm* nuclear charge

atomlaikmets *nm* atomic age

atomledlauzis *nm* nuclear icebreaker

atomlielgabals *nm* nuclear cannon

atommasa *nf* atomic mass

atomnumurs *nm* atomic number

atompatvertne *nf* fallout shelter

atompulkstenis *nm* atomic clock

atomraķete *nf* nuclear rocket

atomreaktors *nm* nuclear reactor

atoms *nm* atom

atomsēne *nf* mushroom cloud

atomskaitlis *nm* atomic number

atomspēkstacija *nf* nuclear power plant

atomsprādziens *nm* nuclear explosion

atomsprāgstviela *nf* nuclear explosive

atomspridzeklis *nm* nuclear warhead

atomsvars *nm* atomic weight

atomtechnika *nf* nuclear technology

atomtrieciens *nm* nuclear attack

atomūdeņradis *nm* atomic hydrogen

atomuzbrukums *nm* nuclear attack

atomzemūdene *nf* nuclear submarine

atonālisms *nm* atonalism

atonāls *adj* atonal

atonija *nf* atony

atonisks *adj* atonic

ators *nm* whirlpool

atpakaļ *adv* back; backwards; (naut.) astern; (of a trip) return; **uz . . . un a.** round trip to . . .

atpakaļadrese *nf* return address

atpakaļatkāpe *nf* (compu.) backspace

atpakaļbiļete *nf* return ticket

atpakaļbrauciens *nm* return trip

atpakaļceļš *nm* trip back

atpakaļdūriens *nm* backstitch

atpakaļejoši *adv* retroactively

atpakaļejošs *adj* retroactive

atpakaļējs *adj* retrograde; retroactive

atpakaļgaita *nf* reverse (gear); reverse motion

atpakaļgājiens *nm* **1.** reverse gear; **2.** march back

atpakaļiedarbība *nf* (phys.) reaction

atpakaļiekļaušana *nf* reincorporation; re-absorption

atpakaļiekļaut *vt* reincorporate; reabsorb

atpakaļiski *adv* backwards

atpakaļkadrs *nm* (of a film) cutback

atpakaļkrava *nf* back freight

atpakaļkrišana *nf* backsliding

atpakaļkritēj/s *nm*, ~a *nf* backslider

atpakaļnāciens *nm* return trip

atpakaļniski *adv* backwards

atpakaļpalicis *adj* backward

atpakaļpirkums *nm* repurchase; (of shares) redemption

atpakaļplūde *nf* backflow

atpakaļplūstošs *adj* return, backflow

atpakaļrāpulība *nf* reactionism

atpakaļrāpulīgs *adj* reactionary

atpakaļrāpulis *nm* reactionary

atpakaļsitiens *nm* (of firearms) recoil

atpakaļskats *nm* view backward

atpakaļskata spogulis *nm* rearview mirror

atpakaļvērsts *adj* retrospective

atpakuloties *vr* frazzle, fray

atpal/i *nm pl* **1.** ebb; **2.** second flooding; ~**iem** (fig.) in large quantities; enough and to spare; more than fully

atpalicēj/s *nm,* ~**a** *nf* **1.** laggard; **2.** straggler

atpalicība *nf* backwardness

atpalicis *adj, part* of **atpalikt 1.** backward (pol.) underdeveloped; **2.** retarded

atpaliem *adv* a lot, plentifully

atpalikt *vi* **1.** lag behind; fall behind; **2.** (of timepieces) be slow

atpals *nm* whirlpool

atpārslošana *nf* deflocculation

atpazīstamība *nf* recognizability

atpazīšana *nf* recognition

atpazīt *vt* recognize

atpēd/as *nf pl* ruts; tracks, footprints; **(atkrist)** ~**ās** (return to) one's old ways; **a. dzīt** trace (back)

atpeldēt *vi* **1.** swim to, float to; **2.** swim away from, float away from

atpeldināt *vt* **1.** float back; **2.** make float away

atpelnīt *vt* (of a debt) work off

atpenterēt *vt* (col.) untangle, untie

atpenterēties *vr* (col.) become untied

atpērties *vr* struggle home, struggle to a place

atpestīt *vt* save, deliver, redeem; free, rescue

atpestīties *vr* get rid of s.o.

atpilde *nf* (el.) recharge

atpuildes spuldze *nf* discharge lamp

atpildīt *vt* (el.) recharge

atpīle *nf* water frozen over ice; icicle; ice-free spring

atpīlis *nm* a second lamb born in the fall

atpiņķerēt *vt* = **atpiņķēt**

atpiņķēt *vt* (col.) disentangle

atpircēj/s *nm,* ~**a** *nf* repurchaser

atpirkt *vt* buy back, repurchase, (of shares) re-deem

atpirkties *vr* buy one's way out

atpirkums *nm* buyback

atpīt *vt* **1.** untwist, (of hair) unplait; **2.** (of horses) untether

atpīties *vr* **1.** untwist; come unplaited; **2.** get untethered

atplaiksna *nf* flash, reflection

atplaiksnījums *nm* flash, reflection

atplaiksnīt *vi* **1.** flash; **2.** reflect; **3.** (fig.) light up, lighten

atplaiksnīties *vr* **1.** flash; **2.** reflect; **3.** (fig.) light up, lighten

atplaisājums *nm* (former) place of attachment

atplaisāt *vi* become detached

atplakšināt *vi* (col.) come clomping

atplakt *vi* **1.** flatten, fall, subside; **2.** fall back

atplāties *vr* dull

atplaucēt I *vt* detach (by scalding)

atplaucēt II *vt* (of blossoms) force

atplaukt *vi* **1.** blossom, (of blossoms) open; **2.** (fig.) dawn; lighten

atplāvošana *nf* (metall.) descaling

atplest *vt* open, spread; **a. muti** gape; ~**ām acīm** goggle-eyed; ~**ām rokām** with open arms

atplesties *vr* open

atplēst *vt* **1.** tear off; **2.** open, tear open

atplēsums *nm* tear, torn spot; scratch, abrasion

atpletums *nm* opening

atplīst *vi* **1.** tear off; split off; **2.** split open, burst open

atplīsums *nm* tear, torn spot

atplīvot *vi* (of flags, banners) arrive with a flutter; (fig.) waft by

atplīvurot *vt* unveil

atplucināt *vt* **1.** open by shredding; **2.** pluck

atplūdi *nm pl* ebb, ebbing

atpludināt *vt* float to

atplūdums *nm* **1.** ebb, ebbing; **2.** efflux; (fig.) letdown

atplūkāt *vt* **1.** pluck open; **2.** tear off

atplūkt *vt* tear off; (of weeds) pull up

atplūst *vi* **1.** (of waves) reach, come up to; (of sounds) float; (of odors) waft; **2.** flow back, rush back; **3.** flow away, (of water, floods) leave

atpļaujas *nf pl* harvest home

atpļaut *vt* clear (by mowing), mow around the edges

atpogaļot *vt* boll, strip bolls from flax

atpogāt *vt* unbutton

atpogāties *vr* unbutton, (of buttons) come un-done

atprasījums *nm* (jur.) replevin

atprasīt *vt* **1.** demand the return of sth.; **2.** ask to recite a lesson

atprasīties *vr* ask for permission to leave or to go

atprast *vi* understand

atprasties *vr* realize

atprecēt *vt* marry and bring home a wife from far away

atprogrammēšana *nf* deprogramming

atpumpurošana *nf* the pruning of buds

atpumpurot *vt* prune buds

atpurināt *vt* **1.** shake to remove sth.; **2.** shake open; **3.** (of one's head in negation) shake

atpūst *vt* **1.** blow to (a place); **kāds vējš tevi atpūtis?** what brings you here? **2.** blow away; **3.** blow open

atpūsties *vr* rest

atpūt *vi* rot off

atpūta *nf* rest, relaxation; recreation

atpūtas ceļojums *nm* pleasure trip

atpūtas diena *nf* day of rest

atpūtas krēsls *nm* easy chair; deck chair

atpūtas laiks *nm* time off

atpūtas nams *nm* resort

atputekļošana *nf* dust removal

atputekļot *vt* remove dust

atputekļotājs *nm* deduster; dust collector

atputēt *vi* **1.** separate as dust; **2.** be blown to

atputināt *vt* (of sand, dust) blow to

atpūtināt *vt* rest, let rest

atpūtnie/ks *nm*, ~**ce** *nf* vacationer; resort guest

atputot *vt* defoam

atputotājs *nm* defoamer

atradēj/s *nm*, ~**a** *nf* finder; ~**a alga** finder's fee, reward

atraden/is *nm*, ~**e** *nf* foundling

atradi *nm pl* relatives of one's deceased wife or husband

atradības *nf pl* **1.** (obs.) finder's fee; **2.** find, finding

atradināt *vt* wean; disaccustom, break s.o. of a habit

atradināties *vr* break a habit, become disaccustomed

atrādīt *vt* show (for checking)

atrādīties *vr* go for a checkup

atradne *nf* **1.** (geol.) deposit, bed; ~**s prasība** claim; **2.** (biol.) aggregation, association

atradums *nm* **1.** find, thing found; **2.** discovery

atradze *nf* (geol.) spur

atradzis *nm* antler

atrafakse *nf* goat's-wheat

atragene *nf* atragene

atraide *nf* rejection, refusal; denial

atraidīgi *adv* negatively

atraidīgs *adj* negative

atraidījums *nm* rejection, refusal; denial

atraidīt *vt* reject, refuse; deny; turn away

atraidoši *adv* in the negative

atraidošs *adj, part* of **atraidīt** negative

atraiknīte *nf* (bot.) viola

ātrais dilonis *nm* galloping consumption

atraisīt *vt* **1.** untie; **2.** unleash, unfetter; **3.** loosen, undo; **4.** free, release

atraisītība *nf* the quality of being unfettered

atraisīties *vr* **1.** get untied, come undone; **2.** get loose, free oneself; **3.** (fig.) loosen up; **4.** (fig., of talent) blossom

atraisīts *adj, part* of **atraisīt 1.** released; **2.** unfettered; **3.** uninhibited, expansive; animated

atraitne *nf* widow

atraitnība *nf* widowhood, widowerhood

atraitnis *nm* widower

atraitnīte *nf* (bot.) viola
ātrāk *adv, comp* of **ātri 1.** faster; **2.** sooner; **ne ā. kamēr** not until; **3.** rather
atrakcij/a *nf* (theat.) attraction
atrakciju parks *nm* amusement park
atrakciju zāle *nf* amusement arcade
atrakņāt *vt* dig up
atrakstīšanās *nfr* (written) regrets
atrakstīt *vt, vi* drop a line, write (and send) a letter
atrakstīties *vr* send regrets
atrakt *vt* dig up; unearth
atrakties *vr* make one's way to (a place) by digging
atraktivitāte *nf* attractiveness
atraktīvs *adj* attractive
atrāpot *vi* come crawling
ātrapstrāde *nf* high-speed processing
atrāpties *vr* **1.** come crawling; **2.** crawl away; crawl aside
atrāpulis *nm* reactionary
atraslis *nm* foundling
atrast I *vt* **1.** find; **a. galu** perish; **a. pret-mīlestību** have one's love returned; **a. riņķa kvadrātūru** square the circle; **atron kā dūci makstī** finding that which was never lost; **2.** discover
atrast II *vi* become disaccustomed
atrasties *vr* **1.** be, be situated; **2.** be found; turn up; **atradies gudrinieks!** (col., cont.) look at the wise guy! **3.** (obs.) be born
atrašanās *nfr* presence, being there; **a. vieta** location, whereabouts; locus; (naut.) fix
ātraudzēj/s *nm*, **~a** *nf* quick growing; (of plants) early
ātraudzība *nf* quick growth; (of plants) earliness
ātraudzīgs *adj* quick growing; (of plants) early
ātraudzis *nm* early maturing plant
ātraudži *nm pl* **1.** scarlet-berried elder; **2.** bourtree; **3. a. kartupeļi** early potatoes

ātraudžu *indecl adj* quick growing; (of plants) early
atraugas *nf pl* belching
atraugāties *vr* belch
atraust *vt* **1.** rake off; **2.** uncover in raking; **3.** rake away, rake aside
atrausties *vr* scoot to, scoot back
atraušanās *nfr* (mil.) breakaway, disengagement
atraut *vt* **1.** tear off; pull off; **2.** pull away, jerk back; **3.** throw open, (of wind) blow open; **a. vaļā** pull open; **4.** (fig., of thoughts) turn away, (of eyes) take off; **5.** interfere with; **6.** (fig.) tear away, separate forcibly; isolate, split off; **~s** isolated; **~i** in isolation; **7.** deny, deprive of, stop giving; cut off; (of support) withdraw; **a. mantojuma tiesu** disinherit; **a. no savas mutes** stint oneself; **a. svaru** give short weight; **8.** (col.) bring s.o. in a hurry
atrauti *adv* separately
atrautība *nf* isolation, detachment
atrauties *vr* **1.** break loose; be torn off; **a. no ienaidnieka** break contact with the enemy; **a. no zemes** (of aircraft) take off; **2.** pull back, pull away from; **3.** tear oneself away from; **4.** isolate oneself from; get out of touch; avoid, stay away
atravēt *vt* weed
atražošana *nf* repetition of the production process
atražot *vt* repeat the production process
ātrbojīgs *adj* perishable
ātrbraucēj/s *nm*, **~a** *nf* fast moving; **ā. vilciens** express train
ātrcietējošs *adj* quick-setting
ātrdabis *nm* hothead
ātrdarbes *indecl adj* high-speed
ātrdarbīgi *adv* at high speed
ātrdarbīgs *adj* high-speed
ātrdarbīgums *nm* high speed
ātrēdis *nm* fast eater
atreferējums *nm* report, account

atreferēt *vt* report on, give an account of

atreibināt *vt* sober up; detoxify

atreibt *vi* sober up

atreizot *vi* (barb.) drop in on s.o.

atrēkt *vi* roar back; (col.) answer in an angry voice

atrēķināt *vt* deduct

atremdēt *vt* cool

ātrene *nf* speedwell

atrēzēt *vt* (reg.) raise

atrežģīt *vt* disentangle, unravel

ātrfermentācija *nf* stormy fermentation

ātrfilmēšana *nf* slow-motion photography

ātrfrēzēšana *nf* high-speed milling

ātrfrēzētāj/s *nm*, ~a *nf* high-speed milling machine operator

ātrgaita *nf* high speed

ātrgājēj/s *nm*, ~a *nf* high-speed (vehicle, device)

ātrgājiens *nm* high speed

ātri *adv* **1.** quickly, fast, swiftly, rapidly; **2.** soon; **ā. vien** soon

atrībēt *vi* rumble

atrībināt *vi* come rumbling

atribūcija *nf* attribution

atribūtika *nf* attributes

atrib[u]tīvs [ū] *adj* attributive

atribūts *nm* attribute

atridāties *vr* (reg.) move in

atrīdīt *vt* drive s.o. (to a place) by siccing a dog

atriebe *nf* revenge, vengeance

atriebēj/s *nm*, ~a *nf* avenger, revenger

atriebība *nf* revenge, vengeance; retaliation

atriebīgi *adv* vengefully, vindictively

atriebīgs *adj* vengeful, vindictive

atriebīgums *nm* vengefulness, vindictiveness

atriebšanās *nfr* revenge, vengeance

atriebt *vt* avenge; take revenge; retaliate

atriebties *vr* **1.** take revenge; **2.** (*3rd pers*) come home to roost

ātriedarbes *indecl adj* quick-start

atriest *vt* rip

atriesties *vr* unravel

atriet *vi* bark in response; (fig.) answer angrily and in a loud voice

atrieties *vr* **1.** get tired of barking; **2.** bark in response

atrietināt *vt* cause milk to flow (from an udder)

atriezt *vt* (of teeth) bare

ātrīgs *adj* quick-tempered

atrijas *nf pl* regurgitated food

ātrijs *nm* atrium

atrikšot *vi* come trotting

ātrināt *vt* hurry

atriņķot *vi* return

atrioventrikulārs *adj* atrioventricular

atripināt *vt* roll to; roll away

atripot *vi* roll to; come rolling; roll back; roll to one side

atrisinājums *nm* **1.** solution (of a problem); **2.** resolution (of a conflict)

atrisināmība *nf* **1.** solvability; **2.** resolvability

atrisināms *adj, part* of **atrisināt 1.** solvable; **2.** resolvable

atrisināt *vt* **1.** (of a problem) solve; **2.** (of a conflict) resolve

atrisināties *vr* **1.** (of a problem) solve itself, be solved; **2.** (of a conflict) resolve itself, be resolved

atrist *vi* get untied, get undone

atrīstīt *vt* **1.** cough up; **2.** regurgitate

atrīt *vt* regurgitate

atritēt *vi* **1.** roll to; **2.** come rolling; **3.** unroll

atritināt *vt* **1.** unroll; unfurl; **2.** roll to; **3.** roll aside

atritināties *vr* **1.** unroll; unfur; **2.** roll to

ātrlaiva *nf* speedboat

ātrlode *nf* soft solder

atrobīt *vt* notch and separate

atroce *nf* rolled-up sleeve

atroceniski *adv* backward; with the back of the hand; palm upward

atrociski *adv* = **atroceniski**

atrocīt *vt* roll up

atrofēties *vr* atrophy

atrofija *nf* atrophy

atrofisks *adj* atrophic

atrokošanās *nfr* handshaking (on parting)

atrokoties *vr* shake hands (on parting)

atrope *nf* alkali grass

atropīns *nm* atropine

atrotīt *vt* roll up (sleeves); unroll

atrotīties *vr* (of sleeves, edges) roll up; unfurl

ātrputra *nf* (col.) hothead

ātrputriņš *nm* (col.) hothead

ātrraksts *nm* stenography

ātrrāvējs *nm* zipper

ātrruna *nf* patter, rapid-fire talk

ātr/s *adj* **1.** quick, fast, swift, rapid, speedy; prompt; **uz ~o** (col.) quick and dirty; **2.** hotheaded, quick-tempered

ātrsirdība *nf* vehemence

ātrsirdīgi *adv* vehemently

ātrsirdīgs *adj* vehement

ātrsirdis *nm* the angry man, irascible person

ātrskrējēj/s *nm*, **~a** *nf* (athlete) runner, sprinter

ātrslēdzējs *nm* zipper

ātrslēdzis *nm* = ātrslēdzējs

ātrslidošana *nf* speed skating

ātrslidotāj/s *nm*, **~a** *nf* speed skater

ātrspēle *nf* lightning chess

ātrspiede *nf* high-speed press

ātršaušana *nf* rapid-fire shooting

ātršāvējs *nm* automatic rifle; rapid-fire

ātršuvējs *nm* loose-leaf binder

atrūgtināt *vt* debitter

atrukšķēt *vi* grunt back

atrūkt *vi* growl in reply, growl back

ātrulis *nm* (col.) hothead

ātruma mērītājs *nm* speedometer

ātruma rādītājs *nm* (aeron.) air speed indicator

ātrumkarba *nf* gear box

ātrumpārslēgs *nm* shift lever, gear shift

ātrum/s *nm* **1.** speed, velocity, rate; **atļautais ā.** speed limit; **lielā ā. preces** express goods; **pirmais kosmiskais ā.** orbital velocity; **otrais kosmiskais ā.** escape velocity; **trešais kosmiskais ā.** escape velocity (for escaping the Solar system) ◊ **~ā** being in a hurry, quickly; **2.** (tech.) gear; **lielais ā.** high gear; **mazais ā.** low gear; **otrais ā.** middle gear; **pirmais ā.** low gear; **tre-šais ā.** high gear; **vidējais ā.** middle gear

ātrumsacensības *nf pl* race

ātrumsacīkstes *nf pl* race

atrun/a *nf* **1.** pretext, excuse, subterfuge; **2. bez ~ām** without reservation; no excuses; **3.** stipulation

atrunāt *vt* **1.** dissuade; **2.** stipulate; specify; **3.** re-ply

atrunāties *vr* **1.** talk oneself out of sth., excuse oneself, make pretexts; **a. ar nezināšanu** plead ignorance; **2. a. pretī** talk back; **3.** tire of talking

atrušināt *vt* uncover (by scraping, pushing aside soil, loose material)

ātrvilciens *nm* express train

ātrvirpošana *nf* (mech.) high-speed turning

ātrvirpotāj/s *nm*, **~a** *nf* high-speed lathe operator

atsacīšanās *nfr* **1.** resignation; abdication; **2.** re-fusal; **3.** giving up

atsacīt *vt, vi* **1.** reply; **2.** refuse; **3.** recite

atsacīties *vr* **1.** refuse, decline; **2.** give up, deny oneself sth.; **3.** deny; **4. a. no amata** step down, resign; **a. no troņa** abdicate

atsaiņot *vt* unwrap

atsaistīt *vt* untie

atsaistīties *vr* get untied; (fig.) get rid of

atsaite *nf* **1.** guy wire, guy cable; **2.** (horse harness) trace; **3.** (el.) decoupling

atsaites enkurs *nm* (tech.) dead man

atsaitēt *vt* (of shoelaces) untie

atsaitēties *vr* become untied

atsākt *vt* resume

atsākties *vr* resume

atsala *nf* = atsals

atsaldēt *vt* 1. freeze; 2. (fig.) turn off; 3. defrost

atsaldināt *vt* sweeten

atsālināšana *nf* desalination

atsālināt *vt* desalt

atsālnis *nm* (tech.) waste liquor

atsals *nm* freeze after a thaw

atsalt *vi* 1. freeze, suffer frostbite; 2. cool (toward a person), become alienated, become estranged; 3. freeze again (after a thaw)

atsalums *nm* (fig.) cooling

atsāļošana *nf* desalinization, desalting

atsāļot *vt* desalt

atsāļoties *vr* desalt

atsāne *nf* (horse harness) trace

atsānis *adv* sideways, aside

atsāpes *nf pl* afterpain

atsargam *adv* in reserve, as a precaution

atsargāt *vt* protect; ward off

atsargāties *vr* 1. abstain from; 2. ward off

atsarka *nf* reddish reflection

atsarkt *vi* begin to redden

atsarkums *nm* reddish reflection, reddening

atsārmot *vt* dealkalize

atsārms *nm* (tech.) waste liquor

atsārņošana *nf* cleanup (of trash)

atsārņot *vt* clean up trash

atsārts *nm* (poet.) reddish reflection

atsārtums *nm* reddish reflection, reddening

atsātināt *vt* desaturate

atsaucams *adj, part* of atsaukt revocable

atsauce *nf* 1. (text) reference; 2. reaction; 3. countersign, password

atsaucība *nf* responsiveness, response

atsauciens *nm* response

atsaucīgi *adv* responsively

atsaucīgs *adj* responsive

atsaucīgums *nm* responsiveness

atsauksme *nf* 1. response, reaction, comment; notice, review; reference (from an empoloyer); 2. countersign, password

atsaukšana *nf* 1. call; summoning; 2. recall, revocation, retraction

atsaukšanas zīme *nf* (mus.) natural

atsaukt *vt* 1. call to (a place); summon, send for; a. atmiņā recollect; 2. call away; (of officials) recall; (of orders) countermand, revoke; (of words) retract; a. trauksmi sound the all-clear

atsaukties *vr* 1. respond; 2. refer to; 3. comment; 4. affect

atsaukums *nm* recall, revocation; retraction, countermand; all-clear signal

atsautēt *vt* steam off

atsavinājums *nm* 1. expropriation; 2. expropriated property

atsavināšana *nf* expropriation

atsavināšanas josla *nf* right-of-way

atsavināt *vt* expropriate; (jur.) condemn

atsavinātāj/s *nm*, ~a *nf* expropriator

atsēda *nf* cold weather (after warm days, hindering the growth of plants)

atsēdēt *vt* 1. (of parts of the body) let go to sleep (by sitting); 2. serve time (in jail)

atsēdēties *vr* sit a long time

atsēdināt *vt* seat; (educ.) make a student repeat a grade

atseglot *vt* unsaddle

atsegsme *nf* (in literary works) disclosure

atsegt *vt* uncover, bare; reveal, expose

atsegte *nf* (weav.) take-up motion

atsegties *vr* uncover oneself; be uncovered; be disclosed

atsegts *adj, part* of atsegt bare

atsegums *nm* (geol.) outcrop

atsēja I *nf* second sowing (of the same crop in the same field or in the same year)

atsēja II (with ê) *nf* (harness) trace

atsēnalot *vt* separate chaff from grain

atsērošana *nf* (of crude oil) sweetening; desulfurization

atsērot *vt* desulfurize

atsēst *vi* sit down

atsēsties *vr* sit down

atsēte *nf* = **atsēja** I

atsevišķi *adv* separately; specially, specifically; **a. stāvošs** isolated

atsevišķs *adj* separate; special; specific, particular

atsiet *vt* 1. untie; 2. tie down, tie back, fasten

atsieties *vr* become untied; get loose

atsijas *nf pl* siftings; bran

atsijāt *vt* sift, screen; separate by sifting

atsijāties *vr* get screened out

atsīkt *vi* come buzzing

atsildīt *vt* rewarm

atsildīties *vr* warm up

atsilt *vi* warm, get warm, warm up, warm to

atsirgt *vi* recover (from an illness)

atsist *vt* 1. knock off; 2. hit, kick to; 3. hit back, kick back; (of a ball) return; 4. ward off; repulse; parry; 5. throw open; 6. (of a part of the body) hit against; stub; 7. make sore (by hitting); 8. be tinged with a color; 9. (of rivets) upset

atsisties *vr* 1. hit, strike; bounce back; 2. be thrown open; 3. bolt back; 4. (col.) take after a relative

atsišķis *nm* (col.) one who takes after an ancestor

atsite *nf* (of firearms) recoil

atsitenis *nm* bulkhead

atsites atspere *nf* counterspring

atisitiens *nm* 1. (phys.) impact; 2. (firearm) recoil; (ball) return

atsitus *adv* at some distance, in a remote location

atskabarga *nf* splinter

atskabargains *adj* splintery; barbed

atskabargainums *nm* susceptibility to splintering

atskābekļot *vt* deoxygenate

atskābēt *vt* deacidify

atskābļošana *nf* deacidification

atskaidrot *vt* sober up; clear up

atskaidroties *vr* sober, become sober; clear up

atskaite *nf* account, report, review; ~s **sistēma** frame of reference

atskaitījums *nm* deduction

atskaitīšana *nf* 1. deduction; 2. (math.) subtraction

atskaitīt *vt* 1. deduct; 2. (math.) subtract; 3. recite

atskaitīties *vr* (col.) report

atskaitot *adv, part* of **atskaitīt** excepting, with the exception of

atskalas *nf pl* (reg.) echo

atskalde *nf* splitting off

atskaldīt *vt* 1. split off; 2. reply curtly

atskaldīties *vr* split off

atskaldnība *nf* cleavability

atskalot *vt* 1. wash ashore; 2. uncover by washing; 3. rinse off; 4. wash away

atskaloties *vr* 1. be washed ashore; 2. be washed away; 3. be uncovered by washing; 4. be rinsed off

atskandināt *vt* (of songs, melodies) repeat

atskanēt *vi* 1. resound, ring out, be heard; 2. echo

atskanīgi *adv* resoundingly

atskanīgs *adj* echoing, resounding

atskaņa *nf* rhyme; **daktiliskā a.** trisyllabic rhyme; **krusteniskās** ~s alternating rhymes; **sie-viskā a.** feminine rhyme; **vīriskā a.** masculine rhyme; ~s (phys., fig.) repercussions; echo

atskaņojums *nm* musical performance

atskaņošana *nf* sound reproduction

atskaņot *vt* 1. (of music) perform, play; 2. rhyme

atskaņotājmāksla *nf* art of muscial performance

atskaņotājmākslinie/ks *nm*, ~**ce** *nf* musical performer

atskaņotāj/s *nm* 1. performer (of music); ~**a** *nf*; 2. (sound) recorder; ~**a galviņa** sound pickup head

atskaņoties *vr* rhyme

atskarāties *vr* hang in tatters

atskarbi *adv* the wrong way; against the grain

atskarpains *adj* barbed

atskarpe *nf* barbed hook, barb; (metall.) fin

atskārsme *nf* understanding; realization

atskārst *vt* grasp, realize

atskārsties *vr* realize

atskārta *nf* insight

atskārtība *nf* understanding; realization

atskārtums *nm* realization

atskatīties *vr* look back; (in negative constructions) unable to take one's eyes off

atskats *nm* look back, retrospective look

atskaust *vt* take (s.o.'s property, prompted by envy)

atskola *nf* continuation school

atskolēns *nm* student in a continuation school

atskrāpēt *vt* scrape off

atskriet *vi* 1. come running; 2. run back, run away from; 3. (of animals) bear young; 4. a. vaļā open

atskrieties *vr* 1. run until exhausted; 2. run, take a run (preparatory to a jump)

atskrubināt *vt* gnaw off

atskrudzināt *vt* (of hair) straighten

atskrūvēt *vt* unscrew

atskrūvēties *vr* come unscrewed

atskujot *vt* remove the needles (from the branches of a needle tree)

atskujotājs *nm* needle remover

atskurbināt *vt* sober up

atskurbt *vi* become sober

atskurbtuve *nf* sobering station

atskurbums *nm* sobering up

atslābināšanās *nfr* relaxation, loosening

atslābināt *vt* relax; loosen

atslābināties *vr* relax

atslābt *vi* relax, slacken, weaken; subside

atslābums *nm* relaxation, slackening, weakening

atslāņojums *nm* (tech.) flaking

atslāņošanās *nfr* flaking; (of the retina) detachment

atslāņot *vt* separate (from other layers)

atslāņoties *vr* separate (from other layers), detach; flake

atslapināt *vt* soak off

atslāt *vt* (com.) come

atslaucīt *vt* 1. sweep away, sweep aside; 2. wipe off

atslaucīties *vr* wipe oneself off

atslaukas *nf pl* sweepings, trash

atslaukties *vr* (of cows) resume yielding milk (after calving)

atslēdziņa *nf dim* of **atslēga**, small key

atslēdznie/ks *nm*, ~**ce** locksmith; mechanic

atslēg/a *nf* 1. lock; **aizšaujamā a.** night latch; **priekškaŗamā** (or **aizkaŗamā, piekaŗamā**) **a.** padlock; ~**s vācele** lock case ◊ **aiz** ~**s** under lock and key; **zem deviņām** ~**ām** well guarded; 2. (instrument; fig.) key; **galvenā a.** master key; **pakaļtaisīta a.** picklock; ~**s gredzens** key ring; ~**s zobi** (key) bit; 3. wrench; 4. (mus.) clef

atslēgas caurums *nm* keyhole

atslēgas akmens *nm* keystone

atslēgas kauls *nm* collarbone

atslēgas nauda *nf* key money

atslēgt *vt* unlock

atslēgties *vr* open up

atsleja *nf* (of chairs, couches) back

atslejus *adv* backward, leaning backwards, pushed back

atslempties *vr* (com.) come

atslēpot *vi* come on skis

atslīdēt *vi* 1. slide to; 2. slide back

atslidot *vi* come skating

atsliept *vi* (col.) come by

atsliet *vt* **1.** lean against; **2.** straighten up

atslieties *vr* **1.** lean against; **2.** straighten up

atslīgt *vi* sink into

atslodze *nf* relief

atslogojums *nm* relief

atslogot *vt* relieve

atsmaidīt *vi* smile back

atsmakot *vt* deodorize

atsmalstīt *vt* dip off

atsmarēot *vi* (of a substance, plant, *3rd pers*) waft its aroma

atsmelt *vt* dip out

atsmiet vi reply laughingly

atsmieties *vr* **1.** reply laughingly; **2.** laugh a long time

atsmīnēt *vi* react with a sneer

atsnauda *nf* nap

atsnausties *vr* take a nap

atsniegt *vt* reach

atsniegties *vr* reach to

atsolot *vi* come marching

atspaidījums *nm* inflammation

atspaidīt *vt* **1.** knead, press (to restore a previous state); **2.** hurt (as a result of prolonged impact)

atspaidīties *vr* begin to hurt

atspaids *nm* **1.** prop; **2.** support; **3.** backshore

atspārdīt *vt* **1.** kick to; **2.** kick off

atspars *nm* counterforce, reaction

atspēcināties *vr* recover (from illness)

atspēkojums *nm* refutation

atspēkot *vt* refute

atspēle *nf* return game

atspēlēt *vt* win back

atspēlēties *vr* (col.) get even

atspere *nf* (mech.) spring; **galvenā a.** mainspring; **~s sloksne** spring leaf

atsperecēšas *nf pl* spring-tooth harrow

atsperēšana *nf* springtoothing

atsperēt *vt* springtooth

atsperība *nf* springiness, elasticity, resilience

atspēriens *nm* (in jumping) takeoff; (soccer) kickoff

atspēries *adj, part* of **atsperties** with all one's might; **labi a.** (col.) doing well for oneself

atsperīgi *adv* resiliently

atsperīgs *adj* springy, elastic, resilient

atsperīgums *nm* springiness, elasticity, resilience

atsperīte *nf dim* of **atspere**, small spring

atsperkultiv[a]tors [ā] *nm* spring-tooth cultivator

atspernazis *nm* switchblade

atspernieki *nm pl* carriage, spring wagon

atsperojums *nm* system of springs

atsperpaplāksne *nf* (mech.) spring washer

atsperrati *nm pl* spring wagon

atsperslodzēts *adj* spring-loaded

atspert *vt* kick to; kick away; kick back

atsperties *vr* **1.** stem oneself against; **2.** (col.) come

atsperuzāle *nf* spleenwort; haircap moss

atsperuzgrieznis *nm* (mech.) spring nut

atspīda *nf* reflection

atspīdēt *vi* **1.** begin to shine; **2.** reflect; **3.** shine, (of light) reach

atspīds *nm* = **atspīdums**

atspīdums *nm* **1.** gleam; **2.** reflection

atspiegt *vi* squeal in reply

atspiest *vt* **1.** lean on; **2.** press open; **3.** make sore (by continuing pressure); **4.** push back; **a. de-fensīvā** put on the defensive

atspiesties *vr* **1.** lean on; **2.** grow sore (from continuing pressure)

atspīguļoties *vr* reflect

atspirdze *nf* refreshment

atspindzēt *vi* whiz by

atspirdzinājums *nm* refreshment

atspirdzināt *vt* refresh

atspirdzināties *vr* refresh oneself, take refreshments

atspirdzinoši *adv* refreshingly

atspirdzinošs *adj, part* of atspirdzināt refreshing

atspirgt *vi* recover, get well; revive

atspirināties *vr* stem oneself against sth.; kick o.s. free

atspīte *nf* retaliation

atspītēt *vi* get back at s.o., retaliate

atspītēties *vr* get back at s.o., retaliate

atspļaut *vi* spit back

atspoga *nf* reflection

atspogāties *vr* be reflected

atspogot *vi* be reflected

atspogs *nm* reflection

atspoguļojums *nm* reflection

atspoguļot *vt* reflect

atspoguļoties *vr* be reflected

atspole *nf* shuttle

atspolēt *vt* unreel

atspolīte *nf dim* of atspole, shuttle

atsprādzēt *vt* unbuckle

atsprādzēties *vr* come unbuckled

atsprāgt *vi* 1. fly open; 2. pop off, split off; 3. be blown to (a place); 4. jump back, recoil

atsprākleniski *adv* (reg.) backwards

atsprāklis or atsprākliski *adv* (reg.) backwards

atsprāklu *adv* backwards

atsprakstēt *vi* (of sparks) fly crackling to

atsprakšķēt *vi* (of sparks) fly crackling

atspraudene *nf* (typ.) composing stick

atspraudīt *vt* stick back; pin up; hitch up

atspraukties *vr* squeeze oneself through to (a place)

atspraust *vt* stick back; pin up; hitch up

atsprēgāt *vi* 1. (of sparks) come flying; 2. peel off

atspridzināt *vt* blast away

atspriedze *nf* relaxation

atspriegums *nm* detente

atspriest *vt* support

atsprindzināt *vt* relax

atspringt *vi* relax

atsprukt *vi* 1. pop open, come loose, come untied; 2. (col.) flee

atspuldzene *nf* (sl.) movie theater

atspulga *nf* reflection

atspulgot *vt* 1. gleam, shine; 2. reflect

atspulgoties *vr* 1. gleam, shine; 2. reflect

atspulgs *nm* reflection

atspulgt *vi* 1. shine; 2. be reflected

atspulgums *nm* reflection

atspurēt *vi* frazzle

atspurgt *vi* (of birds) come fluttering

atspurkšķēt *vi* (of birds) come fluttering

atspuroties *vr* frazzle

atspurt *vi* become frazzled

atstabulēt *vt* entice with pipe playing

atstādinājums *nm* dismissal

atstādināt *vt* dismiss; (educ.) make repeat a grade

atstaigāt *vi* come, sashay over

atstaipīt *vt* stretch

atstaipīties *vr* stretch oneself

atstaļinizācija *nf* de-Stalinization

atstaļinizēt *vt* de-Stalinize

atstarošana *nf* reflection

atstarošanas krāsns *nf* reverberatory furnace

atstarot *vt* reflect

atstarotājs *nm* reflector

atstaroties *vr* be reflected

atstarp/e *nf* 1. distance, space between; ar divām ~ēm double-spaced; 2. interval; pa ~ēm at in-tervals

atstarpināt *vt* space

atstarpinātājs *nm* spacer, furring

atstars *nm* (poet.) reflection

atstāstījuma izteiksme *nf* (gram.) indirect discourse mood, subjunctive

atstāstījums *nm* narration, recounting, retelling; report; account; story

atstāstīt *vt* relate, recount, retell; repeat

atstāsts *nm* story, account

atstāšana *nf* 1. leaving; ~s osta port of embarcation; 2. abandonment

atstāt *vt* 1. leave; **a. bez palīdzības** fail to help; **a. ierindu** (mil.) fall out; **a. kaunā** humiliate; (fig.) betray; **a. neziņā** leave in the dark; **a. pēc stun-dām** keep after school; **a. uz otru gadu** make repeat a grade; **neatstāt akmeni uz akmeņa** devastate; 2. abandon; allow to decay, allow to drift; **a. bez ievērības** disregard; **a. novārtā** neglect; **a. pašplūsmai** allow things to drift; **a. sēdot** leave all dressed up and nowhere to go; 3. save; **a. sev** keep for oneself

atstātība *nf* abandonment

atstāties *vr* go away, leave alone

atstatīt *vt* 1. set back; put back; 2. lean against; 3. remove from office; (jur., of a witness) reject

atstātne *nf* abandoned field, abandoned piece of land; remote place

atstats *adj* remote, distant

atstatu *adv* at a distance

atstatums *nm* distance; space (in time)

atstatus *adv* at a distance

atstaukāt *vt* (of rivets) upset; hot-press; head

atsteberēt *vi* hobble (to a place)

atsteigt *vi* come in a hurry

atsteigties *vr* come in a hurry

atstibīt *vt* (col.) lug (to, here)

atstiept *vt* 1. lug (to, here); 2. stretch out; **a. lūpas** pout; 3. straighten; **a. muguru** (or **kaulus, locek-ļus**) (col.) lie down to rest; **a. asti** (or **ļipu**) die; **a. kājas** a. (com.) die; b. stretch one's legs

atstiepties *vr* 1. straighten up; 2. (col.) stretch out, lie down; 3. (com.) die

atstiklošanās *nfr* devitrification

atstirināties *vr* (com., of animals) die

atstīvēt *vt* (col.) lug (to)

atstope *nf* (in sleds) link (between the front end of a runner and the first standard)

atstote *nf* skirt hem

atstrādāt *vt* work off

atstrādāties *vr* get tired working

atstreipuļot *vi* come staggering

atstūkāt *vt* (metallworking) upset

atstumšana *nf* rejection; **a. no mantojuma** disinheritance

atstumt *vt* 1. push back, push aside; 2. reject, re-buff; **a. no mantojuma** disinherit

atstumtība *nf* rejection

atstumties *vr* 1. push off; 2. come pushing

atstūrēt *vi* come sailing; come driving; steer to (a place)

atstutēt *vt* 1. (barb.) prop up; 2. (barb.) lean against

atstutēties *vr* (barb.) lean against

atsudrabot *vt* desilver

atsukas *nf pl* combings; (of flax) tow

atsukāt *vt* comb back

atsūknēt *vt* vacuum, vacuum-clean; pump out

atsuloties *vr* (of water in food) separate; (of food) become watery

atsust *vi* come off (through the action of steam)

atsutināt *vt* steam off

atsūtīt *vt* send

atsvabināt *vt* free; **a. vietu** make room for

atsvabinātāj/s *nm*, ~a *nf* liberator

atsvabināties *vr* free oneself

atsvabinošs *adj, part* of **atsvabināt** relaxing

atsvaidze *nf* deodorant

atsvaidzināt *vt* refresh, freshen up; **a. zināšanas** brush up one's knowledge

atsvaidzinātājs *nm* deodorant; freshener

atsvaidzināties *vr* refresh oneself

atsvars *nm* weight, counterweight, counterbalance, counterpoise

atsveicināšanās *nfr* leave-taking, parting, farewell

atsveicināt *vi* return a greeting

atsveicināties *vr* take leave, say goodbye

atsveķot *vt* tap resin

atsvempties *vr* come gallumphing

atsvērt *vt* **1.** take out (off) and weigh; **2.** counterbalance; compensate ◊ **ne ar zeltu atsveŗams** worth its weight in gold

atsvērties *vr* **1.** sink back; **2.** lean back, detach oneself from

atsvešināšanās *nfr* alienation

atsvešināt *vt* alienate, estrange

atsvešināties *vr* become alienated, become es-tranged

atsvēte *nf* repeat celebration; a Sunday that follows a major holiday

atsvētīt *vt* celebrate an **atsvēte**

atsvētīties *vr* do enough celebrating

atsviediens *nm* backswing

atsviedīgi *adv* adroitly

atsviedīgs *adj* adroit

atsviest *vt* **1.** throw aside, toss aside; **2.** throw back, toss back

atsviesties *vr* throw oneself back

atsvilpt *vt* **1.** summon by whistling; **2.** whistle back

atsvilpties *vr* reply with a whistle, whistle back

atsvīst *vi* (of light) dawn

atšālējies *adj, part* of **atšālēties** (sl., of beve-rages) stale

atšālēties *vr* (of beverages) become stale

atšalkas *nf pl* (poet.) echo

atšalkot *vi* echo

atšalkt *vi* echo

atšaubeniski *adv* backwards

atšaubiski *adv* backwards

atšaubu *adv* backwards

atšaudināt *vt* (col.) let rest

atšaudīties *vr* fire back, return fire

atšaut *vt* **1.** shoot off; **2.** (of projectiles) reach (the target); **3.** unbolt; **4.** stretch out ◊ **a. asti** (or **ļipu**) (sl.) breathe one's last; **a. lūpu** pout; **5.** (col.) get to a place fast

atšauties *vr* **1.** stretch out; **2.** (col.) come rushing; **3.** cool off; **4.** become stale; **5.** open suddenly

atšiept *vt* (of teeth) bare

atšiepties *vr* bare one's teeth

atšifrējums *nm* decoding

atšifrēšana *nf* decryption, decoding, deci-phering

atšifrēt *vt* decode, decipher

atšķaidāms *adj, part* of **atšķaidīt** dilutable

atšķaidījums *nm* dilution

atšķaidināt *vt* dilute

atšķaidīšana *nf* **1.** dilution; **2.** adulteration

atšķaidīt *vt* **1.** dilute; **2.** adulterate

atšķaidītājs *nm* **1.** thinner; diluent; **2.** diluter

atšķaidīties *vr* become diluted

atšķelšanās *nfr* separation; breakaway

atšķelt *vt* split off, separate

atšķeltība *nf* separation

atšķelties *vr* split off, separate from

atšķēlums *nm* split-off piece

atšķērst *vt* cut open, dissect

atšķēršļošana *nf* (mil.) obstacle clearing, breaching

atšķeterēt *vt* **1.** untwine; unwind; **2.** disen-tangle

atšķeterēties *vr* **1.** untwine; unwind; **2.** become disentangled

atšķetināt *vt* **1.** untwine; unwind; **2.** disen-tangle

atšķetināties *vr* **1.** untwine; unwind; **2.** become disentangled

atšķīdināt *vt* dilute

atšķidrināt *vt* dilute

atšķila *nf* fragment

atšķindēt *vi* hear a clanging sound

atšķipelēt *vt* shovel away, clear (by shoveling)

atšķira *nf* distinction, difference

atšķiras *nf pl* siftings

atšķirība *nf* distinction; difference; **bez ~s** regardless of any differences, indiscrimi-nately

atšķirības zīmes *nf pl* (mil.) insignia

atšķirīgi *adv* distinctly; differently

atšķirīgs *adj* distinct, different

atšķirīgums *nm* distinction, difference

atšķirot *vt* sort and separate

atšķirsme *nf* difference

atšķirt *vt* **1.** distinguish; differentiate; discriminate; **2.** separate; **a. no krūts** wean; **3.** (of pages) open

atšķirtenis *nm* divorced man

atšķirtība *nf* isolation, seclusion; separation; ~s **trauksme** separation anxiety

atšķirties *vr* **1.** differ, stand out; **2.** separate onself (from others), seclude oneself, isolate oneself; **3.** (of books) open

atšķirtne *nf* (of hair) parting

atšķirts *adj, part* of **atšķirt** separate

atšķiru *adv* separately

atšķirule *nf* divorcee

atšķirulis *nm* divorced man

atšķūrēt *vt* (col.) **1.** bring; **2.** shovel free, shovel away

atšķūtēt *vt* (col.) bring

atšļākt *vt, vi* splash at; splash up to

atšļākties *vr* (of waves) reach

atšļukt *vi* slip to (a place)

atšļūkt *vi* slide to (a place); (sl.) come

atšļupstēt *vi* mutter in reply

atšmaukt *vi* come (after slipping away)

atšņākt *vi* **1.** hiss in reply; **2.** hiss back

atšņiebt *vt* (of teeth) bare

atšņorēt *vt* (col.) untie

atšņorēties *vr* (col.) become untied

atštauka *nf* (sl.) **1.** recoil; **2.** retirement

atštaukāt *vt* (col., of rivets) upset

atšūbeniski *adv* backward

atšūpot *vt* bring rocking

atšūt *vt* hem

atšūties *vr*, usu. *imper* **atšujies!** (sl.) get lost!

atšuve *nf* hem

attaisāmais *nom adj* opener

attaisīt *vt* open

attaisīties *vr* open

attaisnojums *nm* **1.** justification; **2.** (jur.) acquittal

attaisnošana *nf* acquittal

attaisnošanās *nfr* excuse

attaisnot *vt* **1.** (jur.) acquit; **2.** justify

attaisnotais *nom adj* the acquitted

attaisnotājs *nm* **1.** justifier; **2.** *adj* justified; valid

attaisnotājs dokuments *nm* voucher

attaisnotājs spriedums *nm* acquittal, verdict of not guilty

attaisnoties *vr* **1.** justify oneself; **a. ar nezināšanu** plead ignorance; **2.** be justified; prove correct

attaka *nf* (of streams) branch, arm, slough

attāle *nf* usu. *loc* **attālē** in the distance

attālējs *adj* distant, remote

attālēm *adv* at some distance

attāli *adv* far off

attāliene *nf* distance

attālināšanās *nfr* **1.** moving away; withdrawal; **2.** estrangement; alienation

attālināt *vt* **1.** move away; **2.** postpone; **3.** estrange; **4.** differentiate

attālināties *vr* **1.** move away; distance oneself from; **2.** become remote (in time); **3.** become estranged, become alienated

attāls *adj* distant, remote

attālu *adv* far off

attāluma deglis *nm* proximity fuse

attāluma mērītājs *nm* odometer

attāluma noteicējs *nm* range finder

attāluma noteikšana *nf* ranging

attālum/s *nm* distance; . . . ~ā at a distance of . . .

attapība *nf* quick wit, ingenuity, resourcefulness

attapīgi *adv* ingeniously, cleverly

attapīgs *adj* quick-witted, ingenious, resourceful

attapīgums *nm* quick wit, ingenuity, resourcefulness

attapt *vi* manage to get to (a place)

attapties *vr* 1. recover (from a surprise); 2. remember suddenly

attarot *vt* empty nets (of fish)

attaukošanās *nfr* weight reduction

attaukot *vt* degrease

attaukoties *vr* 1. slim, reduce; 2. lose fat

attaurēt *vi* call back (using a horn); call together (with a horn)

attaustīties *vr* grope one's way to (a place)

attauvoties *vr* (naut.) cast off

attece *nf* backflow

atteceņus *adv* 1. at a run; 2. at full speed

attecēt *vi* 1. come scurrying; 2. (of streams) branch off; pour back; pour to; 3. (of animals) drop, give birth

atteikšanās *nfr* 1. refusal; 2. renunciation; abandonment; 3. resignation; abdication; 4. (jur.) abjuration; disclaimer

atteikt *vt* 1. reply; come back, retort; 2. cancel; 3. recite; 4. refuse; reject; repudiate; deny

atteikties *vr* 1. refuse; decline; 2. resign; abdicate; **a. no amata** resign; **a. no troņa** abdicate; 3. give up, relinquish

atteikums *nm* refusal

atteka *nf* (of streams) branch, arm, slough; **iz-sīkstoša a.** false channel

attēlojošs *adj, part* of **attēlot** descriptive

attēlojums *nm* depiction, description; portrayal, interpretation

attēlot *vt* depict, describe; portray, interpret; mim-ic; **nepareizi a.** misrepresent

attēlotāj/s *nm*, ~a *nf* portrayer; interpreter

attēloties *vr* 1. be reflected; 2. picture (in one's mind)

attēls *nm* 1. image; reflection; **šķietamais a.** (phys.) virtual image; 2. (graphics) picture, illustration, figure; display; **grafisks a.** graphic representation; **tiešs a.** erect image

attēlu izvērsējs *nm* (compu.) scanner

attenterēt *vi* stagger to, toddle to; stagger back

attiece *nf* 1. attitude; 2. relationship

attiecīb/a *nf* 1. relation, relationship; ~ā uz in re-lation to, with regard to; 2. ratio

attiecību sk[a]la [ā] *nf* (stat.) ratio scale

attiecīgi *adv* appropriately; accordingly; correspondingly

attiecīgs *adj* appropriate; corresponding

attiecinājums *nm* application (bringing to bear)

attiecināt *vt* apply (make use of as suitable)

attieksme *nf* 1. attitude; 2. relationship

attieksmes vietniekvārds *nm* relative pronoun

attie/kties *vr* refer to, concern, apply to; **neattiekties uz lietu** be irrelevant; **kas ~cas uz** as to

attiesājums *nm* (jur.) dispossession

attiesāt *vt* (jur.) dispossess

attikt *vi* 1. get to (a place); 2. come undone

attikties *vr* 1. happen to be at a place; 2. happen; 3. come true; 4. get one's fill, be satisfied; 5. get better; 6. figure out

attiņāt *vt* unwrap

attipināt *vi* trip to, toddle to

attirgus *nm* the day following market day

attirināt *vt* **a. kājas** (com.) kick the bucket

attīrīšana *nf* cleaning, cleansing; purification; (sewage) treatment

attīrīt *vt* 1. clear; clean; 2. treat, purify

attīrīties *vr* be cleansed

attirkšķēt *vi* come rattling

attirpināt *vt* stretch one's legs (after keeping them in the same position a long time)

attirpt *vi* (of limbs gone numb) lose numbness

attīstība *nf* development; ~s novirze developmental deviation

attīstīšana *nf* (photo.) development

attīstīt *vt* 1. develop; 2. unwrap; 3. (of speed) pick up

attīstītāj/s *nm*, ~**a** *nf* (person; photo.) developer

attīstīties *vr* 1. develop; evolve; 2. unwrap

attīt *vt* 1. unwrap; unfurl; 2. untwist

attīties *vr* 1. unwrap; unfurl; 2. untwist

attramdīt *vt* chase to, drive to

attransportēt *vt* transport to

attrāpīt *vt* (of an intended target) hit; hit upon

attraukt *v* 1. *vt* shake down; 2. *vi* retort; 3. *vi* come in a rush

attraukties *vr* come in a rush

attrenk(ā)t *vt* chase to, drive to

attriekt *vt* (of animals, people) drive to; (of an enemy) throw back

attriekties *vr* come traipsing

attrīt *vt* wear down

attrīties *vr* wear down

attrūkt *vi* (of buttons, accessories) come off

attūkt *vi* (of swellings) subside

attuntulēt *vt* (col.) unwrap

attuntuļot *v* 1. *vi* come waddling; 2. *vt* unwrap

attuntuļoties *vr* come waddling

attupināt *vt* (col.) seat

attupties *vr* squat

attura *nf* reservation

atturēšanās *nfr* abstention; abstinence

atturēt *vt* hold back; keep from

atturēties *vr* abstain; refrain

atturgultnis *nm* axial thrust bearing

atturība *nf* 1. modesty; reserve; reticence; 2. abstinence, temperance

atturībnie/ks *nm*, ~**ce** *nf* abstainer; **pilnīgs a.** teetotaler

atturīgi *adv* reservedly; reticently; guardedly, cautiously

atturīgs *adj* 1. reserved, restrained; reticent; 2. temperate, abstemious; 3. guarded, cautious

atturīgums *nm* reserve, restraint

atturis *nm* (mech.) stop

atturķīlis *nm* holding key

atturošana *nf* falsework removal

atturs *nm* (mental) reservation

atturuzgrieznis *nm* stop nut

attvaiks *nm* exhaust steam

atūdeņot *vt* 1. dehydrate; 2. drain

atūdeņošana *nf* dehydration

atūdeņotājs *nm* 1. dehydrating agent; desiccant; 2. drain, drain cock

atūdeņoties *vr* (of whey, watery portion) separate

aturkšķēt *vt*, *vi* grunt in reply

atutīt *vt* = **atutot**

atutīties *vr* = **atutoties**

atutot *vt* delouse

atutoties *vr* get deloused

atvad/as *nf pl* farewell, parting, leave-taking, goodbye; ~**u vārdi** parting words

atvadāties *vr* move in

atvadēties *vr* (of beer) go flat

atvadības *nf pl* farewell party

atvadīšanās *nfr* leave-taking, parting, farewell; **a. viesības** seeing-off party

atvadīt *vt* see s.o. to (a place)

atvadīties *vr* say goodbye, bid farewell, take leave

atvadnieki *nm pl* wedding guests (who accompany the new bride back to her home for her to say goodbye to her family and relatives)

atvaga *nf* a furrow that encircles a field

atvaicāt *vi*, *vt* answer a question with a question

atvaidēt *vi* answer moaning

atvainošanās *nfr* apology

atvaino/t *vt* excuse; ~**jiet!** excuse me! I am sorry!

atvaino/ties *vr* excuse oneself, apologize; ~**jos!** I beg your pardon!

atvaire *nf* defense; deflection

atvairīgi *adv* defensively

atvairīgs *adj* defensive

atvairis *nm* bumper; (naut) fender

atvairīšana *nf* repulsion

atvairīt *vt* 1. repulse; rebuff; parry; 2. keep off, fend off; 3. suppress

atvairīties *vr* 1. fend off, ward off, keep off; 2. parry, repulse

atvākot *vt* (of honeycombs) uncap

atvākt *vt* 1. bring; 2. shove aside

atvākties *vr* (of a household) move to

atvaļa *nf* respite

atvaļinājum/s *nm* vacation; leave; furlough; ~ā on vacation

atvaļināt *vt* retire

atvaļināties *vr* retire

atvarains *adj* full of whirlpools

atvārījums *nm* boiled pan drippings

atvariņš *nm dim* of **atvars**, small whirpool

atvārīt *vt* boil (until meat separates from bone)

atvārīties *vr* come off in boiling

atvars *nm* 1. whirlpool; 2. opening; (of instruments) mouth

atvārsne *nf* opening; foramen

atvārsnis *nm* hole, opening

atvārsnīte *nf* (bot.) stoma

atvāršas *nf pl* repeat wedding feast (celebrated the Sunday after the wedding at the home of the bride's parents)

atvaru *adv* half-open

atvarums *nm* whirlpool

atvarzot *vt* (col.) untie

atvasājs *nm* coppice

atvasara *nf* Indian summer

atvasarīgs *adj* late-summer

atvase *nf* 1. sprout, shoot; 2. (col.) offspring

atvasinājums *nm* derivation; (math.) derivative

atvasināt *vt* derive

atvazāt *vt* drag in

atvazāties *vr* arrive (in gadding about)

atvāzt *vt* open; unclasp

atvažot *vi* (folk.) come riding, come driving

atvēcināt *vt* raise one's arm (for a blow)

atvēcināties *vr* fend off

atvedinājums *nm* derivation; deduction

atvedināt *vt* 1. apply to, relate to; 2. make a deduction; derive; 3. **a. atmiņā** remember

atvēdīt *vt* make waft to

atveide *nf* (poet.) variant

atveidņošana *nf* (metall.) formwork removal

atveidņot *vt* (metall.) remove form, strip form

atveidņotājs *nm* (metall.) form remover, stripper

atveidojums *nm* rendering; interpretation; reproduction, simulacrum

atveidot *vt* render, reproduce

atveidoties *vr* take shape (mentally)

atveids *nm* 1. rendering; interpretation; 2. form; image

atvējot *vi* waft from

atveldze *nf* refreshment; thirst quencher

atveldzēt *vt* refresh

atveldzēties *vr* refresh oneself; quench one's thirst

atveldzinājums *nm* refreshment; thirst quencher

atveldzināt *vt* refresh

atveldzināties *vr* refresh oneself

atvēle *nf* (obs.) permission

atvēlēt *vt* 1. allot; 2. (obs.) permit

atvēlēties *vr* allow oneself

atvelgt *vi* (of plants) recover

atvelt *vt* 1. roll to; 2. roll away

atvelties *vr* 1. roll away; 2. fall back

atvemt *vt* throw up, vomit

atvērā *adv* open

atvere *nf* opening

atvērējs *nm*, ~a *nf* opener

atvērējs pulss *nm* gating pulse

atverkšt *vt* (of teeth) bare

atvērst *vt* 1. ward off; 2. (of eyes) avert; 3. bring back, restore

atvērsties *vr* turn away

atvērt *vt* open; **a. durvis** a. open the door; b. unlock the door; c. answer the door; **a. zaļās ugunis** give the green light

atvērtība *nf* openness; receptiveness

atvērties *vr* open

atvērtne *nf* 1. slit in a skirt; 2. top part of a two-part door

atveru *adv* half-open

atvērums *nm* 1. opening; 2. (of a book) facing pages

atvērzt *vt* (of teeth) bare

atveseļošanās *nfr* convalescence, recuperation; **a. māja** convalescent home

atveseļot *vt* cure

atveseļoties *vr* get better, recover

atvēsināt *vt* cool

atvēsināties *vr* cool off

atvest *vt* bring; (fig.) lead to

atvēst *vi* cool off

atvēstīt *vt* (obs.) call, invite

atvešana *nf* bringing; **piespiedu a.** compelled appearance

atvētīt *vt* separate in winnowing

atvēzeniski *adv* using the backswing

atvēzenisks *adj* backswing

atvēzēt *vt* swing back

atvēzēties *vr* swing back; **a. sitienam** raise one's arm for a blow; **a. (pret kādu) ar zobenu** brandish one's sword at s.o.

atvēziens *nm* backswing

atvēzt *vt* swing back

atvēzties *vr* swing back

atvīdēt *vi* 1. shine dimly; 2. reflect dimly

atvideināt *vi* twitter back, twitter in reply

atviebt *vt* **a. lūpu** pout

atvieglinājums *nm* 1. relief; 2. advantage, privilege

atvieglināt *vt* ease, make easier, facilitate, lighten; alleviate

atvieglināties *vr* (col.) relieve oneself

atvieglojums *nm* 1. relief; 2. advantage, privilege

atvieglot *vt* ligthen, ease; alleviate; **a. sirdi** unburden oneself

atviegloti *adv* with relief

atvieglots *adj, part* of **atvieglot** lightened, eased; alleviated; easier; lighter; (of terms) favorable

atvienojums *nm* (el.) disconnection; power cut

atvienot *vt* disconnect; cut off; **a. strāvu** cut off electricity

atvienoties *vr* get disconnected

atviept *vt* **a. lūpu** pout

atviesoties *vr* 1. repay a visit; 2. say goodbye

atvietot *vt* replace; substitute

atvietotāj/s *nm,* ~**a** *nf* replacement; substitute

atviezt *vt* **a. lūpu** pout; **a. zobus** bare one's teeth

atvilcējmuskulis *nm* (anat.) abductor

atvilceniski *adv* **a. siet** tie a slipknot, tie a hitch

atvīlēt *vt* file down, file off

atvilgt *vi* 1. soften; 2. relax

atvilināt *vt* entice, lure

atvilkšana *nf* (mil.) withdrawal

atvilkšanās *nfr* (mil.) withdrawal

atvilkt *vt* 1. pull to; drag; draw; **a. elpu** a. breathe a sigh of relief; b. take five, rest; 2. pull away, pull aside, pull back; 3. pull open; 4. deduct; 5. (col., of an unwilling person) drag; 6. (col.) (of coats, wraps) take off.

atvilkties *vr* 1. catch one's breath; 2. (of coats, wraps, coll) take off; 3. (com.) come, arrive; 4. pull back

atvilktne *nf* drawer

atvilkums *nm* deduction

atvilnis *nm* reflux; regurgitation

atvilnīt *vi* stream

atvilt *vt* lure away; entice

atviļņi *nm pl* low tide, ebb

atviļņot *vi* reverberate

atviļņoties *vr* reverberate

atvirmot *v* **1.** *vi* flutter down; come fluttering; **2.** *vt* send fluttering

atvirt *vi* boil off

atviru *adv* open

atvirpuļot *v* **1.** *vi* come whirling; **2.** *vt* whirl sth. to

atvirze *nf* deviation; digression

atvirzījums *nm* deviation

atvirzīšanās *nfr* retreat; stepping back

atvirzīt *vt* **1.** move to, move back, move away from; move aside; set back; **2.** postpone

atvirzīties *vr* move to, move back, move away from, move aside

atvīstīt *vt* unwrap

atvīt *vt* untwist, unwind; unfurl

atvīties *vr* **1.** untwist; **2.** wind

atvizēt *vi* **1.** glisten, shimmer; **2.** begin to glisten, begin to shimmer

atvizināt *vt* bring back from a pleasure drive

atvizma *nf* reflection

atvizmot *v* **1.** *vi* glisten, shimmer; **2.** *vi* begin to glisten, begin to shimmer; **3.** *vt* reflect

atvizuļot *v* **1.** *vi* glisten, shimmer; **2.** *vi* begin to glisten, begin to shimmer; **3.** *vt* reflect

atzagt *vt* steal back

atzagties *vr* sneak back

atzāģēt *vt* saw off

atzaiga *nf* reflection

atzaigot *vt* reflect; *vi* be reflected

atzaigoties *vr* be reflected

atzailis *nm* a spot in a winter wheat field showing more vigorous growth

atzala *nf* = **atzale**

atzale *nf* **1.** seedling; **2.** second growth of grass, rowen; **3.** unripe grain stalk

atzalains *adj* containing many seedlings or immature grain stalks

atzalgoties *vr* **1.** begin to shine; **2.** reflect; **3.** shine, (of light) reach

atzaliņa *nf dim* of **atzale**, seedling; rowen; unripe grain stalks

atzaļot *vi* green again

atzare *nf* = **atzarojums**

atzarkabelis *nm* branch cable

atzarojums *nm* **1.** branch, offshoot; (of a road) fork; **2.** (RR) siding; **3.** barb

atzarot *vt* prune

atzaroties *vr* branch off

atzars *nm* = **atzarojums**

atzelt *vi* green again; recover

atzibēt *vi* glitter; shine

atzīdīt *vt* (of animals) wean

atzīdīte *nf* weaned lamb

atziedēt *vi* bloom again

atziema *nf* return of cold weather in early spring

atzīme *nf* **1.** note; ~s uz malas marginal notes; **2.** (educ.) mark, grade

atzīmēt *vt* **1.** note down, record; mark; check; **a. punktus** keep score; **2.** remark on, note; **3.** (of anniversaries) celebrate

atzīmju žurnāls *nm* grade book

atzinība *nf* recognition, appreciation

atzinīgi *adv* appreciatively

atzinīgs *adj* **1.** appreciative; **2.** positive, good

atzinum/s *nm* opinion; finding, conclusion; **pēc mana ~a** in my opinion

atziņa *nf* **1.** conclusion, finding; **2.** cognition

atziņas koks *nm* tree of knowledge

atziņas psīcholoģija *nf* cognitive psychology

atziņas teorija *nf* epistemology

atzīstami *adv* admittedly

atzīstams *adj, part* of **atzīt** admitted

atzīšana *nf* recognition; acknowledgment; admission; **a. par vainīgu** verdict of guilty; **a. par spēkā neesošu** annulment

atzīšanās *nfr* confession

atzīt *vt* recognize, acknowledge, admit; **a. savu vainu** admit one's guilt; plead guilty; **a. par vainīgu** find guilty, reach the verdict of guilty; **a. par labu** approve; **a. par nederīgu** annul, cancel; **a. par vajadzīgu** consider it necessary

atzīties *vr* confess; **a. mīlestībā** make a declaration of love; **a. par vainīgu** plead guilty; **neat-zīties par vainīgu** plead innocent

atzvala *nf* (of chairs) back

atzvanīt *vi* (of telephone) **1.** call back; **2.** (obs.) hang up

atzvans *nm* (of telephone) hanging up

atzvelt *vt* lean back; (of one's head) throw back

atzveltenis *nm* easy chair

atzvelties *vr* **1.** lean back against; recline; **2.** fall back heavily

atzveltne *nf* (of chairs) back

atzveltness krēsls *nm* easy chair, recliner

atzveltnis *nm* easy chair

atzviegt *vi* respond with a neigh

atzviegties *vr* respond with a neigh

atzvilt *vi* **1.** lean back against; recline; **2.** fall back heavily

atzvilu or **atzvilus** *adv* reclining

atzvīņot *vt* scale

atzvīņotājs *nm* scaler

atžadzināt *vi* (of a magpie) call back, answer

atžāvāties *vr* answer with a yawn

atžeibt *vi* come to; recover from a blow

atžilbināt *vt* sober up

atžilbt *vi* come to; recover from a blow

atžirbt *vi* **1.** come to, recover; **2.** sober

atžirgt *vi* recover, get well; revive

atžogot *vt* fence off

atžuburains *adj* branched, forked

aube *nf* coif

aubise *nf* (reg.) poor shotgun

aubriecija *nf* aubrietia

audaļa *nm* diligent, skilled worker

audēj/s *nm*, **~a** *nf* weaver

audekla pauspapīrs *nm* tracing cloth

audekla preces *nf pl* dry goods

audekla veltenis *nm* (weav.) cloth beam

audeklenes *nf pl* linen or cotton pants

audekl/s *nm* linen or cotton fabric; (painter's) canvas; **~a sējums** cloth binding

audene *nf* woven sash

audeniski *adv* rapidly

audenīte *nf dim* of **audene**, sash

audi *nm pl* **1.** (biol.) tissue; **2.** (weav.) weft

audience *nf* (reception, interview) audience

audiēšana *nf* audio-lingual method

audināt *vt* (poet.) weave

audiofrekvence *nf* audio frequency

audiogramma *nf* audiogram

audiokasete *nf* audio cassette

audiometrija *nf* audiometry

audiometrs *nm* audiometer

audiona lampa *nf* detector tube

audiona uztvērējs *nm* grid leak detector

audions *nm* (el.) audion

auditorija *nf* **1.** auditorium; **2.** audience, listeners

auditor/s *nm*, **~e** *nf* (educ.; bus.) auditor

audits *nm* audit

audrums *nm* wild, unruly child or person; brat

audu drellis *nm* weft-faced twill

audumiņš *nm dim* of **audums**, fabric, cloth, material

audummala *nf* selvage

audums *nm* fabric, cloth, material; **pastiprināts a.** double-woven fabric

audu repsis *nm* weft-faced rep

audze *nf* **1.** (forest.) stand; growth; **2.** generation

audzējs *nm* tumor

audzējums *nm* crop

audzēkn/is *nm*, **~e** *nf* **1.** student, pupil, trainee; **bijušais a.** alumnus; **bijušā ~e** alumna; **2.** ward

audzēknītis *nm dim* of **audzēknis**, pupil

audzelība *nf* fast growth; fecundity; prolificacy

audzelīgi *adv* prolifically

audzelīgs *adj* 1. fast growing; fecund; prolific; 2. growth-promoting

audzelīgums *nm* fast growth; fecundity; prolificacy

audzēšana *nf* cultivation, raising, growing; rearing, breeding

audzēt *vt* cultivate, raise, grow; breed

audzētājs *nm*, ~a *nf* grower; breeder

audzētava *nf* nursery; breeding farm

audzināšana *nf* 1. education; ~s iestāde educational institution; 2. upbringing, breeding

audzinā/t *vt* 1. educate; 2. bring up; lab ~ts well-bred; courteous; slikti ~ts ill-bred; rude; grūti ~ms intractable, unmanageable, incorrigible; 3. develop

audzinātāj/s *nm*, ~a *nf* 1. educator; 2. tutor

audzīte *nf dim* of **audze**, forest growth

audžģimene *nf* foster family

audēubērns *nm* foster child

audžubrālis *nm* foster brother

audžudēls *nm* foster son

audžumāsa *nf* foster sister

audžumāte *nf* foster mother

audēžumeita *nf* foster daughter

audēžutēvs *nm* foster father

audžuvecāki *nm pl* foster parents

auga *nf* harvest

augājs *nm* plant cover

augaļa *nf* birch grove; young forest

augēdāj/s *nm*, ~a herbivore

augīts *nm* augite

augkopība *nf* cultivation of plants

augkop/is *nm*, ~e *nf* plant grower

auglenīca *nf* (bot.) pistil

auglība *nf* fertility, fruitfulness, productivity, fecundity

auglīgi *adv* fruitfully, productively

auglīgs *adj* fertile, fruitful, productive, fecund

auglīgums *nm* fertility, fruitfulness, productivity, fecundity

auglinieks *nm* (bot.) pistil

auglis *nm* 1. fruit; see also **augļi**; 2. fetus

auglītis *nm dim* of **auglis**, little fruit

augļaugs *nm* fruit-bearing plant

augļ/i *nm pl* 1. fruit; 2. (bus.) interest; ~u a. compound interest

augļkoks *nm* fruit tree

augļkopība *nf* fruit farming, fruit growing

augļkopības saimniecība *nf* fruit farm

augļkop/is *nm*, ~e *nf* fruit grower

augļkultūra *nf* fruit growing

augļermenis *nm* (bot.) fruiting body

augļlapa *nf* (bot.) carpel

augļošana *nf* usury

augļot *vi* engage in usury

augļotājs *nm* usurer

augļoties *vr* (obs.) be fruitful

augļsikspārnis *nm* flying fox

augļu cukurs *nm* fructose

augļu dārzs *nm* orchard

augļūdens *nm* soft drink

augļu koku mūķene *nf* vaporer moth

augļu koku tīklērce *nf* red spider mite

augmentācija *nf* augmentation

augments *nm* (ling.) augment

augonis *nm* boil, abscess

augoņains *adj* covered with boils, abscessed

augs *nm* plant

augs *adj* See **augu**

augseka *nf* rotation of crops

augsme *nf* growth, development

augsne *nf* soil

augstā abroma *nf* devil's cotton

augstā ežziede *nf* a globe thistle, Echinops ritro

augstais amoliņš *nm* melilot

augstais grīslis *nm* tussock sedge

augstākais *adj, super* of **augsts** highest; supreme; (*adv*, col.) at most

augstākstāvošs *adj* higher (in a hierarchy), superior

augstā žodzene *nf* tall sisymbrium

augstbūve *nf* high-rise building

augstceltne *nf* high-rise building

augstcienīb/a *nf* high regard; ~ā (obs. complimentary close) very truly yours

augstcilnis *nm* high relief

augstciltība *nf* nobility

augstciltīgais *nom adj* nobleman

augstciltīgs *adj* of noble birth, noble

augstciltīgums *nm* nobility

augstciltnieks *nm* nobleman

augstdegunis *nm* (col.) snob

augstdzimis *adj* of noble birth, noble

augstdzimtība *nf* nobility; **Jūsu a.** (in addressing a person) my lord

augstdzimtīgais *nom adj* nobleman

augstdzimušais *nom adj* nobleman

augste *nf* (poet.) heights; summit

augstenes *nf pl* attic

augstfrekvences *indecl adj* high-frequency; (of an electronic filter) high-pass

augstgr[a]dīgs [ā] *adj* high-grade

augsti *adv* high; highly; very

augstība *nf* highness; (Bibl.) the highest; **Jūsu a.** Your Highness

augstiene *nf* upland, high country, plateau

augstiņi *nm pl* centaury; see also **skaistie a.**

augstjaudas *indecl adj* high-power

augstkrastains *adj* having high banks

augstžēcēj/s *nm*, ~a *nf* high jumper

augstžēcīte *nf* (folk., an epithet for the frog) high jumper

augstlēkšana *nf* high jump; **a. no vietas** standing high jump

augstmanība *nf* nobility, aristocracy

augstmanīgi *adv* aristocratically

augstmanīgs *adj* aristocratic

augstman/is *nm*, ~e *nf* noble, aristocrat

augstnesis *nm* (obs.) nobleman

augstnieks *nm* (obs.) nobleman

augstpapēžu *indecl adj* high-heel

augstplāksnis *nm* high-wing monoplane

augstprātība *nf* haughtiness, snobbery, arrogance

augstprātīgi *adv* haughtily, snobbishly, arrogantly

augstprātīgs *adj* haughty, snobbish, arrogant

augstprātīgums *nm* haughtiness, snobbery, ar-rogance

augstprāt/is *nm*, ~e *nf* haughty or arrogant person, snob

augstprātnieks *nm* haughty or arrogant person, snob

augstprocentīgs *adj* high-proof

augstraudzīte *nf* (folk., an epithet for the frog) one that looks up

augstražība *nf* high productivity

augstražīgi *adv* highly productively

augstražīgs *adj* highly productive

augstražīgums *nm* high productivity

augsts *adj* **1.** high; tall; **2.** (of holidays) major; **3.** (of style) lofty, elevated

augstsirdība *nf* magnanimity, generosity

augstsirdīgi *adv* magnanimously, generously

augstsirdīgs *adj* magnanimous, generous

augstsirdīgums *nm* magnanimity, generosity

augstskanīgs *adj* high-flown, high-sounding

augstskola *nf* higher educational institution, university

augstskolnie/ks *nm*, ~ce *nf* university student

augstspiede *nf* letterpress

augstspiediena *indecl adj* high-pressure

augstspieduma madarojums *nm* block printing

augstspiedums *nm* letterpress

augstspriegums *nm* high voltage

augststumbrains *adj* (of trees, forest) tall

augsttīrelis *nm* high moor

augstu *adv* high; highly; very

augstumlīnija *nf* contour (line)

augstummērītājs *nm* altimeter; height finder

augstum/s *nm* **1.** height; altitude; ~i heights; summit; (fig.) acme; **2.** (of sound) pitch

augstumstūre *nf* (aeron.) elevator

augstvērtīgi *adv* valuably

augstvērtīgs *adj* high-quality, highly valuable

augstvērtīgums *nm* high quality

augš/a *nf* **1.** top; **pašā ~ā** at the very top; **no ~as** from above; **2.** attic; loft; **3. uz ~u** up, upward; **pa upi uz ~u** upstream

augšā *adv* **1.** up; **2.** upstairs; overhead; **a. minētais** above-mentioned; **3.** up, awake

augšāmcelšanās *nfr* resurrection

augšāmcelties *vr* rise from the dead

augšana *nf* growth

augšanas konuss *nm* growing point

augšas gaisma *nf* fanlight

augšbaznīca *nf* choir loft

augšbjefs *nm* headrace

augšcilpām *adv* by high leaps

augšdaļa *nf* upper part

augšdelma kauls *nm* humerus

augšdelms *nm* upper arm

augšdevons *nm* Upper Devonian

augšējais *adj* top, upper

augšgaliet/is *nm*, **~e** *nf* an inhabitant of Augš-zeme

augšgalnie/ks *nm*, **~ce** *nf* an inhabitant of Augš-zeme

augšgals *nm* top end, upper end; upland; (of river) upper course, headwaters

augšiene *nf* top

augšistaba *nf* upstairs room; garret

augšklēts *nf* granary loft

augškurzemnie/ks *nm*, **~ce** *nf* Upper Cour-lander

augšlūpa *nf* upper lip

augšļaudis *nm pl* inhabitants of Augšzeme

augšmala *nf* upper edge

augšminētais *adj* above-mentioned

augšnams *nm* (pol.) upper house; (England) House of Lords

augšpalāta *nf* (pol.) upper house

augšpēdu(s) *adv* on one's back

augšpus *adv* above

augšpuse *nf* top side, upper side

augšpusējais *adj* top, upper

augšstāvs *nm* upper floor, top floor

augšstilbs *nm* thigh

augštece *nf* (of a river) upper course

augštilpe *nf* headrace

augšup *adv* up, upward

augšupceļš *nm* progress

augšupeja *nf* growth, development

augšupējais *adj* upper, top; ascending

augšupejā zarna *nf* ascending colon

augšupejošs *adj* rising, ascending

augšupenis *nm* upstroke letter

augšupielāde *nf* (compu.) upload

augšus *adv emph* of **augt**; **a. aug** growing apace

augšvilenis *nm* (weav.) warp beam

augšzeme *nf* upper world

augšzemnie/ks *nm*, **~ce** *nf* **1.** uplander; **2.** inhabitant of Augšzeme; **~ku izloksne** dialect of eastern Latvia

augšzobs *nm* upper tooth

augšžoklis *nm* upper jaw

augt *vi* grow; grow up; increase; (of moon) wax; (of smallpox immunization) take; (of abscesses, boils) develop; **a. augumā** grow, increase in strength

augtene *nf* (bot.) habitat

augtin *adv emph* of **augt**; **a. aug** growing apace

augu *acc sg* of *adj* **augs**, n. u. in other cases; **a. dienu** all day long

augu blusiņa *nf* psylla

augu eļļa *nf* vegetable oil

augulis *nm* a well-developed or thriving animal or person

augulītis *nm dim* of **augulis**

augum/s *nm* **1.** (of persons) height; **liela ~a** tall; **maza ~a** short; **vidēja ~a** of medium height; **(būt kāda) ~ā** (be) of s.o.'s height; **2.** (of persons) figure, build, shape; **slaida ~a** slender; **glīta ~a** nicely built, having a nice figure; **3.** growth; **4.** (obs., Bibl.) generation

augu noteicējs *nm* herbal

augūrija *nf* augury

augūrs *nm* augur

augu sega *nf* vegetation

augu seka *nf* rotation of crops

augustīnietis or augustīns *nm* Augustinian

augusts *nm* August

augu vācējs *nm* herbalist

augu valsts *nf* vegetable kingdom

auka *nf* gale, storm

aukaini *adv* stormily

aukains *adj* stormy

aukla *nf* string, cord; **lecamā a.** skipping rope

auklas keramika *nf* cord-marked ceramics

aukle *nf* (children's) nurse

auklējums *nm* that which has been lovingly nursed, child

auklēt *vt* (of infants) rock; (of small children) take care of

auklēties *vr* (col.) fuss (with a small child)

auklis *nm* (of a plow) brace

auklot *vt* tie, bind

aukot *vi* storm, gust

auklu vieta *nf* place halfway up the calf

auksīns *nm* auxin

aukslējas *nf pl* (anat.) palate

aukslējenis *nm* (ling.) palatal

aukslēju šķeltne *nf* cleft palate

aukso[ch]roma [h] *nf* auxochrome

aukso[ch]roms [h] *adj* auxochromic

aukstasinība *nf* sangfroid

aukstasinīgi *adv* coolly

aukstasinīgs *adj* self-possessed, cool, equanimous

aukstasinīgums *nm* self-possession, composure, coolness

aukstasiņu *indecl adj* (biol.) coldblooded

aukstens *adj* cool

aukstēt *vt* cool, make cold

aukstēties *vr* freeze

auksti *adv* coldly; **man ir a.** I am cold

aukstināt *vt* cool off

aukstlīme *nf* cold-water glue

aukstlūstamība *nf* cold-shortness

aukstnējs *adj* cool

auksts *adj* cold; frigid; chilly; (of colors) cool; **desmit gradi a.** ten degrees below freezing; **a. pa muguru iet** it gives me the creeps

aukstūdeņu *indecl adj* (biol.) cold-water

aukstuma dobe *nf* frost pocket

aukstuma iekārta *nf* air conditioning unit, air conditioning system

aukstumizturība *nf* resistance to cold

aukstumizturīgs *adj* cold-resistant

aukstum/s *nm* cold; ~i shivers

auktors *nm* (jur.) auctor

aukuba *nf* aucuba

aukurs *nm* firewood for the drying kiln (in a threshing barn)

aula *nf* hall, assembly hall

aulaka *nm* (reg.) madcap

aule *nf* (of boots) upper

aulekām *adv* at a gallop

aulekš/i *nm pl* gallop; ~iem at a gallop

aulekšot *vi* gallop

aulekšotājs *nm* (horse) galloper

auliņa *nf* cage

aulis I *nm* beehive (made of bark or a hollowed-out tree trunk)

aulis II *nm* reveler

aulis III *nm* (poet.) run

auls *nm* aul, Caucasian mountain village

auļegle *nf* a spruce with an **aulis (aulis I)**

auļ/i *nm pl* gallop; ~iem or ~os at a gallop; ~u zirgs galloper

auļot *vi* gallop

auļotājs *nm* galloper

auļpriede *nf* a pine with an **aulis (aulis I)**

aumakām *adv* = **aumaļām**

aumaļaini *adv* torrentially

aumaļains *adj* torrential

aumaļām *adv* (of sweating) profusely, (of rain) in torrents

aumaļas *nf pl* downpour

aumaļība *nf* impetuosity, vehemence, excess

aumaļiem *adv* = **aumaļām**

aumaļīgi *adv* impetuously, vehemently; excessively

aumaļīgs *adj* impetuous, vehement, excessive

aumanis *nm* blusterer, maniac

aumašām *adv* = **aumaļām**

aumeistars *nm* (hist.) tutor

aumež *adv* too (excessively)

aumuļi *nm pl* mistletoe

aunāda *nf* fleece

aunagalva *nm* blockhead

aunazirņi *nm pl* chick pea

aunene *nf* cauliflower mushroom

aungalva *nf* globeflower

auniņi *nm pl* fleabane

aunragi *nm pl* water arum

auns *nm* **1.** ram; **2. Auns** Aries

aunu beka *nf* cauliflower mushroom

aunu piere *nf* (geol.) sheep rock, roche moutonnée

aupēties *vr* knock oneself out

aupucis *nm* wild, devil-may-care person

aura I *nf* howling

aura II *nf* aura

aurāts *nm* aurate

aure *nf* bugle

aurēlija *nf* moon jelly

aureols *nm* aureole

aureomicīns *nm* Aureomycin

aurēt *vi* = **aurot**

aurētājs *nm* horn blower

aurēties *vr* = **auroties**

aur/i *nm pl* **1.** hollering, roaring, bellowing; **~os iet** rut; **2.** (of wind) howling, roaring

aurības *nf pl* rut, estrus

auriņš *nm* (reg.) bird house

auris *nm* storm

aurora *nf* (poet.) dawn, aurora

aurot *vi* **1.** holler, roar, bellow; **2.** (of wind) howl, roar

auroties *vr* rut

auru laiks *nm* rutting time

ausa *nf* dawn, sunrise

ausainā aurēlija *nf* moon jelly

ausainais apogs *nm* scops owl

ausainais cīrulis *nm* horned lark

ausainais kārkls *nm* eared willow

ausainā pūce *nf* long-eared owl

ausaine *nf* winter hat (with ear flaps); (mil.) pile cap

ausainis *nm* long-eared animal

ausainīte *nf dim* of **ausaine**, winter hat

ausainītis *nm dim* of **ausainis**, long-eared animal

ausains *adj* long-eared; (of caps, hats) with ear flaps

auseklis *nm* (poet., folk.) morning star

auseklītis *nm dim* of **auseklis**, morning star

auseknis *nm* (folk.) aurora

ausene *nf* winter hat (with ear flaps)

ausīgs *adj* having good ears

ausīt *vt* (of a hot liquid) cool (by dipping and pouring)

ausīties *vr* prick up one's ears, listen attentively

auskariņš *nm dim* of **auskars**, earring

auskars *nm* earring

auskultācija *nf* auscultation

auskultēt *vt* auscultate

ausķīķis *nm* (naut.) crow's nest

auslecīte *nf* birthwort

ausleja *nf* (zool.) bleak

auslis *nm* a horse that pricks up its ears

ausma *nf* dawn; sunrise

auspicijs *nm* auspice

auspufs *nm* (sl.) exhaust pipe

aus/s *nf* **1.** ear; **mākslīgā a.** earphone coupler ◊ **dzirdīgas ~is** receptive audience; **ar biezām ~īm** hard of hearing; **līdz ~īm** up to one's ears; (in love) head over heels; **(nosarkt) līdz ~u galiem** (blush) to the roots of one's hair; **pa ~u galam** (of listening) inattentively; (of hearing) overhear; **~is kust** trying to put one over; **pa vienu ~i iekšā,**

pa otru ārā in one ear and out the other;
2. dogear; flap; 3. mortise

auss eja *nf* auditory canal

auss gliemene *nf* auricle

aust I *vi* 1. dawn; **diena a** it dawns; 2. (of celestial bodies) rise

aust II *vt* weave

austekles *nf pl* (obs.) loom

austene *nf* shawl

austenīte *nf dim* of **austene**, little shawl

austenītisks *adj* austenitic

austenīts *nm* austenite

austenīttērauds *nm* austenite steel

austere *nf* oyster

austies *vr* be woven; **a. cauri** weave through

austiņ/a *nf* 1. *dim* of **auss**, little ear; 2. bootstrap; 3. turned-up coattail; 4. ~**as** a. headphone; b. drawstring holes ◊ **uz ~ām** (of a trade) even

austra *nf* (poet.) aurora, red dawn

austrālāzietis *nm* Australasian

austrālietis *nm*, ~**e** *nf* Australian

Austrālijas dzelzkoks *nm* casuarina

Austrālijas sudrabkoks *nm* honeymyrtle

australopiteks *nm* Australopithecus

austrāls *adj* austral

austrenis *nm* northeasterly wind

austrietis *nm*, ~**e** *nf* Austrian

Austrijas dzelzene *nf* a knapweed, Centaurea austriaca

Austrijas vībotne *nf* an artemisia, Artemisia austriaca

austriņš *nm* easterly wind

Austrumāzijas briedis *nm* sika

austrumbalti *nm pl* Eastern Balts (Lithuanians, Latvians, Cours)

austrumdaļa *nf* eastern region

austrum/i *nm pl* east; the East, the Orient; **uz ~iem** eastward; ~**u** eastern, oriental; easterly

austrummala *nf* the east

austrumnieciski *adv* in an oriental fashion

austrumniecisks *adj* oriental

austrumnie/ks *nm*, ~**ce** *nf* Oriental

austrumu baltā priede *nf* eastern white pine

austrumu bitene *nf* an avens, Geum aleppicum

austrumu dižpērkone *nf* a corn cockle, Bunias orientalis

austrumu dzilnītis *nm* nuthatch

austrumu egle *nf* oriental spruce

austrumu hiacinte *nf* common garden hyacinth

austrumu karūsa *nf* goldfish

austrumu magone *nf* oriental poppy

austrumu platana *nf* oriental plane

austrumu plostbārdis *nm* a goatsbeard, Tragopogon orientalis

austrumu sarkanais ciedrs *nm* eastern red cedar

austrumu žodzene *nf* eastern rocket

austrumzemes *nf pl* the East, the Orient

austuve *nf* weaver's shop, weave shed

ausu aizbāžamais *nm* earplug

ausu krimstala *nf* pinna

ausu mati *nm pl* tragi

ausums *nm* dawn

ausu primula *nf* dusty miller

ausu sērs *nm* earwax

ausu sildītājs *nm* earmuff

ausu skripstiņa *nf* earlobe

ausu sviedri *nm pl* earwax

auša *nm*, *nf* flighty person; scatterbrain

aušana *nf* weaving

aušāties *vr* = **aušoties**

aušība *nf* flightiness

aušīgi *adv* flightily, giddily

aušīgs *adj* flighty, giddy; scatterbrained

aušīgums *nm* flightiness

aušiņa *nf dim* of **auša**, scatterbrain

aušoņa *nm*, *nf* flighty person; scatterbrain

aušoties *vr* act naughty, fool around, romp

aušprātīgi *adv* flightily, giddily

aušprātīgs *adj* flighty, giddy; scatterbrained

aušprātis *nm* scatterbrain

aušulīgs *adj* playful, mischievous

aušul/is *nm*, ~e *nf* (of a person) romp

aut *vt* put on; **a. kājas** put on shoes and socks; (fig.) prepare for a journey; (col.) get ready for; **a. zaķa kājas** take to one's heels

autar|ch|ija [h] *nf* autarchy

autar|ch|iski [h] *adv* autarchically

autar|ch|isks [h] *adj* autarchic

autarķija *nf* autarky

autarķiski *adv* autarkically

autarķisks *adj* autarkic

autbrīdings *nm* outbreeding

autēcisks *adj* autoecious

autentificēt *vt* authenticate

autentiski *adv* authentically

autentisks *adj* authentic

autentiskums *nm* authenticity

autentitāte *nf* authenticity

auties *vr* put on shoes and socks

autiņ/š I (with û) *nm* **1.** *dim* of **auts** I; **2.** diaper; ~i swaddling clothes

autiņš II *nm* (col.) car

autisms *nm* autism

auto *nm indecl* car; **smagais a.** truck; **vaļējs a.** convertible; **a. krava** truckload

autoamatieris *nm* nonprofessional driver

autoatslēdznieks *nm* automotive mechanic

autobānis *nm* (sl.) superhighway

autob|a|ze [ā] *nf* motor depot

autobiogr|a|fija [ā] *nf* autobiography

autobiogr|a|fiski [ā] *adv* autobiographically

autobiogr|a|fisks [ā] *adj* autobiographic

autobiogr|a|f/s [ā] *nm*, ~e *nf* autobiographer

autobloķēšana *nf* (RR) automatic block signal

autobrauciens *nm* motor trip; motor race

autobuss *nm* bus

autobūve *nf* automobile manufacture

autoceltnis *nm* truck-mounted hoist

autoceļš *nm* motor highway

auto|ch|roms [h] *nm* autochrome

auto|ch|toni [h] *adv* autochtonously

auto|ch|tons [h] *nm* autochton

auto|ch|tons [h] *adj* autochtonous

autocisterna *nf* tank truck

autodafē *indecl nm* auto-da-fé

autodidaktiski *adv* autodidactically

autodidaktisks *adj* autodidactic

autodidakt/s *nm*, ~e *nf* autodidact

autodienests *nm* transportation service

autodiģestija *nf* autolysis

autodrezīna *nf* autorail

autodroms *nm* motordrome

autoeļļa *nf* motor oil

autoerotiski *adv* autoerotically

autoerotisks *adj* autoerotic

autoerotisms *nm* autoerotism

autoeskorts *nm* motorcade

autofurgons *nm* camper (vehicle)

autog|a|mija [ā] *nf* autogamy

autog|a|ms [ā] *adj* autogamous

autogarāea *nf* garage

autog|e|ni [ē] *adv* autogenously

autog|e|nisks [ē] *adj* = **autogens**

autog|e|ns [ē] *nm* autogenous welding equipment

autog|e|ns [ē] *adj* autogenous

autografisks *adj* autographic

autografēt *vt* autograph

autogr|a|fs [ā] *nm* autograph

autogramma *nf* autograph (manuscript)

autogravīra *nf* autolithograph

autogreiders *nm* grader (self-propelled)

autoģen|e|ze [ē] *nf* autogenesis

autoh- See **autoch-**

autoiekrāvējs *nm* forklift

autoinspekcija *nf* traffic police

autoinspektors *nm* traffic policeman

autointoksikācija *nf* autointoxication

autokamanas *nf pl* snowmobile

autokārs *nm* small tractor truck

autokatal[i]ze [ī] *nf* autocatalysis
autokatastrofa *nf* automotive accident
autokefālija *nf* autocephaly
autokinētisks *adj* autokinetic
autoklavēt *vt* autoclave
autokl[a]vs [ā] *nm* autoclave
autoklubs *nm* automobile club
autoknipse *nf* (photo.) self-timer
autokolonna *nf* 1. motor pool; 2. truck caravan; truck convoy
autoko[rr]elācija [r] *nf* autocorrelation
autokr[a]tija [ā] *nf* autocracy
autokr[a]tiski [ā] *adv* autocratically
autokr[a]tisks [ā] *adj* autocratic
autokr[a]ts [ā] *nm* autocrat
autokrava *nf* truckload
autokrāvējs *nm* forklift
autokritika *nf* self-criticism
autokritisks *adj* self-critical
autolitogr[a]fija [ā] *nf* autolithography
autol[i]ze [ī] *nf* autolysis
autols *nm* motor oil
autoluminiscence *nf* autoluminescence
automaģistrāle *nf* principal highway
automašīna *nf* motor vehicle; **smagā a.** truck
automašīnu parks *nm* motor pool
autom[a]tika [ā] *nf* 1. automation science; 2. automata
autom[a]tiski [ā] *adv* automatically
autom[a]tisks [ā] *adj* automatic
autom[a]tisms [ā] *nm* automatism
autom[a]tists [ā] *nm* submachine gunner
automatizācija *nf* automation
automatizēt *vt* automate
autom[a]t/s [ā] *nm* 1. automaton; automat, vending machine; 2. submachine gun; automatic rifle; ~**u uz krūtīm, ņem!** port, arms!
auto mazgātava *nf* car wash
autome[cha]niķis [hā] *nm* automobile mechanic

autome[cha]nisks [hā] *adj* car repair
automobi/lis *nm* automobile; **a. preāu izvadāšanai** van; **smagais a.** truck; **vieglais a.** passenger car
automobilisms *nm* motoring
automobilist/s *nm*, ~**e** *nf* motorist
automobiļa vadītājs *nm* driver
automobiļu novietne *nf* parking lot
automodelis *nm* car model
automodelisms *nm* car model building and racing
automodelist/s *nm*, ~**e** *nf* car model hobbyist
automotrisa *nf* railcar
autonomi *adv* autonomously
autonomija *nf* autonomy
autonomists *nm* autonomist
autonoms *adj* autonomous
auto novietne *nf* parking space; **a.** ~**s pulksteni**s parking meter
autooksidācija *nf* auto-oxidation
autoosta *nf* bus terminal
autoparks *nm* motor pool
autopārvadājums *nm* truck transport, shipment by truck
autopiederumi *nm pl* automotive accessories
autopilots *nm* automatic pilot
autoplastika *nf* autoplasty
autoplastisks *adj* autoplastic
autoportrets *nm* self-portrait
autopsija *nf* autopsy
autorallijs *nm* rallye
autorapliecība *nf* certificate of copyright registration
autora procenti *nm pl* royalties
autora tiesīb/as *nf pl* copyright; **a. tiesību aiz-skaršana** a. copyright infringement; b. plagiarism
autoreferāts *nm* author's abstract
autoregresija *nf* autoregression
autoregulācija *nf* autoregulation
autoreksemplārs *nm* author's copy

autorība *nf* authorship

autoriepa *nf* automobile tire

autoritāri *adv* in an authoritarian manner

autoritārisms *nm* authoritarianism

autoritārs *adj* authoritarian

autoritāte *nf* authority

autorit[a]tīvi [ā] *adv* authoritatively

autorit[a]tīvs [ā] *adj* authoritative

autorizēt *vt* authorize

autorkoncerts *nm* one composer's concert

autorloksne *nf* manuscript signature

autorotācija *nf* autorotation

autor/s *nm*, ~e *nf* author

autortiesības *nf pl* copyright

autorūpnīca *nf* motor plant

autorūpniecība *nf* auto industry

autosadursme *nf* automobile collision

autosaimniecība *nf* trucking industry

autosalons *nm* automobile showroom

autosatiksme *nf* motor traffic

autoseroterapija *nf* autoserum therapy

autoserviss *nm* automotive service

autosportists *nm* auto racer

autosports *nm* motor sport, motoring, auto racing

autostopist/s *nm*, ~e *nf* hitchhiker

autostops *nm* hitchhiking

autostrāde *nf* superhighway

autosuģestija *nf* self-suggestion

autotanks *nm* armored car

autotipija *nf* 1. autotypy; 2. autotype

autotipogr[a]fija [ā] *nf* autotypy

autotips *nm* autotype

autotomija *nf* autotomy

autotransform[a]tors [ā] *nm* autotransformer

autotransfūzija *nf* autotransfusion

autotransportdienests *nm* motor transport service

autotransports *nm* motor transport

autotrase *nf* superhighway

autotrofs *adj* autotrophic

autotūrisms *nm* motoring

autotūrist/s *nm*, ~e *nf* motorist

auto vadītājs *nm* driver

autoviesnīca *nf* motel

autovilciens *nm* tandem trailer, articulated truck

autoē[i]rs [ī] *nm* autogiro

auts I *nm* 1. foot-wrapping cloth; 2. (obs.) kerchief; tablecloth; wrap; (fig.) cover (of darkness, fog)

auts II *nm* (sports) out

autskalis *nm* (obs.) thin, store-bought fabric

auzaine *nf* oat stubble

auzaite *nf* (reg.) harvested oat field

auzāj/s *nm* harvested oat field, oat stubble; ~i oat straw

auzas *nf pl* oat; oats

auzene *nf* fescue

auzenīte *nf dim* of **auzene**, fescue

auziņas *nf pl dim* of **auzas**, oats

auzu cietā melnplauka *nf* an oat smut, Ustilago laevis

auzu ķīselis *nm* oatmeal jelly

auzu melnā stobrmuša *nf* frit fly

auzu milti *nm pl* oatmeal

auzu putraimi *nm pl* grits, groats

auzu pārslas *nf pl* rolled oats

auzu rūsa *nf* oat rust

auzu sakne *nf* salsify

auzu spilva *nf* palea

auzu tripsis *nm* a thrip, Stenothrips graminum

auzu zāles *nf pl* corn cockle

aužamā mašīna *nf* power loom

āva *nf* battle ax, halberd

avals *nm* (bus.) guaranty

avangardisks *adj* avant-garde

avangardisms *nm* (pol.) vanguardism; (art) avant-gardism

avangards *nm* vanguard

avanscēna *nf* proscenium

avansējums *nm* advance of funds

avansēt *vt* (of funds) advance

avansēties *vr* advance, get promoted

avanss *nm* (of funds) advance

avansveidā *adv* in advance, on account

avansveidīgi *adv* in advance, on account

avantūra *nf* (political, military) adventure, ad-venturism

avanturīns *nm* aventurine

avantūrisms *nm* adventurism

avantūristiski *adv* in an adeventuristic manner

avantūristisks *adj* adventuristic

avantūrists *nm*, ~e *nf* adventurer

avarējis *adj, part* of avarēt (of motor vehicles) damaged

avarēt *vi* (of motor vehicles) suffer an accident, (of aircraft) crash, (of ships) shipwreck

av[a]r/s [ā] *nm*, ~iete *nf* Avar

av[a]rija [ā] *nf* (of motor vehicles) accident, (of aircraft) crash, (of vessels) shipwreck; (insurance loss) average; da]ējā a. particular average; kopē-jā a. general average

av[a]rijas [ā] automobilis *nm* tow truck

āvējs *nm*, ~a *nf* one that puts on his (her) shoes or clothing

avelītis *nm* (reg.) birdhouse

avenājs *nm* raspberry plant; stand of raspberry bushes

avenāju vabole *nf* raspberry beetle

avene *nf* raspberry

av[e]nija [ē] *nf* avenue

avenīte *nf dim* of avene, raspberry

avenragi *nm pl* 1. water arum; 2. a needlework pattern

avens *nm* ram

aveņkrāsas *indecl adj* crimson

aveņkrūms *nm* raspberry bush

aveņu tārps *nm* raspberry fruit worm

aveņu ziedu smecernieks *nm* raspberry weevil

aveņvabole *nf* raspberry beetle

aversija *nf* aversion

averss *nm* obverse

aviācija *nf* aviation

aviācijas inēenieris *nm* aeronautical engineer

aviācijass medicīna *nf* aviation medicine

Aviācijass ministrija *nf* Air Ministry

aviācijas rūpniecība *nf* aircraft industry; kosmiskās a. r. aerospace industry

aviācijas zinātne *nf* aeronautical science

aviatore *nf* aviatrix

avi[a]tors [ā] *nm* aviator

avicenijas *nf* Avicennia

avieksene *nf* (reg.) raspberry

aviekstene *nf* (reg.) raspberry

aviesene *nf* (reg.) raspberry

aviesnājs *nm* (reg.) raspberry bushes

avietene *nf* (reg.) raspberry

avietnājs *nm* (reg.) raspberry bushes

avifauna *nf* avifauna

āvīgs *adj* (reg.) buffoonish

aviniece *nf* shepherdess

avinieks *nm* shepherd

avioatbalsts *nm* air support

aviob[a]ze [ā] *nf* air base

aviobumba *nf* aerial bomb

aviodesanta *adj* (mil.) airborne

aviodispečers *nm* air traffic controller

aviohorizonts *nm* artificial horizon

avioizlūks *nm* aerial observer

aviokatastrofa *nf* airplane crash

aviokompānija *nf* airline

aviokonstruktor/s *nm*, ~e *nf* airplane designer

aviolainers *nm* airliner

aviolīnija *nf* air route

aviometeoroloģija *nf* aviation meteorology

aviometeoroloģisks *adj* (of weather stations) airport

aviomodelis *nm* airplane model

aviomodelisms *nm* airplane model building

aviomodelist/s *nm*, ~e *nf* airplane model hobbyist

avionika *nf* avionics

aviopārvadātājs *nm* air carrier

aviopasts *nm* airmail

aviorūpnīca *nf* airplane manufacturing plant

aviorūpniecība *nf* aircraft industry

aviosabiedrība *nf* airline

aviosports *nm* sports aviation

aviotransports *nm* air transport

aviotūrisms *nm* air tourism

aviouzļēmums *nm* aerial photograph

aviovēstule *nf* airmail letter

āvis *nm* (reg.) buffoon

avista *nf* bearer check

avitaminoze *nf* avitaminosis

avitaminozs *adj* avitaminotic

āvīties *vr* (reg.) play the fool, engage in buffoonery

avitiļa *nf dim* of **avs**, little sheep

avī/ze *nf* newspaper; **dzīvā a.** informational event; **~žu kiosks** newsstand; **~žu stils** journalese

avizēt *vi* advise, notify

avizo *indecl nm* letter of advice, notice

avīēniecība *nf* journalism

avīžnieciski *adv* journalistically

avīžniecisks *adj* journalistic

avīžnie/ks *nm*, **~ce** *nf* **1.** journalist, newspaperman; **2.** news vendor

avīžpapīrs *nm* newsprint

avīžpīle *nf* canard

avīžraksts *nm* newspaper article

Avogadro skaitlis *nm* Avogadro's number

avok[a]do [ā] *indecl nm* avocado

avoksnains *adj* rich in springs

avoksnājs *nm* springy area

avoksnējs *adj* rich in springs

avotains *adj* springy, rich in springs

avotenes *nf pl* brook grass

avotezers *nm* spring lake

avotiļš *nm* **1.** *dim* of **avots**, little spring; **2.** fontanelle

avotkaļis *nm* freshwater limestone; travertine, calcareous tufa; marl, bog lime

avotrīkle *nf* (col.) blabbermouth, bigmouth

avots *nm* **1.** spring, fountain; **2.** source

avotu palija *nf* brook trout;

avotu veronika *nf* European brooklime

avozeta *nf* avocet

avs *nf* (obs.) sheep

āvs *nm* (reg.) buffoon

avtene *nf* (reg.) raspberry

avuāri *nm pl* assets, holdings

avulzija *nf* avulsion

avunkulāts *nm* avunculate

azafrīns *nm* azafrin

azaidot *vi* eat

azaids *nm* meal, repast; breakfast

āzainītis *nm* (reg.) quarreler

azaleja *nf* azalea

azālija *nf* azalea

azartist/s *nm*, **~e** *nf* gambler

azart/s *nm* excitement, passion; **~a spēles** games of chance, gambling

azbestcements *nm* asbestos-cement

azbestoze *nf* asbestosis

azbests *nm* asbestos

azbolīts *nm* wallboard

āzenis *nm* southeasterly wind

azeotropija *nf* azeotropy

azerbaidžān/is *nm*, **~iete** *nf* Azerbaijani

āzēt *vt* make a fool of s.o., laugh at

āzēties *vr* fool around, play pranks

[a]ziātisks [ā] *adj* Asiatic

[a]ziāt/s [ā] *nm*, **~e** *nf* Asian

azīds *nm* azide

Āzijas bifelis *nm* Asiatic buffalo

Āzijas burunduks *nm* Siberian chipmunk

az[i]ls [ī] *nm* asylum

az[i]ltiesības [ī] *nf pl* asylum rights

azimīna *nf* papaw

azimutāls *adj* azimuthal

azimuts *nm* azimuth; **ačgārnais** (or **pretējais**) **a.** back azimuth; **īstais a.** true bearing; **magnetiskais a.** magnetic bearing

āzis *nm* **1.** billy goat; *gen* **āža** (of voice) reedy; **2.** vaulting horse; **3.** sawhorse; **4.** ridge cross; **5.** (of bridge piers) ice apron, icebreaker; **6.** (aeron.) bumpy landing; **7. Āzis** Capricorn

āzītis *nm* **1.** *dim* of **āzis**, little billy goat; **2.** saw-horse

aznīca *nf* malt drying box

azogrupa *nf* azo group

azoisks *adj* azoic

azojs *nm* Azoic (era)

azokrāsviela *nf* azo dye

azoksigrupa *nf* azoxy group

azolas *nf pl* Azolla

azorelas *nf pl* Azorella

azosavienojums *nm* azo compound

azospermija *nf* azospermia

azotbakters *nm* azotobacter

azote *nf* = **azots**

azotēmija *nf* azotemia

azots *nf* bosom

azurīts *nm* azurite

azūrs *nm* azure

āža bārdiļa *nf* goatee

āža čiploki *nm pl* (bot.) ramson

āži *nm pl* **1.** sawhorse; **2.** animal-shaped cresting at end of a roof ridge; **3.** trestle

ažio *nm indecl* agio

ažiotāža *nf* **1.** agiotage; **2.** agitation

āžloki *nm pl* arrow grass

āžrags *nm* (folk., mus.) horn

ažūrs *adj* a jour, ajouré, open-worked

B

bā *interj* wow

bāb/a I *nf* (com.) common woman; (com., of men) coward; **vecu ~u pasakas** old wives' tales; **ru-nā kā veca b.** he is talking nonsense

bāba II *nf* (naut.) net hauling winch

babene *nf* oxeye daisy

bābietis *nm* (com.) woman; (com., of men) coward

babilonieši *nm pl* Babylonians

Babilonijas vītols *nm* weeping willow

bābiļa *nf* **1.** *dim* of **bāba** I, common woman; **2.** evening star; **3.** (hist.) torch bracket

bābisks *adj* (com.) womanly

bab[i]ts [ī] *nm* babbit

babs *nm* bugbear

babuīns *nm* baboon

babulēt *vi* blab

babulis I *nm* (hist.) an **iebūvietis** who had his own hut and a horse

babulis II *nm* blabber

babulnieks or **babuļnieks** *nm* = **babulis** I

babūns *nm* baboon

bacilis *nm* bacillus; disease germ

bacillārs *adj* bacillary

badacietēj/s *nm*, **~a** *nf* starving person

badadzeguze *nf* hoopoe

badains *adj* (col.) hungry

badakāsis *nm* (col., cont.) **1.** miser; greedy, acquisitive person; **2.** glutton

bada kūre *nf* starving cure

badakslis or **badaksnis** *nm* (col.) glutton

badakšļa *nm* (col.) glutton

bada nāve *nf* death from starvation

badapātaga *nf* (hum.) fishing pole

badapātadznieks *nm* (hum.) angler

bada puķīte *nf* whitlow grass

badastakl/is *nm*, **~e** *nf* (col.) glutton

bada streiks *nm* hunger strike

bada vējš *nm* northeasterly

bāde *nf* (sl.) bath

badeklis I *nm* (col.) glutton

badeklis II *nm* a piercing tool; poker

badeleīts *nm* baddeleyite

badene *nf* whitlow grass

badenis *nm* (col.) greedy, acquisitive person

bādēt *vt* (sl.) bathe

badgalīgs *adj* (col.) greedy

badgalis *nm* (col.) **1.** greedy, acquisitive person; **2.** glutton

badi *nm pl* poverty

badīgi *adv* hungrily; greedily

badīgs I *adj* 1. hungry; 2. gluttonous; 3. (col.) greedy

badīgs II *adj* (of cattle) apt to butt

badīgums *nm* 1. hunger; 2. gluttony; 3. (col.) greed

badīkla *nf, nm* (col.) glutton

badīkle *nf* a butting cow

badīklis *nm* poker; piercing tool; pick

badinät *vt* starve

badināties *vr* 1. starve; fast, diet; 2. stint, be stingy, pinch pennies

badīt *vt* 1. butt; 2. poke, prick

badīties *vr* 1. butt heads; 2. be in the habit of butting

badmintonist/s *nm*, ~e *nf* badminton player

badmintons *nm* badminton

badmira *nf, nm* 1. (col., cont.) starveling; 2. voracious person or animal; 3. miser

badokšļa *nf, nm* miser

badoties *vr* 1. starve; 2. fast, diet

bad/s *nm* hunger; starvation; famine; (fig.) shortage, dearth ◊ ~a alga starvation wages; ~a bērni (col.) indigents; ~a dzīve (col.) poverty; ~a graši (col.) starvation wages; pittance; ~a ļaudis (col.) indigents; ~a maize (col.) poverty; ar ~u uz pusēm lead a hand-to-mouth existence

bagara kauss *nm* scoop

bagarēt *vt* dredge

bagarmašīna *nf* dredge

bagars *nm* dredge

bagase *nf* bagasse

bagātais *nom adj* wealthy person, rich man

bagatelle *nf* bagatelle

bagāti *adv* richly

bagātība *nf* 1. wealth; 2. *pl* ~s riches; 3. abundance, richness, plenty, profusion

bagātīgi *adv* richly, abundantly, bountifully; lavishly; amply; sumptuously

bagātīgs *adj* rich, abundant, bountiful; lavish; ample; sumptuous

bagātīgums *nm* richness, abundance, profusion

bagātinājums *nm* enrichment

bagātinät *vt* enrich

bagātināties *vr* become enriched

bagatirs *nm* (in Russian epic tales) bogatyr; (in Latvian folklore) rich farmer, boyar

bagātnie/ks *nm*, ~ce *nf* a wealthy man; ~ki the rich

bagāts *adj* 1. rich; affluent, wealthy; stāvus b. very rich; 2. (with genitive or instrumental) teeming, full, abounding

bagātums *nm* richness; affluence, wealth

bagāturs *nm* = bagatirs

bagāža *nf* luggage, baggage; garīgā b. mental equipment, store of knowledge

bagāžas kolonna *nf* supply column

bagāžas konduktors *nm* baggagemaster

bagāžas kvīts *nf* claim check

bagāžas nesējs *nm* porter

bagāžas nodaļa *nf* luggage compartment

bagāžas novietne *nf* (automobile) trunk

bagāžas plaukts *nm* baggage rack

bagāžas vagons *nm* baggage car

bagāžas zīme *nf* luggage tag

bagāžnieks *nm* 1. luggage carrier; 2. (automobile) trunk

bagete *nf* beading, casing

bah[āi]sms [aj] *nm* Baha'i

baidarka *nf* kayak

baidas *nf pl* 1. fear; 2. threat; 3. horror

baideklis *nm* scarecrow; fright, bugaboo

baidīgs *adj* (obs.) fearsome, fearful

baidīt *vt* scare, frighten, terrify

baidīties *vr* fear, be afraid; dread; (of animals) shy at; nav ko b. there is nothing to be afraid of; nebaidīties ne velna dare to raise the devil

baids *nm* bogey, bugbear

baids *adj* fearsome

baigais *nom adj* the uncanny

baigais gads *nm* (col.) "year of terror" (the year of fiviet occupation of Latvia, 1940-1941)

baigas *nf pl* fear

baigi *adv* (sl.) awfully, terribly; **b. labs** (sl.) cool; **man metas b.** I have an eerie feeling

baiglis *nm* horror, fearsome thing, monster, ghost

baigs *nm* = **baiglis**

baigs *adj* frightening, dreadful, horrible

baigums *nm* dreadfulness, horribleness; eeriness

Baikala ronis *nm* Baikal seal

bail *adv* **man b.** I am afraid; **viļam kļūst b.** he is getting scared; **ka b.** (sl.) terrific

bail/es *nf pl* fear; **man ir b.** I am afraid; **aiz ~ēm** out of fear

bailība *nf* **1.** timidity, timorousness, shyness; **2.** cowardliness

bailīgi *adv* fearfully, timorously, shyly

bailīgs *adj* **1.** timid, timorous, shy; **2.** cowardly; **3.** (col.) dangerous

bailīgums *nm* **1.** timidity, timorousness, shyness; **2.** cowardliness

bailulis *nm* coward

baiļošanās *nfr* worry, anxiety, uneasiness

baiļot *vt* frighten, scare

baiļoties *vr* **1.** be afraid; **2.** worry, be anxious

baiļpilns *adj* fearful

baiļprātiļš *nm* scaredy-cat

baiļš *adj* fearful, fearsome

baiļu sviedri *nm pl* cold sweat

bairīss *nm* (barb.) lager (beer)

bairītis *nm* lager (beer)

bais *adv* **man b.** I am afraid

baisa *nf* dread

baisi *adv* terrifyingly

baisīgi *adv* fearsomely

baisīgs *adj* fearsome

baisma or **baismas** *nf* **1.** eerie feeling, fear; **2.** terror, horror

baismeklis *nm* fright, bugaboo

baismi *adv* terrifyingly

baismīgi *adv* terrifyingly

baismīgs *adj* terrifying, ghastly, awful

baismīgums *nm* ghastliness, awfulness

baismonīgs *adj* terrifying, ghastly, awful

baisms *adj* terrifying, ghastly, awful

baiss *nm* dread, fear

baiss *adj* terrifying, ghastly, awful

baitmultipleksēšana *nf* byte multiplexing

baits *nm* (compu.) byte

bajad[e]ra [ē] *nf* Hindu dancing girl

bajānist/s *nm*, **~e** *nf* bayan player

bajāns *nm* bayan, accordion with a button keyboard

bajāriene *nf* wife of a **bajārs**

bajārs *nm* **1.** rich farmer; **2.** (in Russia) boyar

bajonete *nf* bayonet

bajonetietvere *nf* (el.) bayonet socket

baka *nf* (naut.) forecastle

bāka I *nf* lighthouse; (aeron.) beacon; **peldoša b.** lightship

bāka II *nf* gasoline tank

bakalaurs *nm* (educ.) bachelor

bakaleja *nf* groceries

bakāns *nm* a large person or animal

bakarā *nf indecl* **1.** baccarat; **2.** baccarat glass

bakas *nf pl* smallpox

bākas sargs *nm* lighthouse keeper

bakāt *vt* stuff; stamp upon

bakborts *nm* (naut.) port (side)

bak[ch]anālijas [h] *nf pl* bacchanal

bak[ch]ante [h] *nf* bacchante

bakelīts *nm* Bakelite

bakenas *nf pl* (sl.) sideburns

bakenbārda *nf* (col.) sideburns

bakh- See **bakch-**

baklaēāns *nm* eggplant

bakrēta *nf* pockmark

bakrētains *adj* pockmarked

bakris *nm* (reg.) ram

baks *nm* **1.** cistern, tank; **2.** (naut.) forecastle

bakstāmais *nom adj* pick

baksteklis *nm* poker

bakstīklis *nm* poker

bakstīt *vt* poke, prod; (of teeth) pick

bakstīties *vr* 1. poke each other; 2. poke, dawdle; 3. b. starpā butt in

bakšišs *nm* baksheesh

bakšķi *nm pl* stuffing material, caulk

bākšķ/is *nm* 1. small bundle of straw; 2. ~i (magic) charms

bakšķošanās *nfr* (reg.) casting of spells

bakšķoties *vr* (reg.) cast spells

bakšteina siers *nm* Backstein cheese

bakt[e]riāls [ē] *adj* bacterial

bakt[e]ricidāls [ē] *adj* bactericidal

bakt[e]ricīds [ē] *nm* bactericide

bakt[e]ricīds [ē] *adj* bactericidal

baktērija *nf* bacterium

baktēriju karš *nm* germ warfare

bakt[e]riofāgs [ē] *nm* bacteriophage

bakt[e]riolo/gs [ē] *nm*, ~ģe *nf* bacteriologist

bakt[e]rioloģija [ē] *nf* bacteriology

bakt[e]rioloģiskais [ē] **karš** *nm* biological warfare

bakt[e]rioloģiski [ē] *adv* bacteriologically

bakt[e]rioloģisks [ē] *adj* bacteriologic

bakt[e]rioze [ē] *nf* bacteriosis

bakt[e]riūrija [ē] *nf* bacilluria

bakt[e]rizācija [ē] *nf* bacterization

bakt[e]rizēt [ē] *vt* bacterize

baktrietis *nm*, ~e *nf* Bactrian

bakurētains *adj* pockmarked

baķis *nm* bolt of cloth

bala *nf* = **balanda**

balāde *nf* ballad, ballade

balādisks *adj* balladic

balādist/s *nm*, ~e *nf* balladist

balagāns *nm* 1. booth, show booth; 2. sideshow; low farce

balalaika *nf* balalaika

balamute *nf, nm* (col.) bigmouth; braggart

balamutēt *vi* = **balamutēties**

balamutēties *vr* (col.) boast, brag, swagger

balamutība *nf* brag, braggadocio

balamutīgi *adv* braggingly

balamutīgs *adj* braggartly, braggadocian

balamutīgums *nm* braggadocio

balanda *nf* 1. goosefoot; 2. garden orache

balansēt *vt, vi* balance

balansiere *nf* 1. (acrobatics) balance pole; 2. (in balances, machinery) beam

balanss *nm* balance

balas *nf pl* (reg.) goosefoot

bālasinība *nf* 1. leukemia; 2. (fig.) anemia, blandness

bālasinīgi *adv* anemically, blandly

bālasinīgs *adj* 1. leukemic; 2. (fig.) anemic, bland

bālasinīgums *nm* 1. leukemia; 2. (fig.) anemia, blandness

balasts *nm* ballast

balasttanks *nm* ballast tank

balastvielas *nf pl* roughage

balata *nf* balata

balbaks *nm* clumsy person

balbieris *nm* (barb.) barber

balda[ch]īns [h] *nm* baldachin, canopy

balderiļš *nm* valerian

balderjāns *nm* valerian

baldriāns *nm* valerian

baldriānskābe *nf* valeric acid

baldriļi *nm pl* corn salad

bālēliļš (also **bālelis, bālelītis, bāleniļš**) *nm, dim* of **bālis**, brother

balenis *nm* linen cloth to be bleached

bālēns *nm* 1. a pale person; 2. wilted and faded leaf

balerīna *nf* ballerina

bālēt *vi* fade

bālēt *vi* 1. grow pale, blanch; 2. fade; 3. be dimly visible

baletdejotāj/s *nm*, ~a ballet dancer

baletfilma *nf* ballet on film

balēties *vr* bleach

baletmeistar/s *nm*, ~e *nf* ballet master, choreographer

baletmūzika *nf* ballet music

baletoman/s *nm*, **~e** *nf* balletomane

baletopera *nf* combined opera and ballet

balets *nm* ballet

baletskola *nf* school of ballet

bālganā zemzālīte *nf* a wood rush, Luzula pallescens

balgani *adv* pallidly; light, pale, whitish

balgans *adj* light, pale; pallid; whitish

bālgans *adj* = **balgans**

balganums *nm* lightness, paleness; pallor; whitishness

bālganums *nm* = **balganums**

balgalvji *nm pl* cotton grass

balgot *vi* shine white

balgs *adj* pale

balgzds *nm* (of a sled) bench

bāli *adv* pallidly; colorlessly, insipidly

balināmā mašīna *nf* bleacher

balināt *vt* bleach

balinātājs *nm* bleach

balinātava *nf* bleaching yard

balināties *vr* bleach

bālins *adj* pale

bāliļ/š *nm* **1.** (folk.) *dim* of **bālis**; brother; **2.** (folk.) unmarried male relative; **~i** male kinfolk

bā/lis *nm* (folk.) brother; **~ļi** male kinfolk

balista *nf* ballista

bālītis *nm dim* of **bālis**, (folk.) brother

balkers *nm* bulk carrier

balkona durvis *nf pl* French window

balkons *nm* balcony; **augšējais b.** (theat.) upper circle; **pirmais b.** (theat.) dress circle

balksne *nf* (obs.) sound, voice; horn

balkšļa *nf* **1.** bleaching; **2.** bleaching yard, bleachfield

balle I *nf* ball, dance party; **beigta b.!** (col.) that's the end of it! that's all!

balle II *nf* (of point scales) point; **desmit ~s stiprs vējš** wind force ten (on the Beaufort scale); (educ.) mark, grade

balle III *nf* (play, sports) ball

balles tērps *nm* evening gown

balles zāle *nf* ballroom

ballēšanās *nfr* partying

ballēt *vi* = **ballēties**

ballēties *vr* go to balls, party; give dancing parties

ballinie/ks *nm*, **~ce** *nf* ballroom guest, party-goer

ballis *nm* ten reams

ballistika *nf* ballistics

ballistiski *adv* ballistically

ballistisks *adj* ballistic

balneolo/gs *nm*, **~ģe** *nf* balneologist

balneoloģija *nf* balneology

balneoloģiski *adv* balneologically

balneoloģisks *adj* balneologic

balneoterapija *nf* balneotherapy

balodains *adj* pigeon-colored

balodas *nf pl* touch-me-not

balodene *nf* orache

balo/dis *nm* pigeon, dove; **~ēu būda** dovecote; **~ēu mēnesis** March; **(dzīvo tik mīļi) kā ~ēi** two lovey-doveys

balodītis *nm dim* of **balodis**, little pigeon, little dove

balometrs *nm* balometer

balongāze *nf* bottled gas

balons *nm* **1.** balloon; **piesiets b.** captive balloon; **2.** round glass flask; carboy; **3.** gas cylinder

balonu aizsprosts *nm* aerial barrage

balot *vi* **1.** fade; **2.** shine white

baloties *vr* = **balot**

balotēšanās *nfr* running for office

balotēt *vi* cast ballots

balotēties *vr* be a candidate, run for an office

balotne *nf* = **balanda**

baloēkrāsas *indecl adj* pigeon-colored

baloēpelēks *adj* dove gray

baloēu ģerānija *nf* long-stalked cranesbill

baloēu rācenis *nm* sedum

baloēu skabioza *nf* small scabious

baloēveidīgie *nom adj* Columbdae

bals *nm* **1.** bleaching; **2.** bleaching yard, bleachfield

bāls *adj* pale, pallid; (fig.) colorless, insipid; **b. kā krīts** pale as a sheet

balsa *nf* balsa

balsekļi *nm pl* vocal cords

balsene *nf* larynx

balsens *adj* light, whitish

balsēt *vi* shine white

balsēties *vr* grow, develop, put on weight

balsiens *nm* syllable

balsīgi *adv* voiced

balsīgs *adj* voiced

balsīgums *nm* voicedness, voice

balsināt *vt* whitewash

balsināties *vr* clean weapons

balsīties *vr* grow, develop, put on weight

balsnēji *adv* in a whitish color

balsnējs *adj* whitish

balsnējums *nm* whiteness, white

balsnēt *vi* shine white

balsnīt *vi* = **balsnēt**

balsns *adj* light, whitish

balsnums *nm* whitishness

balsošana *nf* voting, balloting; **aizklāta b.** secret ballot; **vispārēja b.** universal suffrage

balsošanas pilnvara *nf* proxy

balsošanas urna *nf* ballot box

balsot *vi* vote

balsotāj/s *nm*, **~a** *nf* voter

bals/s *nf* **1.** voice; **dobja** (or **rupja**) **b.** deep voice; **smalka b.** high-pitched voice ◊ **~ī** aloud; **pilnā** (or **visā**) **~ī** loudly, out loud; **ne-labā ~ī** at the top of one's voice; **vienā ~ī** with one voice, in unison; **2.** (mus.) part; **ceturtā b.** bass; **otrā b.** a. alto; **b. harmony**; **(dziedāt) otro ~i** (sing) second; **pirmā b.** a. so-prano; **b. melody**; **trešā b.** tenor; **divām ~īm** two-part; **3.** vote; **~u skaitītājs** teller; **padomdevēja b.** consultative voice;

~is par un pret the ayes and the nays; **~u vairākums** majority vote

balss lūzums *nm* voice change

balss rīkle *nf* larynx

balss saites *nf pl* vocal cords

balss sprauga *nf* glottis

balss tiesības *nf pl* right to vote; suffrage

balss veidošana *nf* phonation

balstakmens *nm* footstone

balstaudi *nm pl* supporting tissue

balstaugi *nm pl* prop plants

balsteklis *nm* prop, support, shore; (constr.) bearing, shoe; abutment

balsteknis *nm* = **balsteklis**

balstenis *nm* (arch.) bracket

balstiekārta *nf* (automobile) suspension

balstiesības *nf pl* right to vote; suffrage

balstiesīgs *adj* having the right to vote

balstīklis *nm* = **balsteklis**

balstiļa *nf dim* of **balss**, voice

balstiļas *nf pl* a meal of boiled lamb's quarters (goosefoot) and dog's mercury

balstiļš *nm* (of string instruments) bridge

balstīt *vt* support, prop up

balstīties *vr* **1.** lean against, lean on; **2.** rest on, be supported by; **3.** (fig.) be based on

balstkoki *nm pl* mine timber

balstmalka *nf* mine timber

balstplātne *nf* (mortar) baseplate

balstritenis *nm* road wheel

balsts *nm* **1.** support, prop, shore, stay; (gun) mount; **divkāju b.** bipod; **2.** (arch.) bearing, abutment, pier; **3.** (fig.) support, bulwark

balstšķīvis *nm* (artillery) footplate

baltā akācija *nf* black locust

baltā apse *nf* white poplar

baltā auzene *nf* tricholoma

baltā balanda *nf* lamb's quarters

baltābols *nm* white clover

baltacainā nira *nf* ferruginous duck

baltā cielava *nf* white wagtail

baltacis *nm* a white-faced person

baltaču pīle *nf* ferruginous duck

baltā driģene *nf* Jimsonweed

baltā dzeguēpuķe *nf* butterfly orchid

baltā egle *nf* = **baltegle**

baltā ezerroze *nf* white water lily

baltā gauriļa *nf* smew

baltā haizivs *nf* great white shark

baltaine *nf* a white **villaine**

baltā irbe *nf* willow grouse

baltais *nom adj* **1.** white (person); **2.** (col.) alcohol, vodka

baltais āboliļš *nm* white clover

baltais amoliļš *nm* white sweet clover

baltais amūrs *nm* grass carp, huan yu

baltais arsenīts *nm* arsenolite

baltais asinsķermenītis *nm* white corpuscle, leucocyte

baltais dadzis *nm* cotton thistle

baltais grifs *nm* Egyptian vulture

baltais grimons *nm* cornel

baltais lācis *nm* polar bear

baltais ozols *nm* white oak

baltais rubenis *nm* willow grouse

baltais sapals *nm* dace

baltais sesks *nm* ferret

baltais stārķis *nm* white stork

baltais ūpis *nm* snowy owl

baltais vītols *nm* white willow

baltais vizbulis *nm* wood anemone

baltais zaķis *nm* Alpine hare

baltaitiļa *nf* (folk.) sheep

baltā jāļuzāle *nf* wild madder, white bedstraw

baltakmens *nm* granulite

baltā lēpa *nf* white water lily

baltā lilija *nf* Madonna lily

baltalksnājs *nm* growth of white alder

baltalksnis *nm* white alder

baltalus *nm* pale Berlin beer

baltā madara *nf* wild madder

baltā mājas piepe *nf* Poria

baltamols *nm* white clover

baltā mušmire *nf* booted Amanita

baltā narcise *nf* narcissus

baltā nātre *nf* dead nettle

baltā panātre *nf* white dead nettle

baltā piestiļa *nf* butterfly orchid

baltā planārija *nf* white planarian

baltā pūce *nf* snowy owl

baltā puķe *nf* **1.** oxeye daisy; **2.** white water lily

baltās dzeguēu zāles *nf pl* hoary whitlow grass

baltā sinepe *nf* white mustard

baltās jāļogas *nf pl* white currant

baltā skudra *nf* termite

baltās lapas *nf pl* sphagnum moss

baltā smilga *nf* redtop

baltā spulgnaglene *nf* white campion

baltastes māļbriedis *nm* Virginia deer

baltā ūdensroze *nf* white water lily

baltauts *nm* white kerchief

baltā vārsma *nf* blank verse

baltā zilrīklīte *nf* white-spotted bluethroat

baltbiksis *nm* white pants (person)

baltdadzis *nm* cotton thistle

baltegle *nf* fir; see also **lielā b.**, **sudraba** (or **vien-krāsas**) **b.**

baltene *nf* milk cap

baltenis *nm* **1.** roach; **2.** white horse

balteļi *nm pl* (butterflies) whites

baltērkšķis *nm* hawthorn

baltēt *vt* whiten, whitewash

baltgalvainā zoss *nf* white-fronted goose

baltgalvas grifs *nm* griffon vulture

baltgalve *nf* **1.** woman with flaxen hair; **2.** white-headed cow

baltgalvis *nm* person with flaxen hair

baltgalvji *nm pl* cotton grass

baltgans *adj* whitish

baltgārnis *nm* white egret

baltgvardi *nm pl* (hist.) White Guards

baltģērētājs *nm* tawer

balti *nm pl* Balts

balti *adv* in white

baltie *nm pl* (race; pol.; pieces in a board game) whites

baltie biškrēsliļi *nm pl* sneezewort

baltie kārkliļi *nm pl* sneezewort

baltieši *nm pl* Baltic peoples

baltie ziedi *nm pl* leukorrhea

Baltijas doļi *nm pl* Baltic rush

Baltijas dzeguēpuķe *nf* Baltic orchid

Baltijas kāpu niedre *nf* Baltic reed

Baltijas menca *nf* Baltic cod

baltin *adv, emph* of **balts**; **b. balts** white as white can be

baltināt *vt* whiten, whitewash

baltiļš *nm* white horse

baltistika *nf* Baltic studies

baltist/s *nm,* ~e *nf* Baltic studies specialist

baltkājains *adj* white-legged

baltkājis *nm* white-legged horse

baltkakla dūkuris *nm* great crested grebe

baltkakla mušķērājs *nm* collared flycatcher

baltkaklis *nm* white-throated black cat

baltkaļis *nm* whitewash

baltkrevju sēnes *nf pl* white rust

baltkriev/s *nm,* ~iete *nf* Belorussian

baltkvēl/e *nf* white heat; ~ē candent

baltlasis *nm* inconnu, nelma

baltļipains *adj* white-scutted, white-tailed

baltļipis *nm* hare, rabbit

baltmaize *nf* white bread

baltmaizīte *nf* (bread) roll

baltmatains *adj* white-haired, flaxen-haired

baltmat/is *nm,* ~e *nf* a flaxen-haired person

baltmatu *indecl adj* white-haired, flaxen-haired

baltmeldri *nm pl* beak rush

baltmet[all]s [āl] *nm* white brass

baltmizis *nm* white alder

baltmugurčakstīte *nf* black-eared wheatear

baltmugurdzenis *nm* white-backed woodpecker

baltmugure *nf* white-backed cow

baltmut/is *nm,* ~e *nf* a person with a clean, beautiful mouth

baltnējs *adj* whitish

baltolo/gs *nm,* ~ģe *nf* Baltic studies specialist

baltoloģija *nf* Baltic studies

baltot *vi vr* shine white

baltoties *vr* shine white

baltpiens *nm* milk curds

baltpieres zoss *nf* white-fronted goose

baltpieris *nm* a horse with a blaze

baltpreces *nf pl* linen goods

baltpuķīte *nf* 1. white flower; 2. darling

baltraibs *adj* white-spotted

baltroce *nf* delicate damsel

baltroc/is *nm* work-shy person, a person of un-sullied hands

balts *adj* 1. white; 2. (of clothes) clean; (of a sheet of paper; of verse) blank; 3. (of skies) clear; 4. (fig.) very; whole; 5. dear

baltsaris *nm* white-maned horse; (folk.) epithet for the horse

baltsārts *adj* pinkish white

baltsej/a *nf,* ~is *nm* (folk.) pretty face

baltskarains *adj* (folk.) white-maned

baltskaris *nm* (folk.) white-maned horse

baltspalvis *nm* (folk.) a white-haired animal

baltspārnu zīriļš *nm* white-winged black tern

baltsprāklis *nm* northern wheatear

baltsprodzīti/s *nm,* ~e *nf* (folk.) white-haired person

baltsprogainis *nm* white-fleeced lamb

baltspure *nf* (folk.) epithet for the oats

baltstarīte *nf* star-of-Bethlehem

baltsvārc/is *nm,* ~e *nf* a white-frocked person

baltsvītru krustknābis *nm* two-barred crossbill

baltu *indecl adj* Baltic

baltūksnējs *adj* whitish

baltum *adv emph* of **balts; b. balts** white as white can be

baltums *nm* whiteness, white; (of tongue) fur

baltvāciet/is *nm* , ~e *nf* Baltic German

baltvācu *indecl adj* Baltic German

baltvaidz/is *nm*, ~e *nf* white-cheeked person

baltvaigu *indecl adj* white-cheeked

baltvaigu zīriļš *nm* whiskered tern

baltvaigu zoss *nf* barnacle goose

baltvalis *nm* white whale, beluga

baltvēdera *indecl adj* white-bellied

baltvēderains *adj* white-bellied

baltvēdere *nf* **1.** white-fronted goose; **2.** coltsfoot; **3.** cinquefoil; **4.** (folk.) white-belly, an epithet for the squirrel

baltvēderiļi *nm pl* cinquefoil

baltvēderis *nm* Eurasian wigeon

baltveļa *nf* (laundry) whites

baltvīns *nm* white wine

baltziedes *nf pl* (bot.) snowflake

baltzilrīklīte *nf* white-spotted bluethroat

baluč/s *nm*, ~iete *nf* Baluchi

bālūksnējs *adj* whitish

bāluliļš *nm dim* of **bālis**, brother

bālumkaite *nf* chlorosis, greensickness

bālums *nm* paleness, pallor

balus *nm* bleaching yard

balustrāde *nf* balustrade; **dekorātīva b.** balconet

balustrs *nm* baluster

balva *nf* **1.** prize, trophy; **ceļojošā b.** challenge trophy; **2.** gift, present

balzama biškrēsliļi *nm pl* costmary

balzamapse *nf* balsam poplar

balzamegle *nf* balsam fir

balzamēt *vt* embalm

balzamīne *nf* garden balsam

balzamkārkls *nm* sweet gale

balzamkoks *nm* balsam tree

balzampīpene *nf* costmary

balzams *nm* balsam; balm

balzenis *nm* **1.** thwart of a sled; **2.** swing seat; **3.** half belt

balziens *nm* = **balzenis**

balzīt *vt* **1.** tuck; **2.** (of a sled) connect opposite struts with seats

baļis *nm* log; beam

baļītis *nm dim* of **baļis**, small log

baļļa *nf* wooden tub; **kā b.** (col.) fat

baļļiļa *nf dim* of **baļļa**, small tub

baļļot *vi* (col.) party

baļļuks *nm* wingding

bambale *nf* (col.) beetle

bambalis *nm* (col.) beetle

bambāt *vi* pound, knock loudly

bambiens *nm* (mus., folk.) time

bamblis *nm* bittern

bambuks *nm* bamboo

bambulis *nm* (col.) **1.** beetle; **2.** potato

bambuslācis *nm* panda

bambusniedre *nf* bamboo cane

bambuss *nm* bamboo

bāmija *nf* okra

banāli *adv* banally, tritely

ban[a]litāte [ā] *nf* **1.** banality; **2.** cliché

ban[a]lizēt [ā] *vt* banalize

banāls *adj* banal, trite

banana *nf* banana

banānenes *nf pl* baggy pants

banānkoks *nm* banana tree

banāns *nm* banana

banāntapa *nf* banana plug

banda I *nf* gang, ring; ~s **vadītājs** ringleader

banda II *nf* **1.** (hist.) land given to a farm worker in tenancy and in lieu of wages, peculium; **2.** (obs.) sideline; second job; ~s **dzīt** snack

bandāēa *nf* **1.** bandage, dressing; **2.** (tech.) strap

bandiniece *nf* wife of a **bandinieks** (**bandinieks** I)

bandinieks I *nm* (hist.) farm worker (who was paid with a tenement of land and seed in lieu of wages)

bandinieks II *nm* (chess) pawn

bandītiski *adv* murderously, brutally

bandītisks *adj* murderous, brutal

bandītisms *nm* banditism, thuggery

bandīts *nm* bandit, thug, brigand, gangster

bandoties *vr* **1.** (hist.) plant a peculium; **2.** hold a second job, moonlight

bandrole *nf* **1.** wrapper; **2.** printed matter, third-class mail

bandubērns *nm* (obs.) illegitimate child

bandūra *nf* bandore

bandūrist/s *nm*, **~e** *nf* bandore player

bandēo *indecl nm* banjo

bang/a *nf* billow; **~s** heavy seas; **~u vāls** wave

bangains *adj* **1.** (of seas) heavy; **2.** (of horses) dappled; **3.** (of skies) overcast

bangot *vt, vi* billow, surge

bangoties *vr* (of seas) run high

bangotne *nf* surf

bangpūtis *nm* (poet.) storm

bangu atbalss *nm* sea clutter

bangu plate *nf* (naut.) wash plate

bānis I *nm* fired clay pot with handles

bā/nis II *nm* pile; **ar ~ni** suddenly; **~ļiem** in gusts

bānis III *nm* (com.) train

banīte *nf* (obs.) bonnet

bānītis *nm* (col.) narrow-gage railroad train

banjans *nm* banyan tree

bank/a I *nf* bank ◊ **kā ~ā!** (sl.) in the bank!

banka II *nf* (med.) cupping glass; **~s** cupping

bankabrošs *nm* (weav.) speeder, speed frame

bankas pārskats *nm* bank statement

bankets *nm* banquet

banknote *nf* bank note; (paper money) bill

banko *indecl nm* bank's price of an obligation

bankomāts *nm* automatic teller machine, ATM

bankrotējis *adj, part* of **bankrotēt** bankrupt

bankrotēt *vi* go bankrupt

bankrots *nm* bankruptcy

Banksa priede *nf* jack pine

banksija *nf* banksia

banksti *nm pl* (of a rafter) collar tie

bankšēt *vi* sound hollow

bankšķēt *vi* = **bankšēt**

banstaklis *nm* hoop driver

bansteķis *nm* wooden barrel hoop

bantains *adj* (col.) beribboned

bante *nf* (col.) ribbon

bantengs *nm* banteng

banti *nm pl* Bantus

baļķieris *nm* banker

baļķis *nm* (barb.) bank (shoal)

baobabs *nm* baobab

baptisms *nm* Baptist teachings

baptist[e]rija [ē] *nf* baptistery

baptist/s *nm*, **~e** *nf* Baptist

baptizija *nf* Baptisia

barabeka *nf* king bolete

bārabērns *nm* (poet.) orphan

bārainis *nm* orphan

baraka *nf* barrack

baranka *nf* bagel

baranko *indecl nm* barranca

baras *nf pl* (obs.) impost of grain

baratrija *nf* barratry

baravika *nf* king bolete

barba *nf* (zool.) barbel

bārbala *nf* **1.** thin flake from birch bark; sliver, frazzle; fringe; **2.** barberry

bārbaļa *nf* = **bārbele**

bārbaļains *adj* tattered

barbariski *adv* barbarously

barbarisks *adj* barbarous

barbariskums *nm* barbarousness

barbarisms *nm* **1.** barbarism; **2.** barbarity

barbaritāte *nf* barbarity

barbarizēt *vt* barbarize

barbars *nm* barbarian

barbe *nf* barbel

bārbele *nf* common barberry; mahonia

barbiturāts *nm* barbiturate

barbiturskābe *nf* barbituric acid

bārda *nf* beard ◊ **gaŗa b.** old chestnut; **2.** wattles

bārdainais akmeļgrauzis *nm* stone loach

bārdainais naktssikspārnis *nm* whiskered bat

bārdainā pūce *nf* great gray owl

bārdainība *nf* beardedness

bārdainis *nm* the bearded one

bārdainums *nm* beardedness

bārdains *adj* bearded

bardaks *nm* (sl.) **1.** mess; **2.** brothel

bārdāma *nf* bar girl

bārdas ķērpis *nm* beard lichen

bārdas na/zis *nm* razor; **b. ~ēa siksna** strop

bārdas tiesa *nf* (hist.) extra grain added to a grain impost by the peasant

bārdas ziepes *nf pl* shaving soap

bārdas zīlīte *nf* = **bārdzīlīte**

bārddzinis *nm* barber

bārdiļa *nf dim* of **bārda**, little beard

bards *nm* bard

bārdskuvis *nm* barber

bardune *nf* (naut.) backstay

bardzība *nf* severity, harshness, sternness

bardzīgi *adv* severely, sternly, harshly

bardzīgs *adj* severe, stern, harsh

bārdzīlīte *nf* bearded tit

bardzināt *vt* scold severely

bāre *nf* orphan

bareljefs *nm* bas-relief

barels *nm* (unit of volume) barrel

bāren/is *nm*, **~e** *nf* orphan; **apaļš b.** complete or-phan

bārenīte *nf* **1.** *dim* of **bārene**, orphan; **2.** pansy

bārenītis *nm dim* of **bārenis**, orphan

bāreļu aizgādnis *nm* guardian

bāreļu nams *nm* orphanage

bāreļu tiesa *nf* orphans' court

barete *nf* beret

bargaliļa *nf* (folk.) harsh, angry woman

bargi *adv* severely; sternly; harshly

bargonis or **bargoļa** *nm* stern, angry man

bargot *vi* behave angrily, be angry

bargoties *vr* behave angrily, be angry

bargs *adj* **1.** severe; **2.** stern; harsh; **3.** (col.) expensive; (of money paid) lots of; **4.** difficult; **5.** inclement

barguliļa *nf* = **bargaliļa**

bargulis *nm* stern, angry man

bargulīte *nf* = **bargaliļa**

bargums *nm* severity; harshness; sternness

barh[a]ns [ā] *nm* barchan

barība *nf* **1.** food; nutrition, nourishment; **2.** feed; **rupja b.** rough forage; **sausā b.** provender

barības galds *nm* feeding rack; feeding trough

barības kule *nf* nosebag

barības līdzekļi *nm pl* provisions

barības vads *nm* gullet, esophagus

barības vērtība *nf* nutritional value

barībviela *nf* nutrient

baricentrs *nm* barycenter, center of mass

bāriens *nm* a scolding

bārija klistīrs *nm* barium enema

bārijs *nm* barium

barikāde *nf* barricade

bārin *adv emph* of **bārt; b. bāra** she scolded severely

baringtonija *nf* Barringtonia

bariļš *nm dim* of **bars**, small group

bāriļš *nm dim* of **bāris**, orphan

bāriļtiesa *nf* custody court

barions *nm* baryon

bār/is *nm*, **~e** *nf* orphan

bārisks *adj* baric

barisf[ai]ra [ē] *nf* barysphere

bārītis *nm dim* of **bāris**, orphan

baritons *nm* baritone

barīts *nm* barite

barjera *nf* **1.** barrier; (RR) gate; **2.** hurdle

barjerrifs *nm* barrier reef

barjerskrējiens *nm* hurdle race, hurdles

barka *nf* barge

barkarola *nf* barcarole

barkass *nm* launch

barkentīna *nf* barkentine

barkstainā mušmire *nf* pine cone amanita

bārkstains *adj* fringed; fimbriate

bārkstiņa *nf* **1.** *dim* of **bārksts**, fringe; **2.** cilium

bārkstnieks *nm* haberdasher

bārksts *nf* fringe; (anat.) villus

bārkšains or bārkšķains *adj* fringed

bārkšķes *nf pl* cow parsnip

barkšķēt *vi* speak rapidly, rattle

barkšķi *nm pl* cow parsnip

bārkšu sakne *nf* fibrous root

bārmenis *nm* bartender

bārņi *nm pl* flour sprinkled under the loaves on a baker's peel

barodinamika *nf* barodynamics

barogr|a|fs [ā] *nm* barograph

barogramma *nf* barogram

barojošs *adj, part* of **barot** nutritious, nourishing

barojums *nm* nutrition

barokāls *adj* baroque

barokamera *nf* altitude chamber

baroklis *nm* porker, market hog

baroks *nm* baroque

baroksnis *nm* = **baroklis**

barols *nm* Barolo (wine)

barometrisks *adj* barometric

barometrs *nm* barometer

baronēns *nm* a baron's underage son

baronese *nf* baroness

baronets *nm* baronet

baronlielskungs *nm* milord

barons *nm* baron

baroskops *nm* baroscope

barošana *nf* feeding; nourishing; (of infants) nursing, suckling, breast-feeding

barot *vt* feed; nourish; **b. ar krūti** suckle, breast-feed; **b. mencas** (hum.) feed the fishes (vomit)

barotāj/s *nm*, ~a *nf* feeder

barotava *nf* feeding station

baroterapija *nf* decompression chamber therapy

baroties *vr* **1.** put on weight; **2.** (*3rd pers*) be fattened; **3.** feed on

barotne *nf* (biol.) culture medium

barotnis *nm* porker, market hog

barreters *nm* barreter

bar/s I *nm* **1.** group; (of women) bevy; (of cattle, ruminants) herd, drove; (of birds, sheep) flock; (of dogs, wolves) pack; (of fish) run, school; (of insects) swarm; ~iem (or ~os, ~u ~iem, ~u ~umis) in great numbers

bars II *nm* **1.** swath; **2.** (reg.) sandbar

b|a|rs [ā] III *nm* (phys.) bar

bārs *nm* (restaurant) bar

bārs *adj* orphaned; (fig.) abandoned

bārslas *nf pl* falling petals or snowflakes

bārsli *nm pl* pourable material

barsonis *nm* carpenter's mallet

bārstelēt *vt* pour; scatter

bārstīt *vt* pour; scatter

bārstīties *vr* **1.** pour, run out; **2.** pour back and forth; **3.** scatter; **b. ar naudu** throw money around

bāršļi *nm pl* cow parsnip

bārt *vt* scold

bārties *vr* **1.** scold; **2.** quarrel, squabble

bārtin *adv emph* of **bārt**; **b. bārt** scold severely

bartonija *nf* Bartonia

bārubērns *nm* (poet.) orphan

barvede *nf* (folk.) lead singer

barvedis *nm* **1.** gang leader; **2.** lead mower

barzāt *vt* (reg.) crumble

bārzda *nf* beard

bārzdiņa *nf dim* of **bārzda**, little beard

barēa *nf* barge

bāŗabērns or bāŗubērns *nm* (poet.) orphan

baseins *nm* **1.** pool; swimming pool; **apakšējais b.** tailwater, lower pool; **augšupējais b.** headwater, upper pool; **2.** (river, coal) basin basets *nm* Basset

basģit|a|ra [ā] *nf* bass guitar

basists *nm* player of a bass instrument

baskājains *adj* barefooted

baskāj/is *nm,* ~e *nf* hobo

basketbolist/s *nm,* ~e *nf* basketball player

basketbols *nm* basketball

baskets *nm* (col.) basketball

basklarnete *nf* bass clarinet

bask/s *nm,* ~iete *nf* Basque

baskvils *nm* pasquinade

bāslis *nm* 1. sorcerer; 2. (fig.) packrat

bas/s *nm* (mus.) bass; basso; ~ā in a deep voice

bass *adj* barefoot

bastards *nm* (col.) mixed-blood; mongrel

bastarda āboliņa smecernieks *nm* clover weevil

bastarda āboliņš *nm* alsike clover;

bastarda balanda *nf* maple-leaved goosefoot

bastarda panātre *nf* cut-leaved dead nettle

basteja *nf* (hist.) bastion

bastene *nf* kerchief of fine cloth

bastions *nm* bastion

bastot *vt* (sl.) miss, fail to attend

bašķ|i|r/s [ī] *nm,* ~iete *nf* Bashkir

bašķošanās *nfr* (reg.) casting of spells

bašķoties *vr* (reg.) cast spells

bašliks *nm* bashlyk

bāšļošana *nf* (reg.) casting of spells

bāšļot *vi* (reg.) cast spells

bāšļoties *vr* (reg.) cast spells

batālija *nf* 1. painting of a battle scene; 2. verbal battle

batālist/s *nm,* ~e *nf* battle scene painter

bataljon/s *nm* batallion; ~a kanceleja (batallion) orderly room

batāl/s *adj* pertaining to battle scene painting; ~ais žanrs battle scene painting

batāte *nf* sweet potato

baterija *nf* 1. (el.; mil.) battery; 2. (col.) flash-light

batiāle *nf* bathyal zone

batigr|a|fija [ā] *nf* deep-sea exploration

batika *nf* batik

batimetrija *nf* bathymetry

batimetrisks *adj* bathymetric

batimetrs *nm* bathymeter

batisf|ai|ra [ē] *nf* bathysphere

batiskafs *nm* bathyscaphe

batists *nm* cambric

batitermogr|a|fs [ā] *nm* bathythermograph

batol|i|ts [ī] *nm* batholith

batometrs *nm* bathometer

batra|ch|oloģija [h] *nf* amphibiology

bāts *nm* baht

batuts *nm* trampoline

baubiens *nm* (mus., folk.) beat

baucene *nf* thick winter hat with earflaps

baud/a *nf* pleasure, enjoyment, relish; ~u cilvēks hedonist

baudāms *adj, part* of baudīt enjoyable; palatable; drinkable, eatable

baudījums *nm* enjoyment

baudīt *vt* 1. enjoy; 2. (col.) eat, drink; take, partake of

baudkāre *nf* sensuality, thirst for pleasure

baudkārīgi *adv* sensually

baudkārīgs *adj* sensual, pleasure-seeking

baudviela *nf* stimulant

bauga *nf* (reg.) junk

baugznes *nf pl* cudweed

bauka *nf* (reg.) shack

baukš *interj* bang

baukšķēt *vi* bang, thud, thwack

baukšķināt *vi* bang, thud, thwack; *vt* bang

baukšķināties *vr* bang

baukšķis *nm* bang, thud, thwack

baumanis *nm* gossip monger

baum/as *nf pl* rumor; ~u birojs (sl.) gossip central

baumot *vi* spread rumors

bauris *nm* bellower; (folk.) epithet for the bull

baurot *vi* bellow; (sl.) sing in a loud and ugly voice; (sl.) bawl

bauslinieks *nm* sanctimonious person, hypocrite

bauslis *nm* (rel.) commandment

baušļaks *nm* 1. shortness of breath; 2. cough

bauze *nf* 1. stick (for striking); (of a flail) swiple; 2. head; top, peak

bauzēt *vt* strike

bauzīte *nf dim* of **bauze**, stick; swiple

bavāriet/is *nm*, **~e** *nf* Bavarian

bazālā membrāna *nf* basilar membrane

bazāls *adj* basilar

bazalts *nm* basalt

bazārs *nm* bazaar

b[a]ze [ā] *nf* 1. base; basis; **~s veikals** post exchange; 2. depot

Bazedova slimība *nf* exophthalmic goiter

bāzeklis *nm* magic object, charm; enchanted object

bazelas *nf pl* Basella

b[a]zeskuģis [ā] *nm* 1. aircraft carrier; 2. factory trawler

bazēt *vt* base

bazēties *vr* be based upon, rest upon

bazīdijs *nm* basidium

bazīdiju sēnes *nf pl* basidiomycetes

bazifikācija *nf* basification

bazilika *nf* basilica

baziliks *nm* basil; see also **parastais b.**

bazilisks *nm* basilisk

b[a]zisks [ā] *adj* alkaline

bāzīt *vt* tuck in; **b. kukuli** bribe

baznīca *nf* church; **akadēmiskā b.** campus chapel; **kaŗojošā b.** church militant

baznīcas dārzs *nm* churchyard

baznīcas dziesma *nf* hymn

baznīcas gads *nm* eccelsiastic year

baznīcas grāmatas *nf pl* parochial register

baznīcas kalps *nm* sexton

baznīcas likumi *nm pl* canon law

baznīcas mūzika *nf* sacred music

baznīcas nodevas *nf pl* church rate

baznīcas rokas grāmata *nf* agendum

baznīcas skola *nf* parochial school

baznīcas slavu valoda *nf* Church Slavonic

baznīcas sols *nm* pew

baznīca svētki *nm pl* religious holiday

baznīcas tiesa *nf* ecclesiastic court

baznīcas trauki *nm pl* sacred vessels

baznīcas valsts *nf* Pontifical State

baznīcas vidus *nm* nave

baznīcas vīns *nm* sacramental wine

baznīcēn/s *nm* churchgoer; **~i** congregation

baznīcgājējs *nm* churchgoer

baznīclaiks *nm* time of church service; Sunday morning

baznīckrogs *nm* tavern near a church

baznīckungs *nm* (obs.) pastor, parish priest

baznīcļaudis *nm pl* congregation

baznīcnieks *nm* churchgoer

baznīctēvs *nm* (hist.) minister

bazofilija *nf* basophilia

bazofils *nm* basophil

bāzt *vt* shove; thrust; push; stick; **b. acīs** (fig.) rub it in; **b. galvu cilpā** (fig.) stick one's neck out; **b. makstī** sheath; **b. visu vienā maisā** (col.) make no distinction; **b. degunu, kur nevajag** poke one's nose into other people's affairs; **b. spieķus riteņos** (col.) put a spoke in s.o.'s wheel; **bāz pats savu asti āliņģī!** pull s.o.'s chestnuts out of the fire

bāzties *vr* 1. (col.) intrude, impose oneself; **ne-bāzies man virsū!** leave me alone! **b. citu da-rīšanās** poke one's nose into other people's af-fairs; 2. **b. ārā** stick out

bāztin *adv emph* of **bāzt**; **b. piebāzts** jam-packed

bazūne *nf* trombone

bazūnēt *vi* (col.) trumpet

bazūnists *nm* trombonist

bāža *nf* 1. meddlesome person; 2. fun-seeking woman

bažas *nf pl* worry, anxiety

bažibozuks *nm* bashibazouk

bažīgi *adv* worriedly, anxiously

bažīgs *adj* worried, anxious; **man b. prāts** I am worried

bažīgums *nm* anxiousness

bažīties *vr* worry, be anxious

bdellijs *nm* bdellium

bē *interj* baa

beatificēt *vt* beatify

beatifikācija *nf* beatification

bēbis *nm* (col.) crybaby

bebrāda *nf* beaver pelt

bebrenāji *nm pl* speedwell

bebrene *nf* beaver hat

bebriņš *nm dim* of **bebrs**, little beaver

bebrkārkliņš *nm* (bot.) bittersweet

bebrs *nm* beaver

bebružurka *nf* coypu

beburs *nm* (reg.) shag, tuft of hair

beciņa *nf dim* of **beka**, little bolete

bēd/a *nf* **1.** care, trouble ◊ ~u dienas bad times, trouble; ~u ļaudis sufferers, the afflicted **kas man ~as!** what do I care! **man maza b.** what do I care! **nav tava b.!** none of your business! **bez** ~u carefree; **2.** ~as grief, sorrow; **aiz** ~ām from grief ◊ ~u dvēsele poor soul; ~u leja vale of tears; ~u liktenis sad fate; ~u luga (obs.) tragedy; ~u mati prematurely gray hair; ~u pilns sorrowful; ~u pūslis (col.) sourpuss; ~u sagrauzts brokenhearted; ~u stāsts tale of woe; hard luck story; ~u vēsts sad news; ~u zeme vale of tears

bēdāt *vi* **1.** worry; **b. bēdas** (folk.) sorrow; **2.** take care of

bēdāties *vr* **1.** grieve; **2.** worry

bedējs *nm* (obs.) gravedigger

bedeklis *nm* (reg.) molehill

bedības *nf pl* (obs.) burial

bēdīgi *adv* **1.** sadly, sorrowfully, mournfully; **2.** pitifully

bēdīgs *adj* **1.** sad, sorrowful, mournful, rueful; **2.** pitiful

bēdīgums *nm* sadness, sorrow

bēdināt *vt* aggrieve; sadden

bedīt *vt* bury

bedlends *nm* badlands

bedlingtonterjers *nm* Bedlington terrier

bēdluga *nf* (obs.) tragedy

bēdnesis *nm* bird of ill omen

bēdnieks *nm* sufferer

bedrains *adj* (of the ground) full of holes, full of potholes

bedre *nf* **1.** hole in the ground, pit; (col.) grave; **2.** pothole

bedrīte *nf* **1.** *dim* of **bedre**, small hole, pit; **2.** dimple; **3.** fossette

bēdrozis *nm* Siberian jay

bēdubrālis *nm* fellow sufferer

beduīn/s *nm*, ~iete *nf* Beduin

bēdulīgs *adj* sad, mournful, sorrowful

bēdul/is *nm*, ~e *nf* sufferer; poor devil

bedumi *nm pl* hog diggings; molehills

bēdze *nf* **1.** flight; **2.** avoidance

bēdzējs *nm* escapee

bēdziens *nm* flight

bēdzīgs *adj* evanescent

bēdzin *adv emph* of **bēgt**; **b. bēga** (he, she) was in full flight

bēdzināt *vt* conceal; (of stolen goods) fence; (of money) embezzle

befstroganovs *nm* beef Stroganoff

bēglis *nm*, ~e *nf* **1.** fugitive; escapee; **2.** refugee

begonija *nf* begonia

bēgšana *nf* **1.** flight; **neorganizēta b.** headlong flight; **2.** escape; **3.** stampede

bēgšus *adv* **1.** running, fleeing; **2.** *emph* of **bēgt**; **b. bēga** he (she) was in full flight

bēgt *vi* **1.** flee; **2.** escape; **3.** avoid; **b. kā no uguns** avoid at all costs

bēgtin *adv emph* of **bēgt**; **b. bēga** (he, she) was in full flight

bēgul/is *nm*, ~e *nf* fugitive

bēguļot *vi* be a fugitive

bēgums *nm* ebb

bēģelis *nm* (obs.) window sill

behemots *nm* hippopotamus

beice *nf* wood stain; (metal) pickle

beicēt *vt* (of wood) stain; (of metal) pickle

beidzam/ais *nom adj* **1.** last; last one; **līdz ~am** to the last; **2.** utter; **noguris līdz ~am** on one's last legs

beidzēj/s *nm*, ~a *nf* **1.** finisher; **2.** graduate

beidzot *adv, part* of **beigt 1.** finally, at last; **2.** in finishing

beig/as *nf pl* end, finish; close; conclusion ◊ **~u ~ās** in the end; at long last; **visam ~as** that is the end; **līdz pašām ~ām** to the very last; **turpmāk ~as** to be concluded; **uz ~ām** toward the end; **~ās** finally

beigizmantošana *nf* (forest.) harvesting of stands that have reached a predetermined age

beigt *vt* **1.** end, finish; complete; conclude; stop; (of a school) graduate from; **b. ciest** die; **2.** do damage; **b. nost** torture

beigties *vr* (*3rd pers*) end, finish, cease, be over **laiks ir beidzies** time is up; **b. nost** be dying; suffer; sweat and strain

beigt/s *adj, part* of **beigt 1.** finished; **2.** dead; **b. kā muša** dead as a doornail; **3.** damaged, ruined, kaput ◊ **b. un pagalam** (col.) gone forev-er; dead and buried; **~a balle!** and that's it

beigu *indecl adj* final

beigugals *nm* end

beigum/s *nm* end; ~ā finally

beiguš/ais *nom adj*, ~ā *f* graduate

beigu vārds *nm* epilogue

beisiks *nm* (compu.) BASIC

beisbols *nm* baseball

bējināt *vi* bleat

bejs *nm* bey

beka *nf* **1.** bolete; **cietā b.** = **baravika**; **2.** an old hat

bekars *nm* (mus.) natural

bekerels *nm* becquerel

bekhends *nm* backhand

bekmanijas *nf pl* Beckmann's grass, slough grass

b[e]koncūka [ē] *nf* export hog

b[e]kons [ē]s *nm* export pork; (col.) export hog

bekot *vi* pick mushrooms; **ej b.!** (col.) pish!

bekotāj/s *nm*, ~a *nf* mushroom picker

beķereja *nf* (col.) bakery

beķer/is *nm*, ~e *nf* (col.) baker

beladonna *nf* deadly nightshade

belcebuls *nm* beelzebub

belemnīts *nm* belemnite

beletāža *nf* **1.** (theat.) dress circle, **2.** first floor

beletristika *nf* belles lettres, fiction

beletristiski *adv* belletristically

beletristisks *adj* belletristic

beletrist/s *nm*, ~e *nf* belletrist, fiction writer

beletrizācija *nf* rendering in a literary style

bēliņģis *nm* attic

belīziet/is *nm*, ~e *nf* Belizean

belkants *nm* bel canto

belladonna *nf* = **beladonna**

bels *nm* (phys.) bel

beludžistān/is *nm*, ~iete *nf* Baluchi

beluga *nf* white sturgeon

belveders *nm* belvedere

belzenis *nm* **1.** breech bolt; **2.** hammerhead

belzeņa dzelksnis *nm* firing pin

belziens *nm* blow, stroke

belznis *nm* = **belzenis**

belzt *vi* strike, hit

beļģi *nm pl* Belgians; (hist.) Belgae

beļģietis *nm*, ~iete *nf* Belgian

beļģiski *adv* in Belgian

beļģisks *adj* Belgian

bembere *nf* (reg.) shorty

bemberis *nm* knotty tree; gnarled birch; knot, gnarl

bemburs *nm* (col.) clumsy person

bēmele *nf, nm* mute; taciturn person

bēmīts *nm* boehmite

bemols *nm* (mus.) flat

bencīns *nm* See **benzīns**

bencīnštelle *nf* (sl.) gas station

bende *nm, nf* **1.** executioner; **2.** killer, butcher

bendes kalniņš *nm* place of execution

bendes kalps *nm* henchman, hatchetman

bendesmaiss *nm* blackguard

bendēt *vt* **1.** kill, butcher; torture; **2.** ruin, wreck

bendētājs *nm* murderer

bendēties *vr* **b. vai nost** nearly kill o.s. working

bendijs *nm* bandy

bendrs *nm* companion

bendzele *nf* (naut.) seizing

bene *nf* beret

benedikcija *nf* benediction

Benedikta dadzis *nm* blessed thistle

benedikti *nm pl* avens

benediktietis *nm* Benedictine (monk)

benediktīns or **benediktīnietis** *nm* Benedictine (liqueur)

benefice *nf* benefit performance

beneficiants *nm* beneficiary

beneficiārs *nm* beneficiary

beneficijs *nm* benefice, fief

beng[a]l/is [ā] *nm*, **~iete** *nf* Bengal

beng[a]liski [ā] *adv* in Bengalese

beng[a]lisks [ā] *adj* Bengal, Bengalese

beng[a]lu [ā] svece *nf* Bengal light

bengulis *nm* (reg., term of endearment) child

bēniņ/i *nm pl* attic; **viss nav ~os** (sl.) not quite right in one's head

benīte *nf dim* of **bene**, beret

bentāle *nf* benthal zone

bentoss *nm* benthos

benzīlamīns *nm* benzylamine

benzīls *nm* benzyl

benzīna pildne *nf* gas station

benzīns *nm* gasoline; **dabiskais b.** natural gasoline

benzoīns *nm* benzoin

benzoldiazonijs *nm* benzene diazonium

benzols *nm* benzene

benzolveidīgs *adj* benzenoid

benzoskābe *nf* benzoic acid

benzosveķi *nm pl* benzoin

beņķ/is *nm* sandbar; (com.) bench; **~i mērīt** (com.) laze

bērais *nom adj* bay, bay horse

bērala *nf* rye bread (made of grain mixed with chaff); **~s** mixed seed cattle feed

be[r]ams [ŗ] *adj, part* of **bērt** pourable, dry, loose

berbele *nf* frazzle, tatter

berbelēt *vi* (col.) jabber, talk incoherently, blabber

berbeļains *adj* frazzled, tattered

berberica *nf* barberry

berber/is *nm*, **~iete** *nf* Berber

berdanka *nf* Berdan's rifle

bērējs *nm* **1.** pourer; **2.** gravedigger

bērene *nf* bay mare

beres *nf pl* (hist.) impost of grain

bēres *nf pl* **1.** funeral; **2.** bier

berete *nf* beret

beretīte *nf dim* of **berete**, beret

bergamoteļļa *nf* bergamot oil

bergamots *nm* bergamot

bergenijas *nf pl* Bergenia

bergsonisms *nm* Bergsonism

bergšrunds *nm* bergschrund

beri *nm pl* (hist.) impost of grain

beri-beri *indecl nm* beriberi

bēriens *nm* a pouring

beri[l]ijs [ll] *nm* beryllium

beri[l]s [ll] *nm* beryl

bērinie/ks *nm*, **~ce** *nf* funeral guest

bēris *nm* bay, bay horse

bērītis *nm dim* of **bēris**, bay, bay horse

bērkambaris *nm* funeral building (in a cemetery); (hist.) ossuary

berklijs *nm* berkelium

berlas *nf pl* dry curds

Berlīnes pankūka *nf* doughnut

berlīniet/is *nm*, **~e** *nf* Berliner

berma *nf* berm

bermontiāde *nf* (hist.) incursion into Courland, in 1919, of Pan-German militarists, led by general Bermont

bermudas *nf pl* Bermuda shorts

bernardīnietis *nm* (dog breed) Saint Bernard

bērnaukle *nf* nurse; wet nurse; dry nurse

bērndārzniece *nf* kindergarten teacher

bērnelis *nm* brat

bērnība *nf* childhood; infancy

bernīdze *nf* mother of many children

bērnīgs *adj* having many children; fertile

bērniņš *nm dim* of **bērns**, small child, baby

bērnistaba *nf* children's nursery

bērniškība *nf* childishness

bērniškīgi *adv* childishly

bērniškīgs *adj* childish

bērniškīgums *nm* childishness

bērnišks *adj* = **bērniškīgs**

bērnmeita *nf* nanny

bērnotība *nf* number of children

bērnoties *vr* (of animals), drop, have young

bērn/s *nm* child; (of animals) young ◊ **~u spēle** child's play; **~a autiņos** in an incipient stage, barely beginning; **uz ~u ~iem** for the coming generations; **no ~u dienām** from early childhood; **no ~a kājas** from childhood; **~a prātā** childish, in one's dotage

bērnu ārsts *nm* pediatrician

bērnubērni *nm pl* grandchildren

bērnudārzs *nm* kindergarten

bērnudienas *nf pl* childhood days

bērnu dzeja *nf* nursery rhyme

bērnu gultiņa *nf* crib

bērnu istaba *nf* 1. community child education center; 2. (police) juvenile division

bērnu josta *nf* swaddling band

bērnuks *nm dim* of **bērns**, small child, kid

bērnu ķērāja *nf* (obs.) midwife

bērnu māte *nf* a mother that takes care of her children

bērnumeita *nf* nurse; nanny

bērnunams *nm* children's home; orphanage

bērnu ratiņi *nm pl* baby carriage

bērnurīts *nm* morning program for children, children's matinee

bērnu saņēmēja *nf* midwife

bērnu silīte *nf* day nursery

bērnu slepkavība *nf* infanticide

bērnu trieka *nf* poliomyelitis

bērs *adj* bay

bērsters *nm* x-ray burster

bērt *vt* 1. pour; 2. (of words) spout; **b. kā no grā-matas** (or **kā pupas**) spout (words, rapidly and fluently); **b. kā no maisa** gibber, rattle away

bērties *vr* pour, be poured

bērtin *adv emph* of **bērt**; **b. bēra** he (she) poured without letup

bertolecijas *nf pl* Bertholettia

Bertolē sāls *nf* potassium chlorate

bēru kase *nf* (hist.) credit union

bērulains *adj* (of bread) baked with chaff, bran, or other additives

berulas *nf pl* water parsnip

bērums *nm* 1. a quantity poured, a quantity dumped; 2. (metall.) burden

berza *nf* 1. spawning ground; 2. friction site between two trees

bērzaine *nf* birch grove

bērzājs *nm* birch grove

berze *nf* 1. friction; 2. grater

berzeklis *nm* 1. scrubber (made of straw or horsehair); 2. spawning ground; 3. a quarrelsome person

berzene *nf* pestle

bērzene *nf* = **bērzlape**

berzenis *nm* **1.** (ling.) fricative; **2.** dark rye bread crumbled into milk or porridge

berzes līste *nf* (naut.) rubbing strake

berzēt *vt* rub

berzēties *vr* rub, rub oneself; (fig.) rub shoulders with

bērziens *nm* birch grove

bērziņš *nm dim* of **bērzs**, little birch

bērzlape *nf* Russula

bērzlapīte *nf dim* of **bērzlape**, Russula

bērzola *nf* (reg.) birch grove

bērzpuķīte *nf* starflower

bērz/s *nm* birch ◊ ~a siers birching

bērzsulas *nf pl* birch sap

berzt *vt* **1.** rub; **2.** chafe; **3.** grind, grate; **4.** scrub, scour

berztala *nf* grate

berzties *vr* **1.** rub, (with **gar**) rub against; **2.** rub oneself, scrub oneself

berztuve *nf* grater; (flax, hemp) brake

bērzu beka *nf* rough boletus;

bērzu gremzdgrauzis *nm* birch bark beetle

bērzu koksnurbis *nm* birch borer

bērzulājs *nm* birch grove

berzumi *nm pl* crumbs

bērzūne *nf* (reg.) birch grove

bērzu vērpējs *nm* a tent caterpillar moth, Eriogaster lanestris

beržamais *nom adj* scrubber

berēu laiks *nm* spawning time

besarabiet/is *nm*, ~e *nf* Bessarabian

bese *nf* (econ.) bear market

Besemera bumbieris *nm* Bessemer converter

best *vt* (obs.) bury

bestiāls *adj* bestial

bestiārijs *nm* bestiary

bestija *nf* predator; (fig.) brutal, depraved, or bestial person

bestrs *adj* healthy; strong; beautiful

bestsellers *nm* bestseller

bešā *adv* (col.) without anything, empty-handed

b|e|šs [ē] *adj* beige

bet *conj* but; **bet toties** yet; **bet arī** but also; **bet ta** (or **tad**) (com.) how

b|e|ta [ē] *nm* beta; **b. dzelz**s beta iron; **b. sabruk-šana** beta decay

b|e|taīns [ē] *nm* betaine

b|e|tatrons [ē] *nm* betatron

beteļpalma *nf* betel palm

beteļpipars *nm* betel pepper

betona nagla *nf* masonry nail

betonēt *vt* concrete, pave with concrete

betonētāj/s *nm*, ~a *nf* concrete worker

betonika *nf* betony

betoniku sārmenes *nf pl* wood betony

betons *nm* concrete; **gaisots b.** air-entrained concrete

betonsitējs *nm* (mil.) concrete-piercing

betulins *nm* betulinol

bevatrons *nm* bevatron

bez *prep* **1.** without; out of; less, minus; **b. tam** in addition, besides; **2.** in addition; not counting, besides, except

bezacis *nm* eyeless person

bezakmens *indecl adj* free of stones

bezakotu *indecl adj* awnless

bezakotu lāčauza *nf* awnless bromegrass

bezakotu lavsonija *nf* henna

bezakotu zāļu auzas *nf pl* awnless bromegrass

bezalgas *indecl adj* unpaid, without pay

bezalkohola *indecl adj* nonalcoholic

bezalkoholisks *adj* nonalcoholic, alcohol-free; (of an establishment) temperance

bez|a|nbrase [ā] *nf* (naut.) crossjack brace

bez|a|nbura [ā] *nf* (naut.) mizzen

bez|a|nmasta [ā] cepure *nf* (naut.) mizzen-truck

bez|a|nmasts [ā] *nm* (naut.) mizzenmast

bez|a|nraja [ā] *nf* (naut.) crossjack yard

bez|a|ns [ā] *nm* mizzenmast

bez[a]nštaga [ā] *nf* mizzen stay

bez[a]nzāliņš [ā] *nm* (naut.) mizzentop

bezapkalpes *indecl adj* unmanned; (of aircraft) pilotless, robot

bezapziņa *nf* the unconscious

bezasinība *nf* bloodlessness

bezasinīgs *adj* 1. bloodless; 2. pallid

bezasiņu *indecl adj* 1. bloodless; 2. pallid

bezastainie abinieki *nm pl* Salientia, salientians

bezastains *adj* tailless

bezaste *nf* 1. tailless one; 2. (folk.) witch

bezastes *indecl adj* tailless

bezatbalss *indecl adj* anechoic

bezatbildība *nf* irresponsibility

bezatbildīgi *adv* irresponsibly

bezatbildīgs *adj* irresponsible

bezatbildīgums *nm* irresponsibility

bezatgrūdes *indecl adj* recoilless

bezatlīdzības *indecl adj* (of a position) unpaid

bezatmaksas *indecl adj* nonprofit

bezatmosf[[ai]ras [ē] *indecl adj* without an atmosphere

bezatsitiena *indecl adj* recoilless

bezatskaņu *indecl adj* unrhymed

bezatspoļu *indecl adj* shuttleless

bezattiecīgs *adj* nonrelational

bezaugsnes *indecl adj* soilless

bezaugu *indecl adj* aphytal

bezav[a]riju [ā] *indecl adj* accident-free, breakdown-free

bezbailība *nf* fearlessness

bezbailīgi *adv* fearlessly

bezbailīgs *adj* fearless

bezbailīgums *nm* fearlessness

bezbailis *nm* fearless person

bezbalsīgs *adj* voiceless, mute

bezbārdains *adj* beardless

bezbārdis *nm* beardless man

bezbēdība *nf* unconcern, light-heartedness

bezbēdīgi *adv* in a carefree manner, light-heartedly

bezbēdīgs *adj* carefree, unconcerned, light-hearted

bezbēdīgums *nm* unconcern, lightheartedness

bezbēd/is *nm*, ~e *nf* devil-may-care person, happy-go-lucky person

bezbēdnie/ks *nm*, ~ce *nf* = bezbēdis

bezbēdu *indecl adj* carefree, unconcerned, lighthearted

bezbēnīte *nf* star-flower

bezbērnība *nf* childlessness

bezbērnis *nm* childless person

bezbērnu *indecl adj* childless

bezberzes *indecl adj* frictionless

bezbiksis *nm* (col.) indigent person, poor devil; (hist.) sansculotte

bezbiļetnie/ks *nm*, ~ce *nf* ticketless passenger; stowaway

bezceļ[a] [u] *indecl adj* roadless

bezcentra *indecl adj* centerless

bezcere *nf* hopelessness

bezcerība *nf* hopelessness

bezcerīgi *adv* hopelessly

bezcerīgs *adj* hopeless

bezcerīgums *nm* hopelessness

bez[ch]lorofilla [h] *indecl adj* achlorophyllous

bezcienība *nf* irreverence

bezcienīgi *adv* irreverently

bezcienīgs *adj* irreverent

bezcukura *indecl adj* sugarless, sugar-free

bezcukura diabēts *nm* diabetes insipidus

bezdarbība *nf* inactivity, idleness; (jur.) inaction

bezdarbīgi *adv* inactively, idly

bezdarbīgs *adj* inactive, idle

bezdarbīgums *nm* inactivity, idleness

bezdarbis *nm* idler

bezdarbniek/s *nm* unemployed person; ~i the unemployed

bezdarbnieku pabalsts *nm* unemployment relief

bezdarbs *nm* unemployment

bezdefektu *indecl adj* defectless
bezdeficīta *indecl adj* no-deficit
bezdelīdzēns *nm* young swallow
bezdelīdziņa *nf dim* of **bezdelīga**, little swallow
bezdelīga *nf* barn swallow
bezdelīgactiņas *nf pl* bird's-eye primrose
bezdelīgaste *nf* dovetail
bezdelīgtārtiņš *nm* pratincole
bezdelīgu piekūns *nm* northern hobby
bezdelīgveidīgie *nm pl* Hirundinidae
bezdels *nm* (vulg.) fart
bezdēt *vi* (vulg.) fart
bezdibena *indecl adj* bottomless
bezdibenīgi *adv* botomlessly
bezdibenīgs *adj* bottomless, abyssal
bezdibenis *nm* abyss
bezdievība *nf* godlessness
bezdievīgi *adv* (col.) to the extreme
bezdievīgs *adj* godless
bezdiev/is *nm*, ~**e** *nf* godless person, atheist
bezdievnie/ks *nm*, ~**ce** *nf* = **bezdievis**
bezdomība *nf* absence of thought
bezdomīgi *adv* unthinkingly
bezdomīgs *adj* unthinking
bezdomīgums *nm* absence of thought
bezdomu *indecl adj* unthinking
bezdrāts *indecl adj* wireless
bezdrudža *indecl adj* free from fever, afebrile
bezdūmu *indecl adj* smokeless
bezdūšelis *nm* milksop, sissy
bezdūšība *nf* timidity, timorousness, craveness
bezdūšīgi *adv* timidly, timorously; cravenly
bezdūšīgs *adj* timid, timorous, craven
bezdvēsele *nf, nm* soulless person
bezdvēseles *indecl adj* soulless
bezdvēselīgs *adj* soulless
bezdvēsel/is *nm*, ~**e** *nf* **1.** tone-deaf person; **2.** cruel, merciless person
bezdzeloņ[a] [u] *indecl adj* stingless
bezdzelzs *indecl adj* iron-free

bezdzimuma *indecl adj* asexual, agamic
bezdzinēja *indecl adj* motorless
bezē *indecl nm* meringue
bezēnu *indecl adj* shadowless
bezērkšķu *indecl adj* thornless
bezformīgi *adv* formlessly
bezformīgs *adj* formless
bezgaisa *indecl adj* airless
bezgala *indecl adj* infinite
bezgala *adv* infinitely; extremely
bezgala sakne *nf* laserwort
bezgale *nf* **1.** blind gut; **2.** chatty woman; **3.** laserwort; **4.** (poet.) infinity
bezgalība *nf* infinity; **līdz ~i** ad infinitum
bezgalīgi *adv* infinitely, endlessly, interminably
bezgalīgs *adj* infinite, endless; interminable
bezgalīgums *nm* infiniteness
bezgalis *nm* glutton
bezgalotnes *indecl adj* **1.** inflectionless, zero-ending; **2.** (of trees) flat-topped
bezgalvains *adj* headless
bezgalvas *indecl adj* acephalous
bezgalvis *nm* headless one
bezgaļas *indecl adj* meatless
bezgaršība *nf* tastelessness
bezgaršīgums *nm* tastelessness
bezgaumība *nf* tastelessness
bezgaumīgi *adv* tastelessly
bezgaumīgs *adj* tasteless
bezgaumīgums *nm* tastelessness
bezgausīgi *adv* gluttonously, insatiably
bezgausīgs *adj* gluttonous, insatiable
bezgausīgums *nm* gluttony
bezgausis *nm* glutton, insatiable person
bezgodība *nf* infamy, dishonorableness
bezgodīgi *adv* dishonorably, disgracefully
bezgodīgs *adj* dishonorable, disgraceful, infamous
bezgodīgums *nm* dishonorableness
bezgod/is *nm*, ~**e** *nf* dishonorable person, infamous person, scoundrel

bezgods *nm* disgrace

bezgrēcība *nf* sinlessness

bezgrēcīgi *adv* sinlessly

bezgrēcīgs *adj* sinless

bezgrēcīgums *nm* sinlessness

bezgribas *indecl adj* will-less

bezģimenes *indecl adj* without a family

bezģimenes nodoklis *nm* bachelor tax

bezidejiski *adv* without principles or ideals

bezidejisks *adj* lacking both principles and ideals

bezidejiskums *nm* lack of principles and ideals

beziemesla *indecl adj* without a reason

bezierunu *indecl adj* unconditional

bezindukcijas *indecl adj* non-inductive

bezīpašnieka *indecl adj* ownerless, (jur.) derelict; **b. manta** (jur.) res nullius

bezīpašumtiesīgs *adj* not having property rights; **b. turēšana** (jur.) adverse possession

bezizeja *nf* impasse; hopless situation; ~s stā-voklī in a hopeless situation, dead end

bezizmēra *indecl adj* unsized

bezizredēu *indecl adj* hopeless

bezizteiksmīgi *adv* expressionlessly

bezizteiksmīgs *adj* expressionless

bezjēdzība *nf* senselessness, absurdity

bezjēdzīgi *adv* senselessly, absurdly

bezjēdzīgs *adj* senseless, absurd

bezjēdzīgums *nm* senselessness, absurdity

bezjēga *nf* (philos.) insensateness

bezjēgas *indecl adj* senseless, absurd

bezjūtība *nf* insensitivity

bezjūtīgi *adv* insensitively

bezjūtīgs *adj* insensitive

bezjūtīgums *nm* insensitivity

bezjūtu *indecl adj* insensitive

bezkaislība *nf* passionlessness, impassiveness

bezkaislīgi *adv* passionlessly, impassively

bezkaislīgs *adj* passionless, impassive

bezkaislīgums *nm* passionlessness, impassiveness

bezkājains *adj* footless, legless; apodous

bezkāj/is *nm*, ~e *nf* legless person

bezkāju *indecl adj* footless, legless; apodous

bezkapacitātes *indecl adj* noncapacitive

bezkarkasa *indecl adj* (arch.) frameless

bezkāta *indecl adj* stemless

bezkāta prīmula *nf* European primrose

bezkaunība *nf* shamelessness, impudence, in-solence

bezkaunīgi *adv* shamelessly, impudently, insolently

bezkaunīgs *adj* shameless, impudent, insolent

bezkaunīgums *nm* shamelessness, impudence, insolence

bezkauņa *nf, nm* shameless, impudent, insolent person ◊ **b.!** what a nerve!

bezkļūdaini *adv* without error

bezkļūdains *adj* errorless

bezkompromisa *indecl adj* no-compromise

bezkondensācijas *indecl adj* non-condensing

bezkonflikt[a] [u] *indecl adj* without conflict

bezkonfliktība *nf* absence of conflict

bezkontaktu *indecl adj* without moving contacts

bezkontrole *nf* lack of supervision

bezkontroles *indecl adj* unchecked

bezkopas *indecl adj* (of sentences) one-word

bezkrāsaini *adv* colorlessly

bezkrāsainība *nf* colorlessness

bezkrāsains *adj* colorless

bezkrāsainums *nm* colorlessness

bezkrāsas *indecl adj* colorless

bezkrasta *indecl adj* shoreless

bezkr[i]žu [ī] *indecl adj* unmarked by crises

bezkrunkains *adj* wrinkleless

bezkunga *indecl adj* (obs.) ownerless

bezķermenisks *adj* incorporeal

bezķermeniskums *nm* incorporeity; disem-bodiment

bezlaicība *nf* timelessness

bezlaicīgi *adv* **1.** timelessly; **2.** prematurely

bezlaicīgs *adj* **1.** timeless; **2.** premature

bezlaicīte *nf* autumn crocus

bezlaika *indecl adj* premature

bezlaikā *adv* before time, prematurely

bezlapains *adj* leafless

bezlape *nf* toothwort

bezlapots *adj* leafless

bezlapu *indecl adj* leafless

bezlaulība *nf* celibacy

bezliesmas *indecl adj* flashless

bezlietains *adj* rainless

bezlietus *indecl adj* rainless

bezlogu *indecl adj* windowless

bezlūp/is *nm,* ~**e** *nf* lipless one

bezļaužu *indecl adj* pertaining to temporary personnel, pertaining to non-staff positions

bezmājas *indecl adj* homeless

bezmākoņu *indecl adj* cloudless

bezmaksas *indecl adj* free, free of charge; (of a worker) unpaid

bezmalas *indecl adj* infinite

bezmantība *nf* indigence

bezmantietis *nm* indigent person

bezmantīgs *adj* indigent

bezmantinieku *indecl adj* (jur.) intestate

bezmantis *nm* indigent person

bezmatains *adj* hairless

bezmātes *indecl adj* motherless; (of bees) queenless

bezmat/is *nm,* ~**e** *nf* hairless one

bezmaz *adv* (col.) almost

bezmēness *indecl adj* moonless

bezmēns *nm* steelyard

bezmēra *indecl adj* immeasurable, very great; excessive

bezmērība *nf* immensity

bezmērīgi *adv* exceedingly

bezmērīgs *adj* immeasurable, very great; excessive

bezmērķa *indecl adj* aimless, purposeless

bezmērķība *nf* aimlessness, purposelessness

bezmērķīgi *adv* aimlessly, purposelessly

bezmērķīgs *adj* aimless, purposeless

bezmērķīgums *nm* aimlessness, purposelessness

bezmērs *nm* steelyard

bezmeža *indecl adj* woodless, treeless

bezmiedzība *nf* sleeplessness

bezmiega *indecl adj* sleepless

bezmiegains *adj* sleepless

bezmiegs *nm* sleeplessness, insomnia

bezmiera *indecl adj* restless

bezmiesība *nf* incorporeality, immateriality

bezmiesīgs *adj* incorporeal, immaterial

bezmiesīgums *nm* incorporeality, immateriality

bezmotora *indecl adj* motorless

bezmugurkaula *indecl adj* invertebrate, spineless

bezmugurkaulainis *nm* invertebrate

bezmugurkaulains *adj* invertebrate, spineless

bezmugurkaulnieks *nm* invertebrate

bezmuitas *indecl adj* duty-free

beznaga *indecl adj* (of headgear) peakless

beznaģe *nf* peakless cap

beznaidība *nf* absence of envy

beznaudas *indecl adj* not involving money; **b. norēķins** (econ.) clearing operation

beznaudīgs *adj* moneyless

beznodevu *indecl adj* duty-free

beznodokļu *indecl adj* tax-free

beznokrišņu *indecl adj* without precipitation

beznorēķina *indecl adj* not requiring an accounting; (bookk., of expenses) uncontrolled

beznosacījuma *indecl adj* unconditional; (physiol.) unconditioned

beznosaukuma *indecl adj* nameless

beznosēšanās *indecl adj* nonstop

beznoteikuma *indecl adj* unconditional

beznoteces *indecl adj* = **beznotekas**

beznotekas *indecl adj* drainless; (of bodies of water) stagnant

beznozīmes *indecl adj* meaningless

bezoarkaza *nf* bezoar goat

bezoderes *indecl adj* unlined

bezosas *indecl adj* (of cups, pitchers) handleless, earless

bezpagātnes *indecl adj* without a past

bezpajumtes *indecl adj* homeless

bezpajumtnie/ks *nm*, ~ce *nf* homeless person

bezpalīdzība *nf* helplessness

bezpalīdzīgi *adv* helplessly

bezpalīdzīgs *adj* helpless

bezpalīdzīgums *nm* helplessness

bezpamata *indecl adj* groundless, unfounded

bezpamatība *nf* groundlessness

bezpapēžu *indecl adj* heelless

bezparaksta *indecl adj* unsigned, anonymous

bezpartejiski *adv* impartially, in a nonpartisan fashion

bezpartejisks *adj* impartial, nonpartisan; non-affiliated

bezpartejiskums *nm* impartiality, nonpartisanship; lack of party affiliation

bezpārtraukuma *indecl adj* uninterrupted

bezpases *indecl adj* passportless

bezpasnie/ks *nm*, ~ce *nf* passportless person

bezpaspēles *indecl adj* sure thing

bezpavalstniecība *nf* statelessness

bezpavalstnie/ks *nm*, ~ce *nf* stateless person

bezpeļņas *indecl adj* non-profit

bezpersonas *indecl adj* (gram.) impersonal

bezpersonība *nf* impersonality

bezpersonīgs *adj* 1. bland, without character; 2. impersonal

bezpersonisks *adj* 1. bland, without character; 2. impersonal

bezpersoniskums *nm* 1. lack of character; 2. im-personality

bezpersonu *indecl adj* pertaining to non-permanent personnel, non-staff

bezperspekt[i]vitāte [ī] *nf* lack of promise

bezperspektīvs *adj* lacking promise

bezpiedurknis *nm* sleeveless jacket

bezpiedurkņains *adj* sleeveless

bezpiedurkņu *indecl adj* sleeveless

bezpietek[as] [u] *indecl adj* without tributaries

bezpigmenta *indecl adj* unpigmented

bezpilota *indecl adj* pilotless

bezpilsonība *nf* statelessness

bezpirkstu *indecl adj* fingerless

bezplāna *indecl adj* planless

bezprāta *indecl adj* crazy, irrational, senseless, madcap

bezprātība *nf* madness, folly

bezprātīgs *adj* crazy, irrational, senseless, madcap

bezprātīgums *nm* madness, folly

bezprāt/is *nm*, ~e *nf* madcap

bezprāts *nm* madness, folly

bezprecedenta *indecl adj* unprecedented

bezpreču *indecl adj* not involving the manufacture of goods

bezpriecīgs *adj* joyless

bezpriedēkļa *indecl adj* unprefixed

bezprieka *indecl adj* joyless

bezpriekšmetīgs *adj* nonrepresentational

bezpriekšmetu darbība *nf* (theat.) pantomime

bezprincipi[a]litāte [ā] *nf* unprincipledness

bezprincipiāli *adv* in an unprincipled way

bezprincipiāls *adj* unprincipled

bezprincipu *indecl adj* unprincipled

bezprocentīgs *adj* interest-free

bezpupe *nf* (folk.) flat-chested girl

bezradu *indecl adj* having no relatives

bezradze *nf* polled cow

bezragu *indecl adj* (of anvils) hornless

bezrakstura *indecl adj* bland, without character

bezrasains *adj* dewless

bezrasas *indecl adj* dewless

bezremanences *indecl adj* non-remanent

bezrobežu *indecl adj* limitless

bezrocība *nf* poverty

bezrocis *nm* 1. indigent person; 2. armless person; 3. tank top

bezroči *nm pl* sleeveless jacket

bezrūpība *nf* unconcern; carelessness

bezrūpīgi *adv* in an unconcerned manner; carelessly

bezrūpīgs *adj* 1. carefree, untroubled, unconcerned; 2. careless; reckless; unconcerned

bezrūpīgums *nm* unconcern; carelessness

bezrūpis *nm* carefree person

bezrūpju *indecl adj* carefree

bezsaikļa *indecl adj* (gram.) asyndetic

bezsaimnieka *indecl adj* ownerless

bezsaistes *indecl adj* (compu.) off-line

bezsakara *indecl adj* unconnected, out of context

bezsakarīgi *adv* incoherently

bezsakarīgs *adj* unconnected; incoherent, jumbled

bezsala *indecl adj* frostless (no freeze)

bezsalnas *indecl adj* frostless (no hoarfrost)

bezsāls *indecl adj* saltless

bezsamaņa *nf* unconsciousness

bezsāpju *indecl adj* painless

bezsapņu *indecl adj* dreamless

bezsaris *nm* bristleless animal

bezsāta *indecl adj* = **bezsātīgs**

bezsātība *nf* 1. (of food) inability to satisfy; 2. (of a person) insatiability

bezsātīgi *adv* insatiably

bezsātīgs *adj* 1. (of food) insubstantial, not nourishing; 2. (of a person) insatiable

bezsātīgums *nm* = **bezsātība**

bezsatura *indecl adj* empty (of content), vapid

bezsaturība *nf* emptiness, vapidity

bezsaturīgi *adv* vapidly

bezsaturīgs *adj* empty (of content), vapid

bezsaturīgums *nm* emptiness, vapidity

bezsaules *indecl adj* sunless

bezseguma *indecl adj* (of bonds, IOUs) unsecured; **b. čeks** bad check

bezsejains *adj* faceless

bezsejība *nf* facelesness

bezsejas *indecl adj* faceless

bezsēkle *nf* seedless fruit, seedless berry

bezsēklu *indecl adj* seedless

bezsekmība *nf* lack of success

bezsekmīgi *adv* unsuccessfully

bezsekmīgs *adj* unsuccessful

bezserdes *indecl adj* coreless

bezsētas *indecl adj* fenceless

bezsirdība *nf* heartlessness

bezsirdīgi *adv* heartlessly

bezsirdīgs *adj* heartless

bezsirdīgums *nm* heartlessness

bezsirdis *nm* heartless person

bezsirds *indecl adj* heartless

bezsižeta *indecl adj* plotless

bezsižetisks *adj* plotless

bezskābekļa *indecl adj* lacking oxygen

bezskaidras naudas maksājums *nm* book transaction

bezskaņas *indecl adj* unvoiced

bezslavītes *nf pl* toothwort

bezslieču *indecl adj* railless

bezsniega *indecl adj* snowless

bezspārnis *nm* wingless animal

bezspārnu *indecl adj* wingless

bezspārnu zvaguļi *nm* a rattle, Rhinanthus apterus

bezspārņi *nm pl* Apterygota

bezspēcība *nf* feebleness, weakness, debility; (fig.) impotence, powerlessness

bezspēcīgi *adv* feebly, weakly; impotently

bezspēcīgs *adj* feeble, weak; impotent, powerless

bezspēcīgums *nm* feebleness, weakness, debility; (fig.) impotence, powerlessness

bezspēks *nm* feebleness, weakness, debility, loss of strength

bezstrāvas *indecl adj* currentless

bezstrīdus *indecl adj* non-actionable; **b. kārtībā** by entering a nolo contendere plea

bezstruktūras *indecl adj* structureless

bezsulu *indecl adj* sapless

bezsvara *indecl adj* weightless; (phys.)
 imponderable; **b. stāvoklis** weightlessness
bezsvina *indecl adj* lead-free; (of gasoline)
 un-leaded
bezšķirnes *indecl adj* unpedigreed
bezšķiru *indecl adj* classless
bezšūnu *indecl adj* noncellular
bezšuves *indecl adj* seamless
beztalantīgs *adj* untalanted
beztaras *indecl adj* tareless
beztelpisks *adj* spaceless
beztermiņa *indecl adj* unlimited, indefinite;
 lifetime; (of loans) permanent
beztiesība *nf* lack of rights
beztiesīgi *adv* without rights
beztiesīgs *adj* without rights, deprived of
 rights
beztiesīgums *nm* lack of rights
beztiesiski *adv* without rights
beztiesisks *adj* without rights
beztiesiskums *nm* lack of rights
beztraucējumu *indecl adj* interference-free
beztrokšņa *indecl adj* noiseless
bezūdens *indecl adj* **1.** waterless; arid; **2.** anhydrous
bezūsains *adj* without a moustache
bezuzraudzība *nf* lack of supervision
bezvadu *indecl adj* wireless
bezvainas *indecl adj* **1.** innocent; **2.** no-fault
bezvainība *nf* innocence
bezvainīgi *adv* innocently
bezvainīgs *adj* innocent
bezvaldība *nf* anarchy
bezvalod/is *nm,* ~**e** *nf* mute, speechless person
bezvalstniecība *nf* statelessness
bezvalstnie/ks *nm,* ~**ce** *nf* stateless person
bezvārdība *nf* namelessness
bezvārda *indecl adj* nameless; (of a check)
 bearer
bezvārdīgi *adv* taciturnly
bezvārdīgs *adj* taciturn

bezvārd/is *nm ,* ~**e** *nf* **1.** anonymous person;
 2. unknown species of tree
bezveida *indecl adj* formless, shapeless
bezveidība *nf* formlessness, shapelessness
bezveidīgi *adv* formlessly, shapelessly
bezveidīgs *adj* formless, shapeless
bezveidīgums *nm* formlessness, shapelessness
bezvēja *indecl adj* windless
bezvējains *adj* windless
bezvējš *nm* calm
bezvērstuvju *indecl adj* (of a plow) without a
 moldboard
bezvērtība *nf* worthlessness
bezvērtīgi *adv* worthlessly
bezvērtīgs *adj* worthless
bezvērtīgums *nm* worthlessness
bezvērts *indecl adj* worthless
bezvēsts *indecl adj* without any news, (of
 absences) unaccounted for; **b. prombūtnē**
 (jur.) missing
bezvēstures *indecl adj* without a history
bezvētru *indecl adj* storm-free
bezvien *adv* solely
bezvietas *indecl adj* unemployed
bezviet/is *nm,* ~**e** *nf* one that has no place
bezviltība *nf* guilelessness
bezviltīgi *adv* guilelessly
bezviltīgs *adj* guileless
bezviltus *indecl adj* guileless
bezvīzu *indecl adj* visa-less
bezzarains *adj* branchless
bezzaris *nm* branchless tree
bezzaru *indecl adj* branchless
bezzemes *indecl adj* landless
bezzemnie/ks *nm,* ~**ce** *nf* landless peasant
bezziedu *indecl adj* nonflowering, crypto-
 gamic
bezzirga *indecl adj* horseless
bezzobains *adj* toothless
bezzob/is *nm,* ~**e** *nf* toothless person
bezzobu *indecl adj* toothless

bezzoles *indecl adj* without a sole

bezzvaigēņains *adj* starless

bezzvīņains *adj* scaleless

bezzvīņu *indecl adj* scaleless

bezžokļu *indecl adj* (tech., of chucks) jawless

bēžs *adj beige*

biandrija *nf* bigamy

biatlons *nm* biathlon

bībele *nf* the Bible; bible

bībeliski *adv* biblically

bībelisks *adj* biblical

bībelnie/ks *nm*, **~ce** *nf* Bible expert; Bible reader

bībelstāsts *nm* Bible story

bibis *nm* **1.** (child.) slight injury, hurt; **2.** simpleton; **3.** comb of a turkey

bībis *nm* **1.** (child.) stranger; **2.** (child.) bogeyman; **3.** clumsy person

bibliobuss *nm* bookmobile

bibliofilija *nf* bibliophily

bibliofils *nm*, **~e** *nf* bibliophile

bibliografēt *vt* enter in a bibliography

bibliogr[a]fija [ā] *nf* bibliograpy

bibliogr[a]fiski [ā] *adv* bibliographically

bibliogr[a]fisks [ā] *adj* bibliographic

bibliogr[a]f/s [ā] *nm*, **~e** *nf* bibliographer

bibliom[a]nija [ā] *nf* bibliomania

bibliom[a]n/s [ā] *nm*, **~e** *nf* bibliomaniac

bibliotēka *nf* library

bibliot[e]kār/s [ē] *nm*, **~e** *nf* librarian

bibliot[e]kārs [ē] *adj* library (*adj*)

bibliski *adv* biblically

biblisks *adj* biblical

biblisms *nm* biblical term or expression

bībops *nm* bebop

bicatāt *vi* (of sheep) pronk

bicepss *nm* biceps

bi[ch]romāts [h] *nm* bichromate

bicināt *vt* (of sheep) stomp

bičolis *nm* beekeeper

bičot *vt* (sl.) beg

bīčvolejs *nm* beach volleyball

bīdāmatslēga *nf* dead bolt

bīdāmdurvis *nf pl* sliding door

bidē *indecl nm* bidet

bīde *nf* (tech.) horizontal shear

bīdeklis *nm* **1.** slide, slider, bolt, bar; (artillery) feed blck actuating slide; **2.** rear sight

bīdele *nf* flour sieve

bīdelēt *vt* (of flour) grind finely

bīdelgaņģis *nm* run of millstones

Bīdermeijera stils *nm* Biedermeier style

bīdes spriegums *nm* shear stress

bīdījiens *nm* push, shove

bīdīt *vt* push, shove

bīdītāj/s *nm*, **~a** *nf* pusher

bīdīties *vr* push oneself; **b. priekšā** push oneself in front of others

bīdmērs *nm* caliper

bīdnis *nm* (artillery) slide, feed block actuating slide

bīdstienis *nm* (tech.) follower

bidulis *nm* (hist.) stylus (used in making bast shoes)

biedēklis *nm* scarecrow; fright, bugaboo

biedēt *vt* frighten

biedīgs *adj* frightening

biedinājum/s *nm* warning; **par ~u** as a warning

biedināt *vt* warn

biedram *adv* for company

biedre *nf* See **biedrs**

biedrene *nf* (obj.) *f* of **biedrs**

biedrība *nf* society, association, union

biedrināt *vt* unite

biedrinie/ks *nm*, **~ce** *nf* companion

biedriski *adv* in a comradely fashion

biedrisks *adj* comradely

biedriskums *nm* comradeship

biedrone *nf* society woman

biedros *adv* for company

biedrošanās *nfr* association, social intercourse, fraternization

biedrošanās brīvība *nf* freedom of assembly

biedrot *vt* associate

biedrotājs *nm* hyphen

biedroties *vr* 1. unite, organize; 2. associate with, mix with, be friends with; 3. (gram.) require

biedrs *nm*, ~e, *nf* 1. comrade, fellow, associate; 2. companion; 3. deputy; 4. member; **b. veicinātājs** supporting member; **(aicināt)** ~os (ask) to join

biedru maksa *nf* membership dues

biedrumis *adv* together

biedrzīme *nf* hyphen

bieds *nm* phantom; bogy, bugbear

biennāle *nf* biennial

biešu dzeltenkāju muša *nf* (imago of) spinach leaf miner

biešu nematods *nm* beet cyst eelworm

biešu smecernieks *nm* sugar beet weevil

biešu spradzis *nm* mangold flea beetle

biete *nf* beet

biezādains *adj* 1. thick-skinned; 2. pachydermatous

biezādis *nm* 1. pachyderm; 2. (col.) lazybones

biezais *nom adj* (col.) rich man

biezājs *nm* thicket

biezausis *nm* a person hard of hearing

biezenīca *nf* porridge

biezenis *nm* puree; paste

biezeņzupa *nf* (cul.) bisque

biezēt *vi* thicken

biezgalvis *nm* 1. (col.) blockhead; 2. (col.) pigheaded person

biezgalvnieks *nm* (col.) pigheaded person

biezi *adv* thickly, densely; (of dressing) warmly

biezība *nf* (population) density

bieziens *nm* thicket

biezin *adv emph* of **biezs**; **b. biezs** very thick

biezināt *vt* thicken

biezlapes *nf pl* crassulae

biezlapji *nm pl* crassulae

biezlapu *indecl adj* fleshy-leaved

biezlapu virza *nf* fleshy stitchwort

biezne *nf* (typ.) point size

biezoknis *nm* thicket

biezpiena rausis *nm* cottage cheese cake

biezpiena siers *nm* curd cheese

biezpienmaize *nf* 1. open sandwich with cottage cheese topping; 2. sweet flatbread with cottage cheese topping

biezpiens *nm* curds

biezputra *nf* porridge, gruel; **(zirņu) b.** (pease) pudding

biezs *adj* thick, dense; (of words) coarse; **kā** (or **ka**) **b.** wall-to-wall; thick with . . .

biezsula *nf* concentrated juice

biezt *vi* thicken

biezuklājs *nm* thicket

biezummērs *nm* thickness gage

biezum/s *nm* 1. thickness, density; 2. thicket 3. ~i sediment; (of coffee) grounds; (of soups, stews) solids

bieži *adv* often, frequently; **b. vien** usually

biežņa *nf* thicket

biežs *adj* frequent

biežums *nm* frequency

bifelis *nm* buffalo

bifeļu zāle *nf* buffalo grass

bifenīls *nm* biphenyl

bifokāls *adj* bifocal

bifora *nf* twin kernel, philippine

bīfstēks *nm* beefsteak

bifšteks *nm* = **bīfstēks**

bifurkācija *nf* bifurcation

big[a]mija [ā] *nf* bigamy

bigamisks *adj* bigamous

bigbends *nm* big band

bigbīts *nm* (mus.) big beat

bīgls *nm* beagle

bignonija *nf* Bignonia

bigoterija *nf* hipocrisy, sanctimoniousness

bigulis *nm* (fire) poker

biguzis *nm* white gravy with bits of bacon and onion;dish of bread crumbs, hot water, milk, potatoes, and onions

bīģelēt *vt* (sl.) iron

biheviorisms *nm* behaviorism

bihromāts *nm* = **bichromāts**

bij *v*, contraction of **bija** was; were

bija *v, past* of **būt** was; were ◊ **b. man to zināt** had I but known it; **nekā nebija!** (col.) I won't do it; **te (tev) nu b.** (col.) well, almost; **b. un izbija** (col.) past and gone

bija *nf* awe, reverence

bijājams *adj, part* of **bijāt** awe-inspiring

bijāšana *nf* (col.) fear and respect

bijāt *vt* fear, hold in awe

bijāties *vr* fear

bijība *nf* awe, reverence

bijīgi *adv* reverently, respectfully

bijīgs *adj* reverential, respectful

bijīgums *nm* awe, reverence

bijis *part* of **būt** been ◊ **b. nebijis** (col.) it makes no difference, I don't care; **kur b., kur nebijis** (col.) suddenly; **kas b., izbijis** let bygones be bygones

bijums *nm* **1.** the past; **2.** trace, sign; **3.** secret

bijušais *adj* former, past; *nom adj* the past

bikarbonāts *nm* bicarbonate

Bikforda deglis *nm* Bickford fuse

bikini *indecl nm* bikini

bikli *adv* shyly, timidly

biklība *nf* shyness, timidity

bikls *adj* shy, timid

biklums *nm* shyness, timidity

bikonisks *adj* biconical

bikonkāvs *adj* biconcave

bikonvekss *adj* biconvex

biksainis *nm* a person wearing trousers; an animal with feathered or furry legs

biksains *adj* trousered; (of animals) with feathered or furry legs

bikses *nf pl* trousers, pants, slacks; **īsas b.** shorts ◊ **b. trīc** (col.) shaking in one's boots

biksīgs *adj* (reg.) quarrelsome

biksīns *nm* bixin

biksītes *nf pl* **1.** *dim* of **bikses**, pants, shorts; **2.** panties

biksteklis or **bikstīklis** *nm* (fire) poker

bikstis *nm* nudger

bikstīt *vt* poke; nudge; (col., fig.) goad

bikstīties *vr* poke each other

bikšainais apogs *nm* Tengmalm's owl

bikšainais klijāns *nm* rough-legged buzzard

bikšains *adj* **1.** trousered; **2.** furry-legged

bikšturi *nm pl* suspenders

biktēt *vt* hear a confession; (fig.) pry

biktētājs *nm* (father) confessor

biktnieks *nm* confessant

bikts *nf* (rel.) confession

biktskrēsls *nm* confessional

biktstēvs *nm* father confessor

bikvadrāts *nm* biquadratic

bikvadrātvienādojums *nm* biquadratic equation

biķeris *nm* (obs.) goblet, chalice; cup; **rūgtais b.** (fig.) the bitter cup

biķerīši *nm pl* columbine

biķerītis *nm* **1.** *dim* of **biķeris**; **2.** (obs. bot.) calix

bilabiāls *adj* bilabial

bilance *nf* (bus.) balance; **aizplīvurota b.** concealed balance sheet

bilances pārskats *nm* balance sheet;

bilancspējīgs *adj* (of an accountant) certified, public

bilaterāli *adv* bilaterally

bilaterāls *adj* bilateral

bilbergija *nf* billbergia

bilde *nf* (col.) picture; **dzīvā b.** tableau; **kā b.** picture-pretty

bildēt *vt* say

bildinājums *nm* marriage proposal

bildināt *vt* 1. propose marriage; 2. address, greet

bildīte *nf dim* of **bilde**, little picture; **novelkamā b.** transfer picture

bīles *nf pl* (obs.) fear

bilharcija *nf* schistosome

bilharcioze *nf* schistosomiasis

bīlīgs *adj* (col.) shy

bilimbi *indecl nm* bilimbi

bilināt *vi* (of wind) blow, whistle

bilineārs *adj* bilinear

bilingvāls *adj* bilingual

bilingvisms *nm* bilinguism

bilingvs *adj* bilingual

bilirubīns *nm* bilirubin

biliverdīns *nm* biliverdin

biljarda salons *nm* pool room, billiard room

biljards *nm* billiards, pool

biljons *nm* billion

bilst *vt* 1. say; **b. starpā** interject; **nebilst ne vār-da** without breathing a word; 2. propose marriage

bilēa *nf* (naut.) bilge

bilžains *adj* covered with pictures, adorned with pictures

bilžu špigats *nm* (naut.) limber hole

bīļa *nf, nm* (com.) crybaby

biļešu kase *nf* box office; ticket counter

biļešu kasier/is *nm,* ~**e** *nf* cashier; ticket agent

biļete *nf* 1. ticket; **b. turp un atpakaļ**; return ticket; 2. (written) examination question

biļetens *nm* 1. bulletin; 2. ballot

biļetieris *nm* ticket clerk

bil|i|na |ī| *nf* bylina

biļļas *nf pl* (com.) wailing

biļļāt *vi* (com.) wail

bimba *nf, nm* (com.) crybaby; *nf pl* ~**s** (com.) tears, crying

bimbalas *nf pl* (col., of bells) peal

bimbalis *nm* (reg.) potato

bimbals *nm* 1. (com.) crybaby; 2. (reg.) horsefly

bimbaļa *nf, nm* (com.) crybaby

bimbam *interj* ding dong

bimbāt I *vi* (com.) weep, whimper, snivel

bimbāt II *vt, vi* strike

bimbazis *nm* (reg.) potato

bimbināt *vi* (col.) ring a bell; (com.) cry

bimbis *nm* 1. (com.) crybaby; 2. cry, crying

bimbot *vi* = **bimbāt** I

bimbulis *nm* (col.) bell

bimet|āl|isks |all| *adj* bimetallic

bimet|āl|isms |all| *nm* bimetallism

bimet|āl|ists |all| *nm* bimetallist

bimet|āl|s |all| *nm* bimetal

bims *nm* (naut.) beam

bimsakmens *nm* pumice

bimšteins *nm* (com.) pumice

bimzole *nf* (col.) inner sole

binārkods *nm* binary code

binārs *adj* binary

binaurāli *adv* binaurally

binaurāls *adj* binaural

binde *nf* tie, ribbon, band; bandage

bindēt *vt* (of wounds) dress

binga *nf, nm* (com.) crybaby

bingas *nf pl* (com.) tears, crying

bingāt *vi* whine, blub

binoklis *nm* binoculars, field glasses; opera glasses

binokulāri *adv* binocularly

binokulārs *adj* binocular

binoma izvirzījums *nm* binomial expansion

binomiāls *adj* binomial

binoms *nm* binomial

binturongs *nm* binturong

binzole *nf* (com.) insole

biobibliogr|a|fija |ā| *nf* biobibliography

biocenoze *nf* biocenosis

bioekoloģija *nf* bioecology

bioelektrisks *adj* bioelectric

bioenerģētika *nf* bioenergetics

biofāgs *nm* biophagous organism

biofites *nf pl* Biophytum

biofizika *nf* biophysics
biofizikāls *adj* biophysical
biofiziķ/is *nm*, ~e *nf* biophysicist
biogāze *nf* biogas
biog[e]ns [ē] *adj* biogenic
biogr[a]fija [ā] *nf* biography
biogr[a]fiski [ā] *adv* biographically
biogr[a]fisk/s [ā] *adj* biographical
biogr[a]f/s [ā] *nm*, ~e *nf* biographer
bioģenētiski *adv* biogenetically
bioģenētisks *adj* biogenetic
bioģen[e]ze [ē] *nf* biogenesis
bioģeocenoze *nf* biogeocenosis
bioģeogr[a]fija [ā] *nf* biogeography
bioherma *nf* bioherm
biokataliz[a]tors [ā] *nm* biocatalyst
bioklimatoloģija *nf* bioclimatology
bioķīmija *nf* biochemistry
bioķīmiķ/is *nm*, ~e *nf* biochemist
bioķīmisks *adj* biochemical
biolits *nm* biolith
biolo/gs *nm*, ~ģe *nf* biologist
bioloģija *nf* biology
bioloģiski *adv* biologically
bioloģisk/s *adj* biological
bioma *nf* biome
biomasa *nf* biomass
biome[cha]nika [hā] *nf* biomechanics
biometeoroloģija *nf* biometeorology
biometrija *nf* biometrics
biomolekula *nf* biomolecule
bionika *nf* bionics
bioniķ/is *nm*, ~e *nf* bionics specialist
biopolimers *nm* biopolymer
biopsija *nf* biopsy
bioritms *nm* biorhythm
biosf[ai]ra [ē] *nf* biosphere
biosintēze *nf* biosynthesis
biostratigr[a]fisks [ā] *adj* biostratigraphic
biostrāva *nf* bioelectricity
biostroma *nf* biostrome
biota *nf* 1. biota; 2. (bot.) Biota

biote[ch]noloģija [h] *nf* biotechnology
biotīns *nm* biotin
biotīts *nm* biotite
biotops *nm* biotope
bipatrīds *nm* person of dual nationality
biplāns *nm* biplane
bipolārs *adj* bipolar
birbīne *nf* oaten reed
birda *nf* drizzle
birde *nf* (weav.) 1. loom; 2. reed
birdelēt *vi* drizzle; flurry
birdināt *vt* scatter; (of tears) shed; *vi* drizzle;
    flurry
birdināties *vr* scatter; (of tears) shed
bire *nf* a pellet of sheep droppings
birete *nf* burette
birga *nf* 1. coal gas fumes, smoke; 2. inebriation;
    3. furrow; 4. haze
birgains *adj* (of air) close, stuffy; filled with
    coal gas
birgot *vi* emit fumes, emit coal gas
birģelis *nm* = birģeris
birģeris *nm* (hist.) homeowner (and citizen of
    a city), burgher
birģermeistars *nm* (hist.) burgomaster
birīgs *adj* productive
birināt *vt* pour; scatter
birka *nf* 1. tag; 2. (hist.) tally
birkavnie/ks *nm*, ~ce *nf* sth. weighing one
    berkovets
birkavs *nm* berkovets (unit of weight)
birkstele *nf* spark
birkstis *nf pl* embers
birkstīt *vt* (of embers, ashes) knock off
birkšķis *nm* (col.) a little bit
birmāniet/is *nm*, ~e *nf* Burmese
biroj/s *nm* bureau; office; ~a darbs white-collar
    job; ~a darbi office work; ~a piederumi
    office supplies
birokr[a]tija [ā] *nf* bureaucracy
birokr[a]tiski [ā] *adv* bureaucratically
birokr[a]tisks [ā] *adj* bureaucratic

birokr[a]tiskums [ā] *nm* bureaucratic nature, bu-reaucratic behavior

birokr[a]tisms [ā] *nm* bureaucracy

birokr[a]t/s [ā] *nm*, ~e *nf* bureaucrat

birste *nf* (com.) brush

birstēt *vt* (com.) brush

birt *vi* pour; (of leaves) fall; (of plaster) flake; (of tears) run; **viņam birst asaras** he is shedding tears; **krusa birst** it is hailing

birteniski *adv* **b. pilns** (of grain) heaping full

birtin *adv emph* of **birt; b. bira** it kept pouring

biru birām or **biru birumiem**) *adv* in quantities, in large numbers; in flocks

birums *nm* 1. (of crops) yield; **liels b.** great many, plenty of; 2. scattering, spread; 3. heap

birzains *adj* sown unevenly, with gaps between adjacent **birzes**

bir/ze *nf* 1. sowing strip, strip of field marked for sowing in one pass; 2. furrow; 3. (in Latgale) strip field; ~**ēu lauki** strip fields; 4. grove

birzens *adj* crumbly

birzēt *vt* mark **birzes** before sowing

birzīgs *adj* crumbly

birzīt *vt* = **birzēt**

birzīte *nf dim* of **birzs**, small grove

birzoklējs *adj* (of a needle tree that has grown in a birch grove and therefore has soft wood) rapid-growth

birzs *nf* birch forest; small stand of hardwood

birzt *vi* crumble

birztala *nf* birch grove

birztaliena *nf* (reg.) birch grove

birztaliņa *nf dim* of **birztala**, birch grove

birztalu drojenes *nf pl* wood whitlow grass

birztalu nārbulis *nm* blue cowwheat

birztalu skarene *nf* wood meadowgrass

birztalu stērste *nf* yellow-breasted bunting

birztalu veronika *nf* germander speedwell

birztalu virza *nf* wood stitchwort

birztalu zemzālīte *nf* forest wood rush

birztiņa *nf dim* of **birzs**, grove

birzumi *nm pl* crumbled hay; fine debris, crumblings

birzums I *nm* porridge of bolted flour, with milk

birzums II *nm* furrow

birža *nf* stock exchange; **melnā b.** illegal currency exchange

biržains *adj* rich in groves

biržas aģents *nm* stockbroker

biržas aģentūra *nm* brokerage firm

biržas kurss *nm* stock prices

biržot *vt* = **birzēt**

bis *interj* encore

bise *nf* shotgun

biseksuālis *nm* bisexual

biseksuālisms *nm* bisexuality

biseksualitāte *nf* bisexuality

biseksuāls *adj* bisexual

bisektrise *nf* (math.) bisector

bisenieks *nm* = **bisinieks**

bisinieks *nm* (hist.) free peasant (allowed to have a shotgun)

bisiņš *nm* false morel

bisīte *nf* 1. *dim* of **bise**, little shotgun; 2. false morel

bīskapija *nf* bishopric

bīskaps *nm* bishop

biskutelas *nf pl* Biscutella

biskvīt/s *nm* 1. cookie; ~**a mīkla** cake dough; 2. bisque

bismutāts *nm* bismuthate

bismutīns *nm* bismuthinite

bismutīts *nm* bismuthite

bismuts *nm* bismuth

bismutzelts *nm* maldonite

bīstaklis *nm* poker

bīstami *adv* dangerously, dangerous, risky

bīstamība *nf* dangerousness, perilousness; riskiness

bīstams *adj* dangerous, perilous; risky

biste *nf* (sculpture) bust

bīsteklis *nm* poker
bīstīties *vr* (obs.) fear
bistro *indecl nm* bistro
bistrs *nm* bister
bisulfāts *nm* bisulfate
bisulfīts *nm* bisulfite
biszāles *nf pl* (obs.) gunpowder
bišaugi *nm pl* nectar-producing plants
bišēdis *nm* bee-eater
biškoks *nm* (obs.) bee gum
biškopība *nf* beekeeping
biškop/is *nm*, **~e** *nf* beekeeper
biškrēsliņi *nm pl* tansy
bīšķarags *nm* poker
bišķērājs *nm* bee-eater
bišķi *adv* (sl.) a little
bīšķis *nm* poker
bišķīt *adv* (sl.) a little
bišsaimniecība *nf* beekeeping
bišu āboliņš *nm* white sweet clover
bišu dārzs *nm* apiary
bišu dzenis *nm* bee-eater
bišu kāļi *nm pl* (reg.) avens
bišu kode *nf* bee moth
bišukoks *nm* = **biškoks**
bišu maize nf bee bread
bišu māte *nf* queen bee
bišu mētra *nf* lemon balm
bišu pieniņš *nm* royal jelly
bišu uts *nf* bee louse
bišu vasks *nm* beeswax
bišu zāle *nf* lemon balm
bišveidīgs *adj* bee-like, apial
bišveidīgie plēvspārņi *nm pl* Apoidea
bite *nf* bee
bīte *nf* (obs.) fear
bitene *nf* avens
bitenie/ks *nm*, **~ce** *nf* beekeeper
bīties *vr* **1.** fear; **2.** avoid; **3.** beware of; **b. lāci au-zās** be jealous
bītīgs *adj* (obs.) fearful
bitinie/ks *nm*, **~ce** *nf* beekeeper

bitisodze *nf* puff adder
bitīte *nf dim* of **bite**, little bee
bītnieks *nm* (hist.) clandestine, non-guild craftsman
bītniks *nm* beatnik
bitovnīts *nm* bytownite
bits *nm* (compu.) bit; **~u ātrums** bit rate; **~u blīvums** bit density
bīts *nm* (mus.) beat
bitumena betons *nm* bituminous concrete
bitumens *nm* bitumen
biurēts *nm* biuret
bivuaks *nm* bivouac
biz *interj* buzz
bizammalvas *nf pl* Abelmoschus
bizams *nm* musk
bizamžurka *nf* muskrat
bizantiet/is *nm*, **~e** *nf* Byzantine
bizantisks *adj* Byzantine
bizarrs *adj* bizarre
bize *nf* braid, tress, pigtail
bizenēt *vi* (col.) **1.** run around, scurry; **2.** imitate the buzzing of horseflies
bizenīgs *adj* (col.) restless
bizināt *vt* make cattle bolt; *vi* imitate the buzzing of horseflies (to make cattle bolt)
bizmanis *nm* bewigged man, man wearing a pigtail wig; (hist.) reactionary (a term of derision for conservative Baltic Germans who wore wigs when acting as city councilors)
bizmārīte *nf* (col.) ladybug
biznesmens *nm* businessman
bizness *nm* business
bizonis *nm* (col.) runabout, gadabout
bizoņa *nf, nm* (col.) runabout, gadabout
bizons *nm* bison
bizot *vi* (of cattle plagued by flying insects) bolt (with tails upright); (col.) run around
bizulis *nm* = **bizonis**
bižains *adj* pigtailed, braided
bižut[e]rija [ē] *nf* bijouterie; costume jewelry
bjefs *nm* (of a river) reach

blāc *interj* thud, kerplunk

blace *nf* = blaka

bladāc *interj* kerplunk

bladāks (or bladākš) *interj* kerplunk

blafs *nm* bluff

blaikš *interj* kerplunk

blaiskums *nm* (obs.) blotch, spot

blaka *nf* defect in a weave (in the form of two adjacent ends in a tabby)

blakām *adv* = blakus

blākns *adj* flat

blāknums *nm* flat terrain

blakš *interj* plunk, clunk

blākš *interj* bang, thud

blakšains *adj* infested with bedbugs (or stink-bugs)

blākšēt *vi* = blākšķēt

blakšķēt *vi* clunk, thump

blākšķēt *vi* bang, thud

blakšķināt *vt* clunk, thump

blākšķināt *vt* bang

blakšķināties *vr* continue making clunking or thumping sounds

blākšķināties *vr* continue banging

blakšķis *nm* thump, thud

blākšķis *nm* bang

blaktene *nf* restharrow

blakt/s *nf* bedbug; stinkbug; ~is Heteroptera

blaku *adv, adj* = blakus

blakus *adv* 1. beside, side by side, next to; cieši b. close by; b. esošs adjacent, neighboring; 2. also, simultaneously

blakus *adj* 1. adjacent, neighboring, next-door; 2. secondary, subsidiary, subordinate, side; additional, extra; collateral

blakusaina *nf* (theat.) byplay

blakusceļš *nm* side road; bypass; (RR) siding

blakusdarbība *nf* (lit., theat.) subplot

blakusdarbs *nm* second job, sideline

blakusdurvis *nf pl* side door

blakusgultne *nf* by-channel

blakusiedzīvotājs *nm* neighbor, fellow tenant

blakusieeja *nf* side entrance

blakusiela *nf* side street

blakusiemītnieks *nm* neighbor, fellow tenant

blakusieņēmums *nm* supplementary income

blakusiezis *nm* country rock

blakusintriga *nf* (theat.) secondary plot

blakusistaba *nf* adjacent room, side room, by-room

blakusizdevumi *nm pl* extra expenses

blakusjautājums *nm* side issue

blakusleņķis *nm* coterminous angle

blakuslīgums *nm* subsidiary agreement

blakuslieta *nf* side issue; minor matter; (jur.) collateral issue

blakuslīnija *nf* collateral line; (RR) siding, parallel track

blakusnodarbošanās *nf* sideline, second job

blakusnostādīšana *nf* comparison

blakusnozare *nf* branch business, sideline; branch (of a field of knowledge)

blakusnozīme *nf* secondary meaning

blakusparādība *nf* side phenomenon

blakuspeļņa *nf* additional earnings; incidental earnings

blakusprasījums *nm* additional claim

blakusprodukts *nm* by-product

blakusrezultāts *nm* side effect

blakussieva *nf* mistress

blakussižets *nm* (lit.) subplot

blakusskaņa *nf* (ling.) adjacent sound

blakusslēgums *nm* (el.) shunt

blakussliedes *nf pl* (RR) siding; (RR) parallel track

blakusstāvētājs *nm* bystander

blakustelpa *nf* adjacent room

blakustiesības *nf pl* subsidiary rights

blakustrepes *nf pl* back stairs

blakusvāģis *nm* sidecar

blāķains *adj* in heaps, in piles

blaķene *nf* (com.) two-barrel shotgun

blāķ/is *nm* 1. heap, pile; ~iem heaped up, in piles; 2. quantity; 3. (col.) obese person, blimp, tub

blamāža *nf* (col.) disgrace, embarrasement; blunder

blamēt *vt* disgrace

blamēties *vr* disgrace oneself

blandīties *vr* (col.) gad about, hang out

blandonība *nf* (col.) gadding about

blandonis *nm* gadabout

blandoņa *nf, nm* (col.) gadabout

blanka I *nf* plank

blanka II *nf* form

blankets *nm* small form

blankisms *nm* Blanquism

blankist/s *nm,* ~e *nf* Blanquist

blankkarte *nf* blank card

blankoakcepts *nm* (bus.) uncovered acceptance

blankokredīts *nm* unsecured credit

blankotrata *nf* (bus.) blank draft

blankovekselis *nm* (bus.) blank check

blankožiro *indecl nm* (bus.) blank endorsement

blanks *nm* spot, blaze

blankstīties *vr* (col.) gad about, hang out

blanķēšana *nf* blackout

blanķēt *vt* black out

blanšēt *vt* (cul.) scald

blarkstoņa *nf* rattle

blarkšēt *vi* rattle

blarkšis *nm* rattle, rattling noise

blarkšķēt *vi* rattle

blarkšķināt *vt* rattle

blarkšķināties *vr* rattle

blarkšķis *nm* rattle, rattling noise

blasfēmija *nf* blasphemy

blastomērs *nm* blastomere

blasts *nm* (mining) blast

blastula *nf* blastula

blašķe *nf* flask, canteen; bottle

blaugznains *adj* dandruffy

blaugznas *nf pl* dandruff

blaugznāt *vi* peel

blaugznāties *vr* peel

blaugznēji *nm pl* cudweed

blaugznot *vt* peel

blaugznoties *vr* peel

blauks *interj* plunk, thwack, bang

blaukš *interj* plunk, thwack, bang

blaukšēt *vi* bang

blaukšķēt *vi* bang

blaukšķināt *vt, vi* bang

blaukšķināties *vr* bang

blaukšķis *nm* bang

blaukt *interj* bang

blauzgas *nf pl* (col.) dandruff

blauznēji *nm pl* = blaugznēji

blaužģēt *vi* clatter; chatter

blāva *nf* 1. wanness, dimness, dullness; 2. spot, blotch; bruise; 3. (reg.) puddle

blāvains *adj* wan, pallid, pale

blāvāt *vi* flash, (of flames) dance

blāvāties *vr* flash, (of flames) dance

blāvbaltums *nm* pale, milky whiteness

blāvēt *vi* = blāvot

blāvi *adv* wanly, dimly, dully

blāvināt *vt* dim

blāvot *vi* shine dimly, shine with a pale light; shimmer; *vt* mottle, spot, blotch

blāvoties *vr* shine dimly

blāvs *adj* wan, dim, dull, lusterless, (of gold) dead

blāvstikls *nm* frosted glass

blāvums *nm* wanness, dimness, dullness

blazēts *adj* blasé

blāzma *nf* glow

blāzmaini *adv* fierily, flamingly, glowingly

blāzmains *adj* (of light) fiery, flaming, glowing

blāzmojums *nm* glow

blāzmot *vi* glow

blāzmoties *vr* glow

blāznīties *vr* (reg.) lie (tell lies))

blāznums *nm* glow

blēdība *nf* deceit; swindle, fraud

blēdīgi *adv* deceitfully; mischievously

blēdīgs *adj* deceitful, cheating; rascally; (of a smile) mischievous

blēdīgums *nm* deceitfulness

blēd/is *nm*, ~e *nf* **1.** cheat, swindler, (in card games) cardsharper; rogue, knave; **2.** mischiefmaker

blēdīt *vi* cheat, deceive

blēdīties *vr* cheat, deceive

blēdnieks *nm* = **blēdis**

blefarīts *nm* blepharitis

blefot *vi* (col.) bluff

blefs *nm* (col.) bluff

bleizers *nm* blazer

blējiens *nm* bleat

blekte *nf* gob, clump; mat; horse collar padding

blektēt *vi* ball up

bleķis *nm* **1.** (col.) sheet metal; **2.** (col.) nonsense, boloney

bleķot *vi* (sl.) pay, foot the bill

blende *nf* (photog.) diaphragm

blendēt *vi* (photog.) change the diaphragm opening

blenkt *vi* gape

blenoreja *nf* blennorrhea

blenst *vi, vt* talk nonsense

blenzis *nm* person with poor eyesight, myope

blenzt *vi* see poorly, strain at seeing; gape

blenža *nf, nm* = **blenzis**

blenžamie *nom adj pl* (com.) eyes, peepers

blēņas *nf pl* **1.** mischief, pranks; **2.** nonsense

blēņdarīgs *adj* mischievous, naughty

blēņdar/is *nm* mischievous, naughty boy, rascal; ~e *nf* mischievous, naughty girl

blēņīgs *adj* mischievous, naughty

blēņoties *vr* **1.** play pranks, be naughty; **2.** fool around

blēņu darbs *nm* mischief, prank

blese *nf* blaze (on the forehead of a cow or horse)

blesis *nm* horse with a blaze

blēt *vi* bleat

blēžoties *vr* cheat, deceive

blicēt *vi* (col.) fire

blicot *vi* (col.) rush, race

blīdums *nm* (reg.) throng

blieķēt *vt* (obs.) bleach

blieķis *nm* (obs.) bleaching yard

bliest *vi* swell

bliete *nf* **1.** tamper; (gun) rammer; **2.** throttle; **3.** lancet

blietes vārsts *nm* throttle valve

blietēt *vt* **1.** tamp; **2.** throttle

blietēties *vr* lie heavy upon

blieziens *nm* (col.) blow

bliezt *v* **1.** *vt* tamp; strike, thrash, (col.) hit; shoot; **2.** *vi* run

blīgzna *nf* goat willow, sallow; bay willow

blīkš *interj* bang

blīkšēt *vi* bang

blīkšķēt *vi* bang

blīkšķināt *vt* (of wings) beat

blīkšķis *nm* (of wings) beat, flutter; (of firearms) bang

blikta *nf* (naut.) upper deck

blindāža *nf* dugout

blīnēt *vi* **1.** look sullenly; **2.** lie awake

bliņas *nf pl* blini

blisenes *nf pl* (com.) eyes, peepers

blisināt *vt* (of eyes) blink

blisināties *vr* (of eyes) blink

blisnīt *vt* (of eyes) blink

blīst *vi* swell; put on weight

bliukš *interj* bang

bliukšēt *vi* bang

bliukšķēt *vi* bang

bliukšķināt *vi iter* bang

bliukšķis *nm* bang

bliukt *interj* bang

blīva *nf* mass

blīvais sorgo *indecl nm* Sudan grass

blīvbloks *nm* solid block

blīvceru *indecl adj* densely branched

blīve *nf* (tech.) packing; seal; gasket

blīvējums *nm* compaction

blīves atspere *nf* gasket spring

blīvēt *vt* (tech.) pack; caulk; seal; compact

blīvēties *vr* crowd; (rare.) compact

blīvgredzens *nm* (of a piston) packing ring; washer; (artillery) obturator

blīvi *adv* densely; tightly; compactly

blīvripa *nf* compact disk

blīvs *adj* **1.** dense; compact; **2.** tight; close

blīvslēgs *nm* stuffing box

blīvstanga *nf* tamping rod

blīvstienis *nm* tamping rod

blīvuguns *nf* high-density fire

blīvums *nm* density

blīvziedu cietķērsa *nf* wild peppergrass

bliza *nf* (reg.) fragment, bit, splinter

blīznis *nm* windfallen trees

blīzns *adj* tight, compact, thick

blīzt *vi* swell

bližģēt *vi* (reg.) shine

blokāde *nf* blockade; (med.) block

blokdiagramma *nf* block diagram

blokēka *nf* apartment block, large apartment building

blokflauta *nf* blockflöte, recorder

blokhauzis *nm* (mil.) blockhouse

blokkondensātors *nm* block capacitor

blokmāja *nf* apartment block, large apartment building

bloknots *nm* small note pad

blokposms *nm* (RR) block section

blokpostenis *nm* (RR) block station

bloks *nm* **1.** (pol.) bloc; **2.** (piece of material; group; simple machine) block; **3.** note pad; **4.** (sports) a. blocking; b. starting block

bloks[ch]ēma [h] *nf* flow chart

bloksignāls *nm* (RR) block signal

bloķēšana *nf* (RR) blocking

bloķēt *vt* block; (mil.) blockade

blondīne *nf* blonde

blondīns *nm* blond

blonds *adj* blond

blondums *nm* blondness

bloškas *nf pl* tiddledywinks

blots *nm* (of fish) dense school

blozga *nf* (sl.) **1.** girl; **2.** sloven

bložs *adj* (reg.) compact, tight

blūdīnas *nf pl* blue jeans

blūgrāss *nm* (mus.) bluegrass

blugēģēt *vi* splash

blūks or **blūkš** *interj* splash

blūkšēt *vi* splash

blūkšķēt *vi* splash

blūkšķināt *vi* splash

blūkšķināties *vr* splash

blūkšķis *nm* big splash

bluķene *nf* dugout

bluķēt *vt* work a field with a roller; thresh with a roller

bluķa zārks *nm* dugout coffin

bluķis *nm* **1.** block; **kuļamais b.** threshing roller; **2.** (col.) awkward man; **3.** (obs.) stocks

bluķītis *nm dim* of **bluķis**, small block

bluķu kāpnes *nf pl* notched-log ladder

bluķu māja *nf* log house

bluķu vakars *nm* burning of the Yule log

blumenba[ch]ijas [h] *nf pl* Blumenbachia

blūmings *nm* (metall.) blooming mill

blumīzeris *nm* (col.) harmonica

blumss *nm* (metall.) bloom

blurkšēt *vi* rattle

blurkšķēt *vi* rattle

blurstiķis *nm* (sl.) hodgepodge

blus/a *nf* flea ◊ **~u kāvējs** (col.) thumb

blusains *adj* flea-infested

blusenāji *nm pl* crowberry

blusenes *nf pl* **1.** (bot.) sweet gale; **2.** fleabane; **3.** nettle rash; **4.** (reg.) measles

blusināt *vt* pick s.o.'s fleas

blusināties *vr* pick fleas

blusiņa *nf* 1. *dim* of **blusa**, little flea; 2. psylla, jumping plant louse

blusiņas *nf pl* 1. (bot.) lady's thumb; 2. maianthemum; 3. crowberry; 4. meadow fescue; 5. tiddledywinks

blusot *vi* (of water) bloom (with pollen from water plants)

blusoties *vr* 1. piddle, dawdle; 2. (of animals) catch fleas

blusu kārkliņš *nm* sweet gale

blusu mētra *nf* pennyroyal

blūze *nf* blouse

blūzga *nm* (reg.) drunk

bluzons *nm* blouson

blūzs *nm* (mus.) blues (song)

blužģēt *vi* glug

bļaudināt *vt* (col.) make a baby cry

bļaujamais *nm* (col.) voice

bļauka *nf, nm* (col.) a loud child

bļaukāt *vi* (col.) yell, holler

bļauris *nm* 1. (col.) yeller; (carnival) barker; 2. howler monkey

bļaurs *adj* mean

bļausteklis *nm* (col.) yeller

bļaustīklis *nm* = **bļausteklis**

bļaustīties *vr* yell, shout, holler

bļaustonis *nm* (col.) yeller

bļausts *nm* (col.) yeller

bļaut *vi* (col.) 1. yell, shout; 2. (of children) bawl; **b. kā teļš** blubber; 3. (of animals) moo, bleat, or bray loudly

bļāva *nf, nm* (col.) yeller

bļāvējs *nm*, ~a *nf* (col.) yeller

bļāveklis *nm* (col.) yeller

bļāviens *nm* yell

bļāvināt *vt* (col.) make a child cry

bļāvonis *nm* (col.) yeller

bļāvrīklis *nm* (col.) yeller

bļenduks *nm* (sl.) pendant; medal

bļitka *nf* (fish lure) spoon

bļitkot *vi* fish under ice (using a spoon lure)

bļitkotāj/s *nm*, ~a *nf* ice fisherman

bļoda *nf* dish, bowl; basin; **mazgājamā b.** wash-bowl

bļodas kauls *nm* innominate bone

bļodiņa *nf* 1. *dim* of **bļoda**, small dish; 2. (bra, acorn) cup

bļodlaiža *nf, nm* lickspittle, toady

bļodnieks *nm* potter

bļodveida *indecl adj* dish-shaped

bļodveidīgs *adj* dish-shaped

boa *indecl nf* (snake; scarf) boa

bobriks *nm* 1. beaver cloth; 2. crew cut

bobs *nm* bobsled

bobslejist/s *nm*, ~e *nf* bobsledder

bobslejkamanas *nf pl* bobsled

bobslejs *nm* 1. bobsledding; 2. bobsled

bobteils *nm* Old English sheepdog

bocis *nm* = **boķis**

bocmanis *nm* boatswain

bocmaņa svilpe *nf* boatswain's pipe

bode *nf* 1. (naut.) hatch; 2. (com.) store; ~s **kungs** (obs.) merchant; ~s **zellis** (obs.) sales clerk

bodibildings *nm* bodybuilding

bodīte *nf* 1. *dim* of **bode**, small shop; 2. (col.) dirty business, shady deal

bodmereja *nf* bottomry

bodnie/ks *nm*, ~ce *nf* (obs.) merchant

bods *nm* (compu.) baud

bodziņa *nf* seed pod

Boforta skāla *nf* Beaufort scale

boga *nf* 1. coppice; 2. flock; bevy; herd; group

bogārzemes *nf pl* dry-farming land

bogens *nm* (sl.) questionnaire

bogheds *nm* boghead coal

bogs *nm* = **boga**

bohēma *nf* Bohemia

bohēmiet/is *nm*, ~e *nf* Bohemian

bohēmisks *adj* Bohemian

boikotēt *vt* boycott

boikots *nm* boycott

boilers *nm* boiler

boja *nf* buoy

bojā *adv* **iet b. 1.** perish; **2.** spoil

bojāeja *nf* destruction; (of ships) shipwreck

bojājums *nm* damage; flaw, defect; injury; **nejaušs b.** incidental damage; **netiešs b.** collateral damage

bojāt *vt* **1.** damage; wreck; **2.** spoil

bojāties *vr* **1.** spoil; **2.** get damaged; **3.** worsen

bojāts *adj, part* of **bojāt 1.** damaged; **2.** spoiled; **3.** out of order

bojeviks *nm* (show business) hit

bojīgs *adj* perishable

bojs *nm* bellboy; (male servant) boy

bokāls *nm* = **pokāls**

bokāt *vt* thresh

bokauts *nm* lignum vitae, guaiacum

bokāēa *nf* hedged farmland

bokser(i)s *nm* (pugilist; breed of dogs) boxer

boksēt *vi* box

boksēties *vr* box

boksīts *nm* boxite

bokss I *nm* boxing

bokss II *nm* **1.** press box; **2.** strongbox; isolation chamber; locker

boksterēt *vi* (obs.) learn to read, spell

bokēt *vi* = **bokīt**

bokis *nm* **1.** (col.) obese person; **2.** salt mortar

bokīt *vi* (com.) look, peer

bole *nf* (beverage) punch

bolero *indecl nm* bolero

bolīds *nm* bolide

bolīgs *adj* goggle-eyed

bolīt *vt* (of eyes) roll; goggle

bolīties *vr* goggle

bolivārs *nm* bolivar

boliviano *indecl nm* boliviano

bolīviet/is *nm*, **~e** *nf* Bolivian

bolometrs *nm* bolometer

boļševiks *nm* Bolshevik

boļševisms *nm* Bolshevism

boļševistiski *adv* in the Bolshevik manner

boļševistisks *adj* Bolshevik

boļševizācija *nf* bolshevization

boļševizēt *vt* bolshevize

boļševizēties *vr* become bolshevized

bombakss *nm* bombax

bombardēt *vt* shell, bombard; bomb

bombardieris *nm* bombardier

bombards *nm* bombard

bombasts *nm* bombast

bombonga *nf* (col.) piece of candy

bomeļļa *nf* wood oil

Bomē skāla *nf* Beaumé scale

bomis *nm* heavy wood pole; club; (col.) gate bar; (weav.) beam

bomītis *nm* **1.** *dim* of **bomis**, small pole, beam; **2.** a dish of ground hemp seeds

bomkante *nf* (of lumber) wane

bomonds *nm* beau monde

boms *nm* (naut.) boom; **izgrūžamais b.** sheer pole

bomzis *nm* transient

bomēs *nm* transient

bona *nf* = **bons**

bonapartisms *nm* Bonapartism

bonapartists *nm* Bonapartist

bonbonga *nf* = **bombonga**

bonēt *vt* (of floors) wax and polish

bonētāj/s *nm*, **~a** *nf* waxer, polisher

bongo I *indecl nm* (zool.) bongo

bongo II *indecl nm* bongo (drum)

bonierēt *vt* = **bonēt**

bonierētājs *nm*, **~a** *nf* = **bonētājs**

bonistika *nf* scripophily

bonitāte *nf* (of forest stands) grade

bonitēt *vt* (of forest stands, livestock) grade

bonne *nf* nanny

bonomija *nf* bonhomie

bons *nm* **1.** (bus.) bond; **2.** emergency paper money

bonuss *nm* bonus

bonviv[a]ns [ā] *nm* bon vivant

bonza *nf, nm* (sl.) fat dog; fat child

bora *nf* (wind) bora

boracīts *nm* boracite

boraks *nm* borax

borāns *nm* borane

borāts *nm* borate

borda *nf* edge

bordāža *nf* boarding (of a ship)

borde *nf* (col.) edging

bordelis *nm* brothel

bordīra *nf* (typ.) border

bordo *indecl nm* Bordeaux (wine)

bordo *indecl adj* dark red

bordosarkans *adj* dark red

bordo šķidrums *nm* Bordeaux mixture

boreāls *adj* boreal

boreās *nm* borage

borēt *v* (sl.) **1.** *vi* tell a story; **2.** *vt* drill

borgiss *nm* (typ.) bourgeois, 9-point type

borids *nm* boride

boris *nm* (barb.) brace; drill

bornāns *nm* bornane

borneols *nm* borneol

bornēts *adj* mentally limited

bornīts *nm* bornite

bors *nm* boron

borskābe *nf* boric acid

boršās *nm* borscht

borta logs *nm* porthole

bortapar[a]tūra [ā] *nf* onboard apparatus

bortiekārta *nf* onboard computer

bortinženier/is *nm*, ~e *nf* flight engineer

bortme[cha]niķ/is [hā] *nm*, ~e *nf* flight mechanic

bortpavadone *nf* flight attendant

bortradist/s *nm*, ~e *nf* radio operator (as a crew member)

bort/s I *nm* (naut.) board; **kreisais b.** port; **labais b.** starboard; **pār ~u** overboard; **uz ~a** on board

borts II *nm* (diamonds) bort

bortsistēma *nf* onboard system

borvazelīns *nm* petroleum jelly with boric acid

borvolfrāmskābe *nf* borotungstic acid

bosaks *nm* (reg.) fire hook

bosanova *nf* bossa nova

boskets *nm* bosket

bosniet/is *nm*, ~e *nf* Bosnian

bosons *nm* (phys.) boson

boss *nm* boss

bostons *nm* (card game; dance) Boston

bosvelijas *nf pl* Boswellia

bot[a]nika [ā] *nf* botany

bot[a]niķis [ā] *nm*, ~e *nf* botanist

botāniski *adv* botanically

bot[a]nisks [ā] *adj* botanical

botanizēt *vi* botanize

botes *nf pl* high rubber overshoes (for women and children)

botforti *nm pl* jackboots

Botkina slimība *nf* infectious hepatitis

botri[ch]ijas [h] *nf pl* grape ferns

bots I *nf* (naut.) boat; **b. āķis** boat hook

bots II *nm* (obs.) **1.** a measure of wine; **2.** (of raw skins) count of 10

botulīns *nm* botulin

botulisms *nm* botulism

boulings *nm* bowling

boze *nf* club

bozeklis *nm* (col.) sourpuss

bozēt *vt* strike, hit

bozīgi *adv* crankily

bozīgs *adj* cranky

bozis *nm* (col.) crab

boznieks *nm* night watchman with a boze

bozt *vt* (of hackles) raise; **b. spalvu** raise the hackles

bozties *vr* raise the hackles, bristle up; (col.) grouse, be cranky

bra *indecl nf* sconce

brabantietis *nm* (horse) Belgian

bra[ch]ikefalija [h] *nf* brachycephaly

bra[ch]ikefals [h] *adj* brachycephalic

bra[ch]ikomes [h] *nf pl* Brachicome

bra[ch]iloģija [h] *nf* brachylogy

bra[ch]iloģisms [h] *nm* brachylogy

bra[ch]iopodi [h] *nm pl* Brachiopoda

bra[ch]iozaurs [h] *nm* brachiosaur

bra[ch]isto[ch]rona [h][h] *nf* brachistochrone

bra[ch]mana [h] *nf* Brahmana

bra[ch]manis [h] *nm* Brahman

bra[ch]manisms [h] *nm* Brahmanism

braciņš *nm* dressing down; thrashing

braāa *nf* viola

braāist/s *nm*, ~e *nf* viola player

braāka *nm* (sl.) brother

bradāc *interj* kerplunk

bradāt *vi* wade

bradenis *nm* beach seine

bradikardija *nf* bradycardia

bradu or bradus *adv* by wading

bradulītis *nm* phalarope

brādzinieks *nm* distiller

brāga *nf* (col.) draff

braģis *nm* = braķis

brah- See brach-

brail/s *nm* Braille; ~a iespiedumā Brailled

brāk *interj* crack

brakas *nf pl* menstrual flow

brakete *nf* (naut.) bracket

brakonjers *nm* poacher

brak/s I *nm* sth. useless, sth. no good; ~a useless, no good

braks II *nm* doubletree

braks *adj* useless, no good

brakstēt *vi* = brakšķēt

br[a]kš [ā] *interj* crack

brakšēt *vi* crack, creak

brākšēt *vi* crack loudly

brakšis *nm* cracking

brākšis *nm* crash

brakšķēt *vi* crack, creak

brākšķēt *vi* crack loudly

brakšķināt *vt* make crack, make creak

brakšķināties *vr* make a racket

brakšķis *nm* cracking

brākšķis *nm* crash

brakšķoņa *nf* (loud) cracking

brakteāts *nm* bracteate

braku *interj* crack

brāķdar/is *nm*, ~e *nf* a worker who fabricates rejects

brāķeris *nm* (obs.) sorter; quality inspector

brāķēt *vt* 1. (obs.) sort, inspect for quality; 2. (col.) find fault with, turn down

brāķētāj/s *nm*, ~a *nf* 1. (obs.) quality inspector; 2. (col.) faultfinder

braķis *nm* 1. (movable) roof over a haystack; 2. drying rack for hay or grain; 3. grate; 4. up-right support of a swing

brāķ/is *nm* 1. reject, rejects; ~a patrona dud round; 2. broken ice

brālaitene *nf* sister-in-law

brālene *nf* niece

brālenis *nm* nephew

brālēns *nm* cousin

brālība *nf* brotherhood; fraternity

brālīgi *adv* in a brotherly fashion; fairly

brālīgs *adj* 1. brotherly; fraternal; 2. fair

brālīgums *nm* brotherliness

brālis *nm* brother; īstais b. whole brother

brālītis *nm dim* of brālis, little brother; brālīt *interj* (col.) man, brother

brālnieks *nm* (reg.) brother

brāļadēls *nm* nephew

brāļameita *nf* niece

brāļasieva *nf* sister-in-law

brāļa slepkavība *nf* fratricide

brāļošanās *nfr* fraternization

brāļoties *vr* fraternize; b. pie pudeles hobnob over a bottle

brāļu kap/s *nm* common war grave; b. ~i war graves (for soldiers of one warring side)

brāļu karš *nm* civil war;

brāļuks *nm* (col.) (younger) brother

brambura *nf* (naut.) topgallant sail

bra[m]anība [mm] *nf* swagger, bluster, bravado

bra[m]anīgi [mm] *adv* in a swaggering, blustering fashion

bra|m|anīgs |mm| *adj* swaggering, blustering

bra|m|anīgums |mm| *nm* swagger, bluster

bra|m|anis |mm| *nm* swaggerer, blusterer, braggart

braminisms *nm* = **brachmanisms**

bramins *nm* = **brachmanis**

brammēt *vt* (reg.) scold, take to task

bramrāja *nf* (naut.) topgallant yard

bramštanga *nf* (naut.) topgallant mast

bran|ch|iobdelas |h| *nf pl* branchiobdelids

brandaviņš *nm* (barb.) liquor

brandavs *nm* (barb.) liquor

brandmajors *nm* (obs.) fire chief

brandmeistars *nm* (obs.) fire brigade leader

brandvīna puķe *nf* Saint-John's-wort

brandvīns *nm* (barb.) liquor

branga *nf* (naut.) frame rib; timber; **galvenā b.** midship section, midship frame

brangi *adv* very well

brangs *adj* 1. (of animals) sturdy, well fed; (col., of people) stout, sturdy; 2. (col.) big, very good, great

brangulis *nm* (col.) plump person

brangums *nm* sturdiness; stoutness, plumpness

brankūzis *nm* (reg.) distillery

brannerīts *nm* brannerite

branša *nf* specialty

brants *nm* 1. (col.) gangrene; 2. dry rot

brasa *nf* communal overnight accomodations

brase *nf* (naut.) brace

brasēt *vi* live it up; show off

brasidīnskābe *nf* brassidic acid

brasilskābe *nf* brassylic acid

braslets *nm* bracelet

brasls *nm* ford

brass *nm* breast stroke

braši *adv* dashingly; energetically

brašmanis *nm* (col.) dashing fellow

brašs *adj* dashing, strapping; energetic; (of bearing) upright

brašule *nf* fine girl

brašulīgs *adj* brash, rash

brašulis *nm* fine fellow

brašums *nm* dashing appearance

brašvīrs *nm* dashing fellow

brātarītis *nm* (folk.) brother

braucamais *nom adj* vehicle

braucamjosla *nf* traffic lane

braucamlīdzeklis *nm* vehicle

braucams *adj, part* of **braukt** fit for driving or riding

braucamzirgs *nm* carriage horse

braucēj/s *nm*, ~a *nf* 1. passenger; 2. driver; **meēā b.** firewood hauler; **tirgū b.** marketer

brauciena maksa *nf* fare

brauciens *nm* trip; ride; drive; run

braucienu grāmata *nf* trip record book

braucienu saraksts *nm* timetable

braucin *adv emph* of **braukt; b. brauca** they kept coming; they came from everywhere

braucīt *vt* 1. stroke, massage; 2. strip

braucītāj/s *nm* massager, masseur; ~a *nf* masseuse

braukalēt *vi* = **braukāt**

braukaļāt *vi* = **braukāt**

braukāt *vi* drive, ride around; drive, ride repeatedly, go back and forth

braukšana *nf* going (in a vehicle), driving, riding, cycling, sailing, flight; (of a vehicle) running

braukšanas apliecība *nf* driver's license

braukšanas apmācība *nf* driver education

braukšanas josla *nf* traffic lane

braukšanas maksa *nf* fare

braukšanas noteikumi *nm pl* traffic rules

braukšanas pavēle *nf* marching orders

braukšanas priekšrocība *nf* right of way

braukšus *adv* in a vehicle

braukt *vi* go, ride, drive, sail, fly; move, slide; **b. automašīnā** ride in a car; **b. ar automašīnu** drive a car; **b. ar autobusu** ride a bus; **b. ar divriteni** ride a bicycle; **b. ar kuģi** sail, go by ship; **b. pa lidlauku** taxi; **b. ar ragaviņām** go sledding; **b. ar slēpēm** ski; **b. ar taksometru** take a taxi, ride in a taxi; **b. ar vilcienu** go by train; **b. ar zirgu** drive a horse; **b. jūrā** go to sea; **b. komandējumā** go on a business trip; **b. at-vaļinājumā** go on vacation; **b. uz** go to; **b. uz leju** worsen; **b. uz mežu pēc malkas** haul firewood from the forest; **b. peļņā** (col.) hire out as a driver; make gainful trips; earn a living as a driver; **b. zaļumos** go on an outing, go on a picnic; **b. kā traks** ride hell for leather; **b. pa virsu** (col.) skim the surface, give the once-over-lightly; **b. ar muti** (com.) bluster, talk big

brauktuve *nf* driveway

braukums *nm* trip

braulēt *vi* be in rut

braulība *nf* ardor; rut

braulīgs *adj* (sexually) excited, hot

braulums *nm* ardor; rut

brauna *nf* (reg.) molted skin; chrysalis, (embry-onic) cowl; ~**s** (reg.) (fish) scales; dandruff

Brauna cietpaparde *nf* prickly shield fern

braunains *adj* scurfy, scabby

braunāt *vt* scuff, scratch

brauniņš *nm* Browning (automatic pistol)

brauņa *nf* = **brauna**

bravo *interj* bravo

bravūra *nf* bravado; bravura

bravūrība *nf* bravado; bravura

bravūrīgi *adv* with bravado

bravūrīgs *adj* bravadoing

bravūrīgums *nm* bravado

brazenijas *nf pl* (bot.) water shield

brāzeniski *adv* rapidly, energetically

brāzienīgs *adj* gusty

brāziens *nm* **1.** wind gust; **2.** scolding, dressing down

brāzienuguns *nf* hammering fire

brazīliet/is *nm*, ~**e** *nf* Brazilian

brāzma *nf* wind gust; (of laughter) peal; (of applause) storm

brāzmainība *nf* gustiness; storminess, tumultuousness; impetuousness

brāzmaini *adv* tumultuously, impetuously

brāzmains *adj* gusty; stormy, tumultuous; im-petuous

brāzmainums *nm* gustiness; storminess, tumultuousness; impetuousness

brāzmot *vi* storm; rage

brāzt *v* **1.** *vi* (of storms) rage; (of waves) smash against; **2.** *vt* smash against; **3.** *vt* scrape, abrade, skin; **4.** *vt* scold

brāzties *vr* **1.** (of wind, water) sweep, rush, smash against; **2.** rush, tear along

brēcēj/s *nm*, ~**a** *nf* crier, yeller, squaller

bre[ch]stanga [h] *nf* (barb.) crowbar

brēciens *nm* cry, scream, yell, squall; screech, bray

brēcīgs *adj* whining, crying

brēcināt *vt* make (a baby) cry

breãa *nf* breccia

breik *interj* (boxing) break!

breiks *nm* break, break dancing

breikšis *nm* noise maker; quarreler

brēka *nf* shouting, clamor, squalling, hullaballoo; **liela b., maza vilna** much ado about nothing

brēkaļāt *vi* = (col.) **brēkāt**

brēkāt *vi* shout, yell, clamor repeatedly

brekãija *nf* = **breãa**

brēkoņa *nf* = **brēka**

breksis *nm* bream

brēkt *vi* cry, yell, scream, shriek, squall; cry out; bray; screech; **b. nelabā balsī** shout at the top of one's voice

brēkulība *nf* tendency to cry

brēkulīgi *adv* whiningly

brēkulīgs *adj* whining, crying

brēkul/is *nm*, ~**e** *nf* (col.) squaller, infant, crybaby

brēkuļot *vi* cry, be a crybaby

brēķis *nm* crier, yeller, squaller

breloks *nm* fob

bremze *nf* (tech.) brake; **pneimatiskā b.** air brake

bremzējošs *adj, part* of **bremzēt** resistive; (physiol.) inhibitory

bremzes cilindrs *nm* brake cylinder

bremzes klucis *nm* (of wagon wheels) brake shoe

bremzes konduktors *nm* (RR) brakeman

bremzes kurpe *nf* brake shoe; brake block

bremzes ķēde *nf* tire chain

bremzes skriemelis *nm* brake pulley

bremzēšana *nf* braking; (physiol., psych.) interference

bremzēt *vi* apply the brakes; *vt* brake; *vt* (fig.) hamper, interfere with; (physiol.) inhibit

bremzētājierīce *nf* braking device

brendijs *nm* brandy

brenne *nf* (sl.) trouble

breolīns *nm* hair pomade, hairdressing

brese *nf* birthmark; liver spot

bresmes *nf pl* inflammation of the udder

bresmis *nm* white bream

brētliņa *nf* sprat

breton/is *nm*, **~iete** *nf* Breton

breve *nf* (papal brief) breve

breviārijs *nm* breviary

breviārs *nm* = **breviārijs**

brezents *nm* tarpaulin

brice *nf* (reg.) scolding

bricelēt *vt* (reg.) scold

bricis *nm* awl, punch

brička *nf* (carriage) britska

bridējputns *nm* wading bird

bridēj/s *nm*, **~a** *nf* wader

bridenis *nm* seine net

brīders *nm* (atomic) breeder

brīdēt *vt* (obs.) warn

bridiens *nm* 1. wading; 2. many, great numbers

bridin *adv emph* of **brist; b. brida** (he, she) waded a long distance, waded all over, slogged

brīdinājums *nm* warning, admonition

bridināt *vt* make wade

brīdināt *vt* warn, caution, admonish

brīdinātāj/s *nm*, **~a** *nf* 1. warner; 2. warning (*adj*)

brīdiņš *nm* 1. *dim* of **brīdis**, moment; 2. (reg.) scolding

bridis *nm* seine net

brī/dis *nm* moment; while; period ◊ **~di pa ~dim** ever so often; **~žiem** once in a while; **kuŗu katru ~di** any moment now; **īstā ~dī** at the right mo-ment; **ik ~di** constantly; **vaļas ~dī** at leisure; **pirms ~ža** a moment ago; **pēc ~ža** presently; **šinī ~dī** at this moment; **visam savs b.** all in good time

bridnis *nm* seine net

bridums *nm* wade

bridža bikses *nf pl* breeches

bridžs *nm* (card game) bridge

brieda *nf* rutting season

briedaļa *nf* 1. a cow in the color of elk; 2. (reg.) hind

briedene *nf* 1. a. champignon, meadow mushroom; b. milky cap; 2. matgrass

briedens *adj* swelling, rising

briedēns *nm* elk calf

briedēt *vt* ripen, further the growth of

briedība *nf* ripeness, maturity, mellowness

briedīgs *adj* 1. quick-rising, quick-swelling; (of flour) high-quality; expansive; 2. furthering growth; (of weather, growth season) generous

briedīgums *nm* ripeness, maturity, mellow-ness

briedināt *vt* 1. let swell; 2. ripen

briedis *nm* elk

briedītis *nm* 1. *dim* of **briedis**, little elk; 2. stag beetle

bried/s *nm* ripeness; ~**ā** (poet.) at the peak of ripeness

briedumķermenis *nm* corpus cavernosum

briedums *nm* ripeness; (fig.) prime of life

briedumzars *nm* water sprout

bries *adv* (obs.) afraid

briesmains *adj* = **briesmīgs**

briesmas *nf pl* **1.** danger, peril; **2.** (col.) horror ◊ **taisni b!** pure horror!

briesmeklis *nm* = **briesmonis**

briesmīgi *adv* (col.) very terribly, dying to (do sth.)

briesmīgs *adj* horrible, terrible, awful

briesmīgums *nm* horror, terror, awfulness

briesmonība *nf* monstrosity

briesmonīgs *adj* cruel

briesmonis *nm* monster; fiend

briesmoņa *nm* fiend

briesmu bremze *nf* emergency brake

briesmu darbs *nm* atrocity

briesmu signāls *nm* distress signal;

briest *vi* **1.** ripen; **2.** swell; **3.** (*3rd pers*, fig. of events) brew, develop

briežāda *nf* buckskin

brieža gaļa *nf* venison

brieža ragi *nm pl* antlers

briežauka *nf* snowstorm

briežkopība *nf* elk raising; reindeer raising

briežkop/is *nm*, ~**e** *nf* elk raiser; reindeer raiser

briežpurns *nm* (bot.) shingled hedgehog

briežraga sāls *nf* ammonium carbonate

briežrag/s *nm* hartshorn

briežsakne *nf* libanotis

briežu kūla *nf* matgrass

briežu ķērpis *nm* reindeer moss

briežu māte *nf* elk cow

briežu rūgtdille *nf* hog's fennel

briežu trifeļi *nm pl* Elaphomyces

briežvabole *nf* stag beetle

brīfings *nm* briefing

briga *nf* (naut.) brig

brigāde *nf* brigade; crew

brigādes ģenerālis *nm* brigadier general

brig[a]dier/is [ā] *nm*, ~**e** *nf* crew foreman

brigantīna *nf* brigantine

brik *interj* crack

brikete *nf* briquette; brick, block

briketēt *vt* briquette

brikets *nm* = **brikete**

brikns *adj* angry

briksiers *nm* brick cheese

briksnājs *nm* scrubland

briksnis *nm* scrubland

brikstalas *nf pl* scrubland

brikstēt *vi* crackle, snap

brikš *interj* crack

brīkš *interj* crash

brikšēt *vi* snap, crackle

brikšķēt *vi* snap, crackle

brīkšķēt *vi* crack, creak

brikšķināt *vt iter* make snap or crackle

brikšķināties *vr* make snap or crackle

brikšķis *nm* snap

brīkšķis *nm* crack, crash

brikšķoņa *nf* snapping, crackling

brīkšķoņa *nf* crashing, creaking

brikšņi *nm pl* scrubland

briku braku *interj* crunch

briljantīns *nm* brilliantine

briljants *nm* brilliant

briljants *adj* brilliant

briljantzaļais *nom adj* (dye) Brilliant Green

brille *nf* (sl.) toilet seat, toilet

brilles *nf pl* eyeglasses; goggles

briļļains *adj* bespectacled

briļļots *adj* bespectacled

briļļu čūska *nf* cobra

brīnišķi *adv* wonderful; wonderfully

brīnišķīgi *adv* wonderful; wonderfully

brīnišķīgs *adj* wonderful

brīnišķīgums *nm* wonderfulness

brīnišķs *adj* wonderful

brīnīties *vr* wonder at, marvel at; **nav ko b.** nothing to be surprised at

brīnoties *vr* = **brīnīties**

brīns *nm* amazement, astonishment

brīnum *adv* wonderfully, wondrously; exquisitely

brīnumaini *adv* 1. mysteriously; miraculously; 2. wondrously

brīnumains *adj* 1. mysterious; miraculous; 2. wondrous, amazing

brīnumārsts *nm* miracle healer, faith healer; quackslaver

brīnumbērns *nm* infant prodigy

brīnumdakteris *nm* (col.) quacksalver

brīnumdarbs *nm* miracle, miraculous deed; chef d'oeuvre

brīnumdar/is *nm*, ~e *nf* miracle worker, magician, wizard

brīnumdarītāj/s *nm*, ~a *nf* = **brīnumdaris**

brīnumjauks *adj* wonderful, gorgeous

brīnumliels *adj* collosal, of prodigious size

brīnumlietas *nf pl* miracles, magic; wondrous things

brīnumpasaka *nf* fairy tale (involving magic and the supernatural)

brīnumputns *nm* magic bird

brīnumrīkste *nf* magic wand

brīnum/s *nm* 1. miracle; wonder; **b., k . . .** it is a wonder that . . .; **tas tik ir b.!** wonders never cease; **tavu ~u!** wonders never cease; **~i gan!** wonder of wonders; **~u ~i** wonder of wonders; **zili ~i** wonder of wonders; marvelous things; **kā par ~u** by some miracle, miraculously; 2. amazement, astonishment; **visiem par ~u** to everyone's astonishment

brīnumskaists *adj* exquisitely beautiful

brīnumspogulis *nm* magic mirror

brīnumsvecīte *nf* sparkler

brīnumvārdi *nm pl* magic words, spell

brīnumzāles *nf pl* magic remedy, magic potion

brīnumzeme *nf* wonderland

brinza *nf* cheese made of sheep's milk

briof[i]lis [ī] *nm* bryophyllum

briolo/gs *nm*, ~ģe *nf* briologist

brioloģija *nf* briology

brionija *nf* bryony

Briseles kāposti *nm pl* Brussels sprouts

brī siers *nm* Brie (cheese)

briskas *nf pl* (reg.) scolding

brīsniņš *nm dim* of **brīdis**, moment

brist *vi* wade; **b. jūrā** (of the sun) set; *vt* wade across

brišus *adv* 1. by wading; 2. *emph* of **brist**; **b. bri-da** waded all over; slogged through

brītiņš *nm dim* of **brīdis**

brits *nm* Briton

brīv *adv* (col.) allowed; **man ir b.** I am allowed

brīvā *adv* idle

brīvais kritiens *nm* free fall

brīvbagāža *nf* no-charge luggage

brīvbandinieks *nm* (chess) free pawn, unchecked pawn

brīvbibliotēka *nf* public library

brīvbiļete *nf* free pass, free ticket

brīvciems *nm* (hist.) cluster of farmsteads (given to free peasants for special services)

brīvdabas *indecl adj* open-air; landscape

brīvdiena *nf* day off; ~s (school) break

brīvdomātājs *nm*, ~a *nf* freethinker

brīvdomība *nf* free thought

brīvdomīgi *adv* like a freethinker

brīvdomīgs *adj* freethinking

brīvdomīgums *nm* free thought

brīvdzimušais *nom adj* a freeborn person

brīve *nf* (poet.) freedom, liberty

brīvē *adv* idle

brīvēdāj/s *nm*, ~a *nf* freeloader

brīvēd/is *nm*, ~e *nf* freeloader

brīveksemplārs *nm* free copy; author's copy

brīvestība *nf* (obs.) freedom, liberty

brīvēt *vt* (poet.) free, liberate

brīvēēa *nf, nm* freeloader

brīvgadi *nm pl* (hist.) free years (the first three years during which a peasant who had arrived fleeing from another area was exempted from corvée labor and contributions in kind)

brīvgaita *nf* (mech.) idling; free motion; free running

brīvgājiena sajūgs *nm* freewheel clutch

brīvgājiens *nm* (mech.) play

brīvgrāmata *nf* (hist.) certificate of manumission; exemption certificate (given to a free peasant stating that he has been exempted from corvée labor and tributes)

brīvi *adv* freely; (of speaking a foreign language) fluently; (fig.) openly, candidly; **b.!** (mil.) at ease!

brīvība *nf* freedom, liberty

brīvības atņemšana *nf* imprisonment

brīvības cīnītājs *nm* fighter in a war of liberation; freedom fighter

brīvības cīņas *nf pl* war of liberation; fight for freedom

brīvības ierobežojums *nm* restriction of liberty

brīvības pakāpe *nf* (stat.) degree of freedom

brīvkapi *nm pl* free cemetery

brīvkarte *nf* free pass

brīvklausītāj/s *nm*, ~a *nf* (educ.) auditor

brīvkundze *nf* baroness, baron's wife

brīvkungs *nm* baron

brīvlaiks *nm* (educ.) break, vacation

brīvlaist *vt* manumit, free

brīvlaistais *nom adj* freedman, emancipated serf

brīvlaišana *nf* manumission, freeing of serfs

brīvlaiža *nf, nm* (col.) freeloader

brīvmāja *nf* (hist.) the farm of a free peasant

brīvmākslinie/ks *nm*, ~ce *nf* (educ., in czarist Russia and in Latvia) degree in music

brīvmetiens *nm* (basketball) free throw

brīvmūrniecība *nf* freemasonry

brīvmūrniek/s *nm* freemason; ~u masonic

brīvnieks *nm* = **brīvzemnieks**

brīvnauda *nf* (hist.) emancipation fee (money paid by a **brīvzemnieks** to achieve his freedom)

brīvnedēļa *nf* (hist.) free week (under the corvée system, a week that was free of compulsory corvée labor)

brīvosta *nf* free port

brīvot *vt* (poet.) free, liberate

brīvpieeja *nf* (compu.) random access

brīvpilsēta *nf* free city

brīvprāt *adv* voluntarily

brīvprātība *nf* voluntariness

brīvprātīg/ais *nom adj*, ~ā *f* volunteer

brīvprātīgi *adv* voluntarily

brīvprātīgs *adj* voluntary

brīvprātīgums *nm* voluntariness

brīvpusdienas *nf pl* free lunch

brīvrats *nm* freewheel

brīvrokas *indecl adj* freehand

brīvrumbas bremze *nf* coaster brake

brīv/s *adj* **1.** free; (col.) single; **b. no dienesta** off duty ◊ **par** ~**u** for free; **pie visa** ~**a** free board and lodging; **2.** liberal; **3.** vacant, unoccupied; (of time) spare

brīvsāni *nm pl* (naut.) freeboard

brīvsānu klājs *nm* freeboard deck

brīvsitiens *nm* (soccer) free kick

brīvskola *nf* free school

brīvslūžas *nf pl* escape sluice

brīvsol/is *nm* route step; **iet** ~**ī** (col.) be absent without leave, go AWOL

brīvstunda *nf* (educ.) recess

brīvterritorija *nf* tax-exempt factories (those exempt from import duties on machinery, raw materials, and packing)

brīvtirdzniecība *nf* free trade

brīvvalsts *nf* free state

brīvvieta *nf* scholarship

brīvzeme *nf* (hist.) free land (in the feudal system, land exempt from statutory labor and taxes)

brīvzemnieks *nm* (hist.) free peasant (one ex-empted from statutory labor and most tributes)

brizants *adj* high-explosive

brizantšāviņš *nm* high-explosive shell

brīze *nf* breeze

brizenes *nf pl* brazilwood

brīzīte *nf dim* of **brīze**, slight breeze

brīžam *adv* = **brīžiem**

brīēiem *adv* once in a while

brodenis *nm* gable vent

brodīgs *adj* = (reg.) **briedīgs**

brodiņš *nm* gable vent

broilers *nm* broiler

brokastis *nf pl* breakfast

brokastlaiks *nm* breakfast time

brokastot *vi* breakfast

brokāts *nm* brocade

brokeris *nm* broker

brokoļi *nm pl* broccoli

broma papīrs *nm* bromide paper

bromapskābe *nf* hypobromous acid

bromāts *nm* bromate

bromelija *nf* bromeliad

bromēt *vt* brominate

brom|i|ds [ī] *nm* bromide

bromometrija *nf* bromometry

broms *nm* bromine

bromskābe *nf* bromic acid

bromsudrabs *nm* silver bromide

bromūdens *nm* bromine water

bromūdeņradis *nm* hydrogen bromide

bromūdeņraēskābe *nf* hydrobromic acid

bron|ch|a [h] *nf* = **bronchs**

bron|ch|iāls [h] *adj* bronchial

bron|ch|iola [h] *nf* bronchiole

bron|ch|ītisks [h] *adj* bronchitic

bron|ch|īts [h] *nm* bronchitis

bron|ch|ogr|a|fija [h]|ā] *nf* bronchography

bron|ch|oskopija [h] *nf* bronchoscopy

bron|ch|oskops [h] *nm* bronchoscope

bron|ch|s [h] *nm* bronchus

brontofobija *nf* brontophobia

brontometrs *nm* brontometer

brontozaurs *nm* brontosaurus

bronza *nf* bronze

bronzējums *nm* bronzing

bronzēt *vt* bronze

broņa *nf* (com.) guaranty

brosls *adj* (reg.) heavy-set

broša *nf* brooch

brošēt *vt* (binding) stitch

brošētāj/s *nm*, **~a** *nf* **1.** stitcher; **2.** stapler

brošētava *nf* book stitching shop

brošēts *adj, part* of **brošēt** paperbound

brošūra *nf* brochure, pamphlet

brovalija *nf* browallia

brozls or **brozs** *adj* (reg.) heavy-set

brr *interj* brr

brūce *nf* wound; **cirsta b.** incised wound; **durta b.** puncture wound; **griezta b.** incised wound; **kosta b.** bite; **plēsta b.** lacerated wound; **sista b.** contused wound; **skrāpēta b.** scratch; **šauta b.** bullet wound

bruceklis *nm* (scythe) rifle

bruceloze *nf* brucelosis

brūcene *nf* hovel

brūces slīmests *nm* blazing drawknife

brūces spogulis *nm* (resin tapping) face

brūcēt *vt* embroider

brucināt *vt* **1.** (of a scythe) whet; **2.** rub, scour, scrape; **3.** scald (to clean, remove, or temper)

brucis *nm* thatched hayrick; haystack

brucīte *nf* bodice

brucīts *nm* brucite

bruģakmens *nm* paving stone, cobblestone

bruģa kungs *nm* (hist.) justice of the highway court

bruģa tiesa *nf* (hist.) highway court (a court among whose functions was the overseeing of road and bridge maintenance)

bruģējums *nm* pavement (of paving stones)

bruģēt *vt* pave (with paving stones)

bruģētājs *nm* paver

bruģis *nm* pavement (of paving stones); roadway

bruka *nf* hernia

brūka *nf* a dish of roasted hemp seeds and bread crumbs

brukas saite *nf* truss

brukas zāle *nf* sanicle

brukasvēders *nm* scrag, starveling

brūklenājs *nm* **1.** growth of mountain cranberries; **2.** mountain cranberry bush

brūklene *nf* mountain cranberry

brūkleņaudze *nf* growth of mountain cranberries

brūkleņu tēviņi *nm pl* pipsissewa

bruksla *nf* scrubland

brukslājs *nm* scrubland

brukstalas *nf pl* scrub; new growth in a softwood forest

brukši *nm pl* **1.** windfallen twigs and branches; **2.** scrub

brukšķināt *vi, vt* rattle, crash, crackle

brukšņi *nm pl* = **brukši**

brukt *vi* **1.** collapse, come down; cave in; (also fig.) fall apart; **2.** slide down, roll down; **3.** (of socks) slip down; **4.** (of colors) run; **5. b. virsū** fall upon, attack

bruku *adv* sloppily

brukulains *adj* sloppily dressed

bruku lapas *nf pl* water arum

brūķēt *vt* (obs.) use; **b. lielu muti** (com., hum.) brag; shoot off one's mouth

brūķis *nm* (col.) use

bruljons *nm* rough draft

brumbetes *nf pl* wood betony

brūnā ābele *nf* Oregonian crabapple

brūnacains *adj* brown-eyed

brūnace *nf* brown-eyed girl

brūnacis *nm* brown-eyed boy

brūnacīte *nf* brown-eyed girl

brūnactiņas *nf pl* coreopsis

brūnā čakste *nf* red-backed shrike

brūnā dižspāre *nf* brown aeschna

brūnā dzeguzene *nf* dark-red helleborine

brūnā dzelzsrūda *nf* geothite

brūnā hiēna *nf* brown hyena

brūnais āboliņš *nm* hop clover

brūnais ibiss *nm* glossy ibis

brūnais lācis *nm* brown bear

brūnais lācītis *nm* woolly bear

brūnais pelikāns *nm* brown pelican

brūnais prusaks *nm* common cockroach

brūnais vizbulis *nm* avens

brūnaļa *nf* brown cow

brūnaļģes *nf pl* brown algae

brūnā meēu skudra *nf* wood ant

brūnā sūna *nf* a sphagnum moss, Sphagnum fuscum

brūnā žurka *nf* ship rat

brunč/i *nm pl* **1.** (col.) skirts; **~u mednieks** (col.) skirt chaser; **2.** debris; **3.** cracklings

brūndzeltenais ērglis *nm* golden eagle

brūnēšanās *nfr* (winemaking) brown casse

brūnēt *vi* brown

brunete *nf* brunette

brunets *adj* dark-haired

brūngalvīši *nm pl* or **brūngalvīte** *nf* (bot.) self-heal

brūnganais grīslis *nm* brownish sedge

brūngans *adj* brownish

brūni *adv* in brown, in a brown color

brūnie dižmeldri *nm pl* brown cyperus

brūnīgsnējs *adj* brownish

brūnināt *vt* brown

brūnis *nm* bay horse

brūnkakla gārgale *nf* red-throated diver

brūnkaklis *nm* common pochard

brunkas *nf pl* (reg.) skirt

brūnkātes *nf pl* broomrape

brūnmat/is *nm* brown-haired man; ~e *nf* brown-haired woman

brūnogles *nf pl* brown coal, lignite

brūnot *vi* appear in a brown color

brūnpelēkā mušmire *nf* booted amanita

brūns *adj* brown; tan; bay

brūnsarkans *adj* brownish red

brūnsiens *nm* partly dried hay

brūnspārnu bezdelīgtārtiņš *nm* collared pratincole

brūnspārnu ķauķis *nm* whitethroat

brūnsvārcis *nm* brown-coated person; brown-coated animal; (folk epithet for the cricket) browncoat

brūnums *nm* brownness

brūnvaidze *nf* brown-cheeked girl

brūnvaidzis *nm* brown-cheeked man (or boy)

brūnvālītes *nf pl* great burnet

brūnzeme *nf* brown soil

bruņas *nf pl* armor; **daudzslāņu b.** compound armor; (zool.) test

bruņcepure *nf* = **bruņucepure**

bruņcepures dzegužpuķe *nf* military orchis

bruņinieks *nm* knight; **b. piedzīvojumu meklē-tājs** knight adventurer; **b. sirotājs** knight errant

bruņinieku kārta *nf* knighthood

bruņinieku muiža *nf* manor

bruņinieku ordenis *nm* knightly order

bruņinieku pieši *nm pl* larkspur

bruņinieku romāns *nm* romance, courtly tale

bruņinieku sols *nm* (hist.) knightage

bruņnesis *nm* armadillo; see also **deviņjoslu b.**

bruņniecība *nf* knighthood

bruņnieciski *adv* in a knightly manner, chivalrously

bruņniecisks *adj* knightly, chivalrous

bruņnieciskums *nm* chivalry

bruņogs *nm* shield

bruņojums *nm* armor

bruņošanās *nfr* arming

bruņošanās rūpniecība *nf* arms industry

bruņošanās sacensība *nf* arms race

bruņot *vt* 1. arm; 2. armor

bruņoties *vr* arm oneself

bruņrupucis *nm* turtle; tortoise

bruņsitamība *nf* armor peneterating capability

bruņuautomobilis *nm* armored vehicle

bruņucepure *nf* helmet

bruņucimds *nm* gauntlet

bruņu kaval[e]rija [ē] *nf* armored cavalry

bruņukrekls *nm* coat of mail

bruņukuģis *nm* battleship, armorclad

bruņukurpe *nf* solleret

bruņuķiverene *nf* (bot.) skullcap

bruņu mašīna *nf* armored car; armored vehicle

bruņunesējs *nm* armor bearer, squire

bruņuplāksne *nf* armor plate

bruņurupucis *nm* turtle, tortoise

bruņusitējs *adj* armor-piercing

bruņutērps *nm* knight's armor

bruņutis *nf pl* scale insects

bruņutornis *nm* turret

bruņutransportieris *nm* armored carrier

bruņuveste *nf* body armor

bruņuvilciens *nm* armored train

bruņuzivs *nf* placoderm

bruņvicaiņi *nm pl* dinoflagellates

brusa *nf* saw-cut timber

bruslāgs *nm* (col.) bodice

brustalas *nf pl* scrubland

brustvērs *nm* parapet, breastwork

brutāli *adv* brutally

brut[a]litāte [ā] *nf* brutality

brutāls *adj* brutal

brūtaļa *nf* (com.) lover

brūte *nf* (obs.) bride; (col.) mistress

brūtgāns *nm* (obs.) bridegroom; (col.) beau, lover

bruto *nm indecl* **1.** gross weight; **2.** gross income

bruto *indecl adj* gross

brutoceltspēja *nf* total lifting capacity

brutocena *nf* total price

brutoienākums *nm* gross receipts

brutokapitāls *nm* total capital

brutopeļņa *nf* gross earnings

brutoreģistra *indecl adj* (of measures of weight) gross register

brutosumma *nf* gross sum

brutosvars *nm* gross weight

brūvējums *nm* brew, concoction

brūvelis *nm* = **brūveris**

brūveris *nm* (col.) brewer

brūvēt *vt* brew

bruzdēt *vi* rumble

brūze *nf* head of a sprinkling can

bruzgans *adj* reddish brown

brūzis *nm* (col.) brewery, distillery

bružāt *vt* crush, rub, scuff

bružāties *vr* be rubbed, be scuffed

bružināt *vt* rub; ruffle

brūžļāt *vt* = **bruēāt**

bū *interj* **ne bū, ne bē** nothing at all; **(neprot) ne bū, ne bē (atbildēt)** he is tongue-tied

būbējums *nm* mold

buberts *nm* custard pudding

būbēt *vi* (reg.) grow moldy, mold

bubināt *vi* **1.** whinny; **2.** murmur

bubināties *vr* **1.** whinny; **2.** murmur

bubonis *nm* (med.) bubo

buboņu mēris *nm* bubonic plague

bubulis I *nm* bogey, bogeyman

bubulis II *nm* knot, (of fabrics) pill

buburene *nf* black currant

bucene *nf* **1.** (reg.) blackberry; **2.** mountain ash

būcenis *nm* hovel; shed

buciņš *nm* **1.** *dim* of **buks**, little buck; **2.** (col.) stool

bucis *nm* **1.** buck; **2.** wicker basket

bucītis *nm* little buck

buča *nf* (col.) kiss

buči *nm pl* (sl.) soccer boots

bučot *vt* (col.) kiss

bučoties *vr* (col.) kiss

būda *nf* hut, cabin

būdams *part* of **būt** being

budāt *vi* wake (over a corpse); be awake

budē/lis *nm* **1.** masked Shrovetide guest, mummer; **~los iet** go merrymaking in disguise during Shrovetide; **2.** (hist.) bailiff; **3.** bogeyman

būdeļnieks *nm* cottager

budināt *vt* (folk.) rouse

būdinieks *nm* cottager

būdiņ/a *nf dim* of **būda**, little hut

būdiņu svētki *nm pl* Feast of the Tabernacle

budisms *nm* Buddhism

budists *nm*, **~e** *nf* Buddhist

budleja *nf* buddleia

būdnieks *nm* cottager

buduārs *nm* boudoir

budūksnis *nm* hovel

budulis *nm* = **budēlis**

budzis *nm* **1.** unripe berry, unripe fruit; **2.** (reg.) abscess; **3.** (cont.) big farmer

budzisks *adj* (cont.) of or pertaining to big farmers

budžeta gads *nm* fiscal year

budžeta projekts *nm* budget estimate

budžets *nm* budget; **kārtējais b.** operating budget

buferatmiņa *nf* (compu.) buffer memory

buferatspere *nf* buffer spring

buferīpašība *nf* (chem.) buffering capacity

buferis *nm* (mech.) bumper

buferizācija *nf* (compu.) buffering

buferkapacitāte *nf* buffer capacity

buferkrātuve *nf* buffer storage

bufers *nm* (chem.) buffer

bufervalsts *nf* buffer state

buferzona *nf* buffer zone

bufete *nf* 1. sideboard; 2. small restaurant (within another enterprise); 3. refreshment counter, snack bar

bufetes vagons *nm* dining car

bufetīte *nf dim* of bufete, sideboard; snack bar

bufetnie/ks *nm*, ~ce *nf* attendant at a bufete 2, 3

bufonāde *nf* buffoonery

bufotenīns *nm* bufotenine

bufs *adj* buffo

buga *nf* (naut.) bow

buganvileja *nf* bouganvillea

bugivugi *nm indecl* boogie-woogie

bugsprits *nm* (naut.) bowsprit

buivols *nm* buffalo

bujums *nm* (obs.) total assets

buka *nf* 1. coach box; 2. hod

būka *nf* 1. damson plum; 2. blackthorn

bukāt *vt* = būkāt

būkāt *vt* (col.) nudge; hit; thresh

bukets *nm* bouquet

bukinists *nm* secondhand book dealer

buklē *nm indecl* bouclé

buklets *nm* pamphlet

bukmeikers *nm* bookmaker

buknīt *vt* (col.) nudge

bukņa *nf* (col.) nudge

bukņīt *vt* = buknīt

bukolika *nf* bucolic

bukolisks *adj* bucolic

buk/s *nm* 1. buck; uz ~a shoddy; 2. side horse; 3. saw-horse

bukse *nf* bushing; liner; sleeve

buksēšana *nf* (of wheels) slippage, (RR) slippage of the drivers

buksēt *v* 1. *vi* (of wheels) slip; 2. *vt* tow

buksieris *nm* (obs.) tugboat

buksis *nm* (bot.) box

bukskoks *nm* box

buksnis *nm* (col.) nudge

buksnīt *vt* (col.) nudge

bukstiņš *nm* 1. (col.) nudge; 2. (factory-made) wool cloth

bukstīt *vt* (col.) nudge

buksts *nm* (col.) nudge

buksuss *nm* (bot.) box

būkš *interj* thud, thump

būkšēt *vi* = būkšķēt

būkšināt *vi* = būkšķināt

būkšis *nm* thud, thump

būkšķēt *vi* thud, thump

būkšķināt *vi* make thumping sounds, make thuds

būkšķis *nm* thud, thump

bukta nf (reg.) rope; towline; hawser; painter

bukt/e I *nf* (col.) energy; ar ~i impetuously, energetically

bukte II *nf* (sl.) crease; dent

buktēt *vt* (sl.) crease; dent

buktīgs *adj* (col.) impetuous, energetic

buku bārzda *nf* matgrass

buku-bē *interj* baa

buku lapas *nf pl* water arum

buku loki *nm pl* wild onion

buku ogas *nf pl* black currants

buku saknes *nf pl* burnet saxifrage

buku vītols *nm* velvet osier

bukūzis *nm* (col.) shed; hovel

būķēt *vt* soak in lye

buķete *nf* (col.) bouquet

būķis *nm* lye

bula *nf* = buls

Bula algebra *nf* Boolean algebra

bulbite *nf* hover fly

bulbokodija *nf* bulbocodium, meadow saffron

bulbulis *nm* a legendary bird that turns people into trees

bulciņa *nf dim* of bulka, small bread roll

buldogs *nm* bulldog

buldozerists *nm* bulldozer operator

buldozers *nm* bulldozer

buldurene *nf* valerian

buldurēt *vi* jabber; (of a turkey) gobble

buldurin̦i *nm pl* valerian

bulduris *nm* jabberer

buldurjān̦i *nm pl* valerian

buldurmēle *nf* (col.) blabber

bulenes *nf pl* marsh marigold

bulgāriski *adv* in Bulgarian, (speak) Bulgarian

bulgārisks *adj* Bulgarian

bulgār/s *nm*, ~iete *nf* Bulgarian

bulīmija *nf* boulimia

bulināt I *vi* wink, send eye signals

bulināt II *vi* coo

buljons *nm* broth

bulka *nf* (col.) (bread) roll

bulla *nf* (papal) bull

bullene *nf* a Cortinarius mushroom

bullēns *nm* bullock

bullis *nm* **1.** bull; **2.** dugout; **3.** plow sleeve (for plowing up potatoes)

bullītis *nm* **1.** *dim* of **bullis**, bullock; **2.** small dugout; **3.** (zool.) ruff; **4.** rocambole

bul/s *nm* sultry air; hot, oppressive weather; ~a **zibens** (col.) sheet lightning

bulta *nf* **1.** arrow; **2.** bolt; **3.** pointer, indicator

bultas gals *nm* arrowhead

bultene *nf* (bot.) arrowhead

bulterjērs *nm* bull terrier

bultēt *vt* bolt

bultin̦a *nf dim* of **bulta**, arrow; pointer, indicator

bultskrūve *nf* carriage bolt

bultu maks *nm* quiver

bultveida *indecl adj* arrow-shaped

bultveidīgs *adj* arrow-shaped

bulvāris *nm* boulevard

bulvā[r]u prese [r̦] *nf* gutter press

bul̦ba *nf* (reg.) potato

bul̦l̦apiere *nf, nm* stubborn person

bul̦l̦u pieres *nf pl* globeflower

bul̦va *nf* (reg.) potato

bumba *nf* **1.** ball; **2.** bomb; **lielkalibra b.** blockbuster; **mazkalibra b.** bomblet; **b. ar laika degli** time bomb; **3.** (col.) fat person

bumbierābele *nf* a variety of apple tree

bumbierābols *nm* a variety of apple

bumbiere *nf* pear tree

bumbieris *nm* **1.** pear (fruit); **2.** punching ball

bumbierkoks *nm* pear tree

bumbie[r]u [r̦] esence *nf* pear oil

bumbie[r]u [r̦] lapu blusin̦a *nf* jumping plant louse

bumbie[r]veida [r̦] *indecl adj* pear-shaped, pyriform

bumbie[r]veida pūpēdis [r̦] *nm* pear-shaped puffball

bumbie[r]veidīgi [r̦] *adv* shaped like a pear

bumbie[r]veidīgs [r̦] *adj* pear-shaped, pyriform

bumbin̦a *nf dim* of **bumba**, little ball; pellet; marble

bumbin̦u spēle *nf* marbles (game)

bumbot *v* **1.** *vt* bomb; **2.** *vi* bowl

bumbotava *nf* bowling alley

bumboties *vr* play with the ball

bumbulēt *vi* (col.) loaf

bumbulis *nm* **1.** tuber; **2.** bump, lump; **3.** little ball; **4.** marsh marigold

bumbul̦ainā gundega *nf* meadow crowfoot

bumbul̦ains *adj* knobby, uneven

bumbul̦augs *nm* tuberous plant

bumbul̦sīpols *nm* (bot.) bulb

bumbul̦u dedestin̦as *nf pl* everlasting pea

bumbul̦u pulkstenīte *nf* rampion

bumbul̦veida *indecl adj* ball-like; tuber-like

bumbul̦veidīgs *adj* ball-like; tuber-like

bumburnieks *nm* = **bandinieks** I

bumburs *nm* **1.** hillock; **2.** bump, hump; **3.** tyke

bumbvedējs *nm* bomber

bumbvedis *nm* = **bumbvedējs**

bumbveida *indecl adj* spherical

bumbveidīgs *adj* spherical

bumerangs *nm* boomerang

bums *interj* bang

bums *nm* boom (fast growth, rise)

būna *nf* groin (breakwater)

buncis *nm* **1.** salt shaker; **2.** bellied wooden vessel; **3.** big-bellied boy

bundeslīga *nf* (German) national league

bundesrāts *nm* Bundesrat

bundestāgs *nm* Bundestag

bundesvērs *nm* Bundeswehr

bundulis *nm* **1.** wooden butterbox; **2.** bundle

bundzinie/ks *nm*, **~ce** *nf* drummer

bundziņa *nf* small tin can

bundzis *nm* (col.) belly

bundž/a *nf* **1.** tin can; **2.** (col.) big-bellied person

bundžiņa *nf dim* of **bundēa**, small tin can

bundžu attaisāmais *nm* can opener

bungādiņa *nf* eardrum

bungādiņas iekaisums *nm* tympanitis

bungalo *nm indecl* bungalow

bung/as *nf pl* (mus.) drum; **~u rīboņa** beat of the drums; drumroll

bungāt *vi* = **bungot**

bungdobuma kāpnes *nf pl* tympanic cavity

bungdobums *nm* (anat.) tympanic cavity

bungot *vi* drum; bang, knock; (laundry) beat; **b. ar pirkstiem** drum on, thrum

bungotājs *nm*, **~a** *nf* drummer; banger, knocker

bungplēvīte *nf* eardrum

bungu āda *nf* drumhead

bungulis I *nm* stick, staff

bungulis II *nm* (col.) stomach, tummy

bungvālī/te *nf* drumstick; **~šu pirksti** clubbed fingers

bunka *nf* (col.) nudge

bunkāt *vt* (col.) nudge

bunkurošana *nf* (naut.) bunkering

bunkurs *nm* (naut., mil.) bunker; (sl.) stomach

buntavniecisks *adj* (obs.) insurrectionary, rebellious

buntavnieks *nm* (obs.) insurgent, rebel; ringleader

bunte *nf* (col.) bunch

buntīgs *adj* (barb.) motley, checkered

buntīte *nf dim* of **bunte**, small bunch

buntoties *vr* (obs.) rebel

buņģis *nm* can

bupleires *nf pl* buplevers

bur/a *nf* sail; **galvenā b.** mainsail ◊ **pilnās ~ās** in full sail, (fig., col.) full steam ahead; **~ās** (col.) intoxicated, under steam

burājums *nm* cruise (on a sailing vessel), sailing

bu[r]amvārdi [ŗ] *nm pl* magic spell

burans *nm* buran

burāšana *nf* sailing, yachting; iceboating

burāt *vi* sail; **b. ar sānu vēju** run free; **b. iepretim vējam** sail to the wind; **b. pa vējam** run before the wind

burātāj/s *nm*, **~a** *nf* yachtsman

burba *nf* **1.** rot, decaying material; **2.** pore

burbains *adj* porous; decayed, rotten

burbēt *vi* decay, rot

burbiņa *nf dim* of **burba**, pore

burbons *nm* bourbon

burbulēt *vi* bubble

burbulis *nm* bubble

burbulītis *nm dim* of **burbulis**, small bubble

burbuļot *vi* bubble

burdons *nm* bourdon

būrēja *nf* sorceress

burgundiet/is *nm* **1.** Burgundian; **~e** *nf*; **2.** Burgundy

burgzdala *nf* water bubble

burgzdalāt *vi* bubble

burinieks *nm* sailing ship

burināt *vi* speak rapidly and indistinctly

būris *nm* cage; coop; hutch

būrītis *nm* **1.** *dim* of **būri**s, small cage; **2.** birdhouse

burjat/s *nm,* ~**iete** *nf* Buryat

burka *nf* glass jar

burkānenes *nf pl* pepper saxifrage

burkāniņš *nm dim* of **burkāns**, little carrot

burkān/s *nm* carrot; ~**u sarkans** carroty, saffron-colored

burkānu mušiņa *nf* carrot rust fly

burkste *nf* throng

burkstēt *vi* = **burkšķēt**

burkšēt *vi* = **burkšķēt**

burkšķēt *vi* **1.** (of the stomach) grumble; (of ma-chinery, devices) makes noises; crackle; **2.** (col.) grumble, growl, mutter

burkšķināt *vt* (of an engine) rev; *vi* = **burkšķēt**

burkšķis *nm* rumble; crackle

burlacība *nf* villainy; baseness

burlaks *nm* holdup man

burleska *nf* burlesque

burlesks *adj* burlesque

burnīt *vt* **1.** crumple; **2.** torment; **3.** cut with a dull knife

burnuss *nm* burnous

burot *vi* = **burāt**

būr/s *nm,* ~**iete** *nf* Boer

bursa *nf* **1.** a. (hist.) Greek Orthodox theological seminary; b. bursa (residence hall for students); **2.** (anat.) bursa

bursaks *nm* (hist.) a **bursa** student

burseras *nf* Bursera

burste *nf* (reg.) (woman's) vest

bursteklis *nm* (col.) magic charm

burstelēt *vi* practice magic, cast spells

buršana *nf* (the practice of) magic, sorcery

buršanās *nfr* casting of spells; mumbo jumbo

buršikozs *adj* free and easy

buršs *nm* **1.** (college) senior; college student; **2.** apprentice

burt *vi* do magic, cast spells, conjure

burta *nf* **1.** lottery ticket; **2.** tally, tally mark; ~**s koks** tally; divining stick; **3.** writing

burtains *adj* **1.** marked with tallies; **2.** curly

burta kalps *nm* pedant

burta kalpība *nf* pedantry

burta rieva *nf* (typ.) nick

burta vieta *nf* (typ.) quad

burte *nf* **1.** = **burta**; **2.** (typ.) column; **3.** curl

burtene *nf* (typ.) type case

burties *vr* **1.** = **burt**; **2.** (col.) study diligently; **3.** murmur

burtin *adv emph* of **burt**; **b. būra** she cast spells diligently

burtiņš *nm dim* of **burts**, letter

burtiski *adv* literally, to the letter

burtisks *adj* literal

burtiskums *nm* literalness

burtlic/is *nm,* ~**e** *nf* (typ.) compositor

burtlietuve *nf* typefoundry

burtnīca *nf* **1.** exercise book, test booklet, notebook; cahier; **2.** issue, number

burtniecība *nf* (obs.) aesthetic folklore

burtnieks *nm* (poet.) wise man; wizard; (folk.) sorcerer, diviner

burtot *vt, vi* spell; decipher

burt/s *nm* **1.** letter; **lielie** ~**i** capital letters; **mazie** ~**i** small letters ◊ **b.** ~**ā** letter by letter, letter perfect; **2.** type; **kursīvie** ~**i** italics; **lielie** ~**i** up-per case type; **mazie** ~**i** lower case type; **netīrs b.** (typ.) pick; **treknie** ~**i** boldface

burtsmetis *nm* diviner

burtstabiņš *nm* (typ.) type

burtu garnitūra *nf* font

burtu griezējs *nm* type cutter

burtu lējējs *nm* typefounder

burtu likšana *nf* typesetting

buru audekls *nm* canvas

buru kuģis *nm* sailing ship

buru laiva *nf* sailboat

buru lidmašīna *nf* sailplane

buru lidošana *nf* sailplane sport

būrums *nm* magic spell

burunduks *nm* chipmunk

buru sports *nm* yachting

buru taisītājs *nm* sailmaker;

buru zivs *nf* sailfish

burve *nf* sorceress

burvekle *nf* sorceress

burveklis *nm* charm, magic object

burvene *nf* sorceress

burvesti *nm pl* magic charms

burvestība *nf* (obs.) magic; witchcraft; spell

burvība *nf* 1. magic; witchcraft; spell; 2. enchantment, charm

burvīgi *adv* wonderfully, heavenly

burvīgs *adj* enchanting; wonderful, heavenly

burvīgums *nm* enchantment, charm

burvilka *nf* (naut.) halyard

burv/is *nm* sorcerer, magician, wizard ◊ **kā uz ~ja mājienu** with a wave of the wand, as if by magic

burvju dārzs *nm* enchanted garden

burvju lazda *nf* witch hazel

burvju loks *nm* magic circle; (fig.) vicious circle

burvju māksla *nf* magic; art of conjuring

burvju mākslinieks *nm* magician, conjurer

burvju vārdi *nm pl* magic spell, incantation

burvju zizlis *nm* magic wand;

burza *nf* press, bustle

burzgas *nf pl* spray

burzgot *vi* bubble, boil

burzgulēt *vi* (of running water) bubble; seethe

burzgu/lis *nm* bubble; ~ļi spray; bubbles

burzguļains *adj* bubbly, frothy

burzguļot *vi* (of running water) bubble; seethe

burzīgs *adj* easily wrinkled, easily crumpled

burzīt *vt* finger; crumple

burzīties *vr* crumple

burzma *nf* = **burza**

burzmains *adj* crowded

burznis *nm* (reg.) throng

burzulis *nm* (col.) crowd, throng

burzums *nm* (col.) crowd, throng

burža *nf* (reg., zool.) perch

buržuā *nm indecl* bourgeois

buržu[a]zija [ā] *nf* bourgeoisie

buržu[a]ziski [ā] *adv* in a bourgeois fashion

buržu[a]zisks [ā] *adj* bourgeois

buržu[a]zisms [ā] *nm* bourgeois world view

buržujiski *adv* (cont.) in a bourgeois fashion

buržujisks *adj* (cont.) bourgeois

buržujs *nm* (cont.) bourgeois

būs- *fut* stem of **būt**, *2nd & 3rd pers sg, pl* **lūdzu, te būs!** here you are! **būsim !** let us be ! **tev nebūs** (+ *inf*) thou shalt not; **nekā nebūs!** nothing doing!

busengoltija *nf* Madeira vine

busido *indecl nm* bushido

busole *nf* surveyor's compass; (mil.) aiming circle

buss *nm* (col.) bus

būsters *nm* (tech.) booster

būšan/a *nf* 1. being, existence; 2. matter; **kas tā par ~u?** what is going on? **nedzirdēta b.** that's unheard of! **sasodīta b.!** what a mess! nasty busi-ness!

bušbēbijs *nm* bush baby

bušelis *nm* bushel

bušlats *nm* pea jacket

bušmen/is *nm*, ~**iete** *nf* Bushman

būšot *fut subj* of **būt**; **viņš b.** it is said that he will be; (*fut act part*) being

būšu *fut* of **būt**, *1st pers sg* I will

būt *vi irr* 1. be; **b. vai nebūt** to be or not to be; sink or swim; **b. par** (with *acc*) be, play the role of; 2. (with *dat*, to possess, keep; as auxiliary verb in perfect tenses) have

butadiēns *nm* butadiene

butaforija *nf* stage property; mock-up

butaforisks *adj* false, false-front

butafors *nm* (theat.) property man

butānietis *nm*, ~**iete** *nf* Bhutanese

butanols *nm* butanol

butāns *nm* butane

bute *nf* = **plekste**

būte *nf* (poet.) being, existence

butele *nf* (barb.) bottle

butenklīveris *nm* (naut.) flying jib

būtīb/a *nf* essence; heart of a matter; **pēc ~as** in essence; **~ā** in essence

butiks *nm* boutique

butilacetāts *nm* butyl acetate

butilēns *nm* butylene

butilēteris *nm* butyl ether

butils *nm* butyl

butīns *nm* butyne

butirometrs *nm* butyrometer

būtiskais *nom adj* essence

būtiski *adv* essentially

būtisks *adj* essential; vital; substantive

būtiskums *nm* essentiality

būtne *nf* (existence; creature) being

būtu *cond, deb* of **būt** were, would be, would have, would have to; **lai nu tas tā b.** be it as it may; **lai b.!** all right! agreed! **lai b. kā būdams** be it as it may

būvakmens *nm* building stone

būvamatniecība *nf* carpentry

būvamatnie/ks *nm*, **~ce** *nf* carpenter

būvaprēēins *nm* building cost estimate

buvardija *nf* bouvardia

būvarodi *nm pl* building trades

būvatļauja *nf* building permit

būvbaļēis *nm* (wooden) beam

būvbedre *nf* foundation pit

būvbrigāde *nf* construction crew

būvbrig[a]dier/is [ā] *nm*, **~e** *nf* foreman of a construction crew

būvceļš *nm* construction road

būvdarbi *nm pl* construction, construction project

būvdetaļa *nf* structural detail

būv/e *nf* **1.** structure; building; **2.** construction; **(strādāt) uz ~ēm** (be employed) as a construction worker

būvējams *adj, part* of **būvēt** under construction

būvelements *nm* structural detail

būves līnija *nf* building line

būvēt *vt* build, construct

būvētāj/s *nm*, **~a** *nf* builder

būvētava *nf* shops of a construction firm

būvēties *vr* build for one's own needs

būvgaldniecība *nf* joinery

būvgaldnieks *nm* building joiner

būvgrāvis *nm* trench

būvgrunts *nf* construction site

būvgruži *nm pl* construction debris

būvģipsis *nm* structural plaster

būviecirknis *nm* (building) lot

būvindustrija *nf* construction industry

būvinspektors *nm* building inspector, construction inspector

būvinženier/is *nm*, **~e** *nf* civil engineer

būvinženier[r]zinātnes [ŗ] *nf pl* civil engineering

būvjosla *nf* building zone

būvkantoris *nm* builder's office

būvkeramika *nf* ceramic building materials, structural ceramics

būvklaušas *nf pl* statute construction labor

būvkoki *nm pl* construction lumber; **ēvelēti b.** dressed lumber

būvkonstrukcija *nf* construction; load-bearing parts of a structure

būvkrāns *nm* construction crane

būvēermenis *nm* building

būvlaukums *nm* building site

būvlikumi *nm pl* building laws

būvmateriāls *nm* building material

būvme[cha]nika [hā] *nf* theory of structures

būvmeistars *nm* master builder

būvmets *nm* architect's sketch

būvniecība *nf* building, construction

būvnoteikumi *nm pl* building code

būvobjekts *nm* building under construction

būvorganizācija *nf* building enterprise

būvpamatne *nf* foundation

būvprojekts *nm* building project, construction project

būvrevident/s *nm*, ~**e** *nf* building inspector, construction inspector

būvsezona *nf* building season

būvstatiēis *nm* structure stress analyst

būvstrādnie/ks *nm*, ~**ce** *nf* construction worker

būvsumma *nf* cost of construction

būvtechniē/is *nm*, ~**e** *nf* construction foreman

būvtraktors *nm* construction tractor

būvuzņēmēj/s *nm*, ~**a** *nf* building contractor

būvuzņēmums *nm* construction firm

būvuzraudzība *nf* inspection of construction sites

būvvadītāj/s *nm*, ~**a** *nf* construction supervisor

būvvalde *nf* city engineering department

būvvieta *nf* building site

būvžogs *nm* hoarding

buzelis *nm* (col.) sourpuss

būzelis *nm* person with shaggy hair

buzis *nm* (col.) sourpuss

bužēt *vt* perform a bouginage

bužī *indecl nf* bougie

bužināt *vt* **1.** ruffle, tousle; **2.** fluff up; (of hair) tease

bužināties *vr* ruffle, tousle

C

cabu/lis *nm* **1.** (col.) chick; **2.** ~**ļi** (child.) legs

cabulītis *nm dim* of **cabulis**; chick; term of endearment for little children

cadra josta *nf* sash, girdle

cainis *nm* (hist.) hoist (used by beekeepers)

caka *nf* pointed fringe

cālēns *nm* chick

cālis *nm* **1.** chick; **beigts c.** (col., fig.) dead duck; **2.** (sl.) D grade

cālītis *nm dim* of **cālis**, (as term of endearment) chuck; chick

cāls *nm* (obs.) a count of 360

cāļagalvas *nf pl* globeflower

cāļu vanags *nm* chicken hawk

cangas *nf pl* (col.) tongs, pliers

capatas *nf pl* **1.** old, worn out clothes or shoes; **2.** crumbs

caponlaka *nf* zapon

caputmortuums *nm* calcothar

carēvičs *nm* czarevitch

cariene *nf* czarina

carisks *adj* czarist

carisms *nm* czarism

cariste *nf* czardom

car/s *nm* czar; ~**a dēls** czarevitch; ~**a meita** czarevna

cauna *nf* sable, marten

caunāda *nf* sable fur

caunene *nf* sable fur cap

caur *prep* through; **c. un ~i** (or **c. ~im**) through and through

caurais *nom adj* = **cauras**

cauras *nf pl* stitches of pain in the sides

caurasiņot *vt* supply with blood

cauraudzis *adj* (of meat) marbled

cauraugušā glīvene *nf* clasping-leaved pondweed

caurauklots *adj* laced

cauraust *vt* interweave

caurbira *nf, nm* **1.** sievings, riddlings; ~**s miegs** restless sleep; **2.** also ~**u maiss** insatiable person; **3.** profligate; **4.** loser in an election

caurbiris *nm* insatiable person

caurbraucams *adj* passable

caurbraucēj/s *nm*, ~**a** *nf* through passenger, transient

caurbraukt *vi* pass through

caurbraukšana *nf* passing through; **c. aizliegta** no through traffic

caurbrauktuve *nf* through passage

caurcaurēm *adv* (col.) thoroughly, through and through

caurceļotāj/s *nm*, **~a** *nf* transient; visitant; passage migrant; (of fish) anadromous

caurdancis *nm* a Latvian folk dance

caurdegums *nm* burn hole

caurdeva *nf* throughput

caurdures *nf pl* stitches of pain in the sides

caurduris *nm* colander

caurduršana *nf* perforation

caurduṛu *indecl adj* push-through

caurduṛu atslēga *nf* (obs.) padlock

caure *nf* pipe, tube

caureja *nf* diarrhea; **~s līdzeklis** purgative

caurejams *adj* passable

caurējs *adj* hollow

caurēm *adv emph* of **caur** or **cauri**

caurgaismīgs *adj* translucent

caurgaita *nf* passage; **~s laiks** (tech.) time of passage

caurgājība *nf* (of vehicles) traction; (of terrain) trafficability

caurgājiens *nm* passage through, run

caurgalis *nm* glutton

cauri *adv, prep* 1. through; 2. out of; over, finished

caurim *adv emph* of **caur**, through and through

caurkaklis *nm* (col.) drunk

caurkomponēts *nm* through-component

caurkrišana *nf* failure; fiasco; flop

caurlaide *nf* 1. capacity (for processing); **augst-frekvences ~s filtrs** high-pass filter; **~s spēja** (communications) throughput; **zemfrekvences ~s filtrs** low-pass filter; 2. pass; 3. (rare.) password

caurlaidība *nf* permeability, perviousness; translucence

caurlaidīgs *adj* permeable, pervious; translucent; **daḷēji c.** semipermeable

caurlaidīgums *nm* permeability; translucence

caurlaidspēja *nf* traffic carrying capacity; discharge capacity

caurlaists *adj* filtered

caurlaušana *nf* (mil.) penetration

caurloza *nf* = **caurdancis**

caurlūkošana *nf* = **caurskate**

caurmēra *adj* average

caurmērs *nm* 1. diameter; 2. average; **~ā** on the average

caurmiegs *nm* restless, fretful sleep

caurplūde *nf* flow, discharge; transfer

caurplūdes krāsns *nf* pusher-type furnace

caurprojekcija *nf* rear projection

caurpūte *nf* (of internal combustion engines) scavenging

caurpūtes vārsts *nm* scavenging valve

caurraksts *nm* copy

caurredzamība *nf* transparency

caurredzams *adj* transparent

caur/s *adj* 1. holey; hollow; (of sleep, col.) restless, fretful; (of bowels) loose; **ar ~u vidu** hollow; **c. kā siets** riddled like a sieve; 2. **~u** (of a time period) the whole

caursalšana *nf* freezing through

caursāpju zāles *nf pl* milk thistle

caursišana *nf* driving through, penetration; holing, punching, puncturing

caursite *nf* puncture

caursites spriegums *nm* puncture voltage

caursitnis *nm* mandrel

caursitspēja *nf* (mil.) piercing capability

caurskatāmība *nf* transparency

caurskatāms *adj, part* of **caurskatīt** 1. to be examined; 2. transparent

caurskate *nf* 1. examination; revision; 2. preview; review; 3. public hearing; 4. X-raying

caurskatis *nm* viewfinder; vision slit

caurskatīšana *nf* 1. examination; 2. revision; 3. preview; 4. public hearing; 5. X-raying

caurskatīt *vt* **1.** examine; revise; **2.** review; preview; **3.** X-ray

caurslēdzams *adj* lockable from both sides

caurspīde *nf* transparency

caurspīdība *nf* transparency

caurspīdīgi *adv* transparently

caurspīdīgs *adj* transparen

caurspīdīgums *nm* transparency

caurspiedīgs *adj* penetrating

caurspiednis *nm* broach

caurstaigājams *adj* traversable; (of rooms) connecting

caurstarot *vt* X~ray

caurstrāvot *vt* permeate, pervade, penetrate

caursūknēšanās *nfr* percolation

cauršauts *adj* shot through

cauršāvums *nm* bullet hole, shell hole

cauršūts *adj* sewn through

caurtece *nf* **1.** rate of flow; **2.** channel

caurteces daudzums *nm* (hydr.) discharge

caurteces dīķis *nm* running-water pond

caurteka *nf* **1.** culvert; **2.** channel

caurule *nf* pipe, tube

caurulīte *nf dim* of **caurule**, small pipe

cauruļatslēdznieks *nm* pipe fitter

cauruļatslēga *nf* pipe wrench

cauruļgrieznis *nm* pipe cutter

cauruļkatls *nm* tubular boiler

cauruļklupe *nf* pipe thread cutter

cauruļknaibles *nf pl* pipe wrench

cauruļlicējs *nm* pipelayer

cauruļpālis *nm* hollow pile

cauruļpasts *nm* pneumatic dispatch

cauruļu rūpnīca *nf* pipe rolling mill

cauruļu skrūvspīles *nf pl* pipe vise

cauruļu uzmava *nf* sleeve coupling

cauruļvads *nm* **1.** pipeline; **2.** conduit line

cauruļveida *indecl adj* tubular

cauruļveidīgs *adj* tubular

caurumains *adj* holey

caurumot *vt* perforate, punch holes

caurumotājs *nm* hole punch, perforator

caurumpiepes *nf pl* bracket fungi

caurums *nm* **1.** hole; **2.** port

caurumsitis *nm* hole punch; mandrel

caurumzāģis *nm* keyhole saw

caururbjoši *adv* penetratingly; piercingly

caururbjošs *adj* penetrating; piercing

caururbšana *nf* (of small arms) penetration

caururbt *vt* perforate; (fig.) pierce

caurvadība *nf* conductivity

caurvadītājs *nm* (tech.) conductor

caurvads *nm* wall bushing

caurvējains *adj* drafty

caurvējš *nm* (breeze) draft

caurviju attīstība *nf* (mus.) thematic development

caurvīts *adj* intertwined with

caušneras *nf pl* zauschnerias

ceanots *nm* redroot

cece muša *nf* tsetse fly

cecere *nf* cockscomb

ceceris *nm* **1.** a withered person or animal; **2.** tree stump with roots

ce|ch|īns [h] *nm* (hist. coin) sequin

ce|ch|/s [h] *nm* (of a factory) department, shop; ~**a priekšnieks** shop foreman

ce|ch|šteins [h] *nm* Zechstein

cedele *nf* (barb.) label

cedents *nm* cedent

cedēt *vt* (bus.) assign, transfer

cedri *nm pl* (reg.) heather

cedriens *nm* (reg.) heath

cedriņi *nm pl* (reg.) heather

cedrons *nm* citron

cefalantera *nf* helleborine

cefalarija *nf* scabious

cefalopods *nm* cephalopod

cefeīda *nf* Cepheid variable

cegums *nm* forelock; mane

ceguna *nf* = **cegums**

ceguns *nm* = **cegums**

ceh- See **cech-**

ceiloniet/is *nm*, ~**e** *nf* Ceylonese

ceimuri *nm pl* Cladonia lichens

ceipa *nf* (reg.) tuft of hair

ceitnots *nm* (chess) running out of time

cekins *nm* (hist. coin) sequin

cekoties *vr* (reg.) fight

cekulainais cīrulis *nm* = **cekulcīrulis**

cekulainais dūkuris *nm* = **cekuldūkuris**

cekulainā nira *nf* = **cekulpīle**

cekulainā ziepenīte *nf* a milkwort, Polygala comosa

cekulainā zīlīte *nf* = **cekulzīlīte**

cekulains *adj* tufted, crested

cekula pīle *nf* = **cekulpīle**

cekulcīrulis *nm* crested lark

cekuldūkuris *nm* great crested grebe

cekuliņi *nm pl* ajuga

cekulmuntēaks *nm* muntjack

cekulotie nārbuļi *nm pl* crested cowwheat

cekulots *adj* tufted, crested

cekulpīle *nf* tufted duck

cekuls *nm* **1.** crest (of an animal; also of a weir); **2.** (of hair) tuft

cekulzīlīte *nf* crested tit

cekulzīriņš *nm* Sandwich tern

cekumi *nm pl* (reg.) pitchfork

cekūna *nf* **1.** crest; **2.** (of hair) tuft

celadons *nm* celadon

celaine *nf* sash, girdle

cēlais *nom adj* the sublime

cēlāj/s *nm*, **~a** *nf* **1.** builder; **2.** (tech.) lifter, digger, remover; **3.** (col.) thief

celastri *nm pl* Celastrus

cēlēj/s *nm*, **~a** *nf* **1.** builder; **2.** (usu. with noun in genitive) originator, raiser; **3.** ferryman

cēlējspēks *nm* (tech.) lift force, (in water) buyoant force; uplift

celestīns *nm* celestite

cēlfinieris *nm* precious veneer

cēlgāze *nf* inert gas

cēli *adv* **1.** nobly, loftily, sublimely; **2.** in a stately, dignified fashion

cēlības *nf pl* **1.** lifting (of a person to honor him or her); **2.** the blessing of a new building; **3.** (hist.) unloading (of a newcomer's belongings on the annual moving day); **4.** recompense for helping to right a toppled wagon; **5.** finder's fee

celibāts *nm* celibacy

cēlieniņš *nm dim* of **cēliens**

cēliens *nm* **1.** lift, lifting; **2.** (time) period (one of the four traditional divisions of the day or night); **3.** (theat.) act

cēlināt *vt* (tech.) ennoble

celiņš *nm* **1.** *dim* of **ceļš**; **2.** footpath; **3.** (of hair) part; **4.** runner (rug); **5.** swimming lane

ce/lis *nm* knee; **līdz ~ļiem** up to one's knees, knee-deep

celīte *nf* **1.** (of hair) parting; **2.** (col.) footpath

cēlkoks *nm* high-grade hardwood tree

cēlkoksne *nf* high-grade hardwood

celksnis *nm* found object

celle *nf* (monastic) cell

ce[ll]obioze [l] *nf* cellobiose

ce[ll]of[a]ns [l][ā] *nm* cellophane

ce[ll]olignīns [l] *nm* lignocellulose

ce[ll]osolvs [l] *nm* Cellosolve

ce[ll]ulārs [l] *adj* cellular

ce[ll]ulāze [l] *nf* cellulase

ce[ll]ulīts [l] *nm* cellulitis

ce[ll]uloīds [l] *nm* celluloid

ce[ll]uloza [l] *nf* cellulose

celmaine *nf* clear-cut area

celmainība *nf* stumpiness

celmainis *nm* clear-cut area

celmains *adj* full of stumps, stumpy

celmainums *nm* stumpiness

celmājs *nm* clear-cut area

celmene *nf* honey mushroom

cēlmet[all]s [āl] *nm* precious metal

celmgals *nm* butt end

celmiens *nm* clear-cut area

celminieks *nm* grubber

celmiņš *nm* **1.** *dim* of **celms**, little stump; **2.** (hort.) stock stump

celmlauz/is *nm*, **~e** *nf* grubber; (fig.) pioneer, trailblazer

celmoksne *nf* clear-cut area

celmots *adj* full of tree stumps

celm/s *nm* **1.** stump; **uz ~a** (sale of) standing timber; **2.** (ling.) stem

celmu laušana *nf* grubbing; stump extraction

celmu mušas *nf pl* robber flies

celmu nauda *nf* price of standing timber

celobioze *nf* = **cellobioze**

celofāns *nm* = **cellofans**

celogīne *nf* coelogyne

celoglossas *nf pl* Coeloglossum

celolignīns *nm* = **cellolignīns**

cēlonība *nf* causality

cēlonības ēēde *nf* causal sequence

cēlonis *nm* cause

cēloniski *adv* causally

cēlonisks *adj* causal

cēloņsakarība *nf* cause-effect relationship

cēloņsakarīgi *adv* causally

cēloņsakarīgs *adj* causally related

celostats *nm* heliostat

celozija *nf* coxcomb

cēlprātība *nf* noble-mindedness

cēlprātīgs *adj* noble-minded

cels *nm* shuttle (for hand-weaving belts, garters)

cēls *adj* **1.** noble, lofty, sublime; **2.** stately, dignified

Celsija skala *nf* Celsius (temperature) scale

cēlsirdība *nf* magnanimity, nobility

cēlsirdīgi *adv* magnanimously

cēlsirdīgs *adj* magnanimous, noble

cēlsirdīgums *nm* magnanimity, nobility

cēlsird/is *nm*, **~e** *nf* magnanimous person

celsme *nf* (poet.) **1.** building; **2.** edification

celsmīgs *adj* edifying

celšana *nf* **1.** lifting, raising, hoisting; **2.** building, erection, construction

celšanās *nfr* rising; (of prices) rise; (of value) appreciation

celšus *adv emph* of **celt**; **c. cēla** they built diligently; they lifted mightily

celt *vt* **1.** lift, raise; hoist; **c. augšā** a. pick up, lift; b. waken, rouse; **c. cepuri** raise one's hat; **c. debesīs** (col.) extoll, praise to high heaven; **c. augstu degunu** (col.) put on airs; **c. gaismā** bring to light; **c. galdā** put on the table; **necelt kāju (kāda mājā)** (col.) not to set one's foot (inside s.o.'s house); **necelt ne ausis** (col.) ignore; **c. negodu** malign; **c. priekšā** a. (of food) serve; b. present, propose; **c. spalvu** raise the hackles; **c. seksti** (or **spuras**) **gaisā** get mad; **c. zirgā** lift into the saddle; **2.** waken, rouse; **3.** ferry; **4.** build, erect, construct; **c. gaisa pilis** build castles in the air; **5.** improve, perfect; **6.** start, trigger, cause; engender; **c. naidu** cause hate, cause enmity; **c. neslavu** defame, slander; **c. pra-sību** file a claim; **c. sūdzību** file a complaint, bring action; **c. traci** kick up a row; **c. trauk-smi** sound the alarm; **7.** honor; **c. godā** a. honor; b. revive, reinstate; **c. padebešos** (or **vai de-besīs**) praise to high heaven; **8.** appoint; **9.** (vol-leyball) set up

celtava *nf* ferry

celtavnieks *nm* = **celtuvnieks**

cēltērauds *nm* refined steel

celties *vr* **1.** rise; **c. (kāda) acīs** rise in s.o.'s estimation; **c. augšā** get up; **c. kājās** (or **stāvus**) rise to one's feet, stand up; **c. mantā** (or **naudā**) acquire wealth; **mati ceļas stāvus** (one's) hair is standing on end; **roka neceļas** I can't bring my-self (to do sth.); **2.** (with **uz**, **pāri**) cross, ferry; **3.** (of wind) spring up, (of a storm) gather; **4.** arise from, spring from

celtne *nf* building

celtniecība *nf* **1.** building, construction; **2.** architecture celtnieciski *adv* architecturally

celtniecisks *adj* 1. pertaining to construction; 2. architectural

celtnie/ks *nm,* ~ce *nf* 1. builder; 2. architect

celtnis *nm* 1. crane, hoist, derrick; 2. elevator

celtspēja *nf* lifting capacity

celtuve *nf* 1. ferry landing; 2. ferry

celtuvis *nm* elevator

celtuvnieks *nm* ferryman

celulārs *adj* = cellulārs

celulāze *nf* = cellulāze

celulīts *nm* = cellulīts

celuloids *nm* = celluloīds

celuloze *nf* = celluloza

cēlums I *nm* lift

cēlums II *nm* 1. nobility, loftiness, sublimity; 2. stateliness, dignity; 3. origin

celzijas *nf pl* Celsia

ceļabiedr/s *nm,* ~e *nf* travel companion; fellow passenger

ceļa bruņas *nf pl* genouilliere

ceļagājējs *nm* traveler, wayfarer

ceļa jūt/is *nf pl* crossroads; c. ~īs a. ready to go, on the start; b. at a crossroads

ceļakāj/a *nf* stirrup cup ◊ uz ~u one for the road

ceļalapas *nf pl* plantain

ceļa locītava *nf* knee joint

ceļamaize *nf* provender for the road

ceļamalks *nm* stirrup cup

ceļamkrāns *nm* crane, hoist, derrick

ceļamoliņš *nm* sweet clover

ceļamskrūve *nf* foot screw

ceļa nauda *nf* travel funds

ceļa nomale *nf* shoulder (of a road)

ceļa palocīšana *nf* genuflection

ceļa piezīmes *nf pl* travel notes

ceļa platums *nm* (RR) gage

ceļa rādītājs *nm* signpost, fingerpost

ceļa skriemelis *nm* kneecap

ceļasoma *nf* traveling bag

ceļa sprosts *nm* roadblock

ceļa staipekņi *nm pl* cinquefoil

ceļavārdi *nm pl* envoi; send-off; parting words

ceļavārpas *nf pl* plantain

ceļa vējš *nm* fair wind; tailwind

ceļavīrs *nm* (obs.) traveler

ceļazīme *nf* 1. pass; (mil.) trip ticket; 2. waybill; 3. road sign

ceļazvaigzne *nf* (poet.) lodestar

ceļa žodzenes *nf pl* hedge mustard

ceļgājis *nm* traveler, wayfarer

ceļgals *nm* kneecap

ceļinie/ks *nm,* ~ce *nf* traveler, wayfarer

ceļkrusti *nm pl* crossroads

ceļlauzis *nm* pathfinder

ceļmal/a *nf* roadside, wayside; ~ā by the roadside

ceļmale *nf* (of a road) shoulder

ceļmalīte *nf* plantain

ceļmallapas *nf pl* plantain

ceļmalu kaulu roze *nf* cheeseflower

ceļojošs *adj, part* of **ceļot** traveling, itinerant, (of actors, musicians, hist.) strolling; (of trophies) challenge

ceļojums *nm* journey, trip, voyage; **ārzemju** c. trip abroad; c. **kājām** walking tour, hike

ceļojumu birojs *nm* travel agency

ceļot *vi* travel

ceļotājputns *nm* migratory bird

ceļotājs *nm,* ~a *nf* traveler, voyager

ceļotājs aģents *nm* traveling agent

ceļotājspāre *nf* migratory dragonfly

ceļotāju koks *nm* traveler's-tree

ceļrādis *nm* signpost

ceļ/š *nm* 1. road; way; route; (RR) track; **apbrau-camais** c. (RR) bypass siding; **apdzīšanas** c. (RR) passing track; **blakus** c. sideroad; service road; **braucamais** c. a. public road; b. rural road; **brīvs** c. open road, clear passage; **brīva** ~a sig- **nāls** (RR) proceed signal; **caurejamais** c. thoroughfare; **garais** c. (checkerboard) double corner; **gluds c.** (fig.) smooth sailing; **iemīts c.** trodden path; **īsākais c.** shortest route, shortcut; **jā-jamais c.** bridle path; **tāls c.** long way ◊ ~**ā** on one's way; **(trīs dienas)** ~**ā** (three days) on the road; the trip took three days; ~**ā uz** on the way to; ~**ā, ~ā!** all aboard! **c. brīvs!** all clear! **c. zem kājām** road ahead, about to take to the road; **nost no** ~**a!** out of the way! **pa** ~**am** a. on the way, en route; b. **(tev ar mums) pa** ~**am** (you are going) our way; **mums viens c.** we are going the same way; **uz pareizā** ~**a** on the right track; **pa kuru** ~**u?** which way? **laimīgu** ~**u!** have a good trip! **labu** ~**a vēju!** bon voyage! **2.** ~**ā** in a . . . way, taking the . . . route; **likumīgā** ~**ā** legally; **netiešā** ~**ā** indirectly, in a roundabout way; **taisnā** ~**ā** directly

celteka *nf* plantain

ceļu departaments *nm* highway department

ceļu grupa *nf* (RR) yard

ceļu klaušas *nf pl* statute labor on roads

ceļu savienojums *nm* crossover

ceļved/is *nm* **1.** guide; ~**e** *nf*; **2.** guide book

ceļvieta *nf* ford

cementa duļķis *nm* cement slurry

cementēt *vt* cement

cementfabrika *nf* cement plant

cementīts *nm* cementite

cements *nm* cement

cemere *nf* water parsnip

cemeriņš *nm* hellebore

cemme *nf* **1.** (mech.) staple; **2.** (col.) anger, resentment

cemmēties *vr* (col.) be angry

cemmīgs *adj* (col.) mad

cemur- See **čemur-**

cen/a *nf* price; **augstā** ~**ā** high-priced; **augstākā c.** top price ◊ **par katru** ~**u** at any price; definitely

cencele *nf* (reg.) thigh

cenkurs *nm* (reg.) cluster

cenoģen[e]ze [ē] *nf* cenogenesis

cenot *vt* price

cenotājs *nm*, ~**a** *nf* pricer

cenoze *nf* biocenosis, biotic community

cenrādis *nm* price list

censība *nf* (obs.) diligence

censīgi *adv* (obs.) diligently

censīgs *adj* (obs.) diligent

censlis *nm* eager beaver, career person

censme *nf* diligence

censonība *nf* endeavor

censonis *nm* striver

censties *vr* endeavor, try; strive; **c. pēc (kā)** seek; **c. līdz** try to keep up with

censulis *nm* striver

centība *nf* diligence

centibārs *nm* centibar

centiens *nm* endeavor

centīgi *adv* diligently

centīgs *adj* diligent

centīgums *nm* diligence

centifolija *nf* centifolia rose

centigrams *nm* centigram

centilitrs *nm* centiliter

centiļons *nm* centillion

centimetrs *nm* **1.** centimeter; **2.** centimeter ruler or tape

centners *nm* centner

centrālapkure *nf* central heating

centrālcietums *nm* central prison

centrāle *nf* central office, central station; (telephone) exchange

centrāli *adv* centrally

centrālisms *nm* centralism

centr[ā]lizācija [a] *nf* **1.** centralization; **2.** (RR) signal tower

centr[ā]lizēt [a] *vt* centralize

centrālkomiteja *nf* central committee

centrālpadome *nf* central council

centrāls *adj* central

centrante *nf* red valerian

centra uzbrucējs *nm* (soccer) center forward

centrbēdze *nf* centifugal force

centrējums *nm* centering

centrēt *vt* center

centrētība *nf* centeredness

centrif[u]ga [ū] *nf* centrifuge

centrifugāli *adv* centrifugally

centrifugāls *adj* centrifugal

centrifugēt *vt* centrifuge

centripetāli *adv* centripetally

centripetāls *adj* centripetal

centrisks *adj* centrist

centrisms *nm* centrism

centrist/s *nm*, ~e *nf* centrist

centrozoma *nf* centrosome

centrs *nm* center

centrtiece *nf* centripetal force

centrurbis *nm* center bit

centruzsites *indecl adj* (of a detonator) center impact

cents *nm* cent

centūrija *nf* (Roman) century

centurions *nm* centurion

cenu pārvalde *nf* price control board

cenzēt *vt* censor

cenzor/s *nm*, ~e *nf* censor

cenzs *nm* (pol.) qualification; (hist.) census

cenzūra *nf* 1. censorate; 2. censorship

ceolīts *nm* zeolite

cepams *adj, part* of **cept** frying, (of sauces) basting

cepējs *nm*, ~a *nf* frier, roaster, baker

cepelīns *nm* dirigible, airship, zeppelin

cepenis *nm* hot, oppressive weather

cepešbļoda *nf* platter

cepeškrāsns *nf* baking oven

cepešpanna *nf* roasting pan, baking pan

cepe/tis *nm* roast; ~ša tauki drippings

cepiens *nm* (of baked goods) batch

cepin *adv emph* of **cept**; **c. cepa** she cooked up a storm

cepināt *vt* roast

cepināties *vr* 1. (*3rd pers*) be roasted; 2. (fig.) roast

cepīte *nf* fried herring

ceplis *nm* 1. kiln; 2. oven; 3. (of baked goods) batch

ceplīšveidīgie *nm pl* Troglodytidae

ceplītis *nm* 1. wren; 2. *dim* of **ceplis**, little oven; 3. (hist.) firebox (small, open clay firebox used to provide light on the threshing floor)

cepoņa *nf* (col.) heat

cept *vt* fry; roast; grill, broil; bake; **c. uz restēm** broil, grill; **ne ~s, ne vārīts** (col.) neither fish nor fowl

cepties *vr* fry; roast; grill, broil; bake

ceptuve *nf* bakery

cepumi *nm pl* pastry; **drupani c.** shortbread

cepums *nm* baking, quantity baked

cepurains *adj* behatted

cepur/e *nf* hat; cap; **bez ~es** hatless ◊ ~i **kuldams** carefree

cepures jumts *nm* cupola

cepurīte *nf* 1. *dim* of **cepure**, little hat; 2. (of mushrooms) cap, pileus; 3. bluebell; 4. (of medical personnel, food workers) cap

cepurniece *nf* milliner

cepurnieks *nm* hatter

cepurots *adj* behatted

cepu[r]u [r] veikals *nm* hatter's, milliner's

cera *nf* hair, tuft of hair

cerains *adj* 1. branched; 2. matted

ceram/s *adj, part* of **cerēt**; **c., ka** . . . it is to be hoped that . . . , let's hope that . . .; ~ā *f nom adj* the intended

ceras *nf pl* (poet.) 1. awe; 2. a. wrath; b. fervor; 3. hope

ceratijas *nf pl* Ceratium

ceratonija *nf* carob tree

ceratozamijas *nf pl* Ceratozamia

ceratozaurs *nm* ceratosaurus

cerba *nf* (reg.) crest; (of hair) tuft

cerbers *nm* cerberus

cēre *nf* distaff

cereālijas *nf pl* cereals (cereal plants)

cerebrālis *nm* (ling.) cerebral

cerebrāls *adj* cerebral

cerebrospināls *adj* cerebrospinal

cerejs *nm* Cereus

ceremonēties *vr* stand on ceremony

ceremoniāli *adv* ceremonially; ceremoniously

ceremoniālmaršs *nm* ceremonial march

ceremoniāls *nm* ceremonial

ceremoniāls *adj* ceremonial; ceremonious

ceremonij/a *nf* ceremony; **bez~ām** a. informally; b. without mercy

cerene *nf* girl, object of a suitor's attention

cerenieks *nm* hopeful; suitor

ceres *nf pl* (poet.) hope

cerēt *vi* hope; (formally, politely) trust

cerēties *vr* (of two people) hope to get married

cerezīns *nm* refined ozocerite, ceresin

ceri *nm pl* steam bath stones

cerīb/a *nf* hope; expectation; **~ā** in the hope (of)

cerīgi *adv* hopefully

cerīgs *adj* hopeful

c[e]rijs [ē] *nm* cerium

cerīnes *nf pl* lilac

cerīni *nm pl* lilac

cerintes *nf pl* Cerinthe

ceriņi *nm pl* lilac

ceriņkrāsa *nf* lilac (color)

ceriņkrūms *nm* lilac bush

ceriņu kode *nf* lilac leaf miner

ceriņu primula *nf* a primula, Primula malacoides

ceriņu sfinga *nf* hawkmoth

ceriņzars *nm* spray of lilac

ceriņziedi *nm pl* lilac blossoms

cerkste *nf* aching joints, arthritic pain

cērme *nf* ascarid

cermets *nm* cermet

cērmju zāles *nf pl* anthelmintic

cermūkša *nf* mountain ash

ceroplastika *nf* ceroplastics

cerot *vi* (of plants) branch

ceroties *vr* (of plants) branch

cerotīnskābe *nf* cerotic acid

cērpa *nf* mound, hummock

cērpājs *nm* row of hummocks

cērpe *nf* shearing of sheep

cērpiņš *nm dim* of **cērps**, little hummock

cērp/s *nm* mound, hummock ◊ **~a galva** mophead, shaggy-haired person

cers *nm* whisk, tuft; whisk-shaped shrub or plant; plant-covered hump in a swamp

cērtamais paveseris *nm* hot chisel

cērte *nf* adz

certifikāts *nm* certificate, voucher

cērtnis *nm* adz

cērtule *nf* chisel

ceru purvu ķauķis *nm* sedge warbler

ceru neaizmirstule *nf* a forget-me-not, Myosotis caespitosa

cerusīts *nm* cerusite

ceru staipeknis *nm* club moss

ceru vistiņa *nf* moor hen

cerūzis *nm* (col.) shock of hair; shock-head

cērve *nf* distaff

cervikāls *adj* cervical

cesija *nf* (bus.) transfer, assignment, conveyance

cesionār/s *nm*, **~e** *nf* transferee, asignee, grantee

cestodoze *nf* cestodiasis

cetaļa *nf* a cow born on a Thursday

cetāns *nm* cetane

cetināt *vt* incite

ceturksnis *nm* quarter; **akadēmiskais c.** quarter of an hour's grace

ceturkšņa *indecl adj* quarterly

ceturtais *adj* fourth

ceturtdalis *nm* quarto

ceturtdaļa *nf* a fourth

ceturtdaļfināls *nm* quarterfinals

ceturtdaļgadsimts *nm* quarter of a century

ceturtdaļnots *nf* (mus.) quarter note

ceturtdaļpauze *nf* (mus.) quarter rest

ceturtdaļstunda *nf* quarter of an hour

ceturtdien *adv* on Thursday

ceturtdiena *nf* Thursday

ceturtējais *adj* quaternary

ceturtkārt *adv* fourthly, in the fourth place

ceturtnieks *nm* (hist.) a peasant working one-fourth of an **arkls**

cezalp[i]nij/a [ī] *nf* brazilwood

cēzarisms *nm* caesarism

cēzaropapisms *nm* caesaropapism

cēzijs *nm* cesium

cezūra *nf* caesura

[ch]alaza [h] *nf* chalazion

[ch]alcedons [h] *nm* chalcedony

[ch]alkopirīts [h] *nm* chalcopyrite

[ch]alkozīts [h] *nm* chalcocite

[ch]alva [h] *nf* halva

[ch]ameleonisks [h] *adj* chameleonic

[ch]ameleons [h] *nm* chameleon

[ch]amsins [h] *nm* khamsin

[ch]aniste [h] *nf* khanate

[ch]anoss [h] *nm* milkfish

[ch]ans [h] *nm* khan

[ch]anuka [h] *nf* Hanukkah

[ch]aoss [h] *nm* chaos

[ch]aotiski [h] *adv* chaotically

[ch]aotisks [h] *adj* chaotic

[ch]aotiskums [h] *nm* chaoticness

[ch]aritas [h] *nf pl* Graces

[ch]arizma [h] *nf* charisma

[ch]arizmātiķis [h] *nm* charismatic

[ch]arizmātiski [h] *adv* charismatically

[ch]arizmātisks [h] *adj* charismatic

[ch]arta [h] *nf* charter

[ch]aulmograskābe [h] *nf* chaulmoogric acid

[ch]edīvs [h] *nm* khedive

[ch]eiromantija [h] *nf* chiromancy

[ch]eiromants [h] *nm*, ~e *nf* chiromancer

[ch]elicerāti [h] *nm pl* Chelicerata

[ch]elidonīns [h] *nm* chelidonine

[ch]emiluminiscence [h] *nf* chemiluminiscence

[ch]emosint[e]ze [h][ē] *nf* chemosynthesis

[ch]emosorbcija [h] *nf* chemisorption

[ch]emotaksija [h] *nf* chemotaxis

[ch]emoterapija [h] *nf* chemotherapy

[ch]emotropisms [h] *nm* chemotropism

[ch]enomele [h] *nf* flowering quince

[ch]erubs [h] *nm* cherub

[ch]i [h] *indecl nm* chi

[ch]iasma [h] *nf* chiasma

[ch]iasms [h] *nm* chiasmus

[ch]iastolits [h] *nm* chiastolite

[ch]i [h] kvadrāts *nm* (stat.) chi square

[ch]iliarchs [h] *nm* chiliarch

[ch]iliasms [h] *nm* chiliasm

[ch]ilopods [h] *nm* chilopod

[ch]ilus [h] *nm* chyle

[ch]im[e]ra [h][ē] *nf* chimera

[ch]im[e]risks [h][ē] *adj* chimerical

[ch]imozīns [h] *nm* rennin

[ch]inaldins [h] *nm* quinaldine

[ch]inas [h] miza *nf* cinchona bark

[ch]inas [h] skābe *nf* quinic acid

[ch]inhidrons [h] *nm* quinhydrone

[ch]inīna [h] koks *nm* genus Cinchona tree

[ch]inīns [h] *nm* quinine

[ch]inolils [h] *nm* quinolyl

[ch]inolīnijs [h] *nm* quinolinium

[ch]inolīns [h] *nm* quinoline

[ch]inons [h] *nm* quinone

[ch]inskābe [h] *nf* quinic acid

[ch]ionodoksas [h] *nf pl* chionodoxa

[ch]iralitāte [h] *nf* chirality

[ch]irāls [h] *adj* chiral

[ch]irogr[a]fs [h][ā] *nm* chirograph

[ch]iromantija [h] *nf* chiromancy

[ch]iromants [h] *nm* chiromancer

[ch]ironomija [h] *nf* chironomy

[ch]iropodija [h] *nf* chiropody, podiatry

|ch|iropods |h| *nm*, ~e *nf* chiropodist, podiatrist

|ch|irotonija |h| *nf* chirotony

|ch|irur/gs |h| *nm*, ~ġe *nf* surgeon

|ch|irurġija |h| *nf* surgery

|ch|irurġiski |h| *adv* surgically

|ch|irurġisks |h| *adj* surgical

|ch|itīns |h| *nm* chitin

|ch|itons |h| *nm* chiton

|ch|itozamins |h| *nm* chitosamine

|ch|lamida |h| *nf* chlamys

|ch|lamīdija |h| *nf* Chlamydia

|ch|listi |h| *nm pl* (rel., hist.) khlysty

|ch|loasma |h| *nf* chloasma, liver spots

|ch|loracetonfenons |h| *nm* chloracetophenone

|ch|lorālhidrāts |h| *nm* chloral hydrate

|ch|lorāls |h| *adj* chloral

|ch|loramīns |h| *nm* chloramine

|ch|loranīls |h| *nm* chloranil

|ch|lorapskābe |h| *nf* hypochlorous acid

|ch|lorāts |h| *nm* chlorate

|ch|lorazīds |h| *nm* chlorazide

|ch|lorbromsudrabs |h| *nm* silver chlorbromide

|ch|lorella |h| *nf* chlorella

|ch|lorēšana |h| *nf* chlorination

|ch|lorēt |h| *vt* chlorinate

|ch|lorētājs |h| *nm* chlorinator

|ch|loretīls |h| *nm* chloroethyl

|ch|lorciāns |h| *nm* cyanogen chloride

|ch|loretiķskābe |h| *nf* chloracetic acid

|ch|lorhidrins |h| *nm* chlorohydrin

|ch|lor|i|ds |h||ī| *nm* chloride

|ch|lorinēt |h| *vt* chlorinate

|ch|lorīts |h| *nm* chlorite

|ch|lorkaļķis |h| *nm* calcium chloride

|ch|lormetilēšana |h| *nf* chloromethylation

|ch|lorofilaze |h| *nf* chlorophylase

|ch|lorofi|ll|s |h||l| *nm* chlorophyll

|ch|loroforas |h| *nf pl* Chlorophora

|ch|loroformēt |h| *vt* chloroform

|ch|loroforms |h| *nm* chloroform

|ch|lorometrija |h| *nf* chlorometry

|ch|loromicetīns |h| *nm* Chloromycetin

|ch|loroms |h| *nm* chloroma

|ch|loroplasts |h| *nm* chloroplast

|ch|loroprēns |h| *nm* chloroprene

|ch|loroze |h| *nf* chlorosis

|ch|lorpārskābe |h| *nf* chloric acid

|ch|lorpaskābe |h| *nf* chlorous acid

|ch|lorpikrīns |h| *nm* chloropicrin

|ch|lors |h| *nm* chlorine

|ch|lorskābe |h| *nf* hydrochloric acid

|ch|lorsudrabs |h| *nm* silver chloride

|ch|lorūdens |h| *nm* chloric water

|ch|lorūdeņradis |h| *nm* hydrogen chloride

|ch|lorzelta |h| skābe *nf* chlorauric acid

|ch|lorzelts |h| *nm* gold chloride

|ch|oāna |h| *nf* choana

|ch|olagoga |h| *nf* cholagogue

|ch|olangīts |h| *nm* cholangitis

|ch|olantrēns |h| *nm* cholanthrene

|ch|olecistīts |h| *nm* cholecystitis

|ch|olekalciferols |h| *nm* cholecalciferol

|ch|olelitiāze |h| *nf* cholelithiasis

|ch|olemija |h| *nf* cholemia

|ch|ol|e|ra |h||ē| *nf* cholera

|ch|ol|e|riķis |h||ē| *nm* choleric

|ch|ol|e|riski |h||ē| *adv* cholerically

|ch|ol|e|risks |h||ē| *adj* choleric

|ch|olesteatoms |h| *nm* cholesteatoma

|ch|olesterīns |h| *nm* cholesterol

|ch|olīns |h| *nm* choline

|ch|olskābe |h| *nf* cholic acid

|ch|ondrila |h| *nf* gum succory

|ch|ondrīns |h| *nm* chondrin

|ch|ondrīts |h| *nm* 1. chondrite; 2. chondritis

|ch|ondrodistrofija |h| *nf* achondroplasia

|ch|ondrodīts |h| *nm* chondrodite

|ch|ondroloġija |h| *nf* chrondrology

|ch|ondroms |h| *nm* chondroma

|ch|ondroze |h| *nf* chondrogenesis

|ch|orda |h| *nf* 1. (geom.) chord; 2. (biol.) noto-
chord

|ch|ordaiņi |h| *nm pl* = chordāti

|ch|ordāti |h| *nm pl* Chordata

|ch|orejs |h| *nm* choreus, trochee

|ch|oreogr|a|fija |h||ā| *nf* choreography

|ch|oreogr|a|fiski |h||ā| *adv* choreographi-
cally

|ch|oreogr|a|fisks |h||ā| *adj* choreographic

|ch|oreogr|a|f/s |h||ā| *nm*, ~e *nf* choreogra-
pher

|ch|oreuts |h| *nm* choreus

|ch|orija |h| *nf* chorea

|ch|orijambs |h| *nm* choriamb

|ch|oriokarcinoma |h| *nf* choriocarcinoma

|ch|oripetāls |h| *adj* choripetalous

|ch|oroloģija |h| *nf* chorology

|ch|oroloģisks |h| *adj* chorologic

|ch|orvātiski |h| *adv* in Croatian

|ch|orvātisks |h| *adj* Croatian

|ch|orvāt/s |h| *nm*, ~iete *nf* Croatian

|ch|restomatija |h| *nf* chrestomathy

|ch|rismons |h| *nm* chrismon, christogram

|ch|ristoloģija |h| *nf* christology

|ch|rizantema |h| *nf* chrysanthemum

|ch|rizēns |h| *nm* chrysene

|ch|rizoberils |h| *nm* chrysoberyl

|ch|rizofīti |h| *nm pl* Chrysophyta

|ch|rizol|i|ts |h||ī| *nm* chrysolite

|ch|rizoprass |h| *nm* chrysoprase

|ch|rizotīls |h| *nm* chrysotile

|ch|romāda |h| *nf* chrome leather

|ch|romafins |h| *adj* chromaffine

|ch|roma |h| krams *nm* chrome chert

|ch|roma |h| oks|i|ds |ī| *nm* chromic oxide

|ch|roma |h| sarkanais *nom adj* chrome red

|ch|romatika |h| *nf* chromatics

|ch|romatīns |h| *nm* chromatin

|ch|romatiski |h| *adv* chromatically

|ch|romatisks |h| *adj* chromatic

|ch|romatiskums |h| *nm* chromaticity

|ch|romatisms |h| *nm* chromaticism

|ch|romatofors |h| *nm* chromatophore

|ch|romatogr|a|fija |h||ā| *nf* chromatogra-
phy

|ch|romāts |h| *nm* chromate

|ch|romēt |h| *vt* chrome

|ch|romīts |h| *nm* chromite

|ch|rommagnēzīts |h| *nm* chromic magnesite

|ch|romofors |h| *nm* chromophore

|ch|romofotogr|a|fija |h||ā| *nf* color pho-
tography

|ch|romogens |h| *adj* chromogenic

|ch|romogr|a|fs |h||ā| *nm* chromograph

|ch|romoksilogr|a|fija |h||ā| *nf* chro-
moxylography

|ch|romolitogr|a|fija |h||ā| *nf* chromoli-
thography

|ch|romoplasts |h| *nm* chromoplast

|ch|romosf|ai|ra |h||ē| *nf* chromosphere

|ch|romoskops |h| *nm* chromoscope

|ch|romosoma |h| *nf* chromosome

|ch|romotipija |h| *nf* color printing

|ch|romotipogr|a|fija |h||ā| *nf* chromoty-
pography

|ch|romotropija |h| *nf* chromotropism

|ch|roms |h| *nm* chrome

|ch|romskābe |h| *nf* chromic acid

|ch|ronika |h| *nf* 1. chronicle; 2. newsreel

|ch|ronikāls |h| *adj* documentary

|ch|roniski |h| *adv* chronically

|ch|ronisks |h| *adj* chronic

|ch|ronist/s |h| *nm*, ~e *nf* chronicler

|ch|ronogr|a|fs |h||ā| *nm* chronograph

|ch|ronoloģija |h| *nf* chronology

|ch|ronoloģiski |h| *adv* chronologically

|ch|ronoloģisks |h| *adj* chronological

|ch|ronometrāža |h| *nf* 1. chronometry;
2. duration; 3. time-and-motion study

|ch|ronometrēt |h| *vt* time

|ch|ronometrs |h| *nm* chronometer

|ch|tonisks |h| *adj* chthonic

ciamelids *nm* cyamelide

cianam|i|ds |ī| *nm* cyanamide

cianāts *nm* cyanate

cianidēšana *nf* cyanide process

cian[i]ds [ī] *nm* cyanide

ci[a]nk[a]lijs [ā][ā] *nm* potassium cyanide

ci[a]nkrāsviela [ā] *nf* cyanine dye

cianometrs *nm* cyanometer

cianotipija *nf* cyanotype, blueprint

cianotisks *adj* cyanotic

cianoze *nf* cyanosis

ci[a]ns [ā] *nm* cyanogen

ci[a]nskābe [ā] *nf* cyanic acid

ci[a]nūdeņradis [ā] *nm* hydrogen cyanide

ciatejas *nf pl* Cyathea

ciba *nf* 1. small linden bast box; 2. chicken

cībants *nm* (col.) bootstrap

cibetkaķis *nm* zibet

cibets *nm* 1. civet; 2. (zool.) zibet

cibināt *vi* 1. peep; 2. (col.) scurry

cibiņa *nf dim* of **ciba**, small linden bast box

cibirkste *nf* (reg.) spark

cibis *nm* (col.) chick

ciborijs *nm* ciborium

cibulis *nm* (col.) chick; (term of endearment)

cicero *indecl nm* (typ.) pica

cicināt *vt* (col.) suckle

cīcītis *nm* (reg.) ladybug

čiči *nm pl* mammae, tits

cidonija *nf* quince; Japanese quince

ciedrs *nm* cedar

ciedru priede *nf* Swiss stone pine

ciedru zīdaste *nf* cedar waxwing

ciekuriņš *nm dim* of **ciekurs**, cone

ciekurītis *nm* 1. *dim* of **ciekurs**, cone; 2. (text.) teasel

ciekurs *nm* = **čiekurs**

ciekurznis *nm* (reg.) cone

cielava *nf* wagtail

cielavenes *nf pl* chickweed

cielaviņa *nf dim* of **cielava**, wagtail

cielavveidīgie *nm pl* Motacillidae

cielēt *vi* (sl.) take a good look

ciemakukulis *nm* gift (usu. edible, given by guest to host or host to guest)

ciemaļa *nf, nm* visitor, guest

ciemamaize *nf* (obs.) gifted food (to a departing guest)

ciematnie/ks *nm*, ~ce *nf* villager

ciemats *nm* hamlet; village, settlement

ciembērns *nm* (of a child) guest, visitor

ciemcilvēks *nm* guest, visitor

ciemene *nf* guest, visitor

ciemiņiene *nf* guest, visitor

ciemiņiete *nf* guest, visitor

ciemiņš *nm* guest, visitor

ciemīte *nf* guest, visitor

ciemkukulis *nm* = **ciemakukulis**

ciemļaudis *nm pl* visitors, guests

ciemmaize *nf* = **ciemakukulis**

ciemmeita *nf* girl, (female from a neighboring farmstead or village)

ciemnieks *nm* guest, visitor

ciemoties *vr* visit, be on a visit, stay

ciempuisis *nm* young man (from a neighboring farmstead or village)

ciem/s *nm* 1. village (consisting of a cluster of farmsteads); ~a iedzīvotājs villager; 2. visit; ~a slota village gossip; aiziet (or braukt) ~ā (or ~os) go and visit

ciemsieva *nf* guest, visitor

ciemvīrs *nm* guest, visitor

cienasts *nm* meal (served to entertain), refreshments

cienāt *vt* entertain with food and drink

cienāties *vr* partake of (as a guest)

cienība *nf* respect, dignity

cienīgā *nom adj* (col.) wife, missus

cienīgais *nom adj* (col.) husband

cienīgmāte *nf* (obs.) wife of **cienīgtēvs**; (in ad-dress) madam

cienīgi *adv* in a dignified manner

cienīgs *adj* 1. worthy, deserving; 2. dignified

cienīgtēvs *nm* **1.** (obs.) minister; **2.** (obs.) title given to a social superior; (in address) sir

cienīgums *nm* dignity; imposing appearance

cienījams *adj, part* of **cienīt** respectable, estimable; **Cienījamais . . .** (in address) Dear . . .

cienīšana *nf* appreciation, fondness

cienīt *vt* respect, esteem; honor; appreciate

cienīt/ais *nom adj* (col.) husband; ~**ā** (col.) wife

cienītāj/s *nm*, ~**a** *nf* respecter; appreciator; (col.) fan, lover

cienīt/s *adj, part* of **cienīt**; **C~ais . . .** (in address, more formal than **cienījamais**) Dear . . .

cienmāte *nf* = **cienīgmāte**

ciens *nm* regard, esteem

cieņ/a *nf* **1.** respect, regard, esteem; **dziļa c.** high esteem; **aiz ~as** out of respect; **būt (lielā) ~ā** be (highly) esteemed, be in demand; **2.** dignity; **3.** meal (served to entertain), refreshments

ciepstēt *vi* chirp

ciept *vi* chirp

cierēt *vi* (barb.) stroll, promenade

ciesa *nf* **1.** bushgrass; **2.** couch grass

ciesains *adj* infested with couch grass

ciest *vt, vi* **1.** suffer; (of damage) sustain; **2.** tolerate; bear, stand; **neva-rēt c.** (col.) hate; **c. badu** starve; **c. klusu** keep silent

ciesties *vr* control oneself; stand, bear

ciešamā kārta *nf* (gram.) passive voice

ciešami *adv* tolerably

ciešams *adj, part* of **ciest 1.** bearable, tolerable; *def* **ciešamais** (gram., of verb voice) passive; **2.** fair, passable

ciešanas *nf pl* suffering

ciešanu laiks *nm* Lent

ciešanu nedēļa *nf* Holy Week

cieši *adv* tightly; closely; firmly; (of being asleep) fast; (of admonishing) urgently

ciešīgs *adj* (col.) frugal

ciešmetrs *nm* stere

cieš/s *adj* **1.** tight; solid; compact; **2.** close; **3.** firm; **4.** (of s.o.'s look) attentive, hard; **5.** tightly woven

cieštilpums *nm* solid volume

ciešul/is *nm*, ~**e** *nf* sufferer

ciet *adv* **1.** shut; **muti c. !** (com.) shut up! **2.** closed; **(deguns ir) c.** (the nose is) stuffed up; **(balss ir) c.** lost (one's voice); **(elpu rauj) c.** (takes one's breath) away; **(ausis krīt) c.** (the noise is) deafening; (my ears are) plugged up; **3.** with verbs signifying to catch, grab, or hold, **ciet** has the same meaning as the verbal prefix **sa-** ; **grābt c.** get hold of, grab; **nu tu esi c.** now I've got you

cietā baravika *nf* king bolete

cietāda *nf* hard leather

cietalva *nf* pewter

cietā pērkonene *nf* a wormseed mustard, Erysimum durum

cietaudzītes *nf pl* (bot.) hawk's beard

ciete *nf* starch

cietējs *nm*, ~**a** *nf* sufferer

cietene *nf* king bolete

cietesaugi *nm pl* starchy plants

cietēšana *nf* hardening

cietēt *vi* harden

cietgalvība *nf* stubborness

cietgalvīgi *adj* stubbornly

cietgalvīgs *adj* stubborn

cietgalv/is *nm*, ~**e** *nf* stubborn person

cietgalvnieks *nm* stubborn person

cietgumija *nf* hard rubber

cieti *adv* **1.** firmly; **2.** solidly

cietība *nf* **1.** hardness, firmness, solidity; **2.** frugality

cietie kvieši *nm pl* durum wheat

cietīgs *adj* **1.** (col.) frugal; **2.** (rare.) patient

cietināt *vt* **1.** harden; **2.** starch

cietinātājs *nm* hardener

cietkausējums *nm* hard alloy

cietkoks *nm* hardwood

cietķermenis *nm* solid

cietķērsa *nf* peppergrass

cietlapains *adj* hard-leaved

cietlapis *nm* hard-leaved evergreen

cietlējums *nm* chilled casting

cietlode *nf* hard solder

cietlodēšana *nf* brazing

cietlodēt *vt* braze

cietmet|all|s |āl| *nm* carbide

cietoksnis *nm* fortress

cietokšņa sods *nm* (hist.) minimum security imprisonment

cietokšņpilsēta *nf* fortress city

cietpaparde *nf* Christmas fern

cietpape *nf* cardboard, boxboard

cietpapīrs *nm* laminated paper

cietpaurains *adj* hard-headed, stubborn; dimwitted

cietpauris *nm* (col.) stubborn person; (col.) dimwit

cietpienes *nf pl* = **cietpieres**

cietpieres *nf pl* hawk's beard

cietpieris *nm* = **cietpauris**

ciets *adj* **1.** hard; firm; (of prices, wages) fixed; (of hair, dough) stiff, wiry; (of character) unbending; (of sleep) sound; (of an egg) hardboiled; (of bowels) constipated; **2.** tight; **3.** solid; **c. ķermenis** (phys.) solid; **4. ~a galva** (mentally) slow

cietsēkles *nf pl* gromwell

cietsirdība *nf* cruelty, hardheartedness

cietsirdīgi *adv* cruelly

cietsirdīgs *adj* cruel, hardhearted

cietsirdīgums *nm* cruelty

cietsirdis *nm* cruel, hardhearted person

cietspārņi *nm pl* Coleoptera, beetles

cietspuru *indecl adj* spiny-finned

cietstāvēšana *nf* no-milking period (period between the time the milking of a cow is stopped and the cow's calving)

cietstāvoša *adj* (of a cow) dry

cietstikls *nm* tempered glass

cietuma biedrs *nm* cellmate

cietuma priekšnieks *nm* warden

cietumpakāpe *nf* degree of hardness

cietumniecība *nf* imprisonment

cietumniecisks *adj* prison

cietumnie/ks *nm*, **~ce** *nf* prisoner

cietums I *nm* prison, jail; **miltārais c.** stockade

cietums *nm* II hardness

cietumsargs *nm* prison guard

cietumsods *nm* prison sentence

cietu/šais *nom adj*, **~sī** *f* victim

cietviela *nf* (phys.) solid

cietvielu fizika *nf* solid state physics

cietzeme *nf* mainland; continent

cigarete *nf* cigarette

cigarills *nm* cigarillo

cigārs *nm* cigar

cigārveida *indecl adj* cigar-shaped

cigārveidīgs *adj* cigar-shaped

cigeika *nf* beaver lamb

cigiņš or **cigliņš** *nm* (col.) colt

ciglis *nm* Eurasian goldfinch

cigoriņi *nm pl* chicory; endive

cigulis *nm* (col.) colt

ciguzis *nm* sparrow

cik *adj, adv* **1.** how much, how many; **2.** as much as; **c. tik** as . . . as; **3.** (in exclamations, with following adjective or adverb) how; **c. pulkstens?** what time is it? **4.** (with **nu, tad, tur**) very little, hardly, barely; **c. tur nu (tās naudas)** there is hardly (any money); **c. tur nu (ko pļaut)** what is there (to mow); **c. tik uziet** lots of; **vai c.** lots of; **c. necik** a little bit; more or less; **kaut c.** a little bit; **lai c. (grūti tas arī nebūtu)** no matter (how hard it might be)

cikāda *nf* cicada

cikāde *nf* = **cikāda**

cikadejas *nf pl* cycads

cikāds *adj* how many (different ones)

cikais *adj* which (in numerical order)

cikām *adv* while, as long as

cīkara *nf* (reg.) sinew

cikiem *adj, pl dat & instr* (in interrogatory phrases) a. **līdz c.?** until when? **ap c.?** around what time? b. for how many?

cikkārt *adv* how often

cikkārtējs *adj* (in questions) how often

cikko *adv* almost

cikl|a|mens [ā] *nm* cyclamen

ciklanteras *nf pl* Cyclanthera

cīkliņš *nm* burnisher

cikliski *adv* cyclically

ciklisks *adj* cyclic, cyclical

ciklizācija *nf* cyclization

ciklobutāns *nm* cyclobutane

ciklogen|e|ze [ē] *nf* cyclogenesis

ciklogramma *nf* cyclogram

cikloīda *nf* cycloid

ciklolize *nf* cyclolysis

ciklonīts *nm* cyclonite

ciklons *nm* cyclone

ciklopentadiēns *nm* cyclopentadiene

ciklopentāns *nm* cyclopentane

ciklopentēns *nm* cyclopentene

ciklopisks *adj* cyclopean

ciklopropāns *nm* cyclopropane

ciklops *nm* (myth., zool.) cyclops

cikloserīns *nm* cycloserine

ciklostrofisks *adj* cyclostrophic

ciklotīmija *nf* cyclothymia

ciklotrons *nm* cyclotron

cikls *nm* cycle; (of lectures, concerts) series

cikos *adj, pl loc* (in interrogatory phrases) **c.?** at what time?

cikreiz *adv* **1.** how many times? **2. c. . . . tikreiz** as many times as

ciksta *nf* corduroy bridge; fascine road

cīkste *nf* match, fight, competition

cikstēt *vi* = **čiepstēt**

cīkstēties *vr* wrestle

cīkstiņš *nm* (obs.) match, fight, competition

cīkstonis *nm* wrestler

ciksts *nm* = (reg.) **ciksta**

ciktāl *adv* as far as

cikurats *nm* ziggurat

ciķelbārda *nf* (sl.) goatee

cila *nf* composing stick

cilas *nf pl* clods

cilāšanās *nfr* (naut.) heaving

cilāt *vt* lift, raise, pick up repeatedly; **c. atmiņas** sift through memories; **c. glāzīti** (col.) crook the elbow; **c. ieročus** brandish weapons; **c. jautāju-mu** bring up a question; **c. karoti** (col.) eat, chow down

cilā/ties *vr* rise and fall, heave, go up and down; **kurpes ~jas** the shoes are too big

cilavas *nf pl* newly plowed virgin land

cilda *nf* (poet.) nobility, loftiness, sublimity

cildas *nf pl* (poet.) praise

cildeni *adv* nobly, loftily, sublimely; in a stately, dignified manner

cildenība *nf* = **cildenums**

cildens *adj* **1.** noble, lofty, sublime; **2.** stately, dignified

cildenums *nm* **1.** nobility, loftiness, sublimity; **2.** stateliness, dignity

cildība *nf* nobleness

cildinājums *nm* praise

cildināms *adj, part* of **cildināt** praiseworthy

cildināt *vt* praise, extol

cildīt *vt* = **cildināt**

cildot *vt* ennoble; improve, enhance; refine, upgrade

cildotā krizantēma *nf* a chrysanthemum, Chrysanthemum indicum

cilds *adj* noble

cildums *nm* nobleness

ciliārs *adj* ciliary

ciliāts *nm* ciliate

cilināt *vt* = **cilāt**

cilindriski *adv* cylindrically

cilindrisks *adj* cylindrical; (of levels) toric

cilindrs *nm* 1. (geom., tech.) cylinder; (tech.) drum; 2. (of an oil lamp) chimney; 3. top hat

cilindrveida *indecl adj* cylindrical

cilindrveidīgs *adj* cylindrical

cilksnis *nm* (pork) hock

cilmatradne *nf* mother lode

cilme *nf* origin

cilmiezis *nm* bedrock

cilnis *nm* 1. (geol.) small rise, elevation; 2. (sculpture) relief

cilnītis *nm dim* of cilnis, small rise

cilpa *nf* 1. loop; ačgārnā c. (aeron.) inverted loop; vertikālā c. (aeron.) vertical loop; 2. noose; 3. snare

cilpains *adj* loopy; (also fig.) knotty

cilpene *nf* candytuft

cilpenis *nm* loop for tree climbing

cilpeniski *adv* like a loop; c. siet tie a bow-knot

cilpenisks *adj* like a loop

cilpiņa *nf* 1. *dim* of cilpa; 2. (boot) tag; 3. (knitting) stitch; 4. (in a hook and eye) eye

cilpisks *adj* = cilpenisks

cilpot *vi* stride, foot it; (of rabbit, hare) lope

cilpotājs *nm* 1. loper; 2. currant moth

cilptinums *nm* lap winding

cilts *nf* 1. tribe; 2. family, clan; 3. (biol.) class

ciltsbrālis *nm* tribesman; clansman

ciltsdarbs *nm* (animal) breeding

ciltsgrāmata *nf* family register; pedigree book, studbook

ciltskoks *nm* 1. genealogical tree; 2. horticultural variety

ciltslopi *nm pl* pedigree cattle

ciltsmāte *nf* foremother

ciltsrakst/s *nm*, usu. *pl* ~i pedigree book, studbook

ciltsšūna *nf* zygote

ciltstēvs *nm* forefather

ciltstiesība *nf*, usu. *pl* ~s tribal rights

cilvēce *nf* humanity, humankind

cilvēcība *nf* humaneness, humanity

cilvēcīgi *adv* humanely

cilvēcīgs *adj* humane

cilvēcīgums *nm* humaneness

cilvēciņš *nm dim* of cilvēks, little man

cilvēciski *adv* humanly

cilvēcisks *adj* human

cilvēciskums *nm* humanity

cilvēka blusa *nf* human flea

cilvēka cērme *nf* ascarid

cilvēka medības *nf pl* manhunt

cilvēka pundurlentenis *nm* dwarf tapeworm

cilvēkbērns *nm* (poet.) child, child of man, human

cilvēkdiena *nf* man-day

cilvēkdievs *nm* god-man

cilvēkēdājs *nm* man-eater, cannibal

cilvēkēšana *nf* cannibalism

cilvēkkapitāls *nm* human capital

cilvēkmīla *nf* (poet.) altruism

cilvēkmīlestība *nf* altruism

cilvēknīdēj/s *nm*, ~a *nf* misanthrope

cilvēknīšana *nf* misanthropy

cilvēk/s *nm* human, human being; person; pazudis c. a. s.o. at the end of one's rope; b. depraved person; studēts c. university graduate; scholar; uz ~u per person; ~i people; ~a human; ~u *pl gen* human

cilvēkstunda *nf* manhour

cilvēktiesības *nf pl* human rights

cilvēkveida *indecl adj* anthropomorphic; (biol.) anthropoid

cilvēkveidīgs *adj* anthropomorphic; (biol.) anthropoid

ciļņots *adj* embossed

ciļņu purga *nf* (tinsmith's) drawing punch

cimbala *nf* = cimbole

cimbalarijas *nf pl* kenilworth

cimbalist/s *nm*, ~e *nf* = cimbolists

cimbīdija *nf* cymbidium

cimbole *nf* cimbalon

cimbolist/s *nm*, **~e** *nf* cimbolist

cimbri *nm pl* Cimbri

cimbulis *nm* dry clod

cimbulītis *nm dim* of **cimbulis**, small clod

cimdains *adj* gloved

cimdiņš *nm dim* of **cimds**, little glove

cimdnie/ks *nm*, **~ce** *nf* glover

cimdots *adj* gloved

cimd/s *nm* glove; **dūraini** (or **bezpirkstu**) **~i** mittens; **glazē ~i** kid gloves ◊ **kā c. ar roku** hand in glove; **~iem ņemams** vulnerable; **kā ar ~iem taisīts** botched

cimene *nf* scruff

cimicifugas *nf pl* bugbanes

cimmers *nm* (obs.) count of 40

cimperlēties *vr* (barb.) stand on ceremony; be finicky

cimperlīgs *adj* (barb.) finicky

cimsla *nf* (reg.) sinew

cimts *nm* cinnamon

cinājs *nm* tussocky ground

cinata *nf* **1.** tussock; **2.** tussocky ground

cin[ch]omeronskābe [h] *nf* cinchomeronic acid

cinene *nf* tufted hair grass

cinerārija *nf* cineraria

cinerīns *nm* cinerin

cinerolons *nm* cinerolone

cinga *nf* scurvy

cingulis *nm* (anat.) hock

cinhomeronskābe *nf* = **cinchomeronskābe**

cīnija *nf* zinnia

ciniķ/s *nm*, **~e** *nf* cynic

cīniņš *nm* (poet.) fight, struggle

ci/nis *nm* tussock; **uz ~ņa** (fig.) out of the woods

ciniski *adv* cynically

cinisks *adj* cynical

ciniskums *nm* cynicism

cinisms *nm* cynicism

cīnītājs *nm*, **~a** *nf* fighter; combatant

cīnīties *vr* fight, struggle; **c. ar trūkumu** keeping the wolf from the door; **c. ar vējdzirnavām** tilt at the windmills; **cīnās kā bads ar nāvi** barely keeping the wolf from the door

cinītis *nm dim* of **cinis**, small tussock

cinka baltums *nm* zinc white

cinka dzelzs *nf* franklinite

cinka dzelzs špats *nm* ferriferous smithonite

cinka māns *nm* zinc sulphide, sphalerite

cinka rūda *nf* zinc ore; **pelēkā c. r.** tennanite; **sarkanā c. r.** zincite

cinka silikātrūda *nf* willemite

cinka skārds *nm* galvanized sheet metal

cinka špats *nm* smithsonite

cinkāts *nm* zincate

cinkogr[a]fija or **[ā]** *nf* **1.** zincography; **2.** zincographer's shop

cinkogr[a]fisks [ā] *adj* zincographic

cinkogr[a]fs [ā] *nm* zincographer

cinkot *vt* zinc, galvanize

cinkotipija *nf* zincography

cinkozīts *nm* zincosite

cinks *nm* zinc

cinkslis *nm* **1.** hamstring; **2.** calf; **3.** (of animals) hind foot

cinkuris *nm* (reg.) cone

cinnas *nf pl* woodreed

cinnēt *vt* (col.) tin

cinnija *nf* zinnia

cinnolīns *nm* cinnoline

cinobrs *nm* cinnabar; (color) vermillion

cintiņa *nf* tussock

cintlaks *nm* (cannon) vent

cintronellāls *nm* cintronellal

cīņa *nf* **1.** fight, struggle; strife; **c. ar kaitēkļiem** pest control; **c. uz dzīvību un nāvi** life and death struggle; mortal combat; **2.** competition; **3.** battle, combat; **~s nespējīgs** disabled; casualty; **~s vieta** scene of action, battle scene; **4.** wrestling; **klasiskā c.** Greco-Roman wrestling; **brīvā**

amerikāņu c. freestyle wrestling, catch-as-catch-can

ciņains *adj* tussocky

cīņasbiedr/s *nm*, **~e** *nf* fellow combatant

cīņas gailis *nm* gamecock

cīņaslauks *nm* battlefield

ciņu grīslis *nm* Goodenough's sedge

ciņu meldri *nm pl* tufted club rush

ciņusmilga *nf* hair grass

ciņuzāle *nf* hair grass

cionisms *nm* Zionism

cionistisks *adj* Zionistic

cionists *nm* Zionist

cipa *nf*, usu. *pl* **cipas** (col.) chicks

cipardati *nm pl* digital data

ciparmodelis *nm* digital model

ciparmodulācija *nf* digitizing

ciparnīca *nf* dial, (clock, watch) face

ciparnieks *nm* dial, (clock, watch) face

ciparotājs *nm* numbering machine

ciparots *adj* numbered

ciparripa *nf* (telephone) dial

cipars *nm* digit; numeral

ciparu dators *nm* digital computer

cipāt *vi* (col.) walk

cipatas *nf pl* **1.** (col.) chicks; **2.** (child.) legs; **3.** cracklings

cīpata *nf* (reg.) sinew

cip cip *interj* chick, chick (call to chickens)

ciprese *nf* cypress

cīpsla *nf* tendon, sinew

cīpslains *adj* sinewy

cīpslene *nf* (anat.) sclera

cīpslots *adj* sinewy

cīpstala *nf* tendon, sinew

cipstēt *vi* chirp

cipstiņš *nm* (zool.) yellowhammer

circenis *nm* (zool.) cricket

circināt *vi* (of a cricket) chirp

cīrēt *vi* cast one's eyes on; scrutinize

cirkalis *nm* stone cutter

cirknis *nm* (bot.) compartment

cirkonāts *nm* zirconate

cirkonijs *nm* zirconium

cirkonīts *nm* zirconite

cirkons *nm* zircon

cirkonskābe *nf* zirconic acid

cirks *nm* circus

cirksnis *nm* **1.** groin; **2.** shrew; **3.** felling; clearcut

cirksta *nf* curl, lock; kink

cirkstājums *nm* flourish

cirkste *nf* **1.** aching bones, gout; **2.** kink

cirkstēt *vi* **1.** crunch, grind; **2.** chirr

cirkšņu trūce *nf* inguinal rupture

cirkulācija *nf* circulation

cirkulāri *adv* circularly

cirkulārs *nm* circular

cirkulārs *adj* circular

cirkulēt *vi* circulate

cirkulis *nm* compasses

cirkuļains *adj* curly

cirkumflekss *nm* circumflex

cirkumpolārs *adj* circumpolar

cirkumspekcija *nf* circumspection

cirkumvallācija *nf* circumvallation

cirkuzis *nm* (reg.) cone

cirmenis *nm* grub, maggot

cirmis *nm* worm

cirmuļains *adj* worm-eaten

ciroze *nf* cirrhosis

cirpe *nf* sickle; (mech.) shear

cirpējēde *nf* ringworm

cirpēj/s *nm*, **~a** *nf* **1.** shearer, clipper; **2.** an apple weevil, Rhynchites conicus

cirpstēt *vi* stridulate

cirpt *vt* shear, clip; trim

cirpuļi *nm pl* cracklings

cirpums *nm* shearing, clipping; clip (of wool)

cirslis *nm* **1.** shrew; **2.** = **cirsma**; **3.** (reg.) groin

cirslītis *nm* pygmy shrew

cirsma *nf* (of timberland destined for cutting) tract, patch; felling; clear-cut

cirsmojums *nm* (forest.) felling series

cirsne *nf* = **cirsma**

cirsnis *nm* = **cirsma**

cirst *vt* **1.** (of firewood) split, chop; **c. pušu** cut in two; (fig., col.) beat (overcome an opponent); **2.** cut (in shaping), hew; carve, sculpture, en-grave; **c. istabu** (obs.) build a dwelling; **c. robu** cut a notch; (fig.) cause a loss or expense; **3.** (of trees) fell, cut, harvest; **c. mežu** cut timber; **4.** slam; stamp (one's foot); **5.** *vi* strike (with a sword or paw); **c. ar pātagu** whip, lash; **c. pliķi** slap; **c. pa pirkstiem** rap s.o.'s fingers; **6.** *vi* make smart, make sting; **c. pretim** retort; **c. pār strīpu** take it too far, go wild

cirsties *vr* **1.** (*3rd pers*, of wind, rain, branches) beat; **2.** (*3rd pers*) slam; **3. c. apkārt** (or **pretī**) whip around; **c. prom** dash away; **c. sāņus** shy; **4.** (obs.) fight (with swords)

ciršus *adv* **1.** by cutting, by hewing; **2.** *emph* of **cirst**; **c. cirst** cut, hew energetically; chop away

cirta *nf* curl, lock; kink

cirtainā malva *nf* whorled mallow

cirtainais pelikāns *nm* Dalmatian pelican

cirtaini *adv* with curls, in curls

cirtains *adj* curly

cirtainums *nm* curliness

cirtāt *vt* = **cirtot**

cirtāties *vr* = **cirtoties**

cirte *nf* timber harvesting, tree cutting

cirtējs *nm*, ~a *nf* cutter, chopper; woodcutter

cirtenisks *adj* (col.) energetic, vigorous

cirtiens *nm* **1.** stroke, blow; **2.** cut; chop; **3.** lash

cirtīgs *adj* pungent

cirtin *adv emph* of **cirst**; **c. cirta** he was chopping away; (the rain) kept beating in the face

cirtmets *nm* (forest.) years to harvest time, rotation

cirtne *nf* quarry

cirtnis *nm* **1.** chisel; **2.** ax-hewn log house

cirtot *vt* curl

cirtoties *vr* curl

cirtums *nm* **1.** cut (made by a cutting tool; amount of timber cut); **2.** (forest.) clearing

cīrulēns *nm* young lark

cīrulis *nm* lark

cīrulīši *nm pl* birthwort

cīrulītis *nm dim* of **cīrulis**, lark

cīruļdziesma *nf* song of the lark

cīruļgalvas *nf pl* avens

cīruļputenis *nm* brief late spring snowstorm

cīruļveidīgie *nm pl* Alaudidae

cīruļzāles *nf pl* birthwort

cirvene *nf* water plantain

cirv/is *nm* ax; hatchet ◊ **kā ar ~i pa pieri** stunned

cis/as *nf pl* **1.** straw or hay for bedding or for stuffing a pallet; **2.** palliasse, pallet; **~u maiss** straw mattress; **3.** bed; **uz nāves ~ām** on one's deathbed

cisāt *vi* (col.) urinate

ciscuņa *nf dim* of **ciska**, thigh

cīsiņš *nm* frankfurter

ciska *nf* thigh

cīsķens *nm* siskin

cīsla *nf* = **cīpsla**

cista *nf* cyst

cisteīns *nm* cysteine

cistercietis *nm* Cistercian

cisterna *nf* **1.** cistern; **2.** tank truck; **laistāmā c.** sprinkler truck

cisternas vagons *nm* (RR) tank car

cisticerki *nm pl* cysticerci

cistiserkoze *nf* cystisercosis

cīsties *vr* endeavor, try; strive

cistīns *nm* cystine

cistīts *nm* cystitis

cistoskopija *nf* cystoscopy

cistoskops *nm* cystoscope

cistusroze *nf* rockrose

cisuskoks *nm* cissus

citācija *nf* citation

citādāk *adv* (col.) **1.** differently, otherwise; **2.** *conj* or, otherwise

citādāks *adj* different

citadele *nf* citadel

citādi *adv* **1.** differently, otherwise; **es nevaru c. kā . . .** I cannot but . . .; **2.** *conj* or, otherwise

citād/s *adj* different

cītara *nf* zither

citāts *nm* quotation

cīte *nf* diligence

citējums *nm* quotation

citēt *vt* quote

cītība *nf* diligence, industry, application

cītīgi *adv* diligently, industriously, assiduously

cītīgs *adj* diligent, industrious, assiduous

cītīgums *nm* diligence

citkārt *adv* at other times; sometimes

citkārtējs *adj*, usu. *defin* **citkārtējais** former

citnovadnieks *nm* a person from another area, outsider

citnovads *nm* outside, another area

citodiagnostika *nf* cytology

citodiagnoze *nf* cytodiagnosis

citoģenētika *nf* cytogenetics

citolizīns *nm* cytolysin

citolo/gs *nm*, **~ģe** *nf* cytologist

citoloģija *nf* cytology

citoloģiski *adv* cytologically

citoloģisks *adj* cytological

citoplazma *nf* cytoplasm

citozīns *nm* cytosine

citpagastnieks *nm* a person from another township, outsider

citrakonskābe *nf* citraconic acid

citrāls *nm* citral

citrāts *nm* citrate

citreiz *adv* **1.** another time; **2.** sometimes

citreizējs *adj* former

citrins *nm* citrine

citronaugs *nm* citrus

citrondzeltenās dienziedes *nf pl* a day lily, Hemerocallis citrina

citrondzeltens *adj* lemon yellow

citroneļļa *nf* lemon oil

citronkoks *nm* lemon tree

citronliāna *nf* schisandra

citronmelisa *nf* lemon balm

citronmētra *nf* lemon balm

cintronmiza *nf* lemon peel

citrons *nm* lemon

citronskābe *nf* citric acid

citronspiede *nf* juicer

citronsorgo *indecl nm* lemon grass

cintronsula *nf* lemon juice

citronūdens *nm* lemonade

citruna *nf* another person's speech or thought

citrusaugs *nm* citrus

citruss *nm* citrus

cit/s *pron* **1.** other, another; **tas vai c.** someone or other; **c. ar ~u** with one another; **c. ~u** one another; **c. aiz ~a** one behind the other; **c. par ~u (lielāks)** one (bigger) than the other; **c. pēc ~a** one after another; **c . . . ., c . . . .** some . . ., some . . .; **c. caur ~u** (of speaking) all at once; **2.** (when used nominally) somebody else, something else; **kāds c.** someone else; **kas c.** something else; who else; **nekas c** nothing else; **neviens c.** nobody else; **starp ~u** by the way, incidently; **3. ~i** others

cittautībnie/ks *nm*, **~ce** *nf* = **cittautietis**

cittautiet/is *nm*, **~e** *nf* foreign national

cittautu *indecl adj* foreign

citticībnieks *nm* adherent of another religion

citudien *adv* next day; the other day

citugad *adv* next year

citur *adv* elsewhere, somewhere else; **kur c.** where else; **nekur c.** nowhere else; **visur c.** everywhere else

citurien/e *nf* another place; **uz ~i** to some other place

citurieniet/is *nm*, ~**e** *nf* newcomer
citurīt *adv* next morning
cituviet *adv* elsewhere
citvalodu *indecl adj* foreign language (*adj*)
citzeme *nf* foreign country
citzemju *indecl adj* of other countries, foreign
citzemnie/ks *nm*, ~**ce** *nf* foreigner
civeta *nf* civet
civethiēna *nf* aardwolf
civ[i]lapģērbs [ī] *nm* civilian clothes
civ[i]latbildētājs [ī] *nm* civil respondent
civ[i]latbildība [ī] *nf* civil liability
civ[i]ldarījums [ī] *nm* civil action
civ[i]ldienests [ī] *nm* civil service
civ[i]liedzīvotājs [ī] *nm* civilian
civ[i]linženieris [ī] *nm* civil engineer
civ[i]list/s [ī] *nm*, ~**e** *nf* civilian
civ[i]lizācija [ī] *nf* civilization
civ[i]liz[a]tor/s [ī][ā] *nm*, ~**e** *nf* civilizer
civ[i]lizēt [ī] *vt* civilize
civ[i]lizēties [ī] *vr* become civilized
civ[i]lkārtība [ī] *nf* civil procedure code
civ[i]lkodekss [ī] *nm* civil code
civ[i]llaulība [ī] *nf* **1.** civil marriage;
    2. common-law marriage
civ[i]llieta [ī] *nf* civil suit
civ[i]llikums [ī] *nm* civil law
civ[i]lliste [ī] *nf* civil list (in England)
civ[i]lnodaļa [ī] *nf* county clerk's office
civ[[i]lpersona [ī] *nf* civilian; (mil.) noncom-
    batant
civ[i]lprasība [ī] *nf* civil suit
civ[i]lprasītājs [ī] *nm* plaintiff in a civil suit
civ[i]lprāva [ī] *nf* civil action
civ[i]lprocess [ī] *nm* civil procedure
civ[i]lprocesuāls [ī] *adj* (of civil actions)
    procedural
civ[i]ls [ī] *adj* civil; civilian
civ[i]lsieva [ī] *nf* common-law wife
civ[i]lspriedums [ī] *nm* civil judgment
civ[i]lstāvoklis [ī] *nm* **1.** marital status;
    2. personal status

civ[i]lstrīds [ī] *nm* controversy before a court
    of civil jurisdiction
civ[i]ltērps [ī] *nm* civilian clothes
civ[i]ltiesa[ī] *nf* civil court
civ[i]ltiesība [ī] *nf*, usu. *pl* ~**s** civil rights
civ[i]ltiesisks [ī] *adj* pertaining to civil law or
    civil rights
civ[i]luzvalks[ī] *nm* civilian clothes
civ[i]lvīrs [ī] *nm* common-law husband
civirksne *nf* European common shrew
cizelējums *nm* chased work
cizelēt *vt* (ornament) chase
cizēt *vi* **1.** crunch; squeak; **2.** chirr
cizināt *vi* **1.** crunch; squeak; **2.** chirr
coberis *nm* (sl.) (grade) D
cohums *nm* (sl.) hole
cokols *nm* **1.** socle; **2.** (of a light bulb) base
cokolstāvs *nm* basement
colla *nf* inch
collāt *vi* (col.) go, walk
collmērs *nm* inch rule; yardstick
collštoks *nm* (sl.) folding inch rule, zigzag
    rule
cope *nf* **1.** (col.) pigtail; **2.** (sl., fishing) bite
copēt *vi* (sl., of fish) bite
cst *interj* sh
cūcenāj/s *nm* blackberry; ~**i** blackberry patch
cūcene *nf* **1.** milk cap; **2.** Russula; **3.** blackberry;
    4. (col.) pig, sow; **5.** (sl.) luck, lucky
    break
cūcēns *nm* shoat
cūcība *nf* (col.) filthiness; obscenity
cūcietis *nm* (col.) hog
cūcīgi *adv* meanly
cūcīgs *adj* (col.) **1.** filthy, dirty; **2.** swinish,
    mean
cūcīgums *nm* filthiness, swinishness
cūciņa *nf* **1.** *dim* of **cūka**, piglet; **2.** mumps
cūcis *nm* shoat
cūcisks *adj* = **cūcīgs**
cui *interj* sic'em
cuidināt *vt* sic

cuidīt *vt* sic

cuināt *vt* sic

cujināt *vt* sic

cūk *interj* sooey

cuka *nf* (sl.) draft

cūk/a *nf* 1. pig, hog, swine ◊ c. maisā pig in a poke; ne mana c., ne mana druva it is none of my business; 2. sow; 3. ~as a card game

cūkactiņas *nf pl* a type of ornamental design

cūkāda *nf* pigskin

cūkainis *nm* milkwort

cūkāmols *nm* self-heal

cūkas cepetis *nm* roast pork

cūkas laime *nf* just lucky

cūkas stilbiņi *nm pl* pettitoes;

cūkausis *nm* epithet for one who talks dirty

cūkausis *nf pl* (sl.) dogears

cūkauši *nm pl* water arum

cūkdelfīns *nm* common porpoise

cūkēdiens *nm* hog feed

cūkeglīte *nf* lousewort

cūkgaļa *nf* pork

cūkgans *nm* swineherd

cūkkopēj/s *nm*, ~a *nf* hog attendant

cūkkopība *nf* hog farming

cūkkopības saimniecība *nf* hog farm

cūkkop/is *nm*, ~e *nf* hog farmer

cūkkūts *nf* pigsty, piggery

cūknātra *nf* figwort

cūkot *vt* (col.) dirty, mess up; (fig.) treat dirty

cūkoties *vr* (col.) dirty oneself; (fig.) treat dirty

cūkpiene *nf* dandelion; see also gludā c.

cūkpipari *nm pl* wild ginger

cūkpupa *nf* broad bean

cūksaknes *nf pl* (bot.) cat's-ear

cūktabaka *nf* figwort

cūku āboliņš *nm* self-heal

cūku bekas *nf pl* slippery jacks

cūku bēres *nf pl* a meal following the slaughter of a pig;

cūku briedis *nm* hog deer

cūku cērme *nf* intestinal roundworm of pigs

cūku lentenis *nm* pork tapeworm

cūku mētra *nf* Japanese peppermint

cūku pipari *nm pl* meadow saxifrage

cukura diabēts *nm* diabetes mellitus

cukurains *adj* sugary

cukura kukainis *nm* silverfish

cukura priede *nf* sugar pine

cukura vārītava *nf* sugarhouse

cukurbiešu smecernieks *nm* sugarbeet weevil

cukurbiete *nf* sugar beet

cukurbiķeris *nm* (obs.) sugar bowl

cukurdoze *nf* sugar bowl

cukurfabrika *nf* sugar refinery

cukurgailītis *nm* lollipop

cukurgalva *nf* sugarloaf

cukurgrauds *nm* sugar cube

cukuriņš *nm* 1. *dim* of cukurs; 2. a variety of apple

cukurkļava *nf* sugar maple

cukurmīlis *nm* silverfish

cukurnīca *nf* sugar bowl

cukurniedre *nf* sugarcane

cukurot *vt* sugar

cukuroties *vr* sugar, granulate

cukurots *adj, part* of cukurot 1. sugared; 2. sugary

cukurpalma *nf* gomuti palm

cukurrūpniecība *nf* sugar production

cukurs *nm* sugar; smalkais c. refined sugar

cukurslimība *nf* diabetes

cukurslimnie/ks *nm*, ~ce *nf* diabetic

cukurtrauks *nm* sugar bowl

cukurūdens *nm* sugar water

cukurviela *nf* carbohydrate

cukurzirņi *nm pl* sweet pea

cūku sakne *nf* figwort

cūku tabaka *nf* figwort

cūku tauki *nm pl* lard

cūku uts *nf* pig louse

cūķis *nm* (of a person) pig

cunami *indecl nm* tsunami

cunfte *nf* (hist.) guild, corporation

cunftīgs *adj* (sl.) skilled

cvancigers *nm* 1. (barb.) a (note of) twenty; 2. (vulg.) spit

cvībaks *nm* (sl.) rusk, zwieback

cvingers *nm* zwinger

Č

čaba *nf* 1. rustle; 2. gabber; 3. ~s a. (big, heavy) peasant shoes; b. poor, inferior grain

čāba *nf, nm* gabber

čabans *nm* shepherd

čābāt *vi* (col.) walk

čabatas *nf pl* (big, heavy) peasant shoes

čabēšana *nf* rustle, rustling

čabēt *vi* rustle

čabināt *vt* rustle, make rustle; (fig.) gab

čabināties *vr* rustle

čabiņa *nf* (col.) gabber

čabis *nm* (col.) gabber

čābiski *adv* badly; shabbily; sloppily

čābisks *adj* (col.) bad; shabby; sloppy

čabīte *nf* (reg.) shorty

čaboņa *nf* rustling

čabu, čabu *interj* pit-a-pat

čabu/lis *nm* 1. poorly developed plant; 2. ~ļi chaffy grain; 3. small, insignificant creature; 4. an old and weak person; 5. (reg.) a term of en-dearment, esp. as *dim* čabulītis

čača *nm* = čačarkls

čāča *nf, nm* (col.) 1. gabber; 2. simpleton

čačača *nf* cha-cha

čačarkls *nm* double-blade hand plow

čāčīgs *adj* (col.) clumsy

čačis *nm* = čačarkls

čadra *nf* chador

čaga *nf* 1. small lump of frazil ice; 2. soft head of cabbage; 3. ~s (of pressed fruit or berries) marc

čagani *adv* porously

čaganība *nf* sponginess, porousness

čagans I *adj* spongy, porous

čagans II *adj* (col.) diligent

čaganums *nm* sponginess, porousness

čāgāt *vi* = čagināt

čagināt *vi* (of birds) chatter

čagums *nm* (of a roof) ridge

čak, čak *interj* 1. (of footsteps) rustle; 2. tsack-tsack (the call of a stonechat)

čakans *nm* mallet

čakarēt *vi* (col.) stir; poke

čakarēties *vr* (col.) stir; poke; (sl.) piddle

čakārnis *nm* snag, tree stub

čakāt *vt* stir; poke

čakli *adv* diligently, industriously

čaklība *nf* diligence, industry

čakls *adj* diligent, industrious

čaklums *nm* diligence, industry

čakona *nf* chaconne

čakra *nf* chakra

čakste *nf* shrike

čakstēns *nm* young shrike

čakstēt *vi* 1. rustle; 2. (of birds) chatter

čākstēt *vi* 1. (of snow) crunch; (of fabrics) rustle; (of voice) wheeze; 2. become porous, spongy

čakstināt *vt, vi* 1. *vt* make rustle; 2. *vt* (of birds) chatter; 3. *vi* a. cluck (one's tongue); b. rustle

čakstināties *vr* = čakstināt

čakstiņš *nm* = čakstīte

čakstīte *nf* (zool.) chat

čakstveidīgie *nm pl* Laniidae

čala *nf* 1. chatter; murmur, hum; 2. gurgle

čalīgs *adj* gabby; talkative

čalināt *vi* (col.) 1. chatter; 2. gurgle

čalis *nm* (sl.) young guy

čalītis *nm* (sl.) suspicious young guy

čalma *nf* turban

čalojums *nm* patter

čaloņa *nf* chatter

čalot *vi* 1. chatter; twitter; 2. gurgle

čama *nf, nm* sloppy person; ~s (reg.) trash and slops

čamdīt *vt* (col.) poke around, prod, finger

čamdīties *vr* (col.) poke around, prod, finger

čamma *nf, nm* (col.) slowpoke, slow and awkward person

čammāt *vt* munch

čammāties *vr* (col.) poke, dawdle, dillydally

čams *nm* 1. tuft, bunch; 2. cluster of filberts; 3. tree stump with new shoots; 4. swarm of bees

čamstināt *vt, vi* = čāpstināt

čandala *nf* chandala

čap, čap *interj* (of footsteps) rustle

čāpāt *vi* = čāpot

čapināt *vi* = čāpot

čāpot *vi* (col.) walk slowly and awkwardly, toddle

čapstināt *vi* = čāpstināt

čāpstināt *vt, vi* smack one's lips; munch

čapstīt *vt, vi* = čāpstināt

čāpstīt *vt, vi* = čāpstināt

čāpt *vi* 1. pant, breathe with difficulty; 2. chatter

čardašs *nm* czardas

čarka *nf* (col.) glass of vodka, shot

čarkstēt *vi* make a crushing or grinding noise; rustle; chatter; rattle

čarkstināt *vi* chatter

čarkstoņa *nf* crunch; rustle; chatter; rattle

čarlstons *nm* (dance) Charleston

čartera partija *nf* charter party

čarterreiss *nm* charter flight

čarters *nm* (bus.) charter

čartēt *vt* charter

čartisms *nm* (hist.) Chartism

čartists *nm* (hist.) Chartist

časkas *nf pl* leftovers, remains

častuška *nf* chastushka

čau *interj* (col.) hi; ciao

čau-čau *indecl nm* chow chow

čaučis *nm* winnowing basket

čauga *nf* crumbling substance

čaugani *adv* porously

čauganība *nf* sponginess, porousness

čaugans *adj* spongy, porous

čauganums *nm* sponginess, porousness

čaugs *adj* = čaugans

čauka *nf* = čaukste

čaukste *nf* a soft head of cabbage

čaukstene *nf* (col.) talebearer, gossip

čaukstens *adj* spongy, porous

čaukstēt *vi* 1. rustle; 2. (col.) tattle

čaukstināt *vt* rustle

čaukstināties *vr* rustle

čaukstoņa *nf* rustling

čaukstošais *nom adj* (col.) dough, lettuce

čauksts *nm* rustling

čauksture *nf* baker's brush

čaula *nf* hull, husk, shell; seed coat; jacket, case, casing; cartridge case; (spent cartridge) brass; ~s cepurīte catridge rim; ~s ķermenis (aeron.) monocoque fuselage

čaulainie *nom adj pl* shellfish

čaulains *adj* shelled (having a shell)

čaulaugļi *nm pl* shell fruit

čaulīšu papīrs *nm* cigarette paper

čaulīte *nf* 1. dim of čaula, hull, husk, shell; cartridge case; 2. cigarette wrapper

čaultveris *nm* brass catcher

čaulveida *indecl adj* shell-like

čaumala *nf* shell

čaumaliņa *nf dim* of čaumala, little shell

čaumalot *vt* shell, peel

čavāt *vi* (col.) chat

čavata *nf, nm* (col.) tattler

če[ch]iski [h[*adv* in Czech, (speak) Czech

če[ch]isks [h] *adj* Czech

če[ch]/s [h] *nm*, ~iete *nf* Czech

čečenietis *nm*, ~**iete** *nf* Chechen
čedarsiers *nm* Cheddar cheese
čeka *nf* Cheka
čekists *nm* Chekist
ček/s *nm* check; **bezvārda č.** bearer check; **č. uz-rādītājam** bearer check; **dzēsts č.** cancelled check; **nesegts č.** insufficient funds, bad check
čeku grāmatiņa *nf* checkbook
čeku konts *nm* checking account
čelesta *nf* celesta
čellis *nm* (sl.) young guy
čellists *nm*, ~**e** *nf* cellist
čellītis *nm* (sl.) suspicious young guy
čello *indecl nm* cello
čells *nm* cello
čembalo *indecl nm* cembalo
čemodāns *nm* (baggage) trunk
čempionāts *nm* championship contest
čempions *nm*, ~**e** *nf* champion
čems *nm* cluster
čemurainā mauraga *nf* narrow-leaved hawk-weed
čemurainā ziemciete *nf* pipsissewa
čemurains *adj* full of clusters; umbellate
čemuriņš *nm* **1.** *dim* of **čemurs**, small cluster; **2.** umbellule
čemurkslis *nm* cluster; tangle
čemurneļķe *nf* sweet William
čemuroties *vr* form clusters
čemurs *nm* **1.** cluster; **2.** umbel; **3.** (of a cannon) cascabel
čemuru augstiņš *nm* centaury;
čemuru baltstarīte *nf* meadow saffron
čemuru falkārija *nf* a falcaria, Falcaria sioides
čemuru ziemciete *nf* pipsissewa
čemurveida *indecl adj* umbellate
čemurveidīgs *adj* umbellate
čemurzieži *nm* Umbelliferae, Apiaceae
čemurziežu blakts *nf* lygus bug
čentezims *nm* centesimo

čer, čer *interj* chirp
čeremiss *nm*, ~**iete** *nf* Cheremis
čerimola *nf* custard apple
čerkeska *nf* cherkeska (Caucasian men's outer garment)
čerkess *nm*, ~**iete** *nf* Circassian
čerkstēt *vi* screech; rasp; stridulate; grit, scratch
čērkstēt *vi* screech; rasp; stridulate; grit, scratch
čerkstoņa *nf* screeching, rasping
červelēties *vr* warp; cockle, pucker, crinkle
červelis *nm* crinkle, cockle
červeļains *adj* rough, bumpy, crinkly
červeļainums *nm* roughness, bumpiness, crinkliness
červoncs *nm* chervonets
červoņecs *nm* chervonets
čestersiers *nm* Chester cheese
četracis *nm* (cards) a four
četrai[ŗ]u [ŗ] *indecl adj* four-oared
četrarpus *indecl adj* four and a half
četrasu *indecl adj* four-axle
četratā *adv* four together, the four of them; **(spē-le) č.** four-handed (game)
četrbalsīgi *adv* **dziedāt č.** (sing a) four-part (song)
četrbalsīgs *adj* (mus.) four-part
četrbalsu *indecl adj* (mus.) four-part
četrcēlienu *indecl adj* four-act
četrceliņu *indecl adj* four-track
četrcilindru *indecl adj* four-cylinder
četrcīņa *nf* a contest of four events, "tet-rathlon"
četrcīņnie/ks *nm*, ~**ce** *nf* contestant in a "tet-rathlon"
četrciparu *indecl adj* four-digit
četrdaļīgs *adj* four-part
četrdesmit *indecl adj* forty
četrdesmit/ais *adj* fortieth; ~**ie gadi** the forties
četrdesmitgadīgs *adj* forty-year old

četrdienu *indecl adj* four-day
četrdurvju *indecl adj* four-door
četrējādi *adv* in four different ways
četrējāds *adj* of four kinds
četrēji *adj* four
četreniski *adv* **1.** four times; **2.** in four parts; **3.** on all fours
četrgadējs *adj* four-year
četrgada *indecl adj* quadrennial
četrgadīgs *adj* **1.** four-year; **2.** four-year old; **3.** quadrennial
četrgadu *indecl adj* four-year
četr/i *adj* **1.** *indecl, decl* four; **pa ~iem** in fours; **uz visām ~ām** on all fours; **2.** (educ.) B (grade); **3.** *decl* four o'clock; **~os** at four
četrinieks *nm* **1.** a four; **2.** team of four, foursome; **3.** B (grade)
četrinieku sacīkstes *nf pl* (boat race) fours
četriski *adv* on all fours
četristabu *indecl adj* four-room
četrīši *nm pl* quadruplets
četrjūgs *nm* (horse team) four-in-hand
četrkājainis *nm* quadruped
četrkājains *adj* four-legged, quadrupedal
četrkājis *nm* quadruped
četrkanšu *indecl adj* four-sided
četrkanšu mieēi *nm pl* irregular barley
četrkantīgs *adj* four-edged
četrkāršojums *nm* fourfold increase
četrkāršot *vt* quadruple
četrkāršoties *vr* quadruple
četrkāršs *adj* **1.** fourfold; **2.** fourply
četrkārt *adv* four times
četrkārtains *adj* four-layer
četrkārtējs *adj* **1.** four-time; **2.** fourfold, quadruple; four-ply
četrkārtīgi *adv* fourfold
četrkārtīgs *adj* **1.** fourfold, quadruple; **2.** four-ply
četrklasīgs *adj* (grade school curriculum) four-year
četrklašu *indecl adj* four-year

četrkrāsains *adj* four-color
četrkrāsu *indecl adj* four-color
četrlampu *indecl adj* **1.** four-bulb; **2.** four-tube
četrlapains *adj* four-leaf
četrlauku *indecl adj* four-field
četrlauku saimniecība *nf* four-year rotation of crops
četrlemešu *indecl adj* (of plows) with four shares
četrmalu *indecl adj* four-sided
četrmastu *indecl adj* four-masted
četrmēnešu *indecl adj* four-month
četrmotorīgs *adj* four-engine
četrmotoru *indecl adj* four-engine
četrnedēļu *indecl adj* four-week
četrnīšu *indecl adj* (weav.) of four warp threads
četrotne *nf* foursome, team of four
četrpadsmit *adj* fourteen
četrpadsmitais *adj* fourteenth
četrpadsmitgadīgs *adj* fourteen-year old
četrpakāpju *indecl adj* four-stage
četrpēdu *indecl adj* four-foot
četrpirkstu *indecl adj* (zool.) four-toed
četrpols *nm* quadrupole
četrpolu *indecl adj* four-pole
četrprocentīgs *adj* four-percent
četrpusējs *adj* four-sided
četrrāpus *adv* on all fours
četrreiz *adv* four times
četrreizējs *adj* four-time
četrrinde *nf* quatrain
četrrindenis *nm* quatrain
četrrindu *indecl adj* four-line
četrriteņu *indecl adj* four-wheel
četrrocīgi *adv* four-handed, using four hands
četrrocīgs *adj* four-handed; (of a sonata) double
četrrūšu *indecl adj* four-pane
četrsējumu *indecl adj* four-volume
četrsēklu vīķi *nm pl* slender vetch

četrsimt *num adj* four hundred

četrsimtais *num adj* four hundredth

četrskaldnis *nm* tetrahedron

četrskaldņu *indecl adj* rectangular, quadrilateral

četrslīpju *indecl adj* four-sloped

četrslīpju jumts *nm* hip roof

četrspārnains *adj* four-winged

četrspārņi *nm pl* Tetraptera

četrstaru galinsoga *nf* a galinsoga, Galinsoga quadriradiata

četrstāvu *indecl adj* four-story

četrstīgu *indecl adj* four-string

četrstū|r|ains [ŗ] *adj* four-cornered, quadrangular; quadrilateral, tetragonal

četrstūris *nm* quadrangle; quadrilateral

četrstū|r|u [ŗ] *indecl adj* four-cornered, quadrangular, quadrilateral, tetragonal

četrstū|r|veida [ŗ] *indecl adj* four-cornered, quadrangular; quadrilateral, tetragonal

četrstū|r|veidīgs [ŗ] *adj adj* four-cornered, quadrangular; quadrilateral, tetragonal

četršķautnains *adj* four-edged

četršķautņu *indecl adj* four-edged

četršķautņu asinszāle *nf* spotted Saint-John's-wort

četrtaktu *indecl adj* (of engines) four-stroke

četrtik *adv* four times (as much, bigger)

četrtonnīgs *adj* four-ton

četrvērtīgs *adj* (chem.) tetravalent

četrvielu *indecl adj* (of alloys) quaternary

četrvietīgs *adj* four-seated

četrvilcis *nm* chess problem in four moves

četrzarains *adj* four-pronged

četrzaru *indecl adj* four-pronged

četrzilbju *indecl adj* four-syllable

četrzīmju *indecl adj* four-digit

četržuburains *adj* four-armed, four-branched

četržuburu *indecl adj* four-armed, four-branched

četveriks *nm* (obs.) a Russian liquid measure

četverts *nm* (obs.) a Russian liquid measure

čības *nf pl* slippers; gym shoes

čibināt *vt* tickle lightly

čibināties *vr* putter

čibīt *vt* (col.) filch, steal

čibu usu. **čibu, čabu** *interj* sound of indistinct footsteps; **ne č., ne čabu** not a sound

čibuks *nm* chibouk

čičerons *nm* cicerone

čīčiņa *nf* (reg.) ladybug

čičisbejs *nm* cicisbeo

čičunčā *nm indecl* pongee

čiekurains *adj* covered with cones

čiekuraugs *nm* conifer

čiekuriņš *nm* **1.** *dim* of **čiekurs**, little cone; **2.** staminate cone

čiekuroga *nf* juniper berry

čiekurots *adj* covered with cones

čiekurs *nm* (bot.) cone

čiekurveida *indecl adj* cone-shaped

čiekurveida dziedzeris *nm* pineal gland

čiekurveidīgs *adj* cone-shaped

čiepstēt *vi* chirp

čiepstiens *nm* chirp

čiepstoņa *nf* chirping

čiepsts *nm* chirp

čiepstulis *nm* (col.) chick

čiept *v* **1.** *vt* (col.) filch, steal; **2.** *vi* chirp

čigānene *nf* **1.** young Gypsy girl; **2.** gypsy mushroom

čigānēns *nm* young Gypsy boy

čigāniski *adv* in Romany

čigānisks *adj* **1.** Gypsy; **2.** Romany

čigān/s *nm*, **~iete** *nf* **1.** Gypsy ◊ **~u saule** (hum.) the moon; **~u vējš** north wind; **2.** **~i** a. Gypsies; b. mummers

čīgas *nf pl* fiddle

čīgāt *vt* (of a violin) scrape

čīgotne *nf* = (col.) **čīkstene**

čikano *indecl nm* Chicano

čiks *nm* trivial yield of mighty labors

čiks *interj* click

čīkstene *nf* sedum

čīkst/ēt *vi* **1.** squeak; **2.** (col.) whine, whimper, complain; ~**i vai nečīksti** like it or not

čīkstiens *nm* squeek

čīkstīgi *adv* in a whiny voice

čīkstīgs *adj* **1.** (col.) whiny; **2.** squeaky

čīkstināt *vt* make squeak

čīkstināties *vr* (*iter*) **1.** make squeak; **2.** squeak a long time

čīkstis *nm* (col.) whiner

čīkstonis *nm* (col.) whiner

čīkstoņa *n* **1.** *nf* squeaking; **2.** *nf, nm* (col.) whiner

čiksts *nm* corduroy road

čīksts *nm* squeak

čīkstulīgs *adj* (col.) whiny

čīkstul/is *nm,* ~**e** *nf* (col.) whiner

čiku, usu. **čiku čaku** *interj* rustle; **ne č. ne grabu** not a sound; unbeknownst

âiles salpetris *nm* Chile saltpeter

âiles zemene *nf* beach strawberry

čiliet/is *nm,* ~**e** *nf* Chilean

čilkstēt *vi* chirp

čina *nf* **1.** (obs.) rank; **2.** (col., iron.) office, position

činavnieks *nm* **1.** (obs.) civil servant; **2.** (col., iron.) official

činčiļļa *nf* chinchilla

činkslis *nm* hamstring

činkstenis *nm* (col.) whiner

činkstēt *vi* **1.** mewl; whine; **2.** jingle

činkstināt *vt* jingle

činkurs *nm* tussock

činkvečentists *nm* cinquencentist

činkvečento *indecl nm* cinquecento

činšs *nm* (hist.) share rent, census

činuks *nm* (wind) chinook

čipata *nf* **1.** tuft, wisp, strand; **2.** pinch, small amount

čipendeils *nm* Chippendale

čips *nm* chip (microchip)

čipsi *nm pl* potato chips

čipsnis *nm* **1.** tuft, wisp, strand; **2.** pinch, small amount

čipste *nf* meadow pipit

čipstēt *vi* chirp

čipstiens *nm* chirp

čipstiņš *nm* = **čipste**

čipu čapu *interj* tap, tap

čir *interj* chirp; crunch

čirināt *vi* chirp, twitter, chirrup

čirka *nf* (com.) curl; (col.) shorty

čirkains *adj* (com.) curly

čirkāt *vt* curl

čirkāties *vr* curl

čirks *interj* (of grease) sputter; (of cut glass) crunch

čirkstēt *vi* **1.** crunch; squeak; grind; **2.** chirr; stridulate

čirkstināt *v* **1.** *vt* grind; make squeak; **2.** *vi* chirp; stridulate

čirkstoņa *nf* **1.** crunching; squeaking; **2.** chirring; stridulation

čirpstēt *vi* chirp

čirpstināt *vi* chirp

čirpstoņa *nf* chirping

čirs *nm* broad whitefish

čistiki *nm pl* European wheat stem sawfly

čita *nf* cheetah

čiukstēt *vi* **1.** chirp; **2.** hiss

čiv čiv *interj* chirp

čivināt *vi* chirp, twitter, chirrup

čivuļot *vi* chirp, twitter, chirrup

čīzburgers *nm* cheeseburger

čočis *nm* little basket

čok čok *interj* (of squirrels) the sound of scolding

čokarains *adj* = **čokurains**

čokarāties *vr* = **čokuroties**

čokars *nm* = **čokurs**

čoks I *nm* (tech.) choke

čoks II *nm* (sl.) slammer

čokstināt *vi* (of squirrels) scold

čoksts *nm* buttock cleft

čokurains *adj* curled; entangled

čokuroties *vr* roll up, curl up; become entangled, become twisted

čokur/s *nm* tangle; ~**ā** rolled up, curled up, en-tangled

čola *nf* small dugout

čoms *nm* (col.) chum, buddy

čoriņš *nm* (reg.) cockle (shell)

čubas *nf pl* straw or hay for bedding or stuffing a pallet

čubināt *vt* **1.** fluff up; **2.** putter, fuss with a baby's crib

čubināties *vr* **1.** putter; **2.** (col.) pet

čubuks *nm* = **čibuks**

čučabīšķis *nm* (col.) fire poker

čučakoks *nm* (col.) fire poker

čučala *nf* (barb.) scarecrow

čučarags *nm* (col.) fire poker

čučēt *vi* (child.) sleep; **iet č.** (child) go beddy-bye

čučināt *vt* (col.) lull to sleep

čučumuiēa *nf* (child.) beddy-bye

čudīt *vt* urge

čufa *nf* chufa, earth almond

čugas *nf pl* drift ice

čugums *nm* **1.** roof ridge; **2.** (of a hearth or range) hood

čuguns *nm* **1.** cast iron; **2.** (sl.) lies

čukāt *vt* (col.) **1.** poke; **2.** dig

čukbānītis *nm* (col.) choochoo

čukč/s *nm*, ~**iete** *nf* Chukchi

čukčukbānītis *nm* (col.) choochoo

čuknīt *vt* (col.) **1.** poke; **2.** dig

čūkslājs *nm* boggy thicket

čūksliena *nf* = **čūkslājs**

čūksliens *nm* = **čūkslājs**

čūkslis *nm* **1.** boggy thicket; **2.** protruding lips

čūksnis *nm* = **čūkslājs**

čūkstēt *vi, vt* whisper; **č. pa kaktiem** gossip

čūkstēt *vi* hiss, sputter

čūkstēties *vr* converse in whisper

čūkstiens *nm* whisper

čukstīt *vt* (col.) poke

čukstoņa *nf* whispering

čuksts *nm* whisper

čukstus *adv* in a whisper, under one's breath

čukšņa *nf* (reg.) remote corner, boondocks

čukums *nm* = **čugums**

čukurains *adj* crooked, gnarled, twisted

čukurs *nm* **1.** roof ridge; **2.** tuft

čūla *nf* ulcer

čūlains *adj* covered with ulcers; ulcerating

čūlāt *vi* = **čūlot**

čulga *nf* blister

čulgains *adj* blistery

čulgāt *vi* blister

čūlot *vi* **1.** ulcerate; (of wounds) seep; **2.** sputter

čum or **čumā** *adv* (sl.) a lot

čuma *nf* swarm

čumeklis *nm* swarm, writhing tangle

čumēt *vi* teem, swarm; **kā** (or **ka**) **čum** a lot

čumiza *nf* foxtail millet

čumuroties *vr* roll up, curl up; become entangled

čumurs *nm* **1.** cluster; **2.** tangle

čunčināt *vi* **1.** (col.) trot; **2.** pamper

čunčiņš *nm* chiffchaff

čunčurs *nm* bundle, tangle

čup/a *nf* heap, pile; (of letters) cluster; ~**u** ~**ām** in heaps; **viss vienā** ~**ā** (col.) in a mess; ~**ā** (com.) done for, ruined

čupata *nf* (reg.) heap

čūpēt *vi* hiss, sputter

čupiņa *nf dim* of **čupa**, small pile

čupoties *vr* (sl.) gather

čupra *nf* = **čuprs**

čuprs *nm* **1.** nape; **2.** tuft of hair

čūpslis *nm* (col.) nipple

čūpsteklis *nm* (col.) nipple

čūpstelis *nm* (col.) nipple

čūpstināt *vi* smack

čura *nf* **1.** puddle; wetness (from a child's urine); **2.** rill

čurāt *vi* (child.) tinkle, pee

čurga *nf* (col.) rill

čurings *nm* churinga

čurināt *vt* (reg., of fat) render

čuriņas *nf pl* (reg.) cracklings

čūr/is *nm* pouting lips; ~i sacelt (or uzmest) (com.) sulk

čurks *interj* sizzle, splatter

čurksla *nf* chatter

čurksle *nf* rill

čurkslis *nm* martin

čurksnis *nm* dirty room

čurkstas *nf pl* (reg.) cracklings

čurkste *nf* 1. common house martin; 2. rill

čurkstēt *vi* 1. gurgle; 2. sizzle

čurkstināt *vt* make sizzle, fry

čurkstināties *vr* gurgle

čurkstīte *nf dim* of čurkste, martin

čurkstoņa *nf* 1. gurgling; 2. sizzle

čurma *nf* (reg.) group; ~u ~ām mixed together

čurmulis *nm* tangle

čurnēt *vi* doze, mope; stand or sit idly or uncomfortably a long time

čūsciņa *nf dim* of čūska, little snake

čūska *nf* snake; ◊ č. azotē viper in one's bosom

čūskāda *nf* 1. snakeskin; 2. slough

čūskērglis *nm* short-toed eagle

čūskiņa *nf dim* of čūska, little snake

čūskliena *nf* snake-infested thicket

čūskmēlīte *nf* (bot.) adder's-tongue

čūskogas *nf pl* herb Paris

čūsku dīdītājs *nm* snake charmer

čūskulāji *nm pl* male orchis

čūskulāj/s *nm* colony of snakes, snake-infested thicket

čūsku lapas *nf pl* coltsfoot

čūskulēns *nm* young snake; (fig.) backbiter

čūsku midzenis *nm* 1. snake pit; 2. (sl.) dirty hole

čūsku puķes *nf pl* male orchis

čūsku sūrene *nf* snakeweed

čūskveida *indecl adj* snakelike, serpentine; sinuous

čūskveidīgi *adv* like a snake

čūskveidīgs *adj* snakelike, serpentine; sinuous

čūskzivs *nf* snake pipefish

čūslains *adj* boggy

čūsliens *nm* scrubland

čuš *interj* (sl.) finished, through

čuvašs *nm*, ~iete *nf* Chuvash

čuža *nf* shrubby cinquefoil

čužas *nf pl* coarse sweepings

čužināt *vt* fluff up

čužināties *vr* dawdle

D

dab/a *nf* 1. nature; ~ā in reality, under actual conditions; **brīvā** ~ā in the open air; in the wild; **klusā d.** still life ◊ **pie** ~**as krūts** (hum.) in the bosom of mother nature; ~**as klēpī** (poet.) in the open air; in the wild; 2. temper, disposition, nature; **ātras** ~**as** quick-tempered; **jautras** ~**as** of cheerful disposition; **labas** ~**as** good-natured; **otrā d.** second nature; **viņam jau tāda d.** it is the nature of the beast

dabas aizsardzība *nf* conservation; **d.** ~**s speciālists** conservationist

dabas bagātības *nf pl* natural resources;

dabasbērn/s *nm* child of nature; ~**i** people living in a natural state

dabasgāze *nf* natural gas

dabas mācība *nf* general science

dabas parks *nm* scenic area

dabas pētnieks *nm* naturalist

dabas piemineklis *nm* protected natural object

dabas rotaļa *nf* freak of nature

dabasskats *nm* landscape

dabasspēki *nm pl* forces of nature

dabas tauta *nf* preliterate society

dabastiece *nf* return to nature

dabaszinātnes *nf pl* natural sciences

dabaszinātnie/ks *nm*, **~ce** *nf* naturalist

dabaszinātnisks *adj* pertaining to the natural sciences; naturalistic

dabāt *vi* please; indulge

dabecijas *nf pl* Daboecia

dabīgi *adv* = **dabiski**

dabīgs a*dj* = **dabisks**

dabīgums *nm* naturalness, artlessness

dabiski *adv* naturally

dabisks *adj* **1.** natural; (of size) life; (of necessity) physical; (of silk) real; **2.** unaffected, artless, natural

dabiskums *nm* naturalness, artlessness

dabls *adj* strong and slender, well developed

dābolaine *nf* (reg.) mowed clover field

dābolains *adj* (reg.) dapple-gray

dābolaita *nf* (reg.) mowed clover field

dābolājs *nm* (reg.) mowed clover field

dāboliņš *nm* (reg.) clover

dābols *nm* (reg.) clover

dābt *vi* (reg.) hit

dabūjams *adj, part* of **dabūt** obtainable; available

dabums *nm* innate trait

dabūt *vt* **1.** get, obtain, receive; (of infectious disease) catch; **d. cauri** accomplish; **d. galu** (col.) perish; **d. gatavu** get sth. built or made; accomplish; **d. kurvi** (col.) be jilted; **d. lietu** get rained on; **d. mācību** learn a lesson; **d. matīt** experience; **d. pa ādu** (or **pa cepuri**) a. (col.) get a beating; get clobbered; b. (col.) be reprimanded; **d. pa biksēm** (col.) get a spanking; **d. pa pirkstiem** (col.) get one's knuckles rapped; **d. (kādu) pie malas** (col.) get rid of (s.o.); **d. pie samaņas** bring around; **d. pigu** (col.) get turned down flat; **d. piparus uz astes**

(col.) get a scolding, get punished; **d. rokā** get hold of, lay one's hands on; **d. savā pusē** win over; **d. savienojumu** get through (on the telephone); **d. savos nagos** (col.) subject to one's will; **d. sūci** spring a leak; **d. sutu** get raked over the coals; **d. vaļā** get open; **d. vārdu** take the floor; **nevar d. vārdus pār lūpām** cannot get a word out; **d. zināt** learn; **2.** have to; **d. trūkties** (col.) have a scary experience

dabūtenis *nm* illegitimate child

dabzinātne *nf* = **dabaszinātne**

dabzinātnie/ks *nm* = **dabaszinātnieks**

dabzinātnisks *adj* = **dabaszinātnisks**

dācīties *vr* antic

dacīts *nm* dacite

dadadzis *nm* agrimony

dadaisms *nm* Dada

dadaist/s *nm*, **~e** *nf* Dadaist

dadzilis *nm* siskin

dadzis *nm* thistle; **kā d. acī** it's a nuisance; eyesore

dadzītis *nm* **1.** *dim* of **dadzis**, thistle; **2.** goldfinch; **3.** agrimony

dadžains *adj* thistly

dadžu lapu uts *nf* a thistle aphid, Brachycaudus cardui

dafnija *nf* water flea

daga *nf* site of a fire, burn

dagerotipija *nf* daguerrotypy

dagerotips *nm* daguerrotype

dagestān/is *nm*, **~iete** *nf* Daghestanian

dagla *nf* punk (made of tinder fungus)

daglains *adj* = **dagls**

daglītis *nm* blueweed

dagls *adj* variegated, (of pigs, dogs) black-and-white spotted, black-and-rust spotted

daidzīt *vt, vi* stitch

daidžests *nm* digest

daiga *nf* long (fishing) pole

daika *nf* (geol.) dike

daikiri *indecl nm* Daiquiri

daiks *nm* = **daikts**

daikts *nm* (col.) tool, gadget

daile *nf* (poet.) **1.** beauty; **2.** art; ~s teātris art theater

dailene *nf* beauty (beautiful woman)

dailietis *nm* (folk.) handsome man

dailīgs *adj* (poet.) beautiful

dailināt *vt* adorn, beautify

dailināties *vr* adorn oneself

dailinieks *nm* (poet.) artist

dailis *nm* (folk.) handsome man

dailule *nf* beauty (beautiful woman)

dailulis *nm* handsome man

daiļamata *indecl adj* applied arts (*adj*)

daiļamatniecība *nf* applied arts, crafting

daiļamatnie/ks *nm*, ~ce *nf* applied arts master

daiļaudzis *nm* (folk.) handsome man

daiļaudzīte *nf* (folk.) beautiful girl

daiļava *nf* beautiful woman, (poet.) fair maiden

daiļdarbs *nm* literary work

daiļdārzniecība *nf* landscaping, landscape architecture

daiļdārznie/ks *nm*, ~ce *nf* landscape architect, landscape gardener

daiļdārzs *nm* ornamental garden

daiļi *adv* beautifully

daiļkrāsošana *nf* decorative painting

daiļkrāsotāj/s *nm*, ~a *nf* painter

daiļlasīšana *nf* recitation, declamation

daiļlasītāj/s *nm*, ~a *nf* reciter, declamator

daiļlēcēj/s *nm*, ~a *nf* (springboard) diver

daiļlēkšana *nf* (springboard) diving

daiļliter[a]tūra [ā] *nf* belles lettres

daiļnieks *nm* (poet.) artist

daiļot *vt* adorn, beautify

daiļoties *vr* adorn oneself

daiļproza *nf* literary prose

daiļrade *nf* artistic creation; writings; **tautas d.** folk art

daiļradis *nm* writer; artist

daiļrakstniecība *nf* calligraphy

daiļrakstnie/ks *nm*, ~ce *nf* calligrapher

daiļraksts *nm* calligraphy

daiļruna *nf* elocution

daiļrunātāj/s *nm*, ~a *nf* elocutionist

daiļrunība *nf* eloquence

daiļrunīgi *adv* eloquently

daiļrunīgs *adj* eloquent

daiļrunīgums *nm* eloquence

daiļskanība *nf* euphony

daiļskaņa *nf* euphony

daiļskanīgi *adv* euphoniously

daiļskanīgs *adj* euphonious

daiļskanīgums *nm* euphoniousness

daiļslidošana *nf* figure skating

daiļslidotāj/s *nm*, ~a *nf* figure skater

daiļš *adj* (poet.) beautiful, lovely

daiļums *nm* (poet.) beauty, loveliness

daiļvijīgs *adj* lissome

d[ai]moniski [ē] *adv* demonically

d[ai]monisks [ē] *adj* demoniac; daemonic

d[ai]monisms [ē] *nm* demonism

d[ai]monoloģija [ē] *nf* demonology

d[ai]mons [ē] *nm* demon

daina *nf* **1.** Latvian folk song; **2.** (poet.) song

dainot *vi* sing

daiņa *nf* = (obs.) **daina**

daiņāties *vr* be restive

daiņot *vi* = (obs.) **dainot**

dairas *nf pl* anxiety; eerie feeling

dairi *adv* fearsomely; **d. mesties** feel uneasy

dairīgi *adv* shyly

dairīgs *adj* shy

dairīties I *vr* **1.** poke, hesitate; **2.** be anxious; **3.** avoid; beware

dairīties II *vr* split

dairs *adj* fearsome

daiva *nf* (anat.) lobe; (of an orange) section, (of a garlic) clove

daivainā cietpaparde *nf* Christmas fern

daivains *adj* lobate

daiviņa *nf* lobule

daivīte *nf* lobule

dajak/s *nm*, ~**iete** *nf* Dayak
dākarēties *vr* (col.) fool around, kid
dakrons *nm* Dacron
dāks *nm* clown
dakstiņš *nm* roof tile
dakstīt *vt* give, give away
dakša *nf*, usu. *pl* ~**s** pitchfork; (mech.) fork
dakšiņa *nf* **1.** *dim* of **dakša**, fork; **noskaņojamā d.** tuning fork; **2.** (el.) plug
dakšot *vt* load with a pitchfork, fork
dakšots *adj, part* of **dakšot 1.** handled with a pitchfork; **2.** branched, forked
dakšradzis *nm* pronghorn
dakšveida *indecl adj* forked
dakšveidīgs *adj* forked
dakterēt *vt* (col.) doctor
dakter/is *nm*, ~**e** *nf* (col.) doctor
daktilisks *adj* dactylic
daktilogr[a]fija [ā] *nf* dactylography
daktilogramma *nf* dactylogram
daktiloloģija *nf* dactylology
daktiloskopija *nf* dactyloscopy
daktiloskopiski *adv* dactyloscopically
daktiloskopisks *adj* dactyloscopic
daktils *nm* dactyl
daktiņš *nm* (reg.) roof tile
dakts *nf* (col.) wick
dalailama *nm* Dalai Lama
dalāmais *nom adj* (math.) dividend; **mazākais kopīgais d.** least common multiple
dalāmība *nf* divisibility
dalāms *adj, part* of **dalīt** divisible
dalba *nf* = **dalbs**
dalbergijas *nf pl* Dalbergia
dalbis *nm* dolphin (for the mooring of boats)
dalbs *nm* **1.** tree trunk; **2.** pole (for punting or handling of boats or rafts; for driving fish into the net)
dālderains *adj* dappled
dālderis *nm* **1.** (hist.) taler; **2.** a type of ornamental design; **3.** dapple
dalenis *nm* (of a bookshelf) divider

dalība *nf* participation; ~**s nauda** participation fee; ~**s zīme** receipt; ticket
dalībnie/ks *nm*, ~**ce** *nf* **1.** participant, party; **2.** ac-complice
dalībvalsts *nf* member state
dālija *nf* dahlia
dalījums *nm* **1.** division; **2.** (math.) quotient
dalīšana *nf* division
dalīšanās *nfr* division
dalīšanas zīme *nf* (math.) division sign
dalīt *vt* **1.** divide; **2.** share; **3.** (of cards) deal; **kam jādala?** whose deal is it?
dalītājs *nm* **1.** divider; **2.** (el.) distributor; **3.** (math.) divisor; **lielākais kopīgais d.** greatest common measure
dalīties *vr* **1.** divide; be divided; **2.** branch out, fork; **3.** be divisible; **12 dalās ar 3 bez atlikuma** 3 is an aliquot part of 12; **4.** (with **ar**) share
dalmācietis *nm* Dalmatian
Dalmācijas kumelīte *nf* Dalmatian pyrethrum
daloties *vr* quarrel, fight
daltonīds *nm* daltonide
daltoniķ/is *nm*, ~**e** *nf* color blind person
daltonisms *nm* color blindness
dalzāt *vi* **1.** fidget; **2.** gad about
daļ/a *nf* **1.** part; portion; **pienācīgā d.** due; **pa** ~**ai** partly; **pa** ~**ām** apart; in parts; (of payments) on the instalment plan; **līdzīgās** ~**ās** share and share alike; **daļu līdzdalība** partnership; **pa lielākai** ~**ai** for the most part, largely; **2.** fraction; **3.** (mil.) unit, division; department, office; ~**as** *pl* troops; **4.** involvement, interest **kas man par** ~**u!** what do I care! **kas tev par** ~**u!** what's it to you! none of your business! **5.** (mus.) movement
daļas komandieris *nm* commanding officer
dāļāt *vt* divide, distribute, give away
daļēji *adv* partially; partly
daļējs *adj* partial
daļģe *nf* (reg.) one-handed scythe

daļģis *nm* (reg.) one-handed scythe

daļiņa *nf* **1.** *dim* of **daļa**, part; portion; fraction; **2.** particle

daļplūsma *nf* (hydr.) open flow

daļskaitlis *nm* (math.) fraction; **bezgalīgais d.** non-recurring decimal; **decimālais d.** decimal fraction; **īstais d.** proper fraction; **jauktais d.** mixed fraction; **neīstais d.** improper fraction; **periodiskais d.** recurrent decimal; **vienkāršais d.** common fraction

dāma *nf* **1.** lady **2.** (chess, cards) queen; (checkers) king

damaksnis *nm* large old growth forest

damakša *nf* (reg.) swamp

damaregle *nf* Agathis

damascēt *vt* damascene

Damaskas plūme *nf* damson plum

Damaskas roze *nf* damask rose

Damaskas tērauds *nm* Damascus steel

damasts *nm* (fabric) damask

dambēt *vt* dam

dambis *nm* dam; levee; breakwater

dambra *nf* (reg.) swamp

dambrete *nf* checkers

dambretes galdiņš *nm* checkerboard

dambretes kauliņš *nm* checker

dambretist/s *nm*, **~e** *nf* checkers player

dambriedis *nm* fallow deer

dāmiņa *nf* **1.** *dim* of **dāma**; **2.** (col., iron.) fine lady

damnifikācija *nf* damnification

damno *indecl nm* (bus.) loss; discount

damperis *nm* (obs.) steamer

dampis *nm* (col.) **1.** steam engine; **2.** car

dāmu deja *nf* ladies' choice

dāmu dubultspēle *nf* women's doubles

dāmu istaba *nf* powder room

dāmu komiteja *nf* ladies' auxiliary

dāmu vienspēle *nf* women's singles

danajiešu dāvana *nf* Greek gift

danaj/ietis or **danaj/s** *nm*, **~iete** *nf* Danaan

dancināt *vt* **1.** (obs.) dance (a female partner); **2.** (of a horse) exercise, make dance; (of a child) dandle; **3.** (col.) have at one's beck and call, make one hop

dancis *nm* Latvian folk dance; (obs.) dance

dancītis *nm* **1.** *dim* of **dancis**; **2.** connecting rod of a spinning wheel

dancot *vi, vt* **1.** (obs.) dance; **2.** jump, hop; **d. pēc kāda stabules** dance to s.o.'s tune

dančka *nf* (reg.) puddle

danda(la) *nf* Gypsy whip

dandziņa *nf dim* of **danga** II, small rut

danga I *nf* felly; rim

danga II *nf* rut

danga III *nf* morass

dangains *adj* rutted

dangāt *vi* stomp, tread; make ruts, rut

dangāties *vr* struggle through the ruts

dān/is *nm*, **~iete** *nf* Dane

dāniski *adv* in Danish, (speak) Danish

dānisks *adj* Danish

d[a]nsings [ā] *nm* dancing hall

dantonija *nf* danthonia

dāņa *nf* (reg.) gift

daņava *nf* (reg.) puddle; sump

dāņu suns *nm* Great Dane

dao *indecl nm* tao

daoisms *nm* Taoism

darām/ais *nom adj* **1.** thing to be done; **darīt savu ~o** do one's thing; **2.** piece of knitting

darāmā kārta *nf* (gram.) active voice

darāms *adj, part* of **darīt**, usu. *defin* **darāmais** to be done; (of verb voice) active

darba aizsardzība *nf* worker protection

darba alga *nf* wage, salary

darba apgāde *nf* labor exchang

darba aprēķins *nm* job estimate;

darbabiedr/s *nm*, **~ene** *nf* fellow worker, colleague

darba birža *nf* labor ex-change

darba bite *nf* (bee) worker

darba cilvēks *nm* workingman, toiler

darba dalīšana *nf* division of labor;

darba devējs *nm* employer

darbadiena *nf* working day

darba dienests *nm* conscript labor; labor service

darba gaita *nf* agenda

darba gājiens *nm* (internal combustion engines) ignition stroke

darbagalds *nm* = **darbgalds**

darba grāmatiņa *nf* employment record (book)

darba jubileja *nf* employment anniversary

darba kārtība *nf* agenda

darba klaušas *nf pl* labor tax

darba kodekss *nm* labor code

darba kolonija *nf* juvenile correctional institution;

darba koplīgums *nm* collective contract;

darbalaiks *nm* **1.** working hours; office hours; **2. karsts d.** very busy time working

darba laipa *nf* (theat.) fly gallery

darbalauks *nm* field of work

darba līgums *nm* employment contract

darba lopi *nm pl* draft animals

darbaļaudis *nm pl* workers, working people

darba nams *nm* workhouse

darba nespēja *nf* disability

darba ņēmējs *nm* employee

darba pārtraukšana *nf* work stoppage

darba pārtraukums *nm* break

darba pētīšana *nf* time and motion studies

darba piedāvājums *nm* position offered

darba pienākum/i *nm pl* job duties; **d. ~u apraksts** job description

darba pieprasījums *nm* position sought

darba psīcholoģija *nf* industrial psychology

darba racionālizācija *nf* streamlining of the work process

darba rezerves *nf pl* labor reserves;

darbarīk/s *nm* tool; **~u kalējs** toolsmith

darbarokas *nf pl* workers, hands, manpower

darbarūķ/is *nm*, **~e** *nf* worker, toiler

darba sieviete *nf* working woman

darba skola *nf* vocational-technical school

darba sols *nm* workbench

darbaspēja *nf* ability to work; efficiency; productive capacity

darbaspējīgs *adj* able to work

darbaspēks *nm* labor force, manpower

darba stāžs *nm* length of service

darba strīds *nm* labor dispute

darbatauta *nf* working class

darbatmiņa *nf* (compu.) working storage

darbaudzināšana *nf* on-the-job training and education of youth

darba uzņēmējs *nm* contractor

darba vadītājs *nm* foreman

darbavieta *nf* place of employment; place of work

darbavīrs *nm* worker

darba zirgs *nm* workhorse, draft horse

darbdevis *nm* employer

darbdiena *nf* weekday

darbdienīgs *adj* workday

darbeklis *nm* a woman's unfinished handicraft item

darbgalds *nm* **1.** work bench; **2.** machine tool

darbība *nf* action; activity; operation; **~s apvidus** (mil.) battlespace

darbības pārskats *nm* report on operations

darbības vārds *nm* verb

darbības vieta *nf* scene of action

darbietilpība *nf* consumption of labor; manhours per unit of output; amount of work

darbietilpīgs *adj* labor-intensive

darbietilpīgums *nm* = **darbietilpība**

darbīgi *adv* actively

darbīgs *adj* active

darbīgums *nm* activity

darbināt *vt* run, make work

darbinie/ks *nm*, **~ce** *nf* worker, employee; **ārštata d.** supernumerary; **atbildīgs d.** high official; **sabiedrisks d.** community activist; **saimniecisks d.** business executive

darbiņš *nm dim* of **darbs**, work

darbistaba *nf* office; study; studio

darbļaudis *nm pl* = **darbaļaudis**

darbmācība *nf* (educ.) shop

darbmašīna *nf* machine (for the transformation or transportation of materials)

darbmūžs *nm* (of a machine) useful life

darbnespēja *nf* inability to work

darbnespējīgs *adj* unable to work

darbnīca *nf* shop, workshop; studio

darbon/is *nm*, **~e** *nf* (cont.) worker

darbošanās *nfr* activity

darboties *vr* **1.** work; act; be active; be occupied with, be engaged in; **d. laikrakstā** contribute to a newspaper; **d. līdz** participate, take part in; **2.** run, operate, function

darb/s *nm* **1.** work; labor, toil; **garīgais d.** white-collar work; **garīgā ~a strādnieks** white-collar worker; **melnais d.** heavy, unskilled work; blue-collar work; **melnā ~a strādnieks** blue-collar worker ◊ **bez ~a** out of work; **būt ~ā** a. be at work; b. be worked on; c. (of machinery) be running; **pie ~a!** hop to it! **d. ~a galā** no end of work; **2.** work, piece of work; **galvenais d.** masterpiece, chef d'oeuvre; **3.** action; act; deed; **labs d.** good deed; **4.** job; employment; **~u apvienošana** holding more than one job; **5.** workmanship

darbspēja *nf* = **darbaspēja**

darbspējīgs *adj* = **darbaspējīgs**

darbstacija *nf* (compu.) work station

darbtauta *nf* = **darbatauta**

darbtiesisks *adj* labor (*adj*)

darbuzņēmējs *nm* contractor

darbuzņēmums *nm* **1.** contract; **2.** contract work

darbvedība *nf* **1.** office management; **2.** main office

darbved/is *nm*, **~e** *nf* office manager, chief clerk

darbvieta *nf* = **darbavieta**

dārcis *nm* streaky horse

dardedze *nf* (reg.) rainbow

dardeģis *nm* distiller, burner

dārdeklis *nm* rattle

dārdekļa čūska *nf* rattlesnake

dārdēt *vi* rumble, thunder, roar

dārdiens *nm* thunderclap, crash, (of drums) rattle

dārdināt *vt, vi* rattle, rumble, thunder

dārdoņa *nf* rattle, rumbling, thundering

dārdoņas filtrs *nm* (el.) rumble filter

dārd/s *nm* thunderclap, crash, (of drums) rattle; **~i** rumble, thunder, clap, roar

dārdzība *nf* high prices, expensiveness; **~s pie-augums** rise in prices; **~s pielikums** cost-of-living allowance

dārgais *nom adj* (term of endearment) dear

dārgakmens *nm* precious stone, gem, jewel

dārgakmeņu slīpētājs *nm* jeweler

dārglieta *nf* jewel; **~s** jewels, jewelry; **neīstas ~s** paste, imitation jewelry

dārgmet[all]s [āl] *nm* precious metal

dārgi *adv* **1.** expensively, costing a lot; **2.** (fig.) dearly

dārgs *adj* **1.** expensive, costly; **2.** dear, precious

dārgumiņš *nm dim* of **dārgums** (term of endearment) dear

dārgum/s *nm* **1.** high prices, expensiveness; **2.** treasure; **~u krātuve** treasure house

darīgi *adv* effectively, efficiently

darīgs *adj* effective, efficient

darījums *nm* **1.** deal; transaction; **2.** action; **3.** meadow (established on cleared forest floor)

darinājums *nm* product, work, piece of work, manufacture

darināšana *nf* (ling.) (new word) formation

darināt *vt* **1.** make, build, prepare, manufacture; **d. pūru** (folk.) make fabrics and clothing items for a dowry; **2.** (ling.) form (new words); **3.** pare, trim, peel; **4.** sharpen; **5.** fix (castrate, spay); **6.** sing; **d. mēli** chat

darīšan/a *nf* **1.** doing; **2.** business; **~u sarak-stīšanās** business correspondence; **nav tava d.** it is none of your business; **3. ~as** dealings; **man ar to nav nekādu ~u** I have nothing to do with it; **4.** (of beer) brewing

darīt *vt, vi* **1.** do, perform, work; make; **d. bēdas** give trouble; **to dara tā** this is how it is done; **d. galu** end; **d. sev galu** commit suicide; **d. godu** bring honor, be a credit; **d. kaunu** bring shame, disgrace; **d. labu** a. do good; b. do s.o. good; **ko lai es daru?** I cannot help it; what shall I do? **nezināt vairs, ko d.** be at one's wit's end; **d. pa prātam** please, satisfy; **d. pāri** do s.o. wrong; **d. pakaļ** imitate; **d. prieku** bring joy; **neko d.** what can you do? there is nothing to be done; **tur nekā nevar d.** it cannot be helped; **d. tāpat** do the same, follow suit; **d. zināmu** make it known; **2.** prepare, make, brew

darītāj/s *nm,* **~a** *nf* **1.** doer; **priecīgs d.** eager beaver; **2.** (obs.) brewer

darītājvārds *nm* (gram.) agent noun

darītava *nf* brewery; bottling plant

darīties *vr* **1.** make oneself (+ adjective), become; **d. zināmu** make oneself known; **2.** do oneself damage; do oneself good; **sev galu d.** do oneself in; **3.** be busy with, work with; **4.** behave; do sth. with; **5.** answer the call of nature; **6.** get done by itself; **7.** act, handle

dārks *adj* variegated; (of horses) spotted, calico

dārķis *nm* spotted horse

darma *nf* dharma

dārnis *nm* straw mat (for covering cold frames)

dārs *nm* smoke vent (in a bathhouse or threshing barn)

darsonvalizācija *nf* diathermy (using d'Arsonval current)

darsonvaliz[a]tors [ā] *nm* diathermy apparatus (that uses d'Arsonval current)

darva *nf* tar; **atšķaidīta d.** cutback

darvains *adj* tarry; pitchy

darvākslis *nm* wood for tar extraction; resinous stick of wood

darvas dedzinātava *nf* tarworks

darvas dedzinātājs *nm* tar distiller

darvas krāsa *nf* coal tar dye

darvas ota *nf* tarbrush

darvas papīrs *nm* tarpaper

darvaspuķe *nf* German catchfly

darvas tecināšana *nf* extraction of tar

darvas ziepes *nf pl* coal tar soap

darvdedzis *nm* = **darvdeģis**

darvdeģis *nm* tar distiller

darvene *nf* tar barrel

darvinieks *nm* tar distiller

darvinijas *nf pl* Darwinia

darvinisms *nm* Darwinism

darvinist/s *nm,* **~e** *nf* Darwinist

darvojums *nm* coat of tar

darvot *vt* tar

darvotājs *nm* tar applicator

dārza ālanta *nf* elecampane

dārza balodene *nf* garden orache

dārza dievkrēsliņš *nm* petty spurge

dārza īriss *nm* German iris

dārzāji *nm* vegetables

dārza kafejnīca *nf* tea garden

dārza kalnumētra *nf* savory

dārza kārveles *nf pl* chervil

dārza ķauķis *nm* garden warbler

dārza magone *nf* opium poppy

dārza mīkstpiene *nf* annual sow thistle

dārza naglene *nf* clove pink

dārza nazis *nm* pruning knife

dārza piesīši *nm pl* nasturtium

dārza puķes *nf pl* cultivated flowers

dārza stērste *nf* ortolan bunting

dārza šķēres *nf pl* pruning shears

dārzaugļi *nm pl* garden fruit

dārzaugs *nm* garden plant

dārza zemene *nf* cultivated strawberry

dārze/nis *nm* vegetable; ~ņi produce

dārzeņkopība *nf* vegetable gardening, vegetable growing

dārzeņkop/is *nm*, ~e *nf* vegetable gardener, vegetable grower

dārzeņpipars *nm* paprika

dārziņš *nm* 1. *dim* of **dārzs**, little garden; 2. circle of game players or dancers

dārzkopība *nf* horticulture

dārzkop/is *nm*, ~e *nf* horticulturist

dārzniecība *nf* 1. gardening; 2. nursery

dārznie/ks *nm*, ~ce *nf* gardener

dārzpilsēta *nf* garden city

dārzpūcīte *nf* cabbage moth

dārzs *nm* 1. garden; **botaniskais d.** botanical garden; **dendroloģiskais d.** arboretum; **zooloģiskais d.** zoo; 2. park; 3. pen (enclosure); 4. (me-teor.) halo

dārzsaimniecība *nf* truck farm

dārzsaknes *nf pl* garden vegetables

dārzu arkls *nm* orchard plow

dārzu atraitnīte *nf* garden pansy

dārzu ērickiņš *nm* redstart

dārzu pilsēta *nf* garden city

dārzu plūme *nf* European plum

dārzu pupa *nf* kidney bean

dārzu salvija *nf* sage

dārzu sausserdis *nm* woodbine

dārzzeme *nf* land alotted to gardening; garden soil

dāsni *adv* generously

dāsnība *nf* (poet.) generosity

dāsns *adj* (poet.) generous, lavish

dāsnums *nm* (poet.) generosity

dāstīt *vt* (reg.) give away

dastmērs *nm* (forest.) calipers

dastot *vt* (forest.) measure with calipers

datele *nf* (fruit) date

dateļpalma *nf* date palm

dateļplūme *nf* persimmon

datēt *vt* date; **d. atpakaļ** predate; **d. uz priekšu** postdate; **kļūdaini d.** misdate

dati *nm pl* data

datiskas *nf pl* Datisca

datīvs *nm* (gram.) dative

datne *nf* (compu.) file

dato *adv* (bus.) beginning with today's date

datorgrafika *nf* computer graphics

datorika *nf* computer science

datorizācija *nf* computerization

datorizēt *vt* computerize

datorrakstīšana *nf* 1. word processing; 2. operating a computer

datorrakstītāj/s *nm* 1. word processor; 2. computer operator; ~a *nf*

datorraksts *nm* computer printout

dator/s *nm* computer; ~a apar[a]tūra [ā] (compu.) hardware

datorspēle *nf* computer game

datorstandarts *nm* (compu.) computing standard

datorte[ch]nika [h] *nf* computer engineering

datortomogr[a]fija [ā] *nf* axial tomography, CAT scan production

datorvaloda *nf* computer language

datorvīruss *nm* computer virus

datorzinātnes *nf pl* computer sciences

datotēka *nf* (compu.) file

datuma robeža *nf* international date line

datum/s *nm* date; **bez** ~a undated; **(mēneša) pirmais d.** first day (of the month); **šīsdienas** ~a of today's date; **ar atpakaļejošu** ~u backdated

dauba *nf* gulch

daudaliņa *nf* a cheerful child

daudz *adv* much; many; **bezgala d.** an infinite quantity, and infinite number; **diezgan d.** quite a bit, quite a number, a lot, (with noun in genitive) many

daudzacains *adj* many-eyed

daudzatomu *indecl adj* polyatomic
daudzauglība *nf* multiparity
daudzauglīgs *adj* multiparous
daudzausains *adj* many-voiced
daudzbalsīgi *adv* harmonizing
daudzbalsīgs *adj* many-voiced; (of a song) part (*adj*)
daudzbalsīgums *nm* part singing
daudzbērnu *indecl adj* of many children; (of a family) large
daudzcēlienu *indecl adj* multiact
daudzcilindru *indecl adj* multicylinder
daudzcīņa *nf* all-around
daudzcīņnieks *nm* all-arounder
daudzciparu *indecl adj* multidigit
daudzdarbis *nm* universal cultivator
daudzdegvielu *indecl adj* multi-fuel
daudzdienu *indecl adj* of several days
daudzdievība *nf* polytheism
daudzdimensiju *indecl adj* multidimensional
daudzdimensionālitāte *nf* mutlidimensionality
daudzdzīvokļu *indecl adj* multi-apartment
daudzdzemdētāja *nf* multipara
daudzēdājs *nm* glutton
daudzēdelība *nf* gluttony
daudzēdis *nm* glutton
daudzējādi *adv* multifariously
daudzējādība *nf* manifoldness, multifariousness
daudzējāds *adj* various, manifold, multifarious
daudzf|a|žu |ā| *indecl adj* (el.) polyphase; polyphasic
daudzgadējs *adj* of many years, of several years' standing
daudzgadīgā airene *nf* ryegrass
daudzgadīgais plūris *nm* perennial satinpod
daudzgadīgā mēnesene *nf* perennial honesty
daudzgadīgs *adj* (bot.) perennial
daudzgadu *indecl adj* of many years
daudzgalvains *adj* many-headed

daudzgalvis *nm* many-headed monster
daudzgalvu *indecl adj* many-headed
daudzgribis *nm* a person who wants everything or too much
daudzgulētāj/s *nm*, ~a *nf* big sleeper
daudzgulis *nm* big sleeper
daudzi *adj* many, numerous
daudzība *nf* plurality, multitude
daudzināt *vt* 1. praise; 2. mention frequently
daudzkājains *adj* many-legged
daudzkāji *nm pl* Myriopoda
daudzkanšu *indecl adj* multi-rowed
daudzkanšu mieēi *nm pl* beardless barley
daudzkāršojums *nm* 1. multiplication; 2. reduplication
daudzkāršošana *nf* (tech.) multiplication
daudzkāršot *vt* multiply
daudzkāršotājs *nm* (tech.) multiplier
daudzkāršoties *vr* be multiplied
daudzkārt *adv* many times, repeatedly
daudzkārtains *adj* multilayer
daudzkārtējs *adj* repeated; frequent
daudzkārtīgi *adv* repeatedly; frequently
daudzkārtīgs *adj* 1. repeated; frequent; 2. many times greater; 3. multilayer
daudzkārtnis *nm* multiple
daudzkārtu *indecl adj* multilayer
daudzkas *pron* much
daudzkausu *indecl adj* (of an excavator) of multiple buckets
daudzkloķu *indecl adj* multicrank
daudzkomponentu *indecl adj* of many components
daudzkrāsaini *adv* in many colors
daudzkrāsainība *nf* many colors
daudzkrāsains *adj* multicolored; polychromatic
daudzkrāsainums *nm* many colors
daudzkrāsu *indecl adj* multicolored; polychromatic
daudzlaidu *indecl adj* (of stairs) multi-flight
daudzlampu *indecl adj* (el.) multitube

daudzlapains *adj* many-leaved, (bot.) polyphyllous, polypetalous

daudzlap/e *nf* water milfoil

daudzlauku *indecl adj* of multiple crops

daudzlauku sistēma *nf* crop rotation system involving multiple crops

daudzlaulība *nf* polygamy

daudzlemešu *indecl adj* (of plows) multibottom

daudzmāju *indecl adj* (bot.) polyoicous

daudzmaz *adv* more or less

daudzmet[all]isms [āl] *nm* multimetallism

daudzmiljonu *indecl adj* multimillion

daudzmotoru *indecl adj* multiengined

daudznāciju *indecl adj* multinational

daudznacionāls *adj* mutinational

daudznīšu *indecl adj* of multiple heddles

daudznīšu audums *nm* warp-faced twill

daudznozaru *indecl adj* manybranched

daudznozīmība *nf* polysemy

daudznozīmīgs *adj* 1. polysemous; 2. ambiguous

daudznozīmīgums *nm* polysemy

daudznozīmju *indecl adj* 1. polysemous; 2. ambiguous

daudzpakāpju *indecl adj* multistage

daudzpavalstniecība *nf* multiple citizenship

daudzpirkstains *adj* polydactyl

daudzplaknis *nm* polyhedron

daudzplakņu *indecl adj* polyhedral

daudzplāksnis *nm* multiplane

daudzpolu *indecl adj* multipolar, multipole

daudzpunkte *nf* suspension points

daudzpunkts *nm* suspension points

daudzpusēji *adv* multilaterally

daudzpusējs *adj* multilateral

daudzpusība *nf* versatility

daudzpusīgi *adv* from all sides

daudzpusīgs *adj* 1. many-sided, multifaceted; 2. versatile

daudzpusīgums *nm* versatility

daudzrakstītāj/s *nm*, ~a *nf* polygraph, voluminous writer

daudzreiz *adv* many times, repeatedly

daudzreizējs *adj* frequent, repeated

daudzrija *nm* (zool.) glutton; wolverine

daudzrindu *indecl adj* of multiple rows

daudzrobu *indecl adj* (of sound film) variablewidth

daudzrokains *adj* many-armed

daudzrunība *nf* talkativeness

daudzrunīgs *adj* talkative

daudzrunīgums *nm* talkativeness

daudzrunātājs *nm*, ~a *nf* great talker

daudzsakņu *indecl adj* many-rooted

daudzsakņu ūdenslēca *nf* greater duckweed

daudzsānis *nm* polygon

daudzsareņi *nm pl* Polychaeta

daudzsaru *indecl adj* many-bristled

daudzsaru tārpi *nm pl* polychaetes

daudzsējumu *indecl adj* multivolume

daudzsekciju *indecl adj* of multiple sections

daudzsēklu *indecl adj* many-seeded

daudzsēklu balanda *nf* many-seeded goosefoot

daudzsievība *nf* polygamy

daudzsievīgs *adj* polygamous

daudzsievis *nm* polygamist

daudzskaitlīgs *adj* numerically large

daudzskaitlinieks *nm* a noun used only in the plural

daudzskaitlis *nm* (gram.) plural

daudzskaldnis *nm* polyhedron

daudzskaldņu *indecl adj* polyhedral

daudzskanīgs *adj* of many voices

daudzslāņu *indecl adj* multilayer

daudzsliežu *indecl adj* multiple-track

daudzsološi *adv* promisingly

daudzsološs *adj* promising

daudzstarains *adj* of many rays

daudzstāvu *indecl adj* multistory; multideck

daudzstobru *indecl adj* multibarreled

daudzstūŗains *adj* polygonal

daudzstūris *nm* polygon

daudzstūŗveida *indecl adj* polygonal

daudzstūŗveidīgs *adj* polygonal

daudzšķautnainība *nf* multifacetedness

daudzšķautnains *adj* multifaceted

daudzšķautņu *indecl adj* multifaceted

daudzšūnains *adj* multicellular

daudzšūnu *indecl adj* multicellular

daudzšūņi *nm pl* multicellular organisms

daudztautību *indecl adj* multiethnic

daudztautu *indecl adj* multinational

daudztūkstošu *indecl adj* of many thousands

daudzum daudz *adv* a great many

daudzums *nm* amount, quantity; number

daudzvaldība *nf* polyarchy

daudzvalodība *nf* polyglotism

daudzvalodīgs *adj* polyglot, multilingual

daudzvalodu *indecl adj* polyglot, multilingual

daudzvārdība *nf* verbosity

daudzvārdīgi *adv* verbosely

daudzvārdīgs *adj* verbose

daudzvārdīgums *nm* verbosity

daudzvārpstu *indecl adj* (tech.) gang, turret

daudzveida *indecl adj* multiform, diverse, manifold

daudzveida ūdenīte *nf* water starwort

daudzveidība *nf* multiformity, diversity, multiplicity

daudzveidīgi *adv* diversely

daudzveidīgs *adj* multiform, diverse, manifold

daudzveidīgums *nm* multiformity, diversity, multiplicity

daudzveidot *vt* diversify, vary

daudzveidoties *vr* become diversified

daudzvērtība *nf* multivalence; polyvalence

daudzvērtīgs *adj* multivalent; polyvalent

daudzvietīgs *adj* multiseater

daudzvilcis *nm* a chess problem of more than four moves

daudzvīrība *nf* polyandry

daudzzarains *adj* many-branched

daudzzaru *indecl adj* many-branched

daudzziedains *adj* multiflorous

daudzziedu *indecl adj* multiflorous

daudzziedu airene *nf* Italian ryegrass

daudzziedu mauraga *nf* smoothish hawkweed

daudzziedu melmeņu zāle *nf* Solomon's seal

daudzziedu mugurene *nf* Solomon's seal

daudzziedu zemzālīte *nf* a wood rush, Luzula multiflora

daudzzilbīgi *adv* polysyllabically

daudzzilbīgs *adj* polysyllabic

daudzzilbju *indecl adj* polysyllabic

daudzzīmīgs *adj* **1.** meaningful, pregnant; **2.** (of numbers) of several figures

daudzzīmju *indecl adj* (of numbers) of several figures

daudzzinis *nm* pundit

daudzžuburains *adj* many-pronged; many-armed; many-branched

daudzžuburs *nm* grappling hook

Daugavas vizbuļi *nm pl* anemone

daugavietis *nm* Daugava shore dweller

daugmalietis *nm* Daugava shore dweller

Dauna slimība *nf* Down's syndrome

Daurijas lapegle *nf* Dahurian larch

dauzeklis *nm* hyperactive child; blustering person

dauzienmasāža *nf* percussion (massage), tapotement

dauzīgs *adj* romping; naughty

dauzīt *vt* **1.** beat, pound, hammer; batter; **2.** bang; **3.** (of feet) stamp

dauzīties *vr* **1.** bang, knock; **2.** hit against; **3.** romp; **4. d. apkārt** gad about

dauzoknis *nm* = **dauzoņa**

dauzonība *nf* rowdiness

dauzonīgi *adv* in a rowdy manner

dauzonīgs *adj* rowdy

dauzonis *nm* = **dauzoņa**

dauzoņa *nf, nm* rowdy, brawler

dauzulis *nm* romper

dauža *nf, nm* rowdy, brawler

dāvājums *nm* gifting

dāvana *nf* gift, present; donation

dāvaniņa *nf dim* of **dāvana**, small gift

dāvanlasis *nm* beggar, panhandler; mendicant

dāvāt *vt* 1. give; grant; bestow; **d. dzīvību** a. give birth; b. grant one's life; **d. uzticību** trust; 2. offer

dāvāties *vr* (folk.) offer oneself

davidijas *nf pl* Davidia

dāvinājums *nm* gifting; donation

dāvināt *vt* give as a gift; donate

dāvinātāj/s *nm*, ~a *nf* giver; donor

dazilirions *nm* dasylirion

dažādi *adv* variously, diversely

dažādība *nf* 1. variety; diversity; 2. difference

dažādlapu dadzis *nm* a thistle, Cirsium heterophyllum

dažādmalu *indecl adj* of unequal sides, (of triangles) scalene

dažādot *vt* diversify; vary

dažāds *adj* 1. various; diverse; 2. different

dažādveida *indecl adj* of various kinds

dažbrīd *adv* at times

daždažādi *adv* in various ways

daždažāds *adj* of all kinds

daždien *adv* sometimes; **kā d.** as usual; **kā jau d. kungs** as is the wont of bosses

dažkārt *adv* sometimes

dažkārtējs *adj* recurring

dažnedažādi *adv* in various ways

dažnedažāds *adj, emph* of **daždažāds** of all kinds

dažreiz *adv* sometimes

dažreizējs *adj* repeated

daž/s *adj* 1. some; ~ā ziņā in a way; 2. **d. labs** a good many; 3. ~i a few

dažubrīd *adv* at times

daēudien *adv* sometimes

dažugad *adv* some years

dažunakt *adv* on some nights, sometimes in the night

dažur *adv* in some places

dažureiz *adv* sometimes

dažurīt *adv* some mornings

dažuviet *adv* in some places, here and there

dažviet *adv* in some places, here and there

deareācija *nf* deareation

debarkaders *nm* floating pier

debates *nf pl* 1. debate; 2. proceedings

debatēt *vi* debate

debatētāj/s *nm*, ~a *nf* debater

debatraksts *nm* debate shorthand

debesbraukšana *nf* (rel.) ascension

Debesbraukšanas diena *nf* Ascension Day

debesis *nm* (obs.) rain cloud

debesjosta *nf* (reg.) rainbow

debesjums *nm* vault of the sky

debeskaza *nf* (zool.) snipe

debesloks *nm* vault of the sky

debesmala *nf* horizon

debespuse *nf* cardinal point

debes/s *nf* 1. sky ◊ **no skaidrām ~īm** out of the blue; **pie ~īm** in the sky; **uz ~īm** skyward; **zem klajām ~īm** in the open air; **ak debess!** good heavens! 2. ~is heaven, heavens ◊ ~u **brīnumi!** wonder of wonders! ~u **tētiņ!** good heavens! **septītās ~īs** in rapture, on cloud nine; **kā no ~īm nokritis** completely at sea; 3. (obs.) thundercloud

debess gosniņa *nf* (reg.) ladybug

debess jums *nm* vault of heavens

debesskrāpis *nm* skyscraper

debess puse *nf* cardinal point

debess zilgme *nf* azure

debestiņa *nf dim* of **debess**, sky; **ak d.!** good heavens!

debesu dāvana *nf* gift from heaven, godsend

debesu grāmata *nf* (folk.) a type of book of magic

debesu ķermenis *nm* heavenly body

debesu lode *nf* sphere of heavens

debesu rasa *nf* (poet.) rain

debesu rija *nf* (folk.) the next world

debesu tēvs *nm* heavenly father

debesu valstība *nf* kingdom of heavens; the next world, paradise

debeszils *adj* sky blue

debešķīgi *adv* (col.) heavenly

debešķīgs *adj* (col.) heavenly

debešup *adv* upward

d[e]betēt [ē] *vt* debit

d[e]betkarte [ē] *nf* debit card

d[e]bets [ē] *nm* debit

debija *nf* debut

debilitāte *nf* 1. debility; 2. (slight) mental retardation

debils *adj* (slightly) mentally retarded

debitante *nf* debutante

debitants *nm* debutant

debitēt *vi* debut

d[e]bitīvs [ē] *nm* (gram.) debitive (mood)

d[e]bitor/s [ē] *nm*, ~e *nf* debtor

debits *nm* (of water, oil, gas wells) production rate

debloķēšana *nf* (bus.) deblocking; (mil.) blockade clearing

debloķēt *vt* deblock

deboļševizācija *nf* debolshevization

debošs *nm* 1. debauch, debauchery; 2. (mil.) de-bouch

decembris *nm* December

decemvīrs *nm* decemvir

decennijs *nm* decennial

decentrācija *nf* (psych.) decentering

decentrālisms *nm* decentralism

decentr[a]lizācija [ā] *nf* decentralization

decentr[a]lizēt [ā] *vt* decentralize

de[ch]lorēt [h] *vt* dechlorinate

deciārs *nm* deciare

decibels *nm* decibel

decigrams *nm* decigram

decile *nf* decile

decilitrs *nm* deciliter

deciljons *nm* decillion

decima *nf* 1. (mus.) tenth; 2. decastich

decimācija *nf* decimation

decimālcipars *nm* decimal digit

decimāldaļskaitlis *nm* decimal fraction

decimāllogaritms *nm* decimal logarithm

decimāls *adj* decimal

decimālsvari *nm pl* decimal balance

decimēt *vt* decimate

decimetrs *nm* decimeter

dedere *nf* gold-of-pleasure

dēderēt *vi* cackle

dedestiņas *nf pl* common meadow vetchling, meadow pea

dēdēšana *nf* 1. pining away; 2. (geol.) erosion

dēdēt *vi* 1. pine away, waste away; 2. idle; 3. (geol.) age, weather, erode

dedikācija *nf* dedication

dedināt *vi* giggle

dēdināt *vi* 1. hollow (a log for a beehive); 2. accustom (hens) to lay in the same place; 3. (of plowshares) lengthen

dedrs *nm* gold-of-pleasure

deducēt *vt* deduce

dedukcija *nf* deduction

deduktīvi *adv* deductively

deduktīvs *adj* deductive

dedveits *nm* deadweight

dedzeklis *nm* burner

dedzība *nf* ardor, fervor

dedzīgi *adv* ardently, fervently

dedzīgs *adj* 1. ardent, fervent; heated; 2. (rare.) urgent; 3. (rare.) (of pain) burning

dedzīgums *nm* 1. ardor, fervor; 2. (rare.) urgency; 3. (rare.) burning sensation

dedzīkla *nf* burner

dedzināšana *nf* 1. burning; 2. arson; 3. (of ceramics) firing; (of bricks) baking; 4. distillation; 5. incineration

dedzināt *vt* 1. burn; (coffee) roast; (ceramics) fire; (bricks) bake; (spirits, tar) distil; (lime) burn; (tech.) calcine; (of sun) be scorching hot; d. eg-līti light the Christmas tree; 2. incinerate; 3. set fire(s)

dedzinātāj/s *nm*, ~**a** *nf* **1.** (person) burner; **2.** distiller; **3.** arsonist, fire setter; **4.** burning pain

dedzinātava *nf* **1.** kiln; **2.** tarworks; **3.** distillery; **4.** incinerator

dedzinošā kariota *nf* fishtail palm

dedzinošs *adj, part* of **dedzināt** (of the sun) scorching; (of pain) burning

deemuļģēšana *nf* demulsification

deeskalācija *nf* de-escalation

de fakto *adv, indecl adj* de facto

defekācija *nf* defecation

defektelektrons *nm* (el.) electron vacancy, hole

defektīvi *adv* defectively

defektīvs *adj* defective

defektolo/gs *nm*, ~**ģe** *nf* specialist in mental defects and physical handicaps in children; special education teacher

defektoloģija *nf* special education

defektoloģisks *adj* special education (*adj*)

defektoskopija *nf* quality inspection

defektoskopist/s *nm*, ~**e** *nf* defectoscope operator

defektoskops *nm* defectoscope

defekts *nm* defect

defensīva *nf* defensive

defensīvs *adj* defensive

deferizācija *nf* deferrization

defētisms *nm* defeatism

defibrers *nm* defibrator

defibrillācija *nf* defibrillation

defibrill[a]tors [ā] *nm* defibrillator

defic[i]ta [ī] preces *nf pl* goods in short supply

defic[i]ts [ī] *nm* deficit; deficiency, shortage

defic[i]ts [ī] *adj* in short supply

defilēt *vi* march by

definējums *nm* definition

definēt *vt* define

definīcija *nf* definition

defin[i]tīvi [ī] *adv* definitively

defin[i]tīvs [ī] *adj* definitive

definīts *adj* definite

defise *nf* hyphen

deflācija *nf* deflation

deflācijas ieplaka *nf* deflation blowout

deflācijas klājs *nm* deflation pavement

deflegmācija *nf* dephlegmation

deflegm[a]tors [ā] *nf* dephlegmator

deflektors *nm* deflector

deflorācija *nf* defloration

deflorants *nm* delowering agent, deflorant

defoliants *nm* defoliant

deformācija *nf* deformation

deformējamība *nf* deformability

deformēt *vt* deform

deformēties *vr* become deformed

defrostācija *nf* defrosting

defrosters *nm* defroster

defrostēt *vt* defrost

dega *nf* burn (in a forest or grass-covered area)

degadēt *vt* shrink (wool fabric by applying hot water or steam)

degadēts *adj, part* of **degadēt** preshrunk

degaine *nf* burn site

degakmens *nm* bituminous rock

degamība *nf* combustibility

degams *adj* combustible

degamspēja *nf* combustibility

degamvērtība *nf* heating value

degaukla *nf* safety fuse

degazācija *nf* **1.** degassing; **2.** decontamination

degaz[a]tors [ā] *nm* decontamination agent

degazēšana *nf* **1.** degassing; **2.** decontamination; ~**s punkts** decontamination station

degazēt *vt* **1.** degas; **2.** decontaminate

degbumba *nf* incendiary bomb

deggāze *nf* fuel gas

degizrakteņi *nm pl* fossil fuels

degjosla *nf* combustion zone

degkamera *nf* fire chamber

deglaciācija *nf* deglaciation

deglis *nm* 1. wick; 2. burner; 3. (welding, soldering) torch; 4. fuse

deglode *nf* incendiary bullet

degmaisījums *nm* fuel mixture

degmāls *nm* terra cotta

degoņa *nf* (col.) hurry

degošs *adj, part* of **degt** 1. (also fig.) burning; 2. flammable

degpudele *nf* Molotov cocktail

degpunkts *nm* focus

degradācija *nf* 1. degradation; 2. demotion

degradēšana *nf* abasement

degradēt *vt* 1. degrade; 2. demote, reduce in rank

degradēties *vr* become degraded

degrupēt *vt* divide into groups

degslāneklis *nm* oil shale

degsme *nf* ardor, fervor

degsmīgi *adv* ardently, fervently, passionately

degsmīgs *adj* ardent, fervent, passionate

degsmīgums *nm* ardor, fervor

degsnis *nm* burn site

degšana *nf* burning; combustion

degšņa *nf* burn site

degt I *vi* 1. burn; **deg** (of fireplaces, hearths, ovens) there is fire in . . .; **viņam zeme deg zem kājām** a. he is in a big hurry; b. the place is getting too hot for him; **pirksti deg** be itching (to do sth.); **papēži deg** I've got to run; 2. (with **par**) be enthused about

degt II *vt* (of fire, candles) light, (of lights) turn on

degteris *nm* distiller of spirits

degtspēja *nf* combustibility

degtuve *nf* furnace, fire flue; combustion chamber

deguma brūce *nf* burn (injury)

deguma puķe *nf* burnt orchis

deguma smaka *nf* burnt smell

deguma zāle *nf* moneywort

degums *nm* burn, burning, fire; burned area, site of fire

deguna dobums *nm* nasal cavity

degungals *nm* tip of the nose

degunkniebis *nm* pince-nez

degunlācītis *nm* coati

degunmērkaķis *nm* proboscis monkey

degunradzis *nm* rhinoceros

degunradžvabole *nf* rhinoceros beetle

degun/s *nm* nose; **strups d.** pug nose; **uzraukts d.** turned-up nose ◊ **ar garu ~u** empty-handed; **no ~a priekšas** (col.) from under one's nose; **~a priekšā** (col.) under one's nose, in the face; **ar ~u grāmatā** (col.) buried in a book; **viņam ir d. uz . . .** he has a nose for . . .; **ar ~u gaisā** (col.) stuck up

deguntiņš *nm dim* of **deguns**, little nose

degustācija *nf* degustation, tasting

degust[a]tor/s [ā] *nm*, **~e** *nf* degustator

degustēt *vt* degust

degutnieks *nm* ground beetle

deguts *nm* birch tar

degviela *nf* fuel

degvīns *nm* spirit, proof spirit; vodka

degzīme *nf* (cattle) brand

deģenerācija *nf* degeneration

deģener[a]tīvi [ā] *adv* degeneratively

deģener[a]tīvs [ā] *adj* degenerative

deģenerāt/s *nm*, **~e** *nf* degenerate

deģenerēties *vr* degenerate

deģis *nm* distiller, burner

dehelmintizācija *nf* deworming

dehermetizācija *nf* loss of hermetic seal

deheroizācija *nf* (art) portrayal of the little man

dehidrācija *nf* dehydrogenation

dehidr[a]tācija [ā] *nf* dehydration

dehidrēt *vt* dehydrate

dehidrogenizācija *nf* dehydrogenation

dehumanizācija *nf* dehumanization

deicija *nf* deutzia

deiderēt *vi* 1. run back and forth; 2. stagger

deideris *nm* staggerer

deiktisks *adj* deictic

deionizēt *vt* deionize

deisms *nm* deism

deistiski *adv* deistically

deistisks *adj* deistic

deists *nm*, ~e *nf* deist

deit|e|rijs [ē] *nm* deuterium

deitrons *nm* deuteron

deja *nf* dance; **saviesīga d.** ballroom dancing

dējala *nf* hollowed-out tree in the woods (for bees to make a nest in)

dejas ceļ/š *nm* (of dancing) line of direction; **d. ~a virzienā** (of dancing) in the line of direction

dejas zāle *nf* dancing hall, ballroom

dējējvista *nf* laying hen

dējeklis *nm* oviduct

dējība *nf* (of a laying hen) productivity

dējīgs *adj* (of a chicken) productive, a good layer

dējīgums *nm* (of a laying hen) productivity

dejisks *adj* **1.** choreographic; **2.** danceable

dejiskums *nm* danceability

dejojums *nm* dance performance

dejot *vi* dance; *vt* (with the name of the dance) waltz, rhumba, etc.

dejotāj/s *nm*, ~a *nf* dancer

dējums *nm* deposit of eggs

de jure *adv, indecl adj* de jure

deju vakars *nm* dancing party, dance

deka I *nf* (mus.) sounding board

deka II *nf* tape deck

dēka *nf* adventure

dekabrists *nm* (hist.) Decembrist

dek|a|d|a| [ā][e] *nf* **1.** ten days, ten-day period; **2.** decade

dekadence *nf* decadence

dekadentiski *adv* decadently

dekadentisks *adj* decadent

dekadentisms *nm* decadentism

dekadent/s *nm* , ~e *nf* decadent

dēkainība *nf* adventurousness

dēkain/is *nm*, ~e *nf* adventurer

dēkaini *adv* adventurously

dēkains *adj* adventurous

dēkainums *nm* adventurousness

dekalitrs *nm* decaliter

dekalogs *nm* decalogue

dekametrs *nm* decameter

dek|a|nāts [ā] *nm* dean's office

dekānols *nm* decanol

dekān/s *nm* **1.** dean; ~e *nf*; **2.** (chem.) decane

dekantēt *vt* decant

dekantēšana *nf* decantation

dekapitācija *nf* decapitation

dekarboksilācija *nf* decarboxylation

dekarbonizācija *nf* decarburization

dekartiet/is *nm*, ~e *nf* Cartesian

dekartisms *nm* Cartesianism

dekatēšana *nf* (text.) decating

dekers *nm* (obs., of skins) count of 10

deklamācija *nf* declamation, recitation

deklam|a|toriski [ā] *adv* in a declamatory manner

deklam|a|torisks [ā] *adj* declamatory

deklam|a|tor/s [ā] *nm*, ~e *nf* reciter;

deklamēt *vt* recite

deklamētāj/s *nm*, ~a *nf* reciter

deklarācija *nf* declaration; pronouncement

deklar|a|tīvisms [ā] *nm* a style dominated by pronouncements

deklar|a|tīvi [ā] *adv* declaratively

deklar|a|tīvs [ā] *adj* declarative

deklarēt *vt* declare, state; pronounce

deklasēties *vr* become declassed

deklasēts *adj* déclassé, declassed

deklasificēt *vt* declassify

deklasifikācija *nf* declassification

deklinācija *nf* **1.** (gram.) declension; **2.** (phys.) declination; ~s leņķis (firearms) angle of depression; **maksimālais ~s leņķis** minimum elevation

deklinēt *vt* (gram.) decline

deklinometrs *nm* declinometer

dēklis *nm* 1. (gram.) affix; 2. hen's nest

dekoders *nm* decoder

dekodēšana *nf* decoding

dekodēt *vt* decode

dekodētāj/s *nm*, ~a *nf* decoder

dekokts *nm* decoction

dekolonizācija *nf* decolonization

dekolonizēt *vt* decolonize

dekoltē *nm indecl* décolletage

dekoltēts *adj* décolleté

dekompensācija *nf* decompensation

dekompensēt *vt* (med.) decompensate

dekompozīcija *nf* decomposition

dekompresija *nf* decompression

dekompresors *nm* decompressor

dekoncentrācija *nf* (mil.) dispersion

dekoncentrēt *vt* (mil.) disperse

dekoncentrētība *nf* deconcentrated state

dekonservācija *nf* end of conservation; reactivation

dekonstrukcija *nf* deconstruction

dekorācija *nf* decoration; window dressing, display; ~s (theat.) sets, decor

dekor|a|tīvi [ā] *adv* decoratively; ornamentally

dekor|a|tīvisms [ā] *nm* 1. decorativeness; 2. ornamentalism

dekor|a|tivistiski [ā] *adv* decoratively

dekor|a|tīvistisks [ā] *adj* decorative

dekor|a|tivitāte [ā] *nf* decorativeness

dekor|a|tīvs [ā] *adj* decorative, ornamental

dekor|a|tor/s [ā] *nm*, ~e *nf* (theat.) scene painter; decorator

dekorējums *nm* decoration, adornment

dekorēt *vt* decorate

dekors *nm* decor

dekortikācija *nf* decortication

dekorts *nm* discount, deduction

dekrements *nm* decrement

dekrešendo *nm indecl* decrescendo

dekrēta atvaļinājums *nm* maternity leave

dekr|e|tālija [ē] *nf* decretal

dekr|e|tēt [ē] *vt* decree

dekrēts *nm* decree

dekrimin|a|lizācija [ā] *nf* decriminalization

deks *nm* (naut.) deck

deksnis *nm* = dega

dekstrāns *nm* dextran

dekstrīns *nm* dextrin

dekstroze *nf* dextrose

dekubits *nm* decubitus

dēku meklētāja *nf* adventuress

dēku meklētājs *nm* adventurer

dekvalificēties *vr* lose one's skills

dekvalifikācija *nf* disqualification

deķelis *nm* (cont.) blanket; (sl.) cap (of a student corps member)

deķis *nm* (col.) 1. blanket; 2. deck

deķītis *nm dim* of deķis, small blanket

dēladēls *nm* grandson

delamais *nom adj* (com.) tuberculosis

delamā kaite *nf* (col.) tuberculosis

dēlamāte *nf* (folk.) mother-in-law

dēlameita *nf* granddaughter

delartiskā komēdija *nf* commedia dell'arte

dēlasieva *nf* daughter-in-law

delators *nm* (hist.) traitor; spy

delbs *nm* upper arm

deldēšana *nf* 1. wear; wear and tear; 2. paying off; amortization; ~s fonds sinking fund

deldēt *vt* 1. wear out; 2. (of debts) pay off; amortize; (velti) mēli d. waste one's breath

deldināt *vt* = deldēt

deldze *nf* wear and tear

dēle *nf* leech

delēcija *nf* (biol.) deletion

delegācija *nf* delegation

delegāt/s *nm*, ~e *nf* delegate

deleģēšana *nf* delegation

deleģēt *vt* delegate

dēlene *nf* 1. daughter-in-law; 2. (reg.) leech

dēlēns *nm* sonny

delf[i]nārijs [ī] *nm* dolphin pool

delfinija *nf* larkspur

delfīns *nm* dolphin; purpoise

delfīnstils *nm* (swimming) fishtail kick, dolphin (stroke)

delga *nf, nm* insistent pleader

delgavot *vi* 1. talk at length; 2. stretch out one's work

delgt *vi* plead insistently

deliberācija *nf* deliberation

dēlietis *nm* (folk.) young man

delikatese *nf* delicacy; ~s delicacies; delicatessen

delikatešu veikals *nm* delicatessen (store)

delikāti *adv* delicately

delikāts *adj* delicate

delikātums *nm* delicateness

delikts *nm* delict, offense, infraction of law

delimitācija *nf* delimitation

delimitēt *vt* (of borders) delimit

delinkvent/s *nm*, ~e *nf* delinquent

dēliņš *nm dim* of **dēls**, sonny

delīrijs *nm* delirium

dē/lis *nm* 1. board; plank; **divšķautņu d.** flitch; **gludināmais d.** ironing board; **lecamais d.** springboard; **mazgājamais d.** washboard; **melnais d.** blackboard; **spundēts d.** tongue and groove board; **uzvelkamais d.** plasterer's darby ◊ **(iet) kā pa ~li** (it is going) without a hitch; 2. (sl.) failure; mess

dēlišķis *nm* (reg.) young man

dēlītis *nm* 1. *dim* of **dēlis**, little board; 2. wood tile

delkr[e]dere [ē] *indecl nm* del credere

delms *nm* upper arm

delna *nf* palm; metacarpus ◊ **kā uz ~s** spread out before you

delnas kauli *nm pl* metacarpals

delnas locītavas kauli *nm pl* carpals

delok[a]lizācija [ā] *nf* delocalization

dēls *nm* son

delta *nf* 1. (Greek letter) delta; 2. river delta

delta dzelzs *nf* delta iron

deltaplanierisms *nm* hanggliding

deltaplāns *nm* hangglider

del[u]viāls [ū] *adj* diluvial

del[u]vijs [ū] *nm* diluvium

delve *nf* big paw

delverēt *vi* 1. romp; 2. stumble

delverēties *vr* 1. romp; 2. stumble

delverība *nf* romping

delverīgi *adv* rompingly

delverīgs *adj* rompish, romping

delveris *nm*, ~e *nf* 1. romp; restless child; 2. noisemaker, drinker

delverīša *nf* romp; restless child

delzt *vi* talk incessantly

dēļ *prep* 1. because of, on account of, owing to; **šī iemesla d.** for this reason; 2. for the sake of; **da-ri to manis d.** do it for my sake; **manis d. dari to** do it, for all I care

dēļot *vt* cover with boards; **d. grīdu** put down floor boards

dēļu aizsargapšuvums *nm* siding

dēļu apšuvums *nm* boarding

dēļuks *nm dim* of **dēls**, sonny

demago/gs *nm*, ~ģe *nf* demagogue

demagoģija *nf* demagoguery

demagoģiski *adv* demagogically

demagoģisks *adj* demagogic

demaizāarters *nm* demise charter

demarkācija *nf* demarcation

drmarkācijas līnija *nf* line of demarcation

demaršs *nm* demarche

demaskēt *vt* unmask

demence *nf* dementia

dementēt *vt* deny, give the lie to

demeredēs *nm* demurrage

demfermagnēts *nm* damping magnet

demilit[a]rizācija [ā] *nf* demilitarization

demilit[a]rizēt [ā] *vt* demilitarize

demimonds *nm* demimonde

deminutīvpiedēklis *nm* diminutive suffix

deminutīvs *nm* (gram.) diminutive

demisezonas *indecl adj* (of fashion) fall, (or) spring

demisija *nf* demission, resignation

demisionēt *vi* demit, resign

demīt *vt* (reg.) pull

demiurgs *nm* demiurge

demobilizācija *nf* demobilization

demobilizēt *vt* demobilize

demobilizētais *nom adj* demobilized soldier

demobilizēties *vr* get demobilized

demodikoze *nf* demodectic mange

demodulācija *nf* demodulation

demodul[a]tors [ā] *nm* demodulator

demogr[a]fija [ā] *nf* demography

demogr[a]fisks [ā] *adj* demographic

demogr[a]fs [ā] *nm*, ~e *nf* demographer

demokr[a]tija [ā] *nf* democracy

demokr[a]tiski [ā] *adv* democratically

demokr[a]tisks [ā] *adj* democratic

demokr[a]tiskums [ā] *nm* democratism

demokr[a]tisms [ā] *nm* democratism

demokratizācija *nf* democratization

demokratizēt *vt* democratize

demokratizēties *vr* become democratic

demokr[a]t/s [ā] *nm*, ~e *nf* democrat, Democrat

demolācija *nf* demolition

demolēt *vt* demolish

demonetizācija *nf* demonetization

demonetizēt *vt* demonetize

dēmoniski *adv* = **daimoniski**

dēmonisks *adj* = **daimonisks**

dēmonisms *nm* = **daimonisms**

dēmonoloģija *nf* = **daimonoloģija**

demonorops *nm* Daemonorops

dēmons *nm* = **daimons**

demonstrācija *nf* (political) demonstration

demonstrant/s *nm*, ~e *nf* demonstrator

demonstr[a]tīvi [ā] *adv* demonstratively

demonstr[a]tīvs [ā] *adj* demonstrative

demonstrātor/s *nm*, ~e *nf* demonstrator

demonstrējums *nm* demonstration (show)

demonstrēt *vi*, *vt* demonstrate

demontāža *nf* dismantling

demontēt *vt* dismantle

demor[a]lizācija [ā] *nf* demoralization

demor[a]lizēt [ā] *vt* demoralize

demor[a]lizēties [ā] *vr* become demoralized

dēmoss *nm* demos

demotisks *adj* demotic

dempfers *nm* damper

dempings *nm* (bus.) dumping

dēms *nm* demos

denacificēt *vt* denazify

denacifikācija *nf* denazification

denacion[a]lizācija [ā] *nf* denationalization

denacion[a]lizēt [ā] *vt* denationalize

denacion[a]lizēties [ā] *vr* become denationalized

d[e]nārijs [ē] *nm* denarius

d[e]nārs [ē] *nm* denarius

denatur[a]lizācija [ā] *nf* denaturalization

denatur[a]lizēt [ā] *vt* denaturalize

denaturāts *nm* denatured alcohol

denaturēt *vt* denature

denaturēties *vr* become denatured

denderēt *vi* 1. (col.) stumble; 2. gad about; create disturbance

denderiski *adv* stumbling

denderisks *adj* stumbling

dendijs *nm* dandy

dendrārijs *nm* arboretum

dendrītisks *adj* dendritic

dendrīts *nm* dendrite; (tech.) tree

dendrobija *nf* dendrobium

dendro[ch]ronoloģija [h] *nf* dendrochronology

dendro[ch]ronoloģiski [h] *adv* dendrochronologically

dendro[ch]ronoloģisks [h] *adj* dendrochronological

dendrogramma *nf* dendrogram

dendrolo/gs *nm*, **~ģe** *nf* dendrologist

dendroloģija *nf* dendrology

dendroloģiskais parks *nm* arboretum

dendroloģisks *adj* dendrologic

dendronisks *adj* dendritic

dendrons *nm* dendrite

dene *nf* **1.** helmsman's seat; **2.** top of a boat's cabin

dēnēt *vi* **1.** wither away; **2.** wait in vain

deniņi *nm pl* (anat.) temple

deniņu kauls *nm* temporal bone

denitrācija *nf* denitration

denitrēt *vt* denitrate

denitrificēt *vt* denitrify

denitrifikācija *nf* denitrification

denjē *nm* (text.) denier

denkts *adj* strapping

denominācija *nf* denomination

denomināls *adj* denominal

denomin[a]tīvs [ā] *adj* denominative

denonsēt *vt* denounce

denotācija *nf* denotation

denotatīvs *adj* denotative

densimetrija *nf* densimetry

densimetrs *nm* densimeter

densitometrija *nf* densitometry

densitometrs *nm* densitometer

denšāiks *nm* (mil.) orderly

dentāls *adj* (ling.) dental

dentikuls *nm* denticule

dentīns *nm* dentine

dentist/s *nm*, **~e** *nf* dentist

denūdācija *nf* denudation

denuncēt *vt* inform against

denuncētāj/s *nm*, **~a** *nf* informer

denunciācija *nf* denunciation

denunciant/s *nm*, **~e** *nf* informer

deņķeļbuks *nm* (barb.) purse, pocketbook

deodara koks *nm* deodar cedar

deokupācija *nf* end of an occupation

deontisks *adj* deontic

deontoloģija *nf* deontology

departaments *nm* department

depe *nf* (reg.) paw

depene *nf* fat girl

depersonalizācija *nf* depersonalization

depeša *nf* (col.) dispatch

depigmentācija *nf* depigmentation

depīgs *adj* stout

depilācija *nf* depilation

depis *nm* **1.** heavy, sturdy boy; **2.** (reg.) toad

depo *nm indecl* **1.** fire station; **2.** roundhouse; machine shed; **3.** depot, store, storage site

depol[a]rizācija [ā] *nf* depolarization

depolimerizācija *nf* depolymerization

deponent/s *nm*, **~e** *nf* depositor

deponēt *vt* deposit

depopulācija *nf* depopulation

deportācija *nf* deportation

deportēt *vt* deport

deportētais *nom adj* deportee

depozitāre *nf* a contracting power, depository of the original of a treaty

depozitārijs *nm* depositary

depoz[i]ts [ī] *nm* deposit

depresants *nm* depressant

depresija *nf* depression

depresīvi *adv* depressively

depresīvs *adj* depressive

depsis *nm* a stout boy

depuris *nm* a stout boy

deputācija *nf* deputation

deputātnieks *nm* (hist.) sharecropper

deputāt/s *nm*, **~e** *nf* **1.** deputy; representative; **2.** (hist.) share of the crop

deputēt *vt* depute, delegate

deramdiena *nf* (hist) hiring day

deranžēt *vt* derange

deratizācija *nf* extermination of rodents

derbijs *nm* derby

derbist/s *nm*, **~e** *nf* (of a horse) derby winner

derdzība *nf* repulsiveness

derdzīgi *adv* repulsively

derdzīgs *adj* repulsive

derdzīgums *nm* repulsiveness

derealizācija *nf* derealization

derelikcija *nf* dereliction

derēt *v* 1. *vi* fit; **tas viņam der** a. it fits him; b. it serves him right; 2. *vi* be suitable, do, come in useful; **tas nekam neder** it is useless; **kur tas der?** what is it good for? 3. **lieti d.** *vi* come in handy, be appropriate; be worth doing, be worth experiencing; 4. *vi* bet; **deru, ka neuzminēsi** I give you three guesses; 5. *vi, vt* (ob.s) hire; (obs.) betroth; pledge; **d. draudzību** pledge friendship; **d. mieru** (obs.) make peace

derglājs *nm* swampy area

derglis *nm* repulsive fellow

dergt *vi* (rare.) detest, loathe

dergties *vr* detest, loathe

derība *nf* (obs.) agreement, covenant; see also **Jaunā d., Vecā d.**

derīb/as *nf pl* 1. bet, wager; ~u **likme** odds; 2. engagement, betrothal

derības šķirsts *nm* ark of covenant

derīgi *adv* usefully

derīgs *adj* 1. fit, suitable; **d. kuģošanai** seaworthy; 2. valid, viable, serviceable; 3. useful; 4. re-commendable; valuable

derīgum/s *nm* 1. fitness, suitability; 2. validity, viability, serviceability; ~a **ilgums** service life; 3. usefulness; value; utility

deriks *nm* derrick

derināt *vt* 1. (obs.) hire; 2. (folk.) betroth

der[i]vācija [ī] *nf* derivation

der[i]vatīvs [ī] *adj* derivative

der[i]vāts [ī] *nm* derivative

derma *nf* derma

dermatīns *nm* Leatherette

dermat[i]ts [ī] *nm* dermatitis

dermatolo/gs *nm*, ~ģe *nf* dermatologist

dermatoloģija *nf* dermatology

dermatoze *nf* dermatosis

dervišs *nm* dervish

derža *nm, nf* (reg.) person performing corvée labor

desa *nf* 1. sausage; 2. ~s a. sausages; b. ticktacktoe

desantdivīzija *nf* marine division

desantēt *vi* (mil.) land

desantka[r]aspēks [ŗ] *nm* 1. landing force; assault force; **gaisa d.** airborne force; **jūras d.** amphibious force; 2. marines

desantkuģis *nm* landing craft

desantkuteris *nm* landing craft

desantlaiva *nf* landing craft

desantnieks *nm* member of a landing force

desantopercija *nf* assault force operation

desants *nm* (mil.) 1. landing; 2. landing force

desāt *vt* whip, beat

descendence *nf* descent

descendents *nm* descendent

desensibilizācija *nf* desensitization

desegregācija *nf* desegregation

desensibilizēt *vt* desensitize

deserts *nm* dessert

deset[i]na [ī] *nf* dessiatine (Russian areal measure)

desētnieks *nm* (hist.) head of a **desmite**

desielocis *nm* hot dog

designēt *vt* designate

desikants *nm* desiccant

desinieks *nm* sausage maker, sausage dealer

desiņa *nf* 1. *dim* of **desa**; 2. hot dog; cocktail sausage

deskripcija *nf* description

deskriptīvi *adv* descriptively

deskriptīvs *adj* descriptive

deskvamācija *nf* desquamation

desmit *adj* 1. *indecl, decl* ten; 2. *decl* ten o'clock; ~os at ten

desmita *nf* (hist.) tithe

desmitacis *nm* (cards) ten

desmitais *adj* tenth

desmitcīņa *nf* decathlon

desmitcīŋnieks *nm* decathlon athlete

desmitdaļa *nf* one tenth

desmite *nf* (hist.) ten farms (a subdivision of a township)

desmitējādi *adv* in ten different ways

desmitējāds *adj* some ten different (things)

desmitgade *nf* decade

desmitgadējs *adj* of ten years' duration

desmitgadīgs *adj* 1. ten-year; 2. decennial; 3. ten-year old

desmitgadu *indecl adj* ten-year

desmitkājis *nm* decapod

desmitkapeika *nf* ten-kopeck piece

desmitkāršojums *nm* tenfold increase

desmitkāršot *vt* increase tenfold

desmitkāršoties *vr* increase tenfold

desmitkāršs *adj* 1. tenfold; 2. of ten layers

desmitkārt *adv* tenfold

desmitkārtēji *adv* tenfold

desmitkārtējs *adj* tenfold

desmitkārtīgi *adv* tenfold

desmitkārtīgs *adj* 1. tenfold; 2. ten-layer

desmitklasīgs *adj* (of schools) ten-year

desmitkolonnu *indecl adj* (arch.) decastyle

desmitnie/ks *nm* 1. a ten; 2. foreman; (mil.) leader of a squad of ten; (hist.) tithing man, township representative; (hist.) a farm hand representing nine others; ~ce *nf*

desmitprocentīgs *adj* ten-percent

desmitreiz *adv* ten times

desmitreizējs *adj* ten-time; umpteenth

desmitrinda *nf* decastich

desmitrubļu *indecl adj* ten-rouble

desmit/s *nm* ten; ~iem (with genitive) scores of

desmitskaldnis *nm* decahedron

desmitstāvu *indecl adj* ten-story

desmitstūris *nm* decagon

desmitzobu prieēu mizgrauzis *nm* a bark beetle, Ips laricis

desmodija *nf* desmodium

desmotropija *nf* desmotropism

desmotropisks *adj* desmotropic

desmotrops *nm* desmotrope

desodorēt *vt* deodorize

desorbcija *nf* desorption

desot *vi* (sl.) run

despotija *nf* despotism

despostiski *adv* despotically

despotisks *adj* despotic

despotiskums *nm* despotism

despotisms *nm* despotism

despot/s *nm*, ~e *nf* despot

destabilizēt *vt* destabilize

dēstījum/s *nm* planting; ~i plant nursery

desti[l]ācija [ll] *nf* distillation; sausā d. destructive distillation

desti[l]ātors [ll] *nm* still

desti[l]āts [ll] *nm* distillate

desti[l]ēšana [ll] *nf* distilling

desti[l]ēšanas [ll] uzņēmums *nm* distillery

desti[l]ēt [ll] *vt* distil

desti[l]ētāj/s [ll] *nm*, ~a *nf* distiller

destinācija *nf* destination

dēstīt *vt* plant

destitūcija *nf* destitution

destrukcija *nf* destruction

destruktīvs *adj* destructive

dēsts *nm* seedling, sprout

dēstu audzētava *nf* seed-bed

desu zāle *nf* (bot.) savory

dešifr[a]tors [ā] *nm* decoder

dešifrēt *vt* decipher, decode, decrypt

dēt *vi* 1. lay eggs; 2. (obs.) weld; 3. (obs.) make sausages; 4. (archa.) make a beehive (by hollowing a tree trunk)

detalisks *adj* devoted to details

detalizācija *nf* specification, detailing

detalizēt *vt* detail, particularize, specify

detalizēti *adv* in detail

detalizēts *adj, part* of detalizēt detailed

detaļa *nf* detail; (of machinery) part, component

detaļplānojums *nm* detailed plans

detaļprojekts *nm* detailed project

detante *nf* detente

detašē *indecl nm* détaché

detekcija *nf* detection

detektēšana *nf* (radio) detection

detektēt *vt* (radio) detect

detektīvfilma *nf* mystery

detektīvliter[a]tūra [ā] *nf* mysteries

detektīvromāns *nm* detective novel, mystery

detektīvs *nm* detective

detektīvsižets *nm* mystery plot

detektīvu birojs *nm* detective agency

detektīvžanrs *nm* mystery genre

detektora uztvērējs *nm* crystal receiver

detektors *nm* detector

detergents *nm* detergent

deteriorācija *nf* deterioration

deteriorātors *nm* deteriorator

determinācija *nf* determination, identification

determinante *nf* determinant

determin[a]tīvs [ā] *nm* determinative

determin[a]tīvs [ā] *adj* determinative

determinēt *vt* determine

determinisms *nm* determinism

dēties *vr* (col.) go; **kur viņš tagad dēsies?** where is he to go now?

detonācija *nf* detonation; **ietekmēta d.** sympathetic detonation; **~s ķēde** series wired explosives

deton[a]tors [ā] *nm* detonator

detonēt I *vi* detonate

detonēt II *vi* be out of tune

detr[i]ts [ī] *nm* detritus

deva *nf* **1.** ration, portion; **2.** dose

devalvācija *nf* (econ.) devaluation

devalvēt *vt* (econ.) devalue

devanāgari *indecl nm* Devanagari (script)

devastācija *nf* devastation

devasts *nm* gift

devēj/s *nm* **1.** giver; donor; **~a** *nf*; **2.** (tech.) transducer

devele *nf* ninth week of the sowing season

deverbāls *adj* derived from a verb

dēvēt *vt* call; nickname

dēvēties *vr* call oneself

deviācija *nf* deviation

deviance *nf* deviance

devība *nf* generosity, liberalness

deviens *nm* rain shower

devīgi *adv* generously, liberally

devīgs *adj* generous, liberal

devīgums *nm* generosity, liberalness

deviņacis *nm* (cards) nine

deviņāds *adj* ninefold

deviņais *nom adj* the devil

deviņdancis *nm* a Latvian folk dance

deviņdesmit *adj* ninety

deviņdesmit/ais *adj* ninetieth; **~ie gadi** the nineties

deviņdesmitgadīgais *nom adj* nonegenarian

deviņdesmitgadīgs *adj* ninety years old

deviņējs *adj* nine

deviņgadīgs *adj* **1.** nine-year; **2.** nine years old

deviņgalvains *adj* nine-headed

deviņgalvis *nm* (folk.) nine-headed devil

deviņ/i *adj* **1.** *indecl, decl* nine; **2.** *decl* nine o'clock; **~os** at nine

deviņjoslu bruņnesis *nm* peba

deviņkārt *adv* nine times

deviņkārtējs *adj* nine-time

deviņkārtīgi *adv* nine times

deviņkārtīgs *adj* ninefold

deviņkārtu *indecl adj* ninefold

deviņklasīgs *adj* (of schools) nine-year

deviņklašu *indecl adj* (of schools) nine-year

deviņnieks *nm* **1.** a nine; **2.** group of nine

deviņpadsmit *adj* nineteen

deviņpadsmitais *adj* nineteenth

deviņpadsmitgadīgs *adj* nineteen years old

deviņreiz *adv* nine times

deviņsimt *adj* nine hundred

deviņsimtais *adj* nine hundredth

deviņstāvu *indecl adj* nine-story

deviņstūris *nm* nonagon

deviņš *nm* (col.) nine

deviņvīruspēks *nm* mullein

devītais *adj* ninth

devītais *nom adj* (folk.) the devil

devītdaļa *nf* one ninth

devītnieks *nm* a nine

dēvits *nm* davit

devīze *nf* 1. motto, device, slogan; pseudonymous title (for a work submitted in a competition); 2. foreign currency

devīžu apsaimniekošana *nf* foreign exchange control

devīžu kurss *nm* rate of exchange

devocija *nf* devotion

devolūcija *nf* devolution

devons *nm* Devonian

devums *nm* yield

dezadaptācija *nf* maladaptation

dezakt[i]vācija [ī] nf decontamination, cleanup

dezakt[i]vizācija [ī] *nf* = **dezaktivācija**

dezakt[i]vēt [ī] *vt* decontaminate, clean up

dezakt[i]vizēt [ī] *vt* = **dezaktīvēt**

dezavuēt *vt* disavow

dezertēšana *nf* desertion

dezertēt *vi* desert

dezertier/is *nm*, ~e *nf* deserter

deziderāts *nm* desideratum

dezinfekcija *nf* disinfection; ~s līdzeklis disinfectant

dezinfektors *nm*, ~e *nf* disinfector

dezinficēt *vt* disinfect

dezinformācija *nf* disinformation

dezinformēt *vt* disinform

dezinsekcija *nf* insect control

dezintegrācija *nf* disintegration

dezintegr[a]tors [ā] *nm* disintegrator

dezodorācija *nf* deodorization

dezodorants *nm* deodorant

dezodor[a]tors [ā] *nm* deodorizer

dezodorēt *vt* deodorize

dezoksidācija *nf* deoxydation

dezoksidēt *vt* deoxydize

dezoksiribonukleīnskābe *nf* deoxyribonucleic acid, DNA

dezoksiriboze *nf* deoxyribose

dezorganizācija *nf* disorganization

dezorganiz[a]torisks [ā] *adj* disorganizing

dezorganiz[a]tor/s [ā] *nm*, ~e *nf* disorganizer

dezorganizēt *vt* disorganize

dezorganizētājs *nm*, ~a *nf* disorganizer

dezorientācija *nf* disorientation

dezorientēt *vt* disorient

dežūr/a *nf* duty, watch; ~ā on duty

dež[u]rants [ū] *nm*, ~e *nf* person on duty

dežūraptieka *nf* drugstore on duty

dežūrārsts *nm*, ~e *nf* doctor on duty

dežūrbrigāde *nf* team on duty

dežūrēdiens *nm* standing dish

dež[u]rēt [ū] *vi* be on duty; **d. pie slimnieka gultas** watch by a patient's bedside

dežūristaba *nf* room for persons on duty; guardroom

dežūrjoks *nm* standing joke

dežūrmāsa *nf* nurse on duty

dežūrpusdienas *nf pl* dinner of the day, today's special

dežūrtelpa *nf* room for persons on duty; guardroom

dežūru saraksts *nm* duty roster

dežūrveikals *nm* store with extended business hours

dežūrvirsnieks *nm* officer on duty

diabazs *nm* (geol.) diabase

diabētiķis *nm*, ~e *nf* diabetic

diabētisks *adj* diabetic

diabēts *nm* diabetes

diabolisks *adj* diabolic

dia[ch]ilonplāksteris [h] *nm* diachylon

dia[ch]ronija [h] *nf* diachrony

dia[ch]roniski [h] *adv* diachronically

dia[ch]ronisks [h] *adj* diachronic

diadēma *nf* diadem

diado[ch]s [h] *nm* diadochite

diafilma *nf* filmstrip

diafīze *nf* diaphysis

diafragma *nf* diaphragm; (photo.) aperture

diafragmēt *vi* (photo.) change the diaphragm
　opening

diagnoscēt *vt* diagnose

diagnosticēt *vt* diagnose

diagnostika *nf* diagnostics

diagnostiķis *nm* diagnostician

diagnostisks *adj* diagnostic

diagnoze *nf* diagnosis

diagnozēt *vt* diagnose

diagonālaudums *nm* twill; whipcord

diagonāle *nf* diagonal

diagonāli *adv* diagonally

diagonāls *nm* (col.) whipcord

diagonāls *adj* diagonal

diagramma *nf* 1. diagram; 2. graph

diaģen[e]tisks [ē] *adj* diagenetic

diaģen[e]ze [ē] *nf* diagenesis

diah- See diach-

diakonija *nf* diaconate

diakon/s *nm*, ~isa, ~ise *nf* deacon

diakritisks *adj* diacritic

dialektāls *adj* dialect (*adj*)

dialektika *nf* dialectics

dialektiķ/is *nm*, ~e *nf* dialectician

dialektiski *adv* dialectically

dialektisks *adj* dialectical

dialektiskums *nm* dialectical quality

dialektisms *nm* dialectalism

dialektolo/gs *nm*, ~ģe *nf* dialectologist

dialektoloģija *nf* dialectology

dialektoloģiski *adv* dialectologically

dialektoloģisks *adj* dialectological

dialekts *nm* dialect

dializ[a]tors [ā] *nm* dialyser

dial[i]ze [ī] *nf* dialysis

dialogs *nm* dialog

diamagnētiķis *nm* diamagnet

diamagnētisks *adj* diamagnetic

diamagn[e]tisms [ē] *nm* diamagnetism

diametrāli *adv* diametrically

diametrāls *adj* diametrical

diametriski *adv* diametrically

diametrisks *adj* diametrical

diametrs *nm* diameter

diamīns *nm* diamine

dianoētika *nf* dianoia

diapauze *nf* diapause

diapazona pārslēgs *nm* band switch, station
　selector

diapazons *nm* range; scope, compass; operating
　range; (el., of waves) band

diapensija *nf* diapensia

diapīra *nf* diapir

diapozitīvs *nm* (photo.) slide

diaprojektors *nm* slide projector

diareja *nf* diarrhea

diaireze *nf* = diereze

diarijs *nm* diary

diartroze *nf* diarthrosis

diaskops *nm* slide projector; filmstrip pro-
　jector

diaspora *nf* diaspora

diast[a]ze [ā] *nf* diastase

diastereoizomers *nm* diastereoisomer

diastils *nm* diastyle

diastole *nf* diastole

diastolisks *adj* diastolic

diastrofisms *nm* diastrophism

diastrofs *adj* diastrophic

diatermija *nf* diathermy

diatermisks *adj* diathermic

diat[e]ze [ē] *nf* diathesis

diatomeja *nf* diatom

diatomisks *adj* diatomic

diatomīts *nm* diatomite

diatonika *nf* diatonicism

diatonisks *adj* diatonic

diatonisms *nm* diatonicism

diatrēma *nf* diatreme

diazonijs *nm* diazonium

diazosavienojums *nm* diazo (compound)

diazotipija *nf* diazo process

diazotizācija *nf* diazotization

dībelis *nm* screw anchor

dibena ripa *nf* (of a barrel) heading

dibena fauna *nf* zoobenthos

dibena ledus *nm* anchor ice

dibenbranga *nf* (naut.) floor timber

dibendurvis *nf pl* back door

dibenējs *adj* (of rooms) back

dibenistaba *nf* back room

dibenlaiža *nm* (com.) brownnose

dibenledus *nm* underwater ice

dibenplāns *nm* background

dibenpuse *nf* backside

dibens *nm* **1.** bottom; **2.** rear; **3.** backside, posterior; (of pants) seat

dibensaneši *nm pl* (geol.) bed load

dibensiena *nf* back wall

dibentelpa *nf* back room

dibentiņš *nm dim* of **dibens**, bottom

dibēt *vi* thunder, sound

dibināt *vt* **1.** found, establish; **2.** ground, base, justify

dibinātājs *nm*, ~a *nf* founder

dibināti *adv* justifiably

dibināties *vr* **1.** be founded, be established; **2.** be grounded in, be based on, rest on

dibināts *adj, part* of **dibināt** justified, well founded, justifiable

dibrom[i]ds [ī] *nm* dibromide

dibutils *nm* dibutyl

dīcēj/s *nm*, ~a *nf* mewler

dīcekl/is *nm*, ~e *nf* mewler

dicele *nf* two-wheeled cart

di[ch]lordifluormetāns [h] *nm* dichlordifluormethane

di[ch]lor[i]ds [h][ī] *nm* dichloride

di[ch]otomi [h] *adv* dichotomously

di[ch]otomija [h] *nf* dichotomy

di[ch]otoms [h] *adj* dichotomous

di[ch]roisms [h] *nm* dichroism

di[ch]romatisks [h] *adj* dichromatic

di[ch]romatisms [h] *nm* dichromatism

di[ch]romāts [h] *nm* **1.** dichromat; **2.** dichromate

diciāns *nm* dicyanogen

dīcības *nf pl* (hist.) extraordinary corvée labor (imposed during the peasant's free week)

dīciens *nm* buzz; quiet moo

dīcinieks *nm* (hist.) a peasant performing **dīcības**

didaktika *nf* **1.** didactics; **2.** didacticism

didaktiķ/is *nm*, ~e *nf* didact

didaktiski *adv* didactically

didaktisks *adj* didactic

didaktiskums *nm* didacticism

didaktisms *nm* didacticism

didas *nf pl* shivers

dīdekl/is *nm*, ~e *nf* (col.) fidgeter

didelēt *vi* fidget

dīdelis *nm* (col.) fidgeter

didināt *vi* shiver

dīdīt *vt* **1.** make run, make jump; (of a horse) prance; **2.** goad, incite, drive; **kāds velns mani dīdīja?** whatever possessed me? **kāds velns tevi dīda?** what has gotten into you? **3.** (obs., of animals) train

dīdītāj/s *nm*, ~a *nf* (obs.) animal trainer

dīdītava *nf* obedience school

dīdīties *vr* **1.** fidget; **2.** romp

dīdoņa *nf, nm* fidgeter

dīdzelība *nf* germinability

dīdzēt *vt* germinate

dīdzība *nf* germinability

dīdzīgs *adj* germinable

dīdzināt *vt* germinate

dīdžejs *nm* deejay, disc jockey

diebt *vi* run rapidly, scurry

di[e]cēze [ē] *nf* diocese

diedelēt *vt, vi* beg; cadge

diedelēties *vr* loiter

diedelis *nm* = **diedelnieks**

diedelnie/ks *nm*, **~ce** *nf* **1.** beggar; cadger;
   2. loiterer

dieds *nm* old man

diedzenes *nf pl* horned pondweed

diedzēt *vt* germinate

diedzētava *nf* germinator

diedzināt *vt* germinate

diedziņ/š *nm* **1.** *dim* of **diegs**, thread; **2.** **~i**
   yarn

diedziņu krusts *nm* cross hairs

diegabikse *nf* (col.) scrag

diegadvēsele *nf, nm* (col.) **1.** scrag; **2.** coward

diegaine *nf* linsey-woolsey

diegains *adj* linen

diegazēns *nm* (col.) scrag

dieg/s *nm* **1.** thread; **piķots d.** waxed end ◊
   baltiem ~iem šūts (col.) it does not hold
   water; transparent subterfuge; **(karāties)**
   ~a galā (hang) by a thread; **kā pa diegu**
   smoothly; **2.** (sl.) timid or incompetent
   person

diegt I *vt* stitch, baste, tack

diegt II *vi* rush, dash

diegu cimds *nm* cotton glove

diegu tārps *nm* threadworm

diegu veltenis *nm* (weav.) warp beam

diegveida *indecl adj* threadlike, filamentous

diegveidīgs *adj* threadlike, filamentous

dielektriķis *nm* dielectric

dielektrisks *adj* dielectric

diemžēl *partic* unfortunately

dien/a *nf* day; daytime; **balta d.** broad daylight;
   baltās ~as halcyone days days of wine and
   roses; **gaŗā d.** dawdler; **izejamā d.** day of;
   liekā d. leap day; **līgstamā d.** (hist.) hiring
   day (of farm hands); **nebalta d.** (fig.) rainy
   day; **nebaltas ~as** hard times; **pastarā**
   d. judgment day ◊ **~ā** a. during daytime; b.
   per day; **~ās** once; **cauru ~u** all day long;
   ~ām un naktīm night and day; **~u iepriekš**
   the day before; **vienas ~as** a. a day's; b. for a

day; **ik ~as** every day; **otrā ~ā** the next day;
pa ~u during daytime; **(pa) ~ām** during the
day, days; **senās ~ās** in olden days; **šajās**
~ās a. lately, these days; b. soon; **vecuma**
~ās in one's old age; **~u ~ā** day in and day
out; **~u no ~as** day in and day out; **kādā**
jaukā ~ā one of these days; **~ām ilgi** for
days on end; **no ~as ~ā** from day to day; **no**
mazām ~ām since childhood; **no jaunām**
~ām since my younger days; **(sūtīt) labas**
~as (send) one's best; **~u mūžu** constantly,
always; **vēl šo baltu ~u** even today; **visu**
mīļu ~u the whole blessed day; **līdz šai**
baltai ~ai to this very day; **(dzīvot) zaļu ~u**
(live) in clover; **jo ~as, jo (stiprāks)** (get
stronger) day by day

dienaļa *nf* a cow born during the day

dienas alga *nf* daily wage

dienas ausma *nf* daybreak

dienas avīze *nf* daily (newspaper); morning
   newspaper

dienas kase *nf* box office

dienasgaisma *nf* daylight

dienas gaitas *nf pl* daily routine

dienasgrāmata *nf* **1.** diary; **2.** journal; **3.** (educ.)
   assignment book

dienas izrāde *nf* matinee

dienas jautājums *nm* burning issue;

dienaskārtīb/a *nf* agenda; **~ā** on the agenda;
   (fig.) topic of the day

dienas laik/s *nm* daytime; **gaišā d. ~ā** in broad
   daylight

dienas lapa *nf* daily (newspaper)

dienas maiņa *nf* daytime shift

dienas nauda *nf* daily allowance

dienas strādnieks *nm* daily worker

dienas tauriņi *nm pl* Rhopalocera, diurnal
   butterflies

dienas vējš *nm* south wind

dienasvidus *nm* midday, noon

dienaszagl/is *nm*, **~e** *nf* loafer, lazybones

diendārzs *nm* corral (in the open pasture)

dienderis *nm* **1.** flunky, toady; **2.** (obs.) hired farm hand

diendienā *adv* day by day, day after day, every day

diendienas *indecl adj* everyday

diendienīgs *adj* everyday

diendusa *nf* siesta, midday rest

dienesta apliecība *nf* official identification

dienesta atzīme *nf* official notation

dienesta ceļojums *nm* official trip

dienesta gaita *nf* career; **d. ~s apraksts** resume

dienesta noslēpums *nm* official secret

dienesta pakāpe *nf* rank

dienesta telefons *nm* government telephone

dienesta telpas *nf pl* offices

dienesta virsnieks *nm* **1.** officer of the day; **2.** officer in active service

dienesta zeme *nf* government land (in use by one in government service)

dienestmeita *nf* maidservant

dienestnie/ks *nm*, **~ce** *nf* (obs.) domestic servant

dienest/s *nm* **1.** service; **~a** official; service; **~a apliecība** identification card; **~a gaitas apraksts** (mil.) service record; **~a lapa** service re-cord; **~a lietošanai** for official use only; **2.** duty; **d. amats** (mil.) duty position; **d. ārpus kārtas** extra duty

dienēt *vi* serve, be in service

diengalis *nm* sth. or s.o. whose days are coming to an end

dieninieks *nm* **1.** day laborer; **2.** (mil.) orderly; (mil.) enlisted man detailed for 24 hours to be in charge of keeping the barracks clean and orderly

dieniņa *nf dim* of **diena**, day

dienišķīgs *adj* everyday

dienišķis *nm* an afternoon or evening meal

dienišķs *adj* daily

diennakts *nf* twenty-four hours

dienonis *nm* (reg.) daily worker

dienvidafrikān/is *nm*, **~iete** *nf* South African

dienvidamerikān/is *nm*, **~iete** *nf* South American

dienvidaustrumi *nm pl* southeast

dienvidblāzma *nf* aurora australis

dienvidenis *nm* south wind

dienvid/i *nm pl* south; **uz ~iem** to the south, southward; south of; **~u** southern

dienvidjūra *nf* southern sea

dienvidnieciski *adv* in a southern fashion

dienvidniecisks *adj* southern

dienvidnie/ks *nm*, **~ce** *nf* southerner

dienvidpols *nm* South Pole

dienvidpuse *nf* south

dienvidrietenis *nm* southwesterly wind

dienvidrietumi *nm pl* southwest

dienvidrītenis *nm* southeasterly wind

dienvidrīti *nm pl* southeast

dienvidsl[a]v/s [ā] *nm*, **~iete** *nf* Yugoslav

dienvidu dižskābardis *nm* evergreen beech

dienvidu lauvronis *nm* southern sea lion

dienvidu magnolija *nf* southern magnolia

dienvidus *nm* **1.** noon; **2.** midday rest, siesta

dienvidu žodzene *nf* a hedge mustard, Sisymbrium loeselii

dienvidvakari *nm pl* southwest

dienvidvējš *nm* south wind

dienvidzeme *nf* the south, southern climes

dienziedes *nf pl* day lily

diereze *nf* = **diaireze**

diet *vi* (poet., folk.) dance (merrily)

diēta *nf* diet

di[e]tārsts [ē] *nm* dietician (physician)

di[e]tētika [ē] *nf* dietetics

di[e]tētisks [ē] *adj* dietary

diētika *nf* dietetics

diētiķ/is *nm*, **~e** *nf* dietician

dietilamīns *nm* diethylamine

dietilēns *nm* diethylene

dietilstilbestrols *nm* diethylstilbestrol

dietin *adv emph* of **diet**; **d. diet** dance exuberantly

diētisks *adj* dietetic, dietary

di|e|tmāsa [ē] *nf* dietician

di|e|tolo/gs [ē] *nm*, **~ģe** *nf* dietician

di|e|toloģija [ē] *nf* dietetics

di|e|toloģisks [ē] *adj* dietetic

diētterapija *nf* dietotherapy

Dieva dāvana *nf* (col.) God's gift (talent); godsend

Dieva dēli *nm pl* (folk., mythological personifications of heavenly bodies) sons of Dievs

dievaines *nf pl* last day of **veļu laiks**

dievainis *nm* old, pious person

dievais *defin adj* good, noble, splendid; utter

dievajosta *nf* (reg.) rainbow

Dieva kārkls *nm* mullein

Dieva laime *nf* (col.) God's blessing, great luck

Dieva noliedzējs *nm* atheist

Dieva pirksts *nm* the hand of God

Dieva rociņa *nf* tubers of the heath spotted orchid

Dieva suns *nm* wolf

dievāties *vr* use God's name

Dieva tiesa *nf* trial by ordeal

Dieva valstība *nf* kingdom of God, paradise

dievāzītis *nm* common snipe

Dieva zosis *nf pl* (folk.) wild geese

dievbijība *nf* piety, devoutness

dievbijīgi *adv* piously, devoutly

dievbijīgs *adj* pious, devout, God-fearing

dievbijīgums *nm* piousness, devoutness

dievdienas *nf pl* (folk.) days when the souls of the deceased were being fed

dievdots *adj* **1.** feebleminded; **2.** godsent

dieve *nf* goddess

dieveklis *nm* idol, deity

dieverene *nf* (wife's) niece

dieverēns *nm* (wife's) nephew

dieveris *nm* **1.** brother-in-law (husband's brother); **2.** (obs.) bridegroom's brother

dievestība *nf* godliness

dievgaldnieks *nm*, **~ce** *nf* communicant

dievgalds *nm* **1.** Communion; **2.** Communion table

dievgosniņa *nf* ladybug

dievgotiņa *nf* ladybug

dievība *nf* deity

dieviete *nf* goddess

dievīgs *adj* divine

dievināt *vt* worship, idolize; deify

dievinātāj/s *nm*, **~a** *nf* idolizer; admirer; deifier

dieviņi *nm pl* (folk.) spirits of the dead

dieviņ/š *nm* **1.** *dim* of **dievs**, god; **bet kur tu die-viņ** but it was not to be; **2.** idol

dievišķi *adv* divinely

dievišķība *nf* divinity

dievišķīgi *adv* divinely

dievišķīgs *adj* divine

dievišķīgums *nm* divineness

dievišķošana *nf* deification

dievišķs *adj* divine

dievkalpojums *nm* worship, service

dievkalpošana *nf* (obs.) worship, service

dievkociņš *nm* **1.** southernwood; **2.** (col.) coward

dievkrēsliņš *nm* sun spurge

dievķepas *nf pl* male orchis

dievlūdzēja *nf* **1.** (female) worshipper; **2.** (zool.) mantis

dievlūdzējs *nm* worshipper

dievlūgšana *nf* (obs., rel.) service

dievmaize *nf* consecrated wafer, altar bread

dievmaizīte *nf dim* of **dievmaize**

dievmāte *nf* Virgin Mary, Madonna, Our Lady

dievnams *nm* church

dievoties *vr* swear (by God)

dievots *adj* **1.** good, noble; **2.** peculiar, weird; **3.** miserable

dievpalīgs *nm* God's help (bidden to a person working)

dievpaļāvība *nf* trust in God

dievredzis *nm* seer; sorcerer

dievreģis *nm* = **dievredzis**

dievrociņa *nf* male orchis

diev/s *nm* god; **Diev/s** God; (folk.) Dievs (chief god) ◊ **D~a darbi!** miracles never cease; **D~a dēļ** (col.) for God's sake; **D~a dots** (col.) simpleton; **D~a kauts** (col., of animals) perished; **D~a svētība** (col.) great quantities; **D~a vārds!** I swear by God! **ak D.!** of, God! **mīļais D.!** good Lord! **no D~a puses** (col.) for God's sake; **lai D. (tev) žēlīgs** (col.) may God have mercy (on you); **paldies D~am!** thanks goodness! **D. palīdz!** God-speed! **lai D. pasargā!** God forbid! **lai D. tevi uzklausa!** God grant it! **D. palīdz!** God help! (a bid of God's help to a person working); **ar D~a palīgu!** Godspeed! **ar D~u uz pusēm** (col.) fair to middling; getting by; **D. un miers** kiss and make up; **D. ar viņu!** let him be! **D. to zina** God only knows; **D. pie-ņēmis** gone to his reward; **kā D~a nepieņemts** God-forsaken; **kā D~a sūtīts** (col.) a godsend; **kā D~a ausī** in clover; in Abraham's bosom; **tas pats d.** (col.) six of one, half a dozen of the other

dievsungan *adv* enough

dievsunītis *nm* (Arctiidae moth caterpillar) woolly bear

dievticība *nf* religiosity; piety

dievticīgi *adv* piously, religiously

dievticīgs *adj* pious, religious

dievtiesīgs *adj* simple (of mind)

dievturība *nf* Dievturiba (a movement that re-vived ancient Latvian religious beliefs)

dievtur/is *nm*, **~e** *nf* an adherent of **dievturība**

dievu dzēriens *nm* (myth.) nectar

dievu ēdiens *nm* (myth.) ambrosia

dievvārdi *nm pl* (rel.) service

dievvārdnie/ks *nm*, **~ce** *nf* 1. churchgoer; 2. leader of a religious service

dievvārds *interj* by God

dievzaimība *nf* blasphemy

dievzaimīgs *adj* blasphemous

dievzemīte *nf* God's (own) country

dievzirdziņš *nm* ladybug

diez *partic* = **diezin**

diezcik *adv* **lai d. (grūts)** however (difficult); **tas nav d. (grūti)** this is not all that (difficult)

diezgan *adv* 1. enough; 2. rather, fairly, pretty, quite

diezin *partic* 1. I wonder; 2. (with kas, kāds, kad, kur, cik, kā) who knows who (or what, when, etc); (with a negation) no (great, big, etc)

diezinkāds *pron* who knows what kind of, some

diezinkas *pron* who knows who, who knows what

diezkā *adv* somehow

diezkur *adv* somewhere

diēzs *nm* (mus.) sharp

difamācija *nf* defamation

difenilēteris *nm* diphenyl ether

difenilmetāns *nm* diphenylmethane

difenils *nm* diphenyl

difeno[ch]lorarsēns [h] *nm* diphenylchlor-arsene, DA

diference *nf* difference

diferencēt *vt* differentiate

diferencētība *nf* differentiated state

diferencēties *vr* differentiate

diferenciācija *nf* differentiation

diferenciāli *adv* differentially

diferenciālis *nm* (math., mech.) differential

diferenciāldiagnoze *nf* differential diagnosis

diferenciālmanometrs *nm* differential ma-nometer

diferenciālnolīdzinājums *nm* = **diferenciālvie-nādojums**

diferenciālrēķini *nm pl* differential calculus

diferenciāls *adj* differential

diferenciālvienādojums *nm* differential equa-tion

diferenti *adv* differently

diferents *adj* different

difilobotrioze *nf* diphylobothriasis

difosgēns *nm* diphosgene

difrakcija *nf* diffraction

difrakcijas režģis *nm* diffraction grating

difterija *nf* diphteria

difterīts *nm* diphteria

diftongisks *adj* diphthongal

diftongizācija *nf* diphthongization

diftongizēties *vr* diphthongize

diftongs *nm* diphthong

difundēt *vt* diffuse

difūzi *adv* diffusely

difūzija *nf* diffusion

dif|u|zionisms [ū] *nm* diffusionism

dif|u|zitāte [ū] *nf* diffusivity

dif|u|zors [ū] *nm* diffuser

difūzs *adj* diffusey

digamma *nf* digamma

digestija *nf* digestion

digit|a|ls [ā] *adj* digital

digitalizēt *vt* digitize

dīglīgs *adj* capable of germinating

dīg/lis *nm* 1. embryo; ~ļa stāvoklī embryonic; 2. (bot., bact., fig.) germ; ~lī (fig.) in the bud

diglosija *nf* (ling.) diglossia

dīgļaizmetnis *nm* embryo

dīgļlapa *nf* cotyledon

dīgļplazma *nf* endosperm

dīgļpumpurs *nm* (bot.) plumule

dīgļsakne *nf* amnion

dīgļsoma *nf* ovary

dīgļstobrs *nm* pollen tube

dīgļstumbrs *nm* epicotyl

dīgļšūna *nf* germ cell

dignājs *nm* bog

digr|a|fs [ā] *nm* digraph

digresija *nf* digression

dīgsme *nf* (poet.) germination

dīgstamība *nf* ability to germinate

dīgstība *nf* ability to germinate

dīgsts *nm* sprout, shoot

dīgt *vi* sprout, germinate

dīgtspēja *nf* ability to germinate

dīgtspējīgs *adj* germinable

dīgums *nm* sprouted field

diģen|e|tisks [ē] *adj* digenetic

diģen|e|ze [ē] *nf* digenesis

dih- See dich-

dihidroergotamīns *nm* dihydroergotamine

dijodīds *nm* diiodide

dīka *nf, nm* (col.) mewler

dīkā *adv* idle

dīkacis *nm* (col.) loafer, idler

dikalcija *indecl adj* dicalcium

dikāt *vi* (col.) scurry

dikcija *nf* diction

dīkdienība *nf* idleness; indolence

dīkdienīgs *adj* idle; indolent

dīkdien/is *nm*, ~e *nf* idler, loafer

dīkdieņot *vi* loaf

dīkers *nm* culvert

diketons *nm* diketone

dīki *adv* idly

dīkonis *nm* = dīkdienis

dīkoties *vr* idle

dīks *adj* idle; unemployed

diksilends *nm* (mus.) Dixieland

diksonijas *nf pl* Dicksonia

dīkstāve *nf* idle time

dīkt *vi* (of insects) buzz; (of cows) moo quietly; (of speech) drone

diktāfons *nm* = diktofons

diktamne *nf* fraxinella, burning bush

dikt|a|toriski [ā] *adv* dictatorially

dikt|a|torisk/s [ā] *adj* dictatorial

dikt|a|tors [ā] *nm*, ~e *nf* (pol.) dictator

diktāts *nm* 1. dictation; 2. dictate

dikt|a|tūra [ā] *nf* dictatorship

diktēt *vt, vi* dictate

diktētājs *nm*, ~a *nf* dictator

dikti *adv* (obs.) **1.** loudly; **2.** very; strongly, hard

diktofons *nm* dictating machine

diktor/s *nm*, **~e** *nf* (radio, TV) announcer; narrator

dikts *adj* (obs.) loud

diktums *nm* dictum

dīķa naktssikspārnis *nm* pond bat

dīķgliemezis *nm* dwarf pond snail

dīķis *nm* pond

dīķkop/is *nm*, **~e** *nf* fish farmer

dīķmala *nf* pond's edge

dīķsaimniecība *nf* **1.** fish-farming; **2.** fish farm

dīķu gliemene *nf* swan mussel

dīķu tilbīte *nf* marsh sandpiper

dilatācija *nf* dilatation

dilatometrija *nf* dilatometry

dilatometrisks *adj* dilatometric

dilatometrs *nm* dilatometer

dil|a|tors [ā] *nm* dilator

dilbs *nm* forearm

dilbt *vi* dash

dilemma *nf* dilemma

dilenijas *nf pl* Dillenia

dīleris *nm* (stock exchange, bus.) dealer

diletantiski *adv* dilettantishly

diletantisks *adj* dilettantish, amateurish

diletantiskums *nm* dilettantism

diletantisms *nm* dilettantism

diletant/s *nm*, **~e** *nf* dilettante, amateur

dilināt *vt* = **deldēt**

dīlings *nm* (bus.) dealing

diližanss *nm* diligence, stagecoach

dilles *nf pl* dill

dilonis *nm* pulmonary tuberculosis, consumption

diloņains *adj* tuberculous

diloņslimnie/ks *nm*, **~ce** *nf* tuberculosis patient, consumptive

diloņslims *adj* consumptive

dilstošs *adj, part* of **dilt 1.** dwindling; **2.** waning

dilt *vi* **1.** wear out; **2.** dwindle; decay; (of the moon) wane; **3.** lose weight

diluma vaina *nf* (col.) consumption

dilums *nm* wear

dilumzāle *nf* (bot.) everlasting

diluviāls *adj* Pleistocene

dil|u|vijs [ū] *nm* ice age, Pleistocene period

dima *nf* rumbling, resounding

dimantkāzas *nf pl* diamond wedding anniversary

dimants *nm* diamond

dimanttērauds *nm* diamond steel

dimantzaļais *nom adj* diamond green

dimb/a *nf*, usu. *loc* **~ā** in a mess, in a tight spot, in trouble

dimda *nf* rumbling, resounding

dimdēt *vi* rumble, resound, ring

dimdiens *nm* rumble, pounding

dimdināt *vt* make resound, make ring; *vi* (of thunder) roll

dimdoņa *nf* rumbling, resounding; sound of heavy footsteps

dimds *nm* rumble, pounding

dimedons *nm* dimedon

dimensija *nf* dimension

dimension|a|litāte [ā] *nf* dimensionality

dimensionāls *adj* dimensional

dimēt *vi* rumble, resound, ring

dimetilamīns *nm* dimethylamine

dimetilsulfāts *nm* dimethyl sulfate

diminuendo *indecl nm* (mus.) diminuendo

dimīt *vt* (reg.) pull

dimorfisms *nm* dimorphism

dimorfs *adj* dimorphous

dimt *vi* rumble, resound

dimza *nm* restive horse

dimzāt *vi* (col.) stamp, be restive

dinamika *nf* dynamics

dinamiski *adv* dynamically

dinamisks *adj* dynamic

dinamiskums *nm* dynamism

dinamisms *nm* dynamism

dinamīts *nm* dynamite

dinamo *nm indecl* dynamo, direct-current
generator

dinamomašīna *nf* (obs.) dynamo

dinamometrs *nm* dynamometer

dinārs *nm* dinar

dinasa ķieģelis *nm* Dinas brick

dinass *nm* Dinas clay

dinastija *nf* dynasty

dinasts *nm* dynast

dinatrons *nm* dynatron

dindēt *vi* rumble, resound

dindins *nm* rumble

dindzēt *vi* buzz; whiz

dineja *nf* public dinner

dingija *nf* dinghy

dingo *nm indecl* dingo

dingt *vi* whiz

dinitrāts *nm* dinitrate

dinitrobenzols *nm* dinitrobenzene

dinitro|ch|lor|ch|idrīns [h][h] *nm* dinitro-
chlorhydrine

dinitrotoluols *nm* dinitrotoluol

dinoficeji *nm pl* Dinophyceae

dinoterijs *nm* dinothere

d|i|nozaurs [ī] *nm* dinosaur

dins *nm* dyne

diņģēties *vr* (barb.) haggle

diode *nf* diode

dioks|i|ds [ī] *nm* dioxide

dionīsiji *nm pl* Dionisia

dionisisks *adj* Dionysian

dionas *nf pl* Dioön

dioneja *nf* Venus's-flytrap

dions *nm* dyon

diopsids *nm* diopsid

dioptrija *nf* diopter

dioptrika *nf* dioptrics

dioptrs *nm* sight vane

diorāma *nf* diorama

diorīts *nm* diorite

diosfenols *nm* diosphenol

dioskoreja *nf* yam

diotisks *adj* diotic

dip, dip *interj* pit-a-pat

dipada, dipada *interj* clop-clop

dipāt *vi* walk (at a child's pace)

dipēt *vi* (of footsteps) sound

dipiens *nm* footfall

dipināt *vi* (of scurrying footsteps) sound; pit-
a-pat, patter

dīpītis *nm* (sl.) displaced person

diplēģija *nf* diplegia

diplodoks *nm* diplodocus

diploīdija *nf* diploidy

diplokoks *nm* diplococcus

diplomand/s *nm*, **~e** *nf* **1.** (educ.) candidate for
a degree; **2.** recipient of a diploma

diplomātija *nf* diplomacy

diplomātika *nf* diplomatics

diplomātiski *adv* diplomatically

diplomātisks *adj* diplomatic

diplomātiskums *nm* diplomacy

diplomāts *nm*, **~e** *nf* diplomat

diplomdarbs *nm* thesis, dissertation; diploma
piece

diplomēt *vt* diploma, grant a diploma

diplomprojekts *nm* thesis project, graduation
project

diploms *nm* diploma

diplopija *nf* diplopia

diplūras *nf pl* diplurans

dipodija *nf* dipody

dipolmoments *nm* dipole moment

dipols *nm* dipole

dipoņa *nf* sound of light running footsteps;
clatter (of hoofs)

dipropils *nm* dipropyl

diprotons *nm* diproton

dipsaks *nm* teasel

dipsomānija *nf* dipsomania

dipšot *vi* run

dipterikse *nf* tonka bean

dipteroloģija *nf* dipterology

dipti[ch]s [h] *nm* diptych

diptināt *vi* (col.) walk

dīrāt *vt* skin, flay; **d. āēus** (col.) throw up

dīrātāj/s *nm*, ~a *nf* skinner

dirba *nf* 1. trembling person; 2. a horse that gives a bumpy ride; 3. ~s shivers

dirbiens *nm* whipping

dirbināt *vi* drizzle

dirbt *vi* run, scurry

direkcija *nf* 1. management; 2. management offices, main office; **galvenā d.** general manager's office

direktīva *nf* directive

direktīvs *adj* directive

direktorāts *nm* directorate

direktore *nf* 1. directress; manageress; 2. headmistress, principal

direktorija *nf* Directoire

direktorijs *nm* (compu.) directory

direktors *nm* director, manager; principal, headmaster; **galvenais d.** general manager, chief executive officer; **otrais d.** assistant manager

direktoru kopa *nf* board of directors

direktrise *nf* 1. director; 2. (math.) directrix

direkts *adj* direct

dirh[e]ms [ē] *nm* dirhem

diriģent/s *nm*, ~e *nf* (mus.) conductor

diriģēt *vt* (mus) conduct; (sl.) order around

dīriķis *nm* (obs.) skinner

dirižablis *nm* dirigible

dirkas *nf pl* Dirca

dirnēt *vi* stand idle, cool one's heels

dirs/a *nf* (vulg.) ass; ~ā (sl.) in deep trouble

dirst *vi* (vulg.) shit

dirši *nm pl* (bot.) chess

disa[ch]arīds [h] *nm* disaccharide

disciplīna *nf* discipline; **humānitārās** ~s the humanities

discipl[i]nāri [ī] *adv* as a disciplinary measure

discipl[i]nārs [ī] *adj* disciplinary

discipl[i]nārsods [ī] *nm* summary punishment

discipl[i]nārtiesa [ī] *nf* summary court martial; ~s **process** summary procedure

discipl[i]nēt [ī] *vt* discipline, accustom to discipline

discipl[i]nēti [ī] *adv* in a disciplined manner

discipl[i]nētība [ī] *nf* disciplined behavior

discipl[i]nēts [ī] *adj, part* of disciplinēt disciplined

disekcija *nf* disection

dīsele *nf* (of a wagon) pole, shaft, thill

disentērija *nf* = dizentērija

disertācija *nf* dissertation

disertant/s *nm*, ~e *nf* person defending a dissertation

disertēt *vi* expound (on a subject)

disfāgija *nf* dysphagia

disforija *nf* dysphoria

disfunkcija *nf* dysfunction

disgr[a]fija [ā] *nf* writing disorder

disharmonēt *vi* disharmonize

disharmonija *nf* disharmony

disharmoniski *adv* disharmonically

disharmonisks *adj* disharmonic

disidents *nm*, ~e *nf* dissident

disilikāts *nm* disilicate

disimilācija *nf* dissimilation

disimilēties *vr* dissimilate

disimulācija *nf* dissimulation

disimulēt *vt* dissimulate

disipācija *nf* dissipation

disipatīvs *adj* dissipative

disjunkcija *nf* disjunction

disjunktīvs *adj* disjunctive

diskābe *nf* diacid

diska mešana *nf* discus throwing

diskanta atslēga *nf* treble clef

diskants *nm* (mus.) treble

diskdzinis *nm* (compu.) disk drive

diskete *nf* (compu.) floppy disk, diskette

disko *nm indecl* disco

diskobols *nm* discobolus

diskogr|a|fija [ā] *nf* discography

diskomforts *nm* discomfort

diskomūzika *nf* disco music

diskontbanka *nf* discount bank, acceptance corporation

diskontēt *vt* discount

diskontinuitāte *nf* discontinuity

diskonts *nm* discount

diskordance *nf* discordance

diskotēka *nf* 1. library of recordings; 2. discotheque, disco

diskrēcija *nf* discretion

diskreditācija *nf* destruction of trust or confidence

diskreditēt *vt* discredit

diskrepance *nf* discrepancy

diskrēti *adv* discretely

diskrētība *nf* discreteness

diskrēts *adj* discrete

diskrētums *nm* discreteness

diskirminācija *nf* discrimination (against)

diskriminantanalīze *nf* discriminant analysis

diskriminante *nf* discriminant

diskrimin|a|tors [ā] *nm* (el.) discriminator

diskriminēt *vt* discriminate

disks *nm* 1. disc, disk; 2. discus

disku arkls *nm* disk harrow

diskursīvs *adj* discursive

diskurss *nm* discourse

diskusija *nf* discussion

diskutabls *adj* disputable, debatable

diskutējams *adj, part* of **diskutēt** disputable, debatable

diskutēt *vt, vi* discuss, debate

diskvalificēt *vt* disqualify

diskvalifikācija *nf* disqualification

diskvedis *nm* (compu.) driver

diskveida *indecl adj* disk-shaped

diskveidīgs *adj* disk-shaped

diskžokejs *nm* disc jockey

disleksija *nf* dyslexia

dislocēt *vt* 1. (of troops) position; 2. dislocate

dislokācija *nf* 1. (mil., of troops) disposition; 2. (geol.) displacement; 3. (med.) dislocation

dismenoreja *nf* dysmenorrhea

disociācija *nf* dissociation

disociējams *adj, part* of **disociēt** dissociative; dissociable

disociēt *vt* dissociate

disolūcija *nf* dissolution

disonance *nf* dissonance

disonanse *nf* = **disonance**

disonants *adj* dissonant

disonēt *vi* (mus.) be dissonant; (fig.) clash with

dispanserizācija *nf* (of medical care) panel system

dispanserizēt *vt* subject to the panel system of medical care

dispansers *nm* panel of doctors; medical center

dispečerizēt *vt* subject to operational control by dispatchers

dispeč/s *nm*, **~e** *nf* dispatcher

dispensācija *nf* dispensation

dispensēt *vt* dispense

dispepsija *nf* dyspepsia

dispeptisks *adj* dyspeptic

disperģēšana *nf* dispersion

disperģēt *vt* disperse

dispersants *nm* dispersant

dispersija *nf* dispersion

dispersitāte *nf* dispersion

dispersoidoloģija *nf* colloid chemistry

disperss *adj* dispersed

displejs *nm* (compu.) display

disponēt *vt* dispose, incline

dispoz|i|cija [ī] *nf* 1. disposition; predisposition; **d. uz saslimšanu** susceptibility to illness; **ie-dzimta d.** constitutional bias; 2. (mil.) disposition

disproporcija *nf* disproportion

disproporcion[a]litāte [ā] *nf* disproportionality

disprosijs *nm* dysprosium

disprozijs *nm* = **disprosijs**

disputants *nm* disputant

disputēt *vi* dispute, debate

disputs *nm* disputation, debate

distance *nf* **1.** distance; **polārā d.** polar distance; **2.** (mil.) range; **3.** (RR) railroad division

distancēties *vr* distance oneself

distanciāls *adj* (tech.) remote

dīstele *nf* (of a wagon) pole, shaft, thill

disti[ch]s [h] *nm* distich

distinkcija *nf* distinction

distole *nf* diastole

distrakcija *nf* (med.) stretching

distress *nm* distress

distribūcija *nf* distribution

distrib[u]tīvi [ū] *adv* distributively

distrib[u]tīvs [ū] *adj* distributive

distrib[u]tors [ū] *nm* (bus.) distributor

distrikts *nm* district

distrofija *nf* dystrophy

distrofisks *adj* dystrophic

distrofs *adj* dystrophic

disulfāts *nm* disulfate

disulfīds *nm* disulfide

dišlers *nm* (obs.) cabinetmaker

dīšļāt *vi* (of horses) stamp

diteisms *nm* ditheism

ditionskābe *nf* dithionic acid

ditirambs *nm* dithyramb

dito *indecl nm* ditto

ditro[ch]ajs [h] *nm* ditrochee

diurētisks *adj* diuretic

diurēze *nf* diuresis

divacis *nm* (cards) deuce

dīvaini *adv* oddly, peculiarly, quaintly, strangely

dīvainība *nf* oddity, peculiarity, quaintness, queerness, strangeness

dīvainis *nm* odd fellow, eccentric

dīvains *adj* **1.** odd, peculiar, quaint, queer, strange; **2.** wondrous

dīvainulis *nm* weirdo

dīvainums *nm* oddity, peculiarity, quaintness, queerness, strangeness

divairu *indecl adj* pair-oared

dīvānkrēsls *nm* chair-bed

dīvāns *nm* **1.** couch, sofa; **2.** (collection of poems) divan

divarpus *adj* two and a half

divasmeņu *indecl adj* double-edged

divasu *indecl adj* two-axle

divatā *adv* two together, in private, tête-à-tête ; **mēs d.** the two of us

divatība *nf* (of two people) togetherness

divatne *nf* tête-à-tête; twosome

divatnējs *adj* **1.** dual; **2.** (rare.) double

divatnīb/a *nf* **1.** duality; **2.** (of two people) togetherness; **~ā** two together, in private

divatnīgs *adj* **1.** dual; **2.** double

divatnis *nm* double

divats *nm* (rare.) twosome

divbalsienu *indecl adj* disyllabic

divbalsīgi *adv* in two voices; **d. dziedāt** sing a duet

divbalsīgs *adj* (mus.) two-part, for two voices

divbalsu *indecl adj* (mus.) two-part, for two voices

divb[a]zisks [ā] *adj* dibasic

divbērnu *indecl adj* two-children

divbridnis *nm* two-man beach seine

divcēlienu *indecl adj* two-act

divceliņu *indecl adj* two-track

divcilindru *indecl adj* two-cylinder

divcīņa *nf* **1.** duel; two-person competition (mil.) pistol and rifle competition; **2.** biathlon

divcīņnie/ks *nm*, **~ce** *nf* biathlon athlete

divciparu *indecl adj* two-digit

divdabība *nf* duality, twofold nature

divdabīgs *adj* dual

divdabis *nm* **1.** participle; **nelokamais d.** verbal adverb; **2.** hypocrite

divdabja teiciens *nm* participal phrase

divdalījums *nm* dichotomy

divdaļīgs *adj* two-part, two-piece

divdaļtakts *nf* (mus.) 2/2 measure

divdaļu *indecl adj* two-part

divdeja *nf* duet, pas-de-deux

divdesmit *adj* twenty

divdesmit/ais *adj* twentieth; ~ie gadi the twenties

divdesmitgadīgs *adj* twenty-year-old

divdesmitkapeika *nf* twenty-kopeck piece

divdesmitplāksnis *nm* icosahedron

divdeviņi *adj* (folk.) twice nine, very many

divdiapazonu *indecl adj* of two frequency bands

divdienu *indecl adj* two-day

divdīgļlapis *nm* dicotyledon

divdimensiju *indecl adj* two-dimensional

divdimensionāls *adj* two-dimensional

divdomība *nf* double entendre

divdomīgi *adv* ambiguously, equivocally

divdomīgs *adj* ambiguous, equivocal; risque

divdomīgums *nm* ambiguity of meaning

divdurvju *indecl adj* two-door

divdzimumu *indecl adj* bisexual; (bot.) monoclinous

divdzīvokļu *indecl adj* two-apartment

divējādi *adv* in two ways

divējādība *nf* duality

divējāds *adj* dual, double, of two kinds

divējādums *nm* duality

divēji *adj* two

dīveldreķis *nm* (archa.) asafetida

diverġence *nf* divergence

diverġēt *vi* diverge

diversant/s *nm*, ~e *nf* diversionist, saboteur, commando, special forces soldier

diversifikācija *nf* diversification

diversija *nf* diversion, sabotage

diversijas desanta nodaļa *nf* commando party

diversitāte *nf* diversity

divertikuls *nm* diverticulus

divertisments *nm* (mus.) divertissement

divf[a]žu [ā] *indecl adj* two-phase

divgade *nf* two-year period

divgadējs *adj* two-year

divgadīgās cietpieres *nf pl* rough hawk's beard

divgadīgs *adj* two-year; two-year old; biennial

divgadu *indecl adj* two-year

divgala *indecl adj* two-ended

divgalvains *adj* two-headed

divgraudkvieši *nm pl* cultivated emmer

divguļams *adj* sleeping two, (of a bed) double

divguļu *indecl adj* (of a bed) double

div/i *adj* 1. *indecl, decl* two; abi d. both (of them, of us); kā d. deviņi like anything, going full tilt, hell-bent; 2. *indecl* (letter grade) D; 3. *decl* two o'clock; ~os at two

dividende *nf* dividend

divinācija *nf* divination

divirbuļu vilkābele *nf* hawthorn

divistabu *indecl adj* two-room

divīzija *nf* (mil.) division

div[i]zions [ī] *nm* (mil., artillery) batallion; (mil., cavalry, aviation, naval) squadron

divjūga *indecl adj* two-horse

divjūgs *nm* carriage and pair; two-horse team

divkājainis *nm* biped

divkājains *adj* bipedal, two-legged

divkājās *adv* (of animals) on hind legs

divkājis *nm* biped

divkāju or divkājus *adv* (of animals) on hind legs

divkanšu *indecl adj* two-edged; (of barley) two-rowed

divkanšu mieži *nm pl* two-rowed barley

divkapeika *nf* two-kopeck piece

divkaplis *nm* pickax

divkārši *adv* doubly, twice

divkāršojums *nm* doubling

divkāršot *vt* double, redouble; (ling.) reduplicate

divkāršoties *vr* double, be doubled

divkāršs *adj* double, twofold; two-ply

divkārt *adv* twice, double

divkārtām *adv* (rare.) twice, double

divkārtēji *adv* twice, doubly

divkārtējs *adj* twice repeated, double

divkārtīgi *adv* twice, doubly

divkārtīgs *adj* double, twofold; two-ply

divkauja *nf* duel, single combat

divklāju *indecl adj* double-deck

divklasīgs *adj* of two grades; of two classes

divklašu *indecl adj* of two grades; of two classes

divkopienu *indecl adj* of two (linguistic) communities

divkopu *indecl adj* (gram.) having a subject and a predicate

divkopu teikums *nm* (gram.) clause

divkosība *nf* duplicity, double-dealing

divkosīgi *adv* duplicitously

divkosīgs *adj* duplicitous, two-faced, double-dealing

divkos/is *nm*, **~e** *nf* double-dealer

divkrāsainais sikspārnis *nm* frosted bat

divkrāsains *adj* two-color, dichromatic

divkrāsu *indecl adj* two-color, dichromatic

divkrāsu kārkls *nm* tea-leaved willow

divkuprains *adj* two-humped

divkupru *indecl adj* two-humped

divkupru kamielis *nm* two-humped camel

divlaidu *indecl adj* (of stairs) two-flight

divlampu *indecl adj* (radio) two-tube

divlapains *adj* bifoliate

divlape *nf* twayblade; see also **ovālā d.**, **sirdsveida d.**

divlapu naktsvijole *nf* butterfly orchid

divlauku *indecl adj* (of crop rotation) two-field

divlaulība *nf* bigamy

divlemešu *indecl adj* (of plows) two-share

divmājnieks *nm* dioecious plant

divmāju *indecl adj* dioecious

divmāju kaķpēdiņas *nf pl* cat's-foot

divmastnieks *nm* two-master

divmastu *indecl adj* two-masted

divmēnešraksts *nm* bimonthly

divmēnešu *indecl adj* two-month, of two months; bimonthly

divmotorīgs *adj* twin-engine

divmotoru *indecl adj* twin-engine

divmute *nf* distome

divnadzis *nm* artiodactyl

divnedēļu *indecl adj* fortnightly

divnieks *nm* **1.** a two; **2.** (letter grade) D; **3.** (cards) deuce; **4.** pair

divnītis *nf pl* plain weave tabby

divnozīmība *nf* ambiguity

divnozīmīgi *adv* ambiguously

divnozīmīgs *adj* ambiguous

divnozīmīgums *nm* ambiguity

divots *adj* dual; divided

divpadsmit *adj* **1.** *indecl* twelve; **2.** *decl* twelve o'clock; **~os dienā** at noon; **~os naktī** at midnight

divpadsmitais *adj* twelfth

divpadsmitdancis *nm* a Latvian folk dance

divpadsmitgadīgs *adj* twelve-year-old

divpadsmitkolonnu *indecl adj* duodecastyle

divpadsmitpirkstu zarna *nf* duodenum

divpadsmitplāksnis *nm* dodecahedron

divpadsmitskaldnis *nm* dodecahedron

divpadsmitskaldņu *indecl adj* dodecahedral

divpadsmitstāvu *indecl adj* twelve-story

divpadsmitstūris *nm* dodecagon

divpakāpīgs *adj* two-stage

divpakāpju *indecl adj* two-stage

divpalātu *indecl adj* (pol.) two-chamber

divpartiju *indecl adj* two-party

divpavalstniecība *nf* dual citizenship

divpēde *nf* dipody

divpēdu *indecl adj* (of verse meter) two-foot

divpēdu jambs *nm* iambic dimeter

divplaknis *nm* dihedral
divplakņu *indecl adj* dihedral
divplāksnis *nm* biplane
divpolu *indecl adj* two-pole
divprocentīgs *adj* two-percent
divpunkte *nf* two suspension points
divpunktu mārīte *nf* two-spot ladybug
divpusēji *adv* on both sides; bilaterally
divpusējs *adj* two-sided; double-faced; bilateral
divpusgriezīgs *adj* two-edged
divpusība *nf* two-sidedness; bilaterality
divpusīgi *adv* on both sides
divpusīgs *adj* two-sided
divputekšlapu grīslis *nm* lesser panicled sedge
divradu *indecl adj* related through one's parents' relatives; **d. māsa** (first) cousin (female); **d. brā-lis** (first) cousin (male)
divragu *indecl adj* (of anvils) two-horned
divrats *nm* (col.) bicycle
divreiz *adv* twice; double; **d. vairāk** twice as much; **d. mazāk** half as much; **d. gadā** biannually; **d. pa trim mēnešiem** biquarterly; **d. tik** twice the amount
divreizējs *adj* two-time
divriči *nm pl* two-wheeled carriage, hansom; two-wheeled cart, dogcart
divrinda *nf* distich, couplet
divrinde *nf* = **divrinda**
divrindenis *nm* distich, couplet
divrindu *indecl adj* of two rows, double row; (of buttons) double-breasted
divritenis *nm* bicycle
divriteņu *indecl adj* two-wheeled
divrocīgs *adj* two-handed
dīvs *nm* wonder
dīvs *adj* wondrous
divsejība *nf* (rare.) duplicity
divsējumu *indecl adj* two-volume
divsēkle *nf* wall rocket
divsēklu grīslis *nm* soft-leaved sedge

divs[e]riju [ē] *indecl adj* (of a series) two-part
divsēžu *indecl adj* two-seated
divsievība *nf* bigamy
divsimt *num adj* two hundred
divsimtais *num adj* two hundredth
divskaitlinieks *nm* (ling.) dual noun
divskaitlis *nm* (ling.) dual (number)
divskaldnis *nm* dihedral
divskaldņu *indecl adj* dihedral
divskanis *nm* diphthong
divskats *nm* (theat.) scene for two actors
divslejīgs *adj* (of writing, print) two-column
divsleju *indecl adj* (of writing, print) two-column
divsliežu *indecl adj* double-track
divslīpju *indecl adj* (of a roof) gable, two-pitched
divspār/nis *nm* dipterous insect; ~ņi Diptera
divspēle *nf* 1. (tennis) double; 2. (theat.) scene for two actors
divstarains *adj* two-pronged
divstatņu *indecl adj* (of planers) double-column
divstāvokļu relejs *nm* flip-flop relay
divstāvu *indecl adj* two-story
divstīgu *indecl adj* two-stringed
divstilbīgs *adj* two-limbed, two-armed
divstobrene *nf* double-barreled shotgun
divstobru *indecl adj* double-barreled
divšķautņains *adj* two-edged
divšķautņu *indecl adj* two-edged
divšķautņu asinszāle *nf* Saint-John's-wort
divtaktu *indecl adj* 1. (mus.) in double time; 2. (internal combustion engines) two-stroke
divtik *adv* twice as much, twice as many
divtonnīgs *adj* two-ton
divtulība *nf* alone together
divvāku *indecl adj* bivalve
divvaldība *nf* diarchy
divvalodība *nf* bilingualism
divvalodu *indecl adj* bilingual
divvalstnieks *nm* dual citizen

divveidība *nf* dimorphism
divveidīgs *adj* dimorphous
divvērtība *nf* bivalence
divvērtīgs *adj* bivalent
divvērtņu *indecl adj* (of doors, windows) two-leaf
divvielu *indecl adj* (of alloys) binary
divvientulība *nf* shared solitude
divvietīgs *adj* 1. (math.) two-place, two-figure; 2. two-seated
divvilcis *nm* chess problem in two moves
divvīrība *nf* bigamy
divviru *indecl adj* (of doors, gates) two-leaf
divviru vārstulis *nm* mitral valve
divvirzienu *indecl adj* (of streets) two-way
divzarains *adj* two-pronged
divzare *nf* forked branch
divzaru *indecl adj* two-pronged
divzilbīgs *adj* two-syllable
divzilbju *indecl adj* two-syllable
divzīmju *indecl adj* (math.) two-figure
divzirdznieks *nm* carriage and pair
divzirgu *indecl adj* two-horse
divzobene *nf* double iron plane
divzvaigzne *nf* binary star
divžuburains *adj* two-pronged, bifurcated, (of candlesticks) two-arm
divžuburu *indecl adj* two-pronged, bifurcated, (of candlesticks) two-arm
diza *nf* disa
dizainers *nm*, ~e *nf* industrial designer
dizains *nm* industrial design
dizartrija *nf* dysarthria
dizažio *indecl nm* disagio
dīzelis *nm* diesel, diesel engine
dīzeļdegviela *nf* diesel fuel
dīzeļdzinējs *nm* diesel engine
dīzeļelektrisks *adj* diesel-electric
dīzeļeļļa *nf* diesel oil
dīzeļkuģis *nm* motor ship
dīzeļlokomotīve *nf* diesel-electric locomotive
dīzeļmotors *nm* diesel engine

dīzeļtraktors *nm* diesel tractor
dīzeļvilciens *nm* diesel engine train
dizent[e]rija [ē] *nf* dysentery
dizosmija *nf* dysosmia
dizūrija *nf* dysuria
dīēa *nf, nm* restless, fidgety person
diēadata *nf* mending needle
dižā ilzīte *nf* English chamomile
dižais ērglis *nm* imperial eagle
dižais piekūns *nm* peregrine falcon
dižaita *nf* adult sheep
dižā jāņeglīte *nf* Charles's scepter
dižakmens *nm* giant boulder
dižans *adj* = **dižens**
dižā prīmula *nf* oxlip
dižā saulsardzene *nf* parasol mushroom
dižā skābene *nf* common sorrel
dižās noragas *nf pl* greater burnet saxifrage
dīžāt *vt, vi* stamp one's feet; be restive, fidget
dižāties *vr* = **dižoties**
dīžāties *vr* 1. stamp one's feet; be restive; be capricious; 2. show off a horse (by riding it back and forth)
dižauzas *nf pl* tall oatgrass
dižbajārs *nm* (folk.) lord, person of rank
dižbāliņš *nm* (folk.) influential kinsman, outstanding compatriot
dižbaznīc/a *nf* ~ā iet take Communion
dižbļāvējs *nm* bigmouth; barker
dižbriedis *nm* elk
dižceļš *nm* highway
diciltība *nf* 1. nobility (of birth); 2. pedigreed origin
dižciltīgais *nom adj* nobleman
dižciltīgi *adv* as behooves nobility
dižciltīgs *adj* 1. of noble birth, noble; 2. pedigreed
dižciltīgums *nm* 1. nobility (of birth); 2. pedigreed origin
dižciltnieks *nm* important person
diždadzis *nm* burdock
diždarbs *nm* feat

diždēls *nm* outstanding son (of a state, area), outstanding citizen

diždrānas *nf pl* Sunday best

diždundurs *nm* horsefly

diždzejnieks *nm* poet laureate

diždzimtīgs *adj* of noble birth, noble

dižēdājs *nm* glutton

dižēdis *nm* glutton

dižegle *nf* fir

dižen *adv* (reg.) very, mighty

diženi *adv* stately; grandly; mightily

diženība *nf* stateliness; grandeur; prominence

dižens *adj* stately; grand; mighty; noble

dižēnums *nm* stateliness; grandeur

dižēvele *nf* long plane

dižgabals *nm* (obs.) cannon

dižgalvis *nm* stubborn person

dižgars *nm* genius

diži *adv* in a grand manner; (reg.) very

dižība *nf* conceit

dižīgi *adv* conceitedly

dižīgs *adj* conceited

dižilkss *nf* (of a wagon) pole, shaft, thill

dižināt *vt* (folk.) praise

dižistaba *nf* (hist.) large common room

dižjūra *nf* high seas

dižkareivis *nm* private first class

dižknābis *nm* hawfinch

dižkoks *nm* remarkable tree

dižkungs *nm* 1. lord (of the manor); 2. nobleman

dižkuņģis *nm* 1. (col.) glutton; 2. (col.) fatty, beerbelly

dižķengurs *nm* kangaroo

dižķieģelis *nm* large-size brick

dižlaiva *nf* barge

dīēlapainā kļava *nf* big-leaf maple

dižlapainā liepa *nf* broad-leaved linden

dižlazda *nf* filbert

dižl[i]lija [ī] *nf* crinum

dižlopi *nm pl* cattle

dižmakr[e]le [ē] *nf* king mackerel

dižmanība *nf* boastfulness; conceit, arrogance

dižmanīgi *adv* boastfully; conceitedly, arrogantly

dižmanīgs *adj* boastful, conceited, arrogant

dižmanis *nm* 1. boastful, conceited, arrogant person; 2. nobleman, person of rank

dižmatrozis *nm* (mil. rank) seaman

dižmedījumi *nm pl* large game

dižmeistar/s *nm*, **~e** *nf* grand master

dižmeita *nf* adult farm hand, maid

dižmeldri *nm pl* cypress grass

dižmeldru grīslis *nm* cyperus-like sedge

dižmežs *nm* old growth forest

dižmuiža *nf* manor

dižmutīgs *adj* bigmouthed

dižmutis *nm* bigmouth

dižošanās *nfr* showing off, flaunting; swagger

dižoties *vr* flaunt; put on airs, show off; swagger

dižozols *nm* mighty oak; (col., fig.) pillar of society

dižpērkone *nf* corn cockle

dižpīle *nf* shelduck

dižpuisis *nm* unmarried farm hand

dižradu *indecl adj* of noble birth

dižraibais dzenis *nm* great spotted woodpecker

dižraibs *adj* (of animals) large-spotted

dižrausis *nm* a type of cake

dižrīkle *nf* loudmouth

dižs *adj* 1. large, big; 2. stately, grand, prominent

dižsaimniece *nf* wife of a **dižsaimnieks**

dižsaimnieks *nm* big farmer

dižsirdība *nf* magnanimity

dižsirdīgi *adv* magnanimously

dižsirdīgs *adj* magnanimous

dižsirdis *nm* magnanimous person

dižskābardis *nm* European beech

dižslieka *nf* night crawler

dižstrādnieks *nm* adult worker

dižtautietis *nm* prominent compatriot

dižteicējs *nm* (col.) great talker

dižtēvs *nm* **1.** well-to-do farmer; **2.** best man

ditītenis *nm* hedge bindweed

dižūdens *nm* big waters

dižūdrs *nm* giant Brazilian otter

dižums *nm* stateliness, grandeur

dižvalod/is *nm*, ~e *nf* big talker, one with the gift of the gab

dižvaronis *nm* superhero

dižvedējs *nm* best man

dižvēderis *nm* (col.) fatty, blimp

dižvīrs *nm* a person with political clout, bigwig

dižzemnieks *nm* big farmer

dižzobainā apse *nf* bigtooth aspen

Djuāra trauki *nm pl* Dewar vessels

do *indecl nf* (mus.) C

dobains *adj* pitted; pockmarked

dobais rumpucis *nm* fluted black elfin saddle

dobe *nf* **1.** garden bed; **2.** pit, hole; grave; ~s varde (col.) dirty fellow

dobens *adj* hollow

dobermanis *nm* Doberman pinscher

dobermanpinčers *nm* Doberman pinscher

dobie cīrulīši *nm pl* a birthwort, Corydalis cava

dobīte *nf* **1.** *dim* of **dobe**; **2.** dimple

dobjains *adj* full of potholes

dobjķieģelis *nm* hollow brick

dobjplaknis *nm* hollow-core slab

dobji *adv* hollowly

dobjš *adj* (of sound) hollow

dobjums *nm* (of sound) hollowness

dobracis *nm* gravedigger

dobradēi *nm pl* Bovoidea

dobs *adj* hollow

dobspiede *nf* intaglio printing press

dobspiedums *nm* intagliotype

dobt *vt* hollow

dobulains *adj* uneven, pitted; with potholes

dobulis *nm* **1.** (eye) socket; **2.** hole, depression, pit

dobulītis *nm* **1.** *dim* of **dobulis**, little pit; **2.** dimple

dobuļains *adj* full of holes or pits

dobumains *adj* hollow

dobumots *adj* hollow

dobumperētāji *nm pl* birds nesting in hollows

dobums *nm* hollow, cavity; (tech.) flaw; (in met-als) honeycomb

dobumspindele *nf* nose bot

dobvārpsta *nf* hollow shaft

dobzieēi *nm pl* Coeloglossum

docent/s *nm*, ~e *nf* (university) lecturer, assistant professor

docentūra *nf* **1.** assistant professorship; **2.** faculty of assistant professors

docēt *vi* lecture

docētāj/s *nm*, ~a *nf* docent; ~i faculty

do[ch]mijs [h] *nm* dochmius

dodekaedrs *nm* dodecahedron

dodekāns *nm* dodecane

dodekateons *nm* dodecatheon

dodekafonija *nf* dodecaphony

dodekafoniķ/is *nm*, ~e *nf* dodecaphonist

dodekafonisks *adj* dodecaphonic

dodekafonist/s *nm*, ~e *nf* dodecaphonist

dodekagons *nm* dodecagon

dodēt *vi* (of swans) sing

dodēs *nm* doge

dofīns *nm* dauphin

dogma *nf* dogma

dogmatika *nf* dogmatics

dogmatiķ/is *nm*, ~e *nf* dogmatist

dogmatiski *adv* dogmatically

dogmatisks *adj* dogmatic

dogmatisms *nm* dogmatism

dogmats *nm* dogma

dogs *nm* Great Dane

doina *nf* doina

dokers *nm* **1.** shipyard worker; **2.** docker, longshoreman

dokēt *vi* (naut.) dock

dokmanis *nm* (hist.) citizens' representative (in Riga)

dokot *vi* = **dokēt**

doks *nm* (naut.) dock

doksogr[a]fija [ā] *nf* doxography

doksogr[a]fs [ā] *nm* doxographer

doksoloģija *nf* doxology

doksoloģisks *adj* doxological

doktorand/s *nm*, ~e *nf* candidate for the degree of Doctor

doktorants *nm* = **doktorands**

doktorantūra *nf* candidacy for the degree of Doctor

doktorāts *nm* a doctor's house

doktorēt *vt* doctor

doktorēties *vr* obtain the degree of Doctor (or PhD)

doktor/s *nm*, ~e *nf* 1. (the degree of) Doctor; 2. physician, doctor

doktrīna *nf* doctrine

doktr[i]nāls [ī] *adj* doctrinal

doktrināri *adv* doctrinarily

doktr[i]nārisms [ī] *nm* doctrinairism

doktr[i]nārs [ī] *nm* doctrinaire

doktr[i]nārs [ī] *adj* doctrinaire

dokumentācija *nf* documentation; ~i for the record

dokumentālisms *nm* documentation

dokumentālistika *nf* document processing

documentālist/s *nm*, ~e *nf* 1. documentarian; 2. documentalist

dokumentalitāte *nf* documentary nature; documentation

dokumentāli *adv* with documents

dokumentāls *ad* documentary, in the nature of a document

dokumentaritāte *nf* documentary evidence

dokumentāri *adv* with documents

dokumentārs *adj* documentary, supported by documents

dokumentēt *vt* document

dokuments *nm* document

doķis *nm* 1. salmon net; 2. old river bed; 3. salt cellar

dol[a]rs [ā] *nm* dollar

dole *nf* polled cow

dolerīts *nm* dolerite

doli[ch|o[k]ef[a]lija [h][c][ā] *nf* dolicocephaly

doli[ch|o[k]ef[a]ls [h][c][ā] *nm* dolicocephal

dolikokefalija *nf* dolicocephaly

dolikokefals *nm* dolichocephal

dolītis *nm* small bucket without a handle

dolmens *nm* dolmen

dolomītkaļķi *nm pl* dolomitic lime

dolomītmerģelis *nm* dolomitic marl

dolomīts *nm* dolomite

doļa *nf* (obs.) Russian apothecary measure; grain

dom/a *nf* 1. thought; idea; 2. opinion; **sabiedriskā d.** public opinion; **pēc manām ~ām** in my opinion; **būt augstās ~ās par . . .** have a high opinion of . . .

domājams *adj, part* of **domāt** thinkable; **d., ka . . .** one would expect that . . .

domājošs *adj, part* of **domāt** thinking; (with a qualifying adverb) -minded

domāšana *nf* 1. thinking; 2. mentality

domā/t *vt, vi* 1. think; **es ~ju gan!** I should think so! **~s darīts** no sooner said than done; **ko domā!** (col.) just think of it! well, what do you know! **d., ka . . .** one would think that . . .; 2. intend, mean; **jādomā** perhaps

domātājs *nm*, ~a *nf* thinker

domāties *vr* (obs.) seem

dombaznīca *nf* cathedral church

dombra *nf* (mus. instrument) dombra

dome *nf* dome, elective council; (hist.) duma, Duma

domēnatmiņa *nf* (compu.) bubble memory

domēne *nf* domain, crown land

domēns *nm* (compu.) domain

domēņu krāsns *nf* blast furnace

domes nams *nm* town hall

domesticēt *vt* domesticate

domestikācija *nf* domestication

domic[i]ls [ī] *nm* domicile

domība *nf* pensiveness

domīgi *adv* pensively

domīgs *adj* pensive

domīgums *nm* pensiveness

dominance *nf* dominance

dominante *nf* dominant

dominants *adj* dominant

dominējošs *adj* dominant

dominēt *vi* dominate, predominate

domīnija *nf* dominion

domīnijs *nm* domain

dominikān/is *nm*, **~iete** *nf* (member of a religious order; inhabitant of the Dominican Republic) Dominican

domino *indecl nm* (costume, domino tile) domino; (game) dominoes

domiņa *nf dim* of **doma**, little thought

domis *nm* deep place in a river

domkapituls *nm* canonical chapter

domkrats *nm* (mech.) jack

domkungs *nm* (rel.) canon

domna *nf* blast furnace

domnieks *nm* member of a **dome**, councilman

dompilns *adj* pensive

domra *nf* (mus. instrument) domra

domraksts *nm* (educ.) composition, essay

domrist/s *nm*, **~e** *nf* domra player

doms *nm* cathedral church, minster

domskola *nf* Latin school

domstarpība *nf* difference of opinion, disagreement

domu aina *nf* mental picture

domubiedrs *nm* a person that holds the same views

domu gaita *nf* train of thought, process of thinking

domugrauds *nm* aphorism

domuzīme *nf* (punctuation mark) dash

dona *nf* heel of a loaf

donācija *nf* donation

done *nf* groove

dongalis *nm* heel of a loaf

dongs *nm* dong

doniņa *nf dim* of **dona**, heel of a loaf

donis *nm* See **doņi**

donja *nf* doña

donkihotisks *adj* quixotic

donkihotisms *nm* quixotism

donkihots *nm* Don Quixote

donna *nf* donna

donor/s *nm*, **~e** *nf* blood donor

dons *nm* don

donžons *nm* donjon

donžuāns *nm* Don Juan, libertine

doņi *nm pl* rush

doņu spartija *nf* saltmeadow cordgrass

dopēt *vt* (of semiconductors) dope

dopings *nm* dopant

dopināt *v* **1.** *vi* pitter-patter; **2.** *vt* dandle

Doplera efekts *nm* Doppler effect

dore *nf* (obs.) hollow of a tree (used as a bee-hive), bee gum

dorespele *nf* doormouse

doriešu stils *nm* (arch.) Doric order

dorie/tis *nm*, **~te** *nf* Dorian

doriknija *nf* dorycnium

dorisks *adj* Dorian; Doric

dormitorijs *nm* (monastery) dormitory

doronika *nf* leopard's-bane

dorsāls *adj* dorsal

dorstenija *nf* dorstenia

dorša *nf* (reg.) cod

dortuārs *nm* dormitory

do[r]u [ŗ] dējējs *nm* (obs.) beekeeper

dosjē *indecl nm* dossier

došanās *nfr* (of a trip) beginning; **d. ceļā** departure

dot *vt irr* give; hand, pass; grant; **d. atsparu** refute; **d. augļus** bear fruit; **nedod Dievs!** God forbid! **d. ceļu** give way, get out of the way; **~s pret ~u** a. I owed you one! b.

tit for tat; **d. drūksti** (reg.) scold; **d. kājām ziņu** take to one's heels; **d. krūti** suckle; **kas to deva!** (col.) it was not to be; **kas to dos!** (col.) fat chance! **d. krāsu** (cards) follow suit; **d. kukuli** bribe; **d. labdienu** greet; **d. liecību** testify; **d. mācību** a. teach (indirectly); b. teach a lesson; **d. maizi** provide for; **d. mājienu** drop a hint; **nedot mieru** a. give no rest; b. bother, pester; c. worry; **d. mutes** (obs.) kiss; **dod nedodams** (of rain) it is coming down; **d. pa ādu** spank, beat; **d. pa ausi** (col.) slap, smack; **d. pa cepuri** (or **mici, kaklu**) beat; **d. pa dibenu** spank; **d. piekrišanu** consent; **d. pi-parus** scold; **d. pretī** talk back; **d. ražu** yield a harvest; **d. rīkstes** switch, spank; **d. rokām vaļu** hit; **d. savu parakstu** make a signed statement; **d. spēku** invigorate; **d. sukas** spank; **d. sutu** scold; **d. tautās** (folk.) marry off; **d. uguni** open fire; **d. vaļu** allow; **d. vārdu** a. name; b. give s.o. the floor; c. give one's word; **d. vietu** make room; give up one's seat; **d. vilka pasi** fire; **d. virsū** (col.) scold; **d. ziņu** send word; **d. zvē-rastu** take an oath; **d. žagarus** birch

dotācija *nf* subsidy

dotības *nf pl* abilities, aptitudes, talent; makings

doties *vr irr* go, depart, make one's way to, make for; **d. atpakaļ** go back, return; **d. ceļā** set out, get on the way, depart; **d. ceļojumā** go on a trip, set out on a journey; **d. jūrā** go to sea; **d. laulībā** marry; **d. pie altāra** get married; **d. nāvē** kill oneself; **d. pie miera** go to bed; **d. par . . .** hire oneself out as, become (a worker, craftsman, person); **d. pazīstamam** introduce oneself, give one's name; **d. pretī** go to meet; face; **d. prom** depart, leave; **d. triecienā** storm; **d. uzbrukumā** attack; **d. uz priekšu** move forward

dotin *adv emph* of **dot**; **d. deva** they gave generously

dots I (with **uo**) *adj, part* of **dot** given

dots II *nm* (mil.) pillbox

dotumi *nm pl* **1.** givens; **2.** talent

doza *nf* = **doze** II

doz[a]tora [ā] aizkars *nm* (mfg.) batching gate

doz[a]tors [ā] *nm* (mfg.) batcher

doze I *nf* small case, box, or tin

doze II *nf* dose, dosage

dozēšana *nf* (mfg.) batching

dozēt *vt* dose; (mfg.) batch

dozimetrija *nf* dosimetry

dozimetrisks *adj* dosimetric

dozimetrist/s *nm*, **~e** *nf* dosimetry specialist

dozimetrs *nm* dosimeter

drabenes *nf pl* = **drabiņas**

drabiņas *nf pl* brewery slops, draff

drabiņu alus *nm* sediment beer

draca *nf* (reg.) hubbub, uproar

dracēna *nf* dracaena

dra[ch]ma [h] *nf* drachma

dracīt *vt* scold

dracīties *vr* rage, storm; romp

dradži *nm pl* cracklings

draga *nf* dredge

dragāt *vt* smash

draglains *nm* dragline

dragomans *nm* dragoman

dragūns *nm* dragoon

draibste *nf* = **draipste**

draipste *nf* hoyden

draiska *nf, nm* romp, imp

draiskāt *vi* wear tatters

draiski *adv* frolicsomely, friskily

draiskot *vi* romp, cavort, frisk

draiskoties *vr* romp, cavort, frisk

draisks *adj* frolicsome, frisky; prankish; gleeful

draiskulība *nf* friskiness; prankishness, pranks

draiskulīgi *adv* frolicsomely, friskily

draiskulīgs *adj* frolicsome, frisky; prankish

draiskulīgums *nm* prankishness; friskiness

draiskul/is *nm*, **~e** *nf* romp, imp

draiskuļot *vi* romp, cavort, frisk

draiskuļoties *vr* romp, cavort, frisk

draiskums *nm* frolicsomeness, friskiness

draislis *nm* romp, imp

draišķīgs *adj* frolicsome, frisky; prankish

draišķis *nm* romp, imp

draišķot *vi* = **draiskot**

draišķoties *vr* = **draiskoties**

draivers *nm* (compu.) driver

draivs *nm* (tennis) drive

drakelēt *vt, vi* (barb.) stitch

drakoniski *adv* draconically

drakonisks *adj* draconian

drakoniskums *nm* draconian nature

drakonisms *nm* draconian nature

drakons *nm* 1. dragon; 2. Draco lizard

drakts *nf* (shirt) yoke

drāma *nf* drama

dr|a|matiķ/is [ā] *nm*, **~e** *nf* dramatist

dr|a|matiski [ā] *adv* dramatically

dr|a|matisks [ā] *adj* dramatic

dr|a|matiskums [ā] *nm* dramatism

dr|a|matisms [ā] *nm* dramatism

dr|a|matizējums [ā] *nm* dramatization

dr|a|matizēt [ā] *vt* dramatize

dr|a|matur/gs [ā] *nm*, **~ģe** *nf* playwright; dramaturge

dr|a|maturģija [ā] *nf* dramaturgy

dr|a|maturģiski [ā] *adv* dramaturgically

dr|a|maturģisks [ā] *adj* dramaturgic

drāna *nf* 1. fabric, material, cloth; 2. piece of cloth; 3. ~s clothes, garments

dranck/as *nf pl* worn clothing, tatters; **~u ~ās** to pieces

drāniņa *nf* 1. *dim* of **drāna**, small piece of cloth; 2. ~s diapers

dranska *nf* (reg.) tatter

draņķēt *vt* (col.) 1. slop; 2. rain and snow

draņķīgi *adv* lousy, very badly

draņķīgs *adj* (com.) lousy, very bad

draņķis *nm* (col.) 1. slops, garbage; 2. dirty water, bad drink; 3. silage; 4. good-for-nothing; 5. snow and rain mixed; 6. afterbirth

draņķubaļļa *nf* slops trough

drapējums *nm* drapery

drapērija *nf* drapery

drapes *nf pl* (obs.) drops

drapēt *vt* drape

draps *nm* (obs., fabric) drab

drasēt *vi* 1. make merry; 2. prance, swagger, strut

drasēties *vr* 1. make merry; 2. prance, swagger, strut

drasīgs *adj* unruly, untamed

draska *nf, nm* 1. hyperactive boy; 2. tatter

draskāt *vt* tear; strip

draskāties *vr* romp

drāslis *nm* unruly person

drāsme *nf* scar, scratch

drasot *vi* (obs.) march, strut

drastīgi *adv* = **drastiski** I

drastīgs *adj* = **drastisks** I

drastiski I *adv* lightheartedly; frolicsomely

drastiski II *adv* drastically

drastisks I *adj* jolly, lighthearted; frolicsome, prankish

drastisks II *adj* drastic

drastiskums *nm* drastic nature

drāšana *nf* (tech.) chipping

drašķis *nm* unruly person

drašķīties *vr* romp

drātēties *vr* (sl., vulg.) screw

drāts *nf* (com.) wire

drātstārps *nm* wireworm

draudēt *vi* threaten, meanace; **d. ar pirkstu** shake one's finger at

draudi *nm pl* threat, menace; threats

draudīgi *adv* threateningly, menacingly; ominously

draudīgs *adj* threatening, menacing; ominous; imminent

draudoši *adv* menacingly

draudošs *adj, part* of draudēt threatening, menacing, ominous; imminent

draudze *nf* 1. congregation; 2. parish; 3. (hist.) voluntary armed force

draudzene *nf* friend, girl friend; laulātā d. wife, spouse

draudzenīte *nf dim* of draudzene, friend

draudzes gans *nm* pastor

draudzes loceklis *nm* parishioner

draudzes nams *nm* parish house

draudzes priekšnieks *nm* president of the congregation (Lutheran)

draudzes skola *nf* (hist.) parish school;

draudzēties *vr* be friends with

draudzība *nf* friendship

draudzīgi *adv* in a friendly manner, amicably

draudzīgs *adj* 1. friendly, amicable; 2. fraternal

draudzīgums *nm* friendliness

draudziņš *nm dim* of draugs, friend

draugaļa *nf* mistress

draug/s *nm* 1. friend; laulātais d. husband, spouse; d. nelaimē a friend in need; 2. lover, aficionado, enthusiast

draugu būšana *nf* favoritism

draugulis *nm* lover, kept man

drauģelis *nm* pal

drausma *nf* 1. menace; 2. dread; 3. terror, horror

drausmaini *adv* terribly, horribly

drausmains *adj* terrible, horrible

drausmi *adv* terribly, horribly

drausmība *nf* horribleness

drausmīgi *adv* terribly, horribly; (col.) very

drausmīgs *adj* terrible, horrible

drausmīgums *nm* horribleness

drausmonis *nm* monster

drausms *adj* terrible, horrible

drava *nf* apiary

drāva I *nf* scolding; punishment; threat

drāva II *nf* hollowed inside of a bee gum

dravēt *vt* 1. collect honey; 2. hollow a tree trunk for use as a beehive

drāvēt *vt* scold; warn

dravid/s *nm*, ~iete *nf* Dravidian

dravniecība *nf* beekeeping

dravnie/ks *nm*, ~ce *nf* beekeeper

drāza *nf* tumult

draz/as *nf pl* sweepings, debris, chips; ~u ~ās to smithereens

drāzējs *nm* whittler

drazgas *nf pl* sweepings, debris, chips

drāziens I *nm* 1. (of air, wind) rush, gust; 2. sprint

drāziens II *nm* 1. dressing down; 2. cut

drāznis *nm* drawknife

drāzt I *vt* 1. cut, pare, whittle; d. zīmuli sharpen a pencil; chip; 2. scold; 3. hit; 4. d. acīs tell in one's face

drāzt II *vi* dash, rush, tear along

drāztele *nf* wood chip

drāztelēt *vt, vi* whittle

drāzties *vr* dash, rush, tear along

drāztīt *vt, vi* whittle

drāztulis *nm* (col.) runabout

dražē *indecl nf* dragée

dražeja *nf* dragée

drebas *nf pl* shivers

drēb/e *nf* 1. fabric, material, cloth; 2. ~es clothes, attire, garments; gatavas ~es ready-made clothes; izejamās ~es Sunday best; ~es pēc mēra made-to-order clothes

drebek/lis *nm* (col.) 1. fidgety person; 2. also pl ~ļi shivers

drebelēties *vr* (col.) speak in a shaky voice

drebelība *nf* shakiness, tremblingness

drebelīgi *adv* shakily; with trembling fingers

drebelīgs *adj* 1. shaky; shivering, trembling; fidgety; (of horses) shy; 2. rash, impetuous

drebelīgums *nm* shakiness, tremblingness

drebel/is *nm*, ~e *nf* (col.) **1.** rash, impetuous, high-strung person; **2.** fast horse

drēberis *nm* (obs.) trotter, harness racer

drebēt *vi* tremble, shiver, quiver; quake, shake; quaver; jiggle; flutter; **d. pie visām miesām** shake all over

drebināt *vt* shake

drebināties *vr* shake, shiver, quiver, shudder; jitter

drēbju kode *nf* clothes moth, webbing clothes moth

drēbju pakaŗamais *nm* **1.** clothes tree; **2.** coat hanger; **3.** tab, hanger

drēbju skapis *nm* wardrobe

drēbju uts *nf* body louse

drēbju vadzis *nm* clothes rack

dreblas *nf pl* shivers

drebļi *nm pl* shivers

drēbniecība *nf* tailoring; dressmaking

drēbnieks *nm* tailor

dreboklis *nm* fidgeter

drebulīgi *adv* trembling, shivering; in a trembling voice

drebulīgs *adj* trembling, shivering

drebulis *nm* (sl.) weak sister

drēbulis *nm* (reg.) large, wet snowflake

drebuļi *nm pl* shivers; tremor

drebuļot *vi* shiver

drebuļoties *vr* shiver

drednauts *nm* dreadnaught

drēgāt *vi* ail

drēgni *adv* (istabā kļuva) **d.** (it turned) cold and damp (in the room)

drēgns *adj* cold and damp

drēgnums *nm* damp cold

drēgs *nm* thaw, slushy weather

dreģis *nm* drag

drēģis *nm* covered body of a sleigh

dreibeņķis *nm* (barb.) lathe

dreifēt *vi* (naut.) **1.** drift; drag the anchor; **2.** tack

dreifs *nm* **1.** (naut., el.) drift; **2.** (naut.) tack

dreijas *nf pl* (obs.) lathe

dreijāt *vt* (obs.) turn (on a lathe); **d. fasonu** (sl.) dress in style

dreiliņš *nm* **1.** (naut.) tow; **2.** lantern pinion

dreimanis *nm* (obs.) driller

drēliņš *nm* lantern pinion

drellēt *vi, vt* (hist.) **1.** work off a debt; **2.** perform corvée labor; **3.** enslave

drellis I *nm* twill

drellis II *nm* (hist.) a Livonian slave

drempelis *nm* roof overhang

drena *nf* drain pipe; drain hose

drenāža *nf* drainage, draining

drenēt *vt* drain

drenu grāvis *nm* drain, drainage ditch

dresēt *vt* (of animals) train, tame

dresētāj/s *nm*, ~a *nf* animal trainer, animal tamer

dresūra *nf* **1.** (of animals) training, taming; **2.** (fig.) drill

drezgas *nf pl* tatters, shreds

drezīna *nf* handcar

driāda *nf* **1.** dryad; **2.** (bot.) dryas, mountain av-ens

driass *nm* Dryas phase (of last ice age)

driblēt *vi* (basketball) dribble

dribls *nm* dribble

drice *nf* (reg.) scolding

drīcekle *nf* wild rose

dricele *nf* dogcart

dricelēt *vt* (reg.) shake

dricināt *vt* (reg.) shake

driepēt *vi* (reg.) hit

drifters *nm* drift boat

driftertīkls *nm* drift net

drifts *nm* (naut.) drift

drigalka *nf* steering oar of a raft

drigants *nm* **1.** stallion; **2.** unruly person

driģene *nf* henbane; **vai esi** ~s **saēdies?** are you nuts?

drīksna *nf* **1.** (bot.) stigma; **2.** line, scratch, score

drīksnains *adj* lined, scratched, scored

drīkst/ēt *vi* **1.** dare; venture; **kā tu ~i!** how dare you! **2.** be allowed; **vai es ~u?** may I?

driķeris *nm* (barb.) door handle

driķēt *vt, vi* (barb.) write in capitals, print

drillēt *vt* (barb.) drill

drillis *nm* (drilling tool) brace

drima *nf* drimys

drimala *nf* (reg.) tiny bit

drimēt *vi* (reg.) tremble, shiver

driopiteki *nm pl* Dryopithecus, dryopithecids

dripe *nf* gear tooth

drīpelēt *vt* (col.) scold

dripsna *nf* (reg.) tiny bit

driska *nf* tatter

driskains *adj* tattered

driskāt *vt* tatter

driskata *nf* (col.) tatter

driskāties *vr* be tattered

drīve *nf* **1.** caulking tool; **2.** caulk

drīvdzelzs *nf* caulking tool

drīveklis *nm* **1.** oakum; **2.** caulker's chisel

drīveris *nm* caulker

drīvēt *vt* **1.** caulk; **2.** (of anchors) come home

drīz *adv* **1.** soon; shortly, presently; **d. vien** pretty soon; **d. jo d.** very soon; **d . . . ., d . . . .** now . . ., now . . .; **d. šis, d. tas** first one thing, then another; **d. še, d. tur** here and there; **2.** *comp* **~āk** a. sooner; b. rather

drīzi *adv* early, promptly

drīzināt *vt* hurry

drīziņš *nm* a Latvian folk dance

drīzs *adj* early, prompt, (of the future) near

drīzuļi *nm pl* early-ripe fruit; early potatoes

drīzumā *adv* soon, before long

drog/a *nf* **1.** dried medicinal plant; **2.** drug; **~u veikals** drugstore

drogist/s *nm*, **~e** *nf* druggist

drojene *nf* whitlow grass

drojenīte *nf* whitlow grass

drojeņu cietķērsa *nf* hoary cress

dromedārs *nm* dromedary

drone *nf* exhausted clearing

dropēt *vt, vi* (col.) drink

drosa *nf* (poet.) courage, bravery

drosele *nf* **1.** throttle valve; **2.** (el.) induction coil, reactor

droseļspole *nf* (el.) reactor

droseļvārsts *nm* throttle valve

drosme *nf* courage, boldness, daring; heart; bravery; **d. skurbulī** Dutch courage

drosmīgi *adv* courageously, bravely, boldly

drosmīgs *adj* courageous, bold, daring; brave

drosmīgums *nm* courage, boldness, daring

drosmināt *vt* encourage, reassure

drosminie/ks *nm* brave man; **~ce** *nf* brave woman

drosms *adj* courageous, bold, daring; brave

drosonis *nm* brave man

dross *adj* courageous, bold

drostala *nf* = **droztala**

drostalāt *vi* = **droztalāt**

drostaliņa *nf* = **droztaliņa**

drostaloties *vr* = **droztaloties**

drosule *nf* brave woman

drosulis *nm* brave man

drošgalve *nf* brave woman

drošgalvīgs *adj* courageous, brave

drošgalvis *nm* brave man

droši *adv* **1.** boldly, bravely; **2.** safely, securely; **d. vien** probably

drošība *nf* **1.** safety, security **~s pēc** to be on the safe side; **2.** deposit, security; forfeit

drošības adata *nf* safety pin

drošības arests *nm* protective custody

drošības nauda *nf* deposit; escrow; (jur.) bond

drošības saliņa *nf* safety island

drošības spilvens *nm* airbag

drošības stikls *nm* safety glass

drošināt *vt* encourage, reassure

drošinātāj/s *nm* **1.** encourager, reassurer; **~a** *nf*; **2.** fuse; (firearms) safety

drošinātājs ventilis *nm* safety valve

drošiniece *nf* brave woman

drošinieks *nm* brave man

droška *nf* droshky

drošprātība *nf* courage

drošprātis *nm* brave man

droš/s *adj* 1. sure, certain, positive; 2. bold, brave; 3. safe, secure; **d. pret** proof against ◊ **d. paliek d.** just to make sure; 4. reliable, trustworthy; 5. unfailing, assured, guaranteed

drošsirdība *nf* courage, valor, bravery

drošsirdīgi *adv* courageously, bravely, valiantly

drošsirdīgs *adj* courageous, brave, valiant

drošsirdīgums *nm* courage, valor, bravery

drošsirdis *nm* brave man

drošticamība *nf* certainty

drošule *nf* brave woman

drošulis *nm* brave man

drošums *nm* 1. = **drošība**; 2. = **drosme**; 3. reliability

drozofili *nm pl* drosophylla

droztala *nf* 1. scrap, tiny bit; 2. (term of endearment for a girl) darling

droztalāt *vi* 1. whittle (a little, now and then); 2. sing beautifully

droztaliņa *nf dim* of **droztala**, darling

droztaloties *vr* (of egg cells) undergo meiosis

drubažas *nf pl* (reg.) bits and pieces, smithereens

drudzene *nf* quaking grass

dru/dzis *nm* fever; **~dēa aukstums** fever chill; **~dža karstums** fever heat

drudžainība *nf* feverishness

drudžaini *adv* feverishly

drudžains *adj* feverish

drudžainums *nm* feverishness

drudža zāles *nf pl* centaury

drūga *nf* mouth of a river

druīdi *nm pl* Druids

druīdisms *nm* Druidism

druka *nf* print; **sīkā d.** fine print; **treknā d.** boldface

drukas darbs *nm* printed matter

drukas kļūda *nf* typographical error

drukas loksne *nf* (typ.) signature

drukāt *vt* (col.) print

drukātava *nf* (col.) printing office

drukknope *nf* (barb.) snap (fastener)

drukns *adj* stocky, thickset

druknums *nm* stockiness

drūkstīt *vt* (reg.) scold

drūksts *nm* (reg.) scolding

drūkstīties *vr* (reg.) be afraid

drumala *nf* (reg.) crumb

drumbetnes *nf pl* wood betony

drūme *nf* gloom

drūmējs *adj* sad

drūmi *adv* gloomily, glumly, morosely, grimly

drūmība *nf* gloominess

drūmīgs *adj* gloomy

drūmīgums *nm* 1. gloom, gloominess, glumness; 2. dreariness, bleakness

drumlins *nm* (geol) drumlin

drūms *adj* 1. gloomy, glum, morose, grim; 2. bleak, dreary, dismal

drūmsejīgs *adj* glum

drumska *nf* (reg.) fragment

drumsla *nf* crumb, bit, piece; fragment

drumslāt *vt* crumble

drumstala *nf* crumb, bit, piece; fragment

drumstalains *adj* crumbly; fragmented

drumstalāt *vt* = **drumstalot**

drumstalot *vt, vi* crumble, break into fragments

drumstaloties *vr* crumble

drumstīt *vt* crumble

drūmums *nm* 1. gloom, gloominess, glumness, moroseness, grimness; 2. dreariness, bleakness

drupača *nf* crumb, bit

drupana *nf* crumb, bit

drupanība *nf* crumbliness

drupans *adj* crumbly

drupanums *nm* crumbliness

drupas *nf pl* ruins; wreckage

drupata *nf* crumb, bit

drupatains *adj* crumby

drupatot *vt* crumble

drupenis *nm* clabbered milk with bits of rye bread

drupens *adj* crumbly

drupīgs *adj* crumbly

drupināt *vt* crumble; crush

drupinātājs *nm* crusher; **koniskais d.** cone crusher

drupināties *vr* crumble

drūpošs *adj, part* of **drupt** crumbly, crumbling

drupstala *nf* crumb, bit, piece; fragment

drupt *vi* crumble

drupu iezis *nm* clastic rock

drupuļains *adj* crumbly

drusciņ *adv* (col.) a little, somewhat; slightly

drusciņa *nf dim* of **druska**, bit, fragment

druscītiņ *adv* (col.) a little, somewhat; slightly

drusk/a *nf* scrap; bit, crumb; smithereen, small piece ◊ **pa ~ai** little by little; **~u ~ās** to smithereens

druskāt *vt* crumble

drusku *adv* a little, somewhat; slightly

druskumiņš *nm* tiny bit

drūsma *nf* gloom

drūsme *nf* (reg.) scolding

druva *nf* field of grain

druvāns *nm* (reg.) fallow

druvenieks *nm* farm laborer

drūvi *adv* somberly

drūvīgi *adv* somberly

drūvīgs *adj* troubled, worried; somber

druviņa *nf* **1.** *dim* of **druva**, field of grain; **2.** (reg.) meadow

druvmala *nf* edge of a field of grain

druvnesis *nm* wooden container for taking meals to workers in the fields

drūvs *adj* troubled, worried; somber

druvu kaulu zāle *nf* field chickweed

druvu plikstiņš *nm* pennycress

drūza *nf* druse; geode

drūzma *nf* throng, crowd

drūzmēties *vr* jostle, throng; **nedrūzmējieties!** break it up!

družīna *nf* **1.** (hist.) a prince's armed force; armed workers' detachment; **2.** squad; team; patrol; militia group

duajēns *nm* doyen

duālis *nm* (gram.) dual (number)

duālisms *nm* dualism

duālistiski *adv* dualistically

duālistisks *adj* dualistic

duālist/s *nm,* ~**e** *nf* dualist

duālitāte *nf* duality

dublant/s *nm,* ~**e** *nf* **1.** (theat.) understudy; **2.** (film) dubber

dublāža *nf* (of films) **1.** dubbing; **2.** take

dublbemols *nm* (mus.) double flat

dubldiēzs *nm* (mus.) double sharp

dublējums *nm* **1.** (of films) dubbing; **2.** (of films) take; **3.** (compu.) backup

dublēšana *nf* redundancy

dublēt *vt* **1.** duplicate; **2.** (theat.) understudy; **3.** (films) dub

dublētājkopija *nf* (compu.) backup copy

dublētāj/s *nm,* ~**a** *nf* **1.** (theat.) understudy; **2.** (film) dubber

dublēties *vr* **1.** replace each other; **2.** duplicate

dublets *nm* doublet, duplicate

dublier/is *nm,* ~**e** *nf* (theat.) stand-in

dublikāts *nm* duplicate

dublis *nm* (films) take

dublons *nm* doubloon

dubls *nm* = **dublis**

dubļains *adj* muddy

dubļi *nm pl* mud

dubļusargs *nm* mudguard, feņder

dubra *nf* (reg.) pit

dubrains *adj* (reg.) full of pits

dubrājs *nm* (reg.) quagmire

dubt *vi* sink into; form a hollow

dubultattēls *nm* double image

dubultbemols *nm* (mus.) double flat

dubultbiezs *adj* of double thickness

dubultbiezums *nm* double thickness

dubultdarbīgs *adj* double-action

dubultdibens *nm* 1. double bottom; double boiler; 2. false bottom

dubultdiēzs *nm* (mus.) double sharp

dubultdurvis *nf pl* double door

dubulteksemplārs *nm* second copy

dubultgrīda *nf* double floor

dubultgulta *nf* double bed

dubulti *adv* doubly

dubultīgi *adv* doubly

dubultīgs *adj* double

dubultklausīšanās *nfr* diplacusis

dubultkloķis *nm* bell crank

dubultkoris *nm* divided choir

dubultkrustiņš *nm* (typ.) double dagger

dubultkvartets *nm* double quartet

dubultlaušana *nf* double refraction

dubultlogs *nm* double window; storm window

dubultloksne *nf* double sheet of paper

dubultnelsons *nm* full nelson

dubultnīca *nf* double-barreled shotgun

dubultnie/ks *nm* 1. (person) double; ~ce *nf* ; 2. duplicate; 3. double consonant

dubultnumurs *nm* double issue

dubultojums *nm* doubling

dubultot *vt* double

dubultoties *vr* double

dubultpielādēšana *nf* double feed

dubultplats *adj* of double width

dubultplatums *nm* double width

dubultporcija *nf* double portion

dubultportrets *nm* double portrait

dubultritenis *nm* dual wheel

dubults *adj* double

dubultsāls *nf* double salt

dubultsiena *nf* double wall

dubultsliedes *nf pl* double tracks

dubultspēle *nf* (sports) doubles

dubultspirāle *nf* (biol.) double helix

dubultšachs *nm* (chess) double check

dubultšāviens *nm* two quick shots

dubulttoņa krāsa *nf* doubletone

dubultzirdziņš *nm* double horsehead pendant (Latvian, 13th-15th cent.)

dubultzods *nm* double chin

dubultzole *nf* clump sole

dubultzvaigzne *nf* binary star

dūce *nf* 1. quagmire; 2. bog with iron-rich scum; 3. humming top

dūceklis *nm* (col.) grouch

dūcenis *nm* (col.) grouch

ducēt *vi* rumble

du[ch]na [h] *nf* fountain grass

du[ch]obor/ecs [h] (*pl* ~ci) *nm* Doukhobor

dūciens *nm* hum

ducīgs *adj* stocky

dūcin *adv, emph* of dūkt; d. dūca it hummed (buzzed, droned) on and on

ducināt or dūcināt *v* 1. *vi* rumble; *vt* make rumble; 2. *vi* hum, buzz; drone; *vt* make sth. hum; (of a horn, siren) blow; (of an organ) play

du/cis *nm* dozen; ~čiem by the dozen

dūcis *nm* (typ.) dagger; (col.) butcher's knife

dūcmanis *nm* (col.) grouch

duče *nm* duce

dūda I *nf* pigeon

dūda II *nf* a Latvian string instrument

dūdas *nf pl* bagpipes

dūdāt *vi* (col.) cry, weep

dudināt *vi* speak softly

dūdināt *vi* coo

dudināties *vr* speak softly

dūdinie/ks *nm*, ~ce *nf* bagpiper

dūdot *vi* coo

dūdrags *nm* a Latvian wind instrument

dūdulis *nm* = dūdrags

dudzēt *vi* rumble, resound

duelants *nm* duelist

duelēties *vr* duel

duelis *nm* duel

duets *nm* duet

duga *nf* scum

dugains *adj* scummy, dirty, slimy

duglāzija *nf* Douglas fir

dūgmanis *nm* sourpuss

dugongs *nm* dugong

dūja *nf* domestic pigeon

dūjiņa *nf dim* of dūja, dove, dovelet

duka I *nf* (col.) nudge

duka II *nf* 1. (com.) stench; 2. breath; 3. (col.) strength; oomph

dūka *nf, nm* grouch

dūkainis *nm* (horse) roan

dūkains *adj* roan

dūkanbēris *nm* (horse) roan

dūkanbērs *adj* roan

dūkanis *nm* roan

dūkans *adj* roan

dūkas *nf pl* bagpipes

dukāt *vt* 1. pummel; 2. knead

dūkāt *vt* pound (with a fist); shake

dukāts *nm* ducat

dukers *nm* duiker

duklaka *nf* spray enamel

duklas *nf pl* bird snare

duknājs *nm* boggy tract of land

dūknējs *adj* boggy

dukņa I *nf* (col.) nudge

dukņa II *nf* (reg.) smoke, fumes

dūkņa I *nf* morass, quagmire

dūkņa II *nf* wood nymph

dukņāt *vt* (col.) nudge

dūkoņa *nf* hum, buzzing; din, drone

dukot *vt* spray-paint

dūkot *vi* 1. play the bagpipes; 2. coo

duksis *nm* Rover, Fido

duksna *nf* (col.) nudge

dūksna *nf* morass, quagmire

dūksnains *adj* boggy

dūksnājs *nm* boggy tract of land

dūksnis *nm* morass, quagmire

duksnīt *vt* (col.) nudge

dūksns *adj* boggy

dūkstains *adj* boggy

dūkstājs *nm* boggy tract of land

dukstiņš *nm dim* of duksts, nudge

dukstīt *vt* (col.) nudge

duksts *nm* (col.) nudge

dūksts *nf* morass, quagmire

dūkstu genciāna *nf* a gentian, Gentiana uligi-nosa

dūkstu grīslis *nm* mud sedge

dūkstu vijolīte *nf* swamp violet

dūkstu virza *nf* bog stitchwort

dūkt I *vi* hum, buzz; drone; ausīs dūc ringing in the ears

dūkt II *vi* become cloudy; fog up

dukurēt *vi* fish with a dip net

dūkuris *nm* grebe

dūkurītis *nm dim* of dūkuris, little grebe

dukurs *nm* 1. dip net; 2. pole for driving fish into a dip net

dūkurveidīgie *nom adj* Podicipedidae

dūķeris *nm* goldeneye

dūlājs *nm* (bee) smoker

dulbāts *nm* row lock

dulburēt *vi* speak poorly; d. (franciski) speak broken (French)

dulburība *nf* witlessness

dulburīgi *adv* witlessly

dulburīgs *adj* witless

dulburis *nm* blockhead

dulcitols *nm* dulcitol

dūlēji *nm pl* spiked speedwell

dūlēt *vi* 1. (of bees) smoke; 2. (of night fishing) burn a light

dūlis *nm* (reg.) (bee) smoker

dulli *adv* crazily

dulliķis *nm* (col.) dolt, blockhead

dullināt *vt* stun; deafen; stupefy; make unconscious

dulloties *vr* rave, rage, bluster

dulls *adj* (col.) **1.** dizzy; **2.** crazy, nutty

dullums *nm* (col.) **1.** dizziness, stupor; **2.** craziness

dulni *adv* = **dulli**

dulns *adj* = **dulls**

dulnums *nm* = **dullums**

duls or **dūls** *adj* (of horses) dark brown

duļbārds *nm* gunwale

duļķaini *adv* turbidly

duļķainība *nf* turbidity, muddiness

duļķains *adj* turbid, muddy; cloudy

duļķainums *nm* turbidity, muddiness

duļķes *nf pl* lees, sediment, matter in suspension; sludge

duļķis *nm* slurry

duļķojums *nm* (of liquids, solids) cloudiness; (of air) polution

duļķošanās *nfr* turning muddy, turbid, or cloudy

duļķošanās temperātūra *nf* cloud point

duļķot *vt* muddy, make turbid

duļķoties *vr* turn muddy, turbid, or cloudy

duļķu maisītājs *nm* blunger

duļļi *nm pl* tholepins, rowlock

dūmaini *adv* smokily

dūmains *adj* smoky; fumy; (of horses) sorrel

dūmaka *nf* haze

dūmakainība *nf* haziness

dūmakaini *adv* hazily

dūmakains *adj* hazy

dūmakainums *nm* haziness

dūmakot *vi* smoke

dūmakoti *adv* hazily

dūmakots *adj* hazy

dūmals *adj* = (reg.) **dūmaļš**

dūmaļa *nf* dark brown cow

dūmaļš *adj* smoke-colored; roan

dumbēris *nm* muddy water hole; small, muddy pond

dumbra *nf* = **dumbrs**

dumbracālis *nm* water rail

dumbrains *adj* boggy, mucky

dumbrājs *nm* quagmire; (forest.) mixed stand type on mucky soil

dumbrājsloka *nf* godwit; see also **melnā d., sar-kanā d.**

dumbrāju zaķpēdiņas *nf pl* wayside cudweed

dumbri *nm pl* lousewort

dumbriens *nm* quagmire

dumbrs *nm* **1.** swamp; water hole in a swamp; **2.** muck

dumbrs *adj* **1.** brown; **2.** dense, dull-witted

dūmbumba *nf* smoke bomb

dūmcaurule *nf* smoke tube

dūmdesa *nf* salami

dūmdevējs *nm* smoke-producing material

dumdumlode *nf* dumdum (bullet)

dūmeklis *nm* **1.** chimney; **2.** (bee) smoker

dūmenīca *nf* smokehouse

dūmenieks *nm* (bee) smoker

dūmenis *nm* smokestack, chimney, flue

dūmeņa rovis *nm* breeching

dūmgāze *nf* flue gas, exhaust gas

dūmi *nm pl* smoke

dumiķis *nm*, **~e** *nf* (col.) dolt, blockhead

dūmiņš *nm dim* of **dūms**, little smoke

dūmistaba *nf* (hist.) smoke room (a room with an open hearth and no flue)

dumji *adv* foolishly, stupidly

dumjība *nf* nonsense; foolishness, stupidity

dumjš *adj* foolish, stupid; silly, inane

dumjums *nm* dumbness, foolishness

dūmmetējs *nm* smoke dispenser

dūmonis *nm* haze

dumortierīts *nm* dumortierite

dūmot *vi, vt* smoke

dūmotava *nf* smokehouse

dumpalma *nf* doom palm

dumpība *nf* rebeliousness, mutinousness

dumpīgi *adv* rebelliously, mutinously

dumpīgs *adj* rebellious, mutinous

dumpīgums *nm* rebelliousness

dumpinie/ks *nm*, **~ce** *nf* rebel, mutineer; insurgent

dumpis I *nm* rebellion, mutiny

dumpis II *nm* bittern; see also **lielais d., mazais d.**

dumpjot *vt* rouse, incite, stir up

dumpjoties *vr* rebel, muntiny

dumpnieciski *adv* (rare.) rebelliously, mutinously

dumpniecisks *adj* (rare.) rebellious, mutinous

dumpot *vt* = **dumpjot**

dumpoties *vr* = **dumpjoties**

dumprātā *adv* (reg.) crazy

dūmrades *indecl adj* smoke-generating

dūmrades patrona *nf* smoke pot

dums *adj* foolish, stupid; silly, inane

dūms *nm* (col.) smoke, cigarette

dūms *adj* (of horses) sorrel

dūmturīgs *adj* smokeproof

dūmu aizsegs *nm* smokescreen; **vertikālais d. a.** smoke curtain

dūmu pagale *nf* (col.) shotgun

dūmu pūpēdis *nm* giant puffball

dūmu svece *nf* smoke pot

dūmvads *nm* smoke flue

duna *nf* rumble, boom, roll

dūna *nf* fluff; usu. *pl* **~as** down

duncis *nm* dagger; carving knife, butcher's knife

duncka I *nf* = **dunka**

duncka II *nf* smew

dunckāt *vt* nudge, poke in the ribs

dunda *nf* rumble; (of bells) peal

dundēt *vi* rumble, resound; (of bells) ring

dundināt *vi* hum, sing

dundurains *adj* infested with horseflies

dundurāji *nm pl* avens

dunduramols *nm* scabious

dundurēt *vi* = **dundurot**

dunduriņš *nm dim* of **dundurs**, little gadfly

dundurjāņi *nm pl* valerian

dundurot *vi* buzz

dundurs *nm* gadfly ◊ **d. galvā** (col.) drunk

dunduru puķes *nf pl* (reg.) avens

dunēt *vi* boom, roll, rumble

dungans *adj* (of horses) roan

dungas *nf pl* rumble, rattle

dungāt *vi, vt* 1. hum; 2. tap, tattoo

dungot *vi, vt* = **dungāt**

dungstēt *vi* ring

dungriņi *nm pl* = **dunguriņi**

dunguriņi *nm pl* (col.) dungarees; overalls

duniens *nm* boom

dunīgi *adv* boomingly

dunīgs *adj* booming

duninät *vi* rumble

dūniņa *nf dim* of **dūna**, fluff

dunīts *nm* dunite

dunka *nf* nudge, poke

dunkāt *vt* elbow, nudge

dunkāties *vr* elbow, nudge each other

dunkot *vt* = **dunkāt**

dunkoties *vr* = **dunkāties**

dunkste *nf* carbon monoxide

dunkstēt *vi* hum, buzz

dunkurēt *vt* fish with a dip net

dunoņa *nf* rumble, boom, rolling

dūnspalvas *nf pl* down

dunsta *nf* (reg.) fumes

dūnu pēlis *nm* featherbed

dūnu sega *nf* down quilt

dūnu zoss *nf* eider

dūnvilna *nf* underwool

duņa *nf* rumble, boom, rolling

dūņainība *nf* muddiness, muckiness

dūņains *adj* mucky

dūņainums *nm* muckiness

dūņājs *nm* mucky place

dūņas *nf pl* ooze

dūņēdājs *nm* saprophagous organism

dūņene *nf* 1. mudwort; 2. alderfly

duņķis *nm* (col.) nudge, poke

dūņšņibis *nm* broad-billed sandpiper

dūņu pīkste *nf* weatherfish

dūņu vanna *nf* mudbath

duodecimāls *adj* duodecimal

duodecimo *indecl nm* duodecimo

duodenāls *adj* duodenal

duodenīts *nm* duodenitis

duole *nf* (mus.) duplet

dupe *nf* crayfish nest

dupleksprocess *nm* (metall.) duplex process

dulpekss *nm* 1. (communications, metallurgy) duplex; 2. split-level apartment

duplekss *adj* duplex

duplekstērauds *nm* duplex steel

duplika *nf* (jur.) (defendant's) rejoinder

duplikāts *nm* duplicate

dups *adj* (reg.) dull

dupsis *nm* (col.) baby's bottom

dupuris *nm* 1. water vole; 2. (col.) chubby person

dūrainieks *nm* mitten

dūrainis *nm* mitten

dūrains *adj* fisted

dūrakords *nm* (mus.) major chord

duraks *nm* (com.) fool, stupe

dūralum[i]nijs [ī] *nm* Duralumin

du[r]amais [ŗ] *nom adj* pricking implement; stabbing weapon; apple corer; weeder

duratīvs *nm* (gram.) durative

durba *nf* bream

dūre *nf* 1. fist; 2. ice chisel; 3. blow

dūrēj/s *nm* 1. stabber, pricker; 2. weevil; 3. also ~i (col.) stitches (of pain)

dūrējuts *nf* sucking louse

dūrenieks *nm* mitten

durēns *nm* durain

dūres varonis *nm* brawler

dūrēt *vi* (col.) last

durians *nm* durio

dūriens *nm* 1. stab; prick; sting; thrust; puncture; 2. (sewing) stitch

duris *nf pl* = durvis

dūris *nm* (archa.) breaker (plow)

dūrīte *nf dim* of dūre, little fist

durk/lis *nm* bayonet; ~ļa turētājs bayonet lug, bayonet stud; ~ļus makstīs! unfix, bayonets! ~ļus uzspraust! fix, bayonets!

durklītis *nm dim* of durklis, bayonet

durkļots *adj* with bayonet fixed

durnēt *vi* 1. dawdle; 2. sulk; 3. mope

durns *adj* 1. benumbed; 2. besotted, crazy

durnums *nm* 1. (of the head) heaviness; 2. muddleheadedness; 3. (of sheep) staggers

durols *nm* durene

dūrs *nm* (mus.) major

dursteklis *nm* prick, punch

durstelēt *vi* (*iter*) poke, stick

durstīgs *adj* 1. prickly; 2. (fig.) piercing

durstīt *vt* prick; stab; poke

durstīties *vr* stab each other

duršlāgs *nm* (barb.) colander, strainer

durt *v* 1. *vt* stab, prick; thrust, stick; skewer, hook; kā ~s (col.) suddenly; 2. *vi* feel a stitch of pain

durteknis *nm* slip, cutting

durteniski *adv* head on

durties *vr* 1. prick; 2. stab one another; 3. d. klāt (col.) touch; d. acīs stand out, be conspicuous

durtin *adv, emph* of durt; d. dūra he (she, it) kept on stabbing

durtiņas *nf pl* (col.) *dim* of duris, little door

dū[r]u [ŗ] cīņa *nf* fisticuffs

dūrums *nm* 1. thrust; 2. stab wound

durvinieks *nm* doorkeeper

durv/is *nf pl* door; lielās d. front door; aiz slēgtām ~īm behind closed doors, privately, (jur.) in camera; būt pie ~īm (of events) be upon s.o.

durvju augša *nf* doorhead

durvju logs *nm* transom window

durvju plāksnīte *nf* doorplate

durvju sargs *nm* doorkeeper; (court) usher

durvju selmenis *nm* door pediment

durvju virsgaisma *nf* transom window; fanlight

durvpriekša *nf* place in front of the door

durvtiņas *nf pl dim* of **durvis**, little door

dus/a *nf* rest, sleep; **saldu ~u!** sweet dreams! **pēdējā ~as vieta** final resting place

dusēt *vi* sleep, rest; **šeit dus** (tombstone inscription) here lies

dūsma *nf* **1.** sound, blast (of sound), roar, droning; **2.** swirl; bustle

dusm/as *nf pl* anger; **lielas d.** rage, fury ◊ **ātrās ~ās** in a temper

dusmība *nf* (obs.) anger

dusmīgi *adv* angrily

dusmīgs *adj* angry

dusmīgums *nm* anger

dusminat *vt* anger, infuriate

dusmīte *nf* crosspatch

dusmonis *nm* crosspatch

dusmoņa *nm* crosspatch

dusmot *vi* be angry

dusmoties *vr* be angry

dusmulis *nm* crosspatch

dusmu pūslis *nm* (col.) sourpuss

dust *vi* pant

dusulēt *vi* (col.) be out of breath

dusulīgs *adj* short of breath

dusulis *nm* **1.** shortness of breath; **2.** cough; **garais d.** whooping cough

duša *nf* shower

dušas bļoda *nf* shower pan

dušas telpa *nf* shower stall

dūš/a *nf* **1.** courage; **~ā** (col.) tipsy; **d. kā miets** (col.) resolved, determined; **d. papēžos** one's heart in one's boots; **2.** appetite; feeling ◊ **man slikta d.** I feel sick; **tukšā ~ā** on an empty stomach; **iet pie ~as** taste good; **plāna d.** feeling queasy

dūšība *nf* (col.) **1.** energy; diligence; **2.** strength, robustness; **3.** pluckiness

dūšīgi *adv* **1.** energetically; diligently; **2.** heartily

dūšīgs *adj* (col.) **1.** energetic, diligent; **2.** strong, strapping, robust; **3.** plucky, brave; **4.** heavy; **5.** hearty

dūšīgums *nm* (col.) **1.** energy; diligence; **2.** strength, robustness; **3.** pluckiness, bravery

dūšināt *vt* encourage

dūšinieks *nm* (col.) brave man

dušoties *vr* take a shower

dute *nf* **1.** stump; **2.** dull tool, dull weapon

duumvirāts *nm* duumvirate

duumvirs *nm* duumvir

dūve *nf* pigeon

duzēt I *vi* sorrow

duzēt II *vi* mold

dūzis *nm* (cards) ace; (col.) big shot; (sl.) cop

duzot *vi* (reg.) sorrow; (obs.) whisper

duzt *vi* **1.** become overcast; **2.** mold, spoil

dvaga *nf* birch tar

dvaka *nf* (com.) stench

dvakot *vi* (com.) stink

dvālekts *nm* a grain measure

dvars *nm* pole fence gate

dvarsā, also **uz dvarsu** *adv* (naut.) athwarts, athwartships

dvaša *nf* breath

dvašojiens *nm* breath

dvašojums *nm* breath

dvašot *vi* breathe

dvēse/le *nf* (rel.) soul; (psych.) mind ◊ **lāga d.** (col.) good person, kind soul; **~les miers** peace of mind; **~les mokas** mental anguish; **~les sāpes** mental suffering; **ar visu ~li** with all one's heart; **ne dzīvas ~les** not a living soul; **(man nav plika graša) pie ~les** (I don't have a cent) on me

dvēseles aizlūgums *nm* office for the dead

dvēselīgs *adj* **1.** spiritual; **2.** mental; **3.** soulful; **4.** sensitive

dvēselīgums *nm* sensitiveness; soulfulness

dvēselisks *adj* **1.** mental; **2.** soulful; **3.** sensitive

dvēseliskums *nm* soulful nature, soulfulness

dvēselīte *nf* **1.** *dim* of **dvēsele**, soul; **2.** (mus., violin) sound post

dvēseļu apkope *nf* care of the souls

dvēseļu gans *nm* pastor

dvēseļu mielasts *nm* (folk.) a yearly meal served for the souls of the dead

dvēseļu revīzija *nf* (hist.) census

dvēseļu tirgotājs *nm* kidnapper

dvēsenis *nm* (ling.) spirant

dvēsiens *nm* **1.** breath; **2.** whisper; **3.** breeze

dvēsle *nf* (poet.) soul

dvesma *nf* breath

dvēsma *nf* breeze

dvesmojums *nm* breath

dvesmot *vi* **1.** blow gently; **2.** waft; **3.** smell

dv[e]st [ē] *vt,vi* **1.** breathe with difficulty; **2.** whisper; **3.** waft; blow gently; **4.** smell; **5.** emanate; radiate; **6.** (poet.) infuse with

dvielis *nm* towel

dvielītis *nm dim* of **dvielis**, small towel

dvieļturis *nm* towel bar

dvikaplis *nm* double-blade hoe

dvīlis *nm* = **dvinga**

dvinga *nf* carbon monoxide; coal gas, exhaust gas; fumes

dvingains *adj* filled with coal gas

dvī/nis *nm*, **~ne** *nf* **1.** twin; **2.** **D~ņi** Gemini

dvinkstēt *vi* jingle, clink

dvīņkrist[all]s [āl] *nm* twin crystal

dvīņubrālis *nm* twin brother

dvīņumāsa *nf* twin sister

dvīņu zvaigzne *nf* binary star

dviriči *nm pl* = **divriči**

dzādze *nf, nm* emaciated person

dzalkstīt *vi* flash

dzānīte *nf* thin layer

dzebru josta *nf* sash

dzedri *adv* **1.** cooly; **2.** austerely

dzedroties *vr* quarrel

dzedrs *adj* **1.** cool; **2.** harsh, austere, strict

dzedrums *nm* **1.** coolness; **2.** harshness, strictness

dzedzieda *nf* fallow

dzega *nf* **1.** cornice; **2.** mantelshelf; **3.** page-wide rule or ornamental line at the beginning of text; **4.** letterhead (in the upper left corner of the page)

dzegakmens *nm* coping stone

dzegēvele *nf* rabbet plane

dzegu/lis *nm* **1.** dovetail; **2.** **~ļi** battlements

dzeguļot *vt* dovetail

dzeguze *nf* **1.** cuckoo ◊ **d. nokūkojusi!** its all over! **2.** (bot.) ragged robin

dzeguzene *nf* helleborine

dzeguzēns *nm* young cuckoo

dzeguzes asaras *nf pl* Solomon's seal

dzeguzes ērkulis *nm* an orchis

dzeguzes kalps *nm* warbler

dzeguzes lini *nm pl* haircap moss

dzeguzes spļaudekļi *nm pl* cuckoo spit

dzeguzes spulgnaglene *nf* (bot.) ragged robin

dzegužkurpīte *nf* (bot.) lady's slipper

dzegužlapa *nf* helleborine

dezgužlini *nm pl* haircap moss

dzegužpiestiņi *nm pl* orchid

dzegužpieši *nm pl* dame's violet

dzegužpodiņi *nm pl* avens

dzegužpuķe *nf* orchid

dzegužu zāles *nf pl* whitlow gras

dzegužveidīgie *nom adj* Cuculiformes

dzeikste *nf* (reg.) whip

dzeinis *nm* **1.** (hist.) hoist (used by beekeepers for climbing trees to reach beehives); **2.** (weav.) warp that is being beamed

dzeja *nf* poetry; **brīvā d.** free verse; **~s teorija** poetic theory

dzejdarība *nf* poetastery

dzejdaris *nm* poetaster

dzejiski *adv* poetically

dzejisks *adj* poetic

dzejiskums *nm* poeticism

dzejnie/ks *nm*, ~ce *nf* poet

dzejojums *nm* piece of poetry; lengthy poem

dzejolis *nm* poem

dzejot *vi* write poetry

dzejrinda *nf* line of poetry

dzejtēls *nm* poetic image

dzelde *nf* carline thistle

dzeldēt *vt* sting

dzeldīgi *adv* bitingly, caustically

dzeldīgs *adj* 1. stinging; 2. biting, caustic

dzeldināt *vt* sting

dzeldināties *vr* get stung by nettles; wallow in nettles

dzeldīt *vt* sting

dzēlējlapsenes *nf pl* aculeates

dzēlējodi *nm pl* culicids

dzēlība *nf* causticity

dzēliens *nm* sting

dzēlīgi *adv* bitingly, caustically

dzēlīgs *adj* 1. stinging; 2. biting, caustic

dzēlīgums *nm* causticity

dzelis *nm* graver, burin

dzēlīte *nf* stinging hair

dzelkne *nf* = dzelknis

dzelknis *nm* 1. milk thistle; 2. thorn

dzelkņgalvji *nm pl* Acanthocephala

dzelksne *nf* (poet.) arrow

dzelksnīgs *adj* thorny

dzelksnis *nm* 1. thorn, prickle, stinger; 2. thistle; 3. firing pin; 4. piton

dzelkstīgi *adv* stingingly

dzelkstīgs *adj* stinging

dzelkšņaini *adv* thornily

dzelkšņains *adj* thorny

dzelkšņainums *nm* thorniness

dzelkvas *nf pl* water elm

dzelmains *adj* deep

dzelmājs *nm* deep

dzelme *nf* abyss, deep

dzelmenis *nm* deep

dzelmīgs *adj* deep

dzelmjains *adj* deep, depthless

dzelonis *nm* 1. stinger; 2. thorn; 3. barb; **d. acī** (fig.) problem, bugbear

dzeloņainais sīkdadzis *nm* spiny cocklebur

dzeloņainā kapera *nf* caper

dzeloņainā mīkstpiene *nf* spiny sow thistle

dzeloņainā ozolpaparde *nf* spinulose shield fern

dzeloņainā roze *nf* Scotch rose

dzeloņaini *adv* thornily

dzeloņains *adj* thorny; barbed; spiked

dzeloņainums *nm* thorniness

dzeloņcūka *nf* porcupine

dzeloņdrāts *nf* barbed wire

dzeloņhaizivs *nf* spiny dogfish

dzeloņplūme *nf* blackthorn

dzeloņspuru izoets *nm* Braun's quillwort

dzeloņstieple *nf* barbed wire

dzeloņstiepļu aizsprosts *nm* barbed wire entanglement

dzeloņzivs *nf* dogfish

dzeloši *adv* stingingly

dzelošs *adj* stinging

dzēls *adj* (poet.) sharp, biting

dzelsnējs *adj* yellowish

dzelsnēt *vi* yellow

dzelstīt *vi* (*iter*) sting

dzelt *vi* sting; (of snakes) bite

dzeltaine *nf* (folk.) light-haired girl

dzeltains *adj* yellow

dzeltāne *nf* orange milk cap

dzeltānis *nm* yellow horse

dzeltāns *adj* yellow

dzeltānums *nm* 1. yellow color; 2. yolk

dzeltas *nf pl* club moss

dzelte *nf* jaundice

dzeltējums *nm* yellowing

dzeltenā akācija *nf* caragana, Siberian pea tree

dzeltenā akmeņlauzīte *nf* yellow marsh saxifrage

dzeltenā asinssāls *nf* potassium ferrocyanide

dzeltenā bērzlape *nf* yellow Russula

dzeltenā cielava *nf* yellow wagtail

dzeltenā dzegužkurpīte *nf* lady's slipper

dzeltenā ilzīte *nf* oxeye chamomile

dzeltenais āboliņš *nm* **1.** hop clover; **2.** black medic

dzeltenais amoliņš *nm* yellow sweet clover

dzeltenais bērzs *nm* yellow birch

dzeltenais drudzis *nm* yellow fever

dzeltenais gārnis *nm* squacco heron

dzeltenais grīslis *nm* green sedge

dzeltenais koks *nm* fustic

dzeltenais laimiņš *nm* stonecrop

dzeltenais rasaskrēsliņš *nm* (bot.) lady's-mantle

dzeltenais tārtiņš *nm* golden plover

dzeltenais vanags *nm* kestrel

dzeltenais vizbulis *nm* black medic

dzeltenā jāņuzāle *nf* yellow bedstraw

dzeltenājs *nm* loosestrife; see also **ložņīgais d.**

dzeltenā kaite *nf* jaundice

dzeltenā kazu bārda *nf* yellow coral mushroom

dzeltenā krustaine *nf* tansy ragwort

dzeltenā kumelīte *nf* oxeye chamomile

dzeltenā lēca *nf* vetchling

dzeltenā lēpa *nf* yellow water lily

dzeltenā lucerna *nf* yellow-flowered alfalfa

dzeltenā lupīna *nf* yellow lupine

dzeltenā madara *nf* yellow bedstraw

dzeltenā narcise *nf* daffodil

dzeltenā nātre *nf* yellow archangel

dzeltenā pīpene *nf* oxeye chamomile

dzeltenā priede *nf* ponderosa pine

dzeltenā pūslene *nf* a bladderwort, Urticularia ochroleuca

dzeltenā rezēda *nf* yellow cut-leaved mignonette

dzeltenā saulrozīte *nf* sunrose, rockrose

dzeltenās dienziedes *nf pl* lemon day lily

dzeltenās dzegužu zāles *nf pl* wood whitlow grass

dzeltenā skabioza *nf* scabious

dzeltenās kaķpēdiņas *nf pl* everlasting

dzeltenā slimība *nf* jaundice

dzeltenās suņkumelītes *nf pl* dyer's chamomile

dzeltenās šķelpes *nf pl* yellow iris

dzeltenā stērste *nf* yellowhammer, yellow bunting

dzeltenās zvaigznītes *nf pl* coltsfoot

dzeltenā vijolīte *nf* pansy

dzeltenā zeltstarīte *nf* yellow star-of-Bethlehem

dzeltenbalts *adj* pale yellow

dzeltenbrūns *adj* yellowish brown, buff

dzeltene I *nf* nettle

dzeltene II *nf* mezeron; globeflower

dzeltenējs *adj* yellowish

dzeltengalvas cielava *nf* citrine wagtail

dzeltengalvis *nm* blond

dzeltengani *adv* in a yellowish color

dzeltengans *adj* yellowish

dzeltengatavība *nf* (of grain crops) stage of yellow ripe

dzelteni *adv* in a yellow color, with a yellow light

dzeltenība *nf* yellowness

dzeltenie akļi *nm pl* bee nettle

dzeltenie saulkrēsliņi *nm pl* yellow meadow rue

dzeltenīgi *adv* in a yellowish color, with a yellowish light

dzeltenīgs *adj* yellowish; sallow

dzeltenis *nm* yellow horse

dzeltenkakla (klaidoņa) pele *nf* yellow-necked mouse

dzeltenkrūtains *adj* yellow-breasted

dzeltenlapu krizantēma *nf* feverfew

dzeltenmaize *nf* saffron bread

dzeltenmatains *adj* blond

dzeltenmatis *nm* blond

dzeltenot *vi* turn yellow

dzeltenpelēki *adv* in a yellowish gray color

dzeltenpelēks *adj* yellowish gray

dzeltenraibi *adv* with yellow spots

dzeltenraibs *adj* yellow-spotted

dzeltens *adj* yellow

dzeltensarkans *adj* yellowish red

dzeltensprogains *adj* with blond curls

dzeltensvītru ķauķis *nm* yellow-browed warbler

dzeltenums *nm* 1. yellow color; 2. yolk

dzeltenzaļš *adj* yellow-green

dzeltenziedains *adj* having yellow flowers

dzeltessakne *nf* ground fir

dzeltēt *vi* 1. turn yellow; 2. appear yellow

dzeltgani *adv* in a yellowish color

dzeltgans *adj* yellowish

dzelties *vr* sting

dzeltot *vi* = **dzeltēt**

dzeltoties *vr* 1. turn yellow; 2. appear yellow

dzeltras *nf pl* club moss

dzeltūksnējs *adj* sallow, yellowish

dzeltu laiks *nm* (reg.) fall, autumn

dzelums *nm* wood carving

dzēlums *nm* sting, bite

dzelve *nf* (reg.) sinkhole in a swamp

dzelzains *adj* (of water) iron-containing

dzelzasu *indecl adj* having steel axles

dzelzbērzs *nm* iron birch

dzelzceļa katastrofa *nf* train wreck

dzelzceļa pavadonis *nm* conductor

dzelzceļa sargs *nm* crossing guard; signalman

dzelzceļa sastāvs *nm* train

dzelzceļa signāli *nm pl* block system

dzelzceļa sliedes *nf pl* railroad track

dzelzceļa stiga *nf* railroad right-of-way; railroad tracks

dzelzceļa uzbērums *nm* railroad bank

dzelzceļa virsvalde *nf* general office of the railroad; central administration of railroads

dzelzceļlīnija *nf* railroad line

dzelzceļmezgls *nm* railroad junction

dzelzceļnie/ks *nm*, **~ce** *nf* railroader

dzelzceļ/š *nm* railroad; **divsliežu d.** double-track railroad; **platsliežu d.** broad-gage railroad; **šaur-sliežu d.** narrow-gage railroad; **viensliedes d.** monorail; **pa ~u** by rail, by train

dzelzceļu tīkls *nm* railroad system

dzelzene *nf* knapweed

dzel/zis *nm* 1. iron (for flattening clothes); 2. **~ži** a. pieces of iron; **veci ~ži** scrap metal; b. irons; c. (col.) bit (of a bridle)

dzelzs *nf* iron; **aplokāmā d.** folding iron; **kalta d.** wrought iron; **laužamā d.** crowbar; **liedējamā d.** soldering iron;

dzelzsbetons *nm* reinforced concrete

dzelzsceplis *nm* blast furnace

dzelzskoks *nm* ironwood

dzelzs laikmets *nm* iron age

dzelzs lējējs *nm* (metall.) founder;

dzelzslietuve *nf* steel mill

dzelzs monoksids *nm* ferrous oxide

dzelzs porcija *nf* emergency rations

dzelzs preces *nf pl* hardware

dzelzsrūda *nf* iron ore

dzelzssārņi *nm pl* slag

dzelzsskapis *nm* safe, strongbox

dzelzsskārds *nm* sheet iron

dzelzs sulfāts *nm* ferrous sulfate

dzelzs špats *nm* siderite

dzelzs tirgotājs *nm* hardware merchant

dzelzs trioksids *nm* ferric oxide

dzelzsūdeņi *nm pl* mineral water with high iron content

dzelzs vitriols *nm* green vitriol

dzelzszāle *nf* 1. knotgrass; 2. sedge

dzelztiņa *nf* 1. *dim* of **dzelzs**, scrap of iron; 2. key plate

dzelžains *adj* iron, made of iron; ferruginous

dzelži *nm pl* See **dzelzis**

dzelžots *adj* ironclad; (of shoes) hobnailed

dzeļmatiņi *nm pl* stinging hairs

dzeļsporaiņi *nm pl* Cnidosporidia

dzēļš *adj* (poet.) sharp, biting

dzemde *nf* uterus, womb

dzemdes dobums *nm* uterine cavity

dzemdes iekaisums *nm* metritis

dzemdes izkrišana *nf* prolapse of the uterus

dzemdes kakls *nf* cervix

dzemdēt *vt* bear, give birth; **d. priekšlaicīgi** miscarry; give birth prematurely

dzemdētāja *nf* woman in childbirth

dzemdības *nf pl* birth, birthing, childbirth, delivery; **straujas d.** precipitated labor

dzemdību palīdzība *nf* obstetrics

dzemdību sāpes *nf pl* labor pain

dzemdināt *vt* give birth; engender

dzemdniecība *nf* obstetrics

dzemdniecības nodaļa *nf* maternity ward

dzenamais *adj, part* of **dzīt** shaving (*adj*); **d. nazis** (col.) razor

dzenāt *vt* drive (from place to place), shoo; **d. ro-kā** look for

dzenāties *vr* chase each other

dzenaukla *nf* = (reg.) **dzeņaukste**

dzenbudisms *nm* Zen Buddhism

dzenēns *nm* young woodpecker

dzenēt *vt* (of the branches of a felled tree) trim

dzenis *nm* woodpecker

dzenītis *nm* 1. *dim* of **dzenis**; 2. kingfisher

dzenkaste *nf* headstock

dzenols *nm* (bot.) shoot

dzenošs *adj, part* of **dzīt** driving, drive

dzenrats *nm* paddle wheel; flywheel

dzensiksna *nf* driving belt

dzenskriemelis *nm* pulley

dzenskrūve *nf* screw propeller

dzenulis *nm* motive, drive; urge

dzenvārpsta *nf* screw propeller

dzeņaukste *nf* tie, tug (that binds a horse's collar to the pole of a wagon)

dzeņauska *nf* = (reg.) **dzeņaukste**

dzeņveidīgie *nom adj* Picidae

dzeņveidīgs *adj* piciform

dzērāj/s *nm*, ~a *nf* drinker; drunkard

dzērāju dziesma *nf* drinking song

dze|r|amais [ŗ] *nom adj* drink, beverage

dze|r|amnauda [ŗ] *nf* tip, gratuity

dze|r|ams [ŗ] *adj, part* of **dzert**, usu. *defin* **dze-ŗamais** 1. drinkable; potable; 2. drinking (*adj*)

dzērēj/s *nm*, ~a *nf* drinker

dzereklis *nm* drink, beverage

dzerens *nm* Mongolian gazelle

dzeres *nf pl* light beer

dzergzde *nf* kink

dzērien/s *nm* drink, beverage; **bezalkoholisks d.** nonalcoholic beverage; **gāzēts d.** carbonated beverage; **reibinošs d.** alcoholic beverage; **stip-ri ~i** alcoholic beverages

dzerkste *nf* (col.) muscle ache

dzeroklis *nm* (anat.) molar

dzersis *nm* kvass

dzeršus *adv emph* of **dzert**; **d. dzert** drink a lot, drink in great gulps

dzert *v* 1. *vt* drink; sip; gulp; **d. malciņiem** sip; **d. laimes** toast; **d. līkopus** toast a deal; **d. uz (kāda) veselību** drink s.o.'s health; **man gribas d.** I am thirsty; 2. *vi* booze, tipple; 3. *vt* celebrate; **d. kāzas** a. celebrate a wedding; b. attend a wedding party

dzertuve *nf* barroom

dzervelce *nf* (reg.) rainbow

dzēruma trakums *nm* delirium; drunken rage;

dzērumbaļļa *nf, nm* (col.) drinker

dzērum/s *nm* drunkenness; ~ā while drunk, in a drunken state

dzērvači *nm pl* gladiolus

dzērve *nf* (zool.) crane

dzērvenājs *nm* 1. cranberry bush; 2. growth of cranberries

dzērvene *nf* cranberry

dzērveņaudze *nf* growth of cranberries

dzērves acis *nf* gladiolus

dzērvīte *nf* 1. *dim* of **dzērve**, crane; 2. connecting rod of a spinning wheel

dzērvjveidīgie *nom adj* Gruidae

dzērvkāja *nf* marsh cinquefoil

dzēse *nf* **1.** gray heron; **2.** black stork

dzesēt *vt* cool; **d. muti** blab, run off at the mouth; waste one's breath; **d. slāpes** quench one's thirst

dzesētājcilindrs *nm* cooling cylinder

dzesētājs *nm* cooler

dzesētava *nf* cooler, refrigerated storage room, cooling room

dzesēties *vr* cool off

dzesināt *vt* cool

dzesinātājs *nm* **1.** cooler, cooling device; **2.** condenser

dzesinātava *nf* cooling room, refrigerated room, cooler

dzesma *nf* breeze

dzesna *nf* twilight

dzēst *vt* **1.** blow out, put out, extinguish; quench; **2.** erase; **3.** (of debts) pay off; **4.** (of stamps) cancel; **5.** (of lime) slake

dzēstra *nf* (bot.) water soldier

dzestre *nf* cool, shady place

dzestri *adv* coolly

dzestrināt *vt* (rare.) cool

dzestrs *adj* cool

dzestrums *nm* coolness

dzēšamgumija *nf* eraser

dzēšampapīrs *nm* blotting paper

dzēšlapa *nf* blotting paper

dzi *interj* listen

dzīdināt *vt* (reg.) shoo

dzīdīt *vt* (reg.) shoo

dzidr/ais *nom adj* **1.** (90-proof, charcoal-filtered) vodka; **2. baltie ~ie** translucent apples

dzidre *nf* (poet.) azure

dzidri *adv* clearly

dzidrināšana *nf* clarification

dzidrināšanas līdzeklis *nm* fining agent

dzidrināt *vt* (of liquids) clarify; fine

dzidrinātājs *nm* clarifier

dzidrināties *vr* (of translucent apples) ripen

dzidrība *nf* clarity

dzidrot *vt* (of liquids) clarify; fine

dzidrs *adj* clear; limpid

dzidruma mērītājs *nm* nephelometer

dzidrums *nm* **1.** clarity; **2.** azure

dzidzināt *vi* chirr

dziedājums *nm* **1.** singing performance; **2.** vocal part; **3.** canto

dziedāšana *nf* **1.** singing; **2.** (educ.) music

dziedāšanas biedrība *nf* choral society

dziedāšanas skolotāj/s *nm*, **~a** *nf* voice teacher; (educ.) music teacher

dziedāt *vt, vi* sing; chant; (of roosters) crow; **d. līdz** sing along; **d. pusbalsī** sing in an undertone; **d. pareizi** sing in tune; **d. nepareizi** sing out of tune; **d. citu dziesmu** change one's tune; **ne gailis pakaļ nedziedās** (col.) no one will be the wiser; **d. savā meldijā** carry one's own tune

dziedātājputns *nm* song bird

dziedātājs *nm*, **~a** *nf* singer

dziedātājsienā/zis *nm* cricket; **~ēi** long-horned grashoppers

dziedātājstrazds *nm* song thrush

dziede *nf* (obs.) medicine

dziedenīte *nf* sanicle

dziedēklis *nm* remedy, medicine

dziedēt *vt* heal, cure

dziedētava *nf* sanatorium

dziedēties *vr* undergo a cure, receive treatment

dziedīgs *adj* healing, curative

dziedināt *vt* heal, cure

dziedinātava *nf* sanatorium

dziedināties *vr* undergo a cure, receive treatment

dziednīca *nf* sanatorium

dziedniecība *nf* **1.** medical arts, therapeutics; **2.** treatment; therapy

dziedniecības amoliņš *nm* sweet clover

dziedniecības avots *nm* curative spring

dziedniecības gurķis *nm* borage

dziedniecības iestāde *nf* hospital, clinic

dziedniecisks *adj* medical; curative

dziednie/ks *nm*, ~ce *nf* healer

dziedon/is *nm*, ~e *nf* professional singer

dziedrenis *nm* azure

dziedrs *nm* 1. crossbeam; (floor) girder; 2. rake bar

dziedrs *adj* clear; azure

dzieds *nm* = dziedrs

dziedze[r]ainā [ŗ] kazroze *nf* northern willow herb

dziedze[r]ains [ŗ] *adj* filled with glands

dziedze/ris *nm* gland; ~ŗi glands; (col.) adenoids

dziedzerītis *nm dim* of dziedzeris, gland

dziedze[r]matiņi [ŗ] *nm pl* (sundew) glands

dziedzināt *vi* (of nightingales) sing

dziemulis *nm* = gāmurs

dziesma *nf* 1. song; tune; daudzbalsīga d. part-song; garīga d. hymn ◊ cita d. (col.) a different story; tā pati vecā d. (col.) the tune the old cow died of; tava d. izdziedāta! it's curtains for you!

dziesminieks *nm*, ~ce *nf* author and singer of folk songs; (poet.) poet, bard

dziesmiņa *nf dim* of dziesma, little song

dziesmot *vi* 1. (poet.) write poetry; 2. sing

dziesmots *adj, part* of dziesmot 1. full of songs; 2. (rare.) given to singing

dziesmu grāmata *nf* hymnal; song book

dziesmu kamols *nm* reel

dziesmuspēle *nf* (theat.) musical

dziesmu svētki *nm pl* choral festival

dziesmu vainags *nm* garland of songs;

dziesna *nf* (poet.) sunset glow

dziesnāt *vi* (poet., of the sun) set

dziestošs *adj, part* of dzist fading; (tech.) dying

dzieša *nf* (reg.) evening star

dziet I *vi* spring up, originate

dziet II *vi, vt* heal

dziets *nm* (poet.) shoot (sprout)

dziezna *nf* = dziesna

dzija *nf* yarn; dabīgā d. natural fiber

dzijtiņa *nf dim* of dzija; short length of yarn or thread; thin yarn

dzīle *nf* depth, the deep; (poet.) the bowels

dziliena *nf* (reg.) depth

dzilināt *vt* sting

dzilkstēt *vi* twitter

dzilna *nf* woodpecker

dzilniņa *nf dim* of dzilna, woodpecker

dzilnītis *nm* Eurasian nuthatch

dziļaršana *nf* subsoil plowing

dziļbumba *nf* depth charge

dziļbūve *nf* underground construction

dziļdomība *nf* profundity

dziļdomīgi *adv* 1. profoundly; 2. thoughtfully, pensively

dziļdomīgs *adj* 1. profound; 2. thoughtful, pensive; 3. eloquent

dziļdomīgums *nm* profundity

dziļdziļš *adj* very deep

dziļi *adv* deeply; profoundly

dziļirdināšana *nf* subsoiling

dziļjūra *nf* deep sea

dziļjūtība *nf* empathy

dziļjūtīgi *adv* with empathy

dziļjūtīgs *adj* deeply sensitive; emphatizing

dziļjūtīgums *nm* empathy

dziļkultūru arkls *nm* breaker (plow)

dziļoksnis *nm* (reg.) 1. thicket; 2. depth

dziļš *adj* deep; profound

dziļūdens *indecl adj* deepwater

dziļuma grafika *nf* fathogram

dziļuma līmeņmērs *nm* depth gage

dziļumbumba *nf* depth charge

dziļumieraksts *nm* vertical recording

dziļumiezis *nm* (geol.) intrusive rock

dziļummērītājs *nm* depth gage

dziļummīna *nf* ground mine

dziļumplūsma *nf* undercurrent

dziļums *nm* depth; profundity

dziļurbis *nm* (oil drilling) deep hole drilling rig

dziļurbums *nm* (oil drilling) deep hole

dzim/is *part* of dzimt born; es esmu d. decembrī I was born in December; viņš ir d. liepājnieks he was born in Liepāja; viņa ir ~usi Zāle her maiden name was Zāle; viņš ir d. vadonis he is a born leader

dzīmis *nm* multitude, myriad

dzimstība *nf* birth rate

dzimšana *nf* birth

dzimšanas apliecība *nf* birth certificate

dzimšanas diena *nf* birthday

dzimt *vi* be born

dzimta *nf* family

dzimtais *def adj* native; of birth

dzimtbūšana *nf* serfdom

dzimtbūšanas atcēlējs *nm* abolitionist

dzimtbūšanas atcelšana *nm* abolition of serfdom

dzimtbūtniecība *nf* serfdom

dzimtbūtniecisks *adj* pertaining to serfdom

dzimtbuve *nf* serfdom

dzimtcilvēks *nm* serf

dzimte *nf* (gram.) gender

dzimtele *nf* bracket

dzimtene *nf* 1. homeland, native country; birthplace, home; (of plants and animals) native to . . . 2. (sl.) moonshine

dzimtenes ilgas *nf pl* homesickness

dzimtenes mīlestība *nf* love for one's native land;

dzimtenīte *nf* 1. *dim* of dzimtene, homeland; birthplace; 2. (sl.) moonshine

dzimtes vārds *nm* (gram.) article

dzimtīpašnie/ks *nm*, ~ce *nf* owner by succession; lord of the manor

dzimtīpašums *nm* hereditary property

dzimtkapi *nm pl* family plot, family vault

dzimtkungs *nm* lord of the manor

dzimtlaiki *nm pl* serfdom

dzimtļaudis *nm pl* serfs

dzimtmājas *nf pl* ancestral homestead; hereditary farmstead

dzimtmuiža *nf* patrimonial estate

dzimtmuižnie/ks *nm*, ~ce *nf* owner of a patrimonial estate, lord of the manor

dzimtniecība *nf* serfdom

dzimtniecisks *adj* pertaining to serfdom

dzimtnie/ks *nm*, ~ce *nf* 1. serf; 2. (hist.) a farmer who had bought his farm from the lord of the manor as hereditary property

dzimtnoma *nf* emphyteusis, hereditary lease

dzimtnomnie/ks *nm*, ~ce *nf* hereditary leaseholder

dzimts *nf* clan

dzimt/s *adj* 1. native; 2. born; (iepirkt) par ~u buy (land) as hereditary property

dzimtsēta *nf* ancestral homestead

dzimtssarakstu nodaļa *nf* bureau of vital statistics

dzimtuve *nf* (reg.) birthplace

dzimtverdzība *nf* serfdom

dzimtzemnie/ks *nm*, ~ce *nf* serf

dzimumakts *nm* sexual intercourse

dzimumattiecības *nf pl* sexual relations

dzimum|ch|romatīns [h] *nm* Barr body

dzimumdiena *nf* birthday

dzimumdziedzeris *nm* sex gland

dzimumdziņa *nf* sex drive

dzimumdzīve *nf* sexual relations, sex life

dzimumgatavība *nf* sexual maturity

dzimumgatavs *adj* sexually mature

dzimumhibridizācija *nf* sexual hybridization

dzimumhormons *nm* sex hormone

dzimumidentitāte *nf* gender identity

dzimuminstinkts *nm* sexual instinct

dzimumloceklis *nm* male member

dzimumlomas *nf pl* gender roles

dzimumnespēks *nm* impotence

dzimumnobriedums *nm* sexual maturity

dzimumnoziegums *nm* sex crime

dzimumorg[a]ns [ā] *nm* sex organ

dzimumpārkāpums *nm* sex offense

dzimumpazīme *nf* sex characteristic

dzimum/s *nm* **1.** sex, gender; **skaistais d.** fair sex; **2.** origin; **augsta ~a** of noble birth; **3.** offspring; **4.** generation; **5.** birth

dzimumsakari *nm pl* sexual relations

dzimumsastāvs *nm* gender structure

dzimumsatiksme *nf* sex act

dzimumspēja *nf* (male) potency

dzimumšūna *nf* sex cell

dzimumtieksme *nf* sexual attraction

dzimumuzbudinājums *nm* sexual excitement

dzimumvairošanās *nfr* sexual reproduction

dzimumzīme *nf* birthmark

dzindras *nf pl* **1.** slag; **2.** oxide film

dzindzināt *vi* buzz

dzīne *nf* shoot, sprout

dzinējass *nf* driving axle

dzinējraķete *nf* propulsion rocket

dzinējrats *nm* = **dzinējritenis**

dzinējritenis *nm* (RR) driver; driving wheel

dzinējs *nm* **1.** driver; drover; beater; **2.** (hist.) messenger; **3.** hound; **4.** engine; **elektriskais d.** electric motor; **reaktīvais d.** jet

dzinējsiksna *nf* driving belt

dzinējskriemelis *nm* pulley

dzinējskrūve *nf* screw propeller

dzinējspēks *nm* motor power

dzinējsuns *nm* hound

dzinēju medības *nf pl* hunting with beaters

dzinējvārpsta *nf* screw propeller

dzinējzobrats *nm* drive gear

dzineklis *nm* drive, urge

dzinis *nm* (compu.) driver

dzinkstēt *vi* = **džinkstēt**

dzinkstināt *vi* (*iter*) clink; tinkle; chink; jingle

dzinkstoņa *nf* clinking; tinkle; chink; jingle

dzintarains *adj* amber-colored

dzintarjūra *nf* Baltic Sea

dzintarkal/is *nm*, **~e** *nf* jeweler (who works in amber)

dzintarots *adj* amber-colored

dzintarpriede *nf* amber tree

dzintars *nm* amber

dzintarskābe *nf* succinic acid

dzintarzeme *nf* land of amber; (folk.) Prussia

dzintele *nf* bracket; (tech.) dog, pawl, catch

dzinulis *nm* drive, urge

dzinums *nm* shoot, sprout

dzinumu kode *nf* incurvariid

dziņa *nf* drive, urge

dzīņošana *nf* (mech.) microdisplacement

dzīparains *adj* embroidered; knitted

dzīparots *adj* embroidered; knitted

dzīpars *nm* dyed woolen yarn

dzīparu kārkls *nm* narrow-leaved osier; violet willow

dzīparu klēts *nf* (hist.) building where a bride's dowry was kept

dzīpsla *nf* (reg.) sinew

dzira I *nf* **1.** slops (thin gruel for animals); **2.** potion, drink

dzira II *nf* intention

dzīras *nf pl* = **dzīres**

dzirdami *adv* audibly

dzirdamība *nf* audibility

dzirdams *adj, part* of **dzirdēt 1.** audible; **2.** it is rumored, they say; **kas d.?** what's new?

dzirde *nf* **1.** hearing; **2.** musicality; **absolūtā d.** absolute pitch; **laba mūzikālā d.** good ear for music; **bez mūzikālās ~s** tone-deaf; **pēc ~s** by the ear

dzirdes atmiņa *nf* aural memory

dzirdes kauliņi *nm pl* auditory ossicles

dzirdes nervs *nm* auditory nerve

dzirdes slieksnis *nm* auditory threshold;

dzirdēšana *nf* hearing; **pirmā d.** (col.) never heard of it

dzirdēt *vt* hear ◊ **kā dzird** it is said; I hear that; **vai tas ir ~s!** whoever heard of such a thing! **d. pa ausu galam** overhear; **nelikties ne dzirdam** pretend not to hear

dzirdētājs *nm*, **~a** *nf* one that hears

dzirdīgi *adv* receptively

dzirdīgs *adj* hearing; (of audiences) receptive

dzirdināt *vt* ply with drinks; (of domestic animals) water, give liquid food

dzirdinātava *nf* = **dzirdītava**

dzirdīt *vt* ply with drinks; (of domestic animals) water, give liquid food

dzirdītava *nf* watering place

dzīrenieks *nm* guest at a feast; reveler, carouser

dzirenis *nm* (reg.) lamb

dzīres *nf pl* feast, banquet

dziris *nm* (reg.) drinker

dzirkalis *nm* stonecutter; millstone dresser

dzirkles *nf pl* shears

dzirklēt *vt* shear

dzirklītes *nf pl* **1.** *dim* of **dzirkles**, shears; **2.** scissors

dzirknes *nf pl* raw edge (of a piece of fabric)

dzirkste *nf* pain in the joints

dzirkstele *nf* spark; ~s gar acīm see stars

dzirkstelīte *nf* **1.** *dim* of **dzirkstele**, sparklet; **2.** (bot.) maiden pink

dzirksteļains *adj* sparky; (of a glance) withering

dzirksteļķērājs *nm* spark arrester

dzirksteļot *vi* spark, emit sparks

dzirksteļstarpa *nf* spark gap

dzirkstenis *nm* fruit soda

dzirkstēt *vi* sparkle, scintillate

dzirkstīgi *adv* scintillatingly

dzirkstīgs *adj* sparkling, scintillating

dzirkstīgums *nm* sparkle, scintillating character

dzirkstījums *nm* sparkle

dzirkstīt *vi* sparkle, scintillate

dzirkstīte *nf* **1.** *dim* of **dzirksts**, sparklet; **2.** (bot.) maiden pink

dzirkstīties *vr* (rare.) sparkle, scintillate

dzirksts *nf* spark; (fig.) talent

dzirnakmens *nm* millstone

dzirnas *nf pl* mill; quern

dzirnav/as *nf pl* mill; quern; ~u acs eye of the upper millstone; ~u dīķis millpond;

~u gaņģis set of millstones; ~u strauts millrace

dzirnavezers *nm* millpond

dzirnaviņas *nf pl* **1.** *dim* of **dzirnavas**, windmill, watermill; **2.** peppermill; coffee grinder; **3.** whirligig

dzirnavnie/ks *nm* miller; ~ce *nf* miller's wife

dzirnavupe *nf* millstream

dzirnums *nm* See **acu dzirnums**

dzirnupe *nf* millstream

dzirnus *nf pl* (obs.) mill; quern

dzīrot *vi* feast; revel, carouse

dzīrotāj/s *nm*, ~a *nf* reveler, carouser; party-goer

dzirties *vr* ready oneself, be about to do sth.

dzirulis *nm* (obs.) drinker

dzisa *nf* (of light) dying out; (fig.) fading, waning

dzisināt *vt* cool; **d. muti** jabber, blab; **nav vērts muti d.** it is not worth wasting your breath

dzīsla *nf* **1.** sinew; **2.** (bot., geol., col. for blood vessel) vein; **slokšņota d.** banded vein

dzīslainais gneiss *nm* flaser gneiss

dzīslains *adj* **1.** sinewy; **2.** veined

dzīslene *nf* (anat.) choroid

dzīsliņa *nf dim* of **dzīsla**, veinlet

dzīslojums *nm* venation

dzīslots *adj* **1.** sinewy; **2.** veined

dzīslu iezis *nm* (geol.) dyke rock, intrusive vein

dzīslulapas *nf pl* plantain

dzist *vi* **1.** cool, turn cold; **2.** (of fire) die, go out; (of light) grow dim, go out; **3.** fade; **4.** sink, go downhill; wane

dzistin *adv emph* of **dzist**; **d. dzisa** it cooled fast

dzisums *nm* (of light) dying out; (fig.) fading, waning

dzīšanās *nfr* (with **pēc**) pursuit of, striving for

dzīšus *adv emph* of **dzīt** I; **d. dzīt** drive relentlessly

dzīt I *vt* drive, chase; **d. asnus** sprout; **d. bārdu** shave; **d. jūgā** exploit; **d. pēdas** track; **d. zirgu** ride a horse hard; **d. pie darba** hurry s.o. on with his or her work; **d. stigu** clear a right-of-way; **d. vagu** plow a furrow; **d. ratā** (col.) send packing; **d. stāvus kapā** (col.) make life intolerable; **d. šeptes** (sl.) wheel and deal; **d. velnu** (or **jokus**) (col.) cut up; play a joke on s.o.

dzīt II (with **î**) *vi* (*3rd pers*) heal

dzītars *nm* amber

dzītava *nf* (folk., of cattle) coming-home time

dzīties *vr* (with **pēc**) strive for, seek after; **d. pakaļ** pursue; tear after; **d. pa pēdām** track; **d. ellē** (col.) travel to the boondocks

dzītin *adv emph* of **dzīt** I; **d. dzina** he (she) drove relentlessly

dzītiņa *nf* short length of yarn or thread; thin yarn

dzīvais ozols *nm* live oak

dzīvdzemdētāja *nf* viviparous animal

dzīve *nf* life; **pēcnāves d.** life after death; **sabied-riskā d.** a. social life; b. public life; **saviesīga d.** party, social; **zaļa d.** bed of roses; **dzīves gud-rība** *nf* practical wisdom; **~es ilgums** longevity; life span; **~s izdevumi** living expenses; **~s pieredze** practical experience; **~s prasības** living requirements; **dzīves proza** *nf* humdrum existence, prosaic nature of life; **~s slogs** the wear and tear of life; **~s spars** vitality, vigor, verve, vim; **~s uzturs** sustenance; **~s vajadzī-bas** necessities of life; **dzīves vakars** *nm* declining years of life; **dzīves ziedonis** *nm* prime of life

dzīves apnikums *nm* weariness of life, ennui

dzīves apraksts *nm* biography

dzīves dārdzība *nf* cost of living

dzīves gājums *nm* course of life

dzīves jēga *nf* meaning of life

dzīves kārta *nf* position in life

dzīves laiks *nm* lifetime

dzīves līmenis *nm* living standard

dzīves māksla *nf* art of living

dzīves mērķis *nm* purpose in life

dzīves minimums *nm* minimum standard of living

dzīves spēja *nf* viability

dzīves standarts *nm* standard of living

dzīves telpa *nf* Lebensraum

dzīves uzskats *nm* world view

dzīves veids *nm* lifestyle

dzīves vieta *nf* residence; **bez noteiktas d. ~s** of no fixed address

dzīvelība *nf* toughness, survivorship

dzīvelīgs *adj* tenacious of life, tough

dzīvelnieks *nm* migratory worker, hired hand

dzīvesbiedrs *nm*, **~e** *nf* spouse

dzīvespriecīgi *adv* joyfully, buoyantly

dzīvespriecīgs *adj* joyful, buoyant

dzīvesprieks *nm* joy of living, buoyancy, vim

dzīvesspējīgs *adj* viable, tenacious of life

dzīvesstāsts *nm* story of life

dzīvesvieta *nf* residence

dzīv/i *adv* quickly; briskly; **~āk!** get a move on!

dzīvība *nf* life (animate being)

dzīvības briesmas *nf pl* mortal peril

dzīvības dziņa *nf* life instinct, survival instinct

dzīvības glābējs *nm* 1. lifeguard; 2. life saver

dzīvības jautājums *nm* question of life and death

dzīvības koks *nm* arborvitae; see also **milzu d. k.**

dzīvības process *nm* life process

dzīvības spēks *nm* vitality

dzīvības zīme *nf* sign of life

dzīv/ie *nom adj pl* the living; **~o atmiņā** in living memory

dzīvīgi *adv* in a lively manner

dzīvīgs *adj* lively

dzīvīgums *nm* liveliness

dzīvildze *nf* (med.) survival

dzīvināt *vt* 1. give life, vivify; 2. enliven

dzīvīte *nf dim* of **dzīve**, life

dzīvmasa *nf* biomass

dzīvnadzis *nm* hangnail

dzīvnieciņš *nm dim* of **dzīvnieks**, little animal

dzīvnieciski *adv* bestially, brutally

dzīvniecisks *adj* animal; bestial, brutal

dzīvnieciskums *nm* bestiality, brutality

dzīvniekkopība *nf* animal husbandry

dzīvniekkopis *nm* animal husbandman

dzīvnieks *nm* animal, beast

dzīvnieku valsts *nf* animal kingdom

dzīvojams *adj, part* of **dzīvot** living, habitable; residential

dzīvok/lis *nm* apartment; **konspiratīvais d.** safe house; **kooperātīvais d.** condominium apartment; **vienistabas d. ar virtuvi** efficiency apartment; **~ļa iekārta** furnishings (of an apartment); **~ļa īpašnieks (īpašniece)** landlord (landlady); **d. ar uzturu** bed and board

dzīvoklītis *nm dim* of **dzīvoklis**, small apartment

dzīvokļa maksa *nf* rent

dzīvokļu celtniecība *nf* housing construction

dzīvokļu fonds *nm* housing resources

dzīvokļu kazarme *nf* tenement block

dzīvokļu kolonija *nf* blocks of apartment houses

dzīvokļu kr[i]ze [ī] *nf* critical housing shortage

dzīvokļu nams *nm* apartment building

dzīvošana *nf* living, life; **mūžīgā d.** life eternal ◊ **d. ar uguni aizgāja** (col.) the house burnt down

dzīvo/t *vi, vt* **1.** live; reside, lodge; **d. augsti** (col.) live high on the hog; **d. bez laulības** cohabit; **d. cepuri kuldams** live in clover; **d. dīkā** live a life of leisure; **d. kā niere taukos** (or **kā azotē**) live the life of Riley; **d. kā pa miglu** be in a fog; **d. labas dienas** lead an easy life; **d. (Lielā) ielā** live on (Main) Street; **lai dzīvo!** long live!

d. uz nebēdu live it up; **d. nesaticīgi** fight (fig.); **d. nometnē** camp out, go camping; **d. noslēgti** live in seclusion; **d. pārticībā** be well off; **d. paša namā** be a homeowner; **d. plaši** live in grand style; **d. kā suns ar kaķi** lead a cat-and-dog life; **d. trūcīgi** lead a precarious existence; **~jiet veseli!** goodbye; farewell; **d. vienkārši** lead a simple life; **d. zaļu dienu** (col.) live it up; **d. no zila gaisa** live on love and fresh air; **kad ~sim, tad redzēsim** wait and see; **2.** carry on

dzīvotāj/s *nm*, **~a** *nf* one that lives; **viņš nebūs ilgi d.** he is not long for this world

dzīvotgriba *nf* will to live

dzīvoties *vr* play, romp

dzīvotpriecīgi *adv* joyfully, buoyantly

dzīvotpriecīgs *adj* joyful, buoyant

dzīvotprieks *nm* joy of living, buoyancy, vim

dzīvotspēja *nf* survivability, viability

dzīvotspējīgs *adj* viable, tenacious of life

dzīvotspēks *nm* vitality

dzīvpumpuru sūrene *nf* Alpine bistort

dzīv/s *adj* **1.** alive, live, living; animate; **kā d.** true to life; **~am esot** during one's lifetime; **ne d., ne miris** more dead than alive; scared stiff; **2.** lively, vivacious; **3.** animated; quick, brisk; (of traffic) busy; **4.** vivid; **5.** (col.) intact; **6.** whole, entire, straight

dzīvsudraba az[i]ds [ī] *nm* mercurous azide

dzīvsudrabs *nm* mercury

dzīvsvars *nm* live weight

dzīvums *nm* **1.** livingness; **2.** liveliness; **3.** aliveness

dzīvžogs *nm* hedge

dzots *nm* (mil.) blockhouse

džainisms *nm* Jainism

džains *nm* Jain

džakuzi *indecl nm* jacuzzi

džambolāna *nf* Java plum

džamboreja *nf* (boy scout) jamboree

džaurs *nm* giaour

Džefrija priede *nf* Jeffrey pine
džeirans *nm* goitered gazelle
džeks *nm* (sl.) guy
džemperis *nm* pullover
džems *nm* jam
džemsesija *nf* jam session
džentlmenis *nm* gentleman
džentlmeniski *adv* in a gentlemanlike manner
džentlmenisks *adj* gentlemanlike
džentrija *nf* gentry
džerkste *nf* **1.** tangle; **2.** arthritic pain
džerkstēt *vi* grate
džerkstoņa *nf* grating
džersijs *nm* jersey (cloth)
džets *nm* jet airplane
džezbends *nm* jazz band
džezmanis *nm* jazzman
džezroks *nm* jazz-rock
džezs *nm* **1.** jazz band; **2.** jazz (music)
dēiga *nf* (dance) jig
džīgas *nf pl* fiddle
džīgāt *vi* fiddle
džigers *nm* (text.) jigger
džigitēšana *nf* Circassian horsemanship
džigitēt *vi* (of a Circassian horseman) display horsemanship
džigits *nm* Circassian horseman
džihada *nf* or **dēihāds** *nm* jihad
džīnas *nf pl* jeans
džindžala *nf* Gipsy whip
džindžēt *vi* jingle, jangle; tinkle
džingls *nm* jingle
džingoisms *nm* jingoism
džinkstēšana *nf* jingling; clinking; buzzing; whizzing; **d. ausīs** ringing in the ears, tinnitus
džinkstēt *vi* jingle; clink; buzz; twang; (of bullets) whizz; (of ears) ring; **(viņam, tev) džinkst** (sl.) off (his, your) rocker
džinkstiens *nm* twang; buzz; whizz
džinkstināt *vt* twang; *vi* jingle, buzz

džinkstoņa *nf* jingling; clinking; buzzing; whizzing; **d. ausīs** ringing in the ears
džinrikša *nm* jinriksha
džins I *nm* gin
džins II *nm* jinn, genie
džins III *nm* (cotton) gin
džiterbags *nm* jitterbug
džiudžitsu *nm indecl* jujitsu
džīps *nm* jeep
džirkstēt *vi* crunch, squeak, grind
džirkstoņa *nf* crunching, squeaking
džokers *nm* (cards) joker
džonglierēt *vi* (sl.) balance
džonka *nf* (water craft) junk
Džoula likums *nm* Joule's law
džouls *nm* joule
džorga *nf* (reg.) puddle
džudist/s *nm*, **~e** *nf* judoka
džudo *nm indecl* judo
džūksliens *nm* (reg.) quagmire
džūkstājs *nm* (reg.) quagmire
džumpot *vi* (sl.) swim
džungļi *nm pl* jungle
džungurs *nm* (sl.) money, pelf
džuta *nf* jute
džuzguns *nm* Calligonum

E

e or **ē** *interj* **1.** (col.) look! hey! **2.** oh, well! **3.** (dis-missal of a notion) ah; **4.** right?
ebenkok/s *nm* ebony; **~i** Diospyros
ebonīt/s *nm* ebonite
ebr[e]j/s [ē] *nm*, **~iete** *nf* Hebrew; Jew
ece *nf* (col.) quarrel
ecēklis *nm* (col.) quarrelsome person
ecēšas *nf pl* harrow; **piekabināmās e.** mounted harrow

ecēšš|ūce *nf* planer

ecēt *vt* harrow

ecēties *vr* (col.) quarrel

e|ch|atoloģija |h| *nf* eschatology

e|ch|idna |h| *nf* echidna

e|ch|inacijas |h| *nf pl* Echinacea

e|ch|inocerejs |h| *nm* echinocereus

e|ch|inokaktuss |h| *nm* echinocactus

e|ch|inokokoze |h| *nf* echinococcosis

e|ch|inokoks |h| *nm* echinococcus

e|ch|īns |h| *nm* echinus

e|ch|oencefalogr|a|fija |h||ā| *nf* echoencepha-
lography

e|ch|ogr|a|fs |h||ā| *nm* echograph

e|ch|olalija |h| *nf* echolalia

e|ch|olots or e|ch|olote) |h| *nm* sonic depth
finder

e|ch|opraksija |h| *nf* echopraxia

ecīgs *adj* quarrelsome

ēciņa *nf dim* of **ēka**, small building

ēcis *nm* (reg.) juniper

ečeverija *nf* echeveria

ēda *nf* bait

edafisks *adj* edaphic

ēdāj/s *nm* **1.** a. eater; big eater b. (family
member) mouth; diner; ~a *nf*; **2.** (obs.)
herpes

ēdamais *nom adj* food, edibles, (col.) eats

ēdamais kastanis *nm* sweet chestnut

ēdamā kolokāzija *nf* taro

ēdamā se|ch|ija |h| *nf* chayote

Edames siers *nm* Edam cheese

ēdamgalds *nm* dining table

ēdamība *nf* (of fodder) taste

ēdamie loki *nm pl* chives

ēdamistaba *nf* dining room

ēdamkarote *nf* soup spoon, (as a measure)
tablespoon

ēdamlietas *nf pl* comestibles

ēdamreize *nf* mealtime

ēdamrīki *nm pl* silverware

ēdams *adj, part* of **ēst** edible

ēdamtelpa *nf* messroom, dining hall

ēdamtrauki *nm pl* dishes

ēdamviela *nf* foodstuff

ēdamvagons *nm* dining car

ēdamzāle *nf* dining hall

ēde *nf* eczema

ēdēj/s *nm* eater; ~a *nf*

ēdelība *nf* greediness, insatiability

ēdelīgi *adv* greedily, insatiably

ēdelīgs *adj* greedy, insatiable

ēdelīgums *nm* greediness, insatiability

ēdelveiss *nm* edelweiss

ēdene *nf* (fig.) garden of Eden, paradise

Edera grīslis *nm* green sedge

ēdesis *nm* hog slops

ēdes zāle *nf* **1.** filago; **2.** cud-weed

edicija *nf* edition

ēdienkarte *nf* menu

ēdienreize *nf* mealtime

ēdiens *nm* meal; dish, course; **otrais ē.** main
course; **saldais ē.** dessert

ēdienu celtnis *nm* dumbwaiter

ēdienvārītāj/s *nm*, ~a *nf* cook

ēdienveikals *nm* diner; cafeteria; restaurant

edikts *nm* edict

ed|i|ls |ī| *nm* aedile

ēdin *adv emph* of **ēst; viņi e. ēda** they ate
heartily

ēdināšana *nf* feeding; **sabiedriskā ē.** community
food service

ēdināt *vt* feed

Edipa komplekss *nm* Oedipus complex

ēdnīca *nf* diner; refectory, messroom; cafeteria

ēdoklis *nm* cud

ēdokslis *nm* cud

ēdri *adv* (reg.) clearly, straightforwardly

edz *interj* (col.) look

efēbs *nm* ephebus

efedras *nf pl* ephedra

efedrīns *nm* ephedrine

ef-ef *indecl adj* **uz ef-ef** *adv* tip-top

|e|feja |ē| *nf* ivy

[e]feju [ē] pelargonija *nf* ivy-leafed pelargonium

[e]feju [ē] sētložņa *nf* field balm

[e]fejvīns [ē] *nm* cissus

efektīgi *adv* effectively

efektīgs *adj* effective, striking

efektīvi *adv* effecticely

efekt[i]vitāte [ī] *nf* effectiveness

efekt[i]vizēt [ī] *vt* increase the effectiveness of

efektīvs *adj* effective, efficacious

efektors *nm* effector

efekts *nm* effect; **nesenais e.** (psych.) recency ef-fect; **sākotnējais e.** (psych.) primacy effect

efemera *nf* mayfly

efemer[i]das [ī] *nf pl* ephemeris

efemerisks *adj* ephemeral

efemers *nm* (bot.) ephemeral

efemers *adj* ephemeral

efendi *indecl nm* effendi

eferents *adj* efferent

efesieši *nm pl* Ephesians

efūzija *nf* effusion

ef[u]zīvs [ū] *adj* effusive

efors *nm* ephor

egalitārisms *nm* egalitarianism

egalitārs *adj* egalitarian

eg[i]da [ī] *nf* aegis

egilopss *nm* Aegilops

eglaine *nf* or **eglainis** *nm* stand of spruce

eglājs *nm* stand of spruce

egle *nf* spruce

eglene *nf* bearded milk cap

eglenes *nf pl* harrow

egliena or **egliene** *nf* stand of spruce

egliens *nm* stand of spruce

eglis *nm* wooden harrow

eglīte *nf* **1.** *dim* of **egle**, spruce, small spruce; **2.** Christmas tree; **3.** (mus. instrument) rattle

eglītes *nf pl* corn spurry

eglonis *nm* (obs.) stand of spruce

egļi *nm pl* corn spurry

egļu astoņzobis *nm* spruce bark beetle

egļu auzas *nf pl* white oats

egļu ciekuru kode *nf* fir coneworm

egļu kazu bārda *nf* green-staining coral mushroom

egļu kode *nf* spruce bud moth

egļu krustknābis *nm* red crossbill

egļu lapu uts *nf* spruce gall aphid

egļu mizgrauži *nm pl* spruce bark beetles

egļu mūķene *nf* tussock moth; gypsy moth

egļu putns *nm* red crossbill

egļu ragaste *nf* horntail

egocentriski *adv* egocentrically

egocentrisks *adj* egocentric

egocentriskums *nm* egocentricity

egocentrisms *nm* egocentricity

egoisms *nm* egotism

egoistiski *adv* egoistically

egoistisks *adj* egotistic

egoistiskums *nm* egotism

egoist/s *nm*, **~e** *nf* egotist

egotisms *nm* egotism

eģe *nf* (col.) selvage

îģiptes žurka *nf* Alexandrian black rat

ēģiptiet/is *nm*, **~e** *nf* Egyptian

ēģiptolo/gs *nm*, **~ģe** *nf* Egyptologist

ēģiptoloģija *nf* Egyptology

eh *interj* eh, oh

eha- See **echa-**

ehei *interj* hey

ehi- See **echi-**

eho- See **echo-**

ei *interj* hey; **ei nu** go on, come on

ei[ch]hornija [h] *nf* Eichhornia

eidāties *vr* swing

eidemonisks *adj* = **eudaimonisks**

eidemonisms *nm* = **eudaimonisms**

eidenieks *nm* (horse) pacer

eideniski *adv* **e. iet** (of horses) pace

eidētika *nf* eidetic imagery

eidētiķis *nm* eidetic

eidētisks *adj* eidetic

eidētisms *nm* eidetic imagery

eidoimetrs *nm* = eudiometrs

eidololatrija *nf* idolatry

eidoss *nm* eidos

eiduks *nm* (hist.) a Polish coin

eifēmiski *adv* = eufēmiski

eifēmisks *adj* = eufēmisks

eifēmisms *nm* = eufēmisms

eifonija *nf* = eufonija

eifonisks *adj* = eufonisks

eiforbija *nf* = euforbija

eiforbijs *nm* = euforbijs

eiforija *nf* = euforija

eiforiski *adv* = euforiski

eiforisks *adj* = euforisks

eiforizēt *vt* = euforizēt

eifotisks *adj* = eufotisks

eifuisms *nm* = eufuisms

eigenika *nf* = eugenika

eigeniķis *nm*, ~e *nf* = eugeniķis

eigenisks *adj* = eugenisks

eigenist/s *nm*, ~e *nf* = eugenists

eigenols *nm* = eugenols

eigeosinklināle *nf* = eugeosinklināle

eiglenas *nf pl* = euglenas

eiglenofīti *nm pl* = euglenofīti

eiharistija *nf* = eucharistija

eiharistisks *adj* = eucharistisks

eihemerisms *nm* = euhemerisms

eihhornija *nf* = eichhornija

eiholoģija *nf* = eucholoģija

eikaīns *nm* = eukaīns

eikalipteļļa *nf* = eukalipteļļa

eikaliptols *nm* = eukaliptols

eikalipts *nm* = eukalipts

eikariots *nm* = eukariots

eikomija *nf* = eukomija

eikosans *nm* eicosane

eikrazija *nf* = eukrazija

eilalija *nf* = eulalija

eiloģija *nf* = euloģija

eima *imper* of **iet**, *1st pers pl* (folk.) let's go

einomija *nf* = eunomija

ein[s]teinijs [š] *nm* einsteinium

einuhoīdisms *nm* = eunūchoīdisms

einuhs *nm* = eunūchs

eipatrīdi *nm pl* = eupatrīdi

eipraksija *nf* = eupraksija

eirāzieši *nm pl* Eurasians

eiriales *nf pl* basket stars

eirihalīns *nm* = eurihalīns

eirija *nf* Eurya

eiriterms *adj* = euriterms

eiritmija *nf* = euritmija

eiro *indecl nm* euro

eirodolārs *nm* eurodollar

eirokom[u]nisms [ū] *nm* Eurocommunism

Eiropas baltegle *nf* silver fir

Eiropas dziedenīte *nf* sanicle

Eiropas ciedru priede *nf* Swiss stone pine

Eiropas lapegle *nf* European larch

Eiropas repsis *nm* vendace

Eiropas sardīne *nf* sardine, pilchard

Eiropas segliņš *nm* spindle tree

iropeīdi *nm pl* Caucasoids

iropeīds *adj* Caucasoid

iropeisks *adj* = eiropisks

iropeizēt *vt* = eiropizēt

iropietis *nm*, ~e *nf* European

iropijs *nm* europium

iropisks *adj* European

iropizēt *vt* Europeanize

eisebija *nf* Eusebian canons

Eistākija kanālis *nm* Eustachian tube

eistatisks *adj* = eustatisks

eita *imper* of **iet**, *2nd pers pl* (folk.) go

eitanazija *nf* = eutanazija

eitektisks *adj* = eutektisks

eitektoidisks *adj* = eutektoidisks

eiterpes *nf pl* Euterpe

eitrofikācija *nf* = eutrofikācija

eitrofisks *adj* = eutrofisks

eitrofs *adj* = **eutrofs**

eiženija *nf* eugenia

eja *nf* passage; aisle; lane

ejakulācija *nf* ejaculation

ejakulāts *nm* ejaculate

ejakulēt *vt, vi* ejaculate

ejkājas *nf pl* walking legs

ejošs *adj, part* of **iet 1.** moving; **2.** marketable, salable; bestselling; **labi e.** (of goods) fast moving

ejot *part* of **iet** going, in going; walking, in walking; on foot

ek *interj* **1.** yuck; **2.** oh; **3.** look

ēka *nf* building; **dižā ē.** all-purpose farm building; **dzīvojamā ē.** residential building

ekers *nm* optical square

ekgonins *nm* ecgonine

ekī *nm indecl* ecu

ekijs *nm* ecu

ekipāža I *nf* crew

ekipāža II *nf* carriage

ekipējums *nm* equipment

ekipēt *vt* equip

ekistika *nf* ekistics

ekistisks *adj* ekistic

eklampsija *nf* eclampsia

eklatants *adj* striking, showy, loud

eklektika *nf* eclecticism

eklektiķ/is *nm*, ~**e** *nf* eclectic

eklektiski *adv* eclectically

eklektisks *adj* eclectic

eklektisms *nm* eclecticism

eklērs *nm* eclair

eklēziasts *nm* **1.** ecclesiast; **2.** ecclesiastic

eklesioloģija *nf* ecclesiology

eklimetrs *nm* clinometer

eklipse *nf* eclipse

ekl|i|ptika [ī] *nf* ecliptic

eklogīts *nm* eclogite

ekoloģija *nf* ecology

ekoloģiski *adv* ecologically

ekoloģisks *adj* ecological

ekonomaizers *nm* (tech.) economizer

ekonomēt *vi* economize

ekonometrija *nf* econometrics

ekonomģeogr|a|fija [ā] *nf* economic geography

ekonomizers *nm* (tech.) economizer

ekonomija *nf* economy; **politiskā e.** (hist.) political economy; economics

ekonomijas fakultāte *nf* School of Business

ekonomika *nf* economics

ekonomiski *adv* economically

ekonomisks *adj* **1.** economic; **2.** economical

ekonomiskums *nm* thriftiness

ekonomisms *nm* economism

ekonomist/s *nm*, ~**e** *nf* economist

ekonomizēt *vt, vi* economize

ekonoms *nm* chief of food service

ekosēze *nf* ecossaise

ekosf|ai|ra| ē| *nf* ecosphere

ekosistēma *nf* ecosystem

ekotips *nm* ecotype

ekotūrisms *nm* ecotourism

ekr|a|nējums [ā] *nm* shielding

ekr|a|nēt [ā] *vt* (tech.) shield

ekrānisks *adj* adapted to the screen

ekr|a|nizācija [ā] *nf* = **ekranizējums**

ekr|a|nizējums [ā] *nm* screening (of a literary work)

ekr|a|nizēt [ā] *vt* screen, make into a screenplay

ekrānpults *nf* (compu.) screen

ekrān/s *nm* **1.** screen; **pirmā** ~**a** (of movies) first-run; **2.** (tech.) shield; **akustiskais e.** baffle

ekremokarps *nm* Eccremocarpus

eksakti *adv* exactly

eksakts *adj* exact

eksaltācija *nf* excitement, exaltation; rapture

eksaltēts *adj* excited, (pathologically) elated; (of style) high-flown

eksāmens *nm* examination; **e. rakstos** written examination eks|a|minācija [ā] *nf* examination

eks|a|minand/s [ā] *nm*, ~e *nf* examinee

eks|a|min|a|tor/s [ā][ā] *nm*, ~e *nf* examiner

eks|a|minējamais [ā] *nom adj* examinee

eks|a|minēt [ā] *vt* examine, give an examination

eks|a|minētāj/s [ā] *nm*, ~a *nf* examiner

eks|a|minēties [ā] *vr* take an examination

eksarācija *nf* quarrying

eksar|ch|ija [h] *nf* exarchate

eksar|ch|s [h] *nm* exarch

ekscentrība *nf* eccentricity

ekscentricitāte *nf* eccentricity

ekscentriķ/is *nm* ~e *nf* eccentric

ekscentriski *adv* excentrically

ekscentrisks *adj* eccentric

ekscentrs *nm* (mech.) eccentric

ekscentrspiede *nf* eccentric press

ekscepcija *nf* exception

ekscepcionāli *adv* exceptionally

ekscepcionāls *adj* exceptional

ekscerpēt *vt* excerpt

ekscerpts *nm* excerpt

ekscesīvi *adv* excessively

ekscesīvs *adj* excessive

ekscess *nm* excess

ekscitēt *vt* excite

ekscīzija *nf* excision

eksčempion/s *nm*, ~e *nf* ex-champion

eksedra *nf* exedra

eks|ēg|ēts [eģ] *nm* exegete

eks|ēg|ēze [eģ] *nf* exegesis

eksekūcija *nf* execution

eksek|u|tīvs [ū] *adj* executive

eksek|u|tor/s [ū] *nm*, ~e *nf* executor

eksekvijas *nf pl* exequies

ekse|l|ence [ll] *nf* excellence; Excellency

ekselēt *vt* cut with a chaffcutter

ekseļi *nm pl* chopped fodder

ekseļmašīna *nf* chaffcutter

eksempcija *nf* exemption

eksemplār/s *nm* 1. (of books, documents) copy; divos ~os in duplicate; 2. specimen

eksemplifikācija *nf* exemplification

eksercicija *nf* exercise

eksfoliācija *nf* exfoliation

ekshalācija *nf* exhalation

ekshibicija *nf* exhibition

ekshibicionist/s *nm*, ~e *nf* exhibitionist

ekshumācija *nf* exhumation

ekshumēt *vt* exhume

eksikators *nm* dehydrator; desiccator

eksils *nm* exile

eksistējošs *adj, part* of eksistēt existing, existent

eksistence *nf* existence

eksistences minimums *nm* living wage

eksistenciālisms *nm* existentialism

eksistenciālistisks *adj* existentialist

eksistenciālists *nm* existentialist

eksistenciāls *adj* existential

eksistēšana *nf* existence; (philos.) subsistence

eksistēt *vi* exist

eksitons *nm* exciton

ekskavācija *nf* excavation

ekskav|a|torist/s [ā] *nm*, ~e *nf* excavator operator

ekskav|a|tors [ā] *nm* excavator

eksklāvs *nm* exclave

eksklūzija *nf* exclusion

ekskluzīvi *adv* exclusively

eksklūzīvitāte *nf* exclusiveness

ekskluzīvs *adj* exclusive

ekskomunicēt *vt* excommunicate

ekskomunikācija *nf* excommunication

ekskrēcija *nf* excretion

ekskr|e|ments [ē] *nm* excrement

ekskrēts *nm* excretion

ekskursant/s *nm*, ~e *nf* excursionist

ekskursija *nf* excursion

ekskurss *nm* excursus, digression

ekskuzācija *nf* excuse

ekslibrist/s *nm,* ~**e** *nf* **1.** bookplate artist; **2.** exlibrist

ekslibrs *nm* bookplate, ex libris

eksmatrikulācija *nf* **1.** leaving (a university); **2.** expulsion (from a university)

eksmatrikulēt *v* **1.** *vi* leave (a university); **2.** *vt* expel (from a university)

eksoderma *nf* exodermis

eksods *nm* exodus

eksoftalmija *nf* exophthalmia

eksog[a]mija [ā] *nf* exogamy

eksog[e]ni [ē] *adv* exogenously

eksog[e]niski [ē] *adv* exogenously

eksog[e]nisks [ē] *adj* exogenous

eksog[e]ns [ē] *adj* exogenous

eksoni *nm pl* (genetics) coding sequences

eksorbitants *adj* exorbitant

eksorbitēt *vi* exorbitate

eksorcisms *nm* exorcism

eksosf[ai]ra [ē] *nf* exosphere

eksoteriski *adv* exoterically

eksoterisks *adj* exoteric

eksotermisks *adj* exothermic

eksoti *nm pl* exotics

eksotika *nf* the exotic, exotic character

eksotiski *adv* exotically

eksotisks *adj* exotic

eksotisms *nm* exoticism

eksotoksīns *nm* exotoxin

ekspansija *nf* expansion

ekspansionisms *nm* expansionism

ekspansionistiski *adv* expansionistically

ekspansionistisks *adj* expansionistic

ekspansīvi *adv* expansively

ekspansivitāte *nf* expansiveness

ekspansīvs *adj* expansive

ekspatriācija *nf* expatriation

ekspatriēt *vt* expatriate

ekspatriēt/ais *nom adj* expatriate; ~**ā** *f*

ekspedēt *vt* dispatch, forward

expedīcija *nf* **1.** expedition; **2.** mailroom

eksped[i]tor/s [ī] *nm,* ~**e** *nf* freight forwarder, forwarding agent; manager or employee of a parcel service or dispatch service

eksperimentāli *adv* experimentally

eksperimentāls *adj* experimental

eksperiment[a]tor/s [ā] *nm,* ~**e** *nf* experimenter

eksperimentēt *vi* experiment

eksperimentētāj/s *nm,* ~**a** *nf* experimenter

eksperiments *nm* experiment

ekspert[i]ze [ī] *nf* **1.** expertise, expert opinion; examination by experts; **2.** panel of experts

ekspermetode *nf* expert method

ekspert/s *nm,* ~**e** *nf* expert

ekspertsistēma *nf* (compu.) expert system

ekspertvērtējums *nm* expert evaluation

ekspiācija *nf* expiation

ekspilācija *nf* expilation

ekspirācija *nf* expiration (breathing out)

ekspiratorisks *adj* expiratory

eksplantācija *nf* explantation

eksplicēt *vt* explicate

eksplicīts *adj* explicit

eksplikācija *nf* explication

eksplik[a]tīvs [ā] *adj* explicative

eksplodēt *vi* explode

eksplozija *nf* explosion

eksplozijas spēja *nf* explosiveness

eksplozīvi *adv* explosively

eksplozīvs *adj* explosive

ekspluatācija *nf* exploitation; utilization; ~**s di-rektors** director of operations

ekspluat[a]toriski [ā] *adv* exploitatively

ekspluat[a]torisks [ā] *adj* exploitative

ekspluat[a]tor/s [ā] *nm,* ~**e** *nf* exploiter

ekspluatēt *vt* **1.** exploit; utilize; **2.** operate, run

eksponāts *nm* exhibit, item on display

eksponējums *nm* **1.** exhibition; **2.** (photo.) exposure eksponenciāls *adj* exponential

eksponentfunkcija *nf* exponential function

eksponents *nm* 1. (math.) exponent; 2. exhibitor

eksponentvienādojums *nm* exponential equation

eksponēt *vt* 1. exhibit; display; 2. (photo.) expose

eksponibls *adj* (philos.) exponible

eksponometrs *nm* (photo.) exposure meter

eksportēt *vt* export

eksportētājs *nm* exporter

eksportieris *nm* exporter

eksportkred|i|ts [ī] *nm* export credit

eksportmuita *nf* export duty

eksportosta *nf* export harbor

eksportpreces *nf pl* export goods

eksports *nm* export

ekspozīcija *nf* 1. exposition; 2. (photo.) exposure

ekspresija *nf* expression

ekspresionisms *nm* expressionism

ekspresionistiski *adv* expressionistically

ekspresionistisks *adj* expressionistic

ekspresionist/s *nm*, ~e *nf* expressionist

ekspresis *nm* 1. drayman; 2. mover; 3. express (express bus, elevator, train)

ekspresīvi *adv* expressively

ekspres|i|vitāte [ī] *nf* expressivity

ekspresīvs *adj* expressive

eksprespasts *nm* express mail

ekspressūtījums *nm* express goods parcel

ekspresvēstule *nf* express letter

ekspresvilciens *nm* express train

eksprešu kantoris *nm* (local) draymen

eksprešu ratiņi *nm pl* dray

ekspromisors *nm* guarantor

eksprompti *adv* impromptu, extemporaneously

eksprompts *nm* impromptu

eksprompts *adj* impromptu; extemporaneous

ekspropriācija *nf* expropriation

ekspropri|a|tor/s [ā] *nm*, ~e *nf* expropriator

ekspropriēt *vt* expropriate

ekstatiķis *nm* ecstatic

ekstatiski *adv* ecstatically

ekst|a|tisks [ā] *adj* ecstatic

ekst|a|ze [ā] *nf* ecstasy

ekstemporālis *nm* unannounced exam, pop quiz

ekstemporēt *vi* extemporize

ekstensija *nf* extension

ekstensitāte *nf* extensiveness

ekstensīvi *adv* extensively

ekstensīvs *adj* extensive

ekstenzors *nm* (biol.) extensor

eksteriorizācija *nf* exteriorization

ekste|r|itori|a|litāte [rr][ā] *nf* exterritoriality

ekste|r|itoriāli [rr] *adv* exterritorially

ekste|r|itoriāls [rr] *adj* exterritorial

eksterj|e|rs [ē] *nm* (of a building) exterior; (of farm animals) externals

eksternalizācija *nf* externalization

eksternāta eksāmens *nm* equivalency examination

eksternāts *nm* external studies

eksterni *adv* externally

ekstern/is *nm*, ~e *nf* external student

eksterns *adj* external

ekstinkcija *nf* (of radiation intensity) extinction

ekstirpācija *nf* extirpation; ablation

ekstirpātors *nm* extirpator

ekstirpēt *vt* extirpate

ekstr|a| [ā] *indecl adj* extra

ekstraģents *adj* extractive

ekstrahēšana *nf* extraction

ekstrahēt *vt* extract; lixiviate, leach

ekstrakcija *nf* extraction

ekstraktīvs *adj* extractive

ekstraktors *nm* extractor

ekstrakts *nm* extract

ekstraktvielas *nf pl* extractives

ekstralingvistisks *adj* extralinguistic

ekstraordinārs *adj* 1. extraordinary; 2. (educ.)
 untenured
ekstrapolācija *nf* extrapolation
ekstrapolēt *vt* extrapolate
ekstrasensitīvs *adj* extrasensory
ekstrasenss *nm* seer
ekstrasistolija *nf* extrasystolic arrythmia
ekstravagance *nf* extravagance
ekstravaganti *adv* extravagantly
ekstravagants *adj* extravagant
ekstraversija *nf* extroversion
ekstravertēts *adj* extroverted
ekstraverts *nm* extrovert
ekstrazonāls *adj* extrazonal
ekstr[e]māls [ē] *adj* extreme
ekstrēmi *adv* extremely
ekstrēmisms *nm* extremism
ekstrēmist/s *nm*, ~e *nf* extremist
ekstr[e]mitāte [ē] *nf* extremity
ekstrēms *nm* 1. extreme; 2. (math.) extremum
ekstrēms *adj* extreme
ekstroversija *nf* extroversion
ekstrovertēts *adj* extroverted
ekstroverts *nm* extrovert
ekstrūders *nm* extruder
ekstrūzija *nf* extrusion
eksudācija *nf* exudation
eksud[a]tīvs [ā] *adj* exudative
eksudāts *nm* exudate
ektāzija *nf* (med.) ectasia
ektoderma *nf* ectoderm
ektoģen[e]ze [ē] *nf* ectogenesis
ektoparazītisks *adj* ectoparasitic
ektoparazīts *nm* ectoparasite
ektopija *nf* ectopia
ektopisks *adj* ectopic
ektoplazma *nf* ectoplasm
ektotrofs *adj* ectotrophic
eku *interj* lo, look
ēku kokgrauzis *nm* house longhorn
ekumene *nf* = oikūmene

ekumenisks *adj* = oikūmenisks
ekumenisms *nm* = oikūmenisms
ēku piepe *nf* house fungus
ekur *interj* lo, look
ekusēze *nf* ecossaise
ekvadoriet/is *nm*, ~e *nf* Equadorian
ekvalaizers *nm* (el.) equalizer
ekv[a]toriāli [ā] *adv* equatorially
ekv[a]toriāls [ā] *adj* equatorial
ekv[a]tors [ā] *nm* equator
ekvilibristika *nf* balancing, rope walking
ekvilibrist/s *nm*, ~e *nf* balancer, equilibrist
ekvinokciāls *adj* equinoctial
ekvinokcij/a *nf* equinox
ekvinokciju apsteidze *nf* precession of the
 equinoxes
ekvipotenciāls *adj* equipotential
ekvivalence *nf* equivalence
ekvivalents *nm* equivalent
ekvivalenti *adv* equivalently
ekvivalents *adj* equivalent
ekzēma *nf* eczema
ekzo[ch]orda [h] *nf* Exochorda
ēķele I *nf* flax comber
ēķele II *nf* (cont.) *dim* of ēka, small, run-down
 building
ēķelēt *vt, vi* (col.) crochet
elaidīns *nm* elaidin
elaidīnskābe *nf* elaidic acid
elamieši *nm pl* Elamites
elastība *nf* elasticity, flexibility
elasticitāte *nf* elasticity, flexibility
elastīgi *adv* elastically, flexibly
elastīgs *adj* elastic, flexible
elastīgums *nm* elasticity, flexibility
elastiski *adv* elastically, flexibly
elastisks *adj* elastic, flexible
elastomērs *nm* elastomer
elastoplastisks *adj* elastoplastic
elaterīts *nm* elaterite
elatīvs *nm* (ling.) elative

Elbingas siers *nm* Wensleydale cheese

eleagns *nm* See **sudraba e., šaurlapu e.**

eleāts *adj* Eleatic

elefantiāze *nf* elephantiasis

elefants *nm* elephant

elegance *nf* elegance

eleganti *adv* elegantly

elegants *adj* elegant

elēģija *nf* elegy

elēģiski *adv* elegiacally

elēģisks *adj* elegiac

eleizine *nf* eleusine

elejietis *nm* Eleatic

elektorāls *adj* electoral

elektors *nm* elector

eleksīrs *nm* elixir

elektorāts *nm* electorate

elektrets *nm* electret

elektrība *nf* **1.** electricity; **2.** (col.) (electric) lights

elektrības iestāde *nf* power plant

elektrības skaitītājs *nm* electric meter;

elektrificēt *vt* electrify, supply with electricity

elektrifikācija *nf* electrification

elektriķ/is *nm*, ~e *nf* electrician

elektriski *adv* electrically

elektrisks *adj* electric, electrical

elektrizācija *nf* **1.** electrification; **2.** treatment with electricity

elektrizēt *vt* **1.** electrify; **2.** treat with electricity

elektrizēties *vr* **1.** be electrified, acquire an electric charge; **2.** undergo electrical treatment

elektroakustika *nf* electroacoustics

ektroakustiski *adv* electroacoustically

elektroakustisks *adj* electroacoustic

elektroanal[i]ze [ī] *nf* electroanalysis

elektroapgāde *nf* electric power supply

elektroautomobilis *nm* electric automobile

elektrobioloģija *nf* electrobiology

elektrobuss *nm* trolley bus

elektroceltnis *nm* electric crane, electric hoist

elektro[ch]romatogr[a]fija [h][ā] *nf* electrochromatography

elektrodekantācija *nf* electrodecantation

elektrodeton[a]tors [ā] *nm* electric detonator

elektrodial[i]ze [ī] *nf* electrodialysis

elektrodinamika *nf* electrodynamics

elektrodinamiski *adv* electrodynamically

elektrodinamisks *adj* electrodynamic

elektrods *nm* electrode

elektrodzinējs *nm* electric motor

elektrodzinējspēks *nm* electromotive force

elektroen[c]efalogr[a]fija [k] [ā] *nf* electroencephalography

elektroen[c]efalogr[a]fs [k] [ā] *nm* electroencephalograph

elektroen[c]efalogramma [k] *nf* electroencephalogram

elektroenerģētika *nf* production and consumption of electric energy

elektroenerģija *nf* electric energy

elektrofiltrs *nm* electrostatic precipitator

elektrofizioloģija *nf* electrophysiology

elektrofons *nm* electrophone

elektroforēze *nf* electrophoresis

elektrofors *nm* electrophorus

elektrofotogr[a]fija [ā] *nf* electrophotography

elektrofotometrs *nm* electric photometer

elektrogr[a]fija [ā] *nf* electrography

elektrogr[a]fiski [ā] *adv* electrographically

elektrogr[a]fisks [ā] *adj* electrographic

elektrogr[a]fs [ā] *nm* electrograph

elektroģenerēšana *nf* electric generation of free radicals

elektroģitāra *nf* electric guitar

elektroiekārta *nf* power equipment

elektroierīce *nf* electric appliance

elektroierosme *nf* electrical induction

elektroietilpība *nf* (electric) capacity

elektroinsta[l]ācija [ll] *nf* electrical wiring

elektrointegr[a]tors [ā] *nm* integrator

elektroinž

enier/is *nm*, **~e** *nf* electrical engineer

elektroizolācija *nf* electric insulation

elektrokalorifers *nm* electric heater

elektrokardiogr|a|fija [ā] *nf* electrocardiography

elektrokardiogr|a|fs [ā] *nm* electrocardiograph

elektrokardiogramma *nf* electrocardiogram

elektrokardiostimulators *nm* pacemaker

elektrokārs *nm* battery-propelled van

elektrokinētika *nf* electrokinetics

elektrokinētisks *adj* electrokinetic

elektrokoagulācija *nf* electrocoagulation

elektroķīmija *nf* electrochemistry

elektroķīmiķ/is *nm*, **~e** *nf* electrochemist

elektroķīmiski *adv* electrochemically

elektroķīmisks *adj* electrochemical

elektrolīnija *nf* power line

elektrol|i|tiski [ī] *adv* electrolytically

elektrol|i|tisks [ī] *adj* electrolytic

elektrol|i|ts [ī] *nm* electrolyte

elektrol|i|ze [ī] *nf* electrolysis

elektrol|i|zers [ī] *nm* electrolyzer

elektrolizēt *vt* electrolyze

elektrolokomotīve *nf* electric locomotive

elektroloks *nm* electric arc

elektroluminiscence *nf* electroluminescence

elektromagnētiski *adv* electromagnetically

elektromagnētisks *adj* electromagnetic

elektromagnētisms *nm* electromagnetism

elektromagnēts *nm* electromagnet

elektromašīna *nf* electric machinery

elektrome|cha|nika [hā] *nf* electromechanics

elektrome|cha|niķ/is [hā] *nm*, **~e** *nf* electromechanics specialist

elektrome|cha|niski [hā] *adv* electromechanically

elektrome|cha|nisks [hā] *adj* electromechanical

elektrometa|ll|urgs [l] *nm* electrometallurgist

elektrometa|ll|urģija [l] *nf* electrometallurgy

elektrometināšana *nf* electric welding

elektrometinātāj/s *nm*, **~a** *nf* electric welder

elektrometrisks *adj* electrometric

elektrometrs *nm* electrometer

elektromobilis *nm* electric car

elektromontāža *nf* assembly of electric equipment

elektromontieris *nm*, **~e** *nf* electrician

elektromotors *nm* electric motor

elektromūzika *nf* electronic music

elektronegatīvs *adj* electronegative

elektronierīce *nf* electronic device

elektronika *nf* electronics

elektroniski *adv* electronically

elektronisks *adj* electronic

elektronlampa *nf* electron tube

elektronmikroskops *nm* electron microscope

elektronogulsnēšana *nf* electrodeposition

elektrons *nm* electron

elektronstars *nm* electron beam

elektronvolts *nm* electron volt

elektrooptika *nf* electrooptics

elektrooptisks *adj* electrooptical

elektroosmoze *nf* electroosmosis

elektropārvade *nf* power transmission

elektropiederumi *nm pl* electric items

elektropiedziņa *nf* electric starting

elektropozitīvs *adj* electropositive

elektropreces *nf pl* electric appliances

elektroratiņi *nm pl* electric truck

elektroretinogr|a|fija [ā] *nf* electroretinography

elektrosildītājsega *nf* electric blanket

elektroskops *nm* electroscope

elektrospēkstacija *nf* power plant

elektrostacija *nf* power plant

elektrostatika *nf* electrostatics

elektrostatiski *adv* electrostatically

elektrostatisks *adj* electrostatic

elektrostimulācija *nf* electrostimulation

elektrošoka terapija *nf* electric shock therapy

elektrošoks *nm* electric shock

elektrotablo *indecl nm* electronic billboard; scoreboard

elektrote|ch|nika [h] *nf* electrotechnology

elektrote|ch|niķ/is [h] *nm*, ~e *nf* electrotechnician

elektrote|ch|niski [h] *adv* eletrotechnically

elektrote|ch|nisks [h] *adj* electrotechnical

elektroterapija *nf* electrotherapy

elektrotērauds *nm* electric steel

elektrotermisks *adj* electrothermal

elektrotīkls *nm* electrical network

elektrotipija *nf* electrotyping

elektrotransports *nm* electric transportation

elektrouzliesmotājs *nm* electric ignitor

elektrovadītspēja *nf* conductivity

elektrovilciens *nm* electric train

elektroviskozs *adj* electroviscous

elektrozāģis *nm* power saw

elementārdaļiņa *nf* elementary particle

elementārlādiņš *nm* elementary charge

elementāri *adv* elementarily

elementārs *adj* elementary

elementārskola *nf* elementary school

elementārstarotājs *nm* elementary radiator

elements *nm* 1. element; 2. electric cell; **sausais e.** dry battery

elengs *nm* milk tree

eleokarps *nm* Brisbane quandong

eleostearīnskābe *nf* eleostearic acid

elerons *nm* aileron

elev|a|tors [ā] *nm* 1. grain elevator; 2. bucket conveyor

elevons *nm* elevon

elfa *nf* elf

elidējums *nm* elision

elidēt *vt* elide

eliksīrs *nm* elixir

eliminācija *nf* elimination

eliminēt *vt* eliminate

elipse *nf* 1. ellipse; 2. ellipsis

elipsogr|a|fs [ā] *nm* ellipsograph

elipsoīds *nm* ellipsoid

elipsveidīgs *adj* ellipsoidal

eliptiski *adv* elliptically

eliptisks *adj* elliptic

eliptiskums *nm* ellipticity

elitārisms *nm* elitism

elitārs *adj* elite

elite *nf* (of raised animals or plants) elite

el|i|zija [ī] *nf* elision

elīzijs *nm* elysium

elkdievība *nf* idolatry

elkdievīgs *adj* idolatrous

elkdievs *nm* idol

elknuši *nm pl* primrose

elko/nis *nm* elbow ◊ **cauri ~ņi** out at the elbows

elkoņbalsts *nm* (of a chair) arm

elkoņkauls *nm* 1. ulna; 2. funny bone

elkoņu bruņas *nf pl* cubitière

elks *nm* idol

elksna *nf* alder growth

elksnaine *nf* alder growth

elksnājs *nm* alder growth

elksnene *nf* red hot milk cap

elksnis *nm* alder

elkši *nm pl* water soldier

elkšņains *adj* overgrown with alders

elku kalps *nm* idolater

elku pielūdzējs *nm* idolater

elle *nf* hell; ~s infernal

elles akmens *nm* lunar caustic

elles mašīna *nf* infernal machine

ellēties *vr* rave, rage, go wild

ellīgi *adv* (col.) very

ellīgs *adj* (col.) riled up, mad

elliņš *nm* slipway

elliski *adv* hellishly

ellisks *adj* hellish

ellišķi *adv* (col.) very

ellišķīgi *adv* (col.) very

ellišķīgs *adj* (col.) infernal

ellišķs *adj* (col.) infernal

elodeja *nf* common waterweed

elokvence *nf* eloquence

elokventi *adv* eloquently

elokvents *adj* eloquent

elongācija *nf* elongation

elpa *nf* breath; ~s **trūkums** shortness of breath; ~s **vilciens** breath, inhalation; **bez** ~s out of breath, breathless

elpe *nf* forage

elpēklis *nm* larynx

elpēties *vr* (reg.) struggle

elpināšana *nf* artificial respiration

elpināt *vt* apply artificial respiration

elpojums *nm* breath

elpošana *nf* breathing, respiration; **apgrūtināta e.** difficulty in breathing; ~s respiratory

elpot *vi* breathe

elpvads *nm* windpipe

ēls *nm* ale

elsa *nf*, usu. *pl* **elsas** sob, sobbing

elsāt *vi* **1.** sob; **2.** pant

elsiens *nm* gasp

elsiņš *nm* (barb.) dickey

elsis *nm* See **elši**

elsojiens *nm* gasp

elsoņa *nf* puffing

elsot *vi* **1.** sob; **2.** pant

elst *vi* breathe heavily, puff, pant, gasp; **elsdams pūzdams** huffing and puffing

elsuļot *vi* puff, pant

elšamā zāle *nf* mullein

elšāt *vi* puff, pant, gasp

elši *nm pl* water soldier

elšu zāle *nf* water soldier

eluents *nm* eluent

eluviāls *adj* eluvial

el[u]vijs [ū] *nm* eluvium

eļļ/a *nf* oil; **ēteriskā e.** essential oil; **kurināmā e.** fuel oil; **smagā kurināmā e.** bunker oil ◊ ~**u ugunī liet** add fuel to the fire

eļļaini *adv* oilily

eļļainība *nf* oiliness

eļļains *adj* oily

eļļainums *nm* oiliness

eļļasaugi *nm pl* oil producing plants

eļļas glezna *nf* oil painting

eļļas koks *nm* olive tree

eļļas krāsa *nf* oil paint

eļļas palma *nf* African oil palm

eļļas rausis *nm* oilcake

eļļas spiedne *nf* oil press

eļļas vanna *nf* oil pan

eļļjaka *nf* oilskin

eļļot *vt* oil

eļļoties *vr* be oiled

eļļveidīgs *adj* oily

ēma *nf* bait

emalja *nf* enamel

emaljēt *vt* enamel

emaljzvīņu *indecl adj* ganoid-scale

emalzvīņu skrimšļu zivis *nf pl* ganoid fishes

emaļa *nf* = **emalja**

emaļēt *vt* = **emaljēt**

emanācija *nf* emanation

emanācijs *nm* emanation (the element Em)

emancipācija *nf* emancipation

emancipēt *vt* emancipate

emancipēties *vr* become emancipated

emanometrs *nm* emanometer

embargo *nm indecl* embargo

emblēma *nf* emblem; logo

embl[e]mātiski [ē] *adv* emblematically

embl[e]mātisks [ē] *adj* emblematic

embolija *nf* embolism

embols *nm* embolus

embotiņ/i *nm pl* **1.** germander; **2.** houseleek

embotiņu veronika *nf* germander speedwell

embrijs *nm* embryo

embrioģen[e]ze [ē] *nf* embryogeny

embriolo/gs *nm*, ~ģe *nf* embryologist

embrioloģija *nf* embryology

embrionāli *adv* embryonically

embrionāls *adj* embryonic

embrionisks *adj* embryonic

embutes *nf pl* = **embotiņi**

embuti *nm pl* = **embotiņi**
emendācija *nf* amendment
emendēt *vt* amend
Ementāles siers *nm* Emmentaler cheese
emeraldīns *nm* emeraldine
emeritēt *vt* retire (with the emeritus status)
emerits *nm* emeritus (professor, official)
emeritūra *nf* emeritus office
emers *nm* emmer
emf[a]tiski [ā] *adv* emphatically
emf[a]tisk/s [ā] *adj* emphatic
emf[a]ze [ā] *nf* emphasis
emfiteuze *nf* emphyteusis
emfizēma *nf* emphysema
emigrācija *nf* emigration
emigrant/s *nm*, **~e** *nf* emigrant
emigrēt *vi* emigrate
emilijas *nf pl* Emilia
eminence *nf* eminence
eminents *adj* eminent
em[i]rāts [ī] *nm* emirate
emīrs *nm* emir
emisārs *nm* emissary
emisija *nf* **1.** (bus.) issue; **2.** (phys.) emission
emitents *nm* issuer
emiters *nm* (transistor) emitter
emitēt *vt* **1.** (bus.) issue; **2.** (phys.) emit
emocija *nf* emotion
emocionāli *adv* emotionally
emocion[a]litāte [ā] *nf* emotionality
emocionāls *adj* emotional
emocionālums *nm* emotionality
emodīns *nm* emodin
emotīvisms *nm* emotivism
empātija *nf* empathy
empiēma *nf* empyema
empīricist/s *nm*, **~e** *nf* empiricist
empīrija *nf* empirics
empīriķ/is *nm*, **~e** *nf* **1.** empiricist; **2.** empiric
emp[i]riokriticisms [ī] *nm* empiriocriticism
emp[i]riokritiķis [ī] *nm* proponent of empirio-
　　criticism

emp[i]riokritisks [ī] *adj* empiriocritical
empīriski *adv* empirically
empīrisks *adj* empirical
empīrisms *nm* empiricism
empīristisks *adj* empiristic
emplektīts *nm* emplectite
empora *nf* choir loft
emu *nm indecl* emu
emulācija *nf* (compu.) emulation
emul[a]tors [ā] *nm* (compu.) emulator
emulg[a]tors [ā] *nm* emulsifier
emuļģējamā mašīna *nf* empulsifier
emuļģēt *vt* emulsify
emuļģēties *vr* become emulsified
emulsificēt *vt* emulsify
emulsija *nf* emulsion
emulsīns *nm* emulsin
ēn/a *nf* shadow; shade; **~s puse** (fig.) downside;
　　~u valsts realm of shadows
ēnaine *nf* shade
ēnaini *adv* shadowily
ēnains *adj* shady; shadowy
ēnainums *nm* shadowiness; shadiness
enantēma *nf* enanthem
enantiomērija *nf* enantiomorphism
enantiomers *nm* enantiomorph
enantiomorfisks *adj* enantiomorphous
enantiomorfisms *nm* enantiomorphism
enantiomorfs *nm* enantiomorph
enantiotropija *nf* enantiotropy
enantiotropisks *adj* enantiotropic
ēnas palma *nf* talipot
ēnaugs *nm* shade plant
ēnava *nf* (poet.) shade
encefalīts *nm* encephalitis
encefalogr[a]fija [ā] *nf* encephalography
encefalop[a]tija [ā] *nf* encephalopathy
encēties *vr* (reg.) quarrel, fight; tease
en[ch]īridijs[h] *nm* enchiridion
enciāns *nm* gentian
ēncietība *nf* tolerance of shade
ēncietīgs *adj* shade-tolerant

enciklika *nf* encyclical

enciklopēdija *nf* encyclopedia

enciklopēdiski *adv* encylopedically

enciklopēdisks *adj* encyclopedic

enciklopēdiskums *nm* encyclopedic character; en-cyclopedic knowledge

enciklopēdist/s *nm*, ~e *nf* encyclopedist

encis *nm* (reg.) quarreler

endarterīts *nm* endarteritis

endēmija *nf* endemic (endemic disease)

endēmiski *adv* endemically

endēmisks *adj* endemic

endēmiskums *nm* endemism

endēms *nm* endemic species

endermisks *adj* endermic

endiobionts *nm* endobiotic organism

endīvija *nf* endive

endoderma *nf* endoderm

endodontika *nf* endodontia

endodontist/s *nm*, ~e *nf* endodontist

endog[a]mija [ā] *nf* endogamy

endog[a]misks [ā] *adj* endogamous

endog[e]ns [ē] *adj* endogenous

endokardīts *nm* endocarditis

endokards *nm* endocardium

endokr[i]nolog/s [ī] *nm*, ~ģe *nf* endocri-nologist

endokr[i]noloģija [ī] *nf* endocrinology

endokrīns *adj* endocrine

endolimfa *nf* endolymph

endometrs *nm* endometrium

endometrīts *nm* endometritis

endomorfija *nf* endomorphism

endomor(isk)s *adj* endomorphic

endoparazītisks *adj* endoparasitic

endoparazīts *nm* endoparasite

endoplazma *nf* endoplasm

endoskopija *nf* endoscopy

endoskops *nm* endoscope

endosperma *nf* endosperm

endotēliāls *adj* endothelial

endotēlijs *nm* endothelium

endotermisks *adj* endothermic

endotoksīns *nm* endotoxin

enduro *indecl nm* enduro

endzeliņš *nm* little finger

ēnene *nf* toothwort

eneol[i]ts [ī] *nm* aeneolithic period

energoapgāde *nf* power supply

energoiekārta *nf* power plant

energomašīnbūve *nf* construction of power generators

energopatēriņš *nm* power consumption

energoresursi *nm pl* energy sources

energosadale *nf* power distribution; power grid

energosaimniecība *nf* power industry

energosistēma *nf* power distribution system

energotechnoloģija *nf* power technology

energouzņēmums *nm* power plant

enerģētika *nf* energetics

enerģētiķ/is *nm*, ~e *nf* energeticist

enerģētiski *adv* energetistically

enerģētisk/s *adj* energetistic

enerģētisms *nm* energism

enerģija *nf* energy

enerģijas nezūdamības likums *nm* law of conservation of energy

enerģijas pastāvība *nf* conservation of energy

enerģiski *adv* energetically

enerģisks *adj* energetic, vigorous; enterprising

enerģiskums *nm* energy

Engelmaņa egle *nf* Engelmann spruce

englaciāls *adj* englacial

enharmonija *nf* enharmonic note

enharmoniski *adv* enharmonically

enharmonisks *adj* enharmonic

enharmonisms *nm* enharmonic

enhiridijs *nm* = enchirīdijs

enigmātiski *adv* enigmatically

enigmātisks *adj* enigmatic

ēniņa *nf dim* of ēna, shadow

enkaustika *nf* encaustic

enkefalīts *nm* encephalitis

enkefalogr[a]fija [ā] *nf* encephalography
enkefalop[a]tija [ā] *nf* encephalopathy
enkl[i]tika [ī] *nf* enclitic
enkl[i]tisks [ī] *adj* enclytic
enkl[i]ze [ī] *nf* enclisis
enkomjenda *nf* encomienda
enkura nodevas *nf pl* anchorage (toll)
enkura trice *nf* cat tackle
enkurboja *nf* buoy
enkurbulta *nf* anchor bolt
enkurceltnis *nm* anchor davit
enkurķēde *nf* chain cable
enkurlaiva *nf* anchor hoy
enkurnieks *nm* raft pilot
enkurot *vt* anchor
enkurplātne *nf* anchor plate
enkur/s *nm* 1. anchor; uz ~a at anchor; 2. (el.)
    armature; 3. (of clocks) crotch; 4. (obs.) a
    measure of wine; 5. (of a magnet) keeper
enkurskrūve *nf* stay bolt
enkurspilve *nf* windlass
enkurtauva *nf* anchor cable
enkurvieta *nf* anchorage
ēnmīlis *nm* shade-loving plant
ēnojums *nm* shading
enolāts *nm* enolate
enoloģija *nf* oenology
enorms *adj* enormous
ēnot *vt* shade
ēnoties *vr* 1. silhouette; 2. cast a shadow
ēnpaparde *nf* saw fern
ēnpelēks *adj* grayish
ēns *nm* apparition, ghost
ēnsmilga *nf* millet grass
entalpija *nf* enthalpy
entāze *nf* entasis
entele[ch]ija [h] *nf* entelechy
enterīts *nm* enteritis
enterobioze *nf* enterobiasis
enterokolīts *nm* enterocolitis
enterovīruss *nm* enterovirus
entoderma *nf* endoderm

entomofāgs *nm* entomophagous organism
entomofilija *nf* entomophily
entomolo/gs *nm*, ~ģe *nf* entomologist
entomoloģija *nf* entomology
entomoloģisks *adj* entomological
entoptisks *adj* entoptical
entropais *defin adj* enthropic
entropija *nf* entropy
entuziasms *nm* enthusiasm
entuziastiski *adv* enthusiastically
entuziastisks *adj* enthusiastic
entuziast/s *nm*, ~e *nf* enthusiast
ēnu attēls *nm* shadowgraph
ēnu kabinets *nm* shadow cabinet;
ēnulīte *nf* hepatica
enurēze *nf* enuresis
envaironmentalisms *nm* environmentalism
enz[i]misks [ī] *adj* enzymatic
enzims or enzīms *nm* enzyme
enzootija *nf* enzootic
enžambements *nm* enjambement
eņģe *nf* hinge
eņģelis *nm* angel
eņģeliski *adv* angelically
eņģelisks *adj* angelic
eņģelītis *nm* 1. *dim* of eņģelis, little angel;
    2. a Latvian folk dance
eņģeļmati *nm pl* angel's hair
eņģīgs *adj* (col.) strong
eocēns *nm* Eocene
eolisks *adj* 1. (mus.) aeolic; 2. (geol.) eolian
eol[i]tisks [ī] *adj* Eolithic
eol[i]ts [ī] *nm* Eolithic period
eol/s *adj* (geol.) 1. eolian; 2. *defin* ~ais Eo-
    lithic
eons *nm* eon
eozinof[i]ls [ī] *adj* eosinophile
eozīns *nm* eosin
eozoisks *adj* Eozoic
eozojs *nm* Eozoic
eozoons *nm* eozoon
epaktas *nf pl* epact

epar|ch|ija |h| *nf* eparchy

eparchs *nm* eparch

e-pasts *nm* e-mail

epeiroģen|e|tisks |ē| *adj* epeirogenic

epeiroģen|e|ze |ē| *nf* epeirogeny

ependima *nf* ependyma

epentetiski *adv* epenthetically

epentetisks *adj* epenthetic

epent|e|ze |ē| *nf* epenthesis

epiblasts *nm* epiblast

epicentrs *nm* epicenter

epicikloīds *nm* epicyloid

epicikls *nm* epicycle

epidēmija *nf* epidemic

epid|e|miologs |ē| *nm*, ~ģe *nf* epidemiologist

epid|e|mioloģija |ē| *nf* epidemiology

epid|e|mioloģisks |ē| *adj* epidemiologic

epid|e|miski |ē| *adv* epidemically

epid|e|misks |ē| *adj* epidemic

epidēmiskums *nm* epidemicity

epidendrs *nm* epidendrum

epiderma *nf* epidermis

epidermisks *adj* epidermal

epidiaskops *nm* slide-opaque projector

epidots *nm* epidote

epif|a|nija |ā| *nf* epiphany

epifenom|e|ns |ē| *nm* epiphenomenon

epifils *nm* crab cactus

epifīts *nm* epiphyte

epifīze *nf* 1. epiphysis; 2. pineal gland

epifora *nf* epistrophe

epiforisks *adj* epistrophic

epiglotis *nm* epiglottis

epigoniski *adv* epigonically

epigonisks *adj* epigonic

epigonisms *nm* epigonism

epigon/s *nm*, ~e *nf* epigone

epigr|a|fija |ā| *nf* epigraphy

epigrafiķis *nm* epigraphist

epigrafisks *adj* epigraphic

epigr|a|fs |ā| *nm* epigraph

epigramma *nf* epigram

epigrammatiķis *nm* epigrammatist

epigrammatisks *adj* epigrammatic

epiģen|e|tisks |ē| *adj* epigenetic

epika *nf* epic poetry

epikūriet/is *nm*, ~e *nf* Epicurean

epikūrisks *adj* Epicurean; epicurean

epikūrisms *nm* Epicureanism; epicurism

epikūristisks *adj* Epicurean; epicurean

epikūrs *nm* epicure

epiķ/is *nm*, ~e *nf* prose writer

epilācija *nf* epilation

epil|a|tors |ā| *nm* epilator

epil|e|psija |ē| *nf* epilepsy

epil|e|ptiķ/is |ē| *nm*, ~e *nf* epileptic

epil|e|ptiski |ē| *adv* epileptically

epil|e|ptisks |ē| *adj* epileptic

epilimnijs *nm* epilimnion

epilogs *nm* epilogue

epimedijas *nf pl* Epimedium

epimers *nm* epimer

epinīkija *nf* eponychium

epipolārs *adj* epipolar

episki *adv* epically

episkopālsistēma *nf* episcopate

episkopāts *nm* episcopate

episkops *nm* opaque projector

episks *adj* epic

epist|e|misks |ē| *adj* epistemic

epistemoloģija *nf* epistemology

epistemoloģiski *adv* epistemologically

epistemoloģisks *adj* epistemological

epists *nm* epic poet

epistolārs *adj* epistolary

epistologr|a|fija |ā| *nf* epistolography

epistulārs *adj* epistolary

epistrofa *nf* epistrophe

epistula *nf* epistle

epit|a|fija |ā| *nf* epitaph

epitaksiāls *adj* epitaxial

epital|a|mija |ā| *nf* epithalamium

epitēlijķermenītis *nm* parathyroid gland

epitēlijs *nm* epithelium

epitēlķermenītis *nm* parathyroid gland

epitēlšūna *nf* epithelial cell

epitermāls *adj* epithermal

epitetisks *adj* epithetic

epitets *nm* epithet

epitome *nf* epitome

epizode *nf* episode

epizodiski *adv* episodically

epizodisks *adj* episodic

epizodiskums *nm* episodic nature

epizods *nm* episode

epizootija *nf* epizootic

epizootisks *adj* epizootic

epizootoloģija *nf* epizootology

epizootoloģiski *adv* epizootologically

epizootoloģisks *adj* epizootological

epo|ch|a |h| *nf* epoch

epo|ch|āls |h| *adj* epoch-making, epochal

epods *nm* epod

epoks|i|dlīme |ī| *nf* epoxy glue

epoks|i|ds |ī| *nm* epoxide

epoks|i|dsveķi |ī| *nm pl* epoxy resin

epolete *nf* epaulet

epon|i|ms |ī| *nm* eponym

epop|e|ja |ē| *nf* epopee

epop|e|jiski |ē| *adv* epically

epop|e|jisks |ē| *adj* epic

eposs *nm* epic poem

eps *nm* epic poem

epsilons *nm* epsilon

epsomīts *nm* epsomite

ēra I *nf* era

ēra II *nf* öre

eragroste *nf* love grass

erante *nm pl* winter aconite

er|a|tisks |ā| *adj* (geol.) erratic

ērbēģis *nm* = ērbērģis

ērbērģis *nm* (hist.) cabin, hut

erbijs *nm* erbium

ērce *nf* 1. tick; 2. mite

ērceklis *nm* sourpuss

ercene *nf* (col.) queen of hearts

erceņģelis *nm* archangel

ērcesis *nm* (reg.) juniper

ērceša *nf* (reg.) quarrelsome woman

ērcēties *vr* fret, chafe

erchercogiene *nf* archduchess

erchercogs *nm* archduke

ērcīgi *adv* (col.) quarrelsomely

ērcīgs *adj* (col.) quarrelsome

ērcināt *vt* tease

ērcis *nm* (reg.) juniper

ērdavs *adj* flexible; adroit; (of speech) fluent

erdelterj|e|rs |ē| *nm* Airedale terrier

ercs *nm* (cards) hearts

erecija *nf* ehretia

erekcija *nf* erection

erem|i|tāža |ī| *nf* hermitage

eremītisms *nm* hermitry

eremīts *nm* hermit

eremofīts *nm* eremophyte, desert plant

eremurs *nm* eremurus

ergastuls *nm* ergastulum

ergatīvs *nm* (ling.) ergative

ērglene *nf* columbine

ērglis *nm* eagle; 2. (game) pitch-and-toss; 3. (of coins) tails

ērglītis *nm dim* of ērglis, little eagle

ērglpaparde *nf* bracken

ērglveidīgie *nm pl* Aquilidae

ergodisks *adj* ergodic

ergogr|a|fs |ā| *nm* ergograph

ergogramma *nf* ergogram

ergokalciferols *nm* ergocalciferol

ergometrija *nf* ergometric measurement

ergometrs *nm* ergometer

ergonomija *nf* ergonomy

ergonomika *nf* ergonomy

ergotamīns *nm* ergotamine

ergotioneīns *nm* ergothioneine

ergotisms *nm* ergotism

ergots *nm* ergot

ergs I *nm* (cgs unit) erg

ergs II *nm* (geol.) erg

ērģeles *nf pl* (mus.) organ

ērģelēt *vi* (col.) play the organ

ērģeļkoncerts *nm* organ concert

ērģeļmāksla *nf* the art of organ playing

ērģeļmūzika *nf* organ music

ērģelnie/ks *nm*, ~ce *nf* organist

ērģeļpunkts *nm* pedal point

erģīties *vr* (reg.) quarrel

eriants *nm* erianthus, plume grass

erickiņš *nm* common redstart

ērikas *nf pl* heath

erines *nf pl* Erinus

eringija *nf* sea holly

eriobotrijas *nf pl* Eriobotrya

erio[ch]loja [h] *nf* dotted millet

eriofiles *nf pl* Eriophyllum

eriokaules *nf pl* pipewort

eristika *nf* eristic

eristisks *adj* eristic

eritēma *nf* erythema

eritēmija *nf* erythema

eritrejiet/is *nm*, ~e *nf* Eritrean

eritri[ch]ija [h] *nf* mountain allocarya

eritrina *nf* erythrina

eritrīts *nm* erythritol

eritroblasts *nm* erythroblast

eritrocīts *nm* erythrocite

eritroze *nf* erythrose

eritruloze *nf* erythrulose

erkera logs *nm* bay window; oriel

erkers *nm* (arch.) bay

erkerveida *indecl adj* (arch.) bay-shaped

ērkšķainība *nf* thorniness

ērkšķains *adj* thorny

ērkšķauzas *nf pl* awnless bromegrass

ērkšķenājs *nm* goosberry bushes

ērkšķene *nf* gooseberry

ērkšķis *nm* thorn

ērkšķoga *nf* gooseberry

ērkšķogulājs *nm* gooseberries (bushes)

ērkšķogulāju kode *nf* 1. gooseberry fruitworm;
2. gooseberry spanworm

ērkšķogulāju lapu uts *nf* gooseberry aphis

ērkšķogulāju miltrasa *nf* gooseberry mildew

ērkšķogulāju sprīžmetis *nm* gooseberry moth

ērkšķogulāju zāģlapsene *nf* gooseberry sawfly

ērkšķu krūms *nm* briar

ērkšķu plūmīte *nf* 1. blackthorn; 2. sloe

ērkšķu roze *nf* dog rose

ērkšķuzāle *nf* prickle fescue

ērkulis *nm* 1. distaff; 2. (of wool, flax, or tow that is set on the distaff for spinning) bunch; 3. (folk.) erkulis (an adorned, sistrum-like musical instrument with bells, used at weddings)

ērķis *nm* (reg.) juniper

ērlifts *nm* air lift

ērmeklīgs *adj* droll; weird

ērmeklis *nm* (col.) weirdo

ērmība *nf* drollness; weirdness

ērmīgi *adv* drolly; weirdly

ērmīgs *adj* droll; weird

ērmīgums *nm* drollness; weirdness

ērmkaķis *nm* (col.) weirdo

ērmnieks *nm* (obs.) monkey

ermo[n]ikas [ņ] *nf pl* concertina

ērmoti *adv* drolly; weirdly

ērmoties *vr* droll

ērmotīgs *adj* (col.) weird

ērmots *adj* droll; weird

ērms *nm* (col.) clown, buffoon; eccentric; weirdo

ērms *adj* droll; weird

ērmulis *nm* weirdo

erodēt *vi*, *vt* erode

erog[e]nisks [ē] *adj* erogeous

erog[e]ns [ē] *adj* erogenous

erotika *nf* 1. eroticism; 2. erotica

erotiķ/is *nm*, ~e *nf* erotic

erotiski *adv* erotically

erotisks *adj* erotic

erotiskums *nm* eroticism

erotisms *nm* eroticism

erotom[a]nija [ā] *nf* erotomania

erozija *nf* erosion

errastība *nf* (obs.) unplesantness

erreklis *nm* (obs.) grouch

errība *nf* peevishness, surliness, crabbiness

errīgi *adv* peevishly, surlily, crabbily

errīgs *adj* peevish, surly, crabby

errīgums *nm* peevishness, surliness, crabbiness

erroties *vr* (col.) fuss, get mad at

ersināt *vt* tease

ērskis *nm* manna-grass

erskoties *vr* (reg.) quarrel

ersteds *nm* oersted

ērti *adv* **1.** comfortably; **2.** conveniently

ērtība *nf* **1.** comfort; **2.** convenience

ērts *adj* **1.** comfortable; **2.** convenient

ērtums *nm* **1.** comfort; **2.** convenience

erudēti *adv* = **erudīti**

erudēt/s *adj* = **erudīts**

erudīcija *nf* erudition

erudīti *adv* eruditely

erudīts *nm* erudite

erudīts *adj* erudite

erudītums *nm* erudition

eruka *nf* garden rocket

erukskābe *nf* erucic acid

erupcija *nf* eruption

eruptīvs *adj* eruptive

ērzelis *nm* stallion

es *pron* I; **es pats** I myself; **es tas esmu** it is I; *indecl nm* I, self, ego

esamība *nf* being, existence

es[ch]atoloģija [h] *nf* eschatology

es[ch]atoloģisks [h]s *adj* eschatological

eseja *nf* essay

esejist/s *nm*, **~e** *nf* essayist

esence *nf* essence

esentiālisms *nm* essentialism

eseris *nm* (hist.) social-revolutionary

esesietis *nm* SS-man

esība *nf* being, existence

eskadra *nf* fleet

eskadriļa *nf* (air force) squadron

eskadrons *nm* squadron; (cavalry) troop

eskalācija *nf* escalation

eskalāde *nf* escalade

eskal[a]tors [ā] *nm* escalator

eskalops *nm* scallopini

eskapāde *nf* escapade

eskarps *nm* scarp

eskimoss *nm*, **~iete** *nf* Eskimo

eskortēt *vt* escort

eskortpatruļa *nf* escort patrol

eskorts *nm* escort

eskudo *indecl nm* escudo

eskulaps *nm* Aesculapius, physician

eskvairs *nm* esquire

esliņš *nm* (reg.) dace

ēslis *nf* **1.** bait; **2.** (col.) food

ēsma *nf* **1.** bait; **2.** (col.) food

esme *nf* being, existence

esošs *adj, part* of **būt** existing

esot *part* of **būt** being; indirect discourse mood of **būt**

espanders *nm* (athletic training equipment) chest pull

esparsete *nf* sainfoin

esperantist/s *nm*, **~e** *nf* Esperantist

esperanto *indecl nm* Esperanto

esplanāde *nf* esplanade

esseksīts *nm* essexite

ēst *vt, vi* **1.** eat; have (a food item); **badīgi ē.** wolf one's food; **ē. kā gailis** eat next to nothing; **ē. no rokas** (fig.) eat out of one's hand; **veseli ēdu-ši!** bon appetit! **2.** (col.) corrode; **3.** (col., fig.) hurt, be mean to so; **4.** (col., of insects) bite, sting

estakāde *nf* trestle bridge

estamps *nm* (art) print

estergumija *nf* ester gum

esterifikācija *nf* esterification

esteris *nm* ester

estētika *nf* = **aistētika**

estētiski *adv* = **aistētiski**

estētisks *adj* = **aistētisks**

estētisms *nm* = **aistētisms**

estētizācija *nf* = **aistētizācija**

estēts *nm*, **~e** *nf* = **aistēts**

estēzija *nf* esthesia, sensibility

ēstgriba *nf* appetite; **~s veicinātājs** appetizer

ēsties *vr* (col.) **1.** (with reference person in dative case) be disgusted, disappointed; **2.** bicker, squabble; **3.** (of acids, effects of friction) eat its way into; **ē. virsū** bother, annoy

estrāde *nf* stage; platform;

estrādes dziesmiņa *nf* popular song

estrādes māksla *nf* variety acts

estrādes mākslinieks *nm* variety artist

estrādes mūzika *nf* light music

estrādes uzvedums *nm* variety show

estradiols *nm* estradiol

estrādisks *adj* (of music) popular

estragons *nm* tarragon

estriols *nm* estriol

estrog[e]ns [ē] *nm* estrogen

estrons *nm* estron

estrs *nm* estrus

estuārs *nm* estuary

ēstuve *nf* diner; refectory, messroom; cafeteria

ēstvārītāja *nf* cook

ešafots *nm* scaffold

ēšana *nf* eating; meal

ēšanās *nfr* bickering, squabble

ešelonēt *vt* echelon

ešelons *nm* (mil.) **1.** echelon; **2.** troop train

ēška *nf, nm* (reg.) glutton

ēšķis *nm* (reg.) glutton

ešolcija *nf* California poppy

etalonaparāts *nm* calibration instrument

etalons *nm* standard

etalontonis *nm* reference tone

etamīns *nm* estamine

etanols *nm* ethanol

etāns *nm* ethane

etap/s *nm* **1.** stage, period; **2.** (sports) stretch, portion of a distance; **3.** (mil.) rear; **4.** (hist.) transportation of convicts; halting place for transported convicts

etaž[e]re [ē] *nf* whatnot

ēterifikācija *nf* etherification

ēteris *nm* (chem.) ether

ēteriski *adv* ethereally

ēterisks *adj* ethereal

ēterizēt *vt* etherize

ēters *nm* (philos., phys.) ether

ēticisms *nm* ethicalness

etīde *nf* **1.** (painting) study; **2.** (mus.) étude

ētika *nf* ethics

etiķa esence *nf* concentrated vinegar

etiķējamā mašīna *nf* labeler

etiķe/te *nf* **1.** label; **~šu piemērošan**a (fig.) labeling; **2.** etiquette

etiķis *nm* vinegar

etiķkaļķis *nm* calcium acetate

etiķkoks *nm* staghorn sumac

etiķskābais mālūdens *nm* Burow's solution

etiķskābais svins *nm* lead acetate

etiķskābe *nf* acetic acid

etiķskāb/s *adj* acetic; *defin* **~ais** acetate

etiķūdens *nm* acetic liquor

etilacetāts *nm* ethyl acetate

etilalkohols *nm* ethyl alcohol

etilbenzols *nm* ethyl benzene

etilbrom[i]ds [ī] *nm* ethyl bromide

etilbutirāts *nm* ethyl butyrate

etilceluloza *nf* ethyl cellulose

etil[ch]lor[i]ds [h][ī] *nm* ethyl chloride

etilēnamīns *nm* ethylamine

etilēnglikols *nm* ethylene glycol

etilēnoks[i]ds [ī] *nm* ethylene oxide

etilēns *nm* ethylene

etilēteris *nm* ethyl ether

etilfluor[i]ds [ī] *nm* ethyl fluoride

etiljod[i]ds [ī] *nm* ethyl iodide

etilnitrīts *nm* ethyl nitrite

etils *nm* ethyl

etilspirts *nm* ethyl alcohol

etimolo/gs *nm*, ~ģe *nf* etymologist

etimoloģija *nf* etymology

etimoloģiski *adv* ethymologically

etimoloģisks *adj* etymological

etimoloģizēt *vt* etymologize

etimons *nm* etymon

etiolācija *nf* etiolation

etioloģija *nf* etiology

etioloģiski *adv* etiologically

etioloģisks *adj* etiological

etiop/ietis or etiop/s *nm*, ~iete, ~e *nf* Ethiopian

ētiski *adv* ethically

ētisks *adj* ethical

etniski *adv* ethnically

etnisks *adj* ethnic

etnocentrisms *nm* ethnocentrism

etnogr[a]fija [ā] *nf* ethnography

etnogr[a]fiski *adv* ethnographically

etnogr[a]fisks [ā] *adj* ethnographic

etnogr[a]f/s [ā] *nm*, ~e *nf* ethnographer

etnoģen[e]ze [ē] *nf* ethnogeny

etnoģeogr[a]fija [ā] *nf* ethnogeography

etnoģeogr[a]fisks [ā] *adj* ethnogeographic

etnolingvistika *nf* ethnolinguistics

etnolo/gs *nm*, ~ģe *nf* ethnologist

etnoloģija *nf* ethnology

etnoloģiski *adv* ethnologically

etnoloģisks *adj* ethnologic

etnomedicīna *nf* ethnomedicine

etnometodoloģija *nf* ethnomethodology

etnom[u]zikoloģija [ū] *nf* ethnomusicology

etnonims *nm* ethnonym

etnops[īch]oloģija [ih] *nf* ethnopsychology

etnops[īch]oloģiski [ih] *adv* ethnopsychologically

etnops[īch]oloģisks [ih] *adj* ethnopsychological

etnoss *nm* ethnos

etoks[i]ds [ī] *nm* ethoxide

[e]tolo/gs [ē] *nm*, ~ģe *nf* ethologist

[e]toloģija [ē] *nf* ethology

[e]toloģiski [ē] *adv* ethologically

[e]toloģisks [ē] *adj* ethologic

ētoss *nm* ethos

etruski *nm pl* Etruscans

etvija *nf* cigarette case; etui

e[uch]aristija [ih] nf eucharist

e[uch]aristisks [ih] *adj* eucharistic

e[uch]oloģija [ih] *nf* euchologion

e[u]d[ai]monisks [i][e] *adj* eudaemonic

e[u]d[ai]monisms [i][e] *nm* eudaemonism

e[u]fēmiski [i] *adv* euphemistically

e[u]fēmisks [i] *adj* euphemistic

e[u]fēmisms [i] *nm* euphemism

e[u]fonija [i] *nf* euphony

e[u]foniski [i] *adv* euphonically

e[u]fonisks [i] *adj* euphonic

e[u]forbija [i] *nf* euphorbia, spurge

e[u]forbijs [i] *nm* euphorbium

e[u]forija [i] *nf* euphoria

e[u]foriski [i] *adv* euphorically

e[u]forisks [i] *adj* euphoric

e[u]forizēt [i] *vt* induce euphoria

e[u]fotisks [i] *adj* euphotic

e[u]fuisms [i] *nm* euphuism

e[u]g[e]nika [i][ē] *nf* eugenics

e[u]g[e]niķ/is [i][ē] *nm*, ~e *nf* eugenicist

e[u]g[e]niski [i][ē] *adv* eugenically

e[u]g[e]nisks [i][ē] *adj* eugenic

e[u]g[e]nist/s [i][ē] *nm*, ~e *nf* eugenicist

e[u]genols [i] *nm* eugenol

e[u]geosinklināle [i] *nf* eugeosyncline

e[u]glenas [i] *nf pl* Eugelena

e[u]glenofīti [i] *nm pl* Euglenophyta

e[u]hemerisms [i] *nm* euhemerism

e[u]kaīns [i] *nm* eucaine

e[u]kaipteļļa [i] *nf* eucalyptus oil

e[u]kaliptols [i] *nm* cineole

e[u]kalipts [i] *nm* eucalyptus

e[u]kariots [i] *nm* eukaryote

e[u]komija [i] *nf* Eucommia

e[u]krazija [i] *nf* eucrasia

e|u|lalija |i| *nf* eulalia

e|u|loģija |i| *nf* eulogy

e|u|nomija |i| *nf* eunomy

e|u|n|ūch|oīdisms |i||uh| *nm* eunochoidism

e|u|n|ū|chs |i||u| *nm* eunuch

e|u|patrīds |ī| *nm* eupatrid

e|u|praksija |i| *nf* eupraxia

e|u|rihalīns |i| *nm* euryhaline

e|u|rija |i| *nf* Eurya

e|u|riterms |i| *adj* eurythermal

e|u|ritmija |i| *nf* eurhythmy, eurythmics

e|u|statisks |i| *adj* eustatic

e|u|tan|a|zija |i||ā| *nf* euthanasia

e|u|tēktisks |i||e| *adj* eutectic

e|u|tēktoīdisks |i||e| *adj* eutectoid

e|u|trofikācija |i| *nf* eutrophication

e|u|trofisks |i| *adj* eutrophic

e|u|trofs |i| *adj* eutrophic

evakuācija *nf* evacuation

evaku|a|tors |ā| *nm* wrecker

evakuēt *vt* evacuate

evakuētais *nom adj* evacuee

evakuēties *vr* evacuate

evalvācija *nf* evaluation

evanģ|e|lijs |ē| *nm* Gospel

evanģelis *nm* Gospel

evanģ|e|liski |ē| *adv* evangelically

evanģ|e|lisks |ē| *adj* evangelical

evanģ|e|list/s |ē| *nm*, ~e *nf* evangelist

evanģelizācija *nf* evangelization

evanģelizēt *vt* evangelize

evaporācija *nf* evaporation

evaporimetrs *nm* evaporimeter

evaporīts *nm* evaporite

evāzija *nf* evasion

ēvele *nf* (tool) plane

ēveles zobs *nm* plane iron

ēvelēt *vt* plane; (of cabbage) shred

ēve|l|galds |l| *nm* joiner's bench

ēvelīte *nf dim* of ēvele, small plane

ēve|l|kalts |l| *nm* plane cutter

ēve|l|mašīna |l| *nf* planer; **radiālā e.** radial planer

ēve|l|nazis |l| *nm* plane iron

ēve|l|sols |l| *nm* joiner's bench

ēve|l|skaidas |l| *nf pl* wood shavings

ēve|l|zobs |l| *nm* plane iron

evenk/s *nm*, ~iete *nf* Evenk, Tungus

eventuāli *adv* eventually; **ja e.** in case

eventu|a|litāte |ā| *nf* eventuality

eventuāls *adj* eventual

ēverģēlība *nf* (col.) prank

ēverģēlīgs *adj* (col.) given to pranks

ēverģēl/is *nm*, ~e *nf* (col.) prankster

evertebrats *nm* invertebrate

evidence *nf* evidence

evidenti *adv* evidently

evidents *adj* evident

evikcija *nf* eviction

evolūcija *nf* evolution

evol|u|cionārs |ū| *adj* evolutionary

evol|u|cionēt |ū| *vi* evolve

evol|u|cionisms |ū| *nm* evolutionism

evol|u|cionist/s |ū| *nm*, ~e *nf* evolutionist

ēze *nf* forge

ēzelis *nm* donkey; ass

ēzelisks *adj* asinine

ēzelītis *nm dim* of ēzelis, little donkey

ezerains *adj* laky

ezera purva ķauķis *nm* reed warbler

ezera rūda *nf* limnic iron ore

ezera rutks *nm* water hemlock

ezera salaka *nf* smelt

ezerdobe *nf* lake basin

ezerenes *nf pl* quillwort

ezergailis *nm* bittern

ezeriņš *nm dim* of ezers, lakelet

ezerkaļķi *nm pl* lake marl

ezermala *nf* lakeshore

ezermaliet/is *nm*, ~e *nf* lakeshore dweller

ezermalnieks *nm* = ezermalietis

ezernieks *nm* = ezermalietis

ezerpils *nm* castle in the lake

ezerrieksts *nm* water chestnut

ezerroze *nf* water lily

ezer/s *nm* lake; **daudzzarains e.** dendritic lake; **~a** lacustrine

ezersaimniecība *nf* aquiculture

ezersala *nf* lake island

ezeru forele *nf* brown trout

ezeru lakstīgala *nf* sedge warbler; (iron.) frog

ezeru meldri *nm pl* bulrush

ezeru strazds *nm* sedge warbler

ezeru varde *nfr* marsh frog

ezervālītes *nf pl* cattail

ezīgi *adv* testily

ezīgs *adj* testy, miffy

ezis *nm* hedgehog

ezītis *nm* **1.** *dim* of **ezis**, young hedgehog; **2.** crew cut

ezoteriski *adv* esoterically

ezoterisks *adj* esoteric

eža I *nf* balk, edge of a field

eža II *nf, nm* glutton

ēža *nf* (reg.) feeding rack

ežadatu lipene *nf* stickseed

ežektors *nm* ejector

eženieks *nm* neighbor, neighboring farmer

ežgalvī/te *nm* burr reed

ežmala *nf* or **ežmalis** *nm* balk, edge of a field

ežu zāle *nf* yarrow

ežziede *nm* globe thistle

F

fa *nf indecl* (mus.) F

fabiāns *nm* Fabian

fabricēt *vt* fabricate

fabrika *nf* factory, mill; **~s darbs** machine-made; **~s preces** factory-made goods

fabrikācija *nf* fabrication

fabrikants *nm*, **~e** *nf* factory owner

fabrikas zīme *nf* trade mark

fabrikāts *nm* manufactured product

f|a|bula [ā] *nf* **1.** fable; **2.** (lit.) plot, story line

f|a|bulist/s [ā] *nm*, **~e** *nf* fabulist

facēlija *nf* wild heliotrope

faciāls *adj* facial

fācija *nf* (geol.) facies

facits *nm* outcome, result

faetons *nm* phaeton

fagocitoze *nf* phagocytosis

fagoc|i|ts [ī] *nm* phagocyte

fagotist/s *nm*, **~e** *nf* bassoonist

fagots *nm* bassoon

fāgs *nm* phage, bacteriophage

fails *nm* (compu.) file

fain- See **fen-**

faivokloks *nm* five o'clock tea

fajanss *nm* faience

fakirs *nm* = **faķīrs**

faksēt *vt* fax

faksimils *nm* facsimile

faksimilsakari *nm pl* facsimile telecommunications

fakss *nm* fax

faktiski *adv* actually, as a matter of fact

faktisks *adj* real, actual, factual; (of proof) material

faktitīvs *adj* factitive

faktogr|a|fija [ā] *nf* (mere) recording of facts

faktogr|a|fisks [ā] *adj* pertaining to the (mere) re-cording of facts

faktoranal|i|ze [ī] *nf* (stat.) factor analysis

faktoriāls *nm* (math.) factorial

faktorija *nf* trading station

faktorings *nm* (bus., jur.) factoring

faktors *nm* factor

faktotums *nm* factotum

fakts *nm* fact ◊ **f. !** (col.) it's a fact!

faktu ekspozīcija *nf* bill of particulars

faktūra *nf* **1.** (mus., art) texture; **2.** invoice

fakt|u|rējums [ū] *nm* texture

fakt|u|rēt [ū] *vt* texture

fakultāte *nf* (subdivision of university) school

fakult|a|tīvi [ā] *adv* optionally; electively

fakult|a|tīvs [ā] *adj* optional; (educ., of courses) elective

faķīrs *nm* fakir

falanga *nf* 1. phalanx; 2. phalange; 3. phalangid

falangist/s *nm*, ~e *nf* Falangist

falce *nf* rabbet, groove

falcēt *vt* rabbet, groove

faleristika *nf* badge collecting

faleristiķ/is *nm*, ~e *nf* badge collector

faliski *nm* Falisci

falkārija *nf* falcaria

falkonets *nm* falconet

falle *nf* (naut.) halyard

falliments *nm* bankruptcy, failure; stoppage of payments

falls *nm* phallus

falltrepe *nf* (naut.) Jacob's ladder

falsets *nm* falsetto

falsgrāfs *nm* palsgrave

falsificējums *nm* forgery, counterfeit

falsificēt *vt* forge, counterfeit; falsify

falsifikācija *nf* forgery, counterfeit; falsification

falsifikātor/s *nm*, ~e *nf* forger, counterfeiter; falsifier

falsifikāts *nm* forgery, counterfeit

falšborti *nm pl* (of a tank) skirting

falšs *adj* (sl.) fake

falte *nf* (barb.) fold

familiaritāte *nf* liberties, unceremoniousness, familiarity

familiāri *adv* unceremoniously

familiārs *adj* unceremonious, familiar

fam|i|lija [ī] *nf* (obs.) family

famozs *adj* famous, legendary

famuls *nm* famulus

fanariots *nm* Phanariot

fanātiķ/is *nm*, ~e *nf* fanatic

fanātiski *adv* fanatically

fanātisks *adj* fanatical

fanātiskums *nm* fanaticism

fanātisms *nm* fanaticism

fandango *indecl nm* fandango

fanerograms *nm* phanerogram

fanerozojs *nm* Phanerozoic

fanfara *nf* 1. trumpet; 2. fanfare

fanfaronāde *nf* fanfaronade

fanfarons *nm* fanfaron, braggart

fanglomerāts *nm* fanglomerate

fantasma *nf* phantasm

fantasmagorija *nf* phantasmagoria

fantastika *nf* fantasy; fantasy fiction; **zinātniskā f.** science fiction

fantasts *nm* fantast, visionary, dreamer

fantazēt *vi* fantasize

fant|a|zija [ā] *nf* fantasy; fancy; (mus.) fantasia

fantoms *nm* phantom

fantomsāpes *nf pl* phantom pain

fanza *nf* 1. fanza (Chinese or Korean peasant dwelling); 2. foulard

Faradeja likums *nm* Faraday's law

faradisks *adj* faradic

faradisms *nm* faradism

faradizācija *nf* faradization

farads *nm* farad

farandola *nf* farandole

faraons *nm* pharaoh

faraonskudra *nf* pharaoh ant

Fārenheita termometrs *nm* Fahrenheit thermometer, Fahrenheit scale

farēri *nm pl* Faeroese

faringīts *nm* pharyngitis

faringoskopija *nf* pharingoscopy

farizejiski *adv* Pharisaically

farizejisks *adj* Pharisaical

farizejiskums *nm* pharisaicalness

farizejisms *nm* pharisaism

farizejs *nm* Pharisee

farma *nf* farm

farmaceitisks *adj* pharmaceutical
farmaceit/s *nm*, ~e *nf* pharmacist
farm|a|cija |ā| *nf* pharmacy (the art or practice of pharmacy)
farmakodinamika *nf* pharmacodynamics
farmakognozija *nf* pharmacognosy
farmakolo/gs *nm*, ~ģe *nf* pharmacologist
farmakoloģija *nf* pharmacology
farmakoloģiski *adv* pharmacologically
farmakoloģisks *adj* pharmacological
farmakopeja *nf* pharmacopoeia
farmakoterapija *nf* pharmacotherapy
farmeris *nm* farmer
farsants *nm* phony
farss *nm* farce
fārvaters *nm* (naut.) fairway
fasāde *nf* front; facade
fasādes kāpējs *nm* cat burglar
fasādes ķieģelis *nm* facing brick
fasciācija *nf* fasciation
fascija *nf* fascia
fascikuls *nm* fascicle
fascinācija *nf* fascination
fascinēt *vt* fascinate
fascis *nm* fasces
fasējums *nm* packaging
fasenda *nf* fazenda
fasēt *vt* pack; bottle
fasētājs *nm*, ~a *nf* packer; bottler
fasētava *nf* packing plant; bottling plant
fasetacs *nf* compound eye
fasete *nf* facet
fasetēt *vt* facet; bevel
fasetfrēzmašīna *nf* (typ.) mitering machine
fasondzelzs *nf* section steel
fasonēvele *nf* molding plane
fasongaldnieks *nm* molder, maker of foundry molds
fasons *nm* fashion, style; cut
fastidiozi *adv* fastidiously
fastidiozs *adj* fastidious
fašīna *nf* fascine

fašings *nm* carnival
fašisms *nm* fascism
fašistiski *adv* fascistically
fašistisks *adj* fascistic
fašist/s *nm*, ~e *nf* fascist
fašizācija *nf* fascistization
fatāli *adv* fatally
fatālisms *nm* fatalism
fatālistiski *adv* fatalistically
fatālistisks *adj* fatalistic
fatālist/s *nm*, ~e *nf* fatalist
fat|a|litāte |ā| *nf* fatality
fatāls *adj* fatal
fatālums *nm* fatality
fatamorg|a|na |ā| *nf* fata morgana
fāters *nm* (barb.) father
fauls *nm* (col.) (sports) foul
fauna *nf* fauna
fauns *nm* faun
favorītisms *nm* favoritism
favorīt/s *nm*, ~e *nf* favorite
favorizēt *vt* favor
fazāns *nm* pheasant
f|a|ze |ā| *nf* phase
fazenda *nf* fazenda
f|a|zēt |ā| *vt* phase
f|a|zētāj/s |ā| *nm*, ~a *nf* animator's assistant
f|a|zgriezējs |ā| *nm* phase shifter
f|a|zīgs |ā| *adj* phasic
f|a|zometrs |ā| *nm* phasemeter
fazotrons *nm* synchrocyclotron
februāris *nm* February
fēces *nf pl* feces
feciāls *adj* fetial
federācija *nf* federation
federāli *adv* federally
federālisms *nm* federalism
federālist/s *nm*, ~e *nf* federalist
feder|a|lizācija |ā| *nf* federalization
feder|a|lizēt |ā| *vt* federalize
federāls *adj* federal
feder|a|tīvi |ā| *adv* federatively

feder[a]tīvs [ā] *adj* federative, federal, federated

federe *nf* (barb.) spring

federrati *nm pl* (col.) carriage

f[e]dings [ē] *nm* (el.) fading

feerija *nf* pantomime show; spectacle

feihoja *nf* feijoa

feins *adj* (barb.) fine

feirāms *nm* (barb.) end of working day

feja *nf* fairy

fekālijas *nf pl* fecal matter

fektēt *vt* (sl.) cadge

felācija *nf* fellatio

felandrāls *nm* phelandral

feldfēbelis *nm* sergeant

feldmaršāls *nm* field marshall

feldšer/is *nm*, ~e *nf* feldsher, medical assistant, paramedic

feldvēbelis *nm* = feldfēbelis

fella[ch]s [h] *nm* fellah

felēma *nf* phelem

felonija *nf* felony

felts *nm* (obs.) a measure of wine

feluka *nf* felucca

feļetonisks *adj* light literary

feļetonist/s *nm*, ~e *nf* feuilletonist

feļetons *nm* feuilleton; sīkais f. topical satire

feļetonu stils *nm* light literary style

feļļa *nf* felly

femin[i]ns [ī] *nm* (gram.) feminine; feminine noun

feminisms *nm* feminism

feministe *nf* feminist

feminizācija *nf* feminization

fenacetins *nm* acetophenetidin

fenatrēns *nm* phenatrene

fenazons *nm* antipyrine

fen[ch]els [h] *nm* fennel

fen[ch]ēns [h] *nm* fenchene

fen[ch]ons [h] *nm* fenchone

fenderēt *vt* (sl.) buy, sell

fenders *nm* (naut.) fender

feneks *nm* fennec

fenetidīns *nm* phenetidine

fenetols *nm* phenetole

fenijs *nm* Fenian

f[ē]nik[s] [e][ss] *nm* phoenix

feniķiet/is *nm*, ~e *nf* Phoenician

fenilalanīns *nm* phenylalanine

fenilbutazons *nm* phenylbutazone

feniletiķskābe *nf* phenylacetic acid

fenilhidrazīns *nm* phenylhydrazine

fenilhidrazons *nm* phenylhydrazone

fenils *nm* phenyl

feniņ/š *nm* pfennig; penny; bez ~a (col.) penniless

fenobarbitāls *nm* phenobarbital

fenoģen[e]tika [ē] *nf* phenogenetics

fenokrists *nm* phenocryst

fenoloģija *nf* phenology

fenoloģiski *adv* phenologically

fenoloģisks *adj* phenological

fenols *nm* phenol

fenomenāli *adv* phenomenally

fenomenālisms *nm* phenomenalism

fenomenāls *adj* phenomenal

fenomenologs *nm* phenomenologist

fenomenoloģija *nf* phenomenology

fenomenoloģiski *adv* phenomenologically

fenomenoloģisks *adj* phenomenological

fenomens *nm* phenomenon

fenotipiski *adv* phenotypically

fenotipisks *adj* phenotypic

fenotips *nm* phenotype

fēns *nm* 1. foehn; 2. hairdrier

feo[ch]romocitoma [h] *nf* pheochromocytoma

feodāli *adv* feudally

feodālis *nm* feudal lord

feodālisms *nm* feudalism

feodāls *adj* feudal

feods *nm* feod

ferāts *nm* = ferrāts

feri- See ferri-

fēri *nm pl* Faeroese

fērija *nf* pantomime show; spectacle

fērlīgs *adj* (sl.) picky

ferma I *nf* farm

ferma II *nf* truss

fermāta *nf* fermata

fermentācija *nf* fermentation

ferment[a]tīvs [ā] *adj* fermentative

fermentēt *vt, vi* ferment

ferments *nm* ferment

fermer/is *nm*, ~e *nf* farmer

fermijs *nm* fermium

fermions *nm* fermion

fero- See ferro-

fe[rr]āts [r] *nm* ferrate

fe[rr]icianīds [r] *nm* ferricyanide

fe[rr]ici[a]nkālijs [r][ā] *nm* potassium ferricyanide

fe[rr]itīvs [r] *adj* ferritic

fe[rr]īts [r] *nm* ferrite

fe[rr]īttērauds [r] *nm* ferrite steel

fe[rr]o[ch]roms [r][h] *nm* ferrochromium

fe[rr]ocian[i]ds [r][ī] *nm* ferrocyanide

fe[rr]oci[a]nkālijs [r][ā] *nm* potassium ferrocyanide

fe[rr]oelektrisks [r] *adj* ferroelectric

fe[rr]omagnētiķis [r] *nm* ferromagnetic

fe[rr]omagnētisks [r] *adj* ferromagnetic

fe[rr]omagnētisms [r] *nm* ferromagnetism

fe[rr]omangāns [r] *nm* ferromanganese

fe[rr]osakausējums [r] *nm* ferroalloy

fe[rr]osilicijs [r] *nm* ferrosilicon

fe[rr]osulfāts [r] *nm* ferrous sulfate

fe[rr]otipija [r] *nf* ferrotype

fertilitāte *nf* fertility

fertils *adj* fertile

ferula *nf* giant fennel

feska *nf* fez

festivāls *nm* festival

fetišisms *nm* fetishism

fetišists *nm* fetishist

fetišizēt *vt* fetishize

fetišs *nm* fetish

fi *indecl nm* phi

fiakrs *nm* fiacre

fiāle *nf* phiale

fiasko *indecl nm* fiasco

fiasks *nm* fiasco

fibra *nf* paperboard

fibrilla *nf* fibril

fibrillācija *nf* (of pulp) fibrillation

fibr[i]nog[e]ns [ī][ē] *nm* fibrinogen

fibr[i]nolizīns [ī] *nm* fibrinolysin

fibr[i]nozs [ī] *adj* fibrinous

fibrīns *nm* fibrin

fibroblasts *nm* fibroblast

fibrogastroskopija *nf* fibrogastroscopy

fibroīds *nm* fibroid

fibrolīts *nm* wallboard

fibroma *nf* fibroma

fibromioma *nf* fibromyoma

fibula *nf* fibula

fice *nf* (barb.) skein

ficelbante *nf* (barb.) ribbon

fideikomisārs *nm* fideicommissary

fideikomiss *nm* fideicommissum

fideikomitents *nm* fideicommissor

fideisms *nm* fideism

fideist/s *nm*, ~e *nf* fideist

fīders *nm* (el.) feeder

fidibusa sērkociņš *nm* fidibus match

fid|u|ciārs [ū] *nm* fiduciary

fid|u|ciārs [ū] *adj* fiducial; fiduciary

fi fenomens *nm* phi phenomenon

fifīgs *adj* (sl.) neat; attractive

figūra *nf* 1. figure; 2. chessman, piece; 3. figurine

fig[u]rācija [ū] *nf* figuration

fig[u]rāli [ū] *adv* figurally

fig[u]rālist/s [ū] *nm*, ~e *nf* figure painter, figure sculptor

fig[u]rāls [ū] *adj* figural

fig[u]rant/s [ū] *nm*, ~e *nf* figurant, ensemble dancer; ~es corps de ballet

fig[u]rēt [ū] *vi* figure

figūriekava *nf* brace (the marks or)

figūriņa *nf dim* of **figūra**, figurine

fikcija *nf* fiction; (jur.) legal fiction

fikcionālisms *nm* fictionalism

fiksācija *nf* **1.** fixation; **2.** (photo.) fixing

fiks|a|tīvs [ā] *nm* fixative

fiks|a|tors [ā] *nm* **1.** fixative; **2.** adjusting knob

fiksāža *nf* (photo.) fixer, fixing bath

fiksēšana *nf* (mil.) containment

fiksēt *vt* **1.** record; **2.** fixate, render immobile; contain; **f. uz vietas** (of enemy force) fix in place; **3.** (photo.) fix

fiksi *adv* (col.) quickly

fikss *adj* (col.) quick

fiktīvi *adv* fictitiously

fiktīvs *adj* fictitious

fikuss *nm* rubber plant

fila *nf* phyle

filadelfs *nm* mock orange

filaments *nm* filament

filantropija *nf* philanthropy

filantropiski *adv* philanthropically

filantropisks *adj* philanthropic

filantrop/s *nm*, ~e *nf* philanthropist

filariotoze *nf* filariasis

filat|e|lija [ē] *nf* philately

filat|e|list/s [ē] *nm*, ~e *nf* philatelist

filcs *nm* felt

fileja *nf* = **filejs**

filejs *nm* **1.** fillet; **2.** sirloin

filēt *vt* fillet

filharmonija *nf* (society) Philharmonic; Philharmonic Hall

filharmonisks *adj* philharmonic

filiāle *nf* branch office

filibustieris *nm* freebooter

filigrāns *nm* **1.** filigree; **2.** watermark

filigrāns *adj* filigreed

filipika *nf* philippic

filipīniet/is *nm*, ~e *nf* Filipino

Filipsa skrūvgriezis *nm* Phillips screwdriver

filistieši *nm pl* Philistines

filistriski *adv* in a Philistine manner

filistrisks *adj* Philistine

filistrs *nm* **1.** senior member of a student corps; **2.** Philistine, Babbitt

filjers *nm* drawplate

fi|l|īts [l] *nm* phyllite

filloksēra *nf* phylloxera

filma *nf* film; **galvenā f.** (of movies) feature; **mē-mā f.** silent film

filmaktieris *nm* movie actor

filmaktrise *nf* movie actress

filmaparāts *nm* movie camera

filmdaris *nm* producer (of films)

filmēt *vt* film, shoot

filmēties *vr* be filmed

filmiski *adv* filmically

filmisks *adj* filmic

filmofonogr|a|fs [ā] *nm* film recorder

filmoskops *nm* film strip projector

filmotēka *nf* film library

filo|ch|inons [h] *nm* phylloquinone

filodendrs *nm* philodendron

filofonija *nf* the collecting of sound recordings

filofoniķ/is *nm*, ~e *nf* phonophile

filoġen|e|tiski [ē] *adv* phylogenetically

filoġen|e|tisks [ē] *adj* phylogenetic

filoġen|e|ze [ē] *nf* phylogeny

filokaktus *nm* orchid cactus

filokartija *nf* card collecting

filokartist/s *nm*, ~e *nf* card collector

filologs *nm*, ~ģe *nf* philologist

filoloģija *nf* philology

filoloģiski *adv* philologically

filoloģisks *adj* philological

filonīts *nm* phyllonite

filos- See **filoz-**

filosta|ch|i [h] *nm pl* Phyllostachys

filozofēt *vi* philosophize

filozofija *nf* philosophy

filozofiski *adv* philosophically

filozofisks *adj* philosophical

filozof/s *nm*, ~**e** *nf* philosopher

filtrācija *nf* filtration

filtrāts *nm* filtrate

filtrēt *vt* filter

filtrēties *vr* filter through

filtrpapīrs *nm* filter paper

filtrprese *nf* filter press

filtrs *nm* filter

filumēnija *nf* collecting of matchboxes

filumēnist/s *nm*, ~**e** *nf* matchbox collector

fimbers *nm* (sl.) A (grade)

fimoze *nf* phimosis

finālcīņa *nf* final match

fināle *nf* (ling.) final

finālist/s *nm*, ~**e** *nf* finalist

fin|a|litāte |ā| *nf* finality

fināls *nm* finale; (sports) finals

fināls *adj* final

finālsacensības *nf pl* (sports) finals

finālskrējiens *nm* final race

finālspēle *nf* finals game

finālturnīrs *nm* final tournament

finan|c|e |s| *nf*, usu. *pl* **finances** finance; finances, money

finan|c|ējums |s| *nm* funding, financing

finan|c|ēt |s| *vt* finance

finan|c|iāli |s| *adv* financially

finan|c|iāls |s| *adj* financial

finan|c|ist/s |s| *nm*, ~**e** *nf* financier

finan|č|u |š| **kapitāls** *nm* financial capital

finan|č|u |š| **gads** *nm* fiscal year

finan|č|u |š| **inspektors** *nm* tax assessor

finan|č|u |š| **ministrija** *nf* Ministry of Finance; Exchequer (in Great Britain); Treasury Department (in USA)

finan|č|u |š| **pārbaude** *nf* audit

finan|č|u |š| **struktūras koeficients** *nm* leverage ratio

finese *nf* subtle nuance; finesse

finglierēt *vi* (sl.) maneuver, try to fix

finierējums *nm* veneer

finierēt *vt* veneer

finie|r|fabrika |ŗ| *nf* plywood mill

finieris *nm* **1.** veneer; **2.** plywood

finie|r|zāģis |ŗ| *nm* scroll saw

finisāēa *nf* (mfg.) finishing

finiša stabs *nm* winning post

finiša taisne *nf* homestretch

finišēt *vi* (sports) finish

finišs *nm* (sports) finish

finīts *adj* (gram., of verb forms) finite

finlandizācija *nf* Finlandization

finna *nf* cysticercus

finnoze *nf* cysticercosis

finta *nf* (sports) feint

finte *nf* twaite shad

finvalis *nm* finback

fiole *nf* vial

fioritūra *nf* (mus.) grace

firma *nf* firm

firmaments *nm* firmament

firmīgs *adj* stylish

fīrers *nm* führer

firniss *nm* varnish

firns *nm* névé

firstiene *nf* the spouse of a prince; princess

firsts *nm* prince, sovereign

firziķis *nm* peach

firziķu laputs *nf* green peach aphid

fisharmonijs *nm* harmonium

fiskāli *adv* fiscally

fiskāls *adj* fiscal

fiskars *nm* (barb.) knife

fisks *nm* fisc, treasury

fistula *nf* fistula

Fišera kritērijs *nm* (stat.) F-ratio

fitings *nm* (tech.) fitting

fitīns *nm* phytin

fitobakterioloģija *nf* phytobacteriology

fitobentoss *nm* phytobenthos

fitocenoze *nf* plant community, phytocoenosis

fitofāgi *nm pl* Phytophaga

fitoftora *nf* phytophthora

fitog|e|ns |ē| *adj* phytogenic

fitoģen|e|ze |ē| *nf* phytogenesis

fitoģeogr|a|fija |ā| *nf* phytogeography

fitolaka *nm* pokeweed

fitol|i|ts |ī| *nm* phytolite

fitols *nm* phytol

fitoncīds *nm* plant bactericide

fitopatolo/gs *nm*, ~ģe *nf* plant pathologist

fitopatoloģija *nf* plant pathology

fitoplanktons *nm* phytoplankton

fitosterīns *nm* phytosterol

fitoterapija nf phytotherapy

fitotoksīns *nm* phytotoxin

fitozojs *nm* zoophyte

fizāle *nf* ground-cherry

fizelāža *nf* fuselage

fizika *nf* physics

fizikāli *adv* physically

fizikālisms *nm* physicalism

fizikālists *nm* physicalist

fizikāls *adj* physical

fizikoķīmiķ/is *nm*, ~e *nf* physical chemist

fiziķis *nm*, ~e *nf* physicist

fizilieris *nm* infantry rifleman

fiziognomija *nf* = fizionomija

fiziognoms *nm* = fizionoms

fiziogr|a|fija |ā| *nf* physiography

fiziogr|a|f/s |ā| *nm*, ~e *nf* physiographer

fizioģeogr|a|fija |ā| *nf* physical geography

fizioģeogr|a|f/s |ā| *nm*, ~e *nf* physical geographer

fizokarps *nm* ninebark

fiziokr|a|tija |ā| *nf* physiocracy

fiziokr|a|ts |ā| *nm* physiocrat

fiziologs *nm*, ~ģe *nf* physiologist

fizioloģija *nf* physiology

fizioloģiski *adv* physiologically

fizioloģisks *adj* physiological

fizionomija *nf* physiognomy

fizionoms *nm* physiognomist

fizioplastisks *adj* physioplastic

fizioterape|i|tiski |u| *adv* phisiotherapeutically

fizioterape|i|tisk/s |u| *adj* physiotherapeutic

fizioterape|i|t/s |u| *nm*, ~e *nf* physical therapist

fizioterapija *nf* physical therapy

fizioterapist/s *nm*, ~e *nf* physical therapist

fiziski *adv* physically

fizisks *adj* physical

fizkultūra *nf* physical culture

fizkultūriet/is *nm*, ~e *nf* physical culturist, athlete

fizkultūrist/s *nm*, ~e *nf* physical culturist, athlete

fizs *nm* fizz

fjelds *nm* fjeld

fjords *nm* fjord

fjūčerss *nm* (bus.) futures

flaga *nf* (naut.) flag; sveša f. flag of convenience

flage|l|ants |ll| *nm* Flagellant; flagellant

flagkuģis *nm* flagship

flagmanis *nm* flag captain

flagmaņkuģis *nm* flagship

flagvirsnieks *nm* flag officer

flakons *nm* vial

flakurtijas *nf pl* Flacourtia

flamenko *indecl nm* flamenco

flamings *nm* flamingo

flamini *nm pl* flamines

flām/s *nm*, ~iete *nf* Fleming; ~u valoda Flemish

flanelis *nm* flannel; flannelette

flanēt *vi* (col.) stroll

flanētāja *nf* flaneuse

flanētājs *nm* flaneur

flangs *nm* (mil.) flank

flankēt *vt* flank

flankgards *nm* flank guard

flankuguns *nf* flanking fire

flanža *nf* butt joint

flanžu kniedējums *nm* butt joint riveting

flaters *nm* (aeron.) flutter

flauta *nf* flute

flautīna *nf* piccolo flute

flautist/s *nm*, ~**e** *nf* flutist

flavons *nm* flavon

flavopurpurīns *nm* flavopurpurin

flažolets *nm* flageolet

fleb|i|ts [ī] *nm* phlebitis

flegma *nf* phlegmatism

flegmatiķ/is *nm*, ~**e** *nf* phlegmatic

flegmatiski *adv* phlegmatically

flegmatisks *adj* phlegmatic

flegmatiskums *nm* phlegmatism

flegmatisms *nm* phlegmatism

flegmona *nf* phlegmon

fleita *nf* flute

fleitists *nm*, ~**e** *nf* flutist

fleksibls *adj* flexible

fleksija *nf* flection, inflection

fleksīvs *adj* inflected

fleksors *nm* (anat.) flexor

fleksūra *nf* flexure

flektīvs *adj* inflected

flibustieris *nm* freebooter

flīģeladjutants *nm* aid-de-camp

flīģelis *nm* grand piano

flikermetrs *nm* flicker photometer

flinte *nf* (barb.) shotgun, rifle

flintstikls *nm* flint glass

flips *nm* (skating) flip

flirtēt *vi* flirt

flirts *nm* flirting

flīsītes *nf pl* (col.) plissé

flīze *nf* glazed tile; masonry panel; flagstone

flīžu knaibles *nf pl* tile cutting nippers

flogistons *nm* phlogiston

flokens *nm* (metall.) fissure

flokši *nm pl* phlox

flomāsters *nm* felt-tip pen, marker

flome *nf* Jerusalem sage

flora *nf* flora

florete *nf* fleuret, fencing foil

floretist/s *nm*, ~**e** *nf* fencer

florīns *nm* florin

floristika *nf* floristics

flors *nm* (fabric) gossamer

flotācija *nf* flotation

flote *nf* fleet

flotes arsenāls *nm* naval yard

flotes atbalsta punkts *nm* naval base

flotile *nf* flotilla

flu|i|dāls [ī] *adj* 1. fluidal; 2. fluid

fluīdi *adv* fluidly

fluīds *nm* fluid

fluīds *adj* fluid

fluksmetrs *nm* fluxmeter

fluktuācija *nf* fluctuation

fluktuēt *vi* fluctuate

fluorēns *nm* fluorene

fluorescence *nf* fluorescence

fluorescēt *vi* fluoresce

fluorescīns *nm* fluorescein

fluorfosforskābe *nf* fluorophosphoric acid

fluor|i|ds [ī] *nm* fluoride

fluorinēt *vt* flourinate

fluorīts *nm* fluorite

fluorogr|a|fija [ā] *nf* photofluorography

fluorogr|a|fisks [ā] *adj* photofluorographic

fluoroplasts *nm* flouroplastic

fluoroskops *nm* fluoroscope

fluors *nm* fluorine

fluorūdeņradis *nm* hydrofluoride

fluorūdeņražskābe *nf* hydrofluoric acid

fluviāls *adj* fluvial

fluvioglaciāls *adj* glaciofluvial

foajē *nm* *indecl* (of a theater) promenade, foyer

fobija *nf* phobia

fogteja *nf* (hist.) office, residence, or jurisdiction of a governor or bailiff

fogts *nm* (hist.) overseer, bailiff, governor, administrator

foiniķieši *nm pl* Phoenicians

fokālā līnija *nf* caustic curve

fokālā plakne *nf* focal plane; ~s ~s **slēdzis** focal plane shutter

fokbura *nf* foresail

fokmasta cepure *nm* foretruck

fokmasts *nm* foremast

fokometrs *nm* focometer

fokraja *nf* (naut.) foreyard

foksterj[e]rs [ē] *nm* fox terrier

fokstrots *nm* fox-trot

fokusa ga[r]ums [r̦] *nm* focal length

fokusēt *vt* focus

fokuss I *nm* focus

fokuss II *nm* (col.) **1.** trick; **2.** whim, caprice

fokzāliņš *nm* (naut.) foretop

foliants *nm* folio

folija *nf* (metal) foil

folijskābe *nf* folic acid

folikulīns *nm* folliculin, estron

folikulīts *nm* folliculite

folikuls *nm* follicle

folio *indecl nm* (paper size; leaf number) folio

folketings *nm* Folketing

folklora *nf* folklore; ~s **krātuve** archives of folklore

folkloriski *adv* folklorically

folklorisks *adj* folkloric

folkloristika *nf* folklorism

folkloristisks *adj* folkloristic

folklorist/s *nm*, ~e *nf* folklorist

folklorizēties *vr* pass into folklore

folkmūzika *nf* folk music

folkroks *nm* folk rock

folverks *nm* (hist., a type of estate or large farm) folwark

fon *prep* von

fonācija *nf* phonation

fondī *indecl nm* fondue

fonds *nm* **1.** fund; resources; collection, body; **2.** foundation

fonēma *nf* phoneme

fon[e]mātisks [ē] *adj* phonematic

fonendoskops *nm* phonendoscope

fonētika *nf* phonetics

fonētiķ/is *nm*, ~e *nf* phonetician

fonētiski *adv* phonetically

fonētisks *adj* phonetic

fonofors *nm* phonophore

fonogr[a]fs [ā] *nm* phonograph

fonogramma *nf* phonogram

fonoieeja *nf* (el.) phono input

fonokardiogramma *nf* phonocardiogram

fonolīts *nm* phonolite

fonoloģija *nf* phonology

fonoloģiski *adv* phonologically

fonoloģisks *adj* phonological

fonometrs *nm* phonometer

fonons *nm* phonon

fonotaka *nf* sound track

fonotēka *nf* library of sound recordings

fons I *nm* background

fons II *nm* phon

fontanella *nf* fontanelle

fontāns *nm* (of liquids) jet

fonts *nm* (typ.) font

foraminīferas *nf pl* foraminifera

fordisms *nm* Fordism

forele *nf* trout

forgals *nm* (naut.) stem

forints *nm* forint

forma *nf* **1.** form; **2.** uniform; **ikdienas f.** undress uniform; **3.** mold

formācija *nf* formation

formaldeh[i]ds [ī] *nm* formaldehyde

formāli *adv* formally

formalīns *nm* Formalin

formālisms *nm* formalism

formālistiski *adv* formalistically

formālistisks *adj* formalistic

formālist/s *nm*, ~e *nf* formalist

form[a]litāte [ā] *nf* formality

form[a]lizācija [ā] *nf* formalization

form[a]lizēt [ā] *vt* formalize

formāls *adj* formal

formam[i]ds [ī] *nm* formamide

formants *nm* formant

formas tērps *nm* uniform

formas virpa *nf* (potter's machine) jolley

form[a]tēšana [ā] *nf* (compu.) formatting

form[a]tēt [ā] *vt* (compu.) format

formāt/s *nm* format, size; **liela ~a** large-sized; **vidēja ~a** medium-sized

formelements *nm* component

formēšana *nf* forming, formation; shaping; mold-ing; raising (an army)

formēšanās *nfr* formation, forming

formēt *vt* form, shape; mold; (mil.) raise (an army)

formētāj/s *nm*, **~a** *nf* molder

formēties *vr* form

formiāts *nm* formate

formtērauds *nm* steel shapes

formols *nm* Formol

formula *nf* formula

formulārijs *nm* formulary

formulārs *nm* (document) form

formulējums *nm* formulation; wording

formulēt *vt* formulate; word, (of a document) draw up

formulisms *nm* formulism

formulist/s *nm*, **~e** *nf* formulist

formalizēt *vt* formalize

formējums *nm* formation

formelements *nm* component

formika *nf* Formica

forons *nm* phorone

forsēt *vt* **1.** force; accelerate; exaggerate; **2.** (mil.) cross (a river under fire)

forsēts *adj, part* of **forsēt** (mil., of a march) forced

forsītija *nf* forsythia

forsmažors *nm* force majeure

forsterīts *nm* forsterite

forši *adv* (sl.) very well, great

foršs *adj* (sl.) good, great, cool

forštate *nf* (sl.) suburbs

forte *nf* (mus.) forte

fortificēt *vt* fortify, build fortifications

fortifikācija *nf* fortification

fortrans *nm* Fortran

forts *nm* fort

fortūna *nf* fortune

fortunella *nf* kumquat

forums *nm* forum

forvarda līgums *nm* (bus.) forward contract

fosa *nf* fossa

fosfatēšana *nf* phosphatization

fosfatēt *vt* phosphatize

fosfat[i]ds [ī] *nm* phosphatide

fosfāts *nm* phosphate

fosf[i]ds [ī] *nm* phosphide

fosfīns *nm* phosphine

fosfīts *nm* phosphite

fosfolip[i]ds [ī] *nm* phospholipide, phosphatide

fosfonijs *nm* phosphonium

fosforējošs *adj* phosphorescent

fosforescence *nf* phosphorescence

fosforescēt *vi* phosphoresce

fosforēt *vi* phosphoresce

fosforil[ch]lor[i]ds [h][ī] *nm* phosphoryl chloride

fosforils *nm* phosphoryl

fosforiski *adv* phosphorescently

fosforisks *adj* phosphorescent

fosforītmilti *nm pl* crushed phosphorite

fosforīts *nm* phosphorite

fosforizēt *vi* phosphoresce

fosforizēts *adj* phosphor-coated, phosphorescent

fosformolibdenskābe *nf* phosphomolybdic acid

fosforpaskābe *nf* phosphorous acid

fosfor/s *nm* phosphorus; **~a** phosphorous; phosphoric

fosforskābe *nf* phosphoric acid

fosforūdeņradis *nm* phosphoreted hydrogen

fosforvolframāts *nm* phosphotungstate

fosforvolframskābe *nf* phosphotungstic acid

fosgenīts *nm* phosgenite
fosg|e|ns [ē] *nm* phosgene
fosilija *nf* fossil
fosilizācija *nf* fossilization
fosils *adj* fossil
fosilūdens *nm* connate water
fosterīts *nm* fosterite
foto *indecl nm* (col.) photo
fotoalbums *nm* photo album
fotoalerģija *nf* photoallergy
fotoamatier/is *nm*, ~e *nf* amateur photographer
fotoaparāts *nm* camera
fotoar|ch|īvs [h] *nm* photographic archive
fotoateljē *indecl nm* photographic studio
fotoattēls *nm* photograph
fotoattīstītājs *nm* (photo.) developer
fotobiogr|a|fija [ā] *nf* photobiography
fotobioloģija *nf* photobiology
fotobiotisks *adj* photobiotic
fotoburt/i *nm pl* type set by a photocomposer;
    ~u saliekamā mašīna photocomposer
foto|ch|romatisks [h] *adj* photochromatic
foto|ch|ronika [h] *nf* story in photo images;
    newsreel
fotocinkogr|a|fija [ā] *nf* photozincography
fotocinkotipija *nf* photozincography
fotodarbnīca *nf* photographic studio
fotodinamika *nf* photodynamics
fotoefekts *nm* photoelectric effect
fotoelektrība *nf* photoelectricity
fotoelektriski *adv* photoelectrically
fotoelektrisks *adj* photoelectric
fotoelektrons *nm* photoelectron
fotoelements *nm* photocell
fotoemulsija *nf* photographic emulsion
fotofilma *nf* photographic film
fotofinišs *nm* photo finish recording camera
fotofobija *nf* photophobia
fotoforēze *nf* photophoresis
fotog|e|ni [ē] *adv* photogenically
fotog|e|niski [ē] *adv* photogenically

fotog|e|niskums [ē] *nm* photogenic quality
fotog|e|ns [ē] *adj* photogenic
fotografēt *vt* photograph, take pictures
fotografēties *vr* be photographed, have one's
    pic-ture taken
fotogr|a|fija [ā] nf 1. photography; 2. photograph
fotogr|a|fiski [ā] *adv* photographically
fotogr|a|fisks [ā] *adj* photographic
fotogr|a|f/s [ā] *nm*, ~e *nf* photographer
fotogramma *nf* photogram
fotogrammetrija *nf* photogrammetry
fotogravējums *nm* photoengraving
fotogravētāj/s *nm*, ~a *nf* photoengraver
fotogravūra *nf* photogravure
fotoizlūkošana *nf* photographic reconnaissance
fotoizstāde *nf* photographic exhibition
fotokamera *nf* photographic camera
fotokatal|i|z|a|tors [ī][ā] *nm* photocatalyst
fotokatal|i|ze [ī] *nf* photocatalysis
fotokatods *nm* photocathode
fotokinētika *nf* photokinetics
fotokonkurss *nm* photography competition
fotokopētājs *nm* photocopier
fotokopija *nf* photocopy
fotoko|r|espondent/s [rr] *nm*, ~e *nf* news
    photographer
fotoķīmija *nf* photochemistry
fotoķīmiski *adv* photochemically
fotoķīmisks *adj* photochemical
fotolaboratorija *nf* photographic laboratory
fotolitisks *adj* photolytic
fotolitogr|a|fija [ā] *nf* photolithography
fotolitogr|a|fiski [ā] *adv* photolithographically
fotolitogr|a|fisks [ā] *adj* photolithographic
fotol|i|ze [ī] nf photolysis
fotoluminiscence *nf* photoluminescence
fotomāksla *nf* photographic art
fotome|cha|nika [hā] *nf* photomechanics
fotome|cha|niski [hā] *adv* photomechanically

fotome|cha|nisks |hā| *adj* photomechanical
fotometrija *nf* photometry
fotometrs *nm* photometer
fotomikroskops *nm* photomicroscope
fotomodelis *nm* (photographer's) model
fotomontāža *nf* photomontage
fotons *nm* photon
fotoobjektīvs *nm* photographic lens
fotopapīrs *nm* photographic paper
fotoperiodisms *nm* photoperiodism
fotoperiods *nm* photoperiod
fotopiederumi *nm pl* photographic equipment
fotoplate *nf* photographic plate
fotorelejs *nm* electric eye
fotoreportāža *nf* photoreport
fotorezistors *nm* photoconductor
fotorobots *nm* photo booth
fotosaliekamā mašīna *nf* photocomposer
fotosaliekams *adj* photocomposition (*adj*)
fotosalikums *nm* photocomposition
fotosf|ai|ra [ē] *nf* photosphere
fotosint|e|tiski [ē] *adv* photosynthetically
fotosint|e|tisks [ē] *adj* photosynthetic
fotosint|e|ze [ē] *nf* photosynthesis
fotospuldze *nf* photoflood bulb
fotostats *nm* photostat
fotostudija *nf* photographic studio
fotošūna *nf* photoelectric cell
fotota|ch|imetrija [h] *nf* phototachymetry
fototaksija *nf* phototaxis
fototēka *nf* photographic library
fototelegr|a|fija [ā] *nf* phototelegraphy
fototelegr|a|fs [ā] *nm* phototelegraph
fototelegramma *nf* phototelegraph
fototerapija *nf* phototherapy
fototipija *nf* phototypography
fototriangulācija *nf* photogrammetric triangulation
fototropija *nf* phototropism
fototropisks *adj* phototropic
fototropisms *nm* phototropism
fotouzņēmums *nm* photograph, snapshot

fotovadītspēja *nf* photoconductivity
fotovitrīna *nf* photographic display case
fots *nm* phot
fovisms *nm* Fauvism
fovists *nm* Fauvist
fragmentācija *nf* fragmentation
fragmentāri *adv* in a fragmentary manner, in fragments
fragmentārisms *nm* fragmentariness
fragmentārs *adj* fragmentary
fragmentists *nm* fragmentist
fragments *nm* fragment
fragrants *adj* fragrant
fraka *nf* tailcoat
frakcij/a *nf* (chem.) fraction; (pol.) parliamentary group; faction; ~u cīņa interfaction struggle
frakcionārisms *nm* factionalism
frakcionārs *nm* factionary, partisan
frakcionārs *adj* factional, factious
frakcionēt *vt* fraction, fractionate; (of crude oil) crack
fraktāls *adj* fractal
fraktāļi *nm pl* fractals
fraktēšana *nf* chartering
fraktēšanas līgums *nm* charter party
fraktēt *vt* (of ships) charter
fraktētājs *nm* charterer
frakts *nf* 1. cargo; freight; 2. freightage; carriage; f. brīva freight paid
fraktūra *nf* 1. German type; 2. fracture
francijs *nm* francium
franciskānis *nm* Franciscan
franciskānisms *nm* Franciscanism
franciski *adv* in French, (speak) French
francisks *adj* French
francūziete *nf* Frenchwoman
francūzis *nm* Frenchman
franči *nm pl* Frenchmen, the French
franču gotika *nf* ogival style
franču raizāle *nf* tall oat grass
franču skābenes *nf pl* French sorrel

frankenija *nf* sea heath

frankēt *vt* prepay, pay postage

frankēts *adj, part* of frankēt postpaid, stamped;
nepietiekami f. insufficient postage

franki *nm pl* Franks

frankist/s *nm*, ~e *nf* Francoist

franklinīts *nm* franklinite

franklinizācija *nf* electrotherapy with electrostatic fields

franko *nm indecl* postage; brīvs f. postage paid,
postpaid; f. kuģī free on board

frankofonisks *adj* French-speaking

frankolīns *nm* francolin

franks *nm* franc

franksēze *nf* (hist.) a dance

franšīze *nf* franchise

frants *nm* dandy

frapants *adj* striking

frāters *nm* (fraternity) brother

fratrija *nf* phratry

fr[a]ze [ā] *nf* phrase; nodrāzta f. platitude,
hack-neyed expression

frazējums *nm* phrasing

frazeoloģija *nf* phraseology

frazeoloģiski *adv* phraseologically

frazeoloģisks *adj* phraseological

frazeoloģisms *nm* expression, phrase

frazēt *vt* phrase

fr[a]žaini [ā] *adv* with fine-sounding phrases

fr[a]žainība [ā] nf phrase-mongering

fr[a]žains [ā] *adj* containing fine-sounding
phrases

fregate *nf* frigate

fregates putns *nm* frigate bird

freidisks *adj* Freudian

freidisms *nm* Freudism

freilene *nf* (barb.) missy

frekvence *nf* frequency

frekvenču josla *nf* (el.) band

frekventatīvs *adj* (ling.) frequentative

frencis *nm* (mil.) tunic; field jacket

frenologs *nm* phrenologist

frenoloģija *nf* phrenology

frenoloģisks *adj* phrenological

freons *nm* Freon

freska *nf* fresco

frēze *nf* 1. milling cutter; 2. milling machine

frēzējums *nm* milled work

frēzes nazis *nm* milling cutter

frēzēt *vt* mill

frēzētāj/s *nm*, ~a *nf* milling machine operator

frēzija *nf* freesia

frēzmašīna *nf* milling machine

friči *nm pl* Fritzes (World War I Latvian
nickname for German soldiers); Boche

frīdžezs *nm* free jazz

frigida *adj* frigid

frīģieš/i *nm pl* Phrygians; ~u Phrygian

frīģisks *adj* Phrygian

frikadele *nf* quenelle, meatball

frikasē *indecl nm* fricassee

frik[a]tīvs [ā] *adj* fricative

frikcija *nf* friction

frišs *adj* (barb.) fresh

fritēt *vt* frit

friti[l]ārija [ll] *nf* checkered lily

frits *nm* frit

frivoli *adv* frivolously

frivolitāte *nf* frivolity

frivols *adj* frivolous

Frīza glīvene *nf* Fries' pondweed

frīze *nf* frieze

frizēt *vt* barber, do s.o.'s hair

frizētava *nf* barbershop; hairdresser's shop

frizēties *vr* have one's hair done

friziere *nf* hairdresser

frizieris *nm* barber

frizija *nf* vriesia

frīz/s I *nm*, ~iete *nf* Frisian

frīzs II *nm* = frīze

frizūra *nf* haircut; hairdo

fronda *nf* 1. the Fronde; 2. unprincipled
opposition

frondists *nm* (hist.) frondeur

frontāli *adv* frontally

frontāls *adj* frontal

fronte *nf* front

frontēšana *nf* (bus.) fronting

frontinieks *nm* frontline soldier

frontispiss *nm* frontispiece

frontoģen|e|ze [ē] *nf* frontogenesis

frontolize *nf* frontolysis

frontons *nm* pediment, fronton

frotē *indecl nm* terry cloth

frotē dvielis *nm* Turkish towel

frotēt *vt* rub down

frug|a|litāte [ā] *nf* frugality

frugāls *adj* frugal

fruktāns *nm* fructan

fruktifikācija *nf* fructification

fruktoze *nf* fructose

ft|a|lāts [ā] *nm* phthalate

ft|a|lazīns [ā] *nm* phthalazine

ft|a|lskābe [ā] *nf* phthalic acid

ftiziatrija *nf* phthisiology

ftiziatr/s *nm*, **~e** *nf* phthisiologist

fuajē *nm* foyer

fūders *nm* (obs.) measure of wine

fufaika *nf* (barb.) quilted jacket

f|u|g/a [ū] *nf* (mus.) fugue; (sl.) flight; **dot ~u** beat it

fūga *nf* (barb.) joint

fugasa bumba *nf* demolition bomb

fugass *nm* fougasse

fugato *indecl nm* (mus.) fugato

fui *interj* phooey

fuksija *nf* fuchsia

fuksīns *nm* fuchsine

fuksis *nm* **1.** (fraternity) pledge; **2.** (col.) handsaw

fuksītis *nm* **1.** *dim* of **fuksis**, fraternity pledge; **2.** (col.) hand saw

fukusi *nm pl* fucuses

fulārs *nm* foulard

fulgurīts *nm* fulgurite

fulmināts *nm* fulminate

fulminēt *vi* fulminate

fulmīnskābe *nf* fulminic acid

fulminurskābe *nf* fulminuric acid

fulrigers *nm* full-rigger

fumarola *nf* fumarole

fumārskābe *nf* fumaric acid

fumigācija *nf* fumigation

fumigants *nm* fumigant

fundācija *nf* founding

fundamentāli *adv* fundamentally

fundamentālisms *nm* fundamentalism

fundament|a|litāte [ā] *nf* fundamentality

fundamentāls *adj* fundamental

fundaments *nm* foundation

fundātor/s *nm*, **~e** *nf* founder

fundēt *vt* found

funerālijas *nf pl* obsequies

fungēt *vi* function

fungicīds *nm* fungicide

funikulārs *adj* funicular

funikulers *nm* funicular, cable railway

funkcija *nf* function

funkcionālanal|i|ze [ī] *nf* functional analysis

funkcionāli *adv* functionally

funkcionālisms *nm* functionalism

funkcionāls *adj* functional

funkcionār/s *nm*, **~e** *nf* functionary

funkcionēt *vi* function

funkija *nf* hosta

funktierēt *vi* (barb.) think, figure

furacilīns *nm* nitrofurazone

furanoze *nf* furanose

furāns *nm* furan

furāža *nf* forage, fodder

furcelārija *nf* furcellaria

furfurīls *nm* furfuryl

furfurols *nm* furfural

furgons *nm* van

f|u|rija [ū] *nf* **1.** Fury; **2.** (fig.) termagant, dragon

furīls *nm* furyl

furiozs *adj* furious

Furjē anal[i]ze [ī] *nf* Fourier analysis

furkroja *nf* Furcraea

furma *nf* blast box

fūrma/nis *nm* (barb.) coachman; ~**ņu valoda** (col.) raw language

furnitūra *nf* accessories

furors *nm* furore, sensation, stir

furunkuloze *nf* furunculosis

furunkuls *nm* furuncle

fustiks *nm* fustic

fušier/is *nm* (barb.) mistake, flop; **izdarīt** ~**i** lay an egg

futbolbumba *nf* soccer ball

futbolists *nm* soccer player

futbolkomanda *nf* soccer team

futbols *nm* soccer; **amerikāņu f.** football

futene *nf* (sl.) soccer, soccer ball

futrālis *nm* case, instrument case, etui

futūriski *adv* futuristically

futūrisks *adj* futuristic

futūrisms *nm* futurism

futūristisks *adj* futuristic

futūrist/s *nm*, ~**e** *nf* futurist

fut[u]roloģisks [ū] *adj* futurological

fut[u]rolo/gs [ū] *nm*, ~**ģe** *nf* futurologist

fut[u]roloģija [ū] *nf* futurology

futūrs *nm* future tense

fuzārija *nf* fusarium

fūzelis *nm* fusel oil; (sl.) moonshine

fūzeļeļļa *nf* fusel oil

fuzēns *nm* fusain

fūzija *nf* merger; (bus., ling.) fusion

G

gabalainība *nf* chunkiness

gabalainis *nm* tireless wheel

gabalains *adj* in pieces, chunky

gabalainums *nm* chunkiness

gabaldarb/s *nm* piecework; ~**a alga** piece rate; ~**a strādnieks** pieceworker

gabalgabalos *adv* in little pieces, to smithereens

gabaliņš *nm* **1.** *dim* of **gabals**; little piece; snippet; **2.** (el.) chip

gabalnieks *nm* (hist.) gabalnieks (under the corvée system, a peasant who worked an assigned piece of the landlord's land; a farm hand who did the corvée work assigned by his employer)

gabalogles *nf pl* lump coal

gabalot *vt* cut

gabaloties *vr* split up

gabalpreces *nf pl* parcel goods, retail goods

gabal/s *nm* **1.** piece; bit; chunk; (of sugar, clay, ore) lump; (of soap) cake; (of bread) slice, hunk; (of land) lot ◊ ~**ā** (of price) apiece, each; **vienā** ~**ā** all of a piece; (col.) uninterruptedly; ~**u pa** ~**am** piece by piece; ~**u** ~**os** in smithereens; **uz** ~**a** (do) piecework; **2.** distance ◊ ~**iem** in places; **pa** ~**u** at a distance, from afar; **būt jau labā** ~**ā** be already some distance away; (of the sun) be already high up

gabalsāls *nf* salt in chunks

gabalu likme *nf* piece rate

gabalziepes *nf pl* cakes of hard soap

gabana *nf* (reg.) stack

gabane *nf* yarrow

gabardīns *nm* gabardine

gabarīt/s *nm* gabarit, clearance diagram; ~**i** di-mensions

gābiķis *nm* miser

gabions *nm* gabion

gabro *nm indecl* gabbro

gadadiena *nf* anniversary; **simtā g.** centennial; **divsimtā g.** bicentennial

gadagājums *nm* **1.** (of periodicals) volume; **2.** age group, cohort

gadagrāmata *nf* **1.** annual, annual review, yearbook; **2.** (obs.) almanac, calendar

gadakalps *nm* farm hand (hired for a year)

gadalaiks *nm* season

gada pārskats *nm* annual report

gadapuisis *nm* farm hand (hired for a year)

gada staipeknis *nm* stiff club moss

gada svētki *nm pl* anniversary

gādāt *vi* **1.** look after, take care of, see to; **2.** get, provide, provide for; **3.** (folk.) think, guess

gadatirgus *nm* fair

gadaudzis *nm* yearling; one-year old

gadenieks *nm* farm hand (hired for a year)

gadenis *nm* (of animals) about a year old

gadgadā *adv* year after year

gādība *nf* care

gādīgi *adv* solicitously, caringly

gādīgs *adj* (of husbands, fathers) good provider; solicitous, caring

gādīgums *nm* care

gadījumatlase *nf* random sample

gadījumcipars *nm* random digit

gadījumkļūda *nf* random error

gadījumlielums *nm* random value; **mainīgs g.** random variable

gadījummeklēšana *nf* random search

gadījumparaugkopa *nf* random sample

gadījumprocess *nm* random process

gadījumsecība *nf* random sequence

gadījumskaitļi *nm pl* random numbers

gadījumsvārstības *nf pl* random variation

gādīgums *nm* solicitude

gadījum/s *nm* **1.** occasion; **pie ~a** on occasion; **2.** opportunity, chance; circumstance; **nekādā ~ā** under no circumstances; **pie ~a** when you have a chance; **3.** (unforeseen) event; occurrence, incident; case; **~a darbi** odd jobs; **~a mērķis** target of opportunity; **~a rakstura** incidental, accidental; **~a sabiedrība** casual company; **~a strādnieks** temporary worker; **~a troksnis** random noise; **ārkārtējā ~ā** in case of emer-gency; **katram ~am** just in case; **~ā, ja** in case;

katrā ~ā in any event; **labākajā ~ā** in the best case, at best; **ļaunākajā ~ā** if worse comes to worst; **pretējā ~ā** otherwise

gadinieks *nm* (hist.) gadinieks (a hired hand on contract for the whole year)

gādiņš *nm* (col.) **1.** care; **2.** that which is provided

gadīt *vi* (of missiles) hit

gadī/ties *vr* happen (by chance); **kā ~sies** will play it by the ear; when there is a chance; **kur ~jies, kur nē** happened to run into (s.o.); **visādi gadās** accidents will happen

gadmija *nf* eve of a new year

gādnie/ks *nm*, **~ce** *nf* provider

gadolīnijs *nm* gadolinium

gadolins *nm* gadolinium

gadriņi *nm pl* grating, grille; louver

gad/s *nm* year; **astronomiskais g.** solar year; **baigais g.** (hist.) year of horror (1940-1941); **garais g.** leap year; **četrsimt ~u jubileja** quadricentennial; **divsimt ~u jubileja** bicentennial; **simts ~u jubileja** centennial; **trīssimt ~u jubileja** tertcentenary; **tūkstoš ~u jubileja** millenary; **~u mijā** on the eve of the new year; **~u tūkstotis** millenium; **ar ~iem** in time; **~u no ~a** year after year; **jau ~os** up in years; **~iem ilgi** for years; **cauru ~u** the whole year; **labi ~os** ad-vanced in years; **manos ~os** at my age; **vidējos ~os** middle-aged

gadsimtens *nm* century

gadsimt/s *nm* century; **~u robeža** turn of the century

gadskaitlis *nm* year (as written)

gadskārt/a *nf* **1.** season; **2.** annual ring; **3.** (poet.) anniversary; **pa ~u** every year

gadskārtējs *adj* annual

gadstrādnieks *nm* farm hand (hired for a year)

gadu gredzeni *nm pl* annual rings

gadumija *nf* New Year

gadu raksti *nm pl* chronicle

gadusimte/nis *nm* century; **~ņu mija** turn of the century

gadusimts *nm* century

gādzināt *vi* (of geese) honk

gafelbura *nf* gaffsail

gafele *nf* (naut.) gaff

gafelšoneris *nm* schooner

gāga *nf* eider; **~s dūnas** eiderdown

gāgans *nm* tom (turkey), gander

gāgas *nf pl* (of geese) honking

gāgāt *vi* (of geese) honk

gāgināt *vi* (of geese) honk

gaiba *nf* silly, talkative woman

gaida *nf* girl scout

gaidas *nf pl* expectations, anticipation, longing

gaid/e *nf* wait; **stāvēt ~ē** (of hunters) lie in wait

gaidele *nf* cowslip

gaidelītes *nf pl* cowslip

gaidīb/as *nf pl* pregnancy; **~ās** pregnant

gaidīgs *adj* expectant, longing

gaidin *adv emph* of **gaidīt**; **g. gaidīja** he (she, they) waited impatiently

gaidisms *nm* girl scout movement

gaidīt *vt, vi* **1.** wait; await; **g. kārtu** wait one's turn; **laiks negaida** time presses; **2.** expect

gaidītāj/s *nm*, **~a** *nf* he who waits (or expects)

gaidpilns *adj* longing, yearning; pining

gaigala *nf* goldeneye

gaigalīši *nm pl* cowslip

gaigalītes *nf pl* cowslip

gaigt *vt* crave

gaija *nf* (naut.) guy, vang

gailardija *nf* gaillardia

gaile *nf* glow; blue flames over embers

gailene *nf* **1.** chanterelle; **2.** primrose; cowslip

gailenīte *nf dim* of **gailene**

gailēns *nm* cockerel

gailestība *nf* (obs.) jealousy

gailēt *vi* glow; smolder

gailēties *vr* glow; smolder

gai/lis *nm* **1.** cock, rooster ◊ **sarkanais g.** fire; **2.** (firearms) hammer; **~ļa sprosts** hammer lug; **3.** animal-shaped cresting at the end of a roof ridge

gailīši *nm pl* **1.** sour milk, yogurt, or sour cream lumps; **2.** top sheaves of straw in a thatched roof; **3.** break in voice (in the upper registers while singing)

gailītis *nm* **1.** *dim* of **gailis**, cockerel; **2.** a Latvian folk dance;

gails *adj* tall, slender

gaiļa āboliņš *nm* yellow-flowered alfalfa

gaiļa paslavas *nf pl* cowslip

gaiļa sekstes *nf pl* **1.** cockscomb; **2.** funnel chanterelle

gaiļa svars *nm* bantam weight

gaiļbikses *nf pl* cowslip

gaiļ/i *nm pl* a crow of the cock ◊ **līdz ar ~iem** (of rising) with the chickens; **ne g. pakaļ nedziedās** no one will be the wiser

gaiļpieši *nm pl* **1.** nasturtium; **2.** primrose; **3.** lark-spur

gaiļsāre *nf* barnyard grass

gaiļugriķi *nm pl* bindweed

gaiļu pelavas *nf pl* cowslip

gaiļuzirņi *nm pl* (bot.) yellow-flowered alphalpha

gainīt *vt* shoo, drive off

gainīties *vr* ward off

gaiņāt *vt* chase; shoo, drive away

gaiņāties *vr* shoo, drive off

gaisa aizsprosts *nm* air barrage

gaisa apkure *nf* space heating; hot air heating

gaisa barjēra *nf* aerial barrage

gaisa bedre *nf* air pocket

gaisa ceļš *nm* airway

gaisa dārzi *nm pl* hanging gardens

gaisa desantniek/s *nm* paratrooper; **g. ~i** paratroops gaisa desant/s *nm* airborne force; g. ~a trieciens airborne assault

gaisa dzelzceļš *nm* elevated railroad

gaisa fotografija *nf* aerial photography

gaisagrābeklis *nm* (col.) thoughtless, imprudent person

gaisagrābslis *nm* (col.) thoughtless, imprudent person

gaisa izpalīgs *nm* antiaircraft battery helper

gaisa kaŗa flote *nf* air force

gaisa lēciens *nm* somersault; caper

gaisa ligzda *nf* air pocket

gaisa līnij/a *nf* beeline; g. ~ā as the crow flies

gaisa osta *nf* airport

gaisa parāde *nf* air display

gaisa pasts *nm* airmail

gaisa pelde *nf* air bath

gaisa pilis *nf pl* castles in the air

gaisa pirāts *nm* airline hijacker

gaisa pūslis *nm* air bladder

gaisa pūslītis *nm* air bubble

gaisa reklāma *nf* aerial advertising

gaisa skūpsts *nm* blown kiss

gaisa slūēžas *nf pl* air lock

gaisa spēki *nm pl* air force

gaisa spiediens *nm* atmospheric pressure

gaisa spilvens *nm* (automobile) airbag

gaisa šautene *nf* airgun

gaisa telpa *nf* airspace

gaisa tilts *nm* 1. suspension bridge; 2. airlift

gaisa trase *nf* air route, airway

gaisa trauksme *nf* air alert

gaisa uzbrukums *nm* air raid

gaisa vilciens *nm* cable car

gaisa vanna *nf* air bath

gaisave *nf* thoughtless, flighty person

gaisaviete *nf* thoughtless, flighty person

gaiseklis *nm* (col.) thoughtless, imprudent person

gaiselīgs *adj* = gaisīgs

gaisene *nf* thoughtless, flighty person

gaisība *nf* 1. whispiness, airiness; 2. frivolity, flightiness

gaisīgi *adv* 1. whispily, airily; 2. frivolously

gaisīgs *adj* 1. light, whispy, airy; 2. frivolous, flighty

gaisīgums *nm* 1. whispiness, airiness; 2. frivolity, flightiness

gaisināt *vt* squander

gaiskuģis *nm* airship

gaiskuģniecība *nf* navigation by airship; aeronautics

gaiskuģotājs *nm* aeronaut

gaislaide *nf* (of an oven) air vent

gaislis *nm* (col.) thoughtless, imprudent person

gaism/a *nf* 1. light; ~as necaurlaidīgs light proof; ar ~u at dawn; 2. (fig.) education, knowledge; 3. ~as (col.) (automobile) lights; priek-šējās ~as headlights; tālās ~as high beam; tu-vās ~as low beam

gaismas bilde *nf* (obs.) lantern slide

gaismas ieguve *nf* luminous efficacy

gaismas iespiedums *nm* collotype

gaismas lietderības koeficients *nm* luminous efficiency

gaisms pils *nf* (poet.) school; educational institution

gaismas svīda *nf* dawn

gaismas tablo *indecl nm* luminous indicator board

gaismas vainags *nm* halo

gaismeklis *nm* light source; light fixture, lamp

gaismēna *nf* chiaroscuro

gaismiņ/a *nf dim* of gaisma; mazā ~ā at daybreak

gaismizturība *nf* lightfastness

gaismizturīgs *adj* lightfast

gaismizturīgums *nm* lightfastness

gaismjutība *nf* photosensitivity

gaismjutīgs *adj* photosensitive

gaismjutīgums *nm* photosensitivity

gaismlaidība *nf* translucency

gaismlaidīgs *adj* translucent

gaismlaidīgums *nm* translucency

gaismmīlis *nm* photophilic plant

gaismojums *nm* 1. light; 2. (photo.) exposure

gaismot *vt* light

gaismoties *vr* turn lighter

gaismprasīgs *adj* photophilic

gaismspēja *nf* (photo., of lenses) speed

gaismspējīgs *adj* (photo., of lenses) fast

gaismturīgs *adj* lightproof

gaisonis *nm* thoughtless, imprudent person

gaisotne *nf* atmosphere

gais/s *nm* 1. air; **tukšs g.** empty space; ~a a. aerial, air; b. overhead; ~a **necaurlaidīgs** airtight ◊ **biezs g.!** look out for squalls! **no zila ~a** out of the blue; **no ~a grābts** made out of thin air; **g. tīrs** (com.) the coast is clear; **pa ~u ~iem** to all winds; **kā no ~a nokritis** completely baffled; ~**a gabals** long distance; ~**a gabalu** (col.) a long way off; **2.** ~**ā** a. in the air; in midair; b. up; **ar kājām ~ā** belly up; upside down

gaissauss *adj* air-dry

gaist *vi* dissipate, vanish, disappear, evaporate, fade away

gaistamība *nf* volatility

gaistošs *adj, part* of **gaist** volatile; dissipating, vanishing, disappearing; fleeting

gaisulis *nm* (col.) thoughtless, imprudent person

gaišais *nom adj* (typ.) lean face

gaišais degunradzis *nm* white rhinoceros

gaišais ķauķis *nm* lesser whitethroat

gaišais ķeģis *nm* arctic redpoll

gaišais šņibītis *nm* sanderling

gaišalus *nm* lager

gaišana *nf* fading, disappearance

gaišbalts *adj* pure white

gaišbrūni *adv* in a light brown color

gaišbrūns *adj* light brown

gaišdzelteni *adv* in a pale yellow color

gaišdzeltens *adj* pale yellow

gaiši *adv* 1. brightly; 2. clearly

gaišība *nf* light, lightness; **Jūsu g.** Your Serene Highness

gaiši dzeltenbrūnā ripene *nf* shaggy-stalked parasol

gaišmatains *adj* blond

gaišmate *nf* blonde

gaišmatis *nm* blond

gaišot *vi* turn lighter

gaišoties *vr* turn lighter

gaišpelēks *adj* light gray

gaišredzība *nf* clairvoyance

gaišredzīgi *adv* clairvoyantly

gaišredzīgs *adj* clairvoyant

gaišreģ/is *nm*, ~e *nf* clairvoyant

gaišrozā *indecl adj* (col.) pale pink

gaišs *adj* 1. (of light soures, sound; fig.) bright; 2. (of color, illumination) light; **jau g.** it is already daylight; 3. clear

gaišsarkans *adj* light red

gaišums *nm* brightness, light

gaišzaļi *adv* in a light green color

gaišzaļš *adj* light green

gaišzilā zīlīte *nf* azure tit

gaišzili *adv* in a light blue color

gaišzils *adj* light blue

gait/a *nf* 1. pace; rate (speed); **pilnā ~ā** at full speed; in full swing; 2. gait; **ļempīga g.** slouch; **ļogana g.** waddle; **viegla g.** light step; 3. course, progress; progression; movement; motion; running; **atgriezniska g.** reciprocating motion; **viss iet savu ~u** all things are going as they should; **pēdējā g.** funeral; 4. a. ~**as** activity; **raibas ~as** adventures; b. corvée

gaitene *nf* (mining) adit, drift

gaitenis *nm* corridor, hallway, passage

gaitīgi *adv* 1. nimbly; 2. quickly, fast

gaitīgs *adj* 1. nimble; 2. quick, fast

gaitnie/ks *nm* 1. serf; farm hand; ~**ce** *nf*; 2. (mil.) enlisted man on barracks duty

gaitot *vi* perform corvée labor

gajals *nm* gayal

gājēj/s *nm*, ~a *nf* **1.** walker, good walker; **2.** pedestrian; **3.** farm hand; **4.** goer; **kaŗā g.** soldier

gājien/s *nm* **1.** march; procession; ~a **izkārtojums** order of march; **2.** walk; **3.** (of a piston) stroke; **atgrieznisks g.** reciprocating stroke; **g. uz augšu** upstroke; **g. uz leju** downstroke; (of screw threads) turn; **tukšs g.** idle movement; **4.** (chess, checkers; fig.) move; **vienā ~ā** at one go; **5.** (fig.) angle, trick; **6.** dance figure

gājīgi *adv* = **gaitīgi**

gājīgs *adj* = **gaitīgs**

gājis *part* of **iet** gone

gājputns *nm* migratory bird

gāju *indecl adj* migratory

gājums *nm* **1.** course; **2.** walk; **3.** (obs.) harvest; **4.** (obs.) class; origin

gājzvaigzne *nf* planet

galā *indecl adj* gala

gala atskaņa *nf* end rhyme

galado *indecl nm* bush baby

galakses *nf pl* galaxes

galaktāns *nm* galactan

galaktika *nf* galaxy

galaktisks *adj* galactic

galaktometrs *nm* lactometer

galaktonskābe *nf* galactonic acid

galaktoze *nf* galactose

galal[i]ts [ī] *nm* Galalith

galamērķis *nm* **1.** final goal; **2.** destination

gala morēna *nf* end moraine

galance *nf* gallantry, chivalry

galant[e]rija [ē] *nf* haberdashery

galanti *adv* gallantly

galants *adj* gallant, chivalrous

galantums *nm* gallantry, chivalry

gala osta *nf* port of destination

gala pārbaudījums *nm* final examination

galaprodukts *nm* end product

galapunkts *nm* end point; destination; terminal

galarezultāts *nm* net result

gala savienojums *nm* butt joint

galasiena *nf* end wall, headwall

galastacija *nf* terminal (station)

galatieši *nm pl* Galatians

galavārds *nm* concluding remarks; final word; epilogue

gala vieta *nf* destination

galdabiedr/s *nm*, ~e *nf* table companion

galda biete *nf* red beet

galda brālis *nm* commensal, messmate

galdains *adj* (obs.) checkered

galda kalns *nm* table mountain

galda karte *nf* place card

galda karote *nf* tablespoon

galda lūgsna *nf* grace

galda nazis *nm* dinner knife

galda piederumi *nm pl* tableware; place setting

galda rīki *nm pl* flatware

galda runa *nf* dinner speech, after-dinner speech

galda spēle *nf* board game

galda telefons *nm* desk telephone

galdauts *nm* tablecloth

galda veļa *nf* table linen

galddrāna *nf* tablecloth

galdienis *nm* terminally ill patient

galdiņa *nf* wooden bowl

galdiņa dancināšana *nf* table turning

galdiņ/š *nm* **1.** *dim* of **galds** ◊ **plānā ~a urbējs** (col.) an educated incompetent (one who, al-though educated, shirks serious work); **2.** checkerboard; **3.** stave; **4.** **aužamais g.** netting (or knotting, tatting) shuttle; **5.** stone tablet

galdīt *vt* (of pods, nuts) shell

galdkalns *nm* mesa

galdklājis *nm* table setter

galdniecība *nf* cabinetmaking, joinery; (col.) cabinetmaker's shop

galdniekmeistars *nm* master cabinetmaker

galdnieks *nm* cabinetmaker, joiner

galds *nm* **1.** table; desk; **aukstais g.** cold buffet; **mazgājamais g.** washstand; **siltais g.** hot dishes; **g. ir klāts** dinner is served; **2.** (obs.) board; **3.** department, bureau

galdsega *nf* table cloth

gāle *nf* **1.** glaze, sleet; **2.** (poet.) icy summit

galega *nf* goat's rue

galēji *adv* to the utmost, to the extreme

galējība *nf* extreme

galējs *adj* **1.** utmost, extreme; **2.** furthest, end, last

galenes *nf pl* oakum

galenis *nm* (of a bread loaf) heel

galeniski *adv* end-on, end-to-end, on end; traversely

galenisks *adj* **1.** butt, abutting; **2.** traverse; crosscut;

galēnisks *adj* Galenic; galenic; **g. preparāts** galenical

galeniskums *nm* abutting

galēnists *nm* Galenist

galenīts *nm* galena

galeons *nm* galleon

galera *nf* galley

galerija *nf* gallery

galerts *nm* jellied meat; jellied fish

galēt I *vt* **1.** bring to an end, finish; **2. g. nost** kill

galēt II *vi* thicken

gālēt I *vi* become covered with sleet, ice over

gālēt II *vi* glow, glimmer

galete *nf* hardtack, galette

galēties *vr* **1.** come to an end; kill oneself; **2.** find refuge; **3.** fight off

galgot *vi* (reg., of geese) honk

galgt *vi* (reg., of ice) crack

galīciet/is *nm*, ~**e** *nf* Galician

galifē *nm indecl*, usu. **g. bikses** riding breeches

galifejas *nf pl* (col.) riding breeches

galīgi *adv* utterly

galīgs *adj* **1.** final; **2.** utter; **3.** finite

galīgums *nm* finiteness

galiliet/is *nm*, ~**e** *nf* Galilean

galināt *vt* kill, torture to death

galināties *vr* kill oneself

galindi *nm pl* Galindians

galinieks *nm* **1.** representative; **2.** leader

galinsoga *nf* galinsoga

galiņš *nm* **1.** *dim* of **gals**, end, tip; **2.** (of a bread loaf) heel

galiski *adv* end-on; traversely

galisks *adj* **1.** end-on; longitudinal; **2.** traverse

galjona *nf* galleon

galli *nm pl* Gauls

gallicisms *nm* Gallicism

Gallijas roze *nf* sweetbrier

gallijs *nm* gallium

gallikānis *nm* Gallican

gallikānisms *nm* Gallicanism

gallisks *adj* Gallic

gallofilija *nf* Francophilia

gallofils *nm* Francophile

gallofobija *nf* Francophobia

gallofobs *nm* Francophobe

gallom[a]nija [ā] *nf* Gallomania

gallons *nm* gallon

galloromāņu *indecl adj* Gallo-Roman

gallusrieksti *nm pl* gallnuts

galluss *nm* gall

gallusskābe *nf* gallic acid

galma apvērsums *nm* court revolution

galma dāma *nf* lady-in-waiting

galminie/ks *nm*, ~**ce** *nf* courtier

galms *nm* court

galoda *nf* whetstone, hone

galons *nm* galloon

galops *nm* gallop

galoša *nf* overshoe, galosh; **pusdziļās ~s** storm rubbers

galot *vt* finish, finish off

galoties *vr* romp

galotne *nf* **1.** top, summit, peak; apex; **2.** end-game; **3.** (gram.) ending; **lokāmā g.** inflexion

galotnes vērtība *nf* peak value

galotņot *vt* top, cut off the top

gal/s I *nm* **1.** end; finish ◊ **~u ~ā** after all, in the long run; **g. klāt** (col.) end of the line; (we are) finished; **bez sava ~a** endlessly; **līdz ~am vaļā** wide open; **no paša pirmā ~a** from the outset; **no viena ~a līdz otram** from end to end; **katra vārda ~ā** after every word; **ne ~a, ne malas** far-flung; a lot and without stopping, copiously; no end in sight; **ak g.! ak g.!** it's a disaster; **no sākta ~a** from the outset, from day one; **ka vai gals** at the top of one's voice; **2.** tip; point; end; butt; **asais g.** point; **resnais g.** butt (end); **tie-vais g.** tip; **3.** top, summit, peak; **4.** end of life; **5.** farm; room, quarters; neighborhood; **6. ~ā** at an end, finished, over; **7. ~ā** (with repeated noun); **(rati ratu) ~ā** one (wagon) after another, numerous (wagons); **8. ~i** (naut.) rigging

gals II *nm* (phys.) gal

galsvēre *nf* (naut.) trim

galtonija *nf* galtonia, summer hyacinth

galv/a *nf* **1.** head; **caura g.** (col.) forgetful person; **gaiša g.** bright intellect, intelligent; **grūta g.** slow learner; **kailu ~u** bareheaded; **liela g.** a. know-it-all; b. stubborn person; **spējīga g.** capable (person); **viegla g.** fast learner; **~as darbs** mental work; **~as tabletes** (col.) headache tablets ◊ **~ā** (have, put) on one's head; **virs ~as** overhead; **no ~as (zināt)** (know) by heart; **no ~as līdz kājām** from head to toe; **kā bez ~as** mindlessly; **uz ~ām** share and share alike;

uz savu galvu on one's own initiative; **uz ~u** (of diving) head first; **~u nost!** off with his (her) head! **~u augšā!** chin up! **pa ~u!** hit him! **man g. griežas** I feel dizzy; **pa ~u, pa kaklu** head over heels; **skaidrā ~ā** sober; **(viņam) g. uz pleciem** (he has a) good head; **kā g. kūp** grinding away (at a mental task); **par ~as tiesu** by a head; **kur tev g.?** don't you know any better? **visā ~ā** at the top of one's voice; **(skriet) ar ~u sienā** run one's head against a brick wall; **ar siltu ~u** intoxicated; **2.** hair; **3.** (of a newspaper, magazine) title, masthead; **4.** chief, head, manager

galvains *adj* (of clouds) puffy, cumulus; with thunderheads

galvanisks *adj* galvanic

galvanisms *nm* galvanism

galvanizācija *nf* galvanization

galvanizēt *vt* galvanize

galvanizētāj/s *nm*, **~a** *nf* galvanizer

galvanokaustika *nf* galvanocautery

galvanomagnētiski *adv* galvanomagnetically

galvanomagnētisks *adj* galvanomagnetic

galvanomatrice *nf* electrotype

galvanometrisks *adj* galvanometric

galvanometrs *nm* galvanometer

galvanoplastika *nf* galvanoplastics

galvanoskops *nm* galvanoscope

galvanostēģija *nf* electrodeposition

galvanote|ch|nika [h] *nf* electrodeposition

galvanotropisks *adj* galvanotropic

galvanotropisms *nm* galvanotropism

galvas āda *nf* scalp

galvasgabals *nm* a piece to be memorized

galvaskaus/s *nm* skull; **~a vāks** calvarium

galvas lakats *nm* kerchief

galvas mājiens *nm* nod

galvasnauda *nf* capitation (tax), head money; poll tax

galvaspilsēta *nf* capital

galvas plikums *nm* pate

galvas rēķins *nm* mental arithmetic

galvas smadzenes *nf pl* cerebrum

galvasrota *nf* head ornament

galvassāpes *nf pl* headache

galvassega *nf* headgear

galvasstāja *nf* headstand

galvas telefons *nm* headphone

galvas uts *nf* head louse

galvasvirsa *nf* top of the head

galvauts *nm* kerchief

galvenais *adj* **1.** main, chief, principal; master; primary; **2.** central; leading

galvenais *nom adj* main thing

galvenājs *nm* bog bilberry bushes

galvene *nf* bog bilberry

galvenis *nm* **1.** letterhead; **2.** head of the table

galvenokārt *adv* mainly, chiefly, principally

galvgabals *nm* a piece to be memorized

galvgalis *nm* head of the bed; headboard

galvīgi *adv* self-assuredly

galvīgs *adj* **1.** self-assured; **2.** smart

galvinie/ks *nm*, **~ce** *nf* **1.** guarantor; sponsor; **2.** head, chief

galviņ/a *nf* **1.** *dim* of **galva**, head, little head; **uz ~ām** share and share alike; **2.** (phono; bot.) head; **dzēšamā g.** erasing head; **ierakstāmā g.** recording head; **3.** (of a pipe) bowl

galviņkāposti *nm pl* cabbage

galviņsalāti *nm pl* head lettuce

galviņurbis *nm* Forstner bit

galviņveida *indecl adj* capitate

galviņveidīgs *adj* capitate

galvkājis *nm* cephalopod

galvkrūts *nf pl* cephalothorax

galvojums *nm* warranty, guaranty; pledge; security, bail

galvošan/a *nf* warranting, guaranteeing; **uz ~u!** (col.) guaranteed! for sure!

galvot *vi* warrant, guarantee; vouch for

galvotāj/s *nm*, **~a** *nf* guarantor; sponsor

galvturis *nm* headrest

galvup *adv* head first; headlong

galvveida *indecl adj* head-shaped

galvveidīgs *adj* head-shaped

galvvidus *nm* top of the head

galvvirsa *nf* top of the head

gaļa *nf* meat; flesh; **auksta g.** headcheese, jellied meat; **liekā g.** proud flesh; **žāvēta g.** dried meat, beef jerky

gaļains *adj* fleshy, meaty; pulpy

gaļas āmurs *nm* steak hammer

gaļas buljons *nm* beef buillon

gaļas ekstrakts *nm* beef buillon

gaļas izcirtējs *nm* meat cutter

gaļas klucis *nm* chopping block

gaļas kombināts *nm* meat packing plant

gaļas konservi *nm pl* canned meat

gaļas lopi *nm pl* beef cattle

gaļas mašīna *nf* meat grinder;

gaļas muša *nf* blowfly; see also **pelēkā g. m.**, **zi-lā g. m.**

gaļas pastēte *nf* minced meat pie

gaļas receklis *nm* headcheese

gaļas skapis *nm* meat safe

gaļas veikals *nm* butcher shop

gaļas vira *nm* beef broth

gaļēdājs *nm* carnivore

gaļēdis *nm* carnivore

gaļēži *nm pl* Carnivora

gaļīgs *adj* fleshy, meaty; pulpy

gaļīgums *nm* fleshiness, meatiness; pulpiness

gaļiņa *nf dim* of **gaļa**, meat

gaļots *adj* fleshy, meaty; pulpy

gāma *nf*, *nm* glutton

gamaša *nf* gaiter; spat

gamba *nf* viola da gamba

gambīts *nm* gambit

gambūzija *nf* gambusia

gamelāns *nm* gamelan

gameta *nf* gamete

gametofīts *nm* gametophyte

gamma I *nf* **1.** (mus.) scale; **2.** (fig.) gamut

gamma II *nf* gamma

gammaglobulīns *nm* gamma globulin

gāmrija *nf, nm* (com.) glutton

gāmrīļa *nf, nm* (com.) glutton

gāmura spogulis *nm* laryngoscope

gāmurenis *nm* (ling.) laryngeal (sound)

gāmurs *nm* larynx

gan *partic* (for emphasis or added meaning of doubt, uncertainty, conviction, or contrast); **es to pārdevu g. !** I did sell it! **labi g. !** all right! **kas g. tur notiek?** I wonder what is happening there; **to g. nezinu** I really don't know; **es tev g.!** (as a warning) just you wait! **ir g.!** (in a contradiction) it is so!

gan *conj* **1. g. . . . g.** both . . . and; now . . . now; **g. šā, g. tā** now one way, now another; **2.** (for contrasting emphasis) but instead; **3.** (with **lai, kaut**) although

gana *adv* enough

ganāmpulks *nm* herd, flock

ganceļš *nm* cowpath

gandarījuma balva *nf* consolation prize

gandarījums *nm* satisfaction; amends

gandarīt *vt* **1.** repay, recompense; give satisfaction; **2.** get back at, repay (for a wrong)

gandarīts *adj, part* of **gandarīt** satisfied

gandēt *vt* (col.) ruin, spoil, damage

gandēties *vr* spoil

gandra *nf* geranium

gandrene *nf* geranium

gandrīz *adv* almost; *adj* quasi; **g. neko** next to nothing

gandrknābis *nm* geranium

gandrs *nm* (reg.) stork

gane *nf* herdgirl

ganekle *nf* pasture

ganeklis *nm* herd

gāneklis *nm* one in the habit of cussing

gangatis *nm* (reg.) glutton

ganglijs *nm* ganglion

ganglioblok[a]tors [ā] *nm* autonomic nervous system blocker

gangrēna *nf* gangrene; **slapjā g.** moist gangrene

gangrēnozi *adv* gangrenously

gangrēnozs *adj* gangrenous

gangste/ris *nm* gangster; **~ŗu pasaule** gangland

gangsterisms *nm* gangsterism

gangveja *nf* gangway

ganības *nf pl* pasture

ganību ālanta *nf* willow-leaved inula

ganību pienenītes *nf pl* hawkweed

ganību tiesības *nf* herbage

ganījums *nm* herding

ganīkla *nf* **1.** pasture; **2.** herd

ganiņš *nm dim* of **gans**, herdboy

ganisters *nm* ganister

ganīt *vt* (of herds, flocks) tend, herd, shepherd

gānīt *vt* call names

ganīte *nf dim* of **gane**, herdgirl

ganīties *vr* graze, pasture

gānīties *vr* cuss, use abusive language

gankulītes *nf pl* (bot.) shepherd's purse

gan/s *nm* **1.** herdsman; **~u tauta** nomadic tribe; **2.** **~i** a. herdsmen; b. tending of herds, herding; **~u ceļš** pasture road; **~u gaitas** herding job; **~os** a. herding; b. out to pasture

ganudiena *nf* herding day

ganumeita *nf* herdgirl

ganuzēns *nm* herdboy

ganoīdu *indecl adj* ganoid

gaņģis *nm* (obs.) **1.** corridor; **2.** run of millstones; **3.** (weav.) set of ends

gar *prep* **1.** along; by, past; **g. zemi** on the ground, to the ground; **2.** (of movement, activity) against, around, with respect to

garabērns *nm* creation, product of creativity

garaiņi *nm pl* vapor, steam

ga[r]ais [ŗ] Indriķis (or **Toms**) *nm* middle finger

ga[r]ais [ŗ] klepus *nm* whooping cough

ga|r|ām |r̩| *adv* 1. past, by; g.! missed! g. ejot in passing, casually; (chess) en passant; 2. over, gone

garamantas *nf pl* (poet.) folklore

ga|r|ā |r̩| Māra *nf* (col.) middle finger

ga|r|āmbraucēj/s |r̩| *nm*, ~a *nf* passing driver, passing motorist

ga|r|āmbraukt |r̩| *vi* drive past

ga|r|āmgājēj/s |r̩| *nm*, ~a *nf* passerby

ga|r|āmiet |r̩| *vi* pass by

garantēt *vt* guarantee

garantētāj/s *nm* ~a *nf* guarantor

garantija *nf* guaranty

garants *nm* guaranty, guarantor

ga|r|ā |r̩| rasene *nf* oblong-leaved sundew

garastāvoklis *nm* mood, humor

ga|r|astainā |r̩| lija *nf* pallid harrier

ga|r|astainais |r̩| zīriņš *nm* arctic tern

ga|r|astains |r̩| *adj* long-tailed

ga|r|astes |r̩| *indecl adj* long-tailed

ga|r|astes |r̩| kaija (or klijkaija) *nf* long-tailed skua

ga|r|astes |r̩| pūce *nf* Ural owl

ga|r|ast/is |r̩| *nm* the long-tailed one; ~e *nf* (folk.) an epithet for the magpie

ga|r|astīte |r̩| *nf* long-tailed tit

ga|r|audzis |r̩| *nm* tall, lanky person; tall plant

ga|r|ausainais |r̩| sikspārnis *nm* long-eared bat

ga|r|ausains |r̩| *adj* long-eared

ga|r|ausis |r̩| *nm* rabbit, hare

ga|r|ausītis |r̩| *nm dim* of ga|r|ausis |r̩|, rabbit, hare

garāža *nf* garage

ga|r|bārdains |r̩| *adj* long-bearded

ga|r|bārdis |r̩| *nm* the long-bearded one

ga|r|bārkstains |r̩| *adj* having long fringes

gārcelēt *vi* croak; caw

garde *nf* guard

gardē *interj* (chess) gardez

gardēd/is *nm*, ~e *nf* gourmet

ga|r|degun/is |r̩| *nm*, ~e *nf* long-nosed person

gard|e|nija |ē| *nf* gardenia

garderobe *nf* 1. cloakroom; ~s pakaramie checkracks; ~s zīme cloakroom check; 2. wardrobe, clothes

garderobist/s *nm*, ~e *nf* cloakroom attendant

gardēža *nf, nm* (col.) gourmand

ga|r|dibene |r̩| *nf* (obs.) top hat

ga|r|dibenis |r̩| *nm* = gardibene

ga|r|diena |r̩| *nf, nm* = gardienis

ga|r|dienis |r̩| *nm* dawdler

gardināt *vt* spice

gardināties *vr* relish (in eating)

gardīne *nf* curtain

gardīņu sprediķis *nm* curtain lecture

gardmarīns *nm* midshipman

gardmēlīgs *adj* dainty, picky

gardmēlis *nm* gourmand

gardmutis *nm* gourmand

gardi *adv* with relish

gards *adj* delicious, tasty, savory; (of laughter) hearty

gardumnieks *nm* gourmand

gardums *nm* 1. delicacy, tasty tidbit; 2. tastiness, savoriness

gārdzēt *vi* rattle in one's throat

gārdziens *nm* rattle (in the throat)

gardzobis *nm* gourmand

gārdzoņa *nf* rattle (in the throat)

garenās smadzenes *nf pl* medulla

garenb|a|ze |ā| *nf* wheelbase

garenēvele *nf* jack plane

garenēvelmašīna *nf* parallel-planing machine

garengriezums *nm* longitudinal cut, longitudinal section; inboard profile

gareni *adv* longitudinally, lengthwise

gareniski *adv* longitudinally, lengthwise; (naut.) fore-and-aft

garenisks *adj* 1. longitudinal; 2. longish, oblong

garenkārta *nf* stretcher course (of bricks)

garenpadeve *nf* longitudinal feed

garenprofils *nm* longitudinal profile

garens *adj* longish, oblong, elongated

garensaists *nm* stringer

garensavienojums *nm* (masonry) stretcher bond

garensija *nf* purlin; (aeron.) longeron

garenšķiedra *nf* long fiber

garenvilnis *nm* longitudinal wave

garenzāģis *nm* pit saw

garē/ties *vr*, only *3rd pers*; **uguns ~jas** the fire is about to go out

ga[r]ēvele [ŗ] *nf* jack plane

ga[r]gabalnie/ks [ŗ] *nm*, **~ce** *nf* long-distance runner

ga[r]gabalu [ŗ] *indecl adj* long-distance

ga[r]gāle [ŗ] *nf* (zool.) diver

ga[r]galv/is [ŗ] *nm*, **~e** *nf* long-headed one

gārgāļveidīgie *nom adj pl* Gaviidae

ga[r]ga[r]š [ŗ][ŗ] *adj* very long

ga[r]gāzeniski [ŗ] *adv* lying down, stretched out

ga[r]gāzu [ŗ] *adv* lying down, stretched out

gārgt *vi* rattle in one's throat

ga[r]gulus [ŗ] *adv* lying down, stretched out

gārguļot *vi* rattle (in respiratory organs)

ga[r]gūra [ŗ] *nf, nm* dawdler

ga[r]i [ŗ] *adv* at length; **g. un plaši** (of speaking) expatiate; at length

garīdzniecība *nf* clergy

garīdznieks *nm* clergyman; priest

gariga *nf* garigue

garīgi *adv* 1. spiritually; 2. mentally

garīgs *adj* 1. spiritual; 2. mental; 3. religious, church, sacred; 4. (of drinks, hum.) alcoholic

garīgums *nm* spirituality

garināt I *vt* 1. lenghen; 2. draw it out

garināt II *vt* cool

gariņš *nm dim* of **gars**, steam; spirit

gariski *adv* lying down

ga[r]kājains [ŗ] *adj* long-legged, lanky, leggy

ga[r]kāji [ŗ] *nm pl* tipulas, crane flies

ga[r]kājis [ŗ] *nm* long-legged person

ga[r]kaklains [ŗ] *adj* long-necked

ga[r]kaklis [ŗ] *nm* 1. long-necked person; 2. northern pintail

ga[r]kātains [ŗ] *adj* 1. long-stemmed; 2. long-handled

ga[r]kāte [ŗ] *nf* long-handled scythe

ga[r]kātis [ŗ] *nm* (col.) long-legged person

ga[r]klucis [ŗ] *nm* log

ga[r]knābis [ŗ] *nm* long-beaked bird

ga[r]knābja [ŗ] *indecl adj* long-beaked

ga[r]knābja [ŗ] gaura *nf* red-breasted merganser

gārkstēt *vi* 1. cackle; 2. rattle in one's throat

gārkstiens *nm* cackle; rattle

gārkstoņa *nf* 1. cackling; 2. rattle (in one's throat)

ga[r]kūļi [ŗ] *nm pl* long sheafs of straw (used in thatching)

ga[r]laicība [ŗ] *nf* boredom

ga[r]laicīgi [ŗ] *adv* boringly; (in predicates) bored

ga[r]laicīgs [ŗ] *adj* boring, dull

ga[r]laicīgums [ŗ] *nm* boringness, dullness

ga[r]laikot [ŗ] *vt* bore

ga[r]laikoties [ŗ] *vr* be bored; **g. līdz nāvei** be bored stiff

ga[r]laiks [ŗ] *nm* boredom

garlaka *nf* See **jūras garlaka**

ga[r]lapu [ŗ] *indecl adj* longleaf

ga[r]lapu [ŗ] gundega *nf* spearwort

ga[r]lapu [ŗ] mētra *nf* horse mint

ga[r]lapu [ŗ] rasene *nf* oblong-leaved sundew

ga[r]lapu [ŗ] veronika *nf* a veronica, Veronica longifolia

ga[r]lapu virza [ŗ] *nf* lesser stitchwort

ga[r]lapu [ŗ] vītols *nm* a willow, Salix dasyclados

ga[r]lielis [ŗ] *nm* long-legged person

ga[r]malka [ŗ] *nf* fireplace logs

ga[r]matain/is [ŗ] *nm*, **~e** *nf* long-haired one

ga[r]matains [ŗ] *adj* long-haired

ga[r]matis [ŗ] *nm* long-haired one

garme *nf* warmth

ga[r]mēlīgs [ŗ] *adj* derisive

ga[r]mēl/is [ŗ] *nm*, ~e *nf* scoffer, ridiculer

garmetis *nm* bucket (for throwing water on hot stones in a sauna)

ga[r]nadzība [ŗ] *nf* petty thievery

ga[r]nadz/is [ŗ] *nm*, ~e *nf* (col.) petty thief

garnējums *nm* (food) garnish

garnele *nf* shrimp

garnēt *vt* (of food) garnish

garnica *nf* (obs.) a Russian measure of volume

garnierēt *vt* (col., of food) garnish

gār/nis *nm* heron; ~ņu kolonija heronry

garnitūra *nf* 1. trimmings; 2. set (of things that belong together); (of type) font

garnizon/s *nm* garrison; ~a dienests garrison duty; ~a priekšnieks garrison commander; ~a slimnīca military hospital

gārņveidīgie *nom ad pl* Ardeidae

garojums *nm* emanation

garot *vi* steam

garoz/a *nf* crust; (anat.) cortex; ~ā kodis (col.) long in the tooth

garozains *adj* crusty

ga[r]pēteris [ŗ] *nm* (col.) middle finger

ga[r]pirkstains [ŗ] *adj* long-fingered, long-toed

ga[r]pirkstis [ŗ] *nm* (col.) thief

ga[r]pirkstnieks [ŗ] *nm* (col.) thief

ga[r]purnis [ŗ] *nm* gray seal

ga[r]radēži [ŗ] *nm pl* long-horned cattle

ga[r]rokains [ŗ] *adj* long-armed

gar/s *nm* 1. steam, vapor; 2. spirit; augstā ~ā high-flown; spirgtā ~ā in high spirits; svētais g. holy spirit; 3. mind; lieli ~i great minds; ~a aptumsums mental disturbance; ~a apvārsnis mental outlook; plašs ~a apvārsnis broad-mindedness; šaurs ~a apvārsnis narrow-mind-edness; ~a bērns intellectual offspring; ~a dar-bība mental

activity; ~a dāvana talent; ~a gaisma education; ~a mantas oral tradition; ~a nabadzība lack of imagination; ~a radniecība congeniality, mental affinity; ~a slimība mental disorder; ~ā slims mentally ill; ~a spējas mental capacity; ~a vājums feeblemindedness; ~ā vājš feebleminded; (redzēt) ~ā (see) in the mind's eye; lēnā ~ā calmly, unhurriedly; vienā-dā ~ā in the same way

gārsa *nf* goutweed

ga[r]skropstains [ŗ] *adj* having long eyelashes

ga[r]skujainā [ŗ] priede *nf* longleaf pine

ga[r]snuķis [ŗ] *nm* weevil

ga[r]spalvains [ŗ] *adj* long-haired

ga[r]spārnains [ŗ] *adj* long-winged

ga[r]spārnis [ŗ] *nm* a long-winged animal

ga[r]stilbains [ŗ] *adj* long-legged

ga[r]stilbis [ŗ] *nm* long-legged person

ga[r]stilbju [ŗ] *indecl adj* long-legged

ga[r]stobra [ŗ] *indecl adj* long-barreled

ga[r]stulmains [ŗ] *adj* (of boots) high-leg

ga[r]stulmu [ŗ] *indecl adj* (of boots) high-leg

ga[r]svārcis [ŗ] *nm* a long-frocked person

ga[r]š [ŗ] *adj* 1. long; cik g., tik plats six of one, half a dozen of the other; 2. (of persons) tall

garša *nf* (sense; sensory quality) taste; flavor

gārša *nf* mixed forest; (forest.) mixed stand type on rich soil

gāršas lācītis *nm* caterpillar of an Arctiidae moth, Pericalli matronula

gāršas striebuļi *nm pl* angelica

garšaugs *nm* herb

garši *adv* heartily, with relish

garšīgi *adv* deliciously

garšīg/s *adj* tasty, delicious, savory, flavorful

garšināt *vt* season

ga[r]šķiedrains [ŗ] *adj* long-fibered

ga[r]šķiedras [ŗ] *indecl adj* long-fibered

ga|r|š|aukus |ŗ| *adv* stretched out (fully on the ground)

garšojams *adj, part* of garšot sapid

garšot *vi, vt* taste; **man garšo ēst** I have a good appetite; **tas man negaršo** I don't like the taste of it; **garšo pēc . . .** it tastes like . . .

garšsaknes *nf pl* savory vegetables

garšviela *nf* spice; ~s spices, seasoning

ga|r|taustes |ŗ| **kodes** *nf pl* gelechiids

garu izdzīšana *nf* exorcism

garu izdzinējs *nm* exorcist

garu mēnesis *nm* October

garu saukšana *nf* necromancy

garu saucējs *nm* necromancer;

ga|r|um |ŗ| *adv emph* of garš; **g. gaŗš** really long

ga|r|ums |ŗ| *nm* **1.** length; **2.** (of persons) height; **3.** longitude

ga|r|umzīme |ŗ| *nf* macron

ga|r|ūsains |ŗ| *adj* long-whiskered

ga|r|valodība |ŗ| *nf* long-windedness

ga|r|valod/is |ŗ| *nm*, ~e *nf* long-winded person

ga|r|vasa |ŗ| *nf* water sprout

garvilka I *nf* ventilation

ga|r|vilka |ŗ| II *nf, nm* slowpoke, dawdler

ga|r|vilnas |ŗ| *indecl adj* long-wool

ga|r|ziedu |ŗ| **lilija** *nf* Easter lily

ga|r|zobis |ŗ| *nm* banterer, scoffer

gaŗ- See gar-

gaspaēa *nf* (obs.) madame

gasterija *nf* gasteria

gastīt *vt* (reg.) entertain with food and drink

gastrāls *adj* gastral

gastraļģija *nf* gastralgia

gastrisks *adj* gastric

gastrīts *nm* gastritis

gastroenterīts *nm* gastroenteritis

gastroenterolo/gs *nm*, ~ģe *nf* gastroenterologist

gastroenteroloģija *nf* gastroenterology

gastrolēt *vi* tour; make guest appearances

gastrolīts *nm* gastrolith

gastromicētes *nf pl* Gasteromycetes

gastronomija *nf* gastronomy

gastronomijas veikals *nm* delicatessen

gastronomisks *adj* gastronomic

gastronom/s *nm*, ~e *nf* gastronomer

gastropods *nm* gastropod

gastroptoze *nf* gastroptosis

gastroskopija *nf* gastroscopy

gastroskops *nm* gastroscope

gastrula *nf* gastrula

gastrulācija *nf* gastrulation

gasts *nm* (reg.) guest

gāšana *nf* overthrow; **g. no troņa** dethronement; ~s ass (geod.) trunnion axis

gāšanās *nfr* fall, tumble

gāšus *adv emph* of gāzt; **g. gāza** he toppled everything; it was coming down in buckets

gatavais *adj* (col.) pure, sheer, real, utter

gatavbetons *nm* ready-mixed concrete

gatavdaļa *nf* prefabricated unit; precast unit

gatavēža *nm* freeloader

gatavība *nf* **1.** preparedness, readiness; willingness; **2.** ripeness, maturity

gatavības apliecība *nf* high school diploma

gatavināt *vt* ripen, age

gatavliets *adj* precast

gatavot *vt* **1.** make; prepare; **2.** coach

gatavotāj/s *nm*, ~a *nf* preparer; maker

gatavoties *vr* **1.** prepare, prepare oneself, get ready; **2.** ripen; **3.** be imminent, be impending; (of storms) gather

gatavplaknis *nm* precast slab

gatavs *adj* **1.** ready, prepared; **2.** finished; ready-made; (of an idea) preconceived; **3.** ripe, mature

gatavums *nm* ripeness

gāte *nf* alley; lane; avenue

gateris *nm* saw frame; sawmill

gātis *nf pl* See gāts

gāts *nf* (exit or entrance) opening; passage

gatuve *nf* = gatve

gatve *nf* alley; lane; avenue

gaučo *indecl nm* gaucho

gaud/as *nf pl* 1. wailing; ~u dziesma plaintive song; 2. howling

Gauda siers *nm* Gouda cheese

gauddienis *nm* a luckless person

gaudēj/s *nm*, ~a *nf* complainer, lamenter; whiner

gaudelība *nf* constant complaining and lamentation

gaudeni *adv* feebly

gaudenība *nf* feebleness, decrepitude, decadence

gaudenīgi *adv* 1. feebly; 2. plaintively

gaudenīgs *adj* 1. feeble; 2. plaintive

gauden/is *nm*, ~e *nf* cripple

gaudens *adj* feeble; crippled

gaudenums *nm* feebleness, decrepitude

gaudi *nm pl* wailing

gaudiens *nm* howl

gaudīgi *adv* plaintively

gaudīgs *adj* 1. wailing; complaining; 2. howling

gaudīt *vt* (reg.) grab, catch

gaudonis *nm* 1. wailer; 2. (com.) crier

gaudoņa *nf* howling

gaudot *vi* 1. howl; 2. (col., cont.) wail

gauds *adj* (folk.) painful, sad

gaudulība *nf* tendency to complain; plaintiveness, dolefulness

gaudulīgi *adv* plaintively; dolefully

gaudulīgs *adj* wailing; plaintive; doleful

gaudulīgums *nm* tendency to complain; plaintiveness, dolefulness

gaudul/is *nm*, ~e *nf* complainer, lamenter; whiner

gauduļot *vi* 1. (col., cont.) wail; 2. howl

gauja *nf* quantity; crowd

gaujmaliet/is *nm*, ~e *nf* dweller on the banks of the Gauja

gaulterija *nf* gaultheria, checkerberry

gaum/e *nf* (aesthetic sense) taste; ar ~i tastefully; cilvēks ar ~i person of taste

gaumēt *v* 1. *vt* take note, observe; 2. *vi* taste

gaumība *nf* tastefulness

gaumīgi *adv* tastefully

gaumīgs *adj* tasteful

gaumīgums *nm* tastefulness

gaunerēties *vr* (barb., com.) be stingy

gaunerīgs *adj* (barb., com.) stingy

gauneris *nm* (barb., com.) miser

gaura *nf* merganser

gaura zāle *nf* corn spurry

gaurenīte *nf* pearlwort

gaurēt *vi* bellow

gauri *nm pl* spurry

gauriņa *nf* smew

gauriņi *nm pl* corn spurry

gauris *nm* 1. corn spurry; 2. lazybones

gaurs *nm* gaur

gausa *nf* 1. moderation; 2. fill, satiety; 3. blessing

gausarausa *nf, nm* (col.) slowpoke

gausdiena *nm, nf* = gausdienis

gausdienis *nm*, ~e *nf* (col.) slowpoke

gauselis *nm* (col.) slowpoke

gausi *adv* slowly, pokingly

gausība *nf* 1. blessing, prosperity; 2. slowness, pokiness

gausīgs *adj* 1. (of food) filling; 2. moderate

gausināt *vt* 1. slow down; 2. sate; lai Dievs gausina! God bless this meal!

gausinie/ks *nm*, ~ce *nf* slowpoke

gausis *nm* (col.) slowpoke

gausmetrs *nm* gauss meter

gausne *nf* (reg.) thistle

gausoties *vr* hesitate

gausrausis *nm* (col.) slowpoke

gauss *adj* 1. slow, poky; lingering; 2. sating, filling; 3. moderate, temperate

gauss *nm* (el.) gauss

gaust *vi* complain, lament, vail

gausties *vr* complain, lament, wail

gausul/is *nm*, **~e** *nf* slowpoke

gausums *nm* slowness, pokiness

gauša *nf, nm* (col.) **1.** slowpoke; **2.** slow and boring speaker

gaušanās *nfr* complaining, complaints

gaušāt *vi* engage in insignificant, boring talk

gaušelis *nm* = **gaušulis**

gaušulis *nm* (col.) slowpoke

gaut *vt* obtain; grab, snatch

gauties *vr* (reg.) seek shelter, take refuge

gautin *adv emph* of **gaut**; **g. gaut** grab, snatch eagerly

gauzt *vi* blab, chatter

gaužām *adv* very, much, greatly

gauži *adv* **1.** bitterly; sorely, badly; **2.** greatly, exceedingly, very

gaužs *adj* **1.** sad, painful; plaintive; (of tears, crying) bitter; **2.** great, exceeding

gavēnis *nm* fast; **lielais g.** Lent

gavēt *vi* fast

gaviāls *nm* gavial

gavi/les *nf pl* jubilation, rejoicing; **~ļu sauciens** cheer

gavilēt *vi* **1.** rejoice, jubilate; **2.** sing (in a manner akin to yodeling)

gaviļaini *adv* jubilantly

gaviļains *adj* jubilant

gavilnie/ks *nm*, **~ce** *nf* jubilarian

gaviļpilns *adj* jubilant

gaviļu gads *nm* jubilee

gavote *nf* gavotte

gazānija *nf* gazania

gāzbetons *nm* air-entrained concrete, Aerocrete

gāze I (with **â**) *nf* downpour

gāze II *nf* gas; **mākslīgā g.** coal gas; **šķidrā g.** liquified petroleum gas

gāze III *nf* gauze

gāzējāds *adj* gaseous

gāzēj/s *nm*, **~a** *nf* upsetter, overturner, overthrower, demolisher, topler

gazele I *nf* gazelle

gazele II *nf* ghazel

gāzelēt *vt* make wobble

gāzelēties *vr* wobble, stagger; rock

gāzelīgi *adv* wobblingly

gāzelīgs *adj* wobbly

gāzeļļa *nf* gas oil

gāzenis *nm* downpour

gāzes fabrika *nf* gasworks

gāzes ģenerātors *nm* gas producer

gāzes pedālis *nm* gas pedal, accelerator

gāzes svira *nf* (auto) throttle

gāzes tvertne *nf* gas-holder

gāzes spuldze *nf* gas discharge lamp

gāzēt *vt* gas; carbonate; aerate

gāzģener[a]tors [ā] *nm* gas producer

gāzholders *nm* gasholder

gāziens *nm* **1.** downpour; **2.** whipping; **3.** blow

gazificēt *vt* gasify

gazifikācija *nf* gasification

gāzīt *vt* make wobble, make teeter

gāzma *nf* downpour

gāzmains *adj* (of rain) heavy

gāzmaska *nf* gas mask

gāzmotors *nm* gas engine

gazolīns *nm* gas oil

gazometrs *nm* gas meter

gazotrons *nm* diode (electron tube)

gāzt *vt* **1.** upset, overturn, tumble; uproot; **g. ārā** dump; **g. darbus** work hard; **g. uz sāniem** turn sth. on its side; **g. baltu** (col.) be pouring down; **g. cauri** fail, flunk; **g. kalnus** accomplish great deeds, move mountains; **g. kaunā** put to shame; **g. māju apkārt** rage; **g. postā** ruin; **2.** overthrow; dethrone; **3.** pile up, push into a pile, dump into a pile; **4.** (of large quantities of a liquid; also *vi*) pour; **g. aumaļām** pour; **gaž kā ar spaiņiem** it is raining cats and dogs; **gāz vaļā!** let it rip! **g. uguni** fire; **5.** *vi* (col.) give a beating

gāzties *vr* **1.** fall, topple; **g. no kājām** a. be unable to stand on one's feet; b. be very tired; **g. kopā** collapse; **g. virsū** throw oneself at (or up-on) s.o.; come down on s.o.; **2.** tumble; **3.** rush

gāzturbīna *nf* gas turbine

gāzturbīndzinējs *nm* gas turbine engine

gāzuļoties *vr* wobble, stagger; rock

gāzums *nm* **1.** a dumping; **2.** large numbers, slew; **3.** clearing; **4.** windfall

gāzveida *indecl adj* gaseous

gāzveidīgi *adv* as a gas

gāzveidīgs *adj* gaseous

Geigera skaitītājs *nm* Geiger counter

geims *nm* (tennis) game

geiša *nf* geisha

geizers *nm* geyser

geizerīts *nm* geyserite

geko *indecl nm* gecko

gekons *nm* gecko

gelada *nf* gelada

gelignīts *nm* gelignite

gels *nm* gel

gēlu valoda *nf* Gaelic

gemals *nm* guemal

geminācija *nf* gemination

gemināta *nf* geminate

geminēt *vt* geminate

gemma *nf* **1.** cameo; intaglio; **2.** gemma

gena *nf* = **gēns**

genciān/a *nf* gentian

geneta *nf* genet

geno[c]īds [s] *nm* genocide

genofonds *nm* gene pool

genoms *nm* genome

genotips *nm* genotype

gēns *nm* gene

gentianoze *nf* gentianose

gentiobioze *nf* gentiobiose

genuīns *adj* genuine

gēnu inženierija *nf* genetic engineering

gepards *nm* cheetah

geranijskābe *nf* geranic acid

geraniols *nm* geraniol

gerbera *nf* gerbera

geriatrija *nf* geriatrics

geriatr/s *nm,* **~e** *nf* geriatrician

g[e]rla [ē] *nf* chorus girl

germānijs *nm* germanium

germ[a]nīts [ā] *nm* germanite

gerontokr[a]tija [ā] *nf* gerontocracy

gerontolo/gs *nm,* **~ġe** *nf* gerontologist

gerontoloģija *nf* gerontology

gerontoloģiski *adv* gerontologically

gerontoloģisks *adj* gerontological

geronts *nm* elder, member of the gerousia

gerūsija *nf* gerousia

gesnerija *nf* gesneria

Gesnera tulpe *nf* Gesner's tulip

gestapo *indecl nm* Gestapo

gestapovietis *nm* Gestapo man

gēste *nf* geest

geštaltps[īch]oloģija [ih] *nf* Gestalt psychology

geštalts *nm* (psych.) Gestalt

geters *nm* (el.) getter

getīts *nm* goethite

geto *indecl nm* ghetto

getra *nf* spat; gaiter

ghaniet/is *nm,* **~e** *nf* Ghanian

giāniet/is *nm,* **~e** *nf* Guianese

gibelīns *nm* Ghibeline

gibons *nm* gibbon

gibsīts *nm* gibbsite

g[i]d/s [ī] *nm,* **~e** *nf* tourist guide

gigahercs *nm* gigahertz

gigakalorija *nf* gigacalorie

gigantiski *adv* gigantically

gigantisks *adj* gigantic

gigantiskums *nm* gigantism

gigantisms *nm* gigantism

gigantomachija *nf* gigantomachy

gigantom[a]nija [ā] *nf* fascination with the gigantic

gigants *nm* giant

gigaoms *nm* gigaohm

gigavats *nm* gigawatt

gigavoltampērs *nm* gigavolt-ampere

gigavoltampērstunda *nf* gigavolt-ampere
hour

gigerls *nm* dandy

gijots *nm* guyot

gilberts *nm* (el.) gilbert

gilija *nf* gilia

gi[lj]otīna [|] *nf* guillotine

gi[lj]otinēt [|] *vt* guillotine

gilsonīts *nm* uintaite, Gilsonite

gimnadenijas *nf pl* Gymnadenia

gimnasijs *nm* (Greek hist.) gymnasium

ginaikokratija *nf* = ginekokratija

ginaikolog/s *nm*, ~ģe *nf* = ginekologs

ginaikoloģija *nf* = ginekoloģija

ginaikoloģisks *adj* = ginekoloģisks

ginaikomastija *nf* = ginekomastija

ginandrija *nf* gynandry

ginecejs *nm* gynoecium

gineja *nf* guinea

ginejiet/is *nm*, ~e *nf* Guinean

ginekokratija *nf* gynecocracy

ginekolo/gs *nm*, ~ģe *nf* gynecologist

ginekoloģija *nf* gynecology

ginekoloģiski *adv* gynecologically

ginekoloģisks *adj* gynecological

ginekomastija *nf* gynecomastia

gingīvīts *nm* gingivitis

ginks *nm* ginkgo

gitija *nf* gyttja, sapropelite

gizotijas *nf pl* Guizotia

gjaurs *nm* giaour

glāba *nf* rescue; salvation; reprieve

glabājamais *nom adj* that which is to be kept
(or safeguarded); (jur.) trust corpus

glabājuma devējs *nm* trustor

glabājuma līgums *nm* trust deed

glabājums *nm* (jur.) trust

glabāšana *nf* 1. custody; storage; 2. burial

glabāt *vt* 1. keep, save; 2. guard, keep out
of harm's way, take good care of; **g. aiz
atslēgas** keep under lock and key; 3. bury

glabātājs *nm*, ~a *nf* keeper, custodian

glabātava *nf* depository, storehouse; treasury;
checkroom

glabāties *vr* 1. be kept; 2. (col.) hide

glābējs *nm* rescuer, saver

glābiņ/š *nm* rescue; salvation; reprieve; **viņiem
nav ~a** they are beyond help

glābšana *nf* saving, rescue

glābšanas josta *nf* life belt, life preserver

glābšanas komanda *nf* rescue party

glābšanas laiva *nf* lifeboat

glābšanas plosts *nm* life raft

glābšanas riņķis *nm* life buoy

glābšanas trepes *nf pl* fire escape

glābšanas veste *nf* life vest

glābšanas virve *nf* (naut.) lifeline

glābt *vt* save, rescue; **g. situāciju** save the day

glābties *vr* save oneself; seek refuge, seek
shelter; **g. bēgot** flee for one's life; **glābjas,
kas var!** every man for himself! run for
your lives!

glaciāls *adj* glacial

glaciofluviāls *adj* glaciofluvial

glaciolakustrīns *adj* glaciolacustrine

glaciolo/gs *nm*, ~ģe *nf* glaciologist

glacioloģija *nf* glaciology

glacioloģisks *adj* glaciological

gladi[a]tors [ā] *nm* gladiator

gladiola *nf* gladiolus

glagolica *nf* Glagolitsa

glagolisks *adj* Glagolitic

glaime *nf* (poet.) bliss

glaimi *nm pl* flattery

glaimi *adv* in a flattering manner

glaimība *nf* flattering manner

glaimīgi *adv* in a flattering manner

glaimīgs *adj* full of flattery

glaimīgums *nm* flattering manner

glaimnie/ks *nm*, **~ce** *nf* flatterer

glaimojošs *adj, part* of **glaimot** flattering

glaimot *vi* flatter

glaimotāj/s *nm*, **~a** *nf* flatterer

glaimoties *vr* make up to, ingratiate oneself with s.o.

glaims *adj* full of flattery

glanc/e *nf* (sl.) **1.** gloss; **2.** style; **ar ~i** with style

glancēt *vt* (photo.) gloss, make glossy

glāsaini *adv* gently, tenderly

glāsains *adj* gentle, tender, caressing

glāsainums *nm* gentleness, tenderness

glasē *indecl adj* glacé

glasēt *vt* glacé

glāsi *adv* (poet.) tenderly

glāsīgi *adv* gently, tenderly

glāsīgs *adj* gentle, tender, caressing

glāsīgums *nm* gentleness, tenderness

glāsināt *vt* (reg.) pamper

glasis *nm* glacis

glāsīt *vt* = **glāstīt**

glāsma *nf* (poet.) caress

glāsmaini *adv* gently, tenderly

glāsmains *adj* gentle, tender, caressing

glāsmīgi *adv* gently, tenderly

glāsmīgs *adj* gentle, tender, caressing

glāsni *adv* tenderly

glāsns *adj* tender

glāss *adj* (poet.) tender

glāstiens *nm* (poet.) caress

glāstīgi *adv* gently, tenderly

glāstīgs *adj* gentle, tender, caressing

glāstīgums *nm* gentlenes, tenderness

glāstījums *nm* caress

glāstīt *vt* stroke, pet, caress, fondle

glāstīties *vr* = **glausties**

glāstoši *adv* gently, tenderly

glāstošs *adj, part* of **glāstīt** gentle, tender, caressing

glāsts *nm* caress

glaubersāls *nf* Glauber's salt

glaucija *nf* glaucium

glauda *nf*, usu. *pl* **glaudas** caress

glaudāt *vi* (obs.) joke, engage in levity

glaudens *adj* **1.** smooth; **2.** cuddlesome

glaudi *nm pl, sg* **glauds** caresses

glaudīgi *adv* snuggling

glaudīgs *adj* snuggling, cuddlesome

glaudīgums *nm* cuddliness

glaudīt *vt* stroke, caress, pet, fondle; **g. galvu** pat on the head; **g. pret spalvu** stroke against the grain; (fig.) rub so the wrong way; **g. pa spalvai** stroke with the grain; (fig.) flatter

glaudīties *vr* snuggle up, (of cats) rub against, (of dogs) fawn on

glauds *nm* caress

glaukoma *nf* glaucoma

glaukonīts *nm* glauconite

glauma *nf* blindworm

glaumeni *adv* smoothly

glaumens *adj* smooth, slick

glaumi *adv* smoothly

glaumiķis *nm* (col.) fop

glaums *adj* smooth, slick

glauns *adj* (col.) fine, elegant

glaunums *nm* (col.) elegance

glaust *vt* **1.** smooth; **2.** cuddle; **3.** caress; **4.** (of ears) flatten

glausties *vr* **1.** snuggle up, (of cats) rub against; (of dogs) fawn on; cuddle; **2.** caress

glazē *indecl adj* glacé

glāze *nf* **1.** glass; **2.** glassful

glazējums *nm* glaze

glāzenājs *nm* growth of bog bilberries

glāzene *nf* bog bilberry

glazēt *vt* **1.** glaze; enamel; **2.** (of cakes) ice

glāzīte *nf* **1.** *dim* of **glāze**; **2.** shot (of liquor)

glāznieks *nm* (obs.) glazier

glāzturis *nm* glassholder

glazūra *nf* **1.** glaze; **2.** icing

glāžaini *adv* glassy-eyed

glāžainība *nf* glassiness

glāžain/s *adj* glassy; ~ām acīm glassy-eyed; ~i *adv* glassy-eyed

glāžainums *nm* glassiness

glāžot *vt* glass

gleča *nf* slack-baked bread

glečeris *nm* glacier

gledicija *nf* honey locust

glei[ch]enijas [h] *nf pl* Gleichenia

glejots *adj* containing gley

glejs *nm* gley

glema *nf*, usu. *pl* glemas slime, mucus

glemains *adj* slimy, mucous

gleme *nf* slime, mucus

glemēt *vi* become covered with slime or mucus

glemi *nm pl* mucus; slime

glemīgs *adj* slimy

glems *adj* slimy

glemzt *vt, vi* (reg.) eat

glemžāt *vt, vi* (reg.) eat

gleti *adv* lifelessly; g. cepts slack-baked

glets *adj* 1. slimy; 2. (of bread) slack-baked, underdone; 3. lax, slack, lifeless; (of clothes) baggy

gletums *nm* sliminess, stickiness

glezains *adj* (reg.) slack-baked, doughy

gleze *nf* slack-baked bread

glezēt *vi* 1. become sticky; 2. ball up, clump, pack; 3. chat; 4. eat slowly

glezna *nf* painting; vienkrāsaina g. monochrome

gleznaini *adv* 1. picturesquely; 2. graphically

gleznainība *nf* picturesqueness

gleznains *adj* 1. picturesque; 2. graphic

gleznainums *nm* picturesqueness

glezni *adv* 1. beautifully, gracefully; 2. delicately

gleznniecība *nf* painting (art form)

gleznniecisks *adj* pictorial

gleznnieciskums *nm* pictorialness

gleznojums *nm* painting

gleznot *vt* paint (paintings); g. uz stikla stain glass

gleznotāj/s *nm*, ~a *nf* painter (artist)

glezns *adj* 1. beautiful, graceful; 2. fine, delicate

gleznums *nm* 1. beauty, grace; 2. delicateness, refinement

glezstājs *nm* easel

glicerāts *nm* glycerate

glicerīds *nm* glyceride

glicerīns *nm* glycerin

glicerols *nm* glycerol

glicīnija *nf* wisteria

glicīns *nm* glycine

glīda *nf* slack-baked bread

gliemains *adj* slimy

gliemas *nf pl* (reg.) slime, mucus

glieme *nf* snail, slug

gliemene *nf* 1. bivalve, mussel; ēdamā g. shellfish; 2. outer ear, pinna

gliemeņvēži *nm pl* Ostracoda

gliemēt *vi* (reg.) turn slimy

glieme/zis *nm* 1. snail, slug; ~ža gaitā at a snail's pace; 2. (anat.) cochlea; 3. (tech.) worm; 4. (of a violin) scroll

gliemežnīca *nf* 1. shell (of a mollusc); 2. (anat.) pinna

gliemežkonvejers *nm* screw conveyor

gliemežpārvads *nm* worm gear

gliemežrats *nm* worm gear

gliemežurbis *nm* spiral drill

gliemežvāks *nm* shell (of a mollusc)

gliemežveida *indecl adj* shell-like

gliemežveidīgs *adj* shell-like

gliemis *nm* mollusc

gliemītis *nm dim* of gliemis, small mollusc

gliftāls *nm* Glyptal

glikagons *nm* glucagon

glik[e]mija [ē] *nf* glycemia

gliko[ch]olskābe [h] *nf* glycocholic acid

glikogēns *nm* glycogen

glikokols *nm* glycine

glikol|i|ze [ī] *nf* glycolysis
glikols *nm* glycol
glikolskābe *nf* glycolic acid
glikoproteīds *nm* glycoprotein
glikozāns *nm* glycosan
glikoze *nf* glycose
glikozīds *nm* glycoside
glikozūrija *nf* glycosuria
glīmains *adj* (reg.) doughy
glīme *nf* (reg.) clay soil
gliptāls *nm* Glyptal
gliptika *nf* glyptic
gliptostrobs *nm* Gliptostrobus
gliptotēka *nf* sculpture gallery
gliseris *nm* (naut.) glider
glīst *vi* become slick
glita *nf* (reg.) slime, mucus
glitains *adj* (reg.) slimy
glitēt *vi* (reg.) turn slimy
glīti *adv* neatly
glītrakstīšana *nf* penmanship
glits *adj* slick; (of potatoes) waxy
glīts *adj* neat; pretty, handsome
glitums *nm* slickness; waxiness
glītums *nm* neatness; prettiness, handsome-
    ness
glīve *nf* plant cover on stagnant water
glīvene *nf* pondweed
glīzda *nf* heavy clay
glīzdaine *nf* heavy clay soil
glīzdains *adj* 1. clayey; 2. slack-baked
glīzdainums *nm* clayey quality
glīzdens *adj* slick
glīzdēt *vi* turn clayey; turn slimy
glīzds *nm* heavy clay
globāli *adv* globally
glob|a|lizācija [ā] *nf* globalization
glob|a|lizēšanās [ā] *nfr* globalization
globālisms *nm* globalism
globāls *adj* global
globīns *nm* globin
globtroters *nm* globe-trotter

globula *nf* Bok globule
globulārija *nf* globe daisy
globulārs *adj* globular
globulīns *nm* globulin
globuss *nm* globe
glodene *nf* blindworm
glodens *adj* (reg.) 1. slippery; 2. nimble
glods *adj* (reg.) slippery
gloksīnija *nf* gloxinia
glomains *adj* (reg.) slimy
glomas *nf pl* (reg.) slime, mucus
glorificējums *nm* glorification
glorificēt *vt* glorify
glorifikācija *nf* glorification
glorija *nf* 1. gloria; 2. (meteor.) glory
gloriola *nf* gloriole
glorioza *nf* gloriosa, climbing lily
gloriozs *adj* glorious
glosa *nf* gloss
glosārijs *nm* glossary
glosārs *nm* glossary
glosātors *nm* glossarist
glosēma *nf* glosseme
glosemātika *nf* glossematics
glosēt *vt* gloss
glosīts *nm* glossitis
glosogr|a|fs [ā] *nm* glossographer
glosolalija *nf* glossolalia
glotoģenēze *nf* glottogony
glūda *nf* clay soil
gludā cūkpiene *nf* red-seeded dandelion
glūdains *adj* clayey
gludais firziķis *nm* nectarine
gludā plekste *nf* common dab
gluddzelzs *nf* iron (flatiron)
gludeklis *nm* iron (flatiron)
gludenā čūska *nf* European smooth snake
gludeni *adv* smoothly
gludens *adj* smooth, slick
gludenums *nm* smoothness
gludgalviņa *nf* (folk.) the smooth-headed one,
    epithet for the wagtail

gludgalvis *nm* one with smooth, slick hair

gludi *adv* smoothly; fluently; without a hitch;
   g. skuvies clean-shaven

gludinājums *nm* ironing, pressing

gludināmais paveseris *nm* blacksmith's flatter

gludināmais veseris *nm* planishing hammer

gludināt *vt* iron, press; smooth, polish

gludinātāja *nf* ironer, presser

gludinātava *nf* ironing room

gludlapu *indecl adj* smooth-leaved

gludlapu pienene *nf* red-seeded dandelion

gludmatains *adj* straight-haired

gluds *adj* **1.** smooth; slick, slippery; (of hair)
   straight; **2.** fluent

gludsala *nf* dry freeze

gludspiede *nf* lithographic press

gludspiedums *nm* lithography; planography

gludspuru izoets *nm* quillwort

gludstobra *indecl adj* smoothbore

gludums *nm* **1.** smoothness; slickness, slipperiness; **2.** fluency

gludveseris *nm* planishing hammer

glūdzeme *nf* clayey soil

glukonāts *nm* gluconate

glukonskābe *nf* gluconic acid

glukozamīns *nm* glucosamine

glukoze *nf* glucose

glume *nf* mucus, slime

glumeklis *nm* mucus, slime

glumene *nf* finishing file

glumenieks *nm* (anat.) rennet bag, abomasum

glumēns *adj* slimy

glumēt *vi* become slippery

glumēvele *nf* smoothing plane

glumgalvīte *nf* (folk.) the smooth-headed one,
   epithet for the wagtail

glumi *adv* adroitly

glumiķis *nm* a slippery one; (col.) toady

glumnieks *nm* = **glumenieks**

glums *adj* slimy; slippery, slick

glumt *vi* become slippery

glumums *nm* sliminess, slipperiness

glumza *nf* (cont.) dumb, awkward woman

glundzīties *vr* choke

glūneklis *nm* **1.** lurker, spy; **2.** reclusive,
   malevolent person

glūnēt *vi* **1.** look sullenly, glower, scowl; **2.** lurk,
   lie in wait; spy, peep

glūnētāj/s *nm*, **~a** *nf* lurker; spy

glūnīgi *adv* surreptitiously

glūnīgs *adj* lurking; surreptitious

glūnīgums *nm* lurking quality; habit of
   lurking

glūniķis *nm* **1.** lurker, spy; **2.** reclusive, malevolent person

glūnis *nm* **1.** lurker, spy; **2.** reclusive, malevolent
   person

glūns *nm* secret malevolence

glūņa *nf, nm* **1.** lurker, spy; **2.** reclusive, malevolent person

glūņāt *vi* **1.** glower; **2.** lurk; spy

gluons *nm* gluon

glupi *adv* (barb.) stupidly

glupība *nf* (barb.) stupidity

glupiķis *nm* (barb.) stupid person

glupjš *adj* = **glups**

glupjums *nm* = **glupums**

glups *adj* (barb.) stupid

glupums *nm* (barb.) stupidity

glutamīns *nm* glutamine

glutamīnskābe *nf* glutamic acid

glutārskābe *nf* glutaric acid

glutenīns *nm* glutenin

glutens *nm* gluten

glūzdēt *vi* (folk., of querns) rumble

glūzdināt *vt* (folk.) make a quern rumble

gluži *adv* quite, completely, entirely

gļēmot *vt, vi* (reg.) eat

gļēvi *adv* **1.** in a cowardly manner; **2.** limply

gļēvnadzis *nm* (col.) butterfingers

gļetns *adj* (reg.) slack; sticky, underdone

gļets *adj* (reg.) slack; sticky, underdone

glēvs *adj* 1. cowardly; 2. limp; 3. tender

glēvulība *nf* cowardice

glēvulīgi *adv* in a cowardly manner

glēvulīgs *adj* cowardly

glēvul/is *nm*, ~e *nf* coward

glēvums *nm* cowardice

gļomains *adj* (reg.) slimy

gļomas *nf pl* (reg.) slime, mucus

gļotāda *nf* mucous membrane

gļotains *adj* mucous, slimy

gļotas *nf pl* mucus, slime

gļotēt *vi* turn slimy

gļotsēne *nf* slime mold

gļotskābe *nf* mucic acid

gļotviela *nf* mucus

Gmelina alises *nf pl* Gmelin's alyssum

gnauzīt *vt* wring, wring out; crumple

gnauzt *vt* wring, wring out; crumple

gnauzties *vr* strain

gneiss *nm* gneiss

gnets *adj* beat, good-looking

gnets *nm* Gnetum

gnēze *nf* 1. (of abird) crest; beak; 2. cabbage stem, cabbage core

gnībeklis *nm* clamp, vice

gnīda *nf* nit; (cont.) lazy, slow, or stingy person

gnīdains *adj* nitty

gnīdausis *nm* riffraff

gnīdīzers *nm* (com.) miser

gnīdlaides *nf pl* botflies

gnome *nf* gnome, aphorism

gnomiķis *nm* aphorist

gnomisks *adj* gnomic

gnomonisks *adj* gnomonic

gnomons *nm* gnomon

gnoms *nm* gnome (dwarf)

gnoseoloģija *nf* = gnozeoloģija

gnoseoloģisks *adj* = gnozeoloģisks

gnosticisms *nm* Gnosticism

gnostiķ/is *nm*, ~e *nf* Gnostic

gnotobionts *nm* gnotobiote

gnotobiotisks *adj* gnotobiotic

gnozeoloģija *nf* epistemology

gnozeoloģiski *adv* epistemologically

gnozeoloģisks *adj* epistemological

gnu *indecl nm* gnu

gņēga *nf, nm* picky eater

gņēgāt *vi* eat pickily

gņūzt *vi* buckle (bend)

goba I *nf* elm

goba II *nf* (hist.) tribute, contribution, tax in kind; ~s zeme leasehold

gobelēnist/s *nm*, ~e *nf* Gobelin tapestry maker

gobelēns *nm* Gobelin (tapestry)

gobija *nf* goby

goblapu spireja *nf* a spirea, Spiraea chamedryfolia

gobzemis *nm* (hist.) leaseholder

gobzinis *nm* (hist.) tax administrator

goda apziņa *nf* rectitude

godabiedr/s *nm*, ~e *nf* honorary member

godājams *adj, part* of godāt honorable; G~ais (in salutations) Dear

godalga *nf* prize

godalgojums *nm* award of a prize

godalgot *vt* award a prize; tikt ~am win a prize

godalgots *adj, part* of godalgot prize-winning

goda mielasts *nm* banquet

godaprāts *nm* rectitude, probity

goda raksts *nm* certificate of appreciation, honor scroll

goda saraksts *nm* honor roll

godasardze *nf* honor guard

godāt *vt* 1. honor; 2. call, title

godāties *vr* boast, display; adorn oneself

godatiesa *nf* court of honor

godavārds *nm* word of honor

goda vārti *nm pl* triumphal arch

godavīrs *nm* man of honor

godbijība *nf* reverence

godbijīgi *adv* reverently

godbijīgs *adj* reverent

godbijīgums *nm* reverence

goddevība *nf* respectfulness, deference

goddevīgi *adv* respectfully, deferentially

goddevīgs *adj* respectful, deferential

godēcija *nf* godetia; farewell-to-spring

godība *nf* glory, grandeur; ~s festival, banquet

godībnie/ks *nm*, ~**ce** *nf* guest at a festivity

godīgi *adv* honestly, honorably; properly, decently

godīgs *adj* **1.** honest, honorable; fair; **2.** proper, decent

godīgums *nm* **1.** honesty; fairness; **2.** decency

godinājums *nm* honor

godināt *vt* honor; pay homage

godīt *vt* call, title

godkāre *nf* ambition

godkāri *adv* ambitiously

godkārība *nf* ambition

godkārīgi *adv* ambitiously

godkārīgs *adj* ambitious

godkārīgums *nm* ambition

godkāris *nm* an ambitious person

godkārs *adj* ambitious

godmīlis *nm* an ambitious person

godpilns *adj* honored

godprātība *nf* decency

godpratīgs *adj* decent

godpratīgums *nm* decency, rectitude

god/s *nm* **1.** honor; reputation; **pēdējais g.** last respects; ~**a** of honor; honorary; ~**a atdošana** salute, saluting; ~**a aizmirsis** re-probate; ~**a laupīšana** a. dishonor; b. defamation; libel; ~**a parādīšana** homage ◊ ~**a vārds!** honest! **uz** ~**a vārdu** (of prisoners) on parole; ~**am** (or **pa** ~**am**) honorably; **par** ~**u** in honor of; **g., kam g. nākas** honor to whom honor is due; **būt** ~**ā** be honored; **g. kā no poda** honors galore; **g.** ~**am** just right, very well, properly; **uz** ~**a** (col.) okay, proper; **2.** rank, position; **3.** also *pl* ~**i**; festivity, celebration, festive occasion (to celebrate a baptism, wedding, or funeral); ~**am** for a festive occasion; for

show; to celebrate; ~**a drēbes** Sunday best; ~**a istaba** guest room

godsirdība *nf* **1.** honesty, fairness; **2.** decency

godsirdīgi *adv* honestly, honorably; fairly

godsirdīgs *adj* honest, honorable; fair

godvieta *nf* place of honor

gofrē *indecl nm* accordion pleats

gofrējums *nm* corrugation

gofrēt *vt* (of sheet metal, cardboard) corrugate; (of fabric) goffer

gogelmogelis *nm* (col.) egg flip

gojs *nm* goy

gokartist/s *nm*, ~**e** *nf* kart driver

gokarts *nm* kart

goldlaks *nm* wallflower

golfa laukums *nm* golf course

golfa nūja *nf* golf club

golfist/s *nm*, ~**e** *nf* golfer

golfs *nm* golf

goliāta ietvere *nf* mogul lamp socket

goliāts *nm* goliath

gols *nm* (soccer) goal

gomele *nf* (reg.) bumblebee

gomfrenas *nf pl* Gomphrena

gomindāns *nm* Kuomintang

gonāda *nf* gonad

gon[a]dotropisks [ā] *adj* gonadotropic

gondola *nf* **1.** gondola; **2.** (of a dirigible) nacelle; **3.** gondola car

gondoljērs *nm* gondolier

gongs *nm* gong

goniometrija *nf* goniometry

goniometrs *nm* goniometer

gonīts *nm* gonitis

gonokoks *nm* gonococcus

gono[r]eja [rr] *nf* gonorrhea

gorals *nm* goral

gorāt *vt, vi* smoke

gorbuša *nf* humpback salmon

Gordija mezgls *nm* Gordian knot

gordiņš *nm* (naut.) buntline

gordonseters *nm* Gordon setter

gorgona *nf* Gorgon, gorgon

gorgonisks *adj* Gorgonian

Gorgonzolas siers *nm* Gorgonzola (cheese)

gorīgi *adv* wobbling; swiveling

gorīgs *adj* fidgety, wriggling; wobbly

gorilla *nf, nm* gorilla

gorīt *vt* (of hips) swivel

gorīties *vr* **1.** wobble; **2.** stretch oneself; posture; fidget, wriggle; **3.** (col.) poke around, dawdle

gorodki *nm pl* skittles (Russian version)

gorodovojs *nm* (hist.) policeman

gorza *nf, nm* one that basks

gosnele *nf dim* of **govs**, little cow

gosniņa *nf dim* of **govs**, little cow

gospelis *nm* gospel music

gotele *nf dim* of **govs**, little cow

gotene *nf* **1.** cow boletus; **2.** heifer; **3.** (col.) cow pie

gotēns *nm* young cow, heifer

goteņu lapas *nf pl* water arum

goti *nm pl* Goths

gotika *nf* (arch.) Gothic

gotiņa *nf dim* of **govs**, little cow

gotisks *adj* Gothic

gotu burti *nm pl* Gothic (lettering)

govgan/s *nm*, ~e *nf* cowherd

govisks *adj* cowy, cowlike

govju bakas *nf pl* cowpox

govju beka *nf* cow boletus

govju dundurs *nm* ox warble fly

govju gans *nm* cowherd

govju gārsa *nf* angelica

govju ķimenes *nf pl* common fenugreek

govju meita *nf* cowgirl

govju mīzenes *nf pl* mayweed

govju peka *nf* cow pie

govju puķe *nf* oxeye daisy

govkope *nf* cowgirl

govkopēja *nf* cowgirl

govkopība *nf* cattle raising

govkopis *nm* cowman

govkūts *nf* cow barn

govmēle *nf* (bot.) shingled hedgehog

govmīze *nf* corn chamomile

govpurne *nf* marsh marigold

govs *nf* cow; **slaucamā g.** milch cow

govslopi *nm pl* cattle

govsmēle *nf* (bot.) shingled hedgehog

govspuse *nf* (com.) lazy girl, lazy woman

govs zobi *nm pl* toothwort

goza *nf, nm* idler

gozains *adj* sunny

goze *nf* heat, sun-heated place

gozēt *vt* sun, expose to the sun

gozēties *vr* bask

graba *nf* lean spring flatfish

grabas *nf pl* junk

grābas *nf pl* rakings

grābāt *vt* **1.** rake lightly; **2.** fumble, grope; **3.** (col.) grab, steal

grābāties *vr* **1.** rake lightly; **2.** fumble, grope

grabaža *nf* piece of junk; ~s junk

grabažkaste *nf* junk box; (sl., of a car) pile of junk

grabažnieks *nm* sundries merchant

grābēj/s *nm*, ~a *nf* **1.** raker; **2.** grabber; gripper

grabeklis *nm* **1.** rattle; a rattling object; **2.** (col.) prattler

grābeklis *nm* rake

grābeklīte *nf* alfilaria

grabeklītis *nm dim* of **grabeklis**, little rattle

grābeklītis *nm dim* of **grābeklis**, little rake

grābens *nm* (geol.) graben

grabēt *vi* **1.** rattle, clatter; **2.** (com.) blab

grabētājs *nm* (com.) blabber

grābiens *nm* grasp, grip; snatch, grab

grabižis *nm* (col.) blabber, prater

grabināt *vt* rattle; *vi* (of rain) beat against

grabināties *vr* rattle

grabis *nm* (col.) prater, blabber

graboņa *nf* rattle, clatter

grābslīgs *adj* (col.) thieving

grābslis *nm* (col.) **1.** grabber; **2.** thief

grābstīgs *adj* (col.) thieving

grābstīt *vt* **1.** rake lightly; **2.** fumble, grope

grābstīties *vr* **1.** grope, fumble; paw; rummage; **2.** engage in petty thievery; **3.** engage in small talk; **g. pa gaisu** talk nonsense

grābstoņa *nf, nm* (col.) thief

grābšķ/is *nm* (col.) **1.** prater; **2.** thief; **3.** ~i a. non-sense; b. gossip; c. (reg.) rakings

grābšļi *nm pl* **1.** (col.) nonsense; **2.** (reg.) rakings

grābt *vt* **1.** rake; **2.** grab, grasp; **g. aiz krāga** collar ◊ **g. Dievam acīs** (col.) be overweening; **g. no (zila) gaisa** spin out of thin air; ~**s no gaisa** figment of one's imagination; **3.** (col.) get hold of

grabu *interj* rattle; **ne čiku, ne g.** not a sound

grabulis *nm* rattle (toy)

grābul/is *nm*, ~**e** *nf* petty thief

grabuļkaste *nf* (col.) jalopy

grabzdiņas *nf pl* (reg.) cracklings

grācija *nf* **1.** grace, gracefulness; Grace; **2.** corset

gracils *adj* gracile

gr[a]ciozi [ā] *adv* gracefully

gr[a]ciozitāte [ā] *nf* grace, gracefulness

gr[a]ciozs [ā] *adj* graceful

gr[a]ciozums [ā] *nm* grace, gracefulness

gradācija *nf* gradation

gradēt *vt* (of salt solutions) graduate

gradients *nm* gradient

grādīgs *adj* (of drinks) hard

gr[a]d/s [ā] *nm* **1.** (geog.; temperature; educ.) degree; ~**u tīkls** (map) grid; **cik ~u ir šodien?** what is the temperature today? **2.** proof (alcohol content); **3.** (typ.) point

graduālis *nm* (rel.) gradual

graduāls *adj* gradual

graduēt *vt* graduate (calibrate)

grafējums *nm* ruling

grafēma *nf* grapheme

grafēmika *nf* graphemics

grafēt *vt* rule (draw lines)

grāfiene *nf* countess

grafika *nf* graphic arts; graphics

grafik/s *nm* **1.** graph; **2.** schedule, timetable; chart; **pēc ~a** on schedule

grafiķ/is *nm*, ~**e** *nf* graphic artist

grafiski *adv* graphically

grafisks *adj* graphic

grāfiste *nf* county

grafiti *nm pl* graffiti

grafitizēt *vt* graphitize

grafīts *nm* graphite; (pencil) lead

grafolo/gs *nm*, ~**ģe** *nf* graphologist

grafoloģija *nf* graphology

grafoloģisks *adj* graphological

grafom[a]nija [ā] *nf* graphomania

grafom[a]n/s [ā] *nm*, ~**e** *nf* graphomaniac

grafometrija *nf* graphometry

grafs *nm* graph

grāfs *nm* count (titled noble)

grafu teorija *nf* graph theory

graize *nf* cut; *pl* ~**s** stomachache

graizes zāle *nf* golden saxifrage

graizīgi *adv* cuttingly, bitingly

graizīgs *adj* cutting, biting

graizījumi *nm pl* clippings, parings

graizīt *vt* **1.** cut, shred; mince; **2.** castigate; **3.** hit

grājas *nf pl* soft rumble

graķītis *nm* (col.) vodka

Grāla biķeris *nm* Holy Grail

grāmat/a *nf* **1.** book; **baltā g.** white paper; **galvenā g.** ledger; **lasāmā g.** reader; **g. ar uzdruku** lettered book ◊ ~**ās** on the books; **pēc ~as** by the book; **kā no ~as** (of speaking) like a book; **2.** (obs.) letter

grāmatas apvalks *nm* dust jacket

grāmatele *nf* (cont.) small, poorly made book or booklet

grāmatgalds *nm* bookstall

grāmatiespiedējs *nm* book printer

gramatika *nf* grammar

gramatiķ/is *nm*, ~e *nf* grammarian

grāmatiņa *nf dim* of grāmata, booklet

gramatiski *adv* grammatically

gramatisks *adj* grammatical

grāmatizdevējs *nm* book publisher

grāmatnesis *nm* (hist.) letter carrier

grāmatnīca *nf* bookstore

grāmatniecība *nf* book publishing

grāmatniecisks *adj* 1. book-publishing; 2. bookish

grāmatnie/ks *nm*, ~ce *nf* 1. book lover, bibliophile; 2. (obs.) literate person, reader; 3. person employed in the publishing business; 4. (anat.) psalterium, manyplies

gramatoms *nm* gramatom

grāmatplaukts *nm* bookshelf

grāmatrūpniecība *nf* book production

grāmatsējēj/s *nm*, ~a *nf* bookbinder

grāmatsiešana *nf* bookbinding

grāmatsietuve *nf* bookbindery

grāmatskapis *nm* bookcase

grāmatspiestuve *nf* book printing plant

grāmattirdzniecība *nf* book business

grāmattirgotāj/s *nm*, ~a *nf* bookseller

grāmattirgotava *nf* bookstore

grāmatu apskats *nm* book review

grāmatu balsts *nm* bookend

grāmatu draugs *nm* book lover

grāmatu nelga *nm*, *nf* bibliomaniac

grāmatu noslēgums *nm* balancing of books

grāmatu pārbaudīšana *nf* auditing

grāmatu pārbaudītājs *nm* auditor

grāmatu rādītājs *nm* booklist

grāmatu skapis *nm* bookcase

grāmatu skarpis *nm* book scorpion

grāmatu soma *nf* book bag

grāmatu tārps *nm* bookworm

grāmatu zīme *nf* 1. bookmark; 2. bookplate

grāmatvedība *nf* bookkeeping; **dubultā g.** double-entry bookkeeping; **vienkāršā g.** single-entry bookkeeping

grāmatved/is *nm*, ~e *nf* bookkeeper; accountant; **zvērināts g.** certified public accountant

grāmatveikals *nm* bookstore

grāmatzīme *nf* 1. bookplate; 2. bookmark

gramba *nf* rut (in the road)

grambains *adj* rutty

gramekvivalents *nm* gram equivalent

gramicidīns *nm* gramicidin

gramīns *nm* gramine

gramions *nm* gram ion

grāmis *nm* heartburn

gramkalorija *nf* gram calorie

grammofons *nm* phonograph

grammolekula *nf* gram molecule

gramnegatīvs *adj* gram-negative

grampozitīvs *adj* gram-positive

grams *nm* gram

gramslīgs *adj* (col.) thieving

gramslis *nm* (col.) thief

gramstīt *vt* (col.) grope, fumble

gramstīties *vr* 1. (col.) grope, fumble, rummage; 2. nibble

gramšķīgs *adj* (col.) thieving

gramšķ/is *nm* (col.) 1. blabber; 2. petty thief; 3. ~i odds and ends; bits and pieces; debris, rem-nants

gramšļi *nm pl* (reg.) odds and ends; bits and pieces; debris, remnants

gramžāt *vt* (*iter*, reg.) scratch

granapipka *nf* (col.) vodka

granāta *nf* 1. grenade, hand grenade; 2. shell

granātābele *nf* pomegranate tree

granātābols *nm* pomegranate

granātkoks *nm* pomegranate tree

granātmetējnieks *nm* mortarman

granātmetējs *nm* 1. light mortar; 2. grenade launcher

granāts *nm* 1. pomegranate; 2. garnet

granātstobrs *nm* bazooka

granātšāvējs *nm* grenadier

granātuztvērējs *nm* grenade sump

granda *nf* rumbling

grandēt *vi* rumble, thunder, roar

grandi *nm pl* rumble

grandien/s *nm* thunderclap; (of a cannon) roar; ~i rumble

grandiozi *adv* grandiosely

grandiozitāte *nf* grandiosity

grandiozs *adj* grandiose

grandiozums *nm* grandiosity

grandīt *vi* slambang; rumble; make a racket

grandīties *vr* 1. toss about; 2. rumble, roll

grandoņa *nf* rumbling

grands *nm* grandee

granītciets *adj* hard as granite

granītols *nm* imitation leather

granīts *nm* granite

granoblastisks *adj* granoblastic

gr[a]nodiorīts [ā] *nm* granodiorite

gr[a]ns [ā] *nm* (weight) grain

grantaine *nf* gravelled area, gravelled road

grantains *adj* gravelly

grantainums *nm* gravelliness

grantēt *vt* gravel

grants *nf* gravel

grantsbedre *nf* gravel pit

grantskalns *nm* gravel hill

grantskarjērs *nm* gravel pit

granula *nf* granule; nodule

granulācija *nf* granulation

granulācijas līkne *nf* sieve analysis curve; grading curve

granulārs *adj* granular

granulēšana *nf* granulation

granulēt *vt* granulate

granulīts *nm* granulite

granulocīts *nm* granulocite

granuloma *nf* granuloma

granulozs *adj* granular

grape *nf* (reg.) rut (in the road)

grāpis *nm* (col.) kettle

graptolīts *nm* graptolite

gra/sis *nm* groschen, groat; mite ◊ **nožēlojami** ~**ši** pittance; **ne plika** ~**ša vērts** not worth

a cent; **(viņam) nav ne plika** (or **sarkana**) ~**ša** (he is) penniless

grasīties *vr* 1. be about to, prepare, make ready; 2. threaten

grāte *nf* (metal.) burr, fin

gratifikācija *nf* bonus

gratis *adv* gratis

gratulācija *nf* congratulation

gratulant/s *nm*, ~**e** *nf* congratulator

gratulējums *nm* congratulation

gratulēt *vt* congratulate

graudaini *adv* granularly

graudainība *nf* granularity, graininess

graudains *adj* granular, grainy

graudainums *nm* granularity, graininess

graudaugs *nm* (bot.) cereal

graudēdājs *nm* granivore

graudēdis *nm* granary weevil

graudenis *nm* bruchus

graudēt *vi* rumble; make loud noises, thunder

graudien/s *nm* thunderclap; (of a cannon) roar; ~i rumbling

graudiņš *nm dim* of **grauds**, little grain; (of medicine) pill

graudkopība *nf* grain growing

graudniece *nf* share-tenant's wife

graudniecība *nf* share-tenancy

graudnieks *nm* share-tenant

graudot *vi* work the land using share-tenants

graudotājs *nm* owner of farmland farmed by share-tenants

graud/s *nm* 1. grain; kernel; **melnie** ~**i** ergot; 2. granule; 3. usu. *loc* ~**ā** (payment) in kind; 4. nugget; pellet; 5. (of firearms) front sight

graudsaimniecība *nf* grain farm

graudu cukurs *nm* granulated sugar

graudu kalte *nf* dryhouse

graudu kode *nf* grain moth

graudu melnplauka *nf* bunt of wheat

graudums *nm* thundering

graudu smecernieks *nm* granary weevil

graudu tēviņi *nm pl* ergot

graudu tīrītājs *nm* winnower

graudveida *indecl adj* granular

graudveidīgi *adv* granularly

graudveidīgs *adj* granular

graudzāles *nf pl* grass family

grauja *nf* destruction; ~s thunderclaps; rumble

graust *vi* thunder; rumble

grausts *nm* **1.** dilapidated building, hovel, shack; **2.** old, teetering person; **3.** coffin

graustu sanācija *nf* slum clearing

graušļāt *vt* chew on, nibble

graušļi *nm pl* debris, rubbish

graut *v* **1.** *vt* demolish, wreck; **2.** *vt* undermine; **3.** *vi* thunder

grauties *vr* thunder

grautiņš *nm* pogrom

grauvake *nf* graywacke

grauzdas *nf pl* cracklings

grauzdēļi *nm pl* cracklings

grauzdēt *vt* roast; toast

grauzdētājs *nm* roaster; toaster

grauzdētava *nf* roasting room, roasting plant

grauzdēties *vr* roast

grauzdiņ/š *nm* **1.** *dim* of **grauzds**, toast; melba toast; rusk; **2.** ~i cracklings

grauzd/s *nm* **1.** toast; melba toast; rusk; **2.** ~i cracklings

grauzdumi *nm pl* cracklings

grauze *nf* (reg.) rut (in the road)

grauzēj/s *nm*, ~a *nf* **1.** gnawer; **2.** rodent

grauzējtipa *indecl adj* (of insect mouth parts) chewing

grauzējutis *nf pl* bird lice

grauzelēt *vt* (*iter*) chew, nibble on

grauzi *nm pl* (reg.) gravel

grauzīt *vt* (*iter*) chew, nibble on

grauznis *nm* bark louse

grauzt *vt* **1.** gnaw; nibble, chew on; eat; chafe; (of nails) bite; (of smoke) sting; **2.** nag at; **3.** rankle

grauzties *vr* gnaw, chew, eat one's way into; fret

grauzums *nm* chewed spot; wormhole

grava *nf* ravine; **aprimusi g.** abated ravine

gravains *adj* raviney

grāvējbumba *nf* wrecking ball

grāvējs *nm* **1.** demolisher, wrecker; **2.** (theat., mus.) hit

gravējums *nm* engraving; etching

grāvene *nf* heath spotted orchid

gravēt *vt* engrave; etch

grāvēt *vt* dig ditches; put in drainage ditches

grāvēties *vr* make a ruckus

gravētāj/s *nm*, ~a *nf* engrave; etcher

grāviens *nm* crash, thunderclap, roll (of thunder); explosion, blast

gravier/is *nm*, ~e *nf* engraver; etcher

gravimetrija *nf* gravimetry

gravimetrisks *adj* gravimetric

gravimetrs *nm* gravimeter

gravīra *nf* engraving; etching; print

gravis *nm* (diacritic mark) grave

grāv/is *nm* ditch; moat; ~ja **vaimanas** (hum.) vodka, liquor

gravitācija *nf* gravitation

gravit[a]tīvs [ā] *adj* gravitational

gravitēt *vi* gravitate

gravitons *nm* graviton

grāvjot *vt* = **grāvot**

grāvmala *nf* side of a ditch, edge of a ditch

grāvot *vt* dig ditches

grāvracis *nm* ditch digger

grazis *nm* capricious, stubborn child

graža *nf* arrogance, conceit

graži *nm pl* caprice, whim

gražība *nf* capriciousness; whimsicality

gražīgi *adv* capriciously; whimsically

gražīgs *adj* capricious; whimsical

gražīgums *nm* capriciousness; whimsicality

gražotāj/s *nm*, ~a *nf* capricious person

graēoties *vr* **1.** be capricious; cut up; **2.** fret

gražu slota *nf* witches' broom

grebe *nf* (reg.) rut, pothole

grebināt *vt* gouge, carve, hollow out; cut

grebjains *adj* (reg.) rutted

greble *nf* (reg.) hole, pothole; rut

greblis *nm* gouge

grebļa *nf* (reg.) rut, pothole

grebt *vt* gouge, carve, hollow out; cut

grebuļaini *adv* unevenly

grebuļains *adj* uneven

grebums *nm* carving, woodcut

grebzdas *nf pl* (reg.) cracklings

grebzdi *nm pl* sapwood, alburnum

grecele *nf* kink in a yarn

grecelēt *vt* (of yarns) spin unevenly

grēcība *nf* sinfulness

grēcīgi *adv* sinfully

grēcīgs *adj* sinful

grēcīgums *nm* sinfulness

grēcinie/ks *nm*, ~ce *nf* sinner

grēciņš *nm dim* of **grēks**, little sin

grēcisms *nm* Grecism

grēda *nf* (of mountains) range; (of wood) pile; (of clouds) bank; stack

grēdot *vt* pile, stack

grēdoties *vr* pile up, stack

grēdveida *indecl adj* stack-like

grēdveidīgs *adj* stack-like

gredzenains *adj* with many rings

gredzenmuskulis *nm* orbicular muscle

gredzenot *vt* **1.** (of birds) band; **2.** (of trees) girdle; **3.** ring

gredzenpirksts *nm* ring finger

gredzens *nm* ring; band; ferrule

gredzentīkls *nm* (compu.) ring network

gredzentinējs *nm* tent caterpillar moth

gredzentiņš *nm dim* of **gredzens**, ringlet

gredzenūbele *nf* collared dove

gredzenveida *indecl adj* ring-shaped, annular

gredzenveidīgi *adv* in the shape of a ring

gredzenveidīg/s *adj* ring-shaped, annular

Gregora kalendārs *nm* Gregorian calendar

gregoriānisks *adj* Gregorian

greičot *vi* (reg.) turn

greiderist/s *nm*, ~e *nf* grader (machine operator)

greiders *nm* grader (machine)

greidi *nm pl* ornamental stripes (along the edges of woven or knit articles); nubs

greids *adj* uneven, textured; grained; nubby; streaky; twisted

greifers *nm* grab bucket, clamshell

greifs *nm* griffin

greilis *nm* (reg.) cripple

greiliski *adv* wrong way, backward, askew

greipfrūts *nm* grapefruit

greizacains *adj* squint-eyed

greizacīgs *adj* squint-eyed

greizacis *nm* squint-eye

greizens *nm* (geol.) greisen

greizgalvis *nm* (folk.) head-muddler, epithet for the hops

greizi *adv* crooked; askance; awry

Greizie rati *nm pl* Great Bear

greizkājains *adj* crippled

greizkājis *nm* bowlegged person

greizkāpe *nf* (mus.) flat

greizs *adj* **1.** crooked, lopsided; **2.** slanting, leaning; oblique; sidelong; **3.** wrong; **4.** wry

greizsirdība *nf* jealousy

greizsirdīgi *adv* jealously

greizsirdīgs *adj* jealous

greizsirdīgums *nm* jealousy

greizskanis *nm* dissonance

greizulis *nm* cripple

greizums *nm* crookedness, skewness, lopsidedness

greižot *vi* move in the wrong direction, awry or obliquely

grejs *nm* (phys.) gray

grēka gabals *nm* scapegrace, scamp

grēka kalps *nm* hardened sinner;

grēkatlaide *nf* remission of sins

grēkāzis *nm* scapegoat

grēkdar/is *nm*, ~e *nf* sinner

grēkos krišana *nf* the Fall

grēkot *vi* sin

grēk/s *nm* sin ◊ ne ~am! not on your life! ~u maiss heavy sinner

grēksūdze *nf* (rel.) confession

grēku atlaišana *nf* remission of sins

grēku nožēlošana *nf* penitence

grēku nožēlotāj/s *nm*, ~a *nf* penitent

grēku plūdi *nm pl* the Flood

grēku sūdzētāj/s *nm*, ~a *nf* confessant

grēmas *nf pl* heartburn

gremdaka *nf* caisson

gremde *nf* (volleyball) spike; (basketball) dunk

gremdēt *vt* 1. sink; 2. (volleyball) spike, (basket-ball) dunk; 3. countersink

gremdētava *nf* (naut.) hold; (theat.) trap; trap room; ~s aila trap opening

gremdēties *vr* immerse oneself

gremdināt *vt* sink

gremdkaste *nf* (tech.) crib

gremdkniede *nf* countersunk rivet

gremdsieniņa *nf* baffle plate

gremdurbis *nm* countersink bit

gremdurbšana *nf* countersinking

gremdurbt *vt* countersink

gremdvirzulis *nm* plunger

grēmenes *nf pl* herb Paris

grēmeņi *nm* (reg.) heartburn

gremojamā zāle *nf* buckbean

gremoklis *nm* cud

gremokslis *nm* cud

gremošana *nf* 1. digestion; 2. rumination; 3. chewing

gremošanas kanāls *nm* digestive tract

gremošanas traucējumi *nm pl* indigestion

gremot *vt* 1. digest; 2. ruminate, chew the cud; 3. (col.) chew

gremotājdzīvnieks *nm* ruminant

gremotājs *nm* ruminant

gremslis *nm* (reg.) 1. poor eater; 2. omnivore; 3. quarreler

gremsties *vr* = gremzties

gremt *vi* = gremzties

gremties *vr* = gremzties

gremzda *nf* heartburn

gremzdains *adj* (of trees) full of sap

gremzdēt *vt* remove sapwood

gremzdgrauži *nm pl* bark beetles

gremzdi *nm pl* sapwood, alburnum

gremzdot *vt* = gremzdēt

gremzt *vt* gnaw

gremzties *vr* fret, worry

gremža *n* 1. *nf, nm* (col.) fretter; 2. unevenly spun yarn

gremžas kaite *nf* hypochondria

gremžība *nf* (col.) peevishness

gremžīgs *adj* (col.) peevish; fretful

grenadieris *nm* grenadier

grenči *nm pl* (reg.) cracklings

grendzele *nf* a pig's curly tail

Grenlandes haizivs *nf* Greenland shark

Grenlandes ronis *nm* harp seal

Grenlandes valis *nm* Greenland right whale

grenlandiet/is *nm*, ~e *nf* Greenlander

grēns *nm* (weight) grain

grepstele *nf* tangle

grevijas *nf pl* Grewia

grevileja *nf* grevillea

grēviņš *nm* net float

grēvis *nm* or grēve *nf* a marine isopod, Mesidotea entomon

grezele *nf* 1. basket (made of vines); 2. (col.) frump

grezelīte *nf dim* of grezele, small basket

grezna *nf* (folk.) 1. piece of jewelry, adornment; 2. a cock's tail feathers

grezneklis *nm* piece of jewelry

grezni *adv* luxuriously; splendidly; magnificently; sumptuously

greznība *nf* luxury; splendor

grezrīgi *adv* bedecked

greznīgs *adj* fond of finery

greznojums *nm* adornment; decoration

greznot *vt* adorn, decorate; **g. ar spalvām** plume

greznoties *vr* adorn oneself, put on one's finery

grezns *adj* luxurious; de luxe; splendid; magnificent; sumptuous

greznumlieta *nf* adornment; piece of jewelry

greznum/s *nm* **1.** luxury; splendor; magnificence; ~a **priekšmets** luxury item; **2.** adornment; **lēts g.** bauble

grib/a *nf* will; **laba g.** goodwill; ~as **piepūle** volitional exertion; **pie labākās** ~as in good conscience, much as I want to; **pret manu** ~u against my wishes

grības *nf pl* cracklings

gribasspēks *nm* willpower

gribēšana *nf* desire

gribēt *vt* **1.** want; **2.** like; **(dariet), kā gribat** (do) as you wish; **es gribētu** I would like; **gribot ne-gribot** willy-nilly; **3.** mean, intend; **4.** (col.) be able; **5.** (col.) be about to (do sth.)

gribēties *vr* want; like; **nav tā, kā gribētos** it is not as one would like it to be; **(pateicos), man vairs negribas** no more for me, (thank you); **man gribas (dzert, ēst)** I am (thirsty, hungry), I would like (sth. to drink, eat)

gribīgi *adv* willingly

gribīgs *adj* willing

grībiņas *nf pl* cracklings

gribugrabas *nf pl* riffraff

gricelēt *vi* (reg.) scrawl

grīda *nf* floor

grīdas durvis *nf pl* trapdoor

grīdas segums *nm* flooring

grīdceliņš *nm* runner (carpet)

grīddēlis *nm* floorboard

grīdiņa *nf dim* of **grīda**, floor ◊ **līdz** ~i! down the hatch!

grīdlīste *nf* baseboard

grīdot *vt* lay a floor

grīdsega *nf* carpet; rug

grieķ/is *nm*, ~**iete** *nf* Greek; ~**u-romiešu cīņa** Greco-Roman wrestling

grieķiski *adv* in Greek, (speak) Greek

grieķisks *adj* Greek, Grecian

griemenes *nf pl* buckbean

griesti *nm pl* ceiling

griests *nm* ceiling joist

griešanās *nfr* turning, rotation; whirling, spinning; **g. tiesā** appeal to the courts

grietiņa *nf* (col.) ladybug

grietiņš *nm* (naut.) grating

grievalga *nf* or **grievalgs** *nm* hame strap

grieza *nf* coulter

griezāji *nm pl* stubble

griezaune *nf* (folk.) temptress; flighty female

grieze I *nf* rotation

grieze II (with **iê**) *nf* corncrake

griezējaparāts *nm* cutter

griezējdaļa *nf* cutting part

griezējdeglis *nm* (metall.) lance; cutting torch

griezējdzelis *nm* cutting stylus

griezējgalviņa *nf* (tech.) cutter

griezējierīce *nf* cutting device

griezējinstruments *nm* cutting implement

griezēj/s *nm*, ~**a** *nf* **1.** cutter; **2.** an apple weevil, Rhynchites conicus

griezējšķautne *nf* cutting edge

griezējzobs *nm* incisor

griezene *nf* fumitory

griezenes *nf pl* rotary sled (sled on a pivoted arm for sledding on ice)

griezenis *nm* **1.** whirlpool; **2.** gouge

griezes pāris *nm* couple of rotation

griezgali *nm pl* cut ends of stalks (in a sheaf of wheat or rye)

griezgalvis *nm* wryneck

griezi *nm pl* stubble

grieziens I *nm* **1.** twist, turn; **2.** viewpoint

grieziens II (with **iê**) *nm* cut; section

griezīgi *adv* shrilly

griezīgs *adj* cutting; sharp; piercing, shrill

griezīgums *nm* shrillness

griezis *nm* single-board plow (for breaking virgin soil), breaker

grieznes *nf pl* **1.** scissors, shears; **2.** rotary sled (on a pivoted arm for sledding on ice)

grieznis *nm* **1.** (mech.) cutter; **2.** (bot,. reg.) rape

griezonis *nm* (of sheep) turning sickness

griezt I *vt* **1.** turn; twist; spin, whirl, twirl; **g. apkārt** turn over; **g. ceļu** give way, step aside; **g. deju** dance; **g. filmu** shoot a film; **g. ilksis atpakaļ** retreat; **g. krūti pretī** resist; **g. lielas lietas** do land-office business; **g. ligzdu** make a nest; **g. par labu** mend matters; turn to the best, turn sth. around; **g. riņķī** turn around; **g. valodu (uz citu pusi)** change the subject; **g. vērību** pay attention; **g. visas malas apkārt** turn everything upside down; **g. zobus** a. grind one's teeth; b. gnash one's teeth; **2.** wring; **3.** (of plants) form (heads, round pods)

griezt II (with **iê**) *vt* **1.** cut, slit; carve, whittle; **g. dones** chamfer; **g. nost** cut off; pare; **g. rīkstes** make a rod; **cita godu g.** slander; **2.** (of strong light) hurt, (of loud sound) grate; **3.** *vi* (of a corncrake) call

grieztaga *nf* (folk.) temptress; flightly female

grieztava *nf* orache

griezties I *vr* **1.** turn, revolve, rotate; whirl, spin; (with **pie**) turn to, appeal to; **galva griežas** feel dizzy; **g. pa labi** turn right; **viņam** (or **viņai**) **griežas** (sl.) he (or she) is out of his (her) mind; **apkārt g.!** about face! **2.** twist; **3.** (of wind) shift; **g. uz labo pusi** take a favorabled turn; **4.** *part* **griezdamies** (of growing) by leaps and bounds

griezties II (with **iê**) *vr* **1.** cut into; (fig.) hurt; **2.** (of sound) grate on the ears

grieztin *adv emph* of **griezt** I ; (with **iê**) *emph* of **griezt** II

griezturētājs *nm* (tech.) turret

grieztuve *nf* windlass, capstan

griezulis *nm* (RR) turntable

griezuma zāle *nf* sea holly

griezums I *nm* turn

griezum/s II (with **iê**) *nm* **1.** cut; **2.** carving; **3.** (tech. drawing) section; **4.** book edge; **5.** ~i chopped fodder

griežamais *nom adj* **1.** strickle; **2.** cutting implement

griežamgalds *nm* turntable

griežams *adj, part* of **griezt** I rotary, swing

griežamtilts *nm* swing bridge

grieži *nm pl* (of the moon) phases; (of the sun) solstice; (of a century) turn

griežveidīgie *nom adj pl* Rallidae

grifele *nf* slate pencil

grifpurna bruņrupucis *nm* alligator snapper

grifs I *nm* **1.** vulture; **2.** griffin

grifs II *nm* fingerboard

grifs III *nm* signature stamp

grigalka *nf* raft oar

Grijēras siers *nm* Gruyère cheese

grikaine *nf* buckwheat field

grikājs *nm* buckwheat field

grikene *nf* knotgrass

griki *nm pl* buckwheat

grilēt *vt* (cul.) grill

grilīgs *adj* = **grīļīgs**

griljāēa *nf* caramel

grīļa *nf, nm* wobbly object; unsteady, staggering person

grīļaini *adv* wobblingly

grīļains *adj* wobbly, rocking, swaying

grīļīgi *adv* wobblingly

grīļīgs *adj* wobbly, rocking, swaying

grilļa *nf* a wobbly object or person

grīļoties *vr* totter, stagger, sway, reel

grīļš *adj* (rare.) wobbly

grima *nf, nm* grouch

grimase *nf* grimace

grimējums *nm* makeup

grimēt *vt* apply makeup

grimētāj/s *nm*, ~a *nf* makeup artist

grimētava *nf* makeup room

grimēties *vr* apply makeup

grimons *nm* dogwood

grimoņu bruņuts *nf* a scale insect, Parthenolecanium corni

grims *adj* (folk.) peevish, mean

grims *nm* 1. makeup; 2. greasepaint

grimšana *nf* sinking; (tech.) subsidence

grimšus *adv emph* of **grimt; g. nogrimt** sink like a rock

grimt *vi* 1. sink; become immersed; 2. be submerged

grimtība *nf* cruelty

grimts *adj* hard, severe, unfriendly

grimulis *nm* sinker

grimža *nf, nm* grouch

grīneklis *nm* sourpuss

grīnēt *vi* sneer

grīni *adv* peevishly; sneeringly

grīnība *nf* peevishness; sneering; anger

grīnīgi *adv* peevishly; sneeringly; angrily

grīnīgs *adj* peevish; sneering; angry

grīnis *nm* (forest.) pine type on poor sandy soil

grīns *adj* 1. peevish; sneering; angry; 2. hard, severe; 3. tightly spun

grinti *adv* peevishly

grints *adj* peevish

grīnums *nm* peevishness; sneering; anger

grinzduļi *nm pl* (reg.) cracklings

grīņu sārtene *nf* cross-leaved heath, bog heather

gripa *nf* grippe, influenza

gripiņa *nf* horseshoe calk

gripozs *adj* influenzal

gripveida *indecl adj* influenza-like

gripveidīgs *adj* influenza-like

grīsla *nf* sedge

grīslaine *nf* sedge-covered area

grīslājs *nm nf* sedge-covered area

grīsliens *nm* sedge-covered area

grīslis *nm* sedge

grīst *vt* lay a floor; lay ceiling boards

grīste *nf* 1. wisp (of straw); twist, braid; 2. swirl; 3. (aeron.) spin; **ačgārna g.** inverted spin; **plakana g.** flat spin

grīsts *nf* 1. swirl; 2. (rare.) wisp (of straw); twist, braid

grīšļains *adj* sedgy

grīšļainums *nm* sedginess

grīšļaugi *nm pl* rushes

grīšļu purva ķauķis *nm* aquatic warbler

grīšļveida *indecl adj* sedge-like

grīšļveidīgs *adj* sedge-like

griuzdiņi *nm pl* (reg.) cracklings

griuždži or **griužģi** *nm pl* (reg.) cracklings

grīva *nf* (of a river) mouth, estuary

grīvis *nm* long, coarse grass

grivna *nf* 1. (hist.) grivna (medieval Russian currency unit); 2. (obs.) 10 kopecks; 3. (hist.) pendant

grizajs *nm* grisaille

grīzeklis *nm* 1. wooden door bolt; 2. a type of baby walker

grīzeknis *nm* whirlpool

grizete *nf* grisette

grizlijs *nm* grizzly bear

grīzte *nf* = **grīste**

grizulis *nm* wooden winnowing pitchfork

grīzulis *nm* 1. whirlpool; 2. tantrum

groba *nf* rut (in the road)

grobulains *adj* bumpy, uneven

grodi *nm pl* 1. wellhead; 2. (of a wooden bridge) floor

grodi *adv* tightly

grods *adj* tightly twisted, plaited

grodums *nm* tight twist

groks *nm* grog

grope *nf* groove

gropene *nf* rabbet plane

gropeslogs *nm* grooved window

gropes savienojums *nm* rabbet joint

gropēt *vt* groove

gropēvele *nf* rabbet plane

gropēvelmašīna *nf* groover

gropzāģis *nm* grooving saw

grosists *nm* wholesale merchant

grosmamma *nf* (barb.) grandma

grospaps *nm* (barb.) grandpa

gross *nm* gross (12 dozen)

groša I *nf* groschen

groša II *nf* (barb.) grandma

grota *nf* grotto

grota brases kāja *nf* main-brace bumpkin

grota gafeltopbura *nf* (schooner) main gaff-topsail

grota marsa štagbura *nf* main topmast stay-sail

grota marsbura *nf* main topsail

grota raja *nf* main yard

grota reilis *nm* main royal

grota skaisele *nf* main skysail

grota štagbura *nf* main staysail; (schooner) main topmast staysail

grota vantu dzelži *nm pl* main chains

grota zāliņš *nm* maintop

grotbura *nf* mainsail

grotburas brases *nf pl* main braces

groteska *nf* **1.** grotesque; **2.** cartoon film; **3.** (typ.) sans serif

groteski *adv* grotesquely

grotesks *adj* grotesque

groteskums *nm* grotesqueness

grotmasta cepure *nf* (naut.) main truck

grotmasts *nm* main mast

grots *nm*, usu. *gen* **grota** (naut.) main

groza līkne *nf* compound curve

grozāmbalsts *nm* ring mount

grozāms *adj, part* of **grozīt 1.** turnable; (of stage, doors) revolving; (of chairs) swivel; **2.** variable, adjustable; **3.** changeable

grozgalvis *nm* **1.** wryneck; **2.** (folk.) wryneck, an epithet for the hops and the horse

grozības *nf pl* **1.** changes; **2.** vicissitudes; **3.** (of the moon) phases

grozīgi *adv* changeably, variably

grozīgs *adj* changeable, variable; fickle

grozīgums *nm* changeability, variability; fickleness

grozījums *nm* alteration, modification, change

groziņš *nm dim* of **grozs**, small basket

groziņu vakars *nm* covered-dish supper

groziņzieēi *nm pl* Compositae, Asteraceae

grozīt *vt* **1.** turn repeatedly; twiddle; **g. galvu** shake one's head; **2.** change, alter, modify

grozītājmuskulis *nm* sternocleidomastoid muscle

grozītāj/s *nm* **1.** turner; **~a** *nf*; **2. lielais g.** great trochanter; **mazais g.** lesser trochanter

grozīties *vr* **1.** turn; toss about; fidget; posture; **2.** shift, change; **3.** be busy, be active; move (in social circles); **4.** (of conversations, with **ap**) turn (on a topic), deal with; **ap ko lieta grozās?** what is it all about?

grozpin/is *nm*, **~e** *nf* basketmaker

grozs *nm* **1.** basket; hamper; **pīts g.** wicker basket; **2.** basketful

groži *nm pl* rein

groži *adv* tightly

grožot *vt* provide with a rein

grožs *adj* tightly twisted, plaited

grūbas *nf pl* pearl barley

grūbe *nf* groove

grubināt *vi* **1.** gnaw; **2.** scrape, hollow

grubucis *nm* bump

grubulis *nm* bump

grubuļaini *adv* unevenly, roughly

grubuļains *adj* bumpy, uneven, rough

grubuļots *adj* bumpy, uneven, rough

grūda *nf* (reg.) **1.** throng; **2.** junk

grūdēj/s *nm*, **~a** *nf* pusher, shover; see also **lodes g.**

grūdenis *nm* **1.** grūdenis (meal of pork, barley groats, crushed peas or beans); **2.** grūdenis (meal of crushed hempseed, peas or beans)

grūdesis *nm* (reg.) hog feed

grūdien/s *nm* **1.** push, shove; jerk, jolt; shock; (el.) surge; **~iem** jerkily, by fits and starts; **2.** rain shower grudināt *vi* rumble

grūds *nm* (poet.) push

grudzināt *vi* 1. whinny softly; 2. laugh softly

grugot *vi* (of cranes) call

gruģināt *vi* 1. whinny softly; 2. laugh softly

grumba *nf* wrinkle, line; crease

grumbaini *adv* in wrinkles

grumbains *adj* 1. wrinkled, lined; 2. (rare.) rutty

grumbāt *vt* wrinkle

grumbiņa *nf dim* of grumba, little wrinkle

grumbojums *nm* wrinkles

grumbot *vt* wrinkle

grumbots *adj, part* of grumbot; 1. wrinkled; 2. (rare.) rutty

grumboties *vr* wrinkle

grumbulis *nm* bump, rough spot

grumbuļaini *adv* unevenly, roughly

grumbuļains *adj* bumpy, uneven, rough

grumbuļainums *nm* bumpiness, unevenness, roughness

grumbuļots *adj* bumpy, uneven, rough

grumdīt *vt* toss around; jostle, press

grumīties *vr* impose oneself, throw oneself at s.o.

grūms *nm* groom (horse attendant)

grumslas *nf pl* debris

grumstalas *nf pl* debris

grumšļi *nm pl* debris

grumties *vr* struggle; g. virsū importune, bother

grundulis *nm* gudgeon

grundži *nm pl* (reg.) cracklings

grunte *nf* (obs.) = grunts

gruntējums *nm* prime coat, priming

gruntene *nf* fishing rod for bottom fishing

gruntēt *vt* (of painting) prime

gruntīgi *adv* (col.) solidly, thoroughly

gruntīgs *adj* (col.) solid

gruntniecība *nf* class of peasant landowners

gruntnie/ks *nm*, ~ce *nf* peasant landowner

grunts *nf* 1. ground; (constr.) soil; 2. (of a body of water) bottom; 3. prime coat

gruntsāķi *nm pl* ledger tackle

gruntsceļš *nm* dirt road

gruntsēsma *nf* ledger bait

gruntsgabals *nm* lot (of land)

gruntskārta *nf* layer of soil

gruntskrāsa *nf* (paint) primer

gruntskungs *nm* landowner

gruntsmakšķere *nf* ledger line

gruntsnoma *nf* (hist.) quitrent, ground rent

gruntsnomnieks *nm* renter

gruntsūdens *nm* groundwater; water table

grupa *nf* group; outfit; (infantry) squad; (cavalry) section; operatīvā g. (mil.) forward echelon; taktiskā g. task force; ~s lidojums formation fligh

grupējums *nm* grouping, group; arrangement

grupēt *vt* group

grupēties *vr* group

grupeto *indecl nm* gruppetto

grupor/gs *nm*, ~dze *nf* group leader

grupu teorija *nf* group theory

grupveida *indecl adj* group

grupveidā *adv* in a group; as a group

grupveidīgi *adv* in a group; as a group

grupveidīgs *adj* group

grūslis *nm* = grūdenis

grūsma *nf* shock, blow, impact; (poet.) gust; throng, crush, press

grūsna *adj* (of mammals) pregnant; in calf, in foal, in lamb

grūsnēja *adj* in calf, in foal, in lamb

grūsnība *nf* pregnancy

grūsnīca *nf* cow in calf

grūst *vt* 1. push, shove; g. ārā push out; (of money) squander; g. darbus work hastily or sloppily; g. lodi put the shot; g. nelaimē plunge into misery; g. postā bring to ruin; g. rīklē (com.) feed; give away (to an unworthy recipient); g. vaļā blurt out; 2. pound, crush

grūsties *vr* **1.** jostle; **g. virsū** press upon; **2.** (col.) rush; **g. uz priekšu** push forward

grūstin *adv emph* of **grūst; g. grūst** push and shove mightily

grūstīt *vt* jostle, push around

grūstīties *vr* jostle, push

grūstuvis *nm* chopper (tool)

grūšana *nf* **1.** pushing, shoving; *see also* **ab-rocīgā g., (lodes) g.; 2.** pounding, crushing

grūši *adv* (reg.) heavily, painfully

grūšus *adv* **1.** by pushing; **2.** *emph* of **grūst; g. grūst** to push mightily

grūt *vi* **1.** collapse; **2.** tumble down; **3.** (of crowds) stream

grūta *adj* (col.) pregnant

grūtdien/is *nm,* **~e** *nf* wretch, unfortunate

grūtība *nf* difficulty; **nav nekādas ~s!** it's no trouble at all!

grūtgalvīgs *adj* (intellectually) slow

grūtgalv/is *nm,* **~e** *nf* slow learner

grūti *adv* hard, difficult

grūtin *adv emph* of **grūts; g. grūts** very difficult

grūtkūstamība *nf* refractoriness

grūtkūstošs *adj* refractory

grūtme *nf* (poet.) difficulty; burden

grūtmūžīte *nf* (poet.) orphan

grūtniece *nf* pregnant woman, expectant mother

grūtniecība *nf* pregnancy

grūtpūtīte *nf* (poet.) orphan

grūtredzēt *vi* (folk.) have troubles

grūtredzīgs *adj* having poor vision

grūt/s *adj* **1.** difficult, hard; arduous, trying; (fig.) heavy; **2.** (intellectually) slow; **3.** *f* **~a** (col.) pregnant

grūtsirdība *nf* low spirits, depression

grūtsirdīgi *adv* in a depressed manner

grūtsirdīgs *adj* in low spirits, down in the dumps, depressed

grūtsirdīgums *nm* low spirits, depression

grūtumi *nm pl* (col.) head cold

grūtums *nm* difficulty; burden; heaviness

gruva *nf* hole (in the ground), pothole; **~s** ruins

gruvains *adj* full of potholes

gruvekļi *nm pl* ruins

gruvešains *adj* littered; polluted

gruveši *nm pl* ruins; (geol.) detritus

gruza *nf* construction debris

gruzdējums *nm* smoldering remains

gruzdēt *vi* smolder

gruzdināt *vt* roast

gruzdiņi *nm pl* cracklings

gruzdumi *nm pl* cracklings

gruzdum/s *nm* burn, scorch; **~a smaka** burnt smell

gruzīns *nm,* **~iete** *nf* Georgian

gruzis *nm* **1.** mote, speck, particle; **2.** gudgeon

grūzis *nm* pilewort

gruzītis *nm dim* of **gruzis,** mote, speck, particle

gruznis *nm* idler

gružaine *nf* dustheap

gružains *adj* littered

gruži *nm pl* rubbish, litter, sweepings

gružiens *nm* dustheap

gružot *vt* litter

grūžu zāle *nf* horsetail

guanidīns *nm* guanidine

guanīns *nm* guanine

guano *indecl nm* = **gvano**

guanozīns *nm* guanosine

guaša *nf* gouache

gub/a *nf* **1.** stack; **2.** pile; **~u ~ām** piled up **ar ~u** replete; **3.** (col.) fatty

gubāt *vt* = **gubot**

gūbāt *vi* lumber

gubenis *nm* shed (or space) for storing unthreshed grain and straw

gubern[a]tors [ā] *nm,* **~e** *nf* governor

gubern[a]tūra [ā] *nf* (political unit) government

guberņa *nf* (hist., political unit in czarist Russia) government

gubiņa *nf dim* of **guba**, small stack

gubmākoņi *nm pl* cumuli

gubot *vt* stack; pile

gubotājs *nm*, ~**a** *nf* stacker

gubt *vi* collapse

gucul/s *nm*, ~**iete** *nf* Huzul

gudāt *vi* (of swans) sing

gudi *nm pl* (obs.) Goths, Swedes (of Gothland), and Vikings

gudr/ais *nom adj* wise man; ~**ie no austrumiem** the Magi

gudrelis *nm* wise guy

gudrgalve *nf* clever girl

gudrgalvis *nm* clever fellow

gudri *adv* wisely, cleverly

gudrība *nf* **1.** wisdom; *pl* ~**s** (col.) clever ideas; **2.** know-how; **3.** cunning

gudrības zobs *nm* wisdom tooth

gudrībniece *nf* clever girl

gudrībnieks *nm* clever fellow

gudriķis *nm* (col.) clever fellow

gudriniece *nf* clever girl; **(lapsa) g.** clever fox

gudrinieks *nm* clever fellow

gudrojums *nm* figuring

gudrons *nm* oil tar

gudrot *vt* figure, figure out, come up with

gudrotājs *nm*, ~**a** *nf* **1.** thinker; **2.** know-it-all

gudrs *adj* **1.** wise; **2.** clever, smart; **es netieku g.** I can't figure it out; **3.** intelligent; **4.** sly, cunning; **5.** sane

gudrums *nm* wisdom

gugatnis *nm* (zool.) ruff

gugoties *vr* complain, fret

guģot *vi* **1.** coo; **2.** murmur; **3.** vail

guģoties *vr* complain, fret

gulags *nm* gulag

gulašs *nm* goulash

gulbēns *nm* cygnet

gulbis *nm* swan

gulbju sakne *nf* white swallowwort

guldenis *nm* gulden

guldības *nf pl* (folk.) bedding (a Latvian wedding tradition)

guldināt *vt* (*iter*) put to bed

guldīt *vt* **1.** put to bed; **2.** lay down; **3.** inter, bury

guldzeknis *nm* **1.** gulp, draft; **2.** glug

guldzenēt *vi* choke

guldzēt *vi* glug

guldziens *nm* **1.** gulp, draft; **2.** glug

guldzināt *vi* **1.** glug; **2.** gobble

guldzīt *vt* wolf down

guldzīties *vr* choke

guldzoņa *nf* glugging

gulējums *nm* sleep

gulene *nf* fallow

gulenis *nm* (col.) sleepyhead

guleniski *adv* horizontally

gulenisks *adj* horizontal

guleniskums *nm* horizontality

gulēt *vi* **1.** sleep; **iet g.** go to bed; **guļ kā nosists** sleeping like a log; **2.** lie; **g. blāķiem** be heaped up, be piled up; **g. uz ausīm** (col.) fail to hear, miss; **3.** be laid up, be down (with a sickness); **g. uz gultas** be bedridden; **4.** rest; **g. uz lauriem** rest on one's laurels

gulētāja žurka *nf* loir, edible doormouse

gulētāj/s *nm*, ~**a** *nf* sleeper

gulētiešana *nf* going to bed; ~**s laiks** bedtime

gulgaini *adv* glugging

gulgāt *vi* choke

gulgāties *vr* choke

gulgi *adv* glugging

gulgot *vi* gurgle, glug

gulgt *vi* gurgle, glug

guliski *adv* stretched out, lying down

gulkoks *nm* = **guļkoks**

gulkstēt *vi* gurgle

gulkšķēt *vi* gurgle

guloņa *nf, nm* (col.) sleepyhead

guļošā gaurenīte *nf* procumbent pearlwort

gulošs *adj, part* of **gulēt 1.** sleeping, dormant; **2.** lying; resting; recumbent; couchant; **3.** (of business partners) silent

guloze *nf* gulose

guls *adj* horizontal

gulskapis *nm* clothes chest

gulsnēt *vi* lie around, lounge

gulsnis *nm* **1.** railroad tie; **2.** joist

gulstavāt *vi* snooze, lounge

gulstavnie/ks *nm*, **~ce** *nf* (col.) sleepyhead

gulšņa *nf, nm* (col.) sleepyhead, big sleeper

gulšņāt *vi* snooze, lounge

gulšņātāj/s *nm*, **~a** *nf* sleepyhead, big sleeper

gulšņava *nf, nm* (col.) sleepyhead

gulšņavāt *vi* snooze, lounge

gult *vi* sink down, sink upon, sink into; descend upon

gulta *nf* bed; bedstead; **divguļama g.** double bed; **saliekamā g.** folding bed; **uz ~s** on the bed; bedridden, confined to bed

gultas apklājs *nm* bedspread

gultas biedrs *nm* bedfellow

gultas blakts *nf* bedbug

gultas drēbes *nf pl* bedclothes

gultas maiss *nm* palliasse

gultas pārklājs *nm* bedspread

gultas pope *nf* matress

gultas režīms *nm* confinement to bed

gultas sega *nf* blanket

gultasvieta *nf* bunk; shared lodging

gultdrānas *nf pl* bed linen

gultekus *adv* horizontally

gulties *vr* **1.** go to bed; **2.** lie down; fall down; **3.** lie upon; **4.** (fig.) rest upon, fall upon

gultiņa *nf* **1.** *dim* of **gulta**, bed; **2.** crib, cot

gultne *nf* bed, riverbed; channel

gultnieks *nm* subtenant (one renting a place for sleeping only)

gultnis *nm* (mech.) bearing; **koniskais g.** taper roller bearing; **stacionārais g.** pillow block

gultņa odere *nf* bushing

gultsega *nf* blanket

gulus (or **gulu**) *adv* = **guļus**

gu|l|žogs [ļ] *nm* split rail fence

guļa *nf* **1.** sleep, sleeping; **2.** lying; **3.** estivation, hibernation; **4.** position, lie

guļamais *defin adj* sleeping (*adj*)

guļamdīvāns *nm* sofa bed, lounge

guļamistaba *nf* bedroom

guļamkorpuss *nm* dormitory

guļamlāviņa *nf* bunk

guļamkrēsls *nm* recliner

guļammaiss *nm* **1.** palliasse; **2.** sleeping bag

guļamsofa *nf* sofa bed, lounge

guļamtelpa *nf* sleeping quarters

guļamtīkls *nm* hammock

guļamuzvalks *nm* pajamas

guļamvagons *nm* sleeping car

guļamvieta *nf* **1.** berth; **2.** sleeping place; bed

guļamzvilnis *nm* sleeping sofa

guļasvieta *nf* sleeping place; bed, couch

guļava *nf, nm* (col.) great sleeper

guļavot *vi* snooze, lounge

guļbaļķis *nm* log (for a log construction)

guļbūve *nf* log construction

guļkoks *nm* log (for a log construction)

guļņa *nf, nm* great sleeper

guļošs *adj, part* of **gulēt** reclining; horizontal

guļsārts *nm* horizontal charcoal pile

guļsēta *nf* split rail fence

guļstrops *nm* horizontal beehive

guļus *adv* lying, reclining; **g. uz vēdera** prone; **g. uz muguras** supine

guļvieta *nf* shakedown, makeshift bed

guļžogs *nm* split rail fence

gumainā cūknātra *nf* figwort

gumains *adj* tuberous

gumba *nf* bump

gumbāt *vi* (col.) stump, gallumph

gumdināt *vt* urge, goad, incite

gumdīt *vt* urge, goad, incite

gumdītāj/s *nm*, **~a** *nf* inciter, instigator

gumiar|a|biks [ā] *nm* gum arabic

gumiguts *nm* ghatti gum

gumija *nf* 1. rubber; dzēšamā g. eraser; kožļā-
jamā g. chewing gum; 2. elastic

gumijas līme *nf* rubber cement

gumijkoks *nm* rubber tree; rubber plant

gumijot *vt* rubberize

gumijsveķi *nm pl* gum arabic

gumiņaugi *nm pl* tuberous plants

gumiņbaktērijas *nf pl* Rhizobium bacteria

gumiņsmecernieks *nm* pea weevil

gumiņš *nm* 1. *dim* of gums, bulb, tuber;
2. (bot.) nodule

gumma *nf* (med.) gumma

gumoze *nf* gummosis

gum/s *nm* bulb, tuber; ~u augi tuberous plants

gumt *vi* bow, stoop, bend

gumu vīgrieze *nf* dropwort

gumveida *indecl adj* tuber-like

gumveidīgs *adj* tuber-like

gumz/a *nf, nm* 1. (col.) clumsy person; 2. (col.)
slowpoke; 3. bend; fold; wrinkle; ~u ~ām
(*adv*) crooked

gumzāt *vt* crumple, crease, wrinkle

gumzāties *vr* poke, dawdle

gumzīgs *adj* wrinkling

gumzīt *vt* crumple, crease, wrinkle

gumzīties *vr* 1. wrinkle; 2. bend

gundega *nf* buttercup

gundene *nf* buttercup

gunderes *nf pl* gill-over-the-ground

gunera *nf* gunnera

guns *nf* (poet., reg.) fire

gunskurs *nm* (poet.) campfire

guntene *nf* (bot.) pink

guntiņa *nf* 1. *dim* of guns, little flame;
2. Brownie

gūņāt *vt* crumple, finger

gupija *nf* guppy

guramija *nf* gourami

gūrāt *vi* = gūrāties

gūrāties *vr* bend and unbend slowly; slowly
move about, stooping

gurdelīgs *adj* sickly

gurdelis *nm* sickly person

gurdenība *nf* weariness, fatigue

gurdeni *adv* wearily

gurdenis *nm* sickly person

gurdens *adj* weary, tired

gurdenums *nm* weariness, fatigue

gurdi *adv* wearily

gurdināt *vt* wear down, tire

gurdme *nf* (poet.) weariness, fatigue

gurds *adj* 1. weary, tired; 2. feeble

gurduļot *vi* (obs.) ail

gurdums *nm* weariness, fatigue

gurdvilnis *nm* spreading wave, slack wave

gurdzelēt *vi* (reg.) choke

gurdzēt *vi* crunch

gurgulis *nm* (reg.) Adam's apple

gūris *nm* loafer

gurkstēt *vi* 1. crunch; 2. growl, gurgle

gurkstoņa *nf* crunching

gurķene *nf* borage

gurkšķēt *vi* = gurkstēt

gurķ/is *nm* 1. cucumber; sālīts g. pickle; skābs
g. pickle; 2. (com.) idler, sluggard; ~u laiks
vacation time

gurķoties *vr* (com.) idle, laze

gurķu magnolija *nf* cucumber tree

gurķu mētra *nf* borage

gurnauts *nm* loincloth

gurns *nm* hip; (meat cut) loin, round; (col.)
ham

gūrs *nm* guhr

gurste *nf* wisp of flax

gurt *vi* get tired, grow weary

gurte *nf* (col.) belt

guru *indecl nm* guru

gurums *nm* tiredness, weariness

gūrums *nm* large quantities, scads

gūstīgs *adj* (obs.) greedy

gūstams *adj, part* of gūt obtainable

gūstek/nis *nm*, ~ne *nf* prisoner, captive

gūstekņu nometne *nf* prisoner-of-war camp

gūstīgs *adj* greedy

gūstīt *vt* try to capture

gūstniecība *nf* captivity

gūsts *nm* captivity

gušņa *nf* (reg.) thistle

gūt *vt* obtain, get; achieve, attain; **g. labumu** profit; **g. pārsvaru** gain the upper hand; **g. sek-mes** progress, advance; **g. uzvaru** be victorious, carry the day

guta *nf* (arch.) gutta

gutācija *nf* guttation

gutaperča *nf* gutta-percha

gūters *nm* one who wants to finish a job quickly, a hurry-it-up guy

gūties *vr* strive for

gūtne *nf* mine

guturāli *adv* gutturally

guturāls *adj* guttural

guvējs *nm*, ~a *nf* getter, attainer

guvernante *nf* governess

guvums *nm* gain, acquisition; achievement, at-tainment

guza *nf* crop; gizzard

guzains *adj* having a prominent crop

guziņa *nf dim* of **guza**, crop, gizzard

guzma *nf* (reg.) pile, heap; throng; large quantities, scads

gūzma *nf* = **guzma**

guzmēties *vr* crowd

guzna *nf* crop, gizzard

gūža I *nf* hip, haunch

gūža II *nf* (reg.) goose

gūžains *adj* hippy

gūžas kauls *nm* hipbone

gvajakols *nm* guaiacol

gvajaks *nm* guaiacum

gvajave *nf* guava

gvajula *nf* guayule

gvalstīt *vi* prattle

gvalstīties *vr* prattle

gvalte *nf* (col.) force

gvanako *indecl nm* guanaco

gvano *indecl nm* guano

gvano nirējpelikāns *nm* Peruvian booby

gvarana *nf* guarana

gvarani *indecl nm* guarani

gvarde *nf* guard; guards

gvardes mīnmetējs *nm* rocket launcher

gvardist/s *nm*, ~e *nf* guardsman

gvards *nm* guardsman, guard

gvarkstēt *vi* blab, prattle

gvatemaliet/s *nm*, ~e *nf* Guatemalan

gvelfs *nm* Guelf

gvelzīgi *adv* talkatively, gabbily

gvelzīgs *adj* (col.) talkative, gabby

gvelšana *nf* (col.) blabber, gabbing, twaddle

gvelzēj/s *nm*, ~a *nf* (col.) gabber

gvelzis *nm* (col.) gabber

gvelzt *vi* (col.) blab, gab

gvelžas *nf pl* (col.) gossip

gvereca *nf* guereza

gvergzdēt *vi* grunt

gverkstēt *vi* grunt

gvinejiet/is *nm*, ~e *nf* Guinean

Ģ

ģaubas *nf pl* complaining; lamentation

ģaubties *vr* **1.** rejoice; **2.** expect; **3.** promise; **4.** complain

ģaurēt *vi* slubber

ģedne *nf* side post of a loom

ģedovščina *nf* (mil. sl.) bullying, harassment (of subordinates)

ģeida *nf* hoyden

ģeķība *nf* (col.) foolishness

ģeķīgi *adv* foolishly

ģeķīgs *adj* (col.) foolish

ģeķīgums *nm* (col.) foolishness

ģeķis *nm* (col.) fool

ģeķot *vt* (obs.) fool

ģeķoties *vr* clown

ģeldēt *vi* (barb.) fit, do, be of use

ģēles *nf pl* (obs.) heartburn

ģēli *nm pl* Gaels

ģēloga *nf* herb Paris

ģelzis *nm* (col.) old, dull knife; a knife without a handle

ģemburot *vi* (reg.) stagger

ģemze *nf* chamois

ģenčiks *nm* (col.) orderly

ģene|a|lo/gs [ā] *nm*, ~ģe *nf* genealogist

ģene|a|loģija [ā] *nf* genealogy

ģene|a|loģiski [ā] *adv* genealogically

ģene|a|loģisks [ā] *adj* genealogical

ģenerācija *nf* generation

ģenerālaģents *nm* agent-general

ģenerālbass *nm* (mus.) continuo

ģenerāldirektors *nm* director general

ģenerālfeldmarš|a|ls [ā] *nm* field marshal-general

ģenerālgubern|a|tor/s [ā] *nm*, ~e *nf* governor-general

ģenerālgubern|a|tūra [ā] *nf* government-general

ģenerāli *adv* generally

ģenerālinspekcija *nf* Office of the Inspector General

ģenerālinspektors *nm* Inspector General

ģenerālis *nm* general; **komandējošais ģ.** general-in-chief

ģenerālisimuss *nm* generalissimo

ģener|a|litāte [ā] *nf* 1. generality; 2. body of generals; general officers

ģener|a|lizācija [ā] *nf* generalization

ģener|a|lizēt [ā] *vt* generalize

ģenerālkauja *nf* decisive battle

ģenerālklauzula *nf* general clause

ģenerālkomandieris *nm* commander in chief

ģenerālkomisij/a *nf* trade distribution; **(N uzņēmuma)** ~ā distributors for the trade, (X company)

ģenerālkonsulāts *nm* consulate general

ģenerālkonsuls *nm* consul general

ģenerālkopa *nf* (stat.) population

ģenerālleitnants *nm* lieutenant general

ģenerāllīnija *nf* party line

ģenerālmajors *nm* major general

ģenerālmantnieks *nm* universal heir

ģenerālmēģinājums *nm* dress rehearsal

ģenerālpārstāvis *nm* general agent

ģenerālpauze *nf* general pause

ģenerālpilnvara *nf* full power of attorney

ģenerālpilnvarnie/ks *nm*, ~ce *nf* chief representative

ģenerālplāns *nm* master plan; big picture

ģenerālprokurors *nm* attorney general

ģenerālpulkvedis *nm* colonel general

ģenerāls *adj* general

ģenerālsapulce *nf* general meeting; annual meeting

ģenerālsekretār/s *nm*, ~e *nf* secretary general

ģenerālstābs *nm* = ģenerālštābs

ģenerālstati *nm pl* = ģenerālštāti

ģenerālstreiks *nm* general strike

ģenerālštāba karte *nf* strategic map

ģenerālštābs *nm* general staff

ģenerālštāti *nm pl* estates general

ģenerāltīrīšana *nf* major cleanup

ģenerāluzbrukums *nm* general offensive

ģenerālvikārs *nm* vicar-general

ģener|a|tīvi [ā] *adv* generatively

ģener|a|tīv/s [ā] *adj* generative

ģener|a|tors [ā] *nm* generator

ģenerēt *vt* generate

ģeneriski *adv* generically

ģenerisks *adj* generic

ģen|e|tika [ē] *nf* genetics

ģen|e|tiķ/is [ē] *nm*, ~e *nf* geneticist

ģen|e|tiski [ē] *adv* genetically

ģen|e|tisks [ē] *adj* genetic

ģen|e|ze [ē] *nf* genesis

ģenga *nf* (sl.) money, moola

ģeniāli *adv* brilliantly

ģeni|a|litāte [ā] *nf* genius; brilliance

ģeniāls *adj* of genius, brilliant

ģ[e]nijs [ē] *nm* genius

ģenitālijas *nf pl* genitalia

ģenitīvs *nm* genitive; **dalāmais ģ.** partitive genitive

ģenotips *nm* genotype

ģeņģerēt *vi* (col.) stagger, totter

ģeņģeris *nm* 1. pacer, ambler; walker; 2. restless child; 3. adventurer; 4. foot

ģeņģeriski *adv* tottering, staggering; (of a horse) pacing

ģeņģeṛu ģeņģeṛiem *adv* staggering

ģeņģes *nf pl* threads

ģeņģīzeris *nm* diestock

ģenuīni *adv* genuinely

ģenuīns *adj* genuine

ģeoantiklināle *nf* geoanticline

ģeobot[a]nika [ā] *nf* phytogeography

ģeobot[a]niķis [ā] *nm*, ~e *nf* phytogeographer

ģeobot[a]nisks [ā] *adj* geobotanical

ģeocentriski *adv* geocentrically

ģeocentrisks *adj* geocentric

ģeocentrisms *nm* geocentrism

ģeo[ch]ronoloģija [h] *nf* geochronology

ģeo[ch]ronoloģiski [h] *adv* geochronologically

ģeo[ch]ronoloģisks [h] *adj* geochronologica

ģeodet/s *nm*, ~e *nf* geodesist

ģeodēzija *nf* geodesy

ģeodēzisks *adj* geodesic; geodetic

ģeodēzist/s *nm*, ~e *nf* geodesist

ģeodimetrs *nm* geodimeter

ģeodinamika *nf* geodynamics

ģeofizika *nf* geophysics

ģeofizikāli *adv* geophysically

ģeofizikāls *adj* geophysical

ģeofiziski *adv* geophysically

ģeofizisks *adj* geophysical

ģeognozija *nf* geognosy

ģeogonija *nf* geogony

ģeogr[a]fija [ā] *nf* geography

ģeogr[a]fiski [ā] *adv* geographically

ģeogr[a]fisks [ā] *adj* geographic

ģeogr[a]f/s [ā] *nm*, ~e *nf* geographer

ģeoīds *nm* geoid

ģeoķīmija *nf* geochemistry

ģeoķīmiķi/is *nm*, ~e *nf* geochemist

ģeoķīmisks *adj* geochemical

ģeolo/gs *nm*, ~ģe *nf* geologist

ģeoloģija *nf* geology

ģeoloģiski *adv* geologically

ģeoloģisks *adj* geological

ģeomagn[e]tisks [ē] *adj* geomagnetic

ģeomagn[e]tisms [ē] *nm* geomagnetism

ģeometrija *nf* geometry; **analitiskā ģ.** analytic geometry

ģeometriski *adv* geometrically

ģeometrisks *adj* geometric

ģeometriskums *nm* geometricity

ģeometrizēt *vt* geometrize

ģeometrs *nm*, ~e *nf* geometrician

ģeomorfolo/gs *nm*, ~ģe *nf* geomorphologist

ģeomorfoloģija *nf* geomorphology

ģeopol[i]tika [ī] *nf* geopolitics

ģeopol[i]tiķ/is [ī] *nm*, ~e *nf* geopolitician

ģeopol[i]tiski [ī] *adv* geopolitically

ģeopol[i]tisks [ī] *adj* geopolitical

ģeorģīne *nf* dahlia

ģeosf[ai]ra [ē] *nf* geosphere

ģeosinklināle *nf* geosyncline

ģeostacionārs *adj* geostationary, geosynchronous

ģeostrofisks *adj* geostrophic

ģeotaksija *nf* geotaxis

ģeote[ch]nika [h] *nf* geotechnics

ģeotermāls *adj* geothermal

ģeotropisms *nm* geotropism

ģēpele *nf* horse treadmill (for operating a thresher)

ģer[a]nija [ā] *nf* 1. geranium; 2. pelargonium

ģērbēja *nf* 1. (theat.) dresser; 2. lady's maid

ģērbējs *nm* (theat.) dresser

ģērbināt *vt* 1. dress in pretty clothes; 2. clean a horse's mouth

ģērbistaba *nf* dressing room

ģērbkambaris *nm* vestry, sacristy

ģerbonis *nm* arms, coat of arms

ģerboņzīmogs *nm* coat of arms seal

ģērbs *nm* apparel, clothing

ģērbt *vt* dress, clothe, (of clothes) put on; ģ. nost take off

ģērbties *vr* dress oneself; dress; wear

ģērbtuve *nf* dressing room; cloak room; locker room

ģērēt *vt* 1. (of skins) tan; ģ. āēus (col.) vomit; 2. (com.) flay

ģērētāj/s *nm*, ~a *nf* tanner

ģērētava *nf* tannery

ģermānijs *nm* germanium

ģērmanis *nm* (obs.) tanner

ģermānisks *adj* Germanic

ģermānisms *nm* Germanism

ģermānistika *nf* Germanistics

ģermānists *nm*, ~e *nf* Germanist

ģerm[a]nizācija [ā] *nf* Germanization

ģerm[a]nizēt [ā] *vt* Germanize

ģerm[a]nizēties [ā] *vr* become Germanized

ģerm[a]nofils [ā] *nm* Germanophile

ģerm[a]nofobija [ā] *nf* Germanophobia

ģerm[a]nofobs [ā] *nm* Germanophobe

ģermāņi *nm pl* Germanic peoples

ģermāņu *indecl adj* Germanic

ģerstele *nf* oven peel

ģērstelēt *vt* (of bread in baking) sprinkle

ģerundijs *nm* gerund

ģerundīvs *nm* gerundive

ģērviela *nf* tannin

ģēse *nf* (reg.) gray heron

ģēvele *nf* (obs.) gable

ģība *nf* (col.) faint

ģībiens *nm* faint

ģībonis *nm* faint

ģībt *vi* faint

ģībulis *nm* (col.) 1. faint; 2. weakling

ģieblis *nm* (col.) crier, crybaby

ģiebulīgs *adj* (col.) weepy, tearful

ģiebulis *nm* (col.) crier, crybaby

ģiedroties *vr* (of the sky) clear up

ģiedrs *adj* (of the sky) clear

ģiest *vt* sense

ģieza *nf, nm* teller of tall tales

ģiezenis *nm* emaciated person

ģiezēties *vr* fret and quarrel without reason

ģiezties *vr* laugh inappropriately at another person's mishap

ģifts *nf* (barb.) poison

ģīga *nf, nm* 1. (com.) crier, bawler; 2. (folk.) single-stringed bowed musical instrument; ~s (cont.) fiddle

ģīgāt *vi* 1. (cont.) fiddle; 2. (com.) weep

ģīģis *nm* (naut.) gaff

ģikts *nf* (obs.) podagra

ģilde *nf* guild

ģildes nams *nm* guildhall

ģilis *nm* (reg.) skin and bones

ģiltenis *nm* (reg.) skeleton

ģilze *nf* (col.) cigarette shell (of a Russian-type cigarette with cardboard mouthpiece)

ģimene *nf* family

ģimenes pavards *nm* (fig.) hearth

ģimenes stāvoklis *nm* marital status

ģimenietis *nm* close relative

ģimenisks *adj* familial; family-oriented

ģīmetne *nf* portrait; photograph (of a person)

ģīmis *nm* (col.) face; ģ. kā mēness moon-faced

ģimnastika *nf* gymnastics

ģimnast/s *nm*, ~e *nf* gymnast

ģimn[a]zija [ā] *nf* high school; humanitārā ģ. (hist.) humanities division of a high school; klasiskā ģ. (hist.) classics division of a high school; praktiskā ģ. (hist.) home economics division of a high school; reālā ģ. (hist.) science division of a high school

ģimn[a]zist/s [ā] *nm*, ~e *nf* high school student

ģīmzieēi *nm pl* Compositae

ģindenis *nm* skeleton

ġinst *vi* perish
ġint *vi* perish
ġints *nf* **1.** (anthr.) kin, clan, family; **2.** (biol.) genus
ġipsējums *nm* plaster cast
ġipsene *nf* chalk plant
ġipsis *nm* gypsum; plaster of Paris
ġipsīts *nm* gypsite
ġipsot *vt* gypsum
ġipstelis *nm* roof tile
ġipša cietapmetums *nm* hardwall plaster stucco
ġipšains *adj* containing gypsum
ġipšakmens *nm* gypsum
ġipšot *vt* gypsum
ġipte *nf* (barb.) poison
ġiptīgs *adj* (barb.) poisonous
ġirbes koks *nm* guelder rose
ġirlicis *nm* European serin
ġirnīt *vt* (reg.) tear
ġirts *adj* (reg.) tipsy
ġirtums *nm* (reg.) tipsiness
ġisme *nf* feeling, awareness
ġist *vi* become aware, sense
ġit|a|ra [ā] *nf* guitar
ġit|a|rists [ā] *nm*, ~e *nf* guitarist
ġuibt *vi* pine away
ġundēt *vi* cuss; mutter; denounce behind one's back
ġunnēt *vt* cuss out

H

habanera *nf* habanera
habenarija *nf* habenaria
haberlejas *nf pl* Haberlea
habilitācija *nf* (educ.) habilitation
habilitēties *vr* (educ.) habilitate
habits *nm* (rel.) habit

habituāls *adj* habitual
habituss *nm* **1.** habitat; **2.** habitus
hadrons *nm* hadron
hādžs *nm* haj
hafnijs *nm* hafnium
hagiogr|a|fija [ā] *nf* hagiography
hagiogr|a|fs [ā] *nm* hagiographer
hagiolatrija *nf* hagiolatry
hagiologs *nm* hagiologist
hagioloġija *nf* hagiology
haiduks *nm* haiduk
haihats *nm* high-hat cymbals
haiku *indecl nf* haiku
haim- See hem-
haimorīts *nm* sinusitis (of the maxillary sinuses)
h|ai|r|e|tiķ/is |e||ē| *nm*, ~e *nf* heretic
h|ai|r|e|tisks |e||ē| *adj* heretic
h|ai|r|e|ze |e||ē| *nf* heresy
h|ai|r|e|zija |e||ē| *nf* heresy
haiteks *nm* high-tech
haitiet/is *nm*, ~e *nf* Haitian
haizivs *nf* shark
hakas/s *nm*, ~iete *nf* Khakas
hakeris *nm* (compu.) hacker
haki *indecl nm* khaki (cloth)
haki *indecl adj* khaki (color)
halāts *nm* dressing gown, robe; smock, lab coat
halaza *nf* = **chalaza**
halcedons *nm* = **chalcedons**
hale *nf* challah
halenija *nf* spurred gentian
halezija *nf* halesia
halfzāle *nf* esparto
halimlapu licija *nf* matrimony vine
halimodendrs *nm* salt tree
halīts *nm* halite
halkopirīts *nm* = **chalkopirīts**
halkozīns *nm* = **chalkozīns**
Halla ābele *nf* Hall's crabapple
halle *nf* hall
hallo *interj* hello

ha|ll|ucinācija |l| *nf* hallucination

ha|ll|ucinēt |l| *vi* hallucinate

ha|ll|ucinog|e|ns |l||ē| *nm* hallucinogenic

ha|ll|ucinog|e|ns |l||ē| *adj* hallucinogenic

halo *nm indecl* halo

halo|ch|romija |h| *nf* halochromism

halofils *nm* halophile

halofīts *nm* halophyte

halogen|i|ds |ī| *nm* halogenide

halogenizācija *nf* halogenation

halogenizēt *vt* halogenate

halog|e|ns |ē| *nm* halogen

halogenūdeņradis *nm* hydrogen halide

halo|i|ds |ī| *nm* halide

halometrs *nm* halometer

haltūra *nf* **1.** potboilers; hackwork; **2.** odd jobs; **3.** slipshod work

halt|u|rēt |ū| *vi* **1.** do shoddy work; **2.** work a second job

haltūrists *nm* potboiler (person); hack

halucinācija *nf* = **halucinācija**

halucinēt *vi* = **halucinēt**

halucinog|ē|ns *nm* = **halucinogēns**

halucinog|ē|ns *adj* = **hallucinogens**

halva *nf* halva

halze *nf* (naut.: course; run; rope) tack; **kreisā h.** port tack; **labā h.** starboard tack

hamada *nf* hammada

hamadrils *nm* sacred baboon

hamburgers *nm* hamburger

hameleonisks *adj* = **chameleonisks**

hameleons *nm* = **chameleons**

hamīti *nm pl* Hamites

hamsins *nm* = **chamsins**

handbols *nm* handball

handikaps *nm* (sports) handicap

haniste *nf* = **chaniste**

hanoss *nm* = **chanoss**

hans *nm* = **chans**

hantele *nf* dumbbell

hant/s *nm,* **~iete** *nf* Ostyak

hanuka *nf* = **chanuka**

hanzeāts *nm* Hanseatic

haoss *nm* = **chaoss**

haotiskums *nm* = **chaotiskums**

haotisks *adj* = **chaotisks**

hapakslegomens *nm* hapax legomenon

haploīdija *nf* haploidy

haploīds *nm* haploid

haploloģija *nf* haplology

haploloģisks *adj* haplological

harakiri *nm indecl* hara-kiri

hārdroks *nm* (mus.) hard rock

har|e|ms |ē| *nm* harem

hariolācija *nf* hariolation

haritas *nf pl* = **charitas**

harizma *nf* = **charizma**

harizmātiķ/is *nm,* **~e** *nf* = **charizmātiķis**

harizmātiski *adv* = **charizmātiski**

harizmātisks *adj* = **charizmātisks**

harlekins *nm* Harlequin

harmala *nf* Syrian rue

harmatans *nm* harmatan

harmonēt *vi* harmonize

harmonija *nf* harmony

harmonijs *nm* harmonium

harmonikas *nf pl* concertina

harmoniskā *nom adj* harmonic

harmoniski *adv* harmonically; harmoniously

harmonisks *adj* **1.** harmonic; **2.** harmonious; (of flavor) balanced

harmoniskums *nm* harmoniousness

harmonist/s *nm,* **~e** *nf* concertina player

harmonizācija *nf* (mus.) part writing, addition of harmony, accompaniment

harmonizējums *nm* harmonization

harmonizēt *vt* **1.** write harmony, write accompaniment; **2.** harmonize, agree with, go with

harpija *nf* harpy

harpsikords *nm* harpsichord

harpūna *nf* harpoon

harp|u|nēt |ū| *vt* harpoon

harta *nf* = **charta**

harza *nf* yellow-throated marten

hasīdi *nm pl* Hassidim

hasīdisms *nm* Hasidism

haskijs *nm* husky

hašišs *nm* hashish

hašura *nf* hachure

haubeks *nm* (col.) halfback

haubice *nf* howitzer; **smagā h.** siege howitzer

haulmograskābe *nf* = **chaulmograskābe**

haustorija *nf* haustorium

Havajas puķe *nf* hibiscus

havajiet/is *nm*, ~e *nf* Hawaiian

havajisks *adj* Hawaiian

havortija *nf* haworthia

hazards *nm* See **azarts**

H dzelzs *nf* H beam

he *interj* pish

hebefr[e]nija [ē] *nf* hebephrenia

hebraistika *nf* Hebraic studies

hebr[i]ds [ī] *nm* hybrid

hečbeks *nm* hatchback

heders I *nm* header (of a combine)

heders II *nm* heder

hedi[ch]ija [h] *nf* hedychium

hedīvs *nm* = **chedīvs**

hedizarija *nf* hedysarum

h[e]doniķ/is [ē] *nm*, ~e *nf* hedonist

h[e]doniski [ē] *adv* hedonistically

h[e]donisks [ē] *adj* hedonistic

h[e]donisms [ē] *nm* hedonism

h[e]donistiski [ē] *adv* hedonistically

h[e]donistisks [ē] *adj* hedonistic

h[e]donist/s [ē] *nm*, ~e *nf* hedonist

hedžra *nf* hegira

hēgeliet/is *nm*, ~e *nf* Hegelian

hēgelisms *nm* Hegelism

h[e]gemonija [ē] *nf* hegemony

h[e]gemoniski [ē] *adv* hegemonically

h[e]gemonisks [ē] *adj* hegemonic

h[e]gemonistiski [ē] *adv* hegemonistically

h[e]gemonistisks [ē] *adj* hegemonistic

h[e]gemons [ē] *nm* hegemon

h[e]gūmena [ē] *nf* Mother Superior (of a monastery)

h[e]gūmens [ē] *nm* Father Superior (of a monastery)

hei *interj* hey

hei[ch]era [h] *nf* heuchera

heijā *interj* whee

heirēka *nf* eureka

heiristika *nf* = **heuristika**

heiristiski *adv* = **heuristiski**

heiristisks *adj* = **heuristisks**

heiromantija *nf* = **cheiromantija**

heiromant/s *nm*, ~e *nf* = **cheiromants**

heisā *interj* heigh-ho

hekatomba *nf* hecatomb

heks *nm* hake

heksabrom[i]ds [ī] *nm* hexabromide

heksa[ch]loretāns [h] *nm* hexachlorethane

heksa[ch]lor[i]ds [h][ī] *nm* hexachloride

heksa[ch]ords [h] *nm* hexachord

heksadecimāls *adj* hexadecimal

heksadekāns *nm* hexadecane

heksaedrs *nm* hexahedron

heksafluor[i]ds [ī] *nm* hexafluoride

heksagonāli *adv* hexagonally

heksagonāls *adj* hexagonal

heksakisoktaedrs *nm* hexakisoctahedron

heksakontāns *nm* hexacontane

heksamet[i]l[ē]ntetramīns [ī][e] *nm* hexa-methyl-enetetramine

heksametrisks *adj* hexameter

heksametrs *nm* hexameter

heksanols *nm* hexanol

heksāns *nm* hexane

heksēns *nm* hexene

heksils *nm* hexyl

heksode *nf* hexode

heksoks[i]ds [ī] *nm* hexoxide

heksoze *nf* hexose

hektāns *nm* hectane

hekt[a]rs [ā] *nm* hectare

hektiski *adv* hectically

hektisks *adj* hectic

hektografēt *vt* hectograph

hektogr[a]fisks [ā] *adj* hectographic

hektogr[a]fs [ā] *nm* hectograph

hektograms *nm* hectogram

hektolitrs *nm* hectoliter

hektometrs *nm* hectometer

helebarde *nf* halberd

helēnija *nf* sneezeweed

helēnisms *nm* = **hellēnisms**

helēnistisks *adj* = **hellēnistisks**

helēnists *nm* = **hellēnists**

helēņi *nm pl* = **hellēņi**

helicerāti *nm pl* = **chelicerāti**

helidonīns *nm* = **chelidonīns**

hēlijs *nm* helium

h|e|likonija [ē] *nf* wild plantain

h|e|likons [ē] *nm* helicon

h|e|likopters [ē] *nm* helicopter

h|e|liocentrisks [ē] *adj* heliocentric

h|e|liocentrisms [ē] *nm* heliocentrism

h|e|liofizika [ē] *nf* solar astronomy

h|e|liogr[ā]fs [ē][a] *nm* heliograph

h|e|liogravīra [ē] *nf* heliogravure

h|e|liometrs [ē] *nm* heliometer

h|e|liostats [ē] *nm* heliostat

h|e|liotakse [ē] *nf* heliotaxis

h|ē|liote|ch|nika [e][h] *nf* solar energy tech-
nology

h|ē|liote|ch|niķ/is [e][h] *nm,* ~e *nf* solar energy
technician

h|e|lioterapija [ē] *nf* heliotherapy

h|e|liotropisms [ē] *nm* heliotropism

h|e|liotrops [ē] *nm* heliotrope

h|e|lioze [ē] *nf* heliosis

h|e|liozoji [ē] *nm pl* Heliozoa

helksine *nf* See **Soleirola helksine**

hellēnisms *nm* Hellenism

hellēnistiski *adv* Hellenistically

hellēnistisks *adj* Hellenistic

hellēnist/s *nm,* ~e *nf* Hellenist

hellēņi *nm pl* Hellenes

hellers *nm* heller

helminti *nm pl* Helminthes

helmintolo/gs *nm,* ~ģe *nf* helminthologist

helmintoloģija *nf* helminthology

helmintoloģisks *adj* helminthological

helmintosporīns *nm* helminthosporin

helmintoze *nf* helminthiasis

helofīts *nm* helophyte

h|e|lots [ē] *nm* Helot

hemaglutinācija *nf* hemagglutination

hematīns *nm* hematin

hematīts *nm* hematite

hemalbumins *nm* hemalbumen

hemamēba *nf* hemamoeba

hemangioma *nf* hemangioma

hemartroze *nf* hemarthrosis

hematog|e|ns [ē] *adj* hematogenous

hematokele *nf* hematocele

hematoksilīns *nm* hematoxylin

hematol[i]tisks [ī] *adj* hematolytic

hematol[i]ze [ī] *nf* hematolysis

hematolo/gs *nm,* ~ģe *nf* hematologist

hematoloģija *nf* hematology

hematoloģiski *adv* hematologically

hematoloģisks *adj* hematologic

hematoma *nf* hematoma

hematomielija *nf* hematomyelia

hematopoēze *nf* hematopoiesis

hematoporfirīns *nm* hematoporphyrin

hematozojs *nm* hematozoon

hematūrija *nf* hematuria

hemeralopija *nf* hemeralopia

hemeritrīns *nm* hemerythrin

h|e|miacetāls [ē] *nm* hemiacetal

h|e|mianestēzija [ē] *nf* hemianesthesia

h|e|mianopsija [ē] *nf* hemianopsia

h|ē|mice|ll|uloz[a] [e][l][e] *nf* hemicellulose

hemiluminiscence *nf* = **chemiluminiscence**

h|e|mimorfīts [ē] *nm* hemimorphite

hemīns *nm* hemin

h|e|miparēze [ē] *nf* hemiparesis

h|e|miplēģija [ē] *nf* hemiplegia

h[ē]misf[ai]ra [e][ē] *nf* hemisphere

h[ē]misti[ch]s [e][h] *nm* hemistich

hemlokegle *nf* hemlock

hemloks *nm* hemlock

hemo[ch]romog[e]ns [h][ē] *nm* hemochromogen

hemodial[i]ze [ī] *nf* hemodialysis

hemodinamika *nf* hemodynamics

hemof[i]lija [ī] *nf* hemophilia

hemof[i]liķis [ī] *nm* hemophiliac

hemoglobīns *nm* hemoglobin

hemogramma *nf* hemogram

hemol[i]tisks [ī] *adj* hemolytic

hemol[i]ze [ī] *nf* hemolysis

hemometrs *nm* hemometer

hemoperikards *nm* hemopericardium

hemor[a]ģija [ā] *nf* hemorrhage

hemor[a]ģisks [ā] *adj* hemorrhagic

hemoroidāls *adj* hemorrhoidal

hemoro[i]ds [ī] *nm* hemorrhoid

hemosf[ai]ra [ē] *nf* mesosphere

hemosporidiji *nm pl* Haemosporidia

hemosintēze *nf* = **chemosinteze**

hemosorbcija *nf* = **chemosorbcija**

hemostaze *nf* hemostasis

hemotaksija *nf* = **chemotaksija**

hemoterapija *nf* hemotherapy

hemotropisms *nm* = **chemotropisms**

hēms *nm* heme

henna *nf* henna

henomele *nf* = **chenomele**

henoteisms *nm* henotheism

henrijs *nm* (el.) henry

hepar[i]ns [ī] *nm* heparin

hepatīts *nm* hepatite

hepenings *nm* (theat.) happening

heptadekāns *nm* heptadecane

heptaedrs *nm* heptahedron

heptagons *nm* heptagon

heptakontāns *nm* heptacontane

heptakords *nm* heptachord

heptametrs *nm* heptameter

heptanols *nm* heptanol

heptāns *nm* heptane

heptasulf[i]ds [ī] *nm* heptasulfide

heptode *nf* heptode

heptoks[i]ds [ī] *nm* heptoxide

heptoze *nf* heptose

heraldika *nf* heraldry

heraldisks *adj* heraldic

herbārijs *nm* herbarium

herbārist/s *nm*, ~e *nf* herbalist

herb[a]rizācija [ā] *nf* herborization

herb[a]rizēt [ā] *vt* herbalize

herbicīds *nm* herbicide

herbivors *nm* herbivore

hercogiene *nf* duchess

hercogiste *nf* duchy

hercogs *nm* duke

hercogvalsts *nf* duchy

hercs *nm* hertz

heremīts *nm* hermit

heress *nm* sherry

her[e]tiķ/is [ē] *nm*, ~e *nf* heretic

her[e]tisks [ē] *adj* heretic

her[e]ze [ē] *nf* heresy

her[e]zija [ē] *nf* heresy

heritijeras *nf pl* Heritiera

herkulisks *adj* Herculean

herma *nf* herm

hermafrodītisms *nm* hermaphroditism

hermafrodīts *nm* hermaphrodite

herm[e]ne[i]tika [ē][u] *nf* hermeneutics

herm[e]ne[i]tisks [ē][u] *adj* hermeneutic

herm[e]ne[i]ts [ē][u] *nm* hermeneut

herm[e]tiski [ē] *adv* hermetically

herm[e]tisks [ē] *adj* hermetic

herm[e]tiskums [ē] *nm* hermetic seal

hermetizācija *nf* hermetic sealing

hermetizēt *vt* seal hermetically

herminija *nf* musk orchis

hernhūtieši *nm pl* Moravian Brethren

hernhūtisks *adj* in the spirit of the Moravian Brethren

hernhūtisms *nm* teachings of the Moravians

h|e|roika [ē] *nf* heroic spirit

heroīns *nm* heroin

h|e|roiski [ē] *adv* heroically

h|e|roisks [ē] *adj* heroic

h|e|roiskums [ē] *nm* heroic character

h|e|roisms [ē] *nm* heroism

h|e|roizācija [ē] *nf* heroization

h|e|roizēt [ē] *vt* heroize

h|e|rojs [ē] *nm* hero

herolds *nm* herald

herpess *nm* herpes; parastais h. herpes simplex

herp|e|tisks [ē] *adj* herpetic

herpetolo/gs *nm*, ~ģe *nf* herpetologist

herpetoloģija *nf* herpetology

herubs *nm* = cherubs

Hesenes ods *nm* Hessian fly

hetēra *nf* hetaera

heteroblastisks *adj* heteroblastic

heterociklisks *adj* heterocyclic

heterodīns *nm* heterodyne oscillator

heterodokss *adj* heterodox

heteroēcisks *adj* heteroecious

heterofi|l|ija [ll] *nf* heterophylly

heterofonija *nf* heterophony

heterogenitāte *nf* heterogeneity

heterog|e|ns [ē] *adj* heterogenous

heterogr|a|fija [ā] *nf* heterography

heteron|i|ms [ī] *adj* heteronymous

heteronomija *nf* heteronomy

heteronoms *adj* heteronomous

heteroplastika *nf* heteroplasty

heteropolārs *adj* heteropolar

heteroseksuāls *adj* heterosexual

heterosillabisks *adj* heterosyllabic

heterotopija *nf* heterotopia

heterotrofisks *adj* heterotrophic

heterotrofs *adj* heterotrophic

heteroze *nf* heterosis

heterozigota *nf* heterozygote

heterozs *adj* manifesting heterosis

heti *nm* Hittites

hetmanis *nm* = hetmans

hetmans *nm* hetman

heuristika *nf* heuristic

heuristisks *adj* heuristic

heveja *nf* hevea

hi, hi *interj* hee-hee

hiacinte *nf* hyacinth

hiacints *nm* (gem) hyacinth

hiādes *nf pl* Hyades

hialinoze *nf* hyalinosis

hialins *nm* hyaline

hialīts *nm* hyalite

hialokrist|āl|isks [all] *adj* hyalinocrystallic

hiasma *nf* = chiasma

hiasms *nm* = chiasms

hiastolīts *nm* = chiastolīts

hiāts *nm* (ling.) hiatus

hibači *nm indecl* hibachi

hibernācija *nf* hibernation

hibisks *nm* hibiscus

hibr|i|ddators [ī] *nm* hybrid computer

hibridizācija *nf* hybridization

hibridizēt *vt* hybridize

hibridog|e|ns [ē] *adj* hybrid-producing

hibr|i|ds [ī] *nm* hybrid

hibr|i|ds [ī] *adj* hybrid

hibr|i|dvārds [ī] *nm* portmanteau word

hidantoīns *nm* hydantoin

hidatog|e|ns [ē] *adj* hydatogenic

hidra *nf* hydra

hidrācija *nf* hydration

hidrants *nm* hydrant

hidrargilīts *nm* hydrargillite

hidrastins *nm* hydrastine

hidratācija *nf* hydration

hidratofīts *nm* hydratophyte

hidrāts *nm* hydrate

hidraulika *nf* hydraulics

hidrauliski *adv* hydraulically

hidraulisks *adj* hydraulic

hidraz|i|ds [ī] *nm* hydrazide
hidrazīns *nm* hydrazine
hidrazonbenzols *nm* hydrazonbenzene
hidrazons *nm* hydrazone
hidr|e|mija |ē| *nf* hydremia
hidrēt *vt* hydrate
hidr|i|ds [ī] *nm* hydride
hidrija *nf* hydria
hidrilas *nf pl* Hydrilla
hidroakustika *nf* echolocation, sonar technology
hidroakustiķ/is *nm*, ~e *nf* sonarman
hidroakustisks *adj* sonar (*adj*)
hidroar|ch|eoloģija |h| *nf* underwater archeology
hidroar|ch|eoloģisks |h| *adj* pertaining to underwater archeology
hidroaviācija *nf* hydroaviation
hidrobiolo/gs *nm*, ~ģe *nf* hydrobiologist
hidrobioloģija *nf* hydrobiology
hidrobioloģisks *adj* hydrobiological
hidrobionts *nm* aquatic organism
hidrocefālija *nf* hydrocephalus
hidrocēle *nf* hydrocele
hidro|ch|inons |h| *nm* hydroquinone
hidrodinamika *nf* hydrodynamics
hidrodinamiski *adv* hydrodynamically
hidrodinamisks *adj* hydrodynamic
hidroelektrisks *adj* hydroelectric
hidroelektrostacija *nf* hydroelectric power plant
hidroenerģētika *nf* hydroelectric power
hidroenerģētisks *adj* driven by hydroelectric power
hidroenerģija *nf* hydroelectric power
hidrofilija *nf* hydrophily
hidrofils *adj* hydrophilic
hidrofīts *nm* hydrophyte
hidrofobija *nf* hydrophobia
hidrofobisks *adj* water-repellent
hidrofobizēt *vt* make water-repellent
hidrofobs *nm* hydrophobe

hidrofobs *adj* water-repellent
hidrofons *nm* hydrophone
hidrogr|a|fija |ā| *nf* hydrography
hidrogr|a|fisks |ā| *adj* hydrographic
hidrogr|a|fs |ā| *nm* hydrographer
hidroģenerātors *nm* hydroelectric power generator
hidroģeolo/gs *nm*, ~ģe *nf* hydrogeologist
hidroģeoloģija *nf* hydrogeology
hidroģeoloģiski *adv* hydrogeologically
hidroģeoloģisks *adj* hydrogeological
hidroīds *nm* hydroid
hidroizolācija *nf* 1. (of buildings) waterproofing; 2. watertight barrier
hidrokefalija *nf* hydrocephaly
hidrokefals *nm* hydrocephalus
hidrokortizons *nm* hydrocortisone
hidroks|i|ds [ī] *nm* hydroxide
hidroksilamīns *nm* hydroxylamine
hidroksilēt *vt* hydroxylate
hidroksilions *nm* hydroxyl ion
hidroksils *nm* hydroxyl
hidroksisavienojums *nm* hydroxy compound
hidrolāze *nf* hydrolase
hidrolizācija *nf* hydrolization
hidrol|i|ze [ī] *nf* hydrolysis
hidrolizēt *vt* hydrolyze
hidrolizēties *vr* hydrolyze
hidrolo/gs *nm*, ~ģe *nf* hydrologist
hidroloģija *nf* hydrology
hidroloģiski *adv* hydrologically
hidroloģisks *adj* hydrologic
hidrolokācija *nf* sonar technology
hidrolok|a|tors |ā| *nm* sonar
hidromantija *nf* hydromancy
hidromasa *nf* dredging spoil
hidromasāža *nf* water jet massage
hidrome|cha|nika |hā| *nf* hydromechanics
hidrome|cha|niski |hā| *adv* hydromechanically
hidrome|cha|nisks |hā| *adj* hydromechanical
hidromedūza *nf* hydromedusa

hidromeliorācija *nf* (of soil) water balance improvement

hidrometa|ll|urģija [l] *nf* hydrometallurgy

hidrometeorolo/gs *nm*, ~ģe *nf* hydrometeorologist

hidrometeoroloģija *nf* hydrometeorology

hidrometeoroloģiski *adv* hydrometeorologically

hidrometeoroloģisks *adj* hydrometeorological

hidrometrija *nf* hydrometry

hidrometrisks *adj* hydrometric

hidrometrs *nm* hydrometer

hidromezgls *nm* hydroelectric power station

hidromonitors *nm* hydraulic mining jet

hidronefroze *nf* hydronephrosis

hydronīmi *nm pl* hydronymy

hidrop|a|tija [ā] *nf* hydropathy

hidrop|a|ts [ā] *nm*, ~e *nf* hydrotherapist

hidroplāns *nm* seaplane

hidropneumotorakss *nm* hydropneumothorax

hidroponika *nf* hydroponics

hidropults *nf* spray can, sprayer

hidrosfēra *nf* hydrosphere

hidrosols *nm* hydrosol

hidrospēkstacija *nf* hydroelectric power plant

hidrostacija *nf* hydroelectric power plant

hidrostatika *nf* hydrostatics

hidrostatisks *adj* hydrostatic

hidrosulf|i|ds [ī] *nm* hydrosulfide

hidrosulfīts *nm* hydrosulfite

hidrote|ch|nika [h] *nf* hydraulic engineering

hidrote|ch|niķ/is [h] *nm*, ~e *nf* hydraulic engineer

hidrote|ch|nisks [h] *adj* pertaining to hydraulic engineering, pertaining to waterworks

hidroterape|i|tisks [u] *adj* hydrotherapeutic

hidroterape|i|t/s [u] *nm*, ~e *nf* hydrotherapist

hidroterapija *nf* hydrotherapy

hidroterapists *nm*, ~e *nf* = hidroterapeuts

hidrotērps *nm* diving suit

hidrotropisms *nm* hydrotropism

hidroturbīna *nf* hydroturbine

hidrovizla *nf* hydromica

hidrozojs *nm* hydrozoan

hidžra *nf* hegira

hiēna *nf* hyena

hiēnsuns *nm* African hunting dog

hierar|ch|ija [h] *nf* hierarchy

hierar|ch|iski [h] *adv* hierarchically

hierar|ch|isks [h] *adj* hierarchical

hierar|ch|iskums [h] *nm* hierarchism

hierar|ch|s [h] *nm* hierarch

hierātisks *adj* hieratic

hieroglifika *nf* hieroglyphic

hieroglifisks *adj* hieroglyphic

hieroglifs *nm* hieroglyph

hierogramma *nf* hierogram

hieromantija *nf* haruspicy

hifa *nf* hypha

higiēna *nf* hygiene

higiēniski *adv* hygienically

higiēnisks *adj* hygienic

higiēnist/s *nm*, ~e *nf* hygienist

higiēniskums *nm* observance of hygiene

higrofils *adj* hygrophilous

higrofīts *nm* hygrophyte

higrogr|a|fs [ā] *nm* hygrograph

higrometrija *nf* hygrometry

higrometrs *nm* hygrometer

higroskopiski *adv* hygroscopically

higroskopisks *adj* hygroscopic

higroskopiskums *nm* hygroscopic quality

higroskops *nm* hygroscope

higrostats *nm* humidistat

higrotermogr|a|fs [ā] *nm* hygrothermograph

higrotermogramma *nf* hygrothermograph chart

hikorija *nf* hickory

hileja *nf* South American tropical rain forest

hiliarhs *nm* = chiliarchs

hiliasms *nm* = chiliasms

hilopods *nm* = chilopods

hiloteisms *nm* hylotheism

hiloteists *nm* hylotheist

hilozoisms *nm* hylozoism

hilozoists *nm* hylozoist

hilus *nm* = **chilus**

himantoglosas *nf pl* Himantoglossum

himenofilas *nf pl* filmy ferns

himenopteri *nm pl* Hymenoptera

himera *nf* = **chimera**

himerisks *adj* = **chimerisks**

himēns *nm* hymen

himna *nf* anthem

himniski *adv* like a hymn

himnisks *adj* hymnic

himniskums *nm* hymnic quality

himozīns *nm* = **chimozīns**

hin- See **chin-**

hindi *nm indecl* Hindi

hinduisms *nm* Hinduism

hinduists *nm* Hindu

hindustāni *indecl nf* Hindustani

hīneraugs *nm* (barb.) corn, clavus

hinterlande *nf* hinterland

hionodoksas *nf pl* = **chionodoksas**

hipabisāls *adj* hypabyssal

hipeastri *nm pl* hippeastrum

hipekojas *nf pl* Hypecoum

hiperaktivitāte *nf* hyperactivity

hiperbatons *nm* hyperbaton

hiperbola *nf* **1.** hyperbola; **2.** hyperbole

hiperboliski *adv* hyperbolically

hiperbolisks *adj* hyperbolic

hiperboliskums *nm* hyperbolic quality

hiperbolizācija *nf* hyperbolization

hiperbolizēt *vt* hyperbolize

hiperboloīds *nm* hyperboloid

hiperemija *nf* hyperemia

hiperestēzija *nf* hyperesthesia

hiperfunkcija *nf* hyperfunction

hiperg[a]mija [ā] *nf* hypergamy

hiperglikēmija *nf* hyperglycemia

hiperhidroze *nf* hyperhydrosis

hiperinflācija *nf* hyperinflation

hiperkapnija *nf* hypercapnia

hiperkinēze *nf* hyperkinesis

hiperkomensācija *nf* overcompensation

hipermnēzija *nf* hypermnesia

hiperons *nm* hyperon

hiperplāzija *nf* hyperplasia

hipersekrēcija *nf* hypersecretion

hiperskaņa *nf* hypersonic sound

hipersomija *nf* hypersomia

hiperstēns *nm* hypersthene

hiperteksts *nm* (compu.) hypertext

hipertelpa *nf* hyperspace

hipertermija *nf* hyperthermia

hipertireoze *nf* hyperthyroidism

hipertonija *nf* hypertonicity; hypertension

hipertoniķ/is *nm*, ~e *nf* hypertensive

hipertonisks *adj* hypertonic; hypertensive

hipertrofēties *vr* hypertrophy

hipertrofija *nf* hypertrophy

hipervitaminoze *nf* hypervitaminosis

hipestēzija *nf* hypesthesia

hipij/s *nm*, ~a *nf* hippie

hipnagoģisks *adj* hypnagogic

hipnopēdija *nf* sleep learning

hipnopēdisks *adj* sleep learning (*adj*)

hipnopompisks *adj* hypnopompic

hipnoterapija *nf* hypnotherapy

hipnotiķis *nm* hypnotizer

hipnotiski *adv* hypnotically

hipnotisks *adj* hypnotic

hipnotisms *nm* hypnotism

hipnotizēt *vt* hypnotize

hipnotizētāj/s *nm*, ~a *nf* hypnotizer

hipnoze *nf* hypnosis

hipobromīts *nm* hypobromite

hipocentrs *nm* hypocentrum

hipo[ch]lorīts [h] *nm* hypochlorite

hipo[ch]ondrija [h] *nf* hypochondria

hipo[ch]rondriķ/is [h] *nm*, ~e *nf* hypochondriac

hipo[ch]rondrisks [h] *adj* hypochondriacal

hipo[ch]ondrs [h] *nm* hypochondriac

hipodiakons *nm* subdeacon

hipodinamija *nf* hypodynamia

hipodorisks *adj* Hypodorian

hipodroms *nm* hippodrome

hipofīze *nf* hypophysis

hipofosfāts *nm* hypophosphate

hipofosforskābe *nf* hypophosphoric acid

hipofrīģisks *adj* Hypophrygian

hipofunkcija *nf* hypofunction

hipoglikēmija *nf* hypoglycemia

hipojodīts *nm* hypoiodite

hipokausts *nm* hypocaust

hipokinēzija *nf* sedentary way of life

hipokrepe *nf* horseshoe vetch

hipokritisks *adj* hypocritic

hipokrits *nm* hypocrite

hipokrize *nf* hypocrisy

hipoksija *nf* hypoxia

hipolidisks *adj* Hypolydian

hipolimnijs *nm* hypolimnion

hipoloģija *nf* hippology

hipom[a]nija [ā] *nf* hypomania

hiponitrīts *nm* hyponitrite

hipoplāzija *nf* hypoplasia

hipopotams *nm* hippopotamus

hiposekrēcija *nf* hyposecretion

hipostatiski *adv* hypostatically

hipostatisks *adj* hypostatic

hipostaze *nf* hypostasis

hipostazēt *vt* hypostatize

hipostils *nm* hypostyle

hiposulfāts *nm* hyposulfate

hiposulfīts *nm* hyposulfite

hipotakse *nf* hypotaxis

hipotalāms *nm* hypothalamus

hipotēka *nf* mortgage

hipot[e]kārs [ē] *adj* hypothecary

hipotēkas parādnieks *nm* mortgagor

hipotēkas turētājs *nm* mortgagee

hipotensija *nf* hypotension

hipotenūza *nf* hypotenuse

hipotermāls *adj* hypothermal

hipotermija *nf* hyothermia

hipot[e]tiski [ē] *adv* hypothetically

hipot[e]tisks [ē] *adj* hypothetical

hipot[e]ze [ē] *nf* hypothesis

hipotireoze *nf* hypothyroidism

hipotonija *nf* hypotonicity

hipotonisks *adj* hypotonic

hipotrofija *nf* hypotrophy

hipovitaminoze *nf* avitaminosis

hipsogr[a]fija [ā] *nf* hypsography

hipsometrija *nf* hypsometry

hipsometrisks *adj* hypsometric

hipsometrs *nm* hypsometer

hipsotermometrs *nm* hypsometer

hipurskābe *nf* hippuric acid

hir- See **chir-**

hirsūtisms *nm* hirsutism

hirudīns *nm* hirudin

histamīns *nm* histamine

histazarīns *nm* hystazarin

histerēze *nf* hysteresis

hist[e]rija [ē] *nf* hysteria, hysterics

hist[e]riķ/is [ē] *nm*, ~e *nf* hysteric

hist[e]riski [ē] *adv* hysterically

hist[e]risks [ē] *adj* hysterical

histidīns *nm* histidine

histiocīts *nm* histiocyte

histoģen[e]ze [ē] *nf* histogenesis

histolo/gs *nm*, ~ģe *nf* histologist

histoloģija *nf* histology

histoloģisks *adj* histological

histons *nm* histone

historiogr[a]fija [ā] *nf* historiography

historiogr[a]fisks [ā] *adj* historiographic

historiogr[a]f/s [ā] *nm*, ~e *nf* historiographer

historisms *nm* historicism

histrions *nm* histrion

hitīns *nm* = **chitīns**

hitleriet/is *nm*, ~e *nf* Hitlerite

hitlerisks *adj* Hitlerian

hitlerisms *nm* Hitlerism

hitons *nm* = **chitons**

hitozamīns *nm* = chitozamīns

hīts *nm* (sports) heat

hjūmisms *nm* Humism

hlamida *nf* = chlamida

hlisti *nm pl* (rel., hist.) khlysty

hloazma *nf* = chloazma

hlor- See chlor-

hm *interj* humph

ho *interj*, usu. repeated ho, ho haw-haw

hobijs *nm* hobby

hodogr[a]fs [ā] *nm* hodograph

hodometrs *nm* odometer

hofmaršals *nm* seneschal

hoftiesa *nf* (hist.) Hofgericht

hokejists *nm* hockey player

hokejs *nm* hockey

holagoga *nf* = cholagoga

holanders *nm* hollander

Holandes liepa *nf* common linden

Holandes slimība *nf* Dutch elm disease

holandiešu savienojums *nm* Flemish bond

holandiet/is *nm* Dutchman; ~e *nf* Dutch woman

holandiski *adv* in Dutch, (speak) Dutch

holandisks *adj* Dutch

holangīts *nm* = cholangīts

holantrēns *nm* = cholantrēns

holarktisks *adj* holarctic

holdingsabiedrība *nf* holding company

hole- See chole-

holīns *nm* = cholīns

holisms *nm* holism

holmijs *nm* holmium

holoce[ll]uloz[a] [l][e] *nf* holocellulose

holocēns *nm* Holocene

holografēt *vt* make a hologram

hologr[a]fija [ā] *nf* holography

hologr[a]fisks [ā] *adj* holographic

hologr[a]fs [ā] *nm* holograph

hologramma *nf* hologram

holokausts *nm* holocaust

holokrist[āl]isks [all] *adj* holocrystalline

holosteja *nf* jagged chickweed

holotūrija *nf* holothurian; sea cucumber

holskābe *nf* = cholskābe

homeoblastisks *adj* homeoblastic

homeop[a]tija [ā] *nf* homeopathy

homeop[a]tiski [ā] *adv* homeopathically

homeop[a]tisks [ā] *adj* homeopathic

homeop[a]t/s [ā] *nm*, ~e *nf* homeopath

homeost[a]ze [ā] *nf* homeostasis

homērisks *adj* Homeric

homiķis *nm* (sl.) homo

homilētika *nf* homiletics

homilētisks *adj* homiletic

homilēts *nm* homilist

hom[i]lija [ī] *nf* homily

homin[i]ds [ī] *nm* hominid

homofonija *nf* homophony

homofonisks *adj* homophonic

homofons *nm* homophone

homofons *adj* homophonic

homoforma *nf* homophone

homog[a]mija [ā] *nf* homogamy

homog[e]nisks [ē] *adj* homogenous

homogenitāte *nf* homogeneity

homogenizēt *vt* homogenize

homog[e]ns [ē] *adj* homogenous

homogr[a]fs [ā] *nm* homograph

homoioterms *adj* homoiothermic

homologs *nm* homologue

homologs *adj* homologous

homoloģija *nf* homology

homoloģisks *adj* homologous

homon[i]mija [ī] *nf* homonymy

homon[i]misks [ī] *adj* homonymous

homon[i]ms [ī] *nm* homonym

homonkuls *nm* homonculus

homoplastika *nf* homoplasy

homopolārs *adj* homopolar

homoseksuāli *adv* homosexually

homoseksuālisms *nm* homosexuality

homoseksūālist/s *nm*, ~e *nf* homosexual

homoseksu[a]litāte [ā] *nf* homosexuality

homoseksuāls *adj* homosexual

homosf[ai]ra [ē] *nf* the five lower regions of the atmosphere

homotētija *nf* homothety

homotētisks *adj* homothetic

homotransplantācija *nf* homotransplantation

homozigota *nf* homozygote

homrūle *nf* home rule

homrūls *nm* home rule

hondr- See **chondr-**

honduriet/is *nm*, ~e *nf* Honduran

honēšana *nf* honing

honēšanas galva *nf* hone

honkenija *nf* seabeach sandwort

honorāciors *nm* local dignitary

honorārs *nm* honorarium, fee; royalties

honorēt *vt* (bus.) honor

hons *nm* hone

hop *interj* up

hopā *interj* up

hopers *nm* (RR) hopper

hopkalīts *nm* Hopcalite

hord- See **chord-**

hore- See **chore-**

horija *nf* = **chorija**

horijambs *nm* = **chorijambs**

horiokarcinoma *nf* = **choriokarcinoma**

horipetāls *adj* = **choripetāls**

horizontāle *nf* horizontal line; contour

horizontāli *adv* horizontally; (in crosswords) across

horizontāls *adj* horizontal

horizonts *nm* horizon

hormonāls *adj* hormonal

hormons *nm* hormone

hormonterapija *nf* hormone therapy

hornblende *nf* hornblende

horns *nm* (geol.) horn

horoloģija *nf* horology

horoloģisks *adj* 1. horological; 2. chorologic

horoskops *nm* horoscope

horsts *nm* (geol.) horst

hortenzija *nf* hydrangea

horvātisks *adv* = **chorvātisks**

horvāts *nm* = **chorvāts**

hose *nf* (bus.) bull market

hospice *nf* hospice

hospitālietis *nm* Hospitaler

hospitālis *nm* military hospital

hospitālisms *nm* hospitalism

hospit[a]lizācija [ā] *nf* hospitalization

hospit[a]lizēt [ā] *vt* hospitalize

hospitants *nm* (educ.) visitor, observer

hospitēt *vi* (educ.) visit (for observation)

hosta *nf* hosta

hostija *nf* (rel.) host

hota *nf* jota

hotelis *nm* hotel

hotentot/s *nm*, ~e *nf* Hotentot

hrestomatija *nf* = **chrestomatija**

hris- See **chris-**

hriz- See **chriz-**

hrom- See **chrom-**

hron- See **chron-**

htonisks *adj* = **chtonisks**

hucul/s *nm*, ~iete *nf* Huzul

hučinsija *nf* hutchinsia

hugenāts *nm* Hugenotism

hugenot/s *nm*, ~e *nf* Huguenot

hulig[a]niski [ā] *adv* in a hoodlumish manner

hulig[a]nisks [ā] *nm* hoodlumish

hulig[a]niskums [ā] *nm* hoodlumism

hulig[a]nisms [ā] *nm* hooliganism, hoodlumism

hulig[a]n/s [ā] *nm*, ~e *nf* hooligan, hoodlum

humāni *adv* humanely

humānisms *nm* humanism

humānistiski *adv* humanistically

humānistisks *adj* humanistic

humānists *nm*, ~e *nf* humanist

hum[a]nitārisms [ā] *nm* humanitarianism

hum[a]nitārs [ā] *adj* humanitarian; (educ.) of humanities

hum[a]nitāte [ā] *nf* humaneness

hum|a|nizēt [ā] *vt* humanize

humāns *adj* humane

hum|i|ds [ī] *adj* humid

humifikācija *nf* humification

humīns *nm* humin

humīts *nm* humite

humorāls *adj* humoral

humoreska *nf* 1. humorous sketch; 2. humoresque

humoriski *adv* humorously

humorisks *adj* humorous

humoriskums *nm* humorousness

humoristiski *adv* humorously

humoristisks *adj* humoristic

humoristiskums *nm* humorousness

humorists *nm*, ~e *nf* humorist

humor/s *nm* humor; ~a izjūta sense of humor

humulēns *nm* humulene

humus *nm* humus

humusskābe *nf* humic acid

hunta *nf* junta

hunveibini *nm pl* (hist.) Red Guards

huņņi *nm pl* Huns

huras *nf pl* Hura

hurakāns *nm* hurricane

h|u|rija [ū] *nf* houri

hurma *nf* Japanese persimmon

hu|s|isms [ss] *nm* Hussitism

hu|s|īti [ss] *nm pl* Hussites

hūte *nf* (col.) hat, fedora

huzārs *nm* hussar

I

i I *interj* phoo

i II *partic* = ir II

ibēre *nm* candytuft

ibēriet/is *nm*, ~e *nf* Iberian

ibēr/s *nm*, ~e *nf* Iberian

ibiss *nm* ibis

ibisveidīgie *nom adj* Threskiornithidae

i|ch|neumons [h] *nm* mongoose

i|ch|tiofauna [h] *nf* ichthyofauna

i|ch|tiolo/gs [h] *nm*, ~ģe *nf* ichthyologist

i|ch|tioloģija [h] *nf* ichthyology

i|ch|tioloģiski [h] *adv* ichthyologically

i|ch|tioloģisks [h] *adj* ichthyological

i|ch|tiols [h] *nm* Ichthyol

i|ch|tiozaurs [h] *nm* ichthyosaur

i|ch|tioze [h] *nf* ichthyosis

icikas *nf pl* Icica

idalgo *nm indecl* hidalgo

īdas *nf pl* ides

ideācija *nf* ideation

ideāli *adv* ideally

ideālisms *nm* idealism

ideālistiski *adv* idealistically

ideālistisks *adj* idealistic

ideālistiskums *nm* idealistic quality

ideālist/s *nm*, ~e *nf* idealist

ide|a|litāte [ā] *nf* ideality

ide|a|lizācija [ā] *nf* idealization

ide|a|lizēt [ā] *vt* idealize

ideāls *nm* ideal

ideāls *adj* ideal

ideāltips *nm* ideal type

ideālums *nm* ideality

ideālreālisms *nm* ideal realism

ideja *nf* idea

idejiski *adv* 1. as far as the main idea is concerned; 2. ideologically

idejisks *adj* 1. (of literary works) pertaining to the basic idea; 2. ideologica

idejiskums *nm* quality and quantity of ideas; ideological content

identi *adv* identically

identificējums *nm* (an instance of) identification

identificēšana *nf* identification

identificēt *vt* identify

identificēties *vr* identify oneself

identifikācija *nf* identification; ~s žetons
  identification tag, dogtag
identiski *adv* identically
identisks *adj* identical
identiskums *nm* identicalness
identitāte *nf* identity
idents *adj* identical
identums *nm* identicalness
ideogr|a|fija [ā] *nf* ideography
ideogr|a|fiski [ā] *adv* ideographically
ideogr|a|fisks [ā] *adj* ideographic
ideogramma *nf* ideogram
ideomotors *adj* ideomotor
idiolekts *nm* idiolect
ideolo/gs *nm*, ~ģe *nf* ideologist; ideologue
ideoloģija *nf* ideology
ideoloģiski *adv* ideologically
ideoloģisks *adj* ideological
ideoloģiskums *nm* ideological content
īdēt *vi* (of calves) bleat
idille *nf* idyll
idilliski *adv* idyllically
idillisks *adj* idyllic
idilliskums *nm* idyllic quality
idiogr|a|fisks [ā] *adj* idiographic
idiolekts *nm* idiolect
idioma *nf* idiom
idiom|a|tika [ā] *nf* 1. idioms; 2. idiomology
idiom|a|tiski [ā] *adv* idiomatically
idiom|a|tisks [ā] *adj* idiomatic
idiop|a|tisks [ā] *adj* idiopathic
idioplazma *nf* idioplasm
idiosinkrātiski *adv* idiosyncratically
idiosinkrātisks *adj* idiosyncratic
idiosinkrāzija *nf* idiosyncrasy
idiotija *nf* idiocy
idiotips *nm* gene pool
idiotiski *adv* idiotically
idiotisks *adj* idiotic
idiotiskums *nm* idioticalness
idiotisms *nm* idiocy
idiot/s *nm*, ~e *nf* idiot

idiš *indecl nf* Yiddish
idišs *nm* Yiddish
ido *indecl nf* Ido
idols *nm* idol
idoze *nf* idose
idra *nf* 1. gold-of-pleasure 2. rotted tree core
idrains *adj* 1. overgrown with gold-of-pleasure;
  2. rotten at the core
idre *nf* = idra
idrialīts *nm* idrialite
idrot *vi* rot at the core
īdus *nm* ides
īdzība *nf* surliness, grumpiness
īdzīgi *adv* surlily, grumpily
īdzīgs *adj* surly, grumpy
īdzīgums *nm* surliness, grumpiness
īdzināt *vt* make grumpy
īdzul/is *nm*, ~e *nf* (rare.) surly, peevish person
ieacot *vt* engraft
ieadījums *nm* knitted patch, knitted inset
ieadīt *vt* 1. knit in(to); 2. begin a knitting
ieadīties *vr* 1. get the knack of knitting; 2. get
  knitted by mistake
ieaicinājums *nm* invitation
ieaicināt *vt* invite, ask in
ieaijāt *vt* lull to sleep
ieaijāties *vr* be lulled to sleep
ieaijināt *vt* lull to sleep
ieairēt *vi*, *vt* row into
ieairēties *vr* 1. row into; 2. learn to row
ieāķēt *vt* put a hook into
ieāķēties *vr* get hooked into
iealoties *vr* (obs.) wander into, stumble into
ieapaļi *adv* in a rounded way
ieapaļš *adj* roundish
ieapaļums *nm* roundishness
ieart *vt* 1. plow in, plow under; cut a furrow;
  2. begin to plow; 3. *vi* stray in plowing
iearties *vr* 1. dig into; 2. plow into too far;
  3. get the knack of plowing
iearums *nm* plowing under
ieasfaltēt *vt* fix in asphalt, asphalt in

ieaudi *nm pl* weft

ieaudums *nm* interwoven pattern, strip, or material

ieaudzēt *vt* acclimatize; (of animals) breed

ieaudzināt *vt* inculcate, breed into

ieaugt *vi* **1.** grow into; **2.** take root; **dziļi ieaudzis** deeply rooted; **3.** become surrounded (by vegetation); **4.** adapt

ieaugties *vr* (of plants) become established

ieaugums *nm* ingrowth

ieauklēt *vt* lull to sleep

ieaulekšot *vi* gallop into

ieauļot *vi* gallop into

ieaurēt *vi* = **ieaurot**

ieaurēties *vr* = **ieauroties**

ieaurot *vi* roar into

ieauroties *vr* utter a roar

ieaust *vt* **1.** weave; **2.** weave into; **3.** begin to weave

ieausties *vr* become interwoven

ieaut *vt* **1.** put one's feet into (footwear); **2.** line footwear

ieauties *vr* put on shoes or socks

ieauzot *vt* feed oats

iebadīt *vt* **1.** butt; **2.** stick into

iebaidīt *vt* **1.** intimidate; **2.** (of fowl) shoo into (a place)

iebakstīt *vt* poke

iebalēt *vi* begin to fade

iebalgani *adv* in a whitish color

iebālgans *adj* whitish

iebalināt *vt* bleach lightly

iebalot *vi* = **iebalēt**

iebāls *adj* somewhat pale

iebalsot *vt* vote in

iebalsoties *vr* (rare.) begin to sound

iebalts *adj* whitish

iebalzamēt *vt* embalm

iebandoties *vr* become well-to-do (as a **bandinieks**), acquire wealth

iebangot *vi* well up

iebangoties *vr* begin to surge or swell

iebarot *vt* **1.** attract by feeding; **2.** feed

iebārstīt *vt* strew in

iebārt *vt* (rare.) scold a little; ~s *part* intimidated

iebaudījis *adj, part* of **iebaudīt** (col.) intoxicated

iebaudīt *vt* taste; partake of; **i. kādu malku** have a little drink

iebauroties *vr* give a bellow

iebāzīt *vt* tuck in, stick in

iebāzt *vt* push in, stick in, tuck in; **i. kabatā** pocket; **i. aiz restēm** (col.) put in jail; **i. (kādu) kabatā** put s.o. in one's pocket; **i. maisā** (col.) beat, surpass; **i. zobenu makstī** sheathe the sword

iebāzties *vr* slip in, get tucked away (unawares)

iebēgt *vi* flee to

iebelzt *vi* give s.o. a punch

iebērt *vt* pour into

ieberzēt *vt* run in; rub into

ieberzēties *vr* rub oneself (with oil, salve)

ieberzt *vt* **1.** crumble (into a container); **2.** rub

ieberzties *vr* **1.** get crumbled into (unintentionally); **2.** create a rubbing sore

ieberzums *nm* abrasion

iebetonēt *vt* **1.** set in concrete; **2.** pour concrete

iebetonējums *nm* **1.** setting in concrete; **2.** poured concrete

iebīdīt *vt* push in; push into; **i. patronu** load a round

iebīdītājs *nm* (firearms) loader

iebīdīties *vr* be pushed into

iebīdnis *nm* **1.** (wooden) bar; tenon; **2.** (mech.) feeder

iebiedēšana *nf* intimidation; (mil.) show of force

iebiedēt *vt* intimidate

iebiedēšana *nf* intimidation; ~s **līdzeklis** deterrent

iebiezināt *vt* (of liquids) condense

iebikstīt *v* **1.** *vi* poke; **2.** *vt* push (by poking)

iebikstīts *adj, part* of **iebikstīt** (col.) intimidated

iebilde *nf* objection

iebildība *nf* (rare.) haughtiness

iebildīgi *adv* haughtily

iebildīgs *adj* (rare.) haughty

iebildums *nm* objection

iebilst *v* **1.** *vi* object; demur; **2.** *vt* remark, add; **i. (kādam) par labu** put in a good word

iebilsties *vr* speak up, observe

iebilšķis *nm* inveterate objector

iebimbāties *vr* (com.) begin to cry

iebirdināt *vt* let fall in, strew in

iebirt *vi* (of friable materials) fall into, get into

iebizot *vi* bolt into

ieblakām *adv* almost side by side

ieblakus *adv* almost side by side

ieblandīties *vr* (col.) wander into

ieblarkšķēties *vr* begin to rattle

ieblaukšķēties *vr* bang (once)

ieblāvi *adv* wanly, dimly

ieblāvoties *vr* begin to dawn

ieblāvs *adj* wan, dim

ieblāzmot *vi* light up, begin to glow

ieblāzmoties *vr* light up, begin to glow

ieblēdīt *vt* obtain by deceit

ieblēdīties *vr* insinuate oneself

ieblenzt *vi* (com.) look into

ieblēties *vr* utter a bleat

ieblietēt *vt* ram into

iebliezt *vi* (col.) strike

ieblīvēt *vt* jam into

iebļaut *vi* shout into

iebļauties *vr* (col.) yell out

iebļāviens *nm* short cry

iebojāt *vt* damage somewhat

iebojāties *vr* (rare.) spoil a little

ieborēt *vi* (barb.) persuade, make believe

iebradāt *vt* trample, trample down, tread in

iebrakšķēties *vr* make a cracking noise

iebraucamā vieta *nf* coaching inn

iebraucams *adj, part* of **iebraukt** drive-in

iebraucējs *nm*, **~a** *nf* **1.** newcomer; visitor; **2.** horse trainer

iebraucīt *vt* sweep into

iebraukāt *vt* **1.** make tracks, blaze a trail; **2.** (of horses) break in; (of machines) run in

iebraukšana *nf* **1.** entrance, entry, arrival; **2.** breaking-in, running-in; **3.** opening up a road, making tracks, blazing a trail

iebraukšanas atļauja *nf* entry permit

iebraukšanas vīza *nf* entrance visa

iebraukt *v* **1.** *vi, vt* drive in, drive into; **i. grāvī** err; **i. laulības ostā** (col.) get married; **i. purvā** (fig.) get mired; **2.** *vi* arrive; **3.** *vt* make tracks, blaze a trail; **4.** *vt* (of horses) break in, (of machines) run in; **5.** *vt* (col.) slide in

iebrauktuve *nf* driveway

iebrāzmot *vi* (of wind; fig.) rush in

iebrāzmoties *vr* storm briefly; (of wind) blow hard a short while

iebrāzties *vr* rush in

iebrēciens *nm* cry

iebrēkt *vi* scream into; trumpet into

iebrēkties *vr* cry out

iebriest *vi* swell

iebrikšķēties *vr* give a crack, snap, start cracking

iebrīkšķēties *vr* creak (briefly)

iebrist *vi* wade in

iebrokastot *vi* have breakfast

iebrucēj/s *nm*, **~a** *nf* invader

iebrucināt *vt* cause a cave-in

iebrukt I *vi* fall in, come down, collapse; cave in

iebrukt II *vi* **1.** invade, break in; **2.** burst in

iebrukums I *nm* collapse; cave-in; (geol.) rift

iebrukums II *nm* invasion; incursion

iebrūnēt *vt* brown a little

iebrūns *adj* brownish

iebrūvēt *vt* brew

iebubināt *vi* mutter into

iebubināties *vr* begin to whinny

iebuknīt *v* = **iebukņīt**

iebukņīt *v* 1. *vi* give a nudge; 2. *vt* beat up on s.o.

iebuksnīt *vi* give a nudge

iebūkšķēties *vr* thud or thump briefly

iebuktēt *vt* (col.) 1. dent; 2. put a crease in pants

iebuldurēt *vt* 1. (col., of reading skil) drill; 2. mumble into

iebuldurēties *vr* 1. gobble briefly; 2. mumble, mutter; 3. learn with effort

iebungāt *vt* (col.) give a whipping

ieburāt *vi* sailt into

ieburbuļot *vi* flow into, bubbling

ieburbuļoties *vr* bubble briefly

ieburkšķēties *vr* 1. grumble or growl briefly; 2. speak up angrily

ieburnīt *vt* wrinkle

ieburzījums *nm* wrinkle, wrinkles

ieburzīt *vt* wrinkle

ieburzīties *vr* get wrinkled

iebūve *nf* built-in

iebūvējums *nm* 1. built-in structure; 2. insertion, installation, building-in

iebūves leņķis *nm* (of kites) angle of attack

iebūvēt *vt* 1. build in; 2. use in building

iebūvēties *vr* establish oneself by building

iebūviete *nf* wife of an **iebūvietis**

iebūvietis *nm* (hist.) peasant farmer who built and farmed on someone else's land; crofter

iebužināt *vt* 1. bury, hide (by ruffling); 2. toussle a little

iecelt *vt* 1. lift into; 2. (of doors, windows) hang; 3. **i. amatā** appoint; **i. bruņinieku kārtā** knight; **i. godā** honor; **i. maizē** provide with livelihood; **i. virsnieka amatā** commission

iecelot *vi* arrive; immigrate, migrate to

iecelotāj/s *nm*, ~a *nf* immigrant

iecementēt *vt* cement in

iecementēties *vr* become rooted

iecentrēt *vt* center

iecept *v* 1. *vt* bake into; 2. *vi* (rare.) bake incompletely

iecere *nf* 1. project, plan; intention; 2. conception, idea

iecerējums *nm* plan; concept

iecerēt *vt* 1. plan; intend; 2. (col.) fall in love and plan to marry

iecerēt/ais *nom adj*, ~**ā** *nf* intended, beloved

iecerēties *vr* remember

iecienīt *vt* esteem; value

iecienīts *adj, part* of **iecienīt** favorite, popular

ieciepties *vr* utter a peep

iecietēt *vi* harden

iecietība *nf* tolerance; indulgence

iecietīgi *adv* tolerantly; indulgently

iecietīgs *adj* tolerant; indulgent

iecietīgums *nm* tolerance; indulgence

iecietinājums *nm* starching

iecietināt *vt* starch

iecilāt *vt* 1. (of recipe ingredients) fold; 2. **i. kājas** limber up, warm up

iecildīgs *adj* conceited

iecildināt *vt* extol

iecildīt *vt* extol

iecilpot *vi* lop into

iecirknis *nm* district

iecirpt *vi* 1. begin to shear; 2. injure in shearing

iecirst *v* 1. *vt* hew in(to); (of a cutting instrument, teeth) sink into; 2. *vt* notch; 3. *vi* cut into; 4. (*vi 3rd pers*, of spices) bite; 5. *vt* hit; **i. pliķi** slap; **i. ar ķepu** paw; **i. glāzīti** (or **čarku**) down a shot (of liquor); 6. *vt* (of one's head) hang

iecirsties *vr* 1. grab (with teeth, talons); 2. (*3rd pers*) cut into; 3. cut one's way into; 4. (fig.) turn stubborn; 5. (of pungent smells) hit the nostrils; 6. (col.) fall in love

iecirtējs *nm* coal hewer

iecirtība *nf* stubborness

iecirtiens *nm* cut, slash, chop

iecirtīgi *adv* stubbornly

iecirtīgs *adj* stubborn

iecirtīgums *nm* stubborness

iecirtot *vt* curl

iecirtuma savienojums *nm* bridle joint

iecirtums *nm* cut

iecistēties *vr* encyst

iecukurot *vt* candy

iecukuroties *vr* absorb sugar

iečabēties *vr* begin to rustle

iečabināties *vr* rustle briefly

iečakstēties *vr* **1.** rustle briefly; **2.** (of birds) chatter briefly

iečakstināties *vr* (of birds) chatter briefly

iečaloties *vr* **1.** begin to chatter; **2.** begin to gurgle

iečāpāt *vi* toddle in

iečāpot *vi* = **iečāpāt**

iečarkot *vr* (col.) have a drink

iečarkoties *vr* (col.) have a drink

iečaukstēties *vr* begin to rustle

iečaulojums *nm* (tech.) cowl, cowling

iečerkstēties *vr* screech briefly, rasp briefly

iečiepstēties *vr* utter a peep

iečiepties *vr* utter a peep

iečīkstēties *vr* creak, squeak

inčinkstēties *vr* (col.) begin to whimper

iečīpstēties *vr* utter a peep

iečirkstēties *vr* squeak, creak; begin to chirp

iečivināties *vr* begin to twitter

iečubināt *vt* (col.) wrap

iečučināt *vt* (child) lull to sleep

iečukstēt *vt* whisper (in s.o.'s ear)

iečukstēties *vr* begin to whisper

iečūkstēties *vr* begin to sputter

iečunčināt *vt* (col.) wrap

iečurkstēties *vr* **1.** begin to gurgle; **2.** begin to sizzle; **3.** begin to chirp

iedaba *nf* natural disposition

iedabāt *vt* (reg.) imagine

iedabāties *vr* become accustomed

iedābt *vi* (reg.) hit

iedabūt *vt* get sth. in; **i. vārdu starpā** get a word in edgewise

iedale *nf* division; subdivision

iedalījums *nm* **1.** division; subdivision; **2.** arrangement; **3.** classification; **4.** assignment

iedalīt *vt* **1.** divide, subdivide; **2.** arrange; **3.** classify; **4.** assign

iedalīties *vr* (*3rd pers*) be divided into

iedaļa *nf* division; subdivision

iedambēt *vt* levee

iedancot *vi* dance into

iedangāt *vt* trample into

iedarbe *nf* influence, effect

iedarbība *nf* influence, effect; **atsitiena ~s** recoil-operated

iedarbīgi *adv* effectively

iedarbīgs *adj* effective

iedarbīgums *nm* effectiveness

iedarbināšana *nf* (of engines) starting

iedarbināt *vt* start, set in motion

iedarboties *vr* **1.** effect, influence, work on; **2.** be-gin to work

iedārdēt *vi* move in with a rumble

iedārdēties *vr* begin to rumble, begin to thunder

iedārdināt *vt, vi* move in with a rumble

iedaris *nm* originator

iedarīt *vt* **1.** do sth. to s.o.; **2.** cast a spell; **3.** begin to do

iedarīts *adj, part* of **iedarīt** routine

iedars *nm* **1.** malt; **2.** unplowed field; **3.** butter churn starter; **4.** one that has begun a job

iedarvojums *nm* tarring, tarring job

iedarvot *vt* tar, impregnate with tar

iedaudzināt *vt* **1.** name; **2.** praise

iedaudzināts *adj, part* of **iedaudzināt** popular, favorite

iedauzīt *vt* crack; dent; **i. caurumu** make a hole

iedauzīties *vr* **1.** become bruised, dented, or cracked; **2.** (col.) wander in

iedāvāt *vt* give as a gift

iedāvināt *vt* give as a gift

iedaža *nf* idea, fancy, notion

iededze *nf* (welding) penetration

iededzīgi *adv* glowingly; passionately

iededzīgs *adj* easily enthused

iededzinājies *adj, part* of **iededzināties** tanned

iededzinājums *nm* burn

iededzināt *vt* **1.** (of candles) light, (of lamps) turn on; (of a fire) start; **i. elektrību** turn on the lights; **2.** burn into; **3.** (of barrels) burn out

iededzināties *vr* get a tan

iededzis *adj, part* of **iedegt** II tanned, sunburnt

iedega *nf* (bot.) blotch

iedegt I *vt* = **iededzināt** 1

iedegt II *vi* tan, acquire a tan; become sunburnt

iedegties *vr* **1.** light up; **2.** flare up; **i. dusmās** become enraged; **3.** catch fire; **4.** get caught up (in an argument, emotion); enthuse

iedegums *nm* suntan; sunburn

iedejot *v* **1.** *vi* enter dancing; **2.** *vt* break in, inaugurate with a dance

iedejoties *vr* become a good dancer

iedejots *adj, part* of **iedejot** well practised

iedēklis *nm* **1.** (ling.) infix; **2.** nest egg

iedelverēt *vi* stumble in

iederēties *vr* fit in

iederība *nf* fittingness, appropriateness

iederīgi *adv* fittingly, appropriately

iederīgs *adj* fitting, appropriate

iederīgums *nm* fittingness, appropriateness

iedēstīt *vt* plant

iedēsts *nm* (rare.) seedling

iedēt *vt* lay (eggs) in(to) a place

iedēvēt *vt* begin to call (by a name), nickname

iedibene *nf* bottom

iedibinājums *nm* introduction (of sth. new)

iedibināt *vt* **1.** introduce (sth. new); **2.** (rare., of an argument) found

iedibināties *vr* become established

iedīdīt *vt* inculcate, drill; (of animals) break in, train

iediebt *vi* run in

iediedzēt *vt* (rare.) sprout

iediegt I *vt* stitch on, attach with stitches

iediegt II *vi* dash into

iedīglis *nm* (fig.) germ

iedīkties *vr* **1.** buzz briefly; **2.** pule briefly

iedilt *vi* wear out a little; wane

iedilums *nm* worn-out spot

iedimdēt *vi* rumble into

iedimdēties *vr* begin to rumble; rumble briefly

iedimdināt *vi* (rare.) rumble into

iedimēt *vi* rumble into

iedipēties *vr* (of muffled footsteps) sound

iedipināt *vi* pit-a-pat in

iedirbe *nf* influence; effect

iedobe *nf* (geol.) kettle; (rare.) dimple

iedobīte *nf dim* of **iedobe**, dimple

iedobs *nm* hollow

iedobt *vt* hollow

iedobulis *nm* small depression (in the ground)

iedobumains *adj* filled with depressions

iedobums *nm* depression, hollow

iedoma *nf* **1.** notion; idea; **2.** whim; **3.** imagination, fancy; **4.** presumption

iedomāt *v* **1.** *vt* recall; **2.** *vt* think of; **3.** *vi* imagine

iedomātais *nom adj* the imaginary

iedomāties *vr* **1.** recall; **2.** think of; **3.** imagine

iedomāts *adj, part* of **iedomāt** imaginary

iedomība *nf* conceit; presumptuousness

iedomīgi *adv* conceitedly; presumptuously

iedomīgs *adj* conceited; presumptuous

iedomīgums *nm* conceit; presumptuousness

iedot *vt irr* give, hand; allot; **i. aprīli** play an April fool on s.o.; **i. kurvīti** jilt

iedragājums *nm* damage

iedragāt *vt* shatter, crack; (fig.) undermine

iedraudzēties *vr* make friends with

iedrāzt *v* 1. *vi* rush in; 2. *vi* smash into; 3. *vt* (of a blow) administer; **i. pliķi** slap

iedrāzties *vr* 1. rush in; 2. smash into

iedrēbe *nf* lining

iedrebēties *vr* shiver briefly

iedresēt *vt* (of animals) train

iedrēzt *vt* (of a match, fire) light

iedrīksnāt *vt* scratch

iedrīkstēties *vr* dare; venture

iedrillēt *vt* (com.) learn (by rote)

iedriskāt *vt* tatter somewhat

iedrosināt *vt* encourage

iedrosmināt *vt* encourage

iedrošinājums *nm* encouragement

iedrošināt *vt* encourage

iedrošināties *vr* dare; venture

iedrukāt *vt* print (in)

iedrupināt *vt* crumble into

iedrupis *adj, part* of **iedrupt** crumbling

iedrupt *vi* 1. begin to crumble; 2. crumble and fall into

iedublējums *nm* dubbing

iedublēt *vt* dub

iedubt *vi* (of eyes, cheeks) sink

ieducināt *vi* move in rumbling

iedūcināt *vi* 1. begin to play (a low-register instrument); 2. move in humming

ieducināties *vr* rumble a little

iedudināt *vi* speak softly into

iedudināties *vr* 1. begin to speak softly; 2. begin to rumble

iedūdot *vi* begin to coo; (of musical instruments) begin to play

ieduknīt *vi* hit, butt

iedūkties *vr* buzz, hum, or drone briefly

iedūmoties *vr* begin to smoke

iedundurojis *adj, part* of **iedundorot** (col.) drunk

iedundurot *vi* (col.) have a few drinks

iedunēt *vi* move in reverberating

iedunēties *vr* rumble, drone briefly

iedungot *vi* hum into

iedungoties *vr* hum briefly

iedunkāt *vt* give a nudge

iedurstīt *vt* 1. pierce (here and there); 2. stick in (here and there)

iedūšināties *vr* summon one's courage

iedūšot *vt* encourage

iedurt *vt, vi* stick (with an instrument), stick in, into; **i. degunu (grāmatā)** (col.) bury oneself in (a book)

iedurties *vr* 1. stick; 2. penetrate; 3. experience sudden sharp pain

iedūšināt *vt* encourage

iedūšojies *adj, part* of **iedūšoties** (col.) intoxicated

iedūšoties *vr* summon up one's courage

iedvašot *vt* 1. inhale; 2. blow one's breath into

iedvesma *nf* 1. inspiration; 2. suggestion

iedvesmēt *vt* = **iedvesmot**

iedvesmīgs *adj* inspiring

iedvesmot *vt* 1. inspire; 2. suggest

iedvesmotāj/s *nm*, ~**a** *nf* inspirer

iedvesmoties *vr* be inspired, draw inspiration from

iedv[e]st [ē] *vt* 1. inspire; **i. cieņu** command re-spect; 2. instill; 3. suggest

iedzalkstīties *vr* flash

iedzelt *vi* sting; bite; (fig.) nettle, pique, stab

iedzeltenais ķaukis (or **smējējķaukis**) *nm* icterine warbler

iedzeltenā rezēda *nf* dyer's rocket

iedzelteni *adv* in a yellowish color

iedzeltenie dižmeldri *nm pl* yellow cyperus

iedzeltens *adj* yellowish

iedzeltēt *vi* turn yellowish

iedzemdēt *vt* (of genetic characteristics) transmit

iedzenāt *vt* (of animals) drive into

iedzērāj/s *nm*, ~**a** *nf* imbiber

iedzēris *adj, part* of **iedzert** tipsy

iedzerklis *nm* bottom (of a cup or other container with a concave bottom)

iedzerksnis *nm* (of a fish trap) trapping funnel

iedzeršana *nf* drinking; drinking party

iedzert *v* **1.** *vt* (of a liquid) take; **2.** *vi* drink; **i. glāzīti** take a drop; **i. uz (kāda) veselību** drink s.o.'s health

iedzerties, usu. *part* **iedzēries** under the influence of alcohol

iedziedājum/s *nm* recording (of a song); . . . **~ā** (song) recorded by . . .

iedziedāt *vt* **1.** record a song; **2.** announce with a song

iedziedāties *vr* **1.** begin singing, burst out in a song; sing briefly; **2.** gain practice singing, im-prove one's singing

iedziļināties *vr* go deeply into; become absorbed in; fathom; make a thorough enquiry; sink deep-er into; **i. sevī** withdraw into oneself

iedzimt *vi* be inborn

iedzimt/ais *nm*, **~ā** *nf* native

iedzimtība *nf* heredity

iedzimts *adj, part* of **iedzimt** hereditary, inborn; **i. ģimenē** running in the family, familial

iedzinkstēties *vr* begin to buzz; buzz briefly

iedzintarojums *nm* inclusion in amber

iedzirdīt *vt* **1.** control s.o.'s behavior (with liquor or magic potions); **2.** (rare.) make s.o. drunk

iedzīres *nf pl* party to inaugurate a new building

iedzirklis *nm* **1.** (of a fish trap) trapping funnel; **2.** auditory meatus; **3.** (geol.) bottom of a basin

iedzirksteļoties *vr* begin to spark

iedzirkstēt *vi* = **iedzirkstīt**

iedzirkstēties *vr* = **iedzirkstīties**

iedzirkstīt *vi* begin to sparkle

iedzirkstīties *vr* begin to sparkle

iedzīt *vt* **1.** drive in(to), push in(to); **i. bailes** instill fear; **i. bankrotā** bankrupt; **i. galvā** (fig.) hammer into s.o.'s head; **i. kapā**

(col.) send to the grave; **2.** catch up with; **3.** (obs.) collect

iedzīties *vr* drive oneself into

iedzītnis *nm* dowel; peg

iedzītņot *vt* dowel

iedzīv/e *nf* belongings, effects; **ar visu ~i** bag and baggage

iedzīvinājums *nm* realization

iedzīvināt *vt* realize, make a reality, call into life; revive

iedzīvināties *vr* revive

iedzīvošanās *nfr* acquisition of wealth; **netaisna i.** unlawful gain

iedzīvot *vt* (rare.) get accustomed to a residence

iedzīvotāj/s *nm*, **~a** *nf* inhabitant; **~i** population

iedzīvoties *vr* **1.** adapt; get used to; acclimatize; **2.** grow into (a role); **3.** acquire wealth; (fig.) get into (debt, trouble)

iedzīvots *adj, part* of **iedzīvot** (of one's living quarters) accustomed

iedžinkstēties *vr* begin to buzz, buzz briefly

ieecēt *vt* work in with a harrow

ieēdināt *vt* **1.** attract by feeding, tame by feeding; **2.** bewitch (by feeding magic food); **3.** feed a little

ieeja *nf* **1.** entrance; entry; **~s punkt**s point of entry; **2.** admission; **i. aizliegta** no admittance; **3.** (compu.) input

ieejas durvis *nf pl* front door

ieejas maksa *nf* (price of) admission

ieekonomēt *vt* economize

ieelpa *nf* inhalation

ieelpot *vt* inhale

ieelsoties *vr* begin to sob, sob briefly

ieelsties *vr* take a few quick breaths

ieeļļot *vt* oil, lubricate; grease

ieēnojums *nm* **1.** shadow; **2.** shading

ieēnot *vt* **1.** darken the background; **2.** increase contrast

ieēnoties *vr* cast a shadow

ieērcināt *vt* provoke

ieēst *vt* **1.** have a bite to eat; **2.** begin to eat; **3.** eat, consume; **(cik viņš) ieēdis** (amount of his) food intake

ieēsties *vr* **1.** eat one's way into; eat into; **2.** jam, seize, wedge; **3.** (col.) have it in for s.o.

ieēšanās *nf* (tech.) jamming

iefiltrēties *vr* inflitrate

iefrēzējums *nm* milled slot

iefrēzēt *vt* mill

iegādāt *vt* **1.** purchase; acquire; **2.** remember

iegādāties *vr* **1.** purchase; acquire; **2.** remember

iegāde *nf* purchase; acquisition

iegadīties *vr* happen, have the occasion (to do sth.)

iegāds *nm* stock

iegādzināties *vr* (of geese) honk briefly

iegāgināties *vr* (of geese) honk briefly

iegailēties *vr* flare up

iegaiņāt *vt* shoo in(to)

iegaismojums *nm* spotlighting

iegaismot *vt* spotlight

iegaismotāj/s *nm*, **~a** *nf* **1.** spotlighter; **2.** spotlight

iegaismoties *vr* light up

iegaiši *adv* in a rather bright light

iegaišs *adj* rather light

iegalve *nf* headboard

iegalvis *nm* **1.** fontanel; **2.** (of sleds) head of a runner

iegalvojums *nm* persuasion, convincing

iegalvot *vt* persuade, convince

ieganīt *vt* **1.** accustom to being grazed; **2.** graze partly; **3.** feed by grazing

ieganīties *vr* become used to being grazed

iegansts *nm* pretext

iegardināt *vt* make s.o.'s mouth water

iegarens *adj* oblong, elongated, longish

iegarenums *nm* oblongness

iegārgties *vr* begin to rattle in the throat

iegaršoties *vr* come to like the taste of

iegātnība *nf* the state of an **iegātnis**

iegātnieks *nm* = **iegātnis**

iegātnis *nm* (hist.) new farmer (a peasant who became the owner of a homestead through mar-riage); a peasant who married a farmer's daughter or widow

iegaudoties *vr* begin to howl; raise a howl

iegaume *nf* retention

iegaumēt *vt* **1.** mark, notice; **2.** retain, memorize

iegavilēties *vr* **1.** begin to exult, rejoice; **2.** begin to sing (**gavilēt**)

iegāzelēties *vr* wobble in

iegāzt *v* **1.** *vt* dump, throw into; **2.** *vt* (col.) do s.o. an ill turn; **3.** *vi* (col.) whack

iegāzties *vr* **1.** fall in(to); **2.** cave in; **3.** flop down; **4.** (col.) burst into

ieglabāt *vt* **1.** hide; **2.** become accustomed to hiding; **3.** pamper; **4.** save

ieglaudīt *vt* (rare.) accustom to being petted

ieglaust *vt* rest on

ieglausties *vr* cuddle up to

iegleznojums *nm* placement (in a painting)

iegleznot *vt* paint in

iegludinājums *nm* pressed-in crease

iegludināt *vt* iron in, press in

ieglūnēt *vi* peer in

iegniezt *vi* (reg.) hit, whack

iegodāt *vt* begin to call (by a name)

iegodināt *vt* begin to call (by a name)

iegore *nf* ravine

iegorīties *vr* wobble in

iegoznis *nm* sunny and windless spot

iegrābāt *vt* rake in

iegrabēties *vr* begin to rattle; rattle faintly

iegrābiens *nm* grab

iegrabināties *vr* rattle briefly

iegrābstīt *vt* rake in

iegrābt *vt* scoop up

iegrābties *vr* **1.** be caught redhanded; **2.** (com.) fall for; make a bad buy

iegraizīt *vt* **1.** cut, score; **2.** cut (and let drop) into

iegramstīt *vt* rake in (a little, superficially)

iegrāmatojums *nm* (bookk.) entry

iegrāmatot *vt* (bookk.) enter

iegrandēties *vr* begin to rumble

iegrausties *vr* begin to rumble

iegraut *vt* make tumble into; make a hole (in a wall)

iegrauties *vr* begin to rumble; rumble briefly

iegrauzt *vt* **1.** gnaw, gnaw into, eat into; **2.** eat a little (hard food); **3.** burrow through; dig through

iegrauzties *vr* eat into; dig into

iegrauzums *nm* burrowing, cut

iegrava *nf* valley

iegravējums *nm* engraving

iegravēt *vt* engrave

iegrāvis *nm* track; rut

iegrebt *vt* carve in

iegrebums *nm* carving

iegremde *nf* **1.** immersion; **2.** submersion

iegremdējums *nm* **1.** immersion; **2.** submersion; submersion; **3.** underground location

iegremdēšana *nf* submersion

iegremdēt *vt* immerse, submerge, sink; lower into

iegremdēties *vr* sink into; (fig.) become engrossed in

iegrib/a *nf* caprice, whim; ~u **apmierināšana** gratification; indulgence

iegribēt *vt* want (on the spur of the moment), desire; demand

iegribēšana *nf* desire

iegribēties *vr* have craving for; have a sudden wish for

iegribīgi *adv* capriciously

iegribīgs *adj* given to caprices, whims

iegriezt I *vt* **1.** screw in; crank in; **2.** (of a car, horse) turn in; **3.** (of dislocated limbs) set; **4.** (weav.) beam

iegriezt II (with iê) *v* **1.** *vt* cut, cut in(to), carve in; **2.** *vi* cut oneself; **3.** *vt* begin to cut; **4.** *vt* slice into; **5.** *vi* (col.) also **i. ķirķi** do s.o. dirt; (com.) get the better of

iegriezties I *vr* **1.** turn into (change direction), turn; (of a conversation) turn to; **2.** stop by, drop in; **3.** (of weather, wind) turn, set in

iegriez/ties II (with iê) *vr* cut into; **man ~ās pirkstā** I cut my finger

iegriezums *nm* cut, notch, incision

iegrīļoties *vr* stagger in

iegrime *nf* **1.** (of soil) settling; **2.** (of ships) draft

iegrimt *vi* sin, sink into; (of soil) subside, (of buildings) settle; **i. domās** become immersed in thought

iegrimums *nm* **1.** sinking; **2.** depression

iegroba *nf* depression, hollow

iegrobe *nf* depression, hollow

iegropēt *vt* groove

iegrozīt *vt* **1.** turn to fit; **2.** (fig., col.) arrange, fix

iegrozīties *vr* **1.** settle in; **2.** manage; **3.** turn out

iegrožojums *nm* reining in, restraint

iegrožot *vt* rein in, restrain

iegrūdiens *nm* push

iegrupēt *vt* assign to a group

iegrūst *vt* **1.** push in(to); **i. nelaimē** (or **postā**) ruin; **2.** give a push; **3.** (col.) nudge; **4.** (col.) stuff, shove in

iegrūsties *vr* run into; **i. prātā** (col.) remember; think of

iegrūt *vi* **1.** fall in, cave in, collapse; **2.** (of persons) fall in (because of ground giving way)

iegruvums *nm* cave-in; sinkhole

iegudrēties *vr* become experienced (in performing a task)

iegudroties *vr* imagine

iegula *nf* **1.** (geol.) mineral deposit; **2.** (reg.) depression

ieguldījums *nm* investment

ieguldināt *vt* put to bed

ieguldīt *vt* 1. lay down; put to bed; 2. invest

ieguldzēties *vr* gurgle briefly

iegulējums *nm* depression (formed by an object lying in it)

iegulēt *vt* 1. form a depression; 2. get used to a resting place

iegulgoties *vr* gurgle briefly

iegulsnēties *vr* be deposited

iegult *vi* 1. settle in; 2. fit; 3. lay into; 4. (of merchandise) fail to move, find no market

iegulties *vr* 1. lie down; take to bed; 2. settle in; 3. form (under pressure); 4. lay into

iegultne *nf* 1. boggy place; 2. old river bed; 3. depression

iegultnis *nm* insole

iegulums *nm* mineral deposit

iegumt *vi* bend in

iegumzījums *nm* wrinkles

iegumzīt *vt* (col.) 1. stuff in; 2. wrinkle; 3. gulp down

iegumzīties *vr* become wrinkled

iegurkstēties *vr* crunch briefly

iegurnis *nm* pelvis

iegurņa dobums *nm* (anat.) basin

iegūstams *adj* obtainable

iegūšana *nf* 1. procurement; 2. extraction (min-ing)

iegūt *vt* 1. get, obtain; acquire; gain; procure; achieve; **mēģināt i. laiku** play for time; **i. atpakaļ** recover; 2. extract, mine; 3. produce; 4. have a woman; 5. *vi* gain

iegūtnēm *adv* 1. in a hurry; 2. during one's free moments

ieguve *nf* production

ieguvēj/s *nm*, ~a *nf* obtainer, acquirer

ieguvum/s *nm* 1. gain; **dilstošs ~a pieaugums** diminishing returns; 2. acquisition

ieģeņģerēt *vi* stagger in

ieģērbt *vt* clothe, dress, attire

ieģērbties *vr* dress oneself (in a certain kind of clothes)

ieģipsējums *nm* plastering

ieģipsēt *vt* cover with plaster; place in a cast

ieģist *vt* 1. memorize; note; 2. imagine

ieģisties *vr* imagine

ieīdēties *vr* bleat briefly

ieiet *vi irr* 1. go in(to), step in(to); move in(to); enter; **i. asinīs** become a habit; **i. azartā** become reckless; **i. galvā** make drunk; **i. grīstē** (aeron.) put into a spin; **i. sievā** marry; **i. tautā** become popularized; **i. vēsturē** go down in history; 2. (col.) be composed of

ieieties *vr* take root, spread

ieildzināt *vt* prolong, draw out

ieilgoties *vr* begin to long for

ieilgt *vi* go on, drag on, (of an illness) linger; (with **līdz**) last till

ieilgums *nm* delay; prolongation

ieinteresēt *vt* interest, arouse the interest of s.o.

ieinteresētība *nf* personal interest; **materiāla i.** material incentive

ieinteresēties *vr* become interested in, take an in-terest in

ieinteresēts *adj, part* of **ieinteresēt** having an in-terest in, interested

ieintriģēt *vt* intrigue

ieirt I *vt* row into

ieirt II *vi* unravel

ieirties *vr* row into, paddle into

iejāde *nf* dressage

iejādīt *vt* (of horses) break in

iejādītājs *nm* horsebreaker, roughrider

iejājēj/s *nm*, ~a *nf* horsebreaker

iejāt *vt* 1. ride in, enter on horseback; 2. (of horses) break in

iejaucēt *vt* accustom

iejaukšanās *nfr* interference, meddling, (pol.) intervention

iejaukt *vt* 1. mix, mix in, stir in; 2. involve, implicate

iejaukties *vr* **1.** interfere; meddle; butt in; intervene; **2.** merge in; (*3rd pers*) get mixed in

iejaut *vt* **1.** mix dough; **2.** mix into

iejautāties *vr* ask a question

iejava *nf* leaven; (brewery) mash

iejavs *nm* leaven; (brewery) mash

iejemt *vt* = **ieņemt**

iejokoties *vr* (rare.) say sth. jokingly

iejoma *nf* framework; area, sphere

iejoms *nm* **1.** small river bend; **2.** limits, confines, frame; **3.** area, sphere

iejoņot *vi* gallop in; come tearing in

iejozt I *vt* **1.** gird; **2.** envelop

iejozt II *vi* dash in

iejūgs *nm* harness

iejūgt *vt* harness; (fig.) tie down, saddle (with work)

iejūgties *vr* **1.** put oneself in harness; **2.** (fig., col.) buckle to; **i. darbā** put one's back into it

iejukt *vi* **1.** merge in; **2.** get mixed in with

iejūkt *vi* become accustomed

iejundēt *vt* (poet.) herald

iejundīt *vt* = **iejundēt**

iejūsma *nf* enthusiasm

iejūsminā t *vt* enthuse

iejūsmība *nf* enthusiasm

iejūsmīgi *adv* enthusiastically

iejūsmīgs *adj* enthusiastic

iejūsmināties *vr* become enthused

iejūsmot *vt* enthuse

iejūsmoties *vr* become enthused

iejusties *vr* **1.** adjust; feel at home; **i. lietas apstākļos** fit oneself into the situation; **i. lomā** live the part; introject; **2.** empathize with

iejūta *nf* empathy

iej|u|tība [ū] *nf* empathy

iej|u|tīgi [ū] *adv* empathically; sensitively

iej|u|tīgs [ū] *adj* empathic; sensitive

iej|u|tīgums [ū] *nm* empathy

iekabe *nf* shackle

iekabināt *vt* hook in(to)

iekairināmība *nf* stimulability

iekairināt *vt* stimulate

iekaisīgs *adj* impulsive

iekaisis *adj, part* of **iekaist 1.** excited, irritated; **2.** inflamed

iekaisīt *vt* strew in, sprinkle in

iekaisme *nf* (rare., fig.) heat

iekaist *vi* **1.** become inflamed, redden; **2.** become irritated, flare up

iekaisums *nm* **1.** inflammation; **2.** (fig.) heat

iekaitināt *vt* annoy

iekaldināt *vt* **1.** inlay, encrust; **2.** chisel into

iekalkulējums *nm* taking into account

iekalkulēt *vt* take into account, reckon in

iekalne *nf* foot of a hill; low hill

iekalnis *adv* gradually uphill

iekaln/s *nm* slope; *pret* ~**u** uphill

iekalnus *adv* gradually uphill

iekalst *vi* **1.** begin to wither; **2.** dry (inside sth.)

iekalt *vt* **1.** inlay, encrust; **2.** put in irons, fetter; **3.** chisel into; **4.** fasten into; **i. ledū** lock in ice; **5.** cram, learn by rote

iekaltēt *vt* **1.** dry and store; **2.** allow to dry

iekalties *vr* **1. i. ledū** be locked in ice; **i. važās** put chains on oneself; **2.** chisel one's way into; **3.** be engraved (in memory)

iekalums *nm* **1.** metal ornamentation; **2.** engraving; chiseled groove

iekam or **iekām** *adv* before

iekampis *adj, part* of **iekampt** (col.) intoxicated

iekampt *vt* **1.** grasp (with the mouth); gasp (for air); **2.** have a quick bite to eat; have a quick drink; **3.** *vi* bite into

iekams or **iekāms** *adv* before

iekapāt *vt* score, chop

iekāpināt *vt* (of a horse) make step back (and between the thills)

iekapsulošanās *nfr* encapsulation

iekapsulot *vt* encapsulate

iekapsuloties *vr* become encapsuled

iekāpšana *nf* boarding

iekāp/t *vi* 1. step in(to), get in(to); board; **i. galvā** go to one's head; **i.!** all aboard! **~is pu-delē** (col.) in one's cups; 2. (col.) stop by

iekārdināt *vt* tempt

iekāre I *nf* 1. desire, lust; 2. greed

iekāre II *nf* tongue of land

iekārība *nf* 1. desire, lust; 2. greed

iekāriens I *nm* (gymnastics) hang

iekāriens II *nm* (col.) desire

iekārīgi *adv* greedily

iekārīgs *adj* 1. greedy; 2. (rare.) lustful

iekarināt *vt* hang in

iekārināt *vt* tempt

iekārkties *vr* rattle in the throat

iekārot *vt* covet; desire

iekāroties *vr* covet; desire; get a craving for

ieka|r|ojums |ŗ| *nm* conquest

ieka|r|ot |ŗ| *vt* 1. conquer; capture; 2. win

ieka|r|otājs |ŗ| *nm* conqueror

iekārpīt *vt* bury by scraping or scratching

iekārpīties *vr* dig oneself into; sink deeper while struggling to get out

iekarplanieris *nm* hangglider

iekars *nm* honeycomb frame

iekarsēt *vt* heat up

iekarsīgi *adv* heatedly

iekarsīgs *adj* irritable, touchy

iekarst *vi* 1. heat up; 2. become excited; become involved (in a game); warm up (to a subject)

iekarsties *vr* 1. heat up; 2. become excited; be-come involved (in a game); warm up (to a subject)

iekarsums *nm* heat, passion

iekārt *vt* hang; hang up; hang in; **i. eņģēs** hinge

iekārta *nf* 1. (pol) order, system; 2. furnishings, contents of a house, personal property; furniture; 3. equipment; 4. stage set

iekārties *vr* 1. hang on to; 2. get caught in; 3. hang down

iekārtnes *nf pl* (hist.) threshing floor hooks (for hanging winnowing screens)

iekārtojums *nm* arrangement; layout

iekārtošana *nf* 1. arrangement; 2. placement; **i. darbā** job placement

iekārtot *vt* 1. equip, furnish; 2. arrange; 3. place (in a job, school)

iekārtoties *vr* 1. settle in; occupy; **i. ērtāk** make oneself comfortable; 2. get a job; 3. move to, take lodgings

iekarus *adv* (of the manner of fastening scythe blades) at a narrow angle

iekasēt *vt* cash in, collect

iekasētāj/s *nm*, **~a** *nf* collector (of bills)

iekāsēties *vr* cough a little; clear one's throat

iekasījums *nm* scraping, traces of scraping

iekasīt vt 1. scrape in, scratch in; 2. bury (with or as if with claws)

iekasīties *vr* get oneself into

iekast *vt* 1. scrape in, scratch in; 2. bury (with or as if with claws)

iekāst *vt* strain into

iekašāt vt bury (with or as if with claws)

iekašņāt *vt* bury (with or as if with claws)

iekauciens *nm* howl

iekaukties *vr* utter a howl; begin to howl

iekausējums *nm* embedment

iekausēt *vt* embed

iekausēties *vr* become embedded

iekaustīt *vt* (col.) whip; beat

iekaut *vt* give a whipping

iekauties *vr* (col.) get into

iekava *nf* parenthesis, bracket, brace; **apaļās ~s** parentheses

iekavējums *nm* delay

iekavēt *vt* delay

iekavēties *vr* be delayed

iekaviņa *nf dim* of **iekava**, parenthesis

ieklabēties *vr* begin to rattle, begin to clatter; give a rattle

ieklabināties *vr* clatter briefly

iekladzināties *vr* cackle briefly

ieklaigāties *vr* utter a shout; cry out

ieklaiņot *vi* wander in

ieklājs *nm* lining

ieklājums *nm* 1. lining; 2. (of an artwork) background layer

ieklakstēties *vr* click briefly

ieklakšķēties *vr* click briefly

ieklārēt *vi* (barb.) persuade; make believe

ieklāstīt *vi* (col.) make s.o. believe a story

ieklāt *vt* line, spread on the inside

ieklaudzēties *vr* begin to clatter, begin to knock; clatter a little

ieklausīties *vr* listen, listen attentively

ieklauvēties *vr* knock on the door briefly

ieklejot *vi* wander in

ieklepoties *vr* cough a little

ieklibot *vi* come in limping, hobble in

ieklīdenis *nm* stray

ieklidzināt *vi* clip-clop in

iekliedziens *nm* shout

iekliegt *vi* shout into

iekliegties *vr* cry out, utter a cry, scream

ieklikstināt *vi* clip-clop in

ieklimst *vi* wander into, walk into

ieklimt *vi* wander into, walk into

ieklinkāt *vi* wobble in

ieklinkšķēties *vr* tinkle briefly

ieklīst *vi* wander in

iekluburot *vi* wamble in

ieklukstēties *vr* cluck briefly

ieklumburot *vi* wamble in

ieklunkšķēties *vr* gurgle briefly

ieklunkšķināt *vt* down a drink

ieklunkurot *vi* wamble in

ieklupt *vi* 1. stumble in; 2. seize; **i. matos** seize by the hair

iekļaut *vt* 1. include; embrace; draw in; 2. incorporate, annex; 3. wrap, surround

iekļauties *vr* 1. fit in(to); 2. join, join in with; 3. become part of

iekļāvums *nm* inclusion

iekļūt *vi* get in(to); **i. finālā** qualify for finals

ieknābāt *vt* 1. peck a little; nibble (in eating); 2. damage by pecking

ieknābt *v* 1. *vi* peck; 2. *vt* damage by pecking

ieknaibīt *vt* damage by pecking

ieknakstēties *vr* make a brief cracking sound

ieknakšķēties *vr* make a brief cracking sound

ieknibināt *vt* pick (a hole); pick here and there

iekniebt *v* 1. *vi* pinch; 2. *vt* punch

iekniebties *vr* dig into (with fingernails); pinch

iekniedēt *vt* (of a rivet) fasten; fasten with a rivet

ieknikstēties *vr* make a slight cracking or clicking sound

ieknikšķēties *vr* crack or click (slightly)

ieknukstēties *vr* grumble or grunt briefly

iekņudēties *vr* tickle briefly

iekņupt *vi* curl up (in a sleeping position)

iekoda *nf* appetizer, snack

iekodām *adv* for an appetizer

iekodība *nf* obstinacy

iekodies *adj, part* of **iekosties** dogged

iekodināt *vt* stain

iekodīt *vt* nibble at

iekods *nm* appetizer, snack

iekokot *vt* (col.) give a whipping

iekomponēt *vt* include in a composition

iekonservēt *vt* preserve, can; protect

iekonservēties *vr* be well preserved

iekonstruēt *vt* (of a structure, drawing) place (in a framework)

iekopēt *vt* copy

iekopt *vt* cultivate, tend

iekoptība *nf* degree of cultivation

iekortelēties *vr* (barb.) settle (comfortably)

iekopties *vr* 1. become established (on a farm); 2. (col.) become experienced (in performing a task); 3. (reg.) eat

iekost *vt, vi* **1.** bite, bite into, bite down on; **i. mēli zobos** (fig.) bite one's tongue; **2.** have a bite to eat; **3.** begin to eat, nibble on; **4.** sting; **5.** (fig.) get at s.o.

iekosties *vr* **1.** sink one's teeth into, bite into; **2.** eat into; **3.** (col., fig.) fall in love; **4.** persevere; **5.** (col.) have it in for s.o.

iekrāciens *nm* brief snore

iekrājums *nm* stock; store; reserve

iekrakstēties *vr* give a creak

iekrakšķēties *vr* give a creak

iekrākties *vr* give a snore

iekrāmēties *vr* (barb.) move in

iekrampēt *vt* **1.** (of gates, doors) hook, fasten with a hook; **2.** lock in (with a hook and eye fastener)

iekrampēties *vr* get caught (tightly)

iekrāsa *nf* nuance, subtle tone

iekrāsojums *nm* stain, tint

iekrāsot *vt* **1.** tint, tinge; **2.** paint; outline with paint

iekrāsoties *vr* tinge, take on a tint

iekrāt *vt* save up; put up a store

iekrāties *vr* accumulate; be saved

iekratināt *vt* pour in

iekratīt *vt* pour in by shaking

iekratīties *vr* **1.** be shaken into; **2.** rattle in

iekrauja *nf* edge of a drop

iekraukāties *vr* clear one's throat

iekraukstēties *vr* crunch briefly

iekraukšķēties *vr* crunch briefly

iekraustīt *vt* load

iekraut *v* **1.** *vt* load; **2.** *vi* (com.) whack

iekrauties *vr* pile around oneself

iekravāt *vt* load, put in

iekravāties *vr* move in

iekrāvēj/s *nm*, **~a** *nf* loader

iekrekstēties *vr* clear one's throat

iekrekšķēties *vr* clear one's throat

iekrekšķināties *vr* clear one's throat

iekremšļoties *vr* clear one's throat

iekrēsla *nf* twilight

iekrikstēties *vr* crack, creak (briefly)

iekrikšķēties *vr* crack, creak (briefly)

iekrimst *vi* gnaw, chew

iekrist *vi* **1.** fall in(to); **i. acīs** (col.) catch one's attention; **i. naudā** (col.) come into money; **i. nelaimē** (col., of misfortune) befall; **i. prātā** (or **galvā**) occur, cross one's mind; **i. starpā** intervene, butt in; **kā akā iekritis** vanished; **2.** (col.) seize; **i. kājās** seize by the leg; **3.** (col.) flop down;**4.**(col.) interrupt; **i. valodā** butt in; **5.** (*3rd pers*) (of cheeks, eyes) sink; **6.** (*3rd pers*) (col., of events) fall on (a date); **7.** (col.) be caught; **8.** (col.) be taken in; fall for it; **9.** (col.) disappear

iekristies *vr* (of eyes) sink

iekristīt *vt* give a name

iekritiens *nm* (mus.) entrance

iekrities *adj, part* of **iekristies** (of eyes, cheeks) sunken

iekritīgi *adv* fittingly

iekritīgs *adj* **1.** fitting; **2.** obliging, complaisant

iekritis *adj, part* of **iekrist 5** sunken

iekritums *nm* dip; recess

iekrokojums *nm* fold, pleat

iekrokot *vt* fold, pleat

iekrokoties *vr* be pleated

iekrustīt *vt* start calling (by a name)

iekruzuļot *vt* ruffle

iekš *prep* (obs.) in, inside

iekš/a *nf* inside; interior; **no ~as** from within; **uz ~u** inside, inward

iekšā *adv* **1.** inside, within; **2.** into; **i. !** come in! **3.** indoors

iekšapšuve *nf* interior lining, paneling

iekšas *nf pl* innards, entrails; giblets, tripe

iekšdarbi *nm pl* interior finish; work inside

iekšdedze *nf* internal combustion

iekšdedzes motors *nm* internal combustion engine

iekšdrēbe *nf* lining

iekšdurvis *nf pl* interior door

iekšējās slimības *nf pl* internal disorders; ~o
~u ārsts internist

iekšēji *adv* internally

iekšējs *adj* **1.** interior; internal; inner; **2.** inland;
domestic

iekšiene *nf* inside, interior

iekšiņa *nf* (of ball point pens) cartridge, refill

iekškabata *nf* inside pocket

iekškontinentāls *adj* intracontinental

iekškvartāls *nm* vacant city lot

iekšķība *nf* inwardness

iekšķīgi *adv* internally

iekšķīgs *adj* internal

iekšķīgums *nm* inwardness

iekšleņķis *nm* internal angle

iekšlietas *nf pl* internal affairs

iekšlietu ministrija Ministry of Internal Affairs;
(in Great Britain) Home Office; (in the
USA) Department of the Interior

iekšlogs *nm* inside storm window

iekšmala *nf* inside edge

iekšmisija *nf* (rel.) home mission

iekšpilsēta *nf* inner city

iekšpol[i]tika [ī] *nf* domestic policy

iekšpus *adv* inside

iekšpus/e *nf* inside; interior; **uz** ~i inward; **no**
~es from within

iekšpusledāja *indecl adj* intraglacial

iekšpusnieks *nm* insider

iekšsiena *nf* inside wall

iekšskats *nm* interior view

iekštaustis *nm* inside caliper

iekštelpa *nf* inner room; *pl* ~s interior

iekšup *adv* inward

iekšupvērsts *adj* turned inward; inward-
looking

iekšzeme *nf* interior (of a country); ~s domestic;
inland; (of a passport) internal

iekuģot *vi* sail in(to)

iekūkoties *vr* (of cuckoos) begin to call

iekūleņot *vi* tumble in, roll in

iekūlības *nf pl* rite celebrating the beginning of
the threshing season

iekult *vt* **1.** stir in; **2.** thresh; **3.** (col.) give a
spanking

iekulties *vr* (col.) get into (trouble); stumble
into

iekultivēt *vt* **1.** put under cultivation; **2.** work in
(with a cultivator)

iekūlums *nm* threshed-out grain

iekundēties *vr* (barb.) settle, establish oneself

iekunkstēties *vr* **1.** utter a groan; **2.** say sth.
with a groan

iekūņoties *vr* **1.** pupate; **2.** (fig.) wrap oneself in

iekūpēt *vi* (of smoke, fog, vapors) move in

iekūpēties *vr* (of dust, smoke) begin to rise;
rise slowly

iekūpināt *vt* (of a cigarette, pipe) light

iekurēties *vr* begin to burn, kindle

iekurināt *vt* kindle a fire

iekuriņš *nm dim* of **iekurs**, kindling

iekurkstēties *vr* croak briefly

iekurkšķēties *vr* croak briefly

iekurkties *vr* croak briefly

iekurnēties *vr* begin to complain

iekurs *nm* kindling

iekurstīt *vt* kindle a fire

iekurt *vt* kindle a fire

iekurties *vr* (of fire) get going

iekurtēt *vi* become pithy; spoil

iekust *vi* **1.** begin to melt; **2.** melt together

iekustēties *vr* begin to move

iekustināt *vt* set in motion; get started, get
going

iekutēties *vr* itch briefly

iekutināt *vt* cause tickling; (fig.) stimulate

iekvaukšēties *vr* (col.) begin to bark

ievaukšķēties *vr* (col.) begin to bark

iekveldēt *vt* (poet.) enkindle

iekveldināt *vt* (poet.) enkindle

iekvēlināt *vt* set aglow; ignite; (fig.) kindle,
enkindle

iekvēloties *vr* begin to glow, begin to burn; (of eyes) light up

iekvenkšķēties *vr* (col.) begin to bark

iekviekties *vr* begin to squeal; utter a squeal

iekķaukstēties *vr* (col.) begin to bark

iekķaukšēties *vr* (col.) begin to bark

iekķēpāt *vt* 1. get to a bad start; 2. place or work in sloppily; 3. get s.o. into trouble

iekķēpāties *vr* get mixed in with s.o.

iekķepēt *vt* (of sth. sticky) stick in

iekķept *vi* get stuck

iekķepuroties *vr* wriggle in; flounder in

iekķēris *adj, part* of iekķert (col.) tipsy

iekķērkstēties *vr* caw; begin to caw; croak

iekķērksties *vr* caw; begin to caw; croak

iekķērkties *vr* caw; begin to caw; croak

iekķert *vt* (col.) eat (on the run); have a snack; have a drink

iekķerties *vr* 1. grab hold of; 2. get caught in; 3. interlock; gear into; 4. (col.) fall in love, fall for

iekķibelēt *vt* (col.) involve

iekķibelēties *vr* get involved

iekķīlāt *vt* pawn; i. uz hipotēku mortgage

iekķīlātājs *nm*, ~a *nf* pawner; mortgager

iekķīlējums *nm* wedging

iekķīlēšanās *nfr* (mil.) penetration

iekķīlēt *vt* wedge

iekķīlēties *vr* (mil.) penetrate; drive a wedge between

iekķitējums *nm* putty job

iekķitēt *vt* putty

iela *nf* 1. street; aklā i. blind alley, dead end street; uz ~s a. in the street; b. on the street; c. outdoors; 2. long wood pile; 3. row of grain sheaves prepared for threshing

ielabināt *vt* entice

ielabojums *nm* 1. soil improvement; 2. correction

ielabot *vt* 1. (of soil) improve; 2. insert a correction

ielāčot *vi* clomp in

ielāde *nf* loading

ielādēt *vt* (barb.) load

ielāgot *vt* make note of; learn; commit to memory

ielaide *nf* (mech.) admission

ielaideni *adv* concavely

ielaidens *adj* concave

ielaidenis *nm* a type of cast net

ielaidu *indecl adj* inlay

ielaidu darbi *nm pl* inlay work

ielaidums *nm* gore, gusset

ielaikus *adv* in time; on time

ielaipot *vi* step in

ielaist *vt* 1. let in, admit; i. pārnakšņot put up for the night; i. uguni light the fire; 2. drop in; put it; insert; fill; i. ūdenī launch; 3. neglect; (of undesirable qualities) allow to continue; 4. (col.) hit (with a projectile); i. sev lodi pierē blow one's brains out; 5. *vi* (col.) drive in, ride in fast

ielaisties I *vr* fly in(to)

ielaisties II *vr* 1. slide into; 2. sink back into; 3. slip into (a state); i. kompromisā compromise; 4. (col.) get mixed up with, have to do with; 5. (col.) enter into (details, conversation)

ielaistīt *vt* pour in

ielaistīties I *vr* 1. be poured in; 2. perfume oneself

ielaistīties II *vr* sparkle briefly

ielaists *adj, part* of ielaist neglected

ielaizīt *vt* lick, lick up

ielaizīties *vr* 1. eat; 2. acquire a taste (for a lickable food)

ielakt *vt* lap a little; (of a person) drink

ielakties *vr* (rare.) lap a little

ielama *nf* nickname

ielāma *nf* low spot, depression (in a meadow or pasture)

ielamāt *vt* begin to call s.o. a name

ielāpains *adj* patched up

ielāps *nm* (mending) patch

ielasījums *nm* woven-in (ornamental) thread or yarn

ielasīt I *vt* 1. gather into (a container); 2. weave in

ielasīt II *vt* begin to read

ielasīties *vr* 1. take to reading; 2. do more thorough reading

ielasmeita *nf* streetwalker

ielāsmēt *vi* = **ielāsmot**

ielāsmēties *vr* = **ielāsmoties**

ielāsmot *vi* light up

ielāsmoties *vr* light up

ielāsoties *vr* light up

ielaspuika *nm* gamin, street urchin, hoodlum

ielas uzvalks *nm* street clothes

ielas tirgotājs *nm* street vendor; hawker;

ielaunadze *nf* meal taken before **launags**

ielaušanās *nfr* 1. break-in, burglarly; 2. invasion; intrusion

ielauzējs *nm* burglar

ielauzīt *vt* 1. bend (in several places); 2. crumble into (a container); 3. drill (so in a task)

ielauzīties *vr* get the hang of it, master (with effort); **i. grāmatā** learn to read (with difficulty)

ielauzt *vt* 1. break (partially), crack; 2. break in, force; 3. (typ.) make up

ielauzties *vr* 1. break in (commit burglary; fig.); 2. invade; 3. gate-crash

ielavīties *vr* sneak in

ielecināt *vt* 1. make jump into; 2. accustom to being dandled

ieleja *nf* valley, dale, vale

ielejas ūdensceļš *nm* thalweg

ielejiņa *nf dim* of **ieleja**, small valley

ielejots *adj* crisscrossed by valleys

ielēkāt *vi* hop into

ielēkšot *vi* gallop into

ielēkt *vi* jump in(to)

ielene *nf* streetwalker

ielenkt *vt* encircle; (mil.) surround, besiege

ielenkums *nm* encirclement; siege

ielīdīgi *adv* in a pushy or obtrusive manner

ielīdīgs *adj* pushy, obtrusive

ielidināt *vt* make fly into; throw, fling

ielidināties *vr* fly into

ielidojums *nm* arrival by air; fly-in

ielidot *vi* 1. fly in; 2. arrive by air

ielīdzīgi *adv* accomodatingly, peaceably

ielīdzīgs *adj* accomodating, peaceable

ieliece *nf* (geol.) depression; bend; sag

ieliedēt I *vt* 1. solder in; 2. incorporate

ieliedēt II *vt* (of a crop) allow to get a little wet

ieliekamais *nom adj* insert

ieliekņa *nf* low spot, depression (in a meadow or pasture)

ieliekt *vt* 1. bend in, depress; 2. dip into

ieliekties *vr* 1. bend in slightly; 2. dip into; 3. wind into

ieliekts *adj, part* of **ieliekt** 1. bent in; 2. concave

ieliekums *nm* inward bend, curve; flexure; sag

ielielīt *vt* (rare.) talk up, promote

ieliesmināt *vt* fire up, enthuse

ieliesmot *vt* fire up, enthuse

ieliesmoties *vt* catch fire

ieliet *vt* pour; pour in(to)

ielieties *vr* be poured

ielietne *nf* = **ielietnis**

ielietnis *nm* funnel, funnel tube; pouring gate

ielīgot *v* 1. *vi* (of heavy objects) move swaying into; 2. *vt* set in swaying motion; 3. *vt* sing Ligo songs on Saint John's eve

ielīgoties *vr* 1. (of heavy objects) move swaying into; 2. begin to sway; 3. begin to sing Ligo songs

ielīki *adv* slightly bent

ielīks *adj* slightly bent

ielīksme *nf* cheerfulness

ielīksmināt *vt* cheer up, gladden

ielīksmot *vt* cheer up, gladden

ielīksne *nf* depression, low spot

ielikt *vt* 1. put, set, or place in(to); insert; **i. kaktā** stand s.o. in the corner; **i. mutē**

(fig.) spell it out (for s.o.); **i. rociņu** (sl.) kick ass; **2.** (of fruits, vegetables) preserve; **3.** (of grades) give; **4.** (col., of money) put up

ielīkt *vi* **1.** bend in; **2.** dip into

ieliktenis *nm* **1.** henchman; appointee; **2.** insole

ielikties *vr* **1.** (col.) lie down; **2.** (col.) fall in; **3.** march in; **4.** be put in

ieliktne *nf* gore, gusset

ieliktnis *nm* (tech.) insert; plug

ielikums *nm* (printed, published) insert

ielīkums *nm* bay, cover; bend

ielīme *nf* tip-in

ielīmēt *vt* paste in, glue in

ielingot *vt* sling into

ielinieki *nm pl* street people

ieliņa *nf dim* of **iela**, narrow street, alley

ielipināt *vt* paste in

ielīst I *vi* **1.** crawl in(to); **i. slapsto**s hide; **2.** sneak in(to); **3.** (sl.) toady

ielīst II *vt* (rare.) begin to clear land

ielīt *vi* rain in; drip, trickle into

ielobīt *vt* **1.** shell into; **2.** begin to shell or peel; **3.** work in with a stubble plow

ielobīties *vr* (col.) acquire practice

ielobt *vi* run in

ieloc/e *nf* fold, bend; pleat; **ar ~ēm** pleated

ielocījums *nm* fold; pleat; bend

ielociņš *nm dim* of **ieloks**, hem, fold

ielocīt *vt* **1.** bend, turn in, fold; **2.** hem; **3.** weave in; **4.** fold into; **5.** (of legs, arms) stretch; **i. kaulus** limber up

ielocīties *vr* **1.** bend, turn in, fold; **2.** become bent; **3.** slither into; **4.** curve into; **5.** become adept at (by bending one's body); limber up

ielodēt *vt* solder in

ielodze *nf* niche, recess; window bay

ielogojums *nm* frame

ielogot *vt* frame

ielogs *nm* frame; window frame; (typ.) box

ieloks *nm* **1.** hem; tuck; **2.** bend; fold; **3.** (fig.) dowry; **4.** (typ.) box

ieloku sols *nm* beading bench

ielolot *vt* lull to sleep

ielūdzējs *nm*, **~a** *nf* inviter

ielu dzelzceļš *nm* streetcar, streetcar line

ielūgt *vt* invite

ielūgties *vr* invite oneself

ielūgums *nm* invitation

ielūkot *vt* fall in love and plan to marry

ielūkoties *vr* **1.** look in(to); **2.** examine; investigate

ielumpačot *vi* tramp in

ielūrēt *vi* (col.) peek in

ielūzt *vi* **1.** break (partially); crack, be fractured; **2.** break through

ielūzums *nm* fracture; breach

ieļepatot *vi* bounce in

ieļēpot *vi* (of animals) stumble in

ieļinkāt *vi* bounce in, lope in

ieļucis *adj, part* of **ieļukt** sagging, drooping, sunken

ieļukt *vi* sag, droop

iemācīt *vt* teach

iemācīties *vr* learn

iemainīt *vt* trade, exchange

iemaisīt *vt* mix in, fold in

iemaisīties *vr* **1.** interfere; butt in; **2.** get mixed up in

iemaitāt *vt* spoil

iemaitāts *adj, part* of **iemaitāt** (of food) tainted

iemājnieks *nm* inhabitant

iemājojošs *adj, part* of **iemājot** indwelling, in-herent

iemājot *vi* dwell in

iemājoties *vr* **1.** take up housekeeping; **2.** nest

iemāklis *nm* intruder

iemaksa *nf* (instalment) payment; down payment

iemaksāt *vt* pay; pay in; pay down

iemākties *vr* invade

iemala *nf* hem

iemaldināt *vt* detour (deceptively) into

iemaldīties *vr* stray into

iemalis *nm* curbstone

iemalkot *vi* (col.) have a drink

iemalt *vt* **1.** grind (a quantity); **2.** allow to get caught (in a wheel))

iemalties *vr* **1.** be ground; **2.** be caught (in a wheel)

iemaļus *adv* aside

iemānīt *vt* lure in(to)

iemanīties *vr* **1.** acquire skill; **2.** sneak in(to)

iemānīties *vr* sneak into

iemantot *vt* **1.** acquire; win; **2.** inherit

iemaņa *nf* skill

iemargoties *vr* light up, begin to shine

iemarinēt *vt* **1.** pickle; **2.** (fig.) shelve, put on ice

iemarinēties *vr* (of pickles) be ready

iemasēt *vt* rub in

iemaršēt *vi* march in

iemaukt *vt* (of hands, feet) put in (shoes, socks, gloves)

iemaukti *nm pl* bridle

iemaukties *vr* (of feet, legs) slip into (shoes, pant legs)

iemauroties *vr* moo, give a moo

iemaut *vt* bridle

iemauties *vr* moo

iemava *nf* bushing; nipple

iemazgāt *vt* soften (by repeated washings)

iemēģināt *vt* try out

iemeimurot *vi* stagger in

iemelnēt *vt* blacken

iemelnēties *vr* (of a dark object) appear

iemelnot *vt* = **iemelnēt**

iemelnoties *vr* = **iemelnēties**

iemelns *adj* blackish

iemelot *vt* talk into, persuade of sth. (by telling lies)

iemeloties *vr* get the knack of lying

iemelst *vt* talk into, persuade of sth. (by telling lies)

iemērcēt *vt* dip in(to)

iemērcēties *vr* submerge oneself, take a dip in

iemērīt *vt* measure out

iemērkt *vt* immerse, dip in

iemērkties *vr* dip into

iemērot *vt* (rare.) measure out

iemēslot *vt* make more fertile (through repeated applications of a fertilizer)

iemesls *nm* reason; **dibināts i.** good reason; **no-pietns i.** valid reason

iemest *vt* **1.** throw, fling, pop, or drop in(to); (of nets, fishing lines) dip; **i. aci** have a quick look; look sth. up; **i. sodu** (basketball) drop a foul; **i. starpā** interject; **2.** (col.) hit; **3.** (col.) down (a drink); tipple

iemesties *vr* **1.** hurry in; fling oneself down; **i. uz galvas** dive in; **2.** take abode; nest; get into, in-fest; **3.** (of birds) alight on; **4.** (of pain) have, get

iemetējs *nm* (col.) tippler

iemetiens *nm* throw

iemeties *adj, part* of **iemesties** (col.) tipsy

iemetinājums *nm* intercalation

iemetināt I *vt* **1.** hang in; **2.** harness; **3.** add, introduce; remark

iemetināt II *vt* weld in

iemetis *adj, part* of **iemest** (col.) tipsy

iemetnis *nm* a type of cast net

iemēzt *vt* sweep in

iemīcīt *vt* knead

iemīdīt *vt* tread; trample down; beat (a path)

iemīdīts *adj, part* of **iemīdīt** (of paths) beaten, well-trodden

iemidzināt *vt* lull to sleep; make sleepy

iemidzinošs *adj, part* of **iemidzināt** sleep-induc-ing, soporific

iemiegt *vt* put tightly between (two things); squeeze in; **i. asti** put one's tail between one's legs

iemiegties *vr* be squeezed in; be caught in

iemielot *vt* (col.) whip

iemiesojums *nm* embodiment, personification; impersonation; **(veselības) i.** the picture of (health)

iemiesot *vt* **1.** embody, personify; impersonate; **2.** represent

iemiesoties *vr* be embodied, be personified

iemiet *vt* drive into the ground

iemieties *vr* be driven into the ground

iemigt *vi* fall asleep

iemīlēj/ies *adj, part* of **iemīlēties** in love; **~ušies** *nom part pl* lovers

iemīlēt *vt* grow fond of, come to love

iemīlēties *vr* **1.** fall in love; **2.** grow fond of, come to love

iemīlināt *vt* make fall in love

iemīļot *vt* grow fond of, come to love

iemīļots *adj, part* of **iemīļot** favorite, popular

ieminēties *vr* mention

iemīņāt *vt* trample down, trample into

iemirdzēties *vr* light up, begin to shine

iemirgoties *vr* twinkle, begin to twinkle

iemirguļoties *vr* twinkle, begin to twinkle

iemirkšķināties *vr* blink an eye

iemirkt *vi* become immersed

iemist *vi* live, dwell

iemīt I *vt* **1.** tread in, trample down (into); **i. dubļos** (fig.) humiliate, abase; **2.** leave footprints; beat a path; **3.** *vt, vi* step into

iemīt II **(iemît)** *vt* exchange, trade

iemitināt *vt* put up, lodge

iemitināties *vr* settle in, take up lodgings

iemītnie/ks *nm*, **~ce** *nf* tenant, occupant

iemizot *vt* (col.) whip, beat up

iemocīt *vt* wrestle in, squeeze in

iemontēt *vt* install

iemudžināt *vt* entangle

iemukt *vi* **1.** flee to, seek refuge in; **2.** sink into

iemulda *nf* valley

iemuldēt *vi* (reg.) stray into

iemuldēties I *vr* (com.) begin to speak (incoherently)

iemuldēties II *vr* (reg.) stray into

iemulst *vi* (col.) stray into

iemurdzīt *vt* (col.) stuff in

iemūrēt *vt* **1.** mortar in, set in with mortar; **2.** wall in, immure

iemurkšķēties *vr* mutter, grumble briefly

iemurmināties *vr* mumble

iemurmuļoties *vr* mutter briefly

iemute *nf* cigarette holder; (of a pipe) mouthpiece

iemutis *nm* cigarette holder

iemutnis *nm* (mus.) mouthpiece

iemūžināt *vt* immortalize

iemūžot *vt* immortalize

ienācēj/s *nm*, **~a** *nf* (new) arrival; immigrant

ienācies *adj, part* of **ienākties** ripe

ienadzis *nm* hangnail

ienaidība *nf* (obs.) enmity

ienaidnie/ks *nm*, **~ce** *nf* enemy

ienaids *nm* enmity

ienākošais *adj, part* of **ienākt** incoming

ienākšana *nf* entry, entrance; **~s osta** port of debarkation

ienākšanās *nfr* ripening

ienākt *vi* **1.** come in, enter; **i. prātā** occur, come to mind; **2.** move in; **3.** arrive

ienākties *vr* ripen

ienākums *nm* income; revenue

ienāši *nm pl* glanders

ienesa *nf* profit

ienēsāt *vt* **1.** (of shoes) break in; **2.** (of diseases) introduce

ienese *nf* (compu.) fetching

ieneses cikls *nm* (compu.) fetch cycle

ienesība *nf* profitability

ienesīgi *adv* profitably, lucratively

ienesīgs *adj* profitable, lucrative; (of a job) well-paid

ienesīgums *nm* profitability

ienest *vt* 1. carry in(to), bring in; 2. bring; 3. (of profit) bring in

ienesties *vr* 1. dash into; 2. crash into

ienesums *nm* 1. honey yield; 2. profit

ienīdēt *vt* (obs.) hate

ieniezēties *vr* begin to itch

ieniknot *vt* provoke

ieniknoties *vr* be provoked

ieniķot *vt* make restive

ienirt *vi* dive in

ienirties *vr* dive in

ienīst *vt* hate

ienīstams *adj, part* of ienīst odious, hateful

ienītīt *vt* (weav.) reed

ieņaudēties *vr* meow; begin to meow

ieņaukstēties *vr* (col.) meow; begin to meow

ieņēmējietaise *nf* intake

ieņēmība *nf* 1. susceptibility; 2. receptivity

ieņēmīgs *adj* 1. susceptible; 2. receptive

ieņemšana *nf* 1. (of a position, place) occupation; 2. conception; bezvainīgā i. Immaculate Conception

ieņemt *vt* 1. take up; take into, (of a person; col. of a garment, money) take in; (of liquids, seat; mil.) take; i. otro vietu be the runner-up; i. poziciju assume an attitude, assume a position; i. pozicijas take positions; i. triecienā take by assault; 2. (of space, volume, position) occupy; i. amatu fill an office; 3. conceive (become pregnant)

ieņemties *vr* 1. take to, get the habit of; 2. de-cide; i. galvā take into one's head

ieņemts *adj, part* 1. *part* of ieņemt; 2. (Bibl.) conceived

ieņēmums *nm* returns, revenue, receipts; take

ieņerkstēties *vr* whimper briefly; begin to whim-per

ieņirbēties *vr* flicker briefly; begin to flicker

ieņirbties *vr* flicker briefly; begin to flicker

ieņirgties *vr* sneer

ieņirkstēties *vr* creak briefly

ieņirkšķēties *vr* creak briefly

ieņurcīt *vt* 1. crumple somewhat; 2. stuff in

ieņurcīties *vr* get somewhat crumpled

ieņurdēties *vr* growl

ieņurkstēties *vr* growl briefly

ieņurkšķēties *vr* growl briefly

ieņurrāties *vr* purr briefly

ieoderēt *vt* 1. line; 2. (col.) feed

ieorientēties *vr* get oriented

ieost *vt* sniff, smell

ieostīt *vt* sniff, smell

iepakaļ *adv* behind

iepakaļā *adv* (col.) behind

iepakaļis *adv* (reg.) behind

iepakaļš *adv* (reg.) behind

iepakaļus *adv* behind

iepakojums *nm* packaging

iepakot *vt* pack

iepakšķēties *vr* patter briefly, thump briefly

iepakšķināties *vr* patter briefly, thump briefly

ieparkšķēties *vr* rattle briefly, chatter briefly

ieparkšķināties *vr* rattle briefly, chatter briefly

iepātagot *vt* whip

iepatikt *vi* 1. take a liking to; begin to like; 2. wish

iepatikties *vr* 1. take a liking to; begin to like; 2. wish

iepaugāt *vt* (col.) give a whipping

iepaukāt *vt* (com.) learn

iepaunāt *vt* (col.) wrap; (of belongings) load

iepaunāties *vr* (col.) get one's belongings into a vehicle; get oneself and one's belongings into a vehicle

iepaust *vt* (rare.) 1. tell, persuade; 2. make part of (a text)

iepazīstinājums *nm* introduction

iepazīstināt *vt* introduce to; acquaint with

iepazīstināties *vr* introduce oneself

iepazīt *vt* become acquainted with; learn about

iepazīties *vr* 1. meet; become acquainted with, come to know; 2. acquaint oneself with; examine; inspect

iepēdot *vt* 1. tread in, trample down (into); 2. track up

iepēkstēties *vr* quack briefly

iepēkšķēties *vr* quack briefly

iepeldēt *vi* swim into, float into; sail into, steam into

iepelēki *adv* in a grayish color

iepelēks *adj* grayish

iepelēt *vi* grow moldy

iepelnīt *vt* earn a little money

ieperēt *vt* begin to sit on eggs

ieperēts *adj, part* of ieperēt (of eggs) addled

ieperforēt *vt* punch in (holes)

ieperināt *vt* hatch

ieperināties *vr* 1. nest, move in; settle in; invade; 2. worm one's way into, insinuate oneself

iepērt *vt* spank

iepērties *vr* (col.) get into, stumble into

iepīckāt *vt* whip

iepīkstēties *vr* squeak; (in negations) utter a word

iepīkt *vi* be somewhat annoyed

iepīkums *nm* annoyance

iepilde *nf* filling

iepildīt *vt* fill; i. mucās barrel; i. pudelēs bottle

iepildīties *vr* fill

iepilēt *vi* (of drops) fall in

iepilināt *vt* (of drops) put in

iepinkšķēties *vr* (col.) begin to whimper

iepiņķēt *vt* entangle

iepiņķēties *vr* get entangled

iepinums *nm* (of woven, plaited items) insert, in-terwoven article

iepiņķerēties *vr* (col.) get oneself into

iepiņķēt *vt* (com.) involve (s.o. in an affair)

iepīpēt *vi* 1. light up; 2. (of a pipe) break in

iepipkāt *vi* (col.) beat up with a truncheon

iepircēj/s *nm*, ~a *nf* shopper; buyer

iepirkšana *nf* purchase, purchasing

iepirkšanās *nfr* shopping

iepirkt *vt* buy, purchase (larger quantities)

iepirkties *vr* 1. shop; 2. make a mistake in shopping

iepirkums *nm* purchase

iepirkumu soma *nf* shopping bag

iepīt *vt* 1. weave in, plait in; (of hair) dress (with ribbons); (of cane-seated furniture) cane; 2. be-gin to weave; 3. (fig.) insert, interweave, sprinkle with; 4. involve

iepīties *vr* get entangled in; (fig.) get involved in, get mixed up in

iepītne *nf* (reg.) hair ribbon

ieplacināt *vt* flatten

ieplaiksnīties *vr* flash briefly; begin to flash

ieplaisāt *vi* crack, (of skin) chap (in spots)

ieplaka *nf* (geol.) depression

ieplakani *adv* flattishly

ieplakans *adj* flattish

ieplakt *vi* 1. sink in; 2. make oneself flat

ieplankot *vt* erect board walls

ieplānot *vt* include in plans

ieplarkšķēties *vr* rattle briefly

ieplaucēt *vt* (of flour) parboil

ieplerkšķēties *vr* rattle briefly

ieplēst I *vt* open wide; i. acis stare, goggle; i. mu-ti gape

ieplēst II *vt* tear, rend, crack

iepl[e]sties [ē] *vr* 1. spread out; 2. open wide

ieplēsums *nm* tear, rent, crack

iepletums or ieplētums *nm* opening

ieplīkšķēties *vr* (of a whip) crack; (of a sail) flap

iepliķēt *vt* slap

ieplinkšķēties *vr* plink briefly

ieplīst *vi* tear, split, crack

ieplīsums *nm* tear, split, crack

iepliukšķēties *vr* (of a whip) crack briefly

ieplūde *nf* (tech.) inlet

ieplūdes vārstulis *nm* inlet valve

ieplūdinājums *nm* merging

iepludināt *vt* float in

ieplūdināt *vt* let in, make flow into; pour into

ieplūdvārsts *nm* inlet valve

iepluinīt *vt* 1. work s.o. over a little; 2. tear a little

ieplunkšķēties *vr* splash

ieplūst *vi* flow in(to), surge into; flock in

ieplūšana *nf* inflow, influx

iepļaukāt *vt* slap

iepļaut *vi* 1. cross a boundary line in mowing; 2. injure with a scythe

iepļauties *vr* learn to use the scythe

iepļerkšķēties *vr* rattle briefly; blare briefly

iepogāt *vt* button in

iepogoties *vr* utter a warble, break into a warble

iepost *vt* 1. fix up; 2. (of the soil) prepare for sowing

ieposties *vr* 1. fix up; 2. settle in

iepotēt *vt* 1. (bot.) engraft; 2. (med.) vaccinate against; 3. (fig.) instill

iepotēts *adj, part* of **iepotēt** 1. grafted; 2. vaccinated; 3. (fig.) ingrained

iepraktizēties *vr* acquire skill; become a skilled hand

ieprasīties *vr* ask, inquire

ieprasties *vr* acquire skill

iepratība *nf* deftness

ieprātīgi *adv* deftly

iepratīgs *adj* deft; quick (to understand)

iepratināties *vr* acquire skill

ieprātot *vt* get an idea

ieprātoties *vr* get an idea

ieprecēt *vt* marry off

ieprecēties *vr* marry into

ieprecināt *vt* marry off

iepresēt *vt* press in

iepretēji *adv* almost oppositely

iepretējs *adj* almost opposite

iepretī *adv, prep* opposite

iepretim *adv, prep* opposite

iepriecēt *vt* 1. delight; cheer up; 2. comfort

iepriecinājums *nm* 1. joy; 2. consolation, comfort

iepriecināt *vt* 1. give joy, delight; cheer up; **i. sirdi** rejoice one's heart; 2. comfort

iepriecinošs *adj, part* of **iepriecināt** comforting

iepriekš *adv* 1. beforehand, in advance; 2. previously

iepriekšapmaksāts *adj* prepaid

iepriekšēj/s *adj* 1. advance, preliminary; 2. premeditated; 3. *defin* ~ais previous; former; preceding, antecedent

iepriekšeksistējošs *adj* preexistent

iepriekšminētais *adj* the above mentioned

iepriekšnosakāms *adj* predictable

iepriekšsagatavošana *nf* prearrangement

iepriekšsagatavot *vt* prearrange

iepriekšsamontēts *adj* preassembled

iepriekšveidošana *nf* preformation

ieprogrammēt *vt* include in a program

ieprojektēt *vt* include in a project

ieprotokolēt *vt* record

iepūderēt *vt* powder lightly

iepukstēties *vr* (of the heart) begin to beat, begin to thump

iepukšķēties *vr* begin to puff

iepulsēties *vr* begin to pulsate

iepumpēt *vt* pump into

iepumpurojums *nm* bud

iepunktēt *vt* mark with a center punch

iepurināt *vt* shake into

iepūšana *nf* (tech.) insuflation

iepūst *vt* 1. blow in(to); breathe into; 2. (fig., com.) put in one's ear; tell a tale

iepūsties *vr* (of whistles, horns) give a toot, whistle

iepūt *vi* begin to rot

iepūtība *nf* conceit, haughtiness

iepūtīgi *adv* conceitedly, haughtily

iepūtīgs *adj* conceited, haughty

ieputināt *vt* **1. i. sniegā** snow in; **i. smiltīs** cover with sand; **2.** drive (snow, sand) into

iepuvis *adj, part* of **iepūt** partly rotten

iepuvums *nm* rotted spot

ieradināt *vt* **1.** accustom; **2.** train

ieradināties *vr* get into the habit of

ieradis *adj, part* of **ierast** accustomed

ierādīt *vt* **1.** allot, alolocate; **2.** show

ierādītāj/s *nm, ~a nf* (usu. with **vietu**) usher

ieraduma tiesības *nf pl* prescriptive rights

ieradums *nm* **1.** custom; **2.** habit

ieradzis *nm* horn core

ieraidīt *vt* **1.** motion (to move into a place), direct into; shoo into; **2.** kick, roll, throw into

ierakāt *vt* cover with dirt (in digging)

ieraknāt *vt* cover with dirt (in digging)

ierakstāms *adj, part* of **ierakstīt 1.** recordable; **2.** recording

ierakstīt *vt* **1.** write in, enter; **i. kontā** enter in ac-count; **2.** inscribe; **3.** put down; record; **4.** get one's hand used to writing; (of a new writing implement) break in; **5.** (of mail) register, certify; **6.** record (on disc, tape)

ierakstīties *vr* enter one's name; enroll, register

ieraksts *nm* **1.** entry; (of real estate) conveyance; **2.** recording; **3.** (computer, documentary) record

ierakt *vt* bury

ierakties *vr* dig in, entrench; (fig.) bury oneself in (books, work)

ierakums *nm* trench

ierāmējums *nm* framing, frame; (typ.) edging

ierāmēt *vt* frame; (typ.) edge

ierāpot *vi* crawl in(to), creep in(to)

ierāpties *vr* crawl in; climb in

ierast *vi* get in the habit of

ierasti *adv* habitually

ierastība *nf* habit

ierasties *vr* come; appear; show up; arrive

ierasts *adj, part* of **ierast** habitual, accustomed

ieraša *nf* custom; habit

ierašanās *nfr* **1.** coming; appearance; arrival; **2.** attendance, presence

ieraudāties *vr* start crying

ieraudzēt *vt* leaven; ferment

ieraudzīt *vt* **1.** see, notice, sight, catch sight of; **2.** (obs.) like; **neieraudzīt ne acu galā** unable to bear the sight of

ieraugs *nm* starting yeast

ieraukties *vr* shrink

ieraust *vt* rake in

ierausties *vr* **1.** bury oneself in; **2.** clamber in(to)

ieraut *vt* **1.** pull in(to); **i. gaisu** gasp; **i. skabargu** get a sliver in one's hand; **ar ~u asti** with one's tail between one's legs; **i. nāsīs** (com.) steal; **2.** tear, gouge; **3.** (col.) make a fast buck; **4.** *vi* (col., of work tempo) step on it; **5.** (col.) also **i. graķīti** tipple

ierauties *vr* pull back into, shrink into; (of fabrics) shrink

ierāvēj/s *nm, ~a nf* greedy person, profiteer

ierāvums *nm* tear, gash

ieraža *nf* custom; habit

iere *nf* **1.** flue; **2.** cleft between heat shafts of an oven; **3.** oven recess, niche

ierecēt *vi* clot, curdle, set (partly)

ierēdniecība *nf* bureaucracy; civil service

ierēdnieciski *adv* officially; bureaucratically

ierēdniecisks *adj* official; bureaucratic

ierēdn/is *nm, ~e nf* employee; clerk; official; civil servant; (RR) agent

ieredzēt *vt* like, esteem; (in passive constructions) be well thought of; (in negations) bear, stand

ieregulēt *vt* adjust, fine-tune

ieregulētāj/s *nm, ~a nf* adjuster

iereģistrēt *vt* record

iereibies *adj, part* of **iereibties** intoxicated

iereibis *adj, part* of **iereibt** intoxicated

iereibt vi become intoxicated

iereibties vr become intoxicated

iereibums nm state of intoxication

iereibu/šais nom adj drunk; ~sī f

ierekstēties vr grunt

ierekšķēties vr grunt

ierekšķināties vr grunt

ierēkties vr give a roar

ierēķināt vt include (in a calculation)

ieremsties vr clamber in

ierētnis nm false cuff, false facing

ierēvēt vt (naut.) reef

ierībēt vi move in with a rumble

ierībēties vr rumble, roll

ierībināt vt, vi move in with a rumble

ierīce nf device, appliance; contrivance

ierīcība nf 1. management; 2. equipment, furniture

ieridāt vt arrange

ierīdīt vt 1. sic into; 2. (of dogs) tease

ieriebt vi rub the wrong way, irritate

ieriebties vr be disgusted by

ieriest I vi (rare., of an udder) fill with milk

ieriest II vt 1. (weav.) beam the warp; 2. (of buds, fruit) begin to form

ieriesties I vr (rare., of an udder) fill with milk

ieriesties II vr 1. (of buds, fruit) begin to form; 2. (of tears) well up

ierietenis nm (of garments) insertion

ierietēt vi 1. (of the sun) sink into; 2. (of an udder) fill with milk; 3. (of tears) well up

ierieties vr begin to bark, give a bark

ierievene nf 1. rabbet plane, grooving plane; 2. washboard

ierievis nm spline; gib

ierievojums nm groove

ierievot vt grove

ieriezt vt = **ieriest** II

ieriezties vr = **ieriesties** II

ierīkojums nm institution

ierīkot vt 1. set up, establish; lay out; 2. arrange; 3. (of nests, dens) make; (den, home); 4. (of land) exploit

ierīkoties vr settle, establish oneself

ierikšot vi trot in

ierikte nf (col.) device, appliance; contrivance

ieriktēt vt (com.) establish, organize

ierinda nf (mil.) formation; **izvērsta i.** extended order; **slēgta i.** close order; **ārpus ~s** out of commission; **~s priekšā** before the troops

ierindas apmācīb/a nf close order drill; **i. ~u laukums** parade ground

ierindas dienests nm active duty

ierindas sastāvs nm rank and file

ierindas virsnieks nm combat officer;

ierindnie/ks nm, **~ce** nf (mil.) private; **~ki** rank and file

ierindot vt 1. place in line; 2. rank; 3. include

ierindoties vr rank, range with

ieriņķot v 1. vi circle into; 2. vt twirl

ieripināt vt roll in(to); set rolling

ieripināties vr roll into

ieripot vi roll in(to)

ieris nm = **iere**

ierisināt vt initiate, start

ierisināties vr start

ierist vi begin to unravel; begin to unreel, unroll

ierīt vt swallow, gulp down

ieritēt vi roll into; **i. vecajās sliedēs** resume the old course

ieritināt vt roll into

ieritināties vr roll up

ierīvēt vt 1. rub in; 2. grate into; 3. chafe

ierīvēties vr 1. rub oneself with; 2. produce by rubbing; 3. eat into

ierobe nf notch, groove

ierobežojums nm limitation, restriction

ierobežot vt limit, restrict

ierobežotība nf limitations

ierobežoties *vr* limit oneself to, restrict oneself to

ierobīt *vt* notch (irregularly)

ierobot *vt* notch (regularly), groove

ierobs *nm* **1.** notch, groove; **2.** object of contention

iero/cis *nm* **1.** weapon; ~**či** weaponry, arms; **akls i.** (fig.) mere tool; **aukstie** ~**či** cold steel; **šau-jamie** ~**či** firearms; **vieglie** ~**či** small arms; ~**ču uguns** gunfire;; **pie** ~**čiem!** to arms!

ieroču atļauja gun license

ieroču biedrs *nm* comrade-in-arms

ieroču izmēģināšana *nf* test firing

ieroču kalējs *nm* gunsmith

ieroču meistars *nm* armorer; firearms technician

ieroču nesējs *nm* **1.** armiger; **2.** weapons platform

ieroču palāta *nf* armory

ieroču pārzinis *nm* armorer

ierosa *nf* **1.** (physiol.) excitation; ~**s ligzda** lo-cus of excitation; **2.** (rare.) initiative; **3.** (rare.) suggestion, proposal

ierosinājum/s *nm* suggestion, proposal; motion; **pats uz savu** ~**u** on one's own initiative

ierosināmība *nf* (physiol.) excitability

ierosināt *vt* **1.** suggest, propose, move; **i. jautājumu** raise a question; **i. sūdzību** (jur.) bring an action; **2.** (of appetite) whet; (of activity, curiosity) stimulate

ierosinātāj/s *nm* **1.** mover; initiator; ~**a** *nf*; **2.** stimulus

ierosinošs *adj, part* of **ierosināt** stimulating

ierosīt *vt* stimulate

ierosīties *vr* become lively

ierosme *nf* **1.** motive; inducement; **2.** impulse; **3.** initiative

ierosmes krist[all]s [āl] *nm* seed crystal

ierosmes strāva *nf* (el.) exciting current

ierosmīgs *adj* of great initiative

ierosmināt *vt* = **ierosināt**

ierotīt *vt* (of a seam) turn

ieroza *nf* **1.** small rise; **2.** bay

ierubināt *vt* nibble, pick

ierubināties *vr* (of male grouse) begin to utter mating calls

ierūcināt *v* **1.** *vi* (of a motorcycle) come roaring; **2.** *vt* (of a device) make buzz

ierūcināties *vr* rumble; begin to rumble

ieruds *adj* of a slightly rusty color

ierūgt *vi* begin to ferment

ierūgteni *adv* (to taste) bitterish

ierūgtens *adj* bitterish

ierūgti *adv* (to taste) bitterish

ierūgts *adj* bitterish

ierukstēties *vr* grunt

ierukšēties *vr* grunt

ierukšķēties *vr* grunt

ierukšķināties *vr* grunt

ierūkt *vi* (rare., of thunder) rumble for the first time in spring

ierūkties *vr* growl; roll, thunder

ierun/a *nf* objection, protest; **bez** ~**ām** unquestioningly; **bez** ~**ām!** no buts about it!

ierunāt *vt* **1.** speak into; **2.** record (one's voice); **3.** tell, convince

ierunāties *vr* speak up, begin to speak

ierūsēt *vi* **1.** grow rusty; **2.** rust in

ierūsējis *adj, part* of **ierūsēt** rusty

ierūsgani *adv* in a slightly reddish brown color

ierūsgans *adj* slightly reddish brown

ierūsināt *vt* allow to rust; allow to rust in

ierušināt *vt* cover up (with sand, dirt, leaves)

ierušināties *vr* cover oneself up (with sand, straw)

iesācēj/s *nm*, ~**a** *nf* beginner

iesacīt *vt* recommend

iesacīties *vr* speak up

iesaiņojamais *nom adj* packing material, wrapping

iesaiņojamā mašīna *nf* packer

iesaiņojum/s *nm* packing, wrapping; **tukšie** ~**i** empties

iesaiņot *vt* pack, wrap

iesaiņotājs *nm*, ~**a** *nf* packer

iesaistījums *nm* involvement; inclusion

iesaistīt *vt* involve; induce to participate; include

iesaistīties *vr* involve oneself, participate; **i. sa-censībā** enter into competition

iesāka *nf* beginning; ~**s burts** initial letter

iesakņot *vt* root (seedlings)

iesakņo/ties *vr* take root, become rooted; **dziļi** ~**jies** deep-rooted, ingrained

iesākt *vt* **1.** begin, start; **vienreiz ir jāiesāk!** all things have a beginning; **ar mani tu neiesāc!** don't you try it on with me! **2.** (with **kas, nekas**) do; **ko lai tagad iesākam?** what are we going to do now? **nezināja, ko i.** didn't know what to do next

iesākties *vr* begin, start

iesākuma *indecl adj* initial

iesākum/s *nm* beginning, start; ~**i** origins, beginnings

iesalasni *nm pl* green malt

iesalcukurs *nm* maltose

iesaldeni *adv* sweetishly

iesaldens *adj* sweetish

iesaldēt *vt* freeze; deep-freeze

iesaldi *adv* sweetishly

iesalds *adj* sweetish

iesālījums *nm* pickle

iesalināt *vt* (of flour) malt

iesalis *adj, part* of **iesalt** frozen; ice-bound

iesālīt *vt* **1.** salt; pickle; **2.** (col.) stuff it; **3.** store

iesālīties *vr* get pickled

iesalkani *adv* sweetishly

iesalkans *adj* sweetish

iesalnīca *nf* place for drying malt

iesalot *vt* malt

iesals *nm* malt

iesalt *vi* freeze in

iesāļš *adj* saltish; briny

iesanēties *vr* begin to buzz, give a buzz

iesānis *adv* askance, sideways

iesāņš *adv* askance, sideways

iesāņus *adv* askance, sideways

iesāpēties *vr* begin to hurt

iesarkani *adv* in a reddish color

iesarkans *adj* reddish

iesarkt *vi* redden

iesārtā glīvene *nf* slender pondweed

iesārtens *adj* pinkish

iesārtis *adj* reddened

iesārtot *vi* redden

iesārtoties *vr* redden, flush

iesārts *adj* pinkish

iesārtums *nm* pinkish color

iesaucamais *nom adj* draftee

iesauciens *nm* cry

iesauka *nf* nickname

iesaukalēt *vt* nickname

iesaukāt *vt* nickname

iesaukšana *nf* draft; ~**s gados** of draft age

iesaukšanas pavēle *nf* draft notice

iesaukt *vt* **1.** call in; **2.** call up, draft; **3.** begin to call (a name), nickname

iesaukties *vr* call out, exclaim

iesaukums *nm* (military) draft

iesavināt *vt* (philos.) acquire

iesēciens *nm* wheeze

iesēdēt *vt* **1.** make a depression (by sitting); **2.** break in (by sitting)

iesēdies *adj, part* of **iesēsties** (col.) accustomed; persisting in memory

iesēdināt *vt* **1.** seat, put in a seat; **i. vilcienā** put on a train; **2.** (col.) put behind bars

iesēdumezers *nm* suffonic lake

iesēdu or **iesēdus** *adv* (rare.) in a reclining position

iesegs *nm* spread (for lining), lining

iesegt *vt* spread out, line (the inside of sth.)

iesegums *nm* lining

iesējums *nm* **1.** (book) binding; **2.** (tech.) joint

iesēkties *vr* wheeze briefly

iesekus *adv* slightly behind

iesērēt *vi* silt up; (of silt) accumulate

iesērt *vt* put to dry in the drying barn

iesēst *vi* sit down

iesēsties *vr* **1.** sit down (in a place); **2.** (col., fig.) get oneself established (in a position); **i. prātā** stick in one's mind; **3.** sink in

iesēt *vt* sow

iesēties *vr* **1.** sow itself; **2.** be sowed

iesiekalot *vt* wet with saliva

iesiešana *nf* **1.** tying up; **2.** bookbinding

iesiet *vt* **1.** tie in; bundle up; (of a scythe) fasten; **2.** make (by tying); hang (by tying up between two points); **3.** (of books) bind

iesieties *vr* **1.** be tied, be fastened; **2.** fasten oneself in

iesijāt *vt* sift into

iesīkstējums *nm* ossified custom, habit

iesīkstēt *vi* ossify; (of a disease) become chronic

iesīksts *adj* somewhat tough

iesīkties *vr* buzz briefly

iesildenis *nm* preheater

iesildīt *vt* warm, warm up; **i. galvu** hava couple of drinks

iesildīties *vr* warm up

iesilis *adj, part* of **iesilt 1.** warm, tepid; **2.** (col.) in one's cups

iesilt *vi* **1.** warm up; (fig.) warm up to; **2.** (col.) have one too many, tipple

iesilts *adj* warmish

iesilums *nm* intoxication

iesirgt *vi* fall ill

iesirmais grīslis *nm* silvery sedge

iesirmot *vi* (of hair) begin to turn gray

iesirms *adj* grayish, (of hair) with streaks of gray, grizzled

iesirst *vi* become angry

iesirsties *vr* become angry

iesist *v* **1.** *vt, vi* strike, hit; **i. galvā** (col., of liquor) hit; **2.** *vt* drive, drive in; **i. vārtus** (soccer, hockey) score a goal; **i. caurumu** perforate; **i. dobumu** dent; **i. rubli** (or **kapeiku**) (col.) make money

iesisties *vr* **1.** strike, hit; **i. galvā** (col., of liquor) hit; rush to one's head; **i. degunā** hit the nostrils; **2.** be driven; **3.** become perforated, become dented; **4.** (of wind) shift suddenly

iesitināt *vt* wrap

ieskābens *adj* sourish

ieskābēt *vt* pickle

ieskābi *adv* sourishly

ieskābs *adj* sourish

ieskābt *vi* turn sour

ieskaidrot *vt* explain; bring home, make understand

ieskaisties *vr* become angry

ieskaite *nf* **1.** (bus.) credit; payment; **2.** (educ.) test, examination

ieskaitījums *nm* addition, inclusion; crediting

ieskait/īt *vt* **1.** count and put into (a place); **2.** in-clude, count in; ~ot including; **i. štatos** put on the staff; **3.** credit

ieskaitīties *vr* include oneself

ieskaits *nm* (educ.) test; (sports) qualifier

ieskaldīt *vt* cut in (with an ax)

ieskalot *vt* wash into

ieskaloties *vr* be washed into

ieskandināt *vt* begin to ring, begin to sound; open (festivities) with the sound of (music, singing)

ieskanēties *vr* **1.** sound, begin to sound; **2.** (of tone of voice) have a touch of an emotion, (of anger, envy) be audible

ieskaņa *nf* **1.** prologue; **2.** (ling.) anlaut, initial sound; **3.** undertone; intonation

ieskaņojums *nm* sound recording

ieskaņot *vt* (of sound recordings) record; (of film) add a sound track

ieskāņš *adj* sourish

ieskapēt *vt* (barb.) procure, provide

ieskarbi *adv* rather harshly

ieskarbs *adj* rather harsh

ieskāt *vt* (of a hair-covered area) scratch, groom

ieskāties *vr* (of birds) preen

ieskatīt *vt* 1. consider, think, hold; 2. become fond of, fall in love with

ieskatīties *vr* 1. look into, take a peek in; **i. par dziļu glāzē** (col.) have one too many; 2. take a casual look at, glance through; 3. examine, take a close look; 4. fall in love

ieskat/s *nm* 1. opinion, view; 2. discretion, judgment; 3. **~am** for inspection, on approval; 4. in-sight; overview

ieskaut *vt* embrace; envelop

ieskicējums *nm* outline, sketch

ieskicēt *vt* sketch

ieskolot *vt* (col.) teach, train

ieskrabēties *vr* crunch briefly

ieskrabināties *vr* scrape briefly

ieskraidīt *vi* run into

ieskrambājums *nm* scratch

ieskrambāt *vt* scratch

ieskrambāties *vr* get scratched; be scratched

ieskrampt *vt* scratch

ieskrāpējums *nm* scratch

ieskrāpēt *vt, vi* 1. scratch in; 2. scratch lightly

ieskrāpēties *vr* be scratched; get scratched

ieskrapstēties *vr* crackle briefly

ieskrapstināties *vr* scrape briefly

ieskrapšķēties *vr* scrape briefly

ieskrējiena ceļš *nm* runway

ieskrējiens *nm* (aeron.) takeoff run; (sports) running start

ieskribināt *vt* begin to nibble

iskribināties *vr* make gnawing sounds briefly

ieskriešan/ās *nfr* running start; **ar ~os** at a run

ieskriet *vi* run into, run in, run inside; **i. prātā** think of suddenly

ieskrieties *vr* take a run; get up speed

ieskrubināt *vt* begin to nibble

ieskrubināties *vr* make gnawing sounds briefly

ieskrūvēt *vt* screw in

ieskrūvēties *vr* be screwed in

ieskubināt *vt* urge to go in

ieskurbis *adj, part* of **ieskurbt** intoxicated

ieskurbt *vi* become intoxicated

ieskurbums *nm* intoxication

ieskurināt *vt* splash into; sprinkle

ieskūt *vt* begin to shave

ieslacināt *vt* splash into; sprinkle

ieslacīt *vt* splash into; sprinkle

ieslacīties *vr* get splashed into

ieslaids *adj* (rare.) fairly slender

ieslaistīties *vr* wander in idly

ieslakāt *vt* splash into; sprinkle

ieslampāt *vi* trudge in

ieslamstīties *vr* wander in idly

ieslānīt *vt* 1. (col.) spank; 2. stack close to-gether

ieslapstīties *vr* sneak into

ieslāņot *vt* stack in layers

ieslapēt *vt* (rare.) moisten

ieslapināt *vt* moisten

ieslapt *vi* get wet

ieslāt *vi* trudge in

ieslaucīt *vt* sweep into

ieslaukt *vt* 1. milk into; 2. begin to milk; (of cows) get used to being milked

ieslavēt *vt* praise; recommend

ieslavēts *adj, part* of **ieslavēt** popular, highly praised; famous

ieslēdzējrelejs *nm* (automobile) starter relay

ieslēdzējs *nm* switch

ieslēdzis *nm* switch

ieslēgt *vt* 1. lock in; lock up; **i. dzelžos** put in chains; handcuff; **i. ledū** ice in; 2. (of lights, appliances) switch on, turn on; 3. (el.) connect; (of a circuit) insert; 4. (mech.) engage, put in gear; **i. ātrumā** put in gear;

5. enclose; embrace; surround; **i. iekavās** put in parentheses

ieslēgties *vr* **1.** lock oneself in; **2.** be turned on, be switched on; **3.** (fig.) join (in)

ieslēguma strāva *nf* inrush current

ieslēgum/s *nm* **1.** turning-on; **2.** inclusion

ieslēpot *vi* ski into

ieslēpt *vt* hide

ieslēpties *vr* hide

ieslīcināt *vt* immerse

ieslīdens *adj* somewhat slippery

ieslīdēt *vi* glide, slide, or slip in(to)

ieslidināt *vt* **1.** slide into; **2.** smooth with skates

ieslīdināt *vt* slide into, let slide into

ieslidināties *vr* skate into

ieslidot *vi* skate into

iesliedēt *vt* make tracks

iesliegties *vr* = **iesliekties**

iesliekties *vr* reach into; jut out; cut into

iesliet *vt* prop up

ieslieties *vr* **1.** reach, reach into; **2.** stand

ieslīgt *vi* sink into

ieslīkt *vi* sink into

ieslīpeni *adv* at a slant, obliquely

ieslīpens *adj* slanting, oblique

ieslīpi *adv* at a slant, obliquely

ieslīps *adj* slanting, oblique

ieslīpu *adv* at a slant, obliquely

ieslīpums *nm* slant, obliqueness

ieslīpus *adv* at a slant, obliquely

ieslīt *vi* slide into

ieslodzījums *nm* detention, imprisonment

ieslodzīt *vt* lock up, imprison

ieslodzīties *vr* lock oneself in

ieslodzīt/ais *nom adj* prisoner; ~ā *f*

iesmacis *adj, part* of **iesmakt 1.** rancid, spoiled, tainted; **2.** slightly hoarse

iesmakt *vi* **1.** become rancid, spoil; (of food) begin to smell; **2.** become slightly hoarse

iesmakums *nm* **1.** rancid or musty smell; **2.** hoarseness

iesmaržināt *vt* perfume lightly

iesmaržināties *vr* perfume oneself lightly

iesmaržot *vt* perfume

iesmaržoties *vr* **1.** begin to smell; **2.** get a whiff (of a smell); **3.** put on scent

iesmdurklis *nm* spike bayonet

iesmējiens *nm* short laughter

iesmēķēt *vt* **1.** (of pipes) break in; **2.** light up

iesmeķēties *vr* get to like; (of taste) grow on one

iesmeldzēties *vr* begin to smart, feel a pang

iesmelgt *vi* begin to smart, feel a pang

iesmelgties *vr* begin to smart, feel a pang

iesmelt *vt* spoon in, spoon up, ladle in, ladle out; scoop up, dip up

iesmelties *vr* **1.** be dipped (spooned, ladled, scooped) up; **2.** (of liquids) get in, ship, take over the side

iesmeltēt *vt* (col.) give a whipping

iesmērēt *v* **1.** *vt* grease, oil, lubricate; **2.** *vt* palm off; **3.** *vi* (col.) grease s.o.'s palm, bribe; **4.** *vi* (sl.) hit

iesmērēties *vr* **1.** anoint oneself; **2.** bribe one's way into

iesmīdināt *vt* make laugh

iesmidzināt *vt* spray in; sprinkle into; (tech.) in-ject

iesmidzināties *vr* sprinkle briefly

iesmieties *vr* begin to laugh; burst out laughing, laugh out

iesmilkstēties *vr* whine

iesmīnēties *vr* smirk

iesmirdēties *vr* smell (badly) briefly

iesm/s *nm* spit; **garā ~a drāzējs** a. pedant; b. slowpoke

iesnains *adj* (of the nose) runny

iesnas *nf pl* head cold

iesnaudināt *vt* make drowsy, put to sleep

iesnaust *vi* doze off

iesnausties *vr* doze off

iesniedzēj/s *nm*, ~a *nf* presenter, introducer; plaintiff; petitioner; claimant

iesniegšana *nf* presentation, submission; introduction

iesniegt *vt* hand in; (of bills) introduce, (of proposals, petitions) submit, present; (of a motion) make; **i. sūdzību** file a complaint; bring a suit against; **i. atlūgumu** hand in one's resignation, resign

iesniegties *vr* reach, reach into; jut out; cut into

iesniegums *nm* application; presentation; petition

iesnigt *vi* snow in; get snowed in

iesnoties *vr* have a head cold

iesnots *adj* (rare., of the nose) running

iesoļot *vi* march in; enter

iespaidība *nf* impressiveness, imposingness

iespaidīgi *adv* impressively; influentially

iespaidīgs *adj* **1.** impressive; imposing; **2.** influential

iespaidīgums *nm* impressiveness; imposingness

iespaidīt *vt* press in

iespaidot *vt* **1.** impress; **2.** influence

iespaidoties *vr* be influenced

iespaids *nm* **1.** impression; **2.** influence

iespārdīt *vt* kick in

iespārdīties *vr* get in by wriggling and jumping

iesparkšķēties *vr* sputter briefly

iespārnot *vt* (poet.) inspire

iesparoties *vr* pull oneself together, pluck up one's courage

iespēcināt *vt* strengthen, invigorate

iespēcināties *vr* fortify oneself

iespēja *nf* **1.** possibility; **pēc ~s drīzi** as soon as possible; **(dot) pēc ~s** (give) as much as one can; **2.** chance, opportunity; **pēdējā i.** last resort

iespējami *adv* possibly; potentially

iespējamība *nf* feasibility; possibility

iespējams *adj* possible; feasible; potential

iespēkoties *vr* recover

iespeķot *vt* lard

iespēlēt *vt* **1.** (of music) record; **2.** play into; **3.** win

iespēlēties *vr* get in form

iespert *v* **1.** *vi, vt* kick; **2.** *vi, 3rd pers* (of lightning) strike; **3.** *vt* put (one's foot) into (in stepping); **4. i. glāzīti** (or **čarku**) (col.) have a drink

iesperties *vr* **1.** (col.) rush into; **2.** put (one's foot) into (in stepping); **3.** stem oneself against

iespēt *vt* **1.** be able; **2.** manage, have time (to do sth.)

iespīdēt *vi* shine in(to)

iespīdēties *vr* (of lights) come on; begin to shine; shine briefly

iespīdināt *vt* shine in

iespiedautomāts *nm* automatic printing press

iespiedburti *nm pl* (typ.) type

iespiedce[ch]s [h] *nm* press room

iespiedcilindrs *nm* (typ.) impression cylinder

iespieddarbs *nm* printed matter

iespiedējs *nm*, **~a** *nf* printer

iespiedforma *nf* stereotype matrix

iespiediekārta *nf* printing device

iespiedkļūda *nf* printer's error, misprint

iespiedloksne *nf* (typ.) signature

iespiedmašīna *nf* printing press

iespiedmeistars *nm* master printer

iespiedpapīrs *nm* printing paper

iespiedprese *nf* printing press

iespiedprodukcija *nf* printed output

iespieduma krāsa *nf* printer's ink

iespiedumrūpniecība *nf* printing business

iespiedums *nm* **1.** depression, dent; **2.** impression; imprint; **3.** print; **gaišais i.** lean face; **pustreknais i.** medium face; **treknais i.** bold face; **4.** (of books) printing; edition

iespiedveltnis *nm* (typ.) impression cylinder

iespiedveltnītis *nm* printing roller

iespiedzīme *nf* (typ.) type

iespiegties *vr* squeal, scream

iespiest *vt* **1.** push, press, or squeeze in(to); **i. piešus sānos** clap spurs; **2.** depress; **3.** impress; impress upon; stamp; **4.** print

iespiesties *vr* **1.** squeeze oneself into; **2.** penetrate; **3.** get stuck; **4.** get dented; **5.** sink into; **6.** leave an impression

iespiestuve *nf* printing department

iespiešanās *nfr* (mil.) penetration

iespietot *vi* (of swarming bees) settle in

iespīguļoties *vr* flash

iespīlēt *vt* put in a vice, clamp in; squeeze in, force in

iespīlēties *vr* squeeze oneself in

iespindzēties *vr* buzz briefly

iespirdzināt *vt* (rare.) refresh

iespirdzināties *vr* (rare.) refresh oneself

iespirgt *vi* (rare.) recover

iespīte *nf* stubborness

iespītēt *vi* spite

iespītēties *vr* become stubborn

iespītība *nf* stubborness

iespītīgi *adv* stubbornly

iespītīgs *adj* stubborn

iespļaut *vt* spit into

iespolēt *vt* spool

iesprādzēt *vt* buckle in

iesprādzēties *vr* buckle oneself in, buckle up

iesprāgt *vt* **1.** crack; **2.** pop in(to), splatter into, (of sparks) fall into

iespraigāt *vi* crack

iesprakstēt *vi* (of sparks) fly into

iesprakstēties *vr* crackle briefly, begin to crackle, sputter briefly

iesprakšķēt *vi* (of sparks) fly into

iesprakšķēties *vr* crackle briefly, begin to crackle, sputter briefly

iesprandzēt *vt* (col.) squeeze in

iespraudenis *nm* insert; filler; (ling.) patch vowel

iespraudīt *vt* stick in

iespraudums *nm* insertion

iespraukt *vt* stick in(to)

iespraukties *vr* squeeze oneself into; elbow one's way into; (mil.) drive a wedge between

iesprauslāt *vt* inject by caughing, sneezing or sputtering

iesprauslāties *vr* **1.** snort; **2.** burst out laughing

iespraust *vt* **1.** stick in(to); **i. rokas sānos** put one's arms akimbo; **2.** insert

iesprausties *vr* stick

iesprausts *adj, part* of **iespraust** (gram.) parenthetical

iesprēgāt *vi* chap

iesprēgāties *vr* crackle briefly; begin to crackle

iesprengt *vt* (col.) squeeze in

iespridzēt *vi* (rare., of sparks) fly into

iespridzēties *vr* (rare.) begin to sparkle

iespridzināt *vt* blow in (as a result of an explosion or breakage)

iespriest *vt* squeeze in; **i. rokas sānos** put one's arms akimbo

iespriesties *vr* stick

iesprikstēt *vi* (rare., of sparks) fly into

iesprikstēties *vr* (rare.) begin to crackle, begin to sputter

iespringt *vi* get stuck

iesprogāt *vt* = **iesprogot**

iesprogot *vt* curl

iesprostīt *vt* = **iesprostot**

iesprostojum/s *nm* confinement; **~ā** caged

iesprostot *vt* cage; pen in

iesprūdis *part* of **iesprūst** stuck; jammed; (of a hernia) strangulated

iesprūdīt *vt* cage; pen in; (col.) lock up

iesprūdīties *vr* squeeze oneself in

iesprūdums *nm* jamming; (med.) strangulation

iesprukt *vi* run and hide; sneak in, whisk into

iesprūst *v* **1.** *vi* get stuck, jam; **2.** *vt* stick in

iespulgoties *vr* begin to shine

iespundēt *vt* (col.) lock up

iespurgt *vi* flutter in; flit in

iespurgties *vr* 1. flutter briefly; 2. give a short burst of laughter

iespurkšķēties *vr* 1. flutter briefly; sputter briefly; 2. (rare.) give a short burst of laughter

iespurkties *vr* 1. flutter briefly; 2. give a short burst of laughter

iestāde *nf* institution; (government) office

iestādījums *nm* institution

iestādīšana *nf* 1. planting; 2. adjusting; adjustment

iestādīt *vt* 1. plant; 2. (med.) implant; 3. adjust; **i. fokusu** focus; **i. uz nulli** zero adjust

iestādītāj/s *nm*, **~a** *nf* adjuster

iestāds *nm* seedling

iestaigāt *vt* 1. tread a path; 2. (of shoes) break in; 3. (col.) stop by

iestaipīt *vt* 1. limber up; 2. (of clothes) stretch

iestaipīties *vr* 1. limber up; 2. (of clothes) get stretched

iestaips *nm* lining

iestājeksāmens *nm* entrance examination

iestājpārbaudījums *nm* entrance examination

iestāju *indecl adj* entrance (*adj*)

iestampāt *vt* stamp in

iestarot *vi* shine in

iestaroties *vr* light up; flash

iestarpinājums *nm* insertion

iestarpināt *vt* insert

iestāst/īt *vt* persuade; make believe; bring home; **~i to citam!** tell it to the Marines!

iestāt *vt* 1. begin, undertake; 2. place oneself (in a position); step into; 3. enroll, join; 4. (of seasons, natural events) begin, set in

iestāties *vr* 1. stand (in a place), place oneself (in a position); step into; 2. (with **par**) stand up for; 3. enroll, join; **i. darbā** get a job; **i. karadie-nestā** enlist; 4. (of seasons, natural events) be-gin, set in

iestatīšana *nf* setting

iestatīšanas skrūve *nf* setscrew

iestatīt *vt* set in, insert

iestāvēt *vt* depress (by standing in one place)

iestāvēties *vr* 1. get used to standing; 2. get used to standing in the same place; 3. spoil; 4. (of smells) cling

iesteberēt *vi* hobble in

iesteigt *v* 1. *vt* hurry up; 2. *vi* hurry in

iesteigties *vr* hurry in

iestenēties *vr* utter a groan

iestērķelēt *vt* starch

iestibāt *vt* (col.) whip

iestīdzēt *vi* stretch into

iestidzis *adj, part* of **iestigt** stuck; (fig.) steeped

iestiepiens *nm* 1. strain; 2. (col.) gulp, go

iestieplot *vt* wire

iestiept *vt* 1. string, (of wires, cables) hang; 2. drag in(to), lug in(to)

iestiepties *vr* reach into; jut out; cut into; (of events) stretch into

iestīgojums *nm* tendrils, runners

iestigot *vt* mark a lane

iestīgot *vi* spread by runners

iestigt *vi* sink into, get mired

iestīgt *vi* stretch into

iestiklojums *nm* glass

iestiklot *vt* glass

iestilpēt *vt* (reg.) squeeze in

iestingt *vi* freeze

iestingums *nm* frozen state

iestīpot *vt* fasten with hoops

iestiprinājies *adj, part* of **iestiprināties** (col.) intoxicated

iestiprinājums *nm* fastening

iestiprināšana *nf* (Catholic) confirmation

iestiprināt *vt* 1. fasten in; **i. dūšu** (col.) have a drink; 2. (rel., Catholic) confirm

iestiprināties *vr* 1. take root; 2. fortify oneself with food; 3. (col.) have a drink

iestiprot *vt* = **iestiprināt**

iestiproties *vr* = **iestiprināties**

iestīvēt *vt* force in

iestīvināt *vt* starch, stiffen

iestrādājamība *nf* workability

iestrādāt *vt* work into; (of soil) cultivate

iestrādāties *vr* acquire skill, acquire experience; (of machinery) get run in

iestrāde *nf* **1.** working in; **2.** processing; production; extra production; **3.** work experience; **4.** acquisition of a skill; **5.** (of a machine) running in

iestrāvot *vi* stream in

iestrēbt *vt* slurp

iestrēbties *vr* slurp

iestrēgt *vi* get stuck

iestreipuļot *vi* stagger in

iestrigt *vi* get stuck

iestrinkšķēties *vr* **1.** strum, twang; **2.** ring briefly, jingle

iestrinkšķināt *vt* strum; jingle

iestrinkšķināties vr **1.** strum, twang; **2.** ring briefly, jingle

iestudējums *nm* (theat.) production

iestudēt *vt* (theat.) rehearse; study one's part; (of a play) produce, stage

iestūkāt *vt* (col.) shove, push, squeeze in

iestūķēt *vt* (col.) shove in, squeeze in

iestumdīt *vt* push in(to)

iestumt *vt* push in(to)

iestumties *vr* push oneself into

iestūrēt *vt, vi* steer in(to)

iestūris *nm* small corner (of a field or forest)

iestūriski *adv* somewhat diagonally

iesturmēt *vt* storm

iestutēt *vt* prop up

iesūdzējams *adj, part* of **iesūdzēt** (jur.) actionable

iesūdzēt *vt* sue

iesukāt *vt* (col.) whip

iesukāties *vr* be combed

iesūknēt *vt* pump in(to)

iesūknēties *vr* infiltrate

iesūkstēties *vr* begin to smart

iesūkt *vt* **1.** suck in(to); **2.** absorb, soak up

iesūkties *vr* seep in(to); soak in

iesūnojis *adj, part* of **iesūnot** moss-covered; (fig.) hoary, obsolete, stagnant

iesūnot *vi* gather moss; (fig.) begin to stagnate

iesūri *adv* somewhat bitterly

iesūrkstēties *vr* begin to smart

iesūrs *adj* somewhat bitter

iesūtījums *nm* contribution, submission

iesūtīt *vt* send in; submit

iesūtītājs *nm* contributor (of a submitted piece of writing)

iesvaidīt *vt* **1.** anoint; **2.** toss in (carelessly and repeatedly)

iesvārstīšanās *nfr* (el.) building up of oscillation

iesvārstīt *vt* set swinging

iesvārstīties *vr* begin to swing (in a certain direction)

iesvēdrāt *vi* crack, develop cracks

iesvelpt *vi* whistle

iesvelpties *vr* give a whistle

iesvelt *v* **1.** *vt* arouse; inflame; **2.** *vi* arise

iesvelties *vr* arise

iesvempties *vr* stump in

iesvērt *vt* weigh out

iesvērties *vr* be weighed out

iesvērums *nm* weighing

iesvēte *nf* dedication (ceremony)

iesvētības *nf pl* (rel., Lutheran) confirmation

iesvētīšana *nf* (of buildings) dedication, consecration; (rel., Lutheran) confirmation

iesvētīšanas mācība *nf* confirmation lesson; (of clergymen) ordination

iesvētīt *vt* (of buildings) dedicate, consecrate; (of clergymen) ordain; (rel., of Lutheran youths) confirm

iesvētīties *vr* (rel., of Lutherans) be confirmed

iesviest *vt* throw in(to)

iesviesties *vr* **1.** throw oneself into; **2.** be thrown

iesviķojies *adj, part* of **iesviķoties** (col.) intoxicated

iesviķot *vi* (col.) do some drinking

iesviķoties *vr* (col.) do some drinking

iesvilpot *vi* **1.** whistle into; **2.** enter whistling

iesvilpoties *vr* whistle briefly

iesvilpt *vi* whistle into

iesvilpties *vr* whistle

iesvilt *vi* catch fire; flare up

iesvilties *vr* catch fire; flare up; **i. dusmās** fly into a rage

iesvīst *vi* become sweaty

iesvītrojums *nm* **1.** outline; **2.** scratches, lines

iesvītrot *vt* scratch in, mark with lines

iešalkot *vi* begin to rustle; (fig.) spread rapidly

iešalkoties *vr* rustle; begin to rustle

iešalkties *vr* rustle; begin to rustle

iešalkt *vi* (of wind) blow in; (fig.) spread rapidly

iešana *nf* walking, going

iešaut *v* **1.** *vt, vi* fire into; hit, wound; **2.** *vt* shove in; **3.** *vi* (col.) strike (suddenly); **i. pa ausi** slap; **4.** *vt* (of tail) put between one's legs

iešauties *vr* **1.** dash in; **i. prātā** come to mind suddenly, flash across one's mind; **i. vidū** inject; **2.** strike

iešautīt *vt* set swinging

iešinēt *vt* splint

iešķaudīt *vi* sneeze into

iešķaudīties *vr* sneeze briefly

iešķēlot *vt* crack

iešķelt *vt* **1.** split partially; **2.** make a split

iešķelties *vr* **1.** split; **2.** be cut into; **3.** (of sparks) be struck

iešķēlums *nm* split; slot

iešķērsām *adv* across

iešķērse *nf* diagonal

iešķērss *adj* cross, diagonal

iešķērsu *adv* across

iešķetināt *vt* begin to spin

iešķetināties *vr* get spun into

iešķībi *adv* obliquely, awry

iešķībs *adj* slanting, oblique, awry, (of a hat) cocked

iešķiebties *vr* bend inward

iešķielēt *vi* look sideways into

iešķiest *vt* splash into

iešķiesties *vr* get splashed into

iešķilt *vt* strike sparks; **i. uguni** strike fire

iešķilties *vr* (of sparks) be struck

iešķindēties *vr* jingle, (of bells) ring; (of swords) rattle

iešķindināt *vt* begin to ring, begin to sound

iešķīst *vi* splash into, splatter into

iešķīt *vt* **1.** (of berries, fruit, legumes) pick; **2.** pick and put into

iešķīvot *vt* plow with a disc plow

iešķūrēt *vt* shove in

iešļakāt *vt* splash into

iešļakāties *vr* splash into

iešļakstēt *vi* splash into

iešļakstēties *vr* make a splash

iešļakstināt *vt* splash into

iešļakstīt *vt* splash into

iešļakstīties *vr* splash ino

iešļākšana *nf* **1.** splashing into; **2.** (fuel) injection

iešļākt *vt* splash into; (tech.) inject

iešļākties *vr* splash into

iešļaubi *adv* at a slant

iešļaubs *adj* sloping, slanting

iešļaupi *adv* at a slant

iešļaups *adj* sloping, slanting

iešļircinājums *nm* injection

iešļircināt *vt* inject

iešļirkt *vi* get squirted into

iešļūkāt *vt* make tracks (by shuffling)

iešļukt *vi* slip in

iešļūkt *vi* shuffle in

iešļupstēties *vr* lisp; babble

iešmaukt *vi* **1.** foist; **2.** sneak in; **3.** (with **pa**, col.) hit, whack

iešmaukties *vr* sneak in

iešmīkstēties *vr* swish

iešmugulēt *vt* (com.) palm off

iešmukt *vi* sneak in

iešņabojis *adj, part* of **iešņabot** (col.) intoxicated

iešņabot *vi* (col.) drink

iešņakstēties *vr* gnash briefly

iešņākt *vi* hiss into

iešņākties *vr* hiss

iešņāpt *vt, vi* cut into

iešņāpties *vr* cut into

iešņāpums *nm* cut

iešņaukt *vt* 1. (of snuff) take; 2. blow one's nose into

iešņava *nf* (obs.) unsalted lard

iešņīpāt *vt* 1. (col.) scribble; 2. scratch

iešņīpāties *vr* 1. (col.) be scribbled; 2. be scratched

iešņirkstēties *vr* crunch; creak

iešņukstēties *vr* begin to sob, sob

iešņūkt *v* 1. *vt* (of snuff) take; 2. *vi* flow into (the nose)

iešpricēt *vt* 1. (barb.) splash into; 2. inject

ieštancēt *vt* press into

ieštaukāt *vt* (com.) beat up

iešūnot *vt* hang honeycombs in frames

iešūpojums *nm* push on a swing

iešūpot *vt* 1. start a swing (or seesaw, rocking chair), get a swing going; 2. rock to sleep

iešūpoties *vr* 1. begin to rock, swing, or sway; 2. move in swaying

iešus *adv* on foot

iešūt *vt* 1. sew in; 2. take in (in sewing)

iešūties *vr* be sewn in

iešuve *nf* tuck, seam, welt

iešuvums *nm* gore, gusset, inset

iešvīkāt *vt* scratch, score

iešvīkstēties *vr* (of garments) rustle; (of a whip) swish

iešvilpt *vt, vi* (col.) have a drink

iešvirkstēties *vr* crackle

iet *vi irr* 1. go; walk; **i. aizsegā** take cover; **i. armijā** joint the army; **i. ar sālsmaizi** go to a housewarming; **i. ar vistām gulēt** keep good hours; **i. atvaļinājumā** take a vacation; **i. au-gumā** increase (in number); **i. blakus** walk side by side; **i. bojā** a. perish; b. spoil; **i. cauri** a. pass through b. succeed; **i. caur kauliem** (of screeching, grating noises) give the shivers; **i. ciemā** visit; **i. ciet** a. (of cows, goats) decrease milk yield (prior to dropping their young); b. close; **i. cisās** go to bed; **i. četrrāpus** go on all fours; **i. čigānos** go merrymaking in disguise; **i. denderu denderiem** stagger; **i. dibenā** sink; **i. dzīvē** get involved (in life); **i. gaitās** (or **darbos**) (hist.) perform corvée labor; **i. ganos** herd; **i. gar** skirt; **i. gar ausīm** be ignored; **i. garām** a. pass by; b. be missed; c. be spared; **i. garu ceļu** a. cover a long distance; b. get lost; **i. greizi** go wrong; **i. gulēt** go to bed; **i. izlūkos** go on patrol; **i. kā adata** scurry; **i. kā dieviņš** he (she) is really moving; **i. kā pa diegu** (col.) things are going swimmingly; everything is hunky-dory; **i. kā pa celmiem** rough going; **i. kā plēsts** (col.) tear around; **i. kā smērēts** (or **kā pulkstenis**) (col., also fig.) run smoothly; **kad jau i., tad i.** in for a penny, in for a pound; **i. kājām** walk, go on foot; **i. karadienestā** enlist; **i. kopā** fit together; **i. kopsolī** march in step; **i. kungos** (hist.) perform corvée labor; **i., kur deguns rāda** follow one's nose; **i. labi** (or **pareizi**) (of timepieces) keeps good time; **i. labumā** a. do good, benefit; b. gain weight; **lai i., kā iedams** whatever happens; let's chance it! **lai i.!** (col.) okay! let's do it! let it rip! **i. lētumā** become cheaper, (of prices) drop; **i. līdz** accompany; **i. liecībās** (hist.) perform extraordinary corvée; **i. ļaudīs** meet people; **i. mācībā** take confirmation lessons; **i. matos** fight; **i. ma-zumā** decrease; **i. meimuriski** stagger; **i. nāvē** kill oneself; **i. nopakaļ** bring up the rear; **(darbs) i. no**

rokas (he, she is) quick (or efficient); **i. nost**
peel, come off; **i. ogās** go berrying; **i. pa**
priekšu walk in front of; **i. pa tiesas ceļu**
take legal measures; **i. palīgā** go to s.o.'s
help; **i. parādē** pass in re-view; parade; **i.**
pāri (col.) boil over; **i. pāri līķiem** stop at
nothing; **par ko i. runa?** what is it about? **i.**
(kāda) pavadā be led by the nose; **i. (kāda)**
pēdās follow s.o.'s footsteps; **i. peļņā** have a
temporary job; **i. pensijā** retire; **i. pie altāŗa**
be wedded; **i. pie dūšas** (or **sirds**) (col.,
of food) like, taste good; **i. pie dievgalda**
take Communion; **i. pie miera** go to bed;
i. pie sirds enjoy; **i. pie tēviem** die; **i. pie**
tiesas (obs.) go to court; **i. pie urnām** go
to the polls; **i. pie vīra** (of women) marry;
i. pretī a. go to meet; b. ob-lige, meet s.o.
halfway; **i. pušu** burst, break; **i. rikšos** trot;
(galva) i. riņķī be dizzy; **i. roku rokā** go
hand in hand; **i. rotaļās** play games; **i. savu**
ceļu go one's own way; **i. savās gaitās** go
about one's business; **i. savu gaitu** run its
course; **i. secen** a. pass by; b. be missed; c.
be spared; **i. sēnēs** go mushroom picking; **i.**
sevis pēc go see a man about a dog, answer
a call of nature; **i. soļos** (of horses) pace;
i. taisnāko ceļu take the shortest route; **i.**
taisnu ceļu be on the straight and narrow; **i.**
tālāk a. go on, proceed, continue; b. go one
step further; **i. talkā** help, pitch in; **i. tālu**
ceļu go on a long trip; **tas neiet** that won't
do; **tā i.** that's what happens; **i. tautās** (folk.,
of women) marry; **i. tenteriski** stagger; **i.**
uz ādas importune; **i. uz augšu** rise; **i. uz**
beigām a. come to an end; b. run short; **i. uz**
berztu (reg.) spawn; **i. uzbrukumā** attack;
i. uz čučumuižu (child.) go beddy-bye; **i. uz**
dusu a. turn in; b. pass away; **i. uz grunti**
(col.) go under, go down; **i. uz labo pusi**
things are improving; **i. uz leju** go down,
deteriorate; **i. uz ļauno pusi** things are going
downhill; **i. uz varītēm** wrestle; **i. uz vienu**

roku join; **i. uz visām četrām** go on all
fours; **i. vairumā** increase; **i. valodas** it is
rumored; **i. vaļā** open; (col.) start; (of a gun)
discharge); **i. vannā** take a bath; **i. viesos**
visit; **i. virsū** (col.) importune; **i. zaldātos**
(obs., col.) enlist; serve in the military; **i.**
zemē (of sun) set; **i. zudumā** be wasted;
ej nu (ej)! come now! **ej nu sazini!** who
knows? **ej pa gaisu!** go fly a kite! **2.** (of
engines, machinery, shows) run; (of news,
moving objects) go, move, travel; **3.** (of
means of transportation) leave, depart; **4.** (in
ex-changes concerning one's wellbeing) do;
kā i.? how are you? **man i. labi** I am well;
tā i., kā i. so-so; **5.** last, take (time en route);
6. (of container capacity) hold; **7.** (of game
moves, with **ar**) move; **8.** (of merchandise)
sell, move; **9.** (of some games) play (**iesim**
vistiņās! let's play blindman's buff! **10.**
(col., of shows) play

ietaise *nf* installation; contrivance

ietaisīt *vt* **1.** make; install; **i. biksēs** (com.) go
in one's pants; **i. dūšu** (or **ķiveri**) booze;
2. preserve; **i. etiķī** pickle

ietaisīties *vr* **1.** make oneself comfortable; make
a place for oneself; **2.** prepare for

ietālēm *adv* a distance away

ietālu *adv* a distance away

ietaļa *nf* (of a husband's brother) brother-in-
law's wife

ietamborēt *vt* **1.** crochet a design; **2.** begin to
crochet

ietapt *vi* **1.** get in; **2.** please

ietarkšķēties *vr* begin to rattle

ietaujāties *vr* ask about

ietaukot *vt* grease

ietauņāt *vt* (col.) wrap, bundle up

ietauņāties *vr* (col.) bundle up

ietaupījums *nm* savings; economy (achieved)

ietaupīt *vt* save; economize

ietaupīties *vr* be saved

ietaurēt *vi* holler (in s.o.'s ear)

ietaurēties *vr* give a blast (on a horn), (of animals) give a roar

ietaustīties *vr* find one's way by groping

ietece *nf* mouth, estuary

ietecējies *adj, part* of **ietecēties** ripe

ietecēt *vi* **1.** pour in; **2.** flow into; **3.** scurry in(to)

ietecēties *vr* ripen

ietecināt *vt* (of viscous fluids) pour into

ieteicams *adj, part* of **ieteikt** recommendable, recommended

ieteicēj/s *nm,* ~**a** *nf* recommender

ieteikt *vt, vi* **1.** recommend; **2.** advise

ieteikties *vr* **1.** mention, raise one's voice; **2.** recommend oneself

ieteikums *nm* **1.** recommendation; **2.** advice

ieteka *nf* mouth, estuary

ietekāt *vt* trod, trample

ietekme *nf* influence; impact

ietekmējams *adj, part* of **ietekmēt** easily influenced

ietekmēšana *nf* influence; **fiziska i.** coercion

ietekmēt *vt* influence, affect; **fiziski i.** coerce

ietekmēties *vr* be influenced

ietekmīgi *adv* influentially

ietekmīgs *adj* influential

ietekmīgums *nm* influence

ieteksne *nf* temporary worker

ietekties *vr* ripen

ietēlot *vt* **1.** portray; **2.** imagine

ietēloties *vr* **1.** be portrayed; **2.** imagine oneself

ietelpt *vt* (philos.) inhabit, pervade

ietēmēt *vi* **1.** aim and shoot; aim and throw; **2.** mark, notice; retain

ietenterēt *vi* stagger in; toddle in

ietepēt *vt* lubricate

ietept *vt* lubricate

ietere *nf* (of a husband's brother) brother-in-law's wife

ietērēt *vt* (rare.) begin to spend

ietērpakmens *nm* face stone

ietērpķieģelis *nm* face brick

ietērps *nm* **1.** clothing, attire; uniform; **2.** artistic design; (stage) setting; **illustrātīvais i.** illustrations

ietērpt *vt* clothe, attire; accouter; **i. vārdos** put in words

ietērpties *vr* clothe oneself, dress up, put on (a garment)

ietēst *vt* **1.** shape (by cutting, hewing); **2.** begin to shape

ietēsums *nm* notch

ietetovējums *nm* tattoo

ietetovēt *vt* tattoo

ietiekties *vr* reach into

ietielēties *vr* be obstinate

ietielība *nf* obstinacy

ietielīgi *adv* obstinately

ietielīgs *adj* obstinate

ietielis *nm,* ~**e** *nf* obstinate person

ietiepība *nf* obstinacy

ietiepīgi *adv* obstinately

ietiepīgs *adj* obstinate

ietiepīgums *nm* obstinacy

ietiepša *nf, nm* obstinate person

ietiepties *vr* be obstinate

ietīkot *vt* covet

ietīkoties *vr* covet

ietikšķēties *vr* tick; begin to tick

ietikt *vi* get in

ietilpība *nf* **1.** capacity; **2.** spaciousness; **3.** labor intensiveness

ietilpīgs *adj* capacious; roomy; spacious

ietilpīgums *nm* **1.** capacity; roominess; spaciousness; **2.** labor intensiveness

ietilpināt *vt* **1.** fit, find room for; **2.** incorporate

ietilpt *vi* **1.** (of containers) hold; **2.** be part of

ietin *adv emph* of **iet**; **mašīna i. iet** the machine is working full blast

ietinamais *adj* wrapping (*adj*)

ietinamais papīrs *nm* wrapping paper

ietinamā mašīna *nf* wrapper

ietinkšķēties *vr* tinkle briefly

ietinums *nm* wrapping

ietipināt *vi* trip in(to); tiptoe in(to); (of toddlers) toddle in(to)

ietirgot *vt* acquire (through trade)

ietirkšķēties *vr* begin to chirr

ietirkšķināt *vt* make chirr

ietīstīt *vt* wrap up (carelessly or poorly), bundle up, swathe

ietīstīties *vr* wrap oneself; bundle up

ietīt *vt* 1. wrap; 2. envelop, shroud

ietīties *vr* 1. wrap oneself; 2. be enveloped, be shrouded

ietne *nf* sidewalk

ietonēt *vt* tint

ietracināt *vt* enrage

ietraips *nm* streak, spot

ietrakoties *vr* begin to go wild

ietrallināties *vr* warble

ietramdīt *vt* frighten, spook

ietrāpīt *vi* hit

ietrāpīties *vr* (col.) happen; turn out

ietraukt *v* 1. *vi* rush in(to); 2. *vt* drive in, blow in

ietraukties *vr* rush in(to)

ietrausties *vr* clamber in(to)

ietrenēt *vt* train

ietrenēties *vr* train oneself

ietrenkāt *vt* (of animals) drive into

ietrenkt *vt* (of animals) drive into

ietrīcēt *vi* = (rare.) **ietrīcēties**

ietrīcēties *vr* tremble; begin to tremble

ietricināt *vt* rattle, shake

ietrīcināt *vt* = **ietricināt**

ietriekt *vt* (of nails, soccer balls) drive in, (of a knife) plunge; **i. lodi pierē** put a bullet in one's head

ietriekties *vr* hurl oneself into; penetrate (by forceful impact)

ietriept *vt* grease; apply grease (on the inside)

ietrinkšķēties *vr* 1. strum, twang; 2. ring briefly, jingle

ietrinkšķināt *vt* strum; jingle

ietrinkšķināties *vr* 1. strum, twang; 2. ring briefly, jingle

ietrīsa *nf* quiver, tremor

ietrīsēt *vi* tremble, begin to tremble

ietrīsēties *vr* tremble, begin to tremble

ietrīsināt *vt* rattle, shake

ietrīsuļoties *vr* begin to vibrate

ietrīt *vt* rub in

ietrizuļoties *vr* begin to shimmer

ietrokšņoties *vr* make noises (briefly)

ietrūdējis *adj, part* of **ietrūdēt** rotten

ietrūdēt *vi* begin to rot

ietrūdināt *vt* make rot, decompose

ietrūkt *vi* snap; crack open

ietrūkums *nm* 1. break; 2. (mfg.) defect in a punched article

ietrunējis *adj, part* of **ietrunēt** rotten

ietrunēt *vi* begin to rot

ietrupēt *vi* begin to rot

ietrupināt *vt* cause dry rot

ietrusnīties *vr* clamber in(to)

ietrusēt *vi* dry out

ietūcīt *vt* (col.) 1. shove in; 2. whip; 3. wrap

ietūkt *vi* swell somewhat

ietumsa *nf* twilight, dusk

ietumst *vi* get dark

ietumšs *adj* swarthy, dusky

ietuntināt *vt* (col.) wrap, bundle

ietuntulēt *v* (col.) 1. *vt* wrap, bundle; 2. *vi* waddle in

ietuntulēties *vr* (col.) 1. bundle up; 2. waddle in

ietuntuļot *v* (col.) 1. *vt* wrap, bundle; 2. *vi* waddle in

ietuntuļoties *vr* (col.) 1. bundle up; 2. waddle in

ietupināt *vt* 1. make squat; place in an uncomfortable position; 2. (col.) jail

ietupt *vi* squat

ietupties *vr* squat

ieturējums *nm* withholding

ieturēt *vt* **1.** (of payments) withhold; **2.** keep, maintain, observe; **i. dietu** diet; **i. takti** (mus.) keep time; **3.** (col., of meals) have, eat; **i. dūšu** a. have a drink; b. eat; **4.** consider, think of

ieturēties *vr* **1.** observe moderation; **2.** have a hearty meal

ieturība *nf* reserve

ieturīgs *adj* reserved, restrained; reticent

ietusnīt *vi* chug in

ietusnīties *vr* **1.** chug in; **2.** pant briefly

ietuvu *adv* (rare.) nearby

ietvaice *nf* partial evaporation

ietvaicēt *vt* evaporate partly

ietvarlīste *nf* casing

ietvar/s *nm* frame; housing, casing; *pl* ~**i** scope

ietve *nf* sidewalk; ~**s mala** curb

ietvere *nf* setting, mounting; socket; clip

ietverīte *nf dim* of **ietvere**, setting, mounting; socket; clip

ietvert *vt* **1.** surround, encircle; frame; clasp; **2.** include; **i. vārdos** put in words

ietverties *vr* **1.** be included; **2.** take the form of; **3.** take hold of

ietvērums *nm* inclusion; fastening

ietvīcis *adj, part* of **ietvīkt** flushed, red in the face

ietvīkt *vi* **1.** flush, blush; **2.** become hot

ieubagot *vt* obtain by begging

ieūjināties *vr* hallo briefly

ieurbināt *vt* **1.** nibble; **2.** prod

ieurbt *vt* drill

ieurbties *vr* bore into; penetrate, pierce

ieurkstēties *vr* grunt briefly

ieurkšķēties *vr* grunt briefly

ieurkšķināties *vr* grunt briefly

ieurķēt *vt* poke back in

ieva *nf* European bird cherry

ievācēj/s *nm*, ~**a** *nf* **1.** collector; **2.** gatherer, picker; reaper

ievadāt *vt* **1.** lure in; **2.** (of an animal) accustom to follow

ievadāties *vr* move in

ievadcaurule *nf* inlet pipe

ievaddaļa *nf* introductory part

ievaddati *nm pl* (compu.) input data

ievade *nf* **1.** (compu.) input; **2.** filling

ievadiekārta *nf* (compu.) input equipment

ievadierīce *nf* (compu.) input device

ievadījums *nm* introduction

ievadīt *vt* **1.** put in, let in; inject, infuse; **2.** introduce; inaugurate; usher in; (of meetings) open; (of suits) bring, file; (of computer data) enter; **i. amatā** install, inaugurate; **i. sākumstāvoklī** (compu.) initialize; **3.** lead; pilot; **4.** introduce to; **i. darbā** show the ropes

ievadizvade *nf* (compu.) input-output

ievadkurss *nm* introductory course

ievadlekcija *nf* introductory lecture

ievadlīnija *nf* (mil.) start line

ievadnie/ks *nm*, ~**ce** *nf* editorial writer

ievadpiezīme *nf* introductory note

ievadraksts *nm* editorial

ievadreferāts *nm* introductory presentation

ievadruna *nf* opening speech

ievads *nm* **1.** introduction; **2.** (tech.) inlet; input device

ievadtonis *nm* **apakšējais i.** subtonic; **augšējais i.** supertonic

ievadvārdi *nm pl* opening remarks

ievagot *vt* furrow

ievaicāties *vr* ask (a question, casually or incidentally)

ievaidēties *vr* utter a moan; say in a moaning voice

ievaimanāties *vr* utter a wail

ievaine *nf* stand of bird cherries

ievainojamība *nf* vulnerability

ievainojums *nm* injury, wound; **virspusējs i.** flesh wound

ievainot *vt* injure, wound

ievainot/ais *nom adj* the wounded man; ~**ā** the wounded woman; ~**ie** the wounded

ievairot *vt* (rare.) increase

ievairoties *vr* (rare.) increase, multiply

ievaislot *vt* (of farm animals) breed

ievaisloties *vr* (of farm animals) breed

ievajadzēties *vr* be in need of

ievājs *nm* stand of bird cherries

ievākojums *nm* covers

ievākot *vt* put in covers

ievākt *vt* **1.** harvest; gather; **2.** collect; **3.** put in

ievākties *vr* move in

ievākums *nm* **1.** (crop) yield; **2.** collection

ievalcējums *nm* rolled shape (groove, depression, cam)

ievalcēt *vt* (tech.) roll in, shape

ievālēt *vi* (col.) strike, whack

ievalka *nf* (of wood) cross-grained place

ievalkaini *adv* (of wood grain) running transversely

ievalkains *adj* cross-grained

ievalkāt *vt* wear in

ievalkāties *vr* become comfortable through wear

ievalks *nm* bootstrap

ievalstīt *vt* (of barrels) roll in

ievaļa *nf* free time, leisure

ievaļīgs *adj* (of time) free

ievandīt *vt* mix in with (sth. else)

ievandīties *vr* get mixed in with; mingle in

ievankšķēties *vr* yap, bark

ievārdot *vt* recommend

ievārījums *nm* preserves

ievārīt *vt* (of fruits) preserve; **i. putru** (or **ziepes**) (col.) complicate things; mess things up

ievārīties *vr* **1.** thicken (in cooking); **2.** be absorbed (in cooking); **3.** settle (on the sides of a cooking vessel)

ievārstīt *vt* **1.** (of hinges) work (until they work smoothly); **2.** lace loosely

ievāršķis *nm* peasant sandal (pastala) lace

ievaskojums *nm* waxing

ievaskot *vt* wax

ievaukšķēties *vr* yap, bark

ievazājums *nm* introduction; introduced species

ievazāt *vt* (of diseases, ideas) introduce; (of dirt) track in

ievazāties *vr* mooch in; (of animals) come in (from the wild)

ievēcināt *vt* (of wings) practice flapping

ievedības *nf pl* welcome (to a new arrival)

ievedināt *vt* lure in(to)

ievēdīt *vt, vi* waft in

ievedmuita *nf* import duty

ievedne *nf* daughter-in-law

ievedtirdzniecība *nf* import trade

ievedums *nm* import

ieveidne *nf* form (mold)

ieveid/nis *nm* form (mold); ~**ņi** formwork

ieveidojums *nm* **1.** (of gems) setting; **2.** shaping

ieveidot *vt* shape; (of hair) set

ieveidoties *vr* be shaped; be set

ieveids *nm* **1.** (of gems) setting; **2.** shaping

ievējot *vi* waft in

ievēkšēties *vr* start crying

ievēkšķēties *vr* start crying

ievēlējamība *nf* election procedure

ievelēt *vt* **1.** (of laundry) soften by pounding; **2. labi** ~**s** (of a laundry pounding stick) much used

ievēlēt *vt* elect; **i. amatā** elect to an office; **i. par priekšsēdētāju** elect chairman

ievelka *nf* **1.** rough, uneven place in wood; **2.** cove

ievelmējums *nm* rolled shape

ievelmēt *vt* (metall.) roll, shape by rolling

ievelt *vt* roll into

ievelties *vr* **1.** roll, roll into; **2.** get caught (in the process of rolling)

ievemt *vt* vomit into

ievērība *nf* attention, notice; ~s **cienīgs** noteworthy

ievērīgi *adv* attentively

ievērīgs *adj* attentive

ievērīgums *nm* attentiveness

ievērojami *adv* considerably

ievērojamība *nf* importance

ievērojams *adj* 1. important; 2. eminent; remarkable; noteworthy; 3. considerable

ievērot *vt* 1. notice; 2. (of laws, customs) observe, keep; **i. distanci** keep one's distance; **i. reglamentu** (of meetings) keep within the time limit; 3. consider; 4. (of applications, petitions) grant

ievērpt *vt* spin into

ievērpties *vr* 1. be spun into; 2. (fig.) begin

ievērst *vt* direct into

ievērt *vt* 1. (of a needle) thread; **i. diegu** thread a needle; 2. pinch (sth. in a door)

ievērties *vr* 1. be threaded, be laced; 2. be pinched

ievēsmot *vi* waft in

ievest *vt* 1. bring in(to) (with a vehicle); 2. show in; lead into; **i. amatā** install, inaugurate; **i. sa-rakstā** enter in the list; **i. valdījumā** (jur.) put in possession; 3. import; 4. (of plants, animals) in-troduce; 5. establish

ievesties *vr* (of introduced plants, animals) become common

ievešana *nf* 1. installation, inauguration; 2. importation; 3. introduction; 4. establishment

ievēzēt *vt* swing (in preparation); (of wings) flap (preparatory to flight)

ievēzēties *vr* take a swing; (of birds) begin to flap one's wings

ievēziens *nm* backswing

ievibrēt *vt* set to vibrate

ievibrēties *vr* begin to vibrate; vibrate briefly

ievicināt *vt* swing (in preparation to striking or flying)

ievicojies *adj, part* of **ievicoties** (col.) intoxicated

ievicot *vi* 1. (col.) drink; 2. switch, whip

ievicoties *vr* (col.) drink

ievidžināties *vr* twitter briefly

ieviest *vt* introduce, establish

ievies/ties *vr* take root; spread, gain ground; in-fest; (of errors, misprints) slip in; **plaši** ~**ies** widespread

ievietot *vt* put in, place; (of articles) publish; in-clude (in a collection, list)

ievietoties *vr* 1. hold, have the capacity; 2. settle, take position; get in

ievijums *nm* intertwining (a thing intertwined)

ievīkstināt *vt* wrap

ievīkstīt *vt* wrap

ievīkstīties *vr* bundle up, wrap oneself

ievīkšķīt *vt* wrap

ievilcējtinums *nm* pull-in winding

ievilcināt *vt* protract, draw out

ievilcināties *vr* drag on

ievīlējums I *nm* filed groove

ievīlējums II *nm* hem

ievīlēt I *vt* mark with a file; file

ievīlēt II *vt* hem

ievīlēties *vr* be filed in

ievilināt *vt* lure in, entice into; entrap, decoy; **i. cilpā** snare

ievilkt *vt* 1. pull in(to); **i. buras** strike sail; **i. dū-mu** (col.) smoke; **i. elpu** take a breath; **i. enkuru** weigh anchor; 2. (of shoes) lace, (of elastic) insert; thread; 3. (of arms, feet) push into (clothing, shoes); 4. (of dislocated limbs) set; 5. (of fabrics) gather; 6. draw a line; **i. sliedes** (of skis, sleds) make tracks; 7. (of electricity, gas, water) install; 8. draw out; 9. (com.) also **i. nāsīs** (or **azotē, degunā**) swipe, filch; 10. (col.) draw into (an argument); 11. (math.) inscribe; 12. (col. *vi*) hit

ievilkties *vr* 1. pull oneself in; (col.) drag oneself in(to), crawl into; 2. (of lines) form; 3. (of infusions) steep; **4.** also **i. garumā** (col.) drag, go on and on; **5.** (col.) move in; **6.** insinuate oneself

ievilkums *nm* (of fabric) gather

ievilnīt *v* **1.** *vi* pour in; **2.** *vt* (of waves) carry into; **3.** *vt* arouse

ievilstīt *vt* lure in, entice into

ievilt *vt* lure in, entice into

ieviļāt *vt* make a depression (by lying)

ieviļināt *vt* roll (in dough, batter)

ieviļņojums *nm* **1.** pouring in; **2.** arousal

ieviļņot *v* **1.** *vi* pour in; **2.** *vt* (of waves) carry into; **3.** *vt* arouse

ieviļņoties *vr* (of waves) begin to arise; (of the heart) palpitate, beat faster

ievingrināt *vt* acquire skill; **i. aci** acquire an eye (for); **i. roku** become a practiced hand

ievingrināties *vr* train oneself, become skillful, acquire the knack

ievīpsnāties *vr* smile ironically

ievirināt *vt* (of hinges) loosen (by working)

ievīrināt *vt* encourage

ievirmot *vi* swirl in

ievirmoties *vr* ripple briefly

ievirot *vt* (of doors, windows) hang

ievirpināt *vt* swirl in

ievirpošana *nf* (pottery) jollying

ievirpot *v* **1.** *vt* cut on a lathe; (pottery) jolly; **2.** *vi* swirl in

ievirpuļot *vi* swirl in

ievirt *vi* **1.** thicken (in cooking); **2.** be absorbed (in cooking); **3.** settle (on the sides of a cooking vessel)

ievirze *nf* **1.** course, tendency, orientation; predisposition; **2.** topic

ievirzes sesija *nf* orientation session

ievirzījums *nm* **1.** direction; **2.** placement; **3.** guidance

ievirzīt *vt* **1.** direct; guide; **i. pareizās sliedēs** bring in line; **i. sliedēs** put on track; **2.** insert; **i. vaigus uz iekšu** suck in one's cheeks

ievirzīties *vr* **1.** slowly move or glide in a given direction; **2.** (of rivers, roads) run (in the direction of or into); **i. vecajās sliedēs** (fig.) get back on track

ievīst *vi* wilt a little

ievīstīt *vt* wrap, bundle up

ievīstīties *vr* wrap oneself up, bundle up

ievīt *vt* **1.** interweave; **2.** (of a nest) make; **3.** (fig, of speeches, songs) inject

ievīteroties *vr* (of birds) sing briefly

ievīties *vr* **1.** intertwine; **2.** meander into; **3.** find its way into

ievizēties *vr* sparkle, glitter briefly

ievizināt *vt* bring in (in a vehicle)

ievizmoties *vr* sparkle, glitter briefly

ievizuļoties *vr* glitter briefly, shimmer briefly

ievoga *nf* bird cherry

ievziedi *nm pl* bird cherry blossoms

iezagšus *adv* (rare.) furtively

iezagties *vr* steal, sneak, or slip in(to); (fig., of doubts) creep in; **i. acīs** (of tears) well up

iezāģējums *nm* saw cut

iezāģēt *vi* **1.** saw, cut with a saw; saw into, cut with a saw into; **2.** (com.) do s.o. dirt

iezaigoties *vr* sparkle, glitter briefly

iezalgoties *vr* sparkle, glitter briefly

iezaļgans *adj* slightly greenish

iezaļot *vi* begin to green

iezāļot *vt* (obs.) embalm

iezaļš *adj* greenish

iezārkot *vt* coffin

iezēģelēt *vi* sail in

iezelt *vi* begin to green

iezeltīt *vt* **1.** gild; **2.** (col.) strike, whack

iezemējums *nm* (el.) grounding

iezemēt *vt* (el.) ground

iezemētājs *nm* (el.) ground plate

iezemiet/is *nm*, ~e *nf* native

iezemojums *nm* (el.) grounding

iezemot *vt* (el.) ground

iezibēt *vi* flash

iezibēties *vr* flash

iezibsnīt *vi* flash

iezibsnīties *vr* flash

ieziemot *vt* winterize

ieziepēt *vt* soap, lather; (sl.) bribe

ieziepēties *vr* soap oneself

ieziest *vt* grease, oil; (of cracks, joints) fill (with a plastic substance)

ieziesties *vr* rub oneself (with oil, ointment)

iezilēt *vi* turn bluish

iezilgans *adj* bluish

iezilgmoties *vr* (of sth. blue or bluish) appear

iezilgs *adj* bluish

iezili *adv* in a bluish color

iezilināt *vt* (of laundry) blue

iezilnēties *vr* (of sth. blue) appear

iezils *adj* bluish

iezīme *nf* 1. mark; 2. characteristic, feature

iezīmējums *nm* 1. design; 2. delineation

iezīmēt *vt* 1. draw; 2. mark; (chem.) tag; 3. outline

iezīmēties *vr* 1. be outlined, show, appear; 2. be marked, be distinguished

iezīmēts *adj, part* of **iezīmēt** (chem.) tracer (*adj*)

iezīmība *nf* characteristic; distinctiveness

iezīmīgi *adv* characteristically; distinctively

iezīmīgs *adj* characteristic, identifying; distinctive

iezināties *vr* (rare.) notice, remember

iezis *nm* rock formation

iezīst *vt* suck in

iezīsties *vr* (of animals with suckers) attach to; (fig., col., of smells) cling to

iezt *vt* (of teeth) bare

iezubrīt *vt* (com.) drill, learn by rote

iezuzēties *vr* begin to buzz; buzz briefly

iezvanīt *vt* ring in, announce by ringing; (fig.) herald

iezvanītāj/s *nm*, **~a** *nf* (fig.) forerunner, herald

iezvanīties *vr* ring (briefly)

iezvejot *vt* (rare.) fish (and fill a container with fish)

iezvelt *v* 1. *vt* (of heavy objects) roll in, dump in; 2. *vi* (col.) strike a heavy blow

iezvelties *vr* 1. plump oneself (into a chair, bed); 2. (col.) wobble in

iezvēroties *vr* flare up

iezvidzēties *vr* flash

iezviegties *vr* neigh

iezvilu *adv* slightly tilted

iezvīļoties *vr* shimmer, begin to shimmer

iežadzināties *vr* (of birds) chatter briefly

iežagarot *vt* (col.) whip, birch

iežagarēt *vt* (col.) whip, birch

iežagoties *vi* hiccup (briefly)

iežaut *v* (com.) 1. *vt* (of liquids) dump; 2. *vi* hit

iežauties *vr* (com.) fall into

iežāvāties *vr* yawn

iežāvēt *vt* dry; begin to dry

iežēla *nf* compassion

iežēlīgs *adj* compassionate

iežēlināt *vt* move to pity

iežēlošanās *nfr* compassion

iežēloties *vr* be moved to pity, feel compassion

iežilbt *vi*, usu. *part* **iežilbis** tipsy

iežļāgt *vt* (com., of liquids) dump in(to)

iežmauga *nf* narrowing, constriction; isthmus, neck of land

iežmaugt *vt* 1. compress; lace in; 2. constrict

iežmaugties *vr* squeeze oneself into

iežmiegt *vt* 1. tuck in; squeeze; clutch; 2. constrict

iežņauga *nf* narrowing, constriction; isthmus, neck of land

iežņaugt *vt* 1. compress; lace in; 2. constrict

iežņaugties *vr* 1. (of laces, belts) cut into; 2. squeeze oneself into; 3. (rare.) get stuck

iežņaugums *nm* narrowing, constriction; isthmus, neck of land

iežogojums *nm* enclosure, fence; hoarding

iežogot *vt* fence in, enclose

iežogs *nm* (fig.) limitation; (rare.) fence

iežūrēt *vi* (com.) peek in

iežūt *vi* 1. dry (inside a place); 2. dry up; 3. shriv-el, shrink in drying

iežuvums *nm* dried-out spot

iežūžināt *vt* lull to sleep

iežūžināties *vr* begin to rustle softly

iežūžot *vt* lull to sleep

iežūžoties *vr* (poet.) begin to rustle softly

iežvadzēties *vr* begin to jingle, clang, or rattle; jingle, clang or rattle a little

iežvarkstēties *vr* rattle briefly

iežvīgoties *vr* begin to rustle

iežvīkstēties *vr* swish, whiz

iežviukstēties *vr* swish, whiz

īga *nf, nm* grouch, crank

īgas *nf pl* surliness, peevishness

igaun/is *nm*, **~iete** *nf* Estonian

igauniski *adv* in Estonian, (speak) Estonian

igaunisks *adj* Estonian

igaunisms *nm* Estonian loan word

īgme *nf* (rare.) surliness, peevishness

īgne *nf* surliness, peevishness

īgnēt *vi* feel disgusted; sicken; resent; *vt* peeve, aggravate

īgnēties *vr* peeve, feel aggravated, show resentment

īgni *adv* surlily, peevishly

ignimbrīts *nm* welded tuff

īgnis *nm* sourpuss, crank

ignorance *nf* ignorance

ignorant/s *nm*, **~e** *nf* ignoramus

ignorants *adj* ignorant

ignorēt *vt* ignore

īgnoties *vr* show resentment, peeve

īgns *adj* surly, peevish

īgnums *nm* surliness, peevishness

īgņa *nf, nm* grouch, crank

īgņoties *vr* show resentment, peeve

īgonis *nm* grouch, crank

īgoņa *nf, nm* grouch, crank

igreks *nm* (the letter) y

īgt *vi* act surly or peevish; grumble

iguāna *nf* iguana

igvartis *nm* (reg.) pond

igvāts *nm* live-box

ij I *partic* (col., reg.) even

ij II *conj* (reg.) 1. and; 2. **ij . . . ij** both . . . and

Ijaba asaras *nf pl* (bot.) Job's-tears

ik *partic* each, every; **ik brīdi** constantly; **ik dienas** every day; **ik pa (gadu)** every (year); **ik pārdienas** every other day; **ik reizes** every time; **ik uz soļa** at every step

īkasts *nm* live-box

ikbrīd *adv* constantly

ikdiena *nf* daily routine; *gen* ~s daily, everyday; (mil.) non-tactical

ikdienas *adv* every day

ikdienēji *adv* in an everyday manner

ikdienējs *adj* everyday

ikdienība *nf* everyday routine, humdrum life

ikdienīgi *adv* in a humdrum manner

ikdienīgs *adj* everyday, ordinary, humdrum

ikdienišķi *adv* in a humdrum manner

ikdienišķs *adj* everyday, ordinary, humdrum

ikdienišķums *nm* everyday routine, humdrum life

ikebana *nf* ikebana

ikgadējs *adj* annual

ikkatr/s *pron* every; *nm* everyone; **~a** *f*

ikku[r]/š [ŗ] *pron* every; *nm* everyone; **~a** *f*

ikmēneša *indecl adj* monthly

iknedēļas *adj* weekly

[i]kon/a [ī] *nf* icon; **~u gleznieсība** icono-graphy

[i]koniski [ī] *adv* iconically

[i]konisks [ī] *adj* iconic

[i]konogr[ā]fisks [ī][a] *adj* iconographic

[i]konogr[ā]fs [ī][a] *nm* iconographer

[i]konoklasms [ī] *nm* iconoclasm

[i]konoklastisks [ī] *adj* iconoclastic

[i]konoklasts [ī] *nm* iconoclast

[i]konolatrija [ī] *nf* iconolatry

[i]konometrija [ī] *nf* iconometry

[i]konometrs [ī] *nm* iconometer

[i]konoskops [ī] *nm* iconoscope

[i]konostass [ī] *nm* iconostasis

īkosaedrisks *adj* icosahedral

īkosaedrs *nm* icosahedron

ikrains *adj* full of roe

ikreiz *adv* every time

ikreizējs *adj* for each occasion

ikreizes *adv* every time

ikreizi *adv* every time

ikri I *nm pl* (anat.) calf

ikr/i II *nm pl* **1.** roe, spawn; **2.** caviar; ~u maizīte caviar sandwich

ikrots *adj* full of roe

ikru bruņas *nf* (armor) jamb

iksa kājas *nf pl* knock-kneed

iksija *nf* ixia, corn lily

ikss *nm* (the letter) x

īkstis I *nm* thumb

īkstis II *nf pl* kidneys

īksts *nf*, usu. *pl* īkstis kidney

īkšķa nospiedums *nm* thumbprint

īkšķa uzmava *nf* thumbstall

īkšķis *nm* thumb

īkšķītis *nm* **1.** *dim* of īkšķis; **2.** Īkšķītis Tom Thumb; **3.** wren

īkšķot *vi* thumb one's way

iktus *nm* ictus

ikucis *nm* **1.** (col.) thumb; (sign of contempt) the fig; **2.** morsel

ikvien/s *pron* every; *nm* everyone; ~a *f*

ilācija *nf* illation

īlaidene *nf* two-hook fishing rod

īlangīlangs *nm* ylang-ylang

ildzināties *vr* hestiate; dawdle, put off

ildziņis *adv* (reg., of time) long

ilecebras *nf pl* Corrigiola

ilegāli *adv* = illegāli

ilegālists *nm* = illegālists

ilegalitāte *nf* = illegālitāte

ilegāls *adj* = illegāls

ilegitims *adj* = illegitīms

īlens *nm* awl

ilgām *adv* long, a long time

ilgana *nf* bitterling

ilgas *nf pl* longing, yearning

ilggadējs *adj* of many years, of long standing

ilggadība *nf* perennation

ilggadīgais sasalums *nm* permafrost

ilggadīgā žultszālīte *nf* perennial knawel

ilggadīgie lini *nm pl* Lewis' wild flax

ilggadīgs *adj* perennial

ilggadu *indecl adj* perennial

ilggulētāj/s *nm*, ~a *nf* long sleeper

ilggul/is *nm*, ~e *nf* long sleeper

ilgguļa *nf, nm* long sleeper

ilgi *adv* a long time; stundām (dienām, gadiem) i. for hours (days, years); i. un gaŗi thoroughly, at length

ilgizturība *nf* elastic limit

ilglaicīgi *adv* in the long term

ilglaicīgs *adj* long-term

ilglaika *indecl adj* long-term

ilglietojams *adj* durable; (mil.) non-expendable

ilgmūža *indecl adj* long-lived

ilgmūžība *nf* longevity

ilgonis *nm* dawdler

ilgošanās *nfr* longing

ilgot I *vt* long for

ilgot II *emph* of ilgoties; i. ilgoties long fervently

ilgoties *vr* long for, yearn for; i. pēc mājām be homesick

ilgotne *nf* (rare.) long period of time

ilgots *adj* longed for, long wished for

ilgperioda *indecl adj* long-period

ilgpilns *adj* longing, yearning; pining

ilgs *adj* (of time) long; protracted

ilgsēdīte *nf* (folk.) epithet for a girl who remains unmarried a long time

ilgspēja *nf* sustainability

ilgspējīgs *adj* sustainable

ilgspēlētājs *nm* long-playing

ilgstamība *nf* durability

ilgstamības pretestība *nf* fatigue strength

ilgstība *nf* duration

ilgstoši *adv* lastingly, protractedly

ilgstošs *adj, part* of **ilgt** lasting; protracted; sustained; (gram., of tenses) continuous

ilgšāviens *nm* hang fire

ilgt *vi* last, continue, go on

ilgtermiņa *indecl adj* long-term

ilgul/is *nm,* ~**e** *nf* dreamer

ilgum *adv emph* of **ilgs; i. ilgs** exceedingly long

ilgums *nm* duration

ilgviļņi *nm pl* permanent wave

ilgviļņot *vt* (of permanent wave) set

ilgziedu begonija *nf* multiflora begonia

iliakāls *adj* ileac

ilicijas *nf pl* Illicium

ilīnijs *nm* illinium

ilīrieši *nm pl* Illyrians

iliterāts *nm* = **illiterāts**

ilknis *nm* fang; tusk

ilkņains *adj* fanged

ilkņzivs *nf* dentex

ilkss *nf* thill

i|llā|tīvs [la] *nm* illative

i|llā|tīvs [la] *adj* illative

i|ll|egāli [l] *adv* illegally

i|ll|egālists [l] *nm* illegal activist

i|ll|egālitāte [l] *nf* illegality

i|ll|egāls [l] *adj* illegal

i|ll|egitīmi [l] *adv* illegitimately

i|ll|egitīms [l] *adj* illegitimate

i|ll|iterāts [l] *nm* illiterate

i|ll|oģiski [l] *adv* illogically

i|ll|oģisks [l] *adj* illogical

i|ll|okūcija [l] *nf* illocution

i|ll|okūtors [l] *nm* illocutor

i|ll|uminācija [l] *nf* illumination

i|ll|umināti [l] *nm pl* Illuminati

i|ll|umin|a|tors [l][ā] *nm* porthole; scuttle

i|ll|uminēt [l] *vt* illuminate

i|ll|ustrācija [l] *nf* illustration

i|ll|ustr|ā|tīvi [l]|a] *adv* illustratively, by way of illustration

i|ll|ustr|ā|tīvisms [l]|a] *nm* pictorialism

i|ll|ustr|ā|tīv/s [l]|a] *adj* illustrative

i|ll|ustr|ā|tor/s [l]|a] *nm,* ~**e** *nf* illustrator

i|ll|ustrējums [l] *nm* illustration

i|ll|ustrēt [l] *vt* illustrate

i|ll|ustrētāj/s [l] *nm,* ~**a** *nf* ilustrator

i|llū|viāls [lu] *adj* illuvial

i|ll|ūvijs [l] *nm* illuvium

i|ll|ūzija [l] *nf* illusion

i|llū|zionisms [lu] *nm* illusionism

i|llū|zionist/s [lu] *nm,* ~**e** *nf* illusionist

i|llū|zoriski [lu] *adv* illusorily

i|llū|zorisks [lu] *adj* illusory

i|llū|zori [lu] *adv* illusorily

i|llū|zors [lu] *adj* illusory

ilmaka *nf, nm* glutton

ilmenits *nm* ilmenite

ilokūcija *nf* = **illokūcija**

ilokūtors *adj* = **illokūtors**

ilum- See **illūm-**

ilustr- See **illustr-**

iluviāls *adj* = **illuviāls**

iluz- or **-ilūz-** See **illūz-**

ilzene *nf* daisy

ilzīte *nf* chamomile

iļģis *nm* ghost of a dead person

imadžisms *nm* imagism

imaginācija *nf* imagination

imaginārs *adj* imaginary

imago *indecl nm* imago

im|a|ms [ā] *nm* imam

imanence *nf* immanence

imanenti *adv* immanently

imanent/s *adj* immanent

imateriāli *adv* immaterially

imateriāl/s *adj* immateria

imateriālisms *nm* immaterialism

imateri|a|litāte [ā] *nf* immateriality

imatrikulācija *nf* (educ.) enrollment

imatrikulēt *vt* (educ.) enroll

imažinisks *adj* imagist

imažinisms *nm* imagism

imbecilitāte *nf* imbecility

imbecils *nm* imbecile

imbibicija *nf* imbibition

imediāts *adj* immediate

imenss *adj* immense

imensitāte *nf* immensity

imersija *nf* immersion

imidazolīns *nm* imidazoline

imids *nm* imide

imigrācija *nf* immigration

imigrant/s *nm*, ~**e** *nf* immigrant

imigrēt *vi* immigrate

imīns *nm* imine

imisija *nf* immission

imitācija *nf* imitation

imit[a]tor/s [ā] *nm*, ~**e** *nf* imitator

imitējums *nm* imitation

imitēt *vt* imitate

imma *nf* tantrum

immāties *vr* throw tantrums

immelmanis *nm* (aeron.) Immelman

immīgi *adv* capriciously

immīgs *adj* capricious

imobilija *nf* real estate

imobilizācija *nf* immobilization

imobilizēt *vt* immobilize

imobils *adj* immobile

imorālisms *nm* immorality

imorteles *nf pl* (bot.) everlasting

impala *nf* impala

impamp/is *nm*, ~**a** *nf* **1.** (folk.) a magical fusion of a living being and an inanimate object; **2.** con-glomerate, congeries

impedance *nf* (el.) impedance

imperatas *nf pl* cogongrass

imper[a]tīvi [ā] *adv* imperatively

imper[a]tīvs [ā] *nm* (gram., philos.) imperative

imper[a]tīvs [ā] *adj* imperative

imper[a]tore [ā] *nf* empress

imper[a]torpingvīns [ā] *nm* emperor penguin

imper[a]tors [ā] *nm* emperor

imperfektīvi *adv* imperfectively

imperfektivitāte *nf* imperfectivity

imperfektīvs *adj* imperfective

imperfekts *nm* (gram.) impefect tense

imperiālisms *nm* imperialism

imperiālistiski *adv* imperialistically

imperiālistisks *adj* imperialistic

imperiālists *nm* imperialist

imperiāls *adj* imperial

impērija *nf* empire

impērijas stils *nm* Empire (style)

impersonāli *adv* impersonally

impersonāls *adj* impersonal

impertinence *nf* impertinence

impertinents *adj* impertinent

impetigo *nm indecl* impetigo

impīčments *nm* impeachment

implantācija *nf* implantation

implantāts *nm* (med.) implant

implantēt *vt* (med.) implant

implicēt *vt* involve

implic[i]ti [ī] *adv* implicitly

implic[i]ts [ī] *adj* implicit

implikācija *nf* implication

imponderābilijas *nf pl* imponderabilia

imponēt *vi* impress, command respect

importēt *vt* import

importētāj/s *nm*, ~**a** *nf* importer

importier/is *nm*, ~**e** *nf* importer

importmuita *nf* import duty

importosta *nf* import harbor

importprece *nf* imported item; *pl* ~**s** imported goods

imports *nm* import, importation

imposts *nm* (arch.) impost

impotence *nf* impotence

impotents *adj* impotent

impozanti *adv* imposingly, impressively

impozants *adj* imposing, impressive

impozantums *nm* imposingness

impregnācija *nf* (tech.) impregnation, infusion, chemical treatment

impregnējums *nm* chemical treatment (of lumber)

impregnēt *vt* (tech.) impregnate, treat (lumber chemically)

impresārijs *nm* impresario

impresija *nf* impression

impresionisms *nm* impressionism

impresionistiski *adv* impressionistically

impresionistisks *adj* impressionistic

impresionist/s *nm* impressionist; ~e *nf*

imprompts *nm* impromptu

improvizācija *nf* improvisation

improviz[a]tor/s [ā] *nm* improviser; ~e *nf*

improvizēt *vi, vt* improvise

improvizētāj/s *nm*, ~a *nf* improviser

improvizēts *adj, part* of **improvizēt** improvised; impromptu; extemporaneous

impulsēt *vt* stimulate, occasion, give rise to

impulsivitāte *nf* impulsivity

impulsīvi *adv* impulsively

impulsīvs *adj* impulsive

impulsīvums *nm* impulsiveness

impulss *nm* 1. impulse; 2. pulse

impulstrokšņi *nm pl* (el.) impulse noise

impulsvilnis *nm* impulse wave

imputābls *adj* imputable

imputācija *nf* imputation

imput[a]tīvi [ā] *adv* imputatively

imput[a]tīvs [ā] *adj* imputative

imputēt *vi* impute

imūndefic[i]ts [ī] *nm* immunodeficiency

imūndepresants *nm* immunosuppressive

imūndepresija *nf* immunosuppression

imūndepresīvs *adj* immunosuppressive

imūnfarmakoloģija *nf* immunopharmacology

imūnglobulīns *nm* immunoglobulin

im[u]nitāte [ū] *nf* immunity

im[u]nizācija [ū] *nf* immunization

im[u]nizēt [ū] *vt* immunize

im[u]noc[ī]ts [ū][i] *nm* immunocyte

im[u]nog[ē]ns [ū][e] *nm* immunogen

im[u]noģen[ē]tika [ū][e] *nf* immunogenetics

im[u]nologs [ū] *nm* immunologist

im[u]noloģija [ū] *nf* immunology

im[u]nosupresīvs [ū] *adj* immunosuppressive

imūnpatoloģija *nf* immunopathology

imūns *adj* immune

imūnserums *nm* antiserum

imūnšūna *nf* immunocyte

imūnterapija *nf* immunotherapy

imūnviela *nf* antibody

inadekvāti *adv* inadequately

inadekvāts *adj* inadequate

inaktivācija *nf* inactivation

inaugurācija *nf* inauguration

inaugurāldisertācija *nf* inaugural dissertation

inaugurālraksts *nm* inaugural paper

inaugurēt *vt* inaugurate

inavigabilitāte *nf* innavigability

incestēt *vi* commit incest

incests *nm* incest

in[ch]oatīvs [h] *adj* inchoate

incidence *nf* incidence

incidents *nm* incident

incis *nm* (col.) pussy

incizija *nf* incision

incu[ch]ts [h] *nm* inbreeding

indaines *nf pl* white swallowwort

indans *nm* indan

inde *nf* poison; venom

indefiniti *adv* indefinitely

indefinits *adj* indefinite

indeklinabils *adj* indeclinable

indek[s] [ss] *nm* index; **apakšējais i.** subscript; **augšējais i.** superscript

indeksācija *nf* indexation

indeks[a]tors [ā] *nm* indexer

indeksēt *vt* index

indemnitāte *nf* indemnity

independenti *adv* independently

independents *nm* (rel.) Independent; *pl* ~i Independency independents *adj* independent

indesķirzaka *nf* Gila monster

indes zobs *nm* (of a snake) fang

indēt *vt* poison

indeterminisms *nm* indeterminism

indēties *vr* take poison

indeve *nf* 1. (obs.) bad habit; 2. ailment

indiān/is *nm*, ~iete *nf* American Indian

indiāņu rīsi *nm pl* wild rice

indicēt *vt* report, denounce, blow the whistle; indicate

indicijas *nf pl* signs, clues, grounds for suspicion

indiet/is *nm*, ~e *nf* East Indian

indiference *nf* indifference

indiferenti *adv* indifferently

indiferentisms *nm* indifferentism

indiferents *adj* indifferent

indīgais suma[ch]s [h] *nm* poison sumac

indigenāts *nm* rights of the native population

indīgi *adv* poisonously; venomously; toxically

indignācija *nf* indignation

indigo *nm indecl* indigo

indigofera *nf* indigo plant

indīgs *adj* poisonous; venomous; toxic

indīgums *nm* toxicity; poisonousness; venomousness

Indijas antilope *nf* black buck

Indijas degunradzis *nm* Indian rhinoceros

Indijas kajans *nm* pigeon pea

Indijas lācis *nm* sloth bear

Indijas mandele *nf* Malabar almond

indijs *nm* indium

indikācija *nf* indication

indik[a]tīvs [ā] *nm* (gram.) indicative

indik[a]tors [ā] *nm* indicator

indikatrise *nf* indicatrix

indirekti *adv* indirectly

indirekts *adj* indirect

indiskrēcija *nf* indiscretion

indiskrēti *adv* indiscreetly

indiskrēts *adj* indiscreet

indiskutabls *adj* not open to discussion

indisponēts *adj* indisposed

indispozīcija *nf* indisposition

indisputabli *adv* indisputably

indisputabls *adj* indisputable

indivīds *nm* individual

individuācija *nf* individuation

individuāli *adv* individually

individuālisms *nm* individualism

individuālistiski *adv* individualistically

individuālistisks *adj* individualistic

individuālist/s *nm*, ~e *nf* individualist

individu[a]litāte [ā] *nf* individuality; self

individu[a]lizācija [ā] *nf* individualization

individu[a]lizēt [ā] *vt* individualize

individuāls *adj* individual

indoāriešu *indecl adj* Indo-Aryan

indoeiropieš/i *nm pl* Indo-Europeans; ~u *indecl adj* Indo-European

indoģermāņu *indecl adj* Indo-European

indoirāņi *nm pl* Indo-Iranians

indoksils *nm* indoxyl

indoktrinācija *nf* indoctrination

indolence *nf* indolence

indolenti *adv* indolently

indolents *adj* indolent

indolīns *nm* indoline

indolo/gs *nm*, ~ģe *nf* Indologist

indoloģija *nf* Indology

indols *nm* indole

indonēziet/is *nm*, ~e *nf* Indonesian

indosabils *adj* endorsable

indosaments *nm* endorsement

indosants *nm* endorser

indosat[a]rs [ā] *nm* endorsee

indosāts *nm* endorsee

indosēt *vt* endorse

inducēt *vt* induce

indukcija *nf* induction

indukcijas spole *nf* inductance coil

induktance *nf* inductance

induktīvi *adv* inductively

indukt|i|vitāte [ī] *nf* (el.) induction
induktīvs *adj* inductive
induktors *nm* inductor, induction motor; inductive heater
induktotermija *nf* inductothermy
indulgence *nf* (rel.) indulgence
indults *nm* (rel.) indulgence
indurācija *nf* induration
industriāli *adv* industrially
industri|a|lizācija [ā] *nf* industrialization
industri|a|lizēt [ā] *vt* industrialize
industriāls *adj* industrial
industrija *nf* industry
indzēt *vi* (rare.) sound
inerce *nf* (phys.) inertia
inerces spēks *nm* momentum
inerciāli *adv* intertially
inerciāls *adj* inertial
inerti *adv* inertly
inertība *nf* inertness
inerts *adj* (phys., chem.) inert; (fig.) sluggish
inertums *nm* inertness; sluggishness
inervācija *nf* innervation
inervēt *vt* innervate
infallibili *adv* infallibly
infallibilisms *nm* infallibilism
infallibilitāte *nf* infallibility
infallibils *adj* infallible
infāmija *nf* infamy
infāms *adj* infamous
infanta *nf* infanta
infanterija *nf* infantry
infanterists *nm* infantryman
infanti|c|īds [s] *nm* infanticide
infantili *adv* in an infantile manner
infantilisms *nm* infantilism
infantils *adj* infantile
infants *nm* infante
infarkts *nm* infarct
infekcija *nf* infection; hospitālā i. nosocomial infection; strutainā i. pyogenic infection; ~s infectious

infekcionist/s *nm*, ~e *nf* infectious disease specialist
infekciozi *adv* infectuously
infekciozs *adj* infectuous
inferiors *adj* inferior
infernāls *adj* infernal
infestācija *nf* infestation
inficēt *vt* infect
inficēties *vr* become infected
infikss *nm* infix
infiltrācija *nf* infiltration
infiltr|a|tīvi [ā] *adv* by infiltration
infiltr|a|tīvs [ā] *adj* infiltrative
infiltrāts *nm* infiltration
infiltrēt *vt* infiltrate
infiltrēties *vr* infiltrate
infinīti *adv* infinitely
infinitīvs *nm* (gram.) infinitive
infinīts *adj* indeterminate, unlimited
inflācija *nf* inflation; slēptā i. latent inflation
infleksibls *adj* inflexible
infleksija *nf* inflection
influence *nf* influenza
informācija *nf* information; ~s atguve information retrieval; ~s ietilpība information capacity; ~s maģistrāle information superhighway; ~s noplūde information leak; ~s pārmērība information redundancy; ~s pārslogojums information overload
informant/s *nm*, ~e *nf* informant
inform|a|tika [ā] *nf* informatics
inform|a|tīvi [ā] *adv* informatively
inform|a|tīvs [ā] *adj* informative
inform|a|tor/s [ā] *nm* 1. informant; information officer; ~e *nf*; 2. information board
informēt *vt* inform
informētājs *nm*, ~a *nf* informant; informer
informētība *nf* store of information
informēties *vr* gather information; inform oneself
infrasarkans *adj* infrared
infraskaņa *nf* infrasound

infrastruktūra *nf* infrastructure
infula *nf* infula
infūzija *nf* infusion
infuzorija *nf* infusorium
infuzoriju zeme *nf* diatomaceous earth
ingredience *nf* ingredients
ingredients *nm* ingredient
ingresija *nf* ingression
ingrosācija *nf* entry in a mortgage register
ingrosēt *vt* enter in a mortgage register
inguš/s *nm*, ~iete *nf* Ingush
ingveralus *nm* ginger beer
ingvera maizīte *nf* gingerbread
ingveraugs *nm* ginger (plant)
ingvercepumi *nm pl* gingerbread
ingvereļļa *nf* ginger oil
ingvers *nm* ginger
inhalācija *nf* inhalation
inhalants *nm* inhalant
inhal[a]tors [ā] *nm* inhalator
inhalēt *vt* inhale vapors
inhērents *adj* inherent
inhibēt *vt* inhibit
inhibicija *nf* inhibition
inhibitors *nm* inhibitor
iniciācija *nf* initiation
iniciālis *nm* initial letter
inicializēšana *nf* (compu.) initialization
iniciāls *adj* initial
inici[a]tīva [ā] *nf* initiative
inici[a]tīvs [ā] *adj* of great initiative
inici[a]tor/s [ā] *nm*, ~e *nf* initiator
iniciēt *vt* initiate
īnītis *nm* (col.) **1.** little finger; **2.** (fig.) insig-
     nificant person
injekcija *nf* injection; **depo i.** depot injection;
     muskulārā i. intramuscular injection;
     venozā i. venous injection; **zemādas i.**
     subcutaneous injection
injektors *nm* injector
injicēt *vt* inject
injūrija *nf* (jur.) injury

inkapacitāte *nf* incapacity
inkapsulācija *nf* incapsulation
inkarnācija *nf* incarnation
inkarnēt *vi* incarnate
inkarnēties *vr* incarnate, become incarnated
inkarvileja *nf* incarvillea
inkasent/s *nm*, ~e *nf* collector; bill collector
inkasēt *vt* collect
inkaso *indecl nm* cash
inkasodarījums *nm* cash transaction
inki *nm pl* Incas
inklinācija *nf* inclination
inklin[a]tors [ā] *nm* inclinometer
inkluzīvi *adv* inclusively
inkluzīvs *adj* inclusive
inkognito *adv* incognito
inkomensurabls *adj* incommensurable
inko[mm]odēt [m] *vt* incommodate
inkompetence *nf* incompetence
inkompetenti *adv* incompetently
inkompetents *adj* incompetent
inkongruents *adj* incongruent
inkonsekvence *nf* inconsistency
inkonsekventi *adv* inconsistently
inkonsekvents *adj* inconsistent
inkonstants *adj* inconstant
inkontinents *adj* incontinent
inkonvenients *adj* inconvenient
inkorporācija *nf* incorporation
inkorporējošs *adj* (ling.) incorporating, poly-
     synthetic
inkorporēt *vt* incorporate
inkorupts *adj* incorrupt
inkriminācija *nf* incrimination
inkriminēt *vt* charge with a crime
inkr[e]ts [ē] *nm* incretion
inkrustācija *nf* inlaid work, inlay
inkrustēt *vt* inlay
inkubācija *nf* incubation
inkub[a]torijs [ā] *nm* incubator house
inkub[a]tors [ā] *nm* incubator
inkubēt *vt* incubate

inkubs *nm* incubus

inkun[a]bula [ā] *nf* incunabulum

inkursija *nf* incursion

inkvizīcija *nf* inquisition

inkviz[i]tors [ī] *nm* inquisitor

inoficiāli *adv* unofficially

inoficiāls *adj* unofficial

inokulācija *nf* inoculation

inokulēt *vt* inoculate

inoportuns *adj* inopportune

inovācija *nf* innovation

inozīns *nm* inosine

inozīts *nm* inositol

insaits *nm* insight

inscenējums *nm* staging, stage production

inscenēt *vt* stage

inscenētāj/s *nm*, ~a *nf* (theat.) producer

insekcēt *vt* (of insects) infest

insektārijs *nm* insectary

insekticīds *nm* insecticide

insekts *nm* insect

inseminācija *nf* insemination

insignija *nf* insignia

insinuācija *nf* insinuation

insinuēt *vt* insinuate

inskripcija *nf* inscription

insolācija *nf* insolation

insolēt *vt* insolate

insolvence *nf* insolvency

insolvents *adj* insolvent

inspekcija *nf* 1. inspection; 2. inspector's office

inspektore *nf* inspectress

inspektors *nm* inspector

inspektrise *nf* inspectress

inspicēt *vt* inspect

inspicient/s *nm*, ~e *nf* inspector

inspirācija *nf* inspiration

inspir[a]tor/s [ā] *nm*, ~e *nf* inspirer; instigator

inspirēt *vt* inspire

inspirētāj/s *nm*, ~a *nf* inspirer

insta[l]ācija [ll] *nf* installation

insta[l]ātor/s [ll] *nm*, ~e *nf* installer

insta[l]ēt [ll] *vt* install

instanc/e *nf* level of authority; **attiecīgā i.** prop-er authority; **augstākā i.** a. highest authority; b. superior court of appeals; **otrās ~es tiesa** court of appeals; **pēdējā i.** last resort; court of ultimate appeal; **caur ~ēm** through channels

instilācija *nf* instillation

instinktīvi *adv* instinctively

instinktīvs *adj* instinctive

instinkts *nm* instinct

institūcija *nf* institution

institucionālisms *nm* institutionalism

institucionalizēt *vt* institutionalize

institucionāls *adj* institutional

instituēt *vt* institute

institūts *nm* institute

instruēt *vt* instruct

instrukcija *nf* instruction

instruktāēa *nf* briefing

instruktīvi *adv* instructively

instruktīvs *adj* instructive

instruktor/s *nm*, ~e *nf* instructor; ~i (mil.) non-commissioned officers

instrumentācija *nf* instrumentation; orchestration

instrumentāli *adv* instrumentally

instrumentālis *nm* (gram.) instrumental case

instrumentālisms *nm* instrumentalism

instrumentālists *nm*, ~e *nf* instrumentalist

instrumentāls *adj* instrumental

instrumentēt *vt* instrument; orchestrate

instrument/s *nm* instrument; tool; **pūšamie ~i** wind instruments; **sitamie ~i** percussion (section)

instrumentu balons *nm* sounding balloon

instrumentu tērauds *nm* tool steel

insubordinācija *nf* insubordination

insuficience *nf* insufficiency

insuflācija *nf* insuflation

insulīns *nm* insulin

insults *nm* cerebrovascular insult

insurekcija *nf* insurrection

insurgent/s *nm*, ~**e** *nf* insurgent

intakts *adj* intact

intalja *nf* intaglio

intarsija *nf* wood inlay

integrācija *nf* integration

integrāli *adv* integrally

integrālis *nm* integral

integrālrēķini *nm pl* integral calculus

integrāls *adj* integral

integrāls[ch]ēma [h] *nf* integrated circuit

integrāls[ch]emote[ch]nika [h][h] *nf* integral circuitry

integrālvienādojums *nm* integral equation

integr[a]tors [ā] *nm* integrator

integrēšana *nf* integration

integrēt *vt* integrate

integritāte *nf* integrity

intelekts *nm* intellect

intelektuāli *adv* intellectually

intelektuāl/is *nm*, ~**e** *nf* intellectual

intelektuālisks *adj* intellectualistic

intelektuālisms *nm* intellectualism

intelektuālist/s *nm*, ~**e** *nf* intellectualist

intelektualitāte *nf* intellectuality

intelektualizēt *vt, vi* intellectualize

intelektuāls *adj* intellectual

inteligibls *adj* intelligible

inteliģence *nf* **1.** intelligence; **2.** intelligentsia; **3.** white-collar workers

inteliģenti *adv* intelligently

inteliģent/s *nm*, ~**e** *nf* **1.** intellectual; **2.** white-collar worker

inteliģents *adj* **1.** intelligent; **2.** cultured, educated

intence *nf* intention

intencija *nf* intention

intencionālisms *nm* intentionalism, act psychology

intencionalitāte *nf* intentionality

intencionāls *adj* intentional

intendants *nm* (mil.) commissary; supply officer; quartermaster; (hist.) intendant; manager (of a theater, television or radio station)

intendantūra *nf* (mil.) commissariat

intendensija *nf* intendencia

intensificēt *vt* intensify

intensifikācija *nf* intensification

intensitāte *nf* intensity

intensīvi *adv* intensely; intensively

intensivitāte *nf* intensiveness; intenseness

intensīvs *nm* (gram.) intensive verb form

intensīvs *adj* intense; intensive

intensīvums *nm* intensiveness; intenseness

interakcionisms *nm* interactionism

interaktīvs *adj* interactive

intercesija *nf* intercession

interdentāls *adj* interdental

interdikts *nm* interdiction

interdisciplinārs *adj* interdisciplinary

interesanti *adv* interesting; interestingly

interesants *adj* interesting

interes/e *nf* interest; **kas man tur par ~i?** where do I come in? ~**es pēc** out of curiosity

interesent/s *nm*, ~**e** *nf* interested party; *pl* ~**i** those interested

interesēt *vt* interest

interesēties *vr* take an interest in, be interested

interfeiss *nm* (compu.) interface

interference *nf* interference

interferometrija *nf* interferometry

interferometrs *nm* interferometer

interferons *nm* interferon

intergalaktisks *adj* intergalactic

interglaciāls *adj* interglacial

interims *adj* interim

interiorizācija *nf* interiorization

interiorizēt *vt* internalize

interjekcija *nf* interjection

interjers *nm* interior

interklubs *nm* international club

interkonfesionāls *adj* interconfessional

interkontinentāls *adj* intercontinental
interkulturāls *adj* intercultural, cross-cultural
interlingvistika *nf* interlinguistics
interloks *nm* (fabric) interlock
interlūdija *nf* interlude
intermeco *nm indecl* intermezzo
interm|e|dija [ē] *nf* interlude
intermet|all|isks [āl] *adj* metallide
intermitējošs *adj* intermittent
intermodulācija *nf* intermodulation
internacionāle *nf* 1. (socialist organization) in-ternational; 2. (hymn) Internationale
internacionāli *adv* internationally
internacionālisms *nm* 1. internationalism; 2. in-ternational loan word
internacionālistiski *adv* internationalistically
internacionālistisks *adj* internationalistic
internacionālists *nm*, ~e *nf* internationalist
internacion|a|lizācija [ā] *nf* internationaliza-tion
internacion|a|lizēt [ā] *vt* internationalize
internacionāls *adj* international
internalizācija *nf* internalization
internāts *nm* boarding house; (school) dormi-tory
internātskola *nf* boarding school
internēšana *nf* internment
internēt *vt* intern
internēt/ais *nom adj* internee; ~ā *f*
interni *adv* internally
internists *nm*, ~e *nf* internist
interns *adj* internal
interpe|l|ācija [ll] *nf* interpellation
interpe|l|ants [ll] *nm* interpellator
interpe|l|ēt [ll] *vt, vi* interpellate
interplanetārs *adj* interplanetary
interpolācija *nf* interpolation
interpolātors *nm* interpolator
interpolēt *vt* interpolate
interpretācija *nf* interpretation
interpret|a|tors [ā] *nm* (compu.) interpreter
interpretējums *nm* interpretation

interpretent/s *nm*, ~e *nf* interpreter
interpretēt *vt* interpret
interpretētāj/s *nm*, ~a *nf* interpreter
interpret/s *nm*, ~e *nf* interpreter
interpunkcija *nf* punctuation
interregns *nm* interregnum
interrogācija *nf* interrogation
interrog|a|tīvs [ā] *nm* intrrogative pronoun
interrog|a|tīvs [ā] *adj* interrogative
interrogēt *vt* interrogate
interrupcija *nf* interruption
interrupts *adj* interrupted
interseksu|a|litāte [ā] *nf* intersexuality
interseksuāls *adj* intersexual
intersensors *adj* intersensory
interstadiāls *adj* interstadial
intersubjektivitāte *nf* interubjectivity
intersubjektīvs *adj* intersubjective
interva|ll|s [l] *nm* interval
interva|ll|sk|a|la [l][ā] *nf* (stat.) interval scale
intervence *nf* intervention
intervencija *nf* intervention
intervents *nm* interventionist
intervēšana *nf* interviewing, interview
intervēt *vt* interview
intervētāj/s *nm*, ~a *nf* interviewer
intervija *nf* interview
intervokāls *adj* intervocalic
intestāts *adj* intestate
int|i|mi [ī] *adv* intimately
intimitāte *nf* intimacy
int|i|ms [ī] *adj* intimate
intoksikācija *nf* poisoning
intolerance *nf* intolerance
intoleranti *adv* intolerantly
intolerants *adj* intolerant
intonācija *nf* 1. vowel quality; lauztā i. rise-fall, glottal stop; stieptā i. long vowel quality; 2. in-tonation
inton|a|tīvi [ā] *adv* intonationally
inton|a|tīvs [ā] *adj* intonational
intonējums *nm* intonation

intonēt *vt* give the keynote, set the pitch

intragalaktisks *adj* intragalactic

intrakardiāls *adj* intracardiac

intramagmātisks *adj* intramagmatic

intramuskulāri *adv* intramuscularly

intramuskulārs *adj* intramuscular

intransigenti *adv* intransigently

intransigents *adj* intransigent

intransitīvi *adv* intransitively

intransitivitāte *nf* intransitivity

intransitīvs *adj* intransitive

intransitīvums *nm* intransitiveness

intravaskulārs *adj* intravascular

intravenozi *adv* intravenously

intravenozs *adj* intravenous

intrazonāls *adj* intrazonal

intriga *nf* **1.** intrigue; **2.** (lit.) plot

intrigants *nm*, ~e *nf* intriguer

intriģēt *vi* intrigue

introducents *nm* introduced plant

introducēt *vt* (bot.) introduce

introdukcija *nf* introduction

introduktīvs *adj* introductory

introjekcija *nf* introjection

introskopija *nf* introscopy

introskops *nm* introscope

introspekcija *nf* introspection

introspektīvi *adv* introspectively

introspektīvs *adj* introspective

introspicēt *vi* introspect

introversija *nf* introversion

introvertēts *adj* introverted

introvert/s *nm*, ~e *nf* introvert

intrudēt *vi* (geol.) intrude

intrūzija *nf* (geol.) intrusion

intr|u|zīvs [ū] *adj* (geol.) intrusive

intubācija *nf* intubation

intu|i|cija [ī] *nf* intuition

intuitīvi *adv* intuitively

intuitīvisms *nm* intuitionism

intuitīvist/s *nm*, ~e *nf* intuitionist

intuitīvs *adj* intuitive

inulins *nm* inulin

invadēt *vt* invade

invaginācija *nf* invagination

invaliditāte *nf* disability, invalidism

inval|i|ds [ī] *nm*, ~e *nf* invalid

inval|i|du [ī] nams *nm* home for the disabled

inval|i|du [ī] ratiņi *nm pl* wheelchair

invariance *nf* invariance

invarianti *adv* invariantly

invariants *nm* invariant

invariants *adj* invariant

invariantums *nm* invariance; invariability

invars *nm* invar

invāzija *nf* invasion

invektiva *nf* invective

invencija *nf* (mus.) invention

inventārgrāmata *nf* inventory record

invent|a|rizācija [ā] *nf* inventorying, inventory taking

invent|a|rizēt [ā] *vt* inventory

inventār/s *nm* inventory; **dzīvais i.** livestock; **nedzīvais i.** dead stock; **ritošais i.** rolling stock; **~a norakstīšanas akts** (mil.) administrative adjustment report

inventūra *nf* taking of inventory; **~s izpārdo-šana** inventory sale

inversi *adv* inversely

inversija *nf* inversion; **militārā i.** reversal

inversors *nm* inverting device

inverss *adj* inverse

invertcukurs *nm* invert sugar

inverters *nm* (el.) inverter

invertēt *vt* invert

investēt *vt* invest, install in office

investīcija *nf* investment

investija *nf* investment

investitūra *nf* investiture

investor/s *nm*, ~e *nf* investor

involūcija *nf* involution

inžektors *nm* injector

inženie|r|celtniecība [ŗ] *nf* architectural engineering

inženie[r]ģeodēzija [ŗ] *nf* soil mechanics
inženierija *nf* engineering
inženier/is *nm,* ~e *nf* engineer; diplomēts i. hold-er of an engineering degree
inženieris celtnieks *nm* civil engineer
inženieris elektriķis *nm* electrical engineer
inženieris ķīmiķis *nm* chemical engineer
inženieris mežkopis *nm* forest engineering specialist
inženie[r]karaspēks [ŗ] *nm* corps of engineers
inženie[r]konstrukcija [ŗ] or *nf* engineered structure
inženie[r]te[h]niski [ŗ][ch] *adv* from the point of view of applied engineering
inženie[r]te[h]nisks [ŗ][ch] *adj* pertaining to applied engineering
inženie[r]zināt/nes [ŗ] *nf pl* engineering sciences; ~ņu fakultāte school of engineering
ionieši *nm pl* Ionians
ionisks *adj* Ionic
ionīts *nm* ion exchanger
ionizācija *nf* ionization
ionizātors *nm* ionizer
ionizēt *vt* ionize
ionizēties *vr* be ionized
ionoforēze *nf* iontophoresis
ionog[e]nisks [ē] *adj* ionogenic
ionog[e]ns [ē] *adj* ionogenic
ionosf[ai]ra [ē] *nf* ionosphere
ionotropija *nf* ionotropy
ions *nm* ion
iontoforēze *nf* iontophoresis
īpašdators *nm* dedicated computer
īpaši *adv* 1. specially; particularly; 2. separately
īpašība *nf* quality; trait; property; raksturīga ī. characteristic
īpašības vārds *nm* adjective; šķiŗamais ī. v. distributive adjective
īpašniecisks *adj* proprietary

īpašnie/ks *nm,* ~ce *nf* owner; proprietor
īpašs *adj* 1. special; particular; 2. separate
īpašum/s *nm* 1. property; estate; kustams ī. movables, personal property; nekustams ī. real es-tate; 2. possession
īpašumtiesības *nf pl* ownership; property rights, title (to a property)
īpašumtiesību ierobežojums *nm* restrictive right of possession
īpašumtiesīgs *adj* having the right to possess
īpašumtiesisks *adj* proprietary
īpašvārds *nm* proper noun
īpašvērtība *nf* (math.) eigenvalue
īpatība *nf* 1. peculiarity; 2. trait, feature
īpatnēji *adv* peculiarly; uniquely
īpatnējs *adj* 1. peculiar; special; unique; 2. (phys.) specific
īpatni *adv* uniquely
īpatnība *nf* 1. peculiarity; 2. trait, feature
īpatnīgi *adv* peculiarly
īpatnīgs *adj* peculiar
īpatnīgums *nm* uniqueness
īpatn/is *nm,* ~e *nf* 1. individual; 2. eccentric; strange person
īpatns *adj* unique
īpatnums *nm* peculiarity
īpats *adj* characteristic
īpatsvars *nm* specific weight
ipekakuana *nf* ipecac
ipomeja *nf* morning glory
iprīts *nm* mustard gas
ipsilons *nm* upsilon
ipsils *nm* upsilon
ir I *conj;* ir . . . ir both . . . and
ir II *partic* 1. also, too; (in negations) either; 2. (col.) even
ir III *3rd pers sg, pl* of būt 1. (he, she, it) is; (they) are; (without pronoun) there is; there are; tā ir, kā ir (col.) things are so-so; things are a bit iffy; 2. (with subject in dative) have, has
ira *nf* existence

irac- See **irrac-**

irad- See **irrad-**

iraid *3rd pers sg, pl* of **būt** *(obs.) emph* of ir III

irakiet/is *nm,* ~**e** *nf* Iraqi

irān/is *nm,* ~**iete** *nf* Iranian

irbe *nf* gray partridge

irbenājs *nm* **1.** guelder rose, snowball; see also **krāšņais i.**; **2.** growth of guelder roses

irbene *nf* growth of guelder roses

irbis *nm* **1.** knitting needle; **2.** skewer; **3.** pointer

irbīte *nf dim* of **irbe**, partridge

irbs *nm* **1.** knitting needle; **2.** skewer; **3.** pointer

irbulene *nf* (bot.) broom

irbulēt *vt* broach (a hole)

irbulis *nm* **1.** pointer; broach; **2.** (bot.) style

irbulītis *nm dim* of **irbulis**

irbuļains *adj* (reg., of bread) porous

irde *nf* **1.** soil; **2.** friable rock

irdenība *nf* looseness; friability, crumbliness

irdens *adj* loose; friable, crumbly

irdenums *nm* looseness; friability, crumbliness

irdināt *vt* loosen; make friable

irdinātājs *nm* soil loosener, cutter

irdnājs *nm* (poet.) soil

irdne *nf* soil

irdns *adj* loose; friable, crumbly

irds *adj* loose; friable, crumbly

irdza *nf* (of water) murmur, purl

irdzēt *vi* purl; bubble, murmur

irdzoņa *nf* purling; bubbling; murmur

īre *nf* rent; lease

ireāl- See **irreāl-**

ired- See **irred-**

iregu- See **irreg-**

irel- See **irrel-**

irep- See **irrep-**

īres bibliotēka *nf* circulating library

īres dzīvoklis *nm* rental apartment

īres hotelis *nm* apartment hotel

īres kariete *nf* hackney coach

īres līgums *nm* rental agreement; lease agreement

īres māja *nf* apartment building

īres maksa *nf* rental

īres nauda *nf* rent

īres valde *nf* office of rent control

īrēt *vt* rent; lease

īrētājs *nm,* ~**a** *nf* renter; tenant

irev- See **irrev-**

irga *nf, nm* (col.) mocker

irgāt *vi* deride, ridicule, mock, taunt

irgāties *vr* deride, ridicule, mock, taunt

irgnēt *vi* deride, ridicule, mock, taunt

irgoņa *nf, nm* (col.) mocker

irgoties *vr* mock

irgt *vi* **1.** bubble, murmur; **2.** titter

iriarteja *nf* stilt palm

irība *nf* (philos.) essence

īrida *nf* (bot.) iris

ir[i]dijs [ī] *nm* iridium

iridociklīts *nm* iridocyclitis

iridoloģija *nf* iridology

iridosmīns *nm* iridosmine

īriens *nm* (of arms, oars) stroke

irig- See **irrig-**

irināt *vi* (of mole crickets) chirp

iris *nm* paddle

īrisdiafragma *nf* iris diaphragm

īriseļļa *nf* orris oil

iriskums *nm* (philos.) being

īriss *nm* **1.** (bot.) iris; **2.** toffee

īrisspiedums *nm* irridescent printing

irit- See **irrit-**

īrizēt *vi* iridesce

irklēt *vi* row

irklis *nm* scull; (poet.) oar

īrnie/ks *nm,* ~**ce** *nf* tenant

irokez/s *nm,* ~**iete** *nf* Iroquoi

ironija *nf* irony

ironiķ/is *nm,* ~**e** *nf* ironist

ironiski *adv* ironically

ironisks *adj* ironic

ironiskums *nm* ironicalness

ironizēt *vi* ironize

i|rr|acionāli |r| *adv* irrationally

i|rr|acionālisms |r| *nm* irrationality

i|rr|acionālistiski |r| *adv* irrationalistically

i|rr|acionālistisks |r| *adj* irrationalistic

i|rr|acionalitāte |r| *nf* irrationality

i|rr|acionāls |r| *adj* irrational

i|rr|adiācija |r| *nf* irradiation

i|rr|adiēt |r| *vi* irradiate

i|rr|eāli |r| *adv* unreally

i|rr|eālisms |r| *nm* nonreferential art

i|rr|ealitāte |r| *nf* irreality

i|rr|eāls |r| *adj* unreal

i|rr|educibls |r| *adj* irreducible

i|rr|egulāri |r| *adv* irregularly

i|rr|egularitāte |r| *nf* irregularity

i|rr|egulārs |r| *adj* irregular

i|rr|elevants |r| *adj* irrelevant

i|rr|eliģiozitāte |r| *nf* irreligiosity

i|rr|eliģiozs |r| *adj* irreligious

i|rr|epar|ā|bilitāte |r||a| *nf* irreparability

i|rr|eparābils |r| *adj* irreparable

i|rr|eversibilitāte |r| *nf* irreversibility

i|rr|eversibls |r| *adj* irreversible

i|rr|igācija |r| *nf* irrigation

i|rr|ig|ā|tors |r||a| *nm* irrigator

i|rr|iģēt |r| *vt* irrigate

i|rr|itācija |r| *nf* irritation

i|rr|itēt |r| *vt* irritate

īr/s *nm* Irishman; **~iete** *nf* Irishwoman

irsis *nm* red deer

irskoties *vr* kid, needle

irstināt *vt* unravel

irt I *vt* row

irt II *vi* 1. unravel; 2. crumble

irties *vr* row, paddle

irtin *adv emph* of **irt** I, **irt** II

irumiezis *nm* (geol.) crumbling formation

īs/ais *nom adj* (col.) 1. short circuit, short; **uz ~o** shorted; 2. short person, shorty

īsastains *adj* short-tailed

īsastes klijkaija *nf* Arctic skua

īsbārdainā kaza *nf* bezoar goat

īscaurule *nf* branch pipe

īsfilma *nf* (film) short subject, short

īsfokusa *indecl adj* short-focus

īsgaitas *indecl adj* (mech.) short-stroke

īsgājiena *indecl adj* (mech.) short-stroke

īsi *adv* short; briefly; **~i un skaidri** in a word, short and sweet

īsinājuma zīme *nf* (mus.) abbreviation

īsinājums *nm* shortening, abbreviation

īsināt *vt* 1. shorten; 2. while away

īsiņš *adj dim* of **īss**

īskājes *nf pl* false bromegrass

īskāte *nf* one-handed scythe

īskonference *nf* briefing

īskņekaru vīķis *nm* bush vetch

īslaicīgi *adv* briefly

īslaicīgs *adj* short-term, short; brief

īslaika *indecl adj* short-term

isl|a|ms |ā| *nm* Islam

Islandes ķērpis *nm* Iceland moss

Islandes lentzivs *nf* snake blenny

Islandes piekūns *nm* gyrfalcon

islandiet/is *nm*, **~e** *nf* Icelander

islandiski *adv* in Icelandic

islandisks *adj* Icelandic

īsļipains *adj* short-scutted

īsmatainie ēibulīši *nm pl* an eyebright, Euphrasia brevipila

īsmatains *adj* short-haired

īsmetrāžas *indecl adj* (of films) short

īsmetrāžas filma *nf* short subject

īsmūēa *indecl adj* short-lived

īsperioda *indecl adj* short-period

īspirkstu mizloda *nf* short-toed treecreeper

israēliet/is *nm*, **~e** *nf* Israelite; Israeli

īsraksts *nm* shorthand

īsredzība *nf* (obs.) short-sightedness

īsredzīgs *adj* (obs.) short-sighted

īsredzīgums *nm* (obs.) short-sightedness

īs/s *adj* **1.** short; **2.** brief; ~**os vārdos** briefly; **tik ī. tik gaŗš** six of one, half a dozen of another

īssavienojums *nm* short circuit

īsskujainā priede *nf* shortleaf pine

īsslēguma strāva *nf* short-circuit current

īsslēgums *nm* short circuit

īsspalvains *adj* (of animals) short-haired

īsspārņi *nm pl* rove beetles

īsstobra *indecl adj* short-barrelled, snub-nosed

īsstobrene *nf* sawed-off shotgun

īsšķiedrains *adj* short-fibered

istaba *nf* room; (obs.) farmhouse; (obs.) heated living room in a farmhouse; **dižā i.** (obs.) principal room in a farmhouse; **dzīvojamā i.** living room; **tumšā i.** darkroom; ~**u sarindojums** en-filaded rooms

istabas antena *nf* indoor antenna

istabas augša *nf* attic

istabas bise *nf* saloon rifle, pistol

istabas iekārta *nf* room furnishings

istabas kļavs *nm* abutilon

istabas kode *nf* clothes moth

istabas liepa *nf* African hemp

istaba muša *nf* housefly; see also **mazā i. m.**

istabas puķes *nf pl* indoor plants

istabas putns *nm* cageling

istabas vecākais *nm* squad room leader

istabaugša *nf* attic

istabene *nf* maid, chamber maid

istablietas *nf pl* room furnishings; furniture

istabpriekša *nf* porch

īstā kumelīte *nf* German chamomile

īstā ķimpene *nf* tinder polypore

īstā madara *nf* yellow bedstraw

īstā sāre *nf* broomcorn millet

īsteni *adv* really, actually; truly

īstenīb/a *nf* reality; ~**ā** in fact

īstenības izteiksme *nf* (gram.) indicative mood

īstenieks *nm* **1.** close blood relative; **2.** (hist.) corvée laborer with a horse

īstenojams *adj, part* of **īstenot** realizable

īstenojums *nm* realization

īstenošana *nf* realization

īstenot *vt* put into practice, realize

īstenoties *vr* come true, be realized

īstens *adj* real, actual; true

īstenums *nm* truth

īstermiņa *indecl adj* short-term

īsti *adv* **1.** really; **2.** genuinely

īstniecība *nf* relationship by marriage

īsts *adj* **1.** real; **2.** genuine, authentic; **3.** correct; **4.** true; **5.** right; (of fractions) proper; **6.** veritable; **7.** (of blood relationships) own (father, brother, etc)

īstums *nm* genuineness, authenticity

īsum/s *nm* **1.** shortness; ~**ā** in short; *pl* ~**i** a. short straw; b. short wool from the legs and belly; **2.** brevity

īsvilnas *indecl adj* (of sheep) having short wool

īsviļņ/i *nm pl* short waves; ~**u** short-wave

īszeķes *nf pl* anklets, ankle socks

īsziņas *nf pl* news in brief

išēmija *nf* ischemia

išiass *nm* sciatica

it *partic* **1.** (in emphases) quite; particularly; at all; **it īpaši** mainly; **it nekas** nothing at all; **it nemaz** not at all; **it neviens** not one; **it sevišķi** especially; **2. it kā** a. as if; b. apparently

itakolumīts *nm* itacolumite

itakonskābe *nf* itaconic acid

it|a|liešu [ā] raizāle *nf* Italian ryegrass

it|a|liešu [ā] streiks *nm* sitdown strike

it|a|lie/tis [ā] *nm,* ~**te** *nf* Italian

It|a|lijas [ā] ciprese *nf* Italian cypress

It|a|lijas [ā] plūme *nf* greengage

It|a|lijas [ā] sarene *nf* Italian millet

it[a]liski [ā] *adv* in Italian, (speak) Italian

it[a]lisks [ā] *adj* Italian

it[a]li [ā] *nm pl* Italic peoples

iteja *nf* Itea

iterācija *nf* iteration

iter[a]tīvi [ā] *adv* iteratively

iter[a]tīvs [ā] *adj* iterative

iterēt *vi* iterate

iterbijs *nm* ytterbium

itin *partic* (in emphases) quite; particularly;
   at all

itrijs *nm* yttrium

īve *nf* English yew

īveles *nf pl* glanders

īveļu zāles *nf pl* herb Paris

īvēt *vt, vi* (naut.) heave

īvju veronika *nf* ivy-leaved speedwell

ivrits *nm* modern Hebrew

iz *prep* from, out of

izacojis *adj, part* of **izacot** porous, spongy

izacot *vt* make porous; *vi* become porous

izadījums *nm* knitting

izadīt *vt* 1. knit; 2. knit designs; 3. use up (yarn)
   in knitting

izadīties *vr* 1. knit a lot; 2. be used up in
   knitting

izaicinājums *nm* challenge

izaicināt *vt* challenge

izaicināties *vr* keep inviting (in vain)

izaicinošs *adj* provocative

izairēt *vt, vi* row out (of a place)

izairēties *vr* 1. row a long time; 2. row out (of
   a place)

izakcentēt *vt* stress, emphasize

izākstīt *vt* make a mockery of

izākstīties *vr* clown

izāķēt *vt* unhook

izālēties *vr* romp, (col.) bluster

izalgot *vt* pay (a wage)

izalkt *vi* get hungry

izalobāra *nf* isallobar

izalot *vt* tunnel; honeycomb

izaloterma *nf* isallotherm

izalvot *vt* tin

izamizēties *vr* enjoy oneself fully

izanalizēt *vt* analyze; parse

izandelēt *vt* (barb.) sell off

izanomāle *nf* isanomal

izara *nf* plowed depression

izārdava *nf* fluent speech

izārdavi *adv* lively, fluently, facilely

izārdavs *adj* (folk., of speech) lively, fluent,
   facile

izārdeni *adv* = **izārdavi**

izārdens *adj* = **izārdavs**

izārdīgi *adv* = **izārdavi**

izārdīg/s *adj* = **izārdavs**

izārdīt *vt* 1. (of seams) rip, undo; 2. (of hay,
   manure) spread, ted; 3. ruin, destroy; (of
   walls, buildings) pull down; 4. take apart,
   dismantle

izārdīties *vr* 1. unravel; 2. fall apart; 3. rave
   and rant

izārstējams *adj, part* of **izārstēt** curable

izārstēt *vt* cure, heal

izārstēties *vr* get well, recover

izart *vt* plow; plow up; **i. vagu** drive a furrow

izarties *vr* plow a long time

izarums *nm* plowed depression

izasarot *vi* cause (temporary) tearing

izasināt *vt* sharpen

izasnot *vt, vi* germinate

izatins *nm* isatin

izaudzēt *vt* (of plants) grow, (of animals)
   breed

izaudzināt *vt* raise, bring up, rear

izaugsme *nf* growth, development

izaugt *vi* 1. grow; grow up; 2. emerge (growing);
   (of boils) come to a head; **i. no drēbēm**
   outgrow one's clothes

izaugums *nm* growth, excrescence; protuberance

izauklēt *vt* nurse, rear, bring up

izauklēties *vr* nurse a long time

izaukstēt *vt* cool, chill

izaukstēties *vr* get chilled

izaukstināt *vt* cool, chill

izaulekšot *vi* gallop out of; gallop through

izauļot *vi* gallop out of; gallop through

izaurēties *vr* holler, roar a while

izaurot *vt* announce with a roar

izauroties *vr* holler (a while, to one's heart's con-tent), roar a while

izaust I *vt* **1.** weave; **2.** use up in weaving; **3.** interweave

izaust II *vi* dawn

izausties *vr* **1.** weave a long time; **2.** be woven

izaušoties *vr* play around enough

izaut *vt* (reg.) **i. kājas** bare one's feet

izauties *vr* (reg.) bare one's feet

izava *nf* worn-out footwear

izāvīt *vt* (reg.) play a trick on s.o.

izāzēt *vt* play a trick on s.o.

izāzēties *vr* fool around a long time

izbadējies *adj, part* of **izbadēties** famished, starving

izbadēties *vr* be hungry, be famished, be starving

izbadināt *vt* starve a long time

izbadināties *vr* starve oneself

izbadīt *vt* **1.** horn; **2.** poke

izbadoties *vr* be hungry, be famished, be starving

izbagarēt *vt* dredge; deepen by dredging

izbaidīt *vt* **1.** scare, startle, frighten; **2.** shoo (out of a place)

izbaidīties *vr* be scared, be startled, be frightened

izbailes *nf pl* fright

izbaiļot *vt* frighten

izbaiļoties *vr* have a fright

izbakstīt *vt* **1.** damage by poking; **2.** make holes; **3.** (of teeth, debris from cracks) pick; **4.** poke through, pierce; **5.** poke around

izbalēt *vi* fade, discolor

izbālēt *vi* fade completely

izbalināt *vt* bleach

izballēties *vr* party (a long time, a lot)

izbalot *vi* fade

izbalsināt *vt* whitewash

izbalsot *vt* vote out; blackball

izbarot *vt* **1.** feed; **2.** keep, provide for

izbārstelēt *vt* scatter

izbārstīt *vt* scatter

izbārstīties *vr* scatter, be scattered

izbārt *vt* scold, dress down

izbārties *vr* do some scolding

izbaudīt *vt* **1.** enjoy, relish; **2.** experience

izbauroties *vr* bellow a long time

izbāzēj/s *nm*, **~a** *nf* taxidermist

izbāznis *nm* stuffed animal

izbāzt *vt* **1.** stick out; put through; **2.** stuff (animals)

izbāzties *vr* stick out

izbazūnēt *vt* (col.) proclaim from rooftops

izbēdāt *vt* **1. i. bēdas** sorrow; **2.** worry about

izbēdāties *vr* worry a lot, worry a long time

izbēgams *adj, part* of **izbēgt** avoidable

izbēgt *vi* **1.** flee, escape from; **2.** avoid

izbēguš/ais *nom adj* escapee; **~ā** *f*

izbeigšanās *nfr* end, expiration

izbeigt *vt* terminate; (of a debate) close; (of a case) dismiss; **izbeidz!** (col.) stop it!

izbeigties *vr* **1.** end; expire; **2.** (of stocks, supplies, time) run out of

izbelzt *vt* knock out

izbērt *vt* **1.** pour out; empty; **2.** spill

izberzējums *nm* rubbed-through spot

izberzēties *vr* **1.** be rubbed through; **2.** rub oneself a lot

izberzēt *vt* **1.** rub out; **2.** rub through; **3. i. acis** rub one's eyes

izberzt *vt* **1.** rub; **i. cauri** rub a hole; **2.** scour, scrub

izberzties *vr* scrub a long time

izberzums *nm* **1.** scrubbing; **2.** rub

izbetonējums *nm* poured concrete

izbetonēt *vt* line with concrete

izbīdams *adj, part* of **izbīdīt** pull-out

izbīdījums *nm* protrusion

izbīdīt *vt* **1.** pull out; **2.** push, shove, or slide (through or forward); **3.** spread out (by pushing, sliding); **4.** make protrude; **5.** nominate

izbīdīties *vr* be pushed out; protrude

izbiedēt *vt* frighten, startle

izbiedināt *vt* frighten

izbieds *nm* fright

izbijis *adj* former, ex-; **kas bijis, tas i.** let bygones be bygones

izbijušais *nom adj* the past

izbikstīt *vt* poke thoroughly

izbīlis *nm* fright

izbiras *nf pl* hayseed

izbirdināt *vt* scatter

izbirināt *vt* scatter

izbirt *vi* spill, scatter; fall out; **i. no galvas** forget

izbirzēt *vt* mark sowing strips

izbirzt *vi* crumble and fall out

izbirzums *nm* crumbled spot

izbīties *vr* get frightened

izbizoties *vr* run around enough

izblamēt *vt* make s.o. look like a fool

izblamēties *vr* disgrace oneself

izblandīties *vr* roam enough

izblāvēt *vi* fade

izblēdīt *vt* cheat out of, swindle out of

izblēdīties *vr* cheat and swindle a long time

izblēņoties *vr* fool around a long time

izblēties *vr* bleat a long time

izblīdis *adj, part* of **izblīst** bloated, fat and flabby

izbliesties *vr* swell

izblietēt *vt* **1.** tamp down; **2.** pound (a hole)

izbliezt *vi* take a shot; *vt* discharge; knock out

izbliezties *vr* swell

izblisināt *vt* **i. acis 1.** blink (upon waking); **2.** stare (in surprise)

izblīst *vi* **1.** swell; become bloated, become fat and flabby; **2.** become waterlogged

izblusināt *vt* deflea

izblusoties *vr* deflea oneself

izbļaustīties *vr* yell enough

izbļaut *vt* yell, call out

izbļauties *vr* yell enough; cry enough

izbojāt *vt* spoil

izbojāties *vr* be spoiled

izboksterēt *vt* (col.) spell

izbolīt *vt*; **i. acis** stare at, goggle at; roll up one's eyes

izbolīties *vr* (of eyes) pop out

izbozt *vt* (of feathers) ruffle, fluff; bristle up

izbozties *vr* be ruffled; bristle

izbradāt *vt* trample down; tramp through

izbradāties *vr* wade through a long time

izbrāķēt *vt* **1.** reject (as defective); **2.** (col.) disdain

izbrauciens *nm* **1.** excursion, outing; **2.** departure

izbraucis *adj, part* of **izbraukt** out of town

izbraucīt *vt* rub, knead

izbraukalēt *vt* travel all over, crisscross in traveling

izbraukāt *vt* travel all over, crisscross in traveling

izbraukāties *vr* **1.** go for a drive (or ride); **2.** drive (or ride) to one's heart's content

izbraukt *v* **1.** *vt, vi* drive out; **2.** *vi* get through; **3.** *vi* leave, depart; **4.** *vt* sightsee driving, do (a town); **5.** *vt* drive over (and damage); rut; **6.** *vt, vi* go for a spin; go on a trip, go out of town; **i. uz ārzemēm** go abroad; **7.** *vt* (of fingers) run through

izbraukties *vr* **1.** go for a drive (or ride); **2.** travel far and wide

izbraukts *adj, part* of **izbraukt** rutted

izbrauktuve *nf* driveway exit

izbraukums *nm* excursion, outing; drive; tour

izbrazdināt *vt* (reg., of roads) rut

izbrāzt *vi* come rushing out; rush through

izbrāzties *vr* come rushing out; rush through

izbrēkāties *vr* cry a good deal

izbrēkt *vt* shout, utter shouts

izbrēkties *vr* 1. cry a good deal; 2. finish crying

izbricelēt *vt* (reg.) take to task

izbriedināt *vt* soak

izbriest *vi* swell

izbrīna *nf* amazement, astonishment

izbrīnēt *vt* amaze, astonish

izbrīnēties *vr* be amazed, be astonished

izbrīnināt *vt* amaze, astonish

izbrīnīt *vt* amaze, astonish

izbrīnīties *vr* 1. be amazed, be astonished; 2. stop being amazed

izbrīns *nm* amazement, astonishment

izbrist *vi* 1. wade through; wade out of; i. malā come ashore; 2. crosscross wading

izbristies *vr* wade a long time

izbrīvēt *vt* free, release; liberate

izbrīvēties *vr* get free

izbrīvot *vt* free, release; liberate

izbrucināt *vt* 1. (of a scythe) whet; 2. scald

izbruģēt *vt* pave

izbrukt *vi* 1. fall out; fall through; 2. sally, make a sortie

izbrukums *nm* 1. breach, gap; 2. sally, sortie

izbrūvēt *vt* brew

izbružāt *vt* rub

izbubināties *vr* have a chat

izbuknīt *vt* nudge, push around

izbuksnīt *vt* nudge, push around

izbuldurēt *vt* (col.) mumble

izbumbot *vt* bomb out

izbundzināt *vt* (col.) advertise

izbungāt *vt* = izbungot

izbungot *vt* 1. plink; bang; 2. (col.) advertise

izburāt *vt* sail all over

izburbējis *adj, part* of izburbēt spongy; decayed

izburbēt *vi* 1. become porous; 2. decay, rot

izburbis *adj, part* of izburbt spongy, decayed, porous

izburbt *vi* 1. become porous; 2. decay, rot

izburbulēt *vi* 1. bubble up; 2. become porous

izburbuļot *vi* bubble up

izburbums *nm* porosity

izburkšķēt *v* 1. *vi* rumble (into, through); 2. *vt* ut-ter in a peeved, growling voice

izburnīt *vt* (reg.) rub

izburt *vt* 1. conjure up; 2. force out magically

izburties *vr* 1. practice magic a lot; 2. extricate oneself; 3. i. cauri (fig.) dig through

izburtot *vt* decipher; spell laboriously

izburzīt *vt* rub (to soften or to clean)

izbūt *irr vi*, usu. as *part* izbijis; See izbijis

izbūve *nf* 1. construction; 2. jetty, projecting portion of a building

izbūvēt *vt* build

izbūvēties *vr* (of settlements) spread, develop

izbužināt *vt* (of hair) ruffle; fluff

izcaurumot *vt* perforate

izcēlājs *nm* potato-digger, sugar beet-digger

izcelsme *nf* origin; birth, parentage

izcelšanās *nfr* 1. origin; 2. contrast; 3. distinction; 4. landing; 5. (of war) outbreak

izcelt *vt* 1. lift out; i. no eņģēm unhinge; 2. land; i. desantu land troops; i. malā put ashore; 3. emphasize; stress, feature; boost

izcelties *vr* 1. originate; start; arise; 2. land; i. malā go ashore; 3. try lifting (unsuccessfully); keep on lifting; 4. stand out

izcēlums *nm* (typ.) display

izceļošana *nf* emigration

izceļot *v* 1. *vi* emigrate; 2. *vt* travel all over, travel through

izceļotājs *nm*, ~a *nf* emigrant

izceļoties *vr* travel to one's heart's content

izcementēt *vt* line with concrete

izcenojums *nm* price, valuation

izcenot *vt* price

izcepināt *vt* (of fat) render; bake slowly

izcepināties *vr* bake slowly

izcept *vt* fry, broil, roast, bake

izcepties *vr* get done (frying, broiling, roasting or baking)

izcerēties *vr* be hoping for a long time

izciemoties *vr* stay a long time (visiting)

izcienāt *vt* wine and dine

izciest *vt* **1.** endure, suffer, bear; **2. i. sodu** serve one's sentence

izciesties *vr* suffer much, have been through a lot

izcieties *adj, part* of **izciesties 1.** long-suffering; **2.** hungry

izcīkstēties *vr* wrestle a long time

izcilāt *vt* lift many times; dig through, ransack

izcilāties *vr* **1.** be lifting a long time; **2.** be lifted

izcildināt *vt* praise

izcili *adv* outstandingly

izcilība *nf* distinction

izcilināt *vt* underscore; single out

izcilnie/ks *nm*, **~ce** *nf* outstanding worker; outstanding student

izcilnis *nm* **1.** projection; cam; **2.** (art) relief

izcilnītis *nm dim* of **izcilnis**, slight projection

izciļņvārpsta *nf* camshaft

izcilpot *vi* **1.** lope out of; **2.** crisscross loping

izcilpoties *vr* lope around a long time

izcils *adj* outstanding; distinguished, prominent, eminent

izcilspiedums *nm* relief printing

izcilus *adv* prominently

izcīnīt *vt* win (by struggling); **i. pirmo vietu** take first place

izcīnīties *vr* struggle, do battle; struggle through

izcīņa *nf* **1.** attainment (through struggle); **2.** contest, competition

izcirksnis *nm* (forest.) clearing

izcirpt *vt* cut out (with shears); shear

izcirst *vt* **1.** fell; **2.** cut out; **3.** carve, sculpture; **4.** cut (a quantity of timber, firewood); **5.** (of meat) carve

izcirsties *vr* **1.** cut (with an ax) a long time; **2.** cut one's way through

izcirtēj/s *nm*, **~a** *nf* cutter

izcirtums *nm* (forest.) clearing, clear-cut

izcūkot *vt* (col.) **1.** spoil; **2.** fool

izčabināties *vr* (col.) have a heart-to-heart talk

izčakarēt *vt* poke, pick, stir thoroughly

izčakarēties *vr* poke through a long time

izčākstējis *adj, part* of **izčākstēt** pithy, spongy

izčākstēt *vi* become spongy, become pithy; (col.) peter out, come to nothing

izčalot *vt* tell all

izčaloties *vr* have a chat

izčamdīt *vt* rummage, ransack, go through

izčāpot *vi* waddle out (of a place)

izčaukstēt *vi* become spongy, pithy

izčaukstināties *vr* rustle a long time

izčibēt *vi* (col.) **1.** vanish; **kaut tu ~u!** to hell with you! **2.** come to nothing

izčiepstēties *vr* chirp a long time

izčiept *vt* pilfer

izčīkstēt *vi* **1.** become squeaky; **2.** obtain by (tear-ful) begging

izčīkstēties *vr* whine a long time

izčinkstēt *vt* (col.) obtain by (tearful) begging

izčinkstēties *vr* whine a long time

izčivināties *vr* chirp a long time

izčubināt *vt* fluff up

izčubināties *vr* fuss around a baby for a long time

izčukstēt *vt* whisper, utter in a whisper

izčūkstēt *vi* (col.) vanish, disappear

izčukstēties *vr* converse in whispers a long time

izčūlāt *vi* come to a head

izčūlot *vi* come to a head

izčūpstināt *vt* (col.) suck out

izčurāties *vr* (child.) urinate, tinkle

izčurināt *vt* (col., of fat) render

izčurkstēt *vi* sizzle while melting

izčurkstināt *vt* (col., of fat) render; fry in sizzling fat

izdabāt *vt* please; indulge

izdabātājs *nm*, ~a *nf* toady, sycophant

izdabīgi *adv* obligingly, complaisantly

izdabīgs *adj* obliging, complaisant

izdabināt *vt* (of children) spoil

izdabis *nm* toady, sycophant

izdabūt *vt* **1.** get out; get through; **2.** obtain (with difficulty); wheedle out

izdailināt *vt* adorn, decorate, beautify

izdaiļot *vt* adorn, decorate, beautify

izdaiļoties *vr* adorn oneself

izdakšot *vt* fork out

izdale *nf* **1.** distribution; **2.** secretion

izdalījumi *nm pl* secretion; discharge

izdalīt *vt* **1.** divide; **2.** distribute; **3.** detail (a group); **4.** award; **5.** secrete, discharge; exude; **6.** isolate; extract; precipitate

izdalītājs *nm* dispenser; distributor

izdalīties *vr* **1.** divide; spread; **2.** stand out, contrast; **3.** be released; (physiol.) secrete, discharge

izdāļāt *vt* give away

izdancināt *vt* **1.** dance (many or for a long time); (of horses) lead on a training rope; **2.** (col.) make jump, order around, overwork

izdancot *v* **1.** *vi* dance out of (a place); **2.** *vt* finish dancing; **3.** *vt* do dance steps

izdancotājs *nm* toady

izdancoties *vr* do a lot of dancing

izdangāt *vt* **1.** rut; **2.** trample

izdarboties *vr* be active a long time

izdārdēt *vi* move out with a rumble

izdārdināt *vi* move out (or through) with a rumble

izdarība *nf* **1.** expeditiousness; efficiency; **2.** be-havior; *pl* ~s doings; ceremony

izdarīgi *adv* expeditiously; efficiently

izdarīgs *adj* expeditious; efficient

izdarīgums *nm* expeditiousness

izdarināt *vt* **1.** make; **2.** trim branches

izdarīt *vt* **1.** do; carry out; perform; (of errors, crimes) commit; (of services) render; (of corrections) make; **i. aprēķinu** a. (bookk., of accounts) settle; b. (of a worker) discharge, fire; **i. pēc sava prāta** have it one's own way; **i. pa prātam** please; **i. sāpes** hurt; **i. secinājumu** draw a conclusion; **i. spiedienu** exert pressure; bring presure to bear; **i. uzņēmumu** take a picture; **2.** finish (doing)

izdarītāj/s *nm*, ~a *nf* perpetrator

izdarīties *vr* **1.** do (a lot, to the point of boredom); **2.** behave arbitrarily

izdastot *vt* (forest.) measure with calipers

izdaudzināt *vt* praise, extol

izdaudzināts *adj, part* of **izdaudzināt** famous

izdauzīt *vt* **1.** knock out; **2.** beat out; thresh; **3.** hammer

izdauzīties *vr* **1.** knock a long time; **2.** (col.) romp to one's heart's content; **3.** gad about

izdāvāt *vt* give away

izdāvināt *vt* give away

izdebatēt *vt* debate

izdebatēties *vr* debate a long time

izdēdējis *adj, part* of **izdēdēt** thin, emaciated; **i. kā līķis** cadaverous

izdēdēt *vi* **1.** emaciate, waste away; **2.** weather

izdedzināt *vt* **1.** burn a hole; **2.** burn out; **3.** use up by burning; **4.** cauterize; **5.** calcinate, roast; (of ceramics) fire; **6.** (of animals) drive out with fire

izdedzis *adj, part* of **izdegt** (of fuses) blown

izdedēi *nm pl* slag; dross; calx; cinder

izdedžu bloks *nm* cinder block

izdega *nf* burn site (in a forest); parched piece of land

izdegsnis *nm* burn site

izdegt *vi* burn out; burn away; (of fire) go out

izdegulis *nm* charred stick of firewood

izdegums *nm* burn site (in a forest); parched piece of land

izdejot *v* **1.** *vi* dance out of (a place); **2.** *vt* finish dancing; **3.** *vt* do dance steps, perform a dance

izdejoties *vr* dance to one's heart's content; enjoy a good, long dance

izdekorēt *vt* decorate

izdeldēt *vt* **1.** wear through; **2.** exterminate, wipe out

izdelverēt *vi* stumble out of (a place)

izdelverēties *vr* romp a long time

izdemolēt *vt* (of the interior of a building) vandalize

izdēnēt *vi* wear out

izdēstīt *vt* (of plants) set out; plant apart

izdēstīties *vr* plant a long time

izdēt *vt* lay an egg

izdevas *nf pl* (folk.) a meal taken on the occasion of giving away a bride's dowry

izdevējdarbība *nf* publishing

izdevējs *nm* **1.** publisher; **2.** attendant (who hands out things, materials)

izdevenes *nf pl* (folk.) wedding at the bride's house

izdēvēties *vr* be referring to s.o. as __ for a long time; *vt* call, refer to

izdevība *nf* opportunity

izdevies *adj, part* of **izdoties 1.** successful; **2.** felicitous, well-turned

izdevīgi *adv* profitably; favorably, advantageously

izdevīgs *adj* **1.** profitable; **2.** favorable, advantageous; **3.** opportune; **4.** convenient

izdevīgums *nm* **1.** profitableness; **2.** advantage, advantageousness; **3.** convenience

izdevniecība *nf* publishing house

izdevum/s *nm* **1.** publication; **2.** edition; **negrozīts i.** printing; **3.** ~**i** expenses; cost; **pieskaitāmie** ~**i** overhead; **tiešie** ~**i** direct costs; ~**u uz-skaite** cost accounting

izdezinficēt *vt* disinfect

izdibināt *vt* find out, establish, get to the bottom of

izdīdīt *vt* **1.** train; **i. pēc notīm** train to perfection; **2.** (col.) order around

izdīdīties *vr* be fidgeting for a long time

izdīdzēt *vt* germinate

izdiebt *vi* rush out

izdiedelēt *vt* cadge

izdiedelēties *vr* be begging for a long time

izdiedzēt *vt* germinate

izdīdzināt *vt* germinate

izdiegt *vi* dash out

izdiena *nf* service time; ~**s uzšuve** service stripe

izdienējis *adj, part* of **izdienēt** retired, superannuated; out of service

izdienēt *vi, vt* **1.** complete a term of service; **2.** earn (by serving, working)

izdienēties *vr* serve (work) a long time

izdiet *v* **1.** *vi* dance out of (a place); **2.** *vt* finish dancing; **3.** *vt* do dance steps, perform a dance

izdieties *vr* dance to one's heart's content; enjoy a good, long dance

izdievoties *vr* swear (by God) repeatedly

izdīgsme *nf* (poet.) sprouting

izdīgt *vi* sprout

izdīkt *vt* cadge

izdīkties *vr* **1.** cry a long time; **2.** go around whining and pleading; **3.** buzz a long time

izdila *nf* worn-out spot, bare spot, hole

izdilas *nf pl* waning phase of the moon

izdilis *adj, part* of **izdilt 1.** emaciated; **2.** worn out, threadbare

izdilt *vi* **1.** waste away, become emaciated; **2.** wear out; wear a hole

izdilums *nm* **1.** worn-out spot; **2.** atrophy

izdimdināt *vt* make resound; make ring a long time

izdimdināties *vr* rumble a long time

izdiņģēt *vt* (com.) cadge, bum

izdipināt *vi* trot out

izdīrāt *vt* cut a slice of skin

izdiriģēt *vt* order around

izdirnēt *vi* (reg.) lose weight, grow thin

izdirnēties *vi* stand around idly a long time, cool one's heels

izdiskutēt *vt* discuss

izdiskutēties *vr* discuss a long time

izdižoties *vr* show off, swagger a lot

izdoba *nf* furrow

izdobe *nf* depression

izdobējis *adj, part* of **izdobēt** hollow

izdobēt *v* **1.** *vi* become hollow; **2.** *vt* hollow out

izdobt *vt* hollow out

izdobts *adj, part* of **izdobt** hollowed-out; con-cave

izdobums *nm* (rare.) depression

izdoma *nf* **1.** imagination; **2.** invention, fabrication

izdomājums *nm* fabrication, invention

izdomāt *vt* **1.** invent; think of; **2.** think out; **3.** make up, fabricate

izdomāties *vr* ponder, think long and hard, rack one's brain

izdošana *nf* **1.** publication; **2.** extradition; **3.** *pl* ~s (col.) expenses, outlays

izdošan/ās *nfr* success; **labu ~os!** good luck!

izdot *vt* **1.** give out, hand out; **i. pie vīra** marry off; **2.** publish; **3.** spend; **4.** give back change; **5.** issue; **6.** rent; **7.** extradite; **8.** betray; **i. līdz-vainīgos** turn state's evidence; **9.** yield (a har-vest); **10.** (of sounds) produce; **11.** (of laws) pass

izdotenes *nf pl* (folk.) beginning of a wedding at the bride's home

izdoties *vr irr* **1.** succeed; **2.** (col.) give a lot of (a thing)

izdraiskoties *vr* romp a long time

izdraiskuļoties *vr* romp a long time

izdraudēties *vr* keep threatening

izdraudzēties *vr* end a friendship

izdrāzt I *vt* whittle, make (by whittling)

izdrāzt II *vi* dash out

izdrāzties *vr* dash out

izdrebēties *vr* shiver a long time

izdrebināt *vt* rattle, shake a lot

izdrebināties *vr* shiver a long time

izdreijāt *vt* turn on a lathe

izdresēt *vt* (of animals) train

izdruka *nf* (compu.) printout

izdrupināt *vt* crumble

izdrupšana *nf* (tech.) pitting

izdrupt *vi* crumble, crumble away; pit

izdrupums *nm* crumbled spot (in a wall, ceiling)

izdubt *vi* become hollow

izducināties *vr* (of thunder) rumble a long time

izdudināties *vr* have a nice, long chat

izdūdot *vt* utter in a cooing voice

izdūdoties *vr* converse in cooing tones

izdūkt *v* **1.** *vt* hum (a tune); **2.** *vi* exit buzzing

izdukurēt *vt* catch with a dipnet

izdūlēt *vt* (of bees) smoke out; (of fish) catch by torchlight

izdūmot *vt* smoke out

izdumpoties *vr* be in rebellion a long time

izdungoties *vr* hum a long time

izdunkāt *vt* pummel

izdunkāties *vr* pummel each other a long time

izdurstīt *vt* prick, stick repeatedly; prick or stick a long time

izdurt *vt* **1.** run through, pierce; **i. caurumu** prick a hole, perforate; **2.** pierce and destroy (all, many); (of weeds) stick

izdurties *vr* pierce

izdusa *nf* rest, respite

izdusēties *vr* have a good sleep

izdusmoties *vr* have a fit of anger

izdvašot *vt* **1.** exhale; **2.** emanate

izdv[e]st [ē] *vt* **1.** whisper; **2.** exhale; **i. nopūtu** sigh; **3.** emanate; **4.** (ling.) aspirate

izdvēsums *nm* **1.** exhalation; **2.** (ling.) aspiration

izdzeltēt *vi* turn yellow

izdzenāt *vt* scatter, drive apart; chase

izdzenāties *vr* chase after (s.o. or sth.) a long time; (of insects) drive away

izdzert *vt* drink, drink up, empty (by drinking)

izdzerties *vr* **1.** drink one's fill; **2.** be consumed (in drinking)

izdzesēt *vt* cool

izdzesināt *vt* cool

izdzēst *vt* **1.** (of lights) turn off; (of fire) put out; **2.** erase; wipe off; blot out, blank

izdzēsties *vr* be putting out a fire for a long time

izdziedāt *vt* **1.** sing; **2.** sing through; **3.** sing out; **4. i. balsi** ruin one's voice singing

izdziedāties *vr* sing to one's heart's content

izdziedēt *vt* cure, heal

izdziedēties *vr* heal, be cured; recover

izdziedināt *vt* cure, heal

izdziedināties *vr* heal, be cured; recover

izdzimt *vi* degenerate

izdzimten/is *nm*, **~e** *nf* degenerate

izdzimtība *nf* degeneracy

izdzimums *nm* monster

izdzinēj/s *nm*, **~a** *nf* (fig.) slave driver

izdzirdēt *vt* hear

izdzirdināt *vt* **1.** (of liquid feed) use up; **2.** feed on milk

izdzirdīt *vt* **1.** feed (liquid food); **2.** feed on milk

izdzirst *vt* (obs.) hear

izdzisināt *vt* cool; allow to get cold

izdzisis *adj, part* of **izdzist 1.** (of lights, fire) gone out; (of eyes) dimmed; **2.** cold; **3.** (of fire, volcano) extinct; **4.** dead

izdzist *vi* **1.** (of lights, fire) go out; **2.** (of food) get cold; **3.** fade, fade away; **4.** (poet.) die

izdzisums *nm* fade-out

izdzīt I *vt* **1.** drive out; turn out; **2.** (of nails) drive through; **3.** push out; **i. atvases** sprout (shoots); **i. vagu** plow a furrow; **4.** (bot.) force; **5.** shave; shape by shaving; **i. stigu** clear an easement; **6.** drive hard; sweat

izdzīt II *vi* heal

izdzīties *vr* **1.** chase after s.o. a long time; **2.** drive oneself ragged by traveling over bad roads

izdzītnis *nm* **1.** shoot; **2.** expellee

izdzīve *nf* debauchery

izdzīvošana *nf* survival

izdzīvot *v* **1.** *vi* survive; **2.** *vt, vi* live, pull through; **viņš ilgi neizdzīvos** he is not long for this world; **3.** *vt, vi* manage, make both ends meet; **4.** *vt* (col.) drive out, force out; **5.** *vt, vi* experience; feel; **6.** *vt* live through; **7.** *vt* squander; **i. prātu** take leave of one's senses

izdzīvoties *vr* **1.** have a great time; **2.** live, stay; **3.** (col.) play with

izdzīvotspēja *nf* survivability

īze *nf* **1.** crack in the ice; **2.** strip (of land, of fabric)

izecēt *vt* **1.** harrow; **2.** scrape

izecēties *vr* **1.** harrow a long time; **2.** quarrel, fight

izēdāj/s *nm*, **~a** *nf* glutton

izēdas *nf pl* (of food eaten by animals) leftovers

izēdināt *vt* **1.** feed; **2.** burn (with a corrosive substance)

izēdināties *vr* feed a long time

izēdums *nm* corroded spot

izeja *nf* **1.** exit; (fig.) way out; **papildus i.** emergency exit; **2.** start; **3.** output; **4.** outing; (mil.) on pass, liberty

izejam/s *adj, part* of **iziet**, usu. *defin* **izejamais 1.** **~ā diena** day of rest; **2.** (of clothing) Sunday, for good

izejas punkts *nm* starting point; point of departure

izejas stāvoklis *nm* starting position

izejas transformātors *nm* output transformer;

izejas uniforma *nf* dress uniform

izejmateriāls *nm* raw material

izejošs *adj, part* of **iziet** (of mail) outgoing

izejpoz[i]cija [ī] *nf* starting position

izejprodukts *nm* primary product

izekscerptēt *vt* excerpt

izejviela *nf* raw material

izelpa *nf* exhalation

izelpojums *nm* exhalation

izelpot *vt* exhale

izelpoties *vr* breathe eagerly

izelsāt *vt* = izelsot

izelsāties *vr* = izelsoties

izelsot *vt* speak between sobs

izelsoties *vr* 1. sob a long time; 2. pant, gasp

izelst *vt* utter with difficulty, gasp

izelsties *vr* pant a long time

izēnot *vt* shade

izentalpisks *adj* isenthalpic

izentropa *nf* isentrope

izentrops *adj* isentropic

izērmot *vt* 1. disfigure; 2. play a joke on s.o.

izērmoties *vr* clown around a lot

izerroties *vr* fuss a long time

izēst *vt* 1. eat up; 2. (of boring insects) eat, eat through; kāpuru ~s worm-eaten; 3. corrode; 4. (col.) drive out, make life unbearable

izēsties *vr* 1. eat one's fill; 2. (of corrosive liquids) eat through; 3. i. cauri work one's way through (a quantity of books, documents)

izēvelēt *vt* shape with a plane

izēvelēties *vr* plane a long time

izfantazējums *nm* product of one's imagination

izfantazēt *vt* make up, concoct, fabricate

izfantazēties *vr* engage in fantasy

izfasēt *vt* pack; bottle

izfilmēt *vt* use up film

izfilmēties *vr* film a lot

izfilozofēties *vr* philosophize a lot

izfiltrēt *vt* filter

izfiltrēties *vr* be filtered

izformēšana *nf* disbandment

izformēt *vt* disband

izfotografēt *vt* use up film

izfotografēties *vr* 1. have pictures taken of oneself; 2. take a lot of pictures

izfrēzēt *vt* shape by milling

izgādāt *vt* procure

izgadīties *vr* 1. appear; 2. happen

izgaidīties *vr* wait a long time; velti i. wait in vain

izgailēt *vi* (of embers) die out

izgainīt *vt* (of animals) shoo, scatter, drive away

izgainīties *vr* (of animals) be shooing for a long time

izgaiņāt *vt* (of animals) scatter, drive away

izgaiņāties *vr* (of animals) be shooing for a long time

izgaisināt *vt* 1. dispel; 2. squander, waste; 3. (col.) lose

izgaismojums *nm* (photo.) exposure

izgaismot *vt* 1. light; (photo.) expose; 2. (fig.) throw light on, elucidate; 3. (compu.) highlight

izgaismotājs *nm* slide viewer, light box

izgaisot *vt* aerate

izgaist *vi* 1. vanish, disappear; 2. perish; 3. die out

izgājiens *nm* 1. (fencing) lunge, thrust; 2. sally

izgājušais *adj* 1. (obs.) past, last; 2. (of papers) outgoing

izgalējies *adj, part* of izgalēties ravenous

izgalēt *vt* exterminate

izgalēties *vr* 1. struggle in vain, labor in vain; 2. romp; 3. become ravenous; 4. avoid

izgalvot *vt* post bail

izgandējis *adj, part* of izgandēt emaciated

izgandēt *vi* 1. perish; 2. starve

izganīt *vt* graze, pasture

izgānīt *vt* cuss out

izganīties *vr* 1. herd a long time; 2. graze a long time

izgānīties *vr* cuss each other out

izgārgt *vt* roar

izgaŗlaikoties *vr* be bored

izgarnēt *vt* (of food) garnish

izgarojumi *nm pl* fumes; vapors

izgarošana *nf* evaporation

izgarošanas mērītājs *nm* evaporimeter

izgarot *v* **1.** *vi* evaporate; transpire; **2.** *vt* exude

izgaršot *vt* taste

izgaršoties *vr* taste repeatedly

izgāšanās *nfr* **1.** failure; **2.** faux pas

izgatave *nf* manufacture

izgatavot *vt* make; prepare; manufacture

izgaudoties *vr* howl a long time

izgausties *vr* complain for a long time

izgavēties *vr* **1.** fast a long time; **2.** not have enough to eat for a long time

izgavilēt *vt* utter in a jubilant voice

izgavilēties *vr* **1.** exult, shout for joy; **2.** sing joyfully

izgāzelēties *vr* waddle out of (a place)

izgāzēt *vt* gas; disinfect with gas

izgāzt *vt* **1.** dump; pour out; **2.** spill; **i. podu** (sl.) make a faux pax; **3.** topple; **4.** fail (on a test); **i. kandidātūru** fail of election; **5.** (of anger) vent; **6.** thrust forward, make protrude

izgāzties *vr* **1.** fall out, spill; **2.** be blown down; **3.** (of a show) flop; (of a test) fail; **4.** (col., of anger) be vented on; **5.** (col.) slouch; **6.** (col.) make a faux pas

izgāztuve *nf* dump; landfill

izgāzums *nm* windfall area

izglabāties *vr* keep safe for a long time

izglābt *vt* save, rescue

izglābties *vr* escape; **tikko i.** have a narrow escape

izglaimot *vt* wheedle out of s.o.

izglaimoties *vr* flatter a lot

izglāstīt *vt* **1.** caress a long time; **2.** smooth

izglāstīties *vr* caress, pet a long time

izglaudīt *vt* **1.** stroke a long time; **2.** smooth

izglaudīties *vr* **1.** stroke a long time; **2.** (of cats) rub against (s.o.'s legs) a long time

izglaust *vt* smooth

izglausties *vr* **1.** (of cats) rub against (s.o.'s legs); **2.** stroke a long time

izgleznojums *nm* **1.** painted details; **2.** depiction

izgleznot *vt* paint (details); decorate with paintings

izglītība *nf* education; **augstākā i.** higher education; **tehniskā i.** technical training; **vidējā i.** secondary education

izglītojošs *adj, part* of **izglītot** educational

izglītot *vt* educate; train

izglītotāj/s *nm*, **~a** *nf* educator

izglītotība *nf* education

izglītoties *vr* get educated; train

izgludināt *vt* iron, press

izgludināties *vr* **1.** smooth out; **2.** be ironed; **3.** be ironing a long time

izglumēt *vi* become slimy (on the inside)

izglūnēties *vr* spy, peep a long time

izgodāt *vt* **1.** praise a lot; **2.** call (by a name); **3.** (obs.) marry off one's daughter

izgodāties *vr* call (s.o. by a name)

izgodēt *vt* = **izgodāt**

izgorīt *vt* (of hips) swivel

izgorīties *vr* **1.** poke around, dawdle; **2.** clamber out

izgoze *nf* sunbath

izgozēties *vr* lie in the sun

izgrābāt *vt* **1.** rake out; **2.** fumble

izgrabāties *vr* fumble (looking for sth.)

izgrabējis *adj, part* of **izgrabēt** rickety

izgrabēt *vi* (rare.) rattle out of

izgrabināt *vt* **1.** find, retrieve; **2.** rattle a long time

izgrabināties *vr* **1.** (col.) talk to one's heart's content; **2.** rattle a long time

izgrābstīt *vt* **1.** rake out; **2.** ransack; fumble

izgrābstīties *vr* fumble (looking for sth.)

izgrābt *vt* **1.** rake out; **2.** (fig, col.) grab

izgrābties *vr* rake a long time

izgraizīt *vt* cut up

izgrāmatot *vt* take off the books

izgrambāt *vt* rut

izgramstīt *vt* ransack

izgramstīties *vr* fumble (looking for sth.)

izgrandēties *vr* rumble a long time

izgraudot *vt* (hist.) work the land using share-tenants

izgraut *vt* breach

izgrauzt *vt* 1. gnaw (a hole); 2. erode

izgrauzties *vr* 1. gnaw through, eat one's way through; 2. gnaw to one's heart's content

izgrauzums *nm* 1. hole; 2. erosion

izgrāvot *vt* crisscross with ditches

izgrebt *vt* gouge out, hollow out

izgreznojums *nm* adornment, decoration

izgreznot *vt* adorn, decorate

izgreznoties *vr* 1. adorn oneself; 2. put on many adornments; spend much time adorning oneself

izgribēties *vr* hanker after

izgribis *nm* glutton

izgriezt I *vt* 1. turn out; 2. unscrew; 3. wring out; 4. (of milk, col.) centrifuge; ~s (col., of milk) skimmed; 5. sprain; 6. (col.) swing one's dance partner

izgriezt II (with iê) *vt* 1. cut, cut out; i. pogas (col.) beat, gain the upper hand; 2. carve, carve out; whittle; 3. clip

izgriezties I *vr* 1. (of vehicles) make a turn; 2. wriggle out of; 3. be turning a long time; 4. come unscrewed; 5. turn out

izgriezties II *vr* cut a long time; carve a long time

izgriezum/s *nm* 1. cut; 2. (newspaper) clipping; 3. neckhole; **(kleita) ar lielu ~u** low-necked (dress)

izgriezumu albums *nm* scrapbook

izgriež amais tilts *nm* swing bridge

izgrīlināt *vt* shake, destabilize

izgrīļojies *adj, part* of **izgrīļoties** wobbly

izgrīļoties *vr* become wobbly

izgrimēt *vt* make up

izgrimēties *vr* make oneself up

izgrozīt *vt* 1. turn this way and that, maneuver; 2. (col., fig.) manipulate

izgrozīties *vr* 1. posture; 2. circulate, move (in certain circles); 3. turn around; 4. evade, dodge; wriggle out (of a jam)

izgrūdējs *nm* (tech.) ejector

izgrūst *vt* 1. push out; 2. (col.) utter (through clenched teeth), blurt out; 3. (fig., col., of money) throw out, waste

izgrūsties *vr* push a long time

izgrūstīt *vt* elbow; push around a long time

izgrūstīties *vr* push each other a long time

izgrūt *vi* (of walls, rock) crumble, form gaps, collapse partially

izgruvums *nm* collapsed portion; landslide; cave-in

izgruzdēt *vi* 1. (of a hole) be burnt; 2. smolder out

izgudrēm *adv* with premeditation; slyly, artfully

izgudrojums *nm* invention

izgudrot *vt* invent; (col.) come up with, figure out

izgudroties *vr* try to figure out

izgudrotājs *nm*, ~a *nf* inventor

izgudrotāju tiesības *nf pl* patent right

izguldināt *vt* bed, bed down, provide sleeping accomodations; (of cattle) allow to rest

izguldīt *vt* bed, bed down, provide sleeping accomodations; (of cattle) allow to rest

izgulējums *nm* bedsore

izgulēt *vt* 1. spend the night; make up for lost sleep; 2. sleep off; i. dzērumu sleep oneself sober; 3. keep to bed; 4. (of matresses, sofas) wear out, flatten; 5. develop bed sores; 6. damage (by lying on top of sth.) 7. sleep in many places sequentially

izgulētāj/s *nm*, ~a *nf* great sleeper

izgulēties *vr* sleep well, have enough sleep

izgulsne *nf* precipitate

izgulsnējums *nm* deposit; precipitate

izgulsnēt *vt* precipitate

izgulsnēties *vr* precipitate; deposit

izgulšņāt *v* **1.** *vi* lie around, nap; **2.** *vt* nap (in several places)

izgulšņāties *vr* lie around, nap

izguļa *nf* great sleeper

izgumt *vi* bulge out

izgumzīt *vt* **1.** crumple; **2.** gulp down

izgurķoties *vr* (com.) loaf

izgūšana *nf* (compu.) retrieval

izgūt *vt* (compu.) retrieve

izgūtnēm *adv* **1.** eagerly; **2.** in snatches, by fits and starts

izgvelzt *vt* blurt out

izģeķot *vt* fool

izģeņģerēt *vi* stagger out

izģērbt *vt* undress; **i. kailu** strip naked

izģērbties *vr* undress; strip

izģērēt *vt* **1.** (of skins) tan; **2.** (col.) flay

izģindis *adj, part* of **izģinst** thin, emaciated

izģinst *vi* emaciate

izieskāt *vt* comb

iziešana *nf* shore leave; weekend furlough; ~s **atļauja** pass; ~s **punkts** exit point

iziet *vi irr* **1.** go out, leave; exit; **i. cilvēkos** go out and meet people; **i. jūrā** put to sea; **i. ļaudīs** become known; **i. no apgrozības** be taken out of circulation; **i. no galvas** forget; **i. no ierindas** fall out; **i. no jēgas** take leave of one's senses; **i. no krastiem** (of rivers, lakes) overflow; **i. no pacietības** lose patience; **i. no pikē** (aeron.) pull out of a dive; **i. no prāta** a. forget; b. lose one's mind; **i. no robežām** pass the limits; **i. no sevis** be beyond oneself; **i. !** dismissed! **tas man neiz-iet no galvas** I can't get it out of my head; **nevar no saviem poldiem i.** she hates to take off her finery; **vēders i.** having a bowel movement; **vai es drīkstu i.?** (educ.) may I be excused? **2.** *vt* walk through, cover (a distance); **3.** keep up with (in walking); **4.** go through, penetrate; **5.** spread; **6.** serve; spend time

(in a pursuit); go through; **i. kursu** take a course; **7.** undergo (a test, inspection); **8.** use up; spend; (of books) go out of print; **9.** cease; (of colors) fade; **i. no modes** go out of fashion; **10. i. pie vīra** (or **tautās; par sie-vu**) marry; **11.** turn out (well, badly); fare; **i. grei-zi** (or **šļūku**) fare badly, make a mistake; **i. sveikā** be none the worse for it; **i. plāni** do not so good, get it; **12.** lead to; face; open to; **13.** start; **14.** al-so *vt* (col.) pass through; **i. labu skolu** be well trained; **i. bargu dzīves skolu** go through the mill; **15. i. cauri** be accepted, go through; **16.** (with **uz**, col.) be given to; engage in

izieties *vi irr* go see sth. or s.o. many times; **i. rotaļā** play a long time

īziņš *nm* twine

izirdināt *vt* (of soil) loosen

izīrēt *vt* rent, let

izīrētāj/s *nm*, ~a *nf* renter, landlord

izirt I *vi* **1.** unravel; **2.** crumble, fall to pieces; (fig.) be ruined; disintegrate

izirt II *vt, vi* row out; row ashore

izirties *vr* row out; row ashore; row through

izirums *nm* disintegration

izjāde *nf* ride (on horseback)

izjādelēt *vt* crisscross on horseback

izjādelēties *vr* ride around

izjādināt *vt* ride (a horse) a long time

izjādīt *vt* **1.** ride (a horse) a long time; **2.** ride through

izjājiens *nm* ride

izjāņoties *vr* celebrate; live it up

izjāt *v* **1.** *vt, vi* ride out of, ride unto; **2.** *vi* go for a ride; **3.** *vt* ride through; **4.** *vt* (sl.) fool; take for a ride

izjāties *vr* ride a long time

izjaucams *adj, part* of **izjaukt** collapsible, knock-down

izjaukšana *nf* disassembly

izjaukt *vt* **1.** disarrange; scatter; break up; (of hair) tousle; rumple; disorder; **i. ierindu**

break the ranks; **i. līdzsvaru** throw off balance; **2.** dismantle, knock down; disassemble; **3.** wreck, spoil

izjautāt *vt* question

izjautātāj/s *nm*, ~**a** *nf* questioner

izjautāties *vr* ask around

izjautināt *vt* question

izjem- See **izņem-**

izjokojums *nm* a trick played on s.o.

izjokot *vt* play a trick on s.o.

izjokoties *vr* joke a long time; **neļauties i.** not allow to be toyed with

izjomot *vt* notch; scallop

izjoņot *vi* **1.** rush out, come tearing out; gallop out, leave in a gallop; **2.** dash back and forth

izjozt *vi* dash out

izjubrs *nm* Manchurian deer

izjūgt *vt* unharness, unyoke

izjūgties *vr* become unharnessed, become un-yoked

izjukt *vi* **1.** (of meetings, marriages, ranks) break up; (of hair) become mussed, become disheveled; **2.** fall apart; **3.** (of plans, intentions) fail, come to naught

izjukums *nm* breakup; unraveling

izjūsmoties *vr* enthuse a lot

izjust *vt* experience (emotionally), feel (keenly)

izjusts *adj, part* of **izjust** heartfelt, deeply felt

izjusties *vr* emphatize

izjūta *nf* sense; feeling, sensibility

izkacināt *vt* (reg.) question s.o.

izkaisām *adv* scattered, dispersed

izkaisīt *vt* scatter; litter (with bedding)

izkaisītājs *nm* spreader

izkaisīties *vr* scatter, get spilled

izkaisu *adv* scattered, dispersed

izkaitināt *vt* tease

izkaitināties *vr* tease a lot

izkakāties *vr* (child.) have a bowel movement

izkaldināt *vt* forge

izkalkulējams *adj, part* of **izkalkulēt** calculable

izkalkulēt *vt* calculate

izkalpība *nf* obligingness

izkalpīgi *adv* helpfully, obligingly

izkalpīgs *adj* helpful, obliging

izkalpināt *vt* exploit

izkalpojums *nm* service, favor

izkalpot *vt* **1.** serve one's time; **i. pensiju** qualify for a pension; **2.** please

izkalpoties *vr* **1.** serve a long time; **2.** (col., cont.) earn (Brownie points or promotion by currying favor)

izkalst *vi* **1.** dry, desiccate, parch; **2.** (fig.) grow thin

izkalt *vt* **1.** forge; mint; **2.** chisel (a hole); **3.** carve (from stone), sculpt

izkaltēt *vt* dry

izkalties *vr* **1.** forge, chisel or peck a long time; **2.** chisel through

izkaltis *adj, part* of **izkalst 1.** dried up; parched; **2.** thin, haggard

izkaļķot *vt* lime; whitewash

izkāmējis *adj, part* of **izkāmēt 1.** thin, haggard; **2.** ravenous

izkāmēt *vi* **1.** grow very thin; **2.** become ravenously hungry

izkāmēties *vr* **1.** grow very thin; **2.** become ravenously hungry

izkampt *vt* grab, snatch (up)

izkapāt *vt* **1.** chop; chop down; damage by chopping; **2.** dig (superficial) holes

izkāpelēt *v* **1.** *vi* climb all over, climb up and down; **2.** *vt* climb (many places)

izkāpaļāt *v* **1.** *vi* climb all over, climb up and down; **2.** *vt* climb (many places)

izkāpaļāties *vr* climb all over, climb up and down

izkāpelēties *vr* climb all over, climb up and down

izkāpinājums *nm* emphasis

izkapināt *vt* (of a scythe) sharpen (by drawing it with a hammer)

izkāpināt *vt* heighten, emphasize

izkāpināties *vr* emote

izkaplēt *vt* hoe

izkāpšana *nf* landing; alighting; disembarkation; ~s **vieta** pier

izkāpt *vi* get out of, step out of; alight, get off; disembark; **i. malā** land, go ashore; **i. no krastiem** (col.) overflow

izkāpties *vr* climb up and down a long time

izkaptnieks *nm* 1. scytheman, mower; 2. (hist.) a peasant armed with a scythe

izkapts *nf* scythe; (as part of a mower or harvester) blade

izkārdināt *vt* tantalize

izkārdināties *vr* tantalize repeatedly

izkārējis *adj* hankering

izkārēt *vt* hanker, crave

izkārēties *vr* hanker, crave

izkariķējums *nm* depiction in caricature

izkariķēt *vt* caricature

izkarināt *vt* hang out, hang up

izkarināties *vr* let oneself hang out, lean far out

izkāris *adj* hankering

izkārnējis *adj, part* of **izkārnēt** (col.) very hungry, starving

izkārnēt *vi* become very hungry

izkārnījuma akmens *nm* caprolith

izkārnījums *nm*, usu. *pl* **izkārnījumi** excrements; droppings

izkārnīšanās *nfr* defecation

izkārnīt *vt* clean

izkārnīties *vr* evacuate, defecate

izka[r]ojums [ŗ] *nm* victory

izka[r]ot [ŗ] *vt* attain; win

izka[r]o/ties [ŗ] *vr* 1. have enough war; ~**jies** having fought; 2. finish fighting

izkāroties *vr* long for sth. for a long time

izkārpīt *vt* scratch, scratch out, dig up

izkārpīties *vr* clamber out

izkarsēt *vt* heat through, warm thoroughly

izkarsēties *vr* get hot

izkarst *vi* 1. get hot; 2. hanker after

izkārst *vt* comb out; card

izkārsties *vr* 1. card a long time; 2. be carded

izkārstīt *vt* hang out, crane

izkārstīties *vr* stick out one's head

izkārt *vt* 1. hang out; 2. post; 3. display, (of flags) fly

izkartēt *vt* chart

izkārties *vr* let oneself hang out; **i. pa logu** lean (far) out the window

izkārtne *nf* 1. signboard; 2. (fig.) facade, window dressing

izkārtojums *nm* arrangement; order

izkārtot *vt* 1. arrange, organize; 2. arrange for

izkārtoties *vr* fall in line

izkāsēt *vt* cough up

izkāsēties *vr* finish coughing

izkasis *nm* small loaf of bread made of dough remnants

izkāsis *adj* (col.) hungry

izkasīt *vt* scrape out, scratch out

izkasīties *vr* 1. finish scratching oneself; 2. (col.) have a quarrel

izkasnis *nm* kneading trough scraper

izkast *vt* scrape out, scratch out

izkāst *vt* strain, filter

izkastrēt *vt* castrate

izkašāt *vt* scrape out, scratch out

izkašāties *vr* scratch a long time

izkašņāt *vt* scrape out, scratch out

izkašņāties *vr* scratch a long time

izkaukt *vt* (col.) obtain by begging

izkaukties *vr* 1. howl a long time; 2. cry a long time

izkaulēt *vt* obtain by haggling; obtain by begging

izkaulēties *vr* 1. haggle a long time; 2. beg a long time

izkaulots *adj* (of meat) boneless

izkaunēties *vr* feel ashamed for a long time

izkaunināt *vt* shame thoroughly

izkausēt *vt* **1.** melt; **2.** dissolve

izkaušanās *nfr* fistfight; **vispārēja i.** free-for-all, battle royal

izkaut *vt* slaughter, exterminate

izkauties *vr* have a fight

izkāzoties *vr* celebrate a wedding

izklabināt *vt* (of a pipe) empty (by knocking); tap (a rhythm)

izklabināties *vr* rattle a long time

izklačot *vt* tattle

izklačoties *vr* gossip a long time

izkladzināt *vt* (col.) **1.** ballyhoo; **2.** blab out

izkladzināties *vr* **1.** cackle a long time; **2.** broadcast (rumors, news)

izklaidām *adv* scattered, dipersed

izklaide *nf* recreation, amusement

izklaidens *adj* absent-minded

izklaides literātūra *nf* light literature

izklaidēšanās *nfr* diversion, amusement

izklaidēt *vt* divert, amuse, entertain

izklaidēties *vr* divert oneself, amuse oneself, have a good time

izklaidība *nf* absentmindedness

izklaidīgi adv absentmindedly

izklaidīgs *adj* absentminded

izklaidīgums *nm* absentmindedness

izklaids *adj* scattered, dispersed; sparse

izklaidsēja *nf* broadcast seeding

izklaidu *adv* scattered, dispersed

izklaidus *adv* scattered, dispersed

izklaigāt *vt* broadcast shouting

izklaigāties *vr* yell to one's heart's content, yell a long time

izklaiņot *vt* roam through

izklaiņoties *vr* roam a long time

izklājlapa *nf* (compu.) spreadsheet

izklājprogramma *nf* (compu.) spreadsheet program

izklājums *nm* **1.** lining, covering; **2.** (geom.) development

izklakšķināt *vt* click (a rhythmic pattern)

izklanīties *vr* bow a lot

izklapatāt *vt* (col.) procure, obtain

izklapēt *vt* (barb., of rugs) beat

izklāstījums *nm* recounting; exposition, outline

izklāstīt *vt* **1.** explain, give an account of, expound; **2.** spread out

izklāsts *nm* recounting; exposition, outline

izklāt *vt* **1.** spread out; **2.** line; cover; **i. ar flīzēm** tile; **i. ar grīdsegu** carpet

izklāties *vr* spread

izklaudzināt *vt* knock, inspect by knocking

izklaudzināties *vr* knock in vain

izklausīšana *nf* auscultation

izklausīt *vt* auscultate

izklausīties *vr* **1.** listen long and hard; listen to one's heart's content; **2.** (*3rd pers*) sound like; **man izklausījās** I seemed to hear; **izklausās ne-ticami** it sounds incredible; **tas ne pēc kā neiz-klausās** it does not sound right

izklaušināt *vt* question; examine

izklaušināties *vr* ask around

izklauvēšana *nf* (med.) percussion

izklauvēt *vt* (med.) percuss

izklauvēties *vr* knock in vain

izklēgāties *vr* shout to one's heart's content

izklejot *vt* roam, roam through

izklejoties *vr* roam far and wide

izklepot *vt* cough up, expectorate

izklepoties *vr* **1.** cough; have a coughing fit; **2.** be through coughing

izklibot *vi* limp out of

izklīdināt *vt* **1.** disperse; scatter; dissipate; **2.** dispel

izklīdu *adv* scattered, sipersed

izklīdus *adv* scattered, dispersed

izklidzināt *vi* clip-clop out of; clip-clop through

izkliede *nf* (ballistics, optics, statistics) dispersion; (phys.) scattering; **ačgārnā i.** backscattering; **~s konuss** cone of dispersion

izkliedes ķermenis *nm* scattering body

iskliedes leņķis *nm* scattering angle

izkliedēt *vt* **1.** scatter; (phys.) disperse; diffuse; (of hay, straw) ted; **2.** dispel

izkliedētājs *nm* spreader

izkliedētā skleroze *nf* multiple sclerosis

izkliedēti *adv* scattered, dispersed

izkliedētība *nf* dispersion, scattering

izkliedēties *vr* disperse, scatter

izkliedsēja *nf* broadcast seeding

izkliedu *adv* dispersed, scattered

izkliedus *adv* dispersed, scattered

izkliedziens *nm* shout, ejaculation

izkliegt *vt* **1.** shout; proclaim noisily; **2. i. balsi** lose one's voice (by shouting)

izkliegties *vr* shout to one's heart's content

izkliest *vt* **1.** scatter; (of hay, straw) ted; **2.** dispel

izklimst *vi* roam all over

izklinkāt *vi* gallumph out of

izklinkstināt *vi* clip-clop out of; clip-clop through

izklīst *vi* scatter; **i.!** (mil.) dismissed! fall out!

izkluburot vi stump out

izklumburot *vi* stump out

izklunkšķināt *vt* gulp down, gurgle while drinking

izklunkurot *vi* stumble out of

izklupiens *nm* (fencing) lunge, thrust

izklupt *vi* **1.** (fencing) lunge; **2.** stumble out, stumble through

izkļauties *vr* bulge out, protrude

izkļūt *vi* get out of, escape

izknāb(ā)t *vt* **1.** peck out; **2.** peck all, peck empty; **3.** peck holes

izknaibīt *vt* pinch all over

izknakstīties *vr* flirt

izknibināt *vt* pick out

izknibināties *vr* tinker, putter, fiddle a long time

izkniebt *vt* **1.** pinch off; **2.** punch (a hole)

izknist *vi* sprout

izknitināt *vt* germinate

izknubināt *vt* pick out

izkodinājums *nm* etched spot; etching

izkodināt *vt* etch; (of corrosive substances) burn

izkodīt *vt* chew

izkodums *nm* bite

izkomandēt *vt* order around

izkombinēt *vt* put together; scheme; (sl.) figure out

izkomplektēt *vt* disband; disperse; dismantle

izkonkurēt *vt* displace (in the course of business competition)

izkonspektēt *vt* make an outline

izkonstruēt *vt* design

izkontrolēt *vt* check

izkopt *vt* cultivate, develop; improve, perfect, refine

izkoptība *nf* refinement

izkopties *vr* develop; refine

izko[r]iģējums [rr] *nm* correction

izko[r]iģēt [rr] *vt* correct

izkost *vt* bite; **i. gabalu** take a bite out of; **i. cau-rumu** bite a hole

izkosties *vr* **1.** bite a long time; **2.** seep through

izkrāmēties *vr* (barb.) move out

izkrāpt *vt* cheat out of

izkrāsot *vt* paint

izkrāsoties *vr* make oneself up

izkrāšņot *vt* adorn

izkratināt *vt* = izkratīt

izkratīt *vt* **1.** shake out; **i. sirdi** unburden oneself to, open one's heart; **2.** search, conduct a search; **3.** shake a long time

izkratīties *vr* shake a long time

izkraukāt *vt* cough up

izkraukāties *vr* hawk a long time

izkraut *vt* unload; **i. par daudz** overland; **i. par maz** shortland

izkrauties *vr* be loading a long time

izkrautne *nf* emporium, mart

izkrautuve *nf* dock, loading platform, sto-wage

izkravāt *vt* **1.** unpack, empty; **2.** spread out

izkravāties *vr* **1.** move out; **2.** rummage a long time

izkrāvēj/s *nm*, ~a *nf* unloader

izkrēpot *vt* cough up

izkrēpoties *vr* expectorate a lot

izkrimst *vt* gnaw (a hole)

izkrist *vi* **1.** fall out, drop; (of hair, teeth) lose; **i. no takts** (col.) miss time; **i. no lomas** act out of character; **2.** (col., of test performance) fail, flunk; **3.** not take place

izkrista|l|izējums [ll] *nm* cristallization

izkrista|l|izēšanās [ll] *nfr* crystallization

izkrista|li|zēt [ll] *vt* crystallize

izkrista|l|izēties [ll] *vr* crystallize

izkristies *vr* lose weight

izkrišana *nf* failure

izkritiens *nm* miss

izkritizēt *vt* criticize thoroughly

izkrokot *vt* put in pleats

izkropļojums *nm* **1.** distortion; **2.** mutilation, disfigurement

izkropļot *vt* **1.** distort; **2.** mutilate, disfigure

izkruķīt *vt* (com.) drive out

izkruzuļot *vt* add frills, frill

izkuģot *vt* **1.** sail through; **2.** crisscross sailing

izkūkot *vt* **i. prātu** (col.) go nuts

izkūkoties I *vr* cuckoo a long time

izkūkoties II *vr* mope around a long time

izkūleņot *vi* come tumbling out

izkūleņoties *vr* tumble a lot

izkuls *nm* yield (of grain in threshing)

izkulstas *nf pl* shives

izkulstīt *vt* swingle

izkult *vt* **1.** thresh; (of dough) beat: **2.** whip

izkulties *vr* **1.** thresh a lot; **2.** get threshed; **3.** get out of (a mess), extricate oneself

izkultivēt *vt* **1.** (of agricultural land) improve; **2.** (of plant varieties) develop

izkūlums *nm* yield (of grain in threshing)

izkunkstēt *vi* utter in a moaning voice

izkunkstēties *vr* moan a long time

izkūņāties = **izkūņoties**

izkūņoties *vr* **1.** leave the cocoon; (fig., col.) shed the wraps; **2.** (fig., col.) develop

izkūpēt *vi* **1.** dissipate; **2.** (fig., col.) go up in smoke; evaporate; **i. gaisā** (col.) melt into the air, go up in smoke

izkūpināt *vt* **1.** (of cigarettes, cigars) smoke (to the end); **2.** smoke out; (fig.) make it too hot for s.o.

izkuplināties *vr* develop

izkurcēt *vi* (of vegetables) become pithy

izkurēties *vr* (of fire in an oven) burn out

izkurināt *vt* **1.** heat; **2.** use up in heating

izkurnēties *vr* grumble, complain a lot

izkurņāt *vt* (col.) dig up

izkurt *vt* heat

izkurtējis *adj, part* of **izkurtēt 1.** rotten; pithy, spongy; **2.** (fig.) corrupt

izkurtēt *vi* **1.** (of vegetables) become pithy; **2.** (fig.) become corrupt

izkurties *vr* (of fire in an oven) burn out

izkurtis *adj* rotten; pithy, spongy

izkūsāt *vi* boil over

izkust *vi* **1.** melt; **2.** dissolve

izkustēt *vi* leave; **i. ļaudīs** go out in the public

izkustēties *vr* **1.** move (from a spot); budge; stir; **2.** move, stretch one's legs; **3.** loosen; **4.** go out in the public

izkustināt *vt* **1.** move, get moving; **2.** loosen; **3.** stretch one's legs

izkusuma morēna *nf* meltout till

izkusums *nm* meltout

izkveldēt *vt* sear

izkveldināt *vt* sear

izkvēlināt *vt* (of embers) let die

izkvēlot *vi* (of fire, embers) die

izkvēpēt *v* **1.** *vt* fumigate; **2.** *vi* smolder

izkvēpināt *vt* **1.** fumigate; **2.** drive out by fumigation; **3.** use up fumigating

izkvernēt *vi* spend time, wait long

izkvernēties *vr* wait in vain

izkviekties *vr* squeal a lot

izķeksēt *vt* **1.** hook, pull out with a hook, fish out; **2.** eat carelessly

izķemmēt *vt* **1.** comb; **2.** comb out

izķemmēties *vr* comb one's hair a long time

izķēmot *vt* disfigure; distort; caricature

izķēmoties *vr* clown a lot

izķencēt *vt* (col.) get out of, fish out of

izķengāt *vt* slander

izķengāties *vr* slander (up and down, a long time)

izķeparāties *vr* scramble out of; extricate oneself

izķēpāt *vt* (col.) **1.** smear all over; **2.** mess up, waste

izķēpāties *vr* mess a long time

izķepēt *vt* **1.** smear, daub all over; **2.** use up by smearing, daubing; **3.** gobble up

izķepuroties *vr* scramble out of; extricate oneself

izķērnāt *vt, vi* (col.) **1.** smear all over; **2.** mess up; waste

izķerrot *vt* **1.** distribute using wheelbarrows; **2.** (hist.) ride out of a factory in a wheelbarrow

izķērstīties *vr* **1.** chase after for a long time; **2.** flirt a lot

izķert *vt* **1.** catch (many, all); **2.** snatch, grab; **3.** (of merchandise) snatch up

izķerties *vr* chase after for a long time

izķēzīt *vt* (com.) **1.** waste; **2.** spoil, damage

izķidāt *vt* (of poultry) draw, eviscerate; (of fish) clean, gut

izķīķēt *vt* (of poultry) draw, eviscerate; (of fish) clean, gut

izķīlāt *vt* redeem a pawned article

izķīvēties *vr* have a quarrel

izķuidīt *vt* (com.) drive out

izlabināt *vt* entice out of (a place)

izlabināties *vr* try to entice s.o. to come out

izlabot *vt* **1.** repair; mend; **2.** correct; **3.** (of a grade) improve

izlāčot *vi* waddle out

izlāde *nf* (el.) discharge

izlādēt *vt* **1.** (of firearms) unloda, clear; defuse; **2.** (el.) discharge; **3.** (col., of loads) unload

izlādēties I *vr* **1.** (el., fig.) discharge; **2.** (col.) fizzle; **3.** (col.) unburden oneself

izlādēties II *vr* cuss

izlaide *nf* **1.** production; **2.** (of crane booms) range

izlaidenis *nm* undisciplined youth

izlaidība *nf* **1.** lack of discipline; **2.** wantonness, licentiousness, dissoluteness

izlaidies *adj, part* of **izlaisties** undisciplined

izlaidīgi *adv* in an undisciplined manner; licentiously

izlaidīgs *adj* **1.** undisciplined; **2.** wanton, licentious, dissolute

izlaidīgums *nm* **1.** lack of discipline; **2.** licentiousness, dissoluteness

izlaidināt *vt* (of fat) render

izlaidum/s *nm* **1.** graduation; **2.** (graduates) class; **3.** (of bank notes, stamps) issue; **4.** (production) series; **5.** omission; (typ.) out; **6.** (of garments, structures) extension; **7.** ~a rampa (RR) runoff ramp

izlaimēties *vr* be lucky

izlaipot *vi* hedge, sidestep, maneuver

izlaipoties *vr* hedge, sidestep, maneuver

izlaist *vt* **1.** let out; **i. balastu** a. discharge ballast; b. cut one's losses; **i. brīvībā** release, set free; **i. gaisu** deflate; **neizlaist no acīm** not leave out of one's sight; **i. no prāta** let slip one's mind; **i. tvaiku** let off steam; **2.** let go; drop; **3.** pass (through a machine, filter); (of milk) skim; **4.** (of children) spoil; **5.** (of bonds, stamps) issue; publish; (of manufactured goods) turn out; **6.** (of hay) ted; **7.** (of hair) let out; **8.** stick out, show; **9.** exude; emit; **i. ikrus** spawn; **10.** (of garments) let out, (of structures) lengthen; **11.** omit; elide; **12.** (of classes, school days, meetings) miss; **13.** (of news, rumors) spread; **14.** graduate; **15.** (col.) throw out (through an opening) ◊ **i. no acīm** lose sight of; **i. līkumu** go for a run; go for a ride; **i. riksi** trot (a horse); run; **i. no rokām** let slip, let go; **i. grožus no rokām** give up the reins; **i. garu** (col.) give up one's ghost; **i. tautās** marry off

izlaisten/is *nm*, ~e *nf* undisciplined, spoiled person

izlaisties I *vr* **1.** fly out of; escape; **2.** fly through

izlaisties II *vr* **1.** stretch out; **2.** (of children) get spoiled; **i. mutē** (col.) use dirty language

izlaistīt *vt* spill

izlaistīties *vr* spill

izlaists *adj, part* of **izlaist** II spoiled, naughty

izlaistuvis *nm* (col.) spoiled brat

izlaizīt *vt* lick clean

izlakt *vt* lap up

izlamāt *vt* cuss out, call names

izlamāties *vr* **1.** swear; **2.** cuss each other out

izlangāt *vt* (reg.) cuss out

izlāpīt *vt* mend

izlāpīties *vr* manage, make do; do without

izlasas *nf pl* leavings, trash

izlase *nf* **1.** selection; *gen* ~s choice; (of teams) select, (of troops) crack; (of timber cutting) selective; (of testing) random; **2.** elite; **3.** (stat.) sample; **nejauša i.** random sample

izlasīt I *vt* **1.** read, read through; **2.** finish reading

izlasīt II *vt* pick out; pick over

izlasīties I *vr* read, read a lot

izlasīties II *vr* (obs.) select

izlasīties III *vr* (col.) beat it, scram

izlāsot *vi* (rare.) percolate; drip

izlaupīšana *nf* plunder

izlaupīt *vt* plunder

izlaupītājs *nm* plunderer

izlaušanās *nfr* breakout; **i. no cietuma** prison break

izlauzīt *vt* **1.** break off; **2.** loosen, shake loose; **3.** crumble; **4.** (of words) twist (to sound differently); **i. galvu** rack one's brain

izlauzīties *vr* struggle with

izlauzt *vt* **1.** break off, break out; (of stumps) uproot; (of doors) force, break open; **2.** brake a hole or passage; **i. ceļu** clear a path, blaze a trail; **i. sev ceļu** (fig.) make a place for oneself in the world, fight one's way to the top

izlauzties *vr* **1.** fight one's way through; break through; break out; (of sighs, cries) escape; **2.** wrestle enough; wrestle a long time; **3.** (of emotions) show, manifest

izlavēt *vi* sail through (by tacking)

izlavierēt *vi* **1.** sail through (by tacking); **2.** maneuver (through, among)

izlavīties *vr* slip out, sneak out; slip away

izlēcējs *nm* one who acts up; spotlight grabber

izlēciens *nm* **1.** spring forward; jumping out; **2.** acting up; outrage; **3.** sudden verbal attack

izlēcīgi *adv* in an attention-getting manner

izlēcīgs *adj* attention-getting

izlecināt *vt* **1.** make jump (out of a place); **2.** dance (many or for a long time)

izleja *nf* drain

izlējums *nm* **1.** spill; **2.** casting

izlēkāties *vr* jump to one's heart's content

izleksēt *vt* (col., of liquid food) eat up

izlēkšana *nf* attention-getting

izlēkšot *vi* **1.** jump out of, jump into; **2.** gallop through; run through

izlēkt *vi* **1.** jump out; **2.** (col.) act conspicuously, make oneself conspicuous

izlēkties *vr* **1.** jump a long time; **2.** (basketball) tip off

izlēmīgi *adv* decisively

izlēmīgs *adj* decisive

izleminät *vt* dislocate

izlemt *vt* decide; **i. par labu** (jur.) find for the accused; **i. par sliktu** find against the accused

izlemtība *nf* decisiveness

izlēņot *vt* (hist.) give as a fee

izlepēt *vt* (col.) eat up

izlepis *adj, part* of **izlept** picky, fastidious

izlepņa *nf, nm* fastidious, demanding person

izlepoties *vr* boast

izlept *vi* become fastidious

izlice *nf* boom (of a crane)

izlicēj/s *nm*, ~a *nf* one that puts out, one that sets

izlidināt *vt* (col.) toss out; make fly

izlidināties *vr* 1. fly out; 2. fly around, fly a long time

izlidleņķis *nm* angle of departure

izlidojums *nm* flight; sortie

izlidot *vi* 1. fly out; 2. (of birds, insects) fledge; begin flying; 3. (of aircraft, birds) leave, take off

izlidoties *vr* fly a long time

izlīdzēj/s *nm*, ~a *nf* 1. conciliator; 2. treacherous appeaser

izlīdzēt *vi* help out

izlīdzēties *vr* 1. manage (to do with less); 2. **savstarpēji i.** help each other

izlīdzīgi *adv* helpfully

izlīdzīgs *adj* helpful

izlīdzinājums *nm* smoothing-out; leveling; alignment; (fig.) reconciliation

izlīdzināt *vt* smooth out, even out; level; align; (aeron.) flatten out; (fig.) reconcile; **i. savu vai-nu** undo a wrong

izlīdzinātāj/s *nm*, ~a *nf* leveler

izlīdzinātība *nf* equilibrium, harmony

izlīdzināties *vr* 1. smooth out, become even; level off; (of scores) become tied; 2. (mil., of a formation) dress; 3. pay restitution

izlīdzinošs *adj, part* of **izlīdzināt** conciliatory

izlīdzniecisks *adj* compromise-seeking

izlīdzsvarot *vt* balance

izliece *nf* deflection; curvature

izliedēt *vt* drench

izliedēties *vr* get drenched

izliegties *vr* keep denying

izliekt *vt* bend; arch

izliekties *vr* 1. bend, curve; 2. lean out

izliekts *adj, part* of **izliekt** 1. bent, curved, arched; 2. convex; spherical

izliekums *nm* bend, curve, curvature

izlielīt *vt* praise, extol

izlielīties *vr* brag, boast

izliesēt *vi* grow thin

izliesmot *vi* (of fire) die down

izliešana *nf* (metall.) teeming

izliet *vt* 1. pour out; spill; (of blood) shed; 2. cast

izlietāt *vt* = **izlietot**

izlieties *vr* spill

izlietne *nf* sink

izlietojums *nm* use, usage; utilization

izlietot *vt* 1. use, utilize; 2. use up

izlietoties *vr* be used up

izlietuve *nf* sink

izlīgot *vi* come out swaying

izlīgoties *vr* 1. come out swaying; 2. sing enough Ligo songs

izlīgt *vi* be reconciled, make it up

izlīgums *nm* reconciliation

izliksis *nm* hypocrite

izlīksmoties *vr* 1. make merry, celebrate a lot; 2. finish celebrating

izlikšanās *nfr* pretence, sham, feint

izlikt *vt* 1. put out; **i. bērnu** abandon a baby, leave a baby at s.o.'s door; **i. posteņus** post sentries; 2. place, arrange; display; 3. evict; 4. (of traps) set, (of snares) lay, (of nets, fishing lines) set out; 5. (of bills, notices) post; 6. face, cover; **i. ar flīzēm** tile; 7. lay out (money), pay (for s.o.); 8. lay out, lay down; **i. kārtis** tell fortune (from cards)

izliktenis *nm* foundling

izlikties *vr* **1.** (*3rd pers*) appear, seem; **2.** pretend; **i. neredzējušam** pretend not to see; **i. par (inva-lidu)** put on the (invalid); **i. par mirušu** play dead; **i. par slimu** feign sickness, malinger

izlīkumojums *nm* curvature

izlīkumot *vt* curve

izlīkumoties *vr* twist and bend

izlīkums *nm* curve

izlīmēt *vt* **1.** (of notices, bills) paste; **i. ar papīru** line with paper; **i. ar tapetēm** paper (a room); **2.** use up in pasting

izliminat *vt* dislocate

izlimt *vi* become dislocated

izlingot *vt* (col.) throw out

izlipinat *vt* post

izlīst *vi* crawl out, slide out; **i. kā no zemes** pop up

izlīt *vi* **1.** pour out; empty; **2.** be drenched

izlīties *vr* **1.** rain a long time; **2.** be drenched

izlobīt *vt* **1.** husk, hull; shell; **2.** make out, understand; **i. lietas kodolu** get at the heart of the matter

izlobīties *vr* emerge

izlobt *vi* dash out, flee

izlocījums *nm* **1.** (of saw teeth) setting; **2.** loop

izlocīšanās *nfr* weaseling out; **bez i.!** don't try to weasel out of this one!

izlocīt *vt* **1.** decline; conjugate; **2.** (of one's limbs) stretch; **3.** (of saw teeth) set; **4.** bend variously; **5.** (of singing voice) vary, modulate

izlocītā ciņuzāle *nf* hair grass

izlocītā ķērsa *nf* wood bitter cress

izlocīties *vr* **1.** evade; weasel out; **2.** meander; **3.** wriggle; **4.** writhe

izlodāt *vt* **1.** crawl through; **2.** (of moles) tunnel; (of worms) eat through; **3.** crisscross

izlodāties *vr* crisscross at length

izloka *nf* bend

izloks *nm* curve, bend

izloksne *nf* dialect

izlolot *vt* bring up lovingly

izlopot *vt* (vulg.) make a fool of s.o.

izloze *nf* lottery, raffle; drawing (of prizes, starting positions)

izlozēt *vt* **1.** win (in a lottery); **2.** raffle; **3.** draw lots

izložņāt *vt* **1.** crawl through; **2.** (of moles) tunnel; **3.** (fig.) pry into, search throughout

izložņāties *vr* snoop around; (fig.) meander

izlūgt *vt* beg for, ask for

izlūgties *vr* **1.** beg for, ask for; **2.** keep begging, keep asking

izlūkdaļa *nf* intelligence unit

izlūkdati *nm pl* intelligence

izlūkdienests *nm* intelligence service

izlūkgājiens *nm* patrol mission

izlūkgrupa *nf* patrol

izlūkhelikopters *nm* observation helicopter

izlūkiebrukums *nm* reconnaissance by force

izlūklidmašīna *nf* reconnaissance plane

izlūklidojums *nm* reconnaissance flight

izlūkmašīna *nf* scout car

izlūkošana *nf* reconnaissance; **~s dienests** intelligence service

izlūkot *vt* reconnoiter, scout

izlūkpatruļa *nf* reconnaissance patrol

izlūks *nm* **1.** reconnoiterer, scout; patroller; **2.** (space, deep ocean) probe

izlūktrieciens *nm* reconnaissance by force

izlūkurbums *nm* exploratory well

izlūkvads *nm* reconnaissance patrol

izlumpačot *vi* lumber out of (a place)

izluncināt *vt* (of one's legs, in walking or dancing) stretch

izluncināties *vr* do a lot of tail-wagging; (fig.) flatter, fawn

izlupināt *vt* peel, shell, hull

izlutināt *vt* spoil, pamper, coddle

izlutināties *vr* get spoiled, grow soft

izlutis *adj* spoiled, pampered, soft

izlūzt *vi* **1.** break off; **2.** (of a break) form; **3.** fall through a break, break through

izļimt *vi* become dislocated

izļepatot *vi* lope out (of, unto)

izļēpot *vi* toddle out, totter out

izļimt vi (reg.) sprain

izļinkāt *vi* lope out (of, unto)

izļipot *vi* lope out (of, unto)

izļodzījies *adj, part* of **izļodzīties** loose, rickety, shaky

izļodzīt *vt* make loose; make rickety

izļodzīties *vr* become loose; become rickety

izļukt *vi* (col.) become loose; become rickety

izļurbot *vt* (vulg.) make a fool of s.o.

izļurcis *adj, part* of **izļurkt** (of garments, footwear) worn shapeless

izļurdzīties *vr* (col.) become loose; become wobbly

izļurkāt *vt* (col.) make loose; make rickety

izļurkāties *vr* (col.) become loose; become rick-ety

izļurkt *vi* (of garments, footwear) wear out shapeless

izmācīt *vt* teach, train

izmācīties *vr* learn

izmadarot *vt* embroider

izmainība *nf* transformation

izmainīt *vt* **1.** trade, exchange; (of money) change; **2.** modify, alter, change

izmainīties *vr* **1.** change; transform; **2.** pass each other (without meeting)

izmaiņa *nf* **1.** change; modification; **2.** exchange

izmaisīt *vt* stir, mix

izmaisīties *vr* **1.** be stirred; **2.** traipse around

izmaitāt *vt* spoil; damage

izmaksa *nf* **1.** payment; **2.** cost; expense

izmaksas diena *nf* payday

izmaksāt *vt* **1.** pay, pay off; **2.** cost; **3.** buy (treat)

izmaksāties *vr* spend a lot

izmakšķerēt *vt* hook, catch

izmaldināt *vt* lead astray; keep s.o. disinformed

izmaldīties *vr* **1.** wander around a long time; **2.** emerge (from a place where one has been lost)

izmalkot *vt* sip

izmalt *vt* **1.** put through the grinder; **i. pienu** (col., of milk) separate; **2.** (col.) roam through, traverse; **3.** grind

izmalties *vr* **1.** be ground; **2.** roam; slog through

izmalts *adj, part* of **izmalt 1.** ground; **2.** rutted

izmalums *nm* yield (of grinding)

izmanevrēt *vi* maneuver

izmanība *nf* agility; skill; resourcefulness

izmanīgi *adv* agilely; skillfully; resourcefully

izmanīgs *adj* agile; skillful; resourceful

izmanīgums *nm* agility; skill; resourcefulness

izmanīt *vt* sense

izmānīt *vt* cheat out of

izmanīties *vr* **1.** slip out; **2.** seize the opportunity

izmānīties *vr* slip out, slip away

izmantojums *nm* utilization; exploitation

izmantošana *nf* use; utilization; **ļaunprātīga i.** abuse; exploitation

izmantot *vt* **1.** use, make use of, utilize; **ļaunprātīgi i.** abuse; **2.** use up; **3.** take advantage of; **i. gadījumu** seize the occasion; make the most of an opportunity; **i. savā labā** turn to one's advantage; **4.** exploit

izmantotājs *nm*, **~a** *nf* exploiter

izmantoties *vr* be utilized

izmaņa *nf* agility; skill; resourcefulness

izmargot *vt* **1.** embroider; **2.** embroider

izmaršēt *vi* march out

izmasēt *vt* massage out

izmasēties *vr* **1.** be massaged; **2.** massage a long time

izmaukt *vt* **1.** put through, slip through; **2. i. stabuli** make a whistle (from a branch)

izmaukties *vr* slip out

izmauroties *vr* moo a long time

izmauties *vr* moo a long time

izmazgāt *vt* wash; wash out; **i. galvu** (col., fig.) take to task

izmazgāties *vr* **1.** be washed; come out in washing; **2.** wash a long time

izmāžot *vt* (col.) disfigure

izmāžoties *vr* clown a lot

izmēbelēt *vt* furnish

izmedīt *vt* hunt to extinction

izmēdīt *vt* jeer at, mock

izmedīties *vr* be hunting for a long time

izmēdīties *vr* mock one another a long time

izmēģinājuma ietaise *nf* pilot plant

izmēģinājuma laiks *nm* probationary period

izmēģinājuma stacija *nf* experimental station

izmēģinājumizdevums *nm* proofing publication

izmēģinājums *nm* test; trial; experiment

izmēģināšana *nf* testing; trial; experimentation

izmēģināt *vt* **1.** test; **2.** try; **i. roku** try one's hand; **3.** experiment with

izmēģinātāj/s *nm*, **~a** *nf* **1.** tester; **2.** experimenter

izmēģināties *vr* try several times, try unsuccessfully

izmeijot *vt* deck with boughs

izmeimurot *vi* stagger out

izmeistarot *vt* make, put together (with simple tools or inexpertly)

izmeklējums *nm* investigation; examination

izmeklēšana *nf* **1.** selection; **2.** (jur.) investigation; inquest; **3.** (med.) examination

izmeklēšanas cietums *nm* pretrial detention

izmeklēšanas tiesnesis *nm* examining magistrate

izmeklēt *vt* **1.** choose, select; **2.** search; **3.** (jur.) investigate; **4.** (med.) examine

izmeklētājs *nm*, **~a** *nf* examiner; (jur.) investigator; (jur.) referee

izmeklēties *vr* **1.** choose, select; **2.** search everywhere

izmeklēts *adj, part* of **izmeklēt** choice, select; fine, refined; recherché

izmeliorēt *vt* effect soil improvement

izmelot *v* **1.** *vi* tell a lie; **2.** *vt* exaggerate; turn one thing into another (in talking)

izmeloties *vr* tell a pack of lies; lie one's way out of

izmelst *vt* blab; tell lies

izmelsties *vr* blab a long time

izmēļoties *vr* talk to one's heart's content

izmērcēt *vt* **1.** drench; **2.** soak, ret, macerate

izmērcēties *vr* get drenched

izmērdēt *vt* starve to death

izmērdēties *vr* starve

izmērdināt *vt* starve

izmērējis *adj, part* of **izmērēt** thin, emaciated

izmērēt *vi* become emaciated

izmērījums *nm* measurement

izmērīt *vt* measure; gage; (of depth) sound, fathom

izmērīties *vr* measure one's own height; compare height measurements

izmērs *nm* **1.** measurement; size; **2.** dimension

izmērzīme *nf* (typ.) trim mark

izmest *vt* **1.** throw out; expel; dump; release (into the air); **i. no galvas** try to forget, put out of one's mind; **i. uz ielas** a. evict; b. fire; **i. pār bortu** (col.) throw overboard; **kā no laivas ~s** like fish out of water; **i. graudus līdz ar pe-lavām** throw out the baby with the bathwater; **2.** (of anchors, fishing lines, nets) cast; **i. krastā** cast ashore; **3.** empty; drink up; **4.** drop; **5.** (fig., of words spoken) toss out; **6.** measure off, pace off; **7.** (basketball) tip off; **i. līkumu** go for a (short) walk; **i. makšķeri** a. (col.) fish; b. (fig.) set out the bait; **i. vilnu** (sl.) have a fight

izmesties *vr* **1.** rush out; **2.** (col.) take off one's clothes; **i. kreklā** take off one's jacket, remain in shirtsleeves; **3.** (basketball) tip off; **4.** (of animals) drop prematurely

izmešanās *nfr* **1.** tipoff, jump ball; **2.** premature birth

izmeši *nm pl* emission; outflow

izmētāt *vt* scatter, fling about

izmētāties *vr* toss in bed

izmete *nf* (compu.) dump

izmetējs *nm* **1.** strawwalker; **2.** (of weapons) ex-tractor

izmetiens *nm* throw

izmetumi *nm pl* droppings

izmēzt *vt* **1.** sweep; **2. i. mēslus** cart out dung

izmeēģījums *nm* dislocation

izmežģīt *vt* dislocate

izmežģīties *vr* get dislocated

izmīcīt *vt* knead thoroughly

izmīcīties *vr* **1.** be kneaded; **2.** slog through

izmīdīt *vt* trample down

izmīdīties *vr* tread in place a long time

izmidzināties *vr* try to make s.o. go to sleep

izmiecēt *vt* tan (leather)

izmiecēties *vr* be tanned

izmiekšķējis *adj, part* of **izmiekšķēt** soft, rain-soaked

izmiekšķēt *vt, vi* soak

izmiekšķēties *vr* soak; soften (in soaking)

izmielot *vt* wine and dine

izmieloties *vr* feast on

izmierināties *vr* try calming s.o.

izmiglot *vt* spray

izmija *nf* (arch.) trimmer; auxiliary beam

izmīkt or **izmīkšt** *vi* (reg.) be soaked, be drenched

izmīlēt *vt* fall out of love

izmīlēties *vr* fall out of love

izmīlināties *vr* pet a long time

izmilzt *vi* (of boils) grow to the point to bursting

izmīļoties *vr* pet a long time

izminēt *vt* solve riddles a long time

izminēties *vr* **1.** mention a few; **2.** solve riddles a long time

izmīņāt *vt* trample

izmīņāties *vr* tread in place a long time

izmiņģēt *vt* (reg.) trample

izmircināt *vt* **1.** drench; **2.** soak, ret, macerate

izmircis *adj, part* of **izmirkt** soaking wet

izmirdzēt *vi* stop shining

izmirgot *vi* stop twinkling

izmiris *adj, part* of **izmirt** extinct; uninhabited

izmirkt *vi* be soaked, be drenched

izmirt *vi* die out; become extinct; (of an area) be-come depopulated

izmirties *vr* **i. badu** starve

izmisa *nf* (poet.) despair

izmisība *nf* (obs.) despair

izmisīgi *adv* desperately, frantically

izmisīgs *adj* desperate, frantic

izmisīgums *nm* desperateness

izmisis *adj, part* of **izmist** I despaired, desperate

izmist I *vi* lose courage, despair

izmist II *vi* get by; live through (the winter)

izmisties *vr* lose courage, despair

izmīstīt *vt* (of flax) brake

izmisum/s *nm* despair; **~a pilns** desperate

izmīt I (with î) *vt* trade, swap

izmīt II *vt* **1.** trample down; **2.** (of a path) beat; **3.** (of footwear) wear out

izmīties I *vr* pass each other

izmīties II *vr* (of footwear) wear out

izmitināšana *nf* keep (means, provisions)

izmitināt *vt* (of animals) keep; provide with food and shelter (temporarily)

izmitināties *vr* live; (of animals) be kept

izmīzties *vr* (com.) pee

izmocīt *vt* **1.** torment, torture; tire out, exhaust; **2.** eat or drink with difficulty; (of words) squeeze out

izmocīties *vr* struggle with; struggle through; suffer through; become exhausted

izmodināties *vr* keep trying to wake s.o. up

izmozēt *vt* (col.) play a trick on s.o.

izmūdīties *vr* slog through, slog out of

izmudžināt *vt* disentangle

izmugurot *vt* make a fool of s.o.

izmukt *vi* **1.** slip out, slip through; **2.** escape

izmuldēt *vt* blurt out

izmuldēties *vr* **1.** talk nonsense; **2.** blab on

izmuļķot *vt* make a fool of s.o.

izmuļķoties *vr* fool around a lot

izmuļļāt *vt* (com., of a road) rut

izmuļļāties *vr* **1.** slog out of; **2.** labor in vain

izmūrējums *nm* masonry

izmūrēt *vt* line with bricks (or stones); (of bricks, stones) shape, make

izmurgot *vt* see in a nightmare; spend time in nightmares

izmurgoties *vr* have nightmares

izmurmināt *vt* mumble

izmurmuļot *vt* mumble

izmutuļot *vi* bubble up; *vt* spew

iznabagot *vt* cadge

iznabagoties *vr* beg a long time

iznaidoties *vr* have a falling out

iznākt *vi* **1.** come out; (of a rash) appear; **i. cauri** come through; **i. priekšā** come forward; **2.** turn out; come of sth.; make; **i. pēc atbildes** (of a problem) get the answer; **cik tev iznāk?** (of a numerical answer) what do you get? **i. čiks** (col.) go pfft; **nekas neiznāks** it won't work; **3.** happen; **4.** be sufficient, suffice; **katram iznāk pa vienam** everybody gets one; **5.** come to; cost

iznākties *vr* come (repeatedly and in vain)

iznākums *nm* result; outcome

iznārstot *vi* finish spawning

iznārstoties *vr* finish spawning

iznasas tirdzniecība *nf* over-the-counter trade

iznašķēt *vt* snack on sweets (and finish them up)

iznašķēties *vr* snack on sweets a lot

iznelgot *vt* make a fool of s.o.

iznerrot *vt* **1.** make a fool of s.o.; **2.** (col.) spoil

iznerroties *vr* tease, mock a long time

iznērst *vt* spawn

iznervozēties *vr* be nervous, have one's nerves on edge

iznesas *nf pl* worn clothes, secondhand clothes

iznēsāt *vt* **1.** carry; deliver; **2.** (of rumors, germs) spread around; **3.** (of babies) carry to term; **4.** (fig., of an idea) nurse; **5.** (col.) wear out

iznēsāties *vr* **1.** carry around a long time; **2.** spread; **3.** get worn out

iznēsātāj/s *nm*, **~a** *nf* carrier; stree vendor

iznesība *nf* good carriage, good bearing; good manners

iznesīgs *adj* of good carriage, of good bearing; well-mannered

iznesīgums *nm* good carriage, good bearing; good manners

iznest *vt* **1.** carry out, bring out; **i. cauri** carry through; **i. krastā** wash ashore; **i. valodas pa-saulē** spread a rumor; **2.** (of currents) carry away, take out; **3.** (sl.) deceive, fool

iznesties *vr* carry oneself

iznests *adj, part* of **iznest 1.** carried out; washed ashore; **2.** (of bridges) out

iznešanās *nfr* (col.) behavior

iznīcība *nf* transitoriness, perishability

iznīcīgs *adj* transitory, perishable

iznīcīgums *nm* transitoriness, perishability

iznīcināšana *nf* destruction; annihilation; (of explosives, arms) disposal

iznīcināt *vt* destroy; annihilate; **i. dīglī** nip in the bud; **pilnīgi i.** wipe out

iznīcinātāj/s *nm* **1.** (person, naval vessel) destroyer; **~a** *nf*; **2.** (airplane) fighter

iznīcinošs *adj, part* of **iznīcināt** destructive; annihilating; (fig., of looks) withering

iznīdēt *vt* exterminate, eradicate

izniecēt *vt* disparage, deprecate

izniecināt *vt* disparage, deprecate

izniekaļa *nf, nm* (folk.) despised person

izniekaļāt *vt* disparage, deprecate

izniekot *vt* **1.** waste; **2.** spoil; **3.** squander; **4.** make a fool of s.o.

izniekoties *vr* trifle, fool around a lot

iznievāt *vt* disparage, deprecate

izniknoties *vr* remain angry

iznīkt *vi* **1.** perish; (of plants) wither away; (of animals) become extinct; (of social phenomena) disappear; **2.** languish a long time

iznīkties *vr* languish a long time

izniķoties *vr* throw tantrums

iznirel/is *nm* upstart; ~e *nf*

iznirt *vi* emerge

iznomāt *vt* rent, lease

iznomātāj/s *nm*, ~a *nf* renter, leaser

izņakāt *vt* (col.) pick one's food, eat mincingly

izņaudēt *vt* meow; (fig., col.) cadge

izņaudēties *vr* **1.** meow a while; **2.** (fig.) complain, wail a long time

izņemot *adv, part* of **izņemt** except; **i. klātesošos** present company excepted

izņemt *vt* **1.** take out; withdraw; **i. iekšas** gut; draw; disembowel, eviscerate; **2.** claim, redeem, pick up; **3.** remove; **4.** (of courses, programs) complete

izņemties *vr* **1.** go at it; **2.** carry on a long time

izņēmuma stāvoklis *nm* state of emergency

izņēmum/s *nm* exception; ~a exceptional

izņergāt *vt* (col.) pick one's food, eat mincingly

izņirgāt *vt* mock, deride, scoff at

izņirgāties *vr* mock, deride, scoff at (a long time)

izņirgt *vt* (col.) jeer at

izņirgties *vr* mock, deride; scoff at (a long time)

izņurdēties *vr* growl a long time

izoanomale *nf* isoanomal

izobaldriānskābe *nf* isovaleric acid

izob[a]ra [ā] *nf* isobar

izobarometrisks *adj* isobarometric

izob[a]rs [ā] *adj* isobaric

izobata or izobate *nf* isobath

izobatiterma *nf* isobathytherm

izobronta *nf* isobront

izobutāns *nm* isobutane

izobutilalkohols *nm* isobutyl alcohol

izocentrs *nm* isocenter

izo[ch]inolīns [h] *nm* isoquinoline

izo[ch]ora [h] *nf* isochor

izo[ch]orisks [h] *adj* isochoric

izo[ch]ors [h] *adj* isochoric

izo[ch]romatisks [h] *adj* isochromatic

izo[ch]rona [h] *nf* isochrone

izo[ch]ronisks [h] *adj* isochronic

izo[ch]ronisms [h] *nm* isochronism

izo[ch]rons [h] *adj* isochronous

izocian[i]ds [ī] *nm* isocyanide

izociklisks *adj* isocyclic

izoderēt *vt* line; pad

izodiametrisks *adj* isodiametric

izodin[a]ma [ā] *nf* isodynamic line

izoets *nm* quillwort

izofona *nf* isophone

izofota *nf* isophote

izogāmija *nf* isogamy

izoglosa *nf* isogloss

izogonisks *adj* isogonic

izogons *nm* regular polygon

izogr[a]fs [ā] *nm* isograph

izogramma *nf* isogram

izoģeoterma *nf* isogeotherm

izohalīna *nf* isohaline

izohēla *nf* isohel

izohiēta *nf* isohyet

izohipsa *nf* contour

izokefālija *nf* isocephaly

izoklīna *nf* isocline

izokstīt *vt* sniff out

izokšķerēt *vt* sniff out

izokšķerēties *vr* snoop around a long time

izolācija *nf* 1. isolation; (med.) quarantine; 2. insulation

izolācijas lenta *nf* friction tape

izolacionisms *nm* isolationism

izolacionists *nm* isolationist

izol[a]tors [ā] *nm* 1. insulator; 2. (med.) isolation ward

izoleicīns *nm* isoleucine

izolējošs *adj, part* of izolēt (ling.) isolating

izolējums *nm* insulation

izolēt *vt* 1. isolate; (med.) quarantine; 2. insulate

izolēti *adv* in isolation

izolētība *nf* isolation

izolēties *vr* isolate oneself

izolēts *adj, part* of izolēt isolated

izolīnija *nf* isogram

izomagnetisks *adj* isomagnetic

izom[e]rija [ē] *nf* isomerism

izom[e]risks [ē] *adj* isomeric

izomerizācija *nf* isomerization

izomerizēt *vt* isomerize

izom[e]rs [ē] *nm* isomer

izometrisks *adj* isometric

izomorfisks *adj* isomorphic

izomorfisms *nm* isomorphism

izomorfs *adj* isomorphic; (chem.) isomorphous

izonefa *nf* isoneph

izoniazīds *nm* isoniazid

izopaga *nf* isopag

izopēkta *nf* isopectic

izoperēt *vt* remove (in an operation)

izopikna *nf* isopycnic

izopira *nf* false rue anemone, isopyrum

izoplapu kamieļzāle *nf* bugseed

izoplēta *nf* isopleth

izopods *nm* isopod

izopora *nf* isopor

izoporisks *adj* isoporic

izopr[e]ns [ē] *nm* isoprene

izopropilalkohols *nm* isopropyl alcohol

izopropils *nm* isopropyl

izops *nm* hyssop

izopulegols *nm* isopulegol

izoritma *nf* izorhythm

izost *vt* sniff out

izostatisks *adj* isostatic

izost[a]zija [ā] *nf* isostasy

izostīt *vt* sniff out

izosviestskābe *nf* isobutyric acid

izošņāt *vt* sniff out

izota[ch]a [h] *nf* isotach

izotera *nf* isothere

izoterma *nf* isotherm

izotermija *nf* homoiothermy

izotermiski *adv* isothermically

izotermisks *adj* isothermal

izotoniski *adv* isotonically

izotonisks *adj* isotonic

izotons *nm* isotone

izotopiski *adv* isotopically

izotopisks *adj* isotopic

izotops *nm* isotope

izotropija *nf* isotropy

izotropiski *adv* isotropically

izotropisks *adj* isotropic

izotropisms *nm* isotropism

izpaicis *adj, part* of izpaikt fastidious, choosy, picky

izpaikt *vi* become fastidious

izpaisīt *vt* (of flax) brake, swingle

izpakot *vt* unpack

izpakoties *vr* unpack

izpalaidņot *vt* squander

izpalīdzēt *vt* help out

izpalīdzētāj/s *nm*, ~a *nf* helper

izpalīdzēties *vr* 1. help oneself; 2. help each other

izpalīdzība *nf* help

izpalīdzīgi *adv* helpfully

izpalīdzīgs *adj* helpful

izpalīdzīgums *nm* helpfulness

izpalī/gs *nm*, ~dze *nf* helper; part-time help

izpalikt *vi* fail to materialize

izpaļa *nf* that which is denigrated, object of a putdown; *pl* ~s bad reputation

izpara *nf* (reg.) old sauna besom

izpārdošana *nf* sale, clearance sale

izpārdot *vt* 1. sell out; 2. sell, have a sale

izpārdots *adj, part* of **izpārdot** sold out; (of books) out of print

izpārslošanās *nfr* flocculation

izpārsloties *vr* flocculate

izpasakoties *vr* (col.) chew the fat

izpatapu *adv* (reg.) slowly

izpaticība *nf* complaisance

izpaticīgi *adv* complaisantly

izpaticīgs *adj* complaisant

izpatikt *vi* please

izpaudums *nm* manifestation, display

izpaunāt *vt* (of belongings) unload

izpaunāties *vr* (of belongings) unload; get out of (a conveyance with one's belongings)

izpausme *nf* manifestation, display

izpaust *vt* 1. make known; divulge; 2. manifest; give vent to

izpausties *vr* manifest, show

izpazīt *vt* become acquainted with

izpēdot *vt* trample

izpeldēt *vt* swim out, swim out of, swim into; float out, float through; emerge

izpeldēties *vr* 1. go for a swim; 2. (col.) get wet

izpeldināt *vt* take for a swim; make swim; give a bath

izpelnīt *vt* earn

izpelnīties *vr* earn; deserve; (cont.) curry favor

izpeļņa *nf* earnings; salary, wages

izpera *nf* (reg.) old sauna besom

izperēt *vt* hatch

izperināt *vt* hatch; incubate

izperināties *vr* be hatched

izpērkams *adj, part* of **izpirkt** redeemable

izpērt *vt* administer a whipping; flap (with a birch besom in a sauna)

izpērties *vr* have a good bath (in a sauna)

izpestīt *vt* save, deliver, release, free

izpestīties *vr* free oneself

izpēte *nf* investigation; (mil.) estimate

izpētīt *vt* explore; investigate; check out

izpikoties *vr* have a snowball fight

izpiķēt *vt* (hort.) prick out

izpildāms *adj, part* of **izpildīt** feasible, practicable; **viegli i.** easily accomplished

izpilddirektor/s *nm,* ~e *nf* managing director

izpilde *nf* fulfilment (of a plan); execution (of an order, job); ~s **iespējamība** feasibility; ~s **pār-baude** performance check

izpildījum/s *nm* performance, execution; N ~ā a. performed by X; b. sung by X; c. played by X

izpildinstitūcija *nf* executive body

izpild/īt *vt* 1. perform, execute; (of a sentence) carry out; do; (of duty) discharge; ~ot **dienesta pienākumus** in the line of duty; 2. (of a wish) grant; **i. lūgumu** comply with a request; 3. (of a plan, wish) fulfill; (of a promise) keep; **i. spaidu kārtā** (jur.) distrain; 4. (of a form) fill out

izpildītājmāksla *nf* performing arts

izpildītāj/s *nm,* ~a *nf* performer; executor; ~u **sa-stāvs** (theat.) cast

izpildkomanda *nf* command of execution

izpildkomiteja *nf* executive committee

izpildnoilgums *nm* deadline

izpildorg|a|ns [ā] *nm* executive branch

izpildraksts *nm* writ of execution, court order

izpildu *indecl adj* executive

izpilduzraksts *nm* (obs.) writ of execution (to collect a debt)

izpildvara *nf* executive power

izpilgt *vi* become picky

izpilēt *vi* drip out

izpilināt *vt* make drip out

izpilkt *vi* become picky

izpilnām *adv* aplenty, plentifully

izpinkāt *vt* 1. untangle; 2. entangle

izpinkšķēties *vr* have a cry

izpīņāt *vt* unbraid

izpiņķēt *vt* untangle, disentangle

izpīpēt *vt* finish smoking; smoke to the end

izpīpēties *vr* have a long smoking session

izpircēj/s *nm*, **~a** *nf* redeemer

izpirkšana *nf* 1. redemption; ransom; 2. expiation, atonement

izpirkšanas vērtība *nf* cash surrender value (of a policy)

izpirkt *vt* 1. buy out; 2. redeem; ransom; buy off; 3. (col.) spend (on purchases); 4. expiate, atone for; 5. (col.) buy (as a treat)

izpirkties *vr* 1. pay ransom; 2. spend all one's money

izpirkums *nm* ransom; buyoff

izpīt *vt* 1. unbraid; 2. weave, make (by weaving)

izpīties *vr* 1. weave, make (wreaths) a long time; 2. disentangle onself; (fig.) extricate oneself

izplacināt *vt* hammer thin

izplandīt *vt* spread out; unfurl

izplandīties *vr* unfurl

izplānojums *nm* plan

izplānot *vt* plan, schedule

izplāt *vt* 1. spread; (of dough) roll out; 2. (fig.) lay it on the table

izplatība *nf* 1. prevalence; distribution; 2. propagation

izplatības josla *nf* range

izplatījums *nm* universe; space

izplatīšanās *nfr* spreading, dissemination, propagation

izplatīt *vt* 1. disseminate, propagate; spread; 2. give off; 3. circulate

izplatītājs *nm*, **~a** *nf* 1. disseminator; spreader; 2. distributor

izplatīties *vr* 1. spread; disseminate; 2. emanate; 3. propagate

izplātīties *vr* boast

izplatīts *adj, part* of **izplatīt** widespread; widely distributed

izplatu(s) *adv* with legs apart

izplaucēt I *vt* scald

izplaucēt II *vt* force into bloom, make bloom

izplaukt *vi* 1. blossom; 2. leaf out

izplenderēt *vt* squander

izplēnēt *vi* (of fire, embers) die away

izplest *vt* 1. spread out, spread; **i. rokas** throw up one's hands; 2. straddle; 3. (of eyes) open wide; 4. distend

izplēst *vt* 1. tear out; 2. make a tear; 3. wrest from

izplestā balodene *nf* halberd-leaved orache

izplesties *vr* 1. expand; dilate; stretch; extend; 2. open up; (of eyes) open wide; 3. straddle; 4. spread oneself out

izplēsties *vr* 1. argue, quarrel; 2. fight, scuffle; 3. (col.) work hard

izplests *adj, part* of **izplest** spread out; wide open; distended; (of angles) straight

izplešanās *nfr* expansion, extension, dilation; **i. koeficients** coefficient of expansion; **i. spēja** expansibility

izpletnis *nm* parachute

izpletņa aukla *nf* ripcord

izpletņa jostas *nf pl* parachute harness

izpletņa kupols *nm* parachute canopy

izpletņu lēcējs *nm* parachutist; paratrooper

izpliķēt *vt* slap

izplinkšķināt *vt* tinkle out

izplīsums *nm* tear, hole

izplīst *vi* tear out, be torn

izplītēt *vt* 1. squander on liquor; 2. beat (the dust) out of (a rug, clothes)

izplosīt *vt* tear up

izplosīties *vr* 1. (of storms) rage; 2. tear around

izplucināt I *vt* (of wool, oakum) pick, (of rags) shred

izplucināt II *vt* scald

izplūde *nf* 1. exhaust; overflow; 2. eluviation

izplūdes caurule *nf* exhaust pipe

izplūdes grīste *nf* contrail

izplūdes vārstulis *nm* exhaust valve

izplūdināt *vt* drain; spill

izplūdis *adj, part* of izplūst 1. blurred, indistinct; vague; runny; 2. prolix, verbose, diffuse; 3. bloated, flabby

izplūdums *nm* effusion; (of blood) hemorrhage; (of emotion) outburst; spill

izpluinīt *vt* tear apart; dishevel

izplūkāt *vt* tear out; tear off, pluck out, pull out

izplūkāts *adj, part* of izplūkāt ragged

izplukt *vi* 1. fall out, fall off; 2. scald

izplūkt *vt* pluck out, pull out, (of weeds) pull up

izplūkties *vr* 1. fight, scuffle; 2. pick (flowers) to one's heart's content

izplukums *nm* scald

izplunčāties *vr* splash; go for a dip

izplūst *vi* 1. flow out; flow from; flow through; emanate; escape; be discharged; 2. run; overrun; spread; 3. grow flabby, spread; 4. (of manner of speaking) ramble; 5. wash out, become indistinct; i. sīkumos go into too much detail; i. asa-rās burst into tears; i. smieklos burst out laughing

izplūšana *nf* 1. outflow; emanation; effluence; discharge; running out; 2. prolixity, verbosity, diffuseness

izpļāpāt *vt* blab

izpļāpāties *vr* 1. blab; 2. have a nice, long chat

izpļaukāt *vt* slap

izpļaustīt *vt* mow (in a limited, confined space)

izpļaut *vt* 1. mow (in a limited, confined space); 2. i. līdzi keep up with s.o.'s mowing

izpļauties *vr* mow a long time

izpļepēt *vt* (com.) blab

izpļerkšķēt *vt* (com.) blab

izpļukstēt *vt* (com.) blab

izpļurkstēt *vt* (com.) blab

izpļurkšķēt *vt* (com.) blab

izpogoties *vr* (of a nightingale) sing

izpost *vt* decorate

izpostīt *vt* destroy; ruin; devastate

izpostītājs *nm*, ~a *nf* destroyer

izpotēt *vt* 1. vaccinate (all, many); 2. finish grafting

izprasījums *nm* request

izprasīt *vt* 1. ask for, request; 2. ask of, inquire

izprasīties *vr* 1. ask around; 2. ask for, beg for

izprast *vt* understand, comprehend

izprašināt *vt* question; pester with questions

izprašņāt *vt* question; pester with questions

izprašņāties *vr* (col.) enquire

izpratīgi *adv* intelligently, smartly

izpratīgs *adj* 1. understanding; 2. intelligent, smart

izpratināt *vt* question; pester with questions

izpratne *nf* 1. understanding; 2. interpretation

izprātot *vt* figure out

izprātoties *vr* talk cleverly, argue

izpraulējis *adj, part* of izpraulēt rotten

izpraulēt *vi* rot from the inside

izprece *nf* marriage

izprecēt *vt* marry off

izprecēties *vr* marry and move elsewhere

izprecināt *vt* marry off

izpreparēt *vt* preserve; mount

izpresēt *vt* press

izprieca *nf* fun, pleasure, amusement; ~s nolūkā for fun

izpriecas brauciens *nm* pleasure trip; outing

izpriecas nodoklis *nm* entertainment tax

izpriecas vilciens *nm* excursion train

izpriecāties *vr* have fun; lieliski i. have the time of one's life

izpriecceļojums *nm* pleasure trip; cruise

izpriecināt *vt* entertain

izprojektēt *vt* design, plan

izprovocēt *vt* provoke

izpucē/ties *vr* dress up; ~jies kā cūka uz zirņiem dressed to the nines

izpūdelēt *vt* (col., of a shot) miss

izpūdēt *vt* rot

izpudurot *vt* (hort.) thin to make clusters

izpuišot *vt* (col.) please

izpukoties *vr* grumble, fuss

izpūlēties *vr* try hard (but in vain)

izpumpēt *vt* pump out

izpumpēties *vr* (col.) 1. tire; 2. spend money

izpurgāt *vt* (sl.) spoil

izpurināt *vt* shake out; shake down

izpurināties *vr* shake

izpūris *adj, part* of **izpurt** disheveled, ruffled

izpurņīt *vt* (com.) toss out

izpurt *vi* become disheveled; bristle

izpurties *vr* struggle to get free

izpūst *vt* 1. blow out; 2. (of soap bubbles, glass, eggs) blow; **i. pēdējo elpu** breathe one's last; 3. ventilate; 4. announce from the rooftops, trumpet

izpūsties *vr* 1. (of wind) blow a long time; 2. blow up

izpuškojums *nm* 1. decoration; adornment; 2.(fig.) embellishment

izpuškot *vt* 1. decorate, adorn; 2. (fig.) embellish

izpuškoties *vr* adorn oneself

izpūt *vi* rot from the inside

izpūte *nf* (tech.) exhaust

izpūtes gāze *nf* exhaust gas

izpūtes vārsts *nm* exhaust valve

izpūtēja caurule *nf* exhaust pipe

izpūtējs *nm* blower; ~a **caurule** exhaust pipe

izputekļošanās *nfr* (tech.) sputtering

izputēt *vi* 1. (of dust) come out of, billow; 2. be ruined, go up in smoke; go bankrupt; 3. scatter; 4. come to nothing; **kaut tu ~u!** the devil take you!

izpūtiens *nm* exhalation

izpūties *vr* rot a long time

izputināt *vt* 1. scatter; 2. squander; 3. ruin (economically)

izputināties *vr* (of snowstorm) blow a long time

izpuvums *nm* rot, rotten spot

izpūžņot *vi* (of suppuration) come to an end

izrāde *nf* performance; show

izrādīt *vt* 1. show; 2. perform (a theater piece)

izrādīties *vr* 1. turn out, prove to be; 2. show oneself; 3. seem, appear

izraibinājums *nm* spots, speckles

izraibināt *vt* spot, speckle

izraibināties *vr* mark oneself with spots; adorn oneself

izraibot *vt* spot, speckle

izraiboties *vr* mark oneself with spots; adorn oneself

izraidījums *nm* banishment

izraidīt *vt* turn out; send out; banish; (of aliens) deport; **i. trimdā** exile

izraisīt *vt* 1. unplait, untwist; 2. arouse; initiate; provoke; cause; (of doubts) raise; (of war, conflict) unleash; **i. apšaudi** draw fire; **i. slāpes** make thirsty; **i. sprādzienu** set off an explosion

izraisītājs *nm* cause; agent; (tech.) trigger

izraisīties *vr* 1. unplait, untwist; unfold; 2. free oneself; 3. begin, arise, develop

izrakāt *vt* 1. dig up; 2. ransack, rummage through

izrakāties *vr* rummage

izrakņāt *vt* 1. dig up; 2. ransack, rummage through

izrakņāties *vr* rummage

izrakstījums *nm* ornamentation; embroidery

izrakstīt *vt* 1. copy out; 2. (of receipts, checks) make out, write; (of medicines) prescribe; 3. check out; take off the register of tenants; discharge (from a hospital); 4. use up (in writing); 5. order, subscribe to; 6. ornament; embroider

izrakstīties *vr* 1. write a lot; 2. check out; be discharged (from a hospital); take one's name off the register of tenants

izraksts *nm* extract (from a document); **i. no slimnīcas** discharge (from a hospital)

izrakt *vt* 1. dig, excavate; **i. aku** sink a well; 2. dig up, dig out; exhume

izrakte/nis *nm* mineral; **derīgi** ~**ņi** mineral de-posits

izrakties *vr* 1. dig oneself out; 2. (with **cauri**) dig through; 3. dig to one's heart's content

izrakum/s *nm* 1. digging, excavation; 2. ~**i** a. excavations; b. archeological findings

izrāpot *vi* crawl out

izrāpoties *vr* crawl a long time

izrāpties *vr* crawl out, climb out

izrasēt *vt* draw, draft

izrasināt *vt* sprinkle

izrasot *vi* secrete in drops

izrasties *vr* arise

izrāt *vt* scold, give a good scolding

izrāties *vr* 1. give a good scolding; 2. have a row

izraudāt *vt* 1. hurt one's eyes by crying; **i. acis** cry one's eyes out; 2. **i. bēdas** ease one's grief by crying

izraudāties *vr* have a good cry

izraudināt *vt* make s.o. cry a lot

izraudzēt *vt* ferment; (of dough) let rise

izraudzīt *vt* select, pick out; **i. par kandidātu** nominate

izraudzīties *vr* select, pick, choose

izraugāties *vr* belch a long time

izraust *vt* rake out

izrausties *vr* scramble out

izraustīt *vt* tear out, pull up; pull out

izraustīties *vr* pull in vain (a long time)

izraušanās *nfr* (mil.) breakout; (sports) spurt

izraut *vt* 1. pull, pull out, pull up; tear out; uproot; (of teeth) extract; tear away from; remove; **i. ar visām saknēm** pull up by the roots, (fig.) eradicate, root out; **kā caur žogu** ~**s** skin and bones; 2. snatch; snatch up; 3. rouse (from sleep, depression); 4. (col.) get, lay one's hands on; 5. wash out; open (a hole)

izrauties *vr* 1. tear away from; (mil.) break out; 2. spurt; 3. be torn off

izravēt *vt* weed, weed out; (fig.) eradicate, root out

izravēties *vr* 1. weed a long time; 2. be weeded out unintentionally

izrāviens *nm* jerk; (sports) spurt; (mil.) thrust, drive, advance

izrāvums *nm* tear, gouge

izreaģēt *vi* (chem.) react completely

izrediģēt *vt* edit

izrēdīt *vt* order, order around

izre/dzes *nf pl* prospect; **ne mazāko** ~**džu** not a chance; **nav** ~**džu, ka . . .** it is unlikely that . . .

izredzēt *vt* 1. intend to marry; 2. choose

izredzēt/ais *nom adj* 1. the intended; 2. the chosen one; ~**ā** *f*

izredzēties *vr* see a lot, experience a lot

izregulēšanās *nfr* loss of adjustment

izregulēt *vt* adjust

izregulēties *vr* 1. get out of adjustment; 2. get adjusted; adjust itself

izreizināt *vt* multiply

izreklamēt *vt* advertise

izreklamēties *vr* advertise oneself

izrēkt *vt* roar

izrēkties *vr* roar a lot

izrēķināšana *nf* 1. calculation, computation; 2. solution

izrēķināšanās *nfr* revenge; reprisal; brutality, vi-olence; **asiņaina i.** massacre, bloody reprisal

izrēķināt *vt* 1. calculate; compute; 2. work out a numerical problem

izrēķināties *vr* 1. get even, take revenge; 2. do away with; get back at; **nežēlīgi i.** deal with brutally

izremontēt *vt* repair; renovate

izremsties *vr* (col.) clamber out

izrentēt *vt* lease, rent

izreti *adv* rarely

izretināt *vt* **1.** (of plants) thin, thin out; (of trees, shrubs) prune, trim; **2.** (of air) rarify; **3.** (mil., of formations) open

izretināties *vr* **1.** (mil., of formations) open; **2.** grow thinner

izretis *adv* rarely

izrētot *vt* scar

izretoties *vr* grow thinner

izretušēt *vt* retouch

izrevidēt *vt* **1.** inspect; audit; **2.** revise

izrībēt *vi* rattle, rumble out of; rattle, rumble through

izrībināt *v* **1.** *vi* rumble out of, rumble through; **2.** *vt* move with a rumble

izrībināties *vr* rattle a long time, rumble a long time

izrīcība *nf* behavior

izrīcīgi *adv* expeditiously; efficiently

izrīcīgs *adj* expeditious; efficient

izridāt *vt* put in order

izrīdināt *vt* sic dogs on s.o., drive out with dogs

izrīdīt *vt* sic dogs on s.o., drive out with dogs

izriebties *vr* engage in magical healing (a long time)

izriest *vt* = **izriezt**

izriesties *vr* = **izriezties**

izrietēt *vi* follow, result from

izrieties *vr* bark a long time

izrievot *vt* groove

izriezt *vt* (of a part of the body) stick out; (of buds, flowers) form

izriezties *vr* **1.** bulge out; **2.** bead

izrīkojums *nm* **1.** assignment; **2.** arrangement; **3.** event; party

izrīkot *vt* **1.** (of tasks, jobs) assign; order, order around; **2.** arrange, organize

izrīkotājs *nm*, **~a** *nf* manager

izrīkoties *vr* do as one pleases, act arbitrarily

izrikšot *vi* trot out

izrikšoties *vr* trot around

izrindot *vt* set up in rows

izrindoties *vr* form a line

izriņķot *vi* **1.** whirl out; **2.** go around in circles

izriņķoties *vr* circle a long time

izripināt *vt* roll out

izripināties *vr* roll out

izripot *vi* roll out

izrisināt *vt* **1.** unwind; **2.** solve

izrisināties *vr* unwind

izrist *vi* come undone

izrīstīties *vr* gag

izrīt *vt* gobble up

izritēt *vi* roll out

izrīties *vr* gobble

izritināt *vt* roll out

izritināties *vr* **1.** roll out; **2.** be rolled out

izrīvēt *vt* **1.** spread; **2.** clean (by rubbing); **3.** ream

izrobīt *vt* jag, notch, serrate; indent, scallop

izrobojums *nm* notching, serration, scallops

izrobot *vt* jag, notch, serrate; indent, scallop

izrosīt *vt* trigger, give rise to

izrosīties *vr* **1.** get ready to leave; **2.** arise

izrotājums *nm* ornamentation, decoration; (mus.) melisma

izrotaļāties *vr* play a long time

izrotāt *vt* ornament, decorate; adorn; embellish

izrotāties *vr* adorn oneself

izrubināt *vt* pick; carve

izrubināties *vr* (of male grouse) utter mating calls

izrūgt *vi* **1.** (of wine) ferment, (of dough) rise; **2.** become waterlogged

izrūkties *vr* grumble a long time; rumble a long time

izrullēt *vt* roll, roll flat, shape by rolling

izrumulēt *vt* splash with water

izrumulēties *vr* have a big water fight

izruna *nf* **1.** pronunciation; **3.** pretext, excuse ◊ **tās ir tikai ~s** nothing but shifts; **tukšas ~s** idle talk; **nav nekādas ~s!** no ifs or buts!

izrunas vārdnīca *nf* pronouncing dictionary

izrunas vieta *nf* (ling.) point of articulation
izrunāšanās *nfr* **1.** conversation, chat; **sirsnīga i.** heart-to-heart talk; **2.** back talk; **3.** mere talk; excuses, shifts; **bez liekas i.** without argument
izrunāt *vt* **1.** pronounce; **i. aplam** mispronounce; **2.** articulate; **3.** utter; **i. pa prātam** talk s.o.'s way; **4.** finish speaking; **neļaut i.** cut short, interrupt; **ļauj man i.!** let me finish! **5.** debate, consider; **6.** say (usu. sth. untrue); **tas ir tikai ~s** it's just talk
izrunāties *vr* **1.** have a talk; **no sirds i.** have a heart-to-heart talk; **2.** talk back, sass; **3.** have one's say; **brīvi i.** speak one's mind, speak freely; **plaši i.** expatiate; **4.** blab out
izrūnīt *vt* (col.) castrate, geld
izrūpēt *vt* (of one's offspring) raise
izrūsēt *vi* rust, rust out, rust through
izrūsināt *vt* rust, rust through
izrušināt *vt* **1.** rake out; **2.** scrape (a hollow in the ground); **3.** (of soil) loosen
izrušināties *vr* (of soil) loosen, dress, cultivate
izsacījums *nm* statement; pronouncement
izsacīt *vt* express; utter; tell; make a statement
izsacīties *vr* express one's opinion; say, put it; **īsi izsakoties** to put it briefly; **piesardzīgi izsakoties** to put it mildly; **i. par (kaut ko)** declare for (sth.); **i. pret (kaut ko)** declare against (sth.); **i. par kādu jautājumu** speak on a question
izsaimniekot *vt* squander
izsaimniekotāj/s *nm*, **~a** *nf* squanderer
izsaiņot *vt* unpack, unwrap
izsaiņoties *vr* unpack
izsaitēt *vt* remove bandages
izsaka *nf* statement
izsakņot *vt* eradicate
izsalcis *adj, part* of **izsalkt** hungry
izsaldēt *vt* freeze out
izsaldēties *vr* get chilled
izsaldināt *vt* sweeten

izsālīt *vt* salt
izsālīties *vr* absorb salt
izsalkt *vi* get hungry
izsalkums *nm* hunger
izsalot *vi* (of snow) become porous (in freezing weather)
izsalšana *nf* winter-kill
izsalt *vi* freeze; freeze out, be killed by the cold; get chilled
izsalties *vr* get chilled
izsamisa *nf* (obs.) despair
izsamist *vi* (obs.) lose courage, despair
izsamisums *nm* (obs.) despair
izsanēt *vi* finish buzzing, finish humming
izsāpēt *vi* (of sight, hearing, teeth) lose (after an interval of pain); *vt* suffer through; (of ideas, artistic creations) feel deeply
izsāpēties *vr* ache a long time
izsapņot *vt* **1.** finish dreaming; **sapnis ~s** the dream is at an end; **2.** imagine
izsapņoties *vr* **1.** dream about (a long time); **2.** imagine
izsargāt *vt* keep from, prevent from
izsargāties *vr* avoid, keep from
izsaucējs *nm* **1.** crier, herald; **2.** exclamation point; **3. i. pulss** tripping pulse
izsaucien/s *nm* exclamation, shout; **~i** outcry
izsaukāt *vt* **1.** call (in vain); **2.** call names
izsaukāties *vr* call (in vain)
izsauksme *nf* interjection
izsauksmes vārds *nm* interjection
izsauksmes zīme *nf* exclamation point
izsaukt *vt* **1.** call (for s.o. to come out); **2.** call up-on, call to the front of the class; summon; call for; send for; **3.** call out; **i. pēc vārdiem** call over a list of names; **4.** challenge; **5.** (col.) buy s.o. a drink; **6.** (obs.) announce
izsaukties *vr* **1.** call out, cry out; **2.** call a long time; **3.** (in playing team games) choose up
izsaukuma teikums *nm* exclamatory sentence
izsaukuma zīme *nf* exclamation point;

izsaukums *nm* **1.** call; **2.** summons; subpoena; **3.** exclamation; **4.** challenge; **5.** toast

izsauļot *vt* expose to sunlight

izsauļoties *vr* sunbathe to one's heart's content

izsausēt *v* **1.** *vt* dry out; **2.** *vi* dry up

izsausināt *vt* dry

izsaust *vi* dry up

izsautēt *vt* steam; stew; soak in hot water; foment

izsautēties *vr* steam

izsecinājums *nm* conclusion

izsecināt *vt* deduce, infer, conclude

izsēdēt *vt* **1.** wear out by sitting; **2.** sit out; **3.** come a conclusion (in a meeting)

izsēdēties *vr* sit a long time

izsēdināšana *nf* **1.** disembarkation; landing; **2.** (of students) change in seating arrangement, separation

izsēdināt *vt* **1.** (of passengers) drop off; put ashore, land; make (s.o.) get off; **2.** seat; **3.** seat apart

izsegt *vt* cover with; line with; spread

izsēja *nf* **1.** sowing; **2.** (med.) spread (of infection)

izsējas norma *nf* standard quantity of seed per unit area;

izsekojums *nm* pursuit

izsekot *vt* **1.** follow; **2.** track; tail; pursue; **3.** trace back

izsekotājs *nm*, **~a** *nf* tail (spy); (tech.) tracer

izselekcionēt *vt* breed

izsenis *adv* since ancient times, historically

izsens *adj* ancient

izsēņot *vt* pick (a place) clean of mushrooms

izsēņoties *vr* pick mushrooms (a long time)

izseparēt *vt* separate out

izsēroties *vr* grieve a long time

izsērsties *vr* **1.** stay for a long visit; **2.** be done visiting

izservēt *vi* (sports) serve

izsēsties *vr* **1.** get off, alight; **2.** sit according to plan

izsēt *vt* **1.** sow; **2.** scatter; **3.** (med.) spread; **4.** (col.) lose; **i. vējā** waste

izsēties *vr* **1.** be sown; **2.** scatter

izsiet *vt* **1.** use up in binding; **2.** (of cheeese or sth. involving binding) make; finish making cheese

izsieties *vr* be tying a long time

izsijas *nf pl* siftings

izsijāt *vt* sift

izsijāties *vr* **1.** be sifted; **2.** (fig.) stand out; be the essence of

izsīkt I *vi* **1.** dry up; run dry; **2.** become exhausted; run short

izsīkt II *vi* stop buzzing

izsīkums *nm* **1.** drying up; **2.** exhaustion; depletion

izsildīt *vt* heat through

izsildīties *vr* warm oneself for a spell

izsilt *vi* heat through

izsirdīties *vr* fret, be angry

izsirgt *vi* overcome an illness

izsirot *vt* maraud

izsiroties *vr* maraud a long time

izsirt *vt* maraud

izsist *vt* **1.** drive out, (with **cauri**) drive through; knock out; **i. korķi** (col.) blow a fuse; **i. no eņģēm** (fig.) unhinge; **i. no ierindas** knock out of action; **i. no pozicijām** dislodge; **i. no sliedēm** (fig.) derail; **2.** tap out (a rhythm); **3.** line; **4.** (col., of money, profit) make; **i. rubuli** (sl.) make money

izsisties *vr* **1.** be knocked out; **2.** break through; **3.** (of a rash, boil) break out; **4.** (col.) make ends meet; **5.** push one's way through; **i. uz augšu** fight one's way to the top, rise from the ranks

izsitnis *nm* (tool) punch

izsitumi *nm pl* rash

izsitumu tīfs *nm* spotted fever

izskaidrojošs *adj, part* of **izskaidrot** explanatory; expositive

izskaidrojums *nm* explanation; elucidation; interpretation; clarification; **nepareizs i.** misinterpretation

izskaidrošanās *nfr* discussion; explanation; **man ar viņu bija i.** I had it out with him

izskaidrot *vt* explain; elucidate; account for; in-terpret

izskaidrotājs *nm*, **~a** *nf* interpreter, expounder, expositor

izskaidroties *vr* **1.** make oneself clear, clarify one's position; **2.** clear up a misunderstanding; have it out

izskaisties *vr* fume a long time

izskaistinājums *nm* **1.** embellishment; **2.** decoration, adornment

izskaistināt *vt* **1.** embellish; **2.** decorate, adorn

izskaistināties *vr* adorn oneself

izskaitīt *vt* count; **i. uz pirkstiem** count on one's fingers

izskaitļojams *adj* calculable

izskaitļojums *nm* calculation

izskaitļot *vt* calculate, figure

izskaldījums *nm* cut (made by cleaving), cleavage

izskaldīt *vt* cut, cleave

izskaldīties *vr* chop a long time

izskalināt *vt* **1.** rinse, rinse out; wash; **2.** wash out, scour, erode

izskalināties *vr* **1.** rinse, wash a long time; **2.** be washed out, be scoured, be eroded

izskalojums *nm* (geol.) scour

izskalošana *nf* leaching; (geol.) avulsion; erosion

izskalot *vt* **1.** rinse, rinse out; wash; **i. kaklu** gargle; **2.** wash out, scour; erode; **3. i. krastā** wash ashore

izskaloties *vr* **1.** rinse, wash a long time; **2.** be washed out, be scoured, be eroded; **3. i. krastā** be washed ashore

izskandēt *vt* recite

izskandināt *vt* **1.** let jingle, let ring; **2.** let resound; **3.** (of news) spread, proclaim

izskandināties *vr* ring (bells) a long time

izskanējums *nm* end, final period

izskanēt *vi* **1.** (of sound) die out, ring out; **2.** (of sound, fame) spread; **3.** sound a note

izskaņ/a *nf* final note; ending; (ling.) terminal sound; **~ā** (ling.) when final

izskatīgi *adv* **i. ģērbies** dressed in good-looking clothes

izskatīgs *adj* good-looking

izskatīgums *nm* good looks, appearance

izskatīšana *nf* **1.** perusal; **2.** consideration, examination; **otrreizēja i.** (jur.) review, retrial

izskatīt *vt* **1.** look through, peruse; **2.** consider, examine; (jur.) review, retry; **i. visas acis** look for far and wide; stare one's eyes out, gawk

izskat/īties *vr* **1.** look through (many items or a long time); **2.** look, appear; **kāds viņš ~ās?** what does he look like? **kāds tu ~ies!** you are a sight! **i. (pēc kāda)** look (like s.o.)

izskat/s *nm* appearance; looks; **~am** just for show; **no ~a** from the looks of it; **(pazīt) pēc ~a** (know) by sight; **aizdomīga ~a** suspicious looking; **bēdīgā ~a bruņinieks** the Knight of the Rueful Countenance

izskaust *vt* exterminate; eradicate, root out; eliminate

izskaušana *nf* extermination; eradication; elimination

izskolot *vt* give an education; **i. par (inženieri)** send to school to become (an engineer)

izskoloties *vr* finish school; **i. par (dārznieku)** learn to be (a gardener)

izskrabināt *vt* gnaw, nibble a long time

izskrabināties *vr* scrape, gnaw a long time

izskraidelēt *vt* run through, run all over

izskraidināt *vt* make s.o. run a long time

izskraidīt *vt* run through, run all over

izskraidīties *vr* **1.** cavort, run around a lot; run oneself ragged; **2.** run around (looking for sth., usu. unsuccessfully)

izskrambāt *vt* scrape all over

izskrāpēt *vt* scratch out; scrape out

izskrāpēties *vr* scratch a long time

izskreja *nf* **1.** beehive entrance; **2.** (of bees) flight

izskrējiens *nm* sally

izskribināt *vt* **1.** gnaw; **2.** scrape clean

izskribināties *vr* nibble, gnaw a long time

izskriet *v* **1.** *vi* run out; **i. cauri** run through **i. no prāta** (col.) forget; **i. no sliedēm** run off the tracks; **2.** *vt* run all over; **3.** *vi* **i. līdzi** keep up with

izskrieties *vr* **1.** have a good run; **2.** run all over

izskrubināt *vt* **1.** gnaw; **2.** scrape clean

izskrubināties *vr* gnaw a long time

izskrūvēt *vt* unscrew

izskrūvēties *vr* unscrew, come unscrewed

izskubināt *vt* urge

izskurināt *vt* shake out

izskūt *vt* shave

izslābt *vi* weaken; decrease; shrink

izslābums *nm* decrease; shrinkage

izslacināt *vt* sprinkle, splash, spray

izslacīt *vt* sprinkle, splash, spray

izslacīties *vr* spill, be spilled

izslaistīties *vr* idle

izslakāt *vt* sprinkle, splash, spray

izslampāt *vi* trudge out

izslamstīties *vr* loaf, hang around a long time

izslāņot *vt* layer

izslāņoties *vr* form layers

izslapēt *vt* wet

izslapināt *vt* wet

izslāpis *adj, part* of **izslāpt** thirsty

izslapstīties *vr* sneak around; hide; avoid

izslāpt *vi* **1.** become thirsty; thirst; **2.** suffocate

izslāpums *nm* thirst

izslāt *vi* shamble out

izslaucīt *vt* sweep, sweep out; wipe, wipe out **tukšs kā i.** completely empty

izslaucīties *vr* **1.** be swept; **2.** be sweeping a long time

izslaukas *nf* sweepings

izslaukt *vt* **1.** milk; (sl., fig.) extort; cheat out of; **2.** finish milking

izslaukums *nm* milking yield

izslavēt *vt* lavish praise, extol

izslavēts *adj, part* of **izslavēt** much praised

izslavināt *vt* lavish praise, extol

izslēdzējs *nm* circuit breaker

izslēgs *nm* switch

izslēgšana *nf* **1.** turning off; cutoff; **2.** expulsion; **3.** exclusion

izslēgt *vt* **1.** (of lights, engines) turn off; disconnect; (of utilities) cut off; **2.** expel; **i. no mantojuma** disinherit; **3.** exclude, preclude; **pilnīgi ~s** out of the question

izslēgties *vr* **1.** turn off; **2.** shut off; shut oneself off

izslepkavot *vt* murder

izslēpot *v* **1.** *vi* ski through; **2.** *vt* ski; **3.** *vt* crisscross skiing

izslēpoties *vr* ski a lot

izslīdēt *vi* slide out, slip out, glide out

izslīdināt *vt* slide out

izslidināties *vr* skate a lot

izslidojums *nm* pass (on skates)

izslidot *v* **1.** *vi* skate out (to); **2.** *vt* skate (a figure)

izslidoties *vr* skate a long time

izsliedēt *vt* make tracks

izsliet *vt* raise; **asti izslējis** with the tail erect; **de-gunu izslējis** with one's nose in the air

izslieties *vr* **1.** pull oneself up; **2.** stand above; project; jut out

izslīgt *vi* **1.** (of fabrics) resume shape; **2.** slide out of

izslīkt *vi* (of plants) die (because of excessive moisture)

izslimot *vt* have an illness

izslinkoties *vr* loaf a long time

izslīpējums *nm* polish

izslīpēt *vt* polish

izsloksnēt *vt* (col.) give a whipping

izsludināšana *nf* announcement; proclamation; publication

izsludināt *vt* announce; proclaim; **i. ārpus likuma** outlaw

izsmalcināt *vt* refine

izsmalcinātība *nf* refinement

izsmalcināties *vr* become refined

izsmalcināts *adj, part* of **izsmalcināt** refined; (of hearing) keen

izsmalstīt *vt* ladle out, spoon out; empty with a spoon

izsmaržināt *vt* perfume

izsmaržot *vi* (of perfume smells, aromas) fade

izsmējēj/s *nm*, **~a** *nf* scoffer, mocker, sneerer

izsmējība *nf* derision

izsmējīgi *adv* derisively, mockingly

izsmējīgs *adj* derisive, mocking

izsmejoši *adv* derisively, mockingly

izsmejošs *adj, part* of **izsmiet** derisive, mocking

izsmēķēt *vt* smoke to the end

izsmēķēties *vr* smoke a long time, smoke to one's heart's content

izsmēķis *nm* (cigarette, cigar) butt

izsmelgties *vr* ache

izsmēlīgi adv exhaustively

izsmēlīgs *adj* exhaustive

izsmelt *vt* **1.** ladle out, spoon out; bail out; **2.** exhaust

izsmelties *vr* **1.** be ladling, spooning or bailing out a long time; **2.** be ladled, spooned or bailed out

izsmeļoši *adv* exhaustively

izsmeļošs *adj, part* of **izsmelt** exhaustive

izsmērēt *vt* (of viscous substances) spread

izsmērēties *vr* be spread

izsmīdināt *vt* make laugh

izsmidzināt *vt* spray (with a sprayer or atomizer)

izsmidzināties *vr* be sprayed

izsmiekl/s *nm* derision, scoffing, mockery; **kļūt par ~u** become a laughing stock; **tīrais i.** it's a laugh

izsmiet *vt* ridicule, laugh at

izsmieties *vr* have a good laugh

izsmilkstēties *vr* whine a long time

izsmirdināt *vt* (hist., pol.) disperse using foul smelling substances

izsmurgāt *vt* (com.) **1.** make a fool of s.o.; **2.** pick, eat mincingly

izsnaicīties *vr* = **izsnaikstīties**

izsnaikstīties *vr* be reaching out for sth. for a long time; be stretching one's neck a long time

izsnaust *vt* sleep off

izsnausties *vr* have a nice nap

izsniegšana *nf* handing out; issue; delivery

izsniegt *vt* hand out; issue; deliver; (of rations) serve

izsole *nf* auction

izsolīt *vt* **1.** (of prizes, rewards) offer; **2.** auction off

izsolīties *vr* promise repeatedly

izsolītāj/s *nm*, **~a** *nf* auctioneer

izsoļot *vi* march out

izsoļoties *vr* walk a long time

izspaidas *nf pl* marc, pomace

izspaidījumi *nm pl* marc, pomace

izspaidīt *vt* **1.** wring out; press out; **2.** massage; **3.** palpate

izspaidīties *vr* be pressed a long time

izspārdīt *vt* kick apart

izspārdīties *vr* be kicking a long time

izspēkoties *vr* wrestle with

izspeķot *vt* lard thoroghly

izspēle *nf* turn to play, (in card games) lead

izspēlēt *vt* **1.** play to the end, finish; **2.** (in card games) play, lead; **3. i. joku** (col.) play a joke; **i. numuru** (col.) do a number on s.o.

izspēlēties *vr* **1.** play a long time, play a lot; **2.** (of actors) show off one's talent

izspēriens *nm* kick

izspert *vt* **1.** kick, kick out, kick off; pop out; overturn with a kick; **i. korķi** (sl.) blow a fuse; **2.** (of feet) put forward

izsperties *vr* **1.** (of feet) step; **2.** sally forth; rush, dash through

izspiedēj/s *nm*, **~a** *nf* blackmailer, extortioner

izspiedums *nm* **1.** protrusion, bulge; **2.** displacement (volume)

izspiegot *vt* spy on

izspiegt *vt* squeal

izspiegties *vr* squeal a lot

izspiest *vt* **1.** squeeze out, press out; **i. pēdējo sulu** (col.) bleed white; **no tā jau nekā neizspiedīsi!** it is like drawing blood from a turnip; **2.** displace; force out; oust; dislodge; **3.** blackmail, extort; **4.** bulge

izspiesties *vr* **1.** ooze through, seep through; permeate; **2.** squeeze through, force one's way through; **3.** (of drops of sweat, tears, blood) form; **4.** bulge out, protrude; **5.** (obs.) get by

izspiešana *nf* **1.** squeezing out, pressing out; **2.** displacement; ouster; **3.** extortion, blackmail

izspietot *vi* swarm

izspīlēt *vt* cause to bulge, cause to protrude

izspīlēties *vr* bulge, protrude

izspīlēts *adj, part* of **izspīlēt** bulging, protruding

izspindzēt *vi* move out (of sth.) buzzing, move through (a place) buzzing

izspītēt *vi* try to achieve sth. by spiting s.o.

izspļaudīt *vt* spit

izspļaudīties *vr* be spitting a long time

izspļaut *vt* spit out; **kā ~s pēc . . .** (col.) the dead spit of . . .

izspļāvas *nf pl* spit

izspodrināt *vt* tidy, clean

izspoguļoties *vr* look at oneself in the mirror

izspokot *vt* (col.) distort, disfigure

izsprāgt *vi* **1.** pop out; **2.** explode; **3.** (of buds) burst open; **4.** (of animals) die out

izspraišļojums *nm* shoring

izsprakstēt *vi* sputter

izsprakšķēt *vi* fly out with a crackle

izspraudīt *vt* **1.** adorn with branches; **2.** (of stakes, branches used to be stuck in the ground or for decoration) use up

izspraukt *vt* push through

izspraukties *vr* force one's way through, squeeze through; burst through

izsprauslot *vt* sputter out

izspraulsoties *vr* snort, sputter a long time

izspraust *vt* decorate (with branches, saplings, flowers)

izsprausties *vr* **1.** adorn oneself (with flowers, twigs); **2.** squeeze through

izsprēgāt *vi* (of sparks) fly out crackling

izspridzināt *vt* blow up; explode

izspriedelēties *vr* have a long discussion

izspriest *vt* decide; **i. tiesu** (of a court, judge) make a decision

izspriesties *vr* discuss a long time

izspruk/t *vi* **1.** get away; flee the coop; (fig.) escape; **viņam ~a** he blurted out; **2.** slip out of, extricate oneself

izspurgt *vi* flutter up from, fly out

izspūris *adj, part* of **izspurt** disheveled, tousled

izspurt *vi* become disheveled, become tousled

izstāde *nf* exhibition, exposition, show

izstādīt *vt* **1.** (of plants) set out; plant widely separated; **2.** exhibit; display

izstādītājs *nm*, **~a** *nf* exhibitor

izstaiga *nf* walk

izstaigāt *vt* walk through, walk along; patrol

izstaigāties *vr* take a long walk

izstaipīt *vt* stretch

izstaipīties *vr* **1.** stretch oneself; **2.** become stretched out

izstampāt *vt* trample down

izstarojums *nm* radiation, emanation, emission

izstarošana *nf* radiation, emanation, emission

izstarot *vt* radiate, emanate, emit

izstaroties *vr* radiate

izstāstīt *vt* tell, relate; blab

izstāsts *nm* narrative

izstāties *vr* leave (formation, an organization), quit, drop out (of school)

izstāvēt *vi, vt* stand a long time; **klāt i.** stand by all the time

izstāvēties *vr* stand a long time; **velti i.** stand in vain

izsteberēt *vi* hobble out

izsteigt *v* **1.** *vt* finish hurriedly; **2.** *vi* hurry out

izsteigties *vr* hurry out; **i. cauri** hurry through

izstenēt *vt* utter (words) with a moan

izstīdzējis *adj, part* of **izstīdzēt** lank; (of plants) leggy

izstīdzēt *vi* grow tall and thin

izstiebrot *vi* shoot into stalk

izstiegrot *vt* rib

izstiepiens *nm* stretch

izstiepjamība *nf* ductility

izstiept *vt* **1.** stretch out; extend; **i. garu kaklu** crane one's neck; **i. ģīmi** pull a long face; **i. ursku** pout; **2.** (col.) drag

izstiepties *vr* **1.** stretch out; **2.** straighten up; **3.** lie down; **4.** (col.) fall flat on one's face; **5.** shoot up

izstiepums *nm* stretch

izstīgojums *nm* (hort.) network of runners

izstigot *vt* clear firebreaks

izstīgot *vi* (hort.) produce runners; (fig.) spread, extend

izstīgt *vi* (hort.) produce runners; (fig.) spread, extend

izstīvēt *vt* drag out

izstīvēties *vr* fight, wrestle

izstomīt *vt* utter sth. hemming and hawing

izstomīties *vr* hem and haw

izstrādājum/s *nm* **1.** manufactured product; **2.** handcrafted article; **3.** ~i processed goods

izstrādāt *vt* **1.** produce; **2.** handcraft; work (carefully, thoroughly); **3.** work out, draw up; **rūpīgi** ~s a. carefully worked out; b. elaborate; **4.** bring off; **i. joku** (col.) play a (practical) joke; **i. muļķību** (col.) do a dumb thing

izstrādāties *vr* **1.** work a long time; work enough; **2.** develop

izstrāde *nf* output

izstrādes diena *nf* unit of daily production

izstrādes norma *nf* production quota

izstrādināt *vt* overwork; exploit

izstrādinātāj/s *nm*, ~a *nf* slave driver, exploiter

izstrādne *nf* development

izstrāvot *vt* radiate

izstrēbt *vt* (of liquid food) eat up, (of a bowl of soup) empty

izstrēbties *vr* (of liquid food) eat a lot, eat enough

izstreipuļot *vi* stagger out

izstrīdēt *vt* dispute, debate

izstrīdēties *vr* have a quarrel

izstrīķēt *vt* whet with a strickle

izstrīpot *vt* cross out

izstrutot *vi* secrete (a lot, all) puss

izstudēt *vt* **1.** study (deeply, thoroughly); **2.** get a degree; **i. par (inženieri)** get a degree in (engineering)

izstumdīt *vt* push out

izstumt *vt* **1.** push out; **2.** banish, drive out; ostracize

izstumtība *nf* ostracism

izstumties *vr* push oneself out

izstūrēt *vt* steer out, steer through; (tech.) control, drive

izstutēt *vt* prop up

izsūcēj/s *nm*, ~a *nf* (fig.) blood sucker

izsūdzēt *vt*; **i. bēdas** pour out one's troubles; **i. grēkus** (rel.) confess

izsukas *nf pl* combings; (of flax) tow

izsūkaļāt *vt* suck out

izsukāt *vt* **1.** comb, brush; comb out; **2.** (col., of food) polish off

izsūkāt *vt* suck out

izsukāties *vr* **1.** comb a long time; **2.** be combed

izsūknēt *vt* pump out; pump dry

izsūknēties *vr* be pumped dry

izsūkstināt *vt* suck out

izsūkt *vt* suck out; suck dry; (fig.) exploit; **i. no pirksta** (fig.) fabricate; **i. spēkus** exhaust

izsūkties *vr* seep out, seep through, percolate

izsunīt *vt* cuss out

izsusēt *vi* become dry, dry up

izsusināt *vt* dry

izsust *vi* **1.** soften (in warm moisture); **2.** stew; **3.** dry

izsusties *vr* **1.** soften (in warm moisture); **2.** stew

izsūtām/ais *nom adj* errand boy; messenger; ~**ā** *f*

izsūtījum/s *nm* **1.** shipment; **2.** exile; ~**ā** deported; in exile

izsutināt *vt* **1.** stew; **2.** soften (in warm moisture); **3.** foment

izsutināties *vr* **1.** take a steam bath; **2.** stew; **3.** soften

izsūtīšana *nf* **1.** sending out; shipping; ~**s paziņojums** advice of shipment; **2.** deportation; banishment; exile

izsūtīt *vt* **1.** send out; dispatch; ship; **2.** deport; banish; exile

izsūtīt/ais *nom adj* deportee; exile; ~**ā** *f*

izsutums *nm* sore (made by moist heat)

izsvaidīt *vt* scatter, fling about

izsvaidīties *vr* throw, toss or fling a long time

izsvarojums *nm* balance

izsvarot *vt* balance; plumb

izsvarotība *nf* balance

izsvārstīt *vt* heft

izsvārstīties *vr* swing a long time

izsvelpt *vt* = **izsvilpt**

izsvelpties *vr* = **izsvilpties**

izsvempties *vr* clamber out

izsvēpēt *vt* fumigate; smoke out

izsvēpināt *vt* = **izsvēpēt**

izsvepstēt *vt* utter with a lisp

izsvērt *vt* **1.** weigh out; **2.** (fig.) weigh, decide

izsvērties *vr* become wobbly

izsvērums *nm* **1.** weighing out; **2.** balance

izsvētīt *vt* celebrate

izsvīdums *nm* secretion

izsviede *nf* (artillery) ejection

izsviedējs *nm* (firearms) extractor

izsviedrēt *vt* make sweat

izsviedrēties *vr* **1.** sweat, make oneself sweat; **2.** take a steam bath

izsviest *vt* **1.** throw out; **i. krastā** cast ashore; **2.** throw away; **3.** separate, centrifuge; **4.** drop

izsvie/sties *vr* **1.** throw a long time; **2.** rush out; rush through; jump out; **3.** lie with arms and legs spread out; **4.** ~**dies kreklā** shirt-sleeved

izsviešana *nf* (artillery) ejection

izsvilināt *vt* burn out; singe; scorch

izsvilpot *vt* whistle (a tune)

izsvilpoties *vr* whistle a lot

izsvilpt *vt* boo, hiss (an actor, speaker)

izsvilpties *vr* whistle a long time (in calling)

izsvilt *vi* burn, get scorched

izsvinēt *vt* celebrate

izsvīst *v* **1.** *vi* sweat thoroughly; **2.** *vt* exude; sweat, sweat out

izsvīsties *vr* sweat thoroughly

izsvītrot *vt* cross out, cross of (a list)

izsvītroties *vr* get crossed out unintentionally

izšalkot *vi* rustle; (of sound) die out; (of a sigh) be heaved

izšalkt *vi* rustle; (of sound) die out; (of a sigh) be heaved

izšaudīt *vt* **1.** kill (all or many by shooting); **2.** use up (in shooting)

izšaudīties *vr* do a lot of shooting
izšaušana *nf* discharge
izšaut *vt* **1.** (of firearms, rockets) fire; discharge; **2.** shoot (many, all); exterminate; **3.** (of ammunition) use up; **4.** shoot (a hole), shoot out; **i. visu pulveri** shoot one's bolt; **5.** stick out (quickly)
izšauties *vr* **1.** leap out; dart out; burst out; (of thoughts) flash across (one's mind); **2.** shoot to one's heart's content
izšāviens *nm* shot
izšķaidīt *vt* **1.** disperse; **2.** smash, splatter; **3.** squander
izšķaidīties *vr* splatter
izšķaudīt *vt* expel (in sneezing)
izšķaudīties *vr* sneeze a long time
izšķelt *vt* separate, cut out
izšķendēties *vr* cuss a long time
izšķērdēt *vt* squander
izšķērdētāj/s *nm*, **~a** *nf* squanderer, spendthrift
izšķērdība *nf* wastefulness; extravagance
izšķērdīgi *adv* wastefully; extravagantly; lavishly
izšķērdīgs *adj* wasteful; extravagant; lavish
izšķērdīgums *nm* wastefulness; extravagance
izšķērdnie/ks *nm*, **~ce** *nf* squanderer, spendthrift
izšķērsot *vt* crisscross
izšķērst *vt* = **1.** squander; **2.** draw, gut, eviscerate
izšķetināt *vt* unwind; untwist, disentangle
izšķetināties *vr* unwind
izšķīdināt *vt* dissolve
izšķiebt *vt* twist, distort
izšķiebties *vr* bend outward, bulge out
izšķiedēj/s *nm*, **~a** *nf* squanderer, spendthrift
izšķiedrot *vt* pulp
izšķiest *vt* **1.** splash; **2.** squander
izšķiesties *vr* **1.** be splashed; **2.** be squandered

izšķilas *nf pl* **1.** shells of hatched eggs; **2.** portion of living father's inheritance bequeathed to a child
izšķilt *vt* **1.** (of sparks, fire) strike; **2.** hatch
izšķilties *vr* **1.** (of sparks, fire) be struck; **2.** hatch
izšķira or **izšķire** *nf* discrimination
izšķīrēj/s *nm*, **~a** *nf* arbitrator; *adj* decisive
izšķirība *nf* **1.** difference; **2.** discrimination; **bez ~s** indiscriminately, without distinction
izšķirības sajutamība *nf* (psych.) discriminability
izšķirības slieksnis *nm* (psych.) difference thresh-old
izšķirīgi *adv* decisively, critically
izšķirīgs *adj* decisive, deciding, critical
izšķiroši *adv* decisively, critically
izšķirošs *adj, part* of **izšķirt** decisive, deciding, critical
izšķirot *vt* sort
izšķirstīt *vt* leaf through
izšķiršana *nf* **1.** separation; parting; **2.** decision; **3.** discrimination, distinction; **~s spēja** a. discriminative ability; b. resolution
izšķiršanās *nfr* **1.** breakup, separation; **2.** decision; **3.** division
izšķirt *vt* **1.** separate, part; **2.** divorce; **3.** decide; **4.** discriminate, distinguish
izšķirties *vr* **1.** break up, separate; **2.** get a divorce; **3.** decide; **4.** be decided; **5.** divide
izšķiru *indecl adj* decisive, deciding, critical
izšķīst *vi* **1.** dissolve; **2.** splash; scatter; **3.** go to pieces
izšķobīt *vt* distort
izšķobīties *vr* become wobbly
izšķūrēt *vt* **1.** shovel (clean); **2.** shovel out
izšķūtēt *vt* **1.** sweep out; **2.** send off
izšli[ch]erēt [h] *vi* (sl.) squeeze through, weasel out of
izšļakstēt *vi* splash out
izšļakstēties *vr* splash out

izšļakstināt *vt* splash out

izšļakstināties *vr* **1.** be splashed; **2.** splash a long time

izšļakstīt *vt* splash out

izšļakstīties *vr* **1.** splash out, be splashed; **2.** splash a long time

izšļākt *v* **1.** *vt* (of liquids) dump (with a splash); **2.** *vi* gush out, spurt out

izšļākties *vr* gush out, spurt out

izšļaucīt *vt* stretch out

izšļaucīties *vr* stretch

izšļaukus *adv* (col.) stretched out (fully on the ground)

izšļircināt *vt* squirt, squirt out

izšļūkāt *vt* damage (by sliding)

izšļukt *vi* slip out; **i. cauri** slip through

izšļūkt *vi* slide out

izšļuncināties *vr* (col.) splash out, spill

izšļupstēt *vt* lisp

izšmaukt *vr* (col.) sneak out, slip away, escape

izšmaukties *vr* (col.) sneak out, slip away, escape

izšmugulēties *vr* (barb.) dodge, escape, weasel out of

izšmukt *vi* (col.) sneak out, slip away, escape

izšmulēt *vt* (col.) spread, smear

izšmurgāt *vt* (of one's meal) mess up

izšņakarēt *vt* snuff; (fig.) ransack

izšņakas *nf pl* leftovers; (col.) leavings

izšņakāt *vt* (col.) pick at one's food, eat mincingly; snuff

izšņākt *vt* hiss, utter with a hiss

izšņāpt *vt* (col.) **1.** cross out; **2.** snip out, cut out (carelessly)

izšņaukt *vt* **i. degunu** blow one's nose

izšņaukties *vr* blow one's nose

izšņergas *nf pl* (com.) leavings

izšņergāt *vt* (com.) pick at one's food

izšņukstēt *vt* utter amidst sobs

izšņukurēt *vt* snuff; (fig.) ransack

izšņūkt *vt* **i. degunu** blow one's nose

izšpricēt *vt* (barb.) spray

izštancēt *vt* punch out

izšūdināt *vt* sew, make (by sewing)

izšūnoties *vr* become honeycombed

izšūpināt *vt* push s.o. on a swing; rock, rock enough

izšūpot *vt* push s.o. on a swing; rock, rock enough

izšūpoties *vr* **1.** swing (on a swing) to one's heart's content; **2.** rock out of; rock through

izšūstīt *vt* embroider

izšūt *vt* **1.** embroider; **2.** use up in sewing; **3.** sew; **4.** face

izšūties *vr* **1.** be sewn; **2.** sew a long time

izšuve *nf* (of brickwork) joint

izšuvju klucītis (or **stienis**) *nm* brick jointer

izšuvot *vt* (of brickwork) point

izšuvum/s *nm* embroidery; embroidered article; ~**i** needlework

izšvirkstēt *vi* fizz out; sputter and die

iztaisīt *vt* **1.** make; **2.** (with accusative or **par**) make into; care, give a hoot; **3.** come to, amount

iztaisīties *vr* **1.** (with **pēc** or **par**, col.) make like s.o., pretend to be; **2.** get ready; **3.** (com.) answer a call of nature

iztaisnojums *nm* straightening out; (el.) rectification

iztaisnot *vt* **1.** straighten out; **2.** (el.) rectify

iztaisnotājs *nm* straightener

iztaisnoties *vr* straighten oneself out, become straight

iztāle *nf* (rare.) distance

iztālēm *adv* from afar, from a distance

iztālis *adv* from afar, from a distance

iztamborēt *vt* crochet

iztapība *nf* obligingness, complaisance; **verdziska i.** servility, obsequiousness

iztapīgi *adv* obligingly, complaisantly

iztapīgs *adj* obliging, complaisant; **verdziski i.** servile, obsequious

iztapīgums *nm* obligingness, complaisance

iztapnie/ks *nm*, **~ce** *nf* toady

iztaponis *nm* toady

iztapoņa *nf, nm* toady

iztapsēt *vt* paper

iztapšņa *nf, nm* toady

iztapt *vi* 1. oblige, please; 2. get out

iztarkšķēt *v* 1. *vi* chug out of (a place); 2. *vt* (col.) blab out

iztarkšķēties *vr* (col.) have a long chat

iztarot *vt* remove fish from a net

iztašķīt *vt* splatter

iztauja *nf* 1. interview; questioning; 2. debriefing

iztaujājums *nm* questioning

iztaujāšana *nf* questioning; interrogation

iztaujāt *vt* 1. question; interrogate; 2. debrief

iztaujātāj/s *nm*, **~a** *nf* questioner; interviewer; interrogator

iztaujāties *vr* ask around

iztaukšķēt *vt* stew

iztaurēt *vt* trumpet, announce with much fanfare

iztaurēties *vr* blow the horn a lot

iztaustīt *vt* feel (with fingers, cane)

iztaustīties *vr* feel around for a long time

iztece *nf* 1. outflow; discharge; 2. outlet

iztecējums *nm* secretion

iztecēt I *vi* 1. pour out; 2. empty; 3. (with **no**, of streams) have its source in . . .; 4. ooze out

iztecēt II *vi* scurry out

iztecēties *vr* be on the go a long time

iztecināt I *vt* 1. (of liquids) let run out; 2. distill; 3. (of meat) render

iztecināt II *vt* (of cutting tools) grind

iztēgāt *vt* (reg.) question

izteicēja *nf* spokeswoman

izteicēja teikums *nm* predicate clause

izteicēj/s *nm* 1. (gram.) predicate; 2. spokesman

izteicien/s *nm* 1. expression; **gleznains i.** figure of speech; picturesque expression; **spārnots i.** catchphrase; **piedodiet ~u** pardon my saying so; 2. statement; **vispārīgos ~os** in general terms

izteika *nf* statement; pronouncement, utterance

izteiksme *nf* 1. (facial, poetic, algebraic) expression; **pilns ~s** pregnant (with meaning); **~s lī-dzeklis** means of expression; **~s spēks** forcefulness; 2. (gram.) mood

izteiksmība *nf* expressiveness

izteiksmīgi *adv* expressively, eloquently; meaningfully

izteiksmīgs *adj* expressive, eloquent

izteiksmīgums *nm* expressiveness, eloquence

izteikt *vt* express, utter, declare, state; **i. brīdinājumu** warn; **i. ar cipariem** digitize; **i. komplimentu** pay a compliment; **i. piezīmi** a. make a re-mark; b. reprove, reprimand; **i. priekšlikumu** make a suggestion; **to nevar vārdos i.** it is more than words can tell

izteikties *vr* 1. express oneself; express one's opinion; state, make comments; **i. gaŗi un plaši** expatiate; **asi i.** talk sharply; **skaidri i.** speak plainly; 2. manifest itself

izteikts *adj* pronounced, marked

izteikums *nm* utterance, statement, pronouncement

izteka *nf* source (of a stream)

iztekāt *vt* scamper all over

iztēle *nf* fantasy, imagination

iztēlojums *nm* depiction, presentation

iztēlot *vt* picture; imagine

iztēloties *vr* picture oneself; imagine

iztēlots *adj, part* of **iztēlot** imaginary

iztelzt *vt* (col.) drink up, swill

iztempt *vt* (col.) drink up, swill

iztenkoties *vr* gossip a lot

iztenterēt *vi* stagger out; toddle out

iztērēt *vt* 1. spend; 2. waste, squander

iztērētāj/s *nm*, **~a** *nf* squanderer

iztērēties *vr* be spent; spend all one's money

iztērgāties *vr* have a nice, long talk

iztērpināt *vt* (reg.) question

iztērzēties *vr* have a nice, long talk

iztēst *vt* roughhew

iztetovēt *vt* tattoo

izticens *adj* (obs.) satisfactory

izticināt *vt* (obs.) provide for

izticis *adj* satisfied with one's lot; doing all right

iztiesāt *vt* (of a case) try

iztiesāties *vr* litigate a long time

iztika *nf* 1. livelihood, living; 2. provisions, groceries

iztikas minimums *nm* living wage

iztīklot *vt* (of nets, networks) spread

iztīksmināties *vr* delight in

iztikšana *nf* (col.) living (means)

iztikt *vi* 1. get by, live on, subsist on; **var i.** (in response to **kā klājas?**) not bad; 2. do with (what one has), do without; 3. get out

iztincināt *vt* (col.) question

iztipināt *vi* trip out; toddle out

iztirdīt *vt* question

iztirgot *vt* 1. sell, sell out; 2. dissipate, squander

iztirgoties *vr* deal, haggle

iztirināt *vt* (with **kājas, rokas**) limber up

iztīrīt *vt* 1. clean; 2. clean out

iztīrīties *vr* be cleansed, become clean

iztirpināt *vt* stretch one's legs (or arms, to rid them of numbness or pins and needles)

iztirzājums *nm* 1. discussion; 2. exposition

iztirzāšana *nf* discussion

iztirzāt *vt* discuss

iztirze *nf* discussion

iztīsis *adj, part* of **iztīst** tall and thin

iztīst *vi* grow tall and thin

iztīstīt *vt* unwrap

iztīstīties *vr* get unwrapped

iztīt *vt* 1. unwrap; unwind; 2. (of skeins, spools) use up

iztīties *vr* get unwrapped; unwrap oneself; unwind

iztracināt *vt* (of animals) excite, tease

iztraipīt *vt* 1. spread, smear; 2. (of a spread, lubricant) use up

iztrakot *vi* 1. (of children) romp, tear about; 2. (of persons, storms) rage; 3. sow one's wild oats

iztrakoties *vr* 1. (of children) romp, tear about; 2. (of persons, storms) rage; 3. sow one's wild oats

iztrallāt *vt* 1. (col.) squander; 2. warble

iztrallināt *vt* 1. (col.) squander; 2. warble

iztrallināties *vr* warble a long time

iztramdīt *vt* (of animals) scare away, (of insects) disturb

iztraucēt *vt* 1. disturb; intrude upon; 2. startle

iztraukt I *vi* rush out, rush through

iztraukt II *vt* rouse

iztraukties *vr* rush out, rush through

iztrausties *vr* clamber out

iztrenkāt *vt* scatter, disperse; drive, chase

iztrenkt *vt* drive out

iztricināt *vt* shake

iztriekt *vt* 1. drive out; **i. cauri** drive through; 2. knock out

iztriekties *vr* 1. drive through; rush out; 2. have a nice, long chat

iztriept *vt* 1. spread, smear; 2. (of spreads, lubricants) use up

iztrinkšķināt *vt* strum

iztriņāt *vt* rub (one's eyes)

iztrīt *vt* sharpen, grind, whet, strop

iztrokšņoties *vr* make a lot of noise

iztrūcināt *vt* startle

iztrūcināties *vr* be startled

iztrūdējis *adj, part* of **iztrūdēt** rotted out

iztrūdēt *vi* rot; rot from inside

iztrūdināt *vt* rot

iztrūkstoš/ais *nom adj* absentee; **~ā** *f*

iztrūkt I *vi* 1. (of buttons, hooks) come off; 2. (of boils) burst

iztrūkt II *vi* **1.** be short of; **2.** be absent; **3.** be missing

iztrūkties *vr* be startled

iztrūkums *nm* shortage, deficit

iztrunēt *vi* (of wood) rot

iztrupēt *vi* (of wood) rot

iztrupt (of wood) rot

iztrusēt *vi* become porous

iztrusnīties *vr* (col.) clamber out

iztukšīt *vt* (obs.) empty

iztukšīties *vr* (obs.) empty

iztukšot *vt* empty

iztukšotība *nf* emptiness, state of depletion

iztukšoties *vr* empty

iztulkojums *nm* interpretation; **nepareizs i.** misinterpretation

iztulkot *vt* **1.** interpret; **2.** translate

iztulkotājs *nm*, **~a** *nf* interpreter

iztūļāties *vr* be pokey about getting ready

iztuntulēt *vi* **1.** trudge, waddle out of; **2.** un-wrap

iztuntulēties *vr* **1.** trudge, waddle out of; **2.** unwrap oneself

iztuntuļot *vi* **1.** trudge, waddle out of; **2.** unwrap

iztuntuļoties *vr* **1.** trudge, waddle out of; **2.** unwrap oneself

izturams *adj* bearable

izture *nf* (sports) hold (pause in movement)

izturēšana *nf* (aeron.) float

izturēšanās *nfr* behavior, conduct; bearing; treatment; **i. modifikācija** behavior modification

izturēt *v* **1.** *vt* endure; bear; stand; withstand; **2.** *vt, vi* keep up (with); keep it up; (mus.) sustain; **3.** *vt* (of a test) pass; **neizturēt kritiku** fail to meet specifications (or expectations); fail the test; **neizturēt pārbaudījumu** fail a test; **4.** (*vi, 3rd pers*) last; **5.** *vt* (of domestic animals) keep

izturētība *nf* **1.** steadiness; **2.** stability

izturēties *vr* behave; conduct oneself; treat; **i. aukstasinīgi** keep one's head; **i. ar neuzticību** mistrust, distrust; **i. atturīgi** keep one's distance; **i. slikti (pret kādu)** maltreat; **i. vēsi** give s.o. the cold shoulder

izturēts *adj, part* of **izturēt 1.** stable, steady; un-flagging; **2.** sustained

izturība *nf* **1.** hardiness, toughness; endurance; **2.** durability; solidity; (of colors) fastness

izturīgi *adv* strongly; durably; solidly

izturīgs *adj* **1.** hardy, tough; **2.** durable; solid; (of colors) fast

izturīgums *nm* durability; solidity

iztušēt *vt* blur

iztvaice *nf* evaporation

iztvaicēšana *nf* evaporation

iztvaicēt *vt* **1.** evaporate; **2.** heat with steam

iztvaicēties *vr* warm up

iztvaikojum/s *nm* **1.** evaporation; **2.** ~i vapor

iztvaikot *vt, vi* evaporate

iztvanēt *v* **1.** *vi* (of fragrances, poet.) evanesce; **2.** *vt* exude a fragrance

iztvarstīt *vt* **1.** buy out (all or most of a merchandise); **2.** catch (all or most of a group of people); **3.** grope, poke

iztvarstīties *vr* persist in going after s.o.

iztveicēt *vt* (of heat) dry out

iztveicēties *vr* get hot

iztvert *vt* pull out; (stat.) sample

iztvērums *nm* (stat.) sample

iztvīkt *vi* be faint with thirst; be parched; (fig.) pine

iztvīkties *vr* be faint with thirst; be parched; (fig.) pine

iztvīkums *nm* thirst (from heat)

izubagot *vt* obtain by begging, cadge

izubagoties *vr* go around begging

izūjināties *vr* hallo a long time

izurbināt *vt* **1.** (of animals) bore; **2.** scrape out

izurbt *vt* drill, bore; (fig.) dig through

izurbties *vr* **1.** drill through; **2.** pierce, penetrate; **3.** (fig.) dig through

izurkņāt *vt* dig up; root up

izurķēt *vt* dig, dig up; make a hole

izūtrupēt *vt* auction off

izvadāt *vt* 1. deliver; 2. show around; 3. (of birds) fledge

izvadāties *vr* show around, show the sights

izvadbuferis *nm* (compu.) output buffer

izvadcaurule *nf* discharge pipe

izvaddatne *nf* (compu.) output file

izvade *nf* 1. posting of sentries; 2. (compu.) output

izvadības *nf pl* funeral procession

izvadierīce *nf* 1. (compu.) output equipment; 2. discharge device, exhaust device

izvadīšana *nf* 1. seeing-off, sending-off; 2. funeral; 3. (physiol.) elimination

izvadīt *vt* 1. see off; 2. guide; pilot; 3. escort out; **i. sardzi** post sentries; 4. attend a funeral; 5. or-ganize a going-away party; 6. (physiol.) eliminate; 7. send to school; 8. (obs.) marry off

izvadītāja kapuce *nf* exhaust hood

izvadītāj/s *nm*, **~a** *nf* reader of funeral orations

izvadkanāls *nm* excretory duct

izvadorg[a]ns [ā] *nm* excretory organ

izvads *nm* 1. excretory duct; 2. exhaust; discharge valve; external lead; (compu.) output device; 3. funeral procession

izvadu *adv* comfortably, unhurriedly

izvagot *vt* furrow

izvaibīt *vt* (of one's face) pull, make

izvaibstīt *vt* (of one's face) pull, make

izvaibstīties *vr* 1. (of a facial expression) produce (**i. smaidā** produce a smile); 2. grimace

izvaicājums *nm* question

izvaicāt *vt* question

izvaicāties *vr* ask around

izvaidēt *vt* moan

izvaidēties *vr* moan a lot

izvaikstīt *vt* (of one's face) pull, make

izvaikstīties *vr* (of one's face) pull, make

izvaimanāt *vt* wail

izvaimanāties *vr* wail a long time

izvainot *vt* find fault, put down

izvaire *nf* escape

izvairelis *nm* shirker, dodger, slacker

izvaires literātūra *nf* escape literature

izvairība *nf* evasiveness

izvairīgi *adv* evasively

izvairīgs *adj* evasive

izvairīgums *nm* evasiveness

izvairīšanās *nfr* avoidance

izvairīšanās gradients *nm* (psych.) avoidance gradient

izvairīt *vt* 1. avoid, keep out of; 2. prevent

izvairīties *vr* avoid; shun; shirk; dodge; escape; evade; elude; **i. no atbildes** equivocate, shuffle

izvajāt *vt* persecute

izvājēt *vi* grow thin

izvākt *vt* remove, get out; evacuate

izvākties *vr* move out; get out

izvalbīt *vt* **i. acis** stare at, goggle at

izvalbīties *vr* (of eyes) pop out

izvalcēt *vt* (tech.) roll

izvālēt *vt* (col.) beat

izvalka *nf* 1. slut; 2. *pl* **~s** worn clothing

izvalkāt *vt* wear out

izvalkāties *vr* 1. get worn out; 2. wear a long time

izvalstīt *vt* (of grass, crops) flatten (by lying or rolling)

izvalstīties *vr* toss in bed

izvaļa *nf* leisure

izvaļām *adv* comfortably, unhurriedly

izvaļāt *vt* 1. roll back and forth; 2. *var* of **izvāļāt**

izvāļāt *vt* (of grass, crops) flatten (by lying or rolling in them)

izvaļāties *vr* roll (in sand, mud, grass), wal-low

izvāļāties *vr* lie in bed, lie around

izvaļīgi *adv* (**dzīvot**) ~**i** (live) a life of leisure

izvaļīgs *adj* free, unconstrained

izvaļīt *vt* (com.) drive out

izvandīt *vt* ransack, rummage through

izvandīties *vr* rummage a long time

izvantēt *vt* (com.) toss out

izvaņķīt *vt* (reg.) beat

izvāpēt *vt* glaze

izvārdzināt *vt* wear out, exhaust; torment

izvārgt *vi* be worn out, be exhausted

izvārgties *vr* 1. suffer; 2. be worn out

izvārīt *vt* 1. boil; 2. cook; 3. boil dry

izvārīties *vr* 1. be boiled; 2. be cooked, be done; 3. boil away

izvarošana *nf* rape

izvarot *vt* rape

izvarotājs *nm* rapist

izvārstīt *vt* 1. thread; 2. open and close (a door) repeatedly

izvārtīt *vt* 1. roll (in dough, snow); 2. (of grass, crops) flatten (by lying or rolling in them), (of beds) mess up

izvārtīties *vr* roll (in sand, snow, grass), wallow

izvazas *nf pl* worn-out footwear

izvazāt *vt* 1. scatter; 2. (of infections) spread

izvazāties *vr* tramp all over

izvēcināt *vt* flap a long time

izvēcināties *vr* flap a long time

izvedība *nf* skill, dexterity

izvedīgi *adv* skillfully, dexterously

izvedīgs *adj* skillful, dexterous

izvedīgums *nm* skillfulness, dexterousness

izvēdināt *vt* air, ventilate

izvēdināties *vr* 1. be aired, be ventilated; 2. go for an airing

izvedmuita *nf* export duty

izvedtirdzniecība *nf* export trade

izvedums *nm* 1. export, amount of goods exported; 2. (math.) derivation (of a formula)

izveicība *nf* skillfulness, dexterity; resourcefulness

izveicīgi *adv* skillfully, dexterously; resourcefully

izveicīgs *adj* skillful, dexterous; resourceful

izveicīgums *nm* skillfulness, dexterity; resourcefulness

izveide *nf* 1. design; 2. shape, form, configuration

izveidojums *nm* 1. design; 2. shape, form, configuration

izveidošana *nf* 1. shaping, formation; 2. organization; 3. development

izveidošanās *nfr* 1. formation; 2. establishment, organization; 3. development

izveidot *vt* 1. shape, form; 2. organize; 3. develop

izveidoties *vr* 1. form, take shape; 2. become established, be organized; 3. develop into

izveids *nm* shape; form

izveiksme *nf* skill, dexterity

izveikties *vr* (obs.) succeed, do well

izvējot *vt* air, ventilate

izvējoties *vr* 1. be aired; 2. cool off

izvelbt *vt* bulge; usu. *part* **izvelbts** (of eyes) bulging

izvelbties *vr* bulge

izvēl/e *nf* choice, selection; **ar** ~**i** discriminately; **pēc** ~**es** as one chooses; **derīgs** ~**ei** eligible

izvēlēšanās *nfr* choice; selection

izvelēt *vt* beat out the washing

izvēlēt *vt* 1. elect; 2. select, choose

izvēlēties *vr* choose; select

izvēlēts *adj, part* of **izvēlēt** elected, elective; chosen

izvēlība *nf* fastidiousness, pickiness

izvēlīgi *adv* fastidiously

izvēlīgs *adj* fastidious, picky, choosy, exacting

izvēlīgums *nm* fastidiousness, pickiness

izvelkams *adj* pull-out, extension

izvēlne *nf* (compu.) menu

izvelmēt *vt* (tech.) roll

izvelt *vt* roll out (from a place); **i. cauri** roll through

izvelties *vr* roll out (from a place); **i. cauri** roll through

izveltnēt *vt* roll out (with a roller)

izvelvējums *nm* vault

izvelvēt *vt* vault, arch

izvemt *vt* throw up, vomit

izvemties *vr* vomit

izverdums *nm* eruption

izverdzināt *vt* drive to exhaustion

izvērējis *adj* (folk.) grown too old

izvērpt *vt* spin; use up in spinning

izvērpties *vr* **1.** spin a long time; **2.** turn out (in spinning)

izvērse *nf* (TV) scan

izvērsējs *nm* expander

izvērsējstars *nm* scanning beam

izvērses iekārta *nf* scanner

izvērst *vt* **1.** expand; (fig.) elaborate on; **2.** turn outward; **3.** turn in-side out, invert; **i. uz kreiso pusi** reverse; **4.** (mil.) deploy; **5.** transform; **6.** (TV, compu.) scan

izvērsties *vr* **1.** expand; **2.** deploy; **3.** turn into, develop into

izvērsums *nm* development; elaboration

izvēršana *nf* **1.** expansion; **2.** inversion; **3.** deployment; **4.** transformation

izvēršanās *nfr* **1.** expansion; **2.** (mil.) deployment; **3.** turning into; transformation; development

izvērt I *vt* **1.** thread, thread through; **2.** pull out (sth. threaded); **kā caur adatas aci ~s** thin as a rail

izvērt II *vt* cook

izvērtējums *nm* evaluation

izvērtēt *vt* evaluate, judge

izvērties *vr* (of sth. threaded) come out

izveseļošanās *nfr* recovery from illness

izveseļoties *vr* recover from illness

izvēsināt *vt* cool

izvēsināties *vr* cool off

izvest *vt* **1.** take out (using a vehicle); move out; **2.** empty (using a vehicle); **3.** take, lead, conduct; **i. no ierindas** put out of action; **i. no pacietības** exasperate, make one lose patience; **4.** export; **5.** (math.) derive

izvēst *vi* cool off

izvesties *vr* **1.** carry (transport) a length of time; **2.** behave

izvešana *nf* exportation

izvētīt *vt* winnow

izvēzt *vt* stick out

izvicināt *vt* brandish a length of time

izvicot *vt* **1.** beat with a switch; **2.** (col.) eat up

izvicoties *vr* beat sth. a long time; have at

izvidžināties *vr* twitter a long time

izviebt *vt* (of one's face) pull, make

izviesoties *vr* have a long visit

izvietne *nf* facility; location

izvietojums *nm* disposition; placement, location; distribution; layout

izvietošana *nf* placing, location; stowage; investment; positioning; billeting; disposal; removal

izvietot *vt* place; locate; dispose, remove; (of cargo) stow; (of capital) invest; (of troops) position; (of troops) billet; **i. barakās** barrack; **i. nometnē** encamp

izvietoties *vr* **1.** take seats; take lodgings; take up positions; **2.** be situated

izvijums *nm* weaving, weave

izvīkstīt *vt* (reg.) unwrap

izvīkstīties *vr* (reg.) unwrap oneself

izvilcēj/s *nm* (tech.) **1.** extractor; **~a aizķere** extractor claw; **2.** puller, stretcher

izvilcējštance *nf* drawing press

izvīlējums *nm* filing job; filed piece

izvīlēt *vt* **1.** file, shape with a file; **2.** sharpen with a file

izvilgt *vi* be soaked, be drenched

izvilināt *vt* **1.** lure from, lure out of; **2.** tease out; **3.** elicit; draw forth

izvilkšana *nf* pulling; extraction; (forest.) skidding; (math.) a. factoring; b. (of roots) extraction

izvilkt *vt* **1.** pull out; extract; (forest.) skid; **i. aiz iekavām** (math.) factor out; **i. cauri** pull through; **i. dzīvību** barely keep body and soul together; **i. garumā** spin out, protract; **i. krastā** (of a boat) beach; pull ashore; **i. labumu** derive profit; **i. no maksts** unsheathe; **i. sakni** (math.) extract a root; **i. saldo** (bookk.) strike the balance; **2.** (of wires, ropes) string, hang, run; **3.** (of lottery tickets, cards) choose; **4.** (of information) tease out; coax out of; **5.** tide over; **6.** (tech.) draw

izvilkties *vr* **1.** slowly pull oneself, drag oneself, slither out of, slither through; **2.** (of odors, moisture) go into, seep through, penetrate; **3.** (*3rd pers*) be pulled out of sth. accidently; **4.** barely manage

izvilkuma darbs *nm* open work

izvilkums *nm* **1.** excerpt; **2.** (chem.) extract

izvilnīt *v* **1.** *vi* come out in waves; **2.** *vt* (of waves) push ashore

izvilt *vt* **1.** lure out of; **2.** swindle s.o. out of sth.

izviļāt I *vt* roll (in dough, snow)

izviļāt II *vt* entice, coax out of

izviļāties *vr* roll (in sand, snow, grass), wallow

izviļināt *vt* roll, make by rolling

izviļņot *v* **1.** *vi* come out in waves; **2.** *vt* (of waves) push ashore

izvingrināt *vt* exercise

izvingrināties *vr* **1.** finish exercising; **2.** be exercised

izvingroties *vr* have a good workout

izvirdumiezis *nm* extrusive rock

izvirdums *nm* eruption

izvirināt *vt* (of doors, gates) open and close repeatedly

izvirmot *vi* rise waveringly

izvirpināt *vt* **1.** turn on a lathe; **2.** hollow out on a lathe

izvirpināt II *vt* whirl out

izvirpot I *vt* **1.** turn on a lathe; **2.** hollow out on a lathe

izvirpot II *vt* whirl out

izvirpuļot *vi* whirl out

izvirst I *vi* **1.** degenerate; **2.** become depraved, become perverted

izvirst II *vi* erupt

izviršana I *nf* degeneration

izviršana II *nf* eruption

izvirt *vi* **1.** erupt; **2.** be cooked, be done

izvirtība *nf* debauchery, depravity, dissolution; perversion

izvirtul/is *nm,* ~**e** *nf* debauchee

izvirums *nm* decoction

izvirze *nf* **1.** statement (of a problem, question); **2.** (phys.) shift

izvirziens *nm* deviation

izvirzījums *nm* **1.** projection, prominence, protuberance; (mil.) salient; (mech.) lug; **2.** (math.) expansion

izvirzīšana *nf* proposal; nomination

izvirzīt *vt* **1.** steer, guide; **2.** put forward; make project; (of a question) raise; (of an idea) advance; **i. priekšplānā** put in the forefront; **3.** propose (a candidate), nominate

izvirzīties *vr* **1.** move out; come forward; **2.** move outward, move ahead; **3.** move to the front ranks, excel; **4.** (of issues, questions) come up

izvīstīt *vt* unwrap; unswaddle

izvīstīties *vr* unwrap oneself

izvīt *vt* **1.** weave, make (an article) by weaving; **2.** use up in weaving

izvītēties *vr* (reg.) sweat; take a steam bath

izvīties *vr* **1.** (of roads, streams) wind; meander; **2.** slip out

izvītņot *vt* cut threads

izvizināt *vt* take for a ride

izvizināties *vr* go for a ride

izzagt *vt* steal (from a place)

izzagties *vr* steal away

izzāģēt *vt* 1. saw, cut out with a saw; 2. make with a saw

izzāģēties *vr* cut (with a saw) a long time

izzaimot *vt* revile

izzākāt *vt* revile

izzarojums *nm* branching, ramification; fork

izzarot *v* 1. *vt* spread branches; 2. *vi* branch, fork

izzaroties *vr* branch, fork

izzaudēt *vt* lose

izzēģelēt *vi* (col.) sail out

izzelēt *vt* (of tobacco) chew (all, a lot)

izzelt *vi* blossom

izzeltīt *vt* gilt (on the inside)

izzibēt *vi* flash

izzīdīt *vt* finish suckling

izziedēt *vi* blossom out, bloom

izziedēties *vr* bloom a long time

izzieķēt *vt* (com.) spread, smear out

izziemot *vi* winter

izziepēt *vt* 1. soap; 2. use up soap

izziest *vt* (of a viscous substance) spread

izzīlēšana *nf* fortune-telling

izzīlēt *vt* tell fortune

izzīlēties *vr* tell a lot of fortunes

izzīmējums *nm* delineation

izzīmēt *vt* 1. draw; delineate; 2. use up in drawing

izzīmēties *vr* draw a long time

izzināmība *nf* cognizability

izzināt *vt* 1. find out, make inquiries; 2. cognize

izziņa *nf* 1. cognition; 2. information; 3. reference; 4. (jur.) preliminary investigation

izziņas teorija *nf* epistemology

izziņot *vt* announce; **i. pa radio** broadcast, announce on the radio; **i. trauksmi** raise the alarm

izziņu birojs *nm* information center

izziņu grāmata *nf* reference volume

izziest *vt* (of a viscous substance) spread

izzīst *vt* suck out; **i. no pirksta** concoct, fabricate, suck out of one's fingers' ends

izzīšļāt *vt* suck out

izzobojums *nm* mockery, scoffing, derision

izzobot *vt* mock, deride, scoff at

izzoboties *vr* scoff at a while

izzortēt *vt* sort out

izzust *vi* fade; vanish, disappear

izzvanīt *vt* 1. (fig.) trumpet, tell everybody; 2. (of a church service) toll out; ring the end of a class session

izzvanīties *vr* be calling (on the telephone) a long time; be ringing the bell a long time

izzvejot *vt* 1. (of fish) catch; 2. fish out; 3. (fig.) fish out from, fish from under

izzvejoties *vr* fish a long time

izzvelties *vr* roll out, fall out

izzvērēties *vr* swear (one's love) constantly

izzviegt *vt* neigh

izzviegties *vr* neigh a lot; guffaw a lot

izžadzināties *vr* chatter a long time

izžagoties *vr* hiccup a lot

izžaut *vt* hang out to dry

izžēāvāties *vr* yawn a lot

izžāvēt *vt* 1. dry; desiccate; (of lumber) season; 2. smoke-dry, cure

izžāvēties *vr* 1. dry oneself; 2. get smoke-dried, get cured

izžēlot *vt* (rare.) feel sorry for

izžēloties *vr* complain at length

izžmaudzīt *vt* wring out

izžmaugt *vt* wring out

izžņaudzīt *vt* wring out

izžņaugt *vt* squeeze out

izžuburots *adj* branched, forked

izžuldzēt *vt* soak
izžulgt vi get soaking wet
izžurgt *vi* get soaking wet
izžūt *vi* dry; dry up, run dry
izžuvis *adj* 1. dry; labi i. (of timber) well-
  seasoned; 2. thin
izžūžot *vt* cradle, nurse

J

ja *conj* if; ja arī even if; ja jau now, if; ja tikai
  provided
jā *partic* yes; jā gan indeed
jā *adv*; kā jā (with nouns) some, terrific,
  magnificent; (with verbs) for sure
jābūtība *nf* (philos.) ought, oughtness
ja[ch]t/a [h] *nf* yacht; ~u sports yachting
ja[ch]tklubs [h] *nm* yacht club
ja[ch]tsmenis [h] *nm* yachtsman
jaciņa *nf dim* of jaka, jacket
jacmašīna *nf* high-hat cymbals
jādeklis *nm* 1. (com.) madcap; 2. hobby
jādelēt *vi* ride about, ride back and forth
jādināt *vt* 1. ride continuously; 2. let ride
  piggyback; dandle
jādīt *vi* ride, ride about
jādīties *vr* fidget; romp
jāds *adj* (com.) rowdy
jafetisks *adj* Japhetic
jafetīti *nm pl* Japhetic peoples
jaguārs *nm* jaguar
jaguārundis *nm* jaguarundi
jaires *nf pl* (reg.) swing
jājam/s *adj* ridable; *defin* ~ais riding, saddle
jājamzirgs *nm* saddle horse
jājēj/s *nm*, ~a *nf* rider, horseman
jājiens *nm* horseback ride
jājampātaga *nf* riding crop
jājums *nm* (folk.) horseback ride

jājamzābaki *nm pl* riding boots
jājamzirdziņš *nm* hobbyhorse
jaka *nf* jacket; cardigan
jakarēt *vt* mess up, jumble together
jakarēties *vr* behave wildly
jakaris *nm* meddler
jāklis *nm* mischief, scamp, rogue
jakobīnis *nm* Jacobin
jaks *nm* yak
jaktene *nf* (col.) shotgun; (sl.) hard salami
jakts *nf* (barb.) hullabaloo
jakut/s *nm*, ~iete *nf* Yakut
jambisks *adj* iambic
jamboza *nf* jambosa
jambs *nm* iamb; četrpēdu j. iambic tetrameter;
  piecpēdu j. iambic pentameter
jampadracis *nm* (com.) row, hullabaloo
jams *nm* yam
jancīgi *adv* strangely; funnily
jancīgs *adj* (col.) 1. strange; 2. funny
jancināt *vt* (of a fleeing hare) call to stop
  ("Jancīt, Jancīt, attupies!")
jandālēt *vi* dance the jandāliņš; dance
jandālēties *vr* 1. dance to one's heart's content;
  2. romp
jandāliņš *nm* 1. a Latvian folk dance, the
  jandāls; 2. *dim* of jandāls, hubbub
jandāls *nm* 1. a Latvian folk dance, the
  jandāliņš; 2. (col.) hubbub
janičārs *nm* Janissary
janis *nm* (in card games) booby, (in schafskopf)
  schneider
jānis *nm* (naut.) schooner
jānīši *nm pl* erigeron, fleabane
jānītis *nm* (hum.) hare
jānudien *adv* (col.) really
janvāris *nm* January
Jāņa āboliņš *nm* hop clover
jāņabērni *nm pl* = jāņubērni
Jāņa paparde *nf* common brake
Jāņa pienītes *nf pl* hawkweed
Jāņa sakne *nf* rhizome of the male fern

Jāņa spuļģis *nm* glowworm

Jāņa ziedi *nm pl* false wintergreen

jāņeglīte *nf* lousewort

Jāņ/i *nm pl* Midsummer Day, summer solstice festival; **~u vakars** Ligo night, Midsummer Eve

jāņmaizīte *nf* carob tree

jāņmētras *nf pl* peppermint

jāņogas *nf pl* currant

jāņogulājs *nm* currant bush

jāņogulāju pelēkais sprīžmetis *nm* V-moth

jāņogulāju zāģlapsene *nf* a sawfly, Pteronidea ribesii

jāņot *vi* celebrate Jāņi

jāņoties *vr* celebrate (Jāņi, other occasions)

jāņtārpiņš *nm* glowworm

jāņubērni *nm pl* celebrants of the Ligo night

jāņuguns *nf* bonfire (lit on Ligo night)

Jāņu roze *nf* peony

jāņusiers *nm* boiled cheese

Jāņu spīgulis *nm* glowworm

jāņuzāle *nf* **1.** any wild flower picked on the eve of Jāņi; **2.** bedstraw; **3.** cowwheat

Japānas apiņi *nm pl* Japanese hop

Japānas aukuba *nf* aucuba

Japānas bārbele *nf* Japanese barberry

Japānas ceriņi *nm pl* Japanese tree lilac

Japānas cidonija *nf* Japanese quince

Japānas kastanis *nm* Japanese chestnut

Japānas krūmcidonija *nf* Japanese quince

Japānas ķirsis *nm* Japanese flowering cherry

Japānas lāčauzas *nf pl* Japanese chess

Japānas lapegle *nf* Japanese larch

Japānas mespils *nm* loquat

Japānas plūme *nf* Japanese persimmon

Japānas segliņš *nm* Japanese spindle tree

Japānas sofora *nf* Japanese pagoda tree

Japānas spireja *nf* Japanese spirea

Japānas sūrene *nf* Japanese knotweed

Japānas vēdekļpalma *nf* hemp palm

japā/nis *nm*, **~niete** *nf* Japanese

japāniski *adv* in Japanese, (speak) Japanese

japānisks *adj* Japanese

japāņu apiņi *nm pl* Japanese hop

japāņu laka *nf* Japanese varnish, japan

japijs *nm* Yuppie

jara *nf* (col.) hubbub, racket

jards *nm* (unit of length) yard

jārēties *vr* (col.) romp, frolick

jārīgi *adv* noisily, boisterously

jārīgs *adj* **1.** frolicky; **2.** noisy, boisterous

jāris *nm* (col.) **1.** quarrel; hubbub; **2.** noise-maker

jarls *nm* jarl

jarovizācija *nf* jarovization

jarovizēt *vt* jarovize

jasmīnkrūms *nm* mock orange bush

jasmīns *nm* **1.** jasmine; **2.** mock orange; **~i** mock orange branches

jasmīnzars *nm* branch of mock orange

jasmīnzieds *nm* mock orange blossom

jasmons *nm* jasmone

jaspiss *nm* jasper

jāšana *nf* horseback riding

jašma *nf* jasper

jašmaks *nm* yashmak

jāšus *adv* mounted, on horseback

jāt *vt, vi* ride (a horse, on horseback); **j. pieguļā** go for a night watch of horses at pasture; **j. zirdziņu** ride one's pet hobby; **j. atkal to pašu ķēvi** playing the same old tune again

jatagans *nm* yataghan

jātavnieks *nm* uncontrollable person

jāteniski *adv* astride

jātenisks *adj* striding

jāties *vr* (sl.) **1.** mess around; **2.** copulate

jātin *adv emph* of **jāt; j. jāja** he rode hell-bent

jātnieciņ/š *nm* **1.** *dim* of **jātnieks; 2.** (balance beam) rider; **3.** braconid

jātnie/ks *nm*, **~ce** *nf* **1.** rider, horseman; **2.** cavalryman; **~ki** cavalry; **3.** (hist.) overseer's assistant

jātnieku bikses *nf pl* riding breeches

jātnieku policija *nf* mounted police

jatrog[e]nija [ē] *nf* iatrogenicity

jatrog[e]nisks [ē] *adj* iatrogenic

jātuve *nf* manege, riding school

jātvingi *nm pl* Jatvingians

jau *adv* already; **j. pēc stundas** in just an hour; **j. rīt** as soon as tomorrow; **j. tā** as it is; **j. tagad** even now, even as we speak; **tur j. viņa nāk** here she comes now

jau *partic* (to emphasize a word, phrase, or clause) really ◊ **kā j.** as always, as is usually the case; **kā j. parasti** as per usual; **kad j., tad j.** in for a penny, in for a pound

jaucamais *nom adj* stirrer; swizzle stick; paddle

jaucēj/s *nm*, ~a *nf* 1. stirrer, mixer, shaker; 2. wrecker

jauceklis *nm* troublemaker

jaucēt *vt* accustom

jaucēties *vr* get used to

jaud/a *nf* 1. might; **viņš skrien, cik ~as** he runs as fast as he can; 2. power; **nominālā j.** rate power; **~s faktors** coefficient of performance; **(braukt) ar pilnu ~u** (go) at full speed; 3. production capacity

jaudām *adv* at times

jaudārzs *nm* (reg.) threshing barn yard

jaudasvīrs *nm* (col.) strongman

jaudāt *vi* be able

jaudīgi *adv* ably

jaudīgs *adj* able

jaudnieks *nm* strongman

jauja *nf* (reg.) threshing barn

jaujas *nf pl* caterwaul

jauji *adv* quickly; steeply

jaujš *adj* 1. quick; 2. steep

jauki *adv* nice, nicely

jauklis *nm* confusion, welter, mess

jauks *adj* nice; lovely

jaukskanība *nf* euphony

jaukskanīgi *adv* euphoniously

jaukskanīg/s *adj* euphonious

jaukskanīgums *nm* euphony

jaukskaņa *nf* euphony

jaukt *vt* 1. mix; (of hair) tousle; (of cards) shuffle; 2. stir; 3. interfere with; **j. (kādam) kārtis** upset s.o.'s applecart; 4. confuse, mix up; 5. **j. ārā** (or **laukā**) disassemble, knock down; 6. **j. nost** dismantle, tear down; 7. **j. iekšā** get (s.o.) involved; **j. pēdas** pull a red herring; **j. prātu** mix (s.o.) up; **j. gaisu** (com., fig.) muddy the waters

jaukten/is *nm*, ~e *nf* 1. mongrel; 2. hybrid

jaukti *adv* in a mixed order

jaukties *vr* 1. mix, mingle; 2. **j. pa kājām** be underfoot; **j. pa vidū** be in the way; 3. interfere, butt in, meddle; **nejaucies starpā!** mind your own business! 4. ransack

jauktin *adv emph* of **jaukt, sajaukt**; **j. sajauca** he really messed it up

jaukts *adj* mixed

jaukumiņš *nm dim* of **jaukums** II, lovely thing

jaukums I *nm* mixture

jaukum/s II *nm* 1. loveliness; attractiveness; 2. ~i beauties

Jaunā derība *nf* New Testament

jaun/ais *nom adj* 1. the young one; **nav nekāds j.** pretty long in the tooth; ~ā *f* ; 2. the new one

jaunaita *nf* ewe lamb

jaunākais *adj, superl* of **jauns** 1. newest; 2. youngest; junior; 3. latest; most recent, recent

jaunaliņa *nf* young woman

jaunaļa *nf* young woman

Jaunanglijas ziemastere *nf* New England aster

jaunapgūstams *adj* (of land) to be opened

jaunapgūts *adj* recently introduced; (of land) newly opened, newly cultivated

jaunarmiet/is *nm,* ~e *nf* (hist.) member of an organized war game group in Soviet public schools

jaunatbraucēj/s *nm,* ~a *nf* new arrival

jaunatklājums *nm* new discovery

jaunatklāsme *nf* new discovery

jaunatklāts *adj* newly discovered

jaunatnācēj/s *nm,* ~a *nf* newcomer

jaunatne *nf* youth, young people; **studējošā j.** college students; **zelta j.** jeunesse dorée; *gen* ~s junior; juvenile

jaunatradums *nm* new discovery

jaunatrasts *adj* newly discovered

jaunattīstības *indecl adj* third-world, developing

jaunatvasinājums *nm* new derivation

jaunatvasināts *adj* newly derived

jaunaudze *nf* new forest; (forestry) plantation

jaunava *nf* young maid, maiden; virgin; **svētā j.** Blessed Virgin; **J.** Virgo

jaunava zaļumos *nf* (bot.) love-in-a-mist

jaunavība *nf* 1. maidenhood; 2. virginity

jaunavīgi *adv* in a maidenly manner; virginally

jaunavīgs *adj* maidenly; virginal

jaunavīgums *nm* maidenliness

jaunbagātnie/ks *nm,* ~ce *nf* nouveau riche

Jaunbeļģijas ziemastere *nf* New York aster

jaunbetons *nm* green concrete

jaunbūve *nf* new construction, newly constructed building

jauncelsme *nf* construction work

jaunceltne *nf* new construction, newly constructed building

jaundadaisms *nm* neo-dada

jaundarbs *nm* new publication

jaundarinājums *nm* neologism

jaundeja *nf* new dance

jaundibināts *adj* newly established, newly founded

jaundzimis *adj* newborn

jaundzimu/šais *nom adj* nenonate, the newborn; ~sī *f*

jaunekle *nf* young woman

jauneklība *nf* youthfulness

jauneklīgi *adv* youthfully

jauneklīgs *adj* youthful

jauneklīgums *nm* youthfulness

jaunek/lis *nm* youth, young man; ~ļa **gadi** years of early manhood

jaunestīgs *adj* virginal

Jaungada kaktuss *nm* Christmas cactus

Jaungada mēnesis *nm* January

Jaungadaa sagaidīšana *nf* New Year's Eve party

Jaungada vakars *nm* New Year's Eve

jaungads *nm* first day of the year; **J.** New Year

jaungaitnieki *nm pl* New Coursists (since 1960, Latvian poets associated with the magazine New Course - Jaunā Gaita)

jaungramatiķis *nm* neogrammarian

jaungrieķu *indecl adj* new Greek

jaungvinejiet/is *nm,* ~e *nf* New Guinean

jaunhēgelietis *nm* neo-Hegelian

jaunhēgelisms *nm* neo-Hegelianism

jaunība *nf* youth

jaunības draugs *nm* school friend

jaunības gadi *nm pl* adolescence

jaunības trakums *nm* sowing one's wild oats

jaunie *nom adj* young people

jauniecelts *adj* newly appointed

jauniegāde *nf* new purchase; (museum, library) recent accession

jauniegūts *adj* newly acquired

jaunienācējs *nm* newcomer

jauniesaucamais *nom adj* draft-age youth

jauniesauktais *nom adj* draftee

jauniesaukts *adj* newly drafted

jauniestudējums *nm* (theat.) revival

jauniešu kārpa *nf* plane wart

jauniešu kopmītne *nf* youth hostel

jaunie/tis *nm*, ~te *nf* youth, adolescent; ~ši young people

jaunievedums *nm* innovation; novelty

jaunievēlēts *adj* newly elected

jaunieviesums *nm* innovation; novelty

jauniķe *nf* (reg.) new bride

jauniķis *nm* (reg.) 1. newlywed; 2. beginner

jauninājums *nm* 1. innovation; 2. novelty

jauninat *vt* 1. make younger; 2. renew

jauniņš *adj* 1. *dim* of **jauns**, young; 2. inexperienced

jaunīte *nf* (reg.) newlywed; daughter-in-law

jaunizcepts *adj* freshly baked

jaunizdevums *nm* new edition

jaunizgudrojums *nm* new invention

jaunizgudrots *adj* newly invented

jauniznācis *adj* recently published

jaunjauns *adj* very young

jaunkalps *nm* young (beginning, inexperienced) farm hand

jaunkantiānisms or jaunkantisms *nm* neo-Kant-ianism

jaunkareivis *nm* army recruit

jaunklasicisms *nm* neoclassicism

jaunkundze *nf* young lady, miss, Miss

jaunkungs *nm* = **jaunskungs**

jaunlaiki *nm pl* modern times; new times

jaunlaiku *indecl adj* modern

jaunlatīņu *indecl adj* Romance

jaunlatvieši *nm pl* "Young Latvians" (nationalistic writers and columnists of the Latvian national revival period of the 1850s and 1860s)

jaunlaulātais *nom adj* newlywed

jaunledus *nm* new ice

jaunlopi *nm pl* young cattle

jaunļaudis *nm pl* young people

jaunmeitene *nf* young girl

jaunmēness *nm* new moon

jaunmāte *nf* stepmother

jaunmatrozis *nm* navy recruit

jaunmežs *nm* new forest

jaunmieži *nm pl* newly harvested barley

jaunmodes *indecl adj* newfangled, novel

jaunmodīgs *adj* newfangled, novel

jaunnedēļ *adv* next week

jaunnedēļa *nf* next week

jaunot *vt* (poet.) renew

jaunpagānisms *nm* neo-paganism

jaunpiedzimis *adj* newborn

jaunpiedzimušais *nom adj* nenonate

jaunpiegriezts *adj* newly converted

jaunpienācēj/s *nm*, ~a *nf* newcomer

jaunpiene *nf* newly calved cow

jaunpiens *nm* beestings, colostrum

jaunplatonisms *nm* neo-Platonism

jaunpuisis *nm* bride's brother

jaunputni *nm pl* young domestic fowl, chickens

jaunrade *nf* creative work

jaunradīt *vt* create sth. new

jaunradītāj/s *nm*, ~a *nf* creative person

jaunreālisms *nm* neorealism

jaunromanticisms *nm* neo-romanticism

jaunromantisms *nm* neo-romanticism

jaunrudzu *indecl adj* (of bread) baked from newly threshed rye

jaun/s *adj* 1. young; 2. new; **no** ~a anew, again; **pa** ~**am** (col.) in a new way; **par** ~**u** again; 3. modern

jaunsaimniecība *nf* new farm (formed as a result of the agrarian reform of 1920 in Latvia), settler's homestead

jaunsaimnie/ks *nm*, ~ce *nf* new farmer, owner of a **jaunsaimniecība**

jauns[ch]olastika [h] *nf* neo-scholasticism

jaunsieva *nf* young bride

jaunskungs *nm* 1. young master; 2. (iron.) young man

jaunsniegs *nm* new snow

jaunstādīts *adj* recently planted

jaunstrāvniecisks *adj* characteristic of New Current or New Currentists (**jaunstrāvnieki**)

jaunstrāvnieks *nm* New Currentist (member of a Latvian socialist movement, 1890-1905)

jaunsudrabs *nm* German silver

jaunšķirne *nf* new variety (of a plant)

jauntēvs *nm* stepfather

jaunul/is *nm,* ~e *nf* beginner

jaunum/s *nm* 1. newness, freshness; 2. novelty; 3. usu. *pl* ~i news

jaunupe *nf* new river

jaunuve *nf* (obs.) daughter-in-law

jaunuzbūve *nf* new construction; reconstruction

jaunuzcelts *adj* newly constructed

jaunuzplēsts *adj* (of soil) newly broken

jaunuzsākts *adj* newly begun

jaunuzvedums *nm* (theat.) new production

jaunvārds *nm* neologism

jaunveidojums *nm* 1. new formation; 2. neologism; 3. neoplasm

jaunvīns *nm* fresh wine

jaunvīrs *nm* newlywed

Jaunzelandes lini *nm pl* New Zealand flax

jaunzelandiet/is *nm,* ~e *nf* New Zealander

jaunzelts *nm* tombac

jaunzemis *nm* settler

jaunzemnieks *nm* settler

jaunzirgs *nm* young horse; colt, filly

jausma *nf* presentiment; foreboding; hunch, no-tion, idea; **par to man nebija ne** ~s I had no idea

jausmīgi *adv* enthusiastically

jausmīgs *adj* (obs.) enthusiastic

jausmojums *nm* supposition

jaust *vt* sense; perceive

jausties *vr* be faintly perceptible

jaušami *adv* perceptibly

jaušam/s *adj, part* of **jaust** perceptible; **tikko j.** faint, barely perceptible

jaušana *nf* (in W. Wundt's psychology) perception

jaut *vt* make dough; add flour

jautājoši *adv* questioningly

jautājošs *adj* questioning

jautājuma teikums *nm* interrogative sentence

jautājuma zīme *nf* question mark

jautājums *nm* 1. question; **tas vēl ir j.** that remains to be seen; 2. issue; matter

jautājumu lapa *nf* questionnaire

jautājumu metode *nf* catechization

jautāt *vt* ask, inquire; question

jautātāj/s *nm,* ~a *nf* inquirer; questioner

jautin *adv, emph* of **jaut**; **j. jaut** prepare dough energetically

jautināt *vt* question

jautraliņa *nf* frolicsome girl

jautraviņa *nf* 1. frolicsome girl; 2. a Latvian folk dance

jautre *nf* joy

jautri *adv* gaily, merrily

jautrība *nf* 1. cheerfulness, gaiety; 2. mirth, hilarity; 3. wakefulness

jautrībnie/ks *nm,* ~ce *nf* merrymaker

jautrināt *vt* entertain

jautrinie/ks *nm,* ~ce *nf* jester

jautrīte *nf* frolicsome girl

jautrītis *nm* lighthearted person

jautrprāte *nf* romp

jautrprātīgi *adv* alertly

jautrprātīgs *adj* alert

jautrprātis *nm* giddy fellow

jautrs *adj* 1. cheerful, gay, merry; 2. funny; 3. (col., of sleep) restless, fretful

jautrul/is *nm,* ~e *nf* fun-loving person

jautrums *nm* 1. cheerfulness, gaiety; 2. mirth, hilarity

java *nf* mortar; plaster

jāvals *nm* slops

jāvārds *nm* consent; acceptance of a marriage proposal

javas apmetums *nm* stucco

javas bigulis *nm* mortar scoop

Javas degunradzis *nm* Javan rhinoceros

javas dēlis *nm* mortarboard

jāveklis *nm* a meal of yogurt and crumbled bread

javnīca *nf* plaster mixture box

javs or **jāvs** *nm* flour mixed in water (as feed)

javturis *nm* plasterer's hawk

jāvums *nm* batch (of dough, plaster, and the like)

jeb *conj* or

jebkad *adv* ever

jebkāds *pron* any; ~a *f*

jebkas *pron* anything

jebkur *adv* anywhere

jebkuŗ/š *pron* anyone; *adj* any; ~a *f*

jebšu *conj* 1. (obs.) although; 2. or else

jeda *nf* 1. a line of connected fishnets; 2. paternoster line

jēdzieniski *adv* conceptually

jēdzienisks *adj* conceptual

jēdziens *nm* concept

jēdzīgi *adv* reasonably, sensibly, logically

jēdzīgs *adj* (col.) reasonable, sensible, logical

jēdzīgums *nm* reasonableness, sensibleness

jefiņš *nm* (sl.) guy

jefreitor/s *nm*, ~e *nf* private first class

jēga *nf* 1. meaning, sense; **(runāt) bez ~s** (talk) nonsense; 2. understanding, idea, notion; **vai tu esi bez ~s?** are you out of your senses? **bez ~s** without measure, no end of, untold quantities; as if there was no tomorrow; (of falling in love) madly

jēgers *nm* (hist.) rifleman

jēgpilnība *nf* meaningfulness

jēgpilns *adj* meaningful

jēgt *vt* (col.) understand, have an idea

jēgties *vr* (col.) cope, struggle with

jēgums *nm* understanding, comprehension

jehovieši *nm pl* Jehovah's Witnesses

jel *partic* 1. (as emphasis of the verb in requests) **esi j. mierīgs!** do be quiet! **dod j. to man!** give it to me, will you? **j. lūdzu!** but please! 2. **kaut j.** (to emphasize a wish or hope) if only

jēlāda *nf* rawhide

jēlakmens *nm* crude matte

jēlaudums *nm* unfinished material

jēlbetons *nm* fresh concrete

jēlbluķis *nm* ingot

jēlcepa *nm* (col.) coward; (com.) galoot

jēlcukurs *nm* unrefined sugar

jēlčaulis *nm* sissy

jēldati *nm pl* raw data

jēldzelzs *nf* pig iron

jele *partic* = (obs.) **jel**

jēlgumija *nf* crude rubber

jēli *adv* obscenely, crudely

jēlība *nf* 1. obscenity; 2. rawness

jēlis *nm* (com.) scrag

jelkad *adv* ever

jelkād/s *pron* any; ~a *f*

jēlkokvilna *nf* lint (staple of cotton fiber)

jēlkula *nf* long straw; wind-dried crop

jēlķets *nm* (metall.) pig

jēlķieģelis *nm* raw brick; adobe

jēlmateriāls *nm* raw material

jēlmene *nf* rawhide

jēlmenis *nm* sissy

jēlmilti *nm pl* raw meal

jēlmina *nf* rawhide; rawhide peasant shoe

jēlmīts *adj* rough tanned

jēlmutis *nm* raunchy, smutty person

jēlnadzis *nm* butterfingers

jēlnafta *nf* crude oil

jēlons *nm* (reg.) heartburn

jēlpape *nf* pulp board

jēlplaknis *nm* slab

jēls *adj* 1. raw; uncooked, undercooked; 2. raw, chafed; 3. crude, obscene

jēlspirts *nm* crude alcohol

jēltauki *nm pl* unrendered fat

jēlums *nm* 1. raw spot; 2. ulcer; 3. rawness

jēlviela *nf* raw material

jēlzīds *nm* raw silk

jēmas *nf pl* liquid cattle feed (made of flour and chaff); revolting semiliquid mixture, gunk

jemeniet/is *nm*, **~e** *nf* Yemenite
jemt *vt* take; see **ņemt**
jena *nf* (monetary unit) yen
jenda *nf* (Scouts) national organization
jenkijs *nm* Yankee (American)
jenotāda *nf* coonskin
jenots *nm* raccoon
jenotsuns *nm* raccoon dog
jeņķis *nm* Yank
jērāda *nf* lambskin
jēradvēsele *nf* (col.) chicken, yellowbelly
jēradvēselība *nf* (col.) cowardice
jēre *nf* ewe
jeremiāde *nf* jeremiad
jērene I *nf* sheepskin cap
jērene II *nf* ewe
jērenīca *nf* sheepskin cap
jērēns *nm* lambkin
jērgaļa *nf* mutton, lamb
Jerikas roze *nf* rose of Jericho
jēriņmākoņi *nm pl* mackerel sky, fleece
    clouds
jēriņš *nm dim* of **jērs**, lambkin
jērkambaris *nm* vestry
jēr/s *nm* lamb ◊ **~a dūša** cowardice
jērulēns *nm* lambkin
jērulis *nm* lambkin
jesauls *nm* (hist.) esaul, Cossack captain
jestri *adv* briskly, friskily
jestrs *adj* **1.** brisk, frisky, lively; **2.** (of fibers)
    coarse; **3.** (of sleep) restless
jestrums *nm* **1.** briskiness, friskiness, liveliness;
    2. (of fibers) coarseness
jetijs *nm* yeti
jezga *nf* bustle, rumpus
juezuītiski *adv* Jesuitically
jezuītisks *adj* Jesuitic
jezuītiskums *nm* Jesuitry
jezuītisms *nm* Jesuitism
jezuīts *nm* Jesuit
jidišs *nm* Yiddish
jiti *nm pl* Jutes

jo *conj* **1.** because; **2. jo . . . jo** the . . . the; **jo**
    labāk so much the better
jo *partic* quite, very
jocīgi *adv* funnily; funny
jocīgs *adj* funny
jocīgums *nm* funniness
jocinieks *nm* wag, joker
jodains *adj* **1.** containing iodine; **2.** stained
    with iodine
joda ola *nf* stinkhorn
joda rociņa *nf* last year's tuber of the heath
    spotted orchid
joda rutks *nm* water hemlock
jodāts *nm* iodate
jodeler/s *nm*, **~e** *nf* yodeler
jodelēšana *nf* yodeling
jodelēt *vi* yodel
jodene *nf* henbane
jod|i|ds **[ī]** *nm* iodide
jodināt *vt* drive, urge
jodizēt *vt* iodize
jodlers *nm* yodel
jodoformisms *nm* poisoning with iodoform
jodoforms *nm* iodoform
jodometrija *nf* iodometry
jodonijs *nm* iodonium
jodpārskābe *nf* periodic acid
jods I (with **uo**) *nm* devil, demon; **pie ~a!**
    hell!
jods II *nm* **1.** iodine; **2.** tincture of iodine
jodskābe *nf* iodic acid
jodūdens *nm* water solution of iodine
jodūdeņradis *nm* hydrogen iodide
jodūdeņražskābe *nf* hydroiodic acid
joga *nf* yoga
jogisms *nm* yoga
jogs *nm* yogin
jogurts *nm* yogurt
johaidī *interj* (sl.) gee
johannieši *nm pl* Knights of St. John of
    Jerusalem (Knights of Malta)
johimbīns *nm* yohimbine

jokaini *adv* funnily

jokains *adj* (col.) funny

jokdaris *nm*, ~e *nf* wag, jester, joker

jokluga *nf* comedy

jokmīlis *nm* lover of jokes

jokot *vi* joke

jokotājs *nm*, ~a *nf* joker, jester, wag

jokoties *vr* joke; trifle with

jok/s *nm* joke; **lielisks j.** big joke; **sekls j.** flat joke; **vecs j.** stale joke; **ar to nav ~i** there is no trifling with it; **~us pie malas** joking apart; **pa ~am** in jest; **bez ~iem** no joking; **~a pēc** just for fun; **ne pa ~am** seriously; **nebūt uz ~iem** not to be in a laughing mood; **labs j. !** that's a good one! **tas jau ir tas j.** there is the rub

jokugailis *nm* joker, wag, buffoon

joku lapa *nf* comics

juku luga *nf* comedy;

jokupēter/is *nm*, ~e *nf* joker, wag, buffoon

jolla *nf* jolly boat

jom/a *nf* 1. haff, lagoon; 2. swale; swash; 3. (of knowledge, skill, expertise) area; **būt savā ~ā** be in one's element

jomains *adj* jagged; (of plants) lobate

jomenrija *nf* yeomanry

jomens *nm* yeoman

joms *nm* 1. (arch.) nave (**vidusjoms**); aisle (**sānu joms**); 2. gap; 3. river bend; 4. stretch, segment; 5. area

jonieši *nm pl* = **ionieši**

jo/nis *nm* 1. spell (time); ~ņiem intermittently; 2. speed; vigor; **ar ~ni** rapidly, suddenly; **pilnā ~nī** at full speed; 3. gust; swoop; **ar vienu ~ni** in one fell swoop; ~ņiem in gusts; **ar ~ni** precipitously; by storm; **uz ~ni** suddenly

jonisks *adj* = **ionisks**

jonīts *nm* = **ionīts**

jonizācija *nf* = **ionizācija**

jonizators *nm* = **ionizātors**

jonizēt *vt* = **ionizēt**

jonosfaira *nf* = **ionosfaira**

jons *nm* = **ions**

jontoforēze *nf* = **iontoforēze**

joņaini *adv* 1. in gusts; laboriously; intermittently; 2. rapidly; explosively

joņains *adj* 1. gusty; labored, intermittent; 2. rapid; explosive

joņiem *adv* intermittently

joņot *vi* (of horses) gallop, (of animals) dash; (of people, vehicles) rush, speed

joņotājs *nm*, ~a *nf* dasher

joprojām *adv* 1. still; 2. **un tā j.** and so on

joprojumis *adv* (reg.) still

jordāniet/s *nm*, ~e *nf* Jordanian

jorģīne *nf* dahlia

josla *nf* 1. zone; 2. belt, strip; lane; **atsavināta j.** right of way; 3. streak; (el.) band; 4. (arch.) frieze; (of a truss) chord

joslains *adj* banded; streaky; divided into zones

joslas filtrs *nm* band-pass filter

joslas platums *nm* band width

josliņa *nf dim* of **josla**, zone; lane

joslu pelargonija *nf* zonal pelargonium

josmenis *nm* = **jozmenis**

josta *nf* belt; sash; **piesprādzējamā j.** safety belt; *gen* ~s (anat.) lumbar; ~s **roze** shingles

jostains *adj* belted

jostas dzīvnieks *nm* armadillo

jostasvieta *nf* waist, waistline

jostene *nf* bracelet Cortinarius

jostiņa *nf* 1. *dim* of **josta**, belt, sash; 2. swaddling band

jostīt *vt* swaddle

jota *nf* iota

jotācija *nf* iotacism

jotēt *vt* (ling.) palatalize with a j

joviāli *adv* jovially

jovi[a]litāte [ā] *nf* joviality

joviāls *adj* jovial

joziens *nm* dash

jozmenis *nm* waist

jozt I *vt* (of a belt) put on; **j. nost** (of a belt) take off; **j. zobenu** don a sword

jozt II *vi* dash

jozties *vr* put on a belt; gird oneself; fasten one's belt

jožus *adv* running, dashing; in a hurry

juaņa *nf* yuan

jubejas *nf pl* Jubaea

jubilācija *nf* (rel. mus.) jubilus

jubilārs *nm*, **~e** *nf* honoree (at an anniversary celebration)

jubileja *nf* anniversary; **četrgadu j.** quadrennial; **desmitgadu j.** decennial; **simtsgadu j.** centennial

juceklība *nf* confusion

juceklīgi *adv* confusedly; chaotically

juceklīgs *adj* confused; chaotic

juceklīgums *nm* confusedness

juceklis *nm* confusion; chaos; jumble

jucekņi *nm pl* stalks of grain left after harvest; grain mixed with chaff (after threshing)

jucenis *nm* confusion; chaos; jumble

juceniski *adv* indiscriminately, in a mixed-up fashion

ju|ch|tāda [h] *nf* Russian leather

juciņi *nm pl* mixed-up straw, straw as found after threshing

jucis *adj* (col.) crazy

jūdaisms *nm* Judaism

Jūdasa graši *nm pl* thirty pieces of silver

Jūdasa koks *nm* Judas tree

Jūdass *nm* Judas, traitor

judra *nf* mark on a horse's incisor

judras *nf pl* (bot.) gold of pleasure

jūds *nm*, **~iete** *nf* Hebrew

jūdze *nf* mile

jūdzēj/s *nm*, **~a** *nf* harnesser

jūdziens *nm* a harnessing job

jūdzin *adv emph* of **jūgt**; **j. jūdza** was busy harnessing

jūga lopi *nm pl* draft animals

jūga vēna *nf* jugular vein

jūgendstils *nm* Jugendstil, art nouveau

jūgēvele *nf* two-person plane

jugliņš *nm* (zool.) bleak

jugosl[a]v/s [ā] *nm*, **~iete** *nf* Yugoslav

jūgrāmis *nm* mountable frame

jūgs *nm* (wooden frame for animals; team of oxen; oppressive agency; hist., cadastral unit) yoke

jūgt *vt* harness

jūgties *vr* put oneself in harness

jūgtuve *nf* tug (part of a horse's harness)

jūgums *nm* a harnessing job

jujuba *nf* jujube

juka I *nf* confusion; chaos; jumble; **~u ~ām** at sixes and sevens, in a jumble; *pl* **~as** (social) disorder

juka II *nf* yucca

jukjukumis *adv* helter-skelter

jūkle *nf* throng, crush

jukli *adv* confusedly, chaotically

jūklis *nm* **1.** throng; **2.** confusion; chaos; jumble

jukls *adj* confused; chaotic

jūkļaini *adv* confusedly, chaotically

jūkļains *adj* confused, chaotic

jūkste *nf* or **jūksts** *nm* (reg.) hubub

jukt *vi* **1.** get mixed up; **viņam jūk solis** he can't keep in step; **2.** mingle; **3.** be jumbled, be confused; **4.** confuse; **man jūk** I am getting it all mixed up; **5. j. ārā** (or **laukā**) fall to pieces; **6.** (of mud, slush) fly; (of people) scatter; **7.** (col.) lose one's mind; **j. prātā** go crazy

jūkt *vi* get accustomed to

juku jukām *adv* helter-skelter

juku laiki *nm pl* turbulent times

jukum/s *nm* confusion; chaos; **~i** mixture of hay and straw (as cattle feed)

jukuris *nm* **1.** dance line (of alternating sexes); **2.** a Latvian folk dance

julga *nf* large numbers, crowd

Jūlijas primula *nf* a primula, Primula juliae

jūlijs *nm* July

juma *nf* frazil ice

jumala *nf* twin fruit

jumaliņa *nf* (folk.) wife of jumis (**jumis 2**)

jumdīt *vt* incite, set on

jumējs *nm* roofer

jumiķis *nm* **1.** roofer; **2.** twin ear of grain

jumis *nm* **1.** twin ear of grain, twin fruit; **2.** (folk.)a deity of the fields

jumols *nm* dome; cupola

jumprava *nf* (obs.) maiden, virgin

jumpravisks *adj* (obs.) maidenly, virginal

jums *nm* (poet.) vault; (poet.) shelter

jums *pron, dat* of **jūs** to you; **ar j.** with you

jumstiņš *nm* roof shingle

jumstiņu gladiola *nf* a gladiolus, Gladiolus imbricatus

jumstiņu ozols *nm* shingle oak

jumt *vt* roof; thatch

jumta acs *nf* circular gable window

jumta antena *nf* overhouse aerial

jumta āzis *nm* ridge cross

jumta čukurs *nm* roof ridge

jumtains *adj* roofed

jumta kore *nf* roof ridge

jumta krēsls *nm* roof framing

jumta noteka *nf* eaves

jumta ornaments *nm* cresting

jumta pape *nf* roofing felt

jumta pienene *nf* hawk's beard

jumta satekne *nf* roof valley

jumta saulrieteņi *nm pl* houseleek

jumta skārds *nm* metal roofing

jumta stāvs *nm* top floor

jumtgale *nf* gable

jumtgals *nm* roof ridge

jumties *vr* (of the sky, clouds, tree branches) spread above

jumtiņš *nm* **1.** *dim* of **jumts**; **2.** haček, wedge; circumflex; **3.** zig, zag

jumtistaba *nf* garret, attic room

jumtlāses *nf pl* **1.** water drips from the roof; **2.** icicles

jumtnieks *nm* roofer

jumts *nm* roof; **četrslīpju j.** hip roof; **divslīpju j.** gable roof; **līmenisks j.** platform roof; **vienslīpes j.** pent roof

jumtu lāčauzas *nf pl* downy chess

jumtveida *indecl adj* roof-shaped

jumtveidīgi *adv* like a roof

jumtveidīgs *adj* roof-shaped

jumtveidā *adv* in the shape of a roof; two-pitched

jumums *nm* roofing

junda *nf* roll call

jundīt *vt* **1.** (poet.) announce; **2.** (rare.) prod, urge

junga *nm* cabin boy, ship boy

jūnija vabole *nf* summer chafer

jūnijs *nm* June

juniors *nm*, **~e** *nf* junior

junkurs *nm* **1.** Junker; **2.** squire; lordling; **3.** (hist.) cadet

jupers *nm* (naut.) deadeye

jupis *nm* devil, evil spirit; **j. parāvis!** (or **j. ar ārā! kad tevi j.!**) oh, hell! **j. viņu sazina!** who the hell knows!

jupiters *nm* floodlight; **J.** Jupiter

jura *nf* Jurassic period

jūra *nf* sea; **~s a.** maritime; marine; sea; nautical; b. naval

jūras adata *nf* pipefish

jūras ainava *nf* seascape

jūras aizsargsiena *nf* seawall

jūras akadēmija nf naval academy

jūras arājs *nm* (poet.) fisherman;

jūras asars *nm* redfish

jūrasbraucējs *nm* mariner, sefarer

jūras brauciens *nm* sea voyage; **pirmais j. b.** maiden voyage

jūras bruņrupucis *nm* tortoise; see also **knābjainais j. b.**

jūrasbu/llis *nm* (zool.) father-lasher; ~**ļļi** sculpins

jūras bungotājs *nm* miller's-thumb

jūras ceļojums *nm* sea voyage

jūrasceļš *nm* sea-lane

jūrascūciņa *nf* guinea pig

jūrascūka *nf* common porpoise

jūras čūska *nf* sea snake

jūras dedestiņas *nf pl* beach pea

jūras ērglis *nm* white-tailed sea eagle

jūras ezis *nm* sea urchin

jūras forele *nf* sea trout

jūras garlaka *nf* black-throated diver

jūras gaŗgāle *nf* black-throated diver

jūrasgrundulis *nm* goby

jūras inženieris *nm* marine engineer

jūrass jūdze *nf* nautical mile

jūras kalns *nm* seamount

jūras kāposti *nm pl* sea kale

jūras karte *nf* chart

jūras kauja *nf* naval engagement;

jūraskrauklis *nm* great cormorant

jūras kuģis *nm* seagoing ship

jūras ķīvīte *nf* grey plover

jūras laupītājs *nm* pirate

jūras lauva *nm* sea lion

jūraslīcis *nm* bay, gulf

jūras līdaka *nf* barracuda

jūras lilija *nf* crinoid

jūras meita *nf* mermaid

jūras mēsli *nm pl* seaware

jūras nēģis *nm* sea lamprey

jūras osta *nf* seaport

jūras parāde *nf* naval review

jūras pīle *nf* sheldrake

jūras plaudis *nm* porgy

jūras putas *nf pl* 1. sea-foam; 2. meerschaum

jūras risks *nm* sea risk

jūras sīpols *nm* squill

jūras skats *nm* seascape

jūrasslimība *nf* seasickness

jūras spēki *nm pl* navy

jūras stagars *nm* sea stickleback

jūras šalkas *nf pl* sound of the surf

jūrasšaurums *nm* straits

jūras šņibītis *nm* purple sandpiper

jūras tārtiņš *nm* Kentish plover

jūras teteris *nm* velvet scoter

jūras tiesības *nf pl* maritime law

jūrastrīce *nf* seaquake

jūras ūdrs *nm* sea otter

jūras vārti *nm pl* sea gate

jūras vējš *nm* sea breeze

jūras velns *nm* frog fish

jūras vērsis *nm* four-horned cottus

jūras vēzis *nm* lobster

jūras vēzītis *nm* shrimp

jūras vilks *nm* old salt

jūrasvīrs *nm* fisherman

jūras zaķis *nm* lump fish

jūraszāle *nf* 1. seaweed; 2. eelgrass

jūras zvaigzne *nf* starfish

jūraszaļš *adj* sea green

jūras zīriņš *nm* arctic tern

jūras zivs *nf* saltwater fish

jūrasžagata *nf* palaearctic oystercatcher

jūrenis *nm* (reg.) westerly

jūrgals *nm* mouth of a river

Jurģi *nm pl* 1. St. George's Day (traditional day for the yearly move of farmhands to another farm); 2. **j.** moving, moving day

jurģinieks *nm* (hist.) a farmhand moving to another farm on St. George's Day

jurģot *vi* (hist., of farmhands) move

juridiskā fakultāte *nf* law school

juridiski *adv* juridically; juristically

juridisks *adj* juridical; juristic; law

jurinejas *nf pl* Jurinea

jūrinis *nm* (reg.) westerly

jūriņa *nf dim* of **jūra**, sea

jurisdikcija *nf* jurisdiction

juriskonsult/s *nm*, ~**e** *nf* legal counselor

jurisprudence *nf* jurisprudence
juristiski *adv* juristically
juristisks *adj* juristic
jurist/s *nm,* **~e** *nf* jurist
jūrlietas *nf pl* naval affairs
jūrmala *nf* **1.** beach, seashore; coast; **2.** seaside
jūrmalas alises *nf pl* sweet alyssum
jūrmalas armērija *nf* thrift
jūrmalas asteres *nf pl* sea starwort
jūrmalas augstiņš *nm* a centaury, Centaurium vulgare
jūrmalas āžloki *nm pl* arrow grass
jūrmalas balodenes *nf pl* halberd-leaved orache
jūrmalas ceļmallapa *nf* sea plantain
jūrmalas dadzis *nm* sea holly
jūrmalas dedestiņas *nf pl* beach pea
jūrmalas grīšļi *nm pl* sedge
jūrmalas kvieši (or **mieži**) *nm pl* wild rye, lyme grass
jūrmalas meldri *nm pl* Canby's bulrush
jūrmalas mirtes *nf pl* sweet gale
jūrmalas pagauri *nm pl* salt-marsh sand spurry
jūrmalas pienzāle *nf* sea milkwort
jūrmalas skābenes *nf pl* golden dock
jūrmalas sūrene *nf* seaside knotweed
jūrmalas vārpata *nf* wheatgrass
jūrmalas vībotne *nf* sea wormwood
jūrmalas zilgalvīši *nm pl* sea holly
jūrmaliet/is *nm,* **~e** *nf* coaster, seacoast dweller
jūrmalnie/ks *nm* **1.** summer resident (on the coast); visitor (at a beach); **2.** coaster, seacoast dweller; **~ce** *nf;* **3.** a Latvian folk dance
jūrniecība *nf* navigation; **~s prasme** seamanship
jūrnieks *nm* sailor
jūrnis *nm* (reg.) westerly
jūrskola *nf* naval academy; nautical school

jūrskolnieks *nm* naval cadet; student at a nautical school
jurta *nf* yurt
jūs *pron, nomin & acc pl* you; **Jūs** polite form of address to one person
jūsēj/ais *nom adj* yours; **esmu j.** I am with you, I am on your side; **~ie** or **J~ie** (when adressing one person) your family (members), yours
jūsējs *pron* yours, your; **Jūsējs** polite form of address to one person
jūsēt *vt* use the polite form of address
jūsināt *vt* use the polite form of address
jusma *nf* presentiment; foreboding; hunch, no-tion, idea
jūsma *nf* enthusiasm
jūsmājas *nf pl* your house
jūsmība *nf* enthusiasm
jūsmīgi *adv* enthusiastically
jūsmīgs *adj* **1.** enthusiastic; **slimīgi j.** exalted; **2.** easily delighted
jūsmīgums *nm* enthusiasm
jūsmināt *vt* delight
jūsmināties *vr* enthuse
jūsmot *vi* enthuse, be enthusiastic about
jūsmotājs *nm* enthusiast; admirer
jūsos *pron, loc pl* of **jūs** in you; **Jūsos** (polite form of reference when addressing one person) in you
jūsot *vt* use the polite form of address
jūsoties *vr* use the polite form of address in ad-dressing each other
jūsprāt *adv* in your opinion
just *vt* feel; sense, have a sensation; **j. līdzi** emphatize, feel for
justēt *vt* check and correct
just[i]cija [ī] *nf* **1.** justice; **2.** (bot.) water willow
justificēt *vt* justify
justifikācija *nf* justification
justies *vr* feel; **j. (kāda) ādā** be in s.o. else's shoes; **j. slikti** not feel good; **j. kā mājās** feel at home; **jūtieties kā mājās!** make

yourself at home! **nejusties formā** be out of form; **j. atkal pēc cilvēka** feel human again; **nejusties savā vietā** feel out of place

jūsu *pron, gen* of **jūs** your, yours

jūsuprāt *adv* in your opinion

jušana *nf* mood, feeling

jūtami *adv* noticeably; perceptibly

jūtams *adj* tangible; noticeable; perceptible

jūtas *nf pl* **1.** feelings; emotions; **2.** haptic sensations

juteklība *nf* sensuality, sensuousness

juteklīgi *adv* sensually, sensuously

juteklīgs *adj* sensual, sensuous

juteklīgums *nm* sensuality, sensuousness

juteklis *nm* sense organ

jutekliski *adv* sensorily; sensually, sensuously

juteklisks *adj* **1.** sensory; **2.** sensual, sensuous

jutekliskums *nm* sensuality, sensuousness

jutelība *nf* oversensitiveness

jūtelība *nf* **1.** sentimentality; **2.** touchiness, irritability

jutelīgi *adv* in an oversensitive way

jūtelīgi *adv* **1.** sentimentally; **2.** touchily, irritably

jutelīgs *adj* oversensitive

jūtelīgs *adj* **1.** sentimental; **2.** touchy, irritable

jūtelīgums *nm* **1.** sentimentality; **2.** touchiness, irritability

jutība *nf* **1.** irritability; delicatness; **2.** sensitivity

jūtība *nf* sensitiveness

jutīgi *adv* sensitively

jūtīgi *adv* sensitively

jutīgs *adj* **1.** irritable; delicate; **2.** sensitiv

jūtīgs *adj* sensitive

jutīgums *nm* sensitiveness

jūtīgums *nm* sensitivity; **pārmērīgs j.** hypersensitivity

jūtin *adv emph* of **just; j.** just feel acutely

jūtis *nf pl* (obs.) crossroads; See **ceļa jūtīs**

jutoņa *nf* mood

jutra *nf* (reg.) whip

jutrenīca *nf* (reg.) whip

juvelie[r]darbs [ŗ] *nm* jewelry

juvelier/is *nm,* ~**e** *nf* jeweler

juvelierisks *adj* jeweler's, of a jeweler

juvelie[r]izstrādājums [ŗ] *nm* piece of jewelry

juvelie[r]māksla [ŗ] *nf* jeweler's art

juvelis *nm* piece of jewelry

juvenālisks *adj* Juvenalian

juvenāls *adj* juvenile

juvenils *nm* juvenile

K

ka *conj* that; **ka vai** (used adverbially, col.) galore; **ka vai nu** (used adverbially, col.) very; a lot

ka *partic* **1.** (at the beginning of optative clauses) here is hoping that (**ka nu vien labi iznāktu!** here is hoping that everything will turn out well!); **2.** (as an expression of allowance or doubt) in case (**ka neuznāk lietus** in case it rains)

kā *adv* **1.** how; **kā tā?** how is that? **un kā vēl!** and how! do I ever! **kā nebūt** somehow; **2.** (in questions) what; **kā, lūdzu?** I beg your pardon? **3.** (in comparisons) as, as if, like; (with verb forms, to express allowance) no matter what (how, who, where), however, whatever, whoever, wherever; **4.** (used as a particle, to emphasize the idea of a temporal adverb) just (**nupat kā** just now); **5.** (used as a particle to express surprise) oh, why; **kā nekā** one way or another, somehow; **lai tur vai kā** no matter what; **kā kuŗu reizi** it depends; **kā un kad** it varies; **kā pagadās** any old way

kā *conj* **1. kā arī** as well as; **2. kā, tā (arī)** both . . . and; **3. kā . . . , tā . . .** (to emphasize the word repeated after both **kā** and **tā**) it just won't . . .; (**kā neiet, tā neiet** it just won't work; **kā sarkans, tā sarkans** it just won't change color)

kā *partic* as, like; **kā kad** as if; **kā tad!** of course! **kā nu ne** of course; **tik labi kā nekad** never better; **kā tik** as soon as

kā *pron, gen* of **kas** whose

kaba *nf* 1. hook-shaped tree root (used in house construction); 2. clothes peg; 3. hook and eye

kabacis *nm* summer squash

kabaks *nm* (barb.) tavern

kabala *nf* cabala

kabalistika *nf* cabalism

kabalistiski *adv* cabalistically

kabalistisks *adj* cabalistic

kabalists *nm* cabalist

kabardiet/is *nm*, **~e** *nf* Kabardin

kabarē *indecl nm* cabaret

kabareja *nf* or **kabarejs** *nm* cabaret

kabata *nf* pocket; **pilna k.** pocketful; **no ~s ārā** out of pocket (expenses) ◊ **būt pa ~i** fit one's budget; **nav pa ~i** too expensive, beyond one's means

kabatas baterija *nf* flashlight

kabatas grāmatiņa *nf* notebook

kabatas lampiņa *nf* flashlight

kabatas nauda *nf* pocket money; allowance

kabatdators *nm* pocket computer

kabatdrāna *nf* handkerchief

kabatēvele *nf* pocket plane

kabatformāts *nm* pocket size

kabatgrāmata *nf* pocket book

kabatiņa *nf dim* of **kabata**, little pocket

kabatlakatiņš *nm* handkerchief

kabatlakats *nm* handkerchief

kabatnazis *nm* pocketknife

kabatportfelis *nm* billfold

kabatzādzība *nf* picking of pockets

kabatzagl/is *nm*, **~e** *nf* pickpocket

kabe *nf* 1. clothes peg; 2. (RR) spike; 3. hook-shaped tree root (used in house construction)

kabelis I *nm* gate hook

k[a]belis [ā] II *nm* cable; **savīts k.** stranded cable

kabeļaka *nf* cable pit

kabeļkurpe *nf* cable lug

kabeļskapis *nm* cable turning section

kabeļskreja *nf* cable run

kabeļtauva *nf* cable's length; hawser

kabeļtelevīzija *nf* cable television

kabenis *nm* a type of dragnet

kabestans *nm* capstan

kabēt *vt* (RR) drive spikes, fasten with spikes

kabīli *nm pl* Kabyles

kabināt *vt* 1. **k. ciet** (also **kopā, klāt**) hook up, hook together, fasten together; 2. **k. vaļā** (or **nost**) unhook, unfasten; 3. hang (on a hook or peg)

kabīne *nf* booth; (ship's) cabin; (of a truck) cab; (of an elevator) car, cage; (of an airplane) cockpit; bathing hut

kabinetklase *nf* dedicated classroom

kabinet/s *nm* 1. study; office; (in medicine) consulting room; (educ.) physics lab (room), chemistry lab; **~a** (of scientists, strategists) armchair; 2. (pol.) cabinet

kabju āmurs *nm* spike maul

kablīgs *adj* (of feet) prehensile

kablis *nm* hook

kablogr[a]fiski [ā] *adv* by cable

kablogr[a]fisks [ā] *adj* cable (*adj*)

kablogramma *nf* cablegram

kabombas *nf pl* Cabomba

kabotāža *nf* coasting trade; **~s kuģis** coaster

kabotēt *vi* engage in coasting trade

kabriolets *nm* cabriolet; convertible

kabstans *nm* capstan

kabuki *indecl nf* kabuki

kabūzis *nm* (col.) 1. closet; cell; 2. dilapidated shack

kabzeķe *nf* sock

kaceniņš *nm dim* of **kacens**, cabbage stump

kacenkāposti *nm pl* fodder cabbage

kacens *nm* cabbage stump

kacēt *vt* (reg.) reach

kacēties *vr* (col.) try to reach

ka[ch]eksija [h] *nf* cachexia

ka[ch]ektisks [h] *adj* cachectic

kacības *nf pl* (reg.) first visit to a woman to see her newborn baby

kacināt *vt* **1.** tease; **2.** question, pepper with questions

kacināties *vr* tease

kačk/s *nm* stick (a short stick used in a Latvian sports game); **~us sist** a Latvian sports game

kačuča *nf* cachucha

kad *adv, conj* **1.** when; (in exclamations or rhetorical questions) when doesn't (hasn't, did he not, etc.); **k. nebūt** whenever; **k. nekad** any time; **kaut k.** some time; **k. vien** whenever; **2.** (col.) ever; **3.** (wth a conjugated verb, participle in **-dams** and **lai**, or just the participle) whenever; **4.** if; **k. tikai** othe condition that; just so that; **k. jau, tad jau** in for a penny, in for a pound; **kā k.** as if; (for emphasis, as first word in a sentence) **k. es jums saku!** I tell you! **5.** *partic.* (with verb in optative mood) if only; I wish; even if; because; so that

kadastrāls *nm* land register

kadastrāls *adj* cadastral

kadastrēt *vt* enter in a cadastre

kadastrs *nm* cadastre

kādējādi *adv* how

kādēļ *adv* why; **k., tādēļ!** just because!

kadence *nf* cadence; cadenza

kādenis *nm* adjective

kadets I *nm* cadet

kadets II *nm* (hist.) Constitutional Democrat

kadetu korpuss *nm* (hist.) military school

kādi *adv* (obs.) how; **kaut k.** somehow

kādība *nf* quality; quale

kādības apstākļa vārds *nm* qualitative adverb

kadijs I *nm* caddy

kadijs II *nm* qadi

kadiķājs *nm* growth of junipers

kadiķa šņabis *nm* gin

kadiķiens *nm* growth of junipers

kadiķis *nm* juniper

kadiķoga *nf* juniper berry

kadiķu irbīte *nf* waxwing

kadiķzars *nm* juniper branch

kadmijēšana *nf* cadmium electroplating

kadmijs *nm* cadmium

kādreiz *adv* **1.** once; (in fairy tales) once upon a time; one day (in the past, future); **2.** some time; **3.** sometimes

kādreizējs *adj, usu. defin* **kādreizējais** former

kadrējums *nm* (film, TV) **1.** shot; **2.** shooting

kadrēt *vt* (film, TV) **1.** frame; **2.** shoot a scene

kadr/i *nm pl* personnel; cadres; **~u sagatavošana** training of specialists

kadriļa *nf* quadrille

kadrinie/ks *nm*, **~ce** *nf* personnel department employee

kadrs *nm* (film, TV) **1.** frame; still; **2.** scene

kadru daļa *nf* personnel department

kāds *pron* **1.** (in questions, exclamations) what; **2.** (in nominal sense) somebody, (in questions) anybody; **3.** (as an attribute) a some, (in questions) any; **k. . . . tāds** like . . . like, as . . . so, such . . . such; **vienalga k.** any; **lai k.** whatever; **k. (nu) kurš** each different

kādubrīd *adv* sometimes

kaducejs *nm* caduceus

kādudien *adv* some day

kādureiz *adv* = **kādreiz**

kādurīt *adv* one morning

kafē *indecl nm* (rare.) cafe

kafeīns *nm* = **kofeīns**

kafejnīca *nf* coffee shop; cafe;

kafers *nm* Kaffir

kafetērija *nf* cafeteria

kafija *nf* coffee; **baltā k.** coffee with cream; **šķīstošā k.** instant coffee

kafijas biezumi *nm pl* coffee grounds

kafijas dzirnaviņas *nf pl* coffee grinder

kafijbrūns *adj* coffee (color)

kafijkanna *nf* coffee pot

kafijkoks *nm* coffee tree

kaft[a]ns [ā] *nm* caftan

kagors *nm* Cahors wine

kahetiet/is *nm*, ~e *nf* Kakhetian

kahetīnietis *nm* Kakhetian wine

kaifa *nf* (col.) (narcotic) high

kaifīgs *adj* (col.) groovy

kaifot *vi* (col.) groove

kaifs *nm* (col.) (narcotic) high

kaija *nf* gull; skua

kaijiņa *nf dim* of **kaija**, little gull

kaijveidīgie *nom adj pl* Laridae

kaika *nf, nm* **1.** lean cow; **2.** tall, long-necked man; **3.** flighty woman

kaikalis *nm* indigent, beggar

kaikaris *nm* ragamuffin

kaikāt *vi* nod (while driving a wagon)

kailā ciprese *nf* bald cypress

kailais kailgliemezis *nm* a field slug

kailatne *nf* bare spot

kailā trūkumzāle *nf* burstwort

kailcirsma *nf* clear-cutting area

kailcirte *nf* clear-cutting (the practice)

kaile I *nf* bare spot

kaile II *nf* (fishnet) dragrope

kailenis *nm* sheepskin coat (with fur on the in-side)

kailēt *vt* **1.** extend a rope in front of a raft; **2.** (of a dragrope) fold

kailfigūra *nf* nude

kailgliemezis *nm* slug

kailība *nf* nakedness, nudity; bareness

kailināt *vt* (typ.) fill with furniture

kailis *nm* sheepskin (to be made into a coat); worn coat

kailķermenis *nm* nude

kailmateriāls *nm* (typ.) furniture

kailot *vi* (of trees, shrubs) lose leaves

kails *adj* naked, bare, nude, (of birds) unfledged, (of mountains) bald; **pilnīgi k.** stark naked

kailsals *nm* dry freeze

kailsēkļi *nm pl* Gymnospermae

kailstumbru magone *nf* Arctic poppy

kailums *nm* nakedness, nudity; bareness

kailvads *nm* (el.) bare conductor

kailvēderis *nm* (col.) indigent

kaimas krūms *nm* (bot.) jethead

kaimans *nm* cayman

kaimene *nf* neighbor

kaimiņattiecības *nf pl* relations between neighbors

kaimiņiene *nf* neighbor

kaimiņmāja *nf* neighbor's house

kaimiņos *adv* next door; (of a farmhouse) in the neighboring farm

kaimiņ/š *nm* neighbor; **k. ~am** neighbor to neigh-bor

kaimiņtauta *nf* neighboring nation

kaimiņvalsts *nf* neighboring country

kaimiņzeme *nf* neighboring state

kaimīte *nf* neighbor

kainīts *nm* kainite

kainozoisks *adj* Cainozoic

kainozojs *nm* Cainozoic era

kaira *nf* guillemot

kaire *nf* **1.** stimulation; **2.** *pl* ~s discord

kaireklis *nm* **1.** stimulus; **2.** irritant

kairestība *nf* stimulability

kairēties *vr* tease

kairi *adv* **1.** temptingly, alluringly; **2.** sensuously

kairīgi *adv* temptingly, alluringly

kairīgs *adj* tempting, alluring

kairinājums *nm* **1.** stimulation; **2.** irritation

kairināmība *nf* stimulability

kairināt *vt* **1.** stimulate; **2.** irritate; **3.** tempt; allure, entice

kairinātāja *nf* temptress

kairinātāj/s *nm* **1.** stimulus; **2.** irritant; **3.** tempter

kairinoši *adv* temptingly

kairinošs *adj, part* of **kairināt** tempting

kairs I *adj* **1.** tempting, enticing, alluring; **2.** passionate; sensuous

kairs II *adj* (dial.) left

kairums *nm* allure

kaisa *nf* (poet.) ardor

kaisi *adv* ardently

kaisīt *vt* scatter, strew; cover (by scattering, strewing); **k. vējā** squander; **k. vārdus vējā** throw one's words to the wind; **k. smiltis acīs** mislead

kaisīties *vr* be scattered, be strewn

kaislā zāle *nf* comfrey

kaisle *nf* (poet.) passion

kaisli *adv* passionately

kaislība *nf* passion

kaislīgi *adv* passionately

kaislīgs *adj* passionate

kaislīgums *nm* passionateness

kaisls *adj* passionate

kaislums *nm* passionateness

kaisme *nf* (poet.) **1.** ardor; **2.** heat

kaismi *adv* ardently

kaismīgi *adv* ardently

kaismīgs *adj* ardent

kaismīgums *nm* ardor

kaisms *adj* ardent

kaiss *adj* ardent

kaist *vi* heat, get hot; begin to glow; (of body heat, passions) burn

kaistin *adv, emph* of **kaist**; **k. kaisa** it got red hot

kaisums *nm* heat, ardor

kaiši *nm pl* litter (for barnyard animals)

kaišļu zāles *nf pl* curled dock

kaitavāt *vi* act capriciously

kaitavāties *vr* (obs.) tease

kaitavīgi *adv* capriciously; cantakerously

kaitavīgs *adj* capricious; cantakerous

kaite *nf* **1.** ailment; **2.** harm, bad thing

kaitējums *nm* harm, injury; detriment, prejudice

kaitēklis I *nm* (insect) pest

kaitēklis II *nm* plaything, toy

kaitēt I *vt* (of metal) heat

kaitēt II *vi* harm, hurt; **k. veselībai** be bad for one's health

kaitēt III *vi* (*3rd pers*) ail; be wrong with; **kas tev kait?** what is the matter with you? **kas kait...** there is nothing wrong with...; **kas nekait...** it is easy for (you) to...; why shouldn't...

kaitētāj/s *nm*, **~a** *nf* harmer

kaitēties *vr* dally

kaitīgi *adv* harmfully

kaitīgs *adj* harmful, injurious; noxious; unhealthy

kaitīgums *nm* harmfulness, injuriousness, noxiousness

kaitin *adv emph* of **kaist**; **k. kaisa** it got red hot

kaitināt *vt* **1.** tease; **2.** irritate, annoy

kaitināties *vr* tease each other

kaitīte *nf dim* of **kaite**, ailment

kaitniecība *nf* sabotage

kaitniecisks *adj* sabotage

kaitnie/ks *nm*, **~ce** *nf* saboteur

kaitulis *nm*, **~e** *nf* a touchy person

kaiva *nf* (reg.) gull

kāj/a *nf* **1.** leg ◊ **plikām ~ām** with bare legs; **uz brīvām ~ām** (col.) free, undetained; **vieglām ~ām** light-footed; **atkal uz ~ām** up and about; **ar izplestām ~ām** with legs apart, straddling; **cik ~s nes** (col.) as fast as one's legs would carry; **ar vienu ~u kapā** half-dead; **ar kreiso ~u no gultas izkāpis** got up on the wrong side of the bed; **2.** foot ◊ *instr* **~ām** on foot; **~ās** up, standing, on

one's feet; **pa ~ām** underfoot; **pa ~u apakšu**
underfoot; **basām ~ām** barefoot; **uz grūtām**
~ām (obs.) in the family way

kājains *adj* legged

kajaks I *nm* common gull, mew

kajaks II *nm* kayak

kājām *adv* on foot

kājāmgājēj/s *nm*, **~a** *nf* pedestrian; walker

kājāmstaigātāj/s *nm*, **~s** *nf* walker

kājapakš/a *nf* **1.** instep; **2. no ~as** from
underfoot; **pa ~u** underfoot

kājas īkšķis *nm* big toe

kājas pirksts *nm* toe

kājas plaukts *nm* instep

kājas starteris *nm* kick starter

kājauts *nm* foot wrapping cloth

kājavi *nm pl* footwear

kājbumba *nf* soccer ball

kājceliņš *nm* **1.** footpath; **2.** runner (carpet)

kājene *nf* (typ.) base, mount

Kajennas pipari *nm pl* Cayenne pepper

kājens *adj* current, customary

kājgalis *nm* foot of the bed

kājīgs *adj* light-footed

kājiņa *nf* **1.** *dim* of **kāja**, leg; foot; **2.** (tech.,
bot.) foot, stalk

kājinie/ks *nm*, **~ce** *nf* (hist.) corvée laborer on
foot (without a horse)

kajīte *nf* cabin, stateroom

kājlaiža *nm, nf* toady

kājmina *nf* **1.** doormat; **2.** (fig., cont.) dirt under
one's feet; *pl* **~s** tracked-in dirt

kājminams *adj* foot-operated, treadle-operated;
(wheel, starter) kick

kājniekot *vi* (col.) walk

kājnie/ks *nm*, **~ce** *nf* **1.** pedestrian; **2.** infantryman; **~i** infantry; **~u kaujasmašīna** armored
personnel carrier; **3.** = **kājinieks**

kājnieku pāreja *nf* crosswalk

kājnieku tilts *nm* footbridge

kājot *vi* foot it, traipse

kajots *nm* cayote

kājpamesl/s *nm* (fig.) dirt; **būt par ~u** (fig.) be
trampled on

kājsargs *nm* shin guard

kājslauka *nf* = **kājslauķis**

kājslauķis *nm* doormat

kājsoliņš *nm* footstool

kājstarp/a *nf* crotch; **pa ~u** (of crawling)
between the legs; **~ā** (putting one's tail)
between the legs

kājstarpe *nf* = **kājstarpa**

kājstidziņa *nf* footpath, trail

kājsvira *nf* foot-operated lever

kājtaka *nf* footpath

kāju dzelži *nm pl* leg irons

kāju nags *nm* toenail

kājup *adv* **1.** (col.) up, awake; **2.** on one's feet

kājvanna *nf* footbath

kājviru *adv* (of open doors) completely, wide

kakadu *nm indecl* cockatoo

kakalijas *nf pl* Cacalia

kakao *nm indecl* cacao; cocoa

kakaokoks *nm* cacao tree

kākarains *adj* (reg.) multicolored

kākars *nm* **1.** ribbon, piece of finery; **2.** thin,
transparent fabric; **3.** (reg.) skin and bones

kakas *nf pl* (child.) poo-poo

kakāt *vi* (child.) make poo-poo

kākaulis *nm* long-tailed duck

kakaža *nf* curved tree root used in shaping
curved pieces of wood

kakemono *indecl nm* kakemono

kakla bruņas *nf pl* gorget

kakla darbs *nm* (obs. col.) felony

kakla dziedzer/i *nm pl* tonsils; **k. ~u iekaisums**
tonsillitis; **k. ~u operācija** tonsillectomy

kakla gauda *nf* (obs.) accusation of a capital
offense

kaklagredzens *nm* neckband

kaklakungs *nm* (cont.) lord and master;
opressor, tyrant

kakla lauzējs *nm* daredevil

kakla lieta *nf* (obs.) capital offense

kaklariņķis *nm* neckband

kaklarota *nf* necklace

kaklasaite *nf* necktie; ~**s adata** necktie pin

kaklkasiksna *nf* (animal) collar

kakla skriemelis *nm* cervical vertebra

kakla tiesa *nf* (hist.) criminal court;

kaklauts *nm* neckerchief, neckcloth; tie; muffler

kaklenīca *nf* (reg.) tie (that fastens a wagon pole to the horse's collar)

kaklinieks *nm* (animal) collar

kakliņš *nm dim* of **kakls**, neck

kakl/s *nm* 1. neck; **ar slēgtu** ~**u** (of a dress) high-necked ◊ **pa** ~**u pa galvu** head over heels, headlong; **(dabūt) nost no** ~**a** (col.) (get) out of one's hair; **(dabūt) pa** ~**u** (get it) in the neck; **būt uz** ~**a** (col.) be a burden; overstay one's welcome; **nost no** ~**a** off one's back; 2. throat; **aplikts k.** strep throat ◊ **līdz** ~**am** (col., of eating) absolutely full; (col., of sth. tedious, boring) fed up, up to here; (of trouble) up to one's neck; **pilnā** (or **visā**) ~**ā** (of laughing) roar (with laughter); (of shouting) at the top of one's voice

kaklsaite *nf* = **kaklasaite**

kakodils *nm* cacodyl

kakofonija *nf* cacophony

kakofonisks *adj* cacophonous

kakomiclis *nm* cacomistle

kākslis *nm* goiter

kaktenieks *nm* shyster

kaktiņš *nm dim* of **kakts**, corner

kakts *nm* corner; **nomaļš k.** (col.) out-of-the-way place

kaktu advokāts *nm* shyster

kaktu balle *nf* clandestine party

kaktu dakteris *nm* quack

kaktusaugi *nm pl* cacti

kaktuss *nm* cactus

kak[u]mināls [ū] *adj* (ling.) retroflex

kaķactiņas *nf pl* 1. (bot.) ragged robin; 2. small (kerosene) lamp

kaķastes *nf pl* (bot.) prince's-feather; love-lies-bleeding

kaķaustiņas *nf pl* a type of ornamental design

kaķe *nf* she-cat

kaķējums *nm* gage markings; scarf

kaķene *nf* 1. she-cat; 2. slingshot; 3. black nightshade

kaķenīca *nf* slingshot

kaķēns *nm* kitten

kaķēt *vt* (carpentry) cog

kaķ/is *nm* 1. cat ◊ **priekš** ~**iem** for the birds; 2. marking gage, parallel marker; 3. cog (tenon); 4. cat-o'-nine-tails

kāķis *nm* pillory

kaķiski *adv* cat-like

kaķisks *adj* cat-like

kaķītis *nm dim* of **kaķis**, kitty

kaķmētra *nf* = **kaķumētra**

kaķoties *vr* trifle, play

kaķpēdiņas *nf pl* cat's-foot

kaķsierīte *nf* dwarf mallow

kaķu koncerts *nm* caterwauling

kaķu laipa *nf* catwalk (across a ditch or creek)

kaķulēns *nm* kitten

kaķumētra *nf* catnip

kaķu pautiņi *nm pl* (bot.) cat's-foot

kaķu siers *nm* dwarf mallow

kaķveidīgie *nom adj pl* Felidae

kaķvilna *nf* cotton grass

kālab *adv* why; *conj* (col.) which is why, for which

kālabad *adv* why

kalabase *nf* calabash

kālabpēc *adv* why

kalada *nf* (reg.) kalada, traditional winter solstice song

kaladijas *nf pl* caladium

kaladot *vi* (reg.) sing kaladas

kalambūrisks *adj* punning

kalambūrist/s *nm*, ~**e** *nf* punster

kalambūrs *nm* pun

kalamitāte *nf* calamity

kalamondīns *nm* calamondin

kalan[ch]oja [h] *nf* kalanchoe

kalandrēt *vt* calender

kalandrinijas *nf pl* Calandrinia

kalandrs *nm* calender

kalante *nf* calanthe

kalcedons *nm* chalcedony

kalcenis *nm* (reg., of clothing, footwear) loop

kalceolarija *nf* slipperwort

kalciferols *nm* vitamin D2

kalcifils *adj* calcicolous

kalcifobs *adj* calcifuge

kalcijs *nm* calcium

kalcimetrs *nm* calcimeter

kalcinācija *nf* calcination

kalcinēt *vt* calcinate

kalcinoze *nf* calcinosis

kalcīts *nm* calcite

kaldārijs *nm* caldarium

kaldera *nf* caldera

kaldieši *nm pl* Chaldeans

kaldinājums *nm* chased metalwork

kaldināt *vt* 1. forge; hammer; 2. ornament with chased metalwork

kaldīt *vt* = kalt

kale *nf* pocket; purse

kaleidoskopiski *adv* kaleidoscopically

kaleidoskopisks *adj* kaleidoscopic

kaleidoskopiskums *nm* kaleidoscopic quality

kaleidoskops *nm* kaleidoscope

kalējdarbnīca *nf* smithy, blacksmith's shop

kalējene or kalējiene *nf* blacksmith's wife

kalējiņš *nm* chiffchaff

kalējmeistars *nm* master smith

kalējplēšas *nf pl* forge bellows

kalējs *nm* smith, blacksmith; (fig.) forger, maker

kalendārijs *nm* (tabular register of days) calendar

kalend[a]rizēt [ā] *vt* schedule

kalendārplāns *nm* time schedule

kalendārs *nm* (calendaric system) calendar; pa-stāvīgais k. perpetual calendar

kalendārs *adj* calendarical

kalendas *nf pl* calends

kaleša *nf* calash

kalēt *adv* (reg.) since; while

kaliantemas *nf pl* Callianthemum

kalībnieks *nm* blacksmith's client; a person sent to the blacksmith's with a job

kalibra mērs *nm* caliper

kalibrēšana *nf* calibration

kalibrēt *vt* calibrate

kalibrometrs *nm* feeler gage, wire gage

kalibrs *nm* caliber, gage, size

kalifāts *nm* caliphate

kalifonijs *nm* colophony, rosin

Kalifornijas piparkoks *nm* pepper tree

kalifornijs *nm* californium

kalifs *nm* caliph

kaligr[a]fija [ā] *nf* calligraphy

kaligr[a]fiski [ā] *adv* calligraphically

kaligr[a]fisk/s [ā] *adj* calligraphic

kaligr[a]fiskums [ā] *nm* calligraphic quality

kaligr[a]f/s [ā] *nm*, ~e *nf* calligrapher

kālija sālszāle *nf* Russian thistle

kālija sārms *nm* caustic potash

kālijmēsli *nm pl* potassium fertilizer

kālijs *nm* potassium

kalikants *nm* Carolina allspice

kalikons *nm* buckram

kalipses *nf pl* (bot.) calypso

kalipso *indecl nm* (mus.) calypso

kālis *nm* (bot.) 1. rape; 2. rutabaga, swede

kalistegija *nf* bearbind

kalistemons *nm* Callistemon

kalitrs *nm* Callitris

kalka *nf* = kalks

kalkot *vt* 1. introduce a foreign word into a language by translating it; 2. trace a copy

kalks *nm* 1. tracing paper; 2. (ling.) translation loan word

kalksnēt *vi* 1. doze, nod; 2. idle, dawdle

kalkulācija *nf* calculation

kalkul[a]tors [ā] *nm*, **~e** *nf* calculator

kalkulēt *vt* calculate

kalkūns *nm* (col.) turkey

kalla *nf* calla

kalluss *nm* callus, callosity

kalmārs *nm* squid

kalme *nf* sweet flag

kalmijas *nf pl* Kalmia

kalmik/s *nm*, **~iete** *nf* Kalmuck

kalnaine *nf* mountainous area, highlands

kalnains *adj* mountainous; hilly

kalnainums *nm* mountainousness; hilliness

kalnājs *nm* **1.** mountain range; **2.** highlands

kalna ozols *nm* chestnut oak

kalna sprediķis *nm* sermon of the mount

kalngalie/tis *nm* (folk.) hill dweller; **~ši** hill folk

kalngals *nm* peak, summit; (fig.) height, zenith

kalniene *nf* mountainous area, highlands

kalniet/is *nm*, **~e** *nf* highlander, mountain dweller, mountaineer

kalniņš *nm dim* of **kalns**, hill, hillock

kalnkāpēj/s *nm*, **~a** *nf* mountain climber

kalnmala *nf* foot of the mountain

kalnotne *nf* hilly, mountainous region

kalnpus *prep* above

kalnpusē *adv* above

kalnracis *nm* miner

kalnraktuve *nf* mine

kalnrūpniecība *nf* mining industry

kalnrūpniecisks *adj* mining

kalnrūpnieks *nm* mine owner, mining executive

kaln/s *nm* mountain ◊ **~ā** up the mountain, up-hill; **aiz ~iem** a. far away; b. gone and forgotten; c. far in the future; **pa ~iem, pa lejām** up hil and down dale; **~u ~iem** lots, mountains of

kalntiesības *nf pl* mineral rights

kalnu aita *nf* argali

kalnu alises *nf pl* alyssum

kalnu baltirbe *nf* ptarmigan

kalnu būda *nf* chalet

kalnu dižķengurs *nm* rock kangaroo

kalnu dzelzene *nf* mountain bluet

kalnugāze *nf* (poet.) mountain slope

kalnu grēda *nf* mountain chain

kalnu grieze *nf* takahe

kalnu inženieris *nm* mining engineer

kalnu irbe *nf* rock partridge

kalnu kaza *nf* Alpine ibex

kalnu kazroze *nf* broad-leaved willow herb

kalnu kļava *nf* sycamore maple

kalnu krist[āl]s [all] *nm* rock crystal

kalnu ķeģis *nm* twite

kalnu lija *nf* griffon vulture

kalnumētra *nf* calamint

kalnu mugura *nf* ridge

kalnu nobrukums *nm* landslide

kalnu norgalvīte *nf* sheep's-bit

kalnup *adv* uphill

kalnu pāreja *nf* mountain pass

kalnupeja *nf* mountain climbing

kalnupejošs *adj* acclivious

kalnu priede *nf* mountain pine

kalnu rūgtdille *nf* mountain parsley

kalnusaule *nf* sun lamp

kalnu slimība *nf* mountain sickness

kalnu strēlnieki *nm pl* mountain troops

kalnu veidošanās *nf* orogenesis

kalnu veronika *nf* mountain speedwell

kalnu žibulīši *nm pl* an eyebright, Euphrasia montana

kalnvirsa *nf* mountaintop

kalnzeme *nf* mountainous region

kalomels *nm* calomel

kalorāža *nf* calorie intake

kalorifers *nm* heat exchanger

kalorija *nf* calorie; **lielā k.** large calorie; **mazā k.** small calorie; **~u vērtība** caloric value

kalorimetrija *nf* calorimetry

kalorimetrisks *adj* calorimetric

kalorimetrs *nm* calorimeter

kalorisks *adj* caloric

kaloristisks *adj* caloristic

kaloritāte *nf* calorie count

kaloša *nf* overshoe, galosh

kalpapuisis *nm* (single) farmhand

kalpasieva *nf* farmhand's wife

kalpavīrs *nm* married farmhand

kalpazēns *nm* (hired) farm boy

kalpība *nf* servitude, bondage

kalpīgi *adv* obligingly

kalpīgs *adj* obliging

kalpināt *vt* exploit; enslave

kalpinātāj/s *nm*, ~a *nf* exploiter; enslaver

kalpiņš *nm* **1.** *dim* of **kalps**, farmhand; **2.** bootjack; **3.** (cards) jack

kalpiski *adv* servilely

kalpisks *adj* servile

kalpmāja *nf* servants' quarters

kalpone *nf* **1.** housemaid; **2.** farm worker

kalponīte *nf dim* of **kalpone**, hired hand

kalpot *vi* serve (also fig.); be employed, work

kalpotāj/s *nm*, ~a *nf* **1.** employee; **2.** servant

kalps *nm* **1.** farmhand; **2.** servant; **3.** (cards) jack

kalpu rinda *nf* (hist.) row housing for farm-hands

kāls *nm* score and a half

kalsenība *nf* thinness, gauntness

kalsens *adj* thin, gaunt, spare

kalsenums *nm* thinness, gauntness

kalsiņš *nm* keelson

kalsnējība *nf* thinness, gauntness

kalsnējs *adj* thin, gaunt, spare

kalsnis *nm* skin and bones

kalsns *adj* thin, gaunt, spare

kalsnums *nm* thinness, gauntness

kalst *vi* **1.** dry; **2.** dry up; wither

kalstīt *vt* (of horses) shoe

kalšana I *nf* drying, withering

kalšana II *nf* forging, hammering; minting

kalt *vt* **1.** forge; **2.** ornament with chased metalwork; **3.** (of horses) shoe; **4.** (of coins) coin, mint; **5.** hammer; chisel; (of stone) dress; sculpt; **6.** (of woodpeckers, also *vi*) peck, excavate; **7.** (col.) cram, grind; **8.** make rhymes

kaltaza *nf, nm* (col.) skin and bones

kalte *nf* **1.** drier; **2.** drying barn, drying room, drying kiln

kaltējamais aparāts *nm* desiccator

kaltenis *nm* copper kettle

kaltēt *vt* **1.** dry; dry-cure; desiccate; **2.** parch

kaltētājtrumulis *nm* dryer

kaltētājventil[a]tors [ā] *nm* drying room fan

kaltētava *nf* drying room, dryhouse

kaltēties *vr* dry

kalties *vr* **1.** have blacksmith's work done for oneself; **2.** forge oneself; **3.** (of blacksmiths) compete, have a contest

kaltināt *vt* dry; dry-cure

kaltiņš *nm dim* of **kalts**, small chisel

kaltnējs *adj* (reg.) thin, gaunt, spare

kaltonis *nm* **1.** (reg.) tuberculosis; **2.** (col.) consumptive

kalts *nm* chisel

kalts *adj, part* of **kalt** **1.** forged; (of iron) wrought, (of gold) beaten; **2.** ornamented with chased metalwork; **3.** shod; **asi k.** roughshod; **ledū k.** (poet.) icebound; **4.** coined, minted; **5.** hammered; chiseled; dressed; sculpted; **6.** ex-cavated, hollowed (by woodpeckers)

kaltuve *nf* **1.** smithy; **2.** stonecutter's shop; **3.** mint

kaltveidīgs *adj* chisel-shaped

kalums *nm* **1.** forging; **2.** coinage

kalva *nf* **1.** low hill; **2.** offing; **3.** (bot.) sweet flag

kalvadoss *nm* calvados

kalve I *nf* forge, smithy

kalve II *nf* sweet flag

kalvene *nf* a place where sweet flag grows

kalvinieks *nm* blacksmith's client

kalvinisms *nm* Calvinism

kalvinists *nm* Calvinist

kalvis *nm* (poet.) smith, forger

kaļadot *vi* chat, blab; quarrel

kaļamība *nf* forgeability, malleability

kaļammašīna *nf* forging machine, machine hammer

kaļams *adj, part* of **kalt** forgeable, malleable

kaļiņa *nf* river sandbar

kaļķains *adj* limy; calcareous

kaļķainums *nm* liminess

kaļķakmens *nm* limestone

kaļķa piens *nm* milk of lime

kaļķarenīts *nm* calcarenite

kaļķaugs *nm* calcicole

kaļķenīca *nf* clay pipe

kaļķiezis *nm* limestone

kaļķ/is *nm, usu. pl* **kaļķi 1.** lime; **dzēsti ~i** slaked lime; **hidrauliskais k.** hydraulic lime; **nedzēsti ~i** quicklime; **sērskābais k.** sulfate of lime; **2.** clay pipe

kaļķītis *nm* clay pipe

kaļķnesējs *nm*, used as *adj* calciferous

kaļķojums *nm* **1.** liming; **2.** whitewash

kaļķot *vt* **1.** lime; **2.** whitewash

kaļķslāpeklis *nm* nitrocalcite

kaļķšpats *nm* calcite

kaļķuceplis *nm* limekiln

kaļķūdens *nm* limewater

kaļķu iezis *nm* lime rock

kaļķu lauztuve *nf* limestone quarry

kaļķu lutīts *nm* calcilutite

kaļķu smilšakmens *nm* calcareous sandstone

kaļķu špats *nm* calcite

kaļķu tufa *nf* calcareous tufa

kaļķu zeme *nf* calcareous earth

kam *pron, dat* of **kas 1.** to whom; **k. nebūt** whomever; **2.** why; **3.** (reg.) if only

kamambers *nm* camembert (cheese)

kaman/as *nf pl* sled, sledge, sleigh; **~u sliece** runner

kamaniņas *nf pl dim* of **kamanas**, sled

kamara *nf* **1.** rind; **2.** crust

kamarainis *nm* crustacean

kamarilja or **kamariļa** *nf* camarilla

kamariņa *nf dim* of **kamara**, little rind

kamaša *nf* gaiter; spat

kamāt *vt* **1.** knead; squeeze; **2.** torment

kamba *nf* turbot

kambaris *nm* **1.** (obs.) small room; (hist.) (unheated) chamber; (hist.) living chamber (con-nected to the bathhouse or heated grain drying barn); **pieliekamais k.** larder, pantry; **2.** (anat.) chamber

kambarītis *nm* **1.** *dim* of **kambaris**; **2.** (col.) toilet

kamba[r]junkurs [r] *nm* chamberlain

kamba[r]meita [r] *nf* chambermaid

kamba[r]kungs [r] *nm* chamberlain

kamba[r]nieks [r] *nm* (hist.) peasant farmer who built and farmed on someone else's land

kamba[r]sulainis [r] *nm* chamberlain; valet

kambartiņš *nm* ossuary

kambijs *nm* cambium

kambīze *nf* (naut.) galley

kambīznieks *nm* assistant ship's cook

kambodiet/is *nm*, **~e** *nf* Cambodian

kamčadāl/s *nm*, **~iete** *nf* Kamchadal

kamdēļ *adv* why

kameja *nf* cameo

kamēlija *nf* camellia

kamembertsiers *nm* Camembert cheese

kamene *nf* **1.** bumblebee; **2.** spruce bark

kamenīte *nf dim* of **kamene**, bumblebee

kamēr *conj* **1.** while; **2.** till; **3.** since

kamera *nf* **1.** camera; **2.** prison cell; **3.** inner tube; bladder; **4.** (tech.) chamber; **saldējamā k.** freezing chamber

kamerālīpašums *nm* (hist.) state property

kamerālisms *nm* cameralism

kamerālistika *nf* cameralistics

kamerāls *adj* 1. cameralistic; 2. (of research, opposite to field) laboratory, desk; 3. (of music) chamber

kamerālvalde *nf* (hist.) crown treasury office in the provinces

kamerālzinātnes *nf pl* cameral sciences

kameransamblis *nm* chamber ensemble

kameransamblist/s *nm*, ~e *nf* member of a chamber ensemble

kamerārija *nf* chamber aria

kamerdīneris *nm* valet

kamerdziedātāj/s *nm*, ~a *nf* = kamerdziedonis

kamerdziedon/is *nm*, ~e *nf* singer of art songs

kamerko[l]ektīvs [ll] *nm* chamber ensemble

kamerkoncerts *nm* chamber music recital

kamerkoris *nm* choral group

kamerluga *nf* intimate play, intimate theater

kamerm[u]zicēšana [ū] *nf* performance of chamber music

kamermūzika *nf* chamber music

kamernie/ks *nm*, ~ce *nf* prison inmate

kameropera *nf* chamber opera

kamerorķestris *nm* chamber orchestra

kamersimfonija *nf* chamber symphony

kamerskaņdarbs *nm* chamber music

kamerspēle *nf* intimate play, intimate theater

kamerstils *nm* intimate style

kamērt *adv* (reg.) while

kamertiesa *nf* (hist.) Supreme Court; Superior Court of Justice

kamertipa *indecl adj* chamber

kamertonis *nm* pitch pipe

kāmēt *vi* grow thin, pine away

kamfēns *nm* camphene

kamforosma *nf* stinking ground pine

kamielenes *nf pl* camel thorn

kamielis *nm* camel

kamielīši *nm pl* raphidians, snake flies

kamieļērkšķi *nm pl* camel thorn

kamieļvilna *nf* camel's hair

kamieļzāle *nf* camel thorn

kamiens *nm* spruce bark

kamiesis *nm* (obs.) shoulder

kamikadze *nm* kamikaze

kamīna dzega *nf* mantelpiece

kamīna režģis *nm* fender; fire screen

kamīns *nm* fireplace

kāmis *nm* 1. hamster; 2. (fig., com.) glutton

kamolainā ežgalvīte *nf* a burr reed, Sparganium glomeratum

kamolainā rūgtlape *nf* a sawwort, Saussurea glomerata

kamolains *adj* (rare., of clouds) puffy

kamolbegonija *nf* a begonia, Begonia tuber-hybrida

kamoliņš *nm* 1. *dim* of kamols, little ball of yarn; 2. a Latvian folk dance

kamols *nm* clew, ball of yarn

kamolu doņi *nm pl* staff rush

kamolu pulkstenīte *nf* clustered bellflower

kamolu radzene *nf* mouse-ear chickweed

kamolveida *indecl adj* ball-shaped

kamolveidīgi *adv* like a ball

kamolveidīgs *adj* ball-shaped

kamolzāle *nf* orchard grass

kamora *nf* camorra

kamorists *nm* camorrist

kampa *nf* hunk (of bread, cheese)

kampanile *nf* campanile

kampaņa *nf* campaign

kampaņveida *indecl adj* occurring in spurts

kampaņveidīgi *adv* in spurts

kampaņveidīgs *adj* occurring in spurts

kampareļļa *nf* camphor oil

kamparkoks *nm* camphor tree

kampars *nm* camphor

kamparskābe *nf* camphoric acid

kamparspirts *nm* solution of camphor in alcohol

kampējs *nm* (col.) thief

kampeškoks *nm* logwood

kampešs *nm* logwood

kampiens *nm* grasp, snatch

kampis *nm* hook

kampstīt *vt* grab (repeatedly)

kampšķis *nm* handful

kampt *vt* grasp, snatch; seize

kampučiet/is *nm*, **~e** *nf* Kampuchean

kams *nm* **1.** clod; **2.** lump; pat; **3.** usu. *pl* ~i balls made of ground peas or roasted grain, soaked in milk

kamsa *nf, nm* glutton

kamslis *nm* glutton

kamšķis *nm* handful

kamucis *nm* lump

kamuflets *nm* camouflet

kamzolis *nm* jacket

Kan[a]das [ā] apse *nf* Canadian poplar

Kan[a]das [ā] egle *nf* white spruce

Kan[a]das [ā] elodeja *nf* common waterweed

Kan[a]das [ā] hemlokegle *nf* eastern hemlock, Canadian hemlock

Kan[a]das [ā] jānīši *nm pl* Canada fleabane

Kan[a]das [ā] plūme *nf* Canada plum

Kan[a]das [ā] zeltgalvīte *nf* Canada goldenrod

Kan[a]das [ā] zoss *nf* Canada goose

kan[a]diet/is [ā] *nm*, **~e** *nf* Canadian

kanaks *nm* **1.** (sl.) soldier, fighter (Latvian, World War II); **2.** (sl.) man; **3.** South Sea Islander

kanālapkure *nf* (piped) hot air heating

kanālis *nm* = **kanāls**

kan[a]lizācija [ā] *nf* sewer system, sewerage

kan[a]lizācijas [ā] caurule *nf* sewer pipe

kan[a]lizācijas [ā] vads *nm* sewer line

kan[a]lizēt [ā] *vt* install a sewer system

kanālmala *nf* canal bank

kanāl/s *nm* **1.** channel; **pa drošiem ~iem** from reliable sources; **2.** canal; **3.** (anat.) tract, canal

kanāls akvadukts *nm* canal aqueduct, flume

kanālstari *nm pl* positive ray

kananga *nf* ilang-ilang tree

kanapē *indecl nm* canapé

kanapejs *nm* sofa

kanārija *nf* Java almond

Kan[a]rijas [ā] miežubrālis *nm* canary grass

kan[a]rijputniņš [ā] *nm* canary

kan[a]rijs [ā] *nm* canary

kancele *nf* **1.** pulpit; **2.** (mil.) turret

kanceleja *nf* (government) office; (of a company, batallion) orderly room

kancelejas piederumi *nm pl* stationery

kancelejas stils *nm* officialese

kancelejas žurka *nf* (cont.) office drudge

kancelejiski *adv* bureaucratically

kancelejisks *adj* bureaucratic, formal, red-tape

kancelejist/s *nm*, **~e** *nf* office worker

kancelejiskums *nm* bureaucratism, red tape

kanceles lielgabalnieks *nm* tail gunner

kancerog[e]nisks [ē] *adj* carcinogenic

kancerog[e]ns [ē] *nm* carcinogen

kancerog[e]ns [ē] *adj* carcinogenic

kanceroģen[e]ze [ē] *nf* carcinogenesis

kancis *nm* (col.) hunk

kancītis *nm* (reg.) little bit

kanclers *nm* chancellor

kancona *nf* canzone

kančuks *nm* a type of whip

kandalas *nf pl* leg and arm shackles

kandava *nf* water-filled pothole

kandavāt *vt* (of horses) beat

kandavnieks *nm* horse beater

kandela *nf* (phys.) candela

kandel[a]brs [ā] *nm* candelabrum

kandidamikoze *nf* candidiasis

kandidāts *nm*, **~e** *nf* **1.** candidate; **2.** doctor of philosophy, PhD

kandid[a]tūra [ā] *nf* **1.** candidacy; **2.** candidate

kandidātvalsts *nf* candidate state

kandidēt *vi* **1.** run for an office; **2.** apply for a position

kandidoze *nf* candidiasis

kandijs *nm* (bee food) candy

kandikas *nf pl* erythronium

kandiscukurs *nm* barley sugar

kandža *nf* (col.) moonshine

kanēlis *nm* cinnamon

kanelūra *nf* cannelure

kanēļeļļa *nf* cinnamon oil

kanēļkoks *nm* cinnamon tree

kanēļmaizīte *nf* cinnamon roll

kaneva *nf* canvas

kangars *nm* 1. row of hills; 2. (sl.) traitor

kanibāliski *adv* cannibalistically

kanibālisks *adj* cannibalistic

kanibālisms *nm* cannibalism

kanibāls *nm* cannibal

kanifass *nm* dimity

kanjons *nm* canyon

kanjonveida *indecl adj* canyon-type

kanjonveidīgs *adj* canyon-type

kankalis *nm* = **kankālis**

kankālis *nm* 1. clod; 2. (reg.) ragamuffin

kankālītis *nm dim* of **kankālis**, small clod

kankals *nm* cow bell

kankaļains *adj* = **kankāļains**

kankāļains *adj* cloddy

kankans *nm* (reg.) skin and bones; jade, hack

kankāns *nm* cancan

kankaraini *adv* in a tattered condition

kankarainība *nf* tattered condition

kankarainis *nm* (col.) tatterdemalion

kankarains *adj* ragged, tattered

kankarainums *nm* tattered condition

kankarbiksis *nm* (col.) tatterdemalion

kankariņš *nm dim* of **kankars**, tatter

kankaris *nm* (col.) tatterdemalion

kankarlācis *nm* (col.) tatterdemalion

kankarnieks *nm* (col.) 1. ragpicker; 2. tatterdemalion

kankars *nm* tatter; ~i rags; tattered clothes

kankāties *vr* work without success

kankle *nf* (Lithuanian) psaltery

kanna I *nf* 1. can; jug; tankard; (tea, coffee) pot; 2. (obs.) a liquid measure

kanna II *nf* canna

kanna III *nf* eland

kannele I *nf* (cont.) can

kannele II *nf* kantele

kanninieks *nm* (hist.) tin caster (caster of tinwork)

kanniņa *nf* 1. *dim* of **kanna** I, little can, tankard, pot; 2. cell of a honeycomb

kanoe *indecl nf* canoe

kanoist/s *nm*, ~e *nf* canoeist

kanonāde *nf* cannonade

kanonieris *nm* artillerist

kanoniķis *nm* canonist

kanoniski *adv* canonically

kanonisks *adj* canonical

kanoniskums *nm* canonicity

kanonizācija *nf* canonization

kanonizēšana *nf* canonization

kanonizēt *vt* canonize

kanons *nm* canon

kanonveida *indecl adj* (mus.) canonic

kanonveidīgs *adj* (mus.) canonic

kanovālija *nf* jack bean

kantains *adj* (col.) angular, edged

kantāķis *nm* cant hook

Kantāla siers *nm* Cantal cheese

kantar[i]da [ī] *nf* Spanish fly

kantaridīns *nm* cantharidin

kantars *nm* kantar

kantāte *nf* cantata

kante *nf* (col.) edge

kantele *nf* kantele

kantēt *vt* (col.) 1. (of a log) square; 2. (of a garment) edge; 3. whip; 4. cant

kantēties *vr* k. klāt (col.) sidle up to

kantiāniet/is *nm*, ~e *nf* Kantian

kantiānisms *nm* Kantianism

kantīgs *adj* (col.) diligent; strong

kantilēna *nf* cantilena

kantilēns *adj* cantilena-like

kantīne *nf* (shop, flask) canteen

kantisms *nm* Kantianism

kantonāls *adj* cantonal

kantonists *nm* (hist.) **1.** (Prussian) conscript; **2.** (Russian) soldier's son

kantons *nm* canton

kantordarbinie/ks *nm*, **~ce** *nf* office worker

kantorgrāmata *nf* register; record book; ledger

kantoris *nm* (business) office;

kantorist/s *nm*, **~e** *nf* office worker

kantor/s *nm*, **~e** *nf* cantor

kantoŗa līme *nf* paper glue

kantoŗa pārzinis *nm* office service supervisor; (RR) chief clerk

kantrīmūzika *nf* country music

kants *nm* chant

kanu laiviņa *nf* canoe

kanva *nf* canvas

kaņepāj/s *nm* **1.** hemp field; **2.** hemp plant; **3.** ~i hemp fiber, hemp

kaņepāju kārkls *nm* common osier

kaņepe *nf* **1.** hemp; **2.** *pl* ~es a. hemp-seed; b. hemp-seed spread

kaņepene *nf* dog's mercury

kaņepītis *nm* linnet

kaņepju putniņš *nm* linnet

kaņons *nm* canyon

kaolinīts *nm* kaolinite

kaolīna māls *nm* china clay

kaolīns *nm* kaolin

kaons *nm* (phys.) muon

kapa I *nf* **1.** (count of) sixty; **2.** (obs.) 1/25th of a **pūrvieta**; **3.** six grain shocks

kapa II *nf* kappa

kāpa *nf* dune; **klejojošā k.** shifting dune; **nekustīgā k.** antidune

kapacitāte *nf* capacity; (el.) capacitance

kapacitīvs *adj* capacitive

kapa dziesma *nf* dirge

kapainis *nm* chopper

kāpains *adj* duny

kapājamais *adj, part* of **kapāt** chopping knife

kapājumi *nm pl* choppings

kapakmens *nm* tombstone

kapa kopiņa *nf* grave mound

kāpaļāt *vi* climb up and down, get up and down on sth.

kaparbrūni *adv* in copper color

kaparbrūns *adj* copper

kaparčūska *nf* blindworm

kapargriezums *nm* copper engraving

kapari *nm pl* = **kaperi**

kapariņš *nm* percussion cap

kaparkalējs *nm* coppersmith

kaparkalums *nm* piece of coppersmith's art; copper relief

kaparkrāsa *nf* coppertone

kaparnauda *nf* copper coins

kaparot *vt* copper

kapars *nm* copper

kāpars *nm* **1.** caterpillar, grub; **2.** larva

kaparsarkans *adj* copper red

kāparu āboliņš *nm* (bot.) scorpion's-tail

kapa runa *nf* funeral oration

kapāt *vt* **1.** chop, hack, mince; **2.** hit (with a whip); beat down; **3.** slash; **4.** (of bullets) riddle; **5.** scourge

kapāties *vr* **1.** hack; **2.** stamp; **3.** beat down; **4.** dig (in the soil); **5.** fight

kapātuvis *nm* chopper

kapaunēt *vt* caponize

kapauns *nm* capon

kapa uzraksts *nm* epitaph

kapavieta *nf* gravesite

kapča *nf* (reg., of potatoes) pile

kape *nf* **1.** (of shoes) quarter, counter; **2.** cap

kāpe *nf* **1.** (aeron.; of screw threads) pitch; **2.** rung; step; ~s stairs, steps; **3.** amplitude

kapeadors *nm* capeador

kāpēc *adv* why; **k., tāpēc!** just because!

kāpecītis *nm* (col.) why-asker

kapeika *nf* kopeck

kāpēj/s *nm*, **~a** *nf* climber

kāpekles *nf pl* ladder

kapela *nf* = **kapella**

kapelāns *nm* = **kapellāns**

kapele *nf* fishline

kāpele *nf* 1. *dim* of **kāpa**; 2. (reg.) heap

kapelēt *vi* fish from a boat with a jig

kāpelēt *vi* climb up and down

kāpelētājaugs *nm* climbing plant

kāpelētāj/s *nm*, ~a *nf* climber

kapella *nf* 1. choir; 2. band, Kapelle; 3. chapel

kapellāns *nm* chaplain

kapelmeistars *nm* band leader, Kapellmeister

kapene *nf*, usu. *pl* **kapenes** 1. burial site; barrow, tumulus; 2. tomb, sepulcher

kāpene *nf* spot on the road not covered with snow

kāpenes *nf pl* stairs; outside stairs at the back of a building; ladder

kapenie/ks *nm*, ~ce *nf* funeral guest

kāpenie/ks *nm*, ~ce *nf* dune dweller

kāpenisks *adj* stepped

kapera *nf* (bot.) caper

kaperēšana *nf* privateering

kaperēt *vt* capture, seize

kaperi *nm pl* (cul.) capers

kaperis *nm* privateer

kaperkrūms *nm* (bot.) caper

kaperkuģis *nm* privateer

kapers *nm* (bot.) caper

kapertiesības *nf pl* letters of marque

kapēt *vt* hoe

kapi *nm pl* cemetery; graveyard; see **kaps**

kāpiens *nm* 1. climb; 2. grade (in a road); 3. step (for climbing)

kāpienveida *indecl adj* stepped

kāpienveidīgi *adv* staggered, in a staggered fashion

kāpienveidīgs *adj* stepped

kapilār- See **kapillār-**

kapi[ll]ārcaurule [l] *nf* capillary tube

kapi[ll]āritāte [l] *nf* capillarity

kapi[ll]ārķīmija [l] *nf* capillary chemistry

kapi[ll]ārs [l] *nm* capillary

kapi[ll]ārs [l] *adj* capillary

kapi[ll]ārūdens [l] *nm* capillary water

kapi[ll]ārvads [l] *nm* capillary

kapi[ll]icijs [l] *nm* capillitium

kāpinājums *nm* rise in intensity; (math) raising to a power

kāpināmais *nom adj* (math.) base

kapināt *vt* (of the blade of a scythe) sharpen (by drawing it with a hammer)

kāpināt *vt* 1. raise (increase; multiply by itself); heighten; 2. catch crayfish with bait; 3. (rare.) make climb

kāpināties *vr* rise

kāpinātāj/s *nm* 1. raiser; ~a *nf*; 2. (math.) exponent

kāpināts *adj, part* of **kāpināt** heightened

kapinie/ks *nm*, ~ce *nf* funeral guest

kapiņš *nm dim* of **kaps**, little grave

kapitālceltniecība *nf* major construction project

kapitāldarbs *nm* major work

kapitāli *adv* mainly; fundamentally

kapitālieguldījums *nm* capital investment

kapitālisms *nm* capitalism

kapitālistiski *adv* capitalistically

kapitālistisks *adj* capitalistic

kapitālist/s *nm*, ~e *nf* capitalist

kapit[a]lizācija [ā] *nf* capitalization

kapit[a]lizēt [ā] *vt* capitalize

kapit[a]lizēties [ā] *vr* become capitalized

kapitālremonts *nm* renovation, major repairs

kapitāl/s *nm* capital; **apgrozāmais k.** working capital; **neaizskarama ~a konts** endowment fund; **nedzīvais k.** dead stock

kapitāls *adj* capital, main; fundamental

kapitālsiena *nf* main wall

kāpīte *nf dim* of **kāpe**, small step

kapitelis *nm* 1. (arch.) capital; 2. capital letter

kapitols *nm* capitol

kapitulācija *nf* capitulation

kapitulantiski *adv* in a capitulatory manner

kapitulantisks *adj* capitulatory

kapitulant/s *nm*, ~e *nf* capitulator

kapitulārvikārs *nm* vicar capitular

kapitulēt *vi* capitulate

kapituls *nm* (rel.) chapter

kapkalns *nm* burial mound, barrow, tumulus

kaplāns *nm* curate

kaplēt *vt* hoe

kaplete *nf* caplet

kapliča *nf* 1. mortuary; 2. vault

kaplis *nm* 1. hoe; mattock; 2. (col.) chisel

kāplis *nm* (reg.) 1. (of a ladder, stairs) step; 2. stir-rup

kaplodziņš *nm dim* of **kaplogs**, small hinged windowpane

kaplogs *nm* small hinged windowpane

kapmirte *nf* periwinkle

kāpnes *nf pl* 1. stairs, stairway; **nolaižamās k.** gangplank; **slīdošās k.** escalator; 2. ladder

kāpnītes *nf pl* ladder; (bot.) Jacob's ladder

kāpņu laukums *nm* landing

kāpņu posms *nm* flight of stairs

kāpņu telpa *nf* staircase

kāpņveida *indecl adj* staired

kāpņveidīgs *adj* staired

kapokkoks *nm* silk-cotton tree

kapoks *nm* kapok

kaponieris *nm* (mil.) salient

kāpostaugs *nm* brassica

kāpostbaļļa *nf* sourkraut tub

kāpostbļoda *nf* pot of cabbage (soup, meal)

kāpostdārzs *nm* cabbage patch

kāpostgalva *nf* 1. head of cabbage; 2. (col.) fool

kāpostgalviņa *nf dim* of **kāpostgalva**, small head of cabbage

kāpostlauks *nm* cabbage patch

kāpostnieks *nm* cabbage vendor

kāpost/s *nm*, usu. *pl* **kāposti** cabbage; **skābie ~i** sauerkraut

kāpostu baltenis *nm* cabbage butterfly, large white

kāpostu blusa *nf* flea beetle

kāpostu cekulainā kode *nf* cabbage moth

kāpostu lapu uts *nf* cabbage aphid

kāpostu muša *nf* cabbage maggot, cabbage fly (adult)

kāpostu odiņš *nm* gall midge

kāpostu pūcīte *nf* a cabbage moth, Barathra brassicae

kāpostu salāti *nm pl* coleslaw

kapracis *nm* 1. gravedigger; 2. burying beetle

kaprālis *nm* corporal; **jaunākais k.** lance corporal

kapriciozi *adv* capriciously

kapriciozs *adj* capricious

kapričo *indecl nm* capriccio

kaprifolija *nf* caprifolium

kaprilskābe *nf* caprylic acid

kaprinskābe *nf* capric acid

kapriola *nf* capriole

kapr[is]e [īz] *nf* caprice, whim

kapr[is]ēt [īz] *vi* be capricious

kapr[is]ēties [īz] *vr* be capricious

kapr[is]i [īz] *adv* capriciously

kapr[is]itāte [īz] *nf* capriciousness

kapr[is]s [īz] *adj* capricious

kapr[is]ums [īz] *nm* capriciousness

kaprolaktāms *nm* caprolactam

kaprolīti *nm pl* caprolites

kaprons *nm* Caprolan

kapronskābe *nf* caproic acid

kap/s *nm* grave; sepulcher; **svētais k.** Holy Sepulcher; **~a** a. (of voice, sounds) sepulchral; b. burial, funeral; c. deathlike; **~i** a. cemetery; b. graves; **līdz ~a malai** to the end of one's days

kapsantīns *nm* capsanthin

kapsele *nf* 1. percussion cap; detonator; 2. kiln

kapseļdeton[a]tors [ā] *nm* firing cap

kapsēta *nf* cemetery

kapsētnieks *nm* funeral guest

kapsis *nm* (reg., of potatoes) pile

kāpsliens *nm* rung (of a ladder)

kāp/slis *nm* 1. stirrup; ~**šļi** climbing irons; 2. step (rise); footboard, running board

kāpslītis *nm* 1. *dim* of **kāpslis**, stirrup; 2. (anat.) stapes

kāpsmildzenes *nf pl* Corynephorus

kapsula *nf* capsule; (pottery) saggar

kapsulveida *indecl adj* capsule-like

kapsulveidīgi *adv* by encapsulating

kapsulveidīgs *adj* capsule-like

kāpšana *nf* (aeron) climb

kāpt *vi* 1. climb; (col., of migratory fish) go upstream; ascend; **k. ārā** get out of; get off, alight; **k. augšā** climb up; **k. augšā pa trepēm** climb the stairs, go upstairs; **k. tronī** ascend the throne; **k. uz ecēšām** (col.) stick one's neck out; **k. uz kakla** (or **galvas**) (col.) lord it over s.o.; **k. uz leju** climb down, descend; **k. uz muguras** (also **ancuka**) (sl.) importune, pester; **k. uz papē-žiem** (col.) breathe down one's neck; 2. (with noun in locative) step into; **k. kuģī** go aboard (ship); **k. lidmašīnā** board a plane; **k. mugurā** mount; **k. virsū** mount; **k. zirgā** mount a horse; 3. (col.) head; walk slowly; 4. rise; **k. galvā** go to one's head; **k. kaklā** (fig.; of food) stick in one's throat; (of nausea) come on; (of bitterness) rise; **ūdens kāpj mutē** (col.) up to one's neck in trouble; 5. **k. bites** (or **medu**) (*vt*, obs., folk.) gather honey

kaptei/nis *nm*, ~**ne** *nf* captain; ~**ņa palīgs** (naut.) mate; **pirmā ranga k.** (Navy) captain; **otrā ran-ga k.** commander; **trešā ranga k.** lieutenant commander

kapteiņa palīgs *nm* (naut.) mate

kapteiņleitnant/s *nm*, ~**e** *nf* lieutenant captain (a grade between those of first lieutenant and captain in the Army); (Navy) lieutenant

kāpties *vr* **k. atpakaļ** step back, move back; (of horses) jib; **k. sānis** move sidewise; step aside

kāptspēja *nf* gradeability

kapu āboliņš *nm* houseleek

kapuce *nf* hood, cowl

kapucietis *nm* Capuchin

kapucīns *nm* 1. capuchin monkey; 2. Capuchin

kapucīte *nf dim* of **kapuce**, little hood, cowl

kapucpērtiķis *nm* capuchin monkey

kāpu grīšļi *nm pl* sedge

kapukalniņš *nm dim* of **kapukalns**

kapukalns *nm* hillside cemetery; (poet.) graveyard

kāpukvieši *nm pl* a beach grass

kapulauks *nm* ancient burial ground

kāpuļot *vi* climb up and down

kāpu mieži *nm pl* wild rye, lyme grass

kāpumlaiks *nm* (el.) rise time

kāpums *nm* 1. climb, ascent; 2. grade (incline); 3. rise

kāpuniedra *nf* beach grass

kāpu pamieēi *nm pl* wild rye, lyme grass

kāpurķēde *nf* caterpillar tread, track

kāpurķēdnieks *nm* caterpillar tractor

kāpurlapsene *nf* ichneumon fly

kāpurmuša *nf* tachina fly

kāpurnieks *nm* caterpillar tractor

kāpurs *nm* 1. caterpillar, grub; 2. larva

kāpuru lapsene *nf* ichneumon fly

kapusvētki *nm pl* memorial service (in a cemetery); All Souls' Day

kaput *adj* kaput

kapu vieta *nf* burial ground

kapzeķe *nf* sock

kara apgabals *nm* = **kaṛa apgabals**

kara atlīdzinājumi *nm pl* = **kaṛa atlīd-zinājumi**

kara aviācija *nf* = **kaṛa aviācija**

karabāze *nf* = **kaṛabaze**

karabiedrs *nm* = **kaṛabiedrs**

karabīn[e] [s] *nf* or *nm* 1. carbine; 2. snap link

karabinieris *nm* 1. carabineer; 2. carabiniere

karačaj/s *nm*, ~**iete** *nf* Karachai

karadarbība *nf* = **kaṛadarbība**

karadienests *nm* = **kaŗadienests**

karadraudze *nf* = **kaŗadraudze**

karadraugs *nm* = **kaŗadraugs**

karafa or **karafe** *nf* decanter, carafe

karaflote *nf* = **kaŗaflote**

karagaitas *nf pl* = **kaŗagaitas**

karagājiens *nm* = **kaŗagājiens**

karagana *nf* caragana

karagūstekn/is *nm* = **kaŗagūsteknis**

karaīb/s *nm*, ~**iete** *nf* Carib

kara iemesls *nm* = **kaŗa iemesls**

karaīmi *nm pl* Karaites

kara invalīds *nm* = **kaŗa invalids**

kara jūrnieks *nm* = **kaŗa jūrnieks**

karakalpak/s *nm*, ~**iete** *nf* Karakalpak

karakalps *nm* = **kaŗakalps**

karakals *nm* caracal

karaklausība *nf* = **kaŗaklausība**

karaklaušas *nf pl* = **kaŗaklaušas**

kara kūdītājs *nm* = **kaŗa kūdītājs**

karakuģis *nm* = **kaŗakuģis**

karakulāda *nf* karakul

karakulaita *nf* karakul sheep

karakuljērs *nm* karakul lamb

karakuls *nm* karakul

karakungs *nm* = **kaŗakungs**

karakurts *nm* karakurt

karalaiks *nm* = **kaŗalaiks**

karalauks *nm* = **kaŗalauks**

kara laupījums *nm* = **kaŗa laupījums**

karaliene *nf* queen

karalietas *nf pl* = **kaŗalietas**

kara likums *nm* = **kaŗa likums**

karalis *nm* king

karaliskā begonija *nf* Rex begonia

karaliskā lilija *nf* regal lily

karaliski *adv* royally; regally

karalisks *adj* royal; regal; kinglike, queenlike

karaliste *nf* kingdom, realm

karaļčūska *nf* boa constrictor

karaļdēls *nm* (folk.) king's son, prince

karaļgalms *nm* king's court

karaļģimene *nf* royal family

karaļkronis *nm* tiger lily

karaļmeita *nf* (folk.) king's daughter, princess

karaļnams *nm* royal house

karaļpalma *nf* royal palm

karaļpāris *nm* royal couple

karaļpingvīns *nm* emperor penguin

karaļūdens *nm* aqua regia

karaļvalsts *nf* kingdom

karamāksla *nf* = **kaŗamāksla**

karamašīna *nf* = **kaŗamašīna**

karamateriāli *nm pl* = **kaŗamateriāli**

karambola *nf* **1.** carom; **2.** (bot.) carambola

karambolža *nf* carom

karambolēt *vt* carom

karambols *nm* carom

karamele *nf* caramel candy

karamelizēšana *nf* caramelization

karamelizēt *vt* caramelize

karamelizēties *vr* caramelize

karamels *nm* caramel

kara musinātājs *nm* = **kaŗa musinātājs**

kara nometne *nf* = **kaŗa nometne**

kara noslēpums *nm* = **kaŗa noslēpums**

karantēna *nf* quarantine

karantīna *nf* quarantine

karaoke *nf* karaoke

kara orķestris *nm* = **kaŗa orķestris**

kara osta *nf* = **kaŗa osta**

kara prokurors *nm* = **kaŗa prokurors**

karapūlis *nm* = **kaŗapūlis**

karapulks *nm* = **kaŗapulks**

kara rags *nm* = **kaŗa rags**

kara sauciens *nm* = **kaŗa sauciens**

karaskola *nf* = **kaŗaskola**

kara slimnīca *nf* = **kaŗa slimnīca**

karaspēks *nm* = **kaŗaspēks**

karaspēle *nf* = **kaŗaspēle**

karastāvoklis *nm* = **kaŗastāvoklis**

kara viltība *nf* = **kaŗa viltība**

karaša *nf* flat, round bread of course-ground wheat or barley

karātavas *nf pl* gallows

karātavnie/ks *nm*, **~ce** *nf* candidate for the gallows

karātavu putns *nm* gallowsbird

karatē *indecl nm* karate

karāties *vr* hang; **k. gaisā** a. be up in the air; b. be imminent; **k. kaklā** be a burden; be de-pendent on; **k. mata galā** hang by a thread

karatiesa nf = **kaŗatiesa**

karatist/s *nm*, **~e** *nf* karate expert

karāts *nm* carat

karavadonis *nm* = **kaŗavadonis**

karavāna *nf* caravan; convoy

karavela *nf* caravel

karavētra *nf* = **kaŗavētra**

karavīrs *nm* = **kaŗavīrs**

kāravs *nm* (cards) diamonds

kara ziņotājs *nm* = **kaŗa ziņotājs**

kārba *nf* box; canister

karbača *nf* a type of whip

karbamīds *nm* urea

karbamīnskābe *nf* carbamic acid

karbēns *nm* carbene

karbīds *nm* carbide

kārbiņa *nf dim* of **kārba**, small box

karbociklisks *adj* carbocyclic

karbohemoglobīns *nm* carbhemoglobin

karboksilāze *nf* carboxylase

karboksilgrupa *nf* carboxyl

karboksilskābe *nf* carboxylic acid

karbolinejs *nm* Carbolineum

karbols *nm* carbolic acid

karbolskābe *nf* carbolic acid, phenol

karbonācija *nf* carbonation

karbonāde *nf* pork chop; veal cutlet

karbonado *indecl nm* carbonado

karbonāri *nm pl* Carbonari

karbonātiezis *nm* carbonate rock

karbonātisks *adj* carbonate

karbonāts *nm* carbonate

karbonils *nm* carbonyl

karbonildzelzs *nf* carbonyl iron

karbonilgrupa *nf* carbonyl

karbonīts *nm* carbonite

karbonizācija *nf* carbonization

karbonizēt *vt* carbonize

karbonizēties *vr* become carbonized

karbons *nm* Carboniferous

karbonskābe *nf* carbonic acid

karborunds *nm* Carborundum

karbunkuls *nm* carbuncle

karburācija *nf* carburetion

karbur[a]tīvs [ā] *adj* carburetive

karbur[a]tormotors [ā] *nm* carburetor engine

karbur[a]tors [ā] *nm* carburetor

karburēšana *nf* carburization

karburēt *vt* **1.** carburet; **2.** carburize

kārbveida *indecl adj* box-shaped

kārbveidīgi *adv* like a box

kārbveidīgs *adj* box-shaped

karceris *nm* solitary confinement cell; lockup

kārciens *nm* croak

karcināt *vt* **1.** wriggle, twitch; **2.** tease

kārcināt *vi* caw

karcināties *vr* wriggle, twitch

karcinoloģija *nf* carcinology

karcinoma *nf* carcinoma

kārdabis *nm* pleasure lover

kardamonaugs *nm* cardamom (plant)

kardamons *nm* cardamom

kardāna gredzens *nm* Cardan suspension

kardāns *nm* Cardan, universal joint; gimbal

kardānsavienojums *nm* Cardan joint

kardānvārpsta *nf* Cardan shaft

karde *nf* card (comb)

kārdeklis *nm* temptation

kardigans *nm* cardigan

kārdinājums *nm* temptation

kardinālbīskaps *nm* cardinal bishop

kardināldekāns *nm* cardinal dean

kardināli *adv* cardinally

kardinālis or **kardināls** *nm* cardinal

kardināls *adj* cardinal

kardinālskaitlis *nm* cardinal number

kārdināšana *nf* temptation

kārdināt *vt* tempt

kārdinātāja *nf* temptress

kārdinātājs *nm* tempter

kārdinoši *adv* temptingly

kārdinošs *adj, part* of **kārdināt** tempting

kardiogr|a|fija [ā] *nf* cardiography

kardiogr|a|fs [ā] *nm* cardiograph

kardiogramma *nf* cardiogram

kardioīda *nf* cardioid

kardioķirur/gs *nm*, ~ģe *nf* heart surgeon

kardioķirurģija *nf* heart surgery

kardioķirurģisks *adj* pertaining to heart surgery

kardiolo/gs *nm*, ~ģe *nf* cardiologist

kardioloģija *nf* cardiology

kardioloģisks *adj* cardiologic

kardioskleroze *nf* hypertrophic cardiomyopathy

kardiospazma *nf* cardiospasm

kardiostimul|a|tors [ā] *nm* 1. pacemaker; 2. defibrillator

kardīts *nm* carditis

kardmašīna *nf* carding machine

kare *nf* (geol.) cirque

karē *indecl nm* (mil.) square

kāre I *nf* desire, craving

kāre II *nf* honeycomb

kareivīgi *adv* valiantly

kareivīgs *adj* 1. warlike, bellicose; 2. valiant, courageous

kareivīgums *nm* 1. bellicosity; 2. valor

kareivis *nm* 1. (mil.) private; 2. soldier; (fig.) fighter

kareiviski *adv* in a soldierly manner, in military fashion

kareivisks *adj* soldierly; military

kareiviskums *nm* soldierly demeanor, military stance

kārējs *nm* hangman

karek/lis *nm* 1. pendant; fob; tag; ~ļi a. (obs.) hinges; b. panicle; 2. clothes peg

kareklītis *nm dim* of **kareklis**, pendant

karel/is or karēl/is *nm*, ~iete *nf* Karelian

karenieks *nm* (obs.) soldier

karēns *nm* carene

kares ezers *nm* tarn

kārestība *nf* (obs.) desire, craving

karete *nf* loggerhead turtle

kargaitis *nm* = **kaŗgaitis**

kāri *adv* greedily, avidly

kari|a|t|ī|de [ā]|[i] *nf* caryatid

kārība *nf* desire, craving

Karibijas priede *nf* slash pine

kārībnieks *nm* pleasure lover

kāriens *nm* hang (on the horizontal bar)

kariess *nm* caries

kariete *nf* carriage, coach

kārīgi *adv* eagerly; covetously; greedily

kārīgs *adj* eager; desirous, covetous, greedy

kārīgums *nm* greed; craving

kārija *nf* hickory

karijs *nm* curry

karikatūra *nf* caricature; (political) cartoon

karikatūriski *adv* in a caricatural (or cartoonish) style

karikatūrisks *adj* caricatural, cartoonish

karikatūrist/s *nm*, ~e *nf* caricaturist; cartoonist

kariķējums *nm* caricature

kariķēt *vt* caricature

kariķēts *adj, part* of **kariķēt** exaggerated

kariljons *nm* carillon

karināmais *nom adj* hanger

karināt I *vt* hang

karināt II *vt* (reg.) tease

karināties *vr* hang out (of, from)

kariņš *nm dim* of **kaŗš**, little war

karioka *nf* carioca

karioloģija *nf* cytology of the nucleus

kariota *nf* Caryota

karioze *nf* caries

kariozs *adj* carious

kārīte *nf dim* of **kāre** II, honeycomb

karj[e]ra [ē] *nf* career

karj[e]risms [ē] *nm* careerism

karj[e]ristiski [ē] *adv* calculated to promote one's career

karj[e]ristisks [ē] *adj* pertaining to the furthering of one's career

karj[e]rist/s [ē] *nm* ~e *nf* careerist

karjers *nm* quarry

karkasmāja *nf* frame house

karkass *nm* **1.** framework, skeleton; **2.** nettle tree; hackberry

kārkāt *vi* croak

kārkaulis *nm* black-throated diver

kārklājs *nm* osiery

kārklaugi *nm pl* salices

kārklene *nf* aster

karkles *nf pl* fodder crib

kārkliens *nm* osiery

kārkliņ/š *nm dim* of **kārkls**, osier

kārkllapu spireja *nf* meadow-sweet

kārkls *nm* osier

kārklu ālants *nm* (reg.) (immature) ide

kārklu bruņuts *nf* scurfy scale

kārklu ķauķis *nm* grasshopper warbler

kārklu sisinātājs *nm* grasshopper warbler

kārkluvācietība *nf* (of a Latvian) pretense to be German

kārkluvāciet/is *nm*, ~e *nf* a Latvian pretending to be German

kārkluvācietisks *adj* pretending to be German, German-sounding

kārklu zvirbulis *nm* reed bunting

karkšķēt *vi* **1.** rattle in the throat; **2.** croak

kārkšķēt *vi* = **karkšķēt**

karkšķināt *vi* **1.** croak; **2.** rattle

karkšķis *nm* frog in the throat

kārkt *vi* **1.** croak; **2.** rattle in the throat

kārkulis *nm* mole cricket

kārlings *nm* (geol.) horn

karludovika *nf* Carludovica

karma *nf* karma

karmaņola *nf* carmagnole

karmelīt/s *nm* , ~e *nf* Carmelite

karmīns *nm* carmine

karmīnsarkans *adj* carmine red

karmīnskābe *nf* carminic acid

karmisks *adj* karmic

karnalits *nm* carnallite

karneols *nm* carnelian

kārnēt *vi* watch greedily; wait in vain

karnete *nf* carnet

karnevāliet/is *nm*, ~e *nf* carnival participant

karnevālisks *adj* carnivalesque

karnevāliskums *nm* carnivalesque character

karnevāls *nm* carnival

kārniņš *nm* roof tile

kārnis *nm* gray heron

kārnīt *vt* **1.** clean, tidy up; **2.** rummage; dig, scratch

kārnīties *vr* dig, scratch

karnitīns *nm* carnitine

karnivori *nm pl* carnivores

karnīze *nf* or **karnīzs** *nm* cornice

karnozīns *nm* carnosine

karns *adj* haggard, gaunt

kārns *adj* (reg.) haggard, gaunt

karnums *nm* haggardness, gauntness

karodziņš *nm* **1.** *dim* of **karogs**, small flag, pennant; **2.** (mus.) flag

karodznieks *nm* **1.** standard-bearer; **2.** flagman

karoga zvērasts *nm* (mil.) oath of allegiance

karogmasts *nm* flagpole

karognesēj/s *nm*, ~a *nf* standard-bearer

karogot *vt* decorate with flags

karog/s *nm* flag; banner; (naut.) ensign; standard; ~a augstums (dimension) hoist; ~a ga-rums (dimension) fly; k. pārvalkā cased colors; k. pusmastā flying the flag at half-mast

karojošs *adj, part* of **karot** = **karojošs**

karos[e]rija [ē] *nf* vehicle body

karot *vi* = **kaṟot**

kārot *vt* desire, crave

karotājs *nm* = **kaṟotājs**

karotāēa *nf* core sampling

karote *nf* **1.** spoon, ladle; **2.** spoonful

kāroties *vr* desire, want

karotinoīdi *nm pl* carotenoids

karotīns *nm* carotene

ka[ro]tīte [ṟ] *nf* **1.** *dim* of **karote**, little spoon, tea-spoon; **2.** scurvy grass

ka[r]otnes [ṟ] *nf pl* scurvy grass

karpa *nf* carp

kārpa *nf* **1.** wart; **2.** birthmark

kārpainais bērzs *nm* wart birch

kārpainais pūpēdis *nm* gemmed puffball

kārpainais segliņš *nm* a euonymus, Euonymus verrucosa

kārpainā pagraba piepe *nf* crust fungus

kārpains *adj* warty

kārpainums *nm* wartiness

Karpatu pulkstenīte *nf* a bellflower, Campanula carpatica

kārpiņa *nf* **1.** *dim* of **kārpa**, wart; **2.** = **garšas k., skaistuma k.**

kārpīt *vt* scrape, scratch; (of horses) paw

kārpīties *vr* **1.** scrape, scratch; **2.** wriggle; **k. pretī** (col.) resist; **3.** work hard at digging, hoeing, or tedding

karpoloģija *nf* carpology

karpoloģisks *adj* carpological

kārpu cūka *nf* wart hog

kārpu zāle *nf* celandine

kārpveida *indecl adj* wart-like

kārpveidīgs *adj* wart-like

karpveidīgs *adj* cyprinid

karre *nf* (geol.) Karren

kars *nm* (geol.) cirque

kārs *adj* greedy; avid; **k. uz saldumiem** he has a sweet tooth

kārsas *nf pl* cress

karsēj/s *nm*, ~a *nf* fan (fanatic)

kārsēj/s *nm*, ~a *nf* carder

karsēt *vt* heat

karsēties *vr* **1.** be heated; **2.** (fig.) fly off the handle

karsiens *nm* (col.) whipping

karsin *adv emph* of **karst**; **k. karsa** it got really hot

karsināt *vt* **1.** tease; **2.** warm, heat

karsonis *nm* fever

karst *vi* heat up, get hot

kārst *vt* card, comb

karstasinība *nf* hot-bloodedness; ardor

karstasinīgi *adv* ardently, passionately

karstasinīgs *adj* hot-blooded; ardent, passionate

karstdabīgi *adv* hotheadedly, impetuously

karstdabīgs *adj* hotheaded, impetuous

karstdab/is *nm*, ~e *nf* hothead

kārstekļi *nm pl* spider webs

karstgalvība *nf* hotheadedness, impetuosity

karstgalvīgi *adv* hotheadedly, impetuously

karstgalvīgs *adj* hotheaded, impetuous

karstgalv/is *nm*, ~e *nf* hothead

karstgriba *nf* desire, craving

karsti *adv* hotly; heatedly; torridly; ardently; fervidly, fervently

karstin *adv emph* of **karst** and **karsts**; **k. karsa** it was getting really hot; **k. karsts** very hot

kārstīt *vt* hang out; (of one's neck) crane, crane out

kārstīties *vr* hang out; (of one's neck) crane, crane out

karstmanis *nm* (col.) hothead

karstprātīgi *adv* hotheadedly, impetuously

karstprātīgs *adj* hotheaded, impetuous

karstputra *nm* (col.) hothead

karstputriņš *nm* (col.) hothead

karsts *adj* hot; heated; torrid; ardent; fervid, fervent

karsts *nm* (geol.) karst

kārsts *nm* drying rack for flax

karstulis *nm* (col.) hothead

karstumguļa *nf* fever

karstumizturība *nf* heat resistance

karstumizturīgs *adj* heat-resistant

karstumizturīgums *nm* heat resistance

karstum/s *nm* **1.** heat; **2.** also *pl* ~i fever

kārstuve *nf* **1.** carding mill; **2.** hackle, comber; **3.** strainer, milk filter

kārstuvis *nm* hackle, comber

karstvīns *nm* mulled wine

karš *nm* = **kaŗš**

kāršaudze *nf* young forest (at the time of thinning)

kāršroze *nf* hollyhock

kāršu licēja *nf* fortune-teller

kāršu mājiņa *nf* chart house

kāršu namiņš *nm* house of cards

kāršu parāds *nm* gambling debt

kāršu pupas *nf pl* string beans

kārt *vt* hang; **k. zobus vadzī** go hungry, tighten one's belt; **k. pie lielā zvana** proclaim to the world

kārt/a *nf* **1.** layer; stratum; ply; (brick) course; (knitting) row; **~u ~ām** one on top of another; **2.** (sequence; biol.) order; **pēc ~as** in order; (so many days) running; **pirmām ~ām** first of all; **galvenām ~ām** mainly; **3.** turn; **4.** ~ā in fashion; **administratīvā ~ā** administratively; **pie-spiedu ~ā** under compulsion; **steidzamā ~ā** urgently; **tādā ~ā** thus; **5.** (hist.) estate; social class; **6.** set of clothes; (col.) suit; **7.** (of competition) round; (of firearms fire) burst; **8.** (gram.) voice; **9.** (obs., gram.) gender; **10. būt ~ā** belong with, be one of (a class of people, young men, adults, women); **11.** position, condition, state

kartāgieši or **kartāģieši** *nm pl* Carthagians

kārtaini *adv* in layers

kārtainība *nf* stratification, layering

kārtains *adj* layered; foliated; stratiform

kārtainums *nm* stratification, layering

kārtājums *nm* second plowing

kārtākslis *nm* (anat.) psalterium, manyplies

kārtas skaitlenis *nm* ordinal number

kārtāt *vt* replow

kārtavnieks I *nm* hangman

kārtavnieks II *nm* card player

karte *nf* **1.** map; (naut.) chart; **sinoptiskā k.** weather chart; **~s ziemeļi** grid north; **2.** card

karteča *nf* **1.** case shot, canister shot; **2.** an early type of machine gun

kartečpielādēšana *nf* breech loading

kārtēj/s *adj,* usu. *defìn* ~ais **1.** regular; usual; recurrent; **2.** current

kartelēt *vt* form a cartel

kartelis *nm* cartel

kartelizācija *nf* formation of cartels

karteris *nm* crankcase

kartēt *vt* chart, map

kartēzietis *nm* **1.** Cartesian; **2.** Carthusian

Kartēzija nirējs *nm* Cartesian diver

karteziānisms *nm* Cartesianism

kartēzisms *nm* Cartesianism

kārtīb/a *nf* **1.** order; **kaut kas nav ~ā** something is wrong; **pie ~as!** order! order! **2.** procedure, course; **3.** custom; **4.** sequence

kārtības dienests *nm* military police service

kārtības rullis *nm* rules of ordera

kārtībassargs *nm* watchman

kārtības sods *nm* disciplinary punishment

kārtības tiesa *nf* (hist.) police court

kārtības traucēšan *nf* disorderly conduct, disturbance of the peace

kārtībnie/ks *nm,* ~ce *nf* (hist.) policeman

kārties *vr* **1.** hang oneself; **2.** hang; **k. kaklā** (col.) a. importune; b. (usu. of women) run after s.o.; **k. vai nost** (col.) work oneself ragged

kārtīgi *adv* really; thoroughly; decently

kārtīgs *adj* **1.** orderly, tidy; **2.** regular; **3.** true, real; **4.** thorough; **5.** decent, honest, respectable

kārtīgums *nm* **1.** orderliness, tidiness; **2.** regularity; **3.** decency, honesty, respectability

kartingist/s *nm*, ~**e** *nf* go-cart racer

kartings *nm* go-cart race

kārtiņa I (with **â**) *nf dim* of **kārta**, layer

kārtiņa II *nf dim* of **kārts** I and **kārts** II, small pole; little card

kartiņš *nm* (col.) potato

kartīte *nf* **1.** *dim* of **karte 2**, little card; **2.** card; postcard; **3.** ration booklet; **4.** snapshot

kārtne *nf* king-post (of a truss)

kārtni *adv* regularly

kārtnie/ks *nm*, ~**ce** *nf* corvée laborer

kārtns *adj* (gram.) regular

kartodiagramma *nf* cartogram

kartodroms *nm* go-cart track

kartografēt *vt* enter on a map

kartogr|a|fija [ā] *nf* cartography

kartogr|a|fiski [ā] *adv* cartographically

kartogr|a|fisks [ā] *adj* cartographic

kartogr|a|f/s [ā] *nm*, ~**e** *nf* cartographer

kartogramma *nf* cartogram

kārtojums *nm* **1.** arrangement, ordering; **2.** a dish consisting of layers of different products; strata

kartomantija *nf* cartomancy

kartonāēa *nf* cardboard articles

kartonāžist/s *nm*, ~**e** *nf* maker of cardboard articles

kartonējums *nm* cardboard binding

kartonēt *vt* bind in cardboard

kartonētāj/s *nm*, ~**a** *nf* **1.** bindery worker; **2.** maker of cardboard articles

kartons *nm* cardboard

kārtot I *vt* **1.** arrange, order; sort; **2.** take care of; (of debts) pay; **3.** regulate, control; **4. k. pār-baudījumus** take examinations

kārtot II *vi* (of weatherbeaten skin) become rough and peel

kartotēka *nf* card index; (loosely) records

kārtoties I *vr* **1.** groom oneself; tidy up; get ready; **2.** draw up, form; line up; **3.** get settled; **4.** get organized

kārtoties II *vr* become arranged in layers

kārtridžs *nm* (compu.) cartridge

karts *nm* go-cart

kārts I *nf* pole

kārts II *nf* card

kārtsgals *nm* end of a pole

kārtslecēj/s *nm*, ~**a** *nf* pole vaulter

kārtslekšana *nf* pole vaulting

kārtula *nf* rule

kartūns *nm* (obs.) calico

kartupelaine *nf* potato field

kartupelājs *nm* potato field (usu. a harvested one)

kartupe/lis *nm* potato; ~**ļi ar mizu** potatoes in their jackets

kartupelītis *nm dim* of **kartupelis**, small potato

kartupeļgrozs *nm* potato basket

kartupeļu biezenis *nm* mashed potatoes

kartupeļūdens *nm* water in which potatoes have been boiling

kartupeļu dēstāmā mašīna *nf* potato planter;

kartupeļu milti *nm pl* potato starch

kartupeļu nematode *nf* golden nematode

kartupeļu rokamā mašīna *nf* potato digger

kartupeļu sfinga *nf* death's-head hawk

kartupeļu vabole *nf* Colorado potato beetle

kartups *nm* (col.) potato

kartuša *nf* cartouche

kartveļi *nm pl* Kartvelians

karulis *nm* pendant; hanging ornament

kārul/is *nm*, ~**e** *nf* gourmand

karulītis *nm dim* of **karulis**, pendant

kārumēd/is *nm*, ~**e** *nf* gourmand

kārumiņš *nm dim* of **kārums**, tasty morsel, delicacy

kārumlaiža *nm* gourmand

kārumnie/ks *nm*, ~**ce** *nf* gourmand

kārums *nm* **1.** delicacy; **2.** craving; greed

karūsa *nf* crucian carp; see also **zelta k.**

karuselis *nm* merry-go-round

karuseļkrāsns *nm* rotary table oven

karuseļstends *nm* carousel

karuseļšūpoles *nf pl* Ferris wheel

karuseļveida *indecl adj* carousel-type

karuseļveidīgs *adj* carousel-type

karuseļvirpa *nf* vertical-turret lathe

karuseļvirpotājs *nm* operator of a vertical-turret lathe

karvakrols *nm* carvacrol

karvedis *nm* = **karvedis**

kārvele *nf* wild chervil

karvomentēns *nm* carvomenthene

karvotanacetons *nm* carvotanacetone

kārzob/is *nm*, ~e *nf* gourmand

ka[ŗ]a [r] akadēmija *nf* military academy

ka[ŗ]a [r] apgabals *nm* 1. military district; 2. theater of war

ka[ŗ]a [r] ārsts *nm* army surgeon; **galvenais k. ā.** surgeon general

ka[ŗ]a atlīdzinājumi *nm pl* war reparations

ka[ŗ]a [r] aviācija *nf* air force

ka[ŗ]ab[a]ze [r][ā] *nf* military base

ka[ŗ]a [r] biedrs *nm* comrade-in-arms

ka[ŗ]adarbība [r] *nf* military operations; hostilities; (nuclear, chemical, psychological) warfare; ~s apgabals war zone, theater of operations

ka[ŗ]adienest/s [r] *nm* military service; **aktīvais k.** active duty; **obligātais k.** mandatory service; ~am nederīgs unfit for military service, 4-F

ka[ŗ]adraudze [r] *nf* armed volunteer force

ka[ŗ]adraugs [r] *nm* (hist.) member of a prince's armed force

ka[ŗ]a [r] flote *nf* navy

ka[ŗ]agaitas [r] *nf pl* military duty

ka[ŗ]agājiens [r] *nm* campaign, military expedition

ka[ŗ]agūstekn/is [r] *nm*, ~e *nf* prisoner of war

ka[ŗ]a [r] iemesls *nm* casus belli

ka[ŗ]a [r] inval[i]ds [ī] *nm* disabled soldier

ka[ŗ]a [r] jūrnieks *nm* navy sailor;

ka[ŗ]akalps [r] *nm* (hist.) mercenary foot soldier

ka[ŗ]aklausība [r] *nf* compulsory military service

ka[ŗ]a [r] klausības apliecība *nf* 1. draft registration card; 2. record of service

ka[ŗ]a [r] klaušas *nf pl* wartime corvée

ka[ŗ]a [r] kūdītājs *nm* warmonger

ka[ŗ]akuģis [r] *nm* warship

ka[ŗ]akuģu [r] remontdarbnīca *nf* navy yard

ka[ŗ]akungs [r] *nm* warlord

ka[ŗ]alaiks [r] *nm* wartime

ka[ŗ]alauks [r] *nm* battlefield

ka[ŗ]a [r] laupījums *nm* spoils of war

ka[ŗ]alietas [r] *nf pl* military affairs; military science

ka[ŗ]a [r] likums *nm* martial law

ka[ŗ]amāksla [r] *nf* the art of warfare

ka[ŗ]amašīna [r] *nf* war machinery

ka[ŗ]amateriāli [r] *nm pl* war matériel

ka[ŗ]a [r] musinātājs *nm* warmonger

ka[ŗ] [r] nometne *nf* cantonment

ka[ŗ]a [r] noslēpums *nm* military secret

ka[ŗ]a [r] orķestris *nm* military band

ka[ŗ]a [r] osta *nf* naval base

ka[ŗ]a [r] prokurors *nm* judge advocate; **galvenais k. p.** judge advocate general

ka[ŗ]apūlis [r] *nm* (cont.) enemy forces

ka[ŗ]apulks [r] *nm* army

ka[ŗ]a [r] rags *nm* bugle

ka[ŗ]a [r] sauciens *nm* war cry

ka[ŗ]askola [r] *nf* military school

ka[ŗ]a [r] slimnīca *nf* military hospital

ka[ŗ]aspēks [r] *nm* army, forces, troops

ka[ŗ]aspēle [r] *nf* war game

ka[ŗ]astāvoklis [r] *nm* 1. martial law; 2. state of war

ka[ŗ]atiesa *nf* court martial

ka[ŗ]a [r] transporta kuģis *nm* troopship

ka[ŗ]avadonis [r] *nm* military commander

ka[ŗ]avētra [r] *nf* (poet.) winds of war

ka[ŗ]a [r] viltība *nf* stratagem

ka|r̦|avīrs |r̦| *nm* soldier; warrior; **bijis k.** war veteran; ex-serviceman; **demobilizēts k.** dischargee; **~u vilciens** military train

ka|r̦|a |r̦| ziņotājs *nm* war correspondent

ka|r̦|gaitis |r̦| *nm* (poet.) warrior

ka|r̦|ojošs |r̦| *adj, part* of **kar̦ot** militant; engaged in war, warring, fighting

ka|r̦|ot |r̦| *vi* wage war, fight

ka|r̦|otājs |r̦| *nm* fighter, warrior

ka|r̦|š |r̦| *nm* war; warfare; **bakterioloģiskais k.** germ warfare; **k. ēterā** jamming war; **īstais k.** shooting war; **kodoltermiskais k.** nuclear war; **ķīmiskais k.** chemical warfare; **lokāls k.** brush fire war; **~a a.** war; **b.** military; **~a vešana** prosecution of the war

ka|r̦|vedis |r̦| *nm* warlord

kas *pron* **1.** (interrogative) who; what; (relative) who; that; **2.** something; anything; **3.** emphasizes a word when placed between the word and its repetition: **tiesa k. tiesa** there is no denying the truth; **tēvs k. tēvs** spitting image of his father; **kungs k. kungs** a real lord; **k. par** a. what kind; b. (in rhetorical questions expressing surprise or admiration) what, what a; c. expresses irony in rhetorical questions that deny the fact stated (**k. nu viņš par . . .** he is no . . .); **k. par to?** what of it? **lai tur vai k.** no matter what; **lai k. tas arī nebūtu** whoever (or whatever) that may be; **k. tur par labumu?** what is the use of it? **k. nebūt** whoever; whatever; **k. nekas** this and that; **k. par to?** so what?

kasācija I *nf* (jur.) cassation, abrogation, nullification

kasācija II *nf* (mus.) cassation

kasācijas tiesa *nf* Court of Cassation, (highest) court of appeal

kasains *adj* (reg.) itchy

kāsalkoks *nm* guelder rose, snowball

kasandra *nf* leatherleaf, cassandra

kas|a|tor/s |ā| *nm*, **~e** *nf* appellant

kasba *nf* casbah

kase *nf* **1.** cash register; **2.** box office; cashier's office, cashier's window; checkout stand; **~s gabals** (col.) box office success; **3.** (bus.) fund, association; **4.** chest, treasury, coffer

kaseklis *nm* **1.** trowel; scraper; **2.** quarreler

kaseklīgs *adj* (col.) quarrelsome

kāsenis *nm* guelder rose

kases grāmata *nf* cash book

kases lodziņš *nm* cashier's window, ticket window

kases revīzija *nf* book audit

kases zīme *nf* voucher

kasēt *vt* (of money) collect

kāsēt *vi* cough

kasete *nf* **1.** casette; **2.** (photo.) plateholder; **3.** (ribbon) cartridge

kasetne *nf* (compu.) cartridge

kasīda *nf* qasida

kasier/is *nm*, **~e** *nf* **1.** cashier, teller; **2.** treasurer

kasīgs *adj* (col.) quarrelsome

kasijas koks *nm* senna

kasījums *nm* **1.** scratch; **2.** erasure

kasīklis *nm* scraper; backscratcher

kasiks *nm* cacique

kasiopejs *nm* lutetium

kasiopes *nf pl* Cassiope

kasis *nm* kneading trough scraper

kās/is *nm* hook ◊ **ar ~i velkams** inefficient

kāsīši *nm pl* columbine

kasīt *vt* **1.** scratch; **2.** scrape

kasiterīts *nm* cassiterite

kasīties *vr* **1.** scratch, scratch oneself; **2.** (col.) quarrel; **3.** (sl.) dawdle; hesitate

kāsītis *nm* **1.** *dim* of **kāsis**, hook; **2.** checkmark; **3.** haček, wedge

kaska *nf* helmet

kaskāde *nf* cascade

kaskadieris *nm* stunt man

kaskādveida *indecl adj* cascade-like

kaskādveidīgs *adj* cascade-like

kaskarilla *nf* cascarilla (bark)

kaskete *nf* cap

kasko *indecl nm* insurance on hull

kaslis *nm* (col.) quarreler

kasnis *nm* scraper

Kaspijas ronis *nm* Caspian seal

kaspins *nm* (reg.) silk headband

kāss *nm* cough

kast *vt* scratch

kāst *vt* filter, strain

kasta *nf* caste

kastanis *nm* chestnut; horse chestnut

kastaņa *nf* chestnut (tree)

kastaņbrūni *adv* in an auburn color

kastaņbrūns *adj* auburn

kastaņetas or kastaņetes *nf pl* castanets

kastaņkoks *nm* chestnut tree

kastaņkrāsa *nf* auburn color

kaste *nf* box; case; bin; (sl.) soccer goal

kastelāns *nm* castellan

kastels *nm* castelet; keep

kastete *nf* knuckle duster

kastigācija *nf* castigation

kastilejas *nf pl* Indian paint brush

kastīliet/is *nm*, ~e *nf* Castilian

kastiloa *indecl nf* Castilloa

kastings *nm* casting competition

kastīte *nf dim* of **kaste**, small box

kastoreļļa *nf* castor oil

kastorins *nm* castor

kastors *nm* beaver cloth

kastrācija *nf* castration

kastrāts *nm* 1. castrate; gelding; 2. castrato

kastrēt *vt* castrate; geld

kastrolis *nm* saucepan; casserole

kāstuve *nf* filter, strainer

kāstuvis *nm* filter, strainer

kastveida *indecl adj* boxlike

kastveidīgi *adv* like a box

kastveidīgs *adj* boxlike

Kasūbijas gundega *nf* a buttercup, Ranunculus
cassubicus

kāsulis *nm* 1. cough; 2. one that coughs;
consumptive

kasus *nm* itch, scabies

kāsus *nm* cough

kašalots *nm* sperm whale

kašāt *vt* (of chickens, birds) scratch, scrape

kašāties *vr* (of chickens, birds) scratch, scrape

kāšgalvji *nm pl* Acantocephala

kāši *nm pl* carrying yoke

kāškrusts *nm* swastika

kašķa ērce *nf* itch mite

kašķains *adj* scabby, mangy

kašķa mārciņa *nf, nm* (col.) quarrelsome
person

kašķene *nf* golden saxifrage

kašķēties *vr* (col.) squabble

kašķība *nf* quarrelsomeness, contentiousness

kašķīgi *adv* contentiously

kašķīgs *adj* quarrelsome, contentious

kašķīgums *nm* quarrelsomeness, contentiousness

kašķinieks *nm* (col.) quarrelsome person

kašķ/is *nm* 1. itch, scabies; scab; mange;
2. (col.) quarrelsome person; ~e *nf*;
3. quarrel, squabble

kāšļāt *vi* cough

kašmiriet/is *nm*, ~e *nf* Kashmirian

kašmirs *nm* cashmere

kašņāt *vt, vi* scratch, scrape; paw, claw; (of
dogs) dig

kašņāties *vr* scratch, scrape; paw; (of dogs)
dig

kašņātājs *nm* scratcher; (of animals) rasorial

kašpo *indecl nm* cache-pot, jardiniere

kašub/s *nm*, ~iete *nf* Kashube

kāšu stakle *nf* hook clincher

kāšveida *indecl adj* hook-shaped

kāšveidīgi *adv* like a hook, in the shape of a
hook

kāšveidīgs *adj* hook-shaped; (of joints) scarf

katabaze *nf* katabasis

katabolisms *nm* catabolism

kata|ch|rēze |h| *nf* catachresis
katafalks *nm* 1. catafalque; 2. hearse
katafor|e|ze |ē| *nf* cataphoresis
katafronte *nf* (meteor.) warm front
kātains *adj* stalky
kataklizma *nf* cataclysm
katakomba *nf* catacomb
katalān/is *nm*, ~iete *nf* Catalan
katalāze *nf* catalase
katal|e|kse |ē| *nf* catalexis
katal|e|ksija |ē| *nf* catalexis
katal|e|ktisks |ē| *adj* catalectic
katal|e|psija |ē| *nf* catalepsy
katal|e|ptisks |ē| *adj* cataleptic
katal|i|tisks |ī| *adj* catalytic
katalizācija *nf* catalysis
kataliz|a|tors |ā| *nm* catalyst; **negatīvs k.**
  inhibitor
katal|i|ze |ī| *nf* catalysis
katalizēt *vt* catalyze
katalogs *nm* catalog
kataloģizācija *nf* cataloging
kataloģizēt *vt* catalog
katalpa *nf* catalpa
katamarāns *nm* catamaran
katamnēze *nf* catamnesis
kataplazma *nf* poultice
kataplēkse *nf* cataplexy
katapulta *nf* catapult
katapultēt *vt* catapult
katapultēties *vr* catapult
katarakta *nf* = katarrakta
katarāls *adj* = katarrāls
katarrakta *nf* (waterfall; disease) cataract
kata|rr|āli |r| *adv* catarrhally
kata|rr|āls |r| *adj* catarrhal
kata|rr|s |r| *nm* catarrh
katars I *nm* = katarrs
katars II *nm* Cathar
katarse *nf* catharsis
katastaze *nf* catastasis
katastrofa *nf* 1. catastrophe; 2. wreck, crash

katastrofāli *adv* catastrophically
katastrofāls *adj* catastrophical
katastrofiski *adv* catastrophically
katastrofisks *adj* catastrophic; disastrous
katastrs *nm* = kadastrs
katatonija *nf* catatonia
katatoniski *adv* catatonically
katatonisks *adj* catatonic
Katavbes rododendrs *nm* Catawba rhododendron
kate|ch|ēts |h| *nm* catechist
kate|ch|ēze |h| *nf* catechesis
kate|ch|ins |h| *nm* catechin
kate|ch|isms |h| *nm* catechism
kate|ch|izēt |h| *vt* cathechize
kate|chu|m|ē|ns |hū||e| *nm* catechumen
katedra *nf* 1. lectern; rostrum; 2. (university)
  department
katedrāle *nf* cathedral
katedrālstikls *nm* cathedral glass
katedras vadītājs *nm* (university) department
  head
kat|e|gorija |ē| *nf* category; (sports) class
kat|e|goriski |ē| *adv* categorically; flatly;
  explicitly
kat|e|gorisks |ē| *adj* categorical; (of refusals)
  flat; (of orders) explicit
kat|e|goriskums |ē| *nm* categorical nature
kat|e|gorizēt |ē| *vt* categorize
katete *nf* (of right triangles) side adjacent to the
  right angle, leg
katetometrs *nm* cathetometer
katetrizācija *nf* catheterization
katetrizēt *vt* catheterize
katetrs *nm* catheter
katica *nf* a type of fish trap
kātiņš *nm* 1. *dim* of kāts, handle; stem; 2. splint
  (of a match); 3. (bot.) petiole; peduncle,
  fruitstalk; 4. part of the mitten below the
  thumb; 5. (of a musical note) stem
kationisks *adj* cationic
kationīts *nm* cation exchanger

kations *nm* cation

katjonisks *adj* = **kationisks**

katjonīts *nm* = **kationīts**

katjons *nm* = **kations**

katķisms *nm* catechism

katla āķis *nm* pothook; trammel

katlakmens *nm* scale, furring, boiler scale

katleja *nf* cattleya

katlenīte *nf* clustered bellflower

katliene *nf* (geol.) kettle

katlinieks *nm* 1. tinker; 2. boilermaker

katliņš *nm* 1. *dim* of **katls**, teakettle; 2. saucepan; 3. messkit; 4. derby hat

katlkalis *nm* boilermaker

katls *nm* 1. kettle; cauldron; 2. pot, saucepan; 3. boiler; 4. (mil.) pocket of resistance

katlu bungas *nf pl* kettledrum

katlu kalējs *nm* boilermaker

katlu labotājs *nm* tinker

katlumāja *nf* boiler house

katlutelpa *nf* boiler room

katlveida *indecl adj* kettle-shaped

katlveidīgs *adj* kettle-shaped

katoda tumšā josla *nf* cathode dark space, Crookes dark space

katodluminiscence *nf* cathodoluminescence

katods *nm* cathode

katodstari *nm pl* cathod rays

katodstaru lampa *nf* cathode ray tube

katolicisms *nm* Catholicism

katolikoss *nm* catholicos

katol/is *nm*, **~iete** *nf* Catholic

katoliski *adv* in a Catholic manner

katolisks *adj* Catholic

katolisms *nm* = **katolicisms**

katoļticība *nf* Catholicism

katoļticīg/ais *nom adj* Catholic; **~ā** *f*

katoļticīgs *adj* Catholic

katoptrika *nf* catoptrics

katoptrisks *adj* catoptric

katoptromantija *nf* catoptromancy

katordznie/ks *nm*, **~ce** *nf* convict serving at hard labor

katorga *nf* penal servitude, hard labor; (fig.) drudgery

kātot *vi* (col.) foot it

katrāds *adj* (reg.) different

katrgadējs *adj* yearly

katrpus *prep* on either side, on both sides, on each side

katrreiz *adv* every time, each time; **k. kad** whenever

katrreizējs *adj* 1. recurrent; 2. (of permits) non-reusable (requiring a new one each time)

katrs *pron* 1. every, each; 2. any

katrubrīd *adv* every time

kāts *nm* 1. handle, haft; 2. (bot.) stem, stalk; (of a column; of a feather) shaft; (of a nail) shank; 3. (com., cont.) leg

katsura *nf* katsura tree

katūns *nm* calico, chintz

kaucēj/s *nm*, **~a** *nf* howler

kauciens *nm* howl

kaucīgs *adj* (com.) weepy

kaucija *nf* security, caution money

kaucināt *vt* (com.) make cry

kaucoņa *nf* howling

kauč or **kaučču** *partic* = (col.) **kaut**

kaučuka funtūmija nf Lagos rubber

kaučuka koks *nm* rubber tree

kaučuka sula *nf* rubber latex

kaučukaugs *nm* rubber plant

kaučuks *nm* natural rubber

kaudāli *adv* caudally

kaudāls *adj* caudal

kaudi[lj]o [ļ] *indecl nm* caudillo

kaudz/e *nf* heap, pile, stack; **~ēm** heaps, piles, stacks of; **ar ~i** heaped, heaping

kauja *nf* battle; combat

kaujas apgabals *nm* combat zone

kaujas apmācība *nf* combat practice

kaujas atspere *nf* (small arms) hammer spring, (artillery) main spring

kaujas biedrs *nm* comrade-in-arms

kaujas darbība *nf* (military) action, combat operations

kaujas gars *nm* fighting spirit

kaujas gatavīb/a *nf* combat readiness; operational readiness; **k. ~ā** combat-ready, in fighting trim, ready for action

kaujas gāze *nf* war gas

kaujas izcilnis *nm* bolt camming lug

kaujas izkārtojums *nm* order of battle

kaujas izlidojums *nm* operational flight

kaujas kārtība *nf* battle formation

kaujas kuģis *nm* battleship

kaujas lauks *nm* battleground

kaujas lidmašīna *nf* warplane

kaujas nogurums *nm* combat fatigue

kaujas patrona *nf* ball ammunition, combat ammunition, live ammunition

kaujas rati *nm pl* chariot

kaujas sauciens *nm* battle cry

kaujasspēja *nf* combat effectiveness

kaujastērps *nm* combat gear

kaujas vienība *nf* combat unit

kaujaszobs *nm* (small arms) sear notch

kaujinieciski *adv* in combat-ready fashion

kaujiniecisks *adj* combat-ready; fighting; militant

kaujinieciskums *nm* combat readiness

kaujinieks *nm* combatant; fighter

kaujlauks *nm* (poet.) battlefield

kaujnieciski *adv* = **kaujinieciski**

kaujniecisk/s *adj* = **kaujiniecisks**

kaujnieciskums *nm* = **kaujinieciskums**

kaukainis *nm* (reg.) toad

kaukales *nf pl* bur parsley

kaukaļi *nm pl* corn cockle

kauk[a]ziet/is [ā] *nm*, **~iete** *nf* Caucasian

Kauk[a]zijas [ā] dzelzkoks *nm* ironwood

Kauk[a]zijas [ā] lilija *nf* Caucasian lily

Kauk[a]zijas [ā] plūme *nf* cherry plum, myrobalan

kaukoņa *nf* howling

kauksma *nf* howling

kaukt *vi* howl; yowl

kaukulis *nm* crybaby

kauķis *nm* zechstein

kaulainā *nom adj* (col.) death

kaulainis *nm* skin and bones

kaulains *adj* bony; (of a look, stare, in phrase **kaulaina acs**) baleful

kaulainums *nm* boniness

kaulājs *nm* skeleton

kaulaudi *nm pl* bone tissue

kaulaža *nf* (col.) skin and bones

kaulenājs *nm* stone bramble

kaulene *nf* 1. stone bramble plant or fruit; 2. dark-brown centipede

kaulenis *nm* 1. drupe; 2. drupaceous tree; 3. (col.) skin and bones

kauleņaugs *nm* drupaceous plant

kauleņkoks *nm* drupaceous tree

kaulēt *vt* pester for; bargain for

kaulēties *vr* 1. haggle, bargain; 2. pester

kaulgriezēj/s *nm*, **~a** *nf* bone carver

kauliflorija *nf* cauliflory

kauliņauglis *nm* stone fruit, drupe

kauliņ/š *nm* 1. *dim* of **kauls**, small bone; 2. (of fruit) stone, pit; 3. (dominoes) tile; (checkers) checker; (other games) man; 4. also **metamais k.** die; 5. (abacus) counter; **skaitāmie ~i** a. abacus; b. abacus counters; 6. (piano, typewriter) key

kaulkambaris *nm* 1. ossuary; 2. (col.) skin and bones

kaulmilti *nm pl* bone meal

kaulmuša *nf* 1. louse fly; 2. sheep ked

kaulradži *nm pl* Cervidae

kaulroze *nf* musk mallow

kaul/s *nm* bone; **~i un āda** skin and bones; **pa ~am** suitable (to one's ability); **līdz ~am** thoroughly, completely

kaulu eļļa *nf* bone oil

kaulu kambaris *nm* 1. ossuary; 2. (col.) skin and bones

kaulu kultūra *nf* bone age

kaulu līme *nf* bone glue

kaulu milti *nm pl* bone meal

kaula porcelāns *nm* bone china

kaulu roze *nf* osteomyelitis

kaulu sakne *nf* wall pepper

kaulu smadzenes *nf pl* bone marrow

kaulu zāle *nf* chickweed

kaulveida *indecl adj*

kaulveidīgi *adv* like a bone

kaulveidīgs *adj* bone-shaped, bone-like

kaulzivis *nf pl* bony fishes

kauna stabs *nm* pillory

kauna zīme *nf* stigma

kaundarīgi *adv* shamefully

kaundarīgs *adj* shameful

kaunelīgi *adv* = **kaunīgi**

kaunelīgs *adj* = **kaunīgs**

kaunēties *vr* **1.** feel ashamed, be ashamed; **kaunies!** for shame! **2.** feel shy, be bashful, be timid

kaunība *nf* shame; diffidence, bashfulness

kaunīgā mimoza *nf* = **kautrā mimoza**

kaunīgi *adv* bashfully, timidly, shyly

kaunīgs *adj* bashful, timid, shy

kaunīgums *nm* bashfulness, timidity, shyness

kauninājums *nm* shame

kaunināt *vt* shame

kaunīte *nf* sensitive plant

kaunpilns *adj* disgraceful, shameful

kaun/s *nm* **1.** shame; **man k.** I am ashamed; ~**a darbs** despicable act; ~**a gabals** (col.) shameless person; ~**a lieta** disgrace; (as an exclamation) it's a shame! ~**a traips** (fig.) blemish, stain; ~**a pilns** disgraceful, shameful ◊ **kā tev nav** ~**a!** shame on you! **taisni k.!** it's a shame! **k. pār visu ģīmi!** shame on you! ~**u apēdis** brazenly shameless; **ne** ~**a, ne labas dienas** poor both in possessions and character; **2.** dishonor; **3.** diffidence, shyness

kaunuma kalns *nm* pubic mound

kaunuma lūpas *nf pl* labiae

kaunuma uts *nf* crab louse

kaunums *nm* pubes, pubic area

kaupa *nf* long-tailed duck

kauperis *nm* = **kaupers**

kaupers *nm* (metall.) Cowper stove, Cowper blast furnace

kaupiņš *nm* (reg.) toad

kaupre *nf* hill; hillcrest; row of hills

kausainās alises *nf pl* yellow alyssum

kausa ķēde *nf* drag chain

kausējamība *nf* melting property

kausējums *nm* **1.** melt; smelt; **2.** alloy

kausenis *nm* crucible

kausēt I *vt* melt; smelt; (glass manufacture) found; thaw; (of cheese) a. melt; b. process; **k. taukus** render

kausēt II *vt* tire

kausētājs *nm* smelter; founder

kausētava *nf* foundry

kausiņš *nm* **1.** *dim* of **kauss**, cup, goblet; **2.** (bot.) calyx; **3.** (hist.) a small medieval silver coin, 1/240th of a mark

kauslapa *nf* sepal

kauslapiņa *nf dim* of **kauslapa**, sepal

kauslapu tofieldija *nf* false asphodel

kauslība *nf* pugnacity

kauslīgi *adv* pugnaciously

kauslīgs *adj* pugnacious

kauslīgums *nm* pugnacity

kausl/is *nm*, ~**e** *nf* pugnacious person, brawler

kauss I *nm* **1.** tankard; mug; (drinking, trophee) cup; goblet; **ceļojošais k.** challenge cup; **2.** ladle; **lejamais k.** foundry ladle, teeming ladle; **3.** (conveyor, excavator) bucket; **4.** (scale) pan; **5.** (bot.) calyx

kauss II *nm* nape, back of he neck

kausskrimslis *nm* (anat.) cervicale

kaust *vt* (reg.) scratch; dig

kaustava *nf* nape, back of the neck

kaustika *nf* (phys.) caustic surface

kaustisks *adj* caustic

kaustīt *vt* (col.) beat up

kaustuve *nf* nape, back of the neck

kausu primula *nf* Japanese primrose

kausveida *indecl adj* cup-shaped

kausveidīgi *adv* like a cup

kausveidīgs *adj* cup-shaped

kauša *nf* grommet

kaušana *nf* slaughter

kaušanās *nfr* fight

kaušļa *nm* (col.) brawler

kaut *vt* 1. slaughter; kill; kazas k. (col.) vomit; 2. (games: of cards, men) take; 3. (col.) whip

kaut *partic* 1. with a verb in the optative mood, emphasizes its meaning (k. viņš nāktu! if only he would come!); 2. used adverbially, emphasizes the meaning of a word and expresses a wish (mini k. vienu piemēru! give me just one example!); 3. *conj* (in optative clauses) that; (es ilgojos, k. lītu I wish that it would rain); 4. (in-troducing a conditional clause) if; 5. even; k. arī (or k. gan) even though; k. cik some, a little bit; somewhat; k. kā a. somehow; b. in any (odd) way; k. kad a. some time; b. at any time; k. kādi a. somehow; b. in any way; k. kāds a. some; b. any; k. kas a something; b. anything; k. kur a. somewhere; b. anywhere; k. kuŗš anybody; k. vai a. even if; b. at least; k. vien if only

kauties *vr* fight; fight with; fight against; battle; k. ar badu go hungry; k. ar bēdām fight off troubles

kautiņš *nm* brawl, fight, fray

kautķermenis *nm* carcass

kautra *nf,* also kautras *nf pl* revulsion

kautrā mimoza *nf* 1. sensitive plant; 2. touch-me-not

kautrēšanās *nfr* bashfulness, diffidence bez k. without ceremony; lūdzu, bez k.! don't stand on ceremony!

kautrēties *vr* be shy (in the presence of others); be hesitant

kautri *adv* shyly, self-consciously; coyly

kautrība *nf* shyness, self-consciousness, bashfulness; hesitancy

kautrīgi *adv* shyly, self-consciously; coyly

kautrīgs *adj* shy, self-conscious; coy

kautrīgums *nm* shyness, self-consciousness, bashfulness; hesitancy

kautrs *adj* shy, self-conscious; coy

kautrums *nm* shyness; self-consciousness; bashfulness; hesitancy

kautsvars *nm* dead weight (of a slaughtered animal)

kautuve *nf* slaughterhouse

kauzāli *adv* causally

kauz[a]litāte [ā] *nf* causality

kauzāls *adj* causal

kauzaļģija *nf* causalgia

kauz[a]tīvi [ā] *adv* causatively

kauz[a]tīvs [ā] *adj* causative

kava *nf* 1. deck of cards; 2. stack, pile, bunch, a number of

kāva *nf* battle

kavākslis *nm* (reg.) pugnacious person, brawler

kaval[e]rija [ē] *nf* cavalry

kaval[e]rists [ē] *nm* cavalryman

kavalier/is *nm* 1. cavalier; 2. gallant; escort; 3. boyfriend; 4. bearer of a decoration; ~e *nf*

kavaljero *indecl nm* caballero

kavaljers *nm* earth waste

kavalkāda or kavalkāde *nf* cavalcade

kavāt *vt* hit repeatedly

kavatīna *nf* cavatina

kavantīne *nf* cavatina

kāvēj/s *nm,* ~a *nf* 1. slayer; 2. slaughterer, butcher

kavējums *nm* 1. delay; 2. absence, nonattendance

kavēklis *nm* hindrance; obstacle

kavents *nm* guarantor

kaverna *nf* (med.) cavity (in the lungs)
kavernozs *adj* cavernous
kaverversija *nf* (mus.) cover version
kavēšana *nf* 1. delaying; 2. hindering; 3. (physiol.) inhibition
kavēšanās *nfr* delay; bez k. without delay, immediately
kavēt *vt* 1. hinder; 2. delay; 3. be late; 4. miss, be absent (from work, school); 5. (of time) waste, kill; k. (kādam) laiku entertain
kavētājs *nm*, ~a *nf* 1. hinderer; 2. shirker; 3. truant
kavēties *vr* 1. linger, stay; 2. hesitate; 3. postpone; 4. be late; be behind schedule; 5. spend time; 6. (with ar, obs.) play
kāvi *nm pl* northern lights
kaviārs *nm* caviar; graudainais k. soft caviar
kāviens *nm* 1. beating; 2. whipping; 3. (card games) trick
kaviļa *nf* feather grass
kavitācija *nf* cavitation
kāvulis *nm* (col.) brawler
kāvums *nm* number (of farm animals) slaughtered
kaza *nf* 1. goat; 2. nanny goat
kazāboliņš *nm* cytisus, broom
kazaciene *nf* (hist.) a court messenger's wife
kazaciete *nf* a Cossack's wife; a Cossack's daughter
kazačoks *nm* a Cossack dance
kazāda *nf* goatskin
kazahs *nm*, ~iete *nf* Kazakh
kaza/ks *nm*, ~ciete *nf* Cossack; (hist.) court messenger
kazaku paeglis *nm* savin
kazanova *nm* Casanova
kazapiņi *nm pl* 1. black bindweed; 2. field bindweed; 3. hedge bindweed
kazarka *nf* ruddy shelduck
kazarm/a *nf* barracks; (RR) line inspector's house; ~u territorija cantonment area

kāzas *nf pl* wedding; zelta k. golden anniversary
kazaskāja *nf* a cigarette rolled in newsprint
kazaslapas *nf pl* plantain
kazbārdiņa *nf* goatee
kazbārdis *nm* (bot.) goatsbeard
kazbuks *nm* billy goat
kaze *nf* (zool.) zieg
kazeīns *nm* casein
kazemāts *nm* casemate
kazenāji *nm pl* 1. dewberry; 2. alder buckthorn; 3. guelder rose
kazenājs *nm* 1. dewberry; 2. dewberry patch
kazenāju roze *nf* willow herb
kazene *nf* 1. dewberry; 2. blackberry; 3. buckthorn
kazi *partic* (obs.) maybe
kazīls *nm* columbine
kāzinie/ks *nm*, ~ce *nf* wedding guest
kaz[i]no [ī] *indecl nm* casino
kaziņa *nf* 1. *dim* of kaza; 2. connecting rod of a spinning wheel
kazisks *adj* goatlike; goatish
kazīši *nm pl* meadow rue
kazkājas *nf pl* goutweed
kazkopība *nf* goat farming
kazkop/is *nm*, ~e *nf* goat farmer
kazlape *nf* honeysuckle
kazlapis *nm* honeysuckle
kazlēns *nm* kid
kazot *vt* whip
kāzot *vi* celebrate a wedding
kāzoties *vr* celebrate a wedding
kazrags *nm* (reg.) stickleback
kazroze *nf* willow herb, fireweed
kazrožu sfings *nm* elephant hawk moth
kazuāls *adj* casual, fortuitous
kazuarīns *nm* casuarina
kazuārs *nm* cassowary
kazu bārda *nf* coral mushroom
kāzu ceļojums *nm* honeymoon trip
kazu griķi *nm pl* bindweed

kazuistika *nf* casuistry
kazuistiski *adv* casuistically
kazuistisks *adj* casuistic
kazuists *nm* casuist
kazu krēsliņi *nm pl* (bot.) lady's mantle
kazu ķiploki *nm pl* ransom
kazu lēpe *nf* scabious
kazulis *nm* corn spurry
kazupis *nm* buckthorn
kazu sieriņš *nm* dwarf mallow
kazu siers *nm* (bot.) shepherd's purse
kāzuss *nm* 1. casus fortuitus; accident; 2. (jur.)
    case
kazu vītols *nm* goat willow
kazu zāle *nf* lady's-mantle
kazvija *nf* field bindweed
kažociņš *nm dim* of kažoks, short fur coat
kažocniecība *nf* furriery
kažocnieks *nm* furrier
kaēokāda *nf* fur
kažokādu izstrādājumi *nm pl* furriery goods
kažokādu tirgotājs *nm* furrier
kažokādu zvēri *nm pl* fur-bearing animals
kažokcepure *nf* fur hat
kažokjaka *nf* fur jacket
kažokmētelis *nm* fur coat
kažokots *adj* fur-coated
kažoks *nm* 1. fur; 2. fur coat
kažoku kode *nf* casemaking clothes moth
kažokveste *nf* fur vest
kažokzvērs *nm* fur-bearing animal
kea *nf* kea
kebračo *indecl nm* quebracho
kebs *nm* cab
kečs I *nm* catch-as-catch-can
kečs II *nm* ketch
kečups *nm* ketchup
kedas *nf pl* (a type of sports shoe) Keds
kedīvs *nm* khedive
kefale *nf* mullet
kefalometrija *nf* cephalometry
kefalometrs *nm* cephalometer

kefīrs *nm* kefir
keikvoks *nm* cakewalk
keinsisms *nm* Keynesianism
kejs *nm* (billiard) cue
kēkss *nm* cake
kelerijas *nf pl* Koeler's grass
kelo[i]ds [ī] *nm* keloid
kelreiterija *nf* goldenrain tree
kelvins *nm* Kelvin
kembrijs *nm* Cambrian (period)
kempings *nm* summer camp; automotive
    campground
kēms *nm* kame
kenafa *nf* gambo hemp
kendira *nf* dogbane
kendo *indecl nm* kendo
kenijiet/is *nm*, ~e *nf* Kenyan
keninghemija *nf* Cunninghamia
kenjiet/is *nm*, ~e *nf* Kenyan
kenofobija *nf* cenophobia
kenotafs *nm* cenotaph
kentijas *nf pl* Kentia
kenotrons *nm* kenotron
kentaurs *nm* centaur
kentumvalodas *nf pl* centum languages
keramika *nf* ceramics; porainas masas k.
    earthenware
keramikas izstrādājumi *nm pl* pottery; stone-
    ware; earthenware
keramiķis *nm*, ~e *nf* ceramist
keramiski *adv* ceramically
keramisks *adj* ceramic
keramzītbetons *nm* ceramic aggregate
keramzīts *nm* bloated clay
keratīns *nm* keratin
keratīts *nm* keratitis
keratoze *nf* keratosis
keriblūterjers *nm* Kerry Blue Terrier
kerija *nf* kerria
kerlings *nm* curling (game)
kermess *nm* kermes
kermeki *nm pl* thrift

kerners *nm* **1.** center punch; **2.** (col.) corner kick

kernēt *vt* mark with a punch

kerns *nm* core sample

keromantija *nf* ceromancy

keroplastika *nf* ceroplastics

kesona slimība *nf* caisson disease, bends

kesons *nm* **1.** caisson; **2.** (arch.) coffer

kešatmiņa *nf* (compu.) cache memory

kešjukoks *nm* cashew

kešjurieksts *nm* cashew nut

keta *nf* dog salmon

ketas kaviārs *nm* red caviar

ketaveja *nf* cutaway coat

ketazīns *nm* ketazine

ketelerijas *nf pl* Keteleeria

ketelēt *vt* chain-stitch

ketēns *nm* ketene

ketgats or **ketguts** *nm* catgut

ketlasis *nm* = **keta**

ketoheksoze *nf* ketohexose

ketons *nm* ketone

ketoze *nf* ketosis

kets *nm* catboat

kēt/s *nm*, **~iete** *nf* Ket

khmer/s *nm*, **~iete** *nf* Khmer

kiangs *nm* kiang

kianīts *nm* cyanite

kianti *indecl nm* Chianti

kibernētika *nf* cybernetics

kibernētiķ/is *nm*, **~e** *nf* cyberneticist

kibernētiski *adv* cybernetically

kibernētisks *adj* cybernetic

kibern|e|tizēt [ē] *vt* introduce cybernetic guidance systems

kibitka *nf* kibitka

kiborgs *nm* cyborg

kibucs *nm* kibbutz

kičīgs *adj* kitschy

kičs *nm* kitsch

kidnapers or **kidnepers** *nm* kidnapper

kidnapings or **kidnepings** *nm* kidnapping

kifoze *nf* kyphosis

kija *nf* (billiards) cue

kikbokss *nm* kickboxing

kikerigā, kikerigī, kikerigū or **kikerikī** *interj* cock-a-doodle-doo

kikstarteris *nm* kick starter

kiligunda *nf* (hist.) armed volunteer force in Estonia and Courland

kilikijs *nm* kylix

kiliks *nm* kylix

kilo I *indecl nm* kilo

kilo II *indecl nm* (canned) sprat

kiloampērs *nm* kiloampere

kilobaits *nm* kilobyte

kilocikls *nm* kilocycle

kilogrammetrs *nm* kilogram-meter

kilograms *nm* kilogram

kilohercs *nm* kilohertz

kilokalorija *nf* kilocalorie

kilolitrs *nm* kiloliter

kilometrāža *nf* mileage

kilometrs *nm* kilometer

kilooms *nm* kiloohm

kiloparseks *nm* kiloparsec

kilotonna *nf* kiloton

kilovats *nm* kilowatt

kilovatstunda *nf* kilowatt-hour

kilovoltampērs *nm* kilovolt-ampere

kilovoltampērstunda *nf* kilovolt-ampere hour

kilovolts *nm* kilovolt

kilvaters *nm* (naut.) wake

kimberlīts *nm* kimberline

kimbri *nm pl* Cimbri

kimogr|a|fs [ā] *nm* kymograph

kimono *indecl nm* kimono

kimri *nm pl* Cymry

kin|e|mātika [ē] *nf* kinematics

kin|e|mātiski [ē] *adv* kinematically

kin|e|mātisks [ē] *adj* kinematic

kin|e|matogr|ā|fija [ē]|a] *nf* cinematography

kin|e|matogr|ā|fiski [ē]|a] *adv* cinematographically

kin|e|matogr|ā|fisks |ē||a| *adj* cinematographic; cinematic

kin|e|matogr|ā|fiskums |ē||a| *nm* cinematic quality

kin|e|matogr|ā|fisms |ē||a| *nm* cinematic quality

kin|e|matogr|ā|fist/s |ē||a| *nm*, ~e *nf* cinematographer

kin|e|matogr|ā|fs |ē||a| *nm* cinema

kin|e|skops |ē| *nm* kinescope, CRT screen

kin|e|stēze |ē| *nf* kinesthesis

kin|e|stēziski |ē| *adv* kinesthetically

kin|e|stēzisks |ē| *adj* kinesthetic

kinētika *nf* kinetics

kinētiski *adv* kinetically

kinētisks *adj* kinetic

kinētostatika *nf* dynamic force analysis

kin|e|toze |ē| *nf* motion sickness

kinēzika *nf* kinesics

kingstons *nm* (naut.) kingston

kiniķi *nm pl* Cynics

kinkāns *nm* kumquat

kino *indecl nm* 1. cinema; the movies; 2. movie theater

kinoaktieris *nm* screen actor

kinoaktrise *nf* screen actress

kinoalmana|ch|s |h| *nm* feature-length film made of related shorts

kinoamatier/is *nm*, ~e *nf* amateur cinematographer

kinoamatierisms *nm* amateur cinematography

kinoaparāts *nm* 1. movie camera; 2. film projector

kinoapar|a|tūra |ā| *nf* filmmaking equipment

kinoapmeklētāj/s *nm*, ~a *nf* moviegoer

kinoapraksts *nm* short documentary

kinoateljē *indecl nm* film studio

kinobiļete *nf* movie theater ticket

kino|ch|ronika |h| *nf* newsreel

kinodarbinie/ks *nm*, ~ce *nf* film industry worker

kinodarbs *nm* film

kinodirekcija *nf* (Soviet) regional film distribution center

kinodokumentālistika *nf* documentary filmmaking

kinodokumentālist/s *nm*, ~e *nf* producer of documentaries

kinodokuments *nm* documentary film

kinodrāma *nf* screenplay

kinodr|a|matur/gs |ā| *nm*, ~ģe *nf* screenwriter

kinodr|a|maturģija |ā| *nf* writing for the screen

kinoekrāns *nm* film screen

kinoepopeja *nf* movie epic

kinofabrika *nf* (obs., Soviet Union) film studio

kinofestivāls *nm* film festival

kinoficēt *vt* equip with facilities for showing films; adapt (a location) for showing films

kinofikācija *nf* spread of facilities for showing films; adaptation for showing films

kinofilma *nf* motion picture

kinofoto *indecl adj* of film and photography

kinofotolaboratorija *nf* photographic lab

kinofotorūpniecība *nf* photographic materials in-dustry

kinogramma *nf* film recording

kinoiekārta *nf* film projector

kinoieraksts *nm* film recording

kinoizmēģinājums *nm* screen test

kinoiznomāšana *nf* film rental

kinoizrāde *nf* (film) show

kinokadrs *nm* film frame, still

kinokamera *nf* film camera

kinoklasika *nf* film classics

kinokomēdija *nf* comedy film

kinokompoz|i|cija |ī| *nf* cinematic composition

kinokoncertzāle *nf* movie and concert theater

kinokritika *nf* film critique

kinokritiķ/is *nm*, ~e *nf* film critic

kinolekcija *nf* film lecture

kinolektorijs *nm* **1.** film series, film lecture serties; **2.** lecture series on cinematography; **3.** lec-ture/film hall

kinolente *nf* film

kinolo/gs *nm*, **~ģe** *nf* cynologist

kinoloģija *nf* cynology

kinoloģisks *adj* cynological

kinoloma *nf* movie role

kinomāksla *nf* cinematic art

kinomākslinie/ks *nm*, **~ce** *nf* **1.** movie actor (act-ress); **2.** cinematographer

kinome|cha|niķ/is [hā] *nm*, **~e** *nf* cinema operator

kinomūzika *nf* motion picture music

kinonams *nm* movie house

kinoobjektīvs *nm* film camera lens

kinooper|a|tor/s [ā] *nm*, **~e** *nf* cameraman

kinopanorāma *nf* wide-screen film

kinoproducent/s *nm*, **~e** *nf* film producer

kinoprodukcija *nf* film production

kinoprojekcija *nf* film projection

kinoprojektors *nm* film projector

kinopublicistika *nf* filming of newsreels

kinopublicist/s *nm*, **~e** *nf* newsreel journalist

kinoražošana *nf* film production

kinoreklāma *nf* cinema advertisement, com-mercial

kinorepertuārs *nm* cinema repertory

kinoreportāža *nf* film reporting

kinoreēisor/s *nm*, **~e** *nf* film director

kinorūpniecība *nf* film industry

kinoscenārijs *nm* script

kinoscenārists *nm*, **~e** *nf* screenwriter

kinoseanss *nm* show, showing of a film

kinostudija *nf* film studio

kinoteātris *nm* movie house

kinote|ch|nika [h] *nf* filmmaking

kinote|ch|nisks [h] *adj* filmmaking

kinouzņēmums *nm* film frame, still

kinovaloda *nf* cinematic language

kinovarone *nf* movie heroine

kinovaronis *nm* movie hero

kinovēsture *nf* history of moviemaking

kinovēsturnie/ks *nm*, **~ce** *nf* cinematic his-torian

kinozāle *nf* movie theater

kinozinātne *nf* cinematography

kinozinātnie/ks *nm*, **~ce** *nf* cinematographer

kinozvaigzne *nf* movie star

kinožanrs *nm* film genre

kinožurnālistika *nf* filming of newsreels

kinožurnālist/s *nm*, **~e** *nf* newsreel journalist

kinožurnāls *nm* newsreel

kinžals *nm* dagger

kiosciņš *nm dim* of **kiosks**, kiosk, newsstand

kiosknieks *nm* newsstand vendor

kiosks *nm* kiosk, newsstand

kiprēgelis *nm* telescope alidade

kirase *nf* cuirass

kirasieris *nm* cuirassier

Kirchhofa likums *nm* Kirchoff's law

kirē *indecl nm* curé

kirēnieši *nm pl* Cyrenaics

kirg[i]z/s [ī] *nm*, **~iete** *nf* Kirghiz

kirī *indecl nm* curie

kirijs *nm* curium

kiri|l|ica [ll] *nf* Cyrillic alphabet

kiri|l|isks [ll] *adj* Cyrillic

kirmašas *nf pl* kermis

kirtometrs *nm* cyrtometer

kirza *nf* kersey

kirzāda *nf* kersey

kīselgūrs *nm* kieselguhr

kišlaks *nm* (village in central Asia) kishlak

kišmišs *nm* sultana (raisins)

kitaibelijas *nf pl* Kitaibelia

kit|a|ra [ā] *nf* cithara

kivete *nf* tray, bath

kivi *nm indecl* kiwi

kizils *nm* cornelian cherry

klaba *nf* clatter

klabačas *nf pl* (reg.) clogs

klabačot *vi* clatter, rattle

klabarkaste *nf* (col.) **1.** jalopy; **2.** chatterbox

klabata *nf* 1. (also *pl* ~s) clapper; 2. chatterbox
klabatiņa *nf dim* of **klabata**; clapper; chatterbox
klabeklis *nm* clapper
klaberjakts *nf* (barb.) hullabaloo
klabēt *vi* 1. rattlle, clatter, (of teeth) chatter;
2. (com., fig. for talk) rattle, chatter; 3. clop
klabiens *nm* knock; clop
klabiķis *nm* (col.) chatterbox
klabināt *vt, vi* clatter, rattle, knock, rap; click
away (on a typewriter); **k. muti** (com.)
shoot off one's mouth, rattle; **k. zobus**
chatter
klabināties *vr* rattle; (fig.) chatter
klabis *nm* (col.) chatterbox
klaboņa *nf* clatter, rattle
klabstēt *vi* clatter
klabu, klabu *interj* clip-clop
klaburčūska *nf* rattlesnake
klaburis *nm* clapper, rattle
klaburot *vi* stumble
klaburs *nm* clapper, rattle
klačas *nf pl* (col.) gossip
klačīgs *adj* gossipy
klačot *vi* (col.) gossip
klačotāj/s *nm*, ~a *nf* gossip, gossipy person
klačoties *vr* (col.) gossip
klačpastala *nf* (com.) gossip, gossipy woman
klaču bāba *nf* (com.) gossip, gossipy woman
klade *nf* notebook; **vaļēju lapu k.** looseleaf
binder
klādināt *vt* spread
Kladnija figūras *nf pl* Chladni figures
kladonija *nf* reindeer moss
kladzināt *vi, vt* 1. cackle; 2. prattle
klaid/a *nf* 1. mistake; 2. drifter; 3. marauding
dog; 4. exile; 5. expanse; ~**u** ~**ām** (of
scattering) widely, helter-skelter
klaidēt *vt* disperse
klaidiens *nm* expanse
klaidīgi *adv* ramblingly

klaidīgs *adj* rambling
klaidīt I *vt* disperse
klaidīt II *vi* wander
klaidīties *vr* wander
klaidonība *nf* vagrancy
klaidonīgi *adv* vagrantly
klaidonīgs *adj* vagrant
klaido/nis *nm*, ~**ne** *nf* vagrant, hobo
klaidoņa *nf, nm* drifter
klaidot *vi* wander
klaidotāj/s *nm*, ~**a** *nf* wanderer
klaids *nm* 1. expanse; 2. spread
klaids *adj* 1. fluid, changing, indefinite , loose;
2. dispersed
klaidstrāva *nf* (el.) drift current
klaidu *indecl adj* = **klaids**
klaidu *adv* back and forth, all over; freely,
loosely
klaidulis *nm* drifter
klaidums *nm* expanse
klaigalēt *vi* shout, clamor
klaiga *nf* 1. shouter, clamorer, crier; 2. shouting,
clamor
klaigas *nf pl* shouting, clamor
klaigāt *vi* shout, clamor
klaigātāj/s *nm*, ~**a** *nf* shouter
klaigonis *nm* crier
klaigulīgs *adj* given to shouting
klaigulis *nm* shouter
klaiņa *nm, nf* tramp
klaiņāt *v* 1. *vi* ramble, tramp; 2. *vt* disperse
klaiņflote *nf* tramp fleet
klaiņojums *nm* wanderings
klaiņot *vi* ramble, rove, tramp
klaiņotājs *nm*, ~**a** *nf* rambler, rover, tramp
klaipa gals *nm* heel of a loaf
klaipu bedre *nf* (metall.) pig bed
klaips *nm* 1. loaf of bread; 2. (iron) pig;
(aluminum) ingot
klaitonija *nf* claytonia
klaja *nf* plain; open fields

klajā *adv* in the open; see **laist klajā**, **nākt klajā**

klāja liekums *nm* (naut.) **gareniskais k. l.** sheer; **šķērsais k. l.** camber

klāja nams *nm* deck house;

klajāns *nm* buzzard

klāja stringers *nm* deck stringer

klājbalsts *nm* (naut.) stanchion

klājdūriens *nm* filling stitches; satin stitches

klājeniski *adv* flat

klājenisks *adj* (of a trajectory) flat; (bot.) recumbent

klaji *adv* openly, frankly

klājiens *nm* **1.** spread; layer; things or material spread out; **2.** grain laid out for threshing; spread-out flax

klajoties *vr* (of the sky) clear

klajotne *nf* open field

klajs *nm* open terrain; expanse, spread

klājs *nm* **1.** deck; **apakšējais k.** lower deck; **augšējais k.** upper deck; **pakaļējais k.** poop deck; **2.** spread; layer; things or material spread out; **3.** open space, range

klaj/š *adj* **1.** (of terrain) open; **~ā laukā** in the open; **zem ~ām debesīm** a. in the open; b. (with **dzīvot**) be homeless; **2.** frank; (of lies) flat

klājuguns *nf* flat (trajectory) fire

klajumains *adj* (of terrain) having open spaces

klajums *nm* open space, range

klājums *nm* layer; coating; covering; facing

klakstēt *vi* click

klakš *interj* click

klakšķēt *vi* click

klakšķiens *nm* click

klakšķināt *vt* click, make click

klakšķināties *vr* (*iter*) click

klakšķis *nm* click

klakt *interj* click

klaķieris *nm* claqueur

klamba *nm* galoot

klambars I *nm* **1.** hair clip; **2.** clasp; **3.** (reg.) clothespin

klambars II *nm* (reg.) **1.** nag; **2.** lumbering person

klambāt *vi* stump, clump, lumber

klamburkāja *nf, nm* (col.) bow-legged person

klamburot *vi* stump, clump, lumber

klamburs *nm* **1.** hair clip; **2.** clasp; **3.** (reg.) clothespin

klampa I *nf* (naut.) cleat

klampa II *nf* hunk

klamsāt *vt, vi* (reg.) eat

klamsts *nm* (col.) gabber, chatterer

klamza *nf, nm* (col.) **1.** nag; **2.** lumbering person

klamzaks *nm* clumsy person, lubber

klamzāt *vi* (col.) lumber

klamzīgs *adj* clumsy

klancis *nm* hunk

klandi *nm pl* clickety-clack, banging

klandoņa *nf* clickety-clack, banging

klandēt *vi* rattle, knock, bang (rhythmically)

klandīties *vr* **1.** (of boats) rock; **2.** (com., usu. with **apkārt**) gad about; **3.** rattle, knock, bang (rhythmically)

klāni *nm pl* marshy meadows; wetlands

klanīgi *adv* obsequiously

klanīgs *adj* obsequious

klaniņa *nf* connecting rod of a spinning wheel

klanis *nm* (mech.) connecting rod

klānis *nm* quantity, spread; (of clouds) bank

klanīšanās *nfr* bowing; (naut.) pitching

klanīt *vt* (of head) nod; bow repeatedly; sway; pump

klanīties *vr* bow; sway; (naut.) pitch

klankstēt *vi* **1.** glug; **2.** (col.) bark

klankšķēt *vi* **1.** glug; **2.** (col.) bark

klankšķināt *v* **1.** *vt* slosh; **2.** *vi* glug

klankšķināties *vr* **1.** slosh; **2.** glug

klankšķis *nm* gurgle

klans I *nm* puddle

klans II *nm* clan

klāns *nm* See klāni

klaņa dakša *nf* crosstail butt of connecting rod

klāņains *adj* (reg., of the growth of crops) uneven

klaņa pirksts *nm* wrist pin, piston pin

klaņķis *nm* (reg.) grey heron

klap *interj*, usu. klap, klap clop-clop; knock-knock

klapata *nf* (barb.) trouble, inconvenience

klapatāt *vi* (barb.) take care of, see to, procure, provide

klapatāties *vr* busy oneself, bustle about; take care of

klape *nf* (com.) lid, flap

klaperis *nm* door knocker

klapēt *vi* 1. knock, tap; 2. pat; 3. clap; k. ar ausīm (col.) ignore

klapkanna *nf* tankard

klapstēt *vi* (col.) 1. bark; 2. blab

klarēns *nm* clarain

klārēt *v* 1. *vi* (sl.) expatiate; 2. *vi* (col.) refine

klarise *nf* Poor Clare

klarkija *nf* clarkia

klarnete *nf* clarinet

klarnetist/s *nm*, ~e *nf* clarinetist

klārs *adj* (sl.) clear

klase *nf* 1. (educ.) grade (year); 2. (educ.) class; classroom; 3. class, category; (naut.) classification

klases *nf pl* hopscotch

klases audzinātāja *nf* homeroom teacher

klasesbiedr/s *nm*, ~e *nf* classmate

klases darbs *nm* 1. classwork; 2. test

klases vecākais *nm* monitor

klases žurnāls *nm* classbook

klasicisms *nm* classicism

klasicistiski *adv* classicistically

klasicistisks *adj* classicistic

klasicist/s *nm*, ~e *nf* classicist

klasificēt *vt* classify

klasifikācija *nf* classification

klasifik[a]tor/s [ā] *nm* 1. classifier; ~e *nf*; 2. classification; 3. sorter; 4. ~i classificatory kinship terms

klasika *nf* classics, classical works

klasiķ/is *nm*, ~e *nf* 1. classic; 2. classicist

klasiski *adv* classically

klasisk/s *adj* 1. classic; 2. classical; 3. (of wrestling style) Greek-Roman

klasiskums *nm* classicality

klasteris *nm* = klasters

klasters *nm* (tech.) cluster

klastisks *adj* clastic

klāstīt *vt* 1. expatiate; expound; 2. spread

klāsts *nm* 1. display; collection; 2. account; 3. flooring

klāt *vt* 1. spread; k. galdu set the table; k. gultu make the bed; k. vaļā (or laukā) (col.) tell everything, unburden oneself; lay it on the line; 2. cover; 3. strike

klāt *adv* 1. up to; close to, close by; near; 2. (with verbs) add, be added; 3. (with forms of būt) a. be present; be here; b. arrive; k. kā likts (or k. kā nagla) (arrive) right on the dot; c. have (sth.) on (one's person); 4. (with certain verbs) on, to (līmēt k. glue on; spiesties k. cling to)

klātbūtne *nf* presence

klātējs *adj* nearby

klātesamība *nf* presence

klātesoš/ie *nom adj pl* those present; present company; ~o pārbaude roll call

klātesošs *adj* present

klātesot *adv* (with subject in dative) present

klātgulētāja *nf* mistress

klātiene *nf* 1. presence; 2. (educ.) residency; ~s students resident student

klāties I *vr* 1. spread; 2. cover; 3. (of table) set itself; galdiņ, klājies! set, table, set!

klāties II *vr* (*3rd pers*, of one's welfare) be, do, fare; kā klājas? how are you? labi k. do well; slikti (or plāni) k. fare badly;

viņam labi ne-klāsies it will turn out badly for him

klāties III *vr* be proper; **tas tā neklājas** it isn't proper; behoove

klātin *adv emph* of **klāt**

klātne *nf* **1.** pavement; **2.** lamina

klātneesošs *adj* absent

klātneesot *part* of **būt klāt** in the absence of, in absentia

klātnie/ks *nm*, **~ce** *nf* resident student

klātņu akmens *nm* flagstone

klātpiegulētāja *nf* mistress

klātpielikts *adj* attached

klatrāts *nm* clathrate

klātums *nm* nearness

klātuvējs *adj* (obs.) nearby

klau *interj* listen; hark

klaudze *nf* (internal combustion engine) knocking

klaudzeklis *nm* door knocker

klaudzēt *vi* **1.** knock, bang; **2.** resound; **3.** chatter, rattle

klaudzien/s *nm* knock, bang; (of hoofs, usu. *pl* ~i) clatter

klaudzināt *vt, vi* knock, bang; click

klaudzināties *vr* (*iter*) bang

klaudzoņa *nf* knocking, banging; clatter

klauģis *nm* **1.** mallet; club, maul; **2.** small wooden block; **3.** braggart, bigmouth

klauks *interj* bang, knock

klaukstēt *vi* knock, bang

klaukšķēt *vi* click

klaukšķināt *vi, vt* click, knock

klaukšķināties *vr* (*iter*) knock

klaukšķis *nm* banging, knocking, bang, knock

klaunāde *nf* clownage

klauniski *adv* clownishly

klaunisks *adj* clownish

klauns *nm* clown

klaupāt *vi* stumble

klausāmais stobriņš *nm* ear trumpet

klausība *nf* **1.** obedience; **2.** obligatory service

klausībnieks *nm* = **klaušinieks**

klausīgi *adv* obediently

klausīgs *adj* obedient

klausīgums *nm* obedience

klausīt *vi, vt* **1.** obey; **k. kā likt**s obey implicitly; **k. (kāda) padomam** follow (s.o.'s) advice; **k. uz vārda** be at one's beck and call; obey at once, jump; **2.** listen; **3.** (obs.) serve; **gaitas k.** perform corvée labor

klausītāj/s *nm*, **~a** *nf* **1.** listener; **~i** audience; **2.** student at a lecture

klausītava *nf* auditorium, lecture room

klausīties *vr* **1.** listen, listen to; **kāri k.** be all ears; **k. ar abām ausīm** be all ears; **k. ar vienu ausi** half-listen; **klausos!** (mil.) yes, sir! **2.** (of a course) take; (of a lecture) attend

klaust *vt* question

klaustrofobija *nf* claustrophobia

klausule *nf* telephone receiver

klauš/as *nf pl* (hist.) corvée; statute labor

klaušinājums *nm* inquiry

klaušināt *vt* question; inquire about

klaušināties *vr* inquire

klaušinātāj/s *nm*, **~a** *nf* questioner

klaušinie/ks *nm*, **~ce** *nf* (hist.) peasant performing corvée labor; person performing statute labor

klaušņāt *vt* ask question, pester with questions

klaušu laiki *nm pl* period of agricultural corvée in Latvia (1817-1863)

klaušu noma *nf* corvées reelles

klauve *nf* accelerated heartbeat; knocking

klauvējiens *nm* knock; rap; tap

klauvēklis *nm* door knocker

klauvēt *vi* knock; rap; tap

klauvēties *vr* **1.** (*iter*) knock; **2.** (of heart) beat fast

klauza *nf* cell; hermitage

klauzula *nf* (jur.) clause

klauzūra *nf* confinement

klauzūras darbs *nm* written test

klavesīnist/s *nm*, ~e *nf* harpsichord player

klavesīns *nm* harpsichord

klavi|a|tūra [ā] *nf* keyboard; keys

klavi|ch|ords [h] *nm* clavichord

klavie|r|darbs [r] *nm* piano piece

klavieres *nf pl* piano

klavie|r|izvilkums [r] *nm* piano score

klavie|r|klase [r] *nf* piano class

klavie|r|koncerts [r] *nm* 1. piano concerto; 2. piano recital

klavie|r|literatūra [r] *nf* piano music

klavie|r|mūzika [r] *nf* piano music

klaviernieks *nm* pianist

klavie|r|partija [r] *nf* piano part

klavie|r|pavadījums [r] *nm* piano accompaniment

klavie|r|skaņdarbs [r] *nm* piano composition

klavie|r|skolotāj/s [r] *nm*, ~a *nf* piano teacher

klavie|r|spēle [r] *nf* piano playing

klavie|r|stunda [r] *nf* piano lesson

klavie|r|te|ch|nika [r][h] *nf* piano technique

klavie|r|vakars [r] *nm* evening piano recital

klāvs *nm* 1. cow barn (in Latgale); 2. a. (wooden) prong (for supporting a fishline); b. roll-line

kleberēt *vi* (col.) drive slowly (a horse-drawn wagon)

kleberēties *vr* (col.) wobble

kleberīgs *adj* (col.) wobbly

klēbēt *vt* (barb.) glue, paste

klēbēties *vr* (barb.) be glued; **k. klāt** make up to

klecene *nf* flour mush

klecēt *vi* (com.) eat

klecīte *nf* game of tag

kledzēt *vi* (com.) eat

klēgāt *vi* (of geese) honk

kleinis *nm* bow-legged man (or boy)

kleinīts *nm* kleinite

kleinkājis *nm* bow-legged man (or boy)

kleins *adj* bow-legged; bowed, bent

kleinums *nm* bow-leggedness

kleistog|a|mija [ā] *nf* cleistogamy

kleists *nm* tramp

kleita *nf* (woman's) dress

klejojošs *adj, part* of **klejot** wandering; (of sand, dunes) shifting; (of dogs) stray; (of ice) drift; (of knights) errant

klejojums *nm* wandering

klejonis *nm* tramp, vagabond

klejoņa *nf, nm* tramp, vagabond

klejot *vi* wander

klejotāja upe *nf* divagative river

klejotājnervs *nm* vagus nerve

klejotāj/s *nm*, ~a *nf* 1. wanderer; 2. nomad; (animal) migrant; traveling

klejotājs sisenis *nm* migratory locust

klejotājtauta *nf* nomadic people

kleknēt *vi* (col.) pine away

kleksis *nm* (barb.) ink blot

kleķe *nf* cow pat

kleķēt *vt* (col.) daub

kleķis *nm* adobe

klematiss *nm* clematis

klemme *nf* (el.) binding post

klemst *vi* 1. (com.) eat; 2. (col.) bark

klemstēt *vi* (col.) bark

klemšāt *vi, vt* (col.) bolt, gobble

klemža *nf, nm* (reg.) glutton

klencēt *vi, vt* (com.) bolt, gobble

klenderēt *vi* gad about

klender/is *nm*, ~e *nf* gadabout

kleņģerēt *vi* gad about

kleome *nf* cleome

klēpāt *vi* (of grain) be beaten down (by rain, wind)

klepelis *nm* lace bobbin

klēpenis *nm* baby

kleperis *nm* jade, hack

klepiņš *nm dim* of **klepus**, little cough

klēp/is *nm* 1. lap; 2. armful; ~jiem by the armful; 3. ~ī in one's arms; (fig.) in the bosom of; 4. womb; 5. (of steam, fog) billow

klēpja bērns *nm* baby, infant

klēpjdators *nm* laptop computer

klēpjot *vi* (reg.) gallop; strut

klepot *vi* cough

klepsēt *vi* (col.) eat noisily

klepsidra *nf* clepsydra

kleptom[a]nija [ā] *nf* kleptomania

kleptom[a]n/s [ā] *nm*, ~e *nf* kleptomaniac

klepus *nm* cough; **stiprs k.** bad cough

klepus konfektes *nf pl* cough lozenges

kl[e]rikāli [ē] *adv* clerically

kl[e]rikāli/s [ē] *nm*, ~e *nf* clericalist

kl[e]rikālisms [ē] *nm* clericalism

kl[e]rikāls [ē] *adj* clerical

kl[e]riķis [ē] *nm* 1. cleric; 2. seminary student

klerks *nm* clerk

klērs *nm* clergy

klesēt *vt, vi* (com.) bolt, gobble

klest *vt, vi* (com.) bolt, gobble

kleškājis *nm* bow-legged man (or boy)

kleteka *nf* (reg.) cowpie

klētiņa *nf dim* of **klēts**, granary

klētnie/ks *nm*, ~ce *nf* granary keeper

kletras *nf pl* Clethra

klēts *nf* granary, garner

klētsapakša *nf* granary crawlspace

klētsaugša *nf* granary loft

klētsdurvis *nf pl* granary door

klēts garsnuķis *nm* a granary weevil

klētsnauda *nf* granary fee (in ancient Latvian wedding tradition, a fee paid by the bridegroom's relatives to the bride's mother for permission to enter the granary where the bride had hidden)

klētspriekša *nf* granary porch

klētssargs *nm* granary guard

klētssiena *nf* granary wall

klētsvīrs *nm* granary guard (on a manor)

kleze *nf* (reg.) porridge

klezēt *vt, vi* (reg.) eat

klib/ais *nom adj* lame person, the lame one; ~ie the lame

klibiķ/is *nm*, ~e *nf* lame person, lame animal

klibiķot *vi* (col.) limp

klibināt *vi* clip-clop

klibis *nm* (col.) lame person, lame animal

klibkājis *nm* (col.) lame person, lame animal

klibot *vi* 1. limp; 2. (fig.) leave much to be desired

klibotājs *nm*, ~a *nf* lame person, limping person

klibs *adj* lame

klibums *nm* lameness

klibzaķis *nm* (col.) 1. lame person; 2. spineless person

kliceņi *nm pl* (reg.) dumplings

klīdēj/s *nm*, ~a *nf* tramp

klīdināt *vt* disperse, dispel

klīdonis *nm* tramp

klidonografs *nm* Klydonograph

klīdoņa *nm, nf* (cont.) tramp

klīdums *nm* spread

klidzēt *vi* = **klidzināt**

klidzināt *vi* (of horse-drawn wagons, carts) drive slowly; go clickety-clack; (of a horse) clip-clop

klidzis *nm* a loose, wobbly object

kliederis *nm* bourtree

kliedēt I *vt* disperse, dispel

kliedēt II *vt* wind (with a wire or string)

kliedēties *vr* disperse

kliediņš I *nm* partition

kliediņš II *nm* (reg.) hay spread for drying

kliedzamais *nom adj* (col.) mouth, throat

kliedzēj/s *nm*, ~a *nf* crier, shouter, yeller

kliedziens *nm* cry, shout, yell, scream; (of an owl) screech; **pēdējais k.** last word; dernier cri

kliedzin *adv, emph* of **kliegt**; **k. kliedza** he (she) kept on shouting, shouted at the top of his (her) voice

kliedzīgs *adj* loud

kliedzināt *vt* make cry

kliedzošs *adj, part* of **kliegt 1.** crying, shrieking, yelling, screaming; **2.** (fig.) loud, gaudy

kliegāt *vi* holler

kliegoņa *nf* shouting, hollering

kliegšus *adv emph* of **kliegt; k. kliedza** he (she) shouted at the top of his (her) voice; he (she) screamed without stopping

kliegt *vi, vt* cry, shout; **spalgi k.** yell, scream

klieģis *nm* crier, shouter, yeller

kliekis *nm* (col.) clay

klieni *adv* thinly

kliens *adj* thin, haggard; spread out thin

klients *nm,* ~**e** *nf* client; patron

klientūra *nf* clientele

kliest *vt* **1.** scatter, disperse, dispel; spread, ted; **2.** hit

kliesties *vr* scatter, disperse, dispel; spread

klifs *nm* (geol.) cliff

klija *nf* (zool.) kite

klijains *adj* mixed with bran

klijāns *nm* Eurasian buzzard

klijas *nf pl* bran

klijkaija *nf* skua

klika *nf, nm* laugher

klikatas *nf pl* **1.** women's wood-soled shoes; **2.** old watermill; **3.** bad luck

klikatiņas *nf pl* women's wood-soled shoes

kliks *interj* click

klikstēt *vi* click

klikstiens *nm* click

klikstināt *vi* (*iter*) click

klikš *interj* click

klikšķēt *vi* click

klikšķināt *vt* click repeatedly

klikšķis *nm* **1.** click; **2.** knife with a loose blade; **3.** clapper

klikt *interj* click

kliķe *nf* clique

klimagramma *nf* climograph

klimakss *nm* climacteric; menopause

klimaktērijs *nm* climacteric; menopause

klimaktērisks *adj* climacteric

klimatiski *adv* climatically

klimatisks *adj* climatic

klimatizēšana *nf* air-conditioning

klimatizēt *vt* air-condition

klimatogr[a]fija [ā] *nf* climatography

klimatogr[a]fiski [ā] *adv* climatographically

klimatogr[a]fisks [ā] *adj* climatographic

klimatogr[a]f/s [ā] *nm,* ~**e** *nf* climatographer

klimatolo/gs *nm,* ~**ģe** *nf* climatologist

klimatoloģija *nf* climatology

klimatoloģiski *adv* climatologically

klimatoloģisks *adj* climatological

klimats *nm* climate

klimatterapija *nf* climatotherapy

klimbucis *nm* (reg.) small piece, morsel

klimpa *nf* dumpling

klimperēt *vt* (sl.) tinkle

klimpināt *vt* (col., cont.) tinkle (the piano)

klimst *vi* **1.** gad about; **2.** wait in vain; dawdle; **3.** talk loudly

klimstēt *vi* (of prolonged, tiresome sounds of barking, coughing, ringing) resound

klimsts *nm* gadabout

klimšķināt *vt* (col., cont., of musical instruments) tinkle

klincis *nm* (reg.) heel of bread

klinča *nf* (naut.) clinch

klinčot *vi* (col.) limp

klinčs *nm* (boxing) clinch

klinču klančām *adv* headlong, stumbling

klindzināt *vt* clink; clank; jingle; (of dishes) clatter

kling *interj* dingdong, ting-a-ling

klingstināt *vt* ring

kl[i]nicist/s [ī] *nm,* ~**e** *nf* clinician

klīnika *nf* clinic

klīnikas ps[īch]olo/gs [ih] *nm,* ~**ģe** *nf* clinical psychologist

klīniski *adv* clinically

klīnisks *adj* clinical

klinkāt *vi* **1.** hobble; **2.** hop

klinkata *nf, nm* lame person, limper

klinkerķieģelis *nm* clinker brick

klinkers *nm* (material) clinker

klinkstēt *vi* clink

klinkstināt *vi* (*iter*) clink; tinkle

klinkšķēt *vi* clink

klinkšķināt *vi* (*iter*) clink; tinkle

kl[i]nometrs [ī] *nm* clinometer

klinšains *adj* rocky

klinšu balodis *nm* rock pigeon

klinšu bluķis *nm* boulder

klinšu ērglis *nm* golden eagle

klinšu ieplaka *nf* rock basin

klinšu ķērpis *nm* crottle

klinšu ložņa *nm* (zool.) wall creeper

klinšu rags *nm* crag, cliff; headland

klinšu siena *nf* cliff

klinšu stabs *nm* (geol.) stack

klintaine *nf* rocky terrain

klintājs *nm* rocky terrain

klintene *nf* cotoneaster

klintiņa *nf dim* of **klints**, small cliff

klints *nf* rock, cliff, crag

klintsbluķis *nm* boulder

klintsradze *nf* crag

klintsrags *nm* promontory

klintzivs *nf* haddock

klīņāt *vi* wander

kliņģeris *nm* 1. pretzel-shaped cake; 2. (folk dancing) figure eight

kliņģerīte *nf* 1. pot marigold; 2. hedgehog mushroom

kliņģerītis *nm dim* of **kliņģeris**; pretzel

kliņķēt *vt* (col.) hook

kliņķi/s *nm* door handle; **līdz ~m** (sl.) completely

klip *interj*, usu. **klip, klip** or **klip-klap** clip-clop

klipa *nf* (col.) 1. trouble; 2. rock; ice block

klipata *nf* (col.) trouble

klipeola *nf* clypeole

kliperis *nm* (naut.) clipper

klipiņš *nm* (reg.) shingle

klips *nm* (film) clip

klipsis *nm* clip-on earring; hair clip

klipstēt *vi* click

klipt *vi* go under, perish

klipu *interj*, usu. **klipu, klipu** or **klipu-klapu** clip-clop

klīrenss *nm* (automobile) clearance

klīrēties *vr* 1. (col.) mince matters; put on airs; 2. (obs., col.) adorn oneself

klirfaktors *nm* (el.) distortion factor

klīrība *nf* affectation, false coyness

klīrīgi *adv* in an affected or mincing manner

klīrīgs *adj* affected; finicky; mincing; falsely coy

klīrīgums *nm* affectation, false coyness

klīrings *nm* (bus.) clearing

klirkstēt *vi* rattle

klirkšķēt *vi* rattle

klīsmeta *nf, nm* (reg.) glutton

klīst *vi* 1. roam, ramble; wander; (with **projām, nost**) wander away; (of clouds) sail; (of rumors) go around; 2. (of fog) lift

klīsterēt *vt* apply paste; (weav.) dress the warp

klīsteris *nm* paste (glue)

klistīrs *nm* enema

klistrons *nm* klystron

klīša *nf* common dab

klišeja *nf* 1. (typ.) cut; electrotype; stereotype plate; 2. (fig.) cliché

klišejisks *adj* stereotyped

klišejists *nm* (typ.) maker of cuts, electrotyper, stereotyper

kl[i]tors [ī] *nm* clitoris

klivāža *nf* (geol.) cleavage

klīverboma tīkls *nm* jib boom net

klīverboms *nm* (naut.) jib boom

klīvergaija *nf* (naut.) jib guy

klīvergaiju boms *nm* (naut.) whisker boom

klīvers *nm* (naut.) jib

klīverštāga *nf* (naut.) jib stay

klīvijas *nf pl* Kaffir lily

klīze *nf* (naut.) **1.** mooring pipe; **2.** hawsehole

klīzes vāks *nm* (naut.) buckler

klizma I *nf* trouble; mishap, accident; breakdown; flat

klizma II *nf* enema

klizmēties *vr* experience trouble, have a mishap; fail

kloāka *nf* **1.** sewer; **2.** cesspool; **3.** cloaca

kloķa klaņturis *nm* crankpin

kloķa plecs *nm* crank web

kloķa vārpsta *nf* crankshaft

kloķis *nm* **1.** handle; lever; **2.** crank; **palaiža-mais k.** crank

kloķītis *nm dim* of **kloķis**, small handle, crank

kloķurbis *nm* brace (tool)

kloķvārpsta *nf* crankshaft

kloķveida *indecl adj* crank-like

kloķveidīgs *adj* crank-like

klona grīda *nf* earthen floor, tamped clay floor

klona maize *nf* rye bread baked in the hearth; country bread

klondaika *nf* (fig.) Klondike

klonēt *vt* (biol.) clone

kloniski *adv* clonically

klonisks *adj* clonic

klonveida *indecl adj* like a tamped clay floor

klonveidīgs *adj* like a tamped clay floor

klons I (with **uo**) *nm* **1.** threshing floor; **2.** floor (usually earthen, made of any material, except boards, in contact with the ground); **peldošais k.** floating screed; **3.** floor of the baking oven, hearthstone

klons II *nm* (biol.) clone

klopfers *nm* (telegraph) sounder

klopsis *nm* ground meat patty

kloste[r]baznīca [ŗ] *nf* chapel

kloste/ris *nm* cloister, monastery, convent; **~ŗa** monastic

klosteŗa brālis *nm* monk

klosteŗa māsa *nf* nun

klosteŗa priekšniece *nf* abbess

klosteŗa priekšnieks *nm* abbot

klotiņš *nm* net float

klozes *nf pl* (sl.) clothes

klozetpods *nm* toilet bowl

klozets *nm* toilet, restroom

kluatrs *nm* cloister courtyard

kluazonē *indecl nf* cloisonné

kluba *nf* (obs.) social with dancing

klubežot *vi* (reg.) stagger

klubkrēsls *nm* easy chair

klubs *nm* **1.** club; **2.** clubhouse

kluburāt *vi* (col.) limp

kluburot *vi* (col.) limp

kluburs *nm* (col.) lame person

kluburu kluburiem *adv* (col.) stumbling, hobbling

klucīgs *adj* clunky; klutzy

klucis *nm* **1.** bolt of wood, wood block; chopping block; **k. saplākšņiem** veneer bolt; **2.** large block (of any material)

klucītis *nm* **1.** *dim* of **klucis**, small block; **2.** toy block

klučains *adj* cloddy

kludzēt *vi* gurgle

kludziens *nm* gulp, swallow

klūdziņa *nf dim* of **klūga**, wicker

klūdziņu kārkls *nm* almond willow

klūdziņu vītols *nm* velvet osier

kluga *nf* (reg.) swallow

klūga *nf* wicker; withe

klūgot *vt* tie with wicker

klūgu grozs *nm* wicker basket

klūgu siena *nf* wattle

kluģis *nm* **1.** wooden block; **2.** wooden handle

kluicens *nm* (reg., zool.) crane

kluiķis *nm* curlew

kluite *nf* curlew

kluknēt *vi* (reg.) sit hunched up; huddle

klukste *nf* clucking hen

klukstēt *vi* cluck

klukstētāja *nf* clucking hen

kluksti *nm pl* (reg.) belching

klukstīte *nf dim* of **klukste**, clucking hen

kluksts *nm* cluck

klukšķēt *vi* 1. gurgle; 2. clunk

klukucēt *vi* (reg.) hiccup

klukuči *nm pl* (reg.) hiccups

klukučot *vi* (reg.) hiccup

klumba *nf* wooden shoe

klumburēt *vi* hobble

klumburis *nm* clumsy person

klumburot *vi* hobble

klumbu|r|u [ŗ] klumbu|r|iem [ŗ] *adv* hobbling

klumpačot *vi* (col.) waddle, toddle

klumpas *nf pl* clogs

klumpis *nm* clumsy person

klumšķis *nm* bunch, tuft, wad

klumzaks *nm* 1. clumsy person, lubber; 2. wad; wadded cloth

klumzāt *vi* (col.) waddle, toddle

klumzīgi *adv* clumsily

klumzīgs *adj* clumsy

klunciens *nm* gulp, swallow

kluncis *nm* 1. hunk; 2. (col.) obese, clumsy person

kluncīt *vt, vi* (com.) eat

klunckāja *nf, nm* fat-legged person

klunčot *vi* (col.) waddle, toddle

klundurēt *vi* (col.) waddle, toddle

klundzēt *vi* glug

klundziens *nm* gulp, swallow

klunkata *nf* gulp, swallow

klunkstēt *vi* glug

klunkstiens *nm* glug

klunkšķēt *vi* glug

klunkšķināt *vt* slosh

klunkšķis *nm* 1. glug; 2. gulp, swallow

klunkurēt *vi* (col.) waddle, toddle

klunkuris *nm* 1. clumsy person; 2. tramp; 3. (cont.) medal

klunkurot *vi* (col.) waddle, toddle

klunku|r|u [ŗ] klunku|r|iem [ŗ] *adv* waddling, toddling

kluņģis *nm* 1. stick; 2. (col.) clumsy person, lubber

klupanodonskābe *nf* clupanodonic acid

klūpdrāts *nf* low wire

klupe *nf* die stock

klupeņot *vi* stumble

klupiens *nm* 1. stumble, false step; 2. (fencing) lunge

klupiņus *adv* stumbling

klūpņāt *vi* stumble

klupšanas akmens *nm* stumbling block

klupšus or **klupšus krišus** *adv* stumbling, headlong

klupt *vi* 1. stumble, trip up; **klupdams krizdams** headlong; 2. **k. klāt** rush to, fall upon; 3. **k. virsū** pounce upon; descend upon; **k. cekulā** (or **krūtīs, matos, saros, vilnā**) (col.) have at, start fighting, attack

klupus *adv* stumbling, headlong

klūrēt *vi* (of cranes) trumpet

klurga *nf* (reg., zool.) crane

klūrgāt *vi* (of cranes) trumpet

klurģis *nm* (reg., zool.) crane

klurkstēt, klurkšēt or **klurkšķēt** *vi* (of cranes) trumpet

klusa *nf* (poet.) silence

klusām *adv* silently, quietly; **k. aiziet** leave quietly; slink away

Klusā oke|a|na [ā] siļķe *nf* Pacific herring

Klusā sestdiena *nf* Holy Saturday

klusatne *nf* (obs.) silence

kluscietīgs *adj* taciturn

kluse *nf* (poet.) silence

klusēšana *nf* silence (keeping of silence)

klusēt *vi* keep silent, be silent; fail to reply, fail to write

klusētājs *nm*, **~a** *nf* silent one, keeper of silence, taciturn person

klusgaitas *indecl adj* (of vehicles) quiet

klusi *adv* 1. silently; 2. quietly

klusīb/a *nf* 1. silence; 2. quiet; ~ā a. silently, in silence; b. secretly, on the sly klusīgs *adj* quiet; reticent

klusinājums *nm* 1. shushing; 2. muffling, damping; muting

klusināt *vt* 1. silence, quiet; shush; 2. muffle, deaden, damp; mute; 3. allay

klusinātāj/s *nm*, ~a *nf* (person; handgun attachment) silencer; (automotive) muffler; (piano) damper; (string or wind instruments) mute

klusināties *vr* become quiet

klusiņām or klusiņi *adv* 1. very quietly, silently; 2. on the sly

klusītēm or klusītiņām *adv* 1. very quietly, silently; 2. on the sly

klus/s *adj* 1. (of sound) soft, low, gentle; 2. quiet; pa ~o secretly, on the sly; 3. silent, noiseless; 4. still; 5. meek; 6. (of business activity) slow

klust *vi* fall silent

klusu *adv* silently, quietly; k.! hush! silence!

klusuciešana *nf* silence (keeping of silence)

klusuciešot *adv* silently

klusums *nm* 1. silence; 2. quiet, calm; hush; 3. standstill, stagnation

kļaut *vt* clasp; k. sev klāt clasp to one's breast, hug

kļauties *vr* cling to

kļava *nf* maple

kļavaine or kļaviene *nf* stand of maples

kļavlapa *nf* maple leaf

kļavs *nm* maple

kļēmēt *vi* (reg., of grass, crops) be beaten down by rain or wind

kļenkstēt *vi* (col.) yap

kļēpa *nf* (col.) wet snow

kļošenes *nf pl* (col.) bell-bottoms

kļūda *nf* mistake, error; rupja k. gross error; blunder

kļūdaini *adv* with errors

kļūdains *adj* faulty; containing errors, full of errors

kļūdīgi *adv* erroneously

kļūdīgs *adj* erroneous, wrong

kļūdiņa *nf dim* of kļūda, little mistake

kļūdīties *vr* make a mistake, be mistaken; k. aprēķinos miscalculate

kļūdu meklēšana *nf* (compu.) debugging

kļūdu teorija *nf* normal law of errors

kļūmains *adj* fatal; precarious, perilous; unfortunate

kļūme *nf* 1. mishap; 2. (mechanical) trouble; 3. misfire

kļūmi *adv* (rare.) mistakenly; unfortunately

kļūmīgi *adv* mistakenly; unfortunately

kļūmīgs *adj* fatal; precarious, perilous; unfortunate

kļūmīgums *nm* precariousness, perilousness

kļūmīte *nf dim* of kļūme, mishap

kļūms *adj* 1. (rare.) fatal; precarious, perilous; unfortunate; 2. (obs.) ominous

kļūt *vi* become, get, grow, turn

knābāns *nm* 1. poor worker; 2. rooster

knābāt *vt* 1. peck (and eat); 2. peck repeatedly

knābāties *vr* peck (and eat) a long time

knābeklis *nm* (pointed) beak

knābiens *nm* peck

knābis *nm* beak, bill

knābītis *nm dim* of knābis, little beak, bill

knābjainais grīslis *nm* yellowish sedge

knābjainais jūras bruņrupucis *nm* hawksbill

knābjainā lazda *nf* beaked filbert

knābjainie tīklspārņi *nm pl* scorpion flies

knābjains *adj* beaked

knablis *nm* clothespin

knābt *vt, vi* peck

knaģis *nm* 1. clothespin; 2. hook, peg; 3. knee timber

knaibīgi *adv* stingingly

knaibīgs *adj* stinging

knaibīt *vt* pinch

knaibīties *vr* pinch each other

knaibles *nf pl* pliers, tongs, tweezers, nippers, pincers

knaidīt *vt* (reg.) crumble

knairīties *vr* (of birds) preen oneself

knaisīt *vt* scratch

knaisīties *vr* scratch oneself

knakstēt *vi* crack

knakstināt *vi* (of squirrels) scold

knakstināties *vr* **1.** flirt; **2.** piddle

knakstīties *vr* **1.** flirt; **2.** piddle

knakš *interj* crack

knakšēt *vi* crack; click

knakšķēt *vi* crack; click

knakšķināt *vt* (*iter*) crack

knakšķināties *vr* make cracking noises

knakšķis *nm* crack

knakšķoņa *nf* cracking noises

knāpe *nf* (reg.) narrow stretch of forest

knapi *adv* (barb.) barely

knapiķis *nm* (barb.) miser

knapināt *vt* (barb.) save

knapināties *vr* (barb.) be stingy

knaps *adj* (barb.) small and narrow

knapsieriņš *nm* (col.) air-dried cheese

knariņš *nm* (sl.) kid, little boy

knarkstēt *vi* grind, crunch

knasters *nm* canaster

knasti *adv* finely; neatly

knasts *adj* fine; neat

knaši *adv* nimbly, quickly

knašība *nf* nimbleness, quickness

knašs *adj* nimble, quick

knašums *nm* nimbleness, quickness

knaucis *nm* (reg.) slice; heel of a loaf

knauks *interj* crack

knaukstēt *vi* crack

knaukš *interj* crack

knaukšēt *vi* crack

knaukšķēt *vi* crack

knaukšķināt *vi* (*iter*) crack

knaukšķināties *vr* make cracking noises (a long time)

knaukšķis *nm* crack

knaukt *interj* crack

knauķis *nm* (col.) tot

knausis *nm* gnat

knauslis *nm* (col.) shrimp, pygmy

knauzerēties *vr* (barb.) stint, pinch pennies

knauzerīgs *adj* (barb.) miserly

knauzeris *nm* (barb.) **1.** miser; **2.** roaster

knēdelis *nm* dumpling

kneija *nf* (naval arch.) knee

kneipe *nf* (col.) tavern

kneipot *vi* (barb.) booze

knesets *nm* Knesset

knets *adj* svelte

knēvelis *nm* (col.) tot

knibāt *vt* (col., of small or sparse berries) pick

knibek/lis *nm* picky, tedious work; ~**ļa darbs** picky, tedious piece of work

knibgalis *nm* (reg.) heel of bread

knibiķis *nm* (col.) dawdler

knibināt *vi* **1.** finger, pick; toy with; **2.** nibble; **3.** do picky work

knibināties *vr* **1.** fumble with; **2.** tinker, putter, fiddle

knibis *nm* heel of bread

knibucis *nm* projection, bump; (col.) doodad

knibulis *nm* bump

knicis *nm* heel of bread

knideklis *nm* itchy place

knidēt *vi* itch

kniebavas *nf pl* pliers

kniebeklis *nm* pliers, pincers

kniebes *nf pl* pliers, pincers

kniebiens *nm* pinch, nip; tweak

kniebīgi *adv* bitingly

kniebīgs *adj* (of cold, freezing weather) biting

kniebīgums *nm* bitingness

kniebles *nf pl* pliers, pincers

kniebt *vt, vi* **1.** pinch, nip; pinch off; tweak; **k. pušu** cut (with cutters); **k. kopā** press together; **2.** punch holes

kniebties *vr* cut into

kniede *nf* rivet

kniedējums *nm* riveting

kniedenes *nf pl* (col.) riveted pants

kniedes kāts *nm* rivet shank

kniedēt *vt* **1.** rivet; **2.** (sl.) a. work; b. eat

kniedētāj/s *nm*, **~a** *nf* riveter

kniedgalva *nf* rivet head

kniedīgs *adj* adroit; strong

kniedīte *nf dim* of **kniede**, rivet

kniedlapa *nf* (compu.) links page

kniepadata *nf* pin

kniepe *nf* pin

kniepēt *vt* fasten with pins, pin together

kniepķens *nm* (col.) stud, double button

knierēt *vt* (reg.) pick berries

kniesēt *vi* itch

kniest *vi, vt* itch

knieta *nf* (reg.) itch

knietēt *vi, vt* germinate

kniezēt *vi* itch

kniežu dzelzs *nf* rivet steel

knifēt *vt* knot (hairs to wig base)

knifs *nm* (sl.) knack

kniksēt *vi* curtsy

kniksis *nm* curtsy

knikstēt *vi* crackle, snap, pop

knikstiņi *nm pl* tricks

knikš *interj* crackle, click; **k. knakš** click, click

knikšēt *vi* crackle, snap, pop

knikšķēt *vi* crackle, snap, pop

knikšķināt *vi* crackle, click

knikšķināties *vr* crackle, click (a long time)

knikšķis *nm* crackle, click

knikšķoņa *nf* crackling, clicking

knīpa *nf, nm* (col., cont.) young girl; young boy

knipele *nf* lace bobbin

knīpele *nf* (col., cont.) young girl

knipelēt *vi* make bobbin lace

knipis *nm* **1.** snap (of fingers); **2.** flick, fillip; **3.** (gesture) fig; **4.** (col.) young boy; **5.** (col.) shorty, shrimp

kniploks *nm* garlic

knipsēt *vi* (col.) take pictures

knīpstangas *nf pl* (col.) pliers

knipu, knapu *interj* knock, knock

knipucītis *nm* bit, morsel

knirkstēt *vi* crackle, snap, pop

knirpis *nm* (cont.) tyke

knisis *nm* = **knislis**

knislis *nm* **1.** gnat, midge; **2.** (fig., cont.) midge, shrimp

knislītis *nm dim* of **knislis**, gnat, midge

knist I *vi* germinate

knist II *vi* itch

knitāji *nm pl* shives

knitināt *vt* germinate

kniukstēt *vi* crackle, snap, pop

kniukstoņa *nf* crackling, snapping, popping

kniukš or **kniukt** *interj* crackle, click, snap

knīveris *nm* (col.) tot

knope *nf* (barb.) button

knopēt *vt* (barb.) button

knopēties I *vr* (barb.) button one's clothes

knopēties II *vr* (of birds) preen

knopsītis *nm* (sl.) button

knoseklis *nm* (col.) dawdler

knosis *nm* (col.) dawdler

knosīt *vt* scratch

knosīties *vr* **1.** scratch oneself; **2.** putter; dawdle; hesitate

knozeklis *nm* beak

knubiķis *nm* projection, bump

knubināt *vt, vi* nibble

knubināties *vr* **1.** tinker with; **2.** tinker, puddle, fiddle

knubucis *nm* bump, rough spot

knubučains *adj* bumpy, rough

knubuķis *nm* projection, bump

knukstēt *vi* **1.** growl; grunt; grumble; (of stomach) rumble; **2.** moan

knūpi *adv* (rare.) at a slant

knupis *nm* **1.** nipple (pacifier); **2.** nightstick; **3.** bundle, bindle

knupītis *nm dim* of **knupis**; nipple (pacifier); bindle

knūps *adj* (rare.) slanted

knupt *vi* hunch

knupu *adv* = kņupus

knupus or knūpus *adv* = kņupus

knusis *nm* gnat, midge

knūst *vi* itch

knutināt *vt* tickle

knužināt *vt, vi* (col.) tickle

kņada *nf* bustle; turmoil, hubbub

kņadīgs *adj* bustling

kņadīgums *nm* noisiness

kņadoņa *nf* bustle; turmoil, hubbub

kņadot *vi* make a noise, cause a commotion

kņāva *nf* booty, spoils; loot; prey

kņaze *nf* princess (unmarried daughter of a knez)

kņaziene *nf* princess (consort of a knez)

kņaziste *nf* principality

kņazs *nm* knez, (Slavic) prince

kņēgāt *vt, vi* (reg.) eat

kņīpa *nf, nm* (col., cont.) young girl; young boy

kņirkstēt *vi* crunch

kņope *nf* = knope

kņopēt *vt* = knopēt

kņopēties *vr* = knopēties

kņubs *adj* (of noses) hooked

kņudas *nf pl* itch

kņudēt *vi* tickle, itch; tingle

kņudināt *vt* tickle

kņudināties *vr* tickle

kņudoņa *nf* tingling

kņudošs *adj, part* of kņudēt tingling

kņupt *vi* hunch

kņupus, kņūpu or kņūpus *adv* 1. hunched up; 2. prone

ko *pron, acc* of kas 1 (interrogative) what; whom; (relative) that, whom, which; ne par ko about nothing; about nobody; (of cost) for nothing; (in answer to "paldies!") don't mention it; 2. *adv* why

koacervācija *nf* coacervation

koacervāts *nm* coacervate

koadjutors *nm* coadjutor

koagels *nm* coagel

koagulācija *nf* coagulation

koagulants *nm* coagulant

koagulāts *nm* coagulum

koagulēt *vi* coagulate

koaksiāli *adv* coaxially

koaksiāls *adj* coaxial

koala *nm* koala

koalescence *nf* coalescence

koal[i]cija [ī] *nf* coalition

koans *nm* koan

koati *indecl nm* coati

kobalamīns *nm* cyanocobalamine

kobalta diarsenīts *nm* smaltite

kobalta stikls *nm* smalt

kobalta ziedi *nm pl* erythrite

kobaltīns *nm* cobaltite

kobalts *nm* cobalt

kobeja *nf* (bot.) cathedral bells

koblers *nm* (drink) cobbler

kobolds *nm* goblin

kobols *nm* (compu.) Cobol

kobra *nf* cobra

kobza *nf* kobza

kobzars *nm* kobzar (Ukranian bard)

kocele *nf* wickerwork basket

kocene *nf* 1. wooden plate; wooden bowl; wooden shoe; 2. (col.) boat

koceris *nm* 1. wooden sheath; 2. needle box

ko[ch]ija [h] *nf* kochia; summer cypress

ko[ch]learija [h] *nf* scurvy grass

ko[ch]s [h] *nm* ship's cook

kocinieks *nm* wooden ship

kocis *nm* beehive

kociņš *nm* 1. *dim* of koks, small tree; 2. stick wand; rādāmais k. pointer

kočiņš *nm* a measure of distilled spirits

koda *nf* coda

kodaliņa *nf dim* of kodaļa, little bunch

kodaļa *nf* bunch (of wool, flax, or tow set on the distaff for spinning)

kodaļāt *vt* chew

kode *nf* moth

kodēdas *nf pl* moth-eaten parts

kodeīns *nm* codeine

kodekss *nm* 1. code; 2. codex

kodelēt *vt* chew

kodeļa *nf* bunch (of wool, flax, or tow set on the distaff for spinning)

koders *nm* (compu.) coder

kodēšana *nf* encoding

kodēt *vt* encode

kodētājs *nm*, ~a *nf* encoder

kodicils *nm* codicil

kodiens *nm* bite

kodificēt *vt* codify

kodifikācija *nf* codification

kodifikātors *nm* codifier

kodīgais kālijs *nm* caustic potash

kodīgais laimiņš *nm* stonecrop

kodīgi *adv* caustically; bitingly; pungently

kodīgs *adj* caustic; biting; acrid; pungent; mordant

kodīgums *nm* causticity; bitingness; acridity; pungency; mordancy

kodinājums *nm* etching

kodināt I *vt* 1. mordant; pickle; 2. stain; 3. etch; 4. (of seeds) sterilize

kodināt II *vt* admonish

kodinātāj/s *nm* 1. pickler; ~a *nf*; 2. mordant; pickling solution

kodīt *vt* chew; bite lightly; champ

kodne *nf* mordant; pickling solution

kodolatbruņošanās *nfr* nuclear disarmament

kodolbrīvs *adj* nuclear-free

kodolbumba *nf* atom bomb

kodoldegviela *nf* nuclear fuel

kodoldrošība *nf* nuclear safety

kodoldzinējs *nm* nuclear-powered engine

kodolelektrostacija *nf* nuclear power plant

kodolenerģetika *nf* nuclear energetics

kodolenerģētisks *adj* nuclear

kodolenerģija *nf* atomic energy

kodolfizika *nf* nuclear physics

kodolfizikāls *adj* pertaining to nuclear physics

kodolfiziķ/is *nm*, ~e *nf* nuclear physicist

kodoliekārta *nf* nuclear energy plant

kodolierocis *nm* nuclear weapon

kodolīgi *adv* concisely; **(runāt)** ~i (put it) in a nutshell

kodolīgs *adj* concise

kodolīgums *nm* conciseness

kodolizmēģinājums *nm* nuclear test

kodolka[r]š [ŗ] *nm* atomic war

kodolkoksne *nf* heartwood

kodolkuģis *nm* nuclear-powered ship

kodolķīmija *nf* radiochemistry

kodolķīmiķ/is *nm*, ~e *nf* nuclear chemist

kodolķīmisks *adj* pertaining to nuclear chemistry

kodollādiņš *nm* nuclear charge

kodollaikmets *nm* nuclear age

kodolledlauzis *nm* nuclear-powered ice-breaker

kodollielgabals *nm* atomic cannon

kodollokomotīve *nf* atomic locomotive

kodolpatvertne *nf* atomic shelter

kodolpētījums *nm* nuclear research

kodolrakete *nf* 1. nuclear missile; 2. atomic-powered rocket

kodolreakcija *nf* nuclear reaction

kodolreaktors *nm* nuclear reactor

kodol/s *nm* 1. kernel; nucleus; ~a sašķelšana nuclear fission; 2. heartwood; 3. essence, core

kodolsēta *nf* nodal farmstead

kodolspēki *nm pl* 1. nuclear forces; 2. atomic arsenal

kodolspēkstacija *nf* nuclear power plant

kodolsprādziens *nm* atomic explosion, nuclear burst

kodolsprāgstviela *nf* nuclear explosive

kodolstarojums *nm* radiation
kodolte|ch|nika [h] *nf* nuclear technology
kodoltermisks *adj* thermonuclear
kodoltrieciens *nm* atomic attack
kodoluzbrukums *nm* atomic attack
kodolvalsts *nf* nuclear power
kodolzemūdene *nf* nuclear submarine
kodolziema *nf* nuclear winter
kodolziepes *nf pl* fatty soap
kodons *nm* codon
kodoskops *nm* overhead projector
kods *nm* code
kodums *nm* bite
koedukācija *nf* coeducation
koeficients *nm* coefficient
koeksistence *nf* coexistence
koeksistēt *vi* coexist
koercitīvs *adj* (phys.) coercive
kofeīnisms *nm* caffeine addiction
kofeīns *nm* caffeine
koferis *nm* suitcase; trunk
koferments *nm* coenzyme
kognātisks *adj* cognate
kognāts *nm* cognate
kognāts *adj* cognate
kognitīvi *adv* cognitively
kognitīvistika *nf* cognitive science
kognitīvs *adj* cognitive
kognoscēt *vt* (jur.) investigate
koh|e|rence [ē] *nf* coherence
koh|e|rents [ē] *nm* laser beam
koh|e|rents [ē] *adj* coherent
kohēzija *nf* cohesion
kohinūrs *nm* Koh-i-noor
kohorta *nf* cohort
koijots *nm* cayote
koika *nf* (sl.) bunk (bed)
koinē *indecl nf* Koine; koine
koja *nf* (naut.) berth
koka *nf* coca
koka āmurs *nm* mallet; beetle
koka asaras *nf pl* crocodile tears

koka bruģis *nm* wood block pavement;
kokagabals *nm* (col.) cruel, hardhearted person
kokaīnaugi *nm pl* Erythoxylaceae
kokainība *nf* woodiness, stiffness
kokaīnisms *nm* cocaine addiction
kokaīnist/s *nm*, ~e *nf* cocaine addict
kokaīnkrūms *nm* cocaine plant
kokains *adj* 1. woody; 2. wooden, stiff; (of face) expressionless
kokaīns *nm* cocaine
kokainums *nm* woodiness, stiffness
koka izstrādājumi *nm pl* woodwork
koka kāja *nf* 1. wooden leg; 2. stilt
kokakola *nf* Coca-Cola
koka konstrukcija *nf* timberwork
kokalis *nm* corn cockle
kokaļains *adj* containing corn cockle seeds
koka māja *nf* frame house
koka masa *nf* wood pulp
koka nagla *nf* treenail
koka pasiena *nf* wood paneling
kokapauris *nm* (col.) blockhead
koka pīle *nf* goosander
kokaplasts *nm* polystyrene-covered plywod
kokapstrādāšana *nf* woodworking
kokapstrādātājs *nm*, ~a *nf* woodworker, mill-man
kokapstrāde *nf* woodworking
kokapstrādes fabrika *nf* planing mill
koka pūtēji *nm pl* woodwinds
koka puve *nf* dry rot
kokarboksilāze *nf* cocarboxylase
kokarde *nf* cockade, cockarde
koka saklātnis *nm* laminated wood
koka skaid/as *nf pl* woodchips; k. ~u plate particle board
koka spirts *nm* methanol
kokasu *indecl adj* wood-axle
koka šķiedr/a wood fiber; k. ~u masa wood pulp; k. ~u plate fiberboard
koka tupele *nf* wooden clog

kokaudze *nf* stand of timber

kokaudzētava *nf* tree farm

kokaugi *nm pl* trees and shrubs

kokbetons *nm* wood-reinforced concrete

kokbūve *nf* wooden structure

kokcīdijs *nm* coccidium

kokc[i]dioze [ī] *nf* coccidiosis

kokdzelēj/s *nm*, ~a *nf* wood-engraver

kokdzelums *nm* wood engraving

kokēži *nm pl* wood moths

kokeļļa *nf* wood oil

kokerspaniels *nm* cocker spaniel

kokgals *nm* treetop

kokgāzējs *nm* 1. lumberjack; 2. toppling fork

kokgrau/zis *nm* woodworm; termite; ~ēi Cerambycidae

kokgrebēj/s *nm*, ~a *nf* wood-engraver

kokgrebums *nm* wood engraving

kokgriezēj/s *nm*, ~a *nf* 1. woodcutter, woodcut maker; 2. woodcarver

kokgriezums *nm* 1. woodcut; 2. wood carving

kokile *nf* (metall.) chillmold

kokizstrādājums *nm* article made of wood, woodcraft article

kokkāpēj/s *nm*, ~a *nf* tree climber

kokle *nf* psaltery, kantele

koklēt *vi* play the psaltery

koklētāj/s *nm*, ~a *nf* psalterer

koklinie/ks *nm*, ~ce *nf* psalterer

kokmasa *nf* groundwood

kokmateriāls *nm* timber; lumber

koknejietis *nm*, ~e *nf* cockney (Londoner)

koknejisms *nm* cockneyism

koknejs *nm* cockney (speech)

kokogle *nf* charcoal

kokons *nm* cocoon

kokonaudējs *nm* cocoon-weaving insect

kokosa šķiedra *nf* coir

kokoseļļa *nf* coconut oil

kokospalma *nf* coconut palm

kokospiens *nm* coconut milk

kokosrieksta piens *nm* coconut milk

kokosrieksts *nm* coconut

kokoss *nm* coco

kokostauki *nm pl* coconut butter

kokot *vt* beat with a stick; cane

kokote *nf* cocotte

kokpiepe *nf* (col.) miser

kokpits *nm* cockpit

kokroze *nf* hollyhock

kokrūpniecība *nf* timber industry

kok/s I (with **uo**) *nm* 1. tree; ~u sagāzums toppled trees; 2. wood; 3. timber; 4. lumber; 5. wood stick; (short for **burtas koks**) tally; ~i caning

koks I I (with **ÿ**) *nm* coccus

koks III (with **ÿ**) *nm* (naut.) ship's cook

koksag[i]zs [ī] *nm* kok-saghyz

koksēt *vt* coke

koksētava *nf* coke oven plant

koksēties *vr* coke

koksirdis *nm* flinthearted person

kokskaida *nf* wood chip

kokskola *nf* tree nursery

kokskrūve *nf* wood screw

koksnaini *adv* woodily

koksnainība *nf* woodiness

koksnains *adj* woody

koksnainums *nm* woodiness

koksne *nf* wood

koksnes puve *nf* sap rot

koksngrauži *nm pl* woodworms

koksnurbji *nm pl* 1. wood borers; 2. wood moths

kokspirts *nm* methanol

kokss *nm* coke (carbonized coal)

kokstrādnie/ks *nm*, ~ce *nf* lumbermill worker

kokšķiedra *nf* wood fiber

kokteilis *nm* cocktail

kokteiļu jaucējs *nm* shaker

koktēlniecība *nf* wood carving

koktēlnie/ks *nm*, ~ce *nf* wood-carver

koktirgotāj/s *nm*, ~a *nf* lumber merchant

koku aizsprosts *nm* abatis

koku blakts *nf* forest bug

koku cirsma *nf* timber cutting area

koku cirtējs *nm* logger, lumberjack

koku čipste *nf* tree pipit

koku dzērve *nf* (reg.) great blue heron

koku magone *nf* bush poppy

koku pētnieks *nm* dendrologist

koku pludināšana *nf* timber floating, rafting

koku pludinātājs *nm* raftsman

kokurbis *nm* wood drill

kokurbji *nm pl* wood borers

koku robeža *nf* timberline

koku sēta *nf* lumberyard

koku šķirotājs *nm* timber grader

kokuts *nf* wood louse

koku utis *nf pl* book lice

kokuvarde *nf* tree frog

kokvedējs *nm* logging truck

kokveida *indecl adj* arboreal; arboreous

kokveida hortenzija *nf* (bot.) hills of snow

kokveida karagana *nf* Siberian pea tree

kokveidīgs *adj* arboreal; arboreous

kokvilna *nf* cotton

kokvilnas krūms *nm* cotton plant

kokvilnas samts *nm* velveteen

kokvilnas vērptuve *nf* cotton mill

kokvirpa *nf* wood lathe

kokzāģētava *nf* sawmill

kokzaru *indecl adj* made of a forked branch

koķete *nf* flirt, coquette

koķetērija *nf* flirting, coquetry

koķetēt *vi* flirt, coquet

koķeti *adv* coquettishly

koķetība *nf* coquettishness

koķetīgi *adv* coquettishly

koķetīgs *adj* coquettish

koķetīgums *nm* coquettishness

koķets *adj* coquettish

koķetums *nm* coquettishness

kola *nf* kola tree

kolabor- See kollabor-

kolāc- See kollāc-

kolag- See kollag-

kolaps- See kollaps-

kolaterāls *adj* = kollaterāls

kolāža *nf* = kollāža

kolba *nf* (laboratory) flask; glass bulb; glass liner (of a vacuum bottle)

kolbiņa *nf dim* of **kolba**, small laboratory flask

kol[ch]icīns [h] *nm* colchicine

kolchoznie/ks *nm* = kolhoznieks; ~ce *nf*

kolchozs *nm* = kolhozs

kolčakietis *nm* (hist.) Kolchakite (member of admiral A. Kolchak's counterrevolutionary army, 1918-1920)

kolčedāns *nm* marcasite

koldkrēms *nm* cold cream

koledža *nf* = kolledža

kolēga *nm*, *nf* = kollēģis

koleģ- See kollēģ-

kolejas *nf pl* coleus

kolekc- See kollekc-

kolekt- See kollekt-

kolembolas *nf* collembolans

kolen[ch]ima [h] *nf* collenchyme

kolēra *nf* cholera

kolhicīns *nm* = kolchicīns

kolhoznie/ks *nm*, ~ce *nf* member of a kolkhoz, collective farmer

kolhozs *nm* kolkhoz, collective farm

kolibaktērija *nf* coli bacillus

kolibri *indecl nm* hummingbird

kolibrijs *nm* hummingbird

kolīdēt *vi* = kollīdēt

kolidins *nm* collidine

kolīdz *conj* as soon as

kolikas *nf pl* colic

kolikvācija *nf* = kollikvācija

kolimācija *nf* = kollimācija

kolimators *nm* = kollimātors

kolinsijas *nf pl* collinsia

kolis *nm* flour moth

kolīts *nm* colitis

kolīzija *nf* = kollīzija
koljē *indecl nm* lavaliere
ko|ll|aboracionisms [l] *nm* collaborationism
ko|ll|aboracionist/s [l] *nm*, ~e *nf* collaborationist
ko|ll|abor|a|tor/s [l][ā] *nm*, ~e *nf* collaborationist
ko|ll|aborēt [l] *vi* collaborate (with the enemy)
ko|ll|ācija [l] *nf* collation
ko|llā|cionēt [la] *vt* collate
ko|ll|agēnoze [l] *nf* collagen disease
ko|ll|agēns [l] *nm* collagen
ko|ll|apsēt [l] *vi* (astron.) collapse
ko|ll|apss [l] *nm* collapse
ko|ll|aterāli [l] *adv* collaterally
ko|ll|aterāls [l] *adj* collateral
ko|ll|āža [l] *nf* collage
ko|ll|edža [l] *nf* college
ko|ll|ēga [l] *nm*, *nf* = kollēģis
ko|llē|ģiāli [le] *adv* collegially
ko|llē|ģiālitāte [le] *nf* collegiality
ko|llē|ģiāls [le] *adj* collegial
ko|ll|ēģija [l] *nf* Collegium; council, board
ko|ll|ēģ/is [l] *nm*, ~e *nf* colleague
ko|ll|ekcija [l] *nf* collection
ko|ll|ekcionārisms [l] *nm* collecting
ko|ll|ekcionārs [l] *nm*, ~e *nf* collector
ko|ll|ekcionēt [l] *vt* collect
ko|ll|ekte [l] *nf* (of money) collection
ko|ll|ektēt [l] *vt* take up a collection
ko|ll|ektīvi [l] *adv* collectively
ko|ll|ektīvisms [l] *nm* collectivism
ko|ll|ektīvistiski [l] *adv* collectivistically
ko|ll|ektīvistisks [l] *adj* collectivist
ko|ll|ektīvist/s [l] *nm*, ~e *nf* collectivist
ko|ll|ekt|ī|vitāte [l][i] *nf* collectiveness
ko|ll|ekt|ī|vizācija [l][i] *nf* collectivization
ko|ll|ekt|ī|vizēt [l][i] *vt* collectivize
ko|ll|ektīvs [l] *nm* collective, collective body; (of workers) all the workers (of an enterprise); (student) body

ko|ll|ektīvs [l] *adj* collective
ko|ll|ektīvums [l] *nm* collectiveness
ko|ll|ektors [l] *nm* 1. (el.) commutator; (person, el.) collector; 2. manifold; 3. repository
kollers *nm* staggers
ko|ll|īdēt [l] *vi* collide
ko|ll|ijs [l] *nm* collie
ko|ll|ikvācija [l] *nf* colliquation
ko|ll|imācija [l] *nf* collimation
ko|ll|im|ā|tors [l][a] *nm* collimator
ko|ll|īzija [l] *nf* collision; conflict; conflict of laws; procesuāla k. (jur.) procedural conflict
ko|ll|odijs [l] *nm* collodion
ko|ll|o|ī|dāli [l][i] *adv* colloidally
ko|ll|o|ī|dāls [l][i] *adj* colloidal
ko|ll|oīdķīmija [l] *nf* colloidal chemistry
ko|ll|oīdķīmisks [l] *adj* colloidal chemistry (*adj*)
ko|ll|oīds [l] *nm* colloid
ko|ll|okvijs [l] *nm* 1. oral examination; 2. colloquium
kolo *nm* (dance) kolo
kolobuss *nm* colobus monkey
kolodijs *nm* = kollodijs
kolofonijs *nm* colophony, rosin
kolofons *nm* colophon
koloid- See kolloid-
kolokāzija *nf* taro
kolokvijs *nm* = kollokvijs
kolombas *nf pl* (bot.) water shield
kolombiet/is *nm*, ~e *nf* Colombian
kolombina *nf* Columbine
kolometrija *nf* colometry
kolonāde *nf* = kolonnāde
koloncipars *nm* page number
koloniālīpašums *nm* colonial property
koloniālisms *nm* colonialism
koloniālpreces *nf pl* colonial goods
koloniāls *adj* colonial
koloniāltirdzniecība *nf* colonial trade
koloniālvalsts *nf* colonial power

kolonija *nf* 1. colony; settlement; 2. nest (of wasps); 3. **(vasaras) k.** summer camp; **(labo-šanas darbu) k.** correctional facility; **(darba) k.** juvenile correctional institution

kolonist/s *nm*, ~e *nf* colonist

kolonizācija *nf* colonization

koloniz[a]toriski [ā] *adv* coloniastically

koloniz[a]torisks [ā] *adj* colonialist

koloniz[a]tor/s [ā] *nm*, ~e *nf* colonizer

kolonizēt *vt* colonize

kolonna *nf* (arch., mil.) column; **četrrindu k.** (mil.) column of fours; **divrindu k.** (mil.) column of twos; **vienrindu k.** (mil.) file; ~**ā pa vienam, soļos marš!** file from the left/right, forward march!

kolonnāde *nf* colonnade

kolonnas galva *nf* capital (of a column)

kolonnas ķermenis *nm* shaft (of a column)

kolonnas pamatne *nf* base (of a column)

kolonnu sistēma *nf* columniation

kolonnveida *indecl adj* columnar

kolonnveidīgs *adj* columnar

kolonnvektors *nm* column vector

kolons I *nm* colon (:)

kolons II *nm* colonus

kolontituls *nm* (typ.) running title

Kolorado vabole *nf* Colorado potato beetle

koloratūra *nf* coloratura

koloratūrsoprāns *nm* coloratura soprano

kolorējums *nm* colorization

kolorēt *vt* color, colorize

kolorimetrija *nf* colorimetry

kolorimetriski *adv* colorimetrically

kolorimetrisks *adj* colorimetric

kolorimetrs *nm* colorimeter

koloristika *nf* color scheme; (mus.) color

koloristiski *adv* coloristically

koloristisks *adj* coloristic

kolorist/s *nm*, ~e *nf* colorist

kolorīti *adv* colorfully

kolorītiski *adv* colorfully

kolorītisks *adj* colorful; color (*adj*)

kolorīts *nm* coloring, color

kolorīts *adj* colorful

kolosāli *adv* colossally

kolosāls *adj* collosal

koloss *nm* colossus

kolportāža *nf* colportage

kolportēt *vt* hawk in books

kolportier/is *nm*, ~e *nf* book hawker

kolrābis *nm* kohlrabi

kols I *nm* colon (:)

kols II *nm* (geol.) col

kolts *nm* Colt revolver

kolumbārijs *nm* columbarium

kolumbīts *nm* columbite

kolumncipars *nm* page number

kolumntituls *nm* (typ.) running title

koluteja *nf* bladder senna

koļēt *vi* (sl.) puke

koļis *nm* (sl.) puke; nausea

koma *nf* 1. (med.) coma; 2. (optics; astron.) coma

komā *nm indecl* (col., of decimal fractions) point

komanda *nf* 1. command; **pēc (kāda) ~s** on (s.o.'s) command; **iepriekšēja k.** preparatory command; 2. party, detachment; commando; brigade; squad; 3. ship's crew; 4. sports team

komandanta stundas *nf pl* curfew

komandant/s *nm* , ~e *nf* commandant

komandantūra *nf* commandant's office

komandas telpa *nf* crew space

komandcentrs *nm* operations center, command center

komandcīņa *nf* team individual competition

komandčempionāts *nm* team championship competition

komandējuma nauda *nf* travel allowance

komandējum/s *nm* business trip; mission; **zinātnisks k.** scientific mission; ~**a izsaukums**

invitational travel order; **(dienas) ~a nauda** per diem; **būt ~ā** be away on business

komandēt *v* **1.** *vi* command, utter commands; **2.** *vt* command, be in charge of; **3.** *vt* order around; **4.** *vt* send on a business trip; send on an official mission

komandfunkcija *nf* command function

komandier/is *nm*, **~e** *nf* commander

komanditāris *nm* (bus.) limited partner, silent partner in a commandite

komanditists *nm* (bus.) limited partner, silent partner in a commandite

komanditsabiedrība *nf* (bus.) limited partnership, commandite

komandkapteinis *nm* team captain

komandķēde *nf* chain of command

komandors *nm* (hist.) military commander (of a castle or district)

komandoss *nm* commando (member of a commando unit)

komandpunkts *nm* command post

komandsastāvs *nm* command structure

komandspēle *nf* team individual competition

komandtiltiņš or **komandtilts** *nm* captain's bridge, navigation bridge

komandturnīrs *nm* team tournament

komandvads *nm* command platoon

komandvērtējums *nm* team standing

komangs or **komāns** *nm* student customs; rule book (of student behavior)

komat- See **kommat-**

kombainier/is *nm*, **~e** *nf* combine operator

kombainis *nm* combine

kombatants *nm* combatant

kombinācija *nf* combination; (sports) play

kombin[a]tīvs [ā] *adj* combinative

kombin[a]torika [ā] *nf* combinatorial analysis

kombin[a]torisks [ā] *adj* combinatorial

kombin[a]tor/s [ā] *nm*, **~e** *nf* schemer

kombināts *nm* group of enterprises; combination

kombinē *indecl nf* chemise

kombinējums *nm* combination

kombinēt *v* **1.** *vt* combine; **2.** *vi* come up with plays (or moves, chess combinations); **3.** *vi* (sl.) figure

kombinēties *vr* combine

kombinezons *nm* coveralls

kombo *indecl nm* (mus.) combo

kombrete *nf* red withe

kom[e]diant/s [ē] *nm*, **~e** *nf* **1.** mountebank, circus comedian; **2.** (fig., cont.) hypocrite

komēdija *nf* comedy

komēdijiski *adv* comedically

komēdijisks *adj* comedic

komēdijiskums *nm* comedic nature

komedons *nm* comedo, blackhead

komelina *nf* commelina; dayflower

komenda *nf* commenda

komendācija *nf* commendation

komens[a]lisms [ā] *nm* commensalism

koment- See **komment-**

komercakts *nm* carrier's statement

komercaritmētika *nf* business arithmetic

komercbanka *nf* commercial bank

komercdarbība *nf* business

komercdirektors *nm* business manager

komerciāli *adv* commercially

komerciālisms *nm* commercialism

komerci[a]lizācija [ā] *nf* commercialization

komerci[a]lizēt [ā] *vt* commercialize

komerciāls *adj* commercial

komercija *nf* commerce

komercinstitūts *nm* business academy

komercizglītība *nf* business education

komerckollēģija *nf* (hist.) board of trade

komerckorespondence *nf* business correspondence

komercraidījum/s *nm* commercial broadcast; **~i** commercial broadcasting

komercreģistrs *nm* commercial register

komercskola *nf* commercial school

komercskolnie/ks *nm*, ~**ce** *nf* commercial school student

komerctiesa *nf* court of equity

komerctiesības *nf pl* law merchant

komercveikals *nm* (hist.) "commercial store" (in Soviet Union, a store that, under conditons of rationing, sold without ration cards but at a higher price)

komercvērtība *nf* commercial value

komersant/s *nm*, ~**e** *nf* businessman

komeršs *nm* Kommers, student revelry

komet *adv* (reg.) while

komēta *nf* comet

komētveida *indecl adj* comet-like

komētveidīgi *adv* like a comet

komētveidīgs *adj* comet-like

komfortabli *adv* comfortably

komfortabls *adj* comfortable

komforts *nm* comfort

kom/i *indecl nm*, ~**iete** *nf* Komi

komiet/is *nm*, ~**e** *nf* Komi

komijs *nm* salesclerk; **ceļojošais k.** traveling salesman

komika *nf* comedy

komiks *nm* comic, comic strip

komiķ/is *nm*, ~**e** *nf* comedian, comic actor

komilitonis *nm* = **kommilitonis**

kominterne *nf* (hist.) Comintern

komis[a]riāts [ā] *nm* commissariat

komisārija *nf* commissary

komisār/s *nm*, ~**e** *nf* commissar

komisija *nf* 1. commission; committee; 2. (bus.) consignment

komisijas līgums *nm* consignment contract

komisionār/s *nm*, ~**e** *nf* middleman

komiskais *nom adj* the comic

komiski *adv* comically

komisks *adj* comical; comic

komiskums *nm* comicality

komisms *nm* 1. the comic; 2. comicality

komisura *nf* commissure

komit[a]ts [ā] *nm* comitatus

komiteja *nf* committee

komitents *nm* 1. consignor; 2. principal (issuing a power of attorney)

komivojažier/is *nm*, ~**e** *nf* traveling salesman, commercial traveler

komjaunatne *nf* Young Communist League

komjauniet/is *nm*, ~**e** *nf* member of Young Communist League, Komsomol

ko[mm]ats [m] *nm* comma; (in decimal fractions) point; **peldošais k.** floating point

ko[mm]atveida [m] *indecl adj* comma-shaped

ko[mm]atveida [m] bruņuts *nf* mussel scale

ko[mm]atveidīgi [m] *adv* like a comma

ko[mm]atveidīgs [m] *adj* comma-shaped

ko[mm]entārs [m] *nm* commentary

ko[mm]ent[ā]tor/s [m][a] *nm*, ~**e** *nf* commentator

ko[mm]entējums [m] *nm* comment; commentary

ko[mm]entēt [m] *vt* comment on, provide commentary

ko[mm]entētāj/s [m] *nm*, ~**a** *nf* commentator

ko[mm]ilitone [m] *nf* sorority sister

ko[mm]ilito/nis [m] *nm* member of a student fraternity, fraternity brother, frater; **ar ~ņu sveicienu** (in writing) fraternally

ko[mm]odāts [m] *nm* (jur.) commodate

ko[mm]oditāte [m] *nf* commodity

ko[mm]unikē [m] indecl nm communiqué

ko[mmū]tācija [mu] *nf* commutation; ~**s panelis** switchboard

ko[mmū]tatīvi [mu] *adv* commutatively

ko[mmū]tātīvs [mu] *adj* commutative

ko[mmū]t[ā]tors [mu][a] *nm* 1. (el.) commutator; 2. local switchboard

ko[mmū]tēt [mu] *vt* commute

komodats *nm* = **kommodāts**

komoditāte *nf* = **kommoditāte**

komodors *nm* commodore

komoners *nm* commoner

komorients *nm* commorient

kompaktdisks *nm* compact disc

kompakti *adv* compactly

kompakts *adj* compact

kompaktums *nm* compactness

komp|a|nija [ā] *nf* (bus.; presence of others) company; ~s pēc to join in (with others); **(tie visi ir) viena k.** (they are all of) the same stripe

kompan|j|on/s [ņ] *nm*, ~e *nf* companion

komparābli *adv* comparably

komparābls *adj* comparable

komparācija *nf* comparison

kompar|a|tīvisms [ā] *nm* comparative approach to literary criticism; comparative historical ap-proach to linguistics

kompar|a|tīvistisks [ā] *adj* comparative

kompar|a|tīvist/s [ā] *nm*, ~e *nf* comparatist

kompar|a|tīvs [ā] *nm* (gram.) comparative

kompar|a|tors [ā] *nm* comparator

kompartija *nf* Communist Party

kompasa salāti *nm pl* prickly lettuce

kompaslampa *nf* binnacle light

kompasmājiņa *nf* binnacle

kompass *nm* compass

kompatibli *adv* compatibly

kompatibls *adj* compatible

kompaundmotors *nm* direct-current machine with compound winding on the field magnet

kompaundtvaikmašīna *nf* compund engine

kompaunds *nm* 1. compound engine; 2. direct-current machine with compound winding on the field magnet

kompaundštance *nf* combination punch

kompendijs *nm* compendium

kompendiozi *adv* compendiously

kompendiozs *adj* compendious

kompensācija *nf* compensation

kompens|a|tori [ā] *adv* in a compensatory manner

kompens|a|toriski [ā] *adv* in a compensatory manner

kompens|a|torisks [ā] *adj* compensatory

kompens|a|tors [ā] *nm* compensator; (firearms) blank firing adapter; *adj* compensating

kompensēt *vt* compensate

kompensēties *vr* be compensated for

kompetence *nf* 1. competence; 2. jurisdiction, powers

kompetenti *adv* competently

kompetents *adj* competent

kompetentums *nm* competence

kompilācija *nf* compilation; pastiche

kompil|a|tīvs [ā] *adj* compilatory

kompil|a|tors [ā] *nm* compiler

kompilēt *vt* compile

kompj|u|ters [ū] *nm* computer

komplanācija *nf* complanation

kompleksi *adv* complexly

kompleksija *nf* complexion

kompleksitāte *nf* complexity

kompleksons *nf* (chem.) complex, coordination compound

komplekss *nm* complex

komplekss *adj* complex

kompleksums *nm* complexity

kompleksveida *indecl adj* complex, combined, composite

kompleksveidā *adv* in a combined (composite) form, as a whole

kompleksveidīgi *adv* in a combined (composite) form, as a whole

kompleksveidīgs *adj* complex, combined, composite

komplektācija *nf* 1. structuring of a complex; 2. manning, staffing

komplektēšana *nf* 1. (of books, collection items) acisition; 2. staffing; recruitment

komplektēt *vt* 1. complete; replenish; supply; acquire a complete set; form a collection; 2. staff; recruit; man

komplektētava *nf* assembly department

komplektēties *vr* consist of, include
komplekti *adv* completely, entirely
komplektība *nf* completeness
komplektizdevums *nm* boxed set
komplekts *nm* 1. complete set; 2. kit; 3. complement (of a ship); staffing; **pilns (darbinieku) k.** fully staffed; 4. (of cards) pack
komplekts *adj* complete, entire
komplektums *nm* completeness, entirety
kompl|e|mentaritāte [ē] *nf* complementarity
kompl|e|mentārkrāsa [ē] *nf* complementary col-or
kompl|e|mentāri [ē] *adv* complementally
kompl|e|mentārs [ē] *adj* complementary
kompl|e|ments [ē] *nm* complement
kompletēt *vt* = **komplektēt**
komplēts *adj* = **komplekts**
komplicēt *vt* complicate
komplicēti *adv* in a complicated manner
komplicētība *nf* complexity
komplicēties *vr* develop complications; become complicated
komplicēts *adj* complicated
komplikācija *nf* complication
kompliments *nm* compliment
komplīss *nm* accomplice
komplots *nm* conspiracy
komponējums *nm* composition; arrangement
komponente *nf* (phys., math.) component
komponents *nm* component
komponēt *vt* compose
komponists *nm*, ~e *nf* composer
kompostēt *vt* compost
kompostēties *vr* compost
kompostier/is *nm* 1. ticket puncher; ~e *nf*; 2. punch
kompostrēt *vt* (of tickets) punch
kompostrētāj/s *nm* 1. ticket puncher; ~a *nf*; 2. punch
kompostrs *nm* cancel
komposts *nm* compost

kompots *nm* stewed fruit, compote
kompoz|i|cija [ī] *nf* composition
kompozicionāli *adv* compositionally
kompozicionāls *adj* compositional
kompoz|i|tmateriāls [ī] *nm* composite (material)
kompoz|i|ts [ī] *nm* composite
kompoz|i|ts [ī] *adj* composite
kompradors *nm* comprador
komprese *nf* compress; **sautējoša k.** poultice
kompresija *nf* compression
kompresijas modulis *nm* bulk modulus
kompresors *nm* compressor
kompromāts *nm* compromisory materials
kompromiss *nm* compromise
kompromitēt *vt* compromise
kompromitēties *vr* compromise oneself
komsorgs *nm* Komsomol organizer; Komsomol secretary (since 1946)
komtese *nf* countess
komtureja *nf* (hist.) commandery
komturija *nf* = **komtureja**
komturs *nm* (hist.) military commander (of a castle or district)
komūna *nf* commune
kom|u|nāli [ū] *adv* communally
kom|u|nāls [ū] *adj* 1. municipal; 2. public; 3. communal
kom|u|nār/s [ū] *nm*, ~e *nf* communard; Communard
komūni *adv* communally
kom|u|nicēt [ū] *vi* 1. commune; 2. communicate
kom|u|nicēties [ū] *vr* communicate
komūnija *nf* Communion
kom|u|nikabilitāte [ū] *nf* communicability
kom|u|nikabls [ū] *adj* communicable
kom|u|nikācija [ū] *nf* communcation
kom|u|nikant/s [ū] *nm*, ~e *nf* communicant
kom|u|nik|a|tīvi [ū][ā] *adv* communicatively
kom|u|nik|a|tīvs [ū][ā] *adj* communicative

kom|u|nik|a|tīvums [ū]|ā] *nm* communicativeness

kom|u|nik|a|tor/s [ū]|ā] *nm*, ~e *nf* communicator

kom|u|nikē [ū] *nm indecl* communiqué

kom|u|nisms [ū] *nm* communism, Communism

kom|u|nistiski [ū] *adv* communistically

kom|u|nistisk/s [ū] *adj* communist, communistic

kom|u|nist/s [ū] *nm*, ~e *nf* communist, Communist

kom|u|nitārisms [ū] *nm* communitarianism

kom|u|nitāte [ū] *nf* community

komūns *adj* common, communal

komutācija *nf* = kommūtācija

komutatīvi *adv* = kommūtātīvi

komutatīv/s *adj* = kommūtātīvs

komutators *nm* = kommūtātors

komutēt *vt* = kommūtēt

konatīvs *adj* conative

koncedēt *vt* concede

koncelebrēt *vt* concelebrate

koncentrācija *nf* concentration

koncentrācijas nometne *nf* concentration camp

koncentr|a|tors [ā] *nm* (compu.) concentrator

koncentrāts *nm* concentrate

koncentrēšana *nf* concentration

koncentrēšanās *nfr* concentration

koncentrēt *vt* concentrate

koncentrētība *nf* concentration

koncentrēties *vr* concentrate

koncentri *nm pl* 1. concentric circles; 2. (educ.) area of concentration

koncentriski *adv* concentrically

koncentrisks *adj* concentric

koncepcija *nf* conception

koncepcijmodelis *nm* conceptual model

konceptīvi *adv* conceptively

konceptīvs *adj* conceptive

konceptpapīrs *nm* bond paper

koncepts *nm* summary

konceptuāli *adv* conceptually

konceptuālisms *nm* conceptualism

konceptuālist/s *nm*, ~e *nf* conceptualist

konceptuāls *adj* conceptual

koncerns *nm* (business) concern

koncertants *nm* concert performer

koncerta apmeklētājs *nm* concertgoer

koncertapvienība *nf* concert organizers

koncertārija *nf* concert aria

koncertbrigāde *nf* concert troupe

koncertceļojums *nm* concert tour

koncertdarbība *nf* concert activity

koncertdzīve *nf* presentation of concerts

koncertestrāde *nf* concert stage

koncertēt *vi* give a concert, give concerts

koncertetīde *nf* concert étude

koncertfilma *nf* filmed concert

koncertflīģelis *nm* concert grand

koncertiestudējums *nm* concert version (of an opera, operetta or literary work)

koncertīna *nf* concertina

koncert|i|no [ī] *indecl nm* concertino

koncertizpildījums *nm* concert performance

koncertklavieres *nf pl* concert piano

koncertlekcija *nf* lecture on music (with musical illustrations)

koncertmeistar/s *nm* 1. concertmaster; 2. accompanist; ~e *nf* concertmistress

koncertmūzika *nf* concert music

koncertnams *nm* concert hall

koncertorganizācija *nf* an organization that organizes concerts

koncertprogramma *nf* concert program

koncertrepertuārs *nm* concert repertoire

koncerts *nm* 1. concert; recital; 2. concerto

koncertsezona *nf* concert season

koncertturneja *nf* concert tour

koncertuzvedums *nm* performance of a concert version (of an opera, operetta or literary work)

koncertvalsis *nm* concert waltz

koncertveida *indecl adj* concert-like

koncertveidīgi *adv* in concert form, as a concert

koncertveidīgs *adj* concert-like

koncertzāle *nf* concert hall

koncesija *nf* concession

koncesionār/s *nm*, ~e *nf* concessionary

kon|ch|oida [h] *nf* conchoid

koncils *nm* (rel.) council

koncipēt *vt* conceive

koncīzi *adv* concisely

koncīzs *adj* concise

končiks *nm* (sl.) cigarette butt

kondemnācija *nf* condemnation

kondensācija *nf* condensation

kondens[a]tors [ā] *nm* 1. condenser; 2. (el.) capacitor

kondensāts *nm* condensate

kondensēt *vt* condense

kondensēties *vr* condense

kondensors *nm* condenser

kond|i|cija [ī] *nf* specifications

kondicionāli *adv* conditionally

kondicionālis *nm* (gram.) conditional

kondicionālisms *nm* (rel.) conditionalism

kondicionāls *adj* conditional

kondicionēt *vt* condition

kondicionētāj/s *nm*, ~a *nf* conditioner

kondicionieris *nm* (col.) conditioner

kondiloma *nf* condyloma

konditoreja *nf* confectionery (store)

konditorejas preces *nf pl* confectionery (goods)

konditor/s *nm*, ~e *nf* confectioner

kondolējums *nm* expression of condolence

kondolence *nf* condolence

kondolents *nm* person offering condolences

kondolēt *vi* condole with

kondomināts *nm* condominium

kondominijs *nm* condominium

kondoms *nm* condom

kondors *nm* condor

kondotjērs *nm* condottiere

kondukcija *nf* 1. conduction; 2. conductance

kondukt|i|vitāte [ī] *nf* conductivity

konduktīvs *adj* conductive

konduktometrija *nf* conductometry

konduktometrs *nm* conductometer

konduktor/s *nm*, ~e *nf* conductor; **jaunākais k.** train guard; **vecākais k.** chief conductor assistant

konduktoru brigāde *nf* train crew

konfabulācija *nf* confabulation

konfederācija *nf* confederation

konfeder[a]tīvs [ā] *adj* confederative

konfederāts *nm* confederate

konfekcija *nf* 1. ready-made clothes; 2. haberdashery

konfekcionārs *nm* outfitter

konfekškoks *nm* hovenia

konfekte *nf* piece of candy

konferansjē *indecl nm*, *nf* master of ceremonies, host (hostess) of a show

konference *nf* conference

konferēt *vi* confer

konfesija *nf* (rel.) denomination; confession, creed

konfesionālisms *nm* confessionalism

konfesionāls *adj* denominational

konfeti *indecl nm pl* confetti

konfidence *nf* confidence

konfidenciāli *adv* confidentially

konfidenciāls *adj* confidential

konfig|u|rācija [ū] *nf* configuration

konfig|u|r[a]tors [ū][ā] *nm* configurator

konfirmācija *nf* confirmation

konfirmands *nm* confirmand

konfirmēt *vt* (rel.) confirm

konfiscēšana *nf* confiscation

konfiscēt *vt* confiscate

konfiskācija *nf* confiscation

konfliktējošs *adj* conflicting, in conflict

konflikts *nm* conflict

konfokāls *adj* confocal

konformācija *nf* conformation

konformācijas analize *nf* conformational analysis

konformāls *adj* conformal

konformēt *vi* conform

konformēties *vr* conform

konformi *adv* conformably

konformisms *nm* conformism

konformist/s *nm*, ~e *nf* conformist

konformitāte *nf* conformity

konforms *adj* conforming; conformable; conformal

konfrontācija *nf* confrontation

konfrontējums *nm* confrontation

konfrontēt *vt* confront

konfrontēties *vr* confront; be confronted

konf[u]ciāniet/is [ū] *nm*, ~e *nf* Confucian

konf[u]ciānisms [ū] *nm* Confucianism

konfūciet/is *nm*, ~e *nf* Confucian

konfūcisms *nm* Confucianism

konfūzi *adv* confusedly

konfūzija *nf* confusion

konfūzs *adj* confused

konga *nf* conga

kongestija *nf* congestion

konglomerācija *nf* conglomeration

konglomerātisks *adj* conglomerate

konglomerāts *nm* conglomerate

kongojiet/is *nm*, ~e *nf* Congolese

kongregācija *nf* congregation

kongreg[a]cionālisms *nm* Congregationalism

kongreg[a]cionālist/s [ā] *nm*, ~e *nf* Congregationalist

kongregāts *nm* congregation

kongresmene *nf* congresswoman

kongresmens *nm* congressman

kongress *nm* congress, Congress

kongruence *nf* congruence

kongruenti *adv* congruently

kongruents *adj* congruent

kongruentums *nm* congruity

kongruēt *vi* congrue, be congruent

kongruisms *nm* (rel.) congruism

konģeni[a]li [ā] *adv* congenially

konģeni[a]litāte [ā] *nf* congeniality

konģeniāls *adj* congenial

konģeniālums *nm* congenialness

konhoida *nf* = konchoida

konīdija *nf* conidium

koniferīns *nm* coniferin

koniski *adv* conically

konisks *adj* conical; taper

koniskums *nm* conicity

konjaciņš *nm dim* of konjaks, (col.) glass of cognac, a little cognac

konjaks *nm* cognac

konjektūra *nf* conjecture

konjugācija *nf* conjugation

konjugātes *nf pl* Zygnemataceae

konjugēt *vt* conjugate

konjunkcija *nf* conjunction

konjunktīva *nf* conjunctiva

konjunkt[i]vīts [ī] *nm* conjunctivitis

konjunktīvs *nm* (gram.) subjunctive (mood)

konjunktūra *nf* situation, conjuncture

konjunktūrisms *nm* opportunism

konjunktūrist/s *nm*, ~e *nf* opportunist

konk[a]vi [ā] *adv* concavely

konk[a]vs [ā] *adj* concave

konkista *nf* Spanish conquest

konkistadors *nm* conquistador

konklāve *nf* conclave

konklāvs *nm* conclave

konklūzija *nf* conclusion

konkordance *nf* concordance

konkordāts *nm* concordat

konkordēt *vi* concord

konkordija *nf* konkordija, a type of Latvian university student organization

konkrēcija *nf* concretion

konkr[e]ments [ē] *nm* concretion

konkrēti *adv* concretely

konkrētība *nf* concreteness

konkrētisms *nm* musique concrète

konkr|e|tizācija [ē] *nf* concretization

konkr|e|tizējums [ē] *nm* concrete instance

konkr|e|tizēt [ē] *vt* concretize

konkr|e|tizēties [ē] *vr* become concrete

konkrēts *adj* concrete

konkrētums *nm* concreteness

konkubīna *nf* concubine

konkub|i|nāts [ī] *nm* concubinage

konkubīne *nf* concubine

konkurence *nf* competition; **ārpus ~s** in a class by itself

konkurent/s *nm*, **~e** *nf* competitor

konkurēt *vi* compete

konkurētspēja *nf* competitiveness

konkurētspējīgs *adj* competitive

konkūrist/s *nm*, **~e** *nf* equestrian

konkūrs *nm* show jumping

konkursa izsludināšana *nf* adjudication of bankruptcy

konkursant/s *nm*, **~e** *nf* competitor (in a test)

konkursa pārbaudījums *nm* competitive examination

konkurs/s *nm* **1.** competition; entrance examination; **ārpus ~a** a. outside of competition, hors concours; b. in a class by itself; **2.** creditors' meeting

konodonts *nm* conodont

konosaments *nm* bill of lading

konotācija *nf* connotation

konotatīvs *adj* connotative

konrektor/s *nm*, **~e** *nf* vice president of a university

konringija *nf* hare's-ear mustard

kons *nm* cone

konsangvinitāte *nf* consanguinity

konsekrācija *nf* consecration

konsekutīvi *adv* consecutively

konsekutīvs *adj* consecutive

konsekvence *nf* **1.** consistency; **2.** consequence

konsekventi *adv* consistently

konsekvents *adj* consistent

konsekventums *nm* consistency

konsenss *nm* consensus

konsensuāli *adv* consensually

konsensuāls *adj* consensual

konservācija *nf* **1.** preservation; **2.** conservation

konservants *nm* preservative

konserv|a|tīvais [ā] *nom adj* (pol.) conservative

konserv|a|tīvi [ā] *adv* conservatively

konserv|a|tīvisms [ā] *nm* conservatism

konserv|a|tīvs [ā] *adj* conservative

konserv|a|tīvums [ā] *nm* conservativeness

konserv|a|torija [ā] *nf* (mus.) conservatory, school of music

konserv|a|torist/s [ā] *nm*, **~e** *nf* music student

konserv|a|tor/s [ā] *nm*, **~e** *nf* (pol.) conservative

konservēt *vt* **1.** can, preserve; **2.** (of lumber) treat; **3.** mothball

konservēties *vr* be preserved

konservi *nm pl* canned food

konservu bundēa *nf* can

konservu fabrika *nf* cannery

konservu rūpniecība *nf* canning industry

konsignācija *nf* consignment

konsignant/s *nm*, **~e** *nf* consignor

konsign|a|tor/s [ā] *nm*, **~e** *nf* consignee

konsignēt *vt* consign

konsilijs *nm* (med.) consultation

konsistence *nf* consistence

konsistenti *adv* consistently

konsistents *adj* consistent

konsistoriāls *adj* consistorial

konsistorija *nf* consistory

konsituācija *nf* context

konsjeržs *nm* concierge

konskripcija *nf* conscription

konsole I *nf* **1.** console; corbel; **2.** console shelf

konsole II *nf* (consolidated government bonds) consol

konsolidācija *nf* consolidation
konsolidēt *vt* consolidate
konsolidēties *vr* consolidate
konsolsija *nf* cantilever
konsonanse *nf* consonance
konsonantisks *adj* consonantal
konsonantisms *nm* consonantism
konsonants *nm* consonant
konsorcijs *nm* consortium
konsorts *nm* member of a consortium
konspektēt *vt* outline, abstract, make a summary of
konspektīvi *adv* concisely, in summary form
konspektīvs *adj* concise, summary
konspekts *nm* abstract, summary; synopsis, digest
konspirācija *nf* 1. conspiracy; 2. conspiracy of silence
konspir|a|tīvi [ā] *adv* conspiratively, conspiratorially; secretly, clandestinely
konspir|a|tīvs [ā] *adj* conspirative, conspiratorial; secret, clandestine
konspir|a|tīvums [ā] *nm* conspiratorial character
konspir|a|tor/s [ā] *nm*, ~e *nf* conspirator, plotter
konspirēt *vt*, usu. as *part* konspirēts concealed, hidden
konstantāns *nm* constantan
konstante *nf* constant
konstanti *adv* costantly
konstants *adj* constant
konstantums *nm* constancy
konstatācija *nf* establishment
konstatējums *nm* finding
konstatēt *vt* ascertain, find; establish, determine; k. nāvi certify death
konstatētājeksperiments *nm* confirming experiment
konstebls *nm* constable
konste|l|ācija [ll] *nf* constellation
konstitūcija *nf* constitution

konstit|u|cionāli [ū] *adv* constitutionally
konstit|u|cionālisms [ū] *nm* constitutionalism
konstit|u|cionālist/s [ū] *nm*, ~e *nf* constitutionalist
konstit|u|cionāls [ū] *adj* constitutional
konstituēt *vt* establish
konstituēties *vr* constitute oneself
konstitutīvs *adj* constituent
konstrikcija *nf* constriction
konstriktors *nm* constrictor
konstruējums *nm* construct
konstruēt *vt* 1. design; 2. construct
konstruēties *vr* (of an elected body) organize itself
konstrukcija *nf* construction; design
konstruktīvi *adv* constructively
konstruktīvisms *nm* constructionism; constructivism
konstruktīvist/s *nm*, ~e *nf* constructionist; constructivist
konstruktīvs *adj* constructive
konstruktīvums *nm* constructiveness
konstruktors *nm* 1. designer; ~e *nf*; 2. (children's) construction set
konstruktoru birojs *nm* engineering design office
konstrukts *nm* construct
konsulārs *adj* consular
konsulāts *nm* consulate
konsulents *nm* (jur.) counselor
konsul/s *nm*, ~e *nf* consul
konsultācija *nf* 1. consultation, advice; (educ.) tutorial; juridiskā k. a. legal advice; b. panel of legal advisors; 2. consulting service, consulting office
konsultants *nm*, ~e *nf* consultant; consulting physician; (educ.) tutor
konsultatīvi *adv* consultatively
konsultatīvs *adj* consultative, advisory
konsultēt *vt* advise
konsultēties *vr* consult
konsuma biedrība *nf* cooperative

konsuma veikals *nm* cooperative store

konsuments *nm* consumer

konsumēt *vt* consume

konsums *nm* consumption

konta izvilkums *nm* statement of account

kontaktalerģija *nf* contact allergy

kontaktaukla *nf* electric cord

kontaktdakša *nf* electric plug

kontaktēt *vi* have contact with

kontaktēties *vr* have contact with

kontaktkopēšana *nf* contact printing

kontaktkopija *nf* contact copy

kontaktlaukums *nm* contact area

kontaktlēca *nf* contact lens

kontaktligzda *nf* electric outlet

kontaktmetināšana *nf* spot welding

kontaktors *nm* contactor

kontaktpersona *nf* contact person

kontaktpoga *nf* pushbutton

kontaktrozete *nf* electrical outlet

kontakts *nm* contact

kontaktsliede *nf* third rail

kontaktstanga *nf* trolley pole

kontaktstienis *nm* trolley pole

kontakttīkls *nm* system of overhead wires (for streetcars)

kontaktvads *nm* overhead wire (for streetcars)

kontaktveida *indecl adj adj* contact

kontaktveidīgs *adj* contact (*adj*)

kont[a]minācija [ā] *nf* contamination

kont[a]minēt [ā] *vt* contaminate

kontants *nm* 1. cash payment; 2. cash customer

konteinerizācija *nf* containerization

konteinerizēšana *nf* containerization

konteinerizēt *vt* containerize

konteinerkuģis *nm* container ship

konteiners *nm* (transportation) container

konteksts *nm* context

kontekstuāli *adv* contextually

kontekstuālisms *nm* 1. pragmatism; 2. operationalism

kontekstuāls *adj* contextual

kontekstūra *nf* contexture

kontemplācija *nf* contemplation

kontempl[a]tīvi [ā] *adv* contemplatively

kontempl[a]tīvs [ā] *adj* contemplative

kontese *nf* countess

kontestēt *vt* contest

kontinentālā platforma *nf* continental shelf

kontinentāli *adv* continentally

kontinentāls *adj* continental

kontinents *nm* continent

kontinentu pārbīdīšanās *nfr* continental drift

kontingence *nf* contingency

kontingents *nm* 1. contingent; 2. quota

kontingēt *vt* impose a quota

kontinuāli *adv* continually

kontinuāls *adj* continual

kontinuēt *vt* continue

kontinuitāte *nf* continuity

kontinuitīvi *adv* continuously

kontinuitīvs *adj* continuous

kontinuums *nm* continuum

kontogrāmata *nf* account book

kontokorents *nm* account current

kontrabanda *nf* 1. contraband; ~s ceļā as a contraband; 2. smuggling

kontrabandist/s *nm*, ~e *nf* smuggler

kontrabasist/s *nm*, ~e *nf* double bass player

kontrabass *nm* double bass

kontracepcija *nf* contraception

kontraceptīvs *adj* contraceptive

kontradikcija *nf* (philos.) contradiction

kontradiktoriski *adv* contradictorily

kontradiktorisks *adj* contradictory

kontradmirālis *nm* rear admiral

kontrafagotists *nm* contrabassoon player

kontrafagots *nm* contrabassoon

kontrafakcija *nf* plagiarism

kontrahent/s *nm*, ~e *nf* contracting party

kontrahēt *vt* 1. contract, make a contract; 2. contract (pull together)

kontrahēties *vr* (physiol.) contract

kontraindikācija *nf* contraindication

kontrakcija *nf* contraction

kontraktācija *nf* contracting, making a contract

kontraktants *nm* contracting party

kontraktēt *vt* contract, make a contract

kontraktils *adj* contractile

kontrakts *nm* contract

kontraktūra *nf* contracture

kontralts *nm* contralto

kontramarka *nf* 1. complimentary pass; 2. counterfoil

kontraposts *nm* contrapposto

kontrapunkta teorija *nf* contrapuntal theory

kontrapunktiski *adv* contrapuntally

kontrapunktisks *adj* contrapuntal

kontrapunkts *nm* counterpoint

kontrāri *nm pl* contraries

kontrāri *adv* contrarily

kontrārs *adj* contrary

kontrasignācija *nf* countersignature

kontrasignatūra *nf* countersignature

kontrasignēt *vt* countersign

kontrastaini *adv* contrastingly

kontrastainība *nf* contrast, contrasting quality

kontrastains *adj* contrasty

kontrastainums *nm* contrasty quality

kontrastējums *nm* contrasting, contrast

kontrastēt *vi* contrast

kontrastēties *vr* contrast

kontrastkrāsa *nf* contrasting color

kontrasts *nm* contrast

kontrastviela *nf* contrast medium

kontražūrs *nm* contre-jour

kontrdancis *nm* = (obs.) **kontrdeja**

kontrdeja *nf* contra dance

kontrekspozīcija *nf* (mus.) counterexposition

kontrforss *nm* (arch.) counterfort

kontrfūga *nf* counterfugue

kontribūcija *nf* war indemnity

kontrib|u|tīvs [ū] *adj* contributive; contributory

kontrindicēts *adj* counterindicated

kontrindikācija *nf* counterindication

kontrkultūra *nf* counterculture

kontrmanevrs *nm* countermove

kontrmīna *nf* countermine

kontrolaka *nf* manhole

kontrolaparāts *nm* monitor

kontrolapar|a|tūra [ā] *nf* control apparatus

kontrolasistent/s *nm*, ~**e** *nf* dairy farm inspector

kontrolbilance *nf* trial balance

kontroldarbs *nm* (educ.) test

kontroldiktāts *nm* test dictation (in foreign language instruction)

kontrole *nf* 1. checking, inspection; control; 2. (col.) a. checkpoint; checker; b. inspector's office; 3. control

kontroleksemplārs *nm* (typ.) control copy, sample copy

kontrolēt *vt* 1. check, inspect; 2. control

kontrolgrupa *nf* control group

kontrolierīce *nf* control (device)

kontrolier/is *nm*, ~**e** *nf* checker; ticket collector; comptroller

kontrolkarte *nf* quality check card

kontrolkomisija *nf* control commission

kontrollaiks *nm* fixed time interval (allowed for the performance of a task)

kontrollers *nm* (el.) controller

kontrolligzda *nf* control nest (for checking the laying rate of chickens)

kontrolnovilkums *nm* (typ.) press proof

kontrolpakete *nf* controlling interest

kontrolpārbaude *nf* proficiency test

kontrolpulkstenis *nm* time clock

kontrolpunkts *nm* 1. reference point; 2. checkpoint

kontrolsaime *nf* (of bees) control colony

kontrolskaitļi *nm pl* production planning figures, production parameters

kontrolslaukums *nm* standard milk yield (from a cow)

kontrolstacija *nf* control station

kontrolstrops *nm* control hive

kontrolsumma *nf* (compu.) check sum

kontrolsvari *nm pl* master scales

kontroltalons *nm* counterfoil

kontroverse *nf* controversy

kontroversi *adv* controversially

kontroversiāli *adv* controversially

kontroversiāls *adj* controversial

kontroverss *adj* controversial

kontrpretenzija *nf* counterclaim

kontrreformācija *nf* counterreformation

kontrrevolūcija *nf* counterrevolution

kontrrevol[u]cionāri [ū] *adv* in a counter-revolutionary manner

kontrrevol[u]cionārs [ū] *nm,* ~e *nf* counter-revolutionary

kontrrevol[u]cionārs [ū] *adj* counterrevolu-tionary

kontrsignāls *nm* countersign

kontrsliede *nf* counterrail

kontrspiede *nf* reversing press

kontruzgrieznis *nm* locknut

kontrvekselis *nm* (bus.) cross-bill

konts *nm* (bus.) account; tekošais k. account current

kontumācija *nf* contumacy

kontūra *nf* contour

kont[u]rāls [ū] *adj* contour

kont[u]rējums [ū] *nm* outline

kont[u]rēt [ū] *vt* contour

kontūrgrāvis *nm* major drainage ditch

kontūrkanāls *nm* drainage canal

kontūrkarte *nf* base map

kontūrlīnija *nf* contour line

kontūrplāns *nm* countour plan

kontūrs *nm* (el.) stage; circuit

kontūrspalvas *nf pl* contour feathers

kontūrzīmējums *nm* contour drawing

kont[u]zēt [ū] *vt* contuse; shell-shock

kontūzija *nf* contusion; shell shock

konubiāls *adj* connubial

konubijs *nm* conubium

konulārija *nf* conulariid

konurbācija *nf* conurbation

konuss *nm* cone

konusveida *indecl adj* conical

konusveidīgi *adv* conically

konusveidīgs *adj* conical

konvalescence *nf* convalescence

konvalescents *adj* convalescent

konveijerizācija *nf* conveyorization

konveijerizēt *vt* conveyorize

konveijers *nm* conveyor; assembly line

konvekcija *nf* convection

konveksi *adv* convexly

konvekss *adj* convex

konvektīvi *adv* convectively

konvektīvs *adj* convective

konvektors *nm* convector

konvencija *nf* convention, agreement

konvencionāli *adv* conventionally

konvencionālisms *nm* conventionalism

konvencionālist/s *nm,* ~e *nf* conventionalist

konvencion[a]litāte [ā] *nf* conventionality

konvencionāls *adj* conventional

konvenēt *vi* 1. convene; 2. be convenient

konvenience *nf* convenience

konvents *nm* convention

konverģence *nf* convergence

konverģenti *adv* convergently

konverģents *nm* converging series; converging integral; converging feature

konverģents *adj* convergent

konverģēt *vi* converge

konversācija *nf* conversation

konversācijas vārdnīca *nf* encyclopedia

konversija *nf* conversion

konvertācija *nf* (of foreign currency) conversion

konverters *nm* (metall.) converter

konvertēt *vt* convert

konvertīts *nm* (rel.) convert

konvertoplāns *nm* convertiplane

konverts *nm* 1. envelope; 2. (bedding) top sheet

konvikts *nm* student dormitory

konvocēt *vt* convoke

konvojēt *vt* convoy

konvojnie/ks *nm*, ~ce *nf* convoy

konvojs *nm* convoy

konvokācija *nf* convocation

konvolūts *adj* convolute

konvulsija *nf* convulsion

kovulsīvi *adv* convulsively

konvulsīvs *adj* convulsive

konzums *nm* consumption

kooperācija *nf* cooperation

kooper|a|tīvi [ā] *adv* cooperatively

kooper|a|tīvs [ā] *nm* cooperative; (col.) cooperative store

kooper|a|tīv/s [ā] *adj* cooperative

kooper|a|tor/s [ā] *nm*, ~e *nf* cooperator

kooperēt *vi* cooperate

kooperēties *vr* cooperate

kooptācija *nf* co-optation

kooptēt *vt* co-opt

koordinācija *nf* coordination

koordināt/a *nf* coordinate; ~u tīkls grid

koordin|a|togr|ā|fs [ā][a] *nm* plotter

koordin|a|tor/s [ā] *nm*, ~e *nf* coordinator

koordinēt *vt* coordinate

koordinēties *vr* coordinate

kopa *nf* 1. group; cluster; 2. pile, mound; 3. (math.) set

kopā *adv* 1. together; (in a summation column) total; 2. entangled; 3. (with verbs meaning deterioration or destruction, stresses the finality of the process) completely

kopādzīvošana *nf* 1. living together, common living; 2. cohabitation

kopaifera *nf* copaiba

kopaina *nf* general impression, total picture

kop|a|ls [ā] *nm* copal

kopapdrošināšana *nf* group insurance

kopapjoms *nm* total amount; overall extent, overall size

kopapmācība *nf* coeducation

kopapstrādāšana *nf* collective cultivation of the soil, collective farming

kopapziņa *nf* sense of community

kopatbildība *nf* joint responsibility

kopatradums *nm* (archeo.) deposit

kopātrums *nm* combined speed

kopattīstība *nf* joint development

kopāturēšanās *nfr* staying together

kopatzinums *nm* consensus

kopaudzināšana *nf* coeducation

kopaudži *nm pl* those grown up together

kopauglis *nm* aggregate fruit

kopautorība *nf* joint authorship

kopbraukšana *nf* joint trip

kopbūve *nf* 1. joint construction project; 2. building complex

kopceļš *nm* same way, same road; common path

kopcikls *nm* combined cycle

kopdarbība *nf* joint action

kopdarbs *nm* teamwork

kopdekorējums *nm* overall decorative scheme

kopdevums *nm* total output

kopdruva *nf* common fields

kopdziedāšana *nf* group singing

kopdzimtes *indecl adj* (gram.) epicene

kopdzimuma *indecl adj* androgynous

kopdzīve *nf* 1. communal living; 2. cohabitation

kopdzīvoklis *nm* multi-family apartment

kopēdināšana *nf* school lunch program

kopēdnīca *nf* communal dining room; cafeteria

kopējamais papīrs *nm* carbon paper

kopējams *adj*, usu. *defin* **kopējamais** copying

kopēji *adv* jointly; in combination

kopēj/s *nm*, **~a** *nf* tender, nurse

kopējs *adj* **1.** common; joint; jointly owned; combined; general; **2.** total

kopernicija *nf* copernicia

kopesamība *nf* (philos.) concomitance

kopēt *vt* **1.** copy; **2.** (photo.) print; **3.** trace

kopētāj/s *nm* **1.** copyist; **~a** *nf*; **2.** copier

kopētava *nf* copying room

kopforma *nf* overall form

kopgaita *nf* (poet.) common path; common task

kopgalā *adv* finally; in sum

kopgalda telpa *nf* refectory

kopgalds *nm* meals taken together; school lunch program; (mil.) mess

kopgalvnie/ks *nm*, **~ce** *nf* cosponsor

kopganības *nf pl* common (common pasture)

kopga[r]ums [ŗ] *nm* total length

kopguvums *nm* total achievement

kophipotēka *nf* **1.** blanket mortgage; **2.** joint and several mortgage

kopība *nf* community (group; mutuality)

kopības vārds *nm* (gram.) collective noun

kopideja *nf* unifying idea

kopiedarbība *nf* joint action

kopieguve *nf* total production

kopieguvums *nm* total production

kopiekūlums *nm* total yield (of grain, legumes after threshing)

kopiena *nf* community; (soc.) Gemeinschaft

kopienākums *nm* total income; total receipts

kopieņēmums *nm* total income; total receipts

kopierīkojums *nm* total installation

kopieskats *nm* collective view, consensus

kopiespaids *nm* general impression

kopiespiedums *nm* joint publication

kopievākums *nm* total harvest

kopīgi *adv* jointly

kopīgs *adj* common, shared; joint; mutual

kopīgums *nm* commonness; community; communality

kopij/a *nf* copy; **zilā k.** blueprint; **ar ~u** in duplicate; **trijās (četrās, piecās) ~ās** in triplicate (quadruplicate, quintuplicate)

kopiņa *nf dim* of **kopa**, small group; stack, heap; mound

kopīpašība *nf* common characteristic

kopīpašnie/ks *nm*, **~ce** *nf* joint owner;

kopīpašums *nm* joint ownership; common property

kopistaba *nf* common room

kopizjūta *nf* general feeling

kopizmaksas *nf pl* total expenses

kopiznākums *nm* total outcome; total amount

kopizstāde *nf* joint exhibition

kopizveids *nm* overall design

kopjauda *nf* total power

kopjēdziens *nm* comprehensive term

kopkajīte *nf* (naut.) messroom

kopkamera *nf* common prison cell

kopkaps *nm* common grave

kopkatalogs *nm* combined (library) catalog

kopkoncerts *nm* joint concert

kopkonstrukcija *nf* unified construction

kopkoris *nm* massed choirs

kopkūts *nf* common barn

kopķis *nm* (sl.) head, noggin

koplaiks *nm* combined time

koplapains *adj* sympetalous

koplapas *nf pl* sympetalous corolla

koplasījums *nm* oral reading (to several listeners)

koplasīšana *nf* oral reading (to several listeners)

koplaulība *nf* plural marriage

koplēmums *nm* joint decision

koplielums *nm* combined magnitude (or size), total number, total amount

koplieta *nf* common cause

koplietošana *nf* common use, communal use; (compu.) sharing

koplietvārds *nm* (gram.) collective noun

koplīgums *nm* collective contract

kopmācība *nf* coeducation

kopmanis *nm* 1. crony; 2. (barb.) merchant

kopmanta *nf* common property

kopmasa *nf* total mass

kopmēģinājums *nm* general rehearsal

kopmetiens *nm* total circulation

kopmielasts *nm* common meal

kopmītne *nf* dormitory

kopmoderniecība *nf* dairy cooperative

kopne *nf* truss

kopnes josla *nf* chord of a truss

kopnes kārtne *nf* king post of a truss

kopnes mezgls *nm* joint of a truss

kopnieks *nm* group leader; foreman

kopnodarītājs *nm* (jur.) accessory

kopnoma *nf* joint lease

kopnomnieks *nm* joint lease holder

kopnorise *nf* general development

kopnosaukums *nm* general title

kopnoskaņa *nf* general feeling

kopnoskaņojums *nm* general mood

kopnovērtējums *nm* overall evaluation

kopnozveja *nf* total catch

kopojamais *def adj, part* of **kopot** (typ.) composing

kopojums *nm* collection

kopolimers *nm* copolymer

koporganisms *nm* composite organism

kopošanās *nfr* copulation

kopot *vt* collect; unite; (typ.) compose

kopotājs *nm*, ~a *nf* collector, gatherer; (of collected works) editor

kopotājveltnis *nm* (typ.) collecting cylinder

kopotie raksti *nm pl* collected works

kopoties *vr* 1. copulate; 2. group, gather; unite

kopots *adj, part* of **kopot** 1. collected; 2. (aeron.) nosing over

koppapīrs *nm* carbon paper

kopparādnieks *nm* bankrupt

kopparāds *nm* total debt

koppārskats *nm* general view; overview

koppasākums *nm* joint enterprise

koppatēriņš *nm* total consumption

koppeļņa *nf* total earnings

koppiederums *nm* joint property

koppienotava *nf* dairy cooperative

kopplāns *nm* joint plan

kopplatība *nf* total area

koppļava *nf* common meadow

kopprasība *nf* principal and charges

kopprodukcija *nf* 1. total production; 2. joint production

kopprodukts *nm* total product; **sabiedriskais k.** gross national product

kopra *nf* copra

koprādītājs *nm* cumulative index

kopraksti *nm pl* edited work, writings from several authors

kopraksts *nm* cursive writing

kopraksturojums *nm* overall characterization

kopraža *nf* total harvest

kopražojums *nm* joint production

koprēdereja *nf* corporation (a type of Latvian corporation combining the features of the ship-owners' company and the limited liability company)

kopredze *nf* binocular vision

koprēķins *nm* (of an addition) total

koprepublikānisks *adj* 1. inter-republic; 2. all-Republic

koprezultāts *nm* total result

koprisinājums *nm* overall solution

koprocesors *nm* (compu.) coprocessor

koprofāgs *nm* coprophagan

kopsabiedrība *nf* corporation (controlled by several other corporate entities)

kopsaime *nf* (poet.) closely knit group

kopsaimniecība *nf* collective farm; collective farming

kopsaimnie/ks *nm*, ~ce *nf* collective farmer

kopsajūta *nf* (psych., Aristotle) common sense

kopsakarība *nf* context; interconnection

kopsakarīgi *adv* contextually

kopsakarīgs *adj* 1. contextual; 2. connected

kopsakars *nm* context; interconnection

kopsapulce *nf* general assembly; general meeting; plenary session

kopsaucējs *nm* common denominator

kopsavilkums *nm* summary

kopsēde *nf* joint meeting

kopsēta *nf* (poet.) collective farm

kopskaits *nm* total, total number

kopskanējums *nm* combined sound

kopskaņa *nf* combined sound

kopskare *nf* contact, connection

kopskats *nm* overall view

kopslaukums *nm* total milk yield

kopsol/is *nm*, usu. *loc* ~ī in step

kopspēks *nm* combined power

kopspēle *nf* (mus.) ensemble

kopsumma *nf* total, sum total

kopsvars *nm* total weight, gross weight

kopš *prep, conj* since

kopšana *nf* 1. nursing, care; 2. cultivation; 3. development

kopt *vt* 1. take care of, care for; nurse; look after; **k. mājas soli** tend to house chores; 2. tend; rear; 3. cultivate; 4. develop; 5. (of concrete) cure

koptelpas *nf pl* common rooms

koptēls *nm* overall character

koptendence *nf* general tendency

kopti *nm pl* Copts

kopties *vr* 1. take care of oneself; 2. do household chores

koptilpums *nm* combined volume

koptirāža *nf* total circulation

koptituls *nm* main title

koptonis *nm* harmony

koptonnāža *nf* total tonnage

koptreniņš *nm* joint training session

kopturis *nm* purlin

kopu *indecl adj* common

kopula *nf* (gram.) copula

kopulācija *nf* copulation

kopul[a]tīvi [ā] *adv* copulatively

kopulatīvs [ā] *adj* copulative

kopul[a]tīvsaliktenis [ā] *nm* (gram.) copulative compound

kopulēt *vt* (bot.) graft

kopulis *nm* (typ.) galley

kopum/s I *nm* 1. complex, combination, aggregate, totality; ~ā in total; 2. corporation-owned land

kopums II *nm* care, caretaking

kopus *adv* together

kopu teorija *nf* theory of sets

kopuzņēmums *nm* joint venture

kopvakariņas *nf pl* joint supper

kopvaloda *nf* common language

kopvalsts *nf* commonwealth

kopvārds *nm* collective name

kopvērtējums *nm* general evaluation

kopvērtība *nf* total value

kopvirtuve *nf* common kitchen, community kitchen

kopzaudējums *nm* total loss; **pieņemtais k.** constructive total loss

kopzeme *nf* jointly owned land

kopzemis *nm* neighbor

kopzemnie/ks *nm*, ~ce *nf* collective farmer

kopzveja *nf* group fishing

kora *nf* roof ridge

korains *adj* peaked; vaulted

Korakanas eleizine *nf* African millet

korālis *nm* hymn; chorale

korallis *nm* coral

koraļļčūska *nf* coral snake

koraļļpolīps *nm* coral polyp

koraļļsakne *nf* coralroot

korāļmeldija *nf* hymn melody

korāļprelūdija *nf* chorale prelude

korāns *nm* koran

korāzija *nf* corrasion

korda *nf* 1. tether; 2. longe

kordebalets *nm* corps de ballet

kordiāls *adj* cordial; sincere

kordierīts *nm* cordierite

kordilīne *nf* cordyline

kordiriģents *nm* = koŗdiriģents

kordīts *nm* cordite

kordodroms *nm* race track for model cars or airplanes

kordonēt *vt* make into a cordon

kordons *nm* cordon

kords *nm* cord (small rope; fabric)

kordziesma *nf* = koŗdziesma

kore *nf* roof ridge

koreāls *adj* = korreāls

koref- See korref-

korejiet/is *nm*, ~e *nf* Korean

korekcija *nf* = korrekcija

korekt- See korrekt-

korel- See korrel-

korepetitor/s *nm*, ~e *nf* = korrepetitors

korespondence *nf* 1. correspondence; 2. report (submitted by a news correspondent)

korespondencraksts *nm* correspondence shorthand

korespondencša[ch]s [h] *nm* chess by mail

korespondentbanka *nf* corresponding bank

korespondents *nm*, ~e *nf* correspondent

korespondēt *vi* correspond, exchange letters

korespondētājlocekl/is *nm*, ~e *nf* corresponding member

korespondētāj/s *nm*, ~a *nf* correspondent; corresponding

koriandrs *nm* coriander

koribants *nm* corybant

koridors *nm* corridor

korifejs *nm* 1. coryphaeus; 2. leader (in science or the arts); 3. leading dancer, male lead

koriģ- See korriģ-

korinte *nf* 1. currant; 2. juneberry

korintieši *nm pl* Corinthians

korintiski *adv* in Corinthian style

korintisks *adj* Corinthian

Koriolisa spēks *nm* Coriolis force

ko/ris *nm* choir, chorus; ~ŗa choral; ~rī *in* chorus

koriski *adv* chorally

korisks *adj* choral

korists *nm*, ~e *nf* chorister, choir singer

korķa goba *nf* cork elm

korķains *adj* corky

korķa josta *nf* lifebelt

korķaudi *nm pl* cork cambium, phellogen

korķa zole *nf* cork platform

korķēt *vt* cork; k. ciet cork up; k. vaļā uncork

korķis *nm* 1. cork; 2. stopper; 3. plug, obstruction; 4. (col.) (electric) fuse; 5. (soccer sl.) corner kick

korķkoks *nm* cork tree

korķozols *nm* cork oak

korķviela *nf* suberin

korķviļķis *nm* corkscrew

kormeistars *nm* = koŗmeistars

kormorāns *nm* cormorant

korners *nm* 1. (bus.) corner; 2. (soccer) corner kick

kornete *nf* (mus.) cornet

kornetists *nm*, ~e *nf* cornet player

kornets *nm* (mil., hist.) cornet

Kornišas šķirne *nf* Cornish (hen)

kornišons *nm* gherkin

korob- See korrob-

korod- See korrod-

korona *nf* corona

koronācija *nf* coronation

koronālā tromboze *nf* coronary occlusion

koronāls *adj* coronary; (ling.) retroflex

koronas izlāde *nf* corona discharge

koronārs *adj* (anat.) coronary

koroners *nm* coroner

koronogr[a]fs [ā] *nm* coronograph

koronopas *nf pl* swine cress

korozija *nf* = korrozija

korozīvs *adj* = korrozīvs

korporācija *nf* 1. corporation; 2. fraternity, sorority, corps

korporants *nm*, ~e *nf* 1. corporator; 2. fraternity brother

korpor[a]tīvisms [ā] *nm* corporatism, corporativism

korpor[a]tīvs [ā] *adj* 1. corporate; 2. pertaining to student organizations

korporel/is *nm* fraternity brother, corpsbruder; ~e *nf* sorority sister

korpulence *nf* corpulence

korpulents *adj* corpulent

korpulentums *nm* corpulence

korpuskula *nf* corpuscle

korpuskulārs *adj* corpuscular

korpuss *nm* 1. body; hull, shell; 2. building (in a group of buildings); 3. corps; **diplomātiskais k.** diplomatic corps; 4. (typ.) long primer, 10-point type

ko[rr]eāls [r] *adj* (jur.) joint and several

ko[rr]eferāts [r] *nm* additional presentation; subsidiary paper

ko[rr]eferents [r] *nm*, ~e *nf* co-lecturer; author of a subsidiary paper

ko[rr]eferēt [r] *vi* act as co-lecturer; present a subsidiary paper

ko[rr]ekcija [r] *nf* correction

ko[rr]ekti [r] *adv* correctly, properly

ko[rr]ektība [r] *nf* correctness

ko[rr]ektīva [r] *nf* correction

ko[rr]ektīvi [r] *adv* correctively

ko[rr]ektīvs [r] *adj* corrective

ko[rr]ektor/s [r] *nm* , ~e *nf* proofreader

ko[rr]ekts [r] *adj* correct, prope

ko[rr]ektums [r] *nm* correctness

ko[rr]ektūra [r] *nf* 1. proofreading; 2. proof sheet; **k. slejās** galley proof; **otrā k.** revise; 3. proofroom; 4. correction, adjustment

ko[rr]ektūras [r] **prese** *nf* proof press

ko[rr]ektūras [r] **tinte** *nf* correction fluid

ko[rr]ektūras [r] **zīmes** *nf pl* proofreader's marks

ko[rr]elācija [r] *nf* correlation; **multiplā k.** multiple correlation; **parciālā k.** partial correlation

ko[rr]el[ā]tīvi [r][a] *adv* correlatvely; correlationally

ko[rr]el[ā]tivitāte [r][a] *nf* correlativity

ko[rr]el[ā]tīvs [r][a] *adj* correlative; correlational

ko[rr]elāts [r] *nm* correlate

ko[rr]elēt [r] *vi* correlate

ko[rr]epetitor/s [r] *nm*, ~e *nf* assistant tutor

korrida *nf* corrida

ko[rr]iģējošs [r] *adj, part* of **korriģēt** corrective

ko[rr]iģējums [r] *nm* correction

ko[rr]iģēt [r] *vt* correct; adjust; **k. uguni** (mil.) adjust the fire; spot

korriģētājs *nm* (mil.) spotter

ko[rr]oborācija [r] *nf* corroboration

ko[rr]oborātīvs [r] *adj* corroborative

ko[rr]oborēt [r] *vt* corroborate

ko[rr]odējamība [r] *nf* corrodibility

ko[rr]odēt [r] *vt, vi* corrode

ko[rr]odēties [r] *vr* corrode

ko[rr]ozija [r] *nf* corrosion

ko[rr]ozīvs [r] *adj* corrosive

korrumpēt *vt* = korumpēt

korrumpētība *nf* = korumpētība

korrumpēties *vr* = korumpēties

korrupcija *nf* = korupcija

korruptants *nm* = koruptants

korrupti *adv* = korrupti

korruptīvi *adv* = koruptīvi

korruptīvs *adj* = koruptīvs

korrupts *adj* = korupts

korsaks *nm* corsac

korsār/s *nm*, ~e *nf* corsair

korsāža *nf* corsage (bodice)

korsete *nf* corset, stays

korsikān/is *nm*, ~iete *nf* Corsican

korso *indecl nm* corso

kortelis *nm* 1. (barb., of clock time) quarter; 2. (col.) fraternity house; 3. (obs.) living quarters

kortelītis *nm* (sl.) one-quarter liter vodka bottle

kortess *nm* cortes

korteēs *nm* cortege

kortikāli *adv* cortically

kortikāls *adj* cortical

kortikostero[i]ds [ī] *nm* corticoid

kortiks *nm* dirk

Korti org[a]ns [ā] *nm* organ of Corti

kortizons *nm* cortisone

korts *nm* (tennis) court

kortuzas *nf pl* bear's-ear sanicle

korumpēt *vt* corrupt

korumpētība *nf* corruption

korumpēties *vr* become corrupt

korunds *nm* corundum

korupcija *nf* corruption

koruptant/s *nm*, ~e *nf* corrupter

korupti *adv* corruptly

koruptīvi *adv* corruptively

koruptīvs *adj* corruptive

korupts *adj* corrupt

korvete *nf* corvette

ko[r]a [r] balkons *nm* choir loft

ko[r]diriģents [r] *nm* choir conductor

ko[r]dziesma [r] *nf* choral composition

ko[r]meistars [r] *nm* choirmaster

kosa I *nf* horsetail

kosa II *nf* 1. horse's neck; 2. mountain ridge

kosa III *nf* jackdaw

kosekanss *nm nf* cosecant

kosinu[s] [ss] *nm* cosine

kosmeja *nf* (bot.) cosmos

kosmētika *nf* 1. cosmetology; 2. cosmetics

kosmētiķ/is *nm*, ~e *nf* cosmetician

kosmētiski *adv* cosmetically

kosmētisks *adj* cosmetic

kosm[e]tolo/gs [ē] *nm*, ~ģe *nf* cosmetologist

kosm[e]toloģija [ē] *nf* cosmetology

kosm[e]toloģiski [ē] *adv* cosmetologically

kosm[e]toloģisk/s [ē] *adj* cosmetological

kosmēts *nm*, ~e *nf* cosmetician

kosmiski *adv* cosmically

kosmisks *adj* 1. cosmic; space; 2. (of velocity) orbital; escape

kosmobiolo/gs *nm*, ~ģe *nf* space biologist

kosmobioloģija *nf* space biology

kosmodroms *nm* spaceport

kosmofizika *nf* astrophysics

kosmofizikāli *adv* astrophysically

kosmofizikāls *adj* astrophysical

kosmofiziķ/is *nm*, ~e *nf* astrophysicist

kosmogonija *nf* cosmogony

kosmogoniski *adv* cosmogonically

kosmogonisks *adj* cosmogonic

kosmogr[a]fija [ā] *nf* cosmography

kosmoķīmija *nf* cosmochemistry

kosmologs *nm* cosmologist

kosmoloģija *nf* cosmology

kosmoloģiski *adv* cosmologically

kosmoloģisks *adj* cosmologic

kosmonautika *nf* astronautics

kosmonauts *nm*, ~e *nf* astronaut

kosmonavigācija *nf* astronautics

kosmonīmija *nf* naming of celestial bodies

kosmoplāns *nm* space shuttle

kosmopolītiski *adv* cosmopolitically

kosmopolītisks *adj* cosmopolitical; cosmopolitan

kosmopolītisms *nm* cosmopolitanism

kosmopolīt/s *nm*, ~e *nf* cosmopolitan

kosmops[īch]oloģija [ih] *nf* psychology of space flight

kosmosf[ai]ra [ē] *nf* globe

kosmoss *nm* (outer) space, cosmos

kosmotelevīzija *nf* transmission of television signals from space

kosmovīzija *nf* = kosmotelevīzija

kosms *nm* = kosmoss

kosubilizācija *nf* cosubilization

kosoviet/is *nm*, ~**e** *nf* Kosovar

kost *vt, vi* **1.** bite ◊ **k. pirkstos** feel like kicking oneself; **k. kaulā** a. chill to the bone; hurt; b. cut to the quick; **k. sīvā ābolā** bite the bullet; **2.** sting; **3.** (of cutting tools) be sharp; **4.** (of freezing temperatures) nip, kill

kostarikiet/is *nm*, ~**e** *nf* Costarican

koste *nf* (sl.) food, board

kosties *vr* **1.** bite each other; **2.** bite into; **3.** (of fish) bite; **4.** (of paints, chemicals) penetrate

kostīmballe *nf* costume ball

kostimērija *nf* outfits; wardrobe

kostimēts *adj* costumed

kostīmfilma *nf* costume movie

kostīmjaka *nf* (women's) suit jacket

kostīmkleita *nf* two-piece dress

kostīms *nm* **1.** costume; (swimming, ski) suit; **2.** women's suit

kostīmsvārki *nm pl* (women's) suit skirt

kosuls *nm* (reg.) beehive

košenile *nf* cochineal

košergaļa *nf* kosher meat

košers *nm* kosher

koši *adv* beautifully; nicely

košināt *vt* beautify

koškrāsaini *adv* in bright colors

koškrāsains *adj* brightly colored

košļājams *adj, part* of **košļāt** (of gum, tobacco) chewing

košļāt *vt* chew

košļāties *vr* bite each other (lightly, playfully)

košs *adj* **1.** (of colors) brilliant; **2.** beautiful; nice

koššarkani *adv* in a bright red color

koššarkans *adj* bright red

košumaugs *nm* ornamental plant

košumdārzs *nm* flower garden

košumkoks *nm* ornamental tree

košumkrūms *nm* ornamental shrub

košums *nm* **1.** (of colors) brilliance; **2.** beauty

košzaļi *adv* in a bright green color

košzaļš *adj* bright green

košzili *adv* in a bright blue color

košzils *adj* bright blue

kotācija *nf* (bus.) quotation

kotangenss *nm* cotangent

kotarnīns *nm* cotarnine

kotedža *nf* cottage

kotedžtipa *indecl adj* cottage-type

kotedžtulpes *nf pl* cottage tulips

kotedžveida *indecl adj* cottagey

kotedžveidīgs *adj* cottagey

kotējums *nm* (bus.) quotation

kotēt *vt* (bus.) quote

kotēties *vr* **1.** (bus) be quoted; **2.** be valued

kotikāda *nf* seal fur

kotiks *nm* fur seal

kotiledons *nm* cotyledon; (plant) Cotyledon

kotiljons *nm* cotillion

kotlešu gaļa *nf* ground meat

kotlete *nf* patty, croquette

kotonēt *vt* cottonize

kotonmašīna *nf* Cotton machine

kotulas *nf pl* mayweed

koturns *nm* cothurnus, buskin

kovalence *nf* covalence

kovalents *adj* covalent

kovariācija *nf* covariation

kovārnis *nm* jackdaw

kovbojs *nm* cowboy

kovboju filma *nf* western (movie)

koveriņš *nm* (naut.) covering

koverkots *nm* covert (cloth)

kozuls *nm* **1.** beehive; **2.** starling house

koža *nf* (col.) grub, eats

kožamais *nom adj* (col.) grub, eats

kožļāt *vt* chew

kožņāt *vt* chew

krā *interj* caw

krabainis *nm* (col.) crawfish

krabiķis *nm* three-legged boat prop

krabināt *vt* rattle

krābiņš *nm* wooden plow

krabis *nm* crab

krāce *nf* rapids

krācēj/s *nm*, ~a *nf* **1.** snorer; **2.** roarer

krācējumi *nm pl* (nasal) sinuses

kra[ch]s [h] *nm* crash, collapse, failure

krāciens *nm* snore

kracis *nm* **1.** drying stand (for crops); **2.** winnow; **3.** jack chain, bull chain

krāčains *adj* full of rapids

krāčainums *nm* multitude of rapids

krači *nm pl* hay and straw fodder

krāču laivošana *nf* whitewater canoeing

krāčupe *nf* (poet.) rapid-studded stream

krāgs *nm* (barb.) collar

kraģis I *nm* nag

kraģis II *nm* stool

krāģis *nm* **1.** low seat; footstool; **2.** trestle; **3.** thin old person; **4.** jade, hack, nag; **5.** collar

krahs *nm* = **krachs**

kraikšķēt *vi* creak

Krainas skopolija *nf* scopolia

kraistīt *vt* skim

kraitāt *vt* stumble, stagger

krāja *nf* **1.** (forest.) (amount of wood in) growing stock; **2.** ~s (rare.) stock; accumulation; savings; resources

krājaizdevu kase *indecl adj* savings and loan association

krājaka *nf* reservoir

krājbanka *nf* savings bank

krājbaseins *nm* sedimentation basin

krājēj/s *nm*, ~a *nf* **1.** saver; **2.** collector

krājgrāmatiņa *nf* passbook

krājība *nf* thrift

krājīgi *adv* thriftily

krājīgs *adj* thrifty

krājkase *nf* savings bank

krājkases grāmatiņa *nf* passbook

krājkasīte *nf dim* of **krājkase**, piggy bank

krājulība *nf* penny-pinching

krājulis *nm* penny-pincher

krājum/s *nm* **1.** collection; stock, store; reserve; ~ā a. in stock; b. in reserve; **neaizskaramais k.** emergency reserve; **2.** deposit; **3.** compendium; anthology;

krākalēt *vi* snore

krākas *nf pl* sputum

krākāt *vi* snore

kraklē *indecl nm* (ceramics) crackle

krākoņa *nf* **1.** roar; **2.** snoring

krākot *vi* snore

krakovjaks *nm* Cracovienne

kraks *interj* crack

krakstēt *vi* crack; creak

krakstināt *vt* (*iter*) crack

krākstīties *vr* choke (on sth.)

krakstoņa *nf* cracking; creaking

kraksts *nm* crack

krakš *interj* crack; crunch

krakšķēt *vi* crack; creak

krakšķiens *nm* crack

krakšķināt *vt* (*iter*) crack

krakšķis *nm* crack

krakšķoņa *nf* cracking; creaking

krākt *vi* **1.** snore; **2.** roar

kraķis *nm* **1.** jade, hack; **2.** thin old person; **3.** low seat; footstool; **4.** (col.) old piece of furniture; old appliance

krākuļot *vi* snore

kraķītis *nm* **1.** *dim* of **kraķis**, low seat; footstool; **2.** (sl.) shot of vodka

krāls *nm* kraal

krama *nf* rash

kramaini *adv* flintily

kramainis *nm* diatomite

kramains *adj* flinty

kramakmens *nm* chert

kramaļģe *nf* diatom

krambambulis *nm* (among university students) strong drink, liquor

krambe *nf* crambe, sea kale

kramenīca *nf* flintlock (musket)

kramerijas *nf pl* Krameria

krāmēt *v* 1. *vt* (col.) pile; **k. nost** remove;
2. *vi* (com.) whack

krāmēties *vr* 1. (col.) busy oneself; mess;
2. (col., with **iekšā, ārā**) move (in, out)

kramgalvis *nm* (col.) pig-headed person

kramgalvnieks *nm* (col.) pig-headed person

krāmi *nm pl* junk, odds and ends

krāmnieks *nm* flea market merchant

krampakausis *nm* (col.) pig-headed person

krampēt *vt* hook, fasten with a hook

krampis *nm* 1. hook; 2. (col.) strength;
3. cramps; 4. (sl.) skinflint

krampītis *nm* 1. *dim* of **krampis**; 2. (col.) shot
(drink, glass)

krampjaini *adv* 1. spasmodically, convulsively;
2. forcedly

krampjainība *nf* forcedness

krampjain/s *adj* 1. spasmodic, convulsive;
2. forced

krampji *nm pl* cramps, spasms, convulsion

krampjveida *indecl adj* cramp-like

krampjveidīgi *adv* like a cramp

krampjveidīgs *adj* cramp-like

kramplauzis *nm* burglar

krampt *vt* grab with one's teeth, snatch

krampuķe *nf* field chamomile

krams *nm* flint

krāms *nm* piece of junk

kramskābe *nf* silica

kramskāb/s *adj*, usu. *defin* ~**ais** (in combination
with the name of an element or compound)
silicate

kramslis *nm* 1. thief; 2. glutton

kramstīt *vt* gnaw

kramstīties *vr* (of horses) pick (with their
teeth)

kramšķināt I *vi* (of ravens) call

kramšķināt II *vi* gnaw, crunch

kramšļi *nm pl* hay or straw debris, sweepings

krāmtirgotāj/s *nm*, ~**a** *nf* junk dealer

krāmu tirgus *nm* flea market

kramzeme *nf* diatomite

krancains *adj* (of a dog) light-collared

krancināt *vi* (of ravens) call

krancis *nm* 1. dog (with a lighter band of hair
around its neck); 2. mut; 3. horse collar
padding

kraniāli *adv* cranially

kraniāls *adj* cranial

krāniņš *nm dim* of **krāns**; small faucet; small
crane

kraniologija *nf* craniology

kraniologiski *adv* craniologically

kraniologisks *adj* craniological

kraniometrija *nf* craniometry

kranioskopija *nf* cranioscopy

krāns *nm* 1. faucet; gate valve, globe valve;
2. crane

krantains *adj* steep, with steep banks

krantmale *nf* steep river bank

krants *nf* steep river bank; drop

krāpīgi *adv* deceitfully

krāpīgs *adj* deceitful

krāpināt *vt* deceive

krapkarmīns *nm* carmine

kraplaka *nf* lac dye

krāpniecība *nf* fraud, swindle

krāpniecīgi *adv* fraudulently

krāpniecīgs *adj* fraudulent

krāpnieciski *adv* fraudulently

krāpniecisks *adj* fraudulent

krāpnie/ks *nm*, ~**ce** *nf* swindler; cheat; deceiver

kraps *interj* scrunch

krapstēt *vi* scrunch

krapstināt *vi* scratch, make scratching noises;
scrunch, make scrunching noises

krapstoņa *nf* scrunching

krapš *interj* scrunch

krapšķēt *vi* scrunch

krapšķināt *vi* scratch, make scratching noises;
scrunch, make scrunching sounds

krapšķis *nm* scrunch

krapšķoņa *nf* scrunching

krapt *interj* gotcha

krāpt *vt* deceive; cheat, cheat on s.o.

krāpties *vr* cheat (habitually)

krapu *interj* See **kripu**

krasa *nf* sharp wind gust

krāsa *nf* 1. color; (psych.) hue; 2. paint; 3. dye

krāsain/ais *nm adj* colored person; *pl* ~ie the colored

krāsaini *adv* colorfully

krāsainība *nf* colorfulness

krāsains *adj* 1. colored; color (*adj*); 2. colorful; 3. (of metals) nonferrous

krāsainums *nm* colorfulness

krāsaugs *nm* a plant that yields a dye

krasi *adv* 1. sharply; 2. suddenly; 3. radically

krāslente *nf* (typewriter, printer) ribbon

krāslis *nm* rouge

krāsmata *nf*, usu. *pl* ~s ruins of a burned-down house

krāsnbedre *nf* hearth (pit)

krāsndurvis *nf pl* stove door, oven door

krāsnesis *nm* corpsbruder, fraternity member

krāsni *adv* = **krāšņi**

krāsniņa *nf* 1. *dim* of **krāsns**; 2. space heater; Franklin stove

krāsnkuris *nm* stoker, fireman

krāsnmūrītis *nm* horizontal heating flue on the floor

krāsnmute *nf* (of ovens, furnaces) throat

krāsnpriekša *nf* hearth (floor area in front of a stove or oven)

krāsns *nf* 1. stove; 2. oven; 3. furnace; **daudzpavardu k.** multi-hearth roasting furnace; 4. kiln

krāsns *adj* = **krāšņs**

krāsns aizsargs *nm* fire screen

krāsnsaugša *nf* top of the oven

krāsns duļķis *nm* kiln wash

krāsnskuris *nm* = **krāsnkuris**

krāsns podiņš *nf* Dutch tile

krāsojums *nm* 1. paint, coat of paint; 2. tint, color

krāsošana *nf* painting

krāsošanas paklājs *nm* drop cloth

krāsot *vt* 1. paint; dye; color; stain; **svaigi ~s** wet paint; **k. eļļām** paint in oils; 2. (of paints, dyes) run (and stain)

krāsotāj/s *nm*, ~a *nf* (house) painter; dyer

krāsotava *nf* dyehouse

krāsoties *vr* 1. turn (change color; **k. zili** turn blue); 2. make up, paint one's face, rouge oneself

krass *adj* 1. (of contrast) sharp; 2. sudden; 3. radical

krasta artilērija *nf* coastal artillery

krasta grīslis *nm* lake bank sedge

krasta līnija *nf* coastline

krasta nodevas *nf pl* wharfage, pierage

krasta tiesības *nf pl* riparian rights

krasta tītenis *nm* hedge bindweed

krasta vējš *nm* offshore wind, land breeze

krasta zīme *nf* (naut.) landmark

krastene *nf* shoreweed

krastkaņepe *nf* hemp agrimony

krastmala *nf* shore, coast; shoreline; bank; quay, dockside

krastmalas *indecl adj* coastal, shore

krastmalnie/ks *nm*, ~ce *nf* shore dweller

krastmalu grīslis *nm* swamp sedge

krastmalu krustaine *nf* marsh fleawort

krastmalu skābene *nf* great water dock

krastnie/ks *nm*, ~ce *nf* shore dweller

krāstonis *nm* hue

krasts *nm* shore; bank

krastu čurkste *nf* sand martin

krastu gliemezis *nm* periwinkle

krāsu aklums color blindness

krāsu dadzis *nm* sawwort

krāsu indigofēra *nf* indigo plant

krāsu krītiņš *nm* colored chalk

krasula *nf* crassula

krāsu miešķi *nm pl* dyer's woodruff

krasums *nm* 1. sharpness; 2. suddenness; 3. radicalness

krāsu tabula *nf* color chart

krāsviela *nf* pigment; dye

krāszieds *nm* tint

krāšļi *nm pl* makeup

krāšļot *vt* put on makeup

krāšļoties *vr* make up (one's face)

krāšmatas *nf pl* ruins (of a burned-down house)

krāšņā ābele *nf* Chinese crabapple

krāšņā pīle *nf* king eider

krāšņais irbenājs *nm* wayfaring tree

krāšņā naglene *nf* fringed pink

krāšņatas *nf pl* ruins (of a burned-down house)

krāšņbruņrupucis *nm* painted turtle

krāšņdzērve *nf* demoiselle crane

krāšņi *adv* splendidly; magnificently; beautifully; sumptuously

krāšņlapsenes *nf* cuckoo wasps

krāšņot *vt* adorn

krāšņoties *vr* adorn oneself

krāšņpūcītes *nf pl* owlet moths

krāšņs *adj* splendid, magnificent; beautiful; sumptuous

krāšņumaugs *nm* ornamental plant

krāšņumdārzs *nm* flower garden

krāšņumkoks *nm* ornamental tree

krāšņumkrūms *nm* ornamental shrub

krāšņums *nm* splendor, magnificence; beauty; sumptuousness

krāt *vt* 1. collect; k. kaudzē pile up, heap; 2. save

kratāmsiets *nm* shaking screen, jig

kratas *nf pl* shivers

krāte *nf* dump

kratekles *nf pl* mixed fodder of hay and straw

krateklis *nm* 1. shaker; (col.) fidgeter; 2. large sieve; winnowing basket

kratenis *nf pl* mixed fodder of hay and straw

krāteris *nm* crater

krāterveida *indecl adj* crateriform

krāterveidīgi *adv* like a crater

krāterveidīgs *adj* crateriform

krāties *vr* collect, accumulate, gather

kratījums *nm* mixed fodder of hay and straw

kratīklis *nm* winnowing basket

kratināt *vt* shake

krātiņš *nm dim* of krāts, cage

kratīšana *nf* 1. shaking; jolting; 2. search; ~s orderis search warrant

kratīt *vt* 1. shake; k. pirkstu wag one's finger; 2. jolt; 3. search

kratītāj/s *nm*, ~a *nf* 1. shaker; 2. (col.) shivers; 3. searcher

kratīties *vr* shake, rattle; be jolted; k. vaļā shake off, try to get rid (of s.o.)

krāts *nm* cage

kratulis *nm* 1. palsy; 2. winnowing screen

krātuve *nf* depository; repository; storehouse; reservoir; (compu.) storage

kraucelēt *vi* keep clearing one's throat

kraucenis *nm* one who keeps clearing his throat

kraucināt *vi* 1. clear one's throat; 2. croak; caw

krauja *nf* steep; scarp

kraujains *adj* with steep banks, with steeps

krauji *adv* steeply

kraujlaukums *nm* storage area

kraujmala *nf* edge of a steep, edge of a riverbank

kraujš *adj* steep

kraujums *nm* 1. steepness; 2. steep; scarp

kraukas *nf pl* 1. hawk; 2. phlegm

kraukāt *vi* 1. hawk; 2. (of ravens) call

kraukatas *nf pl* sputum

kraukāties *vr* (*iter*) hawk

krauklene *nf* baneberry

krauklēns *nm* young raven

krauklēt *vi* (of ravens) call

krauklis *nm* raven

krauklītis *nm dim* of krauklis, raven

kraukļu vārna *nf* carrion crow

krauks *interj* crack, crunch

kraukstēt *vi* crunch

kraukstināt *vt* (*iter*) crunch, crack

kraukstoņa *nf* crunching

kraukš *interj* crack, crunch

kraukšķēt *vi* crunch

kraukšķīgi *adv* crunchingly

kraukšķīgs *adj* crunchy

kraukšķīgums *nm* crunchiness

kraukšķināt *vt* (*iter*) crunch, crack

kraukšķis *nm* crunch

kraukšķoņa *nf* crunching

kraukt *vi* caw

kraukis *nm* (zool.) rook

kraulains *adj* having steep banks, having
steeps

krauli *nm pl* bunt

kraulis *nm* 1. steep, cliff; high shoreline;
2. rotting piece of wood; snag

krauls I *nm* = **kraulis**

krauls II *nm* (swimming stroke) crawl

kraume *nf* heap, a lot, great quantity

krauna I *nf* heap, a lot, great quantity

krauna II *nf* blunt edge of a scythe blade

kraupe *nf* wrinkle

kraupes zāle *nf* buttercup

kraupis *nm* 1. scabies; 2. (plant disease; crust)
scab

kraupainība *nf* scabbiness

kraupains *adj* scabby

kraupainums *nm* scabbiness

kraupi *adv* roughly

kraupjainība *nf* scabbiness

kraupjains *adj* scabby

kraupjainums *nm* scabbiness

kraupja zāle *nf* buttercup

kraups *adj* rough

kraupulis *nm* scab

krause *nf* (reg.) pear tree

krausēt *vt* thresh; strip or crush the beards of
barley ears

krausis *nm* (reg.) pear

kraustīt *vt* (*iter*) stack and restack, shift

kraut *vt* 1. stack, pile (up), heap (up); 2. load;
k. ārā unload; 3. (com.) whack

krautes *nf pl* load-bearing part of a horse
wagon

krautin *adv, emph* of **kraut**; **k. krāva** he was
stacking (piling up things) diligently

krautne *nf* 1. stack; 2. (truck) platform

krautuve *nf* stowage, storage; yard, lot

krava *nf* load, freight; cargo; **derīgā k.**
payload

kravas aģents *nm* freight agent

kravas auto truck

kravas kaste *nf* (truck) stake body

kravas līnija *nf* load line

kravas lūka *nf* cargo hatch

kravaas telpa *nf* hold

kravas tīkls *nm* cargo net

kravas vagons *nm* freight car

kravas zīme *nf* freight bill

kravāt *vt* 1. pack; 2. load; **k. iekšā** load; **k. ārā**
unload; 3. stack; shift, shuffle

kravata *nf* (reg.) pile, heap

kravate *nf* necktie

kravāties *vr* 1. pack; 2. rummage

kravažas *nf pl* junk

krāvējceltnis *nm* forklift

krāvēj/s *nm*, ~a *nf* 1. loader; 2. stevedore

krāviens *nm* 1. (an instance of) loading;
2. blow

kravierīce *nf* loading device, loader

kravietilpība *nf* cargo carrying capacity

kravinieks *nm* truck

kravkoks *nm* derrick

kravnesība *nf* cargo carrying capacity; **pilna k.**
(naut.) deadweight

kravsvars *nm* maximum (cargo) weight

krāvums *nm* pile; cairn

kreacionisms *nm* creationism

kreatin[i]ns [ī] *nm* creatinine

kreat[i]ns [ī] *nm* creatine

kre[a]tīvi [ā] *adv* creatively

kre[a]tivitāte [ā] *nf* creativity

kre|a|tīvs |ā| *adj* creative

kre|a|tūra |ā| *nf* creature

krecele *nf* 1. spiral; 2. corkscrew; 3. (reg.) headcheese

krecelēt *vi* 1. cough lightly, clear one's throat; 2. scribble

krecelīgi *adv* in a scribbly manner

krecelīgs *adj* scribbly

krecelis *nm* 1. cough; 2. one who constantly clears his throat; 3. corkscrew

kreceris *nm* (firearms) cleaning rod

krecēt *vi* clot, congeal, harden

krecināt *vi* cough lightly, clear one's throat

krecumi *nm pl* 1. leftovers; 2. dross; 3. tadpoles

kred|i|tbiedrība |ī| *nf* credit union

kred|i|tbiļete |ī| *nf* bank note

kreditēt *vt* 1. give credit; 2. credit

kreditēties *vr* obtain credit

kred|i|tiestāde |ī| *nf* financial institution

kreditīvs *nm* credentials

kred|i|tkarte |ī| *nf* credit card

kred|i|tkase |ī| *nf* savings and loan association

kred|i|tkooperātīvs |ī| *nm* credit union

kred|i|tlikme |ī| *nf* interest rate

kred|i|tnespēja |ī| *nf* insolvency

kred|i|tnespējīgs |ī| *adj* insolvent

kred|i|toperācija |ī| *nf* credit operation

kreditors *nm*, ~e *nf* creditor

kred|i|trīkotāj/s |ī| *nm*, ~a *nf* treasurer; purser; bursar

kred|i|ts ī| *nm* credit; credit account

kred|i|tspēja |ī| *nf* solvency

kred|i|tspējīgs |ī| *adj* solvent

kred|i|tvēstule |ī| *nf* letter of credit

kred|i|tzīme |ī| *nf* credit voucher

kredo *indecl nm* creed

kreftīgs *adj* (col.) spicy

kreicis *nm* (cards) clubs

kreilība *nf* left-handedness

kreil/is *nm*, ~e *nf* left-hander

kreiliski *adv* k. adīt purl, use the purl stitch

kreilisks *adj* (of knitting) purl

kreilītis *nm dim* of kreilis, left-hander

kreimalaiža *nm* (col.) index finger

kreima puķe *nf* dame's violet

kreima zāle *nf* 1. butterwort; 2. adder's-tongue

kreimene *nf* lily of the valley

kreimot *vt* skim, cream

kreims *nm* cream

kreimule *nf* butterwort

kreisais *nom adj* (pol.) leftist; ~ā *f*

kreiserātrums *nm* cruising speed

kreiseris *nm* cruiser

kreisēt *vi* (naut.) 1. patrol; 2. cruise

kreisi *adv* pa k. to the left; on the left

kreisrocis *nm* left-hander

kreis/s *adj*, usu. *defin* kreisais, *f* ~ā; 1. left, left-hand; uz ~o! left face! 2. (pol.) left-wing; 3. (of fabric side) wrong; 4. (of a side of a wagon or horse) near

kreisums *nm* (pol.) leftism

kreitals *nm* (bot.) lady's-mantle

krejošana *nf* skimming, creaming

krejošanas punkts *nm* creamery

krejot *vt* skim, cream

krejotava *nf* creamery, dairy

krējumains *adj* creamy

krējumkanna *nf* cream jug

krējumkrāsa *nf* cream color

krējumķērne *nf* churn

krējumlaišķis *nm* = krejumlaizis

krejumlaiz/is *nm*, ~e *nf* 1. cream licker; 2. (col.) index finger

krējumlaiža *nm* = krejumlaizis

krējummērce *nf* cream sauce

krējumots *adj* creamy

krējumpods *nm* cream pot

krējums *nm* cream; skābais k. sourcream

krējumsiers *nm* cream cheese

krējumtrauks *nm* cream jug

krējumveida *indecl adj* creamy

krējumveidīgi *adv* like cream

krējumveidīgs *adj* creamy

krēkāt *vi* clear one's throat

krekings *nm* (petroleum) cracking

krekla bikses *nf pl* union suit

krekla priekša *nf* shirt front

kreklbiksītes *nf pl* chemise

krekliņš *nm* 1. *dim* of **krekls**; 2. athletic jersey

krekl/s *nm* shirt; ~**os** in shirt-sleeves; **k. ārā no biksēm** in one's shirttails

kreklu drāna *nm* shirting

kreklveida *indecl adj* shirt-like

kreklveidīgs *adj* shirt-like

krekstēt *vi* clear one's throat

krekšķēt *vi* clear one's throat

krekšķināt *vi* clear one's throat

krekšķis *nm* light cough

krēkt *vi* (of crows, ravens, ducks) call

kreķis *nm* reel

krēķis I *nm* nutcracker

krēķis II *nm* damson

krelle *nf* bead; ~**s** necklace

kreļļains *adj* adorned with beads

kreļļveida *indecl adj* necklace-like

kreļļveidīgi *adv* like a necklace

kreļļveidīgs *adj* necklace-like

kremācija *nf* cremation

kremaļjēra *nf* (mech.) rack

krem[a]torija [ā] *nf* crematorium

krēmbalts *adj* creamy white

krēmdzeltens *adj* creamy yellow

kremelde *nf* meadow mushroom

kremēt *vt* cremate

krēmkrāsa *nf* cream color

kremlis *nm* kremlin, Kremlin

krēms *nm* 1. cream; 2. crème

kremsli *nm pl* remains

kremst *vt* gnaw

kremsties *vr* gripe

kremšķināt *vi* clear one's throat

kremšķis *nm* light cough

kremšļot *vi* clear one's throat

kremzbaltums *nm* Kremnitz white

krencelēt *vi* clear one's throat

krencelis *nm* light cough

krēnēt *vi* wait in vain a long time

kreņķēties *vr* (barb.) worry

kreņķi *nm pl* (barb.) worry

kreņķīgs *adj* (barb.) grouchy

kreolīns *nm* pine oil

kreolisks *adj* Creole; creolized

kreol/s *nm*, ~**iete** *nf* Creole

kreozoteļļa *nf* creosote

kreozots *nm* creosote

krēpainis *nm* the maned one

krēpains *adj* containing sputum

krēpaļāt *vi* hawk

krēpas *nf pl* sputum

krēpāt *vi* hawk

krēpāties *vr* hawk

krepdešīns *nm* crepe de chine

krēpele *nf* doughnut

krēpes *nf pl* mane

krepitācija *nf* (med.) crepitation

krēpjains *adj* bushy-maned

krēpot *vi* expectorate

kreppapīrs *nm* crepe paper

kreps *nm* crepe

krēpuči *nm pl* (reg.) sputum

krepžoržets *nm* Georgette crepe

krese *nf* tall nasturtium

krēsla *nf* twilight, dusk

krēslaine *nf* shade; dusk

krēslaini *adv* duskily

krēslainība *nf* duskiness

krēslains *adj* dusky

krēslainums *nm* duskiness

krēslas dzīvnieks *nm* crepuscular animal

krēsli *adv* duskily

krēslība *nf* twilight

krēslīgi *adv* duskily

krēslīgs *adj* dusky

krēslinieks *nm* chair maker

krēsliņa *nf dim* of krēsla, twilight, dusk

krēsliņš *nm* 1. *dim* of krēsls, little chair; 2. (con-crete pouring) chair

kreslis *nm* = krēslis

krēslis *nm* removable sled seat

krēslojums *nm* twilight

krēslot *vi* get dark (at nightfall)

krēsloties *vr* get dark (at nightfall)

krēsls *nm* chair; braucamais k. wheelchair; pī-tais k. wicker chair; saliekamais k. folding chair

krēsls *adj* dusky

kressalāti *nm pl* watercress

krest *vt* = krēst

krēst *vt* (reg.) 1. shake down, shake off; 2. gulp down

krešendo *nm indecl* (mus.) crescendo

krešķi *nm pl* (col.) dirt

krešu salāti *nm pl* 1. watercress salad; 2. watercress

krešu zāle *nf* watercress

krētainā smilga *nf* silky bent grass

krētainā ziemciete *nf* serrated wintergreen

krētains *adj* bushy-maned

kretīniski *adv* like a cretin

kretīnisks *adj* cretinous

kretīnisms *nm* cretinism

kretīns *nm* cretin

krētis *nf pl* (reg.) mane

kretons *nm* cretonne

kretulis *nm* winnowing pan

kretuls *nm* winnowing pan

kretuļot *vt, vi* winnow

krevaini *adv* scabbily

krevains *adj* scabby

kreve *nf* scab, crust

krevele *nf* scab, crust

kreveļaini *adv* 1. scabbily; 2. roughly, bumpily

kreveļains *adj* 1. scabby, crusty; 2. rough, bumpy

kreveļainums *nm* 1. scabbiness; 2. roughness, bumpiness

krevete *nf* shrimp

krezols *nm* cresol

krēzs *nm* Croesus

kribas *nf* sledge bottom (of bound wooden sticks)

kribināt *vt* gnaw

kribiņš *nm* (col.) little bit, smidgen

kribis I *nm* (col.) little bit, smidgen

kribis II *nm* (reg.) wagon rack

krica *nf* (metall.) bloom

kricelēt *vt, vi* (col.) scribble

kricelīgi *adv* in a scribble

kricelīgs *adj* scribbly

krīcis *nm* (reg.) basket

kridzis *nm* (col.) little bit, smidgen

krieķene *nf* damson

kriens *nm* 1. (folk.) the bridegroom's gift to his bride's parents and relatives; 2. scum, film

kriešu zāle *nf* milkwort

kriet *vt* cream, skim

krietni *adv* considerably, well

krietnība *nf* honesty, decency, (moral) goodness

krietns *adj* 1. honest, decent, (morally) good; 2. considerable, (of amount, length) good

krietnums *nm* honesty, decency, (moral) goodness

krievijnieks *nm* Russian citizen

krieviņi *nm* 1. *dim* of krievi; 2. Votyaks (those taken to Courland as prisoners of war in the 15th century)

krieviski *adv* in Russian, (speak) Russian

krievisks *adj* Russian

krievpiepes *nf pl* crust fungi

kriev/s *nm*, ~iete *nf* Russian

krievu tabaka *nf* makhorka, common tobacco

krievvalodīgs *adj* Russian-speaking

krieze *nf* (reg.) pate

kriezes *nf pl* (reg.) tripe

kriezīte *nf* (reg.) lace

krija *nf* 1. roofing bark; linden bark; 2. (weav.) warp reel

krijgrauži *nm pl* Bostrychidae
krik *interj* crack
krika *nf* (col.) sudden joint pain, sudden back
   pain
krikets *nm* cricket
krīklis *nm* green-winged teal
kriks *interj* crack
kriksis *nm* bit, smidgen
kriksītis *nm dim* of kriksis, tiny bit
krikstēt *vi* crack
krikstināt *vt* (*iter*) make cracking sounds
krikstoņa *nf* cracking
kriksts *nm* crack
krikš *interj* crack
krikšēt *vi* crack
krikšķēt *vi* crack
krikšķināt *vi* 1. make cracking sounds;
   2. giggle; 3. blub
krikšķis *nm* 1. crack; 2. wireworm
krikšķoņa *nf* cracking
krikumains *adj* containing bits
krikum/s *nm* 1. bit, crumb, smidgen, trifle;
   2. ~i odds and ends
kriķis *nm* teal
kriķu pīle *nf* teal
Krimas liepa *nf* Crimean linden
Krimas pīlādzis *nm* Crimean mountain ash
krimelde *nf* = krimele
krimele *nf* 1. a Russula; short-stemmed Russula;
   2. anise mushroom
krimene *nf* = krimele
krimilde *nf* = krimele
kriminālaborts *nm* illegal abortion
kriminālapsūdzība *nf* criminal charges
kriminālatbildība *nf* criminal answerability
kriminālbioloģija *nf* forensic medicine
krimināl[ch]ronika [h] *nf* crime news
kriminālfilma *nf* (movie) mystery
krimināli *adv* criminally
kriminālistika *nf* 1. criminal law; 2. crime
   detection
kriminālistisks *adj* criminalistic

kriminālist/s *nm*, ~e *nf* criminalist
krimin[a]litāte [ā] *nf* criminality
kriminālizmeklēšana *nf* criminal investigation
kriminālkodekss *nm* criminal code
kriminālko[l]ēģija [ll] *nf* criminal division of
   a regional court
krimināllieta *nf* criminal case
krimināllikums *nm* criminal law
kriminālliter[a]tūra [ā] *nf* mysteries (fiction)
kriminālmeklēšana *nf* criminal investigation
kriminālnoziedznie/ks *nm*, ~ce *nf* criminal
kriminālnoziegums *nm* crime
kriminālpārkāpums *nm* criminal offense
kriminālpolicija *nf* crime detection division
   (of the police)
kriminālpolicists *nm* police detective
kriminālprāva *nf* criminal court case
kriminālprocess *nm* criminal procedure;
   criminal case
kriminālprocesuāls *adj* pertaining to criminal
   procedure
kriminālromāns *nm* crime novel, mystery
krimināls *adj* criminal
kriminālsižets *nm* crime story
kriminālsods *nm* criminal penalty
kriminālspriedums *nm* criminal sentence
kriminālstāsts *nm* mystery (novel)
krimināltiesa *nf* criminal court
krimināltiesības *nf pl* criminal law
krimināltiesisks *adj* criminal law (*adj*)
krimināluzraugs *nm* police inspector
kriminālvajāšana *nf* criminal investigation and
   prosecution
kriminālžanrs *nm* mystery genre
kriminog[e]nisks [ē] *adv* criminogenic
kriminog[e]ns [ē] *adj* criminogenic
kriminolo/gs *nm*, ~ģe *nf* criminologist
kriminoloģija *nf* criminology
kriminoloģiski *adv* criminologically
kriminoloģisks *adj* criminological
krimoģen[e]ze [ē] *nf* causes of crime

krimpis *nm* bundle

krimsagizs *nm* krym-saghyz

krimslis *nm* cartilage; gristle

krimslītis *nm dim* of **krimslis**, cartilage; gristle

krimst *vt* gnaw

krimstala *nf* cartilage; gristle

krimstalains *adj* cartilaginous; gristly

krimstaliņa *nf dim* of **krimstala**, cartilage; gristle

krimsties *vr* gnaw

krimstiņa *nf* (reg.) crumb

krimšķēt *vi* crack

krimšķināt *vt* gnaw a long time

krimšķis *nm* little bit

krimšļains *adj* cartilaginous; gristly

krimuldene *nf* = **krimele**

krinkstēt *vi* crunch; crack

krinkšķēt *vi* crunch; crack

krinolīns *nm* crinoline

kriņģelis *nm* 1. pretzel-shaped cake; 2. (folk dancing) figure eight

kriņģelīte *nf* 1. pot marigold; 2. hedgehog mushroom

krioforiski *adv* cryophorically

krioforisks *adj* cryophoric

kriofors *nm* cryophorus

kriog[e]nija [ē] *nf* cryogenics

kriog[e]nisks [ē] *adj* cryogenic

kriog[e]ns [ē] *adj* cryogenic

kriohidrāts *nm* cryohydrate

kriokonīts *nm* cryoconite

krioķirurģija *nf* cryosurgery

kriolits *nm* cryolite

kriolo/gs *nm*, ~ģe *nf* cryologist

krioloģija *nf* cryogenics

krioloģiski *adv* cryologically

krioloģisks *adj* cryologic

kriomagnētisks *adj* cryomagnetic

kriosfēra *nf* cryosphere

krioskopija *nf* cryoscopy

krioskopiski *adv* cryoscopically

krioskopisks *adj* cryoscopic

krioskops *nm* cryoscope

kriostats *nm* cryostat

krioterapija *nf* cryotherapy

kriotrons *nm* cryotron

kripata *nf* bit, crumb

kripatiņa *nf dim* of **kripata**, tiny bit

krips *interj* crack; creak

krīps *nm* (geol.) creep

kripse *nf* crypsis

kripslītis *nm* bit, crumb

kripstēt *vi* crunch; crack

kripstināt *vt* (*iter*) gnaw; crack

kripš *interj* crack; creak

kripšķēt *vi* crunch; crack

kripšķināt *vt* (*iter*) gnaw; crack

kripšķis *nm* crack; crunch

kripšķoņa *nf* cracking; crunching

kript *vi* crack; creak

kripta *nf* crypt

kriptoanal[i]ze [ī] *nf* cryptoanalysis

kriptofīts *nm* cryptophyte

kriptogams *nm* cryptogam

kriptogr[a]fija [ā] *nf* cryptography

kriptogr[a]fiski [ā] *adv* cryptographically

kriptogr[a]fisk/s [ā] *adj* cryptographic

kriptogr[a]f/s [ā] *nm*, ~e *nf* cryptographer

kriptogramma *nf* cryptogram

kriptokrist[āl]isks [all] *adj* cryptocrystalline

kriptomērija *nf* cryptomeria, Japan cedar

kriptonīms *nm* cryptonym

kriptons *nm* krypton

kriptor[ch]isms [h] *nm* cryptorchidism

kriptoskops *nm* cryptoscope

kriptozojs *nm* Precambrian (period)

kripu krapu *interj* click; rattle

krislis *nm* bit; granule, grain; jot, tittle

krist *vi* 1. fall; drop; **k. acīs** (col.) strike, call one's attention; **k. ap kaklu** throw oneself on s.o.'s neck; **k. ceļos** drop to one's knees; **k. ciet** (*3rd pers*, of doors, lids) fall shut, be shut (suddenly); (of ears) a.

become plugged; b. be deafened; (of eyes) be unable to keep open, be very sleepy; **k. grēkos** sin; **k. gūstā** be taken prisoner; **k. izmisumā** abandon oneself to despair; **k. kā no gaisa** (fig.) fall into one's lap; **k. kārdināšanā** yield to temptation; **k. kaunā** be put to shame; **k. kopā** (*3rd pers*, col.) collapse; **k. ļaužu valodās** become a topic of conversation; **k. matos** (or **čuprā, krāgā, vilnā**)) start fighting; **k. nesamaņā** faint; **k. nost** fall off; **k. pār ilksi** (com.) kick the bucket; **k. par upuri** fall a victim; **k. pie kājām** fall down at s.o.'s feet; **k. uz ausīm** (sl., of music) get on one's nerves; **k. uz auss** (col.) go to sleep; **k. uz deguna** be completely exhausted; **k. uz kādu** fall for s.o.; **k. uz kājām** land on one's feet; **k. uz nerviem** (col.) get on one's nerves; **k. vai no kājām zemē** (col.) collapse from fatigue; **k. veldrē** (of hay, crops) flatten; **k. virsū** pounce upon; attack; **krizdams klupdams** head over heels; **2.** (*3rd pers*, with subject in dative) get, receive (by chance), be one's lot

kristal- or **kristāl-** See **kristall-**

krist[all]detektors [āl] *nm* crystal detector

krist[all]cukurs [āl] *nm* crystalline sugar

krist[all]dzidrs [āl] *adj* clear as crystal, perfectly clear

krist[all]dzidrums [āl] *nm* crystal clarity

krist[all]fizika [āl] *nf* physics of crystals

krist[all]fiziķ/is [āl] *nm*, ~e *nf* specialist in the physics of crystals

krist[all]hidrāts [āl] *nm* hydrated crystal

krista[ll]īns [l] *adj* crystalline

krista[ll]īnitāte [l] *nf* crystallinity

krist[all]iski [āl] *adv* in crystalline form

krist[all]isks [āl] *adj* crystalline, crystalliform

krist[all]iskums [āl] *nm* crystallinity

krista[ll]izācija [l] *nf* crystallization

krista[ll]iz[ā]tors [l][ā] *nm* crystallizer

krista[ll]izēt [l] *vt* crystallize

krista[ll]izēties [l] *vr* crystallize

krist[all]ķīmija [āl] *nf* chemistry of crystals

krist[all]ķīmiķ/is [āl] *nm*, ~e *nf* specialist in the chemistry of crystals

krist[all]ķīmisks [āl] *adj* pertaining to the chemistry of crystals

krista[ll]oblastisks [l] *adj* crystalloblastic

krista[ll]oblasts [l] *nm* crystalloblast

krista[ll]ogr[a]fija [l][ā] *nf* crystallography

krista[ll]ogr[a]fiski [l][ā] *adv* crystallographically

krista[ll]ogr[a]fisks [l][ā] *adj* crystallographic

krista[ll]ogr[a]f/s [l][ā] *nm*, ~e *nf* crystallographer

krista[ll]oīds [l] *nm* crystalloid

krista[ll]omantija [l] *nf* crystallomancy

krist[all]optika [āl] *nf* optics of crystals

krist[all]optiķ/is [āl] *nm*, ~e *nf* specialist in the optics of crystals

krist[all]optisks [āl] *adj* pertaining to te optics of crystals

krist[all]režģis [āl] *nm* crystal lattice

krist[all]s [āl] *nm* crystal; crystal glass

krist[all]skaidri [āl] *adv* quite clearly

krist[all]skaidrība [āl] *nf* crystal clarity

krist[all]skaidrs [āl] *adj* clear as crystal

krist[all]skaidrums [āl] *nm* crystal clarity

krist[all]stikls [āl] *nm* crystal glass

krist[all]tīrs [āl] *adj* clear as crystal

krist[all]uztvērējs [āl] *nm* crystal set

krist[all]veida [āl] *indecl adj* crystalliform

krist[all]veidīgi [āl] *adv* in crystalline form

krist[all]veidīgs [āl] *adj* crystalliform

kristāms *adj, part* of **kristīt** (of names) first, given

kristāmtrauks *nm* baptismal font

kristāmzīme *nf* certificate of baptism

Kristiānijas apgrieziens *nm* Christiania turn

kristiānisms *nm* Christianity

kristības *nf pl* baptism

kristībnie/ks *nm*, ~ce *nf* guest at a baptism

kristībvārds *nm* first name

kristībzīme *nf* certificate of baptism

kristies *vr* fall; drop; **k. svarā** (or **miesās**) lose weight

kristietība *nf* Christianity

kristiet/is *nm,* **~e** *nf* Christian

kristietisms *nm* Christianity

kristīg/ais *nom adj* Christian; **~ā** *f*

kristīgi *adv* in a Christian way

kristīgs *adj* Christian

kristīgums *nm* Christian ways

kristin *adv emph* of **krist; k. krist** fall with a thud; fall one after another

kristīt *vt* baptize, christen; (fig., col.) water down

kristīties *vr* **1.** be baptized; **2.** convert to Christianity

kristīts *adj, part* of **kristīt** (of names) given, first; (of milk) watered down

kristobalīts *nm* cristobalite

kristoloģija *nf* Christology

kristoloģisks *adj* Christological

krišana *nf* **1.** falling; dropping; fall; drop; **2.** downfall; **3.** (of cattle) loss; plague

krišanās *nfr* recession

krišanas leņķis *nm* angle of incidence

Kriša zāle *nf* (reg.) baneberry

kriši *nm pl* (reg.) baneberry

krišnaīti *nm pl* Hare Krishnas

krišņi *nm pl* windfall

krišus *adv* **1.** falling, by falling; **k. apsēsties** fall into one's seat; **2.** *emph* of **krist; k. krist** fall with a thud; fall one after another; **3.** headlong

krītains *adj* chalky

krītaka *nf* plunge basin

kritalas *nf pl* windfall, windfallen trees, windfallen branches

kritaļi *nm* = **kritalas**

krītamais *nom adj* (col.) falling sickness, epilepsy

krītamā kaite *nf* epilepsy

krītams *adj, part* of **krist** falling

kritene *nf* sinkhole

krite/nis *nm* **1.** thick forest; **2.** gate pole; **3.** windfallen tree; **~ņi** windfall

kriteniski *adv* vertically

kritenisks *adj* vertical

kritērijs *nm* criterion

krītgultne *nf* (hydrol.) apron

kriticisms *nm* (philos.) critique

kritienleņķis *nm* angle of descent

kritienlīnija *nf* line of fall

kritien/s *nm* fall; **~a zars** descending trajectory arc

kritika *nf* **1.** criticism; **zem ~s** beneath contempt; **2.** critique; re-view; **~s atzinums** judgment of critics

kritiķ/is *nm,* **~e** *nf* critic

kritin *adv emph* of **krist; k. krist** fall with a thud; fall one after another

krītiņš I *nm* colored drawing stick; colored chalk; crayon

krītiņš II (with **î**) *nm* crayfish trap; hoop net

kritis *adj, part* of **krist** fallen; (of fruit, trees) windfallen; **k. uz ausīm** (col.) a. hard of hearing; b. tone-deaf

kritiski *adv* critically, critical

kritisks *adj* critical (pertaining to criticism; pertaining to criticalness)

kritiskums *nm* **1.** critical attitude; **2.** criticalness

kritizēt *vt* **1.** criticize; **2.** critique

kritizētāj/s *nm,* **~a** *nf* faultfinder

kritne *nf* (geol.) fault

kritnis *nm* spillway

krītojums *nm* whitewash

krītot *vt* whitewash

krītpapīrs *nm* coated paper

krīta periods *nm* Cretaceous

krīta raktuve *nf* chalk pit

krītplūsma *nf* gravity flow

krīt/s I *nm* 1. chalk; ~a chalk; cretaceous; uz ~a on credit; 2. crayon; ~a zīmējums drawing in crayons; 3. Cretaceous (period)

krīts II (with î) *nm* hoop net; crayfish trap

krītširmis *nm* (obs.) parachute

krituļu mizgrauzis *nm* a bark beetle, Ips proximus

kritumiņš *nm dim* of kritums, small waterfall

kritumlaiks *nm* (el.) fall time

kritums *nm* 1. drop; (also fig.) fall; waterfall; 2. (rare.) windfall; 3. dead animal

kritu/šais *nom adj* fallen soldier; ~sī *f*; ~šie the fallen

krītvilnis *nm* breaker (wave)

kriuks *interj* crunch

kriukstēt *vi* crunch

kriukš *interj* crunch

kriukšēt *vi* crunch

kriukšķēt *vi* crunch

kriukšķīgs *adj* crunchy

kriukšķināt *vt* (*iter*) crunch

kriukšķis *nm* 1. (col.) shot of liquor; 2. crunch

krivs *nm* criwe (high priest of Old Prussians)

krizantēma *nf* chrysanthemum

krīzdogs *nm* (reg.) a triangular kerchief or scarf

krizdole *nf* (reg.) gooseberry

kr[i]ze [ī] *nf* crisis; ekonomiskā k. (economic) depression

kro[a]t/s [ā] *nm*, ~iete *nf* Croatian

krocetīns *nm* crocetin

krociņa *nf dim* of kroka, wrinkle

krodzinie/ks *nm* innkeeper; ~ce *nf* innkeeper's wife

krodziņš *nm dim* of krogs, tavern, inn

krogistaba *nf* taproom

krogot *vi* (hist.) keep an inn

krog/s *nm* tavern; inn; ~a draugs habitual drinker; ~a papus innkeeper

krogbrālis *nm* habitual drinker, tippler

krogot *vi* (col., hist.) keep an inn

krogus *nm* (obs.) tavern; inn

krogusbrālis *nm* habitual drinker, tippler

krogusmuša *nf* barfly

kroģelis *nm* (cont.) tavern

kroģeris *nm* (obs.) innkeeper

kroģēt *vi* (hist.) keep an inn

kroka *nf* fold; pleat; wrinkle

krokainā glīvene *nf* curly pondweed

krokainais dzelksnis *nm* curled thistle

krokainā kazene *nf* plaited bramble

krokainā roze *nf* rugosa rose

krokaini *adv* in wrinkles; in pleats, gathered

krokains *adj* wrinkled; plicate; pleated, folded, gathered

krokainums *nm* wrinkledness; plicateness

krokas spārns *nm* (geol.) limb of a fold

krokāt *vt* pleat, gather, fold

krokete *nf* croquette

krokets *nm* croquet

krokidolīts *nm* crocidolite

krokjosla *nf* frill

kroklapa *nf* (bot.) lady's-mantle

krokod[i]lāda [ī] *nf* crocodile skin

krokod[i]ls [ī] *nm* crocodile

krokojums *nm* (of fabrics) pleat, gather; fold; plication

krokosmija *nf* crocosmia

krokot *vt* pleat, gather; fold

krokotā skābene *nf* curled dock

krokoties *vr* fall in folds

kroku kalni *nm pl* fold mountains

krokuss *nm* 1. crocus; 2. crocus cloth

kroķe *nf* pleat, gather

kroķēt *vt* (topography) sketch

kromanjonietis *nm* Cro-Magnon

krona *nf* (Swedish) krona, (Norwegian, Danish, Austrian) krone, (Estonian) kroon, (Czech) koruna, (English) crown

kronēt *vt* crown

kronika *nf* = chronika

kronikāls *adj* = chronikāls
kroniski *adv* = chroniski
kronisks a*dj* = chronisks
kronist/s *nm*, ~e *nf* = chronists
kroniņš *nm* curlew
kro/nis *nm* **1.** crown; **nu k.!** that tops it all! **tev k.!** you take the cake! **2.** (fig., obs.) crown, state; **~ņa maizē** (col.) a. in military service; b. in prison; **3.** (obs.) wreath, chaplet
kronītis *nm* **1.** *dim* of **kronis**, coronet (small crown; part of a horse's foot); **2.** (dental) crown
kronšnepe *nf* curlew
kronšteins *nm* (arch.) bracket; (telescope) mount
kroņa laupītājs *nm* usurper
kroņa zvērasts *nm* coronal oath
kroņinieks *nm* (hist.) a peasant who works crown land
kroņlukturis *nm* (obs.) **1.** candelabrum; **2.** chandelier
kroņprincis *nm* crown prince
kroņstikls *nm* crown glass
kroņa palāta *nf* (hist.) crown treasury office in the provinces
kroplains *adj* crippled
kroplība *nf* deformity
kroplīgi *adv* in a deformed, disfigured way
kroplīgs *adj* deformed, disfigured
kroplīgums *nm* deformity, disfigurement
kroplis *nm*, ~e *nf* cripple
kropls *adj* **1.** crippled; **2.** (of trees, shrubs) gnarled; **3.** distorted
kroplums *nm* deformity
kropļojums *nm* **1.** mutilation; **2.** distortion; **3.** (ling.) barbarism
kropļošana *nf* **1.** crippling; **2.** mutilation; disfigurement; **3.** distortion; **4.** (ling.) barbarization
kropļot *vt* **1.** cripple; **2.** mutilate; disfigure; **3.** distort; (ling.) barbarize

krosasemblers *nm* cross assembler
krosbrīdings *nm* cross-breeding
krosingovers *nm* (genetics) crossing over
krosist/s *nm*, ~e *nf* cross-country competitor
kroskonts *nm* cross-country race
kroskompil[a]tors [ā] *nm* cross compiler
kroskulturāls *adj* cross-cultural
kross *nm* **1.** cross-country race; **2.** telephone exchange; **3.** (genetics) cross
krota *nf* steep river bank; drop
krotalarija *nf* crotalaria
krotilalkohols *nm* crotyl alcohol
krotonaldehīds *nm* croton aldehyde
krotons *nm* croton
krotonskābe *nf* crotonic acid
krū *interj* kr-rooh
krubināt *vt* gnaw
kruciferi *nm pl* crucifers, Cruciferae
krucificēt *vt* crucify
krucifikss *nm* crucifix
krucianela *nf* crosswort
kruities *vr* **k. virsū** importune
kruja *nf*, *nm* importuner
krujāties *vr* strive
krūka *nf* jug
krūkle *nf* dwarf elder
krūklenājs *nm* growth of belladonna
krūklene *nf* the berry of **krūkle, krūklenes, krūk-linājs,** or **krūklis**
krūklenes *nf pl* belladonna
krūklinājs *nm* snowball bush
krūklis *nm* alder buckthorn
kruknēt *vi* crouch
Kruksa dzirnaviņas *nf pl* radiometer
Kruksa caurule *nf* Crookes tube
krukšināt *vi* grunt
krukšķināt *vi* grunt
kruķēt *vt* poke, push or rake with a poker
kruķis *nm* **1.** crutch; **2.** fire poker; **3.** (sl.) cop; **4.** (sl., of grades) plus
kruķīt *vt* (barb.) turn, crank

kruķītis *nm* 1. *dim* of **kruķis**, crutch; 2. scythe handle for the left hand; 3. a hook-shaped frog's bone used in magic

krullēt *vt* twist

krūmaine *nf* bushes, shrubs, brushwood; thicket

krūmainība *nf* bushiness

krūmains *adj* bushy, covered with bushes

krūmainums *nm* bushiness

krūmājs *nm* bushes, shrubs, brushwood; thicket

krūmāju sīpoli *nm pl* field garlic

krūmāju strupaste *nf* field vole

krūmāju sūrene *nf* copse buckwheat

krūmāju vīķis *nm* a vetch, Vicia cassubica

krūmāju zīdene *nf* a knapweed, Centaurea phrygia

krūmantilope *nf* bushbuck

krūmaugi *nm pl* shrubs

krūmcedonijas *nf pl* flowering quinces

krūmgriezējs *nm* bush hog

krūmgriezis *nm* bush hog

krūmiene *nf* bushes, brushwood; thicket

krūmiens *nm* bushes, brushwood; thicket

krūmine *nf* (reg.) moonshine

krūmiņš *nm dim* of **krūms**, small bush

krūmmala *nf* edge of shrubbery, edge of brushwood

krumpa *nf* 1. pleat, gather; 2. wrinkle

krumpainais rumpucis *nm* fluted white elfin saddle

krumpains *adj* wrinkly

krumpaiņi *nm pl* (hist.) pleated (men's) frock

krumpe *nf* pleat, gather

krumpēt *vt* wrinkle

krumpot *vt* wrinkle

krūm/s *nm* bush, shrub; ~i bushes, shrubs; brushwood; shrubbery; underbrush

krumslis *nm* 1. cartilage; 2. (col.) ankle, knuckle

krūmsuns *nm* bushdog

krumšķināt *vt* crunch

krumšļains *adj* jagged

krūmu blaktis *nf pl* Scutelleridae

krūmu izkapts *nf* brush scythe

krūmu ķauķi *nm pl* warblers

krumults *nm* (wood) knee

krumuļains *adj* (of roads) rough, rutted

krūmu mežs *nm* brushwood

krūmu skarene *nf* wood meadow grass

krūmveida *indecl adj* shrubby

krūmveida karagana *nf* pea shrub

krūmveida platkājiņi *nm pl* shrubby cinquefoil

krūmveida ziemastere *nf* bushy aster

krūmveidā *adv* as a shrub

krūmveidīgs *adj* shrubby

krunka *nf* wrinkle

krunkaini *adv* in wrinkles

krunkainība *nf* wrinkledness

krunkains *adj* wrinkled

krunkainums *nm* wrinkledness

krunkāt *vt* wrinkle

krunkot *vt* wrinkle

krunkoties *vr* wrinkle

krupis *nm* 1. toad; 2. (sl.) runt, shrimp

krūpis *nm* (reg.) gnome

krupītis *nm dim* of **krupis**, little toad

krupjē *indecl nm* croupier

krupju doņi *nm pl* toad rush

krupozs *adj* croupous

krups *nm* croup

krups *adj* small, short, tiny

krupšķināt *vi* crunch

krupt *vi* 1. pine away; shrink; 2. hunker down; sit motionlessly; stick (in a place without leaving)

krusa *nf* 1. hail; ~s grauds hailstone; 2. chalazion

krusiņa *nf dim* of **krusa**, small hail

krustabas *nf pl* (reg.) baptism

krustābele *nf* hawthorn

krustabnie/ks *nm*, **~ce** *nf* (reg.) guest at a baptism

krustaceļš *nm* Stations of the Cross

krustainā genciāna *nf* crosswort

krustaine I *nf* **lielā k.** Ascension Day; **mazās ~s** the two Thursdays before Ascension Day

krustaine II *nf* groundse

krustainiski *adv* crossing, crossed

krustainisks *adj* cross-shaped

krustains *adj* cross-shaped; ornamented with crosses; with cross designs

krusta izšuvums *nm* needlepoint

krusta karš *nm* crusade

krustakmens *nm* landmark (a stone marked with a cross)

krusta lasis *nm* three-spined stickleback

krusta loks *nm* crossbow

krustām *adv* crosswise; (naut.) abeam; **k. šķērsām** crisscross, in all directions

krustāmzīme *nf* certificate of baptism

krusta nāve *nf* crucifixion

krusta paksis *nm* corner of a log house with projecting log ends

krusta putns *nm* waxwing

krustāre *nf* juncture (of the fields of several farmers)

krusta sējums *nm* by book post

krustā sišana *nf* crucifixion

krusta stacija *nf* station of the cross

krusta velve *nf* cross vault;

krusta zirneklis *nm* garden spider

krustbērns *nm* godchild

krustceles *nf pl* crossroads

krustceļš *nm* crossroad; crossroads

krustcirtnis *nm* cross bit

krustcirtuma vīle *nf* double-cut file

krustdancis *nm* a Latvian folk dance

krustdegunis *nm* crossbill

krustdēls *nm* godson

krustdiena *nf* (rel.) Ascension

krustdūriens *nm* cross stitch

krusteja *nf* cloister (covered passage)

krustenes *nf pl* Saint-John's-wort

krustenis *nm* (RR) frog

krusteniski *adv* across; diagonally

krustenisks *adj* crosswise, crossing, traverse, di-agonal; (of rhymes) alternating

krustgalvis *nm* (mech.) crosshead

krusti *nm, pl* **1.** sacrum; small of the back; (of horses) croup; **2.** crosses; **3.** (cards) clubs

krustības *nf* baptism

krustiem *adv* crosswise

krustiņš *nm dim* of **krusts**, small cross; (typ.) dagger

krustis *adv* across, crosswise

krustiski *adv* crosswise

krustisks *adj* crosswise

krustīt *vt* **1.** cross, make the sign of the cross upon; **2.** baptize

krustīties *vr* cross oneself

krustknābis *nm* crossbill

krustknābītis *nm dim* of **krustknābis**, crossbill

krustkrāvums *nm* crosswise stack

krustkrustām or **krustkrustīm, krustkrustinis, krustkrustumis** *adv* in all directions

krustleņķis *nm* vertical angle

krustmāmiņa *nf dim* of **krustmāte**, aunt; godmother

krustmāte *nf* **1.** aunt; **2.** godmother

krustmeita *nf* **1.** niece; **2.** goddaughter

krustnagliņas *nf pl* cloves

krustnesis *nm* crusader

krustojums *nm* **1.** crossing; crossroads; intersection; **2.** hybrid

krustošana *nf* **1.** crossing; **2.** interbreeding, hybridization

krustošanās *nfr* **1.** crossing, intersection; **2.** interbreeding

krustot *vt* cross; (of arms) fold

krustoties *vr* intersect; cross

krustpārmija *nf* (RR) slip switch

krustpunkts *nm* point of intersection

krust/s *nm* **1.** cross ◊ **k. pāri** this is the end; **būt par ~u** be an intolerable burden; **2.** (cards) clubs

krustsēja *nf* crossrow sowing

kruststrāva *nf* crossflow

krusttētiņš *nm dim* of **krusttēvs**, godfather

krusttēvs *nm* godfather

krustu *adv* across; **k. šķērsu** round about

krustuguns *nf* cross fire

krustu kauls *nm* sacral vertebra

krustu sāpes *nf pl* lower back pain

krustu zāle *nf* goutweed

krustvārdi *nm pl* crossword

krustvārdu mīkla *nf* crossword puzzle

krustvecāki *nm pl* godparents

krustveida *indecl adj* cruciform, cross

krustveidā *adv* in the shape of a cross

krustveidīgi *adv* in the shape of a cross

krustveidīgs *adj* cruciform

krustzieži *nm pl* Crucifera, Brassicaceae

krūšaugstums *nm* breastheight

krūšauts *nm* bib

krūšbomis *nm* (naut.) breast beam

krūšdobums *nm* thoracic cavity

krūšgals *nm* nipple

krūškabata *nf* breast pocket

krūškurvis *nm* = **krūšukurvis**

krūšmētra *nf* spearmint

krušņa *nf* trash pile

krūštēls *nm* = **krūšutēls**

krūšturis *nm* brassier

krūšu balss *nf* chest voice

krūšu bērns *nm* infant

krūšubruņas *nf pl* breastplate, cuirass

krūšu dobums *nm* thoracic cavity

krūšu gabals *nm* brisket

krūšu gals *nm* nipple

krūšu kaite *nf* consumption

krūšu kauls *nm* breastbone

krūšukurvis *nm* rib cage, chest

krūšu plēve *nf* pleura

krūšu putns *nm* dipper

krūšu sērga *nf* consumption

krūšu skriemelis *nm* thoracic vertebra

krūšu stils *nm* breaststroke

krūšu šķērsis *nm* (weav.) breastbeam

krūšu tēja *nf* pectoral herb tea

krūšutēls *nm* bust

krūtains *adj* bosomy; broad-chested

krūteža *nf* **1.** (piece of meat) breast; bust; **2.** dickey

krūtiņa *nf dim* of **krūts**; dickey

krū/ts *nf* **1.** chest, breast; bosom; (zool.) thorax ~šu breast (*adj*); pectoral; thoracic; ~šu augstumā breast-high; iekritušām ~tīm hollow-chested; ar visu (or pilnu) ~ti a. staunchly; b. enthusiastically; **2.** (female) breast; **3.** hillock, hump

krūtsgabals *nm* **1.** dickey; **2.** brisket

krūtsgals *nm* nipple

kruva *nf* (reg.) pile

kruvesis *nm* clod

kruvesītis *nm dim* of **kruvesis**, small clod

kruvešains *adj* cloddy

kruzado *indecl nm* cruzado

krūzains *adj* ruffled

krūze I *nf* jug, pitcher

krūze II *nf* curl

kruzeiro *indecl nm* cruzeiro

krūzene *nf* spearmint

krūzēt *vt* curl

krūzgalv/is *nm*, ~e *nf* curlyhead

krūzīte *nf dim* of **krūze**; small jug, pitcher

krūzmētra *nf* spearmint

krūzots *adj* ruffled

krūzs *adj* curly

kruzulis *nm* frill, ruffle

kruzulītis *nm dim* of **kruzulis**, frill, ruffle

kruzuļainība *nf* frilliness

kruzuļains *adj* frilly, ruffled

kruzuļainums *nm* frilliness

kruzuļots *adj* frilly, ruffled

krūzveida *indecl adj* pitcher-shaped

krūzveidīgi *adv* like a pitcher

krūzveidīgs *adj* pitcher-shaped
ksantīns *nm* xanthine
ksantocers *nm* Xanthoceras
ksantofills *nm* xanthophyll
ksantopurpurīns *nm* xanthopurpurin
ksantoriza *nf* yellowroot
ksantozīns *nm* xanthosine
ksantozoma *nf* yautia
ksendzs *nm* (Roman Catholic) priest
ksenija *nf* xenia
ksenijs *nm* xenial gift
ksenoblastisks *adj* xenoblastic
ksenofobija *nf* xenophobia
ksenofobs *nm* xenophobe
ksenogāmija *nf* xenogamy
ksenol|i|ts [ī] *nm* xenolith
ksenomanija *nf* xenomania
ksenons *nm* xenon
kserantema *nf* xeranthemum
kseroderma *nf* xeroderma
kserofi|ll|s [l] *adj* xerophilous
kserofīts *nm* xerophyte
kseroftalmija *nf* xerophthalmia
kserogr|a|fija [ā] *nf* xerography
kserogr|a|fisks [ā] *adj* xerographic
kserogr|a|fs [ā] *nm* xerox copier
kserokopēt *vt* xerox
kserokopija *nf* xerox (copy)
kserokss *nm* xerox
kserostomija *nf* xerostomia
ksi *nm indecl* xi
ksilāns *nm* xylan
ksilēma *nf* xylem
ksilēns *nm* xylene
ksilitols *nm* xylitol
ksilīts *nm* xylitol
ksilofāgi *nm pl* marine borers
ksilofonist/s *nm*, ~e *nf* xylophonist
ksilofons *nm* xylophone
ksilogr|a|fija [ā] *nf* 1. xylography; 2. xylo-
    graph
ksilogr|a|fisks [ā] *adj* xylographic

ksilogr|a|fs [ā] *nm* xylographer
ksilolīts *nm* xylolite
ksiloloģija *nf* xylology
ksilols *nm* xylene
ksilometrs *nm* xylometer
ksilonskābe *nf* xylonic acid
ksiloze *nf* xylose
kšatriji *nm pl* Kshatriya
ktenoforas *nf pl* Ctenophora
kū *indecl nm* (the letter) q
kuba sakne *nf* cubic root
kubatūra *nf* cubic measure
kubiet/is *nm*, ~e *nf* Cuban
kubikcentimetrs *nm* cubic centimeter
kubikcolla *nf* cubic inch
kubikdecimetrs *nm* cubic decimeter
kubikkilometrs *nm* cubic kilometer
kubikmērs *nm* cubic measure
kubikmetrs *nm* cubic meter
kubikmilimetrs *nm* cubic millimeter
kubikpēda *nf* cubic foot
kubiks *nm* 1. cube; 2. cubic meter
kubikveida *indecl adj* cubical, cube-shaped
kubikvienība *nf* cubic measure
kubiski *adv* cubically
kubisks *adj* cubic, cubical
kubisms *nm* cubism
kubistiski *adv* cubistically
kubistisks *adj* cubistic
kubists *nm*, ~e *nf* cubist
kublains *adj* (reg., of voice) hollow
kubls *nm* wooden tub, wooden tub on stave
    legs
kuboids *nm* cuboid
kuboids *adj* cuboid
kubriks *nm* crew's quarters
kubs *nm* cube
kubucis *nm* large **ciba**; birch bark container for
    berries or tobacco
kubuls *nm* wooden tub, wooden tub on stave
    legs
kubveida *indecl adj* cubical, cube-shaped

kubveidīgs *adj* cubical, cube-shaped

kuce *nf* bitch

kucēniņš *nm dim* of **kucēns**, little cub

kucēnpuika *nm* (col.) small boy, small fry

kucēns *nm* pup, whelp

kucīte *nf* 1. *dim* of **kuce**; 2. socket (piece of wood on the edge of the top stone of a grist mill into which one end of the turning pole is inserted)

kučierēt *vi* (obs.) drive a wagon

kučieris *nm* (col.) coachman

kučkis *adv* (reg.) head over heels

kučkus or **kučkus vāļus** *adv* (reg.) head over heels

kudināt *vt* tickle

kūdināt *vt* incite, instigate, set on

kūdīt *vt* incite, instigate, set on

kūdītāj/s *nm*, ~a *nf* inciter, instigator

kudla *nf* (reg.) tuft

kudlains *adj* (reg.) shaggy

kudlot *vi* (col.) stump, walk

kūdra *nf* peat

kūdraine *nf* area of peat soil

kūdrains *adj* peaty

kūdrājas *nf pl* ground ivy

kūdrājs *nm* area of peat soil

kūdrāju grīslis *nm* Hudson Bay sedge

kūdras bedre *nf* peat bank

kūdras fabrika *nf* peat works

kūdras gabals *nm* turf

kūdras kaudze *nf* peatstack

kūdras plāksne *nf* peat slab

kūdras purvs *nm* peat bog, peat moor

kūdras sūna *nf* peat moss

kūdrinie/ks *nm*, ~ce *nf* peat works worker

kūdrot *vt* work peat into soil

kudu *indecl nm* kudu

kufejas *nf pl* Cuphea

kugra *nf* crucian carp

kuguārs *nm* cougar

kuģa ārsts *nm* ship's surgeon

kuģa biedrs *nm* shipmate

kuģa laipa *nf* gangway

kuģa ļaudis *nm pl* ship's crew

kuģa mašīnas *nf pl* naval engine

kuģa pakaļgal/s *nm* stern; **k.** ~a **kabīne** poop cabin

kuģa piestātne *nf* pier, quay, wharf, jetty

kuģa priekšgals *nm* bow

kuģapuika *nm* shipboy

kuģa skrūve *nf* propeller

kuģa steķis *nm* landing stage

kuģa telpa *nf* stowage, hold

kuģa virtuve *nf* galley

kuģa žurnāls *nm* ship's log

kuģbūve *nf* shipbuilding

kuģbūvniecība *nf* shipbuilding

kuģēvele *nf* circular plane

kuģinie/ks *nm*, ~ce *nf* seaman, mariner

kuģ/is *nm* ship; **apdzīvojamais k.** barracks ship; houseboat; **divklāju k.** double-decker; **divmas-tu k.** two-master; **kosmiskais k.** spaceship; **ma-zie** ~i small craft; ~a **bojā eja** shipwreck

kuģītis *nm* 1. *dim* of **kuģis**, small ship; 2. bobbin case (of a sewing machine); 3. (zool.) Portuguese man-o'-war

kuģniecība *nf* navigation

kuģniecības kantoris *nm* shipping office

kuģniecības sabiedrība *nf* shipping company

kuģojamā ierīce *nf* vessel

kuģojams *adj, part* of **kuģot** navigable

kuģojums *nm* voyage

kuģošana *nf* navigation; **derīgs** ~i seaworthy

kuģot *vi* sail, navigate; **k. gar piekrasti** coast, sail coastwise

kuģotāj/s *nm*, ~a *nf* navigator

kuģu aģents *nm* ship agent

kuģu blokāde *nf* naval blockade

kuģubūve *nf* shipbuilding

kuģubūvētājs *nm* shipbuilder

kuģubūvētava *nf* shipyard

kuģu ceļš *nm* ship lane

kuģu galdnieks *nm* shipwright

kuģu inženieris *nm* naval architect

kuģu ķirmis *nm* teredo, shipworm

kuģu lādēšana *nf* an alphabet game

kuidēt *vt* (reg.) be able

kuiga *nf* 1. coot; 2. woodcock

kuilene *nf* blewit

kuilis *nm* boar

kuilītis *nm dim* of kuilis, little boar

kuitala *nf* western curlew; see also mazā k.

kuitenis *nm* (reg.) thicket

kuiti *nm pl* (reg.) shrubs, bushes, brushwood

kūja *nf* stick, staff, walking stick

kūjinieks *nm* 1. beggar; 2. uninvited guest

kūka *nf* 1. pastry, piece of pastry; 2. veca k. old biddy

kukačās *adv* (col.) piggyback

kukai/nis *nm* insect, bug ◊ ~ņu ciems (col.) cemetery

kukainītis *nm dim* of kukainis, little bug

kukaiņappute *nf* pollination by insects

kukaiņēdējs *nm* insectivore; k. augs insectivorous plant

kukaiņu piekūns *nm* red-footed falcon

kukaprecē *adv* (reg.) piggyback

kukaragās or kukaragās *adv* piggyback

kukaža *nf* crone

kukažiņa *nf dim* of kukaža, crone

kukersīts *nm* oil shale

kukluksklaniet/is *nm*, ~e *nf* Ku Kluxer

kukluksklans *nm* Ku Klux Klan

kuknēt *vi* (reg.) languish

kuknīties *vr* muddle

kukņa *nf* (barb.) kitchen

kukņāties *vr* hunch

kūkojiens *nm* cuckoo call

kūkojums *nm* cuckoo call

kūkot *vi* 1. (of a cuckoo) call; 2. (col.) doze, nod

kuksis *nm* (col., hum.) thumb

kuksnis *nm* (reg.) coppice

kukss *nm* share of mining stock

kukstēt *vi* groan

kukša *nf* (col.) hump, arch

kukšot *vi* (col.) walk

kukt *vi* slump; bend; (of cats) arch

ku-kū *interj* peekaboo; cuckoo

kūkucis *nm* (col.) hunchback

kūku lāpstiņa *nf* cake server

kukulis *nm* 1. loaf; 2. gift; 3. bribe

kukulītis *nm dim* of kukulis, small loaf

kukulsnis nm clod

kukulznis *nm* clod

kukuļdevēj/s *nm*, ~a *nf* briber

kukuļdošana *nf* bribery

kukuļmaize *nf* bread made of fine sifted flour; (obs.) sourdough bread

kukuļnauda *nf* bribe money

kukuļniecība *nf* bribery

kukuļnie/ks *nm*, ~ce *nf* briber

kukuļņēmēj/s *nm*, ~a *nf* bribe taker, bribee

kukuļņemšana *nf* bribe-taking

kukuļošana *nf* bribery

kukuļot *vt* bribe

kūkumainība *nf* humpiness

kūkumains *adj* humped, humpy

kūkumainums *nm* humpiness

kūkumiņš *nm, dim* of kūkums, little hump

kūkumoties *vr* hump, arch

kūkums *nm* hump; arch (in a cat's back); heave (in a roadway)

kukuragās *adv* piggyback

kukurēs *adv* piggyback

kukuriņi *nm pl* leapfrog

kukuriski *adv* head over heels

kūkurot *vi* trudge; stumble

kukurs *nm* 1. hump; 2. clod; boll

kukur[u]za [ū] *nf* Indian corn; k. vālītēs corn on the cob

kukur[u]zas [ū] ciete *nf* cornstarch

kukur[u]zas [ū] milti *nm pl* cornmeal

kukur[u]zas [ū] pārslas *nf pl* corn flakes

kukur[u]zas [ū] vālīte *nf* corncob

kukurzās *adv* piggyback

kukurznis *nm* clod

kukurznītis *nm dim* of **kukurznis**, small clod

kukuržņainība *nf* cloddiness

kukuržņains *adj* cloddy

kukuržņainums *nm* cloddiness

kukuržņots *adj* cloddy

kūķis *nm* a Christmas eve meal (of beans, peas, barley and hog's head)

kūķu vakars *nm* Christmas eve

kulā *adv* (reg.) together

kūla *nf* 1. last year's grass; old, dry grass; 2. (of animals) old hair; (of humans) thick hair

kulainieks *nm* mitten

kulainis *nm* 1. mitten; 2. curlew

kulain/s *adj* 1. covered with last year's growth of grass; 2. hairy; ~i cimdi mittens

kūlāj/s *nm* a place covered with old, dry grass; ~i straw of hemp, flax, peas, or buckwheat

kulaks *nm* (col.) 1. fist; 2. (cont.) kulak, big farmer

kulance *nf* obligingness, accomodation

kul|a|ns [ā] *nm* kulan

kulants *adj* obliging, accomodating

kulba *nf* covered wagon, covered sleigh; covered body of a wagon, sleigh, or truck

kulbārdis *nm* (fish) ruff

kulbas rati *nm pl* covered wagon

kulbene *nf* silene

kulcenis *nm* bolt of wood, wood block

kulciens *nm* gulp

kulcināt *vt* (col., of a tail) swish, wag

kulčināt *vt* (of liquids) slosh, shake

kulda *nf* 1. ash pit; 2. (reg.) glutton

kuldīt *vi* (col.) walk; **k. klāt** catch up with (in walking)

kuldoņa *nf, nm* (reg.) glutton

kulduris *nm* restless person

kuldziens *nm* gulp

kūldžezs *nm* cool jazz

kule *nf* bag, sack; (sl.) scrotum

kūlēj/s *nm* 1. thresher; ~a *nf*; 2. threshing machine

kulenes *nf pl* bagpipe

kūle/nis *nm* 1. tumble; (aeron.) nosing over; ~ņiem tumbling, head over heels; 2. threshing roller

kūleniski *adv* head over heels

kūlenītis *nm* 1. *dim* of **kūlenis**, tumble; 2. (tech.) cam

kūleņošana *nf* tumbling; (of bullets) keyholing

kūleņot *vi* tumble; turn somersaults; (of bullets) keyhole

kūleņoties *vr* stumble

kuličs *nm* Easter cake

kūliens *nm* 1. threshing; 2. (col.) thrashing, whipping

kulīgs *adj* baggy

kūlijs *nm* coolie

kulināri *adv* in a culinary manner; from a culinary viewpoint

kulinārija *nf* 1. culinary art, cookery; cuisine; 2. groceries, food items

kulinārisks *adj* culinary

kulinārs *nm* culinary specialist

kulinārs *adj* culinary

kulināt *vt* (of a tail) wag, swish

kulināties *vr* 1. dangle; 2. slosh, churn

kūliņus *adv* tumbling, headlong

kūlis *nm* sheaf

kulis/e *nf* 1. (theat) wing, side scene; **aiz ~ēm** a. behind the scenes; b. in the wings; 2. (mech.) slotted link, link motion, slips; 3. zone of protective planting; green belt; 4. (trombone) slide

kūliski *adv* head over heels

kulisveida *indecl adj* 1. resembling stage wings; 2. resembling a zone of protective planting

kulisveidīgs *adj* 1. resembling stage wings; 2. resembling a zone of protective planting

kūlīšsējējs *nm* self-binder

kulīte *nf dim* of **kule**, small bag, pouch

kūlītis *nm* 1. *dim* of **kūlis**, small sheaf; 2. sheaf; 3. bundle

kulksnis *nm* (anat.) hock

kulkstēt *vi* gurgle

kulmans *nm* drafting machine

kulminācija *nf* culmination; **apakšējā k.** lower culmination; **augšējā k.** upper culmination; **~s punkts** culmination point

kulminēt *vi* culminate

Kulona likums *nm* Coulomb's law

kulons I *nm* (el.) coulomb

kulons II *nm* gem pendant, lavaliere

kūlot *vi* (of grass) dry out

kuls *nm* earthen floor

kulsma *nf* grain stalks spread out for flailing

kulsnains *adj* rutted

kulstāmmašīna *nf* scutcher (machine)

kulstavnīca *nf* (reg.) scutcher

kulstīkla *nf* scutcher

kulstīt *vt* **1.** scutch; **2.** beat, whip; (of tail) wag; **k. mēli** wag one's tongue

kulstītājs *nm*, **~a** *nf* scutcher

kulstīties *vr* **1.** be scutched; **2.** flutter; **3.** splash; **4.** flap; (of the tongue) wag

kulša *nf* (reg.) flank; hip

kulšņains *adj* rutty

kult *vt* **1.** thresh; **k. tukšus salmus** beat the air; **(dzīvo) cepuri kuldams** (he lives) in clover; **k. niekus** chatter; **2.** churn; **3.** whip, beat

kultene *nf* a fermented drink of flour and water

kultenes *nf pl* catchfly

kultenis *nm* **1.** a dish that requires whipping; usu. **olu k.** scrambled eggs; **2.** **skābputra** made with scalded rye

kultenītis *nm* = **kultenis**

kulties *vr* **1.** churn; **2.** (col.) barely move along, stumble along; **k. apkārt** gad about; **3.** struggle along, muddle through; **k. pa kājām** be in the way; **k. ar bēdām** fight off troubles; **4.** thresh o.s.

kultin *adv emph* of **kult**; **k. kūla** they threshed thoroughly, they threshed a long time

kultiski *adv* following cultic prescription

kultisks *adj* cultic

kultivācija *nf* cultivation

kultiv[a]tors [ā] *nm* cultivator

kultivēt *vt* cultivate

kultor/gs *nm*, **~dze** *nf* (Soviet) recreational director

kults *nm* cult; cultus

kultūra *nf* **1.** culture; **2.** civilization; **3.** crop; **tehniskās ~s** industrial crops

kultūrainava *nf* man-made landscape

kult[u]rāli [ū] *adv* **1.** in a civilized manner; **2.** culturally

kult[u]rālība [ū] *nf* cultural level

kult[u]rāls [ū] *adj* **1.** civilized; **2.** cultura

kult[u]rālums [ū] *nm* cultural level

kultūrarkls *nm* general purpose plow

kultūraršana *nf* plowing with a general purpose plow

kultūras nams *nm* cultural center, civic center

kultūraugs *nm* cultivated plant

kultūraugsne *nf* high-grade soil

kultūrēt *vt* (biol.) culture

kultūrezers *nm* lake stocked with fish

kultūrfilma *nf* documentary (film)

kultūrforma *nf* cultivar

kultūrisms *nm* bodybuilding

kultūrist/s *nm*, **~e** *nf* bodybuilder

kultūrizglītības *indecl adj* cultural and educational

kultūrizglītojošs *adj* cultural and educational

kultūrpol[i]tika [ī] *nf* cultural policy

kultūrpol[i]tisks [ī] *adj* cultural policy (*adj*)

kultūrpreces *nf pl* articles for cultural needs; recreational supplies

kultūrsaimniecisks *adj* cultural and economic

kultūrslānis *nm* archeological layer

kultūršķirne *nf* cultivated variety

kultūršoks *nm* culture shock

kultūrtauta *nf* (highly) civilized people

kultūrte[ch]nika [h] *nf* land reclamation

kultūrte[ch]niķ/is [h] *nm*, **~e** *nf* specialist in land reclamation

kultūrte[ch]nisks [h] *adj* pertaining to land reclamation

kultūrtrēģerība *nf* conceit of a civilizing mission

kultūrtrēģeris *nm* person on a civilizing mission, Kulturträger

kultūrtrēģerisks *adj* of a civilizing mission

kultūrtrēģerisms *nm* conceit of a civilizing mission

kultūrvaloda *nf* language of a civilized people

kultūrvalsts *nf* country with a developed civilization

kultūrvaronis *nm* culture hero

kultūrvērtības *nf pl* cultural values

kultūrvēsture *nf* history of civilization

kultūrvēsturiski *adv* from the history of civilization point of view

kultūrvēsturisks *adj* pertaining to the history of civilization

kultūrvēsturnie/ks *nm*, ~ce *nf* historian of civilization

kuluāri *nm pl* lobby

kuluāru politika *nf* lobbying

kuluāru politiķis *nm* lobbyist

kūlums *nm* yield of threshed grain

kūlvāršus *adv* head over heels

kuļamklons *nm* threshing floor

kuļamlaiks *nm* threshing time

kuļammašīna *nf* threshing machine

kuļamvieta *nf* threshing site

kuļaparāts *nm* threshing mechanism

kuļāt *vt* = **kūļāt**

kūļāt *vt* 1. dangle; wag; 2. slosh; churn

kuļāties *vr* = **kūļāties**

kūļāties *vr* 1. dangle; 2. slosh; churn

kuļičs *nm* koulitch, Russian Easter cake

kuļināt *vt* (of a tail) wag, swish

kuļināties *vr* 1. dangle; 2. slosh

kūļizlāde *nf* (el.) brush discharge

kuļkurvis *nm* (of a thresher) concave

kuļmuca *nf* churn

kūļoties *vr* 1. dangle; 2. slosh

kuļsprauga *nf* gap (between the concave and the threshing cylinder of a thresher)

kuļtrumulis *nm* threshing cylinder

kūļu vāļu *adv* (col.) head over heels

kuma *nf* live box

kūm/a *nf*, *nm* godparent; ~ās iet be a godparent

kumačs *nm* red-headed bunting

kumalīnskābe *nf* coumalic acid

kumarīns *nm* coumarin

kumbračās *adv* (col.) piggyback

kumbraini *adv* bumpily

kumbrains *adj* bumpy

kumbriņš *nm dim* of **kumbrs**, little bump

kumbrs *nm* 1. nape; scruff of the neck; 2. cervical vertebra; 3. rounded elevation; bump

kumēdiņi *nm pl* 1. (col.) caper, antic; 2. (obs.) circus act

kumelēns *nm* young colt

kumelīce or **kumelīdze** *nf* mare in foal

kumeliņš *nm dim* of **kumeļš**, (poet.) horse, steed

kumeliņu zāle *nf* chamomile

kumelīši *nm pl* chamomile

kumelīte *nf* English chamomile

kumelītis *nm dim* of **kumeļš**, foal, colt

kumeļāda *nf* coltskin

kumeļmāte *nf* mare (that has a colt)

kumeļnīcas *nf pl* chamomile

kumeļpauti *nm pl* (reg.) false morel

kumeļpēda *nf* 1. wild ginger; 2. false wintergreen

kumeļ/š *nm* 1. foal, colt ◊ ~a gadi (col.) youth; 2. (poet., folk.) horse, steed

kūmiņš *nm* 1. godfather; 2. sly person, sly fox

kumis *nm* live box

kumiss *nm* koumiss

kūmnie/ks *nm*, ~ce *nf* godparent

kumode *nf* chest of drawers

kumols *nm* cumene

kumosiņš *nm dim* of **kumoss**, little bite, morsel

kumoss *nm* bite, piece; morsel; **kārs k.** tasty tidbit; **rūgts k.** bitter pill; **trekns k. a.** rich food; **b.** (col.) great opportunity; windfall; **k. rīklē** (fig.) lump in the throat

kumpa *nf* hunch, hump

kumpainais rumpucis *nm* fluted white elfin saddle

kumpaini *adv* with a hunched back

kumpainis *nm* hunchback

kumpains *adj* hunched, humped

kumpainums *nm* being hunched

kumpāties *vr* move slowly, stooping

kumpiņa *nf dim* of **kumpa**, small hump

kumpis *nm* **1.** smoked ham; **2.** (col.) hunchback

kumpmuguris *nm* (col.) hunchback

kumps *adj* hunched, humped

kumpt *vi* stoop, hunch one's back

kumpums *nm* hunch, hump

kūms *nm* (obs.) godfather

kumšķaini *adv* mattedly

kumšķains *adj* **1.** matted; **2.** tussocky

kumšķis *nm* tussock

kumšķītis *nm dim* of **kumšķis**, small tussock

kumulācija *nf* cumulation

kumul[a]tīvi [ā] *adv* cumulatively

kumul[a]tīvs [ā] *adj* cumulative; (of an explosive charge) shaped

kumulēns *nm* cumulene

kumulēt *vi* accumulate; (phys.) focus

kumulēties *vr* accumulate; (phys.) focus

kumums *nm* hunch, hump

kumuraini *adv* unevenly, bumpily

kumurains *adj* uneven, bumpy

kumuriņš *nm dim* of **kumurs**, small tangle, ball

kumuris *nm* = **kumurs**

kumurot *vi* = **kumuroties**

kumuroties *vr* **1.** (col.) walk slowly, painfully; dodder; **2.** writhe

kumurs *nm* tangle, wad, ball; cluster; (of people) throng

kunca *nf* (reg.) burbot

kuncele *nf* (reg.) burbot

kuncis *nm* (reg.) vivparous blenny

kunde *nf* (col.) client

kundze *nf* **1.** lady; **2.** mistress (employer, head of a household); **3.** (form of address, title) Mrs, madam, madame; **godātā N k.!** Dear Mrs X; **go-dātā k.!** Dear Madam; **4.** wife, spouse

kundzene *nf* **1.** miss; **2.** lady; **3.** mistress (em-ployer, head of a household); **4.** wife, spouse

kundzenīte *nf dim* of **kundzene**, miss; lady

kundzēns *nm* **1.** (young) master; **2.** (cont.) whippersnapper

kundzība *nf* domination; rule; supremacy

kundzīgi *adv* haughtily; imperiously

kundzīgs *adj* lordly; haughty; imperious

kundziņš *nm* **1.** *dim* of **kungs**, lord; cont. for **kungs**; **2.** (young) master; **3.** orange boletus

kundziski *adv* haughtily; imperiously

kundzisks *adj* lordly; haughty; imperious

kundziskums *nm* lordliness; haughtiness; imperiousness

kundzīte *nf* **1.** *dim* of **kundze**, lady; **2.** employer's young daughter; **3.** young miss; **4.** (cont.) madame

kuneiforms *adj* cuneiform

kunga gaitas *nf pl* corvée

kunga mērs *nm* (hist.) the larger **pūrs** measure (used by the lord of the manor)

kunga novads *nm* a lord's domain

kunga sēta *nf* (hist.) demesne

kunga tiesa *nf* share rent

kunga vārdi *nm pl* a spell (cast by the serfs before seeing their lord);

kungfu *indecl nm* kung fu

kungot *vi* **1.** mister, sir; **2.** act as a boss

kungoties *vr* mister, sir

kung/s *nm* **1.** gentleman; lord; **smalks k.** fine gentleman; **liels k.** great lord, (hum.) pasha ◊ ~**a prātā** drunk as a lord; **mans k. nav tavs sulainis** I am not your servant; **2.** man; **3.** master; lord; **k. un ķēniņš** lord and master; **ak (tu) k.!** Oh, Lord! **būt ~ā** be the master, be in charge; **4.** (form of address, title) mister, Mr, Sir; **Go-dātais N k.!** Dear Mr X; **Godātais k.!** Dear Sir! **5.** (cards) king

kungu frizētava *nf* barber shop

kungu nams *nm* manor house

kungu tauta *nf* ruling nation

kungu vakars *nm* stag party

kunigaite *nf* wife of a **kunigaitis**

kunigaitis *nm* (hist.) war lord (in feudal Lithuania)

kunigaitiste *nf* the territory of a **kunigaitis**

kunilings *nm* cunnilingus

kūniņa *nf* **1.** chrysalis, pupa; **2.** (also ~**s apvalks**) cocoon

kūniņdējējas mušas *nf pl* Pupipara

kūniņdējējs *nm* pupiparous insect

kunkstēt *vi* moan

kunkstiens *nm* moan

kunksts *nm* moan

kunktācija *nf* cunctation, delay, procrastination

kunkt[a]tor/s [ā] *nm*, ~**e** *nf* procrastinator

kunkulis *nm* lump, clot

kunkulītis *nm dim* of **kunkulis**, little lump

kunkuļaini *adv* with lumps, lumpily

kunkuļainība *nf* lumpiness, clottedness

kunkuļains *adj* lumpy, clotted

kunkuļainums *nm* lumpiness, clottedness

kunkuļot *vi* (col.) walk with difficulty, stumble

kunkuļoti *adv* lumpily

kunkuļots *adj* lumpy

kunkurprecē *adv* (col.) piggyback

kunniņš *nm* miller's-thumb

kuņa *nf* (vulg.) bitch

kūņāties *vr* = **kūņoties**

kuņģa čūla *nf* stomach ulcer

kuņģa sula *nf* gastric juice

kuņģis *nm* stomach

kuņģspindele *nf* horse botfly

kūņot *vi* = **kūņoties**

kūņoties *vr* **1.** trudge; stumble; move with difficulty; **2. k. ārā** wriggle out, wriggle free; (of in-sects) molt

kupa *nf* (reg.) mound

kūpainītis *nm* first fluffy snow

kupāēa *nf* **1.** blending; **2.** blend

kupažēšana *nf* blending

kupcis *nm* (barb.) merchant

kupča *nm* (barb.) merchant

kupeja *nf* **1.** (RR) compartment; **2.** coupé

kupelācija *nf* cupelation

kupelēt *vt* cupel

kupena *nf* snowdrift, snowbank

kupenains *adj* covered with snowdrifts

kūpēšana *nf* smoking

kūpēšanas punkts *nm* smoke-black point

kupēt *vt* **1.** blend; **2.** (med.) end, terminate

kūpēt *vi* **1.** (of smoke, steam, dust) rise; steam; **2.** (of candles, lamps, fire) smoke

kupferons *nm* cupferron

kupica *nf* landmark (boundary marker), cairn

kupināt *vt* (of meat) sear, stir-fry; (of milk) curdle

kūpināt *vt* **1.** (of smoke) make; **2.** smoke (cure meat; inhale and exhale smoke)

kūpinātava *nf* **1.** smokehouse; **2.** mantle vault (over a hearth)

kupiņas *nf pl* (reg.) curds

kupīra *nf* **1.** (of texts, films) cut; **2.** coupon bond

kupirēt *vt* (of texts, films) cut

kūpis *nm* moor hen

kuplaste *nf* epithet for the squirrel, bushy-tail

kuplastis *nm* bushy-tailed animal

kupleja *nf* topical song (of a humorous or satirical nature)

kupletists *nm*, ~e *nf* singer (composer) of topical songs

kuplets *nm* couplet

kupli *adv* luxuriantly; (of attendance) in large numbers

kuplinājums *nm* additional attraction

kuplināt *vt* 1. (of hair, skirts) make bouffant; 2. (fig.) enrich, add to

kuplināties *vr* be added to

kuplmat/is *nm*, ~e *nf* bushy-haired person

kuplociņi *nm pl* rocambole

kuplojums *nm* development, increase

kuplot *vi* thrive; green and flourish; (of trees) spread wide

kupls *adj* 1. having dense foliage, branchy, leafy; luxuriant; 2. (of grass, hair) thick; (of tails, eyebrows) bushy; (of hairdos) bouffant; 3. (of skirts, sleeves) full, wide, voluminous, bouffant; 4. puffy; 5. (of numbers of people) large; 6. (col.) well-endowed, corpulent; 7. abundant, bountiful

kuplums *nm* 1. density of foliage; 2. thickness; bushiness; bouffancy; 3. fullness; 4. puffiness; density; 5. endowment; corpulence; 6. abundance; bountifulness

kupoliņš *nm dim* of **kupols**, small dome

kupols *nm* dome; cupola; (of a parachute) canopy

kupolveida *indecl adj* dome-shaped

kupolveidā *adv* like a dome

kupolveidīgi *adv* like a dome

kupolveidīgs *adj* dome-shaped

kuponiņš *nm dim* of **kupons**, coupon

kupons *nm* coupon

kupoross *nm* copperas

kupot *vi* (reg.) foam

kuprainais lasis *nm* humpback salmon

kuprainais valis *nm* humpback whale

kuprainība *nf* humpiness

kuprain/is *nm*, ~e *nf* hunchback; humpbacked animal

kuprains *adj* hunchbacked; humpbacked; (of noses) crooked

kuprainums *nm* humpiness

kuprejs *nm* kouprey

kuprība *nf* humpiness

kupris *nm* 1. hump; hunch; (of cats) arch; 2. hunchback

kuprīt/is *nm*, ~e *nf* 1. *dim* of **kupris**, little hump; 2. (col.) hunchback, humpback

kuprīts *nm* cuprite

kuprlasis *nm* humpback salmon

kuprs *nm* (of cats) arch

kuprs *adj* hunchbacked, humped

kuprums *nm* humpiness

kupsa *nf* (reg.) copse

kūpsis *nm* (reg.) copse

kupt *vi* curdle

kūpt *vi* smoke

kupušpiens *nm* (reg.) curds

kur *adv* 1. where; **k. citur** a. somewhere; b. where else; **kaut k.** somewhere, anywhere; **k. nekur** (col.) somewhere; **k. vien** wherever; **k. kuŗais** each in a different direction, every which way; **k. nu vēl** let alone; **k. bijis, k. ne** suddenly; 2. (in exclamatory phrases and sentences signifying emphasis, impossibility, or negation) never (**k. tas redzēts!** I've never heard of such a thing! **k. nu viņš labosies!** he'll never straighten out!); 3. (in exclamatory sentences signifying emotional evaluation) oh (**k. tās pūles, k. tie izdevumi!** oh, the effort, oh, the expense!)

kura *pron* = **kuŗa**

kurā *pron* = **kuŗā**

kurais *pron* = **kuŗais**

kuramais *nm* = **kuŗamais**

kurante *nf* (mus.) courante

kuranti *nm pl* chimes

kurants *nm* (typ.) brayer

kurāre *nf* curare

kuraste or **kūraste** *nf* creel

kuratela *nf* (jur.) receivers (of a failing company)

kur[a]torija [ā] *nf* board of trustees

kur[a]tor/s [ā] *nm*, ~e *nf* 1. guardian; supervisor; 2. (hist.) superintendent

kurāts *nm* curate

kuraža *nf* 1. covered sleigh, kibitka; 2. removable sleigh seat

kurāža *nf* (obs.) 1. courage; 2. intoxication

kurāžīgs *adj* 1. courageous; 2. intoxicated

kurbete *nf* curvet

kurbetēt *vi* curvet

kurbulēt *vt* (barb.) crank

kurbulis *nm* (barb.) crank

kurcēt *vi* become spongy, become pithy

kurciens *nm* croak

kurcīte *nf* (col.) frog

kurcumi *nm pl* scum (on top of birch sap)

kurdīt *vt* incite, set on

kurd/s *nm*, ~iete *nf* Kurd

kūre I *nf* cure, course of treatment

kūre II *nf* (reg.) crucian carp

kūrēj/s *nm*, ~a *nf* stoker

kureklis *nm* kindling

kureklītis *nm dim* of **kureklis**, little bit of kindling

kurēties *vr* (of fire in a stove or oven) burn

kūrfirstiene *nf* (hist.) elector's wife or daughter

kūrfirst/s *nm* (hist.) elector; ~a **valsts** (hist.) electorate

kurgāns *nm* barrow, tumulus; (mil.) observation mound

k[u]riālisms [ū] *nm* curialism

k[u]riālists [ū] *nm* curialist

k[u]riāls [ū] *adj* curial; **k. stils** officialese

kurien/e *nf*; **uz** ~i where, where to; **no** ~es from where, whence; **līdz** ~ei how far

kūrija *nf* 1. curia; 2. class of voters

kuriķis *nm* (col.) stoker

kurinām/ais *nom adj* fuel; ~ā **padevējs** fuel stoker

kurināms *adj*, usu. *defin* **kurināmais** heating

kurināt *vt* 1. heat; stoke; 2. (fig.) kindle, incite; 3. (col.) smoke

kurinātājs *nm*, ~a *nf* 1. stoker; 2. instigator

kurinātava *nf* heating plant

kuriņš *nm* (reg.) fish-drying hut

kuriozi *adv* curiously, strangely, quaintly

kuriozitāte *nf* curiosity (curious object)

kuriozs *nm* curious (strange) situation; curious (strange) case

kuriozs *adj* curious, strange, quaint

kuriozums *nm* curiousness

kūris *nm* (reg.) large fish basket (for catching Baltic herring)

kurj[e]rdienests [ē] *nm* courier service

kurj[e]r/s [ē] *nm*, ~e *nf* courier, messenger; **ar** ~u special delivery

kurj[e]rvilciens [ē] *nm* express train

kurkstēt *vi* 1. croak; 2. gurgle, rumble

kurkstiens *nm* croak

kurkstoņa *nf* croaking

kurkšķēt *vi* 1. croak; 2. gurgle, rumble

kurkt *vi* 1. croak; 2. gurgle, rumble

kurkulēniņš *nm dim* of **kurkulēns**, tadpole

kurkulēns *nm* tadpole

kurkulis *nm* amphibian eggs

kurkulītis *nm dim* of **kurkulis**, tadpole

kurkuma *nf* turmeric

kurl/ais *nom adj* deaf person; ~ie the deaf; ~ā *f*

kurlausis *nm* (reg.) deaf person

kurliks *nm* laughing gull

kurlis *nm* 1. dove; 2. deaf person

kurlītis *nm dim* of **kurlis 2**, deaf person

kurlmēmais *nom adj* deaf-mute

kurlmēmība *nf* deaf-mutism

kurlmēms *nm* deaf-mute

kurlmēmums *nm* deaf-mutism

kurls *adj* deaf

kurlums *nm* deafness

kūrmāja *nf* 1. pump house (at a spa); 2. spa hotel

kurmēr *adv* **1.** however little; barely; **2.** more or less

kurmet *adv* = **kurmēr**

kurmis *nm* mole

kurmītis *nm dim* of **kurmis**, little mole

kurmjāda *nf* moleskin

kurmjala *nf* **1.** mole hole; **2.** mole drain

kurmja rakums *nm* molehill

kurmjarkls *nm* mole plow

kurmkausis *nm* (reg.) molehill

kurnēt *vi* grumble (complain); mutter

kurņāties *vr* (col.) dig

kuronisms *nm* Curonism (a feature of the Courish language occuring in Latvian)

kuroreiz adv = **kuŗoreiz**

k[u]rortolo/gs [ū] *nm*, **~ģe** *nf* doctor at a health resort

k[u]rortoloģija [ū] *nf* medicine of natural healing agents

kūrortpilsēta *nf* health resort town

kūrortpoliklīnika *nf* health resport polyclinic

kūrorts *nm* health resort, spa

kūrortterapija *nf* therapy administered at health resorts

kurp *adv* where, where to, which way

kurp/e *nf* shoe; slipper; **augstās ~es** high shoes; **zemās ~es** low-cut shoes

kurpīte *nf* **1.** *dim* of **kurpe**, little shoe; **2.** **~s** monkshood, aconite

kurpju karote *nf* shoehorn

kurpju saite *nf* shoelace

kurpju spodrinātājs *nm* shoeshine boy

kurpniekmeistars *nm* master shoemaker

kurpnie/ks *nm* **1.** shoemaker; cobbler; **~ce** *nf* a. female shoemaker; b. shoemaker's wife; **2.** (game) puss in the corner

kurpretī *adv* whereas

kurpretim *adv* whereas

kurs *nm* hearth

kūrs *nm* Cour

kursa darbs *nm* (educ.) thesis

kursant/s *nm*, **~e** *nf* **1.** student, person enrolled in a course; **2.** cadet

kursa svītra *nf* lubber's line

kursenie/ks *nm*, **~ce** *nf*, kursenieks, inhabitant of the dunes around the Kurische Haff, *pl* **~ki**

kursēt *vi* (of ships, vehicles) ply

kur/sis *nm*, **~siete** *nf* Cour; *pl* **~ši** Cours; **~šu valoda** Courish

kursisms *nm* Curonism

kursisks *adj* pertaining to the language of the **kursenieki**

kursist/s *nm*, **~e** *nf* student, course participant

kursīvi *adv* in italics

kursīvs *nm* italics

kursīvs *adj* italic, italicized

kursma *nf* **1.** (of fuel) charge; **2.** heating

kursorbumba *nf* (compu.) trackball

kursorisks *adj* (of reading) uninterrupted

kursors *nm* (compu.) cursor

kursorsvira *nf* (compu.) joystick

kurs/s *nm* **1.** (direction; course of instruction) course; **~i** course(s), instruction; **2.** (educ.) year; **pirmā ~a students** first-year student; **pēdējais k.** graduating year; **3.** curriculum; **4.** (of currencies) rate of exchange, stock price; **~a svārstības** fluctuation in the stock market

kurstīt *vt* tend a fire, poke (a fire)

kurt *vt* **1.** make fire; **2.** (fig.) incite, instigate

kurtāža *nf* brokerage (fee)

kurtēt *vi* become spongy, become pithy

kurties *vr* (of fire in a stove or oven) burn

kurtīne *nf* curtain (wall between two bastions; enclosing curtain)

kurtizāne *nf* courtesan

kurtjē *indecl nm* broker

kurtne *nf* firebox

kurtnieks *nm* (hist.) night watchman (under the corvée system in Livonia)

kurts *nm* greyhound

kurtuve *nf* **1.** firebox; **2.** heating plant

kūrums *nm* (an instance of) making fire

kūrviesis *nm* health resort visitor

kūrvieta *nf* health resort, spa

kurvimetrs *nm* curvometer

kurvis *nm* **1.** basket; hamper; **2.** (col.) creel; **3.** covered sleigh seat

kurvītis *nm* **1.** *dim* of **kurvis**, little basket; **2.** (col.) jilting; **3.** head of a composite

kurvjzieži *nm pl* Compositae, Asteraceae

kurvjvāģi *nm pl* bassinet

kurzemniecisks *adj* Courlandish

kurzemnie/ks *nm* **1.** Courlander; ~ce *nf*; **2.** (sl.) 1/8th-liter vodka bottle

kurzulis *nm* whiny, capricious child

ku[r]a [r] *pron* **1.** *gen* of **kuŗš**; **2.** *f* of **kuŗš**

ku[r]ā [r] *pron* **1.** *loc* of **kuŗš**, *loc* of **kuŗa** 2; **2.** *defin* of **kuŗa** 2

ku[r]ais [r] *pron, defin* of **kuŗš**

ku[r]amais [r] *nom adj* fuel

ku[r]oreiz [r] *adv* each time; from time to time

ku[r]/š *pron* **1.** (interrogative) which; who; **2.** (re-lative) that, which; who; **k. vien** whichever; whoever; **k. ~u** (also **k. ~am, k. ar ~u**) haphazardly, helter-skelter; **k. katrs** anyone; any; **3.** (in-definite) one (**kā nu k. prot** the best one knows how; **kas ~am patīk** whatever one likes); many (~o **reizi es to jau saku!** how many times have I told you! **līst jau ~o dienu** it has been raining these many days); with **kā**, signifies dependence on circumstances; **(dzīvo) kā ~ais** (each lives) according to (his or her) circumstances; **kā ~o reizi** it depends, it is different each time

kūsa *nf* (vulg.) pubic hair

kūsāt *vi* **1.** boil, seethe, boil over; **2.** (fig.) be in full swing

kūsis *nm* = **kūsa**

kusli *adv* weakly

kuslība *nf* weakness, tenderness, delicateness

kusls *adj* weak, tender, delicate

kuslums *nm* weakness, tenderness, delicateness

kusnis *nm* (metall., soldering) flux

kūsot *vi* = **kūsāt**

kust I *vi* thaw; melt

kust II *vi* tire

kustams *adj, part* of **kustēt** movable

kustēt *vi* move; stir

kustēties *vr* move; stir

kustība *nf* **1.** movement; **brīvās ~s** free exercise, Swedish movements; **2.** motion; **apgriezta k.** retrograde motion; **mūžīgā k.** perpetual motion; **turpatpakaļ k.** reciprocation; **3.** traffic

kustības daudzums *nm* momentum

kustīgais atbalsts *nm* tailstock

kustīgi *adv* nimbly, agilely

kustīgs *adj* **1.** mobile, moving; **2.** nimble, agile; active

kustīgums *nm* **1.** mobility; nimbleness, agility; **2.** activity

kustināt *vt* move; (of ears) wiggle; **nekustina ne ausis** he doesn't bat an eyelash

kustods *nm* custodian

kustonis *nm* animal; beast

kustoniski *adv* like an animal

kustonisks *adj* animal-like; beastly

kustoniskums *nm* animal-like behavior

kustoņa *nm* vermin

kustoņu zāle *nf* ground ivy

kūsulis *nm* vortex

kuš *interj* hush

kušana *nf* melting; thawing

kušanas temperātūra *nf* melting point

kušete *nf* couch, day bed

kušināt *vt* soothe (a child)

kušināties *vr* (col.) dig, burrow

kušķains *adj* tufted; bunched

kušķis *nm* bunch; tuft; wad; tussock; clump

kušķītis *nm dim* of **kušķis**, small bunch, tuft

kušņa zāles *nf pl* blueweed

kušņāt *vt* (col.) dig, burrow

kušņāties *vr* (col.) dig, burrow

kušņi *nm pl* (metall., soldering) flux

kuteklis *nm* clitoris

kutelība *nf* ticklishness

kutelīgi *adv* ticklishly

kutelīgs *adj* ticklishy

kutelīgums *nm* ticklishness

kuteris *nm* (naut.) cutter; picketboat

kutēt *vi* tickle

kutikula *nf* cuticle

kutināt *vt* tickle

kūtiņa *nf dim* of **kūts**, small animal barn, stable

kūtniece *nf* cowgirl

kūtri *adv* indolently, lazily

kūtrība *nf* indolence, laziness

kūtrot *vi* loaf, laze

kūtrs *adj* indolent, lazy

kūtrums *nm* indolence, laziness

kūts *nf* animal barn, stable; **dziļā k.** deep barn; **seklā k.** shallow barn

kūtsaugša *nf* hayloft

kūtsdurvis *nf pl* door of an animal barn

kūtsgals *nm* end of an animal barn

kūtsmeita *nf* cowgirl

kūtsmēsli *nm pl* manure, dung

kūtspakaļa *nf* (sl.) homegrown tobacco

kūtspriekša *nf* yard (in front of an animal barn)

kūtssolis *nm* animal barn chores

kūtsstāve *nf* keeping cattle stalled

kuvāde *nf* couvade

kuvērs *nm* place setting; (obs.) envelope

kūvēt *vi* gambol, frolic, cavort

kūvēties *vr* (reg.) gambol, frolic, cavort

kūvīgs *adj* odd, extravagant

kuza *nf* crop; gizzard

kūza *nf* stick, staff, walking stick

kūzinieks *nm* **1.** beggar; **2.** uninvited guest

kuzka *nf* wheat chafer

kužināt *vi* (col.) **1.** tickle; **2.** dig, burrow

kužināties *vr* (reg., of chickens) dustbathe

kuž/is *nm* (sl.) clodhopper; **uz ~iem** in the country

kvā *interj* croak

kvāders *nm* ashlar

kvadr[a]gēna [ā] *nf* quadragesima (the 40 days of Lent)

kvadrants *nm* quadrant

kvadrātcentimetrs *nm* square centimeter

kvadrātdecimetrs *nm* square decimeter

kvadrātdzelzs *nf* steel bar (square bar)

kvadrātiekava *nf* (square) bracket

kvadrātiski *adv* quadratically

kvadrātisks *adj* quadratic, square

kvadrātkilometrs *nm* square kilometer

kvadrātligzda *nf* (agr.) square cluster

kvadrātmetrs *nm* square meter

kvadrātmilimetrs *nm* square millimeter

kvadrātnolīdzinājums *nm* quadratic equation

kvadrāt/s *nm* square; **mazākais k.** (stat.) least square; **~ā** squared

kvadrātsakne *nf* square root

kvadr[a]tūra [ā] *nf* **1.** quadrature; **2.** floor space, area

kvadrātveida *indecl adj* square

kvadrātveidīgi *adv* in the shape of a square

kvadrātveidīgs *adj* square

kvadrātversts *nf* square verst

kvadrātvienādojums *nm* quadratic equation

kvadrātvienība *nf* square measure

kvadrātvīle *nf* square file

kvadriennāle *nf* quadrennial

kvadrika *nf* (math.) quadric

kvadriljons *nm* quadrillion

kvadrinnāle *nf* quadrennial

kvadrinoms *nm* polynomial in four variables

kvadrirēma *nf* quadrireme

kvadrivijs *nm* quadrivium

kvadrofonija *nf* quadraphony

kvadrofoniski *adv* quadraphonically

kvadrofonisks *adj* quadraphonic

kvadrs *nm* ashlar

kvadrumans *nm* quadrumane

kvadrupeds *nm* quadruped

kvadrupols *nm* quadrupole

kvaga *nf* quagga

kvakstēt *vi* quack

kvākstēt *vi* quack

kvākšēt *vi* croak

kvākšķēt *vi* croak

kvakšināt *vi* = **kvakšķināt**

kvakšķināt *vi* (*iter*) **1.** croak; **2.** quack

kvalificēt *vt* **1.** qualify; **2.** classify

kvalificēties *vr* **1.** qualify; **2.** acquire the skills
to qualify

kvalificēts *adj, part* of **kvalificēt** qualified,
skilled, (of seamen) able-bodied

kvalifikācija *nf* **1.** classification; **2.** qualification;
~**s celšana** advanced training

kvalitāte *nf* quality

kvalit|a|tīvi [ā] *adv* qualitatively

kvalit|a|tīv/s [ā] *adj* qualitative

kvalit|a|tīvums [ā] *nm* quality

kvankstēt *vi* (col.) bark, yap

kvankšķēt *vi* (col.) bark, yap

kvantēšana *nf* quantization

kvantēt *vt* quantize

kvantificēt *vt* quantify

kvantifikācija *nf* quantification

kvantisks *adj* quantal

kvantitāte *nf* quantity

kvantit|a|tīvi [ā] *adv* quantitatively

kvantit|a|tīvs [ā] *adj* quantitative

kvantit|a|tīvums [ā] *nm* quantitative character

kvantizēt *vt* quantize

kvants *nm* quantum

kvantu fizika *nf* quantum physics

kvantums *nm* quantity, amount

kvantu pāreja *nf* quantum leap

kvarcdiorīts *nm* quartz-diorite

kvarcīts *nm* quartzite

kvarcot *vt* irradiate with a quartz lamp

kvarcs *nm* quartz; **dūmainais k.** cairngorm,
smoky quartz

kvarks *nm* quark

kvarkstēt *vi* croak

kvārkstēt *vi* **1.** croak; **2.** caw

kvarkstoņa *nf* croaking

kvarkšķēt *vi* croak

kvarkt *vi* croak

kvarta *nf* **1.** (mus.) fourth; **palielinātā k.**
augmented forth; **pamazinātā k.**
diminished fourth; **2.** (hist.) second year of
a Gymnasium; **3.** quat-rain; **4.** (measure)
quart; **5.** (fencing) quarte

kvartāls *nm* **1.** quarter (of a year); **2.** city block,
quarter; **3.** forest section

kvartālstiga *nf* firebreak

kvartāns *nm* (hist.) second-year high school
(Gymnasium) student

kvartārs *nm* Quaternary

kvartārs *adj* Quaternary

kvarte *nf* (fencing) quarte

kvarterklājs *nm* quarterdeck

kvarteronis *nm* quadroon

kvarters *nm* (measure of capacity; unit of
weight) quarter

kvartets *nm* quartet

kvartile *nf* quartile

kvartīrjērs *nm* quartermaster

kvartole *nf* (mus.) quadruplet

kvarts *nm* (of monetary units) quart

kvartsekstakords *nm* (mus.) second inversion

kvasija *nf* Quassia

kvass *nm* kvass

kvašiorkors *nm* kwashiorkor

kvaternārs *adj* quaternary

kvatročento *indecl nm* quattrocento

kvazārs *nm* quasar

kvazidaļiņa *nf* quasiparticle

kvaziharmonisks *adj* quasiharmonic

kvaziperiods *nm* quasiperiod

kvaziperiodisks *adj* quasi-periodic

kvazizinātnisks *adj* quasi-scientific

kvazizvaigzne *nf* quasar

kvēkeris *nm* Quaker

kveksis *nm* **1.** (of dogs) yapper; **2.** trackhound

kveksītis *nm dim* of **kveksis**, yapper

kvekstēt *vi* yap, yelp

kvēkstēt *vi* (com.) cry

kvekšķēt *vi* yap, yelp

kvēkšķēt *vi* (com.) cry

kvekšķināt *vi* (*iter*) yap, yelp

kvekšķis *nm* (of dogs) yapper

kvēkšķis *nm* (com.) 1. yeller; 2. crybaby

kvēlaini *adv* ardently

kvēlainīte *nf* (folk.) impetuous woman

kvēlains *adj* glowing; incandescent; (fig.) ardent, impetuous

kvelde *nf* heat

kveldēt *vt* 1. (of the sun) burn; make burn; heat; make white-hot, incandesce; 2. scald

kveldi *adv* passionately

kvēldiegs *nm* (el.) filament

kveldīgi *adv* hotly, scorchingly

kveldīgs *adj* hot, scorching

kveldināt *vt* 1. heat, burn; sear; 2. scald

kveldot *vi* glow; (fig.) burn

kvelds *adj* passionate

kvēle *nf* 1. glow; 2. (fig.) ardor, heat, passion

kvēlelektrods *nm* hot electrode

kvēles baterija *nf* A battery

kvēles karstums *nm* red heat

kvēles reostats *nm* filament rheostat

kvēles temperātūra *nf* glow temperature, temperature of incandescence;

kvēlēt *vi* glow; (fig.) burn

kvēlgalva *nf* (tech.) hot bulb

kvelgt *vi* (reg.) howl

kvēli *adv* glowingly, ardently; passionately

kvēlīgi *adv* passionately

kvēlīgs *adj* passionate

kvēlīgums *nm* passion

kvēlināt *vt* 1. bring to high heat; 2. (fig.) stoke the fire

kvēlkrāsa *nf* 1. fluorescent pigment, Day-Glo color; 2. temper color

kvelkstēt *vi* 1. yelp; 2. cry silently

kvēlķermenis *nm* incandescent body

kvelmaini *adv* hotly

kvelmains *adj* hot

kvelme *nf* 1. glow; 2. ardor, heat, passion

kvelmot *vi* glow, burn, be hot

kvēlojošs *adj, part* of **kvēlot** glowing; red-hot; fiery; (of coals) live; (fig.) ardent

kvēlojums *nm* glow

kvēlot *vi* glow; (fig.) burn

kvēloties *vr* glow; (fig.) burn

kvēls *nm* glow

kvēls *adj* glowing, fiery; (fig.) ardent; passionate

kvēlspuldze *nf* incandescent bulb

kvelst *vi* (col.) bark, yap

kvēlstrāva *nf* (el.) filament current

kvēltemper[a]tūra [ā] *nf* temperature of incandescence, glow temperature

kvēlums *nm* 1. glow; 2. ardor

kvēlvads *nm* heating wire

kvēlvīns *nm* mulled wine

kvenkstēt *vi* yelp

kvenkšķēt *vi* bark, yap

kvēpaini *adv* sootily

kvēpains *adj* sooty

kvēpainums *nm* sootiness

kvēpekle *nf* = **kvēpeklis**

kvēpeklis *nm* 1. oil lamp, wick lamp; 2. fumigator; 3. censer

kvēpeklītis *nm dim* of **kvēpeklis**, oil lamp

kvēpekļi *nm pl* soot

kvēpele *nf* chimneyless kerosene lamp

kvēpelis *nm* (col.) dirty fellow

kvēpene *nf* oil lamp, wick lamp

kvēpēt *vi* 1. (of fire, candles, lamps) smoke; 2. become covered with soot

kvēpi *nm pl* soot

kvēpināt *vt* 1. soot; 2. (of incense) burn; 3. (col.) smoke (bees, pipe, meat)

kvēpinātāj/s *nm*, ~a *nf* 1. burner; 2. smoker

kvēpis *nm* 1. (col.) dirty fellow; 2. artist's charcoal

kvēplampiņa *nf* oil lamp, wick lamp

kvēpoṇa *nf, nm* **1.** (com.) dirty person; **2.** smoky, sooty place

kvēpot *vi* smoke

kvēpt *vi* **1.** (of fire, candles, lamps) smoke; **2.** become covered with soot

kvercitins *nm* quercetin

kverija *nf* slender-forked chickweed

kverkstēt *vi* (col.) bark, yip

kverkšķēt *vi* (col.) bark, yip

kverkšķināt *vt* **1.** make (a dog) bark; **2.** (col.) interrogate under torture

kverkšķis *nm* yapper

kvērkt *vi* squeal

kverle *nf* waistband

kvernēt *vi* (col.) hang around, idle, dawdle

kverpis *nm* = **kverplis**

kverplis *nm* **1.** (com.) toddler, little boy; **2.** lean shoat; **3.** tiny creature, bug

kverplītis *nm dim* of **kverplis**

kverpt *vi* fail to thrive

kverpucis *nm* = **kverplis**

kverulants *nm* querulant

kvestors *nm* quaestor

kvestūra *nf* quaestorship

kvīcene *nf* porridge with fatty gravy

kvīcināt *vt* make squeal

kvieciens *nm* squeal

kviecināt *vt* make squeal

kviekt *vi* squeal

kviesaine *nf* wheat field

kviesāj/s *nm* wheat field; ~i wheat stalks remaining after harvest

kviesis *nm* wheat

kviešalus *nm* wheat beer

kvieš/i *nm pl* wheat; ~u maize whole-grain wheat bread

kviešu cietā melnplauka *nf* wheat smut

kviētisms *nm* quietism

kviētist/s *nm*, ~e *nf* quietist

kviksteps *nm* quickstep

kvīkstēt *vi* squeal

kvilaja *nf* soapbark

kvinārs *adj* quinary

kvinojbalanda *nf* quinoa

kvinta *nf* (mus.) fifth; **palielinātā k.** augmented fifth

kvintāls *nm* quintal

kvintāns *nm* (hist.) first-year high school (Gymnasium) student

kvintesence *nf* quintessence

kvintets *nm* quintet

kvintiljons *nm* quintillion

kvintole *nf* (mus.) quintuplet

kvirīti *nm pl* Quirites

kvislings *nm* quisling

kvitā *adv* (col.) quits

kvitējums *nm* receipt; signature for money received

kvitēt I *vt* receipt

kvitēt II *vi* (folk.) shine, shimmer

kvīts *nf* receipt; claim check

kviukstēt *vi* (col.) squeal

kvocients *nm* quotient

kvodlibets *nm* quodlibet

kvorums *nm* quorum

kvota *nf* quota

kvotes zeme *nf* (hist.) peasant land annexed by German landlords (1819-1846)

Ķ

ķaukstēt *vi* yelp, yap

ķauķis *nm* **1.** warbler; **2.** (cont.) dumbbell

ķauķītis *nm dim* of **ķauķis**, warbler

ķaulis *nm* **1.** glutton; **2.** clumsy worker

ķauris *nm* myriopod, millipede

ķausēt *vt, vi* **1.** (of liquids) mix; **2.** (com.) eat, gulp down one's food

ķausis *nm* **1.** a meal that has turned out too thick; **2.** glutton ķauzēt *vt, vi* **1.** boil over; **2.** (com.) gulp down one's food

ķeblis *nm* stool, footstool

ķeblītis *nm dim* of ķeblis, footstool

ķeburaini *adv* in a scrawl, in a scrawly handwriting

ķeburains *adj* **1.** crooked, gnarled, twisted; **2.** (of handwriting) scrawly

ķeburīgi *adv* = ķeburaini

ķeburīgs *adj* = ķeburains

ķeburītis *nm dim* of ķeburs, gnarled branch, root

ķeburot *vi* struggle, wriggle, flounder

ķebur/s *nm* **1.** gnarled branch, gnarled root; **2.** usu. *pl* ~i scrawl

ķecerība *nf* heresy

ķecerīgi *adv* heretically

ķecerīgs *adj* heretical

ķecerīgums *nm* hereticalness

ķecer/is *nm*, ~e *nf* heretic

ķēd/e *nf* **1.** chain; **2.** (el.) circuit; **maģistrālā ķ.** trunk circuit; **3.** (mil.) line; **izvērstā ~ē** in a line

ķēdes atslēga *nf* chain tongs

ķēdes dūriens *nm* chain stitch

ķēdes līnija *nf* catenary

ķēdes loceklis *nm* link

ķēdes reakcija *nf* chain reaction

ķēdes ritenis *nm* sprocket

ķēdes suns *nm* **1.** watch dog; **2.** vicious dog

ķēdēt *vt* chain

ķēdveida *indecl adj* chain-like

ķēdveidīgi *adv* like a chain

ķēdveidīgs *adj* chain-like

ķeg/lis *nm* bowling pin; ~ļi bowling (game)

ķegot *vi* (sl.) run

ķegums *nm* **1.** rapids; **2.** roof ridge

ķeģis I *nm* **1.** crutch; cane; **2.** blow

ķeģis II *nm* redpoll

ķeģītis *nm dim* of ķeģis I, crutch; cane

ķeiksmot *vt* (reg.) tease

ķeima zāle *nf* toothwort

ķeipt *vi* pine, languish

ķeire *nf* left hand

ķeirība *nf* left-handedness

ķeir/is *nm*, ~e *nf* left-hander

ķeists *adj* strange

ķeistums *nm* strangeness

ķeizara cirtas *nf pl* haircap moss

ķeizargrieziens *nm* Cesarean section

ķeizariene *nf* empress, kaiserin

ķeizariski *adv* imperially

ķeizarisks *adj* imperial

ķeizariste *nf* empire, kaiserdom

ķeizarkronis *nm* tiger lily

ķeizars *nm* emperor; kaiser

ķeizarvalsts *nf* empire, kaiserdom

ķekarainā ģipsene *nf* (bot.) baby's breath

ķekarainais amarants *nm* spleen amaranth

ķekarainā zeltene *nf* tufted loosestrife

ķekarains *adj* bunchy

ķekarcukurs *nm* glucose

ķekariņš *nm dim* of ķekars, small bunch, cluster

ķekaronis *nm* (bot.) indeterminate inflorescence

ķekarpaparde *nf* grape fern

ķekars *nm* bunch, cluster

ķekaru vībotne *nf* an artemisia, Artmisia paniculata

ķekarveida *indecl adj* clustered

ķekarveidīgs *adj* clustered

ķēkas *nf pl* croquets made of ground peas or beans (with pork, onions, other ingredients)

ķekata I *nf* **1.** stilt; **2.** (cont.) boot

ķekata II *nf* **1.** single file; **2.** mummer; **3.** ~s a. mummery; b. stilts

ķekatnie/ks *nm* **1.** mummer; ~ce *nf*; **2.** a Latvian folk dance

ķekoties *vr* **1.** mum; **2.** play, tease

ķeksēt *vt* **1.** hook; pull or push with a hook; **2.** (col., fig.) fish

ķek/sis *nm* hook; boat hook; grapple; ~ši scrawl

ķeksītis *nm* **1.** *dim* of **ķeksis**, little hook; **2.** checkmark

ķēkša *nf* (obs.) cook

ķekšaini *adv* with hooks; angularly

ķekšains *adj* (of writing) with hooks; angular

ķeķe *nf* bunch, cluster

ķēķene *nf* kitchen maid

ķeķi *nm pl* wonders, curiosities

ķēķis *nm* (obs., col.) kitchen

ķelderis *nm* smock

Ķelnes ūdens *nm* (obs.) cologne

ķelvainis *nm* (husband's) sister-in-law's husband

ķelle *nf* trowel

ķellēt *vt* (com.) **1.** eat; **2.** smear; slap on

ķellēties *vr* mess

ķelneriene *nf* (barb.) waitress

ķelneris *nm* (barb.) waiter

ķelti *nm pl* Celts

ķeltibēri *nm pl* Celtiberians

ķēmarausis *nm* (col., of appearance) fright

ķemberiņš *nm* cambric

ķēmeklis *nm* apparition, ghost

ķemertiņš *nm* (barb.) outhouse

ķēmīgi *adv* errily; grotesquely

ķēmīgs *adj* eerie; grotesque

ķemmašīna *nf* carding machine

ķemmdzija *nf* worsted yarn

ķemme *nf* **1.** comb; **bieza ķ.** toothcomb; **2.** (weav.) reed

ķemmēt *vt* comb

ķemmēties *vr* comb one's hair

ķemmīte *nf dim* of **ķemme**, small comb

ķemmlāde *nf* (weav.) batten

ķemmrats *nm* (obs.) cogwheel

ķemmveida *indecl adj* comb-like

ķemmveida glīvene *nf* fennel-leaved pondweed

ķemmveidīgi *adv* like a comb

ķemmveidīgs *adj* comb-like

ķemmvilna *nf* worsted wool

ķēmošanās *nfr* antics

ķēmoties *vr* clown; **ķ. pakaļ** ape

ķempe *nf* (reg.) conk

ķempelis *nm* stock (wooden block with holes for fastening the butt ends of tree trunks to a wagon or sledge)

ķēms *nm* **1.** apparition, ghost; **2.** (col., of appearance) fright

ķemsis *nm* (reg.) glutton

ķence *nf* goo; thick gravy; flour mush

ķencēt *vt* daub

ķeneris *nm* (com.) expert

ķeng/as *nf pl* slander; **~u raksts** libelious article, libel; **~u lapa** lampoon

ķengāt *vt* slander

ķengātāj/s *nm*, **~a** *nf* slanderer

ķengāties *vr* **1.** slander; **2.** cuss, revile

ķengurēns *nm* joey

ķenguriņš *nm dim* of **ķengurs**, little kangaroo

ķengurs *nm* kangaroo

ķēniņdēls *nm* (folk.) king's son

ķēniņiene *nf* (obs., folk.) queen

ķēniņmeita *nf* (folk.) king's daughter

ķēniņš *nm* (obs., folk.) king

ķēniņvalsts *nf* (folk.) kingdom

ķēniški *adv* royally

ķēniškīgi *adv* royally

ķēniškīgs *adj* royal

ķēnišķs *adj* royal

ķenīte *nf* flour mush with fatty gravy

ķepa *nf* paw

ķēpa *nf* **1.** (col.) slush; **2.** bits of bread in milk; **3.** fuss, trouble; **4.** (com.) mess; **5.** *nf, nm* good-for-nothing

ķepainis *nm* **1.** bear; **2.** teddy bear

ķepains *adj* having paws

ķepaiņi *nm pl* cow parsnip

ķēpājums *nm* mess

ķepals *nm* ball of snow, dough, or clay

ķeparāties *vr* = **ķepuroties**

ķēpāt *v* **1.** *vi* (of wet snow) fall; **2.** *vt* mess up

ķēpāties *vr* mess

ķēpausis *nm* bungler, muff

ķepēt *vt* (col.) **1.** lay on thick; daub; **2.** glue;
   3. (of sticky foods) eat, stuff it in

ķepēties *vr* (col.) eat with one's fingers

ķepīgi *adv* stickily

ķepīgs *adj* sticky, gooey

ķepīgums *nm* stickiness

ķepināt *vt* model, shape

ķepiņa *nf dim* of ķepa, paw

ķēpiņa *nf dim* of ķēpa, slush; bits of bread in
   milk; little mess

ķēpis *nm* (naut.) hawsehole

ķepsele *nf* capstan

ķepsēt *vi* (col.) eat, put away

ķept *vi* stick, stick to, stick together

ķepuroties *vr* struggle, wriggle, flounder; **ķ.**
   pretim fight off (awkwardly)

ķepveida *indecl adj* paw-like

ķepveidīgs *adj* paw-like

ķerainis *nm* **1.** (bot.) burr; **2.** large crayfish;
   3. herb bennet

ķeraiņu madara *nf* (bot.) cleaver

ķerains *adj* shaggy; burred, burry

ķērājs *nm*, ~a *nf* catcher

ķeramtīkls *nm* (spider) snare

ķerbele *nf* (col.) potato basket

ķērciens *nm* croak; caw; screech

ķērcoņa *nf* screeching

ķērcoši *adv* screechingly, raucously

ķērcošs *adj, part* of ķērkt raucous; screeching

ķergalvis *nm* **1.** mophead, shaggy-haired
   person; **2.** curlyhead

ķērien/s *nm* **1.** grasp; **pa ~am** handy; **2.** catch (of
   fish, other things); **3.** skill, knack; **(viņam**
   ir) labs ķ. (he has a) knack for (it)

ķērkoņa *nf* screeching; (of crows) cawing

ķērkstēt *vi* screech; croak; (of crows) caw

ķērkstoņa *nf* screeching; cawing

ķērkstošs *adj, part* of ķērkt raucous; screeching;
   (of human voice) cracked

ķērkši *nm pl* watercress

ķērkt *vi* screech; croak; (of crows) caw

ķerlauks *nm* field of fire

ķerme *nf* problem; bad luck

ķērmeles *nf pl* caraway

ķermelīte *nf* sneezewort

ķerme/nis *nm* body; (aeron.) fuselage; (geom.)
   solid; (phys.) substance; **~ņa piedevas**
   appendages

ķermeniski *adv* bodily; corporeally, materially;
   solidly

ķermenisks *adj* **1.** bodily; **2.** corporeal, material;
   3. solid

ķermeniskums *nm* corporeality

ķermenītis *nm* **1.** *dim* of ķermenis, little body;
   2. corpuscle

ķermuša *nf* ramson

ķērna *nf* dirty fellow

ķērnāt *vt* (col.) mess up

ķērnāties *vr* (col.) mess

ķērne *nf* churn

ķērnes piens *nm* buttermilk

ķērnēt *vt* (obs.) churn (butter)

ķērpis *nm* lichen

ķerpīt *vi, vt* (barb.) stand, suffer

ķērpītis *nm dim* of ķērpis, lichen

ķērpjutis *nf pl* bark lice

ķerra I *nf* wheelbarrow

ķerra II *nf* greater scaup

ķērsa *nf* cardamine; cuckooflower

ķērsiņa *nf dim* of ķērsa, cardamine; cuckooflower

ķērsis *nm* = ķērsa

ķerstelēties *vr* flirt

ķerstīt *vt* catch, try to catch, chase

ķerstīties *vr* **1.** (*iter*) grasp; grope; **2.** flirt

ķeršana *nf* catching; (game) tag

ķeršanās *nfr* (game) tag

ķērši *nm pl* watercress

ķert *vt* **1.** grab; **ķ. ciet** grab, apprehend; **neķer,**
   beķer! keep your hands off! **2.** catch; **ķ.**
   cilpā snare; **ķ. kaulā** (col.) hurt; **ķ. lamatās**
   trap; **ķ. pēc gaisa** gasp for air; **ķ. pēc maka**
   reach for one's purse; **ķ. putnus** fowl; **ķ.**
   slazdā; trap; **ķ. tīklā** net; **ķ. uz muļķa** (col.)

take s.o. in; **ķ. zivis** fish; **ķeriet zagli!** stop thief! **3.** (of projectiles, blows) strike, hit; **ķ. mērķī** hit home; **4.** affect; **viņu ķēra trieka** he had a stroke; **5.** get, obtain; learn

ķerties *vr* **1.** grab, grab hold of; **ķ. klāt** a. go at it, begin; b. (fig.) hurt; **neķeries klāt!** stay away! **ķ. pie goda** (or **pogām**) offend; **ķ. pie kauliem** (of cold) be bone-chilling; **ķ. pie sirds** (or **dūšas**) (fig.) cut to the quick, offend, hurt; **ķ. (kādam) ap kaklu** throw one's arms around s.o.'s neck; **2.** stick, stick to; **3.** be caught in sth., catch; **4.** (of a job, enterprise, with **pie**) start, set to, tackle; (of a tool, implement, or means) take up; resort to; **5.** (of fish) strike; **man labi ķērās** I had a good catch; **6.** (of pens, engines) splutter; **7.** (of voice) catch; **8.** play tag

ķerts *adj, part* of **ķert 1.** caught; **2.** affected; **3.** (col.) a. somewhat (mentally) disturbed, a little off; b. (with **uz**) nuts (about sth.)

ķerubs *nm* cherub

ķērums *nm* catch

ķervele *nf* **1.** a shriveled-up thing; **2.** morel

ķērvele *nf* chervil

ķervelis *nm* morel

ķerveļains *adj* wrinkled, shriveled, rough

ķerzobis *nm* a person with crooked teeth

ķesas *nf pl* (com.) entrails

ķesele *nf* **1.** landing net; fish pot; **2.** gunnysack; nose bag; **3.** hopscotch

ķeselēt *vt* **1.** use crab pots; **2.** take up a collection with a collection pouch

ķeselīte *nf dim* of **ķesele**, landing net

ķesīgs *adj* (reg.) quarrelsome

ķēsis *nm* garfish

ķeskas *nf pl* (com.) entrails

ķest *vt* (com.) **1.** grab; **2.** gobble

ķesteris *nm* sacristan

ķesties *vr* **ķ. virsū** importune

ķeš/a *nf* (barb.) pocket; **(muld) kā pa ~u** (col., of speaking) (he, she is) talking nonsense

ķetna *nf* **1.** paw; **2.** climbing iron; **3.** tenon

ķetnains *adj* with paws

ķetniņa *nf dim* of **ķetna**, little paw

ķetnot *vt* dovetail; tenon

ķets *nm* cast iron; **leģēts ķ.** cast iron alloy

ķēve *nf* mare

ķeverot *vi* (col.) walk

ķcvīte *nf dim* of **ķēve**, filly

ķēvpups *nm* morel

ķeza *nf* quandry, scrape, trouble

ķezbere *nf* (reg.) cherry

ķezberis *nm* cherry tree

ķeziņa *nf dim* of **ķeza**, little trouble

ķēzīt *vt* **1.** soil; **2.** run down, belittle; **3.** waste

ķēzīties *vr* soil oneself; (com.) cuss

ķēžu bloks *nm* chain hoist

ķēžu bruņas *nf pl* chain mail

ķēžu ecēšas *nf pl* chain harrow

ķēžu kalējs *nm* chainsmith

ķēžu kaste *nf* chainlocker

ķēžu likums *nm* chain rule

ķēžu veronika *nf* a veronica, Veronica catenata

ķibele *nf* quandry, scrape, trouble

ķibelēt *vt* bother, make trouble for

ķibelētāj/s *nm*, **~a** *nf* troublemaker

ķibelīgs *adj* involved, complicated, troublesome, tricky

ķibelīte *nf dim* of **ķibele**, little trouble

ķibica *nf* (reg.) sleigh cover

ķibināt *vt* **1.** pick (to open or extract sth.); **2.** glue, paste together; **3.** paw; touch playfully

ķibināties *vr* tinker with

ķibuļi *nm pl* scrawl

ķidas *nf pl* giblets

ķidāt *vt* gut, (of fowl) draw

ķidiņas *nf pl dim* of **ķidas**, giblets

ķieģelis *nm* brick; **caurumotais ķ.** perforated brick; **ugunsizturīgs ķ.** firebrick

ķieģelītis *nm dim* of **ķieģelis**, small brick

ķieģelnieks *nm* brickmaker

ķieģeļceplis *nm* brickkiln

ķieģeļfabrika *nf* brickyard

ķieģeļkrāsa *nf* brick red

ķieģeļnesējs *nm* hod carrier

ķieģeļnīca *nf* brickyard

ķieģeļrūpniecība *nf* brickmaking industry

ķieģeļsārts *adj* pinkish orange

ķieģeļu buka *nf* hod

ķiemeles *nf pl* caraway

ķienains *adj* resinous

ķieņi *nm pl* resinous pinewood

ķigulis *nm* snail; snail shell

ķikāns *nm* common snipe

ķikerikī *interj* cock-a-doodle-doo

ķīkste *nf* (reg.) crab apple tree

ķikukaza *nf* common snipe

ķikurains *adj* wriggler-infested

ķikuri *nm pl* (reg.) cracklings

ķikurigū *interj* cock-a-doodle-doo

ķikurs *nm* wriggler (mosquito larva)

ķikutiņš *nm dim* of ķikuts, great snipe

ķikuts *nm* great snipe

ķīķerēt *vi* (com.) look

ķīķeris *nm* (obs.) telescope

ķīķēt I *vt* (col.) gut, draw

ķīķēt II *vi* (col.) look

ķiķināt *vi* giggle, titter, snicker

ķiķināties *vr* 1. giggle, titter, snicker; 2. flirt

ķīķis *nm* western honey buzzard

ķīķīzeris *nm* (hum.) telescope

ķīla *nf* 1. security, pawn; bail; 2. guaranty, pledge; 3. forfeit

ķīlāt *vt* take as security; attach

ķilava *nf* sprat

ķilavbundēa *nf* sardine can

ķilaviņa *nf dim* of ķilava, sprat

ķild/a *nf* quarrel ◊ ~u ābols apple of discord

ķildība *nf* quarrelsomeness

ķildīgi *adv* quarrelsomely

ķildīgs *adj* quarrelsome

ķildīgums *nm* quarrelsomeness

ķildiņa *nf dim* of ķilda, small quarrel

ķildnie/ks *nm*, ~ce *nf* quarreler

ķildoties *vr* quarrel

ķīlējums *nm* 1. wedging; 2. wedge

ķīlēt *vt* wedge; gib

ķīliņa *nf dim* of ķīla, pawn, forfeit

ķīlis I (with î) *nm* 1. wedge; (tech.) key; 2. wishbone; 3. gusset; 4. vee (formation); 5. (mil.) salient

ķīlis II *nm* 1. keel; 2. (aeron.) fin

ķīlītis *nm dim* of ķīlis I, little wedge

ķilkāns *nm* (reg.) skin and bones

ķīlnie/ks *nm*, ~ce *nf* 1. hostage; 2. (of a forfeits game) forfeiter

ķīlu nams *nm* pawn shop

ķīlu zīme *nf* pawn ticket

ķīļbārda *nf* goatee, imperial

ķīļbārdiņa *nf dim* of ķīļbārda, goatee

ķīļceliņš *nm* keel track

ķīļja[ch]ta [h] *nf* keelboat

ķiļķeni *nm pl* (game) marbles

ķiļķeniņš *nm dim* of ķiļķens, little dumpling

ķiļķens *nm* dumpling

ķīļlīnija *nf* column (line ahead formation of ships

ķīļraksts *nm* cuneiform writing

ķīļrāmis *nm* stretcher frame

ķīļrieva *nf* vee groove

ķīļrievas savienojums *nm* spline joint

ķīļsavienojums *nm* key joint; cotter joint

ķīļsiksna *nf* V-belt

ķīļšķautnis *nm* feather-edged board

ķīļūdens *nm* 1. bilge water; 2. wake

ķīļu savienojums *nm* key joint

ķīļveida *indecl adj* wedge-shaped, V-shaped

ķīļveidīgi *adv* like a wedge

ķīļveidīgs *adj* wedge-shaped, V-shaped

ķimeles *nf pl* caraway

ķimelis *nm* kümmel

ķimenājs *nm* caraway

ķimene I *nf* 1. caraway; 2. ~s caraway seeds

ķimene II *nf* croze

ķimeņatspaids *nm* (naut.) bilge log

ķimeņķīlis *nm* bilge keel

ķimeņkneija *nf* bilge bracket
ķimeņlapu selīnes *nf pl* milk parsley
ķimeņmaizīte *nf* caraway seed roll
ķimeņots *adj* with caraway seeds
ķimeņsieksts *nm* (naut.) bilge block
ķimeņslēpes *nf pl* (naut.) bilge ways
ķimere *nf* (col.) trouble
ķimerēties *vr* (col.) tinker, putter
ķimerīgs *adj* (col.) fussy, complicated
ķīmija *nf* chemistry; ~s **inženierzinātnes** chemical engineering
ķīmijterape|i|tiski |u| *adv* chemotherapeutically
ķīmijterape|i|tisk/s |u| *adj* chemotherapeutic
ķīmijterape|i|t/s |u| *nm*, ~e *nf* chemotherapist
ķīmijterapija *nf* chemotherapy
ķimikālija *nf* chemical
ķimikāts *nm* chemical
ķīmiķ/is *nm*, ~e *nf* chemist
ķīmioterapeitiski *adv* = ķīmijterapeutiski
ķīmioterapeitisks adj = ķīmijterapeutisks
ķīmioterapeit/s *nm*, ~e *nf* = ķīmijterapeuts
ķimioterapija *nf* = ķīmijterapija
ķīmiski adv chemically
ķīmisks *adj* chemical
ķīmisms *nm* chemistry
ķ|i|mizācija [ī] *nf* chemicalization
ķ|i|mizēt [ī] *vt* chemicalize
ķimpene *nf* pore fungus, polypore
ķimsis *nm* stopper
ķimst *vt* stuff; stuff oneself (eating)
ķimulis *nm* goldfinch
Ķīnas astere *nf* China aster
Ķīnas kāposti *nm pl* Chinese cabbage
Ķīnas kastānis *nm* Chinese chestnut
Ķīnas krabis *nm* mitten crab
Ķīnas mīkstbruņrupucis *nm* soft-shelled turtle
Ķīnas plūme *nf* oriental plum, Japanese plum
Ķīnas porcelāns *nm* oriental porcelain
Ķīnas roze *nf* China rose
Ķīnas smilšu bumbiere *nf* Chinese sand pear

Ķīnas vigna *nf* cowpea
Ķīnas zizifa *nf* jujube tree
ķīnie/tis *nm*, ~te *nf* Chinese; **(tā man ir)** ~šu **ābece** it is Greek to me
ķīniski *adv* in Chinese, (speak) Chinese
ķīnisks *adj* Chinese
ķinītis *nm* (sl.) movie theater
ķinka *nf* (reg.) puree; paste
ķiņķele *nf* snag, complication
ķiņķēziņš *nm* 1. hanging room ornamens used on festive occasion; 2. (sl.) gewgaw
ķiņķis *nm* tangle
ķipa *nf* pile, mound
ķīpa *nf* 1. large barrel; 2. hay in a nose bag; 3. palliasse; 4. (tight) bundle; bale; 5. *nf,* *nm* (col.) big and fat person, fatty; 6. count of 600
ķipars *nm* 1. jumping jack; 2. tyke; 3. minnow; 4. epithet for a dog
ķipis *nm* piggin
ķipītis *nm* 1. *dim* of ķipis, piggin; 2. a grain measure
ķiplocene *nf* garlic mustard
ķiplociņš *nm dim* of ķiploks, garlic
ķiplokots *adj* garlicky
ķiploks *nm* garlic
ķiploksēne *nf* garlic mushroom
ķiploku sīpoli *nm pl* rocamble
ķiploku teikrija *nf* wood sage
ķipriet/is *nm*, ~e *nf* Cypriot
ķirbis *nm* pumpkin
ķirbītis *nm dim* of ķirbis, little pumpkin
ķirbjaugi *nm pl* Cucurbitacea, cucurbits
ķirceklis *nm* tease
ķircīgi *adv* teasingly
ķircīgs *adj* teasing
ķircināt *vt* tease
ķircināties *vr* tease; tease each other, banter
ķirelis *nm* mole cricket
ķirģīz/s *nm*, ~iete *nf* = kirgīzs
ķirināt *vt* tease by dangling sth. before one's eyes

ķīris *nm* gull

ķirķis *nm* **1.** cricket; **2.** death watch

ķirla *nf* scrawny domestic animal

ķirlāns *nm* osprey

ķirlis *nm* osprey

ķirmelis *nm,* woodworm

ķirmēt *vi* become worm-eaten

ķirmgrauzis *nm* = **ķirmis**

ķirmināt *vt* (of wood borers) bore

ķirmināties *vr* trifle, piddle

ķirmis *nm* **1.** wood borer, woodworm; **2.** deathwatch

ķirmītis *nm dim* of **ķirmis**, deathwatch

ķirmulis *nm* = **ķirmis**

ķirpa *nf* haystack

ķirpgrauzis *nm* wood borer, wood worm

ķirpiņa *nf dim* of **ķirpa**, little haystack

ķirpis *nm* (reg.) wood borer

ķirpot *vt* stack hay

ķir/sis *nm* cherry (tree or fruit); **~šu sarkans** cherry color, cerise; **~šu šņabis** cherry brandy; **~sī** (col.) drunk

ķirsītis *nm dim* of **ķirsis**, little cherry

ķiršbrūns *adj* maroon

ķirškrāsa *nf* cherry (color)

ķiršoga *nf* cherry

ķiršsarkans *adj* cerise

ķiršu-madaru laputs *nf* black cherry aphid

ķiršu muša *nf* cherry fruitfly

ķiršu pūcīte *nf* gray dagger

ķiršziedi *nm pl* cherry blossoms

ķirurgs *nm* = **chirurgs**

ķirurģija *nf* = **chirurģija**

ķirurģiski *adv* = **chirurģiski**

ķirurģisks *adj* = **chirurģisks**

ķirzaciņa *nf dim* of **ķirzaka**, little lizard

ķirzaka *nf* lizard

ķirzakveidīgs *adj* lizard-like

ķirzata *nf* (reg.) lizard

ķīselis *nm* **1.** fruit juice jelly; **2.** oatmeal pudding

ķisens *nm* (barb.) pillow, cushion

ķīsis *nm* (fish) ruff

ķīsītis *nm dim* of **ķīsis**, ruff

ķiskas *nf pl* (com.) entrails

ķiš *interj* scat

ķit/e *nf* putty; **~ē** (col.) drunk

ķitējums *nm* putty

ķitelis *nm* smock, lab coat

ķitēt *vt* putty

ķītrs *adj* (folk.) bad, evil

ķiukstēt *vi* **1.** yelp; **2.** whiz

ķīve *nf* quarrel

ķīveklis *nm* (col.) quarrelsome person

ķivere *nf* **1.** helmet; **2.** (sl.) a. head; b. hangover

ķiverene *nf* (bot.) scullcap

ķivete *nf* cuvette

ķīvēties *vr* squabble

ķīvīgi *adv* quarrelsomely

ķīvīgs *adj* quarrelsome

ķivināt *vi* (of a lapwing) call

ķīviņš *nm* squabble

ķīvīte *nf* northern lapwing

ķivulis *nm* siskin

ķizināt *vt* (col.) tease (by showing sth. but not giving it)

ķobere *nf* (com.) head, noggin

ķobis *nm* (com.) head, noggin

ķocis *nm* (reg.) basket

ķoķis *nm* = **ķūķis**

ķoniņš *nm* king

ķuidēt *vi* (reg.) be able

ķūķis *nm* **1.** pipe; **2.** thick gruel made of ground barley, with pork

ķūķītis *nm* (reg.) wren

ķūle *nf* = **ķūlis**

ķūlis *nm nf* **1.** (pork cut) hind foot; (poultry) drumstick; **2.** stick, cane; **3.** awkward person, lubber

ķūlītis *nm dim* of **ķūlis**, stick

ķuļķene *nf* (col.) pipe

ķuļķēt *vi* (com.) smoke

ķuļķētājs *nm* (com.) smoker

kuļķis *nm* (col., cont), small clay pipe
kuļķītis *nm dim* of kuļķis, small clay pipe
kurķis *nm* (com.) pen, slammer
kurmis *nm* (barb.) jail
kurza *nf* wrinkle, fold
kutis *nm* (reg.) clumsy person
kuza *nf* trash
kūze *nf* cane

L

la *indecl nf* (mus.) A
labā *prep* **1.** for the sake of; for the benefit (or good) of; for s.o.'s own good; **2.** (of scores) in favor of
labad *prep* for the sake of
labadiena *nf* = labdiena
Labā Indriķa balandas *nf pl* (bot.) Good-King-Henry
lab/ais *adj, defin* of labs **1.** right, right-hand, (side of vehicles, animals) off; (mech.) righthanded; **uz ~o!** right face! **(iet) uz ~o pusi** (it is) improving; **2.** (pol.) right-wing
labāk *adv, comp* of labi **1.** better; **jo l.** so much the better; **jo . . . jo l.** the . . . the better; **vēl jo l.** all the better; **2.** rather; **es gandrīz l.** I would rather
labākais *adj, super* of labs best; **l. ir tas, ka . . .** and the best part of it is that . . .
labāk/s *adj, comp* of labs better; **tā kā nav nekā ~a** for want of anything better
labanakts *nf* good-night
lābans *nm* (col.) clumsy person, booby
labasdienas *nf pl* regards, love (sent through an intermediary)
labdabība *nf* good-naturedness; benignancy
labdabīgi *adv* benignly
labdabīgs *adj* good-natured; benign

labdabīgums *nm* good-naturedness; benignancy
labdabis *nm* good person
labdabls *nm* well-formed plant
labdabls *adj* (of growing plants) well formed
labdare *nf* benefactress
labdarība *nf* charity, philanthropy
labdarības iestāde *nf* charitable institution
labdarīgi *adv* charitably, philanthropically
labdarīgs *adj* charitable, philanthropic
labdar/is *nm*, ~e *nf* **1.** benefactor; **2.** (obs.) folk healer
labdarīt *vi* do good
labdarīte *nf* Jimsonweed
labdien *interj* good morning; hello; (if used in the afternoon) good afternoon
labdiena *nf* (daytime) greeting
labdienoties *vr* greet each other
labdūšas *nf pl* wild marjoram
labdzimtais *nom adj* noble
labdzimtība *nf* **1.** noble birth; **2. Jūsu l.** your Honor
labdzimtīgs *adj* of noble birth
labdzimts *adj* wellborn
labējais *defin adj* **1.** (pol.) right-wing; **2.** *nom adj* rightist, right-winger
labenieks *nm* (folk.) **1.** well-to-do person; **2.** benefactor
labestība *nf* **1.** good-heartedness; **2.** benevolence; **3.** (moral) goodness
labestīgi *adv* good-heartedly; benevolently
labestīgs *adj* **1.** good-hearted; **2.** benevolen
labi *adv* **1.** well; **tev l. runāt** it is easy for you to say; **nu tik ir l. !** this is a fine mess! **2.** all right (of things turning out; agreement); **3.** good; (educ.) with credit; **ļoti l.** (educ.) with honors; **l. daudz** a good many; **tas ir l.** that's good; **tas nav l.** it is no good; **l., ka vēl tā** good thing it isn't any worse; **kā tev l. izgāja?** how did it go? **4. pa l.** to the right; **5.** (for emphasis) **kā l. klājas?** how are you?

labiāli *adv* labially

labiālis *nm* labial

labi|a|lizācija |ā| *nf* labialization

labi|a|lizēt |ā| *vt* labialize

labi|a|lizēties |ā| *vr* be labialized

labiāls *adj* labial

labība *nf* **1.** grain; grain crop;; **2.** crop, harvest

labības augi *nm pl* cereals (plants)

labības izstrādājums *nm* cereal (foodstuff)

labības mēnesis *nm* August;

labības pangodiņš *nm* Hessian fly

labības pļaujmašīna *nf* grain harvester

labības sabērtuve *nf* grain elevator

labības spradzis *nm* flea beetle

labības stiebrlapsene *nf* wheat-stem borer

labības stiebrmuša *nf* a chloropid fly, Chlorops pumilionis

labības vabolīte *nf* wheat chafer

labības zaļace *nf* a chloropid fly, Chlorops taeniopus

labiekārtojums *nm* = **labierīcība**

labiekārtot *vt* = **labierīkot**

labierīcība *nf,* usu. *pl* ~**as** conveniences (usu. found in living quarters); **sabiedriskās l.** public utilities; **(dzīvoklis) ar visām** ~**ām** (an apartment) with all conveniences (electricity, heating, indoor plumbing); **sanitārās** ~**as** indoor plumb-ing

labierīkojums *nm* = **labierīcība**

labierīkot *vt* **1.** equip; **2.** put public utilities in place

labierīkots *adj, part* of **labierīkot 1.** well equip-ped; **2.** (of a town, building) well designed

labiet/is *nm* (folk.) boyar; ~**e** *nf* boyar's wife

labili *adv* unstably

labilitāte *nf* lability

labils *adj* labile

labināt *vt* dispose favorably; mollify, placate; wheedle

labināties *vr* (often with **klāt**) make up to, ingratiate oneself with

labinieks *nm* (folk.) person of rank

labiņais *nom adj* the good one

labiņš *adj dim* of **labs**, good

labiodentāls *adj* labiodental

labirintisks *adj* labyrinthic

labirintodonts *nm* labyrinthodont

labirints *nm* labyrinth

labiski *adv* correctly, in order; right side up

labisks *adj* **1.** (of knitting stitches, opposite to purl) knit; **2.** (of screw threads) right-handed

labklājība *nf* **1.** well-being; welfare; **2.** pros-perity

labojums *nm* **1.** correction; **2.** amendment; **3.** re-pair, mending; **4.** patch

laborant/s *nm* laboratory assistant; ~**e** *nf*

laboratorija *nf* laboratory

laboratoriski *adv* in the laboratory

laboratorisks *adj* laboratorial

labošana *nf* **1.** correction; **2.** amendment; **3.** repair

labošanās *nfr* improvement; reformation

labošanas iestāde *nf* correctional institution

labot *vt* **1.** correct; rectify; **2.** amend; **3.** repair; mend; **4.** improve

laboties *vr* improve; reform

labpatika *nf* pleasure; relish

labpatikt *vi* deign; please

labpatikties *vr* deign; please

labprāt *adv* gladly, willingly, readily; (with a verb in the conditional mode) rather

labprātāk *adv comp* of **labprāt** rather

labprātība *nf* willingness, readiness

labprātīgi *adv* willingly; voluntarily

labprātīgs *adj* willing; voluntary

labprātīgums *nm* willingness, readiness

labradorīts *nm* labradorite

labradors *nm* Labrador retriever

labrīt *interj* good morning

labrīts *nm* morning greeting

lab/s *adj* **1.** good; **2.** in questions, suggests the expectation of a positive answer: **ko tu** ~**u**

dari? what are you up to? **par ~u** (of an outcome, score, testimony) in favor of; for combinations of **par ~u** with verbs, see under the verb in alphabetic order; **dažs l.** good many; **pa ~am** (col.) on good terms; **ar ~u** non-violently, by talking; (of escaping from danger) with a whole skin; **visu ~u!** goodbye! **ar ~u vai ar ļaunu** by hook or by crook; **tas nav uz ~u** it doesn't bode well; **~u ~ais** the best; very good

labsajūta *nf* feeling of comfort, good feeling

labsirdība *nf* good-naturedness; kindheartedness

labsirdīgi *adv* good-naturedly; kindheartedly

labsirdīgs *adj* good-natured; kindhearted

labsirdīgums *nm* good-naturedness; kindheartedness

labsirdis *nm*, **~e** *nf* kindhearted person

labskanība *nf* euphony; harmony

labskanīgi *adv* euphoniously; harmoniously

labskanīgs *adj* euphonious; harmonious

labskanīgums *nm* euphony; harmony

labskaņa *nf* euphony; harmony

labsrīts *nm* = **labrīts**

labsvakars *nm* = **labvakars**

labticība *nf* good faith

labticīgs *adj* bona fide

labum/s *nm* **1.** goodness; for combinations pf labums with verbs, see the appropriate verb; **2.** quality; **augstākā ~a** of superior quality; **pirmā ~a** first-class; **3.** gain, profit, benefit; **man tur nav nekāda ~a** it does not do me any good; it is of no use to me; I do not benefit from it; **4. ~i** a. (with **pasaules**) possessions; b. goodies

labvakar *interj* good evening

labvakars *nm* evening greeting

labvēlība *nf* benevolence; favor; goodwill; **vislielākās ~s princips** most favored nation clause

labvēlīgi *adv* favorably

labvēlīgs *adj* **1.** favorable; **2.** benevolent, favorably disposed

labvēlīgums *nm* favorableness; benevolence

labvēlis *nm*, **~e** *nf* supporter; patron

labzāle *nf* nux vomica

laceklis *nm* dog's water dish

lācenāji *nm pl* cloudberry

lācenājs *nm* cloudberry patch

lācene *nf* **1.** (plant or fruit) cloudberry; **2.** a bolete (Boletus badius); **3.** she-bear; **4. ~s** thick, patched trousers

lacenis *nm* liquid dog food

lācēns *nm* bear cub

la[ch]enalija [h] *nf* lachenalia

la[ch]eze [h] *nf* (zool.) bushmaster

lāciene *nf* she-bear

laciens *nm* (of animals) lap (an act of lapping)

lācīgi *adv* clumsily, awkwardly

lācīgs *adj* clumsy, awkward

lācīgums *nm* clumsiness, awkwardness

lācis *nm* bear

lāciski *adv* bearishly

lācisks *adj* bearish

lacīte *nf* (col.) bib

lācītis *nm* **1.** *dim* of **lācis**, little bear; **2.** bear animalcule; **3.** (garment) sleepers

laco *indecl nm* lazzo

lāčāda *nf* bearskin

lāča miegs *nm* sleeping like a bear

lāča pakalpojums *nm* disservice; bestowing a doubtful benefit

lāča pakaļa *nf* gable hip

lāča saknes *nf pl* spickenel

lāčausis *nf pl* (reg.) mullein

lāčauza *nf* (bot.) chess; bromegrass

lāčauzains *adj* mixed with bromegrass (or bromegrass seeds)

lāčkuskuss *nm* koala bear

lāčķekari *nm pl* bearberry

lāčnagi *nm pl* cow parsnip

lāčnāsis *nf pl* false morel, brain mushroom

lāčogas *nf pl* cloudberry

lāčot *vi* trample; stump; plod

lāčpurns *nm* false morel, brain mushroom

lāčsīpoli *nm pl* (reg.) ramson

lāčsomainis *nm* koala bear

lāčsūna *nf* haircap moss

lāčtauce *nf* pinesap

lāču beka *nf* a bolete, Boletus badius

lāčuks *nm* young bear

lāčumāte *nf* she-bear

lāčzirņi *nm pl* flat pea

lāde *nf* chest, box

lādējums I *nm* 1. loading; 2. charge

lādējums II *nm* curse

lādēt I *vt* (of firearms; col. of vehicles) load; (of explosives, batteries, particles) charge

lādēt II *vt* curse

lādētājs I *nm*, ~a *nf* 1. loader; 2. charger

lādētājs II *nm*, ~a *nf* curser

lādēties *vr* cuss, swear

lādināt *vt* 1. (of dogs) tease, make bark; 2. bark at

lādiņš *nm* (el., weapons) charge; **brizantais l.** high explosive; **kumulatīvais l.** shaped charge; **spridzināmais l.** demolition charge

lādīte *nf dim* of **lāde**, small box, casket

lādzīgi *adv* good-naturedly

lādzīgs *adj* good-natured

lādzīgums *nm* good-naturedness

lafete *nf* gun carriage

laga *nf* (naut.) log (for measuring the speed of a ship)

lāg/a *nf* 1. time (occurrence); 2. (obs., except in **likt ~ā**, to note) insight, understanding; mind

lāga *indecl adj* 1. good, nice; good-natured; 2. (usu. in negatives) decent, proper; *adv* (in negatives) quite, properly, very well

lāgā *adv* (in negations) quite, properly, very well

lagenarija *nf* bottle gourd

lagerstremija *nf* crepe myrtle

lāgiem *adv* (col.) at times

lagoftalmija *nf* lagophthalmos

lāgošana *nf* (compu.) debugging

lagot *vi* (naut.) log

lāgot *vt* (compu.) debug; (mech.) fit

lāg/s *nm* time (occurrence); **pa divi ~i** twice; **pa otram ~am** a second time; **~iem** at times; **~u ~iem** from time to time; **ar ~u** in time

lāg/s *adj* 1. kind, nice; 2. decent; **pa ~u** properly

lagtings *nm* lagting

lagūna *nf* lagoon

lagūnezers *nm* lagoon lake

lagzda *nf* hazel; see **lazda**

lahārs *nm* lahar

lai *partic* 1. (with a verb, expresses encouragement, command, warning, or wish) let (**l. viņš runā** let him speak); **l. dzīvo!** long live! **l. !** let it be! 2. (in interrogative sentences, expresses uncertainty or doubt; **ko nu l. daru?** what shall I do now? **kas to l. zina?** who knows?)

lai *conj* 1. in order, so that, so as; **l. ne** lest; 2. (with **cik, kā, kāds, kas, kur, tur, vai**) no matter (how much, or how, who, where, etc); **l. nu kā** no matter what, whatever; 3. **l. arī** (or **l. gan**) although, even if

laicība *nf* temporality

laicīgi *adv* on time, in a timely fashion

laicīgs *adj* 1. secular; 2. temporal; 3. worldly

laicīgums *nm* 1. worldliness; 2. timeliness

laicināt *vt* 1. protract, draw out; 2. delay

laicināties *vr* hesitate

laiciņš *nm dim* of **laiks**, while, short time

laicīt I *vt* massage

laicīt II *vt* 1. save, keep; 2. give time, wait

laicīties *vr* avoid, evade

laid/a *nf* 1. row; **vienā ~ā** in a row, continuously, incessantly; 2. (of a boat) plank, strake

laidaks *nm* clumsy, lazy person

laidariņš *nm dim* of **laidars**, paddock

laidarniece *nf* cowgirl

laidars *nm* **1.** paddock; **2.** (reg.) large cattle barn

laidava *nf* (reg.) circle

laide *nf* **1.** gun stock; ~**s kakls** small of the stock; **2.** (naut.) strake; **augšējā l.** sheerstrake; **3.** row, string; **4.** insert, inset; **5.** narrow strip of land

laidējs *nm* also **vējā l.** spendthrift

laidelēt *vi* fly around; flutter, hover

laidelēties *vr* fly around; flutter, hover

laidene *nf* jointer, long plane

laideni *adv* smoothly

laidenība *nf* smoothness

laidenieks *nm* (hist.) free peasant

laidenis *nm* **1.** fishing net; **2.** live box; **3.** tedded, broadly spread hay

laideniski *adv* by sliding

laidens *adj* **1.** (of weather) mild; **2.** soft; **3.** sloping; **4.** smooth

laidenums *nm* **1.** smoothness; **2.** softness

laides kakls *nm* small of the stock

laidiem *adv* in gallop

laidiens *nm* **1.** issue (book or pamphlet in a series); **2.** fast drive; (col.) run, dash

laidināt *vt* temper

laidne *nf* gun stock

laidnieks *nm* (hist.) free peasant

laidnis *nm* (chess) bishop

laidns *adj* svelte

laidos *adv* in gallop

laids *nm* **1.** row, string; **2.** tune; **3.** strake; **4.** gallop; **5.** flight of stairs; **6.** span

laids *adj* lazy

laidums *nm* span

laigot *vi* deny; lie

laika *nf* Laika (dog breed)

laikā *adv* **1.** in time; on time; **2.** (of shoes, clothing) fits, fit

laikabiedrs *nm* contemporary

laika deglis *nm* time delay fuse

laika grāmata *nf* (obs.) **1.** chronicle; **2.** calendar

laikāk *adv* sooner

laika kavēklis *nm* passtime

laikam *adv* probably, presumably, very likely; apparently; **l. gan** apparently yes

laikaposms *nm* = **laikposms**

laikapstākļi *nm pl* weather conditions

laikarats *nm* wheel of time

laika skaitīšana *nf* chronology

laika uzņēmums *nm* (photo.) time exposure

laikazobs *nm* signs of age, ravages of time

laikdalība *nf* (compu.) time sharing

laikgrieži *nm pl* seasonal change; turning point

laikiem *adv* at times

laikietilpīgs *adj* time-consuming

laikkavēklis *nm* pastime

laiklaikiem *adv* from time to time

laiklaikos *adv* forever

laiklapa *nf* (obs.) newspaper

laiklīgums *nm* time charter

laikmeta gars *nm* Zeitgeist

laikmeta grieži *nm pl* turn of the century

laikmetīgi *adv* in a manner suited to the age

laikmetīgs *adj* contemporary

laikmetīgums *nm* contemporaneity

laikmetiski *adv* in a manner suited to the age

laikmetisks *adj* contemporary

laikmetiskums *nm* contemporaneity

laikmet/s *nm* age, era, period; **zelta l.** golden age; ~**u** ~**os** forever

laikmūžos *adv* (poet.) forever

laikot *vt* try on

laikposms *nm* period of time

laikrādis *nm* timepiece

laikraksts *nm* newspaper; **mazformāta l.** tabloid

laikrakstu kiosks *nm* newsstand

laikreģis *nm* meteorologist

laik/s *nm* **1.** time; **garš l.** boredom; **melnais l.** time period in the spring after the melting of the snow; **jauno** ~**u vēsture** modern history; **seno** ~**u vēsture** ancient history; **taupāmais**

l. close season; **vecie labie ~i** good old days ◊ **~a gaitā** in the course of time; **bez ~a** prematurely; **īstā ~ā** just in time; **katrā ~ā** at any time; **kopš kuŗa ~a?** since when? **kopš tā ~a** ever since then; **labu ~u pirms** a long time before; **(gada, mēneša) ~ā** within (a year, month); **l. gulēt** bedtime; **l. rādīs** time will tell; **~u ~iem** at times; **~u ~os** forever; **līdz šim ~am** up to now; **~u pa ~am** now and then; **no ~a gala** from time immemorial, always; from day one; **no šī ~a** from now on; **noteiktā ~ā** in due time; **pa to ~u** in the meantime; **pēc neilga ~a** before long; **pēdējā ~ā** lately; **(ir) pēdējais l.** it is high time; **pie l.** (col.) in time; **uz ~u** temporarily; **uz ~u ~iem** forever; **uz visiem ~iem** forever, in perpetuity; **vecos ~os** in olden days, in days of yore; **2.** weather; **gai-dāmais ~s** weather forecast; **3.** (gram.) tense; **sa-likts ~s** perfect tense

laiksakritība *nf* time frame

laiksekā *adv* in order of time

laiksne *nf* water lily

laiksprauga *nf* (compu.) time slot

laiksprīdis *nm* segment of time

laikstarpa *nf* period of time

laiktelpa *nf* space-time

laikumis *adv* (rare.) at times

laikus *adv* in time; on time

laiku saskaņojums *nm* tense shifts

laiku seknība *nf* sequence of tenses

laim/e *nf* **1.** happiness; **daudz ~es (Jaunajā gadā, dzimšanas dienā)** happy (New Year, birthday), (on other occasions) many happy returns; **(dzert) augstas ~es** toast; **2.** luck, good fortune; **uz labu ~i** at random; **par ~i** luckily; **(viņai ir) l.** (she is) lucky

laimes bērns *nm* lucky person, born lucky, fortune's favorite

laimes gadījums *nm* lucky chance

laimes liešana *nf* fortunetelling (by pouring molten lead into water on New Year's eve)

laimes nesējs *nm* lucky charm; mascot

laimes pelēcīte *nf* one-sided shinleaf

laimespuķe *nf* erigeron, fleabane

laimesrats *nm* lottery drum

laimesspēle *nf* game of chance

laimests *nm* prize, winnings; **lielais l.** first prize, grand prize

laimestu izloze *nf* lottery; drawing; **l. ~s tabula** prize list

laimes vēlējums *nm* congratulation, good wishes

laimes zvaigzne *nf* lucky star

laimēt *vt* win

laimētājs *nm*, **~a** *nf* winner

laimēties *vr* be lucky, be lucky enough

laimība *nf* bliss

laimīgi *adv* **1.** happily; **2.** fortunately

laimīgs *adj* **1.** happy; **2.** lucky, fortunate

laimiņš *nm* stonecrop

laimīte *nf* **1.** *dim* of **laime 2**, good luck; **2.** fleabane

laimītis *nm* lucky person

laimot *vt* (rare.) make happy

laimpuķe *nf* fleabane

laineris *nm* ocean liner; airliner

laipa *nf* **1.** catwalk; footbridge; **2.** logs or branches laid down over a muddy footpath

laipiņa *nf dim* of **laipa**, catwalk, footbridge

laipni *adv* kindly; **~i lūdzam!** welcome!

laipnība *nf* kindness

laipnīgi *adv* kindly

laipnīgs *adj* kindly

laipnoties *vr* make up to s.o.

laipns *adj* kind

laipnums *nm* kindness

laipot *vi* **1.** pick one's way (among obstacles); (fig.) maneuver, shuffle; waffle; **2.** walk on a footbridge

laipotājs *nm,* ~a *nf* maneuverer; waffler

laipoties *vr* = **laipot**

laipstules *nf pl* loom

laiska *n* **1.** *nm, nf* lazybones, loafer; **2.** *nf* pillory

laiski *adv* indolently, lazily

laiskonis *nm* lazybones, loafer

laiskot *vi* loaf, be lazy

laiskoties *vr* loaf, be lazy

laisks *adj* indolent, lazy

laiskul/is *nm,* ~e *nf* lazybones, loafer

laiskums *nm* idleness, indolence

laisma I *nf* (reg.) dedication

laisma II *nf* **1.** shine; **2.** (poet.) waft, breeze

laismot *vi* shine

laist *vt* **1.** let; allow, permit; let have (for a price); **l. atmatā** let turn fallow; **l. bojā** let spoil; **l. (ūdeni) cauri** a. be permeable; b. leak; **l. ciet** (of cows and goats) stop milking (before they drop their young); **l. garām** let pass (by); **l. klajā** publish; **l. ļaudīs** a. send into the world; b. publish; **l. ļekas vaļā** (col.) take to one's heels; **l. pār bortu** (col.) vomit; **l. pārdošanā** put up for sale; **l. pār galvu** (or **gar ausīm**) a. turn a deaf ear, disregard; b. make light of; **l. pār kanti** (col.) sell; **l. pār mēli** (col.) vomit; **l. pavedienu** spin; **l. pekas vaļā** take to one's heels; **l. pie šprices** (sl.) let one at it; **l. pie vīra** marry off; **l. pinkšķi (biļļas, bimbas, bingas) vaļā** (col.) be-gin to cry; **l. projām** sell; **l. skolā** send to school; **l. spalvas** (of animals) shed; **l. tauri va-ļā** (col.) begin to talk or cry loudly; **l. tautā** (or **pasaulē**) publish; **l. tautās** (folk.) marry off; **l. valodas** (folk.) converse; **l. vaļā** let go; **l. vaļā balsi** (folk.) raise one's voice; **l. vaļā dūdas** (col.) begin to cry; **l. vaļā vieglos** (col.) take to one's heels; **l. vaļu** give freedom, allow; **l. vieg-los vaļā** (col.) take off, flee; **l. zaķīšus** catch sunbeams

in a mirror; **l. zem āmura** (col.) auction; **2.** start; **l. darbā** a. (of a machine) start; b. start using; **l. uguni klāt** start a fire, set fire; **3.** send; **l. apkārt** pass around; spread around; **bērnus l.** (col., of bees) swarm; **l. dibenā** send to the bottom; **l. pasaulē** send into the world, produce, (of children) bear; **l. ziņu** send word; **4.** (of rafts, toy boats) float, (of ships) launch, (of balloons, kites) fly; (of soap bubbles) blow; **5.** in-sert, put in, drop in; **l. apgrozībā** put in circulation; **l. gaisā** a. let fly; b. (sl.) blow up; **l. kokus** fell trees; **6.** produce; **l. asnus** sprout; **l. ikrus** spawn; **l. miglu** produce fog; **l. miglu acīs** (fig.) produce a smoke screen; **l. dūmus** make smoke; puff (on a pipe); **l. saknes** root; **7.** throw, fling; **8.** *vi* run drive, ride fast; **l. pa diegu** flee; **l. rikšos** trot; **9.** (of liquids) tap, sap, draw, draw off, (of blood) let; **10.** *vi* **l. vaļu** allow, let

laisties *vr* **1.** fly; **2.** let oneself down; **l. dibenā** sink, dive to the bottom; (fig.) give up; **l. guļus** (or **garšļaukus, slīpi**) lie down; **l. lejā** come down, slide down; **l. no kalna** sled down the hill; **l. zemē** come down, (of the sun) set; **3.** al-low; relent; release; (of weather) get warmer; **l. pazīstamam** introduce oneself, give one's name; **l. rokā** allow oneself to be caught; **4.** begin; **l. dejā** begin to dance; **l. miegā** drop off to sleep; **5.** (col.) depart suddenly, run off; **l. lapās** (or **pupās, pa diegu**) (col.) make oneself scarce, beat it, scram; **laidies!** beat it! **6.** (reg.) melt

laistīgs *adj* opalescent, irridescent

laistījums *nm* **1.** sprinkling; **2.** shining

laistīkla *nf* watering can

laistīšanās I *nfr* splashing, pouring of water; water fight

laistīšanās II *nfr* **1.** glistening, sparkling; **2.** iridescence laistīt I *vt* 1. spill; pour repeatedly; 2. water; sprinkle

laistīt II *vt* (of light) cast

laistīties I *vr* 1. splash each other; pour on oneself; 2. spill

laistīties II *vr* glisten, sparkle; iridesce

laišķe *nf* scoop

laišķi *nm pl* (reg.) water lilies

laišķis *nm* toady

laitīt *vt* massage

laitītāj/s *nm* masseur; ~a *nf* masseuse

laiv/a *nf* boat; **akadēmiskā l.** racing rowboat; **izdobta l.** dugout; **plakandibena l.** flat-bottom boat, flatboat; **saliekama l.** faltboat ◊ **mazu ~u stūmējs** educated loafer, educated incompetent

laivascirvju kultūra *nf* Boat-Ax culture

laivas iegultne *nf* boat cradle

laivas mala *nf* gunwale

laivas tauva *nf* painter

laivas trice *nf* boat falls

laivasveida *indecl adj* boat-shaped

laivceltnis *nm* davit

laivinieks *nm* boatman; ferryman

laiviņa *nf* 1. *dim* of **laiva**, little boat; 2. skiff; 3. overseas cap, garrison cap; 4. usu. *pl* ~s pumps (shoes)

laiviņcepure *nf* garrison cap

laiviņveida *indecl adj* boat-shaped

laiviņveidīgs *adj* boat-shaped

laivknābis *nm* boatbill

laivojams *adj* boatable

laivot *vi* boat, canoe

laivu osta *nf* small-craft harbor;

laivu stacija *nf* boathouse, marina

laivveida *indecl adj* boat-shaped

laivveidīgi *adv* like a boat

laivveidīgs *adj* boat-shaped

laizīt *vt* lick; **l. pirkstus** (fig.) lick one's chops

laizītava *nf* lick-log

laizīties *vr* 1. lick one's lips; slaver; 2. (fig.) toady

laiža *nf, nm* 1. gourmand; person with a sweet tooth; 2. toady

laj/s *nm* 1. layman; ~i laity; 2. ignoramus

laka *nf* lacquer; varnish; lac; **caurspīdīga l.** clear varnish

lakači *nm pl* lungwort

lakāda *nf* patent leather

lakatiņš *nm* 1. *dim* of **lakats**, kerchief; neckerchief; 2. (col., WW II) a 50-Reichsmark note

lakatiņveida *indecl adj* kerchieflike

lakatiņveidīgi *adv* like a kerchief

lakatiņveidīgs *adj* kerchieflike

lakatlaiža *nm* (com.) toady

lakatots *adj* scarfed

lakats *nm* kerchief; scarf; **lielais l.** shawl

lakatveida *indecl adj* scarf-like

lakatveidīgs *adj* scarf-like

lakbenzīns *nm* petroleum spirits

lakejs *nm* lackey

lakkrāsa *nf* lacquer

lakkurpes *nf pl* patent leathers

lakmusa ķērpis *nm* lichen (used to produce cudbear)

lakmuspapīrs *nm* litmus paper

lakmuss *nm* litmus

lakojums *nm* lacquering, varnishing, japanning; coat of lacquer, coat of varnish

lakolīts *nm* laccolith

lakoniski *adv* laconically

lakonisks *adj* laconic

lakoniskums *nm* laconism

lakonisms *nm* laconism

lakonizēt *vi* make laconic

lakot *vt* lacquer, varnish, japan

lakotājs *nm*, ~a *nf* varnisher

lakotava *nf* varnishing department

lakrica *nf* licorice

lakricsakne *nf* licorice root

lakrima *nf* Lachryma Christi (wine)

lakrim[a]tors [ā] *nm* lacrimator

lakross *nm* lacrosse

laksiņi *nm pl* pasta

laksis *nm* See **lakši**

lakstains *adj* stalky

lakstaugi *nm pl* caulescent plants

laksti *nm pl* See **laksts**

lakstīgala *nf* nightingale, thrush nightingale

lakstīgs *adj* 1. flirty; 2. superficial; mincing

lakstiņš *nm* 1. *dim* of **laksts**, (of root crops) top;
2. (reg.) handle

lakstīt *vi* jump around, jump up and down;
gambol; flutter about

lakstīties *vr* 1. flirt; 2. flutter about

lakstot *vi* grow stalks, grow tops

lakstoties *vr* flirt

laksts *nm* (of root crops) top

lakstveida *indecl adj* resembling vegetable
tops

lakstveidīgs *adj* resembling vegetable tops

lakši *nm pl* ramson

lakt *vt* (of animals) lap

lakta I *nf* anvil

lakta II *nf* chicken perch

laktācija *nf* lactation

laktas ieliktnis *nm* bottom swage

laktas rags *nm* (anvil) horn

laktas spiede *nf* top swage

lākte *nf* (reg.) burning wood splint

laktāts *nm* lactate

laktāze *nf* lactase

lāktenis *nm* (reg.) lantern

laktīds *nm* lactide

laktiņa *nf* 1. *dim* of **lakta** I or **lakta** II, little
anvil; chicken perch; 2. (anat.) incus

lāktīt *vi* 1. burn with a wide flame, flare;
2. flicker

lāktīties *vr* 1. burn with a wide flame, flare;
2. flicker

laktobacils *nm* lactobacillus

laktometrs *nm* lactometer

laktons *nm* lactone

laktoskops *nm* lactoscope

laktoze *nf* lactose

lākts *nf* 1. burning wood splint; torch; 2. bright
flame

lākturis *nm* 1. hurricane lamp; lantern; 2. torch
holder

lakūna *nf* lacuna

lakustrīns *adj* lacustrine

lakvijole *nf* wall-flower

laķējums *nm* (cont.) embellishment

laķēt *vt* (fig.) varnish, embellish

la[l]ināt [ll] *vi* 1. sing wordlessly; 2. (of babies)
lall

lama I *nf*, usu. *pl* ~s abuse, swear words

lama II *nf* llama

lama III *nm* lama

lāma *nf* 1. large puddle, water-filled depression;
2. spread, stretch

lāmains *adj* covered with large puddles

lamaisms *nm* Lamaism

lamaists *nm* Lamaist

lamantīns *nm* manatee

lamarkisms *nm* Lamarckism

lamarkist/s *nm*, ~e *nf* Lamarckian

lamāt *vt* rail at, cuss; **l. no panckām ārā** (col.)
cuss out

lamat/as *nf pl* trap, snare; ~u licējs trapper

lamāties *vr* cuss, call names, swear; **rupji l.**
swear like a trooper

lamatiņas *nf pl dim* of **lamatas**, little trap

lamatmīna *nf* booby trap

lamatu licējs *nm* trapper

lambada *nf* (dance) lambada

lambārts *nm* (hist.) (court) marshall

lambda *nf* lambda

lambdakisms *nm* lambdacism

lamberts *nm* lambert

lambetvoks *nm* (dance) Lambeth Walk

lamblija *nf* giardia

lamblioze *nf* giardiasis

lambrekens *nm* lambrequin

lamē *nm* lamé

lamele *nf* = **lamella**

lamella *nf* (tech.) leaf, plate; lamina; cooling fin

lamentācija *nf* lamentation

lamentēt *vi* lament

lamento *indecl nm* (mus.) lamento

lamentozs *adj* (mus.) lamentoso

laminārijas *nf pl* laminarias

laminarīns *nm* laminarin

laminārs *adj* (of flow) laminar

laminēšana *nf* lamination

laminēt *vt* laminate

lāmiņa *nf* 1. *dim* of lāma, small puddle; 2. dimple

lāmis *nm* (reg.) windrow

lāmot *vi* form a puddle

lāmoties *vr* form a puddle

lampa I *nf* lamp; (radio) tube

lampa II *nf, nm* (col.) clumsy person

lampačot *vi* (col.) waddle

lampāns *nm* (col.) clumsy person

lampass *nm* leg piping, trouser stripe

lampāt *vi* (col.) trudge

lampata *nf* rag

lampatainis *nm* (col.) ragamuffin

lampatains *adj* (reg.) ragged, tattered

lampatāt *vi* (col.) trudge

lampausis *nm* 1. lop-eared animal; 2. (col.) clumsy person

lampiņa *nf* 1. *dim* of lampa, small lamp; 2. a. radio tube; b. (col.) electric bulb

lampionpuķe *nf* Chinese lantern plant

lampions *nm* lampion; Chinese lantern

lamprofīrs *nm* lamprophyre

lampu aparāts *nm* (radio) tube set

lampu drudzis *nm* stage fright

lāms *nm* meadow

lamsteris *nm* idler

lamstīties *vr* loaf, shirk work; hang around

lamuvārds *nm* cussword

lamza *nm* clumsy, ungainly person, booby

lamzaks *nm* (col.) clumsy, ungainly person, booby

lamzacīgi *adv* clumsily

lamzacīgs *adj* clumsy; ungainly

lamzāt *vi* (col.) trudge

lamzīgs *adj* (col.) clumsy; ungainly

lamža *nm* clumsy person, booby

lamži *nm pl* (folk.) woman's jacket

lancete *nf* lancet

lancetiskā ciesa *nf* purple reed bent

lancetisks *adj* lancet-shaped; lanceolate

lancetnieks *nm* lancelet; amphioxus

lancets *nm* a Latvian folk dance

lancetveida *indecl adj* lancet-shaped; lanceolate

lancetveidīgi *adv* like a lancet

lancetveidīgs *adj* lancet-shaped; lanceolate

lanciņa *nf dim* of lanka, marshy meadow

lancka *nf*, usu. *pl* ~s tatter, rag

lanckarains *adj* tattered

lanckari *nm pl* tatters

landsvērists *nm* member of the Baltische Landeswehr

landesvērs *nm* Baltische Landeswehr (German militia in Latvia, 1918-1920)

landgrāfs *nm* landgrave

landgrāfiene *nf* landgravine

landmaršals *nm* (hist.) president of the landtāgs

lando *indecl nm* landau

landolfija *nf* landolphia

landrāt/s *nm* (hist.) Landrat (member of the governing body of Livonian German nobility, the ~u kollēģija)

landskne[ch]ts [h] *nm* lansquenet

landtāgs *nm* (hist.) Landtag (diet, legislative assembly)

langāt *vt* (reg.) cuss

langāties *vr* (reg.) cuss

langets *nm* fried strip of meat, cutlet

langobardi *nm pl* Lombards

langurs *nm* langur

langusts *nm* langouste, spiny lobster

lānis *nm* 1. large, thick forest; 2. fog bank

lanka *nf* lowland meadow, marshy meadow;
(reg.) river bottom meadow

lankausis *nm* lop-eared animal

lankšķēt *vi* (com.) bark

lanolīns *nm* lanolin

lāns *nm* = **lānis**

lantana *nf* lantana

lantanīdi *nm pl* lanthanides

lantāns *nm* lanthanum

lāņojums *nm* layering, layers

laosiet/is *nm*, ~e *nf* Laotian

lap/a *nf* **1.** leaf **2.** sheet of paper; page; **balta l.**
a. blank page; b. flyleaf; **no ~as** (of playing
mu-sic) at sight; **3.** (printed) form

lāp/a *nf* torch; ~**u gājiens** torchlight procession;
~**as nesējs** torchbearer

lapainis *nm* leafy branch

lapains *adj* leafy; foliate

lāpāmadata *nf* darning needle

lāpāmdiegs *nm* darning thread

lāpām/s *adj*, usu. *defin* ~**ais** darning, mending;
(ling., of sounds, words) expletive, patch
(*adj*)

lāpāmvārds *nm* (ling.) expletive, filler

laparoskopija *nf* laparoscopy

laparoskops *nm* laparoscope

laparotomija *nf* laparotomy

lapas kritiens *nm* (aeron.) falling leaf

lapaspuse *nf* page

lāpāt *vi* (reg.) crawl

lapaugi *nm pl* foliage plants

lapauši *nm pl* lungwort

lapbire *nf* leaf drop

lapegle *nf* larch; tamarack

lapegfains *adj* larchen

lapegļu makstkode *nf* larch casebearer

lapele *nf* **1.** dim of **lapa**, small leaf, leaflet; small
sheet of paper; **2.** (cont. of a periodical) rag;
3. (cont.) flyleaf

lapene *nf* arbor, bower, pergola; **stiklota l.**
gazebo

lapgrauži *nm pl* leaf chafers

lapidācija *nf* lapidation

lapidāri *adv* tersely

lapidārisms *nm* terseness

lapidārs *adj* lapidary, terse

lapiens *nm* (reg.) bushes,brushwood

Lapijas stērste *nf* Lapland bunting

lāpījums *nm* mending, darning

lapills *nm* (geol.) lapillus

lapiņa *nf* **1.** *dim* of **lapa**, small leaf; leaflet; small
sheet of paper; **2.** (bot., zool.) lamella

lapiņu sēnes *nf pl* agarics

lāpīt *vt* mend, darn; patch up; **l. ādu** (col.) whip;
l. muguru (col.) hit, beat; **l. paģiras** (use)
the hair of the hound; **l. slinkumu** loaf

lāpītājs *nm*, ~**a** *nf* mender, darner

lāpīties *vr* **1.** mend, darn (a lot or a long time);
2. make do

lapkāji *nm pl* phyllopods

lapkaktuss *nm* orchid cactus

lapkoks *nm* deciduous tree

lapkritis *nm* fall (season); leaf fall

lapkritnis *nm* fall (season); leaf fall

lapmetis *nm* deciduous tree

lāpnes/is *nm*, ~**e** *nf* torch bearer

lapojums *nm* foliage

lapolits *nm* lapolith

laponis *nm* (bot.) thallus

lapoņaugi *nm pl* Thallophyta

laportejas *nf pl* Laportea

lapot I *vi* leaf out

lapot II *vt* turn over the pages, leaf through

lāpot *vi* **1.** crawl; **2.** pick one's way

lapotne *nf* foliage

lapotnis *nm* foliage

lapots *adj* leafy

lappuse *nf* page; ~**s tituls** running title

lappušatmiņa *nf* (compu.) page memory

lapreņģe *nf* twaite shad

laps *nm*, ~**iete** *nf* Lapp

lāps *nm* mending patch

lapsa *nf* fox

lapsāda *nf* fox fur

lapsas kūmiņš *nm* sly fox; Reynard the Fox

lapsas mātīte *nf* vixen

lapsaste *nf* (bot.) **1.** foxtail; **2.** love-lies-bleeding

lapsene *nf* wasp

lapsenīte *nf* **1.** *dim* of **lapsene**, wasp; **2.** braconid

lapseņu klijāns *nm* honey buzzard

lapsēns *nm* fox cub

lapsīgs *adj* foxy

lapsināties *vr* make up to, ingratiate oneself with s.o.

lapsiņa *nf dim* of **lapsa**, little fox

lapsprādze *nf* (reg.) rudd

lāpsta *nf* **1.** shove, spade; **mechaniskā l.** power shovel; backhoe; **2.** blade, vane

lāpstains *adj* (of antlers) palmate

lāpstiņa *nf* **1.** *dim* of **lāpsta**, small shovel, play shovel; **2.** spatula; **3.** dustpan; **4.** cake server; **5.** scoop; **6.** trowel; **7.** blade, vane; **8.** paddle; **9.** (of anchors) fluke; **10.** shoulder blade

lāpstiņritenis *nm* paddle wheel; impeller

lāpstiņveida *indecl adj* vane-like, blade-like

lāpstiņveidīgi *adv* like a vane, like a blade

lāpstiņveidīgs vane-like, blade-like

lāpstot *vt* shovel

lāpstveida *indecl adj* spade-like, shovel-like

lāpstveidīgi *adv* like a spade, like a shovel

lāpstveidīgs *adj* spade-like, shovel-like

lapsu dzelēi *nm pl* fox trap

lapsu grīslis *nm* soft fox sedge

lapsumāte *nf* vixen (with cubs)

lapsu vīnkoks *nm* chicken grape

lāpturis *nm* torch bracket

lapu atspere *nf* leaf spring

lapu biete *nf* chard

lapu birds *nm* fall (season)

lapu blusiņa *nf* psylla, jumping plant louse

lapu kāposti *nm pl* narrow-stem kale

lapukok/s *nm* deciduous tree; **~u mežs** hardwood forest

lapu ķaukis *nm* willow warbler

lapu laiks *nm* fall (season)

lapu mēnesis *nm* May

lapu mīkla *nf* puff paste

lapu mušas *nf pl* sawflies

lapu pangu ērce *nf* gall mite

lapu salāti *nm pl* leaf lettuce

lapu sinepes *nf pl* Indian mustard

lapu sūnas *nf pl* mosses

lapu tinējs *nm* leaf roller

laputs *nf* aphid

lapveida *indecl adj* leaf-like

lapveidīgi *adv* like a leaf

lapveidīgs *adj* leaflike

Lapzemes kārkls *nm* downy willow

Lapzemes stērste *nf* Lapland bunting

lapžauņi *nm pl* Eulamellibranchia

largeto *indecl nm* larghetto

largo *nm indecl* (mus.) largo

lari *nm pl* lares

laringālis *nm* (ling.) laryngeal

laringāls *adj* laryngeal

laringīts *nm* laryngitis

laringofons *nm* throat microphone

laringolo/gs *nm*, **~ģe** *nf* laryngologist

laringoloģija *nf* laryngology

laringoloģisks *adj* laryngological

laringoskopija *nf* laryngoscopy

laringoskops *nm* laryngoscope

laringotomija *nf* tracheotomy

larkšķēt *vi* (com.) chatter

larkšķ/is *nm*, **~e** *nf* **1.** chatterer; **2.** chatter; clatter

larva *nf* mask

larvicīds *nm* larvicide

larvs *nm* (malevolent spirit) larva

lāsa *nf* **1.** drop (of liquid); **2.** mottle

lāsaini I *adv* with speckles

lāsaini II *adv* iridescently

lāsains I *adj* speckled, spotted; mottled

lāsains II *adj* glittering, glimmering, iridescent

lāsainums *nm* speckledness, spottedness

lasāmatmiņa *nf* (compu.) read-only memory

lasāmgabals *nm* reading assignment

lasāmgalds *nm* reading table

lasāmgrāmata *nf* reader; primer

lasāmierīce *nf* (typ.) reading machine

lasāmība *nf* readability

lasāmmāja *nf* (hist.) library

lasāms *adj, part* of **lasīt** I legible, readable

lasāmviela *nf* reading material

lasāmzāle *nf* reading hall

lasāmzīme *nf* bookmark

lascīvi *adv* lasciviously

lascīvs *adj* lascivious

lāse *nf* 1. drop (of liquid); 2. mottle; 3. bead

lāseklis *nm* gargoyle

lasēns *nm* 1. salmon trout; 2. young salmon

lāsēt I *vi* 1. (*3rd pers*) form icicles; 2. drip, trickle

lāsēt II *vi* glitter, glimmer, irridesce

lāsiens *nm* drop (of liquid)

lasījis *part* of **lasīt** read; **daudz l.** well-read

lasījum/s *nm* 1. reading; 2. interpretation; 3. picking; 4. ~i lecture series

lāsināt *vt* let drops fall, put drops in

lasis *nm* salmon; Atlantic salmon

lasīt I *vt, vi* read; **l. korektūru** read proofs; **l. lekcijas** lecture; **l. morāli** moralize, give a lecture; **l. notācijas** (col.) scold, dress down; **l. sprediķi** preach; (col.) scold, dress down; **l. priekšlasījumu** give a lecture, give a talk; **l. priekšā** read aloud; **l. referātu** give a paper

lasīt II *vt* pick, gather; **l. kopā** gather; **l. vārpas** glean

lasītāj/s I *nm,* ~a *nf* reader

lasītājs II *nm,* ~a *nf* picker, gatherer

lasītava *nf* reading room

lāsīte *nf* 1. *dim* of **lāse**; 2. droplet; (fig., of alcoholic beverages) drop

lasīties *vr* 1. gather; 2. **l. projām** (col.) make oneself scarce; **lasies!** beat it! **lasies ārā!** get out! 3. read

lasītkāre *nf* desire to read

lasītmāka *nf* reading skill

lasītneprasme *nf* illiteracy

lasītprasme *nf* reading skill

lasītprašana *nf* reading skill

lasītnepratēj/s *nm,* ~a *nf* illiterate

lasītpratēj/s *nm,* ~a *nf* literate person

lāsma I *nf* glow

lāsma II *nf* large puddle

lāsmaini *adv* glitteringly, iridescently

lāsmainība *nf* glitter, glimmer, iridescence

lāsmains *adj* glittering, glimmering, iridescent

lāsmainums *nm* glitter, glimmer, iridescence

lasmanis *nm* harbor pilot

lāsme *nf* streak (of another color), mottle

lasmenis *nm* ice hole, air hole

lāsmiņa *nf dim* of **lāsma** I, faint glow

lāsmojums *nm* glitter, glimmer, iridescence

lāsmot *vi* glitter, glimmer, iridesce

lāsmoties *vr* glitter, glimmer, iridesce

laso *indecl nm* lasso, lariat

lāsojums *nm* glitter, glimmer, iridescence

lāsot I *vi* drip, trickle; (of drops of liquid) run down

lāsoties *vr* drip, trickle; (of drops of liquid) run down

lāsot II *vi* glitter, glimmer, iridesce

lāsoties *vr* glitter, glimmer, iridesce

lāsots *adj* speckled, spotted; mottled

lāsteciņa *nf dim* of **lāsteka**, small icicle

lāsteka *nf* 1. icicle; 2. drip

lāstekains *adj* icicle-studded

lastiņš *nm* (fabric) lasting

lasts *nm* last (a liquid measure)

lāsts *nm* curse

lāsumaini I *adv* streakily

lāsumaini II *adv* iridescently

lāsumainība *nf* streakiness, variegation, spottedness, brindle

lāsumains I *adj* streaky, variegated, spotted, brindled

lāsumains II *adj* iridescent

lāsumainums *nm* streakiness, variegation, spottedness, brindle

lāsumiņš *nm dim* of lāsums, small streak, speckle, spot

lāsumojums *nm* glitter, glimmer, iridescence

lāsumoti I *adv* streakily

lāsumoti II *adv* iridescently

lāsumots I *adj* streaky, variegated, spotted, brindled

lāsumots II *adj* iridescent

lāsum/s *nm* streak, speckle, spot; ~i freckles

laškrāsas *adj* salmon-colored

lašņāties *vr* (col.) pick, choose

lāšņot *vi* shimmer

lašu forele *nf* salmon trout

lašzivis *nf pl* salmonids

lāt *vt* (reg.) cuss

lata *nf* lath

latanija *nf* Chinese fan palm

latas nesējs *nm* (geod.) rodman

latatā *adv* (col.) away

lata veikals *nm* (hist.) dime store

latekss *nm* latex

latenti *adv* latently

latents *adj* latent

lāteņi *nm pl* cow parsnip

laterāli *adv* laterally

laterāls *adj* lateral

laterīts *nm* laterite

laterna *nf* lantern; lamp

laternas stabs *nm* lamppost

laternists *nm* (geod.) lightkeeper

latēt *vt* lath

latgalietis *nm*, ~e *nf* Latgallian

latgaliski *adv* in the Latgallian dialect

latgalisks *adj* Latgallian

latgaļi *nm pl* Old Latgallians

latifundija *nf* latifondo, latifundio, (hist.) latifundium

latifundist/s *nm*, ~e *nf* latifundista

latīniski *adv* in Latin

latīnisks *adj* Latin

latīnisms *nm* Latinism

latīnists *nm*, ~e *nf* Latinist

latinizēt *vt* Latinize

latiņa *nf* 1. *dim* of lata, lath; 2. crossbar

latīņamerikān/is *nm*, ~iete *nf* Latin American

latīņi *nm pl* (ancient) Latins

latīņu alfabēts *nm* Roman alphabet

latojums *nm* lathing

latols *nm* gasohol

latot *vt* lath

lats *nm* lat

latu režģis *nm* latticework

latu sēta *nf* lattice fence

latvāņi *nm pl* cow parsnip

latvāņlapu begonija *nf* a begonia, Begonia heracleifolia

latvietība *nf* 1. Latvianism; 2. Latvian

latvie/tis *nm*, ~te *nf* Latvian; *pl* ~ši Latvians; ~šu strēlnieki (hist.) Latvian Rifle Regiments

latv/is *nm*, ~iete *nf* (poet.) Latvian

latviski *adv* 1. in Latvian, (speak) Latvian; 2. according to Latvian custom

latviskojums *nm* 1. Letticized word, Letticized name; 2. Latvian translation

latviskot *vt* 1. Letticize; make Latvian; 2. translate into Latvian

latvisks *adj* Latvian

latviskums *nm* Latvian character

latvji *nm pl, sg* latvis (poet.) Latvians

laucains *adj* spotted

lauce I *nf* a cow or a mare with a blaze

lauce II *nf* glade

laucinieciski *adv* in a rustic manner

lauciniecisks *adj* rural, rustic, country

laucinieciskums *nm* rusticity

laucienie/ks *nm*, ~ce *nf* rustic; rural inhabitant

lauciņš *nm* 1. *dim* of lauks, small field; 2. (garden, agricultural, experimental) plot; 3. (of a game board) square

laucis *nm* 1. a horse or a bull with a blaze; 2. coot

laudanozīns *nm* laudanosine

laudas *nf pl* (rel.) Laudes

laukā *adv* 1. outside, outdoors; 2. out

lauka artil|e|rija [ē] *nf* field artillery

lauka atmatene *nf* meadow mushroom

laukābele *nf* crab apple tree

laukači *nm pl* lungwort

lauka ēze *nf* mobile forge

lauka gulta *nf* cot

lauka hospitālis *nm* field hospital

lauka kaŗa tiesa *nf* summary court martial

lauka katls *nf* field kitchen;

laukakme/ns *nm* boulder; ~ņu mūris rubble wall

lauka lielgabals *nm* fieldpiece

lauka mēle *nf* field scabious

lauka pasts *nm* field post

lauka rācenis *nm* bird rape

laukāre *nf* (reg.) fallow

laukaugi *nm* field crops

laukauši *nm pl* lungwort

lauka uzturdeva *nf* C-ration

laukceļš *nm* country road

laukciemats *nm* village

laukdarbs *nm* field labor

laukdurvis *nf pl* outside door

laukeglīte *nf* wild thyme

laukgals *nm* end of a field

lauk/i *nm pl* country, countryside; ~u rural; uz ~iem in the country; to the country

laukirbe *nf* gray partridge

laukkopība *nf* agriculture, cultivation of field crops

laukkopis *nm* farmer

lauklaidars *nm* (reg.) corral

laukleja *nf* valley (between fields)

laukmāja *nf* farm

laukmala *nf* edge of a field

laukmale *nf* edge of a field

laukmalis *nm* edge of a field

lauknovērojums *nm* field observation

laukpētījumi *nm pl* field research

laukpūcītes *nf pl* owlet moths

laukpuķe *nf* wild flower

lauk/s *nm* field; klajā ~ā in the open

lauks *adj* (of horses, cows) with a blaze

lauksaimniecība *nf* agriculture

lauksaimniecības produkti *nm pl* farm produce

lauksaimniecības te|ch|nikums [h] *nm* agricultural school

lauksaimnieciski *adv* agriculturally

lauksaimniecisks *adj* agricultural

lauksaimnie/ks *nm*, ~ce *nf* farmer

laukskats *nm* landscape

laukskola *nf* rural school

laukskolotājs *nm* rural schoolmaster

laukstrādnie/ks *nm*, ~ce *nf* farm hand, agricultural worker

laukšpats *nm* feldspar

lauku āboliņš *nm* large hop clover

lauku aitene *nf* bugloss

lauku balodis *nm* wood pigeon

lauku blaktene *nf* rest-harrow

lauku cīrulis *nm* Eurasian skylark

lauku čakstiņš *nm* whinchat

lauku čipste *nf* tawny pipit

lauku darbs *nm* farm work

lauku iedzīvotāji *nm pl* rural population; countryfolk

lauku ilzītes *nf pl* field chamomile

lauku irbe *nf* gray partridge

lauku kļava *nf* field maple

lauku kultūra *nf* cultivation

lauku lija *nf* hen harrier

lauku magone *nf* long smooth-fruited poppy

lauku maijvabole *nf* cockchafer

laukumains *adj* spotted; motley, variegated

lauku mājas *nf pl* rural homestead

lauku mājiņa *nf* cottage

lauku mētra *nf* Japanese peppermint

laukumiņš *nm dim* of laukums 2, small square; small playing field

laukumots *adj* motley, variegated

laukum/s *nm* **1.** area; ~a **mērs** areal measure; **2.** square (plaza); (playing) field, court; **3.** spot

lauku neaizmirstule *nf* a forget-me-not, Myosotis intermedia

lauku pašvaldība *nf* communal administration

lauku pele *nf* field mouse

lauku piekūns *nm* common kestrel

lauku pipari *nm pl* yarrow

lauku policija *nf* rural police

lauku puķes *nf pl* wildflowers

lauku pulkstenīte *nf* creeping bellflower

lauku pupa *nf* broad bean

lauku pūtele *nf* a filago, Filago arvensis

lauku riteņspolīte *nf* fumitory

lauku roze *nf* British variety

lauku sārmene *nf* field woundwort

lauku sēta *nf* farmstead

lauku sīkausīte *nf* field vole

lauku sinepes *nf pl* charlock

lauku sīpoli *nm pl* field garlic

lauku skosta *nf* field horsetail

lauku strupaste *nf* vole

lauku suņu kumelītes *nf pl* field chamomile

lauku tītenis *nm* field bindweed

lauku veronika *nf* field speedwell

lauku vībotne *nf* field artemisia

lauku zvirbulis *nm* tree sparrow

lauku žandarmērija *nf* military police

lauķis *nm* (col.) country bumpkin, rube

laulabnieki *nm pl* (reg.) wedding guests

laulājam/ais *nom adj* person to be married; ~ā *f*

laulājam/s *adj*, usu. *defin* ~ais wedding (*adj*)

laulāt *vt* marry

laulāt/ais *nom adj* spouse; ~ie married couple; ~o **kopīpašums** community property; ~o **šķirta dzīve** separation

laulāties *vr* get married

laulene *nf* (col.) wife

laulenis *nm* (col.) husband

laulība *nf* marriage; ~s wedding; ~s **gados** marriagable

laulības apliecība *nf* marriage certificate

laulības biedrs *nm* marriage partner

laulības dzīve *nf* married life

laulības gredzens *nm* wedding ring

laulības jubileja *nf* wedding anniversary

laulības kārta *nf* married state

laulības pārkāpējs *nm* adulterer

laulības pārkāpēja *nf* adulteress

laulības pārkāpšana *nf* adultery

laulības šķiršana *nf* divorce

laulībnie/ks *nm*, ~ce *nf* wedding guest

laulnieki *nm pl* bride and groom

lauma *nf* **1.** witch; **2.** (folk.) earth goddess; **3.** fairy

laumas slota *nf* asparagus

laumēt *vi* cast spells

laumu zāle *nf* baneberry

launadzis *nm* (reg.) south wind, southerly

launagi *nm pl* (reg.) southwest

launaglaiks *nm* afternoon mealtime

launagot *vi* take the afternoon meal

launags *nm* afternoon meal, fours

launteniss *nm* lawn teniss

laupījums *nm* **1.** booty, loot; **2.** prey

laupīšana *nf* **1.** robbery; plunder, looting; ~s **kāre** rapacity; **2.** deprivation

laupīt *vt, vi* **1.** rob; plunder, loot; prey on; **2.** (fig.) deprive, take away, rob of; **l. brīvību** imprison; enslave; **l. godu** a. dishonor; b. de-fame; **l. savai mutei** stint oneself; **3.** peel

laupītājdzīvnieks *nm* animal of prey, predator

laupītājputns *nm* bird of prey

laupītāj/s *nm*, ~a *nf* robber; brigand; plunderer, looter

laupīties *vr* peel

laupītkāre *nf* rapacity, predatoriness

laupītkārs *adj* rapacious, predatory

laupsna *nf* sliver, smidgen

lauraugi *nm pl* laurels

laureāt/s *nm*, ~e *nf* laureate

lauri *nm pl* (fig.) laurels

laurinskābe *nf* lauric acid

laurķirsis *nm* cherry laurel

laurķiršušu ūdens *nm* bay rum

laurlapu kārkls *nm* bay willow

laurs *nm* laurel, bay laurel

lauru lapa *nf* bay leaf

lausciņa *nf dim* of **lauska**, small fragment, potsherd

lauska *nf* fragment, potsherd

lausks *nm* Jack Frost; **l. speŗ** it is crackling with cold

laušana *nf* **1.** breaking; **2.** refraction

laušanās *nfr* wrestling

laušanas leņķis *nm* angle of refraction

laušus *adv* by breaking

lauta *nf* lute

lauva *nm* **1.** lion ◊ ~s **tiesa** lion's share; **2. Lauva** Leo

lauvene *nf* lioness

lauvēns *nm* lion cub

lauviņa *nm dim* of **lauva**, little lion

lauvmutīte *nf* snapdragon

lauvronis *nm* sea lion

lauza *nf* **1.** windfallen branches, windfallen trees; **2.** (col.) aching bones; **3.** (reg.) quantity

lauzējs *nm*, ~a *nf* **1.** breaker, crusher; **2.** grubber; **3.** (with **līguma**, **vārda**) one who fails to perform on a contract, one who breaks his word; **4.** (col.) rheumatic pain; aching bones

lauzīt *vt* **1.** break (repeatedly, in many places); crush, crumble; **l. rokas** wring one's hands; **2.** mangle, distort; **l. (angļu) valodu** speak broken (English); **3.** exert; **l. galvu** rack one's brain

lauzīties *vr* **1.** hem and haw; play hard to get; **2.** struggle with

lauzma *nf* windfall

lauznis *nm* crowbar, wrecking bar

lauzt *vt* **1.** break; **l. burvību** break the spell; **l. ceļu** blaze a trail; **l. kaklu** (or **sprandu**) a. break one's neck; perish; b. fail; **l. kaulus** have aching bones; **l. šķēpus** break a lance; **l. uz rata** rack; **2.** force; **l. celmus** grub; **3.** refract; **4.** (of a contract, one's word) break; violate; **5.** (of mushrooms) pick

lauztās sirdis *nf pl* (bot.) bleeding heart

lauzties *vr* **1.** wrestle; **2.** force one's way (out of, into), try to break in (or out, through); **l. at-vērtās durvīs** force an open door; **2.** (col.) hold back, be stubborn about sth.; play hard to get

lauztin *adv emph* of **lauzt**; **l. lauzt** break with all one's might

lauzts *adj, part* of **lauzt** broken

lauztuve *nf* quarry

lauzum/s *nm* **1.** break; **2.** ~i windfallen branches, windfallen trees

laužņa *nf* windfall

laužņas *nf pl* junk

laužņi *nm pl* (bridle) bit

lava *nf* lava

lāva *nf* pallet bed; (in a sauna) sweating shelf

lavanda *nf* lavender

lavatera *nf* See **Tīringas lavatera**

lavendeleļļa *nf* lavender oil

lavendels *nm* lavender

lavendula *nf* lavender

lavēt *vi* (naut.) tack

lavierēt *vi* **1.** (naut.) tack; **2.** maneuver

lavīna *nf* avalanche

lavināt *vi* (reg.) bark

lavīnsabrukums *nm* avalanche breakdown

lavīnveida *indecl adj* avalanche-like

lavīnveidīgi *adv* like an avalanche

lavīnveidīgs *adj* avalanche-like

lāviņa *nf dim* of **lāva**, pallet bed; sweating shelf

lavīties *vr* sneak (by, out, in); **l. uz kādu** sneak up on; lie in wait for

lavsāns *nm* Dacron

Lavsona paciprese *nf* Port Orford cedar

lavsonija *nf* henna

lazanja *nf* lasagna

lazarete *nf* infirmary; field hospital

lazaretes kuģis *nm* hospital ship

lazaretes vilciens *nm* hospital train

lazd/a *nf* hazel; ~**u rieksts** hazelnut

lazdaine *nf* stand of hazels

lazdājs *nm* stand of hazels

lazdene *nf* blackening Russula

lazdiens *nm* stand of hazels

lazdulājs *nm* stand of hazels

lazdu smecernieks *nm* nut weevil

lazējums *nm* (painting) glaze

lāzeratmiņa *nf* laser storage

lāzerdisks *nm* laser disk

lāzerķirurģija *nf* laser surgery

lāzerprinteris *nm* laser printer

lāzers *nm* laser

lazulīts *nm* lazulite

lazūra *nf* **1.** blue glaze; **2.** azure

lazurīts *nm* lazurite; lapis lazuli

lazūrēt *vt* cover with blue glaze

lazūrkrāsa *nf* azure (color)

lazūrzīlīte *nf* azure tit

laža *nf* **1.** pallet bed; **2.** (cow or horse) feeder

lažiņa *nf dim* of **laēa,** pallet bed

lebeze *nf* **1.** sloven; **2.** flattering gossip

lēc/a *nf* **1.** lens; **ieliekta l.** concave lens; **ieliekti izliekta l.** meniscus convergent lens; **izliekta l.** convex lens; **plakani ieliekta l.** plane concave lens; ~**s** (*gen*) lens, lensatic; **2.** lentil; ~**u virums** (Bibl.) mess of pottage

lecamaukla *nf* jump rope

lecambedre *nf* (sports) pit

lēcējgazele *nf* springbok

lēcējpele *nf* jerboa

lēcēj/s *nm*, ~**a** *nf* jumper

lēcējtipa *indecl adj* adapted for leaping

lēcējzirneklis *nm* wolf spider

lecekšaugi *nm pl* hotbed plants

lecekšu logs *nm* hotbed frame

lecekts *nf* hotbed

lēcenes *nf pl* (reg.) measles

lecideja *nf* Lecidea lichen

lēcien/s *nm* jump, leap, bound; **l. atspeŗoties** vaulting; **l. augstumā** high jump; **l. ar ie-skriešanos** running jump; **l. bez ieskriešanās** standing jump; **l. ar izpletni** parachute jump; **l. ar kārti** pole vault; **l. tālumā** long jump; **l. tumsā** leap in the dark; **l. ūdenī** dive; ~**iem** by leaps and bounds; by fits and starts

lēcienslānis *nm* (hydrological) discontinuity

lēcienveida *indecl adj* **1.** saltatory; leaping; **2.** discontinuous

lēcienveidīgi *adv* discontinuously; by leaps

lēcienveidīgs *adj* **1.** saltatory; leaping; **2.** discontinuous

lēcīgs *adj* **1.** springy; **2.** testy

lecin *adv emph* of **lēkt; l. lēkt** jump up and down

lecināt *vt* **1.** make s.o. jump; **2.** dandle; **3.** (of bark) loosen (by beating)

lecināts piens *nm* curds

leciņus *adv* hopping and skipping

lēcis *nm,* nightjar

lecīte *nf* (col.) frog (as a bait for crayfish)

lecitija *nf* sapucaia

lecitīns *nm* lecitin

lecmīna *nf* bounding mine

lēcveida *indecl adj* lenticular

lēcveidīgi *adv* lenticularly

lēcveidīgs *adj* lenticular

ledaini *adv* icily

ledains *adj* icy; glacial

ledainums *nm* iciness

ledājs *nm* **1.** glacier; **2.** ice sheet

ledene *nf* **1.** icicle; **2.** (col.) sucker, rock candy

ledenīte *nf dim* of **ledene,** rock candy

lederīns *nm* Leatherette

ledgriezis *nm* ice apron

lēdija *nf* lady

ledlauzis *nm* icebreaker

ledot *vi* freeze, form ice

ledteka *nf* icicle

ledus *nm* ice; **aprimis l.** stagnant ice; **caurumains l.** ice potholes; **klejojošais l.** drift ice; **peldošs l.** ice floe; **sadrumstalots l.** brash ice; **sadzīts l.** pack ice; **sagrūsts l.** rafted ice; **l. ielenkts** icebound

ledus adatas *nf pl* ice needles

ledusauksts *adj* ice-cold

ledusbalets *nm* ballet on ice

ledusblāķis *nm* iceberg

ledusburāšana *nf* iceboating

ledusburātāj/s *nm*, ~a *nf* iceboater

ledusceliņš *nm* ice-skating track

leduscirtnis *nm* ice ax

ledus etiķskābe *nf* glacial acetic acid

ledus gabaliņš *nm* ice cube

ledusgabals *nm* block of ice; floating ice

ledus gaigala *nf* loon

ledusgāle *nf* coat of ice

ledushokejs *nm* ice hockey

ledus iešana *nf* ice run, debacle

ledusja|ch|ta [h] *nf* iceboat

ledusjūra *nf* arctic ocean

ledus kaija *nf* Iceland gull

leduskalns *nm* iceberg

ledus kaplis *nm* ice chisel

leduskritums *nm* icefall

leduslācis *nm* polar bear

leduslaikmets *nm* ice age

ledus lauks *nm* ice field

leduslaukums *nm* skating rink

ledusmasa *nf* mass of ice

leduspagrabs *nm* ice cellar

ledus piramīda *nf* serac

ledus plēne *nf* ice rind

leduspuķe *nf* 1. begonia; 2. ~s frost flowers

ledus putniņš *nm* kingfisher

ledus rozes *nf pl* ice flowers

ledus sakustēšanās *nfr* 1. ice push; 2. ice shearing; 3. ice twitch

ledus sastrēgums *nm* ice jam

ledussega *nf* ice sheet; ice cap

ledusskapis *nm* refrigerator

ledusspogulis *nm* smooth sheet of ice

ledusstikls *nm* frosted glass

ledus svars *nm* ice load

ledusūdens *nm* melted ice

ledutiņš *nm* (folk.) *dim* of **ledus**, ice

lēdzeknes *nf pl* thistle

lēdzerkstes *nf pl* thistle

lefkoja *nf* (bot.) stock

legācija *nf* legation

legāli *adv* legally

legālisms *nm* legalism

leg|a|litāte [ā] *nf* legality

leg|a|lizācija [ā] *nf* legalization

leg|a|lizēt [ā] *vt* legalize

leg|a|lizēties [ā] *vr* become legalized

legāls *adj* legal

leg|a|tārij/s [ā] *nm*, ~a *nf* legatee

leg|a|tārs [ā] *adj* legatary

leg|a|tīvs [ā] *adj* legatine

legato *adv, nm idecl* (mus.) legato

leg|a|tor/s [ā] *nm*, ~e *nf* legator

legāts *nm* 1. legate; 2. an item bequeathed; legacy

leghorniete *nf* Leghorn

legists *nm* legist

leguāna *nf* leguan

leg|u|mīns [ū] *nm* legumin

leģele *nf* small wooden tub

leģenda *nf* legend (story; list of symbols)

leģendāri *adv* legendarily

leģend|a|ritāte [ā] *nf* legendary nature; legendary fame

leģendārs *adj* legendary

lēģeris *nm* (barb.) camp

leģēšana *nf* alloyage

leģēt *vt* alloy

leģionārs *nm* legionnaire

leģions *nm* legion

leģislācija *nf* legislation

leġisl|a|tīva [ā] *nf* legislative
leġisl|a|tīvi [ā] *adv* legislatively
leġisl|a|tīvs [ā] *adj* legislative
leġisl|a|tors [ā] *nm*, ~e *nf* legislator
leġisl|a|tūra [ā] *nf* legislature
leġislēt *vt* legislate
leġitimācija *nf* legitimation
leġitimēt *vt* legitimize
leġitimēties *vr* become legitimate
leġit|i|misms [ī] *nm* legitimism
leġitimistisks *adj* legitimist
leġit|i|mist/s [ī] *nm*, ~e *nf* legitimist
leġitimitāte *nf* legitimacy
leġit|i|ms [ī] *adj* legitimate
leibgvarde *nf* household troops
leibgvardists *nm* gentleman-at-arms; Life-
    Guard
leiborisms *nm* Laborism
leiboristisks *adj* laboristic
leiborists *nm* Labourite
leicīns *nm* leucine
leicīts *nm* leucite
leida *nf* 1. (obs.) free, independent existence;
    2. (hist.) (farm) lease, rent; quitrent; ~s vīrs
    = leidenieks
Leidenas trauks *nm* Leyden jar
leidenieks *nm* (hist.) free peasant (one who
    had bought himself freedom from corvée
    obligations); renter
leijerēt *vi* (com.) talk a blue streak
leijerkaste *nf* barrel organ
leijerkastnieks *nm* organ-grinder
leik- See leuk-
leimanis *nm* (hist.) petty Livonian vassal of
    Latvian origin
leinis *nm* bow-legged person
leinītis *nm* dim of leinis
leinkājis *nm* bow-legged person
leins *adj* bow-legged
leiotri|ch|ija [h] *nf* leiotrichy
leiputrija *nf* = Lejputrija
leiširbe *nf* hazel grouse

leišmale *nf* area along the border with
    Lithuania
leišmanija *nf* leischmania
leišmanioze *nf* leishmaniasis
leišu vistiņa *nf* (reg.) golden plover
leitāns *nm* Alpine hare
leitenis *nm* Alpine hare
leitis *nm*, ~tiete *nf* Lithuanian
leitiski *adv* in Lithuanian
leitisks *adj* Lithuanian
leitnants *nm*, ~e *nf* lieutenant; **jaunākais
    l.** second lieutenant; **vecākais l.** first
    lieutenant
leitmotīvs *nm* leitmotiv
lej/a I *nf* 1. valley, dale; 2. lower part; **uz ~u**
    downward; **tur ~ā** down there
leja II *nf* leu
lejā *adv* down, downward, down below;
    downstairs; **pa kalnu (upi, trepēm) l.** down
    the hill (river, stairs)
lejains *adj* with many valleys
lejāk *adv* (col.) lower down
lejamība *nf* castability, pourability
lejasbefs *nm* tailrace
lejasdaļa *nf* lower part
lejasgals *nm* 1. lower end; 2. lower reaches
    of a river
lejaskrautuve *nf* (lumbering) concentration
    point
lejasmala *nf* lower edge
lejas puse *nf* lee side
lejas stāvs *nm* lower floor
lejas vējš *nm* west wind
lejastece *nf* = lejtece
lejastilpe *nf* tailrace
lejasvācu *indecl adj* (of dialect) Low German
lejdaļa *nf* = lejasdaļa
lējējs *nm*, ~a *nf* 1. founder, caster; 2. pourer
lejforma *nf* foundry mold
lejgaliet/is *nm*, ~e *nf* lowland dweller
lejgals *nm* = lejasgals
lejiene *nf* lowland

lējiens *nm* 1. pouring; 2. casing
lejinie/ks *nm*, ~ce *nf* valley dweller
lejiņa *nf dim* of leja, small valley, dale
lejamkanna *nf* watering can
lejkanna *nf* = lejamkanna
lejpus *adv* below, down from
lejpusceļš *nm* downhill road
lejpuse *nf* lower part
Lejputrija *nf* Cockaigne
lejš *adj* low-lying
lejtece *nf* lower reaches of a river; Daugavas
    l. lower Daugava; ~s ūdens downstream
    water
lējums *nm* 1. rain; 2. casting
lejup *adv* 1. down, downward; 2. downstream
lejupceļš *nm* descent
lejupeja *nf* decline
lejupejā zarna *nf* descending colon
lejupejošs *adj* descending
lejupējs *adj* descending
lejupenis *nm* downstroke letter
lejupielāde *nf* (compu.) downloading
lejupkritenis *nm* drop
lejupkrītošs *adj* dropping, falling
lejupslīde *nf* 1. downhill slide; 2. decline
lejupslīdējums *nm* drop, decline
lejupslīdēšana *nf* 1. downhill slide; 2. decline
lejupslīdošs *adj* 1. descending; 2. declining
lejveidne *nf* foundry mold
lejzemnie/ks *nm*, ~ce *nf* lowlander; speaker of
    a lowland dialect
lēka *nf* artery; ~s a. pulse; b. (poet.) veins
lekāls *nm* French curve
lēkaļāt *vi* jump around
lekanoras *nf pl* lecanoras
lēkāšana *nf* (aeron.) bouncing
lēkāt *vi* jump, hop, skip, bounce; (of the heart)
    skip beats
lēkatnes *nf pl* trampolin
lekāža *nf* leakage, wastage
lekāžs *nm* leakage, wastage
lekcija *nf* lecture

lekciju zāle *nf* auditorium
lekits *nm* lecythus
lekmanis *nm* jumper, frog
lēkme *nf* fit, attack, paroxysm; seizure
lēkmjveida *indecl adj* paroxysmal
lēkmjveidīgi *adv* paroxysmally
lēkmjveidīgs *adj* paroxysmal
lēkna *nf* wet meadow
lekni *adv* lushly, luxuriantly
lekns *adj* 1. (of soil) moist and fertile;
    2. (of plants) lush, luxuriant
leknums *nm* 1. fertility; 2. lushness
leks *nm* lek
leksēma *nf* lexeme
leksēt *vi* eat greedily, gobble one's food
leksika *nf* vocabulary
leksikalizācija *nf* word formation
leksikalizēties *vr* become a word
leksikogr[a]fija [ā] *nf* lexicography
leksikogr[a]fiski [ā] *adv* lexicographically
leksikogr[a]fisk/s [ā] *adj* lexicographical
leksikogr[a]f/s [ā] *nm*, ~e *nf* lexicographer
leksikologs *nm*, ~ģe *nf* lexicologist
leksikoloģija *nf* lexicology
leksikoloģiski *adv* lexicologically
leksikoloģisks *adj* lexicological
leksikons *nm* lexicon
leksikostatistika *nf* 1. lexicostatistics;
    2. glotto-chronology
leksiski *adv* lexically
leksisks *adj* lexical
lēkša *nf* lump, cake
lēkšana *nf* (sports) jumping; l. ar slēpēm ski
    jumping
lēkšāt *vi* snow (with large, multiple snow-
    lakes)
lēkšēt *vi* cake, mat, stick together
lēkš/i *nm pl* gallop; usu. *instr* ~iem or *loc* ~os
    at a gallop
lēkšķains *adj* lumpy, caked
lēkšķe *nf* flat lump, piece of caked or matted
    material (snow, mud, hay, feathers)

lēkšņa *nf* large snow flake

lēkšot *vi* gallop

lēkšotājs *nm* galloper

lēkšus *adv* jumping; at a gallop

lēkt *vi* **1.** jump, leap, hop, spring; **l. acīs** (col.) sound off, challenge, contradict, cheek; **l. kājās** jump to one's feet; **l. klases** play hopscotch; **l. no ādas ārā** be hopping mad; **l. uz auguma** (sl.) pick on s.o.; **l. vai gaisā** nearly jump up and down (in joy or frustration); **2.** (of celestial bodies) rise

lēkties *vr* **1.** compete in jumping or hopping; **2.** (col.) happen; **3.** (col.) fare, do; **4.** (col.) get

lēktin *adv emph* of **lēkt; l. lēkt** jump up and down

lektīra *nf* reading material, reading

lektorijs *nm* **1.** lectern; **2.** lecture room; **3.** lecture cycle

lektor/s *nm,* **~e** *nf* lecturer

lektrise *nf* lecturer

lēkts *nm* (of celestial bodies) rise; sunrise, moonrise

leķe *nf* cow pat

leķēt *vi* leak

lēle *nf* (reg.) leach

lelija *nf* laelia

lelilnāt *vt, vi* call the cattle

lēlis *nm* nightjar

lelle *nf* **1.** doll; **2.** puppet; dummy; **3.** (folk.) baby (before baptism)

lellinie/ks *nm,* **~ce** *nf* **1.** puppeteer; **2.** puppet master

lellis *nm* figurehead; (obs.) doll

lellisks *adj* doll-like, dollish;befitting a puppet

lellīte *nf dim* of **lelle**, little doll

lelot *vt, vi* call the cattle; call, holler

lēļveidīgie *nom adj pl* Caprimulgidae

lēmējorg[a]ns [ā] *nm* decision-making body

lēmēj/s *nm,* **~a** *nf* judge; decision maker; ordainer; **~a balss** deciding vote

lēmenis *nm* marshy lakeside

lemesis *nm* plowshare

lemesītis *nm dim* of **lemesis** or **lemess**, plowhsare

lemesnīca *nf* **1.** plowright's shop; **2.** plowshoe

lemess *nm* = **lemesis**

lemešarkls *nm* moldboard plow

lemings *nm* lemming

lemma *nf* lemma

lemperēt *vi* gad about

lemperis *nm* gadabout

lempēt *vi* eat or drink noisily

lempēties *vr* behave clumsily

lempība *nf* boorishness; clumsiness

lempīgi *adv* boorishly; clumsily; awkwardly; gawkily

lempīgs *adj* boorish; clumsy; awkward; gawky

lempīgums *nm* boorishness, clumsiness

lempiķis *nm* (col.) galoot

lempīra *nf* lempira

lemp/is *nm,* **~e** *nf* galoot

lemt *vt* **1.** decide; **2.** usu. *part* **lemts** destined

lēmums *nm* **1.** decision; resolution; judgment; **l. mantas lietā** judgment in rem; **l. personisku saistību lietā** judgment in personam; **2.** decree

lem[u]rs [ū] *nm* lemur

lēna *nf* (reg.) **1.** film; scum; **2.** plant cover (on the surface of water); **3.** groin

lēnains *adj* marshy

lēnām *adv* slowly

lēnaudzīgs *adj* slow-growth

lence *nf* **1.** strap; shoulderstrap; **2. ~s** a. suspenders; b. breeching

lencenieks *nm* bargeman

lencēt *vt* **1.** gulp down one's food; **2.** pump bilge water

lenčs *nm* lunch

lēndabīgi *adv* gently, peaceably

lēndabīgs *adj* mild-mannered, gentle, peaceable
lēndabīgums *nm* mild manner, gentleness
lēndab/is *nm*, ~**e** *nf* gentle person
lendere *nf* hitchrack
lendlers *nm* landler
lendlīze *nf* lend-lease
lendlords *nm* (British) landlord
lēne *nf* (barb.) back of a chair
lēnējs *adj* peaceable
lēngaitas *indecl adj* slow-speed
lēni *adv* 1. slowly; 2. gently; 3. sluggishly
lēnība *nf* 1. gentleness; 2. slowness
lēnica *nf* (reg.) southwesterly
lēniedarbīgi *adv* acting slowly
lēniedarbīgs *adj* slow-acting
lēnīgi *adv* gently; slowly
lēnīgs *adj* 1. gentle; 2. slow
lēnīgsnēji *adv* peaceably, gently
lēnīgsnējs *adj* peaceable, gentle
lēnīgums *nm* 1. gentleness; 2. slowness
lēnināt *vt* slow down
lēnis *nm* (hist.) fief
lēnītēm *adv* slowly
lēnītiņām *adv* slowly
lēnītis *nm* peaceable person
lēnitīvs *adj* lenitive
lēnkrēsls *nm* (barb.) easy chair
lenkt *vt* 1. chase, pursue; 2. follow, shadow
lēnot *vt* slow down
lēnoties *vr* dawdle
lēnplūde *nf* slow flow
lēnprātība *nf* gentleness, meakness
lēnprātīgi *adv* gently, meekly
lēnprātīgs *adj* gentle, meek
lēnprātīgie *nom adj pl* the meek
lēnprātīgums *nm* gentleness, meekness
lēnprātis *nm* peaceable person
lēns *adj* 1. slow; (of fire) small; 2. gentle, peaceable; calm; meek; 3. sluggish
lenšatmiņa *nf* (compu.) tape storage

lenšdzinis *nm* (compu.) tape drive
lenšiekārta *nf* (compu.) tape unit
lente *nf* 1. ribbon, tape; band; 2. (machine, cartridge) belt; **slīdošā l.** conveyor; assembly line
lentenis *nm* tapeworm
lenterēt *vi* toddle
lenterēties *vr* wiggle
lenteris *nm* (barb.) hitchrack; (barb.) banister
lentikulārs *adj* lenticular
lentīte *nf dim* of **lente**, small ribbon
lentmērs *nm* tape measure
lento *adv* (mus.) lento
lentpadeve *nf* belt feed
lentveida *indecl adj* tape-like, ribbon-like
lentveidīgi *adv* like a ribbon
lentveidīgs *adj* tape-like, ribbon-like; (bot.) lig-ulate
lentzāģis *nm* band saw
lentzivs *nf* ribbonfish
lēnu *adv* slowly
lēnulis *nm* peaceable person
lēnums *nm* 1. slowness; 2. sluggishness
lēņa kalps *nm* vassal
lēņu kalpība *nf* feudal service
lēņu kungs *nm* feudal lord
lēņa tiesības *nf pl* feudal law
lenķdzelzs *nf* angle iron
lenķgabals *nm* (pipe) elbow
lenķ/is *nm* angle; **ārējais l.** exterior angle; **iekšējais l.** interior angle; **izplests l.** straight angle; **plats l.** obtuse angle; **saistītie ~i** conjugate angles; **šaurs l.** acute angle; **taisns l.** right angle
lenķa dzelzs *nf* angle iron
lenķa gr[a]ds [ā] *nm* angular degree
lenķa virsotne *nf* vertex
lenķiski *adv* angularly
lenķisks *adj* angular
lenķmērs *nm* 1. protractor; 2. carpenter's square

leņķsvira *nf* toggle lever

leņķtērauds *nm* angle iron

leņķveida *indecl adj* angular

leņķveidīgi *adv* angularly

leņķveidīgs *adj* angular

lēņmuiža *nf* feudal manor

lēņot *vt* (hist.) grant a fee

leonotes *nf pl* Leonotis

leontices *nf pl* blue cohosh

leopards *nm* leopard

lēpa *nf* 1. coltsfoot; 2. water lily; 3. (of an anchor) fluke

lēpe *nf* = lēpa

lēpene *nf* 1. coltsfoot; 2. butterbur

lepēšana *nf* (tech.) lapping

lepēt I *vi* 1. gulp down one's food; 2. snow large flakes

lepēt II *vt* (tech.) lap

lepidīns *nm* lepidine

lepidoblastisks *adj* lepidoblastic

lepieris *nm* (tech.) lapper

lēpis *nm* 1. common nighthawk; 2. clumsy person, lubber

lēpju lapas *nf pl* coltsfoot

lepni *adv* 1. proudly; haughtily; 2. sumptuously; splendidly

lepnība *nf* haughtiness, arrogance

lepnīgi *adv* 1. proudly; 2. haughtily, arrogantly

lepnīgs *adj* 1. proud; 2. haughty, arrogant

lepniķis *nm* (col.) arrogant fellow

lepnis *nm* arrogant person

lepns *adj* 1. proud; 2. haughty, arrogant; 3. rich, luxurious, sumptuous, splendid

lepnulis *nm* arrogant person

lepnums *nm* pride

lepoties *vr* 1. be proud (of sth.); pride oneself (on sth.); 2. boast; strut; display

lepra *nf* leprosy

lepras slimnieks *nm* leper

leprozorijs *nm* leprosorium

leprozs *adj* leprous

lepsis *nm* (col.) small piece

lēpšas *nf pl* (reg., of hares) rut

lept *vi* become spoiled (by being pampered)

lepta *nf* (coin) lepton

leptīts *nm* leptite

leptons *nm* (phys.) lepton

leptospermi *nm pl* Leptospermum

leptospiras [ī] *nf pl* leptospirae

leptospiroze [ī] *nf* leptospirosis

leptotri[ch]i [h] *nm pl* leptotrichia

leptures *nf pl* hard grass

lēpurs *nm* (col.) clumsy fellow

lērums *nm* (col.) 1. ruckus; 2. great quantity, gobs

lēsa *nf* floating island, floating vegetation

lēsans *adj* (reg.) tasteless, flat

lesbiete *nf* Lesbian

lesbisks *adj* Lesbian

lesbisms *nm* Lesbianism

lēse *nf* bill, invoice

leska *nf* (dirty) rag, tatter

leskāt *vi* wade through mud

lespedeza *nf* lespedeza, Japan clover

less *nm* loess

lest *vt* (of birds) peck (at food)

lēst *vt* calculate

lešbomis *nm* (naut.) derrick

lēšķe *nf* lump, cake

letāli *adv* lethally

let[a]litāte [ā] *nf* lethality

letāls *adj* lethal

letarģija *nf* lethargy

letarģiski *adv* lethargically

letarģisks *adj* lethargic

lētaudzis *adj* pampered

letauris *nm* Alpine hare

lētdabība *nf* (obs.) thoughtlessness

lētdabīgi *adv* (obs.) thoughtlessly

lētdabīgs *adj* (obs.) thoughtless

lētdabis *nm* (obs.) thoughtless person

lete *nf* counter

letes kase *nf* cash register

letgaļi *nm pl* = latgaļi
lēti *adv* 1. cheaply, inexpensively; 2. easily;
3. (in negations) soon
lētība *nf* cheapness
leticisms *nm* Letticism
letika *nf* corpus of printed texts in Latvian
lētināt *vt* deprecate
letiņi *nm pl* (sl.) Latvians
lētiņi *nm pl* cow parsnip
letkiss *nm* snake dance; conga
letonika *nf* Lettonica, Latvian studies
lētprātība *nf* (obs.) thoughtlessness
lētprātīgi *adv* (obs.) thoughtlessly
lētprātīgs *adj* (obs.) thoughtless
lētprāt/is *nm*, ~e *nf* (obs.) thoughtless person
lēts *adj* 1. cheap, inexpensive; (of prices,
fees, tariffs) low, reduced; l. un labs (of a
purchase) value, nice and cheap; 2. easy
lētsirdība *nf* 1. gentleness; compassion;
2. ac-comodation; 3. generosity
lētsirdīgi *adv* 1. gently; compassionately;
2. accomodingly; 3. generously
lētsirdīgs *adj* 1. gentle; compassionate;
2. accomodating; 3. generous
lētticība *nf* credulity
lētticīgi *adv* credulously
lētticīgs *adj* credulous
lētticīgums *nm* credulity
lētticis *nm* gull, sucker
lētums *nm* cheapness
le[u]cīns [i] *nm* leucine
le[u]cīts [i] *nm* leucite
le[ukh]ēmija [ik] *nf* leukemia
le[u]kobaze [i] *nf* leuco base
le[u]koblasts [i] *nm* leukoblast
le[u]kocītoze [i] *nf* leukocytosis
le[u]kocīts [i] *nm* leukocyte
le[u]koderma [i] *nf* leukoderma
leukoja *nf* = lefkoja
le[u]kokratisks [i] *adj* leucocratic
le[u]koksens [i] *nm* leucoxene
le[u]koma [i] *nf* leucoma

le[u]kopenija [i] *nf* leukopenia
le[u]koplakija [i] *nf* leukoplakia
le[u]koplasti [i] *nm pl* leucoplasts
le[u]koplasts [i] *nm* adhesive tape
le[u]koreja [i] *nf* leukorrhea
le[u]kosins [i] *nm* leucosin
le[u]koze [i] *nf* leukosis
leva *nf* lev
levāde *nf* levade
lēvenība *nf* obesity
lēvenis *nm* 1. large quantity, pile; 2. layer of
duckweed
lēverainā rudbekija *nf* (bot.) golden glow
lēveraini *adv* in tatters
lēverainība *nf* tatteredness
lēverains *adj* tattered
lēverainums *nm* tatteredness
lēveris *nm* 1. tatter; 2. membrane
leviatāns *nm* leviathan; Leviathan
lēvirāts *nm* levirate
levitācija *nf* levitation
levīts *nm* Levite
levkoja *nf* = lefkoja
levoglukozāns *nm* levoglucosan
levrete *nf* Italian greyhound
lezb- See lesb-
lēze *nf* rut
Lēzeļa lipare *nf* fen orchis
lēzeni *adv* 1. flatly; 2. gently sloping
lēzens *adj* 1. flat; 2. gently sloping
lēzenums *nm* 1. flatness; 2. gentle slope
lēzēt *vt* (weav.) lease
lezgīns *nm*, ~iete *nf* Lezghian
lezginka *nf* lezginka
lēzni *adv* 1. flatly; 2. gently sloping
lēzns *adj* 1. flat; 2. gently sloping
ležņa *nf, nm* (reg.) lie-abed
liāna *nf* liana
liānveida *indecl adj* liana-like
liānveidīgi *adv* like a liana
liānveidīgs *adj* liana-like
liatres *nf pl* liatris

libaniet/is *nm*, ~**e** *nf* Lebanese
libanotes *nf pl* seselis
libella *nf* (instrument) level
liberāli *adv* liberally
liberāl/is *nm*, ~**e** *nf* liberal
liberālisms *nm* liberalism
liber|a|litāte |ā| *nf* liberality
liber|a|lizācija |ā| *nf* liberalization
liber|a|lizēt |ā| *vt* liberalize
liberāls *adj* liberal
liberālums *nm* liberality
liberiņi *nm pl* (sl.) small junk; whatnots, knickknacks
libertārisms *nm* libertarianism
libertīnisms *nm* libertinism
libidināls *adj* libidinal
libido *indecl nm* libido
libietis *nm*, ~**e** *nf* Libyan
lībiet/is *nm*, ~**e** *nf* Liv
līb/is *nm*, ~**iete** *nf* Liv
lībiski *adv* in Livonian
lībisks *adj* Livonian
lībisms *nm* Livonianism
lībķens *nm* (col.) bodice
libociedrs *nm* incense cedar
librācija *nf* libration
libretists *nm*, ~**e** *nf* librettist
librets *nm* libretto
lice *nf* litz wire
licējiņš *nm dim* of **licējs**, (folk.) layer
licejists *nm*, ~**e** *nf* lyceum or lycée student
licejs *nm* lyceum, lycée
licēj/s *nm*, ~**a** *nf* **1.** layer; **2.** commander, ordainer
licence *nf* letters patent; license
licencēt *vt* = **licenciēt**
licenciāts *nm* licentiate
licenciēt *vt* **1.** license; **2.** issue letters patent
līcenis *nm* a curved tool or implement
licente *nf* (hist.) a type of customs tariff
li|ch|enīns |h| *nm* lichenin
li|ch|enologs |h| *nm*, ~**ģe** *nf* lichenologist

li|ch|enoloģija |h| *nf* lichenology
li|ch|ters |h| *nm* (naut.) lighter
licija *nf* matrimony vine
licin *adv emph* of **likt; l. likt** enjoin
līcin *adv emph* of **līkt; l. līkt** bend under a heavy load
līcināt *vt* bend
līcis *nm* bay, gulf; cove, inlet; river bend
līcītis *nm dim* of **līcis**, small bay, cove, inlet
līčains *adj* meandering
līča pļava *nf* water meadow
līča striebuļi *nm pl* garden angelica
ličija *nf* litchi
līčlocis *nm* zigzag
līčločains *adj* zigzag
līčločiem *adv* zigzagging
līčločot *vi* zigzag
līčloču *indecl adj* zigzag; meandering
līčot *vi* wind, meander
līčots *adj, part* of **līčot** winding, meandering
līču loču *adv* zigzag
līčupe *nf* river with many bends
līdaciņa *nf* **1.** *dim* of **līdaka**, pike, little pike; **2.** pickerel; **3.** (diving) back-jackknife; **4.** (col.) shuttle
līdaka *nf* **1.** pike; **2.** (hist., col.) 500-ruble note
līdakveidīgs *adj* pike-like
lidaparāts *nm* aircraft; **kosmiskais l.** space vehicle
lidas *nf pl* (poet.) flight
līdējs I *nm*, ~**a** *nf* **1.** creeper, crawler; **2.** toady
līdējs II *nm* land clearer, grubber
līderīgs *adj* sloppy, messy
līder/is *nm*, ~**e** *nf* leader
līderkomanda *nf* leading team
lidēt *vi* float
līdēt *vt* leave in the rain
lidierīce *nf* aircraft
lidieš/i *nm pl* Lydians; ~**u** Lydian
lidināt *vt* fly; fling
līdināt *vi* drizzle
lidināties *vr* hover; flutter

lidinstruktors *nm* flight instructor

lidķermenis *nm* fuselage

lidlaiks *nm* (of ammunition rounds) flighttime

lidlaiva *nf* flying boat

lidlauks *nm* airfield

lidmašīna *nf* airplane; **bezpilota l.** drone; **reaktīvā l.** jet airplane; **sanitārā l.** ambulance plane; **vertikālstarta l.** vertical takeoff and landing aircraft, VTOL

lidmašīnas apkalpe *nf* aircrew

lidmašīnas pavadonis *nm*, ~**e** *nf* flight attendant

lidmašīnu baze *nf* air base

lidmašīnu bazes kuģis *nm* aircraft carrier

lidmodelis *nm* model airplane

lidmodelisms *nm* model airplane building and racing

lidmodelist/s *nm*, ~**e** *nf* model airplane builder and racer

lidmotors *nm* aviation engine

līdne *nf* manhole

lidnis *nm* glider

lidojums *nm* flight; **ačgārnais l.** upside-down flight; **aklais l.** blindfold flying; **figurāls l.** acrobatic flight; **pikējošs l.** dive; **pirmais l.** maiden flight; **pļaujošs l.** low-altitude flight, hedgehopping; terrain flight

lidon/is *nm*, ~**e** *nf* 1. (poet.) airplane pilot; 2. flier

lidosta *nf* airport

lidot *vi* fly

lidotājputns *nm* flying bird

lidotāj/s *nm*, ~**a** *nf* pilot; flier

lidotājs-izmēģinātājs *nm* test pilot

lidotājs-novērotājs *nm* observer

lidotspēja *nf* ability to fly

lidpasts *nm* airmail

lidplēve *nf* flying membrane (fold, web)

lidspalva *nf* flight feather

lidtaka *nf* flight path

lidul/is *nm*, ~**e** *nf* flighty person

līdumlīdējs *nm* grubber

līdumnie/ks *nm* clearer of woods, grubber; ~**ce** *nf* grubber's wife

līdumošana *nf* grubbing

līdumplēsis *nm* grubber

līdums *nm* 1. woodland turned into arable land; clearing; 2. (col.) quantity

lidus *adv* flying

lidvāvere *nf* 1. polatouche; 2. flying squirrel

līdz I *prep* 1. as far as, up to; (of age) under; 2. until; **l. šim** until now; **l. turpmākam** for the time being; **no . . . līdz** a. from . . . to; b. between . . . and; 3. **l. ar** by (a given time), at the same time as; even with; 4. to

līdz II *adv* 1. along, with (one); (with a verb) join in, accompany; **l. ar ko** whereby; **l. ar šo** herewith; **l. ar to** therewith; thereby; **visi l.** each and everyone; 2. (after numerals) even, exactly; **l. vai lieks?** odd or even?

līdz III *conj* until

līdzaizbildnis *nm* coguardian

līdzaizgādnis *nm* coguardian

līdzās *adv, prep* next to, beside

līdzāspastāvēšana *nf* coexistence

līdzāssēdētāj/s *nm*, ~**a** *nf* neighbor, person sitting next to one

līdzatbildētāj/s *nm*, ~**a** *nf* (jur.) codefendant, correspondent

līdzatbildība *nf* joint responsibility

līdzatbildīgs *adj* jointly responsible, sharing re-sponsibility

līdzatbildīgums *nm* joint responsibility

līdzatnests *adj* brought along

līdzau/dzis *nm* age-mate; ~**dēi** peers

līdzautorība *nf* coauthorship

līdzautor/s *nm*, ~**e** *nf* coauthor

līdzbaudītājs *nm* one enjoying the same pleasures

līdzbiedr/s *nm*, ~**e** *nf* fellow, companion

līdzbraucēj/s *nm*, ~**a** *nf* 1. fellow traveler; travel companion; 2. relief driver; 3. rider (in the sidecar of a motorcycle)

līdzbraukt *vi* go with, travel with, accompany s.o. on a trip

līdzceļotāj/s *nm*, ~a *nf* fellow traveler

līdzcensis *nm* competitor; rival

līdzcenson/is *nm*, ~e *nf* competitor; rival

līdzciest *vi* feel sympathy; express sympathy

līdzcietība *nf* compassion; pity; sympathy; **aiz** ~s out of pity

līdzcietīgi *adv* compassionately, sympathetically

līdzcietīgs *adj* compassionate, sympathetic

līdzcietīgums *nm* compassion; pity; sympathy

līdzciltnieks *nm* fellow tribesman

līdzcilvēks *nm* fellow human being

līdzcīnītāj/s *nm*, ~a *nf* comrade-in-arms

līdzdabūt *vt* obtain (or be given) sth. along with other things

līdzdalība *nf* participation; complicity

līdzdalībnie/ks *nm*, ~ce *nf* 1. participant; partner; 2. accomplice; 3. member of a group in a class action suit

līdzdarbība *nf* cooperation; collaboration; complicity

līdzdarbinie/ks *nm*, ~ce *nf* coworker

līdzdarboties *vr* cooperate; collaborate

līdzdarīšana *nf* being an accomplice in a crime

līdzdeva *nf* dowry

līdzdots *adj* given to take along

līdzdzērājs *nm* drinking companion

līdzdzīvošana *nf* 1. empathy; 2. rooming together

līdzdzīvotāj/s *nm*, ~a *nf* 1. fellow tenant; roommate; 2. emphatizer

līdzēdēj/s *nm*, ~a *nf* table companion, commensal

lidzene *nf* bird's-nest orchid

līdzēj/s *nm*, ~a *nf* 1. hirer; 2. negotiator

līdzek/lis *nm* means; aid; remedy; **braucamie ~ļi** vehicles; **mazgājamais l.** washday product; **no-mierinošs l.** sedative; tranquilizer; **spēcinošs l.** tonic; **uzbudinošs l.** stimulant;

~ļi financial means, money; **apgrozāmie** ~ļi liquidity

līdzeni *adv* evenly, smoothly

līdzenieks *nm* = **līdzinieks**

līdzens *adj* even, flat, smooth

līdzenums *nm* 1. evenness, flatness, smoothness; 2. plain; level ground

līdzestība *nf* compliance

līdzēt *vi* help; be of use; **ko tas līdz?** what is the use of it? **ja nelīdzēs, tad neskādēs** at least it won't hurt anything

līdzēties *vr* help oneself

līdzētāj/s *nm*, ~a *nf* helper

līdzgādība *nf* assistance, help

līdzgādnie/ks *nm*, ~ce *nf* helper

līdzgaitnie/ks *nm*, ~ce *nf* comrade, trusted companion

līdzgājēj/s *nm*, ~a *nf* companion (one walking with another person)

līdzgalvinie/ks *nm*, ~ce *nf* cosponsor, cosigner

līdzgalvotāj/s *nm*, ~a *nf* cosponsor, cosigner

līdzi *adv* along, with (one)

līdzība *nf* 1. similarity; resemblance; 2. parable; 3. likeness; 4. recompense, payment

līdzības nauda *nf* (hist.) composition, restitution, payment for damages

līdziedzīvotāj/s *nm*, ~a *nf* fellow tenant (in the same building)

līdziet *vi irr* accompany

līdzīgi *adv* similarly

līdzīg/s *adj* 1. similar; **būt ~am** resemble; 2. equal; (of money tendered) even; 3. quits; 4. (folk.) easy to live with

līdzīgums *nm* similarity, resemblance

līdzināšanās *nfr* (mil., gymnastics) alinement

līdzināt *vt* 1. level; even out; smooth; 2. (folk.) reconcile, make peace

līdzināties *vr* 1. (mil., gymnastics) aline; **pa labi l.!** dress right, dress! **uz priekšu l.!** (mil.) dress and cover!; 2. resemble; 3. be equal

līdzinie/ks *nm*, ~ce *nf* 1. double; 2. peer, equal; 3. coworker; mate; 4. a close relative of the bride (who takes her to the groom's house and then to church)

līdzīpašnie/ks *nm*, **~ce** *nf* joint proprietor

līdzīpašums *nm* joint property

līdzizdevējs *nm* partner in a publishing house

līdzjust *vt* sympathize

līdzjūta *nf* (poet.) compassion; sympathy

līdzjūtēj/s *nm*, **~a** *nf* sympathizer

līdzjūtība *nf* **1.** compassion; sympathy; **2.** con-dolence

līdzjūtīgi *adv* compassionately; sympathetically

līdzjūtīgs *adj* compassionate; sympathetic

līdzjūtīgums *nm* compassion; sympathy

līdzko *conj* as soon as

līdzmantnie/ks *nm* coheir; **~ce** *nf* coheiress

līdznācēj/s *nm*, **~a** *nf* companion (of one who walks, comes)

līdznākt *vi* come along, accompany

līdznomnie/ks *nm*, **~ce** *nf* joint lessee

līdznoziedznieks *nm* accomplice

līdzņēmējs *nm* (tech.) catcher; clamp

līdzņemts *adj* taken along, brought along

līdzojums *nm* equation

līdzparādnie/ks *nm*, **~ce** *nf* joint debtor

līdzparaksts *nm* signature (that is one in a group of signatures)

līdzpārdzīvojums *nm* emphatic emotional experience

līdzpastāvošs *adj* coexistent

līdzpilsonis *nm* fellow citizen

līdzprasītājs *nm* joint plaintiff

līdzprocesors *nm* (compu.) coprocessor

līdzredaktor/s *nm*, **~e** *nf* coeditor

līdzrunāt *vi* **1.** join in a conversation; **2.** have a say

līdzs *adj* **1.** similar; **2.** even

līdzsaite *nf* (el.) shunt

līdzsānu *indecl adj* (of triangles) isosceles

līdzskanis *nm* consonant; **balsīgs l.** voiced consonant; **eksplozīvs l.** explosive (consonant);

mīkstināts l. palatal consonant; **nebalsīgs l.** voiceless consonant

līdzskaņu dubultojums *nm* gemination

līdzskaņu mija *nf* consonant shift

līdzskrējējs *nm*, **~a** *nf* (pol.) fellow traveler

līdzskriet *vi* **1.** run along, accompany s.o. running; **2.** (pol.) be a fellow traveler

līdzspēlētāj/s *nm*, **~a** *nf* partner (in a game)

līdzspriegums *nm* direct current voltage

līdzstrādāt *vi* work for; contribute to; collaborate

līdzstrādnie/ks *nm*, **~ce** *nf* **1.** contributor (to a publication); correspondent; collaborator; **zi-nātniskais l.** scientific worker; **2.** colleague

līdzstrāva *nf* direct current

līdzstrāvas *indecl adj* **1.** direct current (*adj*); **2.** (mech.) uniflow

līdzsūtīt *vt* send along, send with

līdzsvara akmentiņi *nm pl* statoliths

līdzsvara baļķis *nm* balance beam

līdzsvara org|a|ns [ā] *nm* vestibular system

līdzsvarojums *nm* equilibrium

līdzsvarot *vt* balance; equalize; handicap

līdzsvarotība *nf* equilibrium

līdzsvaroties *vr* **1.** keep one's balance, balance; **2.** be in balance

līdzsvars *nm* balance, equilibrium; **garīgais l.** mental equilibrium

līdzšinējais *defin adj* previous, former

līdztecis *nm* companion

līdztekas *nf pl* parallel bars

līdzteku *indecl adj* parallel

līdztekus *adv* **1.** parallel, in parallel; **2.** simultaneously

līdzteku svītrenis *nm* parallel marker

līdztiesība *nf* equality of rights

līdztiesīgi *adv* with equal rights

līdztiesīgs *adj* having equal rights

līdztiesīgums *nm* equality of rights

līdzvaina *nf* complicity

līdzvainība *nf* complicity

līdzvainīgais *nom adj* accomplice, accessory

līdzvainīgi *adv* as an accessory

līdzvainīgs *adj* accessory (to a crime)

līdzvainīgums *nm* complicity

līdzvaininie/ks *nm*, ~ce *nf* accomplice, accessory

līdzvaldība *nf* regency

līdzvaldnie/ks *nm*, ~ce *nf* regent

līdzveidis *nm* image, likeness

līdzveidotāj/s *nm*, ~a *nf* participant(in the shaping of sth.)

līdzvērtība *nf* equivalence

līdzvērtīgi *adv* equivalently

līdzvērtīgs *adj* equivalent

līdzvērtīgums *nm* equivalence

līdzvest *vt* take along

līdzzinātāj/s *nm*, ~a *nf* accessory, one in the secret

līdzziņojums *nm* subsidiary report

liece *nf* bend, bending, flexion, flexure

liecējmuskulis *nm* flexor

liecēj/s *nm*, ~a *nf* bender

lieces pretestība *nf* (mech.) transverse strength

liecība *nf* 1. testimony; deposition; affidavit; (oral) evidence; **nepatiesa l.** false evidence; 2. report card; 3. usu. *pl* ~as (hist.) extraordinary corvée

liecības šķirsts *nm* ark of covenant

liecībspējīgs *adj* (jur., of a witness) competent

liecinājums *nm* testimony, (oral) evidence

liecināt *vt* 1. give evidence, testify; 2. witness, be evidence of, give proof of

liecinie/ks *nm*, ~ce *nf* 1. witness; **nepatiess l.** false witness; **zvērināts l.** sworn witness; 2. (folk.) outsider; 3. (hist.) a peasant sent to perform extraordinary corvée

liecinieku uzpirkšana *nf* subornation

liečis *adv* extra

liedags *nm* beach

liedāmurs *nm* soldering iron

liede *nf* molten solder

liedējamais *defin adj* soldering (*adj*)

liedens *adj* 1. svelte; 2. slippery

liedēt I (with **iê**) *vt* leave in the rain, make wet

liedēt II *vt* solder, (fig.) weld

liedēties *vr* be out in the rain, get wet

liedināt *vt* (of a metal article) cast

liedzēj/s *nm*, ~a *nf* 1. denier (one that disavows); 2. forbidder

liedzīgi *adv* denyingly

liedzīgs *adj* denying; forbidding

liedzin *adv emph* of **liegt**

liegani *adv* gently, tenderly

liegans *adj* (rare.) gentle, tender

liegas *nf pl* (poet.) gentleness

liegi *adv* gently, tenderly

lieglaime *nf* bliss

lieglaimība *nf* bliss

lieglaimīgi *adv* blissfully

lieglaimīgs *adj* blissful

liegprātība *nf* (obs.) thoughtlessness

liegprātīgi *adv* thoughtlessly

liegprātīgs *adj* (obs.) thoughtless

liegprātis *nm* (obs.) thoughtless person

liegs *adj* gentle, tender

liegšanās *nfr* 1. denial; 2. refusal

liegšus *adv emph* of **liegt**; **l. liegt** stubbornly de-ny

liegt *vt* deny; forbid

liegties *vr* 1. deny; 2. refuse

liegtin *adv emph* of **liegt**; **l. liegt** stubbornly de-ny

liegums *nm* 1. denial; 2. (forest, wetland, wildlife) preserve

liekači *nm pl* 1. low count cards (that are not used in certain games); 2. net mesh

liekatnes *nf pl* 1. extra work; 2. snack

liekēdājs *nm* parasite, sponger

liekēdība *nf* parasitism, sponging

liekēd/is *nm*, ~e *nf* parasite, sponger

liekēžaugs *nm* parasitic plant

lieki *adv* unnecessarily; **l. sacīt** I need not say

liekkauls *nm* bony spur, exostosis

lieklaizis *nm* (col.) sponger

lieklaiža *nm, nf* (col.) sponger

liekmaņi *nm pl* surplus things or persons; inferior parts of a slaughtered animal

liekna *nf* **1.** swale; **2.** (forest.) mixed stand type on mucky soil

liekne *nf* **1.** large, low-lying meadow; **2.** (reg.) water meadow

liekniņa *nf dim* of **liekne**, little water meadow

liekņa *nf* = **liekna**

lieks *adj* **1.** superfluous; redundant; unwanted; unnecessary; needless; (of flesh, with **gaļa**) proud; **2.** spare, extra; left over; (of a horse) free, unburdened; (of days) intercalary, (of years) leap; (of socks, gloves without a mate) odd; **3.** (of teeth, hair, beard) false

lieksvars *nm* overweight

liekšēt *vi* (reg.) feel sick

liekšķere *nf* scoop

liekšķerēt *vt* scoop

liekšķerīte *nf dim* of **liekšķere**, little scoop

liekšķerlāpsta *nf* scoop (deep shovel)

liekšus *adv* by bending

liekt *vt* bend, curve; bow; **l. muguru** (fig.) grovel; **l. ragā** (col.) subdue, overpower

liekties *vr* bend, bow; **l. ap stūri** turn a corner; **l. trijos līkumos** grovel

liektuve *nf* a device for bending wood

liekuguns *nf* will-o'-the-wisp

liekulība *nf* hypocrisy

liekulīgi *adv* hypocritically

liekulīgs *adj* hypocritical

liekulīgums *nm* hypocrisy

liekul/is *nm,* ~e *nf* hypocrite

liekuļot *vi, vt* dissemble, feign

liekuļoti *adv* in a feigned manner, disembling

liekuļots *adv, part* of **liekuļot** disembled, feigned, false, sham

liekums I *nm* bend

liekum/s II *nm* **1.** superfluity; **2.** ~i a. trivia; b. (of slaughtered animals) guts, giblets, inferior parts

liekvārdība *nf* verbosity; redundancy

liekvārdīgi *adv* verbosely; redundantly

liekvārdīgs *adj* verbose; redundant

lielā astrancija *nf* masterwort

lielā baltegle *nf* grand fir

lielā brūngalvīte *nf* a self-heal, Prunella grandiflora

lielacains *adj* big-eyed

lielac/is *nm,* ~e *nf* big-eyed person

lielā čakste *nf* great gray shrike, butcher-bird

lielā čipste *nf* Richard's pipit

lielā dīķu gliemene *nf* swan mussel

lielā dzelzene *nf* scabious knapweed

lielā gaišā tilbīte *nf* common greenshank

lielā gaura *nf* goosander

lielais *defin adj* (of letters) capital; (of prizes) first; (of a toe) big; (of a musical interval) major; (of a door) front; (postpositionally, in titles) the Great; **L-ā iela** Main Street; *nom adj* (in Schafskopf game) player; **(saiet)** ~ajā have words with s.o.

lielais asinsloks *nm* systemic circulation

lielais balodis *nm* wood pigeon

lielais baltais gārnis *nm* great white egret

lielais diždadzis *nm* great bur

lielais dumpis *nm* Eurasian bittern

lielais dundurs *nm* horsefly

lielais egļu lūksngrauzis *nm* a bark beetle, Dendroctonus micans

lielais egļu mizgrauzis *nm* a bark beetle, Ips typographus

lielais koksngrauzis *nm* a sawyer beetle, Monochamus sutor

lielais kudu *nm* greater kudu

lielais ķeģis *nm* linnet

lielais ķīris *nm* black-headed gull

lielais liela kauls *nm* shinbone

lielais mārsils *nm* larger wild thyme

lielais naktssikspārnis *nm* brown bat

lielais ošu lūksngrauzis *nm* a bark beetle, Hylesinus crenatus

lielais pelēkais strazds *nm* mistle thrush

lielais peļu vanags *nm* buzzard

lielais priežu mizgrauzis *nm* a bark beetle, Ips sexdentatus

lielais priežu smecernieks *nm* pine weevil

lielais purvuķauķis *nm* great reed warbler

lielai sikspārnis *nm* brown bat

lielais susuris *nm* edible dormouse

lielais šņibītis *nm* knot

lielais tritons *nm* crested newt

lielais vizbulis *nm* snowdrop anemone

lielais zīriņš *nm* Caspian tern

lielā jūras adata *nf* great pipefish

lielāk/ais *adj, superl* of **liels**; ~o **tiesu** (abb. **l. t.**) mostly

lielākais *adv* at most, at the most

lielā klijkaija *nf* great skua

lielā kosa *nf* great horsetail

lielākoties *adv* for the most part

lielāk/s *adj, comp* of **liels** larger; **(nopirkt)** ~u (buy it) on the large side **pa ~ai daļai** for the most part, largely

lielā kuitala *nf* curlew

lielākums *nm* greater part, majority

lielā lauku magone *nf* long smooth-fruited poppy

Lielā lūdzamā diena *nf* Ash Wednesday

lielā maijpuķe *nf* Solomon's seal

lielā mēŗa puķe *nf* sweet coltsfoot

lielā meēu kazroze *nf* fireweed

lielā nātre *nf* stinging nettle

Lielā piektdiena *nf* Good Friday

lielā pīpene *nf* oxeye daisy

lielā polārkaija *nf* glaucous gull

lielā purvu vijolīte *nf* peat violet

lielā pūslene *nf* a bladderwort, Urticularia neglecta

lielā ragaste *nf* horntail

lielās ceļmallapas *nf* plantain

lielā sīga *nf* great bustard

lielā smilga *nf* common redtop

lielās noragas *nf pl* greater burnet saxifrage

lielā stērste *nf* corn bunting

lielās vātis *nf pl* (obs.) syphilis

lielā šķirzutne *nf* crested newt

lielātruma *indecl adj* high-velocity

lielaugļu *indecl adj* macrocarpous

lielaugļu ķirbis *nm* winter squash

lielaugļu lazda *nf* filbert

lielā ūdenszāle *nf* a waterweed, Glyceria maxima

lielausis *nm* big-eared animal

lielā zilgalvīte *nf* self-heal

lielā zīlīte *nf* great tit

lielā zirdzene *nf* garden angelica

lielā zirgu skudra *nf* horse ant

lielbagātniek/s *nm* superrich man; ~i the superrich

lielbagāts *adj* superrich

lielbārzdis *nm* man with a large beard

lielbloku *indecl adj* concrete-block

lielburžu[a]zija [ā] *nf* upper middle class

lielcekule *nf* (folk.) large-crested one (epithet for the hen, the owl, and the partridge)

lielceļmala *nf* side of a highway

lielceļš *nm* (unpaved) highway

lielceļu laupītājs *nm* highwayman

lielcilvēks *nm* adult

lieldarbs *nm* feat

lieldaris *nm* braggart

lieldators *nm* mainframe computer

lieldegunis *nm* 1. big-nosed person; 2. conceited person

Lieldienas *nf pl* Easter

lieldzērājs *nm* big drinker

lielēdājs *nm* big eater

lielēdis *nm* big eater

lielene *nf* footless knee sock

lielestība *nf* (obs.) boastfulness

lielestis *nm* (obs.) braggart

lielforma *nf* 1. major hypsometric unit; 2. large-scale artwork

lielformāta *indecl adj* large-scale; oversize

lielgaballaiva *nf* gunboat

lielgabalnieks *nm* (obs.) artilleryman, gunner

lielgabals *nm* cannon; **bezatsitiena l.** recoilless rifle

lielgabalu gaļa *nf* cannon fodder

lielgads *nm* leap year

lielgaida *nf* ranger (senior girl scout)

lielgalvains *adj* big~headed

lielgalvas bruņrupucis *nm* highheaded turtle

lielgalvas pīle *nf* red-crested pochard

lielgalvība *nf* stubborness

lielgalvīgs *adj* stubborn

lielgalvis *nm* **1.** stubborn man; **2.** red-crested poachard

lielgalvnieks *nm* stubborn man

lielgruntniecība *nf* class of big landowners

lielgruntnie/ks *nm*, **~ce** *nf* big landowner

lielguļa *nm* (col.) big sleeper

lielguzains *adj* large-cropped

lielģimene *nf* extended family

lielhercogiene *nf* grand duchess

lielhercogiste *nf* grand duchy

lielhercogs *nm* grand duke

lielība *nf* **1.** boastfulness, bragging; **2.** (col.) braggart

lielības gailis *nm* (col.) braggart

lielībnie/ks *nm*, **~ce** *nf* braggart

lielie *nom adj pl* (child.) adults; **l. un mazie** young and old

Lielie greizie rati *nm pl* Ursa Major

lielie vāverāji *nm pl* sweet gale

lielie virši *nm pl* cross-leaved heath

lielie zilauši *nm pl* candle larkspur

lielīgi *adv* boastfully

lielīgs *adj* boastful

lielīgums *nm* boastfulness

lielindustrija *nf* large-scale industry, wholesale manufacture

lielinieciski *adv* in the Bolshevik fashion

lieliniecisks *adj* Bolshevik

lielinieks *nm* Bolshevik

lieliņš *adj dim* of **liels**, big

lielīpašnie/ks *nm* rich proprietor; **~ce** *nf*

lieliski *adv* splendidly, magnificently; **l.!** terrific!

lielisks *adj* excellent, splendid, magnificent, great; terrific

lieliskums *nm* excellence, splendor, magnificence

lielistaba *nf* (hist.) common room (in a peasant farmer's house)

lielīt *vt* praise, extol

lielīties *vr* boast, brag; swagger

lieljaudas *indecl adj* high-power

lieljūra *nf* high seas

lielkāja *nf, nm* (folk.) bigfoot (epithet for the bear)

lielkalibra *indecl adj* large-caliber

lielkalps *nm* farm hand

lielkapitālist/s *nm*, **~e** *nf* big capitalist

lielkarteča *nf* grapeshot

lielkaulis *nm* big-boned person, big-boned animal; plant with a hard stalk

lielkņaziene *nf* wife of a grand duke (in Russia)

lielkņaziste *nf* grand duchy (in Russia)

lielkņazs *nm* grand duke (in Russia)

lielkravas *indecl adj* of large load-carrying capacity

lielkrievi *nm pl* Great Russians

lielkundze *nf* lady, lady of the manor

lielkundzēns *nm* young nobleman

lielkundziski *adv* in a manner typical of nobility

lielkundzisks *adj* typical of the nobility

lielkungs *nm* = **lielskungs**

liellaiva *nf* barge

liellapainā aristolchija *nf* Dutchman's pipe

liellapainā hortenzija *nf* hortensia

liellapains *adj* large-leaved

lielloki *nm pl* Welsh onion

liellop/s *nm*, usu. *pl* **~i** cattle; **~u gaļa** beef; **~u novietne** holding pen; **~u saimniecība** cattle ranch

lielmanība *nf* pomposity, airs, conceit

lielmanīgi *adv* in a conceited, pompous manner

lielmanīgs *adj* conceited, pompous

lielmanīgums *nm* pomposity, airs, conceit

lielman/is *nm* 1. important personage; ~e or ~īša *nf*; 2. lord, noble

lielmaņa *nm* = **lielmanis**

lielmāte *nf* lady of the manor, madam; wife of a rich farmer

lielmeistars *nm* (chess) grand master

lielmestrs *nm* (hist.) Grand Master (of an order)

lielmežs *nm* great forest, old growth forest

lielmiedzīgs *adj* big sleeper

lielmolekulārs *adj* macromolecular

lielmute *nf, nm* bigmouth

lielmutība *nf* big talk, boastfulness

lielmutīgi *adv* boastfully

lielmutīgs *adj* boastful

lielmutīgums *nm* boastfulness

lielmutis *nm* bigmouth

lielnoliktava *nf* wholeseller's warehouse

lielogas *nf pl* cloudberry

lielpanelis *nm* (prefabricated) slab

lielpēdis *nm* bigfoot

lielpilsēta *nf* city

lielpilsētniecisks *adj* metropolitan

lielpilsētnie/ks *nm*, ~ce *nf* city dweller

lielprātība *nf* (col.) conceit

lielprātīgi *adv* conceitedly

lielprātīgs *adj* (col.) conceited

lielrads *nm* distinguished relative

lielragainis *nm* big-horned animal

lielragains *adj* big-horned

lielrakstains *adj* large-patterned

lielražošana *nf* mass production

lielrunātāj/s *nm*, ~a *nf* big talker

lielrūpniecība *nf* large-scale industry

lielrūpnieks *nm* industrialist; tycoon

lielrūtains *adj* having large checks

liels *nm* (anat.) shank, shin; (of a top boot) leg

liel/s *adj* 1. large, big, great; (of a person) tall; **tikpat l.** of the same size; (of people) of the same height; 2. important; **kas nu tur l. !** that's no big deal! (col.) haughty, high and mighty; 3. (of differences, intervals) wide; (of speed) high; (of time) long; 4. grown-up, adult; ~i un mazi young and old; **kad es būšu l.** when I grow up;

lielsaimniecība *nf* 1. large-scale farming; 2. large farm

lielsaimnie/ks *nm*, ~ce *nf* large farmer

lielsaišķis *nm* garter

lielsēklu *indecl adj* large-seeded

lielsirdība *nf* willfulness

lielsirdīgs *adj* willful; (col.) angry

lielsirdis *nm* arrogant person

lielskungs *nm* lord, lord of the manor

lielšķiedrains *adj* coarse-fiber

lieltilpuma *indecl adj* large-capacity

lielturītis *nm* (reg.) wolf

lieltirdzniecība *nf* wholesale trade

lieltirgotava *nf* wholesale outlet

lieltirgotājs *nm* wholesale dealer

lieltonnāžas *indecl adj* large-tonnage

lielu bruņas *nf pl* cuisse

lielūdens *nm* flood

lielum *adv*; **l. liels** very large, huge; over-whelming; **l. lielā (daļa)** greatest (part)

lielumis *adv* broadly, in general

lielumm[a]nija [ā] *nf* delusion of grandeur

lielum/s *nm* 1. greatness, largeness, bigness; 2. size; **dabiskā** ~ā life-size; 3. quantity; magnitude; **bezgalīgi mazs l.** infinitesimal; **mainīgs l.** variable; **atkarīgais mainīgais l.** dependent variable; **vidējais l.** mean; 4. major part, majority

lieluzņēmējs *nm* captain of industry

lieluzņēmums *nm* large business

lielvalod/is *nm*, ~e *nf* great talker

lielvalstisks *adj* great power (*adj*)

lielvalsts *nf* (pol.) great power

lielvara *nf* (pol.) great power

lielvaris *nm* mighty one

lielvēderains *adj* potbellied, paunchy

lielvēderīgs *adj* potbellied, paunchy

lielvēderis *nm*, ~e *nf* potbelly

lielzemnieks *nm* big peasant farmer

lielziedainā sārmene *nf* a hedge nettle, Stachys grandiflora

lielziedains *adj* large-flowered

lielziedu *indecl adj* large-flowered

lielziedu filadelfs *nm* large-flowered syringa

lielziedu genciāna *nf* marsh gentian

lielziedu purveglīte *nf* Charles's scepter

lielziedu uzpirkstīte *nf* a foxglove, Digitalis grandiflora

lielziedu vīgrieze *nf* meadowsweet

lielziedu vijolīte *nf* common dog violet

liemenis *nm* **1.** carcass (of a slaughtered animal); **2.** body

lienēt *vt* (col.) borrow

liepa *nf* linden; ~u **mēnesis** July

liepaine *nf* linden grove

liepains *adj* (rare.) having the odor or linden blossoms

liepājs *nm* linden grove

liepaudze *nf* linden grove

liepene *nf* **1.** cloudy clitocybe; **2.** linden grove

liepiena *nf* or **liepiens** *nm* linden grove

liepiņa *nf dim* of **liepa**, linden tree

liepkoks *nm* linden (wood)

liepūksnājs *nm* (reg.) stand of lindens

liepula *nf* (reg.) linden grove

liepulājs *nm* (reg.) linden grove

liepzars *nm* linden branch

liepziedains *adj* the color of linden blossoms

liepziedi *nm pl* linden blossoms

liesa *nf* spleen

liesas sērga *nf* anthrax

liesas zāle *nf* golden saxifrage

liesēt *vi* lose weight, grow thin

liesi *adv* meagerly

liesināt *vt* **1.** make lose weight; **2.** make thinner; (of concrete mixture) add aggregate

liesinātājs *nm* aggregate (to a concrete mixture)

liesm/a *nf* flame; ~**ās** ablaze; ~**as caurumiņš** flash hole

liesmaini *adv* flamingly, in flames

liesmainība *nf* fieriness

liesmains *adj* flaming, blazing; fiery

liesmainums *nm* fieriness

liesmiņa *nf dim* of **liesma**, small flame

liesmkamera *nf* firebox

liesmojums *nm* flame, flaming

liesmot *vi* flame, blaze; burn

liesmumetējs *nm* flame thrower

liesmu slāpētājs *nm* fire extinguisher

liess *adj* lean, meager; (typ.) plain

liesta or **lieste** *nf* last, shoe tree

liesums *nm* **1.** leanness, meagerness; **2.** lean meat

liešanās *nfr* water fight

liešķere *nf* scoop

liešus *adv* by pouring; *emph* of **liet; l. liet** pour by the bucket

liet *vt* **1.** pour, pour out; water; (of light, blood, tears) shed; **l. eļļu ugunī** add fuel to the fire; **l. pilnu** fill; **tukšu l.** blab; **2.** cast, found; mould; **l. laimes** tell fortune (from the shape of molten lead poured into water); **l. čugunu** (sl.) lie

liet/a *nf* **1.** thing; object; **l. par sevi** thing in itself; ~**as** matériel; **2.** matter; affair; business; **droša l.** sure thing, air-tight case; **nepatīkama l.** a. unpleasant matter; b. home truth; **slapjā l.** (sl.) murder; ~**as apstākļi** state of affairs; ~**as būtība** heart of the matter; **pie** ~**as!** keep to the point! question! ~**as kursā** be up on (a subject), be in the know; **kas par** ~**u?** what is the matter? **tā jau ir tā l.** that's just it; **l. ir tāda** here is the deal; here is what's happening; **(sākt runāt) par** ~**u** (get down to) brass tacks; **liela l.!** big deal! **3.** subject; **pie** ~**as nepiederīgs** impertinent, irrelevant; **4.** cause; **par**

savu ~u **drošs** sure of one's ground;
5. file, dossier; **6.** (jur.) case; action; **7.** tool;
8. value, usefulness, good thing

lietains *adj* rainy

lietainums *nm* raininess

lietaskoks *nm* timber; (fig.) the right stuff

lietāt *vt* use

lietavas *nf pl* rainy period, incessant rain

lietavot *vi* rain a long time

lietderība *nf* usefulness; suitability; efficiency;
~s **koeficients** efficiency (coefficient)

lietderīgi *adv* usefully; efficiently

lietderīgs *adj* useful; suitable; efficient; functional

lietderīgums *nm* usefulness; suitability; efficiency

lietene *nf* **1.** a short whip; **2.** cleg

lietenis *nm* ingot

lietēt *vt* sprinkle

lietētājs *nm* sprinkler system

lieti *adv* efficiently; suitably; **l. derēt** be useful, come in handy

lieties *vr* **1.** pour; **2.** splash each other, have a water fight

lietīgi *adv* usefully

lietīgs *adj* useful

lietiņa *nf* **1.** *dim* of **lieta**, little thing; **2.** knick-knack

lietiņš *nm dim* of **lietus**, light rain

lietiski *adv* materially

lietiskošana *nf* reification

lietiskot *vt* reify

lietisks *adj* material

lietiskums *nm* **1.** materiality; **2.** businesslike manner

lietišķi *adv* in a businesslike manner

lietišķība *nf* businesslike manner; matter-of-factness

lietišķīgi *adv* in a businesslike manner

lietišķīgs *adj* businesslike; matter-of-fact

lietišķs *adj* **1.** businesslike; matter-of-fact;to the point; **2.** applied

lietišķums *nm* businesslike manner; matter-of-factness

lietkoks *nm* = **lietaskoks**

lietkoksne *nf* lumber

lietne *nf* watering can

lietnis *nm* ingot; **apspaidīts l.** (metall.) bloom

lietojamība *nf* usability

lietojams *adj, part* of **lietot** usable

lietojums *nm* use

lietonis *nm* (reg.) nightmare; tormenting spirit

lietošana *nf* use; utilization; **kopēja l.** (compu.) sharing; **vispārējas** ~s general purpose; **vispārējai** ~i for general use; ~i **nederīgs** unserviceable

lietošanas pamācība *nf* directions; instructions, instruction manual

lietošanas tiesība *nf* right to use, usufruct

lietot *vt* use; utilize; employ

lietotājdraudzīgs *adj* user friendly

lietotāj/s *nm*, ~a *nf* user

lietots *adj, part* of **lietot** used; second-hand

lietpratēj/s *nm*, ~a *nf* expert

lietpratība *nf* expertise, expertness, know-how

lietpratīgi *adv* expertly

lietpratīgs *adj* expert

lietpratīgums *nm* expertness

lietprat/is *nm*, ~e *nf* expert

lietuļot *vi* drizzle

lietu rādītājs *nm* subject index

lietu pārvaldnieks *nm* business manager

lietu pakļautība *nf* assignment of jurisdiction

lietu piekritība *nf* (jur.) competence

lietus *nm* rain; **aklais l.** rain with sunshine; **sīks l.** drizzle

lietus dundurs *nm* cleg

lietusgāze *nf* downpour

lietus mēnesis *nm* October

lietusmērs *nm* rain gage

lietusmētelis *nm* raincoat

lietus mežs *nm* rain forest

lietuspuķe *nf* African daisy

lietus putns *nm* woodcock

lietussargs *nm* umbrella

lietus tārps *nm* earthworm

lietusūdens *nm* rainwater; **l. muca** rainbarrel

lietus vanags *nm* gray plover

lietutiņš *nm dim* of **lietus**, light rain

lietuvainis *nm* whimbrel

lietuve *nf* foundry

lietuvēna krusts *nm* pentacle

lietuvēns *nm* nightmare; incubus; tormenting spirit

lietuviet/is *nm*, **~e** *nf* Lithuanian

lietuviski *adv* in Lithuanian, (speak) Lithuanian

lietuvisks *adj* Lithuanian

lietuvji *nm pl* Lithuanians

lietvārds *nm* noun

lietvedība *nf* **1.** business correspondence, paperwork; **2.** chargé's d'affaires office; **3.** management

lietved/is *nm*, **~e** *nf* **1.** office manager, administrative secretary; **2.** chargé d'affaires

lieva *nf* heartwood

lievenes *nf pl* porch; front steps

lievenis *nm* porch; front steps

lievs *adj* (of wood) hard

līferants *nm* **1.** deliveryman; **2.** supplier

līferēt *vt* (sl.) deliver

liftnie/ks *nm*, **~ce** *nf* elevator operator

lifts *nm* elevator

liga *nf* **1.** misfortune; **2.** (obs.) illness

līga I *nf* league

līga II *nf* (distance measure) league

līga III *nf* (mus.) ligature

līga IV *nf* feather grass

ligaments *nm* ligament

līgani *adv* springily; swayingly; shakily

līganība *nf* elasticity; springiness; shakiness

līgans *adj* elastic, springy; yielding; swaying; shaky

līganums *nm* elasticity; springiness; shakiness

līgas *nf pl* **1.** wild flowers picked on St. John's eve; **2.** singing of Ligo songs

ligāt *vi* (obs.) ail

ligatūra *nf* **1.** master alloy; **2.** additive (to a noble metal); **3.** (med., typ.) ligature

līgaste *nf* equality, parity

līgava *nf* bride

līgavainis *nm* bridegroom

līgavaiņa brālis *nm* best man

līgavas bērni *nm pl* illegitimate children

līgavas māsa *nf* bridesmaid

lignīns *nm* lignin

lignīts *nm* lignite

lignocerīnskābe *nf* lignoceric acid

līgns *adj* (poet.) yielding; swaying

līgo *interj* (refrain to Ligo songs) Ligo; **l. vakars** Ligo festival (night of June 23rd)

ligodijas *nf pl* Lygodium

līgodziesma *nf* Ligo song

Līgosvētki *prop nm pl* Ligo festival

līgot I *v* **1.** *vt* rock; **2.** *vi* undulate

līgot II *vi* sing Ligo songs

līgotājs *nm*, **~a** *nf* singer of Ligo songs

līgoties *vr* sway; totter, stagger

līgotne *nf* **1.** bog; **2.** cradle pole; **3. ~s** a. a swing used on Easter Sunday; b. Ligo songs

līgotnis *nm* bog

ligroīns *nm* naphtha

līgstam/s *adj, part* of **līgt** hiring; **~ā diena** (hist.) hiring day

līgšņa *nf* morass, quagmire

līgt *v* **1.** *vt* hire; **2.** *vi* a. hire out; b. conclude a treaty; **l. mieru** make peace

ligula *nf* (zool.) ligula

ligulārija *nf* ligularia, leopard plant

līgumattiecības *nf pl* contractual obligations

līgumdarbs *nm* contracted work

līgumdiena *nf* (hist.) hiring day

līgumiski *adv* contractually

līgumisks *adj* contractual

līgumorganizācija *nf* contracting organization

līgums *nm* agreement; contract; treaty; pact

līgumsaistības *nf pl* contractual obligations

līgumslēdzējs *nm* contracting party

līgumsods *nm* penalty for non-fulfillment, penalty clause

līgumteorija *nf* social contract theory

ligūri *nm pl* Ligurians

ligusti *nm pl* lovage

ligustrs *nm* privet

ligzda *nf* 1. nest; 2. (el.) socket; 3. cluster; 4. (mil.) emplacement

ligzdbēgļi *nm pl* precocial birds, nidifugous birds

ligzdene *nf* bird's-nest orchid

ligzdguļi *nm pl* altricial birds, nidicolous birds

ligzdiņa *nf dim* of **ligzda**, little nest

ligzdot *vi* nest, make a nest

ligzdotāj/s *nm*, ~a *nf* nest maker, nestler

ligzdsēja *nf* cluster sowing

ligzdveida *indecl adj* nest-shaped, nest-like

ligzdveidīgi *adv* like a nest

ligzdveidīgs *adj* nest-shaped, nest-like

liģens *adj* bedridden

liģeri *nm pl* (hist.) medieval Latvian guild of dock workers

liģēt *vt* (cul.) thicken

lih- See **lich-**

lija I *nf* harrier

lija II *nf* soft rain

lijiens *nm* rain shower

lijin *adv emph* of **līt**; **l. lija** it rained hard; it rained a long time

lijums *nm* rainfall

līkāns *nm* a person of twisted figure

likastes *nf pl* Lycaste

līkāt *vi* bob; stoop

līkāties *vr* (*iter*) bob; stoop

līkaupi *nm pl* (obs.) closing a deal

līkdegun/is *nm*, ~e *nf* hook-nosed person

līki *adv* curved, crooked, bent

līkirbuļa vikābele *nf* a hawthorn, Crataegus kyrtostyla

līkkājains *adj* bowlegged

līkkājis *nm* bowlegged person

līkkātains *adj* having a bent (or crooked) handle, having a crooked stem

līklīnija *nf* curve

līklocis *nm* wavy line; meandering line

līkločaini *adv* meanderingly

līkločains *adj* wavy, meandering

līkločiem *adv* meanderingly

līkločot *vi* meander

līkloču or **līkločus** *adv* meanderingly

likma *nf* decree

likme *nf* 1. rate; 2. (in games) stakes

likmēt *vt* (of taxes) assess; fix the rate

līkmugurains *adj* hunch-backed

līkmugur/is *nm*, ~e *nf* hunchback

līknadzis *nm* taloned animal

līkne *nf* (graphic) curve

liknis *nm* composing stick

līkņa *nf* marshy grassland (on the shore of an overgrown lake)

līkņāt *vi* bob; stoop

līkņāties *vr* (*iter*) bob; stoop

līkņveidīgi *adv* curvilinearly

līkņveidīgs *adj* curvilinear

līkop *interj* agreed! it's a deal!

līkopi *nm pl* (obs.) closing of a deal

likopodijs *nm* club moss

likra *nf* Lycra

līkradz/is *nm*, ~e *nf* an animal with curved horns; (folk.) epithet for the goat or cow

līks *adj* curved, crooked, bent; bowed

līksma *nf* (obs.) joy, rejoicing

līksme *nf* joy, rejoicing

līksmi *adv* joyfully, joyously

līksmība *nf* joy, rejoicing

līksmīgi *adv* joyfully, joyously

līksmīgs *adj* joyful, joyous

līksmināt *vt* gladden

līksmot *vi* rejoice

līksmoties *vr* rejoice

līksms *adj* joyful, joyous

līksnis *nm* morass, quagmire

liksoze *nf* lyxose

liksta *nf* trouble, mishap; ~s tribulation, adversity

likste *nf;* ~s **mēle** (folk.) flatterer

līkste *nf* **1.** pole; **2.** cradle pole

līkstoņa *nf* morass, quagmire

līksts *nf* **1.** pole; **2.** cradle pole

līkšņa *nf* morass, quagmire

līkšņains *adj* boggy

līkšņainums *nm* swampiness

līkšņājs *nm* morass, quagmire

līkšņibītis *nm* curlew sandpiper

likt I *vt* **1.** put; place; set; apply; (of traps) set out; **l. aiz auss** mark well, take good notice; **l. apsmieklā** make a laughing stock of s.o.; **l. ārā** a. put out; b. evict; **l. atzīmi** give a grade; **l. bankas** (med.) cup; **l. blakus** consider the equivalent of, consider to be comparable to; **l. eksāmenu** take an examination; **l. elpu ciet** choke; **l. gulēt** out to bed; **l. iekšā** a. put in; b. (col. of food) stuff it in; **l. kāju priekšā** trip; **l. kaktā** stand in the corner; **l. kārtis** tell fortune (from cards); **l. kaudzē** heap, pile, stack; **l. kaunā** put to shame; **l. lāgā** note; **l. laukā** (col.) pour it out, unburden oneself; **l. lietā** put to good use; **l. lombardā** pawn; **l. mierā** leave alone; **nelikt mierā** a. bother, pester; importune; b. urge; **l. nelietā** spoil; **l. nobalsot** put to the vote; **l. novārtā** neglect; **l. omā** (obs.) take note; **l. pasjansu** play solitaire; **l. pie kauna staba** pillory; **l. pie malas** set aside; **l. pie sirds** impress upon s.o., lay to heart; **l. prātus kopā** (col.) put our (their) heads together; **l. pretim** a. offer as an equivalent; b. contrast; **l. priekšā** propose; **l. ribās** (col.) stuff oneself; **l. roku uz sirds** swear to the truth; **l. sienu** move hay (to the barn); **l. soļus** (or **soli**) take steps (in walking, skating); **l. uz kādu visas kārtis** bet everything on s.o.; **l. uz zoba** taste; **l. vaļā** pour it out, unburden

oneself; **l. vārdu** name; **l. vērā** take note; **kā ~s** exactly; you can bet on it; **2.** (of floors, tiles, tracks) lay, put down, set; **3.** (with **pie, klāt**) a. add; b. touch; **4.** use for, do sth. with; **5.** *vi* (col.) whack; **l. pa ausi** slap; **6.** *vi* (col.) take off, dash off; **7.** stake; pledge; **l. cerības** stake one's hopes on (sth. or s.o.); **l. uz spēles** stake; **l. visu uz vienas kārts** stake one's all; **l. galvu ķīlā** stake one's life; **l. roku ugunī** stake one's life

likt II *vt* order; make, compel; **l. sveicināt** (col.) send greetings; **l. saprast** give to understand; imply; **l. trūkties** frighten; **kā likts** for sure, sure enough; **lika (drusku) pagaidīt!** (col.) not so fast!

līkt *vi* **1.** bend; **2.** get tired

liktenība *nf* (rare.) fate

liktenīgi *adv* fatally

liktenīgs *adj* fatal

liktenīgums *nm* fatefulness

liktenis *nm* fate; destiny; lot, fortune

likteņa dieves *nf pl* the Fates

likteņa lēmējs *nm* ruler of destiny

likteņceļš *nm* (poet.) course of destiny

likteņgaitas *nf pl* (poet.) course of destiny

likteņgrieži *nm pl* (poet.) historical turn of events

likteņkopība *nf* common destiny

likteņstāsts *nm* (poet.) story of one's destiny

likteņtēma *nf* theme of one's life

likteņtraģēdija *nf* Greek tragedy

likteņupe *nf* river of destiny (poet. epithet for the Daugava)

likteņvējš *nm* (poet.) winds of fate

likteņvētra *nf* (poet.) winds of war

likties I *vr* **1.** lie down; throw oneself down; **l. garšļauku** stretch out, lie down; **l. gulēt** go to bed; **l. uz auss** (also **uz acs, uz vaiga, cisās, migā, slīpi**) turn in; **liecies mierā!** be quiet! leave me alone! **nelikties mierā** persist; **l. uz enkura** drop an anchor; **l. virsū** attack; **2.** dash (away, at, through,

in); **3.** (with **kur**) a. fit; find shelter; b. hide,
escape from; c. find sth. to do; **4.** (col.)
begin, get down to; **5.** get into, be into sth.;
6. command, order, make

likties II *vr* **1.** seem; **kā liekas** apparently,
seemingly, evidently; **l. zināt** show interest;
2. pretend; **nelikties ne zinis** ignore, pretend
not to notice; **nelikties dzirdam** pretend
not to hear

likties III *vr* make, let, allow, usu. in negative
form **nelikties: nelikās divreiz lūgt** he
did not have to be asked twice; **neliecies
traucēties!** don't let us bother you!

liktin *adv emph* of **likt**

līktin *adv emph* of **līkt, nolīkt, salīkt**

liktors *nm* lictor

liku likām *adv* enough and to spare, plenty

līkločū *indecl adj* winding, meandering

līkucis *nm* inlet

līkumainā zarna *nf* ileum

līkumaini *adv* sinuously, winding, curving,
me-andering

līkumainība *nf* windingness, curvature,
sinuosity

līkumains *adj* winding, curving, sinuous,
meandering

līkumainums *nm* windingness, curvature,
sinuosity

likumdevējaa iestāde *nf* legislature

likumdevēja sapulce *nf* legislative assembly

likumdevēj/s *nm*, **~a** *nf* legislator

likumdošana *nf* legislation

likumgrāmata *nf* law book

likumība *nf* **1.** legality; **2.** lawfulness; regularity

likumīgi *adv* **1.** legally; **2.** legitimately;
3. lawfully

likumīgs *adj* **1.** legal; **2.** legitimate; **3.** lawful

likumīgums *nm* **1.** legality; **2.** legitimacy;
3. lawfulness

likumisks *adj* **1.** legal; **2.** lawful

likumkrājums *nm* (legal) code

likumnieks *nm* (obs.) jurist

likumnoteikums *nm* **1.** statute; **2.** legal provision

līkumot *vi* wind, curve, meander

līkumoties *vr* wind, curve, meander

līkumots *adj, part* of **līkumot** winding, curving,
sinuous, meandering

likumpamatots *adj* based in law

likumpārkāpējs *nm* lawbreaker

likumpārkāpums *nm* lawbreaking

likumpratējs *nm*, **~a** *nf* legal expert

likumprojekts *nm* (pol.) bill

likum/s *nm* **1.** law; act; statute; **rakstīti ~i**
statutory law ◊ **~a burts** letter of the law; **~a
pirksts** long arm of the law; **2.** rule

līkums *nm* **1.** curve, bend, turn; **2.** detour,
roundabout way; **tas ir liels l.** this is quite
out of the way; **3.** elbow; loop; curved piece;
(of sausage) link

likumsakarība *nf* lawfulness, regularity

likumsakarīgi *adv* lawfully, regularly

likumsakarīgs *adj* lawful, regular

likumsakarīgums *nm* lawfulness, regularity

likvācija *nf* liquation

likvidācija *nf* liquidation; elimination

likvid[a]tor/s [ā] *nm*, **~e** *nf* liquidator

likvefaktors *nm* liquefacient

likvidambars *nm* liquidamber

likvidēt *vt* **1.** liquidate; **2.** eliminate; abolish;
stamp out; **l. pārrāvumu** close a breach; **l.
šķēršļus** clear and obstacle

likvidēties *vr* liquidate; go out of business;
clear accounts

likviditāte *nf* liquidity

likv[i]ds [ī] *nm* (ling.) liquid

likv[i]ds [ī] *adj* (econ.) liquid

likvors *nm* cerebrospinal fluid

līķa skate *nf* coroner's inquest

līķa nesējs *nm* pallbearer

līķa skatītājs *nm* coroner; medical examiner

līķauts *nm* shroud

liķie[r]a [ŗ] konfekte *nf* liqueur chocolate

liķieris *nm* liqueur

līķis *nm* corpse, (dead) body, cadaver; **dzīvs l.** walking corpse

līķrati *nm pl* hearse

līķu inde *nf* ptomaine

līķu kambaris *nm* (obs.) **1.** mortuary; **2.** vault

lilija *nf* **1.** lily; **2.** (heraldry) fleur-de-lis

lilijveida *indecl adj* lilylike

lilijveidīgi *adv* like a lily

lilijveidīgs *adj* lilylike

liliputs *nm*, ~e *nf* midget; Lilliputian

lillā *indecl adj* (col.) violet

limakoloģija *nf* malacology

limanda *nf* common dab

limāns *nm* liman

limbo *indecl nm* (dance) limbo

limbs *nm* (astron.; angular scale) limb

Limburgas siers *nm* Limburger (cheese)

līme *nf* glue, paste, mucilage

līmen/is *nm* **1.** level; **vienā ~ī** level with; **2.** surface; **3.** standard (of living)

līmeniski *adv* horizontally

līmenisks *adj* horizontal

līmeniskums *nm* horizontality

līmens *adj* (reg.) **1.** drunk; **2.** full to the brim

līmeņa lēciens *nm* leap of level

līmeņa pašrakstītājs *nm* level recorder;

līmeņmērs *nm* gage, watermark post

līmeņrādis *nm* level (leveling instrument)

limerika *nf* limerick

līmes krāsa *nf* casein paint

līmēt *vt* glue, paste

līmetnis *nm* surveyor's level

līmetņot *vt* level

limfa *nf* lymph

limfadenīts *nm* lymphadenitis

limfangīts *nm* lymphangitis

limf[a]tisks [ā] *adj* lymphatic

limfmezgls *nm* lymph gland, lymph node

limfocīts *nm* lymphocyte

limfogranulomatoze *nf* lymphogranuloma-tosis

limfoidāls *adj* lymphoid

limfvads *nm* lymphatic (vessel)

līmīgs *adj* gluey

limitācija *nf* limitation

limit[a]tīvi [ā] *adv* limitatively

limit[a]tīvs [ā] *adj* limitative

limitēt *vt* limit

limitrofs *nm* limitrophe

limits *nm* limit; limitation

līmlente *nf* adhesive tape

limnantems *nm* floating heart

limnisks *adj* limnic

limnoglaciāls *adj* glaciolacustrine

limnogr[a]fs [ā] *nm* limnimeter

limnolo/gs *nm*, ~ģe *nf* limnologist

limnoloģija *nf* limnology

limnoloģiski *adv* limnologically

limnoloģisks *adj* limnological

limnoplanktons *nm* limnic plankton

limonāde *nf* lemonade

limonīts *nm* limonite

limons *nm* limon

limpatu lampatu *adv* (col.) stumbling

līmspiede *nf* gluing press

līmspīles *nf pl* gluing clamp

limt *vi* fold; collapse

limts *nf* straw blanket, straw cover

limuzīns *nm* sedan, limousine

līmveida *indecl adj* glue-like

līmveidīgi *adv* like glue

līmveidīgs *adj* glue-like

līmviela *nf* adhesive

linaita or linaite *nf* (reg.) flax field

linājs *nm* flax field

linaudekls *nm* linen cloth

linaudums *nm* linen

linaudzēšana *nf* cultivation of flax

linaudzētāj/s *nm*, ~a *nf* flax grower

linauts *nm* linen kerchief, linen tablecloth

linbalts *adj* flaxen

linča tiesa *nf* lynch law

linčot *vt* lynch

lindera *nf* spicebush
lindraki or **lindruki** *nm pl* (obs.) skirt
līne *nf* (naut.) line
lineāri *adv* linearly
lineāls *nm* ruler
lineārisms *nm* linearity
line[a]ritāte [ā] *nf* (mus.) linear counterpoint
lineārs *adj* linear
lineļļa *nf* linseed oil
linete *nf* lunette
linga *nf* 1. sling; 2. (col.) go-getter, live wire
lingafonija *nf* language instruction (via recordings); ~**s kabinets** language laboratory
lingafons *nm* tape recorder
linga franka *nf* lingua franca
linglangot *vi* (col.) jingle, ring
lingot *v* 1. *vt* sling; 2. *vi* (col.) stride
lingotāj/s *nm*, ~**a** *nf* slinger
lingvāli *adv* lingually
lingvāls *adj* lingual
lingvistika *nf* linguistics
lingvistiski *adv* linguistically
lingvistisks *adj* linguistic
lingvists *nm*, ~**e** *nf* linguist
lingvoģeogr[a]fisks [ā] *adj* pertaining to linguis-tic geography
lini *nm pl* flax
līnij/a *nf* 1. line; **līka l.** curve; **vienrindu l.** single rank; **lielās** ~**ās** in bold outline; **uz vienas** ~**as** a. all along the line; b. ranges with the best; 2. a Russian linear measure
līnijas režīms *nm* (compu.) on-line processing
līnijburtnīca *nf* ruled exercise book
līnijdroška *nf* (type of carriage) brake
līnijkope *nf* (mus.) staff, stave
līnijkuģis *nm* ship of the line, battleship
līnijmērs *nm* linear measure
līnijnie/ks *nm*, ~**ce** *nf* parade organizer
līnijot *vt* rule (draw lines)
līnijpapīrs *nm* ruled paper
līnijrati *nm pl* (type of carriage) brake

līnijspektrs *nm* line spectrum
līnijtiesa *nf* court of public transportation
līnijtiesnes/is *nm*, ~**e** *nf* linesman
līniju sānskats *nm* (naut.) sheer plan
līniju zīmējums *nm* (naut.) lines plan
līnijveida *indecl adj* linear
līnijveidīgi *adv* linearly
līnijveidīgs *adj* linear
liniments *nm* liniment
liniņi *nm pl* purging flax
līnis *nm* tench
linkāt *vi* lope
linkopība *nf* cultivation of flax
linkopis *nm*, ~**e** *nf* flax grower
linkrusts *nm* linoleum-like wall covering
linlape *nf* bastard toadflax
linmatains *adj* (of hair color) flaxen
linmate *nf* girl with flaxen hair
linmatis *nm* man with flaxen hair
linneja *nf* twinflower
Linneja ozolpaparde *nf* oak fern
linogravīra *nf* linocut
linogrebums *nm* linocut
linogriezēj/s *nm*, ~**a** *nf* linocut artist
linogriezums *nm* linocut
linoksīns *nm* linoxyn
linolejs *nm* linoleum
linolēnskābe *nf* linolenic acid
linolskābe *nf* linoleic acid
linotipists *nm*, ~**e** *nf* linotyper
linotips *nm* Linotype
linpaisis *nm* flax scutch
linsēkla *nf* flaxseed
linsēklu eļļa *nf* linseed oil
linsēklu milti *nm pl* linseed meal
linsēklu rauši *nm pl* linseed cake
linšķiedra *nf* flax fiber
linšot *vt* (folk.) beribbon
linte *nf* ribbon
linu audums *nm* linen
linu idra *nf* a false flax, Camelina linicola
linu kulstāmā lāpstiņa *nf* scutching blade

linu kulstāmā mašīna *nf* scutcher
linu mīstiklas *nf pl* flax brake
linums *nm* mesh, netting
linu plūcamā mašīna *nf* flax puller
linu pogaļa *nf* flax ball
linu pūcīte *nf* flax plusia
linu raizāle *nf* a ryegrass, Lolium remotum
linu starenīte *nf* flaxseed
linu stiebriņi *nm pl* flax stocks
linu vērptuve *nf* flax mill
linu vija *nf* flax dodder
linzīds *nm* silk and linen blend
linzied/i *nm pl* flax flowers; ~u krāsa flax-flower blue
līņāt *vi* drizzle
liofilizācija *nf* lyophilization
liofilizēt *vt* lyophilize
liofils *adj* lyophilic
liofobs *adj* lyophobic
liotrops *adj* lyotropic
līpamība *nf* adhesive power
lipans *adj* sticky
lipare *nf* twayblade
liparīts *nm* rhyolite
lipāze *nf* lipase
līpdadzis *nm* burdock
lipeklīgs *adj* sticky
lipeklis *nm* 1. gluten; 2. decal, sticker; 3. adhesive
lipekļviela *nf* gluten-containing substance
lip[e]mija [ē] *nf* lipemia
lipene *nf* stickseed
līpenēt *vi* flicker
līpeni *adv* stickily
līpens *adj* sticky
līpēt *vi* 1. fly, flutter, stream; 2. flicker
līpēties *vr* 1. fly, flutter, stream; 2. flicker
lipīds *nm* lipid
lipīgā krustaine *nf* viscous groundsel
lipīgā spulgotne *nf* catchfly
lipīgi *adv* stickily
lipīgs *adj* 1. sticky; 2. contagious, infectious

lipīgums *nm* 1. stickiness; 2. contagiousness, in-fectiousness
lipijas *nf pl* Lippia
līpiķis *nm* (col.) flatterer
lipināt *vt* 1. paste, stick; 2. shape (using plastic material); 3. flutter; 4. (of walking) mince
līpināt *vi* 1. fly, flutter, stream; 2. flicker; 3. jog
lipināties *vr* stick to; (fig.) hang around; l. klāt (col.) make up to, ingratiate oneself with
līpināties *vr* 1. climb; 2. stick around; 3. flicker
lipīt *v* 1. *vi* climb; 2. *vi* walk fast; 3. *vt* light; 4. *vt* hit
liplente *nf* Velcro
lipņāt *vi* stick to
lipoma *nf* lipoma
liposoma *nf* liposome
lipotimija *nf* lipothymia
lipotrops *adj* lipotropic
lipšķināties *vr* (col.) make up to, curry favor
lipšķis *nm* (col.) flatterer
lipšus *adv emph* of lipt; l. lipt stick fast
lipt *vi* stick, adhere; l. pie nagiem (col., fig.) have sticky fingers
liptin *adv emph* of lipt; l. lipt be very sticky
lira I *nf* lyre
lira II *nf* lira
lirasputns *nm* lyrebird
lirastis *nm* lyrebird
lirika *nf* lyric poetry
liriķ/is *nm*, ~e *nf* lyric poet
lirināt *vt* warble
liriski *adv* lyrically
lirisks *adj* lyrical
liriskums *nm* lyricism
lirisms *nm* lyricism
liroepika *nf* lyrico-epic poetry
liroepiķ/is *nm*, ~e *nf* lyrico-epic poet
liroepisks *adj* lyrico-epic
lirveida *indecl adj* lyriform
lirveidīgi *adv* in the shape of a lyre

lirveidīgs *adj* lyriform
Lisažū figūras *nf pl* Lissajou figures
lisimetrs *nm* lysimeter
līst I *vi* **1.** creep, crawl; **l. acīs** (col.) make oneself very visible, call attention to oneself; **l. cilpā** stick one's neck out; **l. cisās** (or **migā**) go to bed; **l. virsū** thrust oneself upon s.o.; **2. l. ārā** a. crawl out; b. protrude; **l. (vai) no ādas ārā** (col.) lean over backwards; **lien kā adata** (it) slips in easily; **3.** (col.) go into, fit; **cik tik lien** as much as possible; (of eating) as much as one can; (of stuffing) as much as it will hold; **4.** (col.) grovel, fawn; **l. uz vēdera** (col.) grovel, fawn; **l. bez ziepēm** brownnose
līst II *vt* **1.** clear land (to make it tillable); **2.** grub
liste *nf* list
līste *nf* lath; batten
listerioze *nf* listerellosis
listers *nm* lister
listīte *nf dim* of **liste**, short list
līstīte *nf dim* of **līste**, thin lath
lišķēt *vi* flatter, adulate
lišķētāj/s *nm*, **~a** *nf* flatterer
lišķība *nf* flattery, adultation
lišķīgi *adv* flatteringly, ingratiatingly
lišķīgs *adj* flattering, ingratiating
lišķīgums *nm* servility
lišķ/is *nm*, **~e** *nf* flatterer, adulator; toady
lišķmē/lis *nm*, **~e** *nf* (col.) flatterer
lišķmut/is *nm*, **~e** *nf* (col.) flatterer
līšus *adv* crawling, creeping, on all fours
līt *vi* **1.** pour, stream, run; **l. pāri** overflow; **2.** rain
lit|a|nija [ā] *nf* litany
litauris *nm* (folk.) gray (Lithuanian) hare
lītavas *nf pl* prolonged rain
litenietis *nm* a Latvian folk dance
litera *nf* (typ.) type
literāri *adv* literarily
literāriski *adv* literarily

literārisks *adj* literary
liter|a|rizēt [ā] *vt* make literary; include in a literary work; render in a literary style
literārkritisks *adj* = **literātūrkritisks**
literārs *adj* literary
literas biļete *nf* military personnel ticket
literāt/s *nm*, **~e** *nf* man of letters, writer, litterateur
liter|a|tūra [ā] *nf* literature; **ieteicama l.** books recommended
liter|a|tūras [ā] saraksts *nm* bibliography
liter|a|tūrkritika [ā] *nf* literary criticism
liter|a|tūrkritiķ/is [ā] *nm*, **~e** *nf* literary critic
liter|a|tūrkritiski [ā] *adv* from the point of view of literary criticism
liter|a|tūrkritisks [ā] *adj* of literary criticism
liter|a|tūrteorētiķ/is [ā] *nm*, **~e** *nf* literary theorist
liter|a|tūrteorētisks [ā] *adj* of literary theory
liter|a|tūrteorija [ā] *nf* theory of literature
liter|a|tūrvēsture [ā] *nf* history of literature, literary history
liter|a|tūrvēsturiski [ā] *adv* from the point of view of the history of literature
liter|a|tūrvēsturisks [ā] *adj* pertaining to the history of literature
liter|a|tūrvēsturnie/ks [ā] *nm*, **~ce** *nf* literary historian
liter|a|tūrzinātne [ā] *nf* study of literature
liter|a|tūrzinātnie/ks [ā] *nm*, **~ce** *nf* specialist in literature, literary scholar
liters *nm* (RR) free pass
litijs *nm* lithium
lītin *adv emph* of **līt**; **l. lija** it poured
lītis *nf pl* (reg.) ice floes
litisks *adj* lytic
lītņa *nf* (reg.) prolonged rain
litofāgi *nm pl* stone destroying organisms
litofīts *nm* lithophyte
litoglifija *nf* lithoglyptics
litoglifs *nm* lithoglyph
litografēt *vt* lithograph

litogr|a|fija |ā| *nf* 1. lithography; 2. lithograph

litogr|a|fiski |ā| *adv* lithographically

litogr|a|fisks |ā| *adj* lithographic

litogr|a|f/s |ā| *nm,* ~e *nf* lithographer

litoġen|e|ze |ē| *nf* lithogenesis

litoksils *nm* lithoxyl

litoloġija *nf* lithology

litopans *nm* lithopone

litorāls *nm* littoral

litorāls *adj* littoral

litosf|ai|ra |ē| *nf* lithosphere

litota *nf* litotes

litotomija *nf* lithotomy

litotriptisks *adj* lithontriptic

litrāža *nf* capacity in liters, capacity of liters

litrīgs *adj* one-liter

litrs *nm* liter

lits *nm* lit

līts *nf* chunk of ice

lituānisms *nm* Lithuanism

liturgs *nm* liturgist

liturġētika *nf* liturgiology

liturġija *nf* liturgy

liturġisks *adj* liturgical

līvis *nm* a type of seine net

livistona *nf* Chinese fan palm

Livonijas ordenis *nm* Teutonic Order of Knights

livra *nf* livre

livreja *nf* livery

livrs *nm* livre

līvs *nm* (obs.) Liv

lizd- See **ligzd-**

lize *nf* peel (bread shovel)

līze *nf* lysis

lizimetrija *nf* lysimetry

lizimetrs *nm* lysimeter

līzings *nm* leasing

lizīns *nm* lysine

lizols *nm* Lysol

līžņa *nf, nm* toady

līžņāt *vi* creep, crawl; slither

ljē *indecl nf* league

loaza *nf* loasa

loazelerija *nf* Alpine azalea

lobārs *adj* lobate

lobēlij/a *nf* lobelia

lobiens *nm* (col.) run

lobijs *nm* (pol.) lobby

lobījums *nm* 1. shelling, husking, peeling; 2. stubble plowing

lobisms *nm* lobbying, lobbyism

lobists *nm* lobbbyist

lobīt *vt* 1. shell, hull; husk; peel; 2. plow down the stubble, stir

lobītājs *nm* 1. sheller, husker, peeler; ~a *nf*; 2. stubble plow

lobītava *nf* (foundry) dressing shop

lobīties *vr* peel; (of cement) spall

loblolli priede *nf* loblolly pine

lobmašīna *nf* veneer lathe

lobt *vi* (col.) run

lobties *vr* (reg.) have success

lobulārs *adj* lobular

locekl/is *nm* 1. limb; 2. member; ~e *nf*; 3. (of a chain) link; 4. part

loceklītis *nm* 1. *dim* of **loceklis**, little limb; 2. (bot.) rachilla

locenieks *nm* 1. maker of shaft bows; 2. archer

lo|ch|ijas |h| *nf pl* lochia

locija *nf* 1. pilotism; 2. pilot chart

locījums *nm* 1. fold, bend; 2. (gram.) case

locīkla *nf* joint

locīklsavienojums *nm* articulated coupling

lociņi *nm pl dim* of **loki**, chives

lociņinstruments *nm* bowed string instrument

lociņš *nm dim* of **loks**, (mus.) bow

locis I (with ô) *nm* bend

locis II *nm* 1. (naut.) pilot; 2. pilot fish

locīšana *nf* 1. declension; 2. conjugation; 3. (in folk singing) modulation

locīt *vt* 1. fold; **l. iekšā** (col.) eat, put away; **l. pūru** (folk.) make one's trousseau; 2. bend;

bow; **l. ceļus** genuflect; (fig.) kowtow; **3.** (in folk singing) modulate; **4.** (gram.) decline; **5.** (gram.) conjugate

locītāja *nf* (in folk singing) modulator

locītāj/s *nm*, **~a** *nf* folder, bender

locītava *nf* joint

locītavu stingums *nm* anchylosis

locīties *vr* **1.** bend; bow; sway; **2.** writhe

locmanis *nm* (naut.) pilot

ločains *adj* curving, meandering

lodalva *nf* solder

lodāmurs *nm* soldering iron

lodāt *vi* (of small animals) crawl back and forth, scurry

loddeglis *nm* soldering torch

lo/de I *nf* **1.** sphere; ball; **2.** (sports equipment) shot; **3.** bullet; (artillery) shell; **~žu necaurlai-dīgs** bulletproof; **zem ~dēm** under fire; **4.** plumb bob

lode II *nf* solder

lodējamība *nf* solderability

lodējums *nm* soldering, soldered place

lodeklis *nm* plumbline

lodens *adj* (reg.) smooth

loderēt *vi* (barb.) loaf, laze

loderis *nm* (barb.) lazy bum

lodes grūdēj/s *nm*, **~a** *nf* shot-putter

lodes grūšana *nf* shot put

lodes savienojums *nm* ball and socket joint

lodes vējš *nm* (reg.) northwesterly

lodēt *vt* solder; braze

lodētājs *nm*, **~a** *nf* solderer; brazer

lodis *nm* (reg.) northwesterly

lodīšspalva *nf* ballpoint pen

lodīšu gultnis *nm* ball bearing; **aksiāls l. g.** thrust ball bearing

lodīte *nf dim* of **lode** I, small ball; bead; globule; pellet

lodlampa *nf* blowtorch

lodmērs *nm* plumb line

lodmet[all]s [āl] *nm* solder

lodoicejas *nf pl* Lodoicea

lodūdens *nm* flux

lodveida *indecl adj* spherical, globular, ball-shaped

lodveidīgi *adv* spherically

lodveidīgs *adj* spherical, globular, ball-shaped

lodziņš *nm dim* of **logs**, small window, ticket of-fice window, teller's window

lodžija *nf* loggia

lofants *nm* giant hyssop

logaile *nf* window opening

logains *adj* checkered

loga režģis *nm* sash

logaritmēt *vt* find the logarithm of

logaritmiski *adv* logarithmically

logaritmisks *adj* logarithmic

logaritms *nm* logarithm

logaritmu lineāls *nm* slide rule

loga spraislis *nm* muntin

loga statnis *nm* mullion

logāt *vt* (naut., of a ship's speed) log

logats or **logāts** *nm* **1.** frame; **2.** (arch.) coffer

loga vāks *nm* (naut.) deadlight

loga vērtnis *nm* casement

logdurvis *nf pl* French window

logers *nm* (naut.) lugger

logkars *nm* curtain

logo *indecl nm* (typ.) logotype

logodedalija *nf* logodaedaly

logodiareja *nf* logorrhea

logogr[a]fs [ā] *nm* logograph

logogrifs *nm* logogriph

logoma[ch]ija [h] *nf* logomachy

logoneiroze *nf* stuttering

logop[a]tija [ā] *nf* speech defect

logop[a]ts [ā] *nm*, **~e** *nf* person with a speech defect

logopēdija *nf* logopedics

logopēdiski *adv* logopedically

logopēdisks *adj* logopedic

logopēd/s *nm*, **~e** *nf* speech therapist

logoss *nm* Logos

logotips *nm* logotype

logs *nm* window; **dubultais l.** storm window; **priekšējais l.** windshield; **uzbīdāms** (or **ceļams**) **l.** sash window; **virsdurvju l.** transom

logsega *nf* curtain

logsna *nf* windowsill

logsols *nm* windowsill

logšķērsis *nm* mullion

loģicisms *nm* logicism

loģika *nf* logic

loģiķ/is *nm*, **~e** *nf* logician

loģiski *adv* logically

loģisks *adj* logical

loģiskums *nm* logicality

loģisms *nm* logical conclusion

loģistika *nf* **1.** mathematical logic, logistic; **2.** logistics

loģistiski *adv* logistically

loģistisks *adj* logistic

loģist/s *nm*, **~e** *nf* logician

lojāli *adv* loyally

loj[a]litāte [ā] *nf* loyalty

lojāls *adj* loyal

lojālums *nm* loyalty

loka *nf* (barb.) curl

lokācija *nf* location

loka cirkulis *nm* bow compass

lokaila *nf* vaulted passage; opening with an arched lintel

lokains *adj* (barb.) curly

loka kanāls *nm* (anat.) semicircular canal

loka lampa *nf* arc lamp

lokāli *adv* locally

lokālisms *nm* localism

lok[a]litāte [ā] *nf* locality

lok[a]lizācija [ā] *nf* localization

lok[a]lizējums [ā] *nm* localization

lok[a]lizēt [ā] *vt* localize

lok[a]lizēties [ā] *vr* become localized

lokālpatriotiski *adv* in a narrowly patriotic way

lokālpatriotisks *adj* narrowly patriotic

lokālpatriotisms *nm* narrow patriotism

lokālpatriot/s *nm*, **~e** *nf* narrow patriot

lokāls *nm* local bar; local restaurant

lokāls *adj* local

lokālums *nm* localness

loka mērs *nm* circular measure

loka metināšana *nf* arc welding

lokāmība *nf* **1.** flexibility, pliability; **2.** (fig.) tractability, manageability; **3.** (gram.) declinability

lokāms *adj, part* of **locīt 1.** flexible, pliable; **2.** tractable, manageable; **3.** (gram.) declinable

lokanā najāda *nf* a naiad, Najas flexilis

lokani *adv* flexibly, pliantly; supplely

lokanība *nf* flexibility, pliancy; suppleness

lokans *adj* flexible, pliant; supple

lokanums *nm* flexibility, pliancy; suppleness

lokāt *vt* (barb.) curl

lokāties *vr* (barb.) curl

lok[a]tīvs [ā] *nm* (gram.) locative case

lokators *nm* locator

lokaugļu zvērene *nf* yellow rocket

lokauts *nm* lockout

lokgabals *nm* curved piping

loki *nm pl* green onions

lokizlāde *nf* arc discharge

lokmala *nf* undressed side of lumber

lokomobile *nf* locomobile, threshing engine

lokomotīve *nf* locomotive, engine

lokomotīves vadītājs *nm* locomotive engineer

lokomotīvist/s *nm*, **~e** *nf* locomotive engineer

lokomotīvju halle *nf* locomotive shed

lokot *vt* (barb.) curl

lokoties *vr* (barb.) curl

loks *nm* **1.** arc; arch; bow; loop; **2.** shaft bow; **3.** range; **4.** circle; circular route; **apburtais l.** vicious circle; **polārais l.** Arctic Circle; **~ā** in a circle

loksne *nf* (paper, glass, metal) sheet

loksnes korektūra *nf* page proof

loksnīte *nf dim* of **loksne**, small sheet

loksodrome *nf* loxodrome, rhumb line

loksodromisks *adj* loxodromic

loksokosms *nm* loxocosm

lokspuldze *nf* arc lamp

lokšķēres *nf pl* curling iron

lokšņgriezis *nm* (typ.) sheeter

lokumaini *adv* sinuously, winding

lokumain/s *adj* winding, curving

lokumoti *adv* sinuously, winding

lokumots *adj* winding, curving

lokums *nm* curve, bend, turn

lokuss *nm* locus

lokveida *adj* arched, bow-shaped

lokveidā *adv* in a curve, arched

lokveidīgi *adv* in an arc

lokveidīgs *adj* arched, bow-shaped

lokzāģis *nm* web saw

lokzarna *nf* colon

lolojums *nm* **1.** pet, darling; **2.** cherished thing or idea

lolot *vt* **1.** nurse; **2.** pamper; **3.** cherish

lom/a *nf* role, part, character; **l. bez vārdiem** walk-on; **galvenā l.** leading role, lead; **galvenās ~as tēlotājs** leading man; **galvenās ~s tēlotāja** leading lady; **mainītās ~ās** (fig.) the tables are turned

lombarda kvīts *nf* pawn ticket

lombardēt *vt* pawn

lombards *nm* pawnshop

lombrs *nm* (card game) ombre

lomiem *adv* (obs.) at times

lomīgs *adj* (reg.) successful

loms *nm* **1.** (of fish) catch; harvest; **2.** (obs.) while, spell; **3.** (reg.) (hay) mow

londoniet/is *nm*, **~e** *nf* Londoner

lone *nf* (barb.) wage

lonēt *vi* (barb., *3rd pers*) **lonē** it pays

longans *nm* longan

longete *nf* (med.) plaster cast

longitudināls *adj* longitudinal

lonēa *nf* **1.** suspension harness; **2.** longe

lonžerons *nm* (aeron.) longeron; spar

loparīts *nm* loparite

lopārstniecība *nf* large animal veterinary medicine

lopārst/s *nm*, **~e** *nf* large animal veterinary

lopbarība *nf* cattle feed, forage, fodder

lopbarības augi *nm pl* fodder crops;

lopbarības b[a]ze [ā] *nf* forage reserve

lopbarības biete *nf* mangel-wurzel

lopbarības rauši *nm pl* cattle cakes

lopceļš *nm* cow path, pasture road

lopdzinējs *nm*, **~a** *nf* cattle driver

lopēdiens *nm* (obs.) cattle feed

lopezijas *nf pl* Lopezia

lopgans *nm*, **~e** *nf* cattle herder

lopība *nf* brutishness

lopiski *adv* brutally, brutishly

lopisks *adj* brutal, brutish

lopiskums *nm* brutality, brutishness

lopkautuve *nf* slaughterhouse

lopkopēj/s *nm*, **~a** *nf* cowman, livestock tender, stockkeeper

lopkopība *nf* stock raising

lopkopības banka *nf* livestock bank

lopkopības farma *nf* ranch

lopkopības saimniecība *nf* livestock farm

lopkop/is *nm*, **~e** *nf* **1.** stockbreeder; **2.** = **lopkopējs**

lopmuižiņa *nf* (hist.) small livestock farm

lop/s *nm* **1.** animal; **~i** livestock, cattle; **2.** (fig.) beast, brute

lopu ārsts *nm* (large animal) veterinary

lopu biete *nf* mangel-wurzel

lopu ceļš *nm* cowpath, pasture road

lopu dārzs *nm* corral

lopu deķis *nm* blanket for carrying mowed grass

lopu dundurs *nm* botfly

lopu farma *nf* ranch

lopu gatve *nf* cattle path

lopu izstāde *nf* livestock show

lopu krišana *nf* loss of cattle, cattle plague

lopu meita *nf* cowgirl

lopu mēris *nm* rinderpest;
lopu rācenis *nm* turnip
lopu sērga *nf* cattle disease
lopu tirgotājs *nm* cattle dealer
lopu vagons *nm* stockcar
lopu zīme *nf* brand
lopuž/i *nm pl*; ~os iet (folk.) drive the bride's cattle to the bridegroom's house
lorants *nm* loranth
lorbēres *nf pl* bay leaves
lordkanclers *nm* lord chancellor
lordmērs *nm* lord mayor
lordoze *nf* lordosis
lords *nm* lord
lordu palāta *nf* House of Lords
lorencijs *nm* lawrencium
lorijs *indecl nm* lory
loris *nm* loris
loriņi *nm pl* (sl.) junk, stuff
lornete *nf* lorgnette
losains *adj* spotted
losions *nm* lotion
losis *nm* dun horse
losītis *nm* dun horse
losjons *nm* lotion
losms *nm* tall, thin person
loss *adj* dun
losums *nm* dun color
lote I *nf* (naut.) sounder; counterweight
lote II (with uo) *nf* Russian ounce
loterija *nf* lottery
lotlīne *nf* sounding line
loto *nm indecl* lotto
lotospuķe *nf* lotus
lotoss *nm* lotus
lourensijs *nm* lawrencium
lovelass *nm* lothario
lozberlapas *nf pl* bay leaves
loze *nf* lottery ticket; lot; **pilna l.** prize-winning ticket; **tukša l.** blank
lozēt *vi* draw lots
lozungs *nm* slogan; catchword

lož/a I *nf* 1. theater box; ~u slēdzējs boxkeeper; 2. lodge
loža II (with uo) *nf, nm* snooper
ložberis *nm* (poet.) machine gun
ložmetējlente *nf* machine gun belt
ložmetējligzda *nf* machine gun emplacement
ložmetējnie/ks *nm*, ~ce *nf* machine gunner
ložmetējrati *nm pl* wheeled machine gun
ložmetējs *nm* machine gun
ložmetis *nm* (obs.) machine gun
ložņa *nf, nm* 1. snooper; 2. teal
ložņāt *vi* 1. creep, crawl; slither; 2. snoop around
ložņātājs *nm*, ~a *nf* snooper
ložņaugs *nm* (bot.) creeper
ložņīgais dzeltenājs *nm* moneywort
ložņīgais kārkls *nm* creeping willow
ložņīgā vīrcele *nf* pale-blue toadflax
ložņīgie platkājiņi *nm pl* wood cinquefoil
ložņīgs *adj* (bot.) creeping
ložņu *indecl adj* (bot.) creeping
ložņu blaktene *nf* restharrow
ložņu cekuliņi *nm pl* bugle
ložņu gundega *nf* creeping buttercup
ložņu saulenīte *nf* rattlesnake plantain
ložu dzirnas *nf pl* ball mill
ložu slēdzējs *nm* boxkeeper
luba *nf* 1. spruce or linden bark; 2. roof shingle
lubenīca *nf* (col.) literary trash
lubinieks *nm*, ~ce *nf* producer of trashy literature or art
lubiņa *nf* 1. *dim* of luba, piece of spruce or linden bark; 2. roof shingle
lubraks *nm* (com.) clumsy oaf
lubrik[a]tors [ā] *nm* lubricator
lubstājs *nm* eaves beam (a combination of eaves board and gutter in rural shake roof construction)
lubu literātūra *nf* literary trash
lubu romāns *nm* dime novel
lucerna *nf* alfalfa
lucernas blakts *nf* alfalfa plant bug

luciferīns *nm* luciferin

lūcinieks *nm*, **~ce** *nf* barker (one that removes bark)

lūciņš *nm dim* of **lūks** I, bast

lucis *nm* = **lucītis**

lucītis *nm* viviparous blenny

lucs *nm* Lutz

lučiņa *nf* (barb.) pacifier

ludotēka *nf* therapeutic playroom

lūdzam/s *adj, part* of **lūgt** **1.** prayer (*adj*); **~ā die-na** day of penitence; **2. ne l.** even if you plead-ed with him; **3.** *interj* please

lūdzēj/s *nm*, **~a** *nf* supplicant; applicant; petitioner

lūdzin *adv emph* of **lūgt**

ludziņa *nf* playlet

lūdzoši *adv* pleadingly

lūdzošs *adj, part* of **lūgt** pleading

lūdzu *interj* **1.** please; **2.** you are welcome; **3.** (in giving, handing over) here you are

luess *nm* syphilis

lufa *nf* luffa

lufars *nm* bluefish

luga *nf* (theat.) play

lugiņš *nm* viviparous blenny

lūgsna *nf* prayer

lūgsnu grāmata *nf* book of prayers

lūgšana *nf* prayer, praying

lūgšanās *nfr* pleading; entreaty, supplication

lūgšanu krelles *nf pl* rosary, prayer beads

lūgšus *adv* **1.** *emph* of **lūgt**; **2.** by asking, by pleading

lūgt *vt* **1.** ask, ask for, beg; **laipni lūdzam** you are welcome; **l. dāvanas** beg, panhandle; **l. vārdu** (parl.) ask to be recognized; **2.** invite; **l. viesos** invite (to one's house); **l. pusdienās** ask to dinner; **l. pie galda** ask to table; **l. uz deju** ask to dance; **l. roku** ask for a woman's hand; **3.** plead with; **l. par kādu** plead for s.o.; **4. l. Dievu** pray (to God)

lūgties *vr* plead with, plead for (mercy, forgiveness); entreat, implore

lūgtin *adv emph* of **lūgt**; **l. lūgt** entreat

lūgtum *interj* please

lūgumraksts *nm* petition; application

lūgums *nm* **1.** request; **2.** appeal; **3.** petition

lugu rakstnieks *nm* playwright

luģe *nf* (reg.) ski; snowshoe

luidors *nm* luis d'or

luizīts *nm* lewisite

lūk *interj* look; there; lo; behold

lūka *nf* trapdoor; hatch, hatchway; scuttle

lukarna *nf* dormer window

lūkas *nf pl* (reg.) baby shower

lūkauts *nm* (naut.) lookout, crow's nest

lūkības *nf pl* (reg.) baby shower

lūkkurpīte *nf* columbine

lūkmanis *nm* (folk.) one who is looking for a wife

luknība *nf* flexibility

lukns *adj* flexible

luknums *nm* flexibility

lūkojums *nm* essay

lūkot *vt* (col.) **1.** look at, check to see; **ar grei-zu aci l.** look askance; cast a baleful eye; **2.** try, attempt

lūkotava *nf* observatory

lūkoties *vr* look at; **sievas l.** (obs.) look for a wife

lūk/s I *nm*, usu. *pl* **~i** bast; **~u vīzes** bast shoes; **pilns kā l.** drunk as a lord

lūks II *nm* scout; one looking for a bride

luksācija *nf* luxation

luksemburģietis *nm*, **~e** *nf* Luxembourger

luksmetrs *nm* luxmeter

lūksna or **lūksne** *nf* living bark, phloem; bast

lūksngrauži *nm pl* bark beetles

luksofors *nm* traffic signal

lukss I *nm* lux

lukss II *nm* luxury

luksts I *nm* broad-leaved wetland plant

luksts II *nm* lowland meadow, marshy meadow

lukstu čakstīte *nf* whinchat

lukstu purva ķauķis *nm* marsh warbler

luksusa *indecl adj* luxurious, deluxe

luksuss *nm* luxury

lūkša *nf*, usu. *pl* ~**as 1.** blacksmith's tongs; **2.** (of animals) front teeth

lukta *nf* choir loft; loft above the threshing floor

lukturis *nm* **1.** lantern; lamp; **2.** candlestick

lukturītis *nm* **1.** *dim* of **lukturis**, little lantern; **2.** flashlight; **3.** (of automotive vehicles) light, side marker light, tag light

lukubrācija *nf* lucubration

lukulliski *adv* in a lucullan manner

lukullisks *adj* lucullan

lūku vīzes *nf pl* bast shoes

lulināt *v* **1.** *vi* sough; **2.** *vt* (reg.) pamper

lūlināt *vi* (of wind instruments) blow, play

lullināt *vt* (of a baby) rock

lūlot *vi* (of wind instruments) blow, play

lumbago *indecl nm* lumbago

lūmens *nm* lumen

lumināls *nm* Luminal, phenobarbital

lumin[a]tors [ā] *nm* luminescent object or substance

luminescence *nf* luminescence

luminescents *adj* luminescent

luminescēt *vi* luminesce

luminofors *nm* phosphor

lumme *nf* guillemot

lumpačot *vi* (col.) waddle

lumpenizācija *nf* reduction to the state of lumpenproletariat

lumpis *nm* galoot

lumpurīgi *adv* gawkily, clumsily

lumpurīgs *adj* ungainly, gawky, clumsy

lumstīties *vr* **1.** make up to s.o.; **2.** (of dogs) wag one's tail, act friendly

lumsts *nm* **1.** (weav.) lease rod; **2.** pine splint

lumza *nm* klutz

lumzaks *nm* (col.) klutz

lumzāt *vi* (col.) toddle

lumzīgi *adv* clumsily

lumzīgs *adj* (col.) clumsy

lumža *nm* = **lumza**

lunaparks *nm* amusement park

lunārijs *nm* lunarium

lunārs *adj* lunar

lunātiķ/is *nm*, ~**e** *nf* lunatic

lunātisms *nm* **1.** lunacy; **2.** somnambulism

lunceklis *nm* (col.) **1.** flatterer; **2.** toady

luncīgi *adv* obsequiously

luncīgs *adj* (col.) obsequious

luncināt *vt* (of one's tail) wag

luncināties *vr* **1.** (of dogs) wag one's tail, act friendly; **2.** make up to, ingratiate oneself with

lunete *nf* lunette

lunīts *nm* moonrock

lunka *nf* (reg.) fishing boat harbor

lunkani *adv* flexibly, pliantly, supplely

lunkanība *nf* flexibility, pliancy, suppleness

lunkans *adj* flexible, pliant, supple

lunkanums *nm* flexibility, pliancy, suppleness

lunkāt *vi* (reg.) drag

lunkmēl/is *nm*, ~**e** *nf* (col.) flatterer

lunomobilis *nm* lunar exploratory vehicle

luņķis *nm* **1.** (of sausage) piece, link; **2.** cigar

lupa *nf* magnifying glass

lūpa *nf* lip; **gaŗā l.** long face

lupanārs *nm* lupanar

lūpas šķeltne *nf* harelip

lupat/a *nf* **1.** rag; ~**u** ~**ās** or ~**u lēveros** in tatters; **2.** (cont.) coward

lupatainis *nm* tatterdemalion

lupatains *adj* tattered

lupatdeķis *nm* (obs.) rag rug

lupatlas/is *nm*, ~**e** *nf* ragpicker, tatter

lupatlēveros *adv* in tatters

lupatnieks *nm* ragpicker, tatter

lūpenis *nm* (ling.) labial

luperkāliji *nm pl* Lupercalia

lupīna *nf* lupine

lupināt *vt* **1.** peel, shell; **2.** (of food) crumble, nibble at

lups *nm* lupus

lupsna *nf* **1.** bark; spruce bark (for use in tanning); **2.** sliver

lupstājs *nm* lovage

lupt *vi* peel, come off

lūpu krāsa *nf* lip gloss

lūpu lācis *nm* sloth bear

lupulīns *nm* lupulin

lupuss *nm* lupus

lūpu zīmulis *nm* lipstick

lūpzieēi *nm pl* Labiatae, Lamiaceae

lūrēt *vi* (col.) peer, spy

lūriķis *nm* (col.) lurker, spy

lūrmanis *nm* (col.) lurker, spy

lūsināties *vr* (col.) look

lūsis *nm* lynx

lust *vi* hang limply

lūstamība *nf* breakability, (of metals) shortness

luste *nf* (barb.) desire; enjoyment

lustes *nf pl* (bot.) chess

lustēt *vi* = **lustēties**

lustēties *vr* (barb.) enjoy oneself, have fun

lustīgi *adv* (barb.) merrily

lustīgs *adj* (barb.) merry

lustināt *vt* (obs.) entertain

lūstošs *adj, part* of **lūzt** breakable, brittle, fragile; breaking

lustra *nf* chandelier

lūšāda *nf* lynx fur

lūškas *nf pl* (reg.) blacksmith's tongs

lutausis *nm* lop-eared animal; lop-eared person

lut|e|cijs [ē] *nm* lutetium

luteīns *nm* lutein

lutekl/is *nm*, **~e** *nf* pet, favorite

luteolīns *nm* luteolin

luterān/is *nm*, **~e** *nf* Lutheran

luterāniski *adv* in the Lutheran manner

luterānisks *adj* Lutheran

luterānisms *nm* Lutheranism

luteriet/is *nm*, **~e** *nf* Lutheran

luteriski *adv* according to Lutheranism

luterisk/s *adj* Lutheran

luterisms *nm* Lutheranism

luterticība *nf* Lutheranism

luterticīgs *adj* Lutheran

lutināt *vt* pamper, spoil

lutināties *vr* pamper oneself

lutīts *nm* lime mud

lūvēt *vi* (naut.) luff

lūza *nf* windfall

luzbas *nf pl* fragments

luzbot *vi* split off

lūzeni *adv* brittly, fragilely

lūzens *adj* brittle, fragile

lūzīgi *adv* brittly, fragilely

lūzīgs *adj* brittle, fragile

lūzin *adv emph* of **lūzt; sirds viņai l. lūza** she was heart-broken

lūzma *nf* (col.) pile, heap, large quantity

lūznājs *nm* pile of junk; junk yard

lūzt *vi* **1.** break; be refracted; **lai tur lūst vai plīst** no matter what, at any cost; **2. l. no (kā)** be jam- packed with, be crammed

lūztin *adv emph* of **lūzt**, (of breaking) completely, clear through

lūzums *nm* **1.** break, fracture; **2.** (sudden) change, turn

luža *nf* wooden clog (without heel or counter)

lūžņa *nf* **1.** junk pile; junk yard; **2.** windfallen trees and branches

lūžņains *adj* junky

lūžņas *nf pl* (reg.) blacksmith's tongs

lūžņi *nm pl* scrap

Ļ

ļakačas *nf pl* gossip

ļana *nf* llano

ļanosi *nm pl* llanos

ļāpāt *vi* (col.) walk

ļapata *interj* See ļipata

ļaras *nf pl* (com.) gossip

ļaudava *nf* (folk.) bride, betrothed

ļaudaviņa *nf dim* of ļaudava, bride

ļaudīgums *nm* population density

ļau/dis *nm pl* 1. people; jaunie ļ. a. young people; b. newlyweds; vienkārši ļ. simple folk ◊ ~žu valodas people talking, what people are saying, talk of the town; kādu ~žu? from what parts? tādu ~žu (obs.) pregnant; 2. (folk.) lower upper class (free, non-indentured persons); hired hands, servants

ļaugani *adv* flabbily, flaccidly, limply

ļaugans *adj* flabby, flaccid, limp

ļauja *nf* (obs.) permission, leave

ļauki *adv* floppily

ļauks *adj* floppy

ļaunā gundega *nf* celery-leaved crowfoot

ļaunais *nom adj* the evil one, Satan

ļaundabība *nf* malignancy

ļaundabīgi *adv* malignantly

ļaundabīgs *adj* malignant

ļaundabīgums *nm* malignancy

ļaundabis *nm* evil person

ļaundarība *nf* villainy, evil deed, crime

ļaundarīgi *adv* villainously, maliciously

ļaundarīgs *adj* villainous, malicious

ļaundar/is *nm*, ~e *nf* evildoer, malefactor, villain

ļaundarīt *vi* wrong

ļaundomīgi *adv* suspiciously

ļaundomīgs *adj* suspicious

ļauneklis *nm* evil person

ļaunestība *nf* malice, malevolence

ļaun/i *adv* 1. badly; jo ~āk so much the worse; 2. maliciously; 3. angrily

ļaunība *nf* malice, malevolence

ļaunīgi *adv* maliciously; viciously

ļaunīgs *adj* evil; malicious; vicious

ļaunoties *vr* 1. be angry with s.o.; 2. take offense

ļaunpieminīgi *adv* by way of remembering wrongs

ļaunpieminīgs *adj* remembering wrongs

ļaunprātība *nf* malice

ļaunprātīgi *adv* maliciously

ļaunprātīgs *adj* malicious

ļaunprātīgums *nm* maliciousness

ļaunprāt/is *nm*, ~e *nf* malicious person

ļaunpriecīgi *adv* delighting in others' misfortune

ļaunpriecīgs *adj* delighting in others' misfortune

ļaun/s *adj* 1. evil; kas tur ļ.? what's the harm? 2. bad; ill; unlucky; 3. malicious; 4. (col.) an-gry; 5. *pl* ~ie evil persons, evildoers

ļaunticība *nf* bad faith

ļaunticīgs *adj* bad faith (*adj*)

ļaunums *nm* 1. evil; 2. harm

ļaunumzāle *nf* baneberry

ļaunvēlība *nf* malevolence, ill will

ļaunvēlīgi *adv* malevolently

ļaunvēlīgs *adj* malevolent

ļaunvēlīgums *nm* malevolence

ļaunvēl/is *nm*, ~e *nf* ill-wisher

ļaupata *nf* flap

ļaut *vt* allow, permit; let; ļ. vaļu give vent to; give free rein to

ļauties *vr* 1. yield to, give way to; abandon oneself to; 2. allow

ļautiņi *nm pl dim* of ļaudis, good folks

ļautiņputra *nf* a dish of curdled milk and ground roasted rye

ļaužu bende *nm* sweater, exploiter

ļaužu istaba *nf* (hist.) servants' room

ļaueu ķēķis *nm* soup kitchen

ļaužu skaitīšana *nf* census

ļavēt *vi* quiver

ļāvīgi *adv* permissively; yieldingly

ļāvīgs *adj* permissive; yielding

ļebene *nf* slouch hat

ļegani *adv* limply; flabbily; flaccidly

ļegans *adj* limp; flabby; flaccid

ļegatas *nf pl* (com.) gossip, tales

ļeka I *nf* dab, lump, pat

ļeka II *nf* loop

ļeka III *nf,* usu. *pl* ~s feet (in col. phrase **laist**
~s **vaļā** take to one's feet)

ļekans *adj* **1.** limp, flabby; **2.** (col.) wet

ļekāt *vi* (col.) **1.** walk fast; **2.** run, lope

ļekata *nf* foot

ļekatas I *nf pl* tatters

ļekatas II *nf pl* (reg.) gossip

ļekatāt *vi* toddle

ļekāties *vr* wobble

ļekatot *vi* toddle

ļekausis *nm* floppy-eared one

ļekot *vi* (col.) **1.** walk fast; **2.** run, lope

ļekstēt *vi* bark

ļembasts *nm* (com.) hullabaloo

ļempurot *vi* (com.) toddle

ļengani *adv* limply; flabbily; flaccidly

ļengans *adj* limp; flabby; flaccid

ļenganums *nm* limpness, flabbiness; flac-
cidity

ļengāties *vr* wobble

ļeniniāna *nf* Leniniana

ļeninietis *nm,* ~e *nf* Leninist

ļeniniski *adv* following Lenin's doctrine, in a
Leninist manner

ļeninisks *adj* Leninist

ļeninisms *nm* Leninism

ļenkani *adv* limply; flabbily; flaccidly

ļenkans *adj* limp; flabby; flaccid

ļenkaras *nf pl* tatters

ļenkausis *nm* floppy-eared one

ļepa *nf* (vulg.) face, mug

ļēpa *nf* **1.** (col.) lout, slouch; **2.** large snowflake

ļēpāt *vi* snow with large, wet snowflakes

ļepatāt *vi* toddle

ļepatot *vi* toddle

ļepausis *nm* floppy-eared one

ļēpīgi *adv* (col.) clumsily

ļēpīgs *adj* (col.) clumsy

ļēpot *vi* (col.) trudge

ļeras *nf pl* (com.) gossip, tales

ļerbas *nf pl* (com.) gossip, tales

ļerga *nf* (com.) moonshine

ļerināt *vi* (com.) blab

ļerkstēt *vi* = ļerkšķēt

ļerkšķēt *vi* **1.** (com.) blab; **2.** (of a liquid)
swash

ļerkšķis *nm* **1.** rattle; **2.** blabber

ļezgas *nf pl* (com.) gossip, tales

ļihačs *nm* (obs.) driver of smart cab (in
Russia)

ļimt *vi* sink down, collapse, (of knees) give
way

ļinkāt *vi* lope

ļipa *nf* scut

ļipainis *nm* (col.) hare

ļipains *adj* with a scut

ļipata *interj* ļ., ļ. or ļ., ļapata lope; gallumph

ļipiņa *nf* **1.** *dim* of ļipa, little scut; **2.** (with
auss) earlobe

ļipot *vi* lope

ļirināt *vi* twitter, sing

ļirkstēt *vi* (com.) laugh

ļodze *nf* buckling

ļodzīgi *adv* unsteadily, wobblingly, totteringly

ļodzīgs *adj* unsteady, wobbly, tottery, rickety

ļodzīgums *nm* wobbliness

ļodzīt *vt* loosen

ļodzīties *vr* sway; (of legs) wobble, give way;
(of furniture) be rickety

ļogani *adv* **1.** unsteadily; **2.** limply, flaccidly

ļogans *adj* **1.** unsteady, wobbly, tottery; rickety;
2. limp, flaccid

ļogāt *vt* shake loose

ļogu ļogām *adv* wobblingly

ļoti *adv* very; highly, greatly, extremely; very
much; badly; **cik ļ. mēs arī gribētu** much
as we we would like

ļudzināt *vt* (col.) shake loose

ļukāt *vt* (col.) shake loose

ļukausis *nm* lop-eared animal or person

ļukt *vi* sag

ļūļa *nm* (com.) klutz

ļuļķene *nf* (col., cont.) pipe

ļuļķēt *vi, vt* (com.) smoke

ļuļķētājs *nm* (com.) smoker

ļuļķis *nm* (col., cont.) pipe, old pipe; pipe or cigarette that is held constantly in the mouth

ļumausis *nm* 1. lop-eared animal or person; 2. (col.) klutz

ļumdēt *vi* quiver

ļumdīt *vt* shake loose

ļumeklis *nm* (com.) tub, fatty

ļumēt *vi* quiver

ļumīgi *adv* wobblingly

ļumīgs *adj* wobbly, wobbling, jiggly

ļumināt *vt* (col.) shake loose

ļumt *vi* buckle; cave in; sag

ļurba *nm* (com.) klutz, lout, meathead

ļurdzīties *vr* wobble, be loose

ļurgāt *vt* (col.) shake loose

ļurināt *vi* 1. play montonously; 2. blab

ļurkabikse *nm* (com.) coward

ļurkāt *vt* (col.) shake loose

ļurkāties *vr* wobble, be loose

ļurkstēt *vi* (com.) blab

ļurkšķēt *vi* slosh, squish

ļutausis *nm* lop-eared animal or person

ļuvenis *nm* (reg.) quagmire

ļuvens *adj* (reg.) boggy, miry

M

maca *nf* matzo

mācāmība nf learning ability

mācāms *adj, part* of mācīt teachable; to be taught

mācāmstunda *nf* study hall (in boarding schools or schools with extended hours)

macas *nf pl* matzoth

macerācija *nf* maceration

maces *nf pl* matzoth

māceklis *nm*, ~e *nf* 1. apprentice; 2. disciple; pupil

macerācija *nf* (med.) maceration

macerāls *nm* maceral

macerāts *nm* macerate

macerēt *vt* macerate

macerēties *vr* macerate (*vi*)

mācēt vt 1. know; know how to; **m. no galvas** know by heart; 2. be able; **(skrien) ko māk** he (she) runs as fast as his (her) legs will carry him (her)

ma[ch]inācija [h] *nf* machination

ma[ch]in[ā]tor/s [h][a] *nm*, ~e *nf* machinator

ma[ch]isms [h] *nm* Machism

ma[ch]ist/s [h] *nm*, ~e *nf* Machian

mācīb/a *nf* 1. teaching, doctrine; 2. course; 3. *pl* ~as instruction, studies; (mil.) exercise, training, drill; ~u **manēža** drill hall; 4. training, apprenticeship; **būt** ~ā be apprenticed; 5. (col.) lesson (to be learned from experience); **tas būs par** ~u that will serve as a lesson

mācības bērni *nm pl* confirmands

mācībgrāmata *nf* textbook

mācībnie/ks *nm*, ~ce *nf* confirmand

mācībpriekšmets *nm* (academic) subject

mācībspēk/s *nm* teacher, instructor, professor; ~i faculty; teaching staff

mācībstunda *nf* class (class time)

mācību bataljons *nm* training batallion

mācību filma *nf* educational film

mācību gads *nm* school year, academic year

mācību iestāde *nf* educational institution; **augstākā m. i.** institution of higher learning

mācību kombināts training center

mācību laukums *nm* exercise ground

mācību lidmašīna *nf* trainer (plane)

mācību līdzekļi *nm pl* instructional aids

mācību nauda *nf* tuition

mācību plāns *nm* syllabus; program of instruction

mācību programma *nf* curriculum

mācību taka *nf* nature trail

mācību telpa *nf* classroom

mācību trauksme *nf* practice alert

mācību viela *nf* (educ.) material

maciņš *nm dim* of **maks**, little purse

mācīšana *nf* 1. teaching; instruction; 2. training; 3. coaching

mācīšanās *nfr* 1. learning; **programmēta m.** pro-grammed learning; 2. studies; 3. memorization

mācīšanas teorija *nf* theory of instruction

mācīšanās teorija *nf* theory of learning

mācīt *vt* 1. teach; instruct; 2. train; 3. coach

mācītais *nom adj* pundit

mācītāja ļaudis *nm pl* (hist.) peasants working for a pastor

mācītāja tiesa *nf* (hist.) rectorial tithes

mācītāja vietnieks *nm* curate

mācītājcienīgtēvs *nm* (obs.) reverend

mācītājiski *adv* ministerially

mācītājisks *adj* ministerial

mācītājmāja *nf* parsonage

mācītājmuiža *nf* (hist.) glebe

mācītāj/s *nm*, **~a** *nf* 1. pastor, minister; clergyman; (Catholic) priest; 2. teacher

mācītība *nf* learnedness

mācīties *vr* 1. learn; **m. amatu** learn a trade, be apprenticed; **m. no galvas** learn by heart, memorize; 2. study; **m. lomu** (theat.) study a part; **m. universitātē** study at a university

mācītprasme *nf* teaching ability

mācīts *adj, part* of **mācīt** learned, erudite; trained

mačete *nf* machete

mačiņš *nm* ouzel

mačisms *nm* machismo

mačka *nf* 1. old woman; 2. slut

mačo *indecl nm* macho

mačs *nm* (sports) match

mačturnīrs *nm* (chess, checkers) tournament

madagaskariet/is *nm*, **~e** *nf* Madagascan

madāma *nf* (col.) lady, big shot, madam

madapolams *nm* madapollam

madara *nf* madder

madarains *adj* 1. filled with madder; 2. tie-dyed; 3. (obs.) ornamented

madarnieks *nm* madder-dyer

madarojums *nm* 1. dyeing; 2. printing

madarot *vt* 1. dye with madder; 2. pick madder plants; 3. (obs.) ornament

madaru sfinga *nf* madder hawk

madeira *nf* Madeira (wine)

madernieks *nm* bungler

madija *nf* melosa

madonna *nf* Madonna

madrace *nf* matress

madrepora *nf* madrepore

madrig|a|ls [ā] *nm* madrigal

mādzeris *nm* wood with spiral grain

mādža *nf* (**M. Marge**) **garā m.** (col.) middle finger

madženta *nf* magenta

madžongs *nm* mah-jong

maestro *indecl nm* maestro

mafija *nf* Mafia

mafiozo *indecl nm* mafioso

mafiozs *adj* organized-crime, Mafioso

māga *nf* (col.) stomach

magarič/as *nf pl* 1. toast, drink (on the closing of a deal or as a reward); 2. **uz ~ām** (col.) for good measure, into the bargain

māgars *nm* (reg.) easterly

magazīna *nf* 1. (tech.) magazine; **~s ligzda** magazine well; 2. (obs.) warehouse; 3. (obs., serial publication) magazine

Magelāna sūna *nf* a sphagnum moss, Sphagnum magellanicum

magma *nf* magma

magmatisks *adj* magmatic

magmatisms *nm* magmatic process

magnālijs *nm* magnalium

magnāts *nm* magnate

magnētiķis *nm* magnetic material

magnētiski *adv* magnetically

magnētisks *adj* magnetic

magnētisms *nm* magnetism

magn|e|tīts [ē] *nm* magnetite

magn|e|tizācija [ē] *nf* magnetization

magn|e|tizēšana [ē] *nf* magnetization

magn|e|tizēt [ē] *vt* magnetize

magn|e|tizēties [ē] *vr* become magnetized

magn|e|to [ē] *nm indecl* magneto

magn|e|todzinējspēks [ē] *nm* magnetomotive force

magn|e|toelektriski [ē] *adv* magnetoelectrically

magn|e|toelektrisks [ē] *adj* magnetoelectric

magn|e|tofons [ē] *nm* tape recorder

magn|e|togr|ā|fija [ē||a] *nf* magnetic ink printing

magn|e|togr|ā|fs [ē||a] *nm* magnetograph

magn|e|togramma [ē] *nf* magnetogram

magn|e|tohidrodināmika [ē] *nf* magnetohydrodynamics

magn|e|tohidrodināmisks[ē]*adj* magnetohydrodynamic

magn|e|toķīmija [ē] *nf* magnetochemistry

magn|e|toķīmiski[ē]*adv* magnetochemically

magn|e|toķīmisks[ē] *adj* magnetochemical

magn|e|tola [ē] *nf* radio casette recorder

magn|e|tometrija [ē] *nf* magnetometry

magn|e|tometrisks [ē] *adj* magnetometric

magn|e|tometrs [ē] *nm* magnetometer

magn|e|tons [ē] *nm* magneton

magn|e|tooptika [ē] *nf* magneto-optics

magn|e|tooptiski [ē] *adv* magneto-optically

magn|e|tooptisks [ē] *adj* magneto-optic

magn|ē|tosf|ai|ra [e||ē] *nf* magnetosphere

magn|e|tostatika [ē] *nf* magnetostatics

magn|e|tostatiski [ē] *adv* magnetostatically

magn|e|tostatisks [ē] *adj* magnetostatic

magn|e|tostrikcija [ē] *nf* magnetostriction

magn|e|tostriktīvi [ē] *adv* magnetostrictively

magn|e|tostriktīvs [ē] *adj* magnetostrictive

magn|e|tpulveris [ē] *nm* magnetic powder

magn|e|trons [ē] *nm* magnetron

magnēt/s *nm* magnet; ~a magnetic

magn|e|tskārds [ē] *nm* magnetic core sheet

magn|e|ttērauds [ē] *nm* magnetic steel

magn|e|ttinte [ē] *nf* magnetic ink

magneziāls *adj* magnesian

magnēzija dūmi *nm pl* magnesia

magnēzijs *nm* **1.** magnesium powder; **2.** magnesium salt

magnezīts *nm* magnesite

magnija oks|i|ds [ī] *nm* magnesia

magnijs *nm* magnesium

magnificence *nf* magnificence

magnifikāts *nm* magnificat

magnitūda *nf* (Richter scale) magnitude

magnolija *nf* magnolia

magone *nf* poppy

magoņkoks *nm* mahogany

magoņmaizīte *nf* poppy-seed roll

magots *nm* Barbary ape

mags *nm* magician, wizard

maģār/s *nm*, ~iete *nf* Magyar

maģija *nf* magic

maģiski *adv* magically

maģisks *adj* magic; magical

maģiskums *nm* magical quality, magic

maģistrāle *nf* (RR) main line; numbered highway; arterial street; main route (water, gas, electric) main

maģistrāls *adj* main; (of cables) trunk

maģistrants *nm* master's degree graduate student

maģistrantūra *nf* (educ.) masters program

maģistrāt/s *nm* **1.** city council; ~a loceklis councilman; **2.** magistrate; **3.** magistracy

maģistr|a|tūra [ā] *nf* magistracy

maģistrs *nm*, ~e *nf* (academic degree) master

mahagonijkoks *nm* mahogany tree

mahagonijs *nm* mahogany (wood)

mahagons *nm* mahogany tree

mahar|a|dža [ā] *nm* maharaja

mahar|a|ne [ā] *nf* maharani

mahariši *indecl nm* maharishi

mahatma *nm* mahatma

mahdī *indecl nm* Mahdi

mahinācija *nf* = **machinācija**

mahinators *nm* = **machinātors**

mahisms *nm* = **machisms**

mahists *nm* = **machists**

mahonija *nf* Oregon grape

mahorka *nf* makhorka

maiandrs *nm* meander

maicēna *nf* corn starch

maida *nf* (reg.) pole, rod, stake

maidavas *nf pl* (weav.) treadles

maidīt *vt* stake out, mark with stakes

maidzīt *vt* squeeze, knead

maie|i|tika [u] *nf* maieutics

maigā sūrene *nf* mild water pepper

maigi *adv* gently, tenderly; mildly; softly

maigie doņi *nm pl* slender rush

maigle *nf* 1. bifurcated pole, fork; 2. ~s pincers; tongs; (of crayfish) claws

maigoties *vr* (col.) pet

maigs *adj* gentle, tender, mild; soft; delicate; **m. kā jērs** meek as a lamb

maigste *nf* support pole, prop

maigums *nm* gentleness, tenderness; mildness; softness

Maija svētki *nm pl* May Day

maijmaizīte *nf* open-face sandwich (with cottage cheese and green onions or radishes)

maijpuķīte *nf* lily of the valley

maijpulkstenīši *nm pl* or **maijpulkstenīte** *nf* lily of the valley

maijroze *nf* Scotch rose

maijrozīte *nf* Scotch rose

maijs *nm* May

maijvabole *nf* cockchafer

maikatene *nf* substitute hostess

maikats *nm* substitute host

maiksne *nf* support pole, prop

maikste *nf* 1. support pole, prop; 2. (geod.) range pole

maikstīte *nf dim* of **maikste**, thin pole, thin prop

maikstīties *vr* reach for

maiksts *nf* = **maikste**

maile *nf* (zool.) bleak

mailīte *nf* minnow

mainība *nf* 1. changeability, variability; mutability; 2. fickleness

mainīgā bērzlape *nf* graying Russula

mainīgais *nom adj* variable

mainīgā lāčauza *nf* hairy chess

mainīgā vainadzīte *nf* axseed, crown vetch

mainīgi *adv* variably

mainīgs *adj* 1. changeable, changing, variable; mutable; 2. fickle

mainīgums *nm* 1. changeability, variability; mutability; 2. fickleness

mainīt *vt* 1. change; **m. dzīvokli** move to another apartment; 2. exchange; trade; 3. vary; 4. (of guards, observers) relieve

mainītājs *nm*, ~a *nf* changer

mainītava *nf*, usu. **naudas m.** money changer's business

mainīties *vr* 1. change; 2. exchange, swap; 3. alternate; 4. vary

maiņ/a *nf* 1. change; **uz ~ām** alternately; 2. exchange; 3. (work) shift; (of guards, observers) relief; ~**as vecākais** shift boss; (mil.) commander of the relief; **jaunā m.** the new generation; 4. inning

maiņas kantoris *nm* exchange agency

maiņas līdzeklis *nm* means of exchange

maiņas tirdzniecība *nf* barter trade

maiņas vērtība *nf* exchange value

maiņgriezis *nm* inverted rectifier

maiņkondensators *nm* variable capacitor

maiņleņķa *indecl adj* adjustable-angle

maiņlielums *nm* alternating quantity

maiņplūsma *nf* two-way traffic

maiņslēdzis *nm* change-over switch

maiņspriegums *nm* alternating current voltage

maiņstrāva *nf* alternating current

maiņstrāvas ģener|a|tors |ā| *nm* alternator

maiņus *adv* alternately

maiņvērsējs arkls *nm* plow with a slotted moldboard

maiņzvaigzne *nf* variable star

maisadata *nf* large needle, packing needle

maisāmais *nom adj* stirrer, ladle

maisaudekls *nm* burlap

maisaudums *nm* burlap

maiseklis *nm* stirrer, agitator

maisīgi *adv* baggily

maisīgs *adj* baggy

maisījums *nm* mixture

maisīklis *nm* stirrer

maisiņš *nm dim* of **maiss**, small bag, sack

maisīšanās *nfr* interference

maisīt *vt* **1.** stir; **2.** mix; **3.** (col.) involve; **4.** bother, interfere with, mess up

maisītāj/s *nm*, **~a** *nf* stirrer, agitator

maisīties *vr* **1.** be stirred; **2.** be mixed in with; mingle with; **m. pa kājām** be in the way; **3.** in-terfere; **4. m. apkārt** wander

mais/s I *nm* **1.** sack, bag ◊ **caurais m.** (fig.) glutton; bottomless pit; **caurbiru m.** one who eats a lot but does not put on weight; **vienā ~ā bāžami** two of a kind; **pilns kā m.** drunk as a lord; **kā ~ā** (col.) in the dark **tas pats, tikai no cita ~a** six of one a dozen of the other; **2.** (mil.) pocket

maiss II (two syllables) *nm* maize, Indian corn

maisudrēbe *nf* burlap, sacking

maisveida *indecl adj* bag-shaped, sacciform

maisveidīgi *adv* like a sack

maisveidīgs *adj* bag-shaped, sacciform; baggy

maišelis *nm* small bag

maišelnie/ks *nm*, **~ce** *nf* **1.** black marketeer; **2.** scrounger (a city dweller scrounging

for food in the country during a food shortage)

maišķis *nm* (col.) stirrer

maišu *indecl adj* mixed; **m. labība** mixed seed crop; **m. tauta** people of mixed stock; **m. valoda** slang, cant

maišu maišām *adv* helter-skelter

maita *nf* **1.** dead animal, carcass; carrion; **2.** (com. cussword) bastard, cad

maitasgabals *nm* bum

maitasputns *nm* vulture

maitāt *vt* spoil

maitāties *vr* spoil

maitātāj/s *nm*, **~a** *nf* spoiler

maitēdējs *nm* scavenger, scavenging animal

maitu lija *nf* cinereous vulture

maitu vabole *nf* carrion beetle

maiz/e *nf* **1.** bread; **grauzdēta m.** toast; **melnā m.** whole-grain rye bread; **rupjā m.** rye bread; **sald-skāba m.** sourdough bread; **2.** livelihood; **sve-šā ~ē** be provided for by strangers; **savā ~ē** earning one's own living; **3.** breadgrain ◊ **~es zemīte** good arable land; **līdz jaunai ~ei** until next year's crop, when the new harvest is brought in

maizes cikadeja *nf* Kaffir bread

maizesdarbs *nm* job (that one makes one's living from)

maizes devējs *nm* employer

maizes klēts *nf* granary

maizeskoks *nm* breadfruit-tree

maizes labība *nf* breadgrain

maizes lāpsta *nf* oven peel

maizes naids *nm* professional competition professional jealousy

maizes pātaga *nf* (hist.) the whipping of peasants (administered at the discretion of the lord of the manor)

maizes pelnītājs *nm* breadwinner;

maizes soma *nf* knapsack

maizes tēvs *nm* provider

maizgriezis *nm* bread slicer

maizīte *nf* **1.** *dim* of **maize**, bread; **2.** roll, bun; scone; **3.** canapé

maiznīca *nf* bakery

maiznie/ks *nm*, ~**ce** *nf* baker

māj/a *nf* **1.** house; **dzīvojamā m.** home; ~**as zī-me** property mark (of a family); **pilna m. (viesu)** a houseful (of guests); **2.** home; *gen* ~**as** domestic; ~**ās** at home; **uz** ~**ām** home, homeward; ~**ās gatavots** homemade; **viņam visi nav** ~**ās** (col.) he has a screw loose; **3.** *pl* ~**as** farm, farmstead

mājamatniecība *nf* home industry; handicraft

mājamatniecisks *adj* home industry (*adj*)

mājamatnie/ks *nm*, ~**ce** *nf* homeworker; handicraftsman

mājas apogs *nm* little owl

mājas aptieka *nf* medicine chest

mājas balodis *nm* domestic pigeon

mājas bērns *nm* a child that lives at home

mājas cauna *nf* stone marten

mājas circenis *nm* house cricket

mājas cirslis *nm* musk shrew

mājasdarbs *nm* **1.** housework; **2.** homework

mājas draugs *nm* family friend

mājas drēbes *nf pl* at home clothes

mājasdzīvnieks *nm* = **mājdzīvnieks**

mājas grāmata *nf* house register

mājas kārtīb/a *nf* rules of the house; **m.** ~**ā** informally; locally

mājas kungs *nm* **1.** master of the house; **2.** (folk.) tutelary spirit, lar

mājas kurpes *nf pl* house slippers

mājas līdzeklis *nm* home remedy

mājas ļaudis *nm pl* household

mājas mācība *nf* home instruction

mājasmāte *nf* hostess

mājas miers *nm* domestic tranquility

mājas muša *nf* **1.** housefly; **2.** stable fly

mājas pārmācība *nf* (hist.) disciplinary punishment (ordered by the lord of the manor);

mājas pārvaldnieks *nm* building superintendent

mājas pele *nf* house mouse

mājas piepe *nf* house fungus

mājas pīle *nf* domestic duck

mājas plūme *nf* European plum

mājas solis *nm* housework

mājas strazds *nm* common starling

mājas suns *nm* **1.** dog; **2.** indoor dog

mājas svārki *nm pl* housedress, housecoat

mājas svētība *nf* aspidistra

mājastēvs *nm* host

mājās tupētājs *nm* homebody

mājasvieta *nf* = **mājvieta**

mājas vizīte *nf* house call

mājas zīme *nf* property mark (of a family)

mājaudums *nm* homespun

mājaudzināšana *nf* home education

mājdzīvnieks *nm* domestic animal

majeitisks *adj* maieutic

majestāte *nf* majesty

majestātiski *adv* majestically

majestātisks *adj* majestic

majestātiskums *nm* majesty

mājība *nf* homeyness, coziness

mājiens *nm* **1.** wave; wink, nod; **2.** hint

mājīgi *adv* cozily

mājīgs *adj* homey, cozy

mājīgums *nm* homeyness, coziness

mājinie/ks *nm*, ~**ce** *nf* = **mājnieks**

mājiņa *nf dim* of **māja**, little house

mājīpašnie/ks *nm*, ~**ce** *nf* homeowner

mājīpašums *nm* owned home

mājiski *adv* domestically

mājisks *adj* domestic

mājiskums *nm* domesticity

mājkalpotāja *nf* domestic, maid

mājkalpotājs *nm* (rare.) domestic servant

mājkopība *nf* housekeeping

mājkurpes *nf pl* house slippers

mājkustonis *nm* domestic animal

mājlietas *nf pl* household items

mājlopi *nm pl* cattle

mājļaudis *nm pl* household

mājmācība *nf* homebound instruction

mājnie/ks *nm*, ~ce *nf* **1.** member of a household; **2.** ~ki those remaining at home (as opposed to those who have left)

mājoklis *nm* dwelling, lodgings; abode

mājoklītis *nm dim* of **mājoklis**, dwelling place

majolika *nf* majolica

majonēze *nf* mayonnaise

majorāneļļa *nf* marjoram oil

majorāns *nm* marjoram

majorāts *nm* **1.** right of primogeniture; **2.** estate devolving by primogeniture

majordoms *nm* majordomo

majoritāte *nf* majority

majorizēt *vi* obtain a majority of votes

major/s *nm*, ~e *nf* major

mājot *vi* dwell, live

mājotne *nf* dwelling, dwelling place, residence

mājputns *nm* domestic fowl

mājražošana *nf* home industry

mājražotāj/s *nm*, ~a *nf* home worker

mājrūpals *nm* cottage industry complex

mājrūpniecība *nf* home industry, cottage industry

mājrūpniecisks *adj* home industry (*adj*)

maj/s *nm*, ~iete *nf* Mayan

mājsaimniece *nf* **1.** housewife; **2.** house owner

mājsaimniecība *nf* **1.** housekeeping; **2.** household

mājsaimnie/ks *nm*, ~ce *nf* **1.** house owner; householder; **2.** landlord

mājskolotāja *nf* governess

mājskolotājs *nm* tutor

mājstrādniece *nf* domestic servant

mājturība *nf* **1.** housekeeping; **2.** home economics

mājturībniece *nf* home economics specialist

māju čurkste *nf* martin

mājulība *nf* homeyness

mājup *adv* home, homeward

mājupceļš *nm* way home, way back, homeward trek

majuskulis *nm* capital letter

māju zvirbulis *nm* house sparrow

mājvārds *nm* name of a farmstead

mājvieta *nf* **1.** lodging; abode; **paliekama m.** permanent abode; **2.** (hist.) coaching inn

māka *nf* skill

makabrs *adj* macabre

makačāt *vt* spin unevenly

makadamija *nf* macadamia tree

makadams *nm* macadam

makadata *nf* pipe cleaner

makaks *nm* macaque

makāns *nm* (col.) **1.** large animal; large and heavy object; **2.** smooth operator

makao *indecl nm* (zool.) macao

makarandiba *nf* massaranduba

makarēt *vi* act deceitfully, machinate

makaroni *nm pl* macaronis

makaronisks *adj* macaronic

makaronisms *nm* mixture of two languages

makars *nm* (col.) sly fox, scamp

makartisms *nm* McCarthyism

maketējums *nm* **1.** maquette; **2.** (typ.) dummy; layout

maketēt *vt* prepare a mockup, prepare a dummy (or layout)

makets *nm* maquette; mockup of a stage set; model

mak[i]avellisks [j] *adj* Machiavellian

mak[i]avellisms [j] *nm* Machiavellianism

makija *nf* (scrubby underbrush) maquis

makijāža *nf* makeup, maquillage

makintošs *nm* raincoat

maklejas *nf pl* Macleaya

mākler/is *nm*, ~e *nf* broker

māklis *nm* **1.** (cont) expert; **2.** trick; **3.** importuner maklura *nf* Osage orange

makmutis *nm* (col.) bigmouth, braggart

mako *indecl nm* maco, Egyptian cotton

māko/nis *nm* cloud; kārtainie ~ņi strati; sudrabainie ~ņi noctilucent clouds; bez ~ņiem cloud-less

mākoņainība *nf* cloudiness

mākoņains *adj* cloudy

mākoņainums *nm* cloudiness

mākoņaitiņas *nf pl* fleece clouds

mākoņpelēks *adj* grayish

mākoņsprauga *nf* break in the clouds

mākoņstūmējs *nm* Don Quixote, quixotic enthusiast

mākoņu augstuma mērītājs *nm* ceilometer

mākoņu daudzums *nm* cloudiness

mākoņu grēda *nf* cloud bank

mākoņu mērītājs *nm* nephelometer

mākoņveida *indecl adj* cloud-like

mākoņveidīgi *adv* like a cloud

mākoņveidīgs *adj* cloud-like

makovice *nf* variegated bolete

makramē *indecl nm* macrame

makrele or makrēle *nf* mackerel

makroanalīze *nf* macroanalysis

makroasambleris *nm* (compu.) macro-assembler

makrobiotika *nf* macrobiosis

makrocefālija *nf* macrocephalus

makroekonomika *nf* macroeconomics

makroekonomisks *adj* macroeconomic

makrofāgs *nm* histiocyte

makrofosilija *nf* macrofossil

makroinstrukcija *nf* (compu.) macroinstruction

makrokefalija *nf* macrocephaly

makrokefals *nm* macrocephalus

makroklimats *nm* macroclimate

makrokosmisks *adj* macrocosmic

makrokosms *nm* macrocosm

makrokristallisks *adj* macrocrystalline

makroķīmija *nf* macrochemistry

makrol[i]ts [ī] *nm* Neolithic stone tool

makroloģija *nf* pleonasm

makromolekula *nf* macromolecule

makromolekulāri *adv* macromolecularly

makromolekulārs *adj* macromolecular

makropasaule *nf* macroscopic world

makropodijas *nf pl* Macropodium

makroprogrammēšana *nf* macroprogramming

makroreljefs *nm* gross planetary features

makroskopiski *adv* macroscopically

makroskopisks *adj* macroscopic

makrostruktūra *nf* macrostructure

makrostrukt[u]rāls [ū] *adj* macrostructural

makrovaloda *nf* (compu.) macrolanguage

makrozamija *nf* macrozamia

maks *nm* purse; pouch; (fig.) pocketbook, wallet

maks/a *nf* 1. pay; ne par kādu ~u not for anything; 2. fee; dues; braucamā m. fare; 3. cost

maksājams *adj, part* of maksāt payable; kļūt m. (bus.) a. become due; b. mature

maksājums *nm* payment

maksājums uz priekšu *nm* payment in advance, prepayment

maksājumu bilance *nf* balance of payments

maksas aprēķins *nm* cost estimate

maksāšana *nf* paying, payment; m. pa daļām payment in instalments; m. naturā payment in kind

maksāšanas termiņš *nm* due date

maksāt *vt* 1. pay; m. dzīvu naudu (col.) pay a pretty penny; m. graudā pay in kind; 2. cost; cik tas maksā? how much is it? lai maksā ko maksādams whatever the cost

maksātājs *nm*, ~a *nf* payer

maksātnespēja *nf* insolvency

maksātnespējīgs *adj* insolvent

maksātspēja *nf* 1. solvency; 2. purchasing power

maksātspējīgs *adj* **1.** solvent; **2.** having purchase power

maksi *indecl adj* maxi

maksilarija *nf* maxillaria

maksima *nf* maxim

maksimāli *adv* maximally

maksimālisms *nm* **1.** extremism; **2.** (hist.) maximalism

maksimālistisks *adj* **1.** extreme; **2.** maximalist

maksimālist/s *nm*, ~**e** *nf* maximalist

maksim[a]lizēt [ā] *vt* maximalize

maksim[a]lizēties [ā] *vr* be maximalized

maksimāls *adj* maximal, maximum

maksimāltermometrs *nm* maximum thermometer

maksimizācija *nf* maximization

maksims I *nm* Maxim gun

maksims II *nm* maximum

maksimums *nm* maximum

maksimumstunda *nf* rush hour

māksla *nf* **1.** art; **brīvās** ~**s** liberal arts; **tēlojošās** ~**s** fine arts; **2.** skill; **tā nav nekāda m.** that's easy enough, piece of cake

mākslas amatniecība applied art, industrial art

mākslas audums *nm* woven artwork

mākslas cienītāj/s *nm*, ~**a** *nf* art lover

mākslas darbs *nm* artwork

mākslas dārzniecība *nf* landscape architecture

mākslas dārznieks *nm* landscape architect

mākslas iespiedums *nm* de luxe edition

mākslas iestādes *nf pl* museums, galleries, and schools of art

mākslas mūzejs *nm* art museum

mākslas priekšmets *nm* objet d'art

mākslas reprodukcija *nf* art print

mākslas rokdarbi *nm pl* fancywork

mākslas zinātne *nf* art history and theory

mākslīgās asinsrites aparāts *nm* heart-lung machine

mākslīgi *adv* artificially

mākslīgs *adj* artificial; imitation (*adj*); synthetic; (of teeth) false; (of gems) paste

mākslīgums *nm* artificiality

mākslinieciski *adv* artistically

māksliniecisks *adj* artistic

mākslinieciskums *nm* artistic value

mākslinieka daba *nf* artistic temperament

mākslinieka darbnīca *nf* studio;

māksliniek/s *nm*, ~**ce** *nf* **1.** artist; painter; **2.** performer

mākslot *vt* feign, affect, pretend

māksloti *adv* affectedly

mākslotība *nf* artificiality; affectation; mannerism

mākslots *adj, part* of **mākslot** artificial; affected, unnatural; forced

mākslotums *nm* artificiality; affectation; mannerism

makstainais grīslis *nm* sheathed sedge

makstainā spilve *nf* sheathed cotton grass

makstains *adj* sheathed

makstene *nf* **1.** (bot.) grisette; **2.** caddisworm, caddis fly

makstīte *nf dim* of **maksts**, small scabbard

makstkode *nf* casebearer moth

maksts *nf* **1.** sheath; scabbard; holster; **2.** vagina

maksts tri[ch]onoma [h] *nf* trichomonad

maksvels *nm* maxwell

makšķerāķis *nm* fishhook

makšķeraukla *nf* fishing line

makšķere *nf* fishing pole, fishing rod

makšķeres kāts *nm* fishing pole, fishing rod

makšķerēšana *nf* fishing (angling); ~**s piederumi** fishing tackle

makšķerēt *v* **1.** *vi* fish (angle); **2.** *vt* fish for

makšķerīte *nf dim* of **makšķere**, fishing pole

makšķerkāts *nm* fishing pole, fishing rod

makšķerniecība *nf* fishing (angling)

makšķernie/ks *nm*, ~**ce** *nf* angler

mākt *vt* **1.** oppress, weigh heavy upon, afflict; **2.** torment, bother

makten *adv* (barb.) very

maktens *adj* (col.) **1.** great; **2.** big

mākties *vr* **1.** become cloudy; **2. m. virsū** a. im-portune; b. (of emotion, fatigue, sleep) overcome

maktīgi *adv* (barb.) very, powerfully

maktīgs *adj* (barb.) powerful

makts *nf* power

makulatūra or **makulātūra** *nf* **1.** (printed) waste paper; **2.** (fig.) pulp (literature)

mākulis I *nm* small rain cloud

mākulis II (with **â**) *nm* (col.) expert, one with the know-how

mākuļains *adj* cloudy

mākuļot *vi* become cloudy

maķedoniet/is *nm*, **~e** *nf* Macedonian

maķenīt or **maķenītiņ** *adv* (col.) a tiny bit

mal/a *nf* **1.** edge; rim, brim; brink; **2.** side; **kreisā m.** (naut.) port; **labā m.** (naut.) starboard; **3.** margin; **4.** edging, border; **5.** (of rivers, lakes) bank; shore; **6.** (col.) area, territory, parts; **svešā ~ā** in a foreign land; **visas ~as** (also **~u ~as**) all over, everywhere; **pie ~as** aside; **no visām ~ām** from all sides, from every corner; **pa ~u ~ām** everywhere

malā *adv* **1.** aside; **2.** ashore

mālābele *nf* apple tree that produces the **mālābols** variety of apples

mālābols *nm* a Latvian apple variety

mala[ch]īta [h] zaļais *nm* malachite green

mala[ch]īts [h] *nm* malachite

mala[ch]ītzaļš [h] *adj* malachite green

malacīgs *adj* (col.) strapping, dashing

malacis *nm* (col.) fine fellow; brave young man; good boy; **m.!** attaboy, attagirl

māla duļķis *nm* slip

malaga *nf* Malaga (wine)

malagas/s *nm*, **~iete** *nf* Malagasy

malahīts *nm* = **malachīts**

malahītzaļš *adj* = **malahītzaļš**

mālaine *nf* loam

mālainis *nm* loam

mālainītes *nf pl* coltsfoot

mālains *adj* clayey; loamy

mālainums *nm* clayiness; loaminess

māla izstrādājumi *nm pl* earthenware

Malajas lācis *nm* sun bear

malajiet/is *nm*, **~iete** *nf* Malayan

malaj/s *nm*, **~iete** *nf* Malay

mālājs *nm* **1.** loam; **2.** clayey area

māla kleķis *nm* adobe

mālakmens *nm* mudstone

malakoloģija *nf* malacology

malārija *nf* malaria

malārijas ods *nm* malaria mosquito

malas piezīmes *nf pl* marginal notes

malas veidojums *nm* (geol.) lateral moraine

malas vējš *nm* (reg.) easterly

māla trauki *nm pl* pottery, earthenware; stoneware

malāts *nm* malate

mālaugsne *nf* clay soil

malaviet/is *nm*, **~e** *nf* Malawian

mālbalodis *nm* clay pigeon

mālbaložu katapults *nm* trap

mālbaložu šaušana *nf* skeet shooting

mālbedre *nf* clay pit

mālbetons *nm* clay concrete

malciena *nf* woodyard

malcinieks *nm* **1.** woodcutter; **2.** firewood vendor

malciņa *nf dim* of **malka**, firewood

malciņš *nm dim* of **malks**, small sip, mouthful

māldegas *nf pl* flux

mālderis *nm* (obs. or cont.) painter

maldi *nm pl* error; delusion; fallacy; **optiskie m.** optical illusion

maldība *nf* **1.** error; **2.** fallibility

maldīgi *adv* erroneously

maldīgs *adj* erroneous, false, wrong, fallacious; fallible

maldīgums *nm* 1. erroneousness, falseness; **2.** fallibility

maldināšana *nf* deception; ~s (mil.) diversionary; ~s **makets** decoy

maldināt I *vt* mislead, delude, deceive, lead astray

maldināt II *vt* (folk.) make s.o. grind (using the grist mill)

maldinātāj/s *nm*, ~a *nf* deceiver

maldinoši *adv* misleadingly, deceptively

maldinošs *adj, part* of **maldināt** misleading, deceptive

maldīšanās *nfr* 1. wandering about; **2.** error, mistake

maldīt *vt* (poet.) mislead, delude, deceive, lead astray

maldīties *vr* 1. wander about (having lost one's way); **2.** be mistaken

maldonis *nm* one that leads astray

malds *nm* See **maldi**

maldu ceļ/š *nm* wrong path; **(staigāt) m.** ~us (go) wrong, (go) astray

malduguns *nf* ignis fatuus, will-o'-the-wisp

maldu mācība *nf* false doctrine, heresy

maldu mācītājs *nm* heretic

maldu tēls *nm* phantom

maldu viesis *nm* (of birds) accidental

maleīnhidrazīds *nm* maleic hydrazide

maleīnskābe *nf* maleic acid

malējais *defin adj* outer

malējs *adj*, usu. *defin* **malējais** outer

malēj/s *nm*, ~a *nf* 1. miller; **2.** miller's customer

mālene *nf* coltsfoot

malēnietis *nm* 1. inhabitant of Maliena (in the southeastern part of Latvia); **2.** provincial, backwoodsman

mālēt *vt* (barb.) paint

malgašs *nm*, ~iete *nf* Malagasy

mālgrauzis *nm* (col.) cricket

mālgrauznis *nm* = **mālgrauzis**

maliān/is *nm*, ~e *nf* Malian

maliena *nf* = **maliene**

maliene *nf* borderland, province, outlying district

maliens *nm* grist

māliens *nm* loam

malignizācija *nf* metastasis

maliņa *nf dim* of **mala**, edge; rim, brim; side

mālis *nm* (folk.) grist

malka *nf* firewood, stovewood; **salasīta m.** windfall; **zaļa m.** green firewood

malkas apkure *nf* heating by woodburning stoves

malkas cirtējs *nm* woodcutter

malkas grēda *nf* woodpile

malkas klucis *nm* wood block

malkas laukums *nm* woodyard

malkas pagale *nf* billet

malkas šķūnis *nm* woodshed

malkcirknis *nm* forest area designated for firewood cutting

malkcirsma *nf* cutting of firewood

malkcirsna *nf* woodshed

malkcirsnis *nm* woodshed

malkcirtis *nm* 1. timberman; **2.** long-horned beetle

malkot *vt* sip

malks *nm* draft, gulp; sip; mouthful

māllēpe *nf* coltsfoot

māllēpene *nf* coltsfoot

māllēpīte *nf* coltsfoot

mallofagi *nm pl* Mallophaga

malms *nm* (geol.) malm

malonskābe *nf* malonic acid

malopes *nf pl* Malope

māls *nm* clay; **blietēts m.** pisé; **dedzināts m.** baked clay; **liess m.** short clay; **merģeļains m.** calcareous clay; **rupjgraudu m.** primary clay; **smalkgraudains m.** secondary clay; **smilšanais m.** sandy loam; **zilais m.** blue clay

mālsmilts *nf* sandy loam

malstīties *vr* gad about

malt *vt* **1.** grind, mill; mince; **2.** drone; **m. niekus**
   chatter, talk nonsense; **3.** (of cats) purr

Maltas krusts *nm* Maltese cross

maltavas *nf pl* (reg.) mill

maltāze *nf* maltase

maltēns *nm* maltene

malties *vr* **1.** be ground, be milled; **2. m. apkārt**
   gad about; mill around

maltiet/is *nm*, ~**e** *nf* Maltese

maltin *adv emph* of **malt**; **m. malt** grind
   away

maltīte *nf* meal

maltoze *nf* maltose

maltretēt *vt* maltreat

malt/s *adj, part* of **malt** ground; minced; *defin*
   ~**ais** (col., of milk) skimmed

maltusisms *nm* Malthusianism

maltuve *nf* flour mill, millhouse; mill room

mālūdens *nm* See **etiķskābais m.**

malumakšķernie/ks *nm*, ~**ce** *nf* poacher

malumedības *nf pl* poaching

malumedniecība *nf* poaching

malumednie/ks *nm*, ~**ce** *nf* poacher

malu mētāšana *nf* "throwing around" (an
   ancient Latvian wedding custom that
   required the bride to place offerings to
   the tutelary deity at various sites in her
   new home and give gifts to relatives and
   wedding guests)

malum/s *nm* **1.** grist; grind; **rupja** ~**a** coarsely
   ground; **smalka** ~**a** finely ground;
   2. melder

malup *adv* aside

maluzvejniecība *nf* poaching

maluzvejnie/ks *nm*, ~**ce** *nf* poacher

malva *nf* dwarf mallow

malvāzija *nf* malmsey

mālviela *nf* clay material

mālzeme *nf* **1.** alumina; **2.** loam

maļamais *nom adj* grist

maļamība *nf* grindability

māļi *nm pl* meal moths

māma *nf* mother

mamaplastika *nf* mammoplasty

mamba *nf* mamba

mambo *indecl nm* mambo

mameluks *nm* Mameluke

māmicīte *nf* (col.) mommy

mamilārija *nf* mammilaria

māmiņa *nf* **1.** *dim* of **māma, māte**, mother,
   mommy; **2.** elderly woman, granny

māmīte *nf* (col.) *dim* of **māte**, mother,
   mommy

mamma *nf* **1.** (col.) mother; mamma; **2.** (com.)
   obese woman

mammicīte *nf* (col.) mommy

mammiņa *nf* mamma

mammīte *nf* (col.) *dim* of **māte**, mother,
   mommy

mammuce *nf* (col.) mommy

mammucīte *nf* (col.) mother, mommy

mamogr[a]fija [ā] *nf* mammography

mamons *nm* Mammon

māmucīte *nf* (col.) mother, mommy

māmuliņa *nf* mother

māmulīte *nf* (col. *dim* of **māmuļa**) mother,
   mom-my

māmuļa *nf* mother

mamuta koks *nm* big tree (sequoia)

mamuts *nm* mammoth

mamzele *nf* (barb.) young lady

man *pron, dat* of **es** **1.** to me; **2.** used for
   emphasis in expressing threat or reproach:
   nu tu m. da-būsi! now you'll get it!

manāmi *adv* perceptibly; noticeably

manāms *adj, part* of **manīt** perceptible;
   noticeable

mancipācija *nf* mancipation

mančestrs *nm* Manchester goods

mandags *nm* (hist.) hiring day (a Monday);
   zilais m. blue Monday

mandala *nf* mandala

mandant/s *nm*, ~**e** *nf* **1.** mandator; **2.** constituent;
   ~**ti** constituency

mandarīnpīle *nf* mandarin duck

mandarīns *nm* mandarin (fruit; Chinese official)

mand[a]tār/s [ā] *nm*, ~e *nf* mandatary

mand[a]tor/s [ā] *nm*, ~e *nf* mandator

mandāt/s *nm* mandate; (in phrase **nolikt ~u**) seat (in a parliament)

mandātte[r]itorija [rr] *nf* mandate territory

mandātvalsts *nf* mandatary power

mandātzeme *nf* mandate (mandate territory)

mandele *nf* 1. almond; 2. tonsil

mandels *nm* (obs.) (count of) fifteen

mandeļeļļa *nf* almond oil

mandeļiezis *nm* amygdaloid

mandeļkoks *nm* almond tree

mandeļkūka *nf* almond cake

mandeļu iekaisums *nm* tonsillitis

mandeļu operācija *nf* tonsillectomy

mandeļveida *indecl adj* almondlike

mandeļveidīgi *adv* like an almond

mandeļveidīgs *adj* almondlike

mandola *nf* mandola

mandolīna *nf* mandolin

mandolīnist/s *nm*, ~e *nf* mandolinist

mandragora *nf* mandrake

mandrils *nm* mandrill

mandž[u]r/s [ū] *nm*, ~iete *nf* Manchu

manēj/ais *nom adj* 1. mine; 2. (col.) my husband; ~ā (col.) my wife; 3. ~ie my folks, my family

manēj/s *pron*, usu. *defin* ~ais mine

maneken/s *nm* 1. mannequin; ~e *nf*; 2. dummy

māneklis *nm* 1. decoy, lure; 2. deceiver, swindler; 3. phantom; 4. pacifier

manevrēšana *nf* maneuvering; ~s spēja maneuverability

manevrēt *vi* maneuver; (of trains) switch

manevr/s *nm* maneuver; ~i. (mil.) maneuvers; (RR) switching

manevrspējīgs *adj* maneuverable

manevru vilciens *nm* switch train

manevru sliedes *nf pl* sidetrack, siding

manēža *nf* 1. manege, riding hall, horse training arena; 2. (circus) ring

mangabejs *nm* mangabey

mangale *nf* mangle

mangalēt *vt* press (with a roller)

mangalis *nm* 1. laundry-pressing roller; 2. laundry beater

mang[a]nāts [ā] *nm* manganate

mangāndzelzs *nf* ferromanganese

mang[a]nīts [ā] *nm* manganite

mangānpārskābe *nf* permanganic acid

mangānpaskābe *nf* manganous acid

mangāns *nm* manganese

mang[a]nsil[i]cijs [ā][ī] *nm* silicomanganese

mangānskābe *nf* manganic acid

mangāntērauds *nm* manganese steel

mangānvaŗš *nm* cupromanganese

mango *indecl nm* mango

mangokoks *nm* mango tree

mangolds *nm* chard

mangostāns *nm* mangosteen

mangot *vt* (col.) beg for, cadge

mangotājs *nm*, ~a *nf* cadger

mangrove *nf* mangrove

mangulis *nm* mangle

mangusts *nm* mongoose

mani *pron, acc* of **es** me

manī *pron, loc* of **es** in me

maniakāls *adj* manic

maniaks *nm* manic

manība *nf* adroitness

mani[ch]eisms [h] *nm* Manichaeism

mani[ch]ejs [h] *nm* Manichaean

maniere *nf* manner; habit; mannerism; *pl* ~s manners

manierēties *vr* put on airs

manierība *nf* affectation

manierīgi *adv* in an affected manner

manierīgs *adj* affected; stilted

manierīgums *nm* affectation

manierisms *nm* mannerism; Mannerism

manierist/s *nm*, ~e *nf* Mannerist
manifestācija *nf* **1.** demonstration; **2.** manifestation
manifestant/s *nm*, ~e *nf* demonstrant
manifestēt *v* **1.** *vi* demonstrate; **2.** *vt* manifest
manifests *nm* manifesto; (naut.) manifest
manīgi *adv* adroitly; sneakily
mānīgi *adv* deceptively
manīgs *adj* **1.** adroit; **2.** sneaky
mānīgs *adj* deceptive
manīgums *nm* **1.** adroitness; **2.** sneakiness
mānīgums *nm* deceptiveness
maniheisms *nm* = **manicheisms**
manihejs *nm* = **manichejs**
m|a|nija [ā] *nf* mania
manījums *nm* sensation
manikīre *nf* manicurist
manikirēt *vt* manicure
manikīrs *nm* manicure
manilkara *nf* bully tree
manim *pron, instr* of **es**; **ar m.** with me
manioka *nf* = **manioks**
manioks *nm* cassava
manipulācija *nf* manipulation
manipul|a|tor/s [ā] *nm*, ~e *nf* manipulator
manipulēt *vt* manipulate
manipuls *nm* (Roman legion subdivision) maniple
manis *pron, gen* of **es** of me, my; **m. dēļ** (or **pēc**) on my account; for my sake; for all I care
mā/nis *nm* **1.** apparition, phantom, ghost; **2.** de-ceiver, swindler; **3.** ~ņi a. superstition; b. illusion; hallucination; ~ņu cerības false hope; c. phantoms, spooks
manīt *vt* **1.** sense; **likt m.** make (s.o.) feel, hint; **2.** notice
mānīt *vt* deceive
mānītāj/s *nm*, ~a *nf* deceiver
manīties *vr* **1.** contrive, manage; **2.** sneak
mānīties *vr* tell lies; deceive
manko *indecl nm* (bus.) shortage
mankurtisks *adj* illiberal, stingy

manna *nf* farina, cream of wheat; (Bibl., bot.) manna
mannāns *nm* mannan
mannitols *nm* mannitol
mannonskābe *nf* mannonic acid
mannoze *nf* mannose
manometrisks *adj* manometric
manometrs *nm* manometer
mans *pron* my, mine; **pa manam** (com.) I think, in my opinion
māns *nm* **1.** phantom, apparition; **2.** illusion; hallucination
mansarda istaba *nf* garret room
mansarda jumts *nm* gambrel roof
mansarda logs *nm* dormer window
mansards *nm* mansard
mans/s *nm*, ~iete *nf* Vogul
manšafte *nf* (sl.) team
manšete *nf* cuff; ~s poga cuff link
manšetveida *indecl adj* cuff-like
manšetveidīgi *adv* like a cuff
manšetveidīgs *adj* cuff-like
mant/a *nf* **1.** property; **aizstājamas ~as** fungibles; **atstāta m.** derelict property; **bezmantnieka m.** intestate property; **kustama m.** personal property; **nekustama m.** real estate; **2.** fortune; treasure; **apslēpta m.** hidden treasure; (jur.) treasure trove; **3.** pl ~as things, possessions, be-longings; **zagtas ~as** stolen goods; **zagtu ~u slēpējs** (or **uzpircējs**) receiver of stolen goods, fence; **4.** item (in a catalog), thing
mantāgs *nm* (hist.) meeting of vassals
mantas cenzs *nm* property evaluation; property qualification, income qualification
mantaskāre *nf* = **mantkāre**
mantas kopība *nf* joint tenancy
mantas novēlētāja *nf* testatrix
mantas novēlētājs *nm* testator
mantas racējs *nm* treasure hunter
mantas šķirtība *nf* severalty
Mantegacas latvāņi *nm pl* cartwheel flower

mantelis *nm* (barb.) overcoat

manteļskurstenis *nm* chimney

mantguvīgi *adv* greedily

mantguvīgs *adj* greedy

mantguv/is *nm*, ~e *nf* moneygrubber

mantība *nf* property, belongings

mantida *nf* mantis

mantīgs *adj* well-to-do, wealthy; propertied

mantīgums *nm* wealth

mantija *nf* **1.** robe; **2.** (clothing; geol., biol.) mantle

mantika *nf* mantic

mantiļa *nf* mantilla

mantiniece *nf* heiress

mantinie/ks *nm* heir; **likumīgais m.** rightful heir; **neatraidāms m.** forceful heir

mantinieku atstumšana *nf* disinheritance

mantiņa *nf* **1.** *dim* of **manta**; **2.** (col.) toy; **3.** ~s things, possessions, belongings

mantisa *nf* mantissa

mantiski *adv* in regard to property

mantisks *adj* property (*adj*); in rem

mantkāre *nf* greed

mantkāri *adv* greedily

mantkārība *nf* greed

mantkārīgi *adv* greedily

mantkārīgs *adj* greedy

mantkārīgums *nm* greediness

mantkārs *adj* greedy

mantkasis *nm* (col.) miser, moneygrubber

mantnesis *nm* (folk.) a treasure-bearing imp

mantnīca *nf* **1.** treasure vault; **2.** (mil.) warehouse

mantnieciski *adv* = **mantiski**

mantniecisks *adj* = **mantisks**

manto *indecl nm* mantle

mantojamība *nf* heritability

mantojams *adj, part* of **mantot** heritable

mantojuma atstājēja *nf* testatrix

mantojuma atstājējs *nm* testator

mantojuma masa *nf* estate

mantojums *nm* inheritance; legacy; **vēsturisks m.** heritage

mantošana *nf* inheritance

mantošanas tiesības *nf pl* hereditary right

mantot *vt* inherit

mantplēsis *nm* (col.) miser, moneygrubber

mantra *nf* mantra

mantracis *nm* treasure hunter

mantrausība *nf* greed

mantrausīgi *adv* greedily

mantrausīgs *adj* greedy

mantrausīgums *nm* greediness

mantrausis *nm* moneygrubber

mantu glabātuve *nf* lost and found office

mantu kambrais *nm* treasure vault

mantu maiss *nm* duffel bag

mantu soma *nf* knapsack, backpack

mantzin/is *nm*, ~e *nf* **1.** treasurer; purser; **2.** quartermaster

manuāli *adv* manually

manuālis *nm* **1.** manual; **2.** keyboard

manuāls *adj* manual

manufaktūra *nf* **1.** hand manufacture; **2.** textile mill; **3.** textiles, fabrics

manufaktūras veikals *nm* fabric store

manufaktūrist/s *nm*, ~e *nf* textile merchant

manufaktūrveikals *nm* fabric store

manuls *nm* manul

manuprāt *adv* in my opinion, to my mind

manuskripts *nm* manuscript

maņa *nf* **1.** (col.) awareness; **2.** sense

maņas org[a]ns [ā] *nm* sense organ

māņbasaringa *nf* thamin

māņbriedis *nm* See **baltastes m., melnastes m.**

māņi *nm pl* See **mānis**

mānkājiņa *nf* pseudopodium

māņlecējpeles *nf pl* jumping mice, Zapodidae

māņticība *nf* superstition

māņticīgais *nom adj* superstitious person

māņticīgi *adv* superstitiously

māņticīgs *adj* superstitious

māņticīgums *nm* superstitiousness

māņoties *vr* (of ghosts) appear; be haunted

māņzirnekļi *nm pl* (zool.) harvestmen

maoisms *nm* Maoism

maoistisks *adj* Maoist

maoist/s *nm*, ~e *nf* Maoist

maor/s *nm*, ~iete *nf* Maori

mape *nf* portfolio

mara *nf* mara

mārābols *nm* sweet clover

marabu *indecl nm* marabou

marabuts *nm* Marabout

maraka *nf* maraca

māraka *nf* horse radish

maralbriedis *nm* maral

marals *nm* maral

marana *nf* madder

maranots *adj* maroon

maranta *nf* arrowroot

Mā[r]as [ŗ] āboliņš *nm* 1. rabbit-foot clover;
     2. sweet clover; white sweet clover;
     3. bird's-foot trefoil

Mā[r]as [ŗ] dadzis *nm* milk thistle

Mā[r]as [ŗ] kārkls *nm* goat willow

marasmatisks *adj* marasmic

marasms *nm* marasmus

Mā[r]as [ŗ] plekste *nf* plaice

Mā[r]as [ŗ] smilga *nf* sweet grass

Mā[r]as [ŗ] vītols *nm* goat willow

Mā[r]as [ŗ] zāle *nf* thyme

marašino *nm indecl* maraschino

maratijas *nf pl* Marattia

maratonisks *adj* marathonic

maratonist/s *nm*, ~e *nf* marathoner

maratons *nm* marathon

maratonskrējēj/s *nm*, ~a *nf* marathon runner

maratonskrējiens *nm* marathon race

mārcains *adj* (of horses) streaked

mārciņa *nf* (weight, currency) pound

marcipāns *nm* marzipan

mārcis *nm* rammer

mare *nf* haff

marengo *indecl nm* Oxford gray fabric

mārenīca *nf* chickweed

marenīte *nf* bird's-eye primrose

mareogr[a]fs [ā] *nm* marigraph

mārga *nf* (reg.) (single) female

margapmale *nf* (naut.) gunwale; rail

margarīns *nm* margarine

margarīnskābe *nf* margaric acid

margas *nf pl* 1. banisters; railing; handrail;
     2. hitch-rack

marginālijas *nf pl* marginalia

margin[a]litāte [ā] *nf* marginality

margin[a]lizācija [ā] *nf* marginalization

margināls *adj* marginal

margojums I *nm* ornamental design

margojums II *nm* twinkling

margot I *v* 1. *vi* twinkle; 2. *vt* ornament

margot II *vi* (*3rd pers*) drizzle

margots *adj, part* of margot I decorated with
     ornamental designs

margrieta *nf* daisy

margrietiņa *nf* daisy

margsiena *nf* bulwarks

margu balsts *nm* rail stanchion

marģināli *adv* marginally

marģināls *adj* marginal

mariāņi *nm pl* Marianists

mariet/is *nm*, ~e *nf* Mari

marihu[a]na [ā] *nf* marihuana

marimba *nf* marimba

marīna *nf* seascape

marināde *nf* marinade; (biešu) m. pickled
     (beets)

marinēt *vt* marinate

marīnisms *nm* 1. striving for hegemony on
     the sea; 2. (rare.) the genre of seascape
     painting

marīnist/s *nm*, ~e *nf* seascape painter

marīns *adj* marine

māriņš *nm* woodruff

marionešu valdība *nf* puppet government

marionete *nf* marionette, puppet

mārīte *nf* 1. ladybug; see also **divpunktu m.**;
2. daisy

marka *nf* 1. postage stamp; 2. (currency) mark;
3. brand, make; 4. token; 5. **dižā m.** (hist.)
mark (land held in common by a village);
6. load line mark

markanti *adv* markedly; saliently; pro-
nouncedly

markants *adj* marked; salient; pronounced

markazīts *nm* marcasite

marketērija *nf* marquetry

mārketings *nm* marketing

marketrija *nf* marquetry

markgrāfiene *nf* margravine

markgrāfiste *nf* margravate

markgrāfs *nm* margrave

markgravijas *nf pl* Marcgravia

markitanta veikals *nm* canteen

markitants *nm* sutler

markīza *nf* awning

markīze I *nf* marchioness

markīze II 1. marquee; 2. awning

markizets *nm* marquisette

markīzs *nm* marquis

markojums *nm* 1. stamps; 2. labeling

markot *vt* 1. put a stamp on; 2. label

Markova ķēde *nf* Markov chain

mārks *nm* retting pond; **pilns kā m.** drunk as
a skunk

marksisms *nm* Marxism

marksisms-ļeņinisms *nm* Marxism-Leninism

marksistiski *adv* in the spirit of Marxism,
according to Marxist doctrine

marksistisks *adj* Marxist

marksist/s *nm*, ~e *nf* Marxist

mārksna *nf* double chin

marķējums *nm* 1. labeling; markings;
2. stamps; 3. dissembling

marķēt *vt* 1. mark, label; 2. put on stamps;
3. dissemble

marķētājs *nm* (billiards, bus., tool) marker;
label paster

marķieris *nm* (billiards, bus., tool) marker;
label paster

marķīze *nf* = **markīze** I

marķīzs *nm* = **markīzs**

marle *nf* gauze; cheesecloth

marlēt *vt* marl

marlijs *nm* mull

marlina *nf* marlin

marlīne *nf* marline

marmelāde *nf* marmalade

marmorējums *nm* marbling

marmorēt *vt* marble

marmorgrīda *nf* (rare.) marble floor

marmorlauztuve *nf* marble quarry

marmorpapīrs *nm* marbleized paper

marmors *nm* marble

marmorziepes *nf pl* marbled soap

marnakas *nf pl* catchweed, cleavers

marodēt *vi* maraud

marodieris *nm* marauder

marokān/is *nm*, ~iete *nf* Moroccan

marokens *nm* 1. marocain; 2. morocco leather

maronīts *nm* Maronite

marote *nf* 1. bauble, fool's scepter; 2. marotte

mārpuķe *nf* daisy

mārpuķīte *nf* daisy

mārrozīte *nf* daisy

mārrutks *nm* horse radish

mārs *nm* (geol.) maar

marsbura *nf* topsail

marseljēze *nf* the Marseillaise

marsietis *nm* Martian

marsilejas *nf pl* Marsilea

mārsiliņi *nm pl* thyme

mārsils *nm* thyme

mārsilu veronika *nf* thyme-leaved speedwell

mārsmilga *nf* sweet grass

mārsniņš *nm* gift (of food from guest to host
or host to guest)

mārsns *nm* bundle, armful

Marss *prop nm* Mars

marss *nm* (naut.) masthead, top

marš *interj* march; **forsēts m.** forced march; **m. ārā!** get out! out you go! **m. gultā!** off to bed!

mārša I *nf* sister-in-law (brother's wife)

mārša II *nf* tidal flat

maršals *nm* marshall

maršancija *nf* marchantia

marša vienība *nf* (mil.) operative unit

maršēšana *nf* marching

maršēt *vi* march

maršrota *nf* (mil.) trained replacement company

maršrutizācija *nf* routing

maršrutizēt *vt* route

maršruts *nm* intinerary; route

maršs *nm* march

maršveida *indecl adj* in march tempo

maršveidīgs *adj* in march tempo

martagonlilija *nf* Turk's-cap lily

martence[ch]s [h] *nm* opean-hearth furnace department

martenceplis *nm* (obs.) open-hearth furnace

martenkrāsns *nf* open-hearth furnace

martenprocess *nm* open-hearth process

martens *nm* (rare.) open-hearth furnace

martensīts *nm* martensite

martentērauds *nm* open-hearth steel

martinija *nf* martynia

mārtiņbērni *nm pl* mummers (at Martinmas time)

Mārtiņdiena *prop nf* Martinmas

Mārtiņi *prop nm* Martinmas

mārtiņroze *nf* small-blossomed variety of chrysanthemum

mārtiņvakars *nm* Martinmas eve

mārtiņzoss *nf* Martinmas goose

martirijs *nm* martyrdom

martirologs *nm* passional

martiroloģija *nf* martyrology

martirs *nm*, **~e** *nf* martyr

marts *nm* March

marubija *nf* horehound

marža *nf* (bus.) margin

masa *nf* 1. mass; 2. slurry; paste; pulp

māsa *nf* 1. sister; 2. (col.) medical nurse; **žēlsirdīgā m.** (obs.) medical nurse

masala *nf* gnat

masalas *nf pl* measles

masaliņas *nf pl* 1. German measles; 2. gnats

mas/as *nf pl* masses; **~u** mass, massed

māsasdēls *nm* nephew (sister's son)

māsasmeita *nf* niece (sister's daughter)

masas pārvade *nf* mass transfer

masas punkts *nm* particle;

māsasvīrs *nm* brother-in-law

masāža *nf* massage

māsene *nf* niece (sister's daughter)

māsenis *nm* nephew (sister's son)

māsēns *nm* cousin (father's sister's son or mother's sister's son)

masēt *vt* massage

masētāja *nf* masseuse

masētājs *nm* masseur

masēties *vr* be massaged

māsīca *nf* 1. cousin (father's brother's daughter or father's sister's daughter; mother's brother's daughter or mother's sister's daughter); 2. sister-in-law

masiere *nf* masseuse

masieris *nm* masseur

māsiņa *nf* 1. *dim* of **māsa**, sister, little sister; 2. (col.) streetwalker

masisks *adj* mass (*adj*)

masīvi *adv* massively

masivitāte *nf* massiveness

mas[i]vizācija [ī] *nf* massing (of fields, plots into larger units)

masīvs *nm* 1. massif; 2. mass, large tract

masīvs *adj* massive

masīvums *nm* massiveness

maska *nf* 1. mask; 2. disguise

maskaļi *nm pl* (folk.) Muscovites

maskarāde *nf* masquerade

maskaviet/is *nm*, **~e** *nf* Muscovite

maskējums *nm* camouflage; coverup

maskēšanās *nfr* (mil.) camouflage

maskēt *vt* 1. mask, disguise; 2. camouflage

maskēties *vr* 1. put on a mask; disguise oneself; 2. camouflage oneself

maskot *vt* = **maskēt**

maskoties *vr* = **maskēties**

masku balle *nf* fancy-dress ball

masku tērps *nm* fancy dress

maskulinizācija *nf* masculinization

maskulinizēties *vr* be masculinized

maskulīns *nm* (gram.) masculine

masons *nm* freemason

masonisms *nm* freemasonry

masora *nf* Masorah

masorēts *nm* masorete

masspektrogr|a|fs [ā] *nm* mass spectrograph

masspektrometrija *nf* mass spectrometry

masspektrometrs *nm* mass spectrometer

masspektrs *nm* mass spectrum

masta grozs *nm* (naut.) crow's nest

masta kok/s *nm* spar; **m. ~i** mast timber

mastifs *nm* mastiff

mastika *nf* mastic

mastikss *nm* 1. mastic tree; 2. mastic

mastīts *nm* mastitis

mastodonts *nm* mastodon

mastoidīts *nm* mastoiditis

mastot *vi* hunt with beaters, participate in a battue

masts I *nm* mast; **galvenais m.** mainmast **pagaidu m.** jury mast; **pakaļējais m.** mizzenmast; **priekšējais m.** foremast; **vairākgabalu m.** made mast; **viengabala m.** pole mast

masts II *nm* beat (the area covered by a battue)

masts III *nm* (of cards) suit

masturbācija *nf* masturbation

masturbēt *vi* masturbate

masu kaps *nm* common grave

masu slepkavība *nf* mass murder, massacre

masveida *indecl adj* mass, massed

masveidā *adv* in a mass

masveidība *nf* mass character

masveidīgi *adv* in a mass

masveidīgs *adj* mass (*adj*), massed

masveidīgums *nm* mass character

maša *nf* bast or reed mat

mašas slota *nf* mop; swab

māšele *nf* (col.) little (younger) sister

mašikuli *indecl nf* machicolation

mašīna *nf* 1. machine; engine; 2. machinery; 3. (col.) car; (mil.) vehicle; **sanitārā m.** ambu-lance; 4. (col.) typewriter

mašīnadījums *nm* piece of machine-knitting

mašīnadīšana *nf* machine knitting

mašīnatslēdznieks *nm* fitter, machinist

mašīnbirojs *nm* typing service

mašīnburtlic/is *nm*, **~e** *nf* linotype operator

mašīnbūve *nf* machine building

mašīnbūvētāj/s *nm*, **~a** *nf* machine builder

mašīnbūvniecība *nf* machine building

mašīndaļa *nf* machine part

mašīndarbnīca *nf* engine shop

mašīndetaļa *nf* machine part

mašīndūrieni *nm pl* basic backstitch

mašīnelements *nm* machine element

mašīneļļa *nf* lubricating oil

maš|i|n|ē|rija [ī][e] *nf* machinery

mašīnindustrija *nf* machine building industry

mašīninformācija *nf* computerized information

mašīninženier/is *nm*, **~e** *nf* mechanical engineer

mašīnist/s *nm*, **~e** *nf* 1. machinist; 2. locomotive engineer

maš|i|nizācija [ī] *nf* mechanization

maš|i|nizēt [ī] *vt* mechanize

mašīnizšuvums *nm* machine embroidery

mašīnkalējs *nm* forging press operator

mašīnkods *nm* (compu.) machine code

mašīnkomanda *nf* (naut.) engine crew

mašīnlaiks *nm* effective machine time

mašīnlasāms *adj* machine-readable

mašīnmācība *nf* practical mechanics; *pl* ~s machine-assisted instruction

mašīnmāja *nf* enginehouse

mašīnmeistars *nm* master mechanic

mašīnpiķis *nm* packing putty

mašīnpistole *nf* submachine gun

mašīnrakstīšana *nf* typing

mašīnrakstītāj/s *nm*, ~a *nf* typist

mašīnrakstītāj/s kantorist/s *nm* , ~a ~e *nf* clerk typist

mašīnrakst/s *nm* typing, typed material; ~ā typed

mašīnrūpniecība *nf* machine production

mašīnstrādnie/ks *nm*, ~ce *nf* machine operator

mašīnšķūnis *nm* machine shed

mašīntelpa *nf* engine room

mašīntulkojums *nm* machine translation (machine-translated item)

mašīntulkošana *nf* machine translation

mašīnvaloda *nf* (compu.) machine language

mašīnzāle *nf* engine room

māt *v* 1. *vi, vt* wave; **m. ar acīm** wink; **m. ar galvu** nod; **m. ar roku** wave; 2. *vi* signal

matadata *nf* hairpin, bobby pin

matador/s *nm*, ~e *nf* matador

matainais āboliņš *nm* rabbit-foot clover

mataina mauraga *nf* mouse-ear hawkweed

matainā sīkgalvīte *nf* a galinsoga, Galinsoga ciliata

matainā vijolīte *nf* hairy violet

matainība *nf* hairiness

matain/is *nm*, ~e *nf* long-haired person

matains *adj* hairy

matainums *nm* hairiness

matatspere *nf* hairspring

mataukla *nf* hair ribbon

mata vilciens *nm* hair stroke

matceliņš *nm* (of hair) parting

māte *nf* 1. mother; 2. (of animals) she- (**vilku m.** she-wolf); (of bees) queen bee; **svešā**

m. (folk.) stepmother; **vientuļā m.** single mother ◊ ~s **brunči** mother's apron strings; ~s **cerībās** ex-pecting, pregnant; ~s **miesās** in the womb

matē *nf indecl* maté

matējums *nm* (of glass) frosting

mateļļa *nf* hair oil

mat|e|m|ā|tika [ē]|[a] *nf* mathematics; **augstakā m.** higher mathematics

mat|e|m|ā|tiķ/is [ē]|[a] *nm*, ~e *nf* mathematician

mat|e|m|ā|tiski [ē]|[a] *adv* mathematically

mat|e|m|ā|tisks [ē]|[a] *adj* mathematical

mat|e|matizācija [ē] *nf* mathematicization

mat|e|matizēt [ē] *vt* mathematicize

mat|e|matizēties [ē] *vr* be mathematicized

matene *nf* hairbrush

matenis *nm* hairworm

mātere *nf* motherwort

materiāli *adv* materially

materiālietilpība *nf* material used per production unit

materiālietilpīgs *adj* requiring a large amount of material per production unit

materiālisms *nm* materialism

materiālistiski *adv* materialistically

materiālistisks *adj* materialistic

materiālists *nm*, ~e *nf* materialist

materiālitāte *nf* materiality

materiālizācija *nf* materialization

materi|a|lizējums [ā] *nm* realization; embodiment

materi|a|lizēt [ā] *vt* materialize

materi|a|lizēties [ā] *vr* materialize

materiālmācība *nf* materials science

materiāls *nm* material; **dedzināmais m.** fuel; **pār-sienamais m.** bandages, dressing

materiāls *adj* 1. material; 2. economic

materiālu pretestība *nf* strength of materials

mat|e|rija [ē] *nf* matter

maternitāte *nf* maternity

mātesaugs *nm* rootstock; stock plant

mātesbrālis *nm* uncle

mātes kanniņa *nf* (of bees) brood cell

māteskoks *nm* mother tree

mātesmāsa *nf* aunt

mātesmāte *nf* grandmother

mātes mētra *nf* one-flowered pyrola

mātesmeita *nf* (folk.) maiden; farmer's daughter

mātesšūna *nf* mother cell

mātestēvs *nm* maternal grandfather

mātes valoda *nf* mother tongue

mātes vārdi *nm pl* (col.) fighting words

mātes zāle *nf* fumitory

matēt *vt* matte, (of metals) deaden, (of glass) frost

matēts *adj, part* of matēt matte, (of gold) dead, (of glass) frosted; (of photographic screens) ground

matgalvis *nm* nematode

mat/i *nm pl* See also mats I; hair (hair covering); hairs; aiz ~iem pievilkts (col.) far-fetched, contrived

mātica *nf* (wife's) mother-in-law

matineja *nf* matinee

matiņš *nm* 1. *dim* of mats; 2. (bot., zool.) hair

matiola *nf* stock, gillyflower

mātiski *adv* in a motherly way

mātisks *adj* motherly

mātišķi *adv* in a motherly way

mātišķīgi *adv* in a motherly way

mātišķīgs *adj* motherly

mātišķs *adj* motherly

matīt *vt* (obs.) 1. see; 2. feel

mātīte *nf* 1. (of animals) female; dam, hen, cow, doe, hind; 2. (sl.) termagant, virago

matjessiļķe *nf* immature herring

matkrāsa *nf* hair dye

matlīnija *nf* hairline

matojums *nm* amount of hair; hair covering

matonis *nm* hairworm

matot *vt* checkmate

matots *adj* hairy

matpapīrs *nm* tracing paper

matpina *nf* hair ribbon

matpīne *nf* tress

matplaisa *nf* fine crack, hairline; ~s crackle

matrace *nf* matress

matracis *nm* matress

m[ā]triar[ch]āts [a][h] *nm* matriarchate

m[ā]triar[ch]ija [a][h] *nf* matriarchy

matrica *nf* (math.) matrix

matrice *nf* (mold) matrix; ~s RNS messenger RNA

matricēt *vt* make a matrix

matricprinteris *nm* matrix printer

matrikula *nf* (educ.) rolls, register

matrikulācija *nf* enrollment

matrikulēt *vt* enroll

matrilineāri *adv* matrilineally

matrilineārs *adj* matrilineal

matrilokāls *adj* matrilocal

matrimoniāli *adv* matrimonially

matrimoniāls *adj* matrimonial

matrona *nf* matron; dowager

matrozis *nm* seaman; sailor; pirmās klases m. able-bodied seaman

matrožcepure *nf* sailor's hat

mat/s I *nm* See also mati; hair (a single strand) ◊ uz ~a (col.) to a hair, to a tee; m. ~ā (col.) to a tee; uz ~a līdzīgs for all the world like; ne par ~u not a whit; (karāties) ~a galā (hang) by a thread; par ~a galu (also par ~a tiesu, par ~a platumu) close shave, hairbreadth (*adj*); par ~u no nāves within a hair's breadth from death

mats II *nm* mate, checkmate

mats *adj* matte

matspuldze *nf* frosted light bulb

matstikls *nm* frosted glass; (photo.) ground glass

mātšūna *nf* mother cell

mattārps *nm* hairworm

matu āboliņš *nm* sweet clover

matu audzēšanas līdzeklis *nm* hair restorer

matūdens *nm* hair lotion

matu griežamā mašīna *nf* hair clipper

matu maksts ērce *nf* follicle mite

matu nodzīšanas līdzeklis *nm* depilatory

matu ota *nf* hair pencil

matu pīne *nf* tress

mat[u]ritāte [ū] *nf* maturity

matu sakārtojums *nm* hairdo

matu skaldīšana *nf* hairsplitting

matu stiebrs *nm* hair shaft

matu tīkliņš *nm* hairnet

matuzāle *nf* fumitory

mātuzņēmums *nm* parent company

matvads *nm* capillary

matveida *indecl adj* hairlike

matveida grīslis *nm* hairlike sedge

matveida ūdensgundega *nf* white water crowfoot

matveidīgi *adv* like hair

matveidīgs *adj* hairlike

maucība *nf* whoredom, whoring

maucinieks *nm* whorer

mauja *nf* bellow, moo

mauka *nf* whore

maukļi *nm pl* wood bulrush

maukna *nf* spruce bark

maukoties *vr* whore

maukt *vt* (of tightly fitting things) put on; **m. ādu** skin (an animal); **m. ādu pār acīm** (col.) exploit mercilessly; **m. nost** take off; **m. stabuli** make a whistle

maule *nf* (reg.) hub

mauraga *nf* hawkweed

maurains *adj* lawny

maura kumelīte *nf* rayless chamomile

maura platkājiņi *nm pl* silverweed

maura retējs *nm* cinquefoil

maura skarene *nf* 1. annual meadow grass; 2. rough-stalked meadow grass

maura sūrene *nf* knot-grass

mauricija *nf* miriti palm

mauriņš *nm dim* of **maurs**, lawn

mauriņu sūrene *nf* 1. knotgrass; 2. cinquefoil

mauris *nm* white bream

mauritānis *nm*, ~iete *nf* Mauritanian

maurloki *nm pl* chives

maurot *vi* moo, bellow

maurs I *nm* lawn

maur/s II *nm*, ~iete *nf* Moor; *pl gen* ~u Moorish; ~u stils moresque

maut I *vt* = **maukt**

maut II *vi* moo

maut III *vi* (reg.) swim; dive

mauties *vr* (reg.) 1. become overcast; 2. compete in swimming

mauzeris *nm* Mauser pistol

mauzolejs *nm* mausoleum

māva *nf* bellow, moo

māviens *nm* bellow, moo

maz *adv* (with verb or noun in singular) little; (with noun in plural) few; **par m.** too little; **m. pamazām** little by little

maz *partic* at all; **vai m.** if at all

mazā adatzivs *nf* snake pipefish

mazā ausainā pūce *nf* scops owl

mazactiņa *nf* dianthus

mazā dzeltenā lēpa *nf* least yellow water lily

mazā ēdes zāle *nf* field filago

mazā ežgalvīte *nf* small burr reed

mazā gaišā tilbīte *nf* wood sandpiper

mazā gaura *nf* smew

mazā govju gārsa *nf* angelica

mazais *nom adj* the little one; child; (as a name) Tiny, Shorty

mazais alks *nm* little auk

mazais apogs *nm* pygmy owl

mazais asinsloks *nm* pulmonary circulation

mazais baltais gārnis *nm* little egret

mazais diždadzis *nm* common burdock

mazais dūkuris *nm* little grebe

mazais dumpis *nm* little bittern

mazais dzenis *nm* lesser spotted woodpecker

mazais dzeroklis *nm* bicuspid

mazais eglu mizgrauzis *nm* a bark beetle, Pitygoes chalcographus

mazais ērglis *nm* lesser spotted eagle

mazais gulbis *nm* tundra swan

mazais jūrasgrundulis *nm* freckled goby

mazais kudu *nm* lesser kudu

mazais ķīris *nm* little gull

mazais krustknābis *nm* red crossbill

mazais kurliks *nm* little gull

mazais liela kauls *nm* fibula

mazais loris *nm* lesser slow loris

mazais mārsils *nm* wild thyme

mazais muškērājs *nm* red-breasted flycatcher

mazais niedrcālis *nm* little crake

mazais ormanītis *nm* little crake

mazais peļu vanags *nm* kestrel

mazais priežu lūksngrauzis *nm* a bark beetle, Blastophagus minor

mazais raibais dzenis *nm* lesser spotted woodpecker

mazais sikspārnis *nm* common pipistrelle

mazais stagaris *nm* nine-spined stickleback

mazais strazds *nm* song thrush

mazais susuris *nm* hazel dormouse

mazais svilpis *nm* scarlet rosefinch

mazais šņibītis *nm* red-necked stin

mazā istabas muša *nf* lesser housefly

mazais tritons *nm* smooth newt

mazais vakarsikspārnis *nm* Leisler's bat

mazais zīriņš *nm* little tern

mazaizsalstošs *adj* nearly ice-free

mazā jūras adata *nf* straight-nosed pipefish

mazāk *adv, comp* of **maz** less

mazākais *adj, super* of **mazs** least; littlest

mazākais *nom adj* the least, the last thing; the slightest; **tas jau ir m. !** that's the least of my worries!

mazākais *adv* at least

mazā kalnu mētra *nf* basil-thyme

mazākprasītājs *nm* lowest bidder

mazāksolīšana *nf* Dutch auction

mazākturīgs *adj* low-income

mazā kuitala *nf* whimbrel

mazākums *nm* minority

mazākumtautība *nf* ethnic minority

mazākvērtīgs *adj* of lesser value

mazā ķirzaka *nf* viviparous lizard

mazā lēpa *nf* frogbit

mazalkoholisks *adj* of low alcohol content

mazā lucerna *nf* hop clover

mazā mauraga *nf* mouse-ear hawkweed

mazambriedis *nm* brocket

mazā nātre *nf* small nettle

mazapdāvināts *adj* untalented; dull, slow

mazapdzīvots *adj* sparsely populated

mazā pele *nf* harvest mouse

mazapgaismots *adj* poorly lit

mazā plūme *nf* damson plum

mazapmeklēts *adj* unfrequented, rarely visited

mazā polārkaija *nf* Iceland gull

mazā puskuitala *nf* Terek sandpiper

mazā pūslene *nf* lesser bladderwort

mazā pūtele *nf* slender cudweed

mazapzinīgi *adv* unconscientiously

mazapzinīgs *adj* unconscientious

mazā raganzālīte *nf* smaller enchanter's nightshade

mazarom[a]tisks [ā] *adj* lightly scented

mazā sanguisorba *nf* salad burnet

mazās brūnvālītes *nf* salad burnet

mazā sīga *nf* little bustard

mazasinība *nf* anemia

mazasinīgs *adj* anemic

mazā skābene *nf* sheep sorrel

mazās smadzenes *nf pl* cerebellum

mazā stērste *nf* little bunting

mazā šķirzutne *nf* smooth newt

mazatalgots *adj* poorly paid

mazatne *nf* early childhood

mazattīstīts *adj* undeveloped

mazā ūdenslēpa *nf* broad-leaved pondweed

mazauto *indecl nm* small car; runabout

mazauglīgs *adj* low-yield; not very fruitful

mazauguma *indecl adj* short

mazautobuss *nm* microbus

mazautomobilis *nm* small car

mazā zoss *nf* lesser white-fronted goose

mazbaldriāns *nm* corn salad

mazbērnība *nf* **1.** infancy; **2.** low birth rate

mazbērn/s *nm* **1.** toddler; **2.** ~i grandchildren

mazbērnu barība *nf* baby food

mazbērnu novietne *nf* day nursery

mazbērnu sētiņa *nf* playpen

mazbībele *nf* New Testament

mazbrālītis *nm* little brother

mazbrokasts *nf* first breakfast, early breakfast

mazceļš *nm* dirt road

mazcienība *nf* contempt

mazcienīgi *adv* contemptuously

mazcienīgs *adj* contemptuous

mazdaisms *nm* Mazdaism, Zaroastrianism

mazdēls *nm* grandson

mazdarbīgs *adj* inactive

mazdārziņš *nm* family garden plot

mazderīgs *adj* of little use

mazdilstošs *adj* wearproof

mazdrusciņ *adv* a little bit

mazdūšelis *nm* coward

mazdūšība *nf* faint-heartedness, cowardice

mazdūšīgi *adv* in a cowardly manner

mazdūšīgs *adj* faint-hearted, cowardly

mazdziņš *nm dim* of **mazgs**, small knot

mazefekt[i]vitāte [ī] *nf* low efficiency

mazefektīvi *adv* inefficiently

mazefektīvs *adj* of low efficiency, inefficient

mazelastīgs *adj* low-elasticity

māzerainība *nf* gnarliness

māzerains *adj* knaggy, gnarled

māzeris *nm* gnarl

māzers *nm* maser

mazformāta *indecl adj* small-size

mazgabarīta *indecl adj* small-size

mazgadība *nf* minority, nonage

mazgadīgais *nom adj* minor, juvenile

mazgadīgo tiesa *nf* juvenile court

mazgadīgs *adj* juvenile

mazgājamā mašīna *nf* washing machine

mazgājamība *nf* washability

mazgājamizturība *nf* washability

mazgājams *adj, part* of **mazgāt** washable; wash, washing, washday (*adj*)

mazgāt *vt* wash; **m. galvu** a. wash one's hair; b. (com.) dress down, haul so over the coals; **m. rokas nevainībā** wash one's hands of guilt; **m. traukus** do the dishes; **m. veļu** wash clothes, do the laundry; **m. vešu** (col.) wash one's dirty linen (in public)

mazgātāja *nf* laundress, washerwoman

mazgātājs *nm* washer; (tech.) scrubber

mazgātava *nf* laundry; laundry room; **(auto) m.** carwash

mazgā/ties *vr* **1.** wash oneself, bathe, take a bath; **2. labi ~jas** (of fabrics) washes easily

mazgātne *nf* washer (washing device)

mazgruntniecība *nf* **1.** small landownership; **2.** small landowners

mazgruntnie/ks *nm*, ~ce *nf* small landowner

mazgs *nm* (reg.) knot

mazgulis *nm* scrubber

mazģimenes *indecl adj* small-family

mazie biškrēsliņi *nm pl* groundsel

maziedarbīgi *adv* ineffectively

maziedarbīgs *adj* ineffective

maziedarbīgums *nm* ineffectiveness

Mazie greizie rati *nm pl* Ursa Minor

maziene *nf* childhood

mazienesīgs *adj* low-yield, low-profit

mazie saulkrēsliņi *nm pl* lesser meadow rue

mazietekmīgs *adj* uninfluential

mazietilpīgs *adj* small-capacity

mazinājums *nm* (math.) result (of a subtraction)

mazināmais *nom adj* minuend

mazināt *vt* reduce; diminish

mazinātājs *nm* subtrahend

mazināties *vr* decrease

mazinieks *nm* (hist.) Menshevik

maziņais *nom adj* little one

maziņš*adj* tiny

maziski *adv* in a mean way; pettily

mazisks *adj* mean, base; petty

maziskums *nm* meanness, baseness; pettiness

mazītiņām *adv* little by little

mazītiņš*adj* teensy-weensy

mazizglītots *adj* semiliterate

mazizmēra *indecl adj* small-size

mazizpētīts *adj* little explored, little investigated

mazizturīgs *adj* not durable

mazjānis *nm* (col.) little finger

mazjaudas *indecl adj* low-powered

mazjutība *nf* low sensitivity

mazjūtība *nf* insensitivity

mazjutīgs *adj* of low sensitivity

mazjūtīgs *adj* insensitive

mazjutīgums *nm* low sensitivity

mazjūtīgums *nm* insensitivity

mazkalibra *indecl adj* small-caliber; small-bore

mazkambaris *nm* (hist.) small bedroom

mazkompetenti *adv* incompetently

mazkompetents *adj* incompetent

mazkriev/s *nm*, ~iete *nf* Ukrainian

mazkustība *nf* 1. low mobility; 2. sedentary way of life

mazkustīgs *adj* not very mobile; (of life style) sedentary

mazkustīgums *nm* 1. low mobility; 2. sedentary way of life

mazkvalificēts *adj* unqualified

mazlācītis *nm* raccoon

mazlapains *adj* small-leaved

mazlauku sistēma *nf* crop rotation system involving few crops

mazlēpe *nf* frogbit

mazlēpīte *nf* frogbit

mazliesmains *adj* small-flame

mazliet or mazlietiņ *adv* a little, somewhat

mazlietots *adj* 1. almost new; 2. rarely used, not much in use

mazlitrāžas *indecl adj* (of cars, car engines) small

mazlodziņš*nm* small, hinged windowpane (used for airing)

mazlops *nm* small farm animal

mazmācīts *adj* semiliterate

mazmāja *nf* cottage

mazmājas *nf pl* small farm

mazmājiņa *nf dim* of **mazmāja**, outhouse, privy

mazmājnieks *nm* cottager

mazmazbērns *nm* great-grandchild

mazmazdēls *nm* great-grandson

mazmazmeita *nf* great-granddaughter

mazmazs *adj* tiny

mazmeita *nf* granddaughter

mazmetrāžas *indecl adj* of small area

mazmežains *adj* sparsely wooded

mazmolekulārs *adj* small-molecule

mazmuiža *nf* (hist.) subsidiary property (of a lord of the manor)

maznieciņ *adv* a little bit

maznoderīgs *adj* of little use

maznodrošināts *adj* indigent

maznozīmība *nf* inconsequentiality

maznozīmīgi *adv* inconsequentially

maznozīmīgs *adj* inconsequential

maznozīmīgums *nm* inconsequentiality

mazo[ch]isms [h] *nm* masochism

mazotne *nf* early childhood

mazpamazām *adv* little by little

mazpamazītēm *adv* little by little

mazpamazītiņām *adv* little by little

mazpazīstams *adj* little known

mazpienīgs *adj* of low milk yield

mazpienīgums *nm* low milk yield

mazpieredzējis *adj* inexperienced

mazpilsēta *nf* small town

mazpilsētniecisks *adj* small-town, provincial

mazpilsētnieks *nm*, **~ce** *nf* small-towner, provincial

mazpilsonība *nf* petty bourgeoisie

mazpilsonis *nm* petty bourgeois

mazpilsonisks *adj* petty bourgeois (*adj*)

mazprasīgi *adv* in an undemanding manner

mazprasīgs *adj* undemanding

mazprātība *nf* feeble-mindedness

mazprātīgs *adj* feeble-minded

mazprātiņš*nm* (col.) **1.** stupid person; **2.** feeble-minded person

mazproduktīvs *adj* of low productivity

mazpuika *nm* little boy

mazpuisis *nm* farm hand (who does not do heavy work)

mazpuķīte *nf* little flower

mazpulcēns *nm* member of the mazpulki youth organization

mazpulki *nm pl* mazpulki, a Latvian youth organization

mazpurnīte *nf* pilewort

mazputniņš*nm* (folk.) little bird

mazražīgs *adj* unproductive

mazrocība *nf* indigence

mazrocīgs *adj* indigent

mazrunātājs *nm* (**latviešu valodas**) **m.** one who speaks little (Latvian)

mazrunība *nf* taciturnity

mazrunīgi *adv* taciturnly

mazrunīg/s *adj* taciturn

mazrunīgums *nm* taciturnity

maz/s *adj* small; little; (of speed) low; (of time, stature) short; (of ideas, mistakes) slight; *defin* **~ais** minor

mazsaimniecība *nf* small farm

mazsaimnieks *nm* small farmer

mazsālīts *adj* lightly salted

mazsaprotams *adj* unintelligible

mazsaraiņi *nm pl* Oligochaeta

mazsaru *indecl adj* short-bristled

mazsaru tārpi *nm pl* oligochaetes

mazsaturīgs *adj* insubstantial; insipid

mazsekmīgs *adj* **1.** (educ.) of low achievement; **m. skolēns** low achiever; **2.** unsuccessful

mazsirdība *nf* small-mindedness

mazsirdīgi *adv* in a small-minded way

mazsirdīgs *adj* small-minded

mazskauts *nm* cub scout

mazsniegains *adj* of little snowfall

mazspēcība *nf* powerlessness, faintness

mazspēcīgi *adv* powerlessly, faintly

mazspēcīgs *adj* powerless, faint

mazspēja *nf* (med.) insufficiency

mazspējība *nf* weakness

mazstāvu *indecl adj* one—and two-story

mazsvarība *nf* inconsequentiality

mazsvarīgi *adv* inconsequentially

mazsvarīgs *adj* of little importance, inconsequential

mazsvarīgums *nm* inconsequentiality

mazsvītrains *adj* paucistriate

mazticams *adj* doubtful

mazticība *nf* faintheartedness

mazticīgi *adv* faintheartedly

mazticīgs *adj* of little faith, fainthearted

maztirāēas *indecl adj* low-circulation; limited-edition

maztoksisks *adj* low-toxicity

maztonnāēas *indecl adj* low-tonnage

mazturība *nf* indigence

mazturīgs *adj* indigent

mazturīgums *nm* indigence

mazubrīd *adv* briefly

mazūdenīgs *adj* arid

mazūdens *nm* low water level, aridity

mazuliet *adv* = **mazliet**

mazulis *nm* **1.** infant; baby; **2.** (of animals) young; fry; cub; calf; **3.** (col.) little finger

mazulītis *nm dim* of **mazulis**; little one

mazumiņš*nm dim* of **mazums**, little bit; sth. put aside

mazum/s *nm* **1.** smallness, littleness; **2.** small way; small amount; **ne m.** not a few, not a little; **3.** **~a** retail

mazumtirdzniecība *nf* retail business

mazūrijs *nm* technetium

mazurka *nf* mazurka

mazuties *adv* a little

mazuts *nm* mazut

mazvācieši *nm pl* (hist.) poor and uneducated Germans

mazvakariņas *nf pl* evening snack

mazvalkāts *adj* little worn

mazvārdains *adj* of few words, laconic

mazvārdība *nf* laconism

mazvārdīgs *adj* of few words, laconic

mazvārdīgums *nm* laconism

mazvarība *nf* powerlessness

mazvarīgs *adj* powerless

mazvelosip|e|ds [ē] *nm* small bicycle

mazvērtība *nf* inferiority

mazvērtīgs *adj* inferior

mazvērtīgums *nm* inferiority

mazvietīgs *adj* (of vehicles) having few seats, small

mazvīrcele *nf* small snapdragon

mazvirsa *nf* egg-and-cream glaze for bread

mazvirtuve *nf* kitchenette

mazzālains *adj* of sparse grass growth

mazzarains *adj* having few branches

mazzarots *adj* having few branches

mazzemnieks *nm* small farmer

mazziedains *adj* 1. pauciflorate; 2. parviflorate

mazziedu *indecl adj* 1. pauciflorate; 2. parviflorate

mazziedu grīslis *nm* few-flowered sedge

mazziedu pameldri *nm pl* few-flowered club rush

māžeklis *nm* (col.) clown, buffoon

māžīgs *adj* (col.) clownish

mažorīgi *adv* in a major scale

mažorīgs *adj* (mus.) major

mažoritārs *adj* majoritarian

mažors *nm* (mus.) major

mažors *adj* (mus.) major

māžoties *vr* (col., cont.) 1. clown 2. play pranks

māž/s *nm* 1. (col., cont.) clown, buffoon; 2. ~i ghosts, spooks

mē *interj* baa

meanders *nm* meander

meandrēt *vi* meander

meandrs *nm* meander

mēbele *nf* piece of furniture; *pl* ~s furniture; iebūvētas ~s built-ins; mīkstās ~s upholstered furniture

mēbelējums *nm* furniture

mēbelēt *vt* furnish

mēbeļaudums *nm* upholstery fabric

mēbeļdrāna *nf* upholstery fabric

mēbeļgaldniecība *nf* 1. cabinetmaking; 2. cabinetmaker's shop

mēbeļgaldnieks *nm* cabinetmaker

mēbeļnieks *nm*, ~ce *nf* 1. cabinetmaker; 2. furniture merchant

mēbeļrūpnīca *nf* furniture factory

mēbeļrūpniecība *nf* furniture manufacture

mecenāt/s *nm*, ~e *nf* patron of the arts

me|cha|nicisks [hā] *adj* (philos.) mechanistic

me|cha|nicisms [hā] *nm* (philos.) mechanism

me|cha|nicists [hā] nm (philos.) mechanist

me|cha|nika [hā] *nf* mechanics

me|cha|niķ/is [hā] *nm*, ~e *nf* mechanic

me|cha|niski [hā] *adv* mechanically

me|cha|nisks [hā] *adj* mechanical, mechanic

me|cha|nisms [hā] *nm* mechanism

me|cha|nistiski [hā] *adv* mechanistically

me|cha|nistisks [hā] *adj* mechanistic

me|ch|anizācija [h] *nf* mechanization

me|ch|aniz[ā]tors [h][a] *nm* 1. specialist in mech-anization; 2. machine operator

me|ch|anizēt [h] *vt* mechanize

me|ch|anoterapija [h] *nf* mechanotherapy

mecosoprāns *nf* mezzo-soprano

mecotinta *nf* mezzotint

medainība *nf* honeyedness

medains *adj* honeyed; mellifluous

medainums *nm* honeyedness; mellifluousness

medaljons *nm* 1. locket; 2. medallion

medalus *nm* mead

medaļa *nf* medal; ~s otrā puse reverse (of a medal); (fig.) the other side of the coin; ~s seja obverse

medaļnie/ks *nm*, ~ce *nf* recipient of a medal

medaunieks *nm* honeyjar

mede *nf* hunt

medene *nf* 1. (bot.) shingled hedgehog; 2. mallard; 3. sweet alyssum

medenes *nf pl* good things, goodies

medenis *nm* capercaillie

mediācija *nf* mediation

mediāli *adv* medially

mediāls *adj* 1. medial; 2. (gram., of voice) reflexive

mediāna *nf* (geom.) median

medianta *nf* mediant

mediastins *nm* mediastinum

medi[a]tizēt [ā] *vt* mediatize

medi[a]tizācija [ā] *nf* mediatization

mediators *nm* 1. pick, plectrum; 2. (chem.; intervener) mediator

medības *nf pl* hunt, hunting

medību atļauja *nf* hunting license

medību bise *nf* shotgun; fowling piece

medību dzīvnieki *nm pl* game

medību nazis *nm* hunting knife

medību piekūns *nm* gyrfalcon

medību putni *nm pl* game birds

medību spieķis *nm* shooting stick

medību suns *nm* hound

medicīna *nf* medicine; ~s medical

medicīnas dēle *nf* medicinal leech

medicīnas māsa *nf* registered nurse

medicīniski *adv* 1. medically; 2. medicinally

medicīnisks *adj* 1. medical; 2. medicinal

medieši *nm pl* Medes

medievistika *nf* medieval studies

medievist/s *nm*, ~e *nf* medievalist

medīgs *adj* good hunter; m. kaķis good mouser

mēdīgi *adv* mockingly

mēdīgs *adj* mocking

medijs *nm* 1. (spiritualistic) medium; 2. (ling.) reflexive voice

medījums *nm* game (quarry; flesh of game animals)

medikamentozi *adv* medicinally

medikamentozs *adj* medicinal; drug (*adj*)

medikament/s *nm*, usu. *pl* ~i medicine, remedies

mediķ/is *nm*, ~e *nf* 1. physician; 2. medical student

mediodentāls *adj* interdental

medīt *vt, vi* hunt

mēdīt *vt* mock

meditācija *nf* meditation

mēdītājs *nm* mocker

mēdītājs putns *nm* mockingbird

medit[a]tīvi [ā] *adv* meditatively

medit[a]tīv/s [ā] *adj* meditative

mediterrāns *adj* Mediterranean

meditēt *vt* meditate

mēdīties *vr* 1. mock; 2. mock one another

medmaize *nf* bread and honey

medmāsa *nf* registered nurse

mednese *nf* (poet.) bee

medniecība *nf* huntsmanship

medniekdesiņa *nf* hard salami (stick)

mednie/ks *nm*, ~ce *nf* hunter

mednieku desa *nf* hard salami

mednis *nm* capercaillie

medoks *nm* Médoc (wine)

medot *vi* produce nectar

medots *adj* honeyed

medpunkts *nm* medical treatment facility

medrese *nf* madrasah

medspiedne *nf* honey press

medsviede or medsviedne *nf* honey separator

medullārs *adj* medullary

medus *nm* honey

medus āpsis *nm* ratel
medusaugi *nm pl* nectar plants
medus blusiņas *nf pl* psyllas
medus kāre *nf* honeycomb
medusmaize *nf* bread and honey
medusmēle *nf, nm* (col.) flatterer
medus mēnesis *nm* honeymoon
meduspuķes *nf pl* madder
medus rasa *nf* honeydew
medusrausis *nm* honey cake
medussalds *adj* honey-sweet
medus stevija *nf* stevia
medus uts *nf* pear sucker
medus vīns *nm* mulset
meduszāle *nf* velvet grass
medusziedi *nm pl* sweet clover
medutiņš*nm dim* of **medus**, honey
medūza *nf* jellyfish
medvīns *nm* honeyed wine
medžl[i]ss [ī] *nm* mejlis
mefistofelis *nm* Mephistopheles, the devil
mefistofeliski *adv* in a Mephistophelian fashion
mefistofelisks *adj* Mephistophelian
megaampērs *nm* megaampere
megabaits *nm* megabyte
megafons *nm* megaphone, bullhorn
megahercs *nm* megahertz
megal[i]tisks [ī] *adj* megalithic
megal[i]ts [ī] *nm* megalith
megalokefalija *nf* megacephaly
megalom[a]nija [ā] *nf* megalomania
megalom[a]niski [ā] *adv* megalomaniacally
megalom[a]nisks [ā] *adj* megalomaniac
megalopole *nf* megalopolis
megarieši *nm pl* Megarians
megaskops *nm* magnifier
megatonna *nf* megaton
megavats *nm* megawatt
megavoltampērs *nm* megavolt-ampere
megavoltampērstunda *nf* megavolt-ampere hour

megavolts *nm* megavolt
megera *nf* shrew, scold
megommetrs *nm* megohmmeter
megoms *nm* megohm
mēgt *vt def* be in the habit of, be used to (doing); **kā mēdz teikt** as the saying goes
megzt *vt* (reg., of fishnets) weave
mēģene *nf* test tube
mēģinājums *nm* 1. try, attempt; 2. experiment; 3. rehearsal
mēģināt *v* 1. *vt* try, attempt; 2. *vt* rehearse; 3. *vi* experiment
mēģināties *vr* practice; try, attempt
meiča *nf* girl, lass
meiers *nm* = **meiris**
meija *nf* bough, birch bough (cut for decoration)
meijot *vt* deck with boughs
meikaps *nm* makeup
meiksts *nf* pole (with one end split crosswise)
meimuriem *adv* staggering
meimuris *nm* staggerer
meimuriski *adv* staggering
meimurot *vi* stagger
meirāns *nm* marjoram
meiris *nm* (hist.) steward, overseer
meisele *nf* (barb.) chisel
meistardarbnīca *nf* (educ.) master class
meistardarbs *nm* masterpiece
meistardziedonis *nm* 1. star singer; ~**e** *nf*; 2. Meistersinger
meistare *nf* 1. master craftswoman; 2. forewoman; 3. champion
meistarība *nf* 1. mastery; workmanship; 2. championship
meistariene *nf* = **meistare**
meistarīgi *adv* in a masterly fashion
meistarīgs *adj* masterly
meistarīgums *nm* masterliness
meistariski *adv* in a masterly fashion
meistarisks *adj* masterly
meistariskums *nm* masterliness

meistarkandidāts *nm* (sports) master's candidate

meistarklase *nf* champion class

meistarkomanda *nf* champion team

meistarojums *nm* contrivance

meistarot *vt* tinker, make (incompetently, with primitive means)

meistars *nm* **1.** master, master craftsman; **vecs m.** old hand, past master; **2.** pro; **3.** foreman; **4.** champion

meistarsacīkstes *nf pl* championship contest

meistarstiķis *nm* (col.) masterpiece

meistaru sakne *nf* masterwort

meistarvienība *nf* champion team

meisteris *nm* (obs.) master

meita *nf* **1.** daughter; **īstā m.** (folk.) own daughter; **2.** girl; single female; **3.** maid, maidservant

meitas bērns *nm* (col.) illegitimate child

meitasdēls *nm* grandson

meitās iešana *nf* (folk.) looking for a bride

meitasmeita *nf* granddaughter

meitasšūna *nf* daughter cell

meitas uzvārds *nm* maiden name

meitasvīrs *nm* son-in-law

meitele *nf* (col.) girl

meitene *nf* girl

meitenīgi *adv* girlishly

meitenīgs *adj* girlish

meitenīgums *nm* girlishness

meitenīte *nf dim* of **meitene**, little girl; girlie

meitēns *nm* (col.) girl

meiteņu pīpene *nf* feverfew

meitie/tis *nm* (com.) woman; **~ša cilvēks** (com.) woman

meitinieks *nm* womanizer

meitiņa *nf dim* of **meita**, daughter; girl, little girl

meitišķis *nm* (col.) female

meitsabiedrība *nf* subsidiary

meitšūna *nf* daughter cell

meituģēģeris *nm* (com.) skirt chaser

meitu māja *nf* (sl.) brothel

meitumednieks *nm* (col.) skirt chaser

mējiens *nm* (com.) blow

mējināt *vi* bleat

meklējum/s *nm*, usu. *pl* **~i** search, seeking; quest; **nejaušo ~u metode** heuristic method

meklēšana *nf* search

meklēšanās *nfr* heat, rut; **~s laiks** rutting time

meklēt *vt* look for, search, seek; (in wanted ads) want(ed); **ko tu te meklē?** what do you want here? **saknēm saknes m.** be nitpicking

meklētājprogramma *nf* (compu.) browser

meklētāj/s *nm*, **~a** *nf* **1.** seeker, searcher; **2.** (tech.) finder

meklēties *vr* **1.** seek for oneself; **2.** search; **3.** be in heat, rut

meknis *nm* glutton

meknīt *vi* dig through, rummage

mekonopsis *nm* meconopsis

meksikān/is *nm*, **~iete** *nf* Mexican

Meksikas fizāle *nf* Mexican ground cherry

mekšināt *vi* bleat

mekšķināt *vi* bleat

mekucis *nm* soft, slippery lump

melafīrs *nm* melaphyre

melan[ch]olija [h] *nf* melancholy

melan[ch]oliķ/is [h] *nm*, **~e** *nf* melancholic

melan[ch]oliski [h] *adv* melancholically

melan[ch]olisks [h] *adj* melancholic

melan[ch]oliskums [h] *nm* melancholiness

melanēziet/is *nm*, **~e** *nf* Melanesian

melanh- See **melanch-**

melan[i]ns [ī] *nm* melanine

melanisms *nm* melanism

melanokratisks *adj* melanocratic

melanoma *nf* melanoma

melanoze *nf* melanosis

melanža *nf* (mixture; yarn) mélange

melase *nf* molasses

mel[ch]iors [h] *nm* German silver

melderiene *nf* (obs., col.) miller's wife; miller

melderis *nm* (obs., col.) miller

meldermeitiņa *nf* (folk.) miller's daughter

melderzellis *nm* (obs.) miller's helper, miller's apprentice

meldes *nf pl* orache

meldēt *vt* (barb.) report

meldija *nf* (col.) melody

meldiņš *nm* (col.) tune

meldrains *adj* overgrown with bulrushes

meldrājs *nm* rushes

meldri *nm pl, sg* **meldrs** bulrush

meldru kosa *nf* sedge-like equisetum

mēl/e *nf* 1. tongue (organ, tongue-like object, language); *pl* ~es gossip; **aplikta m.** furred tongue; **(viņam) gaŗa m.** (he is a) blabber; **lunkana m.** soft soap; **ļauna m.** wicked tongue; ~es galā (also uz ~es) at the tip of the tongue; **m. niez** (col.) can't wait to tell about it; **m. kā piesieta** tongue-tied; **vai tev m. piesieta?** cat got your tongue? **ar divi ~ēm runāt** speak with a forked tongue; **2.** (mil.) identification prisoner; **3.** tenon

mēlene *nf* blue shawl

mēlenis *nm* (ling.) lingual sound

mēleņi *nm pl* tongue worms

mēles I *nf pl* woad

mēles II *nf pl* (col.) gossip, talk

mēles saitīte *nf* frenum

mēles vālene *nf* (bot.) goat's beard

mēlgale *nf* 1. red-breasted merganser; 2. scoffer, mocker

mēlgalība *nf* mockery

mēlgalīgi *adv* mockingly

mēlgalīgs *adj* mocking

mēlgal/is *nm*, ~e *nf* scoffer, mocker

mēlgaļot *vt* mock

melhiors *nm* = **melchiors**

mel/i *nm pl* lie; **balti m.** sheer lies; a lie with a hatchet; **salti m.** out-and-out lie; **nevainīgi m.** white lie, fib; ~u stāsts made-up story; **no ~iem ausis kust** liar, liar, pants on fire!

melība *nf* mendacity

melibioze *nf* melibiose

melīgi *adv* mendaciously

melīgs *adj* mendacious, lying

mēlīgi *adv* gabbily; talkatively

mēlīgs *adj* gabby; talkative

melīgums *nm* mendacity

mēlīgums *nm* gabbiness, talkativeness

melija *nf* Melia

melinīts *nm* melinite

meliorācija *nf* land improvement; land reclamation

melior[a]tīvs [ā] *adj* meliorative

melior[a]tor/s [ā] *nm*, ~e *nf* specialist in land reclamation

meliorēt *vt* drain; (of soil) improve

mel/is *nm*, ~e *nf* liar

melisa *nf* (bot.) balm

melisīnskābe *nf* melissic acid

melismātiski *adv* melismatically

melismātisks *adj* melismatic

melisms *nm* (mus.) melisma

meliss *nm* melis

melitas *nf pl* bastard balm

mēlīte *nf* 1. *dim* of **mēle**, tongue, little tongue; 2. trigger; ~s aizsargskava trigger guard; 3. detent; 4. clapper, tongue; 5. (mus.) reed; 6. (of scales) tongue, pointer

mēlītes *nf pl* starflower

melkulība *nf* mendacity

melkulīgi *adv* mendaciously

melkulīgs *adj* mendacious, lying

melkulīgums *nm* mendacity

melkulis *nm*, ~e *nf* liar

mellenājs *nm* 1. blueberry plant; bilberry plant; 2. blueberry patch; bilberry patch

mellenāju kārkls *nm* bog willow

mellene *nf* (American) blueberry; (European) bilberry

mellenīte *nf dim* of **mellene**, blueberry; bilberry

melleņaudze *nf* blueberry patch; bilberry patch

melleņmelns *adj* blackish blue

melleņoga *nf* blueberry; bilberry

melluža *nf* 1. dark-haired or dark-complexioned woman; 2. dark-colored cow

melmeļi *nm pl* darkling beetles

melmeņi *nm pl* lower back

melmeņsērdzīgs *adj* suffering from lower backpain

melmeņu sērga nf lower back pain

melmeņu zāle *nf* Solomon's seal

melnā apse *nf* black poplar

melnā birža *nf* illegal currency exchange

melnacains *adj* dark-eyed

melnace *nf* dark-eyed girl

melnacis *nm* dark-eyed man

melnādains *adj* black-skinned

melnā dēle *nf* horse leech

melnā driģene *nf* henbane

melnā dumbrājsloka *nf* black-tailed godwit

melnā dzilna *nf* black woodpecker

melnā egle *nf* black spruce

melnā gobija *nf* black goby

meln/ais *nom adj*, ~ā *f* black

melnais alksnis *nm* black alder

melnais amūrs *nm* black amur, ching yu

melnais Apolons *nm* Apollo butterfly

melnais bērzs *nm* black birch

melnais deviņvīruspēks *nm* black mullein

melnais erickiņš *nm* black redstart

melnais grifs *nm* cinereous vulture

melnais gulbis *nm* black swan

melnais jūras grundulis *nm* black goby

melnais mačiņš *nm* ouzel

melnais meža strazds *nm* blackbird

melnais mušķērājs *nm* pied flycatcher

melnais ozols *nm* black oak

melnais paltuss *nm* Greenland halibut, black halibut

melnais piparkrūms *nm* black pepper plant

melnais platsmecernieks *nm* a weevil, Otiorrhynchus niger

melnais plūškoks *nm* bourtree

melnais priežu sakņgrauzis *nm* black pine beetle

melnais prusaks *nm* common cockroach

melnais rubenis *nm* black grouse (blackcock or gray hen)

melnais sakņgrauzis *nm* a rootworm, Hylastes cunicularis

melnais stārķis *nm* black stork

melnais strazds *nm* common starling

melnais valrieksts *nm* black walnut

melnais zīriņš *nm* black tern

melnā kaija *nf* Pomarine skua

melnā kazene *nf* blackberry

melnā klija *nf* black kite

melnalksnājs *nm* (forest.) alder type

melnalksnis *nm* black alder

melnā mamba *nf* black mamba

melnā mangana rūda *nf* hausmannite

melnā naktene *nf* nightshade

melnā paparde *nf* male fern

melnā pīle *nf* common scoter

melnā pinne *nf* blackhead

melnā plūme *nf* Canada plum

melnā priede *nf* Austrian pine

melnapse *nf* black poplar

melnā puskuitala *nf* black-tailed godwit

melnā sinepe *nf* black mustard

melnās jāņogas *nf pl* black currant

Melnās jūras brētliņa *nf* Caspian sprat

melnā skudra *nf* black ant

melnā sotņa *nf* (hist.) Black Hundred

melnastes māņbriedis *nm* mule deer

melnā stiebrmuša *nf* frit fly

melnaugļu *indecl adj* bearing black fruit

melnaugļu aronija *nf* black chokeberry

melnā vārna *nf* carrion crow

melnā velnoga *nf* belladonna

melnā zīlaine *nf* black horehound

melnāžurka *nf* ship rat

melnbalts *adj* 1. black-and-white; 2. piebald

melnbārdains *adj* black-bearded

melnbārdis *nm* black-bearded man

melnbrūns *adj* raw umber

melnceres *nf pl* bog rush

melncirtains *adj* dark-curled

melnējošais vītols *nm* whortle-leaved willow

melnējošās dedestiņas *nf pl* black pea

melnējošā zeltkātene *nf* glutinous gomphidius

melnējs *adj* blackish, dusky; swarthy

melnelksnis *nm* black alder

melnene *nf* blueberry; bilberry

mēlnesība *nf* talebearing

mēlnesīgi *adv* gossipingly

mēlnesīgs *adj* talebearing

mēlnesīgums *nm* talebearing

mēlnes/is *nm*, ~e *nf* talebearer

mēlnešot *vi* tell tales, gossip

melnēt *vi* = melnot

melnfigūru *indecl adj* black-figure

melngalvainais ķauķis *nm* blackcap

melngalvains *adj* blackhead (*adj*)

melngalvas gārgale *nf* great northern diver

melngalvas kaija *nf* Mediteranean gull

melngalvas stērste *nf* black-headed bunting

melngalvas zoss *nf* brant

melngalve *nf* goosander

melngalv/is *nm* 1. black-headed person; black-headed animal; 2. ~ji (hist.) Moor's Heads (a guild of clerks and officials; a guild of German merchants)

melngalvīši *nm pl* blooming cotton grass

melnganā dzelzene *nf* a knapweed, Centaurea nigriscens

melngani *adv* in a blackish color

melnganpelēks *adj* dark gray, charcoal gray

melngans *adj* blackish

melnie *nom adj pl* blacks; (chess) Black

melnie ātraudēi *nm pl* bourtree

mēlnie/ks *nm*, ~ce *nf* talebearer

melnie rudzu graudi *nm pl* ergot

melnīgi *adv* in a blackish color

melnīgs *adj* blackish

melnīgsnēji *adv* in a dark color

melnīgsnējs *adj* swarthy

melnīgsnēt *vi* turn blackish

melnin *adv emph* of melns; m. melns pitch-black

melnināšana *nf* oxide coating

melnināt *vt* blacken

melnis *nm* black horse

melnišķe *nf* dark-haired woman, dark-complexioned woman

melnīte *nf* blueberry; bilberry

melnkaite *nf* black root (disease)

melnkāja *nf* black root (disease)

melnkājība *nf* black root (disease)

melnkājis *nm* 1. black-footed one; one with dirty feet; 2. Blackfoot

melnkakla *indecl adj* black-throated; black-necked

melnkakla dūkuris *nm* black-necked grebe

melnkalniet/is *nm*, ~e *nf* Montenegrin

melnkoks *nm* ebony

melnkreklis *nm* Blackshirt

melnmatains *adj* black-haired

melnmate *nf* black-haired woman

melnmatis *nm* black-haired man

melnmelns *adj* pitch-black

melnmutis *nm* dirty fellow

melnodzene *nf* bladder campion

melnot *v* 1. *vi* show itself black or dark, loom black or dark; 2. *vi* (poet., of darkness) fall; be very dark; 3. *vt* paint black

melnoties *vr* = melnot 1, 2

melnpelēks *adj* charcoal gray

melnpieres čakste *nf* lesser gray shrike

melnplankumains *adj* black-spotted

melnplauka *nf* (bot.) smut; bunt

melnplaukains *adj* infested with smut or bunt

melnraibi *adv* spotted with black and white

melnraibs *adj* piebald

melnraksts *nm* (rough) draft; (of a project) working paper

melnrīkles *indecl adj* black-throated

melnrīkles čakstīte *nf* common stonechat

melnrīkles strazds *nm* black-throated thrush
meln/s *adj* **1.** black; **m. uz balta** in black and white; **kā** (or **ka**) **m.** a lot; **m. un maziņš**(col.) submissive; **2.** (col.) dirty; **cik m. aiz naga** one tiny bit; **3.** (of work) heavy, unskilled
melnsakne *nf* black salsify
melnsēklītes *nf pl* love-in-a-mist
melnsimtniecisks *adj* reactionary
melnsimtnieks *nm* (hist.) **1.** member of the Black Hundred; **2.** extreme reactionary
melnspārnu *indecl adj* black-winged
melnspārnu bezdelīgtārtiņš*nm* black-winged pratincole
melnspārnu kaija *nf* greater black-backed gull
melnspārnains *adj* black-winged
melnspīdīgs *adj* black and shiny
melnstrādnie/ks *nm*, **~ce** *nf* unskilled worker
melnsvārcis *nm* **1.** (cont.) blackcoat; **2.** black bird
melnūksnējs *adj* swarthy
melnulis *nm* dark-colored animal
melnum *adv emph* of **melns; m. melns** pitch-black
melnumains *adj* **1.** stained, dark-spotted; **2.** dirty
melnum/s *nm* **1.** blackness; **2.** black object, sth. black; (metall.) blackwash; **3.** stain, dirt spot; **~i** dirt, stains
melnzaļi *adv* in a blackish green color
melnzaļš*adj* blackish green
melnzeme *nf* black earth, chernozem
melnzili *adv* in a blackish blue color
melnzils *adj* blackish blue
melodeklamācija *nf* poetry reading to music
melodija *nf* melody
melodiķ/is *nm*, **~e** *nf* melodist
melodiski *adv* melodiously
melodisks *adj* melodious
melodiskums *nm* melodiousness
melodrāma *nf* melodrama

melodr[a]matiski [ā] *adv* melodramatically
melodr[a]matisks [ā] *adj* melodramatic
melodr[a]matisms [ā] *nm* melodramatics
melofons *nm* mellophone
melogr[a]fs [ā] *nm* melograph
melom[a]nija [ā] *nf* melomania
melom[a]n/s [ā] *nm*, **~e** *nf* melomaniac
melone *nf* melon, muskmelon; cantaloupe
meloņkaktuss *nm* melon cactus
meloņkoks *nm* papaya tree
meloss *nm* melos
melot *vi* lie; **m. kā ausis kust** lie in one's teeth; **m., acīs skatīdamies** tell barefaced lies
melsīgi *adv* chattily
melsīgs *adj* chatty
melsis *nm* **1.** liar; **2.** (col.) blabber
melsonis *nm* liar
melst *vi* talk nonsense; gossip
melsties *vr* talk nonsense; gossip
melša *nf, nm* gossipmonger
melšas *nf pl* (col.) gossip
melšāt *vi* (col.) **1.** gab; **2.** gossip
meluģis *nm* (reg.) liar
mēlveida *indecl adj* tongue-shaped
mēlveidīgs *adj* tongue-shaped
mēlziede *nf* ligularia
mēļi *adv* in violet (color)
mēļot *vi* **1.** gossip; **2.** gab
mēļotāj/s *nm*, **~a** *nf* glib talker
mēļoties *vr* **1.** gossip; **2.** gab
mēļsarkani *adv* in a violet red color
mēļsarkans *adj* violet red
mēļš*adj* violet
mēm/ais *nom adj*, **~ā** *f* mute
mēmāputra *nm* (col.) tight-lipped person
membrāna *nf* membrane; diaphragm
membrānpumpis *nm* diaphragm pump
mēmi *adv* mutely, speechlessly; silently
mēmiķis *nm* (col.) mute
mēmis *nm* mute
memme *nf* (col.) mother
memmele *nf* (col.)mother

memmesdēliņš *nm* (iron.) mother's boy, sissy

memmesmeitiņa *nf* (iron.) mother's darling

memmiķis *nm* (col.) sissy

memmis *nm* (col.) **1.** sissy; **2.** coward

memmiņa nf (col.) mother

memmīte *nf* (col.) mother

memorands *nm* memorandum

memorēt *vt* memorize

memoriāli *adv* memorially

memoriālm|u|zejs |ū| *nm* memorial museum

memoriālplāksne *nf* memorial plaque

memoriāls *nm* **1.** memorial; **2.** journal

memoriāls *adj* memorial

mēms *adj* **1.** mute, dumb; speechless; **2.** silent

memuāri *nm pl* memoirs

memuāristika *nf* autobiographic materials

memuārist/s *nm*, **~e** *nf* memoirist

mēmulis *nm* mute

mēmums *nm* muteness

mēmuris *nm* (col.) mute

menāda *nf* maenad

menāža *nf* **1.** castor; **2.** food carrier; **3.** ménage, household

menažerija *nf* ménagerie

menca *nf* cod

mencelija *nf* mentzelia

mencveidīgās zivis *nf pl* Gadidae

mencveidīgs *adj* cod-like

menčīgi *adv* funnily; adroitly

menčīgs *adj* **1.** funny; **2.** adroit

mendelevijs *nm* mendelevium

mendelisms *nm* Mendelism

menedžer/is *nm*, **~e** *nf* manager

mēnesene *nf* (bot.) honesty

mēne/sis *nm* month; **~šiem ilgi** for months; **ik ~si** monthly; **~ša laikā** within a month; **pirms ~ša** a month ago; **pēc ~ša** in a month

mēnesnīca *nf* **1.** moonlight; **2.** moon; **3.** (col.) moonfaced person; **4.** (sl.) moonshine; **5.** (sl.) pate

mēnesrags *nm* cup of the (crescent) moon

mēness *nm* moon; **apaļais m.** a Latvian folk dance; **neīsts m.** paraselene, mock moon; **m. ap-gaismots** moonlit

mēnessakmens *nm* moonstone

mēness aptumsums *nm* lunar eclipse

mēness atspīdums *nm* moonglade

mēnessbāls *adj* pale as the moon

mēnesseja *nf* face of the moon

mēnessērdzība *nf* somnambulism

mēnessērdzīg/ais *nom adj*, **~ā** *f* somnambulist, sleepwalker

mēnessērdzīgs *adj* somnambulistic

mēness gads *nm* lunar year

mēnessgaisma *nf* moonlight

mēness grieži *nm pl* phases of the moon

mēnessirpis *nm* crescent

mēnesskrēsla *nf* moonlight

mēnessnakts *nf* night of full moon

mēness mītības *nf pl* (col.) phases of the moon

mēness ripa *nf* disc of the moon

mēness sirpis *nm* crescent

mēness stabs *nm* moon pillar

mēnesstars *nm* moonbeam

mēnessvaigs *nm* face of the moon

mēnesszivs *nf* moonfish

mēnestiņš *nm* **1.** *dim* of **mēness**, moon; **2.** (of fingernails) lunule, half-moon; **3.** pate

menestrels *nm* minstrel

mēnešains *adj* moonlit

mēnešalga *nf* monthly salary

mēnešbiļete *nf* monthly commuter ticket

mēnešgrieži *nm pl* phases of the moon

mēnešmaksa *nf* **1.** monthly payment; **2.** monthly charge (or rent, fee, cost)

mēnešraksts *nm* monthly (publication)

mēnešreizes *nf pl* menstruation

mēnešsirpis *nm* crescent of the moon

mēnešzemenes *nf pl* remontant variety of strawberries

mēnešziedi *nm pl* menstruation

menhīrs *nm* menhir

menijs *nm* menu

meniķis *nm* sluice gate

meningīts *nm* meningitis

meningokoks *nm* meningococcus

menisks *nm* meniscus

menisperms *nm* moonseed

menonītisms *nm* Mennonitism

menonīts *nm* Mennonite

menopauze *nf* menopause

menoraģija *nf* menorrhagia

menstruācija *nf* menstruation

menstruācijas saite *nf* sanitary napkin

menstruāls *adj* menstrual

menstruēt *vi* menstruate

mensula *nf* plane table

mentālisms *nm* mentalism

ment[a]litāte [ā] *nf* mentality

mentālrezervācija *nf* mental reservation

mentāli *adv* mentally

mentāls *adj* mental

mente *nf* stirrer, mixer, spatula

mentenols *nm* menthenol

mentēt *vt* stir, twirl, mix

mentne *nf* stirrer, mixer, spatula

mentols *nm* menthol

mentons *nm* menthone

mentors *nm* mentor

menuets *nm* minuet

menza *nf* (arch., rel.) mensa

menzula *nf* plane table

menzūra *nf* 1. measuring glass, graduate; 2. (mus.) mensuration (in mensural music); 3. student duel

menzurāls *adj* (mus., of notation) mensural

meņģēt *vt* rummage, mess up

meņģēties *vr* (col.) play, romp

meņģīgs *adj* (reg.) happy, joyful

meņševiks *nm* Menshevik

meņševisms *nm* Menshevism

meņševistiski *adv* in a Menshevist manner

meņševistisks *adj* Menshevist

mēraparāts *nm* measuring instrument

mērapar[a]tūra [ā] *nf* measuring equipment

mērapjoms *nm* measuring range

mēra puķe *nf* = mēŗa puķe

mēra putns *nm* = mēŗa putns

mēra zāle *nf* = mēŗa zāle

mēraukla *nf* standard

mērbulta *nf* (typ.) arrowhead

mērce *nf* 1. gravy; sauce; 2. (salad) dressing

mērceklis *nm* (cul.) dip

mercene *nf* mallard

mērces trauks *nm* gravy boat

mērcēt *vt* 1. soak; steep; (of flax) ret; (of pottery) slake; 2. dip, dunk

mērcētava *nf* soaking vat; retting pond

mērcēties *vr* soak; steep; ret

mērciens *nm* (com.) blow

mērcilindrs *nm* graduated cylinder

mērcirkulis *nm* dividers

mērcputriņa *nf* (cul.) dip

mērde *nf* (col.) poison

mērd[e]klis [ē] *nm* (col.) poison

mērdelēt *vt* (col.) starve

mērdelēties *vr* (col.) starve oneself

mērdelis *nm* (com,) bag of bones

mērdene *nf* insect collecting jar

mērdēt *vt* starve

mērdēties *vr* starve oneself

mērdināt *vt* starve

mēreni *adv* moderately

mērenība *nf* moderation

mērens *adj* moderate, (of climate) temperate

mērenums *nm* moderation

mereoloģija *nf* mereology

merga *nf* (col., cont.) gal

mērga *nm, nf* (com.) scrag

mergas *nf pl* banisters; railing; handrail

mērglāze *nf* graduated beaker; (with **lietus**) rain gage

mērglis *nm* (com.) 1. starveling; 2. coward

merģele *nf* (reg.) girl

merģelis *nm* marl; **blīvs m.** marlstone

merģelis *nm* (com.) starveling

merģeļains *adj* marly

meridiānriņķis *nm* meridian circle

meridiāns *nm* meridian

meridionāls *adj* meridional

mēriekārta *nf* measuring equipment

mērierīce *nf* measuring device

mērija *nf* mayor's office

mērījums *nm* measurement

merīnaita *nf* merino

meringija *nf* sandwort

merīns *nm* merino

mērinstruments *nm* measuring instrument

mēriņš *nm dim* of **mērs I 2**, measure; (col.) shot of liquor

mēris *nm* pestilence, bubonic plague

meristēma *nf* meristem

mērīt *vt* 1. measure; (of depth) sound; **m. temperātūru** take s.o.'s temperature; 2. (col.) aim

mērīties *vr* measure oneself; compare one's height with another's

mērītājs *nm*, ~a *nf* 1. mesuring instrument, gage, meter; 2. measurer

meritokr[a]tija [ā] *nf* meritocracy

mērkaķis *nm* monkey

mērkaķiski *adv* in a monkey-like fashion

mērkaķisks *adj* monkeyish

mērkaķītis *nm* 1. *dim* of **mērkaķis**, little monkey; 2. marmoset

mērkaķoties *vr* 1. clown; 2. ape

merkantilisms *nm* mercantilism

merkantilistiski *adv* in the mercantilist fashion

merkantilistisks *adj* mercantilist

merkantilists *nm* mercantilist

merkantils *adj* mercantile

merkaptāns *nm* mercaptan

mērkārts *nf* sounding rod

mērkaza *nf* = **mērkaziņa**

mērkaziņa *nf* common snipe

mērkoks *nm* yardstick

mērkolba *nf* graduated flask

mērkt *vt* 1. dip; 2. soak; ret; 3. (com.) hit, whack

mērkties *vr* 1. be soaking, be retting; 2. dip (into a liquid)

merkuriālisms *nm* mercurialism

Merkurs *nm* Mercury

mērķa lente *nf* goal ribbon

mērķa stabs *nm* winning post

mērķdotācija *nf* earmarked subsidy

mērķēde *nf* surveyor's chain

mērķēk/lis *nm* rear sight; **atklātais m.** open sight; **dioptriskais m.** peep sight, aperture sight; **neregulējams m.** fixed sight; **~ļa komplekss** in-tegrated sight unit

mērķēklītis *nm* lateral adjustment of a rear sight

mērķēšana *nf* aiming; target acquisition; **~s tālums** gun range

mērķēt *vi* take aim; (with **uz**) aim at, (fig.) drive at

mērķ/is *nm* 1. aim, end, object, purpose; 2. goal, finish line; 3. target; **~a virzienā** down range; **~a notveršana** (artillery) bracketing; **~u noteikša-nas** uguns marking fire

mērķlīnija *nf* gun-target line

mērķnorāde *nf* target designation; **~s punkts** target reference point

mērķprogramma *nf* special purpose program

mērķtiece *nf* = **mērķtiecība**

mērķtiecība *nf* purposefulness; goal-directedness

mērķtiecīgi *adv* purposefully

mērķtiecīgs *adj* purposeful; goal-directed

mērķtiecīgums *nm* purposefulness

merlangs *nm* (zool.) whiting

mērlata *nf* leveling rod

mērlente *nf* tape measure

mērlineāls *nm* measuring ruler

mērlogs *nm* (compu.) status box

merlūza *nf* hake

mērnēt *vi* starve

mērniecība *nf* surveying

mērnieka ķēde *nf* surveyor's chain

mērnieks *nm* surveyor

mēroga lineāls *nm* scale rule

mēroga saucējs *nm* scale factor

mērog/s *nm* (of maps, plans) scale; **lielā ~ā** on a large scale

meropija *nf* meropia

mērot *vt* 1. walk, cover a distance; 2. measure

mērotājs *nm*, **~a** *nf* measurer

mēroties *vr* compete; **m. spēkiem** measure swords with s.o.

mērpulkstenis *nm* dial indicator distance gage

mērrīks *nm* measuring device

mērrutks *nm* horse radish

mēr/s I *nm* 1. measure; **~a rīkste** (obs.) a measure of linear distance; 2. measuring stick; measuring tape; measuring cup; 3. limit; **ar ~u** in moderation; **līdz zināmam ~am** to a certain extent; up to a point; **pilnā ~ā** fully; **lielā ~ā** highly, to a great extent; **ne mazākā ~ā** not in the least; **vislielākā ~ā** extremely; **pāri ~am** excessively; **pār ~u** excessively; **bez ~a** beyond all bounds; 4. (col.) size; **pēc ~a** to measure

mērs II *nm* mayor

merserizācija *nf* mercerization

merserizēt *vt* mercerize

mērskaitlis *nm* (stat.) relative; index

mērsloksne *nf* measuring tape

meršķis *nm* straw mat for hotbeds

mērtechnika *nf* measuring technique

mērtiltiņš *nm* measuring bridge

mērtrauks *nm* graduated vessel

mērveltnītis *nm* (typ.) metering roller

mērvienība *nf* unit of measure

mē[r]a [ŗ] puķe *nf* coltsfoot

mē[r]a [ŗ] putns *nm* waxwing

mē[r]a [ŗ] zāle *nf* yarrow

mēs *pron* we; **m. abi** both of us; **m. paši** we ourselves; **m. vieni paši** only ourselves

mesa *nf* 1. (rel., mus.) mass; 2. fair

mese I *nf* (naut.) officers' mess

mese II *nf* fair

mesendēers *nm* (naut.) messenger

mesiānisks *adj* messianic

mesiānisms *nm* messianism

mesija *nf* messiah

mesjē *indecl nm* monsieur

meskalīns *nm* mescaline

mēslaine *nf* dump, refuse pile

mēslains *adj* dirty; littered

mēslājs *nm* dump, refuse pile

mēslenīca *nf* (reg.) dump, refuse pile

mesli *nm pl* 1. tribute; 2. (obs.) dice

mēsli *nm pl* 1. excrement; 2. dung, manure; **mākslīgie m.** fertilizer; 3. refuse; sweepings; 4. (col.) unpleasantness, trouble

mēsliene *nf* dump, refuse pile

meslinieks *nm* (hist.) tribute payer

mēslinieks *nm* trash collector

mēslojums *nm* fertilizer; manure

meslot *vi* draw lots

mēslot *vt* fertilize

mēslu kaste *nf* trash bin

mēslu kaudze *nf* dunghill

mēslvabole *nf* dung beetle; dorbeetle

mesmerisms *nm* mesmerism

mespils *nm* medlar

mest *vt* 1. throw; cast; **m. atspīdumu** reflect; **m. burbuļus** bubble; **m. dzirksteles** spark; **m. garu** throw water on hot bathhouse stones; **m. krustu** cross oneself; **m. kūkumu** (of cats) arch one's back; **m. kūleņus** tumble; **m. līkumu** a. make a turn; b. go out of one's way; **m. lokus** circle; **m. pār bortu** throw overboard; jettison; **m. viļņus** billow; **m. zemē** a. throw down; b. throw away; (fig.) squander; **m. acis (uz kādu)** have one's eyes (on s.o.); **m. acīs** cast in one's teeth, re-proach; **m. cilpu** a. loop; b. (aeron.) loop the loop; **m. cilpas** (of the hare) double; **m. cilpu kaklā** hang oneself; **m. laipu** (fig.)

build bridges; **m. mieru** stop, cease, call
it quits; **m. mirgas** glitter; **m. naudu** toss
a coin; **m. nost** a. throw off; throw away;
b. (of garments) take off; **m. pa ausi** (col.)
slap; **m. plinti krūmos** (col.) give up; **m.
pie malas** stop; **m. prātu ar mieru** give
up an idea (as impossible); **m. preces
tirgū** undersell; **m. riteni** turn cartwheels;
m. sprunguļus ceļā put obstacles in the
way; **nav zemē metams** (col.) not to be
disdained; **2.** make (by throwing together;
3. shed, moult; **m. ādu** slough; **4.** *vi* **m. ar
acīm** wink at; **m. ar roku** (or **ar galvu, ar
acīm**) signal; **5.** (col.) have a few drinks; **m.
ogu** (sl.) drink; **m. pa lampu** (com.) drink;
6. (weav.) draw in the warp;

mestavas *nf pl* (weav.) **1.** warp; **2.** batten

mesties *vr* **1.** throw oneself at (or upon); rush,
rush into; **m. ap kaklu** throw one's arms
around s.o.'s neck; **m. (kāda) apkampienos**
fall into s.o.'s arms; **m. bēgt** dash away, take
off; **m. ceļos** kneel down; **m. iekšā** plunge
into; **m. klāt** rush up to; **m. peldus** plunge
into the water; **m. pulkā** a. join together;
b. butt in, interrupt; **m. ragos** a. attack;
come to blows; b. contest; **m. rāpus** drop
to one's hands and knees; **m. runā** join in
the conversation; **m. starpā** a. intervene b.
butt in, interrupt; **m. uz vienu roku** band
together; **m. virsū** (or **uz**) rush at, attack,
pounce upon; **m. zemē** a. sink to one's
knees, drop to one's hands and knees; b.
sit on the ground, lie down on the ground;
2. (of color, weather) turn; **3.** (*3rd pers*, of
voice; hang up on) catch; develop a snag;
4. *(3rd pers*, of fruit, grain) form, develop;
m. vārpās ear, form ears; (of fire) catch;
5. (*3rd pers*) set in, become; **metas raibs
gar acīm** getting dizzy; **metas tumšs** it is
getting dark; **man metas auksti** I am getting
cold; **man metas bail** I am gettingt scared;
viņai matos metas sirmums her hair is

turning gray; **6.** (*3rd pers*) become infested
with; **7.** (of wood) warp

mestrs *nm* (hist.) Grand Master (of the Livonian
order state)

mešana *nf* (sports) throwing, (javelin, hammer,
disc) throw

mešus *adv emph* of **mest; m. mest** fling

mēt *vi* bleat

metaatmiņa *nf* metamemory

metab|a|ze [ā] *nf* metabasis

metabolija *nf* metamorphosis

metaboliski *adv* metabolically

metabolisks *adj* metabolic

metabolisms *nm* metabolism

metabolīts *nm* metabolite

metabolizēt *vt* metabolize

metaborāts *nm* metaborate

metacentrisks *adj* metacentric

metacentrs *nm* metacenter

metaētika *nf* metaethics

metaf|a|ze [ā] *nf* metaphase

metafilozofija *nf* metaphilosophy

metafizika *nf* metaphysics

metafiziķ/is *nm*, **~e** *nf* metaphysician

metafiziski *adv* metaphysically

metafizisks *adj* metaphysical

metafora *nf* metaphor

metaforiski *adv* metaphorically

metaforisks *adj* metaphorical

metaforiskums *nm* metaphoricalness

metaforizēšana *nf* formation of metaphors; use
of metaphors

metafosfāts *nm* metaphosphate

metafosforskābe *nf* metaphosphoric acid

metafr|a|ze [ā] *nf* metaphrase

metagalaktika *nf* metagalaxy

metagalaktisks *adj* metagalactic

metaġen|e|ze [ē] *nf* metagenesis

metāl- See **metall-**

metalepse *nf* metalepsis

met|all|apstrādāšana [āl] *nf* metalworking

met|all|apstrāde [āl] *nf* metalworking

met|all|a [āl] pūtēji *nm pl* brass (instrument play-ers)

met|all|audums [āl] *nm* wire mesh, wire screen

met|all|darbs [āl] *nm* metalware

met|all|darinājums [āl] *nm* metal article

met|all|detaļa [āl] *nf* metallic detail

met|a|llējējs [ā] *nm,* ~a *nf* foundryman

met|a|llējums [ā] *nm* metal casting

met|all|fizika [āl] *nf* physics of metals

met|all|fizikāls [āl] *adj* pertaining to the physics of metals

met|all|furnitūra [āl] *nf* metal accessories

met|all|galantērija [āl] *nf* metal haber-dashery

met|all|griešana [āl] *nf* metal cutting

met|a|lliešana [ā] *nf* metal casting (process)

met|all|ietilpība [āl] *nf* amount of metal required (for manufacture)

met|all|ietilpīgs [āl] *adj* requiring a large amount of metal

met|a|llietuve [ā] *nf* foundry

met|all|iski [āl] *adv* metallically

met|all|isks [āl] *adj* metallic

met|all|iskums [āl] *nm* metallicity

met|all|ist/s [āl] *nm,* ~e *nf* metalworker

meta|ll|izācija [l] *nf* metallization

meta|ll|izējamība [l] *nf* ability to be metal-lized

meta|ll|izējums [l] *nm* metal coating

meta|ll|izēt [l] *vt* metallize

met|all|izstrādājumi [āl] *nm pl* metalware

met|all|kalēj/s [āl] *nm,* ~a *nf* metalsmith

met|all|kalšana [āl] *nf* metalworking

met|all|kaltuve [āl] *nf* metalworks

met|all|kalums [āl] *nm* decorative metalwork

met|all|kausēšana [āl] *nf* smelting

met|all|keramika [āl] *nf* powder metallurgy

met|all|keramisks [āl] *adj* powder-metallurgical

met|all|konstrukcija [āl] *nf* metal structure

met|all|mācība [āl] *nf* metallurgy

met|all|māksla [āl] *nf* decorative metalwork

met|all|mākslinie/ks [āl] *nm,* ~ce *nf* metal craftsman; metal sculptor

met|all|mazietilpīgs [āl] *adj* requiring little met-al (for manufacture)

met|all|nauda [āl] *nf* specie; coins

meta|ll|ofons [l] *nm* glockenspiel

meta|ll|og|e|nija [l][ē] *nf* origin of ores

meta|ll|og|e|nisks [l][ē] *adj* pertaining to the origin of ores

meta|ll|ogr|a|fija [l][ā] *nf* metallography

meta|ll|ogr|a|fisks [l][ā] *adj* metallographic

meta|ll|ogr|a|fs [l][ā] *nm* metallograph

meta|ll|oīds [l] *nm* metalloid

met|all|org|a|nisks [āl][ā] *adj* organometallic

meta|ll|otermija [l] *nf* reduction (of ores)

meta|ll|otropisms [l] *nm* metallotropism

meta|ll|oplastikāts [l] *nm* plastic-coated sheet metal

met|all|plasts [āl] *nm* plastic-coated sheet metal

met|all|preces [āl] *nf pl* hardware

met|all|pūšams [āl] *adj* (of wind instruments) brass

met|all|rūda [āl] *nf* metal ore

met|all|rūpnīca [āl] *nf* metalworks

met|all|rūpniecība [āl] *nf* metal industry

met|all|rūpnieks [āl] *nm* owner of a metal working plant

met|all|/s [āl] *nm* metal; **krāsainie** ~i non-ferrous metals; **liedējamais m.** solder; **melnie** ~i ferrous metals; **nicināmais m.** filthy lucre

met|all|spiede [āl] *nf* forming press, punch press

met|all|strādnie/ks [āl] *nm,* ~ce *nf* metal-worker

met|all|suka [āl] *nf* wire brush

met|all|termija [āl] *nf* reduction (of ores)

met|all|u [āl] **noteicējs** *nm* metal detector

meta|ll|urgs [l] *nm* metallurgist

meta|ll|urģija |l| *nf* metallurgy; **melnā m.**
　metallurgy of ferrous metals
meta|ll|urģisks |l| *adj* metallurgical
met|a|llūžņi |ā| *nm pl* metal scrap
met|all|valūta |āl| *nf* metal currency
met|all|veida |āl| *indecl adj* metallic
met|all|veidīgs |āl| *adj* metallic
met|all|veidne |āl| *nf* mold, chill mold, die
met|all|velmēšana |āl| *nf* metal rolling
met|all|vilna |āl| *nf* steel wool
met|all|virpošana |āl| *nf* milling
met|all|virpotava |āl| *nf* milling department
met|all|zāģis |āl| *nm* hacksaw
metaloģika *nf* metalogic
metaloģiski *adv* metalogically
metaloģisks *adj* metalogical
metamagnētisks *adj* metamagnetic
metamais *nom adj* missile
metamat|e|mātika |ē| *nf* metamathematics
metamerija *nf* metamerism
metamerisks *adj* metameric
metamers *nm* metamer
metamorfiski *adv* metamorphically
metamorfisks *adj* metamorphic
metamorfisms *nm* metamorphism
metamorfizēties *vr* undergo metamorphism
metamorfizēts *adj* metamorphic
metamorfoze *nf* metamorphosis
metamorfs *adj* metamorphic
metam/s *adj*, often *defin* ~ais throw (*adj*),
　throwing (*adj*)
metanīts *nm* metallized thread
metanols *nm* methanol
metāns *nm* methane
metapl|a|zija |ā| *nf* metaplasia
metaps|īch|oloģija |ih| *nf* metapsychology
metasilicijskābe *nf* metasilicic acid
metasilikāts *nm* metasilicate
metasomatisks *adj* metasomatic
metasomatisms *nm* metasomatism
metasomatoze *nf* metasomatosis
metastab|i|ls |ī| *adj* metastable

metast|a|tisks |ā| *adj* metastatic
metast|a|ze |ā| *nf* metastasis
metastazēties *vr* metastasize
mētāt *vt* **1.** toss; **2.** toss down
metateorēma *nf* metatheorem
metateorija *nf* metatheory
metat|e|ze |ē| *nf* metathesis
mētāties *vr* **1.** toss, toss at each other; (fig.) toss
　out (words, rashly); **m. ar naudu** throw
　away money; **m. rokām** wave one's arms;
　2. (of a vessel) roll, toss; **3.** lie scattered;
　4. (col.) gad about; **m. pa pasauli** change
　one's residence frequently; travel around
metavaloda *nf* metalanguage
metavalodisks *adj* metalingustic
metavanadāts *nm* metavanadate
metavolframāts *nm* metatungstate
metavolfrāmskābe *nf* metatungstic acid
metazinātne *nf* philosophy of science
metazoji *nm pl* Metazoa
metējs *nm*, ~a *nf* **1.** thrower; **2.** (col.) drinker
metek/lis *nm* **1.** nailer stud; **2.** ~ļi (obs.) impost,
　duty
mētelis *nm* topcoat
mētelītis *nm dim* of **mētelis**, child's coat
mēteļdrāna *nf* coating (material)
mēteļkleita *nf* coatdress
metemp|i|risks |ī| *adj* metempirical
metemps|īch|oze |ih| *nf* metempsychosis
metenis *nm* **1.** Shrovetide; **2.** cast net
meteņdiena *nf* Shrovetide
meteņu mēnesis *nm* February
meteopavadonis *nm* weather satellite
meteorisks *adj* meteoric
meteorisms *nm* (med.) tympanites
meteorītika *nf* meteoritics
meteorīts *nm* meteorite
meteorogr|a|fija |ā| *nf* meteorography
meteorogr|a|fs |ā| *nm* meteorograph
meteorogramma *nf* meteorogram
meteorolo/gs *nm*, ~ģe *nf* meteorologist
meteoroloģija *nf* meteorology

meteoroloģiski *adv* meteorologically

meteoroloģisks *adj* meteorological, weather (*adj*)

meteors *nm* meteorite; meteor

meteostacija *nf* weather station

meti *nm pl* (weav.) warp

metieniņš *nm* 1. *dim* of metiens, throw; 2. a Latvian folk dance

metiens *nm* 1. throw, cast, fling; 2. litter; 3. circulation; (of books) edition (of x copies); 4. (col.) blow; 5. (obs.) grain spread on the threshing floor for threshing

metier/is *nm*, ~e *nf* (typ.) maker-up

metikulozi *adv* meticulously

metikulozs *adj* meticulous

met[i]lacetāts [ī] *nm* methyl acetate

met[i]lbrom[ī]ds [ī][i] *nm* methyl bromide

met[i]lcelluloza [ī] *nf* methyl cellulose

met[ī]l]l[ch]lor[i]ds [i][h][ī] *nm* methyl chloride

met[i]lēngrupa [ī] *nf* methylene

met[i]lēns [ī] *nm* methylene

met[i]lēnzilais [ī] *nm* methylene blue

met[i]lēteris [ī] *nm* methyl ether

met[i]lgrupa [ī] *nf* methyl

met[i]ljodīds [ī] *nm* methyl iodide

met[i]loranža [ī] *nf* methyl orange

met[i]lpiridīns [ī] *nm* methylpyridine

met[i]ls [ī] *nm* methyl

met[i]lspirts [ī] *nm* methyl alcohol

metinājum/s *nm* weld; ~a šuve welded joint

metināmība *nf* weldability

metināms *adj, part* of metināt 1. weldable; 2. welding

metināšana *nf* welding; aukstā m. cold welding; autogenā m autogenous welding; elektriskā m. arc welding; m. kaļot forge welding

metināt *vt* 1. weld; 2. baste (in sewing); 3. hook; 4. harness

metinātāj/s *nm*, ~a *nf* welder

metionīns *nm* methionine

metisācija *nf* mestization

metis/s *nm*, ~e *nf* mestizo

metode *nf* method

metodika *nf* methods, methodology

metodiķ/is *nm*, ~e *nf* methodologist

metodiski *adv* methodically

metodisks *adj* methodical

metodiskums *nm* methodicity

metodisms *nm* Methodism

metodist/s *nm*, ~e *nf* Methodist

metodoloģija *nf* methodology

metodoloģiski *adv* methodologically

metodoloģisks *adj* methodological

metols *nm* Metol

meton[i]mija [ī] *nf* metonymy

meton[i]miski [ī] *adv* metonymically

meton[i]misks [ī] *adj* metonymic

metopa or metope *nf* metope

mētra *nf* mint; usu. *pl* ~s lingonberry bush, bilberrry bush

mētrains *adj* covered with mint, full of mint; covered with (or full of) lingonberry or bilberry plants

mētrājs *nm* (forest.) pine type

metramērs *nm* meterstick

metrāža *nf* length in meters; (of film length) footage

metrdotels *nm* maître d'hôtel

metrese *nf* mistress

metrīgi *adv* (col.) hugely

metrīgs *adj* (col.) huge

metrika *nf* 1. metrics; 2. entry (in the bureau of vital statistics)

mētriņa *nf dim* of mētra I or II, mint; lingonberry bush, bilberry bush

metriski *adv* metrically

metrisks *adj* 1. metric; 2. metrical

metrīts *nm* metritis

metrizēt *vt* metricize

metrmērs *nm* meterstick

metro *indecl nm* subway

metrolo/gs *nm*, ~ģe *nf* metrologist

metroloģija *nf* metrology

metroloģiski *adv* metrologically

metroloģisks *adj* metrological

metrom[a]nija [ā] *nf* metromania

metronomiski *adv* metronomically

metronomisks *adj* metronomic

metronoms *nm* metronome

m[e]tropole [ē] *nf* metropolis

m[e]tropolija [ē] *nf* metropolitan see

metropolitēns *nm* subway

m[e]tropolīts [ē] *nm* metropolitan

metrorāģija *nf* metrorrhagia

metroritmika *nf* (mus.) timing and rhythm

metroritmisks *adj* (mus.) of timing and rhythm

metrostacija *nf* subway station

metrovilciens *nm* subway train

metrs *nm* 1. meter (unit of length; mus.; poetry); 2. meter stick

metrumērs *nm* meterstick

mets *nm* sketch; design

metšaušana *nf* snap shooting

metšāviens *nm* snap shot

metums *nm* 1. dam; 2. cast-on row of knitting

mezalianse *nf* mésalliance

mezanīns *nm* mezzanine

mezentērijs *nm* mesentery

mezglainā gaurenīte *nf* knotted pearlwort

mezglaini *adv* knottily

mezglainība *nf* knottiness; nodosity

mezglains *adj* knotty; knobbed; gnarled; nodose

mezglainums *nm* knottiness; knobbiness; nod-osity

mezgla plātne *nf* gusset plate

mezgliņš *nm dim* of **mezgls**, little knot

mezglojums *nm* 1. (fancywork) knottings; 2. knot, gnarled roots or branches, tangle; 3. (fig.) entanglement

mezglot *vt* knot

mezgloti *adv* knottily

mezglots *adj, part* of **mezglot** knotty; knobbed; gnarled; nodose

mezgloties *vr* knot

mezgls *nm* 1. (intertwining; velocity) knot; 2. junction; junction point; juncture; 3. center; **sanitārais m.** bathroom; 4. node; 5. ganglion

mezglu sūrene *nf* a polygonum, Polygonum nodosum

mezglveida *indecl adj* knot-shaped

mezglveidīgi *adv* like a knot

mezglveidīgs *adj* knot-shaped

mezika *nf* woodruff

mezoderma *nf* mesoderm

mezofils *nm* mesophyll

mezofils *adj* mesophylic

mezofīts *nm* mesophyte

mezokarpijs *nm* mesocarp

mezokefals *nm* mesaticephalic person

mezokrist[āl]isks [all] *adj* mesocrystalline

mezol[i]tisks [ī] *adj* Mesolithic

mezol[i]ts [ī] *nm* Mesolithic (period)

mezomerija *nf* mesomerism

mezomorfisks *adj* mesomorphic

mezomorfs *adj* mesomorphic

mezonīns *nm* mezzanine

mezons *nm* meson

mezosf[ai]ra [ē] *nf* mesosphere

mezotrops *adj* mesotrophic

mezozoisks *adj* Mesozoic

mezozojs *nm* Mesozoic (period)

mēzt *vt* 1. clean the stable; 2. sweep

meža atmatene *nf* bleeding agaric

meža avenes *nf pl* wild red raspberry

meža balodis *nm* stock pigeon

meža balzamīnes *nf pl* touch-me-not

mežābele *nf* crab apple tree

mežābols *nm* crab apple

mežabrālis *nm* 1. a revolutionary hiding in the forest (after the 1905 revolution); 2. guerrilla; 3. forest-dwelling bandit

meža bumbiere *nf* choke pear

meža cauna *nf* pine marten
meža ceriņi *nm pl* mezeron
meža cirslis *nm* European common shrew
mežacūka *nf* wild boar
meža dadzis *nm* carline thistle
meža darbi *nm pl* forest exploitation
meža dedestiņas *nf pl* flat pea
meža dienas *nf pl* Arbor Days
meža dzīvnieks *nm* wild animal
meža eglītes *nf pl* germander
meža gabals *nm* wood lot
meža gailis *nm* capercaillie
meža ģeranija *nf* wild geranium
meža iecirknis *nm* forest range
mežaine *nf* woodland
mežainis *nm* **1.** wild man; **2.** wild creature
mežains *adj* wooded, forested
mežainums *nm* forested area
meža īskāje *nf* false bromegrass
meža izpostīšana *nf* forest devastation, destructive lumbering;
mežājs *nm* forest stand
meža junkurs *nm* (col.) wolf
mežakaķis *nm* wildcat
meža kaķpēdiņas *nf pl* cudweed
meža kaza *nf* deer
meža klaušas *nf pl* statute labor in forests
meža kosa *nf* wood horsetail
meža krustaine *nf* wood groundsel
mežaks *nm* **1.** forest dweller; **2.** poorly, sloppily dressed person
mežakuilis *nm* wild boar
meža ķērsa *nf* (bot.) lady's-smock
meža ķirzaka *nf* viviparous lizard
meža lecējpele *nf* birch mouse
mežaļaudis *nm pl* forest dwellers
meža maijvabole *nf* cockchafer
mežamāte *nf* (folk.) a forest deity
meža materiāli *nm pl* forestry products
meža mauraga *nf* a hawkweed, Hieracium lachenali
mežameita *nf* fairy

meža meldri *nm pl* wood bulrush
meža mētra *nf* horse mint
meža miegonis *nm* forest doormouse
meža mirtes *nf pl* wintergreen
meža naglene *nf* grass pink
meža nārbulis *nm* small-flowered cowwheat
meža neaizmirstule *nf* wood scorpion grass
mežānietis *nm* (reg.) **1.** woodsman; **2.** wolf
meža paķērsa *nf* creeping yellow watercress
mežaparks *nm* parkland, forest park
meža pastinaks *nm* wild parsnip
meža pele *nf* long-tailed field mouse
meža pīle *nf* mallard
meža pipari *nm pl* water avens
meža plūmāji *nm pl* blackthorn
meža pļava *nf* forest glade
meža prusaks *nm* wood cockroach
meža pūce *nf* tawny owl
meža purveglīte *nf* lousewort
mežaroze *nf* dog rose
meža salvija *nf* a sage, Salvia nemorosa
meža sārmene *nf* hedge nettle
meža sausserdis *nm* European fly honeysuckle
meža sicista *nf* birch mouse
mežaskola *nf* sanatorium school
meža skosta *nf* wood horsetail
meža skudra *nf* wood ant
meža spriganes *nf pl* touch-me-not
mežastepe *nf* forest-steppe
meža stērste *nf* rustic bunting
meža strazd/s *nm* blackbird; **m. ~i** thrushes
meža strupaste *nf* bank vole
meža suns *nm* wolf
meža susuris *nm* forest doormouse
meža tilbīte *nf* green sandpiper
meža tulpe *nf* wild tulip
mežatundra *nf* forest-tundra
mežaudze *nf* forest type
meža varde *nf* tree frog
meža vējš *nm* easterly
meža veronika *nf* speedwell

meža vijolīte *nf* wood dog violet

meža vīķi *nm pl* wood vetch

meža vīnogas *nf pl* traveler's-joy

meža vīnogulājs *nm* Virginia creeper

mežavīns *nm* = **mežvīns**

mežavīrs *nm* **1.** woodsman; **2.** guerrilla; **3.** (reg.) wolf

meža virzas *nf pl* greater stitchwort

meža vizbulis *nm* wood anemone

mežavots *nm* forest spring

meža zeme *nf* woodland

meža zeltstarīte *nf* gagea

meža zemene *nf* woodland strawberry

meža zīlīte *nf* coal tit

meža zirdzene *nf* wild angelica

mežāzis *nm* **1.** wild goat; **2. M.** Capricorn

mežazoss *nf* graylag

meža zvaigzne *nf* starwort

mežazvērs *nm* wild beast

meža žibulīši *nm pl* an eyebright, Euphrasia nemorosa

meža žurka *nf* bank vole

mežbogs *nm* (reg.) coppice

mežcirtējs *nm* woodcutter; logger

meždega *nf* burnt-out area in a forest

mežeglīte *nf* wall germander

meženis *nm* **1.** (plant, fruit) wilding; **2.** crab stock; **3.** (reg.) wolf

mežezers *nm* forest lake

mežgaliet/is *nm*, **~e** *nf* woodlander

mežģains *adj* tangled

mežģījums *nm* **1.** dislocation; **2.** weave

mežģ[i]nes [ī] *nf pl* lace

mežģis *nm* tangle

mežģīt *vt* **1.** crochet; (of nets) weave; **2.** sprain; **3.** tangle; **4.** confuse

mežģī/ties *vr* **1.** become entangled; **2.** viņam mēle ~jas he falters, he stammers

mežģot *vt* = **mežģīt**

mežierīcība *nf* forest management, forestry

mežierīkotāj/s *nm*, **~a** *nf* specialist in forest management

mežinie/ks *nm*, **~ce** *nf* **1.** woodlander, woodsman; **2.** timber worker; **3.** guerrilla

mežiņš *nm dim* of **mežs**, coppice

mežirbe *nf* hazel grouse

mežizstrāde *nf* timber production

mežkopība *nf* silviculture

mežkopis *nm*, **~e** *nf* silviculturist

mežkungs *nm* (obs.) district forester

mežlemings *nm* red-backed lemming

mežloks *nm* ramson

mežmala or **mežmale** *nf* edge of a forest

mežmaliet/is *nm*, **~e** *nf* dweller at the edge of the forest

mežmateriāli *nm pl* timber

mežniecība *nf* forest district

mežnora *nf* forest glade

mežolietis *nm* (reg.) dweller at the edge of the forest

mežonēns *nm* **1.** wild child; (of a girl) tomboy; **2.** very shy child

mežonība *nf* savagery; wildness

mežonīgi *adv* wildly; savagely; ferociously; (of laughing) fiendlishly

mežonīgs *adj* wild; savage; ferocious; (of laughter) fiendish

mežonīgums *nm* wildness; savageness; ferocity

mežon/is *nm*, **~e** *nf* savage

mežoniski *adv* wildly

mežonisks *adj* wild

mežotne *nf* forest stand

mežpārkāpums *nm* violation of forest laws

mežpuķīte *nf* hepatica

mežpurvs *nm* **1.** swamp in a forest; **2.** wet forest

mežputni *nm pl* Tetraonidae

mežradznie/ks *nm*, **~ce** *nf* French horn player

mežrags *nm* French horn

mežragspēle *nf* performance on the French horn

mežroze *nf* wild rose

mežrozīte *nf* wild rose

mežrūpniecība *nf* timber industry

mežrūpnie/ks *nm*, **~ce** *nf* timber merchant

mež/s *nm* wood, forest; **~a** wood (*adj*), wild; **jaukts m.** mixed hardwood and softwood forest ◊ **~ā būdams, ~u meklē** he can't see the forest for the trees

mežsaimniecība *nf* forestry

mežsaimniecisks *adj* forestry (*adj*)

mežsaimnieks *nm* forester

mežsalāti *nm pl* wall lettuce

mežsargmāja *nf* forest ranger's house

mežsargs *nm* forest ranger

mežstrādnieks *nm* timber worker

mežstrādnieku nometne *nf* logging camp

mežte[ch]nika [h] *nf* forest technology

mežu izstrāde *nf* lumbering

mežu mieži *nm pl* ancestral two-rowed barley

mežu ūdenszāle *nf* a waterweed, Glyceria lithuanica

mežvidus *nm* middle of the forest

mežvīns *nm* Virginia creeper

mežvīteņi *nm pl* virgin's bower

mežzemnieks *nm* (reg.) woodlander

mežzinātnes *nf pl* forestry sciences

mežzinātnie/ks *nm*, **~ce** *nf* forestry science specialist

mežzinība *nf* silvics

mežzinis *nm* district forester

mi *indecl nf* (mus.) E

mialģija *nf* myalgia

miasmatisks *adj* miasmic

miasms *nm* miasma

miastēnija *nf* myasthenia

mice *nf* **1.** (folk.) a married woman's headgear; **2.** (col.) cap; **3.** (col.) noggin

micēlijs *nm* mycelium

micella *nf* micelle

micelle *nf* micelle

mīcenis *nm* mashed potatoes

mīcīt *vt* knead

mīcītava *nf* kneading room

micīte *nf dim* of **mice**, little cap

mīcīties *vr* struggle (to get out of a sticky substance); jostle, press

mičela *nf* partridgeberry

mičman/is *nm*, **~e** *nf* midshipman

mičot *vt* (folk.) put on a **mice** (a wedding tradition: inducting the bride into the married state by putting a married woman's headgear on her)

mičumačs *nm* mélange; jumble, snarl

miču maču *adv* (col.) haphazardly

mičuriniet/is *nm*, **~e** *nf* Michurinist

mičurinisks *adj* Michurinist

mīdeklis *nm* **1.** clay puddle; **2.** grain trod out by horses

midi *indecl adj* midi

mīdija *nf* mussel

mīdīt *vt* trample; **m. kājām** tread under foot; (of laws) violate

mīdīties *vr* tread in place, stamp

midzenis *nm* lair; den; pit; nest

midzināt *vt* put to sleep

midzis *nm* lair; den; pit; nest

miecaugi *nm pl* plants yielding tannin

miece *nf* tanning (process)

miecējums *nm* tanning (outcome of tanning)

miecēklis *nm* tanning agent

miecēt *vt* (of hides) tan

miecētājaugi *nm pl* plants yielding tannin

miecētājmiza *nf* tanning bark

miecētāj/s *nm*, **~a** *nf* tanner

miecētājviela *nf* tannin; tanning agent

miecētava *nf* tannery

miecēties *vr* get wet

miecmateriāls *nm* tanning agent

miecmiza *nf* tanning bark

miecskābe *nf* tannic acid

miecviela *nf* tannin; tanning agent

miedzīgi *adv* sleepily

miedzīgs *adj* sleepy

miedziņš *nm dim* of **miegs**, sleep

miedža *nf* (reg.) sleeper

miega artērija *nf* carotid (artery)

miegacis *nm* (col.) **1.** sleepyhead; **2.** lie-abed

miegaini *adv* sleepily

miegainība *nf* sleepiness

miegainis *nm* (col.) **1.** sleepyhead; **2.** lie-abed

miegains *adj* sleepy

miegainums *nm* sleepiness

miegaļa *nf* sleepy, slow female

miegamaiss *nm* lie-abed

miegamice *nf, nm* (col.) **1.** sluggard; **2.** sleepyhead; **3.** lie-abed

miegapūzn/is *nm,* ~**e** *nf* (col.) **1.** sleepyhead; **2.** lie-abed

miegarausis *nm* lie-abed

miega slimība *nf* sleeping sickness

miega zāles *nf pl* sleeping pills

miegogas *nf pl* **1.** herb Paris; **2.** berries of herb Paris

miegonis *nm* **1.** (col.) lie-abed; **2.** doormouse

miegoties *vr* fight sleepiness

miegpilns *adj* sleepy

mieg/s *nm* sleep; **caurs m.** restless sleep; **ciets m.** sound sleep; **pa** ~**am** in one's sleep; **man nāk m.** I am getting sleepy

miegt *vt* **1.** squeeze, press; (of eyes) close; **2.** (col.) hit; **3.** (col.) run

miegties *vr* blink

miegulība *nf* sleepiness

miegulīgi *adv* sleepily

miegulīgs *adj* sleepy

miegul/is *nm,* ~**e** *nf* (col.) sleepyhead

mieguža *nm, nf* (reg.) sleepyhead

miekšēt *vt* **1.** soak; soften; **2.** (col.) hit

miekšēties *vr* soak

miekšis *nm* (col.) **1.** rainy weather; **2.** rain-drenched person; **3.** drunk

miekšķēt *vt* **1.** soak; soften; **2.** (col.) hit

miekšķēties *vr* soak

miekšķis *nm* (col.) **1.** rainy weather; **2.** rain-drenched person; **3.** drunk

mielasts *nm* banquet, feast

mieles *nf pl* dregs

mielināt *vt* serve food

mielīns *nm* myelin

mielīts *nm* myelitis

mieloma *nf* myeloma

mielot *vt* treat, entertain, feast; **m. acis** feast one's eyes; **Dievs mielo viņa dvēseli!** may God bless his soul!

mieloties *vr* feat; feast on

mieļains *adj* dreggy

mieļu tapa *nm* (col.) drinker, drunk, drunkard

miemuri *nm pl* ties (that connect the front axle of a wagon to the thills)

miera dibinātājs *nm* peacemaker

miera karogs *nf* white flag

miera laušana *nf* breach of peace

mieramika *nm* (col.) peaceable person

miera osta *nf* haven

miera vieta *nf* cemetery

mierīgi *adv* quietly; calmly

mierīgs *adj* **1.** quiet; still; calm; **2.** peaceful; **3.** untroubled; without worry; **esiet** ~**i!** don't worry! **4.** (metall.) killed

mierīgums *nm* **1.** quietness; stillness; calmness; **2.** peacefulness

mierinājums *nm* comfort, consolation

mierināt *vt* comfort, console; calm

mierinātāj/s *nm,* ~**a** *nf* comforter, consoler

mierizlīgums *nm* settlement

mierlaika *indecl adj* peacetime

mierlīgums *nm* peace treaty

miermīlība *nf* peaceableness; love of peace

miermīlīgi *adv* peaceably

miermīlīgs *adj* peaceable; peace-loving; pacific

miermīlīgums *nm* peaceable disposition

miermīlis *nm* peaceable person

mierprātīgi *adv* peaceably

mierprātīgs *adj* peaceable; peace-loving; pacific

mier/s *nm* **1.** peace ◊ **m. un Dievs!** Friends? **m. viņa pīšļiem!** may he rest in peace! **mīļā** ~**a labad** for the sake of peace and quiet; **būt ar** ~**u** agree; **būt** ~**ā** be content; **2.** quiet;

tranquility; calm, stillness; rest; ~ā (mil.)
at attention; ~ā! (mil.) attention! esi ~ā! be
quiet! vienā ~ā very calm-ly; ~a stāvoklī
(phys.) at rest

mierstarpnieks *nm* (hist.) arbitrator

miertiesa *nf* justice court

miertiesnesis *nm* justice of the peace

mies/a *nf* **1.** flesh; ~**as krāsā** flesh-colored; **m.
un asinis** flesh and blood; **2.** body ◊ **melnās
~ās** (of working) very hard, like a slave;
(drebēt) pie visām ~ām (tremble) all over;
ar ~u un dvēseli body and soul

miesas ārsts *nm* physician in ordinary, personal
physician

miesas bojājumi *nm pl* bodily injury; battery

miesas būve *nf* bodily built, constitution

miesaskārība *nf* lust, carnal desire

miesas kārībnieks *nm* lecher

miesaskārīgi *adv* = **mieskārīgi**

miesaskārīgs *adj* = **mieskārīgs**

miesaskrāsa *nf* flesh tones

miesassardze *nf* bodyguards

miesassargs *nm* bodyguard

miesassods *nm* corporal punishment

miesas spēks *nm* physical strength

miesas veļa *nf* underwear

miesīgi *adv* **1.** bodily; **2.** physically

miesīgs *adj* **1.** bodily, physical; **2.** (of blood-
related relatives) own

miesiski *adv* **1.** carnally; **2.** somatically

miesisks *adj* **1.** carnal; **2.** somatic

miesiskums *nm* carnality

mieskārīgi *adv* lustfully, carnally

mieskārīgs *adj* lustful, carnal

mieslotāj/s *nm*, ~**a** *nf* (reg.) one that snacks on
goodies

miesloties *vr* **1.** (Bibl.) rejoice; **2.** (Bibl., reg.)
make love; **3.** (reg.) snack on goodies

miesmetis *nm* Shrovetide

miesnie/ks *nm*, ~**ce** *nf* butcher

miesniekzellis *nm* butcher's apprentice

miestiņš I *nm dim* of **miests** I, unincorporated
town; village

miestiņš II *nm dim* of **miests** II, homemade
beer

miestnie/ks *nm*, ~**ce** *nf* inhabitant of an
unincorporated town

miests I *nm* **1.** unincorporated town; **2.** village

miests II *nm* homemade beer

miešķāns *nm* townsman

miešķis I *nm* woodruff

miešķis II *nm* stirrer

miet *vt* set posts

mietēt *vt* (col.) hit, strike

mieti I *nm pl* **1.** horse trading; **2.** hiring of new
servants

mieti II (with **iê**) *nm pl* of **miets**

mietiņš *nm dim* of **miets**, small peg; stake; **dēs-
tāmais m.** dibble

mietiņu režģis *nm* grillage of pegs

mietne *nf* (of a sled or sleigh) standard, strut

mietnieks *nm* horse trader

mietot *vt* set posts

mietpilsonība *nf* Philistinism, Babbitry

mietpilsonīgi *adv* in a Philistine way

mietpilsonīgs *adj* Philistine

mietpilson/is *nm*, ~**e** *nf* Philistine, Babbit

mietpilsoniski *adv* in a Philistine way

mietpilsonisks *adj* Philistine

mietpilsoniskums *nm* Philistinism, Babbitry

mietpilsonisms *nm* Philistinism, Babbitry

miet/s *nm* pole, post, stake, picket, pale; prop;
~**u žogs** paling; **kā ar ~u pa galvu** stunned;
kā ~u norijis he has swallowed a stake

mietsakne *nf* taproot

mieturaiņi *nm pl* Equisetales

mieturalgas *nf pl* chara

mieturis *nm* **1.** umbel; **2.** stirrer, beater

mieturveida *indecl adj* umbellate

mieturveidīgi *adv* like an umbel

mieturveidīgs *adj* umbellate

mietuŗu daudzlape *nf* water milfoil

mietuŗu mētra *nf* a mint, Mentha verticillata

mietuŗu mugurene *nf* whorled Solomon's seal

mietuŗu salvija *nf* wild sage

mietveida *indecl adj* pole-like

mietveidīgi *adv* like a pole

mietveidīgs *adj* pole-like

miezaine *nf* = miezājs

miezaite *nf* = miezājs

miezāj/s *nm* 1. harvested barley field; 2. ~i barley straw

miezeris *nm* mortar (grinding bowl)

miezerķūlis *nm* pestle

mieziķi *nm pl* woodruff

mie/zis *nm*, usu. *pl* ~ēi barley

miezītis *nm* homemade beer

mieža strutene *nf* St.-John's-wort

miežabrālis *nm* = miežbrālis

miežauzas *nf pl* a mixture of barley and oats

miežbrālis *nm* canary grass; see also parastais m.

miežgrauds *nm* sty

miežgraudiņš *nm dim* of miežgrauds, sty

miež/i *nm pl* barley; ~u grauds barleycorn; ~u Miķelis (col.) fool; ~u putraimi barley groats

miežubrālis *nm* = miežbrālis

miežu cietās melnplaukas *nf pl* barley smut

miežu melnā stiebrmuša *nf* a chloropid fly, Oscinella pusilla

miga *nf* den, lair

migacis *nm* (col.) 1. sleepyhead; 2. lie-abed

migaža *nm, nf* (col.) 1. sleepyhead; 2. lie-abed

migl/a *nf* fog, mist; haze; klājeniskā m. ground fog; ~ā tīts befogged, shrouded in mist ◊ kā pa ~u (col.) in a daze

miglaini *adv* foggily; hazily; vaguely, nebulously

miglainība *nf* fogginess; haziness; (fig.) vagueness

miglains *adj* foggy, misty; hazy; vague, nebulous

miglainums *nm* fogginess; haziness

miglājs *nm* 1. fog, fog bank; 2. nebula; 3. galaxy

miglas aizkars *nm* fog screen

miglas bilde *nf* (obs.) lantern slide

miglas kamera *nf* cloud chamber

miglas taure *nf* foghorn

miglāt *v* = miglot

miglausis *nm* (col.) deaf person

miglināt *vi* 1. be foggy; drizzle; 2. spray

migliņa *nf dim* of migla, light fog

miglojums *nm* 1. fog; 2. spraying

miglot *v* 1. *vi* (3rd pers, of fog, mist) rise; 2. *vi* (3rd pers) drizzle; 3. *vt* spray

miglotāj/s *nm*, ~a *nf* sprayer (person, device)

migloties *vr* fog up

miglots *adj, part* of miglot foggy

miglveida *indecl adj* fog-like

miglveidīgi *adv* like fog

miglveidīgs *adj* fog-like

migmatīts *nm* migmatite

migoņa *nf, nm* (col.) 1. sleepyhead; 2. lie-abed

migot *vi* blink

migrācija *nf* migration

migrant/s *nm*, ~e *nf* migrant

migrēna *nf* migraine

migrēt *vi* migrate

migt *v* 1. *vi* fall asleep; 2. *vt* put to sleep

migties *vr* fall asleep

migulis *nm* 1. young animal (that sleeps in its mother's den); 2. (col.) sleepyhead; 3. (col.) lie—abed

miguzis *nm* (col.) 1. sleepyhead; 2. lie-abed

miguža *nm, nf* (col.) 1. sleepyhead; 2. lie-abed

miģeles *nf pl* biting midges

mija *nf* change; alternation; interchange; shift

mijattiecība *nf* reciprocity

mijējs *nm*, ~a *nf* trader

mijības *nf pl* change; alternation; interchange; shift

mijiedarbe *nf* interaction

mijiedarbība *nf* interaction

mijiedarbīgi *adv* interactively

mijiedarbīgs *adj* interactive

mijimpedance *nf* interaction impedance

mijkrēsla *nf* dusk, twilight

mijkrēslis *nm* dusk, twilight

mijkrēšļaini *adv* duskily

mijkrēšļains *adj* dusky

mijnorāde *nf* cross-reference

mikado *indecl nm* mikado

Mīkālis *prop nm* Michaelmas

mīkla I *nf* dough; batter; paste

mīkla II *nf* 1. riddle, puzzle; 2. mystery; enigma

mīklaini *adv* mysteriously

mīklainība *nf* mysteriousness

mīklains I *adj* doughy

mīklains II *adj* mysterious; puzzling; enigmatic

mīklainums *nm* mysteriousness

mīklas virtulis *nm* doughnut

mīklenāji *nm pl* cloudberry

mīklenājs *nm* 1. mulberry; 2. hawthorn

mīklene *nf* 1. mulberry; 2. hawthorn;hawthorn fruit

mikli *adv* damply, humidly

miklot *vt* moisten; *vi* turn humid

mikls *adj* damp, humid

miklums *nm* dampness, humidity

mikobaktērija *nf* mycobacterium

mikoloģija *nf* mycology

mikoloģisks *adj* mycologic

mikoriza *nf* mycorrhiza

mikotrofisks *adj* mycotrophic

mikotrofs *adj* mycotrophic

mikoze *nf* mycosis

mikrēslis *nm* dusk, twilight

mikroampērmetrs *nm* microammeter

mikroampērs *nm* microampere

mikroanal|i|tiski [ī] *adv* microanalytically

mikroanal|i|tisks [ī] *adj* microanalytic

mikroanal|i|ze [ī] *nf* microanalysis

mikroasambleris *nm* (compu.) microassembler

mikroautobuss *nm* microbus

mikroautomobilis *nm* go-kart

mikrobarogr|a|fs [ā] *nm* microbarograph

mikrobiāls *adj* microbial

mikrobīde *nf* microdisplacement

mikrobiolo/gs *nm*, ~ģe *nf* microbiologist

mikrobioloģija *nf* microbiology

mikrobioloģiski *adv* microbiologically

mikrobioloģisks *adj* microbiological

mikrobs *nm* microbe

mikrocefālija *nf* microcephaly

mikrodaļiņa *nf* subatomic particle

mikrodators *nm* microcomputer

mikrodeformācija *nf* microdeformation

mikrodiorīts *nm* microdiorite

mikrodzinējs *nm* micromotor

mikroelektrods *nm* microelectrode

mikroekonomika *nf* microeconomics

mikroekonomisks *adj* microeconomic

mikroelektrodzinējs *nm* small electric motor

mikroelektromotors *nm* small electric motor

mikroelektronika *nf* microelectronics

mikroelektroniski *adv* microelectronically

mikroelektronisks *adj* microelectronic

mikroelements *nm* trace element

mikrofāgs *nm* microphage

mikrofarads *nm* microfarad

mikrofauna *nf* microfauna

mikrofilma *nf* microfilm

mikrofiša *nf* microfiche

mikrofīts *nm* microphyte

mikroflora *nf* microflora

mikrofons *nm* microphone

mikrofosilija *nf* microfossil

mikrofotogr|a|fija [ā] *nf* 1. microphotography; 2. photomicrograph

mikrofotokopija *nf* microreproduction

mikrofotometrs *nm* microphotometer

mikrofotouzņēmums *nm* microdot; microprint

mikrogr|a|fija |ā| *nf* micrography
mikrograms *nm* microgram
mikrogranīts *nm* microgranite
mikroģen|e|ze |ē| *nf* (psych.) microgenesis
mikroģeogr|a|fija |ā| *nf* microgeography
mikrohenrijs *nm* microhenry
mikroheterogenitāte *nf* microheterogeneity
mikroinfarkts *nm* microinfarct
mikroinstrukcija *nf* (compu.) microinstruction
mikroizcilnis *nm* microgroove
mikrokarte *nf* miniature map
mikrokefalija *nf* microcephaly
mikrokefals *nm* microcephalus
mikroklimatisks *adj* microclimatic
mikroklimats *nm* microclimate
mikroklīns *nm* microcline
mikrokods *nm* microcode
mikrokoks *nm* micrococcus
mikrokopija *nf* microcopy
mikrokosms *nm* microcosm
mikrokrist|āl|isks |all| *adj* microcrystalline
mikroķīmija *nf* microchemistry
mikroķīmisks *adj* microchemical
mikroķirurģija *nf* microsurgery
mikrolitrāžas *indecl adj* (of engine cylinders) small-displacement
mikrolitrs *nm* microliter
mikrol|i|ts |ī| *nm* microlith
mikromanipul|a|tors |ā| *nm* micromanipulator
mikromanometrs *nm* micromanometer
mikromērītājs *nm* micrometer caliper
mikromēsli *nm pl* trace element fertilizer
mikrometa|ll|urģija |l| *nf* micrometallurgy
mikrometrija *nf* micrometry
mikrometrisks *adj* micrometrical
mikrometrs *nm* (instrument; unit of length) mi-crometer
mikrominiaturizācija *nf* microminiaturization
mikrominiatūrs *adj* microminiature

mikromolekula *nf* micromolecule
mikronēziet/is *nm*, ~e *nf* Micronesian
mikrons *nm* micron
mikrooms *nm* microohm
mikroorganisms *nm* microorganism
mikropaleontoloģija *nf* micropaleontology
mikropasaule *nf* microcosm
mikropiedziņa *nf* microdrive
mikropile *nf* micropyle
mikropora *nf* micropore
mikroporains *adj* microporous
mikroprocesors *nm* microprocessor
mikroprogramma *nf* microprogram
mikroprojekcija *nf* microprojection
mikrorajons *nm* microdistrict
mikroreljefs *nm* microrelief
mikros|ch|ēma |h| *nf* microcircuit
mikrosekunde *nf* microsecond
mikrosīmenss *nm* microsiemens
mikroskopija *nf* microscopy
mikroskopiski *adv* microscopically
mikroskopisks *adj* microscopic
mikroskopiskums *nm* microscopic size
mikroskops *nm* microscope
mikrosociolo/gs *nm*, ~ģe *nf* microsociologist
mikrosocioloģija *nf* microsociology
mikrosocioloģisks *adj* microsociological
mikrospora *nf* microspore
mikrostruktūra *nf* microstructure
mikrosvari *nm pl* microbalance
mikrotermisks *adj* microthermal
mikrotipija *nf* microprint
mikrotoms *nm* microtome
mikrotrons *nm* microtron
mikrovats *nm* microwatt
mikrovide *nf* microenvironment
mikroviļņi *nm pl* microwaves
mikrovoltmetrs *nm* microvoltmeter
mikrovolts *nm* microvolt
miksedēma *nf* myxedema
mikseris *nm* (metall.; device, appliance) mixer

miksēt *vt* (el.) mix

miksīnas *nf pl* Myxine

mīksnājs *nm* bog, mire

mīksne *nf* bog, mire

mīksnējs *adj* 1. soft; 2. wet, well watered; 3. juicy

mīksnis *nm* bog, mire

miksobaktērijas *nf* myxobacteria

miksolidisks *adj* Mixolydian

miksovīruss *nm* myxovirus

mikspikļi *nm pl* mixed pickles

mīkstādains *adj* soft-skinned

mīkstā gandrene *nf* dove's-foot

mīkstais *nom adj* (sl.) homo

mīkstā lāčauza *nf* soft cheat

mīkstā madara *nf* wild madder

mīkstā nātre *nf* dead nettle

mīkstā paparde *nf* lady fern

mīkstā roze *nf* downy rose

mīkstās cietpieres *nf pl* hawk's beard

mīkstbarība *nf* mash (poultry feed)

mīkstblaktis *nf pl* Miridae

mīkstčaula *nf* soft-shelled egg

mīkstčaulība *nf* cowardice

mīkstčaulīgi *adv* in a cowardly manner

mīkstčaulīgs *adj* cowardly

mīkstčaul/is *nm*, ~e *nf* coward

mīksti *adv* softly, tenderly; mildly; m. vārīts soft-boiled

mīkstie kvieši *nm pl* common wheat

mīkstinājuma zīme *nf* mark of palatalization

mīkstinājums *nm* 1. softening; mitigation; extenuation; 2. (ling.) palatalization

mīkstināšana *nf* 1. softening; mitigation; ~s temperātūra softening point; 2. (ling.) palatalization

mīkstināt *vt* 1. soften; temper; mitigate; 2. (ling.) palatalize

mīkstinātāj/s *nm*, ~a *nf* softener

mīkstinošs *adj, part* of mīkstināt softening, emollient; mitigatory; (jur.) extenuating

mīkstkoks *nm* softwood

mīkstlapains *adj* soft-leaved

mīkstlapis *nm* soft-wooded tree

mīkstlode *nf* soft solder

mīkstlodēšana *nf* soft soldering

mīkstmēl/is *nm*, ~e *nf* (col.) flatterer

mīkstmiesīgs *adj* (of bodies) soft

mīkstmies/is *nm* 1. mollusc; 2. (col., cont.) softy; ~e *nf*

mīkstnieks *nm* (col.) softy

mīkstpēdiņš *nm* (col.) coward

mīkstpiene *nf* sow thistle

mīkstroc/is *nm*, ~e *nf* person shirking physical work

mīksts *adj* 1. soft, tender; mild; (of furniture) upholstered; (of railroad cars) soft-seated; 2. (col.) flattering

mīkstsirdība *nf* soft-heartedness

mīkstsirdīgi *adv* in a soft-hearted way

mīkstsirdīgs *adj* soft-hearted

mīkstsirdīgums *nm* soft-heartedness

mīkstsird/is *nm*, ~e *nf* soft-hearted person

mīkstspārņi *nm pl* Cantharidae

mīkstspuru *indecl adj* soft-finned

mīkstspuru zivis *nf pl* Malacopterygii

mīksttapšana *nf* softening

mīksttapšanas temperātūra *nf* softening point

mīksttūba *nf* soft felt

mīkstulība *nf* cowardice

mīkstulīgi *adv* weakly

mīkstulīgs *adj* weakly

mīkstulīgums *nm* weakliness

mīkstulis *nm* coward

mīkstums *nm* 1. softness, tenderness; 2. soft parts, (of fruit) flesh

mikstūra *nf* 1. (pharm.) mixture; 2. (mus.) mixture stop

mīkt *vi* soften

mīkūnas *nf pl* (hist.) hiring day

miķelene *nf* Michaelmas daisy

miķelīši *nm* Michaelmas daisy

miķelīte *nf* Michaelmas daisy

miķelnīca *nf* Michaelmas daisy
Miķeļdiena *nf* Michaelmas
Miķeļi *nm pl* Michaelmas
miķeļpuķes *nf pl* Michaelmas daisy
mila *nf* (fabric) mull
mīla *nf* (poet.) love
mīlams *adj, part* of **mīlēt** lovable
mīlas bulta *nf* Cupid's arrow
mīlas dēka *nf* love affair
mīlas dzēriens *nm* love potion
mīlas pāris *nm* lovers
mīlas puķe *nf* oxeye daisy
milda *nf* (sl.) five-lat piece
mīle *nf* clay puddling pit
milēdija *nf* milady
milenārisms *nm* millenarianism
milenārs *adj* millenarian
mīlestība *nf* love; **nelaimīga m.** unrequited
    love; **veca m.** old flame
mīlestības darbs *nm* labor of love
mīlēt *vt* love; **mīl, nemīl** she (he) loves me, she
    (he) loves me not
mīlētājs *nm* lover; **pirmais m.** (theat.) romantic
    lead
mīlēties *vr* make love
milētieši *nm pl* Milesians
miliampērmetrs *nm* milliammeter
miliampērs *nm* milliampere
miliārs *adj* milliary
mīlība *nf* lovableness, sweetness
milibārs *nm* millibar
milicija *nf* 1. militia; 2. police
milice *nf* policewoman
milicis *nm* 1. militiaman; 2. policeman
milicionārs *nm* militiaman
mīlīgi *adv* 1. affectionately, sweetly; 2. gently
miligrams *nm* milligram
mīlīgs *adj* 1. affectionate, sweet; 2. mild,
    gentle
mīlīgums *nm* lovableness, sweetness
milihenrijs *nm* millihenry
mililitrs *nm* milliliter

milimetrīgs *adj* (rare.) millimeter, millimetric
milimetrpapīrs *nm* millimetric cross-section
    grid
milimetrs *nm* millimeter
milimikrons *nm* millimicron
mīlin *adv, emph* of **mīlēt; m. mīlēt** to love
    passionately
mīlinājuma vārd/s pet name; **m. ~i** terms of
    endearment
mīlinājums *nm* endearment
mīlināms *adj* pettable, lovable
mīlināt *vt* pet
mīlināties *vr* pet
milioms *nm* milliohm
milisīmenss *nm* millisiemens
militārā policija *nf* military police; **~s ~s**
    priekš-nieks provost marshall
militāri *adv* militarily
militāriski *adv* militarily
militārisks *adj* military
militārisms *nm* militarism
militāristiski *adv* militaristically
militāristisks *adj* militaristic
militārist/s *nm,* **~e** *nf* militarist
milit[a]rizācija [ā] *nf* militarization
milit[a]rizēt [ā] *vt* militarize
milit[a]rizēties [ā] *vr* become militarized
militārpersona *nf* military man, military; **~s** *pl*
    military personnel
militārps[īch]oloģija [ih] *nf* military psy-
    chology
militārrūpniecisks *adj* miliary-industrial
militārs *adj* military
mīlītis *nm, usu. voc* **mīlīt** dear one, dear
milivats *nm* milliwatt
milivoltmetrs *nm* millivoltmeter
milivolts *nm* millivolt
miljardais *adj* billionth
miljarddaļa *nf* one-billionth
miljardier/is *nm,* **~e** *nf* billionaire
miljards *nm* billion
miljēma *nf* mil

miljonais *adj* millionth

miljonār/s *nm*, **~e** *nf* millionaire

miljondaļa *nf* one-millionth

miljons *nm* million

millenārisms *nm* millenarianism

millerīts *nm* millerite

milna *nf* **1.** club; **2.** hand mill pole; **3.** punting pole

mīlniek/s *nm* gallant, lady-killer, paramour; **~i** lovers

milnot *vt* club

milonitizācija *nf* mylonitization

milonīts *nm* mylonite

milords *nm* milord

milreiss *nm* milreis

milstīties *vr* **1.** move, stir; **2.** idle; **3.** wag one's tail

miltainais deviņvīruspēks *nm* white mullein

miltaini *adv* floury; mealy

miltains *adj* **1.** floury; **2.** (of fruit, potatoes) mealy

miltainums *nm* mealiness

miltāt *vi* turn mealy

miltēdiens *nm* farinaceous food; flour gravy; gruel

miltenājs *nm* **1.** bearberry; **2.** bearberry patch

miltene *nf* bearberry

miltenīca *nf* pap

milti *nm pl* flour; meal; **baltie m.** fine wheat flour

miltīt *vi* (col.) hit

miltots *adj* with flour added; floured

miltrasa *nf* mildew

miltrūpniecība *nf* flour mindustry

miltu biezputra *nf* pap

miltu cukurs *nm* powdered sugar

miltūdens *nm* gruel

miltu ērce *nf* flour mite

miltu klīsteris *nm* paste

miltu kode *nf* Mediterranean flour moth

miltu kukainis *nm* confused flour beetle

miltu melmelis (or **melnulis**) *nm* meal worm beetle

miltumiņš *nm dim* of **miltums 3**, tiny bit, smid-gen

miltums *nm* **1.** mealiness; **2.** mealy pulp; **3.** smid-gen

miltu svilnis *nm* meal moth

miltu zupa *nf* gruel

miltveida *indecl adj* floury

miltveidīgs *adj* floury

milubriedis *nm* Père David's deer

mīlul/is *nm*, **~e** *nf* darling, pet; favorite

milze *nf* **1.** swelling; **2.** gangrene

milzene *nf* giantess

milzenīgi *adv* very

milzenis *nm* giant

milzīgi *adv* hugely, enormously; immensly, vastly

milzīgs *adj* huge, gigantic, enormous; immense, vast

milzīgums *nm* hugeness; enormity; immensity, vastness

milzis *nm* giant; **m. cilvēkēdājs** ogre

milzonīgi *adv* very

milzonis *nm* giant

milzt *vi* **1.** tumefy, swell; **2.** grow

milzu *indecl adj* huge, gigantic, giant, enormous

milzu čūska *nf* boa constrictor

milzu dzīvības koks *nm* giant arborvitae

milzu haizivs *nf* basking shark

milzum *adv* very; **m. daudz** lots and lots

milzumīgs *adj* large, giant, vast

milzums I *nm* vast amount, vast numbers

milzums II *nm* tumefaction, swelling

milzu pūpēdis *nm* giant puffball

milzu sekvoja *nf* giant sequoia

milžbruņrupucis *nm* giant tortoise

mīļ/ais *nom adj*, **~ā** *f* beloved; (in address) dear

mīļākā *nf* mistress

mīļākais *nom adj* lover

mīļbērniņš *nm* pet, pampered child

mīļi *adv* lovingly; cordially

mīļot *vt* love; pet, caress

mīļot/ais *nom adj*, ~ā *f* love, beloved

mīļotājs *nm*, ~a *nf* lover, fancier; viņš ir liels . . .
  m. he is very fond of . . .

mīļots *adj, part* of mīļot beloved

mīļprāt *adv* willingly, gladly

mīļš *adj* 1. dear, beloved; 2. sweet, lovable;
  3. (in polite speech) kind; 4. favorite

mīļumiņš *nm* dear one; *voc* mīļumiņ dearest

mīļum/s *nm* sweetness, lovability

mimeogr[a]fs [ā] *nm* mimeograph

mimeografēt *vt* mimeograph

mīmika *nf* facial expression, portrayal of
  emotion

mīmikrija *nf* mimicry

mīmiķis *nm* mimic, mime

mīmiski *adv* mimetically

mīmisks *adj* mimic, mimetic

mimoz/a *nf* mimosa

mīm/s I *nm*, ~a *nf* mime

mīms II *nm* meme

mimuzops *nm* Mimusops

mina *nf* 1. (stair) step; 2. footprint

mīna I *nf* 1. mine; maskēta m. booby trap; pel-
  došā m. buoyant mine; 2. mortar shell

mīna II *nf* root cellar

minamais I *nom adj* riddle

minamais II *nom adj* treadle

minarets *nm* minaret

mincis *nm* (col.) kitty

mīne *nf* clay puddling pit

minējums *nm* 1. guess, conjecture; 2. mention,
  citation

minerālaugsne *nf* mineral soil

minerālavots *nm* mineral spring

minerālbarība *nf* mineral supplement

minerāleļļa *nf* mineral oil

minerālisks *adj* mineral

miner[a]lizācija [ā] *nf* mineralization

miner[a]liz[a]tors [ā][ā] *nm* mineralizer

miner[a]lizēt [ā] *vt* mineralize

miner[a]lizēties [ā] *vr* become mineralized

minerālmēsli *nm pl* mineral fertilizer

minerālmēslojums *nm* mineral fertilizer

miner[a]lo/gs [ā] *nm*, ~ģe *nf* mineralogist

miner[a]loģija [ā] *nf* mineralogy

miner[a]loģisks [ā] *adj* mineralogical

minerāls *nm* mineral

minerāls *adj* mineral

minerālsāls *nf* mineral salt

minerālskābe *nf* mineral acid

minerālūdens *nm* mineral water

minerālvate *nf* fiberglass

minerālviela *nf* mineral substance, mineral

minēt *vt* 1. guess; riddle, solve; trīsreiz brīv
  m. I give you three guesses; 2. mention,
  name; cite; blakus minot by the way;
  iepriekš ~ais above-mentioned; turpmāk
  ~ais mentioned below

mīnēt *vt* mine

minētāj/s *nm*, ~a *nf* riddler, solver (of riddles)

mīnētājs *nm* miner (one that lays mines)

minete *nf* minette ore

minēties *vr* (rare.) try to guess

mini *indecl adj* mini

miniator/s *nm*, ~e *nf* miniaturist

miniatūra *nf* miniature

miniatūrist/s *nm*, ~e *nf* miniaturist

miniaturizācija *nf* miniaturization

miniaturizēt *vt* miniaturize

miniatūrs *adj* miniature

minidators *nm* minicomputer

mīnijs *nm* red lead, minium; ~a sarkans
  miniaceous

minima *nf* minim

minimakss *nm* (math.) minimax

minimālalga *nf* minimum wage

minimāli *adv* minimally

minim[a]lisms [ā] *nm* minimalism

minimālist/s *nm*, ~e *nf* minimalist

minim[a]litāte [ā] *nf* minimal nature

minim[a]lizācija [ā] *nf* minimization

minim|a|lizēt |ā| *vt* minimize
minim|a|lizēties |ā| *vr* be minimized
minimāls *adj* minimal, minimum
minimāltermometrs *nm* minimal thermometer
minimode *nf* mini fashion
minims *nm* minimum
minimums *nm* minimum; **techniskais m.** minimum of technical knowledge
mīnis *nm* clay puddling pit
ministeriālis *nm* (hist.) ministerial
ministrants *nm* altar boy
ministra vietnieks *nm* Deputy Minister, (in Great Britain or the USA) Undersecretary
ministrija *nf* ministry, (in the USA) department
ministr/s *nm*, ~e *nf* Minister, (in Great Britain) Secretary of State), (in the USA) Secretary
ministru kabinets *nm* cabinet of ministers
ministru padome *nf* council of ministers
ministru prezidents *nm* Prime Minister
minjons *nm* (typ.) minion, 7-point type
minka *nf* (col.) pussy
mīnmetējnie/ks *nm*, ~ce *nf* mortarman
mīnmetējs *nm* mortar
minnartijas *nf pl* Minnartia
minnezengers *nm* minnesinger
minori *adv* in a minor key; melancholily
minorīgi *adv* in a minor key
minorīgs *adj* (mus.) minor
minoriski *adv* in a minor key
minorisks *adj* (mus.) minor
minoritāte *nf* minority
minorīts *nm* Minorite
minors *nm* (mus.) minor
minors *adj* (mus.) minor; melancholy
Minsteres siers *nm* Munster cheese
minstināt *vt* stumble over words
minstināties *vr* hesitate, waver, hem and haw
minstīties *vr* shift from one foot to the other; fidget; stamp

minuends *nm* minuend
mīnukuģis *nm* minesweeper
mīnulauks *nm* minefield
mīnu meklētājs *nm* mine detector
minums *nm* (weav.) shedding order
mīnus *adv* **1.** (math.) minus; **2.** (of temperature) below freezing
minuskulis *nm* (typ.) small letter
mīnuss *nm* **1.** minus sign; **2.** minus, drawback
minūte *nf* minute
miņa *nf* **1.** awareness; **2.** trace; **3.** (obs.) memory
mīņa *nf* **1.** tramped-down place in a crop field; **2.** root cellar; **3.** grain spread out on the threshing floor; **4.** slow person, muff
mīņāt *vt* trample
mīņāties *vr* shift from one foot to the other; fidget; stamp; **m. uz vietas** tread in place
miņķins *nm* = **miņķis**
miņķis *nm* (reg.) **1.** hypocrite; **2.** cheat, rogue
miocēns *nm* Miocene
miofibrilla *nf* myofibril
mioglobīns *nm* myoglobin
mioģeosinklināle *nf* miogeosyncline
miokardīts *nm* myocarditis
miokarda infarkts *nm* fracture of the myocardium
miokards *nm* myocardium
mioloģija *nf* myology
mioma *nf* myoma
mions *nm* muon
miop|a|tija |ā| *nf* myopathy
miopija *nf* myopia
miorelaksants *nm* muscle relaxant
miostimulācija *nf* electric muscle stimulation
miozīns *nm* myosin
miozīts *nm* myositis
mira I *nf* moment of death
mira II *nf* (TV) test pattern
mirabele *nf* mirabelle
mirabile *nf* (bot.) four-o'clock
mirabilīts *nm* mirabilite

m|i|r|a|kls [ī]|ā] *nm* miracle play
mirāēa *nf* mirage
mircināt *vt* soak
mirda *nm* (com.) starveling
mirdināt *vt* 1. starve; 2. anesthetize
mirdza *nf* brilliance
mirdzaritmija *nf* fibrillation
mirdzēt *vi* shine
mirdzīgi *adv* brightly
mirdzīgs *adj* bright
mirdzin *adv emph* of **mirdzēt**; **m. mirdzēt**
   shine brightly
mirdzināt *v* 1. *vt* flash; 2. *vi* shimmer, twinkle;
   3. *vi* (*3rd pers*) drizzle
mirdzināties *vr* (*iter*) 1. flash; 2. shimmer,
   twinkle
mirdzoši *adv* brightly, brilliantly
mirdzošs *adj, part* of **mirdzēt** bright, shining,
   brilliant
mirdzspuldze *nf* glitter lamp
mirdzulis *nm* spangle
mirdzums *nm* shine, brilliance
mirēj/s *nm*, ~a *nf* dying person
mirelis *nm* (com.) starveling
mirenis *nm* (com.) starveling
mirga *nf* 1. brilliance; 2. glitter; 3. drizzle
mirgāt *vi* drizzle
mirgizlāde *nf* glow discharge
mirgizlādes lampa *nf* glow-discharge tube
mirgojums *nm* twinkling, flicker
mirgošana *nf* twinkling, flicker
mirgošanas aritmija *nf* fibrillation
mirgot *vi* 1. glimmer, glitter; flicker, twinkle;
   2. drizzle
mirgulis *nm* spangle
mirguļojums *nm* twinkling, flicker
mirguļot *vi* sparkle; glitter
miriāde *nf* myriad
mirikarija *nf* German tamarisk
mir/is *adj, part* of **mirt**, ~usi *f* died; dead
miritīnskābe *nf* myristic acid
mirklīgi *adv* momentarily

mirklīgs *adj* momentary
mirkl/is *nm* moment, instant; **vienā ~ī** in an
   in-stant; suddenly
mirkoņa *nf* prolonged rain
mirkšķināt *vt* 1. blink; **acis nemirkšķinot**
   without batting an eyelid; 2. wink
mirkšķināties *vr* blink
mirkt *vi* soak, be soaked; **m. asarās** be drenched
   in tears; **m. sviedros** be soaking wet with
   perspiration
mirla *nf, nm* (cont.) starveling
mirmekodijas *nf pl* Myrmecodia
mirmekoloģija *nf* myrmecology
mirmekofīlis *nm* myrmecophile
mirmināt *vi* drizzle
mironīgi *adv* cadaverously
mironīgs *adj* cadaverous
mironis *nm* corpse, dead body
mironītis *nm dim* or **mironis**, the deceased
mirongalva *nf* 1. skull; **m. ar kauliem** skull and
   crossbones; 2. death's-head hawkmoth
mirongalvis *nm* death's-head hawkmoth
mironkauls *nm* exostosis, spavin
miroņu nesējs *nm* pallbearer
miroņu pogas *nf pl* (reg.) field scabious
miroņu puķe *nf* toadflax
mirres *nf pl* myrrh
mirstams *adj, part* of **mirt** dying, death (*adj*)
mirstība *nf* mortality
mirstības putns *nm* waxwing
mirstīgais *nom adj* mortal
mirstīgs *adj* mortal
mirstīgums *nm* mortality
miršan/a *nf* dying, death ◊ **līdz ~as dienai** to
   one's dying day; **būt pie ~as** be dying; **uz**
   ~u gravely ill
miršanas apliecība *nf* death certificate
mirt *vi* die; **m. ātrā nāvē** die suddenly; **m. badā**
   (or **badu m.**) starve to death; **m. dabiskā**
   nāvē die a natural death; **m. traģiskā nāvē**
   die in an accident; **m. varoņa nāvē** die

the death of a hero; **m. no gaŗlaicības** be
bored to death

mirte I *nf* death, dying

mirte II *nf* myrtle

mirtin *adv, emph* of **mirt**; **ļaudis m. mira**
people were dying all over

miru/šais *nom adj,* **~sī** *f* the deceased; **~šie**
the dead

miru zāle *nf* (reg.) field scabious

mirza *nf* mirza

mis *indecl nf* Miss

misa *nf* sweetwort

misāle *nf* missal

mise *nf* (rel.) mass

misējums *nm* error, mistake

misēklis *nm* slip, mistake, blunder

misēt *vt* miss, fail to be on time

misēties *vr, 3rd pers* only; **man misējās** I missed
the mark, I made a mistake

misija *nf* **1.** mission; **2.** legation

misināt *vt* (obs.) lead astray

misiņa skārds *nm* brass plate

misiņbārdis *nm* (folk.) devil

misiņbronza *nf* composition metal

misiņgrauzējs *nm* (hum.) brass instrument
player

misiņot *vt* cover with brass

misiņsmilga *nf* heath grass

misiņ/š I *nm* brass; **~a skārds** brass plate

misiņš II *nm* (col.) messboy

misionārisms *nm* missionary work

misionārs *nm,* **~e** *nf* missionary

misione *nf* (obs.) mission

misis *indecl nf* Mrs.

misīt *vi* miss, fail to be on time

misīties *vr, 3rd pers* only; **man misējās** I missed
the mark, I made a mistake

miskaste *nf* (sl.) trash can

mispels *nm* medlar

mist *vi* live, dwell

mistērija *nf* **1.** mystery; **2.** miracle play

mist[e]riozi [ē] *adv* mysteriously

mist[e]rioz/s [ē] *adj* mysterious

misters *nm* mister

misticisks *adj* mystic

misticisms *nm* mysticism

mistificēt *vt* mystify

mistifikācija *nf* mystification

mistifik[a]tor/s [ā] *nm,* **~e** *nf* mystifier

mistika *nf* **1.** mysticism; **2.** mystery

mīstīkla *nf, nm* chatterer, gabber

mīstīklas *nf pl* (flax, hemp) brake

mistiķ/is *nm,* **~e** *nf* mystic

mistiski *adv* mystically

mistisks *adj* mystical

mīstīt I *vt* (of flax) brake

mīstīt II *vt* trade, exchange; **m. vārdus**
misspeak

mīstītava *nf* (flax, hemp) brake

mistraine *nf* a field of mixed crops

mistrains *adj* mixed

mistrājs *nm* (forest.) mixed stand

mistrāls *nm* mistral

mistraudze *nf* (forest.) mixed stand

mistri *adv* confusedly, helter-skelter, in a mixed-
up fashion

mistrojums *nm* **1.** mixture; **2.** mixup, confusion;
3. mongrel, mixed breed

mistrot *vt* mix (in sowing or planting)

mistroties *vr* be mixed

mistrs *nm* **1.** mixture; jumble; **2.** mixed seed;
mixed seed crop

mistrus *nm* mixture; jumble

miša *nf* (rel.) mass

mīšana I *nf* tanning

mīšana II *nf* exchange

mīt I *vt* **1.** tread; **m. atpēdas** retrace one's steps;
m. uz papēžiem tread upon s.o.'s heels; **m.
plēšas** blow the bellows; **2.** step on; **m. uz
kājām** step on s.o.'s toes; **3.** (of fowl) cover,
tread; **4.** (of hides, skins) tan

mīt II *vt* **1.** replace; **2.** trade, swap, exchange;
m. uz austiņām do an even trade

mīt III *vt* guess, solve a riddle

mita *nf* cessation; **bez ~s** incessantly

mītavas *nf pl* **1.** exchange, trade, barter; celebration of a barter; **2.** crosspiece of a bench

mīte *nf* (col.) rent

mites *nf pl* trade, barter

miteklis *nm* dwelling, home; (of animals) den, lair

mitelšnaucers *nm* standard schnauzer

mītene *nf* tanned skin or hide

mitenieks *nm* horse trader

mītenis *nm* traded (inferior) horse

mitēšanās *nfr* cessation; **bez m.** without stopping, incessantly

mītēt *vt* (col.) rent

mitēties *vr* stop, cease

mītības *nf pl* celebration of a closed barter

mīties *vr* **1.** alternate; **2.** swap, trade, exchange

mitināt *vt* board

mitināties *vr* dwell, stay, live

mītiņot *vi* attend rallies (repeatedly, regularly)

mītiņš *nm* (political) meeting, rally

mītis *nf pl* joint

mītisks *adj* mythical

mitkals *nm* muslin

mītne *nf* **1.** dwelling, dwelling place; **2.** lodging; quarters; shelter; **(virspavēlnieka) galvenā m.** (mil.) general headquarters

mītnes zeme *nf* host country

mītnieks I *nm* (obs.) horse trader

mītnie/ks II *nm*, **~ce** *nf* (obs. col.) tenant

mītnis *nm* (of birds) breastbone

mītņi *nm pl* lower back

mito|ch|ondrijs [h] *nm* mithochondrion

mito|ch|ondrisks [h] *adj* mitochrondrial

m|i|tologs [ī] *nm*, **~ģe** *nf* mythologist

m|i|toloģija [ī] *nf* mythology

m|i|toloģiski [ī] *adv* mythologically

m|i|toloģisks [ī] *adj* mythological

mitot *vt* (reg.) exchange

mitoties *vr* (reg.) exchange

mitotiski *adv* mitotically

mitotisks *adj* mitotic

mitoze *nf* mitosis

mitra I *nf* (headdress) miter

mitra II *nf* (bot.) box

mitraljēze *nf* mitrailleuse

mitrāls *adj* mitral

mitraudzis *nm* hydrophyte

mitrene *nf* wood louse

mitrenīte *nf dim* of **mitrene**, wood louse

mitri *adv* humidly, moistly, damply

mitrība *nf* humidity; moistness; dampness

mitriķis *nm* (col., tech.) nut

mitrinājums *nm* moistening

mitrināt *vt* humidify; moisten, moisturize

mitrinātājs *nm* humidifier

mitrināties *vr* be humidified; be moisturized

mitrot *vt* humidify; moisten, moisturize; *vi* be-come damp

mitroties *vr* become damp

mitrs *adj* humid, moist, damp

mitrumcaurlaidīgs *adj* permeable

mitrumcaurlaidība *nf* permeability

mitrumietilpība *nf* absorbency

mitrumietilpīgs *adj* absorbent

mitrumizturība *nf* resistance to water

mitrumizturīgs *adj* water-resistant

mitrumizturīgums *nm* resistance to water

mitrumkapacitāte *nf* absorbency

mitrumnecaurlaidība *nf* moistureproofness

mitrumnecaurlaidīgs *adj* moistureproof

mitrumprasīgs *adj* requiring moisture

mitrums *nm* humidity, moistness, dampness

mitrumsaturs *nm* water content

mitrzemes *nf pl* wetlands

mīts *nm* myth

miza *nf* bark; rind; peel, skin; *pl* **~s** a. parings; b. (col.) whipping

mizains *adj* barky; unpeeled

mīzali *nm pl* urine

mīzalpūslis *nm* urine bladder

mīzalskābe *nf* uric acid

mīzalvads *nm* ureter

mīzalviela *nf* urea

mizanscēna *nf* mis-en-scéne

mizantropija *nf* misanthropy

mizantropiski *adv* misanthropically

mizantropisks *adj* misanthropic

mizantrop/s *nm*, ~e *nf* misanthrope

mīzeklis *nm* (col.) urethra

mīzene *nf* pismire

mizenes *nf pl* (col.) spanking

mizer[a]bli [ā] *adv* miserably

mizer[a]bls [ā] *nm* miserable

mizēt *vi* set one's teeth on edge

mizete *nf* musette

mizēties *vr* skin over

mizgrauži *nm pl* bark beetles

mīziens *nm* (com.) pee

miziņš *nm* (col.) spanking

mizloda *nf* common treecreeper

mizložņa *nf* = mizloda

mizogamija *nf* misogamy

mizoginija *nf* misogyny

mizoloģija *nf* misology

mizot *vt* 1. bark; peel, pare; 2. (com.) whip; 3. (col.) beat, hit; 4. (col.) hoof it; 5. (col.) pour down

mizoties *vr* peel

mīzt *vi* (com.) pee

mn[e]monika [ē] *nf* mnemonics

mn[e]moniski [ē] *adv* mnemonically

mn[e]monisks [ē] *adj* mnemonic

mn[e]monist/s [ē] *nm*, ~e *nf* mnemonist

mn[ē]mote[ch]nisks [e][h] *adj* mnemotechnical

mn[ē]mote[ch]nika [e][h] *nf* mnemonics

mn[ē]mote[ch]niķ/is [e][h] *nm*, ~e *nf* mnemonist

mobili *adv* mobilely

mobiliārs *nm* household goods

mobilijas *nf pl* movable property

mobilitāte *nf* mobility

mobilizācija *nf* mobilization

mobilizēt *vt* mobilize

mobilizēties *vr* be mobilized

mobils *adj* mobile

mocekl/is *nm*, ~e *nf* martyr

mocība *nf*, usu. *pl* mocības torment, torture

mocīgi *adv* tormentingly

mocīgs *adj* tormenting

mocīt *vt* torture; torment

mocītāj/s *nm*, ~a *nf* torturer; tormentor

mocīties *vr* 1. suffer; **m. ar neziņu** be worried by uncertainty; 2. struggle

moda *nf* (stat.) mode

modā *adv* awake

modāli *adv* modally

mod[a]litāte [ā] *nf* modality

modāls *adj* modal

mod/e *nf* fashion; **valdošā m.** leading fashion ◊ **pēdējais ~es sauciens** dernier cri; **pēc ~es** fashionable, stylish; **tas nav ~ē** it is out of fashion

modelējums *nm* modeling; model

modelēšana *nf* modeling

modelēt *vt* 1. make models; draw a model; draw fashions; 2. model (do research using models)

modelētājs *nm*, ~a *nf* patternmaker

modelis *nm* model; pattern; artist's model

modelisms *nm* model-building

modelist/s *nm*, ~e *nf* 1. model-builder; 2. patternmaker

modeļapavi *nm pl* fashionable footwear

modeļgaldnieks *nm* pattern-maker

modeļnieks *nm* patternmaker

modeļplate *nf* pattern base

modems *nm* (compu.) modem

modenis *nm* (col.) alarm clock

moderato *adv* (mus.) moderato

moder[a]tors [ā] *nm* (piano) damper

modere *nf* (obs.) dairy maid

moderni *adv* modernly

moderniecība *nf* (obs.) dairy

modernieks *nm* (obs.) dairyman

modernisms *nm* modernism

modernistiski *adv* modernistically

modernistisks *adj* modernistic

modernists *nm*, ~**e** *nf* modernist

modernizācija *nf* modernization

modernizējums *nm* modernized feature

modernizēt *vt* modernize

modernizēties *vr* become modernized

moderns *adj* modern

modernums *nm* modernity

modes āksts *nm* fop

modes artiķelis *nm* novelty item

modes ateljē *nm* fashion house

modes dāma *nf* fashion plate (person)

modes ilustrācija *nf* fashion plate

modes teiciens *nm* tag line

modees untums *nm* fashion fad

modees žurnāls *nm* fashion magazine

modēt *vt* wake, awaken

modificēt *vt* modify

modificēties *vr* become modified

modifikācija *nf* modification

modifik[a]tors [ā] *nm* (chem.) modifier

modīgi *adv* strangely, weirdly

modīgs *adj* (col.) strange, weird

modiljons *nm* modillion

modinājums *nm* wake-up

modināt *vt* wake, awaken

modinātājpulkstenis *nm* alarm clock

modinātāj/s *nm* 1. wakener, awakener; ~**a** *nf*; 2. alarm clock

modiste *nf* modiste; milliner

modr/e *nf* (obs.) watch; **stāvēt** ~**ē** stand watch

modrēties *vr* (obs.) be awake, be alert

modri *adv* vigilantly, watchfully, alertly

modrība *nf* vigilance, watchfulness, alertness

modrīgi *adv* vigilantly, watchfully, alertly

modrīgs *adj* vigilant, watchful, alert

modrīgums *nm* vigilance, watchfulness, alertness

modrināt *vt* cheer up, buoy up

modrs *adj* vigilant, watchful, alert; **esi m.!** (mot-to) be prepared!

modrums *nm* vigilance, watchfulness, alertness

mods *nm* 1. mode; 2. (gram.) mood

modulācija *nf* modulation

modulārs *adj* modular

modul[a]tors [ā] *nm* modulator

modulējums *nm* modulation

modulēt *vt* modulate

modulis *nm* 1. modulus; 2. module

modžahedi *indecl nm* mujahedin

mofeta or **mofete** *nf* mofette

mogols *nm* Mogul

mogula ietvere *nf* mogul base

mohārs *nm* foxtail millet

mohēra *nf* mohair

mohikān/is *nm*, ~**iete** *nf* Mohican

moira *nf* Moira

moka *nf* mocha coffee

mok/as *nf pl* 1. torture; torment; 2. agony; **ar lie-lām** ~**ām** with great effort; 3. crucifix at a crossroads

mokasīns *nm* moccasin

mokciet/is *nm*, ~**e** *nf* sufferer

mokpilns *adj* agonizing

mokša *nf* moksha

moku kambaris *nm* torture chamber

moku sols *nm* rack

mola līnija *nf* bulkhead line

mol[a]litāte [ā] *nf* molality

molāls *adj* molal

mol[a]ritāte [ā] *nf* molarity

molārs *adj* molar

molases *nf pl* (geol.) molasse

molberts *nm* easel

moldāviet/is *nm*, ~**e** *nf* Moldavian

molekula *nf* molecule

molekulāri *adv* molecularly

molekulārs *adj* molecular

molekulārspektroskops *nm* molecule spectroscope

molekulmasa *nf* molecular mass

molekulsvars *nm* molecular weight

moleskins *nm* moleskin

molibd|e|nāts [ē] *nm* molybdate

molibd|e|nīts [ē] *nm* molybdenite

molibdēns *nm* molybdenum

molibdēnskābe *nf* molybdic acid

molibdēntērauds *nm* molybdenum steel

molinija *nf* moor grass

moliņš *nm* pier

mollese *nf* effeminacy

mollīgi *adv* (col.) plumply

mollīgs *adj* (col.) plumpish

molls *nm* (mus.) minor

molmasa *nf* molar mass

molo|ch|s [h] *nm* Moloch

mols I *nm* breakwater

mols II *nm* (chem.) mole

moltilpums *nm* molar volume

molucelas *nf pl* Moluccella

molusks *nm* mollusc

moļa *nf* (reg.) strength

momēlis *nm* uvula

momentāli *adv* momentarily

momentāls *adj* momentary

momentāni *adv* 1. momentarily; 2. instantaneously

momentāns *adj* 1. momentary; 2. instantaneous

momentānums *nm* momentariness

moments *nm* moment; **atbildīgs m.** crucial point

momentuzņēmums *nm* snapshot

mona|ch|isms [h] *nm* monasticism

monacīts *nm* monazit

mon|a|da [ā] *nf* monad

monadisks *adj* monadic

monadoloģija *nf* monadology

monar|ch|ija [h] *nf* monarchy

monar|ch|iski [h] *adv* monarchically

monar|ch|isks [h] *adj* monarchical

monar|ch|isms [h] *nm* monarchism

monar|ch|istisks [h] *adj* monarchial

monar|ch|ist/s [h] *nm*, ~e *nf* monarchist

monar|ch|/s [h] *nm*, ~e *nf* monarch

monardas *nm* horsemint

moncijas *nf pl* (bot.) blinks

mondamīns *nm* corn flour

monēta *nf* coin

mon|e|tārisms [ē] *nm* monetarism

mon|e|tārs [ē] *adj* monetary

mongolīd/s *nm*, ~e *nf* Mongoloid, person with the Down's syndrome

mongolis *nm*, ~iete *nf* Mongol, Mongolian

mongoloīdi *nm pl* Mongoloids

mongoloīds *adj* Mongoloid

moninieks *nm* (hist.) married farm hand (who, together with his wife, worked for payment in kind)

monisms *nm* monism

monistiski *adv* monistically

monistisks *adj* monistic

monist/s *nm*, ~e *nf* monist

monitorings *nm* monitoring

monitors *nm* monitor

monoaurāls *adj* monaural

monoaldehīds *nm* monoaldehide

mono|ch|lorids [h] *nm* monochloride

mono|ch|ords [h] *nm* monochord

mono|ch|romatiski [h] *adv* monochromatically

monochrom|a|tisk/s [ā] *adj* monochromatic

mono|ch|romi [h] *adv* monochromatically

mono|ch|romiski [h] *adv* monochromatically

mono|ch|roms [h] *adj* monochromatic

monocikls *nm* unicycle

monodija *nf* monody

monodrāma *nf* monodrama

monofāgs *nm* monofagous organism

monofāgs *adj* monofagous

monof|āg|ija [aģ] *nf* monophagy

monofilija *nf* monogenesis

monofizītisms *nm* Monophysitism

monofizīts *nm* Monophysite

monofobija *nf* monophobia

monofonija *nf* monophonic sound transmission

monofonisks *adj* monophonic, monaural

monoftongisks *adj* monophthongal

monoftongizācija *nf* monophthongization

monoftongizēties *vr* be monophthongized

monoftongs *nm* monophthong

monog|a|mija [ā] *nf* monogamy

monog|a|mists [ā] *nm* monogamist

monog|a|ms [ā] *adj* monogamous

monog|e|nisms [ē] *nm* monogenism

monoglicerīds *nm* monoglyceride

monogr|a|fija [ā] *nf* monograph

monogr|a|fisks [ā] *adj* monographic

monogr|a|fist/s [ā] *nm*, ~e *nf* monographer

monogramma *nf* monogram

monoģen|e|tiski [ē] *adv* monogenically

monoģen|e|tisks [ē] *adj* monogenic, monogenetic

monoh- See **monoch-**

monohidrāts *nm* monohydrate

monokarpisks *adj* monocarpous

monokarps *nm* monocarp

monokarps *adj* monocarpous

monoketons *nm* monoketone

monoklināle *nf* monocline

monoklinisks *adj* monoclinic

monoklis *nm* monocle

monokotiledoņi *nm pl* Monocotyledoneae

monokrats *nm* monocrat

monoks|i|ds [ī] *nm* monoxide

monokulāri *adv* monocularly

monokulārs *nm* monocular

monokulārs *adj* monocular

monokultūra *nf* monoculture

monolitāte *nf* monolithism

monolitēt *vt* create a monolithic structure

monol|i|ts [ī] *nm* monolith

monol|i|ti [ī] *adv* monolithically

monol|i|ts [ī] *adj* monolithic

monol|i|tums [ī] *nm* monolithism

monologs *nm* monologue

monoma|ch|ija [h] *nf* monomachy

monom|a|nija [ā] *nf* monomania

monomērs *nm* monomer

monomērs *adj* monomeric

monomet|āl|isks [all] *adj* monometallic

monomet|āl|isms [all] *nm* monometallism

monominerālisks *adj* monomineralic

monomolekulārs *adj* monomelcular

monoms *nm* monomial

mononitrotoluols *nm* mononitrotoluol

monoplāns *nm* monoplane

monopolapvienība *nf* monopolistic conglomerate

monopolcena *nf* monopolistic price

monopolīpašums *nm* monopolistic property

monopolistiski *adv* monopolistically

monopolistisks *adj* monopolistic

monopolist/s *nm*, ~e *nf* monopolist

monopolizācija *nf* monopolization

monopolizēt *vt* monopolize

monopols *nm* monopoly

monopoltiesības *nf pl* monopoly

monorims *nm* monorhyme

monosa|ch|arīds [h] *nm* monosaccharide

monosēmija *nf* singuarity of meaning, univocality

monosēmiski *adv* univocally

monosēmisks *adj* of one meaning, univocal

monosillabiski *adv* monosyllabically

monosillabisks *adj* monosyllabic

monosillabisms *nm* monosyllabicity

monoskābe *nf* monoacid

monoskops *nm* monoscope

monosomisks *adj* monosomic

monospermija *nf* monospermy

monosulfīds *nm* monosulfide

monoškiedra *nf* single fiber; monofilament

monoteisms *nm* monotheism

monoteistiski *adv* monotheistically

monoteistisks *adj* monotheistic

monoteist/s *nm*, ~e *nf* monotheist

monotipija *nf* monotype technique

monotipist/s *nm*, ~e *nf* Monotype operator

monotips *nm* Monotype

monotoni *adv* montonously

monotonība *nf* monotonousness

monotonija *nf* monotony

monotoniskums *nm* monotonicity

monotons *adj* monotonous

monotonums *nm* monotonousness

monpansjē *nm indecl* fruit drops, lozenges

mons *nm* (hist.) a farm hand's (**moninieks**) payment in kind

monsiņors *nm* monsignor

monstera *nf* monstera

monstrance *nf* monstrance

monstrozi *adv* monstrously

monstrozs *adj* monstrous

monstrs *nm* monster

monsūns *nm* monsoon

montāns *adj* montane

montānvasks *nm* mountain wax

montāēa *nf* 1. assembly, mounting; 2. montage; 3. (theat.) production, adaptation; (film) editing

montāžas ce[ch]s [h] *nm* assembly shop

montāžas konveijers *nm* asembly line

montāžist/s *nm*, ~e *nf* (film) editor

montbr[e]cija [ē] *nf* montbretia

montējums *nm* 1. assembling, mounting; 2. editing

montekristo *nf indecl* air rifle

montereisiers *nm* Monterey cheese

montēt *vt* 1. assemble, mount; 2. edit; cut and paste

montētāj/s *nm*, ~a *nf* assembler

montieratslēdznieks *nm* fitter

montieris *nm* 1. (mech.) fitter; 2. electrician

montijas *nf pl* Montia

montmorilonīts *nm* montmorillonite

monumentāli *adv* monumentally

monumentālisms *nm* monumentalism

monumentālist/s *nm*, ~e *nf* producer of monumental artworks

monument[a]litāte [ā] *nf* monumentality

monument[a]lizēt [ā] *vt* monumentalize

monumentāls *adj* monumental

monuments *nm* monument

monzonīts *nm* monzonite

mopēdisms *nm* moped riding

mopēdist/s *nm*, ~e *nf* moped rider

mopēds *nm* moped

mopsis *nm* 1. pug; 2. (sl.) blockhead

morāle *nf* 1. morals, morality; moral philosophy; ~s līmenis a. moral standards; b. morale; 2. morale

morāli *adv* morally

morālfilozofija *nf* ethics; (hist.) moral philosophy

morāliski *adv* morally

morālisks *adj* moral

morālisms *nm* moralism

morālist/s *nm*, ~e *nf* moralist

mor[a]litāte [ā] *nf* morality

moralitē *indecl nf* morality play

mor[a]lizēt [ā] *vi* moralize

morāls *adj* moral

morālspriedums *nm* moral judgment

moratorijs *nm* moratorium

morāviet/is *nm*, ~e *nf* Moravian

mordants *nm* (mus.) mordant

mordviet/is *nm*, ~e *nf* Mordvin

mordvīn/is *nm*, ~e *nf* Mordvin

morejs *nm* parsnip

morelle *nf* morello (cherry)

morēna *nf* moraine; (glacial sediment) till; ūdenī nogulsnēta m. waterlain till

morēnas līdzenums *nm* till plain

moreska *nf* moresque

morfēma *nf* morpheme

morfijs *nm* morphine

morf[i]nisms [ī] *nm* morphinism

morf[i]nist/s [ī] *nm*, ~e *nf* morphinist

morf[i]ns [ī] *nm* morphine

morfoġen[e]tiski [ē] *adv* morphogenetically

morfoġen[e]tisks [ē] *adj* morphogenetic

morfoġen|e|ze [ē] *nf* morphogenesis
morfolo/gs *nm*, **~ġe** *nf* morphologist
morfoloġija *nf* morphology
morfoloġiski *adv* morphologically
morfoloġisks *adj* morphological
morfometrija *nf* morphometry
morfonēma *nf* morphophoneme
morfonoloġija *nf* morphophonemics
morfonoloġisks *adj* morphophonemic
morgan|a|tisks [ā] *adj* morganatic
morgens *nm* morgen
morgs *nm* morgue
morindons *nm* morindone
Morinella tārtiņš *nm* dotterel
moris *nm* Moor, blackamoor
morisks *nm* Morisco
morītes *nf pl* burnet saxifrage
mormon/is *nm*, **~e** *nf* Mormon
mormonisms *nm* Mormonism
mors *nm* (fabric) moire
morss *nm* fruit juice, fruit drink
mort|a|litāte [ā] *nf* mortality
mortificēt *vt* 1. mortify; 2. invalidate; cancel
mortifikācija *nf* 1. mortification; 2. amortization
mortīra *nf* (mil.) mortar
Morzes ābece *nf* Morse code
Morzes aparāts *nm* telegraph
moskīts *nm* blackfly
moskītu zāle *nf* grama
most *vt* (obs.) 1. sense; 2. wake
mosties *vr* 1. wake up; awake; 2. (fig.) arise
mošeja *nf* mosque
mošk *adv* (barb., sl.) maybe
mošķeni *nm pl* mashed potatoes
mošķ/is *nm* 1. goblin, evil spirit; 2. pest; 3. **~i** magic charms
mošķoties *vr* cut up, clown
mošus *nm* musk
mošusbriedis *nm* musk deer
mošus kaula roze *nf* musk mallow
mošusvērsis *nm* musk-ox

motelis *nm* motel
motete *nf* motet
motets *nm* motet
mot|i|vācija [ī] *nf* motivation
mot|i|vējums [ī] *nm* 1. justification; 2. motivation
mot|i|vēt [ī] *vt* justify, give reasons
motīviski *adv* in terms of motifs; **m. bagāts** showing motivic richness
motīvisks *adj* motivic
motīvs *nm* 1. motive; 2. motif; 3. tune
moto *indecl nm* motto
motobolists *nm* motorcycle soccer player
motobols *nm* motorcycle soccer
motobraucēj/s *nm*, **~a** *nf* motorist
motobrauciens *nm* motor ride; motor race
motocikletist/s *nm*, **~e** *nf* motorcyclist
motociklets *nm* motorcycle
motociklist/s *nm*, **~e** *nf* motorcyclist
motocikls *nm* motorcycle
motodroms *nm* motordrome
motokamanas *nf pl* snowmobile
motokārs *nm* small tractor truck
motokrosist/s *nm*, **~e** *nf* motor cross-country racer
motokross *nm* motor cross-country race
motome|ch|anizācija [h] *nf* motorization
motome|ch|anizēt [h] *vt* motorize
motora kļūme *nf* engine failure
motorallijs *nm* (automobile) rally
motorarkls *nm* motorized plow
motora vāks *nm* (car) hood
motorburnieks *nm* motor sailer
motorbūve *nf* motor building
motoreļļa *nf* motor oil
motoresurss *nm* (of a vehicle or engine) time between repairs
motorika *nf* motor behavior
motoriski *adv* motorically
motorisks *adj* (physiol.) motor , motoric
motoriskums *nm* motoric nature
motorist/s *nm*, **~e** *nf* motor mechanic

817

motorizācija *nf* motorization

motorizēt *vt* motorize

motorja[ch]ta [h] *nf* motor yacht

motorkamanas *nf pl* snowmobile

motorkuģis *nm* motor ship

motorlaiva *nf* motorboat

motorollerist/s *nm*, ~e *nf* motor scooter rider

motorollers *nm* motor scooter

motorragavas *nf pl* snowmobile

motorrati *nm pl* (col.) car

motorremonts *nm* automotive repair

motors *nm* motor; engine

motors *adj* motor

motorstrēlnieki *nm pl* motorized riflemen

motorstunda *nf* one hour of engine operation

motorsūknis *nm* motor pump

motortelpa *nf* engine room

motorūpnīca *nf* motorcyle, moped and motor bicycle factory

motorūpniecība *nf* two-wheeled motor vehicle industry

motorvagons *nm* motorcar

motorvāģis *nm* motorcar

motorvilcējs *nm* small motor-driven locomotive

motorzāģis *nm* power saw

motosacīkstes *nf pl* automotive race

motosportist/s *nm*, ~e *nf* motor sports athlete

motosports *nm* motor sports

mototransports *nm* two-wheeled transportation

mototreks *nm* motorcycle racetrack

motovelosip[e]dist/s [ē] *nm*, ~e *nf* motorbiker

motovelosip[e]ds [ē] *nm* motorbike

mozaīka *nf* mosaic; inlaid work; marquetry

mozaīkas akmentiņš *nm* tessera

mozaīkveida *indecl adj* mosaic-like

mozaīkveidīgi *adv* like a mosaic

mozaīkveidīgs *adj* mosaic-like

mozaiķ/is *nm*, ~e *nf* mosaicist

mozaiski *adv* mosaically

mozaisks *adj* mosaic

mozaist/s *nm*, ~e *nf* mosaicist

mozambikietis *nm*, ~e *nf* Mozambican

mozarella siers *nm* mozarella (cheese)

moze *nf* pulp, mash, mush, purée

Mozeles vīns *nm* Moselle

mozers *nm* mortar

mozēt *vt* (col.) 1. tease, torment; 2. gulp down one's food; 3. spank; 4. bring about, manage

mozēties *vr* 1. fool around, play pranks; 2. stuff oneself

mozusticība *nf* Jewish faith

mozusticīg/ais *nom adj*, ~ā *f* adherent of the Jewish faith

moži *adv* lively, energetically

možs *adj* lively, energetic

možums *nm* liveliness

mu *indecl nm* mu

mū *interj* moo

muarē *indecl nm* moiré

muc/a *nf* 1. barrel; ~ā audzis gauche; 2. (aeron.) barrel roll; ātrā m. snaproll; 3. (col.) fatty; 4. (obs.) a measure of volume

mucas galdiņš *nm* stave

mucas gals *nm* barrelhead

mucasvieta *nf* (obs.) a measure of area

muceklis *nm* boggy place

muciens *nm* flight

mucīgi *adv* like a barrel

mucīgs *adj* barrel-like

mucinieks *nm* cooper

mucīns *nm* mucin

muciņa *nf dim* of **muca**, keg; firkin

mucīši *nm pl* jumpers (child's one-piece coverall)

muckulis *nm* tangle

mucniecība *nf* cooperage

mucveida *indecl adj* barrel-shaped

mucveidīgi *adv* like a barrel

mucveidīgs *adj* barrel-shaped

mučele *nf* (cont.) keg

mudas *nf pl* (reg.) seaweed (that has been washed ashore)

mude *nf* slogan

mudehārs *nm* Mudejar

mudžt I *vi* teem

mudžt II *vi* spoil, mold

mūdēt *vi* (reg., of bells) ring

mudīgi *adv* nimbly, quickly, swiftly

mudīgs *adj* nimble, quick, swift

mudīgums *nm* nimbleness, quickness, swiftness

mudinājums *nm* urging, spurring on, encouragement

mudināt *vt* urge, spur on; stimulate

mudinātāj/s *nm*, ~a *nf* motivator

mūdiņš *nm* (folk.) life

mudīt *vt* urge, spur on; stimulate

mudīties *vr* hurry

mūdīties *vr* (reg.) drag oneself; drudge, labor; go around in circles

mudot *vi* rave, be delirious

mudri *adv* (reg.) quickly, lively; adroitly

mudrināt *vt* urge, spur on; stimulate

mudrs *adj* (reg.) quick, lively; adroit

mudrums *nm* (reg.) quickness, liveliness; adroitness

mūds *nm* (reg.) gnat

mudurains *adj* (of a skirt) gored

muduraiņi *nm pl* frock, a type of peasant garb

muduris *nm* gore

mudzēt *vi* teem, swarm

mudzināt *vt* tangle

mūdzis *nm* vermin

mudžas *nf pl* 1. tangle; 2. refuse

mudžeklīgi *adv* confusedly, chaotically

mudžeklīgs *adj* confused, chaotic

mudžeklis *nm* 1. tangle; 2. throng

mudžekļaini *adv* in a tangled manner

mudžekļains *adj* tangled

mudžēt *vi* teem, swarm

mudžināt *vt* tangle

mudžināties *vr* become entangled

mudžoņa *nf* throng

mudžums *nm* throng

mudžurs *nm* (reg.) tangle

muedzins *nm* muezzin

mufe *nf* sleeve

mufelis *nm* (tech.) muffle

mufeļceplis *nm* muffle furnace

mufeļkrāsns *nf* muffle furnace

muflons *nm* mouflon

muftijs *nm* mufti

mugulis *nm* (reg.) tangle

mugur/a *nf* 1. back; no ~as from the back; at the back; aiz ~as behind one's back; uz ~as on one's back, supine; (swimming style) back stroke; ~ā (of a garment) on; 2. (of mountains) ridge

mugurdancis *nm* a Latvian folk dance

mugurējs *adj* back, rear

mugurene *nf* (bot.) Solomon's seal

mugurgabals *nm* tenderloin; fillet

muguriņa *nf* 1. *dim* of mugura; 2. (of a book) spine

mugurkabata *nf* hip pocket

mugurkaula smadzenes *nf pl* spinal cord

mugurkaulainie *nom adj pl* vertebrates

mugurkaulāja šķeltne *nf* spina bifida

mugurkaulājs *nm* backbone

mugurkaula smadzenes *nf pl* spinal cord

mugurkaulnieks *nm* vertebrate

mugurkauls *nm* backbone, spine

mugurkauļi *nm pl* (bot.) Solomon's seal

mugurpelde *nf* back swimmer

mugurpuse *nf* back; no ~s from behind

mugursiena *nf* back wall

mugursoma *nf* knapsack

mugursomiņa *nf dim* of mugursoma, knapsack

mugurspura *nf* back fin

muhamedān/is *nm*, ~iete *nf* Muslim

muhamedānisms *nm* Islam

muit *vt* 1. gum (chew with the gums); 2. (reg.) torment

muita *nf* 1. customs; 2. customs duty, tariff;
3. (col.) customhouse

muitas aģents *nm* customhouse broker

muitas aizliegums *nm* tariff wall

muitas apskate *nf* customs inspection

muitas dārzs *nm* customhouse yard

muitas kaŗš *nm* tariff war

muitas nodoklis *nm* customs duty

muitas savienība *nf* customs union;

muities *vr* (reg.) 1. struggle in vain; 2. be in the
way; 3. hang around

muitnīca *nf* customhouse

muitnie/ks *nm*, **~ce** *nf* customs officer; (Bibl.)
publican

muitojams *adj, part* of **muitot** subject to
customs duties; **(vai jums kas) m.?** (have
you anything) to declare?

muitot *vt* impose a customs duty, tax

muiž/a *nf* demesne; estate; country seat; manor
house; **~as gaitas** = **klaušas**; **~as kalpi**
(hist.) paid agricultural laborers working
for the lord of the manor; **~as ļaudis** (hist.)
servants and artisans working for the lord
of the manor; **liela m.** ! (col.) big deal! **nāc
uz ~u!** (in card games) play a card!

muižgalieši *nm pl* those living near the manor
house

muižiņa *nf dim* of **muiža**, small estate; manor
house

muižkungs *nm* (hist.) manager of a demesne

muižniece *nf* wife of the lord of the manor

muižniecība *nf* nobility; landed gentry

muižnieciski *adv* in the manner of the gentry

muižniecisks *adj* nobiliary; of the gentry

muižnieks *nm* nobleman; landowner; squire;
lord of the manor

muižnieku zeme *nf* landed estate

muižtur/is *nm*, **~e** *nf* owner of an estate

mūjābels *nm* (sl.) dumbbell

mujāties *nf* (reg.) 1. struggle in vain; 2. muddle
through

mujeklis *nm* 1. dawdler, poor worker; 2. ruined
piece of work

muk/a *nf* 1. mire, bog; 2. sth. easily stripped,
peeled, or skinned; **vienā ~ā** uninterruptedly;
in one piece

mukla *nf* mire, bog

muklaine *nf* mire, bog

muklains *adj* miry, boggy

muklājs *nm* mire, bog

mukliens *nm* mire, bog

mūklis *nm* mire, bog

mukls *adj* miry, boggy

muklums *nm* boggy place

muko|i|ds [ī] *nm* mucoid

mukonskābe *nf* muconic acid

mukopolisa[ch|ar|i]ds [h||ī] *nm* mucopoly-
saccharide

mūk/s *nm* monk; **~a, ~u** monastic; **~a tērps**
habit

mūkšķis *nm* tangle

mukt *vi* 1. slip through, break through, get
stuck; 2. **m. nost** slip off; 3. (col.) flee, take
to one's heels

mūķējamais *nom adj* picklock

mūķene *nf* 1. nun; **~s tērps** habit; 2. tussock
moth; nun moth

mūķēt *vt* pick a lock

mūķiene *nf* nun

mukis *nm* (col.) purse

mūķis *nm* picklock

mūķīzeris *nm* picklock

mūlāps *nm* (com.) lubber; stupe

mulats *nm*, **~e** *nf* mulatto

mulāža *nf* cast, life-size model, moulage

mulāžist/s *nm*, **~e** *nf* cast maker

mulča *nf* mulch

mulčējums *nm* mulch

mulčēt *vt* mulch

mulčkūdra *nf* mulching peat moss

mulčpapīrs *nm* mulching paper

mulda *nf* 1. depression, hollow; (geol.) syncline;
2. trough

muldamdzejoļi *nm pl* game songs

muldeklis *nm* (com.) blabber

muldēt *vi, vt* (com.) 1. twaddle; 2. rave, talk in a delirium

muldēties *vr* (com.) 1. twaddle; 2. rave, talk in a delirium

muldīgs *adj* (com.) twaddly

muldiņa *nf dim* of mulda, small depression; small trough

muldonis *nm* (com.) twaddler

muldoņa *nf* (com.) 1. twaddle; 2. *nf, nm* twaddler

mulgedijas *nf pl* blue lettuce

mulinē *indecl nm* colored twist yarn

muliņš *nm* pier

mūlis I *nm* mule

mūlis II *nm* (com.) face, mug

mulla *nm* mullah

mullīts *nm* mullite

mulmēt *vi* stutter

mulmis *nm* stutterer

mulsa *nf* confusion; bewilderment; perplexity

mulsināt *vt* confuse, bewilder, perplex

mulss *nm* confusion; bewilderment; perplexity

mulss *adj* shy; confused, bewildered

mulst *vi* become confused

mulsums *nm* confusion; bewilderment; perplexity

multiapstrāde *nf* multiprocessing

multigr[a]fs [ā] *nm* Multigraph

multilaterāli *adv* multilaterally

multilaterāls *adj* multilateral

multilingvāls *adj* multilingual

multilingvisms *nm* multilingualism

multilingvs *adj* multilingual

multimetrs *nm* multimeter

multimiljardier/is *nm, ~e nf* multibillionaire

multimiljonār/s *nm, ~e nf* multimillionaire

multinacionāls *adj* multinational

multipleksers *nm* multiplexer

multipleksēšana *nf* multiplexing

multipleksēt *vt, vi* multiplex

multipleksors *nm* multiplexor

multiplicēt *vt* (photo.) animate

multiplikācija *nf* (photo.) animation

multiplikācijas filma *nf* animated cartoon

multiplikands *nm* factor, multiplicand

multiplik[a]tor/s [ā] *nm* 1. (photo.) animator; ~e *nf*; 2. animation camera; 3. (el.) multiplier

multipli *adv* multiply

multipls *adj* mutiple

multivibr[a]tors [ā] *nm* multivibrator

multivide *nf* (compu.) multimedia

mūļa *nm* (com.) lubber; ~s (com.) mouth

muļķadesa *nm* (col.) jackass

muļķība *nf* 1. foolishness, stupidity; folly; 2. often *pl* ~s nonsense, rubbish

muļķīgi *adv* 1. foolishly, stupidly; 2. nonsensically

muļķīgs *adj* 1. foolish, stupid, silly, dumb; 2. nonsensical

muļķi/s *nm, ~e nf* 1. fool; (es esmu) m. (I am) stupid; 2. simpleton; ~m laime dumb luck

muļķiski *adv* foolishly, stupidly

muļķisk/s *adj* (rare.) foolish, stupid

muļķīt/is *nm, ~e nf* 1. dim of muļķis; mazais m. ! little silly! 2. simpleton; (folk.) third (foolish) son of a father

muļķošanās *nfr* tomfoolery

muļķot *vt* fool, dupe

muļķoties *vr* fool around, play the fool

muļķu ķērājs *nm* hoodwinker

muļļa *nf, nm* (com.) dawdler

muļļāt *vt* (com.) chew

muļļāties *vr* (com.) 1. dawdle; 2. mess

mumificēt *vt* mummify

mumificēties *vr* mummify

mumifikācija *nf* mummification

mūmija *nf* (preserved body) mummy

mūmijisks *adj* mummy-like

mūmijs *nm* (substance) mummy

mumio *indecl nm* (concoction, pigment) mummy

mums *pron, dat* of **mēs** to us; **ar m.** with us; **m. līdzīgie** such as we, our equals

muncis *nm* child's smock

mundieris *nm* uniform

mundierots *adj* uniformed, dressed in a uniform

mundri *adv* sprightily

mundrība *nf* liveliness, sprightliness

mundrināt *vt* cheer up, buoy up

mundrs *adj* lively, sprightly

mundrums *nm* liveliness, sprighliness

mun[i]cija [ī] *nf* ammunition; ordnance; ~s pienesējs ammunition bearer

mun[i]cijas [ī]s pagrabs *nm* ammunition depot

municip[a]litāte [ā] *nf* municipality

municip[a]lizācija [ā] *nf* 1. (of a town) incorporation; 2. exappropriation, municipalization

municip[a]lizēt [ā] *vt* 1. (of a town) incorporate; 2. exappropriate, municipalize

municipālpadome *nf* municipal council

municipālpadomnieks *nm* city councilor

municipāls *adj* municipal

municipija *nf* municipality (in Latin American countries)

mūnisti *nm pl* Moonies

munsturēt *vi* 1. (mil.) dril; 2. recruit

munsturis *nm* 1. (mil.) drill; 2. a Latvian folk dance

munsturrullis *nm* muster roll

munštuks *nm* (barb.) cigarette holder

muntžaks *nm* muntjack

muraga *nf* mousetail

muralist/s *nm*, ~e *nf* muralist

murāties *vr* toil in hot weather

murcīt *vt* ruffle, squeeze (in petting)

murdēt I *vi* 1. murmur; 2. mumble

murdēt II *vi* teem

murdoksnis *nm* (reg.) quagmire

murdoņa *nf* hubbub, noise

murds *nm* fish basket; eelpot; bow net

murdslazds *nm* box trap (for birds)

murdzināt *vt* ruffle, squeeze

murdzīt *vt* ruffle, squeeze

murdzīties *vr* jostle

mūrdzītne *nf* screw anchor

mūrējums *nm* masonry

murēna *nf* moray eel

mūrēšana *nf* bricklaying

mūrēt *vt* build in stone (or bricks); construct; m. no ķieģeļiem lay bricks

murgaini *adv* nightmarishly

murgainība *nf* nightmarishness

murgains *adj* nightmarish

murgainums *nm* nightmarishness

murgi *nm pl* 1. nightmare; delirium; 2. phantoms

murgojums *nm* ravings

murgoņa *nm* gusher (enthusiast)

murgot *vi* talk in a delirium, rave

murgpilns *adj* nightmarish

murgs *nm* phantom

murināt *vi* 1. numble, murmur; 2. purr

muris *nm* 1. cat; 2. mumbler

mūris *nm* stone wall, brick wall; **akls m.** dead wall; **bezlogu m.** blind masonry; **jaukts m.** composite masonry

murīt *vt* (reg.) torment

mūrītis *nm* hearth ledge (horizontal heating flue on the floor)

mūrjava *nf* mortar

mūrkaļķi *nm pl* lime mortar

murkšķēt *vi* (col.) mumble, mutter; grumble

murkšķināt *vi* (col.) mumble, mutter; grumble

murkšķis *nm* 1. marmot; 2. (col.) grumbler; 3. (reg.) tangle

murkšķīties *vr* get tangled

murkšļāt *vt, vi* champ

murķelis *nm* (reg.) morel

mūrķieģelis *nm* brick

murķis *nm* (reg.) morel

mūrlata *nf* wall plate

mūrlauzis *nm* battering ram

mūrmāja *nf* stone house

murminãt *vi, vt* mutter; **m. bārdā** mutter under one's breath

mūrmuiža *nf* (hum.) jail

murmulēt *vt, vi* (col.) mutter

murmulis *nm* **1.** marmot; **2.** mutterer; **3.** (folk.) epithet for the billy goat; **4.** bubble

murmulītis *nm dim* of **murmulis**

murmuļot *vi* **1.** mutter; **2.** murmur, bubble

mūrniecība *nf* masonry

mūrnieka āmurs *nm* mason's ax

mūrnieka divkaplis *nm* mason's pick

mūrnieka pušķis *nm* plasterer's brush

mūrnieka veseris *nm* bricklayer's hammer

mūrniekmeistars *nm* master bricklayer

mūrnie/ks *nm*, **~ce** *nf* bricklayer

murogas *nf pl* mousetail

murr *interj* purr

murrāt *vi* purr

murskulis *nm* tangle

murskuļoties *vr* become tangled

muršķis *nm* marmot

murzāties *vr* work at sth. unsuccessfully, mess with

murzīt *vt* rub, crush; vex

mūra darbs *nm* masonry

mūra urbis *nm* masonry chisel; masonry bit

mūru balanda *nf* nettle-leaved goosefoot

mūru divsēkle *nf* sand rocket

mūru ķirzaka *nf* wall lizard

mūru mauraga *nf* wall hawkweed

mūru sīkpaparde *nf* wall rue

mūru veronika *nf* wall speedwell

mūru vīrcele *nf* Kenilworth ivy

mūs *pron, acc* of **mēs** us

mūsa *nf* fly

mūsainība *nf* speckledness; freckledness

mūsains *adj* speckled; freckled

mūsainums *nm* speckledness; freckledness

mūsciemie/ši *nm*, **~tes** *nf* fellow villagers

mūsciems *nm* our village

mūsdienas *nf pl* the present

mūsdienās *adv* nowadays

mūsdienība *nf* modernity

mūsdienīgi *adv* in a contemporary, modern fashion; to fit the current scene

mūsdienīgs *adj* current; contemporary, modern

mūsdienīgums *nm* currency; contemporaneity, modernity

mūsdienu *indecl adj* contemporary, modern

mūsēj/ais *nom adj*, **~ā** *f* one of us; **~ie** our own people

mūsēj/s *adj* our, ours; *defin* **mūsējais** ours

musinājums *nm* instigation, incitement

musināt *vt* instigate, incite; set on

musinātāj/s *nm*, **~a** *nf* instigator, inciter

mūsiņa *nf dim* of **mūsa**, little fly

muskardinoze *nf* muscardine

muskares *nf pl* grape hyacinth

muskarīns *nm* muscarine

mūskārtas *indecl adj* of our class

muskataknas *nf pl* (med.) nutmeg liver

muskata ķirbis *nm* winter crookneck

muskata salvija *nf* clary

muskatels *nm* muscatel

muskatkoks *nm* nutmeg tree

muskatrieksts *nm* nutmeg

muskats *nm* **1.** (grape) muscat; **2.** (wine) muscatel

muskatvīnogas *nf pl* muscatel grapes

muskatvīns *nm* muscatel

muskete *nf* musket

musketieris *nm* musketeer; Mousquetaire

muskovīts *nm* **1.** Muscovite; **2.** muscovite

muskulatūra *nf* musculature

muskulis I *nm* muscle

muskulis II *nm* **1.** tangle; **2.** swarm

muskulītis *nm dim* of **muskulis** II, small tangle

muskuļainība *nf* muscularity

muskuļains *adj* muscular

muskuļainums *nm* muscularity

muskuḷaudi *nm pl* muscle tissue

muskuḷkuņģis *nm* craw, crop

muskuḷots *adj* muscular

muskuḷšķiedras *nf pl* muscle fiber

muskusa hibisks *nm* abelmosk

muskusbriedis *nm* musk deer

muskuss *nm* musk

muskusvērsis *nm* musk-ox

mūslaiki *nm pl* the present age

mūslaiku *indecl adj* contemporary, modern

muslīns *nm* muslin

mūsḷaudis *nm pl* our folks

mūsmājas *nf pl* our house

mūsmājinieki or **mūsmājnieki** *nm pl* our folks

mūsmāte *nf* our mother

musonāls *adj* monsoonal

musons *nm* monsoon

mūsos *pron, loc* of **mēs** in us

mūsots *adj* speckled, freckled

mūspasaule *nf* this world

mūspasaulīgs *adj* of this world

mūspuse *nf* our parts

mūspusnie/ks *nm*, ~**ce** *nf* someone from our parts

mustains *adj* black-muzzled

mustaḷa *nf* black-muzzled cow

mustangs *nm* mustang

mustavas *nf pl* (reg.) batten

mustis *nm* black-muzzled dog

musturains *adj* (col.) patterned

musturis *nm* pattern, design

musturots *adj* (col.) patterned; **viegli m.** with a light pattern, with a small print

musturs *nm* pattern, design

mūsu *pron, gen* of **mēs** our, ours; **m. dēḷ** for our sake; **m. starpā** between us, among us; **m. vidū** in our midst, among us

musulman/is *nm*, ~**iete** *nf* Muslim

musulmanisms *nm* Islam

mūsuprāt *adv* in our opinion

mūs(u)tēvs *nm* Paternoster, Lord's Prayer

muš/a *nf* fly ◊ ~**u no deguna nenodzen** butter wouldn't melt in his mouth; **no** ~**as ziloni iztaisīt** make a mountain out of a molehill

mušains *adj* speckled; freckled

mušas svars *nm* flyweight

mušele *nf* (cont.) little fly

mušiņa *nf* **1.** *dim* of **muša**; little fly; **2.** slub

mušīt *vt* (sl.) **1.** kill; **2.** pet

muškadrilis *nm* a Latvian folk dance

mušķērājs *nm* **1.** flycatcher; **2.** sundew

mušķērājveidīgie *nom adj* Muscicapidae

mušmire *nf* amanita

mušpapīrs *nm* flypaper

mušu sitējs *nm* flyswat

mušu traips flyspeck

mušveida *indecl adj* fly-like

mušveidīgs *adj* fly-like

mušveidīgie *nom adj* Brachycera

mut[a]bilitāte [ā] *nf* mutability

mutācija *nf* mutation; bud sport

mut[a]g[ē]ni [ā][e] *adv* mutagenically

mut[a]g[ē]niski [ā][e] *adv* mutagenically

mut[a]g[ē]nisks [ā][e] *adj* mutagenic

mut[a]g[ē]ns [ā][e] *nm* mutagen

mut[a]g[ē]ns [ā][e] *adj* mutagenic

mut[a]ģen[ē]ze [ā][e] *nf* mutagenesis

mutainis *nm* glib talker

mutains *adj* mouthy, voluble

mutants *nm* mutant

mutants *adj* mutant

mut[a]rotācija [ā] *nf* mutarotation

mut[a]tīvs [ā] *adj* mutative

mutautiņš *nm* handkerchief

mutauts *nm* handkerchief

mut/e *nf* **1.** mouth ◊ **no** ~**es mutē** by word of mouth; **ar gardu** ~**i** with relish; ~**i atplētis** agape; **m. līdz ausīm** a. (col.) having a very wide mouth; b. bigmouthed; **m. ciet** that shut him (her) up; ~**i ciet!** shut up! **vienā** ~**ē** in unison; **m. viņam īstā vietā** he says the right thing at the right time; **liela m.** back talk; **nav uz** ~**es kritis** ready-witted,

ready with a comeback; **uz ~es kritis** (or
sists) speechless; **2.** (col.) face; **netīru ~i**
dirty-faced; **uz ~tes** a. face down, prone;
b. up-side down; **3.** *pl* **~es** (obs.) kiss;
4. opening

mutelīgi *adv* talkatively; chattily

mutelīgs *adj* talkative, chatty

muteniski *adv* prone

mutere *nf* (sl.) mother

mutesbajārs *nm* bigmouth, braggart

mutesbļoda *nf* washbowl

mutes dobums *nm* oral cavity

mutes harmonika *nf* harmonica

mutes organi *nm pl* (insect) mouthparts

mutes un nagu sērga *nf* hoof-and-mouth
disease

mutes ūdens *nm* mouthwash

mutes varonis *nm* blowhard

mutēt I *vt* (obs.) kiss

mutēt II *vi* mutate

mutēties I *vr* **1.** (col.) converse; chat; **2.** (obs.)
exchange kisses

mutēties II *vr* mutate

mūties *vr* (reg.) **1.** struggle in vain; **2.** be in the
way; **3.** hang around

mutīgi *adv* talkatively; chattily

mutīgs *adj* talkative; chatty

mutīgums *nm* talkativeness, chattiness

mutiski *adv* orally

mutisks *adj* oral; (jur., of evidence) parol

mutiskums *nm* (jur.) priciple of oral proceedings

mutisms *nm* mutism

mutslaucis *nm* (col.) handkerchief

mutslauks *nm* (col.) handkerchief

mutslauķis *nm* (col.) handkerchief

mutuāli *adv* mutually

mutuālisms *nm* mutualism

mutuālist/s *nm*, **~e** *nf* mutualist

mutuāls *adj* mutual

mutulis *nm* eddy, swirl; (of smoke) billow,
cloud

mutulītis *nm dim* of **mutulis**, little eddy; little
billow

mutuls *nm* mutule

mutuļains *adj* **1.** eddying, swirling; **2.** tumul-
tous

mutuļot *vi* **1.** swirl, eddy; billow; **2.** seethe

muturs *nm* (barb., mech.) nut

mutvārd/i *nm pl* words; **~iem** or **~os** orally;
~u oral

mūza *nf* Muse

m[u]zejisks [ū] *adj* museum-like

m[u]zejs [ū] *nm* museum

muzgulis *nm* bundle

m[u]zicēt [ū] *vi* make music, play music

mūzika *nf* music; **~s pavadījums** accompaniment

m[u]zikāli [ū] *adv* musically

m[u]zikālijas [ū] *nf pl* sheet music

m[u]zikāliju [ū] **veikals** *nm* music shop

m[u]zikāliski [ū] *adv* musically

m[u]zikālisks [ū] *adj* musical

m[u]zikalitāte [ū] *nf* musicality

m[u]zikāls [ū] *adj* musical

m[u]zikant/s [ū] *nm*, **~e** *nf* player (of music);
~u gaļa jellied meat

mūzikas skola *nf* school of music

mūzikhols *nm* music hall

mūzikls *nm* musical

m[u]zikologs [ū] *nm*, **~ģe** *nf* musicologist

m[u]zikoloģija [ū] *nf* musicology

m[u]zikoloģiski [ū] *adv* musicologically

m[u]zikoloģisks [ū] *adj* musicological

mūziķ/is *nm*, **~e** *nf* musician

muža *nf* (col.) **1.** mouth; **2.** kiss; **3.** mouthful,
something to eat

mūža cerība *nf* life expectancy

mūža draugs *nm* spouse

mūža gājums *nm* course of life

mūža ilgums *nm* life span

mūža katorga *nf* penal servitude for life

mūžam *adv* always; ever, forever; **m. ilgi** for
ages

mūžamaize *nf* pension

mūža māja *nf* (poet.) coffin

mūžamežs *nm* primeval forest, virgin forest

mūža miegs *nm* eternal sleep

mūžamzaļš *adj* evergreen

mūža novakars *nm* declining years

mūža pensija *nf* life annuity

mūždien *adv* always

mūžīb/a *nf* eternity; veselu ~u an eternity, ages, for ages

mūžīgi *adv* eternally; always, incessantly; m. mū-žam for ever and ever

mūžīg/s *adj* eternal; everlasting; immortal; (of motion) perpetual; ~ai lietošanai for use in perpetuity; uz ~iem laikiem forever; padarīt ~u immortalize

mūžīgums *nm* perpetuity

mužiks *nm* muzhik

mūžiņa *nf dim* of muža, kiss

mūžiņš *nm dim* of mūžs, life

mūžmežs *nm* = mūžamežs

mūž/s *nm* life, lifetime ◊ visu ~u all life long; ne savu ~u never; uz ~u forever; for life; uz ~u ~iem for ever and ever; ~u ~os for all eternity; ~u dienu always; (in negations) never; ak (tu) ~s! oh, my goodness!

mūžsens *adj* ancient

mūžudien *adv* = mūždien

mužurs *nm* (reg.) tangle

mūžvecs *adj* ancient

mūžzaļš *adj* evergreen

LaVergne, TN USA
19 August 2009
155363LV00007B/48/P

9 781436 340328